PRODUCTION & OPERATIONS MANAGEMENT

PRODUCTION & OPERATIONS MANAGEMENT

A Life Cycle Approach

Richard B. Chase
University of Southern California

Nicholas J. Aquilano
University of Arizona

Sixth Edition

IRWIN

Homewood, IL 60430
Boston, MA 02116

To our wives
  Harriet and Nina
and to our children
  Laurie, Andy, Glenn, and Rob
  Don, Kara, and Mark

 This symbol indicates that the paper in this book is made from recycled paper. Its fiber content exceeds the recommended minimum of 50% waste paper fibers as specified by the EPA.

© RICHARD D. IRWIN, INC., 1973, 1977, 1981, 1985, 1989, and 1992

Sponsoring editor: Richard T. Hercher, Jr.
Developmental editor: Karen Eichorst
Project editor: Susan Trentacosti
Production manager: Diane Palmer
Designer: Jeanne M. Rivera
Compositor: Better Graphics, Inc.
Typeface: 10/12 Bembo
Printer: R. R. Donnelley & Sons Company

Library of Congress Cataloging-in-Publication Data

Chase, Richard B.
    Production and operations management : a life cycle approach /
Richard B. Chase, Nicholas J. Aquilano.—6th ed.
        p.   cm.
    Includes indexes.
    ISBN: 0-256-10039-X (student ed. : alk. paper).—ISBN
0-256-11309-2 (instructor's ed. : alk. paper)
    1. Production management.   I. Aquilano, Nicholas J.   II. Title.
TS155.C424   1992
658.5—dc20   91-32076

Printed in the United States of America
1 2 3 4 5 6 7 8 9 0 DOC 9 8 7 6 5 4 3 2

Preface for the Student
(By a student)

Operations Management (OM) has seen a resurgence of interest in recent years, returning to a position of critical importance in business. Competitive pressures for quality, time-based competition, and international production have demonstrated that excellent management of the operations function is vital to the survival of the firm. The modern field of Operations Management is broad in scope, ranging from automated manufacturing to high-touch services. An understanding of the operations function is now a necessary part of any good business education.

As a student, I have enjoyed OM. One experiences the intellectual challenge of using mathematical tools such as linear programming and queuing theory to solve problems as varied as locating a plant, scheduling workers, and producing products "just-in-time."

In the text, Dr. Chase and Dr. Aquilano provide coverage of the time-tested approaches, coupled with additional material on current business practices. There are numerous current examples of breakthrough ideas in services, total quality management, continuous improvement, and synchronous manufacturing. I feel that as a student you will find this text interesting, as well as relevant, to all areas of Business Administration, and that you will find studying Operations Management to be as productive and exciting an experience as I have.

Marcella Liem
Student, School of Business Administration
University of Southern California

Preface for the Instructor

The tremendous growth in interest in OM courses at business schools has resulted in attracting individuals from other disciplines to teach it. If you fall into this category this year, we would like to welcome you to this fascinating subject. If you are an old pro, we hope that the sixth edition captures, to your satisfaction, the new developments in the field since 1989.

Adopting the notion of "continuous improvement" as our philosophy, we have made the following changes in this edition:

1. Beefed up our treatment of quality. This involved:
   a. A total revision of what is now our TQM chapter.
   b. Adding a chapter-length supplement on the Baldrige National Quality Award (one of us served as a Baldrige examiner primarily to develop materials to use in this book).
   c. Adding a new chapter on continuous improvement, which is now part of the quality approaches of most world-class companies.

2. Added material dealing with how operations is done in other countries and implications of globalization for U.S. competitiveness.

3. Introduced some new ideas in service management including service guarantees and a four-stage model of service firm competitiveness.

4. Refined the chapter on synchronous manufacturing and discussed its applicability in many other parts of the book. (The other author held a seminar on the subject, also with the objective of bringing the largest applications into the book.)

5. Provided detailed discussions of such contemporary issues as time-based competition, concurrent engineering, design for manufacture (DFM), quality function deployment (QFD), activity-based costing, competitive benchmarking, the Shingo system, and so on.

6. Heavily revised virtually every chapter to ensure that it is both topical and teachable. Our pedagogical goal, by the way, has always been to provide enough material on a technique to enable the student to solve a realistic problem using it.

Teaching aids available with this text include:

- *Study Guide and Lotus Templates* by Singhal, Aquilano, and Pope.
- *Instructor's Manual and Transparency Masters.*
- *Test Bank* by Delurgio, Foster, Chase, and Aquilano.
- *Computerized Testing Software.*
- *Decision Support Systems for Production and Operations Management* by Lofti and Pegels.

Also, we've done our best to make the book interesting reading. Disraeli once said, "The way to become rich is to be an expert on a dull subject." We hope that this book helps accomplish the former without suffering the latter.

ACKNOWLEDGMENTS

We would first like to thank L. J. Chase and L. R. Chase, Chase et Fils Consultants for their many contributions to the book. We are grateful to Doug Stewart, Bill Youngdahl, Andreas Soteriou, and Arvinder Loomba (all from USC) and Joe Pope (University of Texas–El Paso) for help in proofreading and library research, and to Jack Yurkiewicz (Pace University) and Jeongeun Kim (Pennsylvania State University) for checking calculations in examples and problems. We would like to give a special thanks to Danie Mann and Krystie Stout for their help in all aspects of manuscript production.

We would also like to thank the following reviewers for their many thoughtful suggestions: Wayne Cunningham, University of Scranton; Edward Gillenwater, University of Mississippi; Satish Mehra, Memphis State University; Graham Morbey, University of Massachusetts at Amherst; R. Natarajan, Tennessee Technological University; Fred Raafat, San Diego State University; and Edward Rosenthal, Temple University.

We would again like to thank those individuals whose input over the past editions have helped evolve the book to its present form: David Booth, Kent State University; Thomas Cywood, University of Chicago; Mike Martin, Dalhousie University; James Perry, George Washington University; Dan Rinks, Louisiana State University; Raj Srivastavo, Marquette University; Robert Trend, University of Virginia; Everette Adam, University of Missouri–Columbia; Lawrence Bennigson, Harvard University; John G. Carlson, University of Southern California; Amiya K. Chakravarty, University of Wisconsin–Milwaukee; Joel Corman, Suffolk University; Robert B. Fetter, Yale University; William A. Fischer, University of North Carolina; Dale R. Flowers, Case Western University; Carter Franklin III, Houston Baptist University; Oliver Galbraith III, California State University–San Diego; Stanley J. Garstka, University of Chicago; Michael Hotenstein, Penn

State University; Gordon Johnson, California State University–Northridge; Frank L. Kaufman, California State University–Sacramento; Lee Krajewski, Ohio State University; Hugh V. Leach, Washburn University; John D. Longhill, East Carolina University; John R. Matthews, University of Wisconsin; Brooke Saladin, University of Georgia; Ted Stafford, University of Alabama–Huntsville; Trevor Sainsbury, University of Pittsburgh; Chuck Baron Shook, University of Hawaii at Manoa; John E. Stevens, Lehigh University; Jesse S. Tarleton, College of William and Mary.

Thanks too to our faculty colleagues—K. Ravi Kumar, S. Rajagopalan, Norm LaFond, and John Yormark—for their helpful comments on what works and doesn't work in their teaching of OM.

Last, but certainly not least, we would like to thank our families who for the sixth time let the life cycle of the book disrupt theirs.

Richard B. Chase
Nicholas J. Aquilano

Contents in Brief

Contents

Chapter 5
Design for Total Quality Management

Chapter 13
Inventory Systems for Independent Demand   640

Chapter 16
Materials Management and Purchasing   828

SECTION VI
IMPROVING THE SYSTEM   873

Chapter 17
Continuous Improvement   874

Chapter 18
Synchronous Production   906

SECTION I

THE NATURE AND CONTEXT OF OPERATIONS MANAGEMENT

How we manage our productive resources is critical to our productivity growth and competitiveness as a nation. Operations management is the managing of these productive resources. It entails the design and control of systems responsible for the productive use of raw materials, human resources, equipment, and facilities in the development of a product or service. This section addresses the issues of productivity and competitiveness and how the field of operations management can provide direction in gaining and maintaining competitive advantage.

Chapter 1

Introduction and Overview

EPIGRAPH

The Operations Challenge:
Now corporate offices are focusing on deter-
mining what customers really value. This is a
good step, but not good enough. Customers do
not pay corporations for discovering what they
value, but for delivering that value bettter
than the competition.

Arun N. Maira, Director of the Operations
Management Consulting Practice for
Arthur D. Little, *Los Angeles Times*,
May 1, 1991, p. D3.

2

KEY TERMS

Five P's of Operations Management

Operations Objectives

Transformation Process

Life Cycle Approach

Scientific Management

Just-in-Time (JIT)

Total Quality Control (TQC)

Computer-Integrated Manufacturing (CIM)

*R*unning a business requires three basic functions: finance, operations, and marketing. Finance deals with getting the capital and equipment to start the business, operations deals with making the product, and marketing deals with selling and distributing it. This book discusses the fundamental concepts necessary to understand the nature and management of the operations function.

The need to learn about operations has become quite evident in light of the following developments:

1. International competition, especially from the Japanese, has compelled North American companies to "raise the level of their game" to remain competitive in world markets. Producing high-quality products that can be sold at competitive prices is the basic responsibility of the operations area.

2. New operations technologies and control systems are significantly affecting the way firms conduct their businesses. No matter what the business specialty happens to be, a knowledge of operations is critical in making informed managerial decisions.

3. Operations management is critical to service companies as well as manufacturing firms. Take a look at the Fortune 500 service businesses; the vast majority achieved their success through well-run

At the Graduate School of Business

The Christian Science Monitor, November 24, 1987. Danziger © 1987. Reprinted with permission.

operations. Indeed, no service firm can be called excellent without superior operations management.

4. Entrepreneurs, if they are to survive, must have a thorough knowledge of how their organizations make their products. This is particularly true for new service businesses, where quality of operations is frequently the only thing that separates one firm from another.

5. The concepts and tools of operations management (OM) are widely used in managing other functions of the business as well. For example, every manager is concerned with quality and productivity issues—topics presented in this book.

6. Operations management offers an interesting and rewarding career. It requires a broad set of skills that, if mastered, makes you a very attractive candidate for jobs in a wide range of organizations.

1.1 SPECIFIC OBJECTIVES OF THE BOOK

The specific objectives of the book are: (1) to explain how the operations function is managed; (2) to introduce some OM tools and concepts that you can apply on the job; (3) to help you develop an appreciation for the interaction of this management activity with other management systems within the organizations; (4) to introduce some *new* concepts in the field; and (5) to provide an understanding of the field as a totality.

With respect to the last objective, we intend to show that operations management is not just a loosely knit aggregation of tools but rather a *synthesis* of concepts and techniques that relate directly to productive systems and enhance their management. This point is important because operations management (OM) is frequently confused with operations research (OR) (or its synonym, management science [MS]), and with industrial engineering (IE). The critical difference is this: OM is a field of management, whereas OR is a branch of applied mathematics and IE is an engineering discipline. Thus, while operations managers use the tools of OR (such as linear programming) in decision making, and are concerned with many of the same issues as IE (such as factory automation), OM has a distinct management role that differentiates it from both OR and IE.

1.2 OPERATIONS MANAGEMENT DEFINED

Operations management (or *production management,* as it is often called) may be defined as the management of the direct resources required to produce the goods and services provided by an organization. Exhibit 1.1 presents a summary model of the field in a broad business context.

The marketplace—the firm's customers for its products or services—shapes

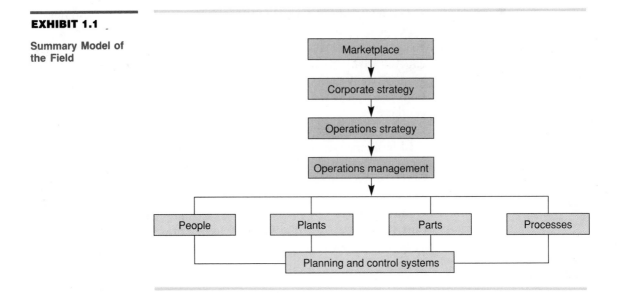

the corporate strategy of the firm. This strategy is based on the corporate mission, and in essence reflects how the firm plans to use all its resources and functions (marketing, finance, and operations) to gain competitive advantage. The operations strategy specifies how the firm will employ its production capabilities to support its corporate strategy. (We discuss the extent to which operations influences corporate strategy in subsequent chapters.)

Operations management deals with the direct production resources of the firm. These resources may be thought of as the **five P's of operations management**—People, Plants, Parts, Processes, and Planning and control systems. The people are the direct and indirect work force; the plants include the factories or service branches where production is carried out; the parts include the materials (or in the case of services, the supplies) that go through the system; the processes include the equipment and the steps by which production is accomplished; and the planning and control systems are the procedures and information used by management to operate the system.

1.3 THE OPERATIONS FUNCTION AND ITS ENVIRONMENT

In most organizations, operations is an internal function that is buffered from the external environment by other organizational functions. Consider the relationship between the operations and other organization functions and the environment shown in Exhibit 1.2. Orders are received by the sales department, which is an arm of the marketing function; supplies and raw materials are obtained through the purchasing function; capital for equipment purchases comes from the finance function; the labor force is obtained through the personnel function; and the product is delivered by the distribution function.

EXHIBIT 1.2   **Relationship between the Operations Function, Other Organization Functions, and the Environment**

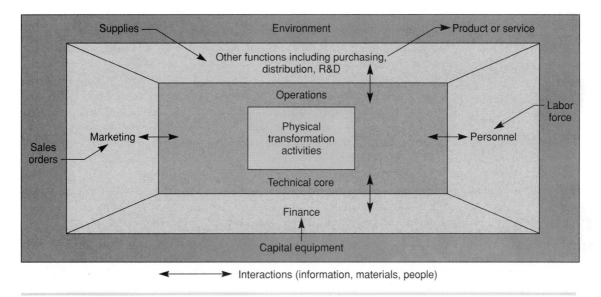

Thus, while there may be a good deal of interaction between the firm and its environment, the production function is rarely involved in it directly.

Buffering the production function (or, as it is sometimes called, the *technical core*) from direct environmental influence has been traditionally seen as desirable, for several reasons:

1. Interaction with environmental elements (e.g., customers and salespeople on the production floor) can be a disturbing influence on the production process.
2. The direct production process is often more efficient than the processes required for obtaining inputs and disposing of finished goods.
3. In certain technologies (for example, assembly lines and petroleum refining), maximum productivity can be achieved only by operating as if the market could absorb all the product being manufactured and at a continuous rate. This means that the production process must shift at least some of the input and output activities to other parts of the firm.
4. The managerial skills required for successful operation of the production process are often different from those required for successful operation of the boundary systems of marketing and personnel, for example.

There are some inherent disadvantages to production being an internal function, however. One is that information lags between production and the so-called boundary functions; this inevitably leads to inflexibility. Another is that for high-tech products in particular, communications between the shop floor and the customer can be extremely valuable in solving technical problems during production. Finally, some companies, such as Tektronix, have found that interaction between the person using the product and the person producing it helps to establish a strong relationship between them and, hence, between their respective organizations as well. (See the Insert.)

We have identified the location of production activities in four different types of organizations in Exhibit 1.3: three service firms (A, B, and D) and one manufacturing company (C). Aside from differences in terminology, the nonmanufacturing organizations also differ from the manufacturing firm in structure. In the manufacturing company, production functions are grouped in one department. In the service firms, certain production activities are scattered throughout the organization. This does not mean that the activity is any less a production one, but only that it is deemed best performed under the aegis of a different department. Note also that the position of plant manager is used in manufacturing to administer the various support activities required for production. Assuming that these organizations are typical of their industries in the way they function, some commonalities would be the fact that production activities account for the lion's share of capital investment and work force.

Jobs Related to the Operations Function

Exhibit 1.4 lists some line and staff jobs that are frequently viewed as relating to the operations function. There are more staff specializations in manufacturing than in services because of the focus on materials management and control.

INSERT   **Linking the Shop-Floor Worker to the Customer**

Tektronix, a manufacturer of electronic equipment, has pioneered direct communication between customers and shop-floor employees. Into the shipping carton of every oscilloscope it sells, the company inserts a postcard listing the names of the workers who built the scope along with an "800" number to a phone on the shop floor. Every day the factory gets several calls from customers; the six people working in the repair area who answer them have all received telephone training.

Customers call for various reasons: questions about the use of their oscilloscopes, requests for information about other Tektronix products, and to see if "they can really talk to the person who made their product." Workers and managers meet daily to discuss these calls; if necessary, further conversations with the customer follow up the meetings. In some cases, workers will call customers six months after delivery to find out how well their products are performing.

Source: R. B. Chase and D. A. Garvin, "The Service Factory," *Harvard Business Review*, July–August 1989, pp. 65–66.

EXHIBIT 1.3   Sample Organization Charts of Four Diverse Firms

Chart (A): Airline

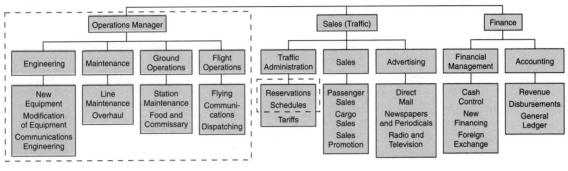

Chart (B): Commercial bank branch

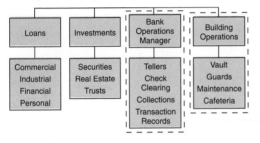

Chart (C): Manufacturing firm

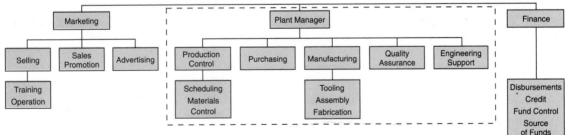

Chart (D): Department store

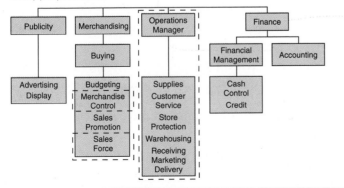

EXHIBIT 1.4

Line and Staff Jobs in Operations Management

Organizational Level	Manufacturing Industries	Service Industries
Upper	Vice president of manufacturing	Vice president of operations (airline)
	Regional manager of manufacturing	Chief administrator (hospital)
Middle	Plant manager	Store manager (department store)
	Program manager	Facilities manager (wholesale distributor)
Lower	Department supervisor	Branch manager (bank)
	Foreman	Department supervisor (insurance company)
	Crew chief	Assistant manager (hotel)
Staff	Production controller	Systems and procedures analyst
	Materials manager	Purchasing agent
	Quality manager	Inspector
	Purchasing agent	Dietician (hospital)
	Work methods analyst	Customer service manager
	Process engineer	

1.4 OPERATIONS OBJECTIVES

The general **objectives** of operations management are to produce a specified product, on schedule, at minimum cost. Most organizations, however, use additional criteria for purposes of evaluation and control. Typical criteria for a manufacturing firm include:

1. Volume of output.
2. Cost (materials, labor, delivery, scrap, etc.).
3. Utilization (equipment and labor).
4. Quality and product reliability.
5. On-time delivery.
6. Investment (return on assets).
7. Flexibility for product change.
8. Flexibility for volume change.

Several of these measures are internally oriented, and thus are of little concern to the customer. However, Richard Schonberger observes that the very best companies (he calls them "world-class manufacturers") use customer-oriented performance measures at the corporate level. These are typically summarized as cost (to the customer), lead time, quality, and flexibility.[1]

---

[1] Richard J. Schonberger, *World Class Manufacturing, The Lessons of Simplicity Applied* (New York: Free Press, 1986), p. 205.

In actually applying these objectives, it is necessary to recognize that not all of them can be achieved with the same level of success. In many cases, low cost must be sacrificed for the flexibility necessary to customize products, or to deliver products within a very short lead time. Even quality, which has reached the level of a religious commandment in many firms, sometimes must be sacrificed to meet lead-time pressures. A case in point would be a hospital supplier delivering a state-of-the-art laboratory device for analyzing blood samples. The hospital may insist on having it immediately, even though it has scratches or minor operating problems. Thus, despite the laudable goal of wanting to excell on all objectives, situations can force trade-offs and priorities, at least in the short run.

Operations objectives are cascaded through the organization and are translated into measurable terms that become part of the operating goals for production-related departments and their managers.

Most companies also have developed a statement of corporate philosophy, or mission, to which operating objectives are closely tied. IBM's corporate philosophy centers on the concept of "customer service;" Hewlett-Packard Company emphasizes "customer satisfaction." A company that describes its objectives as "success factors" is Allen-Bradley, known for state-of-the-art industrial control equipment (see Insert).

INSERT   Success Factors at Allen-Bradley Industrial Control Group

What are the key success factors in manufacturing? Which should a company point toward in its strategic planning of the manufacturing function? Which goals should it set to indicate where it wants manufacturing to be so that it can best serve the overall business objectives? [The vice president of the Industrial Control Group, Larry Yost] lists them as follows:

- Competitive delivery.
- Asset utilization.
- Quality.
- Cost.
- New-product introduction.
- Business systems.
- Human resources.

Competitive delivery means that promised dates are met. Lead times must accurately reflect manufacturing requirements. And delivery compliance must be effected in this post-mass-production age, where manufacturing capability is a hybrid of volume output and flexible product mix.

Asset utilization has become a key indicator in evaluating the performance of a company, right up there with market share, sales volume, and profits. While the "hot buttons" seem to change weekly in industry—inventory is too high, profits are too low, and so forth—return on assets is an approach that keeps everything balanced.

If that is in fact the focus, then what manufacturing can do to help the company is optimize its inventory and the utilization of its fixed assets.

Element number three, quality, must be approached from two angles: customer perception and the internal cost of maintaining quality. As for cost, manufacturing must contribute to a cost equation that is competitive worldwide as well as manageable throughout the different phases of the business cycle. Anyone can make money when business is good; the trick is to be able to do it during a downturn.

New-product introductions are an extremely important gauge of a successful manufacturing operation. In the good old days, five to eight years would transpire from the marketing idea to the sale of the first product. That product in turn would have a 20-year life cycle.

Now, product life cycles can be less than two years. There is no future without new products, and manufacturing's role within the division is to deliver them in a timely manner, to the planned volumes, with respect to both the introduction process and the actual production cost of the item itself.

Finally, manufacturing must be effectively integrated within the business systems and must successfully manage its human resources, including both hiring and training its people for the current and future skills that will be required to fulfill the strategic plan.

Source: Extracted from John M. Martin, "Strategic Planning for Manufacturing," *Manufacturing Engineering*, November 1987, pp. 45–50.

1.5 PRODUCTION SYSTEMS

Operations management manages production systems. A production system may be thought of as a set of components whose function is to convert a set of inputs into some desired output through what we call a **transformation process.** A component may be a machine, a person, a tool, or a management system. An input may be a raw material, a person, or a finished product from another system. Some transformations that take place are:

- Physical, as in manufacturing.
- Locational, as in transportation.
- Exchange, as in retailing.
- Storage, as in warehousing.
- Physiological, as in health care.
- Informational, as in telecommunications.

These transformations, of course, are not mutually exclusive. For example, a department store is set up to enable shoppers to compare prices and quality (informational), to hold items in inventory until needed (storage), and to sell goods (exchange). Exhibit 1.5 presents sample input–transformation–output relationships for typical systems. Note that only the direct production components are listed; a complete system description would, of course, also include managerial and support functions.

EXHIBIT 1.5

Input–Transfor-
mation–Output
Relationships for
Typical Systems

System	Primary Inputs	Components	Primary Transformation Function(s)	Typical Desired Output
Hospital	Patients	MDs, nurses, medical supplies, equipment	Health care (physiological)	Healthy individuals
Restaurant	Hungry customers	Food, chef, waitress, environment	Well-prepared food, well served; agreeable environment (physical and exchange)	Satisfied customers
Automobile factory	Sheet steel, engine parts	Tools, equipment, workers	Fabrication and assembly of cars (physical)	High-quality cars
College or university	High school graduates	Teachers, books, classrooms	Imparting knowledge and skills (informational)	Educated individuals
Department store	Shoppers	Displays, stock of goods, sales clerks	Attract shoppers, promote products, fill orders (exchange)	Sales to satisfied customers
Distribution center	Stockkeeping units (SKUs)	Storage bins, stockpickers	Storage and redistribution	Fast delivery, availability of SKUs

1.6 THE LIFE CYCLE APPROACH

The Operations Management Association has defined the OM subject areas listed in Exhibit 1.6. Although it is useful as a topical checklist, an organizing structure for teaching purposes is needed to (1) allow us to view the field of OM as more than a collection of loosely related topics and (2) mirror the decision hierarchy and sequence actually used in the practice of OM. The structure we have adopted for this book seems to meet these requirements in a straightforward way. This structure, which we have termed the **life cycle approach,** follows the progress of the productive system from its inception to its termination—a concept that we feel reflects the true breadth of the area. The following discussion illustrates how a productive system evolves through its life cycle.

Let us assume that an idea for a product or service is proposed. Questions of marketability, producibility, capital requirements, and so on are examined. If the decision is made to produce this good or service, the final form of the product, the location of the producing facility, the building, and the floor layout all must be specified. The required equipment must be purchased and the production, inventory, and quality control systems designed. The

---

EXHIBIT 1.6

**Subject Areas in
Operations
Management**

1. Operations strategy.
2. Inventory control.
3. Aggregate planning.
4. Forecasting.
5. Scheduling.
6. Capacity planning.
7. Purchasing.
8. Facility location.
9. Facility layout.
10. Process design.
11. Maintenance and reliability.
12. Quality control.
13. Work measurement.

Source: Modified from Operations Management Association, *The Operations Management Newsletter* 1, no. 1 (May–June 1979), p. 14.

---

particular tasks to be done must be designed, the functional groups staffed, and production initiated. Quite likely, there will be problems in this startup phase requiring design changes, re-layout, and personnel adjustments. Once the facility is in operation, problems become more of the day-to-day type, requiring decisions on scheduling priorities, minor changes to remove inefficiencies, and maintenance to ensure continued operation. We term this stage the *steady state*.

This steady-state operating condition may be changed in a number of ways: new products may come into the system or a new service may be offered; new developments may cause significant changes in methods; markets may shift or even cease to exist. If these changes are moderate, a slight revision may be all that is necessary to bring the system into line. At times, though, the needed revisions are of such magnitude that certain phases of the life cycle must be repeated, probably calling for new designs, more or less extensive restaffing, and restarting the revised system. If the system cannot adjust to the stimulus that has generated the need for revision, then, in the extreme case, the enterprise will die (through liquidation) or cease to exist as a separate entity (through sale or merger).

In reality, most enterprises operate within this dynamic life cycle. A system, whether it is a manufacturing firm, service business, or government agency, is born of an idea, passes through a growth stage, and continually changes to meet new demands. And sometimes, of course, it is deliberately terminated.

Exhibit 1.7 lists some of the key decision areas at the various stages in a system's life cycle and the chapter where each is emphasized. Remember that this is a dynamic process, and several phases in the life cycle may occur simultaneously. Indeed, many firms allocate a large portion of their resources to foster a continual rebirth or rejuvenation program through research and development staffs. Further, although no interconnections are shown in the exhibit, in actuality such interconnections are common. The introduction of a

EXHIBIT 1.7   **Key Decisions in the Life of a Productive System**

Stages	Key Decision	
BIRTH of the system	What are the goals of the firm?	Chapters 1, 2
	What product or service will be offered?	Chapters 1, 2
PRODUCT DESIGN and PROCESS SELECTION	What is the form and quality of the product?	Chapters 3, 4, 5
	Technologically, how should the product be made?	Chapters 3, 4, 5
DESIGN of the system	How do you design for Just-in-Time production?	Chapter 6
	How do you determine demand for the product or service?	Chapter 7
	What capacity do you need?	Chapter 8
	Where should the facility be located?	Chapter 8
	What physical arrangement is best to use?	Chapter 9
	What job is each worker to perform?	Chapter 10
	How will the job be performed and measured?	Chapter 10
	How will the workers be compensated?	Chapter 10
STARTUP of the system	How do you get the system into operation?	Chapter 11
	How long will it take to reach desired rate of output?	Supplement to 11
The system in STEADY STATE	How do you manage day-to-day activities?	Chapters 12–16
	How can you improve the system?	Chapters 17, 18
	How do you revise the system in light of changes in corporate strategy?	Chapter 19

new product, for example, might cause the system to loop back to basic product design, followed by the activities of process selection, new system design, staffing, and startup.

Exhibit 1.8 shows a graphic example of such rejuvenation. In this illustration we have assumed that redesign of the system is undertaken during the steady state and termination phases of the initial system's life cycle. This might be a reasonable strategy in that it permits startup of the revised system to begin as soon as operations of the initial system are terminated. We have also assumed (for simplicity) that only one new product is to be produced by the redesigned system and that the life cycle curves for both product and system are roughly equivalent to those of their original counterparts. In actuality, of course, these assumptions are highly restrictive since most manufacturing firms produce several products rather than one, and we would not expect any two system life cycles or any two product life cycles to be identical.

We emphasize that this text is not built around the life cycle of any one system. On the contrary, we have intentionally sought illustrations from a variety of products and services. By doing this, we hope to emphasize the fact that production and operations management is essential in such diverse systems as hospitals, supermarkets, banks, universities—and, of course, factories.[2]

---

[2] See Roger W. Schmenner, "Every Factory Has a Life Cycle," *Harvard Business Review* 61, no. 2 (March–April 1983), pp. 121–29.

EXHIBIT 1.8   **Rejuvenation with Design and Startup of Revised System Begun during Latter Phases of Original System**

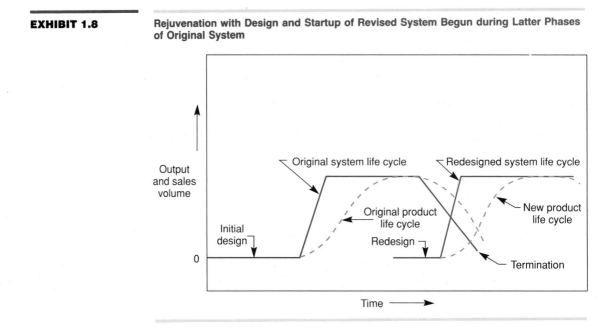

1.7 OPERATIONS MANAGEMENT AND OTHER BUSINESS SPECIALTIES

Operations management is a required course in many business schools not only because it deals with the basic question of how products and services are created but also because it affects every other field of business in the real world.

Accountants, be they internal or external to the firm, need to understand the basics of inventory management, capacity utilization, and labor standards to develop accurate cost data, perform audits, and prepare financial reports. Cost accountants in particular must be aware of how Just-in-Time (JIT) and computer-integrated manufacturing (CIM) work.

Financial managers can use inventory and capacity concepts in judging the need for capital investments and forecasts of cash flow and in the management of current assets. Further, there is a mutual concern between OM and finance in specific decisions such as make-or-buy and plant expansion.

Marketing specialists need an understanding of what the factory can do relative to meeting customer due dates, product customization, and new product introduction. In service industries, marketing and production often take place simultaneously, so a natural mutuality of interest should arise between marketing and OM.

Personnel specialists need to be aware of how jobs are designed, the relationship of standards to incentive plans, and the skills required of the direct work force.

MIS specialists often install manufacturing information systems that they themselves design or that are developed as off-the-shelf software by computer companies. Moreover, a major application of computers in business is in the area of production control.

1.8 HISTORICAL DEVELOPMENT OF OM

Exhibit 1.9 gives a timeline of the history of the field of OM. We now highlight some of the major concepts and their developers.

Scientific Management

Although operations management has existed since people started to engage in production, the advent of **scientific management** around the turn of the century is probably the major historical landmark for the field. This concept was developed by Frederick W. Taylor, an imaginative engineer and insightful observer of organizational activities.

The essence of Taylor's philosophy was that scientific laws govern how much a worker can produce per day and that it is the function of management to discover and use these laws in the operation of productive systems (and the function of the worker to carry out management's wishes without question). Taylor's philosophy was not greeted with approval by all his contemporaries. On the contrary, some unions resented or feared scientific management—and with some justification. In too many instances, managers of the day were quick to embrace the mechanisms of Taylor's philosophy—time study, incentive plans, and so forth—but ignored their responsibility to organize and standardize the work to be done. Hence, there were numerous cases of rate cutting (reducing the payment per piece if the production rate were deemed too high), overwork of labor, and poorly designed work methods. Such abuses resulted in overreaction, leading to the introduction of a bill in Congress in 1913 to prohibit the use of time study and incentive plans in federal government operations. The unions advocating the legislation claimed that Taylor's subject in several of his time-study experiments, a steelworker called "Schmidt," had died from overwork as a result of following Taylor's methods (in evidence whereof they even distributed pictures of Schmidt's "grave"). It was later discovered that Schmidt (whose real name was Henry Nolle) was alive and well and working as a teamster.[3] Ultimately, the bill was defeated.

Note that Taylor's ideas were widely accepted in contemporary Japan, and a Japanese translation of Taylor's book, *Principles of Scientific Management* (titled *The Secret of Saving Lost Motion*), sold more than two million copies. To this

---

[3] Milton J. Nadworny, "Schmidt and Stakhanov: Work Heroes in Two Systems," *California Management Review* 6, no. 4 (Summer 1964), pp. 69–76.

EXHIBIT 1.9

Historical Summary

Year	Concept or Tool	Originator or Developer
1911	*Principles of Scientific Management*; formalized time-study and work-study concepts	Frederick W. Taylor (United States)
1911	Motion study; basic concepts of industrial psychology	Frank and Lillian Gilbreth (United States)
1913	Moving assembly line	Henry Ford (United States)
1914	Activity scheduling chart	Henry L. Gantt (United States)
1917	Application of economic lot size model for inventory control	F. W. Harris (United States)
1931	Sampling inspection and statistical tables for quality control	Walter Shewhart, H. F. Dodge, and H. G. Romig (United States)
1927–33	Hawthorne studies' new light on worker motivation	Elton Mayo (United States)
1934	Activity sampling for work analysis	L. H. C. Tippett (England)
1940	Team approaches to complex system problems	Operations research groups (England)
1947	Simplex method of linear programming	George B. Dantzig (United States)
1950s–60s	Extensive development of OR tools of simulation, waiting line theory, decision theory, mathematical programming, computer hardware and software, project scheduling techniques of PERT and CPM	United States and Western Europe
1970s	Development of a variety of computer software packages to deal with routine problems of shop scheduling, inventory, layout, forecasting, and project management; rapid growth of MRP	Computer manufacturers, researchers, and users in the United States and Western Europe
		Joseph Orlicky and Oliver Wight (United States)
	Manufacturing strategy paradigm for using manufacturing as a competitive weapon	Harvard Business School faculty
1980s	Extensive use of JIT, TQC, and factory automation (CIM, FMS, CAD/CAM robots, etc.)	Tai-ichi Ohno of Toyota Motors (Japan), W. E. Deming, J. M. Juran (United States); engineering disciplines
	Service quality and productivity; introduction of mass production in the service sector	McDonald's restaurants

day, there is a strong legacy of Taylorism in Japanese approaches to manufacturing management.[4]

Notable co-workers of Taylor were Frank and Lillian Gilbreth (motion study, industrial psychology) and Henry L. Gantt (scheduling, wage payment plans). Their work is well known to management scholars. However, it is probably not well known that Taylor, a devout Quaker, requested "cussing lessons" from an earthy foreman to help him communicate with workers; that Frank Gilbreth defeated younger champion bricklayers in bricklaying contests

---

[4] Charles J. McMillan, "Production Planning in Japan," *Journal of General Management* 8, no. 4, pp. 44–71.

by using his own principles of motion economy; or that Gantt won a presidential citation for his application of the Gantt chart to shipbuilding during World War I.

Moving Assembly Line

The year 1913 saw the introduction of one of the machine age's greatest technological innovations—the moving assembly line for the manufacture of Ford automobiles.[5] Before the line was introduced, in August of that year, each auto chassis was assembled by one worker in about 12½ hours. Eight months later, when the line was in its final form, with each worker performing a small unit of work and the chassis being moved mechanically, the average labor time per chassis was 93 minutes. This technological breakthrough, coupled with the concepts of scientific management, represents the classic application of labor specialization and is still common today.

Hawthorne Studies

Mathematical and statistical developments dominated the evolution of operations management from Taylor's time up to around the 1940s. An exception was the Hawthorne studies, conducted in the 1930s by a research team from the Harvard Graduate School of Business Administration and supervised by the sociologist Elton Mayo. These experiments were designed to study the effects of certain environmental changes on the output of assembly workers at the Western Electric plant in Hawthorne, Illinois. The unexpected findings, reported in *Management and the Worker* (1939) by F. J. Roethlisberger and W. J. Dickson, intrigued sociologists and students of "traditional" scientific management alike. To the surprise of the researchers, changing the level of illumination, for example, had much less effect on output than the way in which the changes were introduced to the workers. That is, reductions in illumination in some instances led to increased output because workers felt an obligation to their group to keep output high. Discoveries such as these had tremendous implications for work design and motivation and ultimately led to the establishment of personnel management and human relations departments in most organizations.

Operations Research

World War II, with its complex problems of logistics control and weapons-systems design, provided the impetus for the development of the interdisciplinary, mathematically oriented field of operations research. Operations research (OR) brings together practitioners in such diverse fields as

---

[5] Ford is said to have gotten the idea for an assembly line from observing a Swiss watch manufacturer's use of the technology. Incidentally, all Model-T Fords were painted black. Why? Because black paint dried fastest.

mathematics, psychology, and economics. Specialists in these disciplines customarily form a team to structure and analyze a problem in quantitative terms so that a mathematically optimal solution can be obtained. As mentioned earlier in the chapter, operations research, or its approximate synonym management science, now provides many of the quantitative tools used in operations management as well as other business disciplines.

OM Emerges as a Field

In the late 1950s and early 1960s, scholars began to write texts dealing specifically with operations management as opposed to industrial engineering or operations research. Writers such as Edward Bowman and Robert Fetter (*Analysis for Production and Operations Management* [1957]) and Elwood S. Buffa (*Modern Production Management* [1961]) clearly noted the commonality of problems faced by all productive systems and emphasized the importance of viewing production operations as a system. In addition, they stressed the useful applications of waiting line theory, simulation, and linear programming, which are now standard topics in the field. In 1973, Chase and Aquilano (*Production and Operations Management: A Life Cycle Approach*) stressed the need "to put the management back into operations management" and suggested the life cycle as a means of organizing the subject.

Computers and the MRP Crusade

The major development of the 1970s was the broad use of computers in operations problems. For manufacturers, the big breakthrough was the application of materials requirements planning (MRP) to production control. This approach ties together in a computer program all the parts that go into complicated products. This program then enables production planners to quickly adjust production schedules and inventory purchases to meet changing demands for final products. Clearly, the massive data manipulation required for changing schedules on products with thousands of parts would be impossible without such programs and the computer capacity to run them. The promotion of this approach (pioneered by Joseph Orlicky of IBM and consultant Oliver Wight) by the American Production and Inventory Control Society (APICS) has been termed *the MRP Crusade*.

JIT, TQC, and Factory Automation

The 1980s have seen a revolution in the management philosophies and the technologies by which production is carried out. **Just–in–Time (JIT)** production is clearly the major breakthrough in manufacturing philosophy. Pioneered by the Japanese, JIT is an integrated set of activities designed to achieve high-volume production using minimal inventories of parts that arrive at the workstation "just-in-time." This philosophy, coupled with **total quality control (TQC)** which aggressively seeks to eliminate causes of production defects, is now a cornerstone in the production practices of many manufacturing firms.

As profound as the impact of JIT has been, factory automation in its various forms promises to have even greater impact on operations management in the decades beyond. Such terms as **Computer-integrated manufacturing (CIM),** flexible manufacturing systems (FMS), and factory of the future (FOF) are already familiar to many readers of this book and are becoming everyday concepts to practitioners of OM.

Manufacturing Strategy Paradigm

The late 1970s and early 1980s saw the development of the Manufacturing Strategy Paradigm by researchers at the Harvard Business School. This work by professors William Abernathy, Kim Clark, Robert Hayes, and Steven Wheelwright, built on earlier efforts by Wickham Skinner, emphasized how manufacturing executives could use their factories' capabilities as strategic competitive weapons. The paradigm itself identified the ways in which the five P's of production management can be analyzed as strategic and tactical decision variables. Central to their thinking was the notion of factory focus and manufacturing trade-offs. They argued that because a factory can't excel on all performance measures, its management must derive a focused strategy, creating a focused factory that does a limited set of tasks extremely well. This raised the need for making trade-offs among such performance measures as low cost, high quality, and high flexibility in designing and managing factories. In today's manufacturing environment, the notion of trade-offs is often criticized as inherently limiting management's vision about what is really possible in a factory's performance. So-called "world-class" manufacturers make a big point about doing everything well, and argue that automated, flexible technologies make this objective possible. In fact, however, no company can really be the simultaneous price, quality, and flexibility leader in its industry. Thus, though many give good value on all of these dimensions, trade-offs still have to be made.

Service Quality and Productivity

Quality and productivity represent challenges to today's service firms; whatever new tools are developed to meet these challenges will take their place in the history of OM. The great diversity of service industries—ranging from airlines to zoos, with about 2,000 different types in between—precludes identifying any single pioneer or developer that has made a major impact across the board in these areas. However, there is one service company whose unique approach to quality and productivity has been so successful that it stands as a reference point in thinking about how high-volume standardized services can be delivered: McDonald's. In fact, so successful is McDonald's operating system that the president of Chaparral Steel used it as a model in planning the company's highly efficient minimills.

1.9 CONCLUSION: CURRENT ISSUES IN OPERATIONS MANAGEMENT

We conclude our introduction with a listing of the major current issues that face operations management executives today. All of these issues are interrelated and are addressed as we move through the system life cycle.

1. Speeding up the time it takes to manufacture new products and introduce new services.
2. Achieving and sustaining high quality while keeping costs down.
3. Integrating new technologies and control systems into existing production systems.
4. Obtaining and training qualified workers and managers.
5. Working effectively with other functions of the business (marketing, engineering, finance, and personnel) to accomplish the goals of the firm.
6. Controlling production and service activities at multiple sites in decentralized organizations.
7. Working effectively with suppliers and being user-friendly for customers.
8. Working effectively with new partners formed by strategic alliances (for example, IBM and Apple Computers).

The major current issue for operations management is being able to do all of these at a level that is competitive primarily with the Japanese in both international and domestic markets. This is the competitiveness issue raised in the next chapter.

1.10 REVIEW AND DISCUSSION QUESTIONS

1. What is the difference between OM and OR? Between OM and IE?
2. How would you distinguish OM from management and organizational behavior as taught at your college?
3. Why might "buffering the technical core" be an undesirable strategy for a manufacturing firm?
4. Take a look at the want ads in *The Wall Street Journal* and evaluate the opportunities for an OM major with several years of experience.
5. What are the major factors leading to the resurgence of interest in OM today?
6. Which operations objectives seem to drive your university?
7. Using Exhibit 1.5 as a model, describe the input–transformation–output relationships found in the following systems:
   a. An airline.
   b. A state penitentiary.
   c. A branch bank.
   d. The home office of a major banking firm.

8. What is the life cycle approach to production/operations management? Does it make sense to you? Could it be applied to any other fields you are studying?

9. What are the implications for marketing of Tektronix's "hot-line" to the shop-floor worker?

10. Suppose that *Variety*, the Hollywood trade paper noted for its colorful jargon, presented the following headlines relating to OM. What particular historical events or individuals would they be referring to?

FRED RISKS X-RATING TO GET ACROSS PRINCIPLES

HAWTHORNE WORKERS DO IT FASTER IN THE DARK

STEEL KING VISITS GOLDEN ARCHES

MATERIALS MANAGEMENT MAVENS GET WITH THE PROGRAM

INVENTORY—OH NO!

FRANKY BURIES YOUNG STUDS AT BRICKOFF

CLOCKWISE HENRY BECOMES MARVEL OF MOTOWN

P.S.M. TOPS CHARTS IN GINZA

HERO MEDAL FOR HANK AS BOAT BIZ BOOMS

CRIMSON GANG SEEKS COMPROMISE ON SHOP FLOOR

1.11 SELECTED BIBLIOGRAPHY

Buffa, Elwood S. *Modern Production Management*. New York: John Wiley & Sons, 1961.

Chase, Richard B., and Eric L. Prentis. "Operations Management: A Field Rediscovered." *Journal of Management* 13, no. 2 (October 1987), pp. 351–66.

Chase, Richard B., and David A. Garvin. "The Service Factory." *Harvard Business Review* 67, no. 4 (July–August 1989), pp. 61–69.

Deming, W. Edwards. *Out of the Crisis*. Cambridge, Mass.: Massachusetts Institute of Technology Center for Advanced Engineering Study, 1986.

Goldratt, Eliyahu M., and Jeff Cox. *The Goal*. Croton-on-Hudson, N.Y.: North River Press, 1986.

Hayes, Robert H.; Steven C. Wheelwright; and Kim B. Clark. *Dynamic Manufacturing*. New York: Free Press, 1988.

Schonberger, Richard J. *World Class Manufacturing: The Lessons of Simplicity Applied*. New York: Free Press, 1986.

Skinner, Wickham, "Manufacturing—Missing Link in Corporate Strategy," *Harvard Business Review*, May–June 1969, pp. 136–45.

————. "The Focused Factory." *Harvard Business Review*, May–June 1974, pp. 113–21.

Chapter 2

Productivity and Competitiveness

The wealth and power of the United States depends upon maintaining mastery and control of production.

Stephen S. Cohen and John Zysman, *Why Manufacturing Matters: The Myth of the Post-Industrial Economy* (New York: Basic Books, 1987).

In the next century, the United States will be our farm and Western Europe our boutique.

Attributed to a Japanese minister of trade in Gore Vidal, "Rebirth of a Nation: Why Italy Works," *Los Angeles Times*, May 1, 1988.

CHAPTER OUTLINE

KEY TERMS

Competitiveness

International Competition

Productivity

Effectiveness

Efficiency

Competitive Priorities of Manufacturers

Four Stages of Manufacturing Operations
Strategic Role

Competitiveness refers to the relative position in the marketplace and productivity usually refers to output per unit input. This chapter discusses the interrelationship of competitiveness and productivity, with particular emphasis on manufacturing.

2.1 COMPETITIVENESS DEFINED

Competitiveness is a term that is often used but rarely defined. Business managers talk of discovering and strengthening competitive advantages, the United States bemoans its lack of competitiveness in world markets, and instructors ponder about how to prepare their students for an increasingly competitive future.

Competitiveness is about winning. A boxing match is an example of competition. The person with the most points or the one left standing at the end of the match wins. The sides and the rules of the game are easily defined. What about business? Defining sides, or competitors, and rules of the game becomes much more difficult when considering global markets than when talking about a boxing match.

Share prices and return on equity (ROE) are the key financial indicators that determine whether profit-seeking corporations are winning or losing. As seen in Exhibit 2.1, the ROE and share prices that lead to continuing survival and prosperity depend on many factors. The emphasis of the 1990s will be on speed, or short cycle management. The ability to rapidly develop and produce new products depends heavily on the operations function of the firm. Quality, price, dependability, and reponsiveness are all indicators of the job a company is doing at converting inputs into outputs. This conversion process, thus competition, occurs at different levels.

Firms within a given industry compete with one another for market share. Nations also compete with one another for shares of global markets. In 1985, the President's Council on Industrial Competitiveness offered this definition of **international competition:**

> Competitiveness for a nation is the degree to which it can, under free and fair market conditions, produce goods and services that meet the test of international markets while simultaneously maintaining and expanding the real incomes of its citizens.

Productivity is often discussed with competitiveness and is, of course, a major contributor to a country's, industry's, or company's competitive position. However, as many are too quick to note, a nation's ability to compete in a global market is also affected by wage rates, patents, trade barriers, local labor content laws, and the like.

At the company level, productivity is part of the domain of the operations manager. It is his or her job to manager the conversion of inputs into outputs. When the value of the ouputs is greater than the value of the inputs, the

EXHIBIT 2.1

A Competitiveness Roadmap

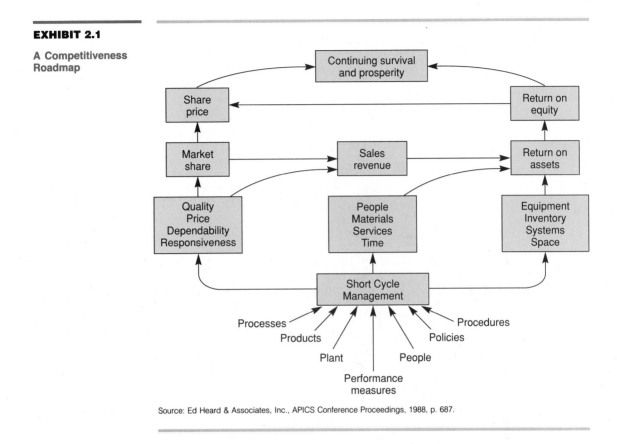

Source: Ed Heard & Associates, Inc., APICS Conference Proceedings, 1988, p. 687.

production system is said to be productive. Balancing the pressure to achieve certain ouput levels while encountering resource (input) constraints is a major challenge facing operations managers.

2.2 PRODUCTIVITY MEASUREMENT AND TRENDS

Productivity Measurement

Productivity in its broadest sense is defined as follows:

$$\text{Productivity} = \frac{\text{Outputs}}{\text{Inputs}}$$

A goal of productivity management is to make the ratio as large as practical; that would indicate the highest output return for given inputs. See the examples of outputs and inputs in Exhibit 2.2.

EXHIBIT 2.2

Examples of Inputs and Outputs Used in Productivity Measurement

Outputs	Inputs
Number of satisfied customers	Hours of customer-service training
Number of printed wiring boards produced	Total costs of producing the printed wiring boards
Number of report pages typed	Secretarial hours

Outputs represent desired results. Inputs represent the resources used to obtain those results. In all cases, outputs and inputs must be quantifiable measures to obtain meaningful productivity ratios. However, a caveat in dealing with productivity is to avoid blind management by the numbers. Many productivity programs have failed because managers zealously strove to increase productivity ratios at the expense of effectiveness.

Effectiveness and efficiency

Effectiveness is obtaining desired results; it may reflect output quantities, perceived quality, or both. **Efficiency** occurs when a certain output is obtained with a minimum of input. Consider the output, number of report pages typed, from Exhibit 2.2. By cutting coffee breaks from the secretaries' daily routine, the number of pages (output) might increase. From the same eight-hour day, more output is achieved resulting in more efficient report production. However, the number of errors might also increase as a result of fatigue. The production system might efficiently produce ineffective reports. In order to assure that productivity measurement captures what the company is trying to do with respect to such vague issues as customer satisfaction and quality, some firms redefine productivity as follows:

$$\text{Productivity} = \frac{\text{Effectiveness}}{\text{Efficiency}} \quad \text{or} \quad \frac{\text{Value to customer}}{\text{Cost to producer}}$$

where effectiveness is doing the right things, and efficiency is doing things right.

As presented in Exhibit 2.3, productivity may be expressed as partial measures, multi-factor measures, or total measures. If we are concerned with the ratio of output to a single input, we have a *partial productivity measure*. If we want to look at the ratio of output to a group of inputs, but not all inputs, we have a *multi-factor productivity measure*. If we want to the express the ratio of all ouputs to all inputs, we have a *total measure of productivity* that might be used to describe the productivity of an entire organization, or even a nation.

A numerical example of productivity measures is presented in Exhibit 2.4. The data reflects quantitative measures of input and output associated with the production of a certain product. Notice that for the multi-factor and partial

EXHIBIT 2.3

**Examples of
Productivity
Measures**

Partial measure

$$\frac{\text{Output}}{\text{Labor}} \text{ or } \frac{\text{Output}}{\text{Capital}} \text{ or } \frac{\text{Output}}{\text{Materials}} \text{ or } \frac{\text{Output}}{\text{Energy}}$$

Multi-factor measure

$$\frac{\text{Output}}{\text{Labor + Capital + Energy}} \text{ or } \frac{\text{Output}}{\text{Labor + Capital + Materials}}$$

Total measure

$$\frac{\text{Output}}{\text{Inputs}} \text{ or } \frac{\text{Goods and services produced}}{\text{All resources used}}$$

Source: David J. Sumanth and Kitty Tang, "A Review of Some Approaches to the Management of Total Productivity in a Company/Organization," *Institute of Industrial Engineering Conference Proceedings*, Fall 1984, p. 305. Copyright Institute of Industrial Engineers, 25 Technology Park/Atlanta, Norcross, Georgia 30092.

measures it is not necessary to use total ouput as the numerator. Often it is desirable to create measures that represent productivity as it relates to some particular output of interest. For example, as shown in Exhibit 2.4, total units might be the output of interest to a production control manager whereas total output may be of key interest to the plant manager. This process of aggregation and disaggregation of productivity measures provides a means of shifting the level of analysis to suit a variety of productivity measurement and improvement needs.

Productivity Trends and Global Competition

Much of the reason for tracking productivity is to assess relative productivity growth or decline, an indicator of competitive position. Exhibit 2.5A shows the productivity growth rate for the United States, West Germany, and Japan from 1950 through 1989. This disturbing picture is mirrored by Exhibit 2.5B which displays the share of world exports of these three nations. As national productivity increases, a nation is able to provide higher quality products at lower prices than those provided by less productive nations.

The decline in export share for the United States has begun to reverse in recent years due in part to quality and productivity efforts and to a weaker dollar. Again, accepting that such factors as currency trade rates are out of the control of operations managers, the focus remains on improvement of operations. Several companies have succeeded in long-term improvement efforts; some of these companies are highlighted later in the chapter. How has the United States done in recent years in improvement efforts? Exhibit 2.6 presents the results of a survey conducted by Deloitte & Touche in 1990. Notice that United States manufacturers have given themselves overall C− scores when it comes to improvement efforts. What has caused this lack of competitiveness on the part of the United States? What can be done to improve? These are the topics of the next section.

EXHIBIT 2.4

Numerical Example of Productivity Measures

Input and Output Production Data $

Output
1. Finished units	10,000
2. Work in process	2,500
3. Dividends	1,000
4. Bonds	
5. Other income	
Total output	13,500

Input
1. Human	3,000
2. Material	153
3. Capital	10,000
4. Energy	540
5. Other expense	1,500
Total input	15,193

Productivity Measure Examples

Total measure:

$$\frac{\text{Total output}}{\text{Total input}} = \frac{13,500}{15,193} = .89$$

Multi-factor measures:

$$\frac{\text{Total output}}{\text{Human} + \text{Material}} = \frac{13,500}{3,153} = 4.28$$

$$\frac{\text{Finished units}}{\text{Human} + \text{Material}} = \frac{10,000}{3,153} = 3.17$$

Partial measures:

$$\frac{\text{Total output}}{\text{Energy}} = \frac{13,500}{540} = 25$$

$$\frac{\text{Finished units}}{\text{Energy}} = \frac{10,000}{540} = 18.52$$

EXHIBIT 2.5   **National Productivity Growth and World Export Comparisons**

A. National productivity growth

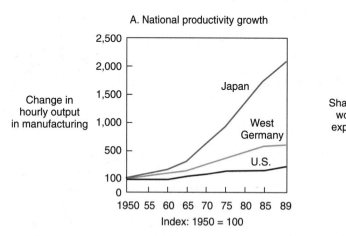

Change in hourly output in manufacturing

Index: 1950 = 100

B. World exports

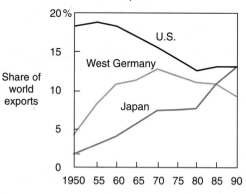

Share of world exports

Source: *Fortune* Special Issue, Spring/Summer 1991.

EXHIBIT 2.6   **Commitment to Improvement Programs over the Past Three Years: Industry Self-Assessment Report Card**

	INDUSTRY						
Program Area	Food	Basic	Fab Metal	Machine Tools	Electronic	Transp./ Auto	Aircraft/ Aerospace
Product and process	D+	C−	C−	C−	C−	C	C−
Human resources	C	C	C	C	C	C	C
Organization	C	C	C	C	C	C−	C
Supply chain	C−	C−	C−	C−	C	C−	C−
Facilities	D+	D+	D+	D+	D+	D+	D+
Overall grade	C−	C−	C−	C−	C−	C	C−

Grading scale:

A = Significant commitment   C = Moderate commitment   F = No commitment
B = Above average commitment   D = Below average commitment

Source: Deloitte & Touche, 1990.

2.3 GENERAL CAUSES AND SOLUTIONS TO THE COMPETITIVENESS PROBLEM

Taken together, productivity data and market-share loss indicate rather clearly that the United States has a serious competitiveness problem. Rationalizations abound. Some claim with a good deal of justification that manufacturing lacks the government support provided to its competitors. See, for example, the Insert on how Japan built a computer industry. Also, a large portion of the blame is frequently put on the relative strength of the dollar against foreign currencies. However, the U.S. trade deficit increased during the 1970s when the dollar depreciated by 15 percent. Thus, although the 1988 weakness in the dollar stimulated exports, long-term reliance on a cheaper dollar is a risky solution at best.

INSERT   How Japan Built a Computer Industry

In the late 1950s, Japanese government officials recognized the strategic importance of computers: their overall impact on industrial productivity and their potential spillover into related industries like telecommunications. Over time, both government and business leaders recognized the computer industry as the *driver* of other strategic areas such as artificial intelligence and aerospace—that is, as an important industry in its own right.

The government employed four public-policy directives to nurture the industry from its embryonic beginnings to a competitive juggernaut: protectionist regulation, a computer rental company, cooperative R&D projects, and heavy subsidies.

Though its power has waned in recent years, the Ministry of International Trade and Industry (MITI) has played a critical role in promoting computers.

In the early years, MITI's hand was heavy and crude. It imposed tariffs and arbitrary regulations to control foreign investment and imports. It pressured IBM to give Japanese companies access to basic patents at low rates in exchange for granting IBM permission to produce in Japan. MITI also controlled the type and volume of computers IBM produced and required the company to export a large proportion of its production.

IBM was then one of Japan's largest earners of foreign exchange. Yet the company was at the mercy of MITI bureaucrats. Strict control of foreign computers, matched with government procurement of some 20 percent to 25 percent of all Japanese-made computers, helped a domestic industry take root. Foreign market share plunged from a high of 93 percent in 1958 to 48 percent by 1965. Today it stands at about 35 percent.

While Japanese companies flourished under MITI's protective umbrella, it was clear to all that these same companies would be crushed if Japan opened its markets—as the government knew it would eventually have to do. The companies would have to be fully competitive with IBM, which meant offering rentals. So in 1961, MITI and seven computer companies established the Japan Electronic Computer Company (JECC), a computer rental company that bought systems from Japanese vendors and rented them to domestic companies at rates far below IBM's. Some $2 billion in low-interest government loans were funneled into JECC between 1961 and 1981. JECC stimulated both the supply and demand for Japanese computers.

JECC paid computer companies up front—essentially an interest-free loan—enabling them to invest heavily in future models. In the 1960s, Japan's computer makers were losing money, and private banks were unwilling to lend more. JECC's up-front cash kept the industry alive. In fact, in the 1960s, JECC fed $270 million to the six makers, almost as much as the $289 million the computer makers invested in R&D and plant and equipment during that period. JECC also set computer prices and prohibited discounts. This forced the companies to compete not on price but on technology, quality, and manufacturing.

Japanese companies still faced enormous competitive disadvantages in production scale and technology during these years. Japanese computer makers' production volume was, on any given model, 1 percent to 2 percent that of IBM, and their technology was far inferior. MITI responded by sponsoring cooperative R&D projects: the labor was divided and the results pooled. In the early 1970s, the government gave money to Fujitsu and Hitachi to develop large computers, NEC and Toshiba to work on midsize machines, and Oki and Mitsubishi to work on small machines for specialized uses. No single Japanese company had the resources to develop a full line, but by dividing up the market temporarily, the industry as a whole was able to offer a product line as broad as IBM's offerings. Similarly, MITI tried to leapfrog IBM and the VLSI project, aimed at building the technology needed to make more densely integrated chips. To avoid redundant research, MITI had three groups try a total of seven different technological approaches.

From 1961 to 1981, the Japanese government put some $6 billion into the industry for R&D, new equipment, and working capital—a huge amount relative to what the companies themselves were investing. In the 1960s, it was 188 percent of the companies' investments; from 1970 to 1975, it was 169 percent; and from 1975 to

1981, 92 percent. The timing of aid has also been critical. Generally, it has come on the heels of an IBM announcement of a new computer.

It should be stressed that MITI has only partially protected Japan's computer makers from foreign competition and has actively encouraged domestic competition. JECC helped the companies rent their computers, but it only bought computers that users requested; it forced computer companies to be responsive to the market.

Finally, subsidized R&D was tied to performance. If a company failed to commercialize a project's results or became uncompetitive, it could expect to be excluded from the next project. And companies were pushed to do risky research they would otherwise have avoided (the VLSI project, for example). The government helped the companies advance in this area but left them to compete in commercializing R&D and going to market. For every company there is a time to compete and a time to cooperate. That is the lesson worth learning.

Source: Charles H. Ferguson, "Computers and the Coming of the U.S. Keiretso," *Harvard Business Review,* July–August 1990, p. 65.

Some say that reliance on manufacturing is outdated and given our shift to services, there *is* no problem. And, indeed, exported services have produced a surplus in the trade-balance equation. However, even here, the trend has been moving toward a deficit. While business services do not constitute all services, they do include the major services traded in international markets, such as travel, transportation (both passenger and cargo), construction, engineering, consulting, banking, communications, and insurance.

Moreover, those who see a shift to the service economy as a salvation miss two crucial points. First, service and manufacturing are linked. Many services are purchased by manufacturing firms, for example, advertising, legal, health care, and accounting services. The United States cannot be supported only by a strong service sector. Second, although foreign purchase of services is high at the present time, it is naive to believe that foreign manufacturers and the societies that are developing around them will forever rely on U.S. services. Japan is building a strong financial base that is already competing with the United States in both the world and domestic marketplaces. For example, the 10 largest banks (in asset base) in the world are Japanese-owned. In fact, the United States has no institutions in the top 25, with Citibank, the nation's largest, having fallen from 17th in 1986 to 28th (according to a survey published in the *American Banker,* July 1988).

Another rationalization for the disappointing performance of the United States in the global marketplace is that the poor performers are just isolated industries and that overall performance is what really matters. This might be true; a dollar's worth of exported wheat has the same value as a dollar's worth of electronics. Unfortunately, the poor performance is not isolated in just a few industries. Portfolio theory has taught us the benefits of diversification. The United States needs a diversified picture in exports, and an increasing number of U.S. goods are not competitive.

U.S. business leaders and policymakers have been slow to recognize that the superiority of industry cannot be taken for granted. The global marketplace is a reality, and we are not competitive. According to the MIT Commission on Industrial Productivity, there are five basic causes of this:

1. American business decisions have been frequently characterized by *short time horizons,* and a related tendency to give excessive weight to financial relative to other criteria. This preoccupation with short-term financial results has had among its consequences a lack of staying power on the part of affected firms, reflected in underinvestment in R&D [research and development] and the physical and human capital needed to maintain technological leadership in a field once the first big returns have been captured. A related tendency has been to diversify away from established businesses in which expertise has been accumulated over a long period into activities that are more profitable in the short term.

2. *Strategic weaknesses* among American companies have arisen particularly as a consequence of parochial attitudes, which have frequently led these firms to pay insufficient attention to the capabilities and intentions of foreign competitors, and to the opportunities presented by foreign markets. Intensifying international competition has forced U.S. companies in a broad range of industries to become less insular, but many firms still seem to be poor imitators even when imitation would be advantageous. Neglect of the manufacturing function relative to other functional areas has been another area of strategic weakness. Despite the strategic benefits conferred by manufacturing excellence, many firms have underinvested in both the human and physical capital needed to build up and sustain a competitive manufacturing capability.

3. *A lack of cooperation* in individual and organizational relationships within and among U.S. firms has been another key barrier to improved productivity performance. Within firms there are often organizational "walls" separating product design, process design, manufacturing, marketing and R&D; and individuals, often highly trained professionals, have frequently been unable to work in teams. Decisions which should have been unified have instead been subdivided and made sequentially, resulting in delay and inefficiency. Similarly, arms-length contractual relationships with a minimum of information flow between the parties have typically been favored over long-term, cooperative relations between companies and their suppliers. As a result, feedback about market preferences has been inhibited and the introduction of new product and process technologies impeded. Very often the obstacles to closer cooperation seem to have resulted from an excessively narrow or short-term perception of self-interest. In some cases the problem has been aggravated by excessive specialization and compartmentalization of individual and departmental functions.

4. *Weaknesses in human resource management and organization* have prevented the full benefits of technical change from being realized. Firms have tended to view labor more as a cost factor to be minimized than as a productive, evolving resource. The importance of a well-trained, well-motivated, and adaptable work force to firm performance has frequently been underestimated.

5. The commission has also found evidence of *recurring weaknesses in technological practice.* While U.S. companies in many industries have made key technological advances, weaknesses in designing simple, reliable, and manufacturable products, failures to build quality into products at the design stage, weaknesses in the design of

manufacturing processes and in production operations, and a related tendency to overinnovate on product but underinnovate on process have often led to a loss of market position, or in some cases an inability to establish one. The inventiveness of American industry has rarely been in question. But technical abilities to reduce new concepts to commercial practice quickly and efficiently, and in embodiments that are responsive to customer demands, have fallen behind international standards of best practice in a number of industries.[1]

The solutions to the competitiveness problem appear to lie in reversing the attitudes and strategies enumerated in the MIT Commission report. That is,

1. Place less emphasis on short-term financial payoffs and invest more in R&D.

2. Revise corporate strategies to include responses to foreign competition. This in turn calls for greater investment in people and equipment to improve manufacturing capability.

3. Knock down communication barriers within organizations and recognize mutuality of interests with other companies and suppliers (the former relative to international competition, in particular).

4. Recognize that the labor force is a resource to be nurtured, not just a cost to be avoided.

5. Get back to basics in managing production operations. Build in quality at the design stage. Place more emphasis on process innovations rather than focusing sole attention on product innovations.

In sum, we must become better at managing our productive capabilities in all dimensions—in strategy and in the five P's of operations: people, plants, parts, processes, and planning and control systems.

2.4 PRODUCTIVITY AND COMPETITIVENESS

"The Productivity Paradox," an article written by Wickham Skinner, discusses the causes of decline in competitiveness in a number of American manufacturing companies.[2] In the late 1970s and early 1980s, major U.S. industries experienced a loss of market share in worldwide markets. To regain their competitive edge, many companies embarked headlong into productivity improvement programs.

One manufacturing company, for example, appointed a corporate productivity manager, established productivity committees, carried out operations analyses to improve efficiency levels and simplify jobs, retrained employees,

---

[1] Lester Thurow et al., "Interim Results of the MIT Commission on Industrial Productivity," AAAS Annual Meeting, Boston, February 15, 1988.

[2] Wickham Skinner, "The Productivity Paradox," *Harvard Business Review* 64, no. 4 (July–August 1986), pp. 55–59.

streamlined work flow, and installed a computerized production control system. The result was that productivity increased only 7 percent over three years, while profits remained low and market share continued to decline.

The reason for this poor competitive performance, according to Skinner, was the company's focus on cost-cutting techniques and conventional productivity measures. Like many U.S. manufacturers, they looked only at short-term results and failed to plan strategically for the long-term results. They targeted direct costs, and therefore direct labor, as the element to control. They saw investing in capital as a means to save on labor, rather than as a means for enhancing production capabilities. Like many other U.S. manufacturing concerns, they overlooked the fact that laying off workers to enhance productivity figures came at the expense of quality and flexibility.

Skinner argues that a better "productivity" strategy is to invest in capital equipment to improve product quality and responsiveness to the market. By focusing on high quality, scrap and rework are reduced and low costs usually follow. In any event, productivity programs per se have fallen into disrepute as *the* solution to competitiveness problems.

2.5 COMPETITIVE PRIORITIES

In the preceding section, we discussed the MIT Commission's priorities for becoming competitive as a nation in manufacturing. In this section, we present **competitive priorities of manufacturers:** what manufacturing executives themselves see as priorities for their firms.

In a 1988 survey by Boston University, senior manufacturing executives were asked to rate the importance of 11 designated manufacturing capabilities. The ranking of these capabilities is shown in Exhibit 2.7. The relative change of eight of these capabilities since 1984 is displayed in Exhibit 2.8.

Conformance quality tops the list of capabilities important to U.S. manufacturing managers. What is top on the Japanese manager's list? Price. The reason: The Japanese have already achieved consistent conformance quality and are looking at the next level of challenge—low prices. Also of interest is the increasing attention being paid to time-based capabilities (Exhibit 2.8). Customers want to be reponsively provided with a variety of products and order volumes. In addition, they increasingly expect service along with their products.

2.6 MEETING THE COMPETITIVE CHALLENGE

There are many examples of United States firms that have risen to the competitive challenge. Monroe Auto Equipment, for example, has succeeded at producing such high-quality shock absorbers that one of its customers, Toyota of Japan, recently gave an appraisal of "defects—zero" in a shipment

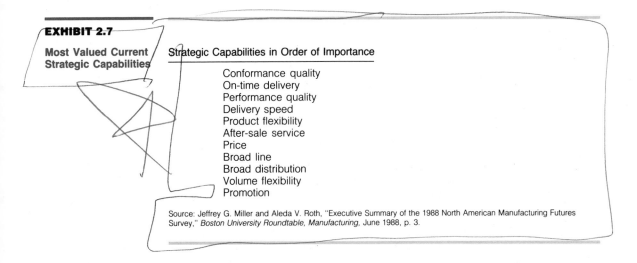

EXHIBIT 2.7

Most Valued Current Strategic Capabilities

Strategic Capabilities in Order of Importance

Conformance quality
On-time delivery
Performance quality
Delivery speed
Product flexibility
After-sale service
Price
Broad line
Broad distribution
Volume flexibility
Promotion

Source: Jeffrey G. Miller and Aleda V. Roth, "Executive Summary of the 1988 North American Manufacturing Futures Survey," *Boston University Roundtable, Manufacturing,* June 1988, p. 3.

EXHIBIT 2.8

Time-Based Capabilities Are Becoming More Important

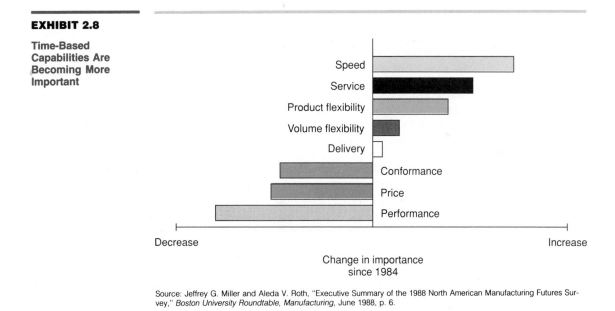

Source: Jeffrey G. Miller and Aleda V. Roth, "Executive Summary of the 1988 North American Manufacturing Futures Survey," *Boston University Roundtable, Manufacturing,* June 1988, p. 6.

of 60,000 shocks. Exhibit 2.9 illustrates how a number of companies are improving the time they take to get their new products to market.

The Insert describes how Compaq Computer managers focus on quality through and with their suppliers and even with their competitors to maintain and enhance the timing, quality, and marketability of their products.

EXHIBIT 2.9

Shortening Product Cycle Times

Company/Product	Product Cycle Time Reduction
General Motors	
New Buick model	60 to 40 months
Hewlett-Packard	
Computer printer	52 to 24 months
IBM	
Personal computer	48 to 13 months
Honeywell	
Thermostat	48 to 12 months
Ingersoll Rand	
Air grinder	42 to 12 months
Warner Electric	
Clutch brake	36 to 10 months

Source: Data from *Developing Products in Half the Time* by Donald Reinersen and Preston Smith (New York: Van Nostrand Reinhold, 1990), reported in *Boardroom Reports,* June 15, 1991, p. 7.

INSERT   Compaq Computer

Swaying from the ceiling at its Houston factory is a white banner that reads:
WE AT COMPAQ COMPUTER ARE ABSOLUTELY COMMITTED TO PROVIDE DEFECT-FREE PRODUCTS AND SERVICES TO OUR CUSTOMERS.

The message jibes with what one sees below: a sparkling assembly line, surrounded by potted ficus trees and ferns, washed with light from vast skylights, that looks more like an expensive health club than a factory. Founded in 1982, the company has its ideal inscribed in its name, an amalgam of the words *computer, compact,* and *quality.*

A maker of IBM-compatible PCs as well as ultrafast computers that manage data on office networks, Compaq has grown into an 11,800-employee business that last year earned $455 million on $3.6 billion in sales. It commands 20 percent of the world PC market, compared with 25 percent each for IBM and Apple Computer, and has almost no foreign rivals, except in the fast-growing field of laptop PCs. Still, competition is ferocious—fighting for sales, Compaq cut prices on its computers this spring as much as 34 percent and warned that second-quarter earnings would drop 80 percent.

Part of Compaq's success derives from its speed at offering the latest processor chips, disk drives, and display screens in its products. Yes, even faster than IBM. A major challenge, says CEO and co-founder Rod Canion, is to keep a breakneck pace of innovation across burgeoning product lines—nine new ones last year alone.

When the company was small, speeding products to market seemed a breeze. Today Compaq tries to maintain its entrepreneurial edge through small product-development teams that include marketers, designers, engineers, and manufacturing experts. Rather than moving a new computer step by step from drawing board to the factory, explains Canion, "the secret is to do all things in parallel."

Compaq's greatest advantage, Canion believes, is that it buys most components rather than making them itself: "Vertical integration is the old way of doing things. The way to succeed in the 1990s is to be open to technology from anywhere in the world." (Japanese competitors, such as Toshiba, continue to make nearly all their components.)

When Compaq needed a hard disk drive for its first laptop in 1986, it considered building one itself. Instead, it helped finance Conner Peripherals, a Silicon Valley startup with a disk drive already under way. "We worked so closely with Conner that they were literally an extension of our design team," says Canion. "We got all the benefits but weren't tied down. If another company had come along with a better drive, we'd have bought from them as well."

In March [1991], Compaq began a nervy foray beyond the realm of PCs into the $7.5-billion-a-year market for powerful desktop workstations used primarily by scientists and engineers. Rather than attacking market leaders Sun Microsystems and Hewlett-Packard head-on, Compaq assembled more than a dozen hardware and software companies, including Microsoft and Digital Equipment Corp., in an alliance. The group aims to win by defining a new technical standard for high-speed desktop computing, much like the IBM standard in PCs. Any workstation designed in accordance with the standard would work with any other. That would free customers to buy the latest, fastest machine without fear of being wedded to a single manufacturer.

Industry experts think rivalry among participants may tear the alliance apart. Observes Dick Shaffer, editor of *Computer Letter:* "All the participants are entrepreneurial companies with big egos." The group's prospects may not become clear until late next year, when Compaq and other members are due to roll out the new computers and software. If the products all work together, Compaq's workstation could be a winner. If not, says Stewart Alsop, publisher of *PC Letter,* Compaq may have to lower its sights: "As a $3.6 billion company, Compaq can't keep up a high rate of growth anymore just by building PCs."

Source: "The New American Century," *Fortune,* Special Issue, Spring/Summer 1991, p. 27.

2.7 MANUFACTURING OPERATIONS' ROLE IN CORPORATE STRATEGY

To achieve success in the global marketplace, a manufacturing firm must have an appreciation of the part operations plays, how it fits into a corporation, and the unique capabilities it brings to supporting and influencing the corporation's overall strategic goals. In the competitive environment that exists today, no business can afford to not use all its resources. If the operations function is not allowed to contribute—or, put more strongly, not expected to contribute—to the development of the goals of the company, there is not much hope for long-term success.

Steven Wheelwright and Robert Hayes have described **four stages of manufacturing operations strategic role** in the overall support of corporate

EXHIBIT 2.10

**Stages in Operations
Manufacturing
Strategic Role**

Stage 1	Minimize manufacturing's negative potential: "internally neutral"	Outside experts are called in to make decisions about strategic manufacturing issues. Internal, detailed management control systems are the primary means for monitoring manufacturing performance. Manufacturing is kept flexible and reactive.
Stage 2	Achieve parity with competitors: "externally neutral"	"Industry practice" is followed. The planning horizon for manufacturing investment decisions is extended to incorporate a single business cycle. Capital investment is the primary means for catching up with competition or achieving a competitive edge.
Stage 3	Provide credible support to the business strategy: "internally supportive"	Manufacturing investments are screened for consistency with the business strategy. A manufacturing strategy is formulated and pursued. Longer-term manufacturing developments and trends are addressed systematically.
Stage 4	Pursue a manufacturing-based competitive advantage: "externally supportive"	Efforts are made to anticipate the potential of new manufacturing practices and technologies. Manufacturing is involved "up front" in major marketing and engineering decisions (and vice versa). Long-range programs are pursued in order to acquire capabilities in advance of needs.

Source: Reprinted by permission of the *Harvard Business Review*. An exhibit from "Competing through Manufacturing" by Steven C. Wheelwright and Robert H. Hayes (January/February 1985). Copyright © 1985 by the President and Fellows of Harvard College; all rights reserved.

goals. Top management and production managers view the decisions and choices that must be made in these stages very differently. A summary of these stages is found in Exhibit 2.10.

Stage 1: Internally neutral.   Manufacturing operations capability is viewed as the result of a few simple decisions about capacity, location, technology, and vertical integration. Typically, top management makes these decisions with the aid of consultants. The company's own production staff handles only day-to-day, "get-the-product-out-the-door" decisions. The workers and managers in the operations departments tend to be low-skilled. There is constant performance measurement because top management wants to be aware of any variance quickly to take corrective action. Operations' potential negative impact needs to be minimized. Innovation in process technology is very slow. Management takes few investment risks in the manufacturing area.

Stage 2: Externally neutral.   This stage is seen in manufacturing-intensive organizations or America's smokestack industries, such as steel. Here operations is viewed as relatively standardized and unsophisticated. Investment in process technology is made only when competitors make changes. Top management is most concerned with decisions about resource allocation (capital investments), with primary consideration to economy-of-scale criteria. In acquiring new technologies, parity with competitors is sought and new technologies are purchased rather than developed. America's failing smokestack industries and the loss of markets to foreign competition are evidence of the effectiveness of this stage.

Stage 3: Internally supportive.   In this stage—a considerable change from the neutrality of the preceding stages—all the manufacturing operations decisions are used to support corporate strategy. The operations staff is given the authority to make decisions, and those decisions are expected to be consistent with overall goals. The corporate strategy is translated into terminology that is meaningful to manufacturing. A longer-term, creative view of the operations function is taken, but only as long as the creative direction is consistent with already existing strategy.

Stage 4: Externally supportive.   In this stage, operations is expected not only to support corporate strategy but also to contribute to its development. The operations function gives the company its competitive advantage, such as low cost or high quality. The scope of decisions is long-term. Investment is made not only in the capital resources but also in work force and systems.

In a true Stage 4 company, the operations function, like all other business functions, takes a proactive role. The formal and informal communication between finance, marketing, accounting, personnel, and other functions is considerable. There is a horizontal structure, with no one function being more important than another.

2.8 OPERATIONS' ROLE IN SERVICE FIRM COMPETITIVENESS

The competitiveness of a service firm is generally *more* dependent on the strength of its operations capabilities than is a manufacturing company. That is, a manufacturing company may be outstanding in its design capabilities but only so-so in its operations, yet still be a market leader. Such is not the case in services where the operations activities constitute all or part of the product. (See Chapter 3 for an elaboration on this point.) This inseparability of product from process means that service firm competitiveness and operations competitiveness are always closely linked. The nature of this linkage relative to operations strategy and philosophy is shown in the four-stage model given in Exhibit 2.11.

EXHIBIT 2.11 Stages of Service Firm Competitiveness

SERVICE DIMENSIONS

Stage	Service Quality	Back Office	Customer	Introduction of New Technology	Work Force	First-Line Management
I. Available for service	Subsidiary to cost: ■ High variability	Counting room	Satisfy unspecified customer at minimum cost	When necessary for survival: ■ Under duress	Negative constraint	Controls workers
II. Journeyman	Attempts to identify and meet customer expectations: ■ Consistent on one or two key dimensions	Contributes to service; plays important role in total service: ■ Given attention, but still a separate role	Market segment whose basic needs are understood	When justified by cost savings	Efficient resource; disciplined (follows procedures)	Controls process
III. Distinctive competence achieved	Exceeds customer expectations: ■ Consistent on multiple dimensions	Equally valued with front office; plays integral role	Collection of individuals whose various needs are understood	When promises to enhance service	Adaptive—permitted to select among alternative procedures	Listens to customers; coaches/facilitates workers
IV. World-class service delivery	Raises customer expectations; seeks challenges: ■ Continuous improvement	Proactive—develops own capabilities, generates opportunities	Source of stimulation, ideas, and opportunity	Source of first-mover advantages, creates ability to do things competitors can't do	Innovative—creates procedures	Listened to by top management as source of new ideas; mentors workers to enhance career growth

Source: R. B. Chase and R. H. Hayes, "Beefing-Up Operations in Service Firms," *Sloan Management Review*, Fall 1991, pp. 17–28.

INSERT   **Four Stages of Service Firm Competitiveness**

Stage	Characteristics
I. Available for service	▪ Firm survives for reasons other than performance (e.g., a government agency) ▪ Operations reactive, at best
II. Journeyman	▪ Firm neither sought out nor avoided ▪ Operations reliable but uninspired
III. Distinctive competence achieved	▪ Firm sought out based on reputation for meeting customer expectations ▪ Operations continually excels, reinforced by management and systems supporting intense customer focus
IV. World-class service delivery	▪ Firm name synonymous with service excellence; exceeds customers' expectations, delighting rather than satisfying; leaves competitors in the dust ▪ Operations is quick learner, fast innovator; masters every step of service delivery process; provides capabilities superior to competitors

Source: R. B. Chase and R. H. Hayes, "Beefing-Up Operations in Service Firms:, *Sloan Management Review,* Fall, 1991, pp. 17–28.

The first column of the exhibit lists four proposed stages of service firm competitiveness (defined in the Insert). Across the top are the major service dimensions that operations executives must address in strategy development. The entries in the table reflect our interpretation of the views held by senior management of companies that fit into each stage.

Some additional comments about the framework: First, the stage attained by any given firm is a composite. Every service delivery system embodies a unique set of choices about service quality, work force policies, and so forth. A company may be at a different stage for a given dimension, or have service units that are further or less advanced than others. What determines a firm's overall stage is where the balance falls along these different dimensions— where, in a sense, the firm's center of gravity lies. Second, a firm can be very competitive (Stage III or even Stage IV) even if it is not outstanding on all dimensions. This could happen when it is doing an exceptional job on its critical success factors. Third, it is difficult or impossible to skip a stage in moving up the ladder. A company obviously must achieve journeyman performance before distinctive competence, and distinctive competence before becoming world class. (It is, however, possible to move through the stages relatively rapidly. For example, Scandinavian Airlines System (SAS) instituted some 120 service improvements which moved it from Stage I to Stage III within the space of a year and a half.) Finally, it is all too easy to slip back a stage. The Los Angeles Police Department (LAPD), for example, was viewed as being equivalent to a Stage III law enforcement organization before the Rodney King beating was made public.[3]

2.9   CONCLUSION

Competitiveness and productivity are what operations management is all about. Whether American industry settles for niche markets, catch-up strategies, and "hollow corporations" (manufacturing companies that don't manufacture but merely coordinate the work of other companies), or decides to get back into the production game and play it well, ultimately depends on its operations capability. The next chapter discusses the process technology that is a central part of this capability in manufacturing. Chapter 4 addresses process design issues in services.

2.10   REVIEW AND DISCUSSION QUESTIONS

1. What is productivity? Explain partial, multi-factor, and total-factor productivity.
2. What is competitiveness?
3. How can the United States become more competitive in the national and international marketplace?
4. During 1988, the dollar showed relative weakness with respect to foreign currencies, such as the yen, mark, and pound. This stimulated exports. Why would long-term reliance on a lower-valued dollar be at best a short-term solution to the competitiveness problem?
5. The MIT Commission on Industrial Productivity identified "preoccupation with short-term financial results" as one of five recurring weaknesses leading to the decline in competitiveness of U.S. industry. If you assume that every U.S. firm's existence is dependent on its financial survival, would the MIT Commission's conclusion lead to the demise of American industry?
6. You are the president of a computer chip manufacturing firm and your firm's market share is being threatened by overseas manufacturers operating at lower cost with higher-quality products. Your manufacturing plant is operating at Stage 1 as defined by the Wheelwright-Hayes model in Exhibit 2.10. Would you change the stage that manufacturing operates in? If so, which organizational and strategic changes would be needed to support your decision?

---

[3] One of the authors of this book had the unique experience of lecturing on service quality to 100 of the LAPD's senior staff, including the chief, during the height of the King controversy.

7. Do business schools have competitive priorities?

8. Contrast the two four-stage models of manufacturing and services. What parallels and differences do you see relative to the role of operations in the two models?

2.11 PROBLEMS

1. A furniture manufacturing company has provided the following data. Compare the labor, raw materials and supplies, and total productivity of 1987 and 1990.

		1987	1990
Output:	Sales value of production	$22,000	$35,000
Input:	Labor	10,000	15,000
	Raw materials and supplies	8,000	12,500
	Capital equipment depreciation	700	1,200
	Other	2,200	4,800

2. Two types of cars, X and Y, were produced by a car manufacturer in 1990. Quantities sold, price per unit, and labor hours follow. What is the labor productivity for each car? Explain the problem(s) associated with the labor productivity.

	Quantity	$/Unit
X Car	4,000 units sold	$8,000/car
Y Car	6,000 units sold	$9,500/car
Labor, X	20,000 hours	$12/hour
Labor, Y	30,000 hours	$14/hour

3. Exhibit 2.4 illustrates various productivity measures. Calculate human and capital partial and multifactor productivity measures for output measured as work in process plus finished unit.

4. A U.S. manufacturing company operating a subsidiary in an LDC (less developed country) shows the following results:

	U.S.	LDC
Sales (units)	100,000	20,000
Labor (hours)	20,000	15,000
Raw materials (currency)	$ 20,000	FC 20,000
Capital equipment (hours)	60,000	5,000

a. Calculate partial labor and capital productivity figures for the parent and subsidiary. Do the results seem misleading?

b. Now compute multi-factor labor and capital productivity figures. Are the results better?

c. Finally, calculate raw material productivity figures (units/$ where $1 = FC 10). Explain why these figures might be greater in the subsidiary.

2.12 CASE: LIFE IN A SOVIET FACTORY

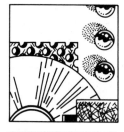

"President Bush should just order some American companies to give us products to make. We want to work, but we need products. The West has plenty of new products. Why can't we make some of them?" The question comes from Mr. Valery Lafazan, a burly man with a large black moustache, who is the chief of welding at the Tula Combine Factory. He is not angry, but genuinely puzzled.

Told that neither Mr. Bush nor any other Western leader could tell companies to do any such thing, Mr. Lafazan simply cannot believe it. What about the embargo against Iraq? If Mr. Bush can order American companies to stop doing business with Iraq, surely he can tell them to do business with a factory in Tula? "We don't want charity. But we need help. And we won't be able to forget that no one in the West was willing to lend us a hand." he says darkly.

Thus runs a typically unsettling conversation with a senior manager at the combine-harvester factory in Tula, a city 150 miles south of Moscow. The factory's managers are struggling to keep production going amid the growing chaos of the Soviet economy, while trying to fathom what will be expected of them when the long-promised free market arrives.

* * * * *

Mr. Lafazan's factory is typical of tens of thousands of middle-ranking enterprises in the Soviet Union. In recent years a team of managers in their 30s and 40s have taken over from the geriatric leadership of the past. The top two managers have been elected by the 11,000-strong work force (4,000 of whom are managers and office workers). The officials whom they, in turn, have appointed to senior posts seem as committed to their jobs as any workaholic in the West. They regularly put in 12-hour days and then plough through paperwork on the weekend.

* * * * *

A Typical Day

Like commuters everywhere, most of the workers are half-asleep as they pass the factory's clinic, hairdresser, and clothing shop. It is cold and there is mud everywhere. Office workers and factory hands alike shuffle through the gates under the suspicious eye of a guard, who checks everyone's identity. Gigantic propaganda posters still greet the workers inside, exhorting them to fulfill the plan, but their heroic messages are now faded and streaked with grime.

Mr. Lafazan arrives at 8 A.M., still groggy. He was at the factory until past midnight the evening before, trying to sort out a problem on the night shift. He perks up after switching on the intercom. Every morning and evening the factory's 30 top managers hold an hour-long meeting by intercom to resolve production problems. Managers in offices scattered all over the sprawling

Source: Adapted from "Life in a Soviet Factory," *The Economist*, December 22, 1990, pp. 21–23.

complex of buildings argue, complain, or defend themselves into a small box on their desk while the discussion is refereed by a dispatcher. As these voices drone on, visitors begin to wander into Mr. Lafazan's office, seemingly at random. Informality reigns; subordinates, workers, or officials from other enterprises need no appointment to see Mr. Lafazan or any other senior manager. Larger meetings are arranged at short notice.

Throughout the morning, engineers arrive with bits of metal, blueprints, and floor plans. They invariably look to Mr. Lafazan for a solution, rarely offering one of their own. Much of this morning is devoted to a snag encountered in the design of the new welding machine, which is Mr. Lafazan's pet project. His two assistants are sullen and discouraged. Mr. Lafazan scolds, cajoles, bullies, pleads. He suggests various ways around the problem. His assistants are skeptical. They complain of a shortage of parts. Mr. Lafazan stresses that they must build a prototype before the end of the year to get any money for further development. Deadlines are being missed. He asks why these problems were not shown to him weeks ago. No one seems to share his sense of urgency.

Over the next few hours Mr. Lafazan must also deal with a number of calls about the need to send workers from the welding department to the local collective farm to help harvest the cabbage crop. A list of names is drawn up. A section chief comes in to complain that he cannot spare the people. Mr. Lafazan sympathizes; but, pounding his desk, he declares that the crop must be harvested. Every department has to take turns sending people. This may play havoc with the factory's schedules, and the workers dread spending a grim day in the cabbage fields; but if the crop rots, they could go hungry this winter. The shops in Tula are already empty and basic necessities like sugar and butter are rationed.

After much talk, a list of those going to the farm is drawn up. To set an example, Mr. Lafazan will go too. Everyone will bring his own kitchen knives to cut the cabbage. Dismayed, an engineer complains that he does not have a big enough knife. Everyone laughs.

Mr. Lafazan sets out for the factory's welding laboratory, across half a mile of mud, past hundreds of finished harvesters, weaving between warehouses and machine shops. Like factories in many places, the Tula complex is a noisy, dirty, and dreary place. But, more than most Western factories, it is clogged with boxes of parts and finished goods. The enterprise, in this nation of queues, is drowning in inventory.

The laboratory is a small building crammed with lathes, drills, and welding gear. Mr. Lafazan holds a series of meetings in the lab director's dusty office. Using a fatherly tone, he gets one worker to agree to do a welding job which the factory has offered to complete for another enterprise. The worker will get paid extra. Mr. Lafazan then explains to a small group of machinists how important it is to make the prototype of the new welding machine as quickly and accurately as possible. "Our future depends on it," he explains. Everyone nods silently.

More meetings in more offices. Then lunch in the canteen: cabbage soup, cabbage salad, meat with stewed cabbage. Mr. Lafazan wolfs his food down before rushing back to his office for an afternoon of meetings, telephone calls, and mini-crises. He is particularly frustrated at the paucity of information about other Soviet enterprises or foreign firms. He does not know where to find parts-suppliers, partners, or customers for his pet project, the new welding machine. Mr. Lafazan's telling suggestion: the government should set up one huge computer database in Moscow to keep track of all the information he needs. Asked if this might not create a shortage of the right information and a surplus of the useless sort, just as decentralisation has for most other things in the Soviet Union, he concedes that this correspondent may have a point. Shortages are something he understands.

* * * * *

The Curse of the System

In a free market the Tula factory would have some things going for it—not least the phenomenal energy and commitment of men like Mr. Lafazan. The factory management is also startlingly open and free of hierarchy. The era when Soviet factories were full of informers and spies is long gone. Subordinates argue openly with bosses. Meetings that begin with shouting frequently end in explosive mirth.

But after a lifetime in a centrally planned economy, the managers are ill-equipped for any sudden switch to a free market. Because they spend so much of their time wading through a mire of petty legalisms, they have become addicted to rules. One of the longest and liveliest meetings that your reporter attended was about petty changes to the factory's "constitution." Predictably, it ended with a telephone call to Moscow for guidance.

A perplexing interview with the factory's finance director reveals that he does not understand such basic concepts as sales, profits, or costs. He has no way of calculating these beyond what is laid down in the ministry's plan. Though he admits the factory is heavily in debt, he happily lends money to other factories below the interest rate charged by the state bank in order to help them out. When he needs cash; they do the same. The factory's debts, he explains, are a secret—because, if they were disclosed, suppliers might not extend credit to the factory. Other finance directors must simply trust him because he is "honest."

Such attitudes may seem comically wrong-headed to a Westerner, but they make perfect sense to someone reared in the Soviet system. In an economy of shortages, raw materials or finished goods are "money in the bank," capable of being bartered for anything. Real money in a real bank is virtually worthless.

Small wonder, then that the factory's managers have no clear grasp of capitalism's cut-and-thrust. They refer constantly to cooperation. The idea of competition makes them acutely uncomfortable. The idea that, in future, the

Tula factory might try to take business away from the Soviet Union's other two combine-harvester factories horrifies Mr. Klikov. These other factories are friends.

* * * * *

Asked whether the Tula factory will survive if a free market is introduced in Russia, the question strikes Mr. Logvinov as ridiculous. "Of course," he replies. "Our country needs harvesters."

QUESTION

What are your prescriptions for Mr. Lafazan given the breakup of the USSR? Should he worry about competitiveness?

2.13 CASE: SPLASH-N-WIPE MANUFACTURING

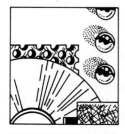

Jim Andrews, director of manufacturing at Splash-N-Wipe, sits at his desk pondering the role of his organization. Splash-N-Wipe, a producer of automobile wiper blades, was recently acquired by Robocar, a Japanese automobile manufacturer. Since the acquisition, Robocar executives have been constantly seeking information regarding the details of Splash-N-Wipe's manufacturing processes and strategies. Several months ago, Jim was given a corporate-level directive to solve any problems that might have attract the interest of Robocar's executives.

Andrews came to Splash-N-Wipe last year after a career in the military. The primary goal of the director of manufacturing, as stated by his predecessor, is to report production status to top management at staff meetings. He only dared to present good news. Bad news had to be solved at the plant through overtime and constant establishment of rush priorities. The corporate office's primary interest is production output. Robocar's interest in manufacturing processes and strategies was foreign to Andrews.

Jim Andrews was quick to implement many process and control improvements to eliminate a troublesome back order of wiper blades. He also developed a five-year manufacturing plan outlining the strategic goals of his organization. Despite the progress, Robocar's presence has increased rather than decreased.

Andrews now feels he is in a no-win situation. Splash-N-Wipe executives continue to be infuriated by the increasing level of Robocar's involvement in Splash-N-Wipe manufacturing. He cannot understand why Robocar does not back off because Splash-N-Wipe manufacturing has never been in better shape.

QUESTIONS

1. Explain Jim Andrews' dilemma in terms of the four stages in manufacturing's strategic role.
2. Why is senior management hostile toward Robocar's interest in Splash-N-Wipe's manufacturing processes and strategies?

2.14 SELECTED BIBLIOGRAPHY

Cohen, Stephen S., and John Zysman. *Why Manufacturing Matters: The Myth of the Post-Industrial Society*. New York: Basic Books, 1987.

Giffy, C.; A. V. Roth; and G. M. Seal. *Competing in World-Class Manufacturing*. National Center for Manufacturing Sciences. Homewood, Ill.: BUSINESS ONE IRWIN, 1990.

Hayes, Robert H.; Steven Wheelwright; and Kim B. Clark. *Dynamic Manufacturing: Creating the Learning Organization*. New York: Free Press, 1988.

Miller, Jeffrey G.; Jinchiro Nakane; and Thomas Vollmann. "The 1985 Global Manufacturing Futures Survey." Manufacturing Roundtable Research Series, Boston University, Boston, 1986.

Miller, Jeffrey G., and Aleda V. Roth. "Report on the 1988 North American Manufacturing Futures Survey." *Boston University Manufacturing Roundtable,* Boston, June 1988.

Productivity Perspectives. Houston, Tex.: American Productivity Center, January 1985.

Skinner, Wickham. *Manufacturing: The Formidable Competitive Weapon*. New York: John Wiley & Sons, 1985.

————. "The Productivity Paradox." *Harvard Business Review* 64, no. 4 (July–August 1986), pp. 55–59.

Starr, Martin K. "Global Production and Operations Strategy." *Columbia Journal of World Business* 19, no. 4 (Winter 1984), pp. 17–32.

————. *Global Competitiveness: Getting the U.S. Back on Track*. New York: W. W. Norton & Co., 1988.

Swaim, Jeffery C., and D. Scott Sink. "Current Developments in Firm or Corporate Level Productivity Measurements and Evaluation." *Issues in White Collar Productivity*. Atlanta, Ga.: Institute of Industrial Engineering, 1984, pp. 8–17.

Wheelwright, Steven C., and Robert H. Hayes. "Competing through Manufacturing." *Harvard Business Review,* January–February 1985.

SECTION II

PRODUCT DESIGN AND PROCESS SELECTION

The first decision in creating a production system is selecting and designing the product or service to be produced. The second decision is defining the process technology and supporting organization by which production is to be carried out. The third decision is developing a quality philosophy and integrating it into the operations of the firm. Section II considers these subjects in two main categories of industry—manufacturing and services.

Chapter 3

Product Design and Process Selection— Manufacturing

EPIGRAPH

The following poem is credited to Mr. Kenneth Lane, a design engineer at General Electric Company:

As Some Men See Us

The Designer bent across his board
Wonderful things in his head were stored
And he said as he rubbed his throbbing bean
"How can I make this thing tough to machine?
If this part here were only straight
I'm sure the thing would work first rate,
But 'twould be so easy to turn and bore
It never would make the machinists sore.
I better put in a right angle there
Then watch those babies tear their hair
Now I'll put the holes that hold the cap
Way down in here where they're hard to tap.
Now this piece won't work, I'll bet a buck
For it can't be held in a shoe or chuck
It can't be drilled or it can't be ground
In fact the design is exceedingly sound."
He looked again and cried—"At last—
Success is mine, it can't even be cast."

We rediscovered this gem cited in Elwood S. Buffa, *Modern Production Management* (New York: John Wiley and Sons, 1961), p. 343, originally from J. P. Hahir, "A Case Study in the Relationship between Design Engineering and Production Engineering," *Proceedings, 5th Annual Industrial Engineering Institute,* University of California, Berkeley–Los Angeles, 1953.

KEY TERMS

Industrial Design

Product Specifications

Continuous Processes

Repetitive Processes

Intermittent Processes

Machining Centers

Numerically Controlled (NC) Machines

Industrial Robots

Computer-Aided Design and Manufacturing
(CAD/CAM)

Flexible Manufacturing Systems (FMS)

Computer-Integrated Manufacturing (CIM)

Break-Even Analysis

Process Flow Design

Manufacturing Cycles

Business Week, April 29, 1991.

*I*n recent years, companies have been so caught up with technological efforts and advances—especially in the field of electronics—that somewhere along the line consumers were forgotten. The cover of *Business Week* magazine demonstrates some consumers' frustrations and points to the importance of good product design.

A good manufacturer's competitive weapons should consist of a range of items: the ability to generate good product ideas and to turn these good ideas into good functional designs and user-friendly operation; a thorough understanding of production flows; and the talent to choose appropriate production processes and the correct level of technology.

This chapter presents some of the basics of product design, manufacturing technology, and material flow processes. We show some product/process interrelationships and some features of automation which include CAD/CAM and flexible manufacturing systems (FMS). In this chapter's supplement we present some introductory material in computer-integrated manufacturing (CIM).

3.1 PRODUCT DESIGN AND DEVELOPMENT SEQUENCE

The three phases to designing a product are the functional (or breadboard) design, industrial (aesthetics and user oriented) design, and design for manufacturability (cost, materials, process choices, etc.).

Functional Design

The use of *breadboard* as a slang term for functional design likely originated in the electronics field when electronic components were assembled and connected to terminals attached to flat boards. These were reminiscent of boards used by grandmothers or great-grandmothers in making bread. The major intent of a functional design is to develop a working functional model of the product, without regard for what it will finally look like.

Industrial Design

Designing for aesthetics and for the user is generally termed **industrial design.** Industrial design—is probably the most abused area by manufacturers. When frustrated with products—setting the VCR, working on the car, or operating a credit card telephone at the airport—most of us have said to ourselves, "The blankety blank person who designed this should be made to work on it!" Often, parts are inaccessible, operation is overly complicated, or there is no logic to setting or controlling the unit. Sometimes even worse conditions exist: metal edges are sharp and consumers cut their hands trying to reach in for adjustments or repairs.

Many products have too many technological features—far more than necessary. The fact is that most purchasers of electronic products cannot fully operate them and only use a small number of the available features. This has occurred because computer chips are inexpensive and adding more controls has negligible cost. Including an alarm clock or a calculator on a microwave oven would be little added cost. But, do you need it? What happens when you lose the operator's manual to any of these complex devices?

So many features have been added to VCRs, for example, that they have been rendered not only unusable but also unreadable. Exhibit 3.1 shows two VCR controls. The one on the left is obviously overpowering, but in reducing the complexity of design, the pendulum seems to have swung too far in the oversimplified control shown on the right. On-screen programming has removed much of the confusion with remote controls.

Written instructions in the operating manuals are often of little help in using the electronic unit. Exhibit 3.2 is an explanation of how to set channels for a VCR. Can you figure it out?

Procedures to use technologically advanced devices are often very inadequate. For example, using a phone to call firms that force us to do our own routing through their system by way of touch tones often has two common frustrations: (1) If we make a mistake we can't backtrack; and (2) we may reach a dead end where none of the choices apply. After several minutes of button pushing on long distance and no option for a live person at the other end, we're disconnected.

One of the best-rated industrial designers is Harmut Esslinger of frogdesign studios (with a small *f*) in Menlo Park, California. Esslinger's studio has

EXHIBIT 3.1

**Simplifying a VCR
Remote Control**

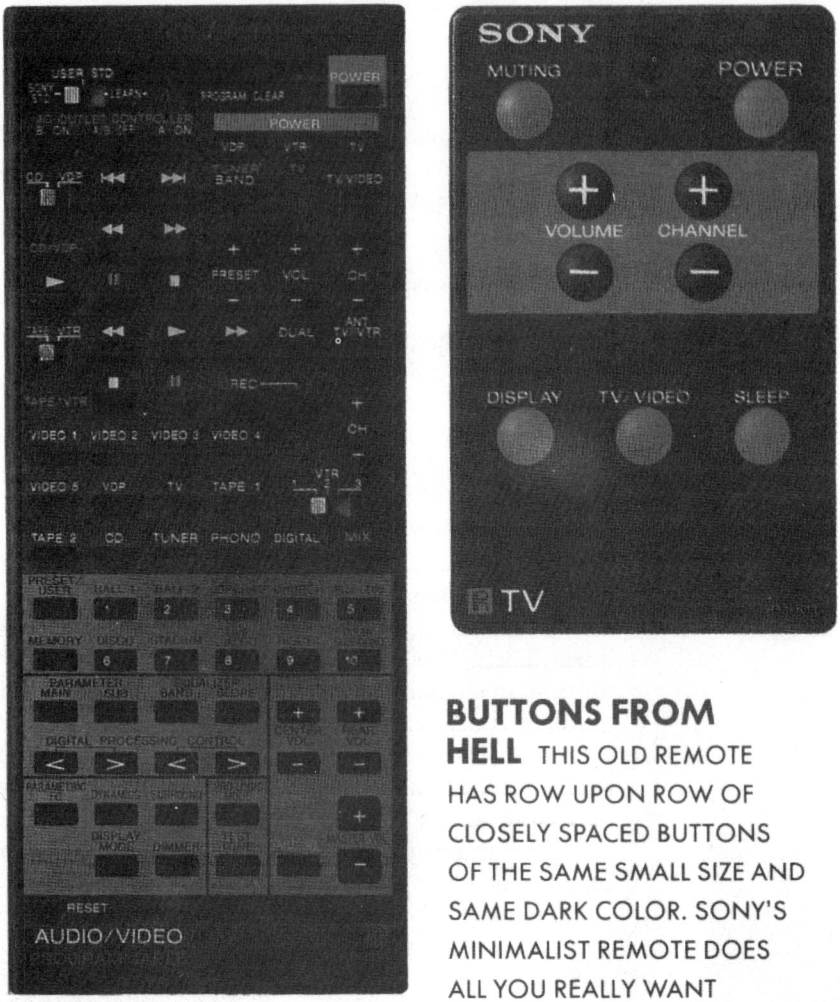

**BUTTONS FROM
HELL** THIS OLD REMOTE
HAS ROW UPON ROW OF
CLOSELY SPACED BUTTONS
OF THE SAME SMALL SIZE AND
SAME DARK COLOR. SONY'S
MINIMALIST REMOTE DOES
ALL YOU REALLY WANT

Source: John W. Verity and Jessie Nathans, "I Can't Work This Thing!" *Business Week*, April 29, 1991, p. 59.

produced designs for General Electric Company, Eastman Kodak, Company, 3M Company, Apple Computer, NeXt Computer, and Sony Corporation. Exhibit 3.3 shows some designs and Esslinger's comments. He was recently commissioned to design the new answering machine for AT&T, shown in Exhibit 3.4. Simplicity was incorporated in operating the machine. A blue button on top is the "play" button.

EXHIBIT 3.2

Directions to Set the
Channels on a VCR
(Can you follow
them?)

> After pre-tuning, if you wish to change the real channel number
> to correspond to the actual pre-tuned station, press the CH NO.
> SET button after calling up the corresponding channel position
> number on the display and enter the desired channel number
> using the READ OUT buttons ("10" and "1"). The "1" button
> changes the figures of the units digit: numerals 0 to 9 are available.
> The "10" button changes the figure of the tens digit: blank,
> numerals 1 to 9, U and C are available.

Source: John W. Verity and Jessie Nathan, "I Can't Work This Thing!" *Business Week*, April 29, 1991, p. 60.

Design for Manufacturability

In translating the functional product design into a manufacturable product, designers must consider many aspects. They can use many ways and many materials to make a product. Material choices can be ferrous (iron and steel), aluminum, copper, brass, magnesium, zinc, tin, nickel, titanium, or several other metals. The nonmetals include polymers (thermoplastics, thermosetting plastics, and elastomers), wood, leather, rubber, carbon, ceramics, glass, gypsum, concrete, as well as several others. Further, all of these materials can be formed, cut, and shaped in many ways. There are extrusions, stampings, rolling, powder-metal, forgings, castings, injection molding, along with a very large variety of machining processes.

In selecting any design for manufacturability, the designers must follow certain rules, depending on the process selected. Many of these rules of design are obvious. For example, Exhibit 3.5 shows two designs to be created through an extrusion process. In an extrusion, the procedure is similar to squeezing toothpaste from a tube. Material squeezed through a die comes out of the other side in the desired shape. To make the squeezing easier, metals are usually heated. A good design avoids sharp points and sharp corners and contains a balance in the pattern. Examples of extrusions are metal screen doors, windows and picture frames.

In designing for manufacturability, it is also desirable to minimize the number of separate parts. In electronics, manufacturers combine circuits that have been in different components into larger and larger integrated circuits. Not only does this increase speed because electrons don't have to travel as far but it also reduces the physical size and increases reliability. Designers increase reliability by eliminating the many connections necessary when circuits were in separate parts. Exhibit 3.6 shows how to reduce a simple bracket from five parts to one by focusing on the purpose of the part, the fabrication, and the assembly procedure used for its manufacture.

EXHIBIT 3.3   Some Examples of Good and Bad Product Designs

THE WORLD ACCORDING TO ESSLINGER: DESIGN DO'S AND DON'TS

Most consumers are barely aware of the products surrounding them. Tools, toys, and transportation fade into the cluttered background of the material world. But when Hartmut Esslinger looks at products, they often set off passionate reactions. To him, form follows emotion. A sampling of what Esslinger loves—and loathes:

MAZDA MIATA "I love it. It's a wonderful translation of soft shapes from the '50s to the proportions of the '90s. In the '50s, it would have been sleeker, but now it's like a chubby child—much more emotional, like the '90s."

IBM PC "Bland. Just a shame. It's not representing what its company should be. IBM's logo is classy, and it demonstrates what its products could be, but the design has no advantage over any clone."

RAY-BAN SUNGLASSES (aviator style) "They have a drama and a competence because they were invented for the pilots. Vuarnets, I think, are just a little too mean. And Cartiers—just stupid. They have no design."

BRAUN RAZOR "I use it because I'm afraid of cutting myself. It's tactile. It has good technology."

ROLEX OYSTER WATCH "It's a macho watch. It says self-confidence, like a Porsche, but if you don't have confidence, it's phony."

MAYTAG WASHERS "The company talks about quality, but the product doesn't say it. You don't want to touch it because it's so edgy and full of chrome panels."

LEVI'S 501 JEANS "The best American product ever. They're global and a symbol of freedom, ironically made for gold diggers."

1954 CADILLAC "A great statement of the fun of driving. Today's Cadillacs have no emotion. A monument to themselves. They're not dynamic, and you cannot imagine young people being joyful in them."

Source: Joan O'C. Hamilton, " Rebel with a Cause," *Business Week*, December 3, 1990, p. 135.

EXHIBIT 3.4

AT&T's 1337 Answering Machines

Source: Joan O'C. Hamilton, "Rebel with a Cause," *Business Week,* December 3, 1990, p. 133.

EXHIBIT 3.5   **Good and Bad Practice in the Design of Cross Sections to be Extruded.**

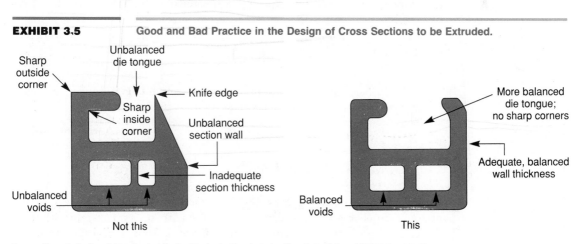

Source: James L. Bralla, ed. *Handbook of Product Design for Manufacturing* (New York: McGraw-Hill, 1986), pp. 3–10.

EXHIBIT 3.6

**Design Change to
Reduce the Number
of Parts in a Bracket**

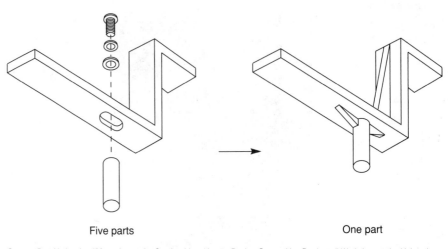

Five parts   One part

Source: Bart Huthwaite, "Managing at the Starting Line: How to Design Competitive Products," Workshop at the University of Southern California—Los Angeles, January 14, 1991, p. 7.

The output of the product design activity is the **product's specifications.** These specifications provide the basis for production-related decisions such as the purchase of materials, selection of equipment, assignment of workers, and the size and layout of the production facility. Product specifications, while commonly thought of as blueprints or engineering drawings, often take other forms ranging from precise quantitative and qualitative statements to rather fluid guidelines. Physical products tend to have traditional blueprint specifications, while a service firm's design specifications tend to be more general.

While designing for manufacturability, we must still remember to design for the consumer.

A basic rule in design is to:

Be obvious. Design a product so that a user can look at it, understand it, and figure out how to use it—quickly, and without an instruction manual.

3.2 FREQUENCY OF DESIGN CHANGES

Should products be changed every year, twice a year, every two years? How often a firm changes design depends, in large part, on its marketing strategy. An example of very frequent design changes is Sony Corporation and its Walkman cassette player. (See Exhibit 3.7.)

EXHIBIT 3.7

The Total Number of
Different Walkman-
type Cassette Players
Produced
by Several
Manufacturers

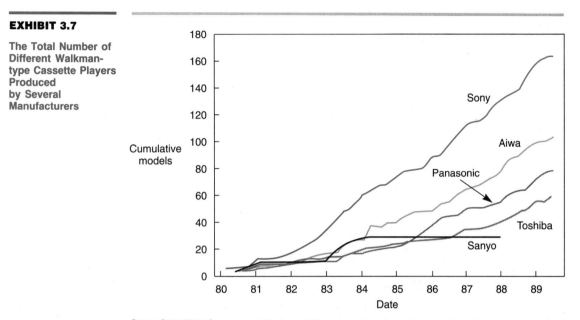

Source: Susan Walsh Sanderson and Vic Uzumeri, "Strategies for New Product Development and Renewal: Design-Based Incrementalism," Center for Science and Technology Policy, School of Management, Rensselaer Polytechnic Institute, Troy, NY 12180.

Sony introduced its Walkman to the market in 1979. It was an immediate success. Two years later, Sony brought out a new model to keep ahead of its competitors. Since 1979, the rate of new Walkman products introduced by Sony has accelerated; Sony has brought out more than 160 models of the Walkman.

Sony has relied on "design-based incrementalism." That is, product families are upgraded and enhanced throughout their life cycles. Such changes are small, frequent, and both technological and topological. *Technological innovation* is introducing new technology that enhances the function, adds higher quality, or lower production cost (for example, developing a new motor). *Topological design* is the rearrangement or remanufacture of well-understood components (for example, making smaller parts, a more compact unit, easier functioning, more appealing, or creating product distinction, etc.).

Due to its policy of incrementalization, Sony could bring out its "My First Sony" line for children in less than one year because it was built on existing products. One of the authors was at a Sony dealer recently; and the dealer stated that there were more than 30 current models of the Walkman! The result is that the average life of a Walkman model is less than 18 months. Sony's other product lines have also been very prolific.

EXHIBIT 3.8

Cost Committed and
Cost Expended from
Product Concept to
Production

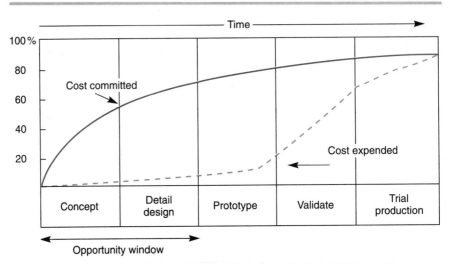

Source: Bart Huthwaite, "Managing at the Starting Line: How to Design Competitive Products," Workshop at the University/Southern California—Los Angeles, January 14, 1991, p. 3.

Opportunity for Product Design Change

Exhibit 3.8 shows the design-to-production phases. This cycle extends from concept through full production. Note that Concept and Design commits about 70 percent of the manufacturing cost while expending only about 5 percent of the total cost. Often, manufacturers spend far too little time finding all the flaws during the design stage of a new product. Therefore, prudent operation might suggest expending a bit more to assure a good sound user-friendly design and expecting to profit through reduced committed cost. Committed cost means the production costs directly resulting from the design. These include materials, processes, and so forth.

Concurrent Engineering

A major trend in manufacturing is early and continuing involvement with new products by production, materials planning, and engineering support groups to ensure that the products are effectively managed throughout their life cycles. At Hewlett-Packard, this responsibility is seen as carrying through product development, transition to manufacturing, volume production, and obsolescence (see Exhibit 3.9).

Concurrent engineering can be used interchangeably with the terms *simultaneous engineering* or *concurrent design*. It also refers to the design team often

EXHIBIT 3.9

Hewlett-Packard Life Cycle Involvement Activities

	DEVELOPMENT	TRANSITION TO MANUFACTURING	VOLUME PRODUCTION	OBSOLESCENCE	END SUPPORT LIFE
Product development	We're responsible for design of the product →————————————————————————→				
Manufacturing engineering	We're responsible for design and support of the processes ——————————→				
Materials/ materials engineering	We're responsible for sourcing/ management of vendor resources ———————→				
Production	We're responsible for building the product ————————————————————→				
Marketing	We're responsible for support of the product ————————————————————→				

used by firms. Obviously, as these terms imply, continual interaction and parallel actions are necessary throughout the entire product design to the production process. Other areas such as marketing and purchasing need to be involved and interact with all phases of design and development. Their input is critical concerning production planning, productive capacity, and the availability of parts and materials. The sequence from product design to delivery to the market place is not a consecutive series of steps. Continual interaction throughout the process assures that a well-designed product is released to the market at a good price and on time.

3.3 ORIGIN OF THE PRODUCT IDEA

Every new product starts with an idea. Exhibit 3.10 outlines the steps leading from the idea stage to actual production. While these steps are not clear-cut increments, nevertheless they do define a flow or a general sequence of phases involved in the process.

Typically, most American firms generate the majority of their product ideas by listening to their customers. Additionally, many companies encourage their own employees to generate new product ideas and to contribute to the development of those currently being investigated. At Hewlett-Packard, for example, product design engineers leave whatever they are working on out on their desks so that others may come by and tinker with their projects.

EXHIBIT 3.10   Product Design and Development Sequence

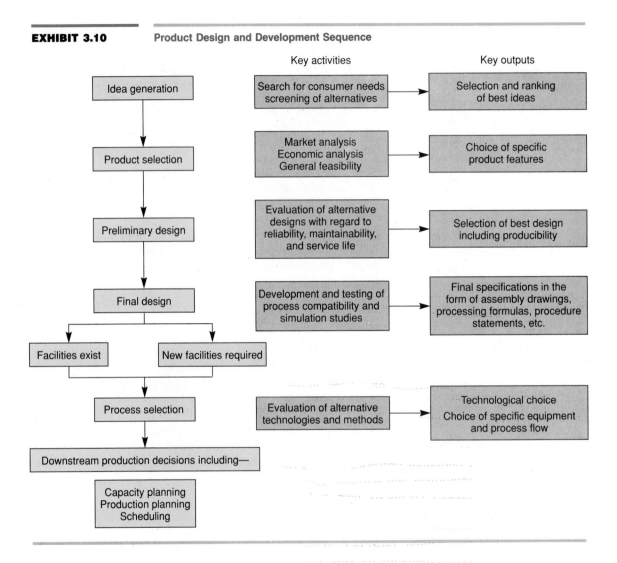

Choosing among Alternative Products

The idea-gathering process often leads to more ideas than can be translated into producible products, so a screening procedure is instituted to eliminate those ideas that clearly are infeasible. In this screening process, some ideas are rejected because they do not meet the company's objectives or its marketing, operations, or financial criteria. Marketing criteria include competition, ability to cross sell, promotional requirements, and distribution considerations. Operational criteria include compatibility with current processes, equipment, facilities, and suppliers. Financial criteria combine marketing and operational concerns and focus on risk, investment requirements, cost accounting, antici-pated profit margin, and length of life cycle.

If the product passes the screening procedure, more rigorous analysis of its cost and revenue characteristics is undertaken. Here the tools of financial analysis—break-even charts and rate-of-return calculations—come into play (see Appendix A). The major problem associated with these tools is that their value is limited to short-run evaluation of the product alternatives, because in many cases long-term developments in costs, the competition, and the econ-omy make the numerical inputs inaccurate within a year.

Financial analysis generally yields information on how many units must be sold. Meanwhile, the marketing department runs studies of potential demand to determine how many units are *likely* to be sold, and conducts marketing-mix analyses, which attempt to determine *how* they are to be sold. This process can be quite involved, however. Some recent thinking has raised the point that existing organizations and procedures stifle creativity and new-product development. We need a new way of thinking about how new-product development can best be done.

3.4 PROCESS SELECTION

Process Structures

Manufacturing operations, in the general sense of transforming some material input into some material output, can be categorized into three types of process structures.

Continuous processes
Continuous processes must be carried out 24 hours a day to avoid expensive shutdowns and startups. These are typified by *process industries* such as steel, plastics, chemicals, beer, and petroleum.

Repetitive processes
In repetitive processes, items are produced in large lots over a significant period following the same series of operations as the previous items. These are typified by *mass production* using production lines in such industries as auto-mobiles, appliances, electronic components, ready-to-wear clothing, and toys.

Intermittent processes
In intermittent processes, items are processed in small lots or *batches,* often to a customer's specifications. These are typified by *job shops,* which in turn are characterized by individual orders taking different work-flow patterns through the plant and requiring frequent starting and stopping. Common examples are repair facilities, capital-equipment manufacture, and custom clothing. Also under the heading of intermittent is *unit* production: one-of-a-kind items or items made one by one. Unit production is typified by large

turbine, airplane, and ship manufacture, and by major *projects* such as those found in construction.

Continuous-process industries *generally* provide fewer operations options because the technology is often analogous to one big machine, rather than a linkage of several individual machines. Intermittent and some repetitive processes often can be decoupled into discrete processing stages and, as a result, present management with more production alternatives. One framework for generating and evaluating production alternatives is presented in an article by Singhal, et al.[1]

Product-Process Matrix

The relationship between process structures and volume requirements is often depicted on a matrix such as the widely cited Hayes and Wheelwright product and process matrix shown in Exhibit 3.11. The way to interpret this matrix is that as volume increases and the product line narrows, (the horizontal dimension), specialized equipment and standardized material flows (the vertical dimension) become economically feasible. Since this evolution in process structure is frequently related to the product's life cycle stage (introduction, growth, and maturity), it is termed a *product-process matrix*.

The industries listed within the matrix are presented as ideal types that have found their process niche. It certainly is possible for an industry member to choose another position on the matrix, however. For example, Volvo makes cars on movable pallets rather than an assembly line. Thus, on the matrix it would be at the intersection of process stage II and product stage III. Volvo's production rate is lower than its competitors because it is giving up the speed and efficiency of the line. On the other hand, the Volvo system has more flexibility and easier quality control than the classic automobile production line. Similar kinds of analysis can be carried out for other types of process-product options through the matrix.

It may be a little easier to understand the logic of a product-process matrix if we divide it into some component parts and simplify the final result. Exhibit 3.12A shows a traditional product life cycle from product conception through product termination. Exhibit 3.12B relates the frequency of changes made in the product design to the stages of the product life cycle. Logically, most of the product changes occur during the initial stages of the life cycle, before major production starts. The product tends to go through many changes—simplification, adding features, newer materials, and so forth. The motivation here is for more performance and perhaps for a broader market. During the maturity stage of the product and during its decline, very few additional changes are made (unless the product undergoes intentional redesign which then places it on another new product cycle).

---

[1] J. Singhal, K. Singhal, and J. K. Weeks, "Long-Range Process Design and Compatability among Operations," *Management Science* 34, no. 5 (May 1988), pp. 619–32; erratum p. 1033.

EXHIBIT 3.11   **Matching Major Stages of Product and Process Life Cycles**

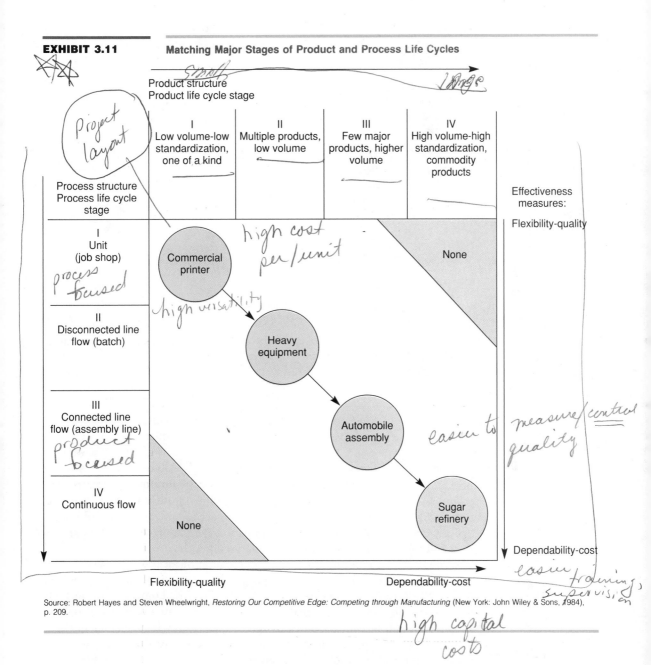

Source: Robert Hayes and Steven Wheelwright, *Restoring Our Competitive Edge: Competing through Manufacturing* (New York: John Wiley & Sons, 1984), p. 209.

Changes in the production process, as shown in Exhibit 3.12C, occur most rapidly during the early stages of production design and startup. This is where choices are made in the production layout, equipment choices, tooling, and so on. The intention here is to reduce production cost. Also, both product and process engineers work together to reduce costs and increase product perfor-

EXHIBIT 3.12   Product and Process Life Cycles

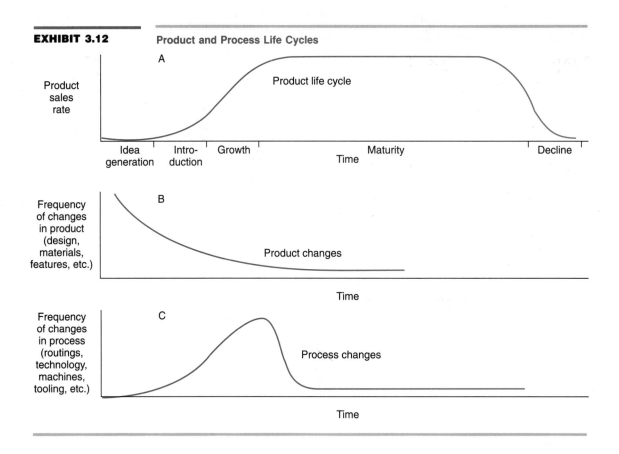

mance through joint efforts in material changes for easier manufacture, and redesign for simpler manufacturing. When full production occurs, few additional changes are made. During the termination phase, some additional process changes occur; these are due in part to switching the smaller production volumes to different equipment and facilities.

Exhibit 3.13 shows the type of production layout during the product life cycle. During the early stages when production is small (certainly during the product research and development stages), the production of the product likely takes place in a functional type layout, which we usually call the job shop layout. All similar machines and processes are grouped together and used for many different products. As production increases, machines and processes may be grouped to simplify the product flow for a particular product (flow shop), or techniques such as flexible manufacturing systems (covered later in this chapter), Just-in-Time systems (covered in Chapter 6), and assembly lines are used. Moving from the functional layout where product moves to the different required processes to an assembly line or JIT system is usually not a single large jump. The best policy is to introduce JIT and assembly lines to those portions of the production process as opportunities arise.

EXHIBIT 3.13

Production-Process Layout over the Product Life Cycle

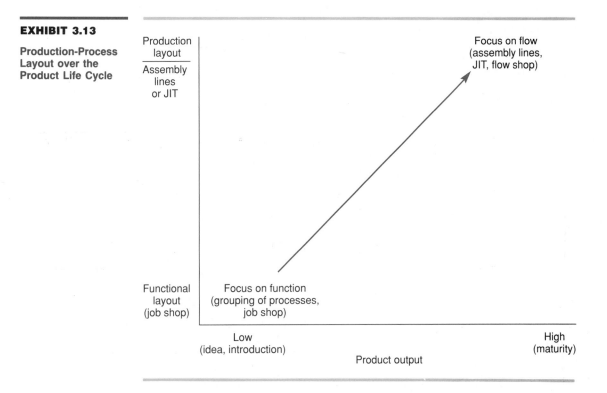

Production layout
_____
Assembly lines or JIT

Focus on flow (assembly lines, JIT, flow shop)

Functional layout (job shop)

Focus on function (grouping of processes, job shop)

Low (idea, introduction)

High (maturity)

Product output

Specific Equipment Selection

The choice of specific equipment follows the selection of the general type of process structure. Exhibit 3.14 shows some key factors that should be considered in the selection decision. Firms may have both general-purpose equipment and special-purpose equipment. For example, a machine shop would have lathes and drill presses (general-purpose) and could have transfer machines (special-purpose). An electronics firm may have a single-function test module to perform only one test at a time (general-purpose) and may have a multifunction test unit to perform multiple tests at the same time (special-purpose). As computer-based technology evolves, however, the general-purpose/special-purpose distinction becomes blurred, since a general-purpose machine has the capability to produce just as efficiently as many special-purpose ones.

Process Technology Evolution

Soon after the Industrial Revolution, machines were substituted for human labor, and mechanized technology replaced many manual tasks. As the volume of standardized products grew, it became more economical to design special-purpose machines dedicated to the production of a single part or product. Ultimately, in discrete-parts manufacturing, these machines became

EXHIBIT 3.14

**Major Decision
Variables in
Equipment Selection**

Decision Variable	Factors to Consider
Initial investment	Price
	Manufacturer
	Availability of used models
	Space requirements
	Need for feeder/support equipment
Output rate	Actual versus rated capacity
Output quality	Consistency in meeting specs
	Scrap rate
Operating requirements	Ease of use
	Safety
	Human factors impact
Labor requirements	Direct to indirect ratio
	Skills and training
Flexibility	General-purpose versus special-purpose equipment
	Special tooling
Setup requirements	Complexity
	Changeover speed
Maintenance	Complexity
	Frequency
	Availability of parts
Obsolescence	State of the art
	Modification for use in other situations
In-process inventory	Timing and need for supporting buffer stocks
Systemwide impacts	Tie-in with existing or planned systems
	Control activities
	Fit with manufacturing strategy

linked through material-handling devices. Now, both material movement and direct production can be performed automatically through automation.

Before the 1960s, the state of the art in manufacturing was the mechanized assembly line used by automobile manufacturers. Now, although many car companies still use many of the same processes, leading-edge applications of technology are found in other industries. This is particularly true in metal fabrication and electronic component manufacturing, where the objective is to approach the flexibility and speed of process industries such as chemicals and foods. Process industries are held up as a model because their processes require no hands-on production by workers. All operations are built into the machine and can be changed by turning a dial or altering a computer code.

3.5 AUTOMATION

The term *automation* is familiar to all, but a commonly agreed-upon definition still eludes us. Some authorities view automation as a totally new set of concepts that relate to the automatic operation of a production process; others view it as simply an evolutionary development in technology in which machinery performs some or all of the process-control function. Automation is a set of concepts, but it is also evolutionary in the sense that it is a logical and predictable step in the development of equipment and processes.

Some major developments in manufacturing automation include machining centers, numerically controlled machines, industrial robots, computer-aided design and manufacturing systems, flexible manufacturing systems, computer-integrated manufacturing, and islands of automation.

Machining centers not only provide automatic control of a machine but carry out automatic tooling changes as well. For example, a single machine may be equipped with a shuttle system of two worktables that can be rolled into and out of the machine. While work is being done at one table, the next part is mounted on the second table. When machining on the first table is complete, it is moved out of the way and the second part is moved into position.

Numerically controlled (NC) machines are under the control of a digital computer. Feedback control loops determine the position of the machine tooling during the work, constantly compare the actual location with the programmed location, and correct as needed. This eliminates time lost during setups, and applies to both high-volume, standardized types of products and low-volume, customized products.

Industrial Robots

Industrial robots are substitutes for human manipulation and other highly repetitive functions. A robot is a reprogrammable machine with multiple functions that can move devices through specialized motions to perform any number of tasks. It is essentially a mechanized arm that can be fitted with a variety of handlike fingers or grippers, vacuum cups, or a tool such as a wrench. Robots are capable of performing many factory operations ranging from machining processes to simple assembly.

Exhibit 3.15 examines the human motions a robot can reproduce. Advanced capabilities have been designed into robots to allow vision, tactile sensing, and hand-to-hand coordination. In addition, some models can be "taught" a sequence of motions in a three-dimensional pattern. As a worker moves the end of the robot arm through the required motions, the robot records this pattern in its memory and repeats them on command.

Robots are expensive but usually can be economically justified because production time is decreased as accuracy and consistency are increased. (See the Insert for a formula to evaluate a robot investment.) At the Fort Worth General Dynamics plant, the computerized Milicron T–3 drills holes at a rate of 24 to 30 parts per shift with no defects. A human worker can produce only six parts per shift, with a 10 percent rejection rate. Even though the robot cost $60,000, it saved the company $90,000 the first year.

As productivity increases with robots, workers can be eliminated. Current estimates set worker displacement at anywhere from 1.7 to 6.0 employees per robot; the potential is especially high in the metalworking industry. It seems

EXHIBIT 3.15

**Typical Robot Axes
of Motion**

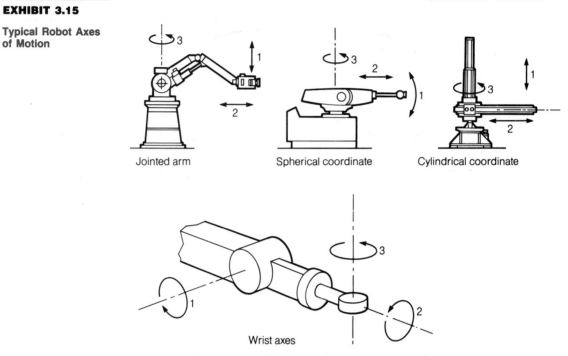

Jointed arm　　Spherical coordinate　　Cylindrical coordinate

Wrist axes

Source: L.V. Ottinger, "Robotics for the IE: Terminology, Types of Robots," *Industrial Engineering*, November 1981, p. 30. Reprinted with Permission.

just a matter of time before sophisticated robots with vision systems will be viable for assembly and sensitive-touch jobs in other industries. Some experts estimate these robots of the future could replace as many as 3.8 million workers. There are, however, some things a robot will probably never be able to do (see Exhibit 3.16).

INSERT　**Formula for Evaluating a Robot Investment**

Many companies use the following modification of the basic payback formula in deciding if a robot should be purchased:

$$P = \frac{I}{L - E + q\,(L + Z)}$$

where

P = Payback period in years

I = Total capital investment required in robot and accessories

L = Annual labor costs replaced by the robot (wage and benefit costs per worker times the number of shifts per day)

E = Annual maintenance cost for the robot

q = Fractional speedup (or slowdown) factor

Z = Annual depreciation

Example:

I = $50,000

L = $60,000 (two workers @ $20,000 each working one of two shifts; overhead is $10,000 each)

E = $9,600 ($2/hour × 4,800 hours/year)

q = + 150% (robot works half again as fast as a worker)

Z = $10,000

then

$$P = \frac{\$50,000}{\$60,000 - \$9,600 + 1.50(\$60,000 + \$10,000)} = \tfrac{1}{3} \text{ year}$$

Computer-Aided Design

One of the major contemporary approaches to the product design process is computer-aided (or -assisted) design (CAD). *CAD* may be defined as carrying out all structural or mechanical design processes of a product or component at a specially equipped computer terminal. Engineers design through a combination of console controls and a light pen that draws on the computer screen or electronic pad. Perspectives can be visualized by rotating the product on the screen, and individual components can be enlarged to examine particular characteristics. Depending on the sophistication in software, on-screen testing may replace the early phases of prototype testing and modification.

CAD has been used to design everything from computer chips to potato chips. Frito-Lay, for example, used CAD to design its O'Grady's double-density, ruffled potato chip. The problem in designing such a chip is that if it is cut improperly, it may be burned on the outside and soggy on the inside, it may be too brittle (and shatter when placed in the bag), or display other characteristics that make it unworthy for, say, a guacamole dip. However, through the use of CAD, the proper angle and number of ruffles were determined mathematically, and the O'Grady's model passed its stress test in the infamous Frito-Lay "crusher" and is now on your grocer's shelf.

CAD is now being used to custom design swimsuits. Measurements of the wearer are fed into the CAD program, along with the style of suit desired. Working with the customer, the designer modifies the suit design as it appears on a humanform drawing on the computer screen. Once the design is decided upon, the computer prints out a pattern, and the suit is cut and sewn on the

EXHIBIT 3.16

Tasks Robots Can Do and May Be Able to Do

Things Present (or Past) Robots Can Do	Things Next Generation Robots Will Be Able to Do	Things a Very Sophisticated Future Robot May Be Able to Do	Things No Robot Will Ever Be Able to Do (Probably)
Play the piano	Vacuum a rug (avoiding obstructions)	Set a table	Cut a diamond
Load/unload CNC machine tools	Load/unload a glass blowing or cutting machine	Clear a table	Polish an opal
Load/unload die casting machines, hammer forging machines, molding machines, etc.	Assemble large and/or complex parts, TVs, refrigerators, air conditioners, microwave ovens, toasters, automobiles	Juggle balls	Peel a grape
Spray paint on an assembly line	Operate woodworking machines	Load a dishwasher	Repair a broken chair or dish
Cut cloth with a laser	Walk on two legs	Unload a dishwasher	Darn a hole in a sock/sweater
Make molds	Shear sheep	Weld a cracked casting/forging	Play tennis or Ping Pong at championship level
Deburr sand castings	Wash windows	Make a bed	Catch a football or a Frisbee at championship level
Manipulate tools such as welding guns, drills, etc.	Scrape barnacles from a ship's hull	Locate and repair leaks inside a tank or pipe	Pole vault
Assemble simple mechanical and electrical parts: small electric motors, pumps, transformers, radios, tape recorders	Sandblast a wall	Pick a lock	Dance a ballet
		Knit a sweater	Ride a bicycle in traffic*
		Make needlepoint design	Drive a car in traffic*
		Make lace	Tree surgery
		Grease a continuous mining machine or similar piece of equipment	Repair a damaged picture
		Tune up a car	Assemble the skeleton of a dinosaur†
		Make a forging die from metal powder	Cut hair stylishly
		Load, operate, and unload a sewing machine	Apply makeup artistically
		Lay bricks in a straight line	Set a multiple fracture
		Change a tire	Remove an appendix
		Operate a tractor, plow, or harvester over a flat field	Play the violin‡
		Pump gasoline	Carve wood or marble
		Repair a simple puncture	Build a stone wall
		Pick fruit	Paint a picture with a brush
		Do somersaults	Sandblast a cathedral
		Walk a tightrope	Make/repair leaded glass windows
		Dance in a chorus line	Deliver a baby
		Cook hamburgers in a fast-food restaurant	Cut and trim meat
			Kiss sensuously

*Assuming the other vehicles are not robot controlled.
†Admittedly a computer could provide very valuable assistance.
‡But it could "synthesize" violin music.

Source: Robert U. Ayres and Steven M. Miller, *Robotics: Applications and Social Implications* (Cambridge, Mass.: Ballinger Publishing, 1983), p. 25.

"Seems like only yesterday it was serving drinks and doing little chores around the house."

"The Art of Product Design," HBR Photo File, *Harvard Business Review,* November–December 1990, p. 107.

spot. A good example of a CAD-designed product is Motorola's new Wrist Watch Pager (see Exhibit 3.17). In addition to receiving and holding phone number messages, the unit also tells time.

A practical limitation of CAD is the extensive programming time required to introduce all parts of a complicated product into the database program. Still, virtually every major manufacturer, from Apple to Xerox, has CAD as one of its priority areas of technical development.

Computer-aided design and manufacturing (CAD/CAM) uses a computer to join part design and processing instructions. In current CAD/CAM systems, when the design is finalized, the link to CAM is made by producing the manufacturing instructions. Because of the efficiency of CAD/CAM systems, design and manufacture of small lots can be low in cost.

Even though CAD/CAM systems are usually limited to larger companies because of the high cost, they do increase productivity and quality dramatically. More alternative designs can be produced, and the specifications can be more exact. Updates can be readily made, and cost estimates can be drawn easily. In addition, computer-aided process planning (CAPP) can shorten or in some cases eliminate traditional process planning.

Flexible Manufacturing Systems

A **flexible manufacturing system** (FMS) actually refers to a number of systems that differ in the degree of mechanization, automated transfer, and computer control. Andrew Kusiak has nicely defined and shown five systems and how they usually related to the annual production and number of different parts used.[2] These systems are the flexible manufacturing module, cell, group, production system, and line. (See Exhibits 3.18 and 3.19.)

---

[2] Andrew Kusiak, "Flexible Manufacturing Systems: A Structural Approach," *International Journal of Production Research* 23, no. 6 (1985), pp. 1057–73.

EXHIBIT 3.17

Motorola's Wrist Watch Pager

PAGER ASSEMBLY

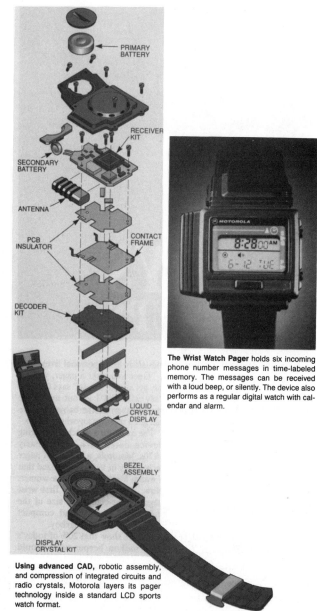

The Wrist Watch Pager holds six incoming phone number messages in time-labeled memory. The messages can be received with a loud beep, or silently. The device also performs as a regular digital watch with calendar and alarm.

Using advanced CAD, robotic assembly, and compression of integrated circuits and radio crystals, Motorola layers its pager technology inside a standard LCD sports watch format.

Source: Dana Gardner, "Tech Toys for Grownups," *Design News*, December 3, 1990, p. 64.

EXHIBIT 3.18

Relationships of
Different Classes of
FMSs, Number of
Different Parts, and
Annual Production of
Parts

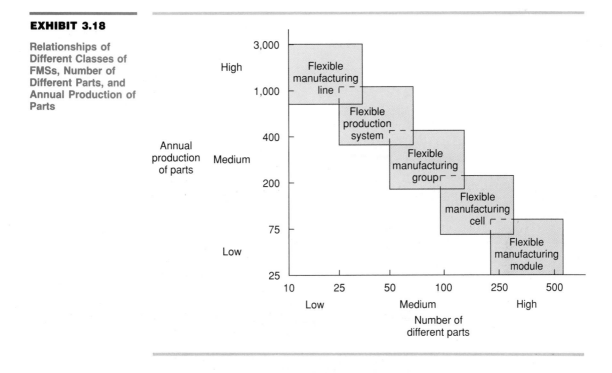

A flexible manufacturing module is a numerically controlled (NC) machine supported with a parts inventory, a tool changer, and a pallet changer. A flexible manufacturing cell consists of several flexible manufacturing modules organized according to the particular product's requirements. A flexible manufacturing group is a combination of flexible manufacturing modules and cells located in the same manufacturing area and joined by a material handling system, such as an automated guided vehicle (AGV).

A flexible production system consists of flexible manufacturing groups that connect different manufacturing areas, such as fabrication, machining, and assembly. A flexible manufacturing line is a series of dedicated machines connected by automated guided vehicles (AGVs), robots, conveyers, or some other type of automated transfer devices.

While the conventional belief is that flexible manufacturing systems are best used in low volume and with a low number of different parts, Cummins Engine Company claims a high degree of success and cost savings using FMS in high volumes.[3]

Computer-integrated manufacturing (CIM) integrates all aspects of production into one automated system. Design, testing, fabrication, assembly,

---

[3] Ravi Venkatesan, "Cummins Engine Flexes Its Factory," *Harvard Business Review,* March–April 1990, pp. 120–27.

EXHIBIT 3.19   Different Flexible Manufacturing Systems

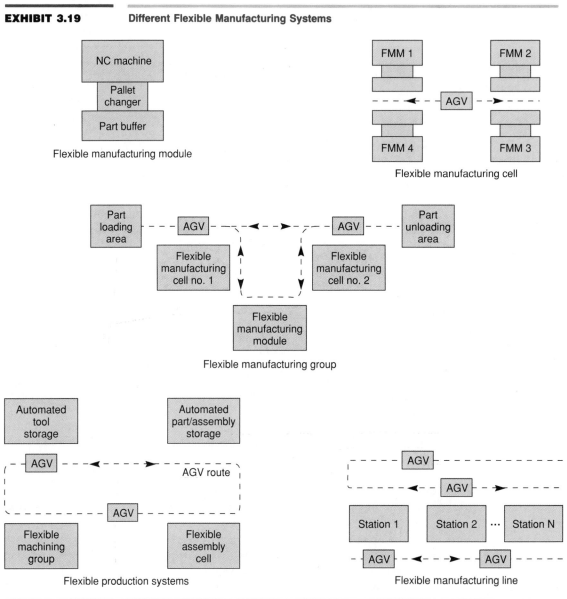

Flexible manufacturing module

Flexible manufacturing cell

Flexible manufacturing group

Flexible production systems

Flexible manufacturing line

inspection, and materials handling may all have automated functions within the area. However, in most companies, communication between departments still flows by means of paperwork. In CIM, these islands of automation are integrated, thus eliminating the need for the paperwork. A computer links all sectors together, resulting in more efficiency, less paperwork, and less personnel expense. (See the supplement to this chapter for further development of this idea.)

Islands of automation refers to the transition from conventional manufacturing to the automated factory. Typical islands of automation include numerically controlled machine tools, robots, automated storage/retrieval systems, and machining centers.

Choosing among Alternative Processes and Equipment

A standard approach to choosing among alternative processes or equipment is **break-even analysis.** A break-even chart visually presents alternative individual and relative profit and losses due to the number of units produced or sold. The choice obviously depends on anticipated demand. The method is most suitable when processes or equipment entail a large initial investment and fixed cost, and when variable costs are reasonably proportional to the number of units produced. By way of example, suppose a manufacturer has identified the following options for obtaining a machined part: It can buy the part at $200 per unit (including materials), it can make the part on a numerically controlled semiautomatic lathe at $75 per unit (including materials), or it can make the part on a machining center at $15 per unit (including materials). There is negligible fixed cost if the item is purchased; a semiautomatic lathe costs $80,000, and a machining center costs $200,000.

Whether we approach the solution to this problem as a cost minimization or as profit maximization really makes no difference, as long as the relationships remain linear; that is, variable costs and revenue are the same for each incremental unit. Exhibit 3.20 shows the break-even points for each of the processes. If demand is expected to be more than 2,000 units (point A), the machine center is the best choice since this would result in the lowest total cost. If demand is between 640 (point B) and 2,000 units, the NC lathe is the cheapest. If demand is less than 640 (between 0 and point B), the most economical course is to buy the product.

Consider the effect of revenue, assuming the part sells for $300 each. As Exhibit 3.20 shows, profit (or loss) is the distance between the revenue line and the alternative process cost. At 1,000 units, for example, maximum profit is the difference between the $300,000 revenue (point C) and the semiautomatic lathe cost of $160,000 (point D). For this quantity the semiautomatic lathe is the cheapest of the alternatives available. The optimal choices for both minimizing cost and maximizing profit are the lowest segments of lines: origin to B, to A, and to the right side of the exhibit.

EXHIBIT 3.20

Break-Even Chart of Alternative Processes

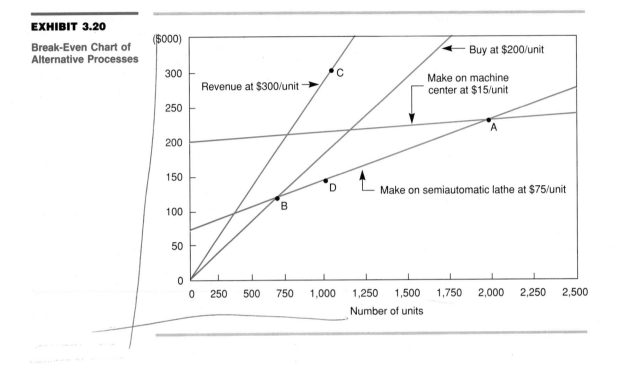

3.6 PROCESS FLOW DESIGN

Process flow design focuses on the specific processes that raw materials, parts, and subassemblies follow as they move through the plant. The most common production management tools used in planning the process flow are assembly drawings, assembly charts, route sheets, and flow process charts. Each of these charts is a useful diagnostic tool and can be used to improve operations during the steady state of the productive system. Indeed, the standard first step in analyzing any production system is to map the flows and operations using one or more of these techniques. These are the "organization charts" of the manufacturing system.

An *assembly drawing* (see Exhibit 3.21) is simply an exploded view of the product showing its component parts. An *assembly chart* (Exhibit 3.22) uses the information presented in the assembly drawing and defines (among other things) how parts go together, their order of assembly, and often the overall material flow pattern.[4] An *operation and route sheet* (Exhibit 3.23), as its name implies, specifies operations and process routing for a particular part. It conveys

---

[4] Also called a *Gozinto chart*, named, so the legend goes, after the famous Italian mathematician Zepartzat Gozinto.

EXHIBIT 3.21

Plug Assembly Drawing

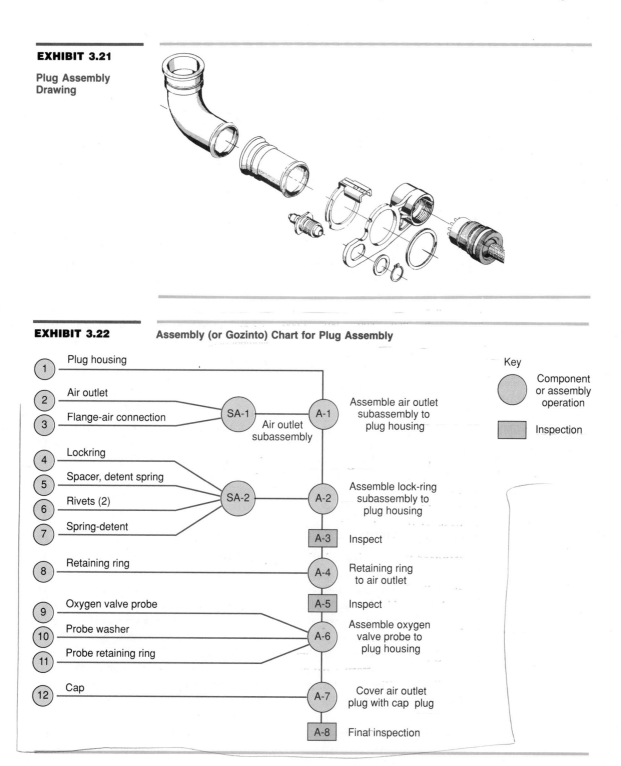

EXHIBIT 3.22   **Assembly (or Gozinto) Chart for Plug Assembly**

1 — Plug housing
2 — Air outlet
3 — Flange-air connection
SA-1 — Air outlet subassembly
A-1 — Assemble air outlet subassembly to plug housing

4 — Lockring
5 — Spacer, detent spring
6 — Rivets (2)
7 — Spring-detent
SA-2
A-2 — Assemble lock-ring subassembly to plug housing
A-3 — Inspect

8 — Retaining ring
A-4 — Retaining ring to air outlet
A-5 — Inspect

9 — Oxygen valve probe
10 — Probe washer
11 — Probe retaining ring
A-6 — Assemble oxygen valve probe to plug housing

12 — Cap
A-7 — Cover air outlet plug with cap plug

A-8 — Final inspection

Key

Component or assembly operation

Inspection

EXHIBIT 3.23

Operation and Route Sheet for Plug Assembly

			Part Name	Plug Housing		Part No.	TA 1274	

Material Specs. _____			Part Name	Plug Housing		Part No.	TA 1274
Purchased Stock Size _____			Usage	Plug Assembly		Date Issued	
Pcs. Per Pur. Size _____			Assy. No.	TA 1279		Date Sup'd.	
Weight _____			Sub. Assy. No. _____			Issued By	

Oper. No.	Operation Description	Dept.	Machine	Set Up Hr.	Rate Pc/Hr.	Tools
20	+.015 Drill 1 hole .32 -.005	Drill	Mach 513 Deka 4	1.5	254	Drill Fixture L-76, Jig #10393
30	+.015 Deburr .312 -.005 Dia. Hole	Drill	Mach 510 Drill	.1	424	Multi-Tooth burring Tool
40	Chamfer .900/.875, Bore .828/.875 dia. (2 Passes), Bore .7600/.7625 (1 Pass)	Lathe	Mach D109 Lathe	1.0	44	Ramet-1, TPG 221, Chamfer Tool
50	Tap Holes as designated - 1/4 Min. Full Thread	Tap	Mach 514 Drill Tap	2.0	180	Fixture #CR-353, Tap. 4 Flute Sp.
60	Bore Hole 1.133 to 1.138 Dia.	Lathe	H & H E107	3.0	158	L44 Turrent Fixture, Hartford
						Superspacer, pl. #45, Holder #L46,
						FDTW-100, Inser #21, Chk. Fixture
70	Deburr .005 to .010, Both Sides, Hand Feed To Hard Stop	Lathe	E162 Lathe	.5	176	Collect #CR179, 1327 RPM
80	Broach Keyway To Remove Thread Burrs	Drill	Mach. 507 Drill	.4	91	B87 Fixture, L59 Broach, Tap. .875120 G-H6
90	Hone Thread I.D. 822/.828	Grind	Grinder		120	
95	Hone .7600/.7625	Grind	Grinder		120	

such information as the type of equipment, tooling, and operations required to complete the part.

A flow process chart such as Exhibit 3.24 typically uses standard American Society of Mechanical Engineers (ASME) symbols to denote what happens to the product as it progresses through the productive facility. The symbols for the various processes are explained at the side of the chart. As a rule, the fewer the delays and storages in the process, the better the flow.

The Manufacturing Cycle

As we previously stated, interaction must continue during the product design and process selection. During the **manufacturing cycle,** the production function interacts with virtually every other function of the enterprise (see Exhibit 3.25). Because we examine the activities that take place during the cycle throughout this text, we won't explain all of them here. It is desirable at this point, however, to highlight some of the major organizational interrelationships that have an ongoing impact on production.

First, there are two engineering groups—manufacturing engineering and industrial engineering. Manufacturing engineering's major responsibilities typically include (1) advising the product design group on producibility of the product, (2) planning process flow along the lines mentioned earlier, (3) specifying the tooling and equipment required, and (4) updating the bill of materials (BOM, the listing of parts that make up the product). Industrial

EXHIBIT 3.24

Flow Process Chart of Plug Housing from Plug Assembly

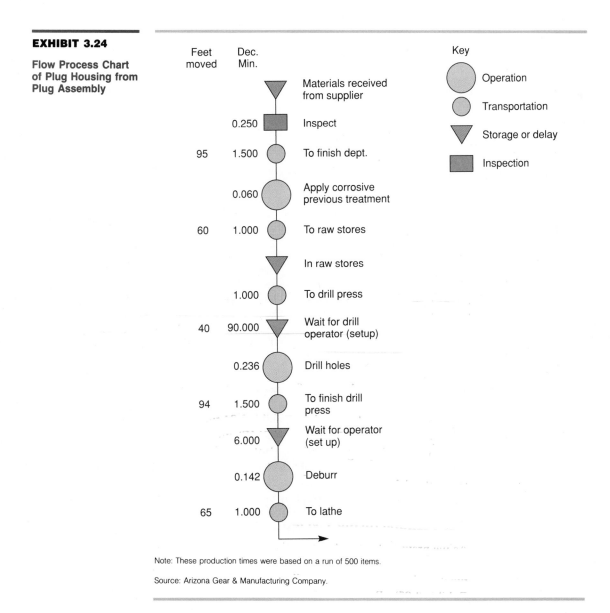

Feet moved	Dec. Min.		
		▽	Materials received from supplier
	0.250	▨	Inspect
95	1.500	◯	To finish dept.
	0.060	◯	Apply corrosive previous treatment
60	1.000	◯	To raw stores
		▽	In raw stores
	1.000	◯	To drill press
40	90.000	▽	Wait for drill operator (setup)
	0.236	◯	Drill holes
94	1.500	◯	To finish drill press
	6.000	▽	Wait for operator (set up)
	0.142	◯	Deburr
65	1.000	◯	To lathe

Key

◯ Operation

◯ Transportation

▽ Storage or delay

▨ Inspection

Note: These production times were based on a run of 500 items.

Source: Arizona Gear & Manufacturing Company.

engineering's major responsibilities typically include (1) determining work methods and time standards, (2) developing the specifics of the plant layout, (3) conducting cost and productivity improvement studies, and (4) implementing operations research projects.

Second, it is common to refer to all functions shown in the exhibit, other than sales and marketing, product design, and production per se, as manufacturing

EXHIBIT 3.25   **The Manufacturing Cycle**

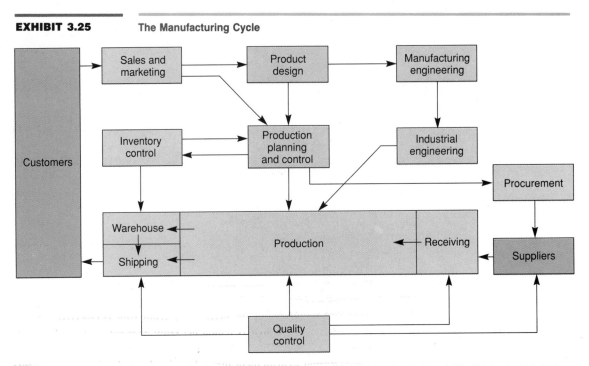

Source: Modified from Mikell P. Groover, *Automation, Production Systems, and Computer-Aided Manufacturing* (Englewood Cliffs, N.J.: Prentice Hall, 1980).

support groups. This conveys the idea that the role of these activities is, quite simply, to help in the frequently complicated task of manufacturing.

Finally, the plant manager is responsible for coordinating these groups, the production manager is responsible for coordinating the direct production work force, and, in multisite firms, the vice president of manufacturing is responsible for coordinating the manufacturing activities thoroughout the plant network.

3.7 CONCLUSION

It is becoming more and more apparent that successful manufacturing firms are not simply a collection of vaguely related activities, but rather well-integrated production machines. Indeed, just like a physical machine, each part of the manufacturing system—labor, equipment, and management—has an important role to play in achieving that success. It is also apparent that computer-based technology will be altering the ways products and factories are designed and manufacturing processes are carried out. How much of an impact such innovations will have across all industries is one of the most intriguing questions to be answered in the coming years.

3.8 REVIEW AND DISCUSSION QUESTIONS

1. Which factors in the economy have led to the renewed interest in manufacturing technology, in your opinion?
2. Discuss the product design phases of functional design, industrial design, and design for manufacturability. Which do you think is the most important?
3. Discuss "design-based incrementalism," which is the frequent product redesign throughout the product's life. What are the pros and cons of this idea?
4. What is the primary production document derived from the product design process? What other types of document does one require to make a product?
5. Why is daily contact between engineering and production groups so important in making early involvement effective?
6. Dennis Heard, Frito-Lay's vice president of R&D, though pleased with O'Grady's, is still seeking to develop the ultimate potato chip. Develop a list of characteristics that would define the perfect chip from your perspective.
7. What is the product-process matrix telling us? How does automation change its basic premise?
8. Why is manufacturing management more than simple production management?
9. Assume that a firm would like to manufacture a new product. What are the areas of responsibility for each of the functional areas (marketing, finance, accounting, personnel, production)?
10. There are two schools of thought about new-product introduction. One is to space bringing out newer replacement products in the family with significant time between products. This school maintains strong and continuous support of existing products. The other school introduces products frequently and continuously. Relatively little support is given to existing products since they will soon be off the market. While replaced products still have a relatively long functional life, they have a very short life in the marketplace.
     What are the pros and cons of each approach?
11. Discuss concurrent engineering and how it can benefit a production system.
12. What is a flexible manufacturing system (FMS)?

3.9 PROBLEMS

1. A computer manufacturer is considering using a robot to spray paint side panels of its tape drives. Given the following information, should the company make the investment if it requires a payback period of one year or less?

Cost of robot and accessories is $75,000.

Annual cost of manual spray painting (by one person) is $20,000.

Annual robot maintenance cost is $10,000.

A robot spray painting works about 25 percent faster than a human. Annual depreciation on the robot is $12,000.

2. *a.* List specific products that you especially like. What do you like most about them?

   b. Create a list of products that you dislike or are unhappy with. What don't you like about them?

   c. Are there some common reasons for your lists? For example, is it more important for products which you don't see or see very little to be functional rather than being attractive (such as the furnace or air conditioning in the house, the transmission or engine in the car)? Is it more important for things to be well designed that other people see and relate to you such as your car, your clothes, your apartment or home furnishings?

   Can you formulate some general design guidelines based on your answers?

3. Pick a product and make a list of issues that need to be considered in its design and manufacture. The product can be something like a stereo, a telephone, a desk, a kitchen appliance, etc. Consider the functional and aesthetic aspects of design as well as the important concerns for manufacturing.

4. Mary Entrepreneur is considering introducing a new novelty item for sale to summer visitors in the Catskill Mountains in upstate New York: a wraparound belt with pockets in which vacationers could carry their suntan lotion, playing cards, and snacks. The belt, which she will market as the "Borscht Belt," was greeted with great enthusiasm by members of a local health club.

   The prototype model consists of six identical naugahyde pockets sewn onto a terrycloth belt, and a metal buckle available in the shape of different astrological signs. Once production begins, Mary will obtain naugahyde and terrycloth in bulk rolls, and buckles will be supplied by a local machine shop. Mary has two heavy-duty sewing machines and a stud-riveting machine (left over from her Bruce Springsteen Levi pants production) to attach the belt buckles. Before entering production, she would like to know:

   a. What an assembly chart for the belts would look like.

   b. What a flow process chart for the entire operation, from raw materials receipt to final inspection, would look like.

5. SYSTEM DESIGN EXERCISE

   The purpose of this exercise is to gain experience in setting up a manufacturing process. (We suggest that this be done as a team project.)

   Assignment:

   a. Get one Ping Pong paddle.

   b. Specify the type of equipment and raw materials you would need to manufacture that paddle, from the receipt of seasoned wood to packaging for shipment.

   c. Assume that one unit of each type of equipment is available to you and is already placed in a rented hangar at your local airport. Further assume that you have a stock of seasoned wood and other materials needed to produce and box

100 paddles. Making reasonable assumptions about times and distances where necessary,

(1)   Develop an assembly drawing for the paddle.
(2)   Prepare an assembly chart for the paddle.
(3)   Develop a flow process chart for the paddle.
(4)   Develop a route sheet for the paddle.

3.10   READING: JAPANESE MANUFACTURING

In the United States, many writers have written books and articles, given lectures, and consulted on the various secrets to Japan's success. A recent article by Kuniyasu Sakai gives a startling revelation about Japanese manufacturing. We quote only a section of this article as he has stated his point of concern so clearly.

THE FEUDAL WORLD OF JAPANESE MANUFACTURING*

In my conversations with Americans and other foreign businesspeople, I am constantly amazed at how little they seem to know about the realities of Japanese industry. At a time when Japan accounts for 15 percent of the global economy and Japanese executives are busily studying U.S. and European industry, it seems both foolish—and in some ways dangerous—for Western executives to have such a tenuous understanding of their Japanese trading partners.

Over the past four decades, I have built up a group of several dozen small and midsize companies in a wide variety of businesses, most related to electronics manufacturing. I know well the real world of Japanese manufacturing. I also know that foreign executives have no idea how it works.

My businesses produce high-tech products for some of the best known companies in Japan—all of which are familiar to customers around the world. Yet my companies' names remain unknown, as they should. They exist to support the efforts of the larger companies that can afford to advertise and distribute the products we make. I am happy to leave that business to them. I do not even mind that customers the world over buy products that one of my companies designed and built, all the time praising some famous Japanese company whose logo is on the switch. That is the nature of my business, and I really do not expect consumers to know or even care who built their television or their computer.

I do, however, expect Western executives in important manufacturing industries to know. And what astounds me—and my Japanese colleagues—is that, despite so much "revisionist" thinking about Japan, so many Western businesspeople still know so little about corporate Japan. It seems that the myths of the 1960s are still alive and well. The most prominent and enduring of these myths is the notion that Japanese industry is

* Kuniyasu Sakai, "The Feudal World of Japanese Manufacturing," *Harvard Business Review,* November–December 1990, pp. 38–39.

made up of a handful of powerful giants with factories spanning the nation and workers forming an army of loyal employees who are cared for until retirement by a paternalistic corporation.

This is absolute nonsense.

The Secret Revealed

The giant Japanese manufacturers have become household names worldwide. Companies like Matsushita, Toshiba, NEC, Hitachi, Sony, and Fujitsu have become strong because they produce what the world wants to buy. Their reputations for advanced R&D, innovative products, low-cost and high-quality manufacturing are legendary. Moreover, they seem to have an uncanny ability not just to invent remarkable new products but also to borrow ideas, rework them, tinker with them, and produce something totally "new" from a product concept that originated elsewhere. More often than not, they shrink the new product, add a few gadgets, and find a way to sell it for half what the industry was expecting. A year later, they bring out a newer model and cut prices on the old one before anyone else even has a copy on the market.

How do they do that? What is their secret?

How can the giant Japanese manufacturers, big and resourceful as they are, continue to come up with one idea after another, make a quantum jump from theoretical to applied technology in a single year, and squeeze production costs below what should be economically feasible? And how do they do it year after year, growing more profitable at every step along the way?

The answer is simple: they don't.

Like the wizard of Oz, Japan's giant industrial combines are not what they appear to be. They do not develop all of their own product line, nor do they manufacture it. In reality, these huge businesses are more like "trading companies." That is, rather than design and manufacture their own goods, they actually coordinate a complex design and manufacturing process that involves thousands of smaller companies. The goods you buy with a famous maker's name inscribed on the case are seldom the product of that company's factory—and often not even the product of its own research. Someone else designed it, someone else put it together, someone stuck it in a box with the famous maker's name on it and then shipped it to its distributors.

Does this operation sound unnecessarily complex? Obviously, these huge corporations have their own factories and workers. So why don't they employ their own resources to produce the goods they sell?

They do, of course—but only partially. For instance, it would make very little sense for an electronics giant like Matsushita to farm out the design, manufacture, and assembly of a refrigerator or microwave oven. These products are ideally suited to mass production in the kind of large, highly automated factories that the giant companies can afford. Their factories produce hundreds of thousands of these units every year.

But what about products that companies must continually redesign to compete for public acceptance—like headphone stereos, small compact disk players, or personal computers? Redesigning means retooling a production line. It means sourcing new parts and lots of other things. For a typical product, a company might expect to sell 30,000 units in a few months, retool, sell another 50,000 units, redesign some basic components, retool again, see what the competition brings out, retool again, and on and on, throughout the life cycle of the entire product line. Although some of the giant makers are now employing the newest flexible manufacturing systems (FMS) to allow them more freedom in production, this retooling process is something many big companies want to eliminate.

Thus they farm out much of this business to subcontractors—smaller companies they can depend on. These companies in turn, faced with redesigning and producing a product three or four times a year, will subcontract the design or manufacture of a dozen key components to still smaller companies.

How extensive is this subcontracting pyramid? Would you guess a few dozen companies? A few hundred? Think again. One electronics company I know has well over 6,000 subcontractors in its industrial group, most of them tiny shops that exist just to fill a few little orders for the companies above them.

Welcome to the real world of Japanese manufacturing.

QUESTION

Relate the various phases of the entire process from idea generation through design for manufacturability as covered in this chapter to Kuniyasu's comments about current Japanese manufacturing. How do you think American firms should react or respond to this? Or should they?

3.11 READING: THE BEST-ENGINEERED PART IS NO PART AT ALL*

Putting together NCR Corp.'s new 2760 electronic cash register is a snap. In fact, William R. Sprague can do it in less than two minutes—blindfolded. To get that kind of easy assembly, Sprague, a senior manufacturing engineer at NCR, insisted that the point-of-sale terminal be designed so that its parts fit together with no screws or bolts.

The entire terminal consists of just 15 vendor-produced components. That's 85 percent fewer parts, from 65 percent fewer suppliers, than in the company's previous low-end model, the 2160. And the terminal takes only 25 percent as much time to assemble. Installation and maintenance are also a breeze, says Sprague. "The simplicity flows through to all of the downstream activities, including field service."

The new NCR product is one of the best examples to date of the payoffs possible from a new engineering approach called "design for manufacturability," mercifully shortened to DFM. Other DFM enthusiasts include Ford, General Motors, IBM, Motorola, Perkin-Elmer, and Whirlpool. Since 1981, General Electric Co. has used DFM in more than 100 development programs, from major appliances to gearboxes for jet engines. GE figures that the concept has netted $200 million in benefits, either from cost savings or increased market shares.

Nuts to Screws

One U.S. champion of DFM is Geoffrey Boothroyd, a professor of industrial and manufacturing engineering at the University of Rhode Island and the co-founder of

* Otis Port, "The Best-Engineered Part Is No Part at All," *Business Week,* May 8, 1989, p. 150.

Boothroyd Dewhurst Inc. This tiny Wakefield (R.I.) company has developed several computer programs that analyze designs for ease of manufacturing.

The biggest gains, notes Boothroyd, come from eliminating screws and other fasteners. On a supplier's invoice, screws and bolts may run mere pennies apiece, and collectively they account for only about 5 percent of a typical product's bill of materials. But tack on all of the associated costs, such as the time needed to align components while screws are inserted and tightened, and the price of using those mundane parts can pile up to 75 percent of total assembly costs. "Fasteners should be the first thing to design out of a product," he says.

Had screws been included in the design of NCR's 2760, calculates Sprague, the total cost over the lifetime of the model would have been $12,500—per screw. "The huge impact of little things like screws, primarily on overhead costs, just gets lost," he says. That's understandable, he admits, because for new-product development projects "the overriding factor is hitting the market window. It's better to be on time and over budget than on budget but late."

But NCR got its simplified terminal to market in record time without overlooking the little details. The product was formally introduced last January, just 24 months after development began. Design was a paperless, interdepartmental effort from the very start. The product remained a computer model until all members of the team—from design engineering, manufacturing, purchasing, customer service, and key suppliers—were satisfied.

That way, the printed-circuit boards, the molds for its plastic housing, and other elements could all be developed simultaneously. This eliminated the usual lag after designers throw a new product "over the wall" to manufacturing, which then must figure out how to make it. "Breaking down the walls between design and manufacturing to facilitate simultaneous engineering," Sprague declares, "was the real breakthrough."

The design process began with a mechanical computer-aided engineering program that allowed the team to fashion three-dimensional models of each part on a computer screen. The software also analyzed the overall product and its various elements for performance and durability. Then the simulated components were assembled on a computer workstation's screen to assure that they would fit together properly. As the design evolved, it was checked periodically with Boothroyd Dewhurst's DFM software. This prompted several changes that trimmed the parts count from an initial 28 to the final 15.

No Mock-up

After everyone on the team gave their thumbs-up, the data for the parts were electronically transferred directly into computer-aided manufacturing systems at the various suppliers. The NCR designers were so confident everything would work as intended that they didn't bother making a mock-up.

DFM can be a powerful weapon against foreign competition. Several years ago, IBM used Boothroyd Dewhurst's software to analyze dot-matrix printers it was sourcing from Japan—and found it could do substantially better. Its Proprinter has 65 percent fewer parts and slashed assembly time by 90 percent. "Almost anything made in Japan," insists Professor Boothroyd, "can be improved upon with DFM—often impressively."

QUESTIONS

1. What tools in this chapter is NCR using?
2. How important is the simplicity of design throughout all aspects of the product use: design, manufacture, use by customer, product service, and maintenance?

3.12 SELECTED BIBLIOGRAPHY

Adler, Paul S.; Henry E. Riggs; and Steven C. Wheelwright. "Product Development Know-How: Trading Tactics for Strategy." *Sloan Management Review,* Fall 1989, pp. 7–17.

Boggs, Robert N. "Rogues' Gallery of 'Aggravating Products'." *Design News,* October 22, 1990, pp. 130–33.

Bolwijn, P. T., and T. Kumpe. "Manufacturing in the 1990's—Productivity, Flexibility, and Innovation." *Long Range Planning* 23, no. 4 (1990), pp. 44–57.

Dixon, John R., and Michael R. Duffy. "The Neglect of Engineering Design." *California Management Review,* Winter 1990, pp. 9–23.

Drucker, Peter F. "The Emerging Theory of Manufacturing." *Harvard Business Review,* May–June 1990, pp. 94–102.

Edmondson, Harold E., and Steven C. Wheelwright. "Outstanding Manufacturing in the Coming Decade." *California Management Review,* Summer 1989, pp. 70–90.

Gardner, Dana. "Tech Toys for Grownups." *Design News,* December 3, 1990, pp. 63–66.

Hamilton, Joan O'C. "Rebel with a Cause." *Business Week,* December 3, 1990, pp. 130–33.

Hammer, Michael. "Reengineering Work: Don't Automate, Obliterate." *Harvard Business Review,* July–August 1990, pp. 104–12.

Huthwaite, Bart. *Design for Competitiveness: A Concurrent Engineering Handbook.* Institute for Competitive Design, 530 N. Pine, Rochester, Mich.

Jonas, Norman. "Can America Compete?" *Business Week,* April 20, 1987, pp. 45–69.

Machlis, Sharon. "Three Shortcuts to Better Design." *Design News,* November 19, 1990, pp. 89–91.

Main, Jeremy. "Manufacturing the Right Way." *Fortune,* May 21, 1990, pp. 54–64.

Nussbaum, Bruce, and Robert Neff. "I Can't Work This Thing!" *Business Week,* April 29, 1991, pp. 58–66.

Pare, Terence P. "Why Some Do It the Wrong Way." *Fortune,* May 21, 1990, pp. 75–76.

Roehm, Harper A.; Donald Klein; and Joseph F. Castellano. "Springing to World-Class Manufacturing." *Management Accounting,* March 1991, pp. 40–44.

Sakai, Kuniyasu. "The Feudal World of Japanese Manufacturing." *Harvard Business Review,* November–December 1990, pp. 38–49.

Sanderson, Susan Walsh, and Vic Uzumeri. "Strategies for New Product Development and Renewal: Design-Based Incrementalism." Center for Science and Technology Policy, School of Management, Rensselaer Polytechnic Institute, May 1990.

Spenser, William J. "Research to Product: A Major U.S. Change." *California Management Review,* Winter 1990, pp. 45–53.

Wheelwright, Steven C., and W. Earl Sasser, Jr. "The New Product Development Map." *Harvard Business Review,* May–June 1989, pp. 112–27.

Ziemke, M. Carl, and Mary S. Spann. "Warning: Don't Be Half-Hearted in Your Efforts to Employ Concurrent Engineering." *Industrial Engineering,* February 1991, pp. 45–49.

Supplement

Computer-Integrated Manufacturing

EPIGRAPH

An interview with J. Tracy O'Rourke, CEO of Allen-Bradley Company:

Mr. O'Rourke, you have been described as an evangelist for computer-integrated manufacturing. Are you?

O'Rourke: No, I'm a businessman, a shrewd one, I hope. . . . If you're behind world competition, apply to manufacturing the best technology you can. . . . It leads you to conclude that computer-automation is our only weapon.

Adapted from Bernard Avishai, "A CEO's Common Sense of CIM: An Interview with J. Tracy O'Rourke." *Harvard Business Review*, January–February 1989, pp. 110–117.

KEY TERMS

Computer-Integrated Manufacturing (CIM)

Computer-Aided Design (CAD)

Group Technology (GT)

Manufacturing Planning and Control Systems (MP&CS)

Automated Materials Handling Systems (AMH)

Computer-Aided Manufacturing (CAM)

Robotics

Computing Technology

As we discussed in Chapter 2, international and domestic competition is becoming more intense with each passing day. Product life cycles now average 12 to 18 months, and they continue to get shorter.[1] Consumers and end users of manufactured products are demanding more individually customized products to suit their own needs. With these pressures facing them, manufacturers are searching out new ways to improve their competitive position.

The answer for many companies lies in automation technologies. Automated manufacturing systems have the potential for providing a heretofore unmatched level of manufacturing performance along the four strategic dimensions of cost, quality, delivery, and flexibility.[2] In the 1960s, manufacturers began using computers to automate financial transactions and later to control inventory, production scheduling, and parts routing. The earliest applications of computers to the actual manufacturing process were the computer-aided design (CAD) systems first introduced in the aerospace and defense industries. Computer automation then moved to the machines used in the manufacturing process to create computer-aided manufacturing (CAM). Automation has now created a host of systems and devices to improve the effectiveness of the entire manufacturing process.

In addition to improving productivity, automation has also improved product quality and made possible rapid design and manufacture of new products. However, automation by itself is not sufficient to assure a competitive manufacturing system. While computer automation alone can make improvements through so-called islands of automation, it is not until these islands are linked and coordinated that an automated system achieves its maximum potential. The approaches taken to achieve such linkages go under several names: *total factory automation,* the *factory of the future,* and *computer-integrated manufacturing.*

S3.1 COMPUTER-INTEGRATED MANUFACTURING

Computer-integrated manufacturing (CIM) is an automation version of the generic manufacturing process (see Exhibit S3.1), with each function replaced by a set of automated technologies.[3] In addition, the traditional integration mechanisms of oral and written communication are replaced by computing technology. With CIM, the three major manufacturing functions—product and process design, planning and control, and the manufacturing process itself—are replaced by six functional areas: computer-aided design,

---

[1] James R. Koelsch, "Robots: The Keystone of Flexible Assembly," *Production Engineering,* February 1986, pp. 36–40.

[2] Kalyan Singhal, "Introduction: The Design and Implementation of Automated Manufacturing Systems," *Interfaces* 17, no. 6 (November–December 1987), p. 1.

[3] The material in this section is drawn from the Arthur D. Little report "The Strategic Benefits of Computer Aided Manufacturing" (Cambridge, Mass.: Arthur D. Little, 1985).

EXHIBIT S3.1

Generic
Manufacturing

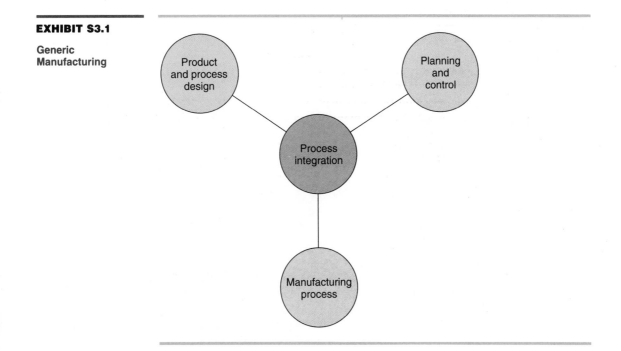

group technology, manufacturing planning and control systems, automated materials handling, computer-aided manufacturing, and robotics. (See Exhibit S3.2.)

Computer-aided design (CAD) covers several automated technologies in addition to the computer graphics systems used to design geometric specifications of a part. CAD includes computer-aided engineering (CAE), used to evaluate and conduct engineering analyses on a part. CAD also includes two technologies associated with manufacturing process design. CAD can be used to design numerically controlled part programs, which give instructions to computer-controlled tools, and to design the use and sequence of machine centers.

Closely associated with CAD in the process design is **group technology (GT),** a production methodology that uses a computer system for classifying, coding, and grouping parts and processes based on the geometry of parts. It is widely used in identifying cells of groups of machinery that are closely associated with each family of parts (see Chapter 9).

Automated **manufacturing planning and control systems (MP&CS)** are simply computer-based information systems. They plan and schedule operations, compare alternatives, update data continuously, monitor operations, and project operating results. More sophisticated manufacturing planning and control systems also include order-entry processing, shop-floor control, purchasing, and cost accounting.

EXHIBIT S3.2

Computer-Integrated Manufacturing

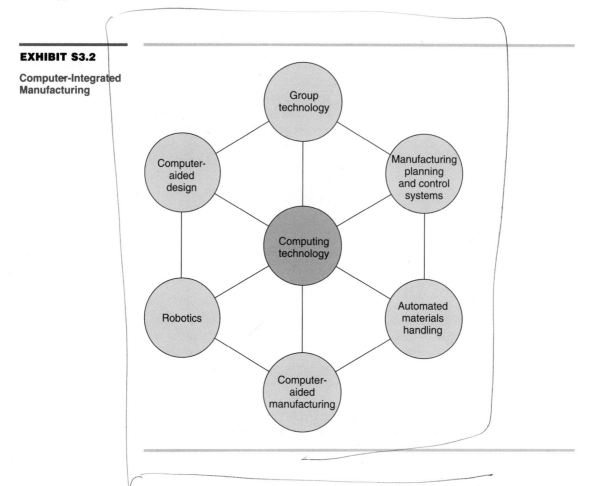

Closely related to MP&CS are **automated materials handling (AMH)** systems. These systems include automated storage and retrieval systems (ASRS) in which computers direct automatic loaders to pick items from bulk and return remainders to storage. AMH systems also include automatic guided vehicle (AGV) systems, which use embedded floor wires to direct driverless trucks to various locations around the factory, delivering materials.

Computer-aided manufacturing (CAM) includes several technologies used in manufacturing: computer-run machine tools, flexible manufacturing systems (FMS), and computer-aided inspection. Computer-run machine tools include numerically controlled machine tools, which can be programmed to perform tasks either directly, on the shop floor, or with a disc or tape. FMS is an integrated system using several automation technologies to create the flexibility of a job-shop operation with the low costs of mass production. FMS links together the machine centers and materials handling system, limiting human involvement to part fixturing and system maintenance. Computer-aided inspection automatically collects and analyzes quality control information and can establish a statistical database and isolate production process problems.

Robotics is closely associated with CAM. A robot is a reprogrammable, multifunctional manipulator with an end effector (such as a gripper, welder, or sprayer) used in a variety of factory tasks that can be segmented as stand-alone operations. Robots are often used for spot welding and assembly.

All these CIM technologies are tied together in a communications link made possible by **computing technology.** The emphasis here is on linking databases of the different components together, because this is where the power of CIM is unleashed. With data integration, CAD systems can be linked to CAM numerical-control parts programs, and MP&CS can be linked to AMH systems to further enhance parts pick-list generation. In a fully integrated system, each automated technology will be able to interface with each of the other technologies through advanced computing technology. (See Exhibit S3.3, which sketches the physical features of a CIM factory.)

S3.2 BENEFITS OF CIM

The benefits of the six CIM technologies are too numerous to discuss in detail. However, a brief overview of the major advantages would be useful.

The primary benefit of a CAD system is higher design productivity. However, CAD can result in many other benefits, such as better design quality, significantly less time spent on prototypes (parts fit can be verified by computer), and an engineering database with an accurate description of each part. The advantages of group technology include reduction of the number of parts in a database, reduced parts introduction costs, higher machine use factors, and reduced overall setup time.

MP&CS produces quantitative and qualitative benefits. Typical quantitative benefits include reduction of inventory errors, overall inventory reductions, higher productivity, fewer late shipments, shorter delivery lead times, and fewer stockouts. Qualitative benefits include improved customer relations, better functional communications, and more professional management (see Exhibit S3.4). Typical automated materials handling benefits include higher inventory record accuracy, reduced storage space requirements, higher labor productivity, increased safety and stockroom security, reduced product damage, and the coordination of material movement with material handling equipment.

CAM systems have many benefits similar to those already mentioned, such as increased labor productivity, increased product quality, and less setup time. Robotics provides many of these same benefits as well, but also substitutes for humans at dirty, dangerous, and dull tasks. In addition, robots can provide higher flexibility, higher reliability, and significant savings in space, materials, heating, and lighting.

The real advantages of CIM, however, are not in the sum of the benefits of each separate technology, although that sum is very significant. The real advantage of CIM lies in the integration of these component technologies. The long-term benefits of a data-integrated system like CIM are the individual

EXHIBIT S3.3   The Automated Factory

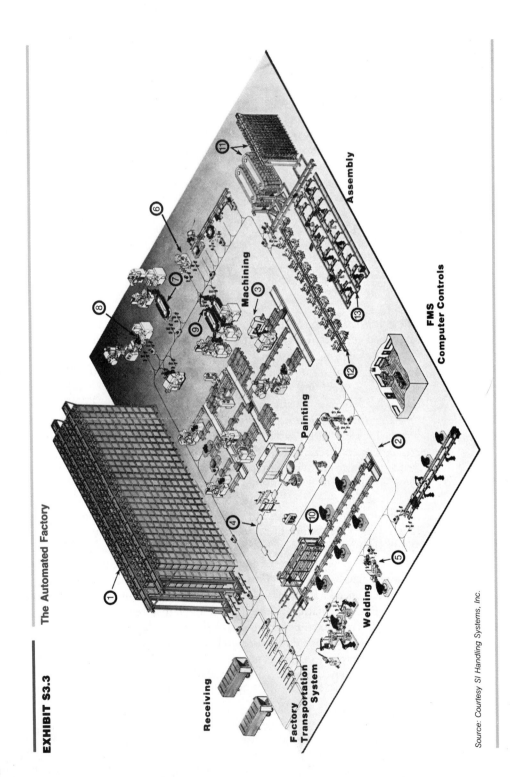

Source: Courtesy SI Handling Systems, Inc.

EXHIBIT S3.4

Qualitative Benefits of MP&CS

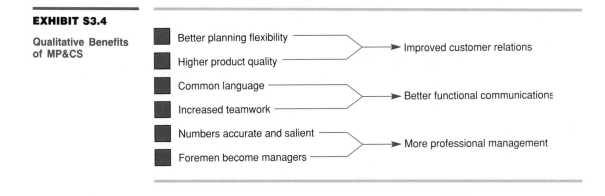

benefits amplified geometrically by the benefits of integrating each component into a common system (see Exhibit S3.5). Integration leads to better management of the flow of manufacturing data, better interdepartmental communications, and better resource utilization, all of which can result in major gains in product quality and production efficiency. Consider these examples of benefits achieved by partial implementation of CIM in five companies:[4]

Achievement	Range of Improvement
Reduction in engineering design cost	15–30%
Reduction in overall lead time	30–60%
Increased product quality as measured by yield of acceptable product	2–5 times previous level
Increased capability of engineers as measured by extent and depth of analysis in same or less time than previously	3–35 times
Increased productivity (complete assemblies)	40–70%
Increased productivity (operating time) of capital equipment	2–3 times
Reduction of work-in-process	30–60%
Reduction of personnel costs	5–20%

As you might surmise, all the component technologies of CIM are further along in their product life cycles than is CIM as a whole (see Exhibit S3.6). Since data integration is the essence of CIM, a key to its widespread application will be the refinement and standardization of the programing languages that provide the linkages. Four key management factors will ultimately determine the speed of implementation and with it a company's success:

1. The articulation of a CIM strategy that recognizes CIM's impact on overall corporate competitiveness, not just its short-run financial implications. This means that the company must clearly identify how it competes (its relative emphasis on price, quality, flexibility, dependability) and how CIM will specifically contribute to its competitiveness.

---

[4] Thomas G. Gunn, *Manufacturing for Competitive Advantage* (Cambridge, Mass.: Ballinger, 1987), p. 171.

EXHIBIT S3.5

Synergistic Effects of A CIM System

CIM benefits	=	Benefits of each separate technology	×	Benefits of data integration

EXHIBIT S3.6   Computer-Integrated Manufacturing

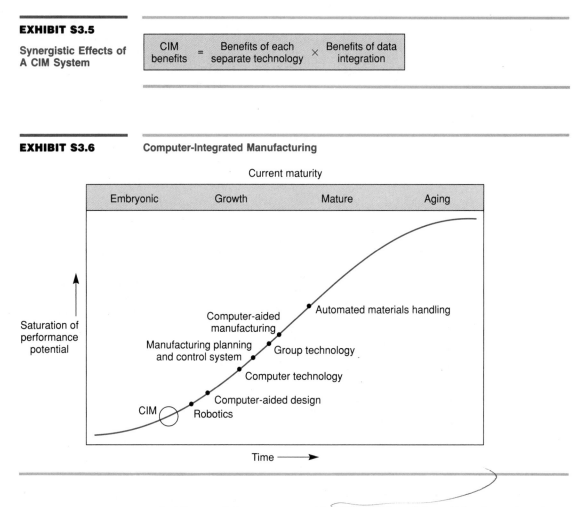

2. The need for companywide planning involving all business functions. The best way to plan for CIM is usually through a multidisciplinary task force, with direct involvement of top management.

3. The recognition that the administrative structure and the jobs of the work force may well have to be changed to take full advantage of CIM's capability. CIM is both a new philosophy and a new technology that breaks down departmental barriers and requires new job skills. It is well known that an essential requirement for effective CIM use is close interaction between engineering and manufacturing, resulting in team structures. Similar kinds of groupings or new forms of organizational linkages among marketing and engineering and manufacturing are also required.

The jobs of the work force obviously become more computer based, requiring information-processing skills rather than direct production skills. This clearly affects workers in the trades, such as machinists. Finally, there is evidence that CIM leads to job enlargement, and hence new and fewer job titles. According to John Ettlie, "In some [modernized] plants, over 100 job categories have been collapsed into 5 or even 3 broad job titles."[5]

4. The recognition that various activities will have to be modified to support CIM technologies. A new GT cell, for example, will require changes in work standards, maintenance procedures, tooling (jigs, dies, and fixtures), and so on. Exhibit S3.7 identifies a series of activities that must be modified to fully use CIM technologies.

S3.3 EXAMPLES OF CIM

Competition has led many companies to install computer-integrated manufacturing (CIM) systems into the manufacturing facilities. It has long been felt that CIM is a trend for the factory of the future, but to use the cliché, the future is now. Each year *Electronic Business* and *Electronic Packaging & Production* grant their Electronic Factory Automation Award to the U.S.-owned plant which they believe is the best example of automation in the electronics industry.[6] Past awards went to the IBM plant in Charlotte, North Carolina; Westinghouse Electric Corporation in College Station, Texas; and Texas Instruments in Johnson City, Tennessee. These three installations are discussed next, along with the automated Fanuc Company factory.

IBM's University Research Park Proprinter Plant

In 1983, IBM designed a highly automated facility to use computer-integrated manufacturing to produce printers that would be cost competitive with foreign manufacturers. IBM designed its printer with automated assembly in mind, so that the factory could be designed around the assembly process. Of the nine assembly stations along the assembly lines that build and test a printer, seven are robotic systems. IBM also uses an automated inventory storage and retrieval system and an automated materials handling system, and ties everything together with its own manufacturing, accounting, production, and inventory control system (MAPICS) software.

By removing much of the direct labor, using the automated technologies of CIM, and designing its product with simplicity of manufacturing in mind, IBM was able to build a factory of the future that is able to compete on an international level. IBM's proprinter has only about one third the parts of the competition's printers, which means it can be produced from raw materials in

---

[5] John Ettlie, speech before the Center for Operations Management Education and Research, University of Southern California, June 27, 1987.

[6] Tony Greene, "CIM Savvy, Tennessee Style," *Electronic Business,* March 6, 1989, pp. 31–36.

EXHIBIT S3.7

Activities Modified to Accommodate and Fully Utilize New Computer-Aided Manufacturing Processes (57 projects)

	Mean Score*
Work measurement and standards	2.0
Quality control and inspection	2.0
Product control and recordkeeping	1.9
Routing	1.9
Maintenance	1.9
Scheduling	1.7
Dispatching	1.7
Design of jigs, dies, and fixtures	1.7
Product design	1.7
Expediting	1.6
Material handling	1.6
Performance evaluation	1.6
Receiving and shipping	1.3
Incentive and reward systems	1.2

*Key: 1 = Not modified
     2 = Somewhat modified
     3 = Completely modified

Source: Stephen R. Rosenthal, "Progress toward the 'Factory of the Future'," *Journal of Operations Management,* May 1984, pp. 203–29.

one day and assembled from parts in 20 minutes. With the communication and coordination benefits of CIM, IBM has been able to minimize the number of its vendors and use the concept of Just-in-Time manufacturing to cut inventory inside the factory to about a day and a half's worth of production.

Westinghouse's College Station Electronic Assembly Plant

Westinghouse committed to investing in CIM after discovering that only 15 to 20 percent of its printed circuit boards were ready for shipping after only one pass through the manufacturing loop, as contrasted to 98 to 100 percent in the plants of its Japanese competition. Westinghouse implemented a sophisticated computing network that tied together several levels of computing technologies in a hierarchical data system. This data system is accessed by a central control system that manages one integrated database. A CAD/CAM subsystem was installed to generate machine data and speed up the assembly process. Westinghouse's own engineers developed six different robots that can perform variable sequential tasks in assembling a circuit board.

The resulting gains in efficiency are impressive. The percentage of printed circuit boards that are ready to be shipped after only one pass through the manufacturing loop has risen to 95 percent. The amount of time from receipt of order to shipment of product is down from 12 weeks to 2. In all, the improvements in quality and efficiency have saved Westinghouse an estimated $19 million and have saved the Air Force (one of its important customers) an estimated $37 million.

Texas Instruments' Johnson City Circuit Board Facility

In responding to customer demands for higher quality in printed circuit boards and management's demands for higher return on investment, Texas Instruments, (TI) created and installed a Surface Mount Technology (SMT) line. The SMT line produces more than 30 types of boards ranging from simple automotive window controllers to high-resolution graphic boards for computer workstations.

The project started with the installation of a flexible electronic manufacturing assembly cell (FEMAC) to produce printed circuit board assemblies. This was to be done with state-of-the-art equipment combined with automated materials handling, machine programming—all controlled with computers. The facility has worked out so well that other TI plants will install similar lines. TI was also able to enter into the contract business.

On this surface mount technology (SMT) line, throughput increased by 21 percent while increased quality improved the yield rate by 20 percent. Electrical rejects decreased from 1,700 ppm to 200 ppm. Cycle time from raw materials to shipping has been reduced from five days to three days. Cycle time reduction was due in part to the setup time required to change to different boards being reduced to less than one hour.

The line consists of two assembly lines and one soldering line in parallel, connected by an overhead conveyer running perpendicular to the ends of the three lines. The first step is to apply solder paste to the bare copper pads where the electrical components mounted on the surface must make contact. The components are then dipped in solder paste and then automatically picked up and correctly placed by a machine. The remaining components also assembled automatically on the board. The boards are then soldered, cleaned, and subjected to electrical tests.

The entire process is controlled by computers with minimal human interaction. The system is tied into Texas Instruments's main computer system so that new designs from computer-aided design (CAD) can be quickly transmitted and to allow for design changes and quick introduction of new products.

TI managers have the attitude that factory automation is a continuous process, and not one which ends when some level of automation is installed. The project leader has the belief that computer-integrated manufacturing (CIM) is a moving target and, although they thought they had a 100 percent installation three years ago, right now they think it is 60 percent CIM. This gives them the feeling that the opportunity exists now to add more improvements and automation to the line.

Fujitsu Fanuc's Robot Factory

Fujitsu Fanuc has put into operation an entire factory for producing robots, small machining centers, and wire-cut electrodischarge machines. The machining section of the factory operates almost wholly unattended on the night shift. (See Exhibit S3.8.)

EXHIBIT S3.8

**Ghost Shop:
Fanuc Co.**

Fanuc Co. is the world leader in developing fully automated factories like the one shown. Working three shifts a day, the robots produce various machines—and other robots. Human workers appear only to service the machines.

Courtesy of Fanuc Co.

There are 29 machining cells (22 machining centers served by automatic pallet changes and 7 robot-served cells), each consisting of one or more NC machine tools and a robot or pallet changer to keep the machine or machines loaded with parts during the night. Workpieces on pallets are transported to and from the cells and to and from computer-controlled automatic stacker cranes by computer-controlled, wire-guided carts.

During the day there are 19 workers on the machining floor. On the night shift no one is on the machining floor, and there is only one worker in the control room. ("I had some difficulty scheduling a time to visit the plant . . . because the company's managers were concerned about protocol: There would be no one senior enough to receive a visitor on the site during 10 of its 15 operating shifts.")[7] In a 24-hour period, machine availability is

---

[7] Gerald K. O'Neill, "Robots Who Reproduce," *Across the Board,* June 1984, p. 37.

running close to 100 percent, and machine use is averaging 65 to 70 percent. As a result, this 2,050-square-meter factory is producing 100 robots, 75 machining centers, and 75 electrodischarge machines each month.

S3.4 CONCLUSION

The benefits derived from the implementation of CIM can be profound. Each CIM technology is a powerful tool by itself, but when linked to a shared database the power of each technology is amplified geometrically. The actual benefits of CIM can be seen immediately, but in a financial analysis, CIM benefits are often realized only on a long-term basis. This is because advantages of CIM can often be intangible and not easily quantified. Furthermore, typical cost accounting methods and ROI analyses do not lend themselves easily to measuring the long-term benefits of CIM.

The decision to implement a CIM system is a large commitment (sometimes called "you bet your company"). For many companies the financial investment required by CIM is out of reach. However, as technologies continue to improve, costs of implementing CIM will continue to drop and place CIM within the reach of many medium-sized firms. Because of the financial commitments required and the long-term return provided by CIM, corporate decision makers and other management members must have a long-term perspective of CIM and how it can benefit their organizations.

S3.5 READING: MAP PILOT PAYS OFF FOR LOCKHEED*

Burbank, California—Using MAP [Manufacturing Automation Protocol] technology and Japanese-style management, Lockheed Corp. has built a system that cuts the time it takes to make airplane parts from two months to two days.

The system is being pilot-tested here in a factory, dubbed the computer-aided layout and fabrication (CALFAB) facility. It promises to improve the speed and efficiency of Lockheed's entire manufacturing operation.

Currently, the system is used to manufacture 15 percent of the medium-sized sheet metal parts—such as brackets in steering systems and braces to hold seats in cockpits—that the company makes for its airplanes.

Previously, Lockheed took as long as 52 days to make these parts. According to Gary Garrow, chief manufacturing research engineer for Lockheed's Aeronautical Systems Co. here, the company plans to expand the system to most of Lockheed's manufacturing operations.

---

* Source: Barton Crockett, "MAP Pilot Pays Off for Lockheed," *Network World*, May 30, 1988. Copyright 1988 by Network World Publishing Inc. Framingham, MA 01701—Reprinted from *Network World*.

Lockheed spent $3.5 million in one year to build the CALFAB prototype. CAL-FAB, which became operational in January, produces more than 1,500 different sheet metal parts for the aerospace company.

A key component of the manufacturing system is Manufacturing Automation Prototcol networking. Using MAP technology, Lockheed has made CALFAB an entirely computer-controlled, paperless factory.

The CALFAB MAP network links engineering workstations above the manufacturing floor to an IBM 3090 mainframe in a corporate office 2½ miles away. The IBM mainframe transmits data to a Digital Equipment Corp. VAX 8200—which serves as a process controller on the factory floor—over a MAP Version 2.1 network running at 1.54M bit/sec. The mainframe and minicomputer are linked using channel-attached equipment the company is beta-testing here.

The VAX controls factory operations by sending and receiving instructions over a MAP local network with Intel Corp. 80386-based workstations used to run machinery such as presses and metal cutters on the factory floor.

The workstations are manufactured by a potpourri of companies. One, called a Trumpf workstation, comes from a West German company. Another, called an LVD workstation, was built in Belgium. The remaining workstations are from a variety of U.S. companies. Garrow said the flexibility of the MAP protocols made it much easier to build an efficient network linking these disparate machines.

"My estimate is that, had we not used MAP, we could have accomplished the same end, but it would have been far more complex technically and a lot more expensive," Garrow said. "We'd have ended up using multiple networks and, in some cases, running a single [type of] machine on a net because of the proprietary nature of the equipment."

The MAP network, Garrow conceded, has had its problems. One serious glitch that still needs to be worked out is a bottleneck that slows the movement of data. Garrow refused give further details, however, or explain how Lockheed hopes to resolve the problem. Garrow said that such information is "highly competitive," and added, "I want my competitors to figure this one out for themselves."

Yet despite the problems, Garrow argued that innovations in CALFAB, if applied in industries throughout the nation, can improve the way the U.S. does business. "I think the concepts used in CALFAB could cut manufacturing costs in this country 50% across the board and increase our competitiveness by a couple of orders of magnitude," he said.

Lockheed clearly stands to gain from the CALFAB project. The metal products that CALFAB now produces in two days still take 40 or 50 days to fabricate at rival aerospace companies, Garrow said.

Lockheed plans to use its manufacturing edge as a weapon in the battle for a multibillion dollar contract to build 750 YF-22A advanced tactical aircraft for the Air Force. A Lockheed spokesman said CALFAB was "optimized" to build parts for those airplanes.

Meanwhile, Garrow said CALFAB embraces a fundamentally new manufacturing concept for Lockheed, one based on integration. Disparate manufacturing steps have been consolidated into a single area.

Garrow said the increased integration helps Lockheed practice personnel management techniques used by Japanese companies. One concept, in particular, is a team management approach, in which employees take greater responsibility for decision making on the factory floor and quality control.

"The industry gets all excited about the technology, but the biggest success in CALFAB is with the people," he said. "Each member works as part of a team. They take pride in their product. They solve problems without help from their supervisors. Previously, supervisors spent all eight hours of the day watching employees. Now they spend only 20 minutes. That's absolutely amazing."

Increased Efficiency

The technological changes make the manufacturing process tremendously more efficient, Garrow said. Previously, he explained, Lockheed believed the most efficient way to manufacture was to perform similar operations for different products close together. This approach often made it necessary to move items more than 2,500 feet on a crowded factory floor.

With CALFAB, however, all the manufacturing processes for a given product are handled at a single cell, 40 ft. wide and 140 ft. long. This cell is manned by seven to eight workers, who know how to operate every piece of machinery used to produce the product.

Design and manufacturing engineers, who previously worked in separate offices, now work side by side in an office overlooking the factory floor.

With CALFAB, design and manufacturing engineers design new products and the manufacturing techniques used to produce them. They transmit that data from their workstations to the IBM mainframe, which runs engineering and materials control programs like MRP II, CADAM, and Artemis.

From here, information about what kinds of products and how many the factory should produce is routed from the mainframe to the VAX controller on the shop floor. The VAX then tells the workstations which programs to run to produce the various sheet metal parts.

From beginning to end, the entire process is computerized.

Previously, Garrow said, instructions would have been delivered to floor supervisors, who would then give orders to machine operators in different areas on the shop floor. From there, workers would have loaded floppy disks into machines to tell them which operation to conduct.

Garrow said this system lets the company cut the number of steps used to manufacture the sheet metal products from 47 to 8. He also said that product quality has dramatically improved, although he would not describe how.

S3.6 REVIEW AND DISCUSSION QUESTIONS

1. Exhibit S3.7 illustrates a series of activities that must be modified to fully utilize CIM activities. Work measurement and standards have a rating of 2.0 (the highest in the list). Why does this activity have to be modified?

2. What are the advantages and disadvantages of CIM?

3. Is CIM appropriate mainly for products that have short life cycles and that are constantly changing?

4. Automation is replacing workers. How should these workers be retrained so that they can cope effectively in a new environment?

5. By implementing CIM, Westinghouse's probability of shipping PCBs after one pass of the manufacturing loop had risen to 95 percent from 15 to 20 percent. The time taken from order to shipment had decreased from 12 weeks to 2 weeks. Calculate separately the productivity gain for assembly and production.

6. The MAP pilot project at Lockheed shows how CIM is applicable to the defense industry. Discuss how the elements of CIM apply to the case.

S3.7 SELECTED BIBLIOGRAPHY

Alden, P. S. "Managing Flexibility." *California Management Review*, Fall 1988.

Avishai, Bernard. "A CEO's Common Sense of CIM: An Interview with J. Tracy O'Rourke." *Harvard Business Review,* January–February 1989, pp. 110–117.

Brody, H. "Overcoming Barriers to Automation." *High Technology*, May 1985, pp. 41–46.

Greene, Tony. "CIM Savvy, Tennessee Style." *Electronic Business,* March 6, 1989, pp. 31–36.

Gunn, Thomas G. *Computer Applications in Manufacturing*. New York: Industrial Press, 1981.

———. "The Mechanization of Design and Manufacturing." *Scientific American* 247, no. 3 (September 1982), pp. 3–49.

———. "The CIM Connection." *Datamation*, February 1, 1986, pp. 50–58.

———. "Integrated Manufacturing's Growing Pains," Electronic Engineering Manager. *Electronic Engineering Times*, February 1986, pp. 1–8.

Haas, E. "Breakthrough Manufacturing." *Harvard Business Review* 2 (March–April 1987), pp. 75–81.

Hales, H. L. "How Small Firms Can Approach, Benefit from Computer-Integrated Manufacturing Systems." *Industrial Engineering*, June 1984, pp. 43–51.

Harrington, Joseph J. *Understanding the Manufacturing Process*. New York: Marcel Dekker, Inc., 1984.

Jacobsen, Gary, and John Hillkirk. *Xerox: American Samurai*. New York: Macmillan Publishing Company, 1986.

Chapter 4

Product Design and Process Selection— Services

EPIGRAPH

After paying for dinner at a restaurant, I asked the cashier who took my money in stony silence why she didn't at least say thank you. "Why should I?" she asked, "It says thank you on your check doesn't it?"

Comedian Jay Leno, on the "Tonight Show"

110

CHAPTER OUTLINE

KEY TERMS

Service Package

Facilities-Based Services

Field-Based Services

Customer

High and Low Contact

Service Focus

Service-System Design Matrix

Service Blueprint

Service Guarantee

Internal Services

*W*hy do we go out for breakfast and pay $4.75 for eggs, toast, and coffee, when we can make this at home for 75 cents? Obviously, what we are really buying is 75 cents worth of product and $4.00 worth of service. Recognize, though, that the service includes the environment, waiters and waitresses, other customers, and so on. Karl Albrecht and Ron Zemke's *Service America!* gets to the heart of the issue of managing service operations in stating: Every time a customer comes into contact with any aspect of the company it is a "moment of truth," and it can create either a positive or a negative impression about the company.[1] How well these moments of truth are managed depends on a carefully designed service delivery system.

In this chapter, after some preliminary comments about services, we address the issue of service delivery system design, starting with the notion of customer contact as a way of classifying service operations. Next, we discuss service organization design, service strategy, and service focus, and describe how marketing and operations interrelate to achieve (or fail to achieve) competitive advantage. We also look at a service system design matrix that can define the broad features of a service process, and at service blueprints as a way of designing the precise steps of a process. In the latter part of the chapter, we present three service designs used in service industries, discuss how service gurarantees can be used as "design drivers," and offer some general comments on designing internal services. At the end of the chapter we provide a case study of a service organization familiar to many readers of this book—Kinko's Copier Stores.

4.1 THE NATURE AND IMPORTANCE OF SERVICES

Our study of the nature of services leads to seven generalizations about what must be considered a vast topic.

1. Everyone is an expert on services. We all think we know what we want from a service organization and, by the very process of living, we have a good deal of experience with the service creation process.

2. Services are idiosyncratic—what works well in providing one kind of service may prove disastrous in another. For example, consuming a restaurant meal in less than half an hour may be exactly what you want at Jack-in-the-Box but be totally unacceptable at an expensive French restaurant.

---

[1] Jan Carlzon, president, Scandinavian Airlines System, quoted in Karl Albrecht and Ron Zemke, *Service America! Doing Business in the New Economy* (Homewood, Ill.: Dow Jones-Irwin, 1985), p. 19.

3. Quality of work is not quality of service. An auto dealership may do good work on your car, but it may take a week to get the job done.
4. Most services contain a mix of tangible and intangible attributes that constitute a **service package,** and this package requires different approaches to design and management than the production of goods.
5. High-contact services (described later) are *experienced*, whereas goods are *consumed*.
6. Effective management of services requires an understanding of marketing and personnel, as well as operations.
7. Services often take the form of cycles of encounters involving face-to-face, phone, electromechanical, and/or mail interactions. (The term *encounter,* by the way, is defined as "meeting in conflict or battle" and hence is often apt as we make our way through the service economy.)

The Insert presents some assorted facts about the impact of services on our economy.

INSERT   Some Facts about Services

- In 1990, 71 percent of the U.S. GNP resulted from services—a 4 percent increase in 10 years. During the same time the contribution from manufacturing decreased by 2 percent.
- In 1986, the number of persons employed increased by 2.5 million; 87 percent of this increase was in services.
- In 1989, 77 percent of all U.S. workers were employed in service-producing jobs.
- Services have increased their employment share 6 percent between 1975 and 1985.
- More than half of all U.S. service workers are employed in white-collar, often highly skilled, occupations.
- Foreign trade in 1986:
  - The United States reported $133.8 billion of service trade.
  - Services netted a $33.1 billion surplus.
  - The trade surplus in services has grown by 200 percent since 1976.
- Of the total investment in new plants and equipment made in 1985, 73 percent was from the service sector.
- In 1986, the number of service companies rose by 2.4 percent and accounted for every one of the 10 fastest-growing business categories. The top five were health clubs (28 percent increase), beauty shops (16 percent), doctors/health services (15 percent), investment management/other (14 percent), and hotels/lodging (12 percent).

- Mac attack (some statistics on McDonald's):
  - Average number on payroll: 500,000 people.
  - Number of workers employed over past 30 years: 8 million (7 percent of the entire U.S. work force, or 1 out of every 15 American workers).
  - Largest job training organization in the United States (the U.S. Army is number two).

Source: From various issues of the *Monthly Labor Review*.

Service Businesses and Internal Services

Service operations management issues exist in two broad organizational contexts:

1. Service business, the management of organizations whose primary business requires interaction with the customer to produce the service. These include such familiar services as banks, airlines, hospitals, law firms, retail stores, restaurants, and so on. Within this category, we can make a further major distinction: **facilities-based services,** where the customer must go to the service facility, and **field-based services,** where production and consumption of the service take place in the customer's environment (e.g., cleaning and home repair services).

Technology has allowed for the transfer of many facility-based services to field-based services. Dental vans bring the dentist to your home. Some auto repair services have repair-mobiles. Telemarketing brings the shopping center to your TV screen.

2. Internal services, the management of services required to support the activities of the larger organization. These services include such functions as data processing, accounting, engineering, and maintenance. Their customers are the various departments within the organization that require such services. Incidentally, it is not uncommon for an internal service to start marketing its services outside the parent organization and become a service business itself.

Our emphasis in this chapter is on service businesses, but most of the ideas apply equally well to internal services.

A Contemporary View of Service Management

A glance at the management book section in your local book store gives ample evidence of the concern for service among practitioners. The way we now view service parallels the way we view quality: The **customer** is (or should be) the focal point of all decisions and actions of the service organization. This philosophy is captured nicely in the service triangle shown in Exhibit 4.1.

EXHIBIT 4.1

The Service Triangle

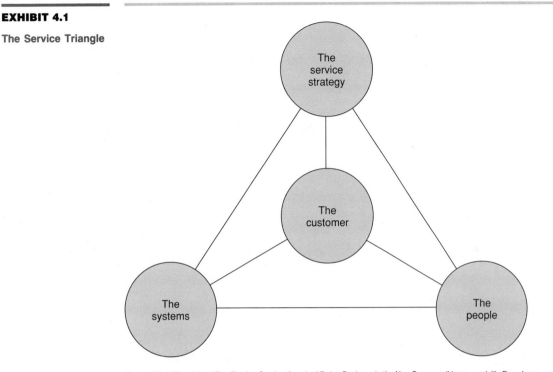

Source: Karl Albrecht and Ron Zemke, *Service America! Doing Business in the New Economy* (Homewood, Ill., Dow-Jones Irwin. 1985), p. 41.

Here, the customer is the center of things—the service strategy, the systems, and the people who serve him or her. From this view, the organization exists to serve the customer, and the systems and the people exist to facilitate the process of service. Some suggest that the service organization also exists to serve the work force because they generally determine how the service is perceived by the customers. Relative to the latter point, the customer gets the kind of service that management deserves; in other words, how management treats the worker is how the worker will treat the public. That is if the work force is well trained and well motivated by management, they will do good jobs for their customers.

The role of operations in the triangle is a major one. Operations is responsible for service systems (procedures, equipment, and facilities) and is responsible for managing the work of the service work force who typically comprise the majority of employees in large service organizations. However, before we discuss this role in depth, it is useful to classify services to show how the customer affects the operations function.

4.2 AN OPERATIONAL CLASSIFICATION OF SERVICES

Services systems are generally classified according to the service they provide (financial services, health services, transportation services, and so on). These groupings, though useful in presenting aggregate economic data, are not particularly appropriate for OM purposes because they tell us little about the process. In manufacturing, by contrast, there are fairly evocative terms to classify production activities (such as *intermittent* and *continuous production*); when applied to a manufacturing setting, they readily convey the essence of the process. While it is possible to describe services in these same terms, we need one additional item of information to reflect the fact that the customer is involved in the production system. That item, which we believe operationally distinguishes one service system from another in its production function, is the extent of customer contact in the creation of the service.

Customer contact refers to the physical presence of the customer in the system, and *creation of the service* refers to the work process that is involved in providing the service itself. *Extent of contact* here may be roughly defined as the percentage of time the customer must be in the system relative to the total time it takes to perform the customer service. Generally speaking, the greater the percentage of contact time between the service system and the customer, the greater the degree of interaction between the two during the production process.

From this conceptualization, it follows that service systems with a **high degree of customer contact** are more difficult to control and more difficult to rationalize than those with a **low degree of customer contact.** In high-contact systems, the customer can affect the time of demand, the exact nature of the service, and the quality of service since the customer is involved in the process.

Exhibit 4.2 describes the implications of this distinction. Here we see that each design decision is impacted by whether or not the customer is present during service delivery. We also see that when work is done behind the scenes (in this case in a bank's processing center), it is performed on customer surrogates—reports, databases, and invoices. We can, therefore, design it according to the same principles we would use in designing a factory. That is, to maximize the amount of items processed during the production day.

Obviously, there can be tremendous diversity of customer influence and hence system variability within high-contact service systems. For example, a bank branch offers both simple services such as cash withdrawals that take just a minute or so, and complicated services such as loan application preparation which can take in excess of an hour. Moreover, these activities many range from being self-service through an ATM, to coproduction where bank personnel and the customer work together as a team to develop the loan application. We have more to say on the ways to configure service activities in subsequent sections of this chapter.

EXHIBIT 4.2

Major Differences between High- and Low-Contact Systems in a Bank

Design Decision	High-Contact System (A branch office)	Low-Contact System (A check processing center)
Facility location	Operations must be near the customer.	Operations may be placed near supply, transport, or labor.
Facility layout	Facility should accommodate the customer's physical and psychological needs and expectations.	Facility should focus on production efficiency.
Product design	Environment as well as the physical product define the nature of the service.	Customer is not in the service environment so the product can be defined by fewer attributes.
Process design	Stages of production process have a direct, immediate effect on the customer.	Customer is not involved in majority of processing steps.
Scheduling	Customer is in the production schedule and must be accommodated.	Customer is concerned mainly with completion dates.
Production planning	Orders cannot be stored, so smoothing production flow will result in loss of business.	Both backlogging and production smoothing are possible.
Worker skills	Direct work force constitutes a major part of the service product and so must be able to interact well with the public.	Direct work force need only have technical skills.
Quality control	Quality standards are often in the eye of the beholder and hence variable.	Quality standards are generally measurable and hence fixed.
Time standards	Service time depends on customer needs, and therefore time standards are inherently loose.	Work is performed on customer surrogates (e.g., forms), thus time standards can be tight.
Wage payment	Variable output requires time-based wage systems.	"Fixable" output permits output-based wage systems.
Capacity planning	To avoid lost sales, capacity must be set to match peak demand.	Storable output permits capacity at some average demand level.

4.3 DESIGNING SERVICE ORGANIZATIONS

Designing a service organization entails the execution of four elements of what James Heskett refers to as the "Strategic Service Vision."[2] The first element is identification of the target market (Who is our customer?); the second is the service concept (How do we differentiate our service in the market?); the third

---

[2] James Heskett, "Lessons from the Service Sector," *Harvard Business Review,* March–April 1987, pp. 118–26.

is the service strategy (What is our service package and the operating focus of our service?); and fourth is the service delivery system (What are the actual processes, staff, and facilities by which the service is created?).

Choosing a target market and developing the service package are top management decisions setting the stage for the direct operating decisions of service strategy and delivery system design.

Several major factors distinguish service design and development from typical manufactured product development. First, the process and the product must be developed simultaneously; indeed, in services the process is the product. (We make this statement with the general recognition that many manufacturers are using such concepts as concurrent engineering and DFM (design for manufacture) as approaches to more closely link product design and process design.)

Second, although equipment and software that support a service can be protected by patents and copyrights, a service operation itself lacks the legal protection commonly available to goods production. Third, the service package, rather than a definable good, constitutes the major output of the development process. Fourth, many parts of the service package are often defined by the training individuals receive before they become part of the service organization. In particular, in professional service organizations (PSOs) such as law firms and hospitals, prior certification is necessary for hiring. Fifth, many service organizations can change their service offerings virtually overnight. Routine service organizations (RSOs) such as barbershops, retail stores, and restaurants, have this flexibility.

Service Strategy: Focus and Advantage

Service strategy begins by selecting the operating focus by which the service firm will compete. These include:

1. Treatment of the customer in terms of friendliness and helpfulness.
2. Speed and convenience of service delivery.
3. Price of the service.
4. Variety of services (essentially a one-stop shopping philosophy).
5. Quality of the tangible goods that are central to or accompany the service. Examples include a "world-class" corned beef sandwich, eyeglasses made while you wait, or an understandable insurance policy.
6. Unique skills which constitute the service offering, such as hair styling, brain surgery, or piano lessons.

Exhibit 4.3 presents what we view as the operating **service focus** choices of a number of well-known companies. If our interpretation is correct, it indicates that most companies choose to compete on no more than one or two dimensions—that trade-offs have been made.

EXHIBIT 4.3   Operations Focus of Selected Service Firms

	Treatment	Speed/ Convenience	Price	Variety	Unique Skills/ Tangibles
Nordstrom Department Stores	X				
Federal Express Corporation	X	X			
Merrill Lynch & Company (Cash Management Account)		X		X[a]	
Crown Books			X		
Wal-Mart Stores	X		X[b]	X	
Price Club			X[c]		
Disneyland	X				X
American Express Company	X	X			
McDonald's Corporation		X	X		
Domino's Pizza		X[d]	X		
Marriott Corporation	X				
Club Med Resorts	X[e]		X		
American Airlines		X[f]		X	
Singapore Airlines	X				
Southwest Airlines			X[g]		
Riverside Methodist Hospitals (Columbus, Ohio)	X[h]				
H & R Block		X	X		
American Automobile Association		X[i]			

[a] A cash management account includes checkbook, credit card, money market fund, and other services in one account.

[b] Wal-Mart controls cost of inventory by driving tough bargains with suppliers.

[c] Price Club converts shoppers into warehouse order pickers in exchange for low-priced volume purchases.

[d] First to use the automated pizza maker where an attendant puts a raw pie in one side and pulls out a cooked pie on the other.

[e] All-inclusive, low-cost resorts where staff known as Gentils Organisateurs (GOs) coproduce a fun vacation with the guests, Gentils Membres (GMs).

[f] Sabre reservation system makes it easy for travel agents to book seats and for the company to instantaneously change prices to counter competitors' rates.

[g] No-frills service (i.e., no computerized reservation system, no assigned seating, and no meals) allows lowest prices in the industry.

[h] Riverside Hospital treats patients and their families like customers—give adult heart patients teddy bears to hold and colorful smocks with hearts imprinted on them. Holding a teddy bear feels good and helps the healing process.

[i] AAA phone/computer network uses the number of the phone a customer is calling from anywhere in the United States to pinpoint the nearest AAA garage.

Integrating marketing and operations to achieve competitive advantage
Achieving competitive advantage in services requires integration of service marketing with service delivery to meet or exceed customer expectations. This holds true no matter which competitive dimensions are emphasized. Companies that do extremely well (or extremely poorly) in this process, create legends and nightmares (Exhibit 4.4).

An overview of the elements leading to service advantage and service oblivion is shown in Exhibit 4.5. As can be seen in the diagram, marketing typically has responsibility for communicating the service promise to the customer and thereby creating customer expectations about service outcomes. Operations is responsible for the actions executing the promise and managing

EXHIBIT 4.4   **Levels of Satisfaction Achieved Due to Service Performance**

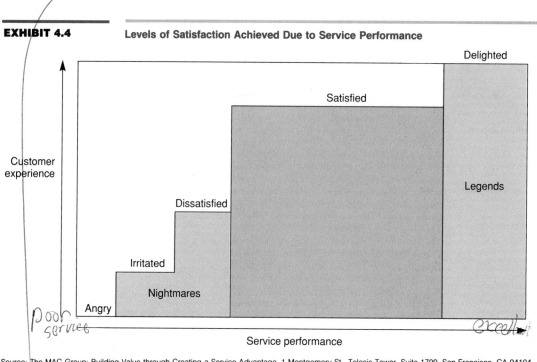

Source: The MAC Group: Building Value through Creating a Service Advantage, 1 Montgomery St., Telesis Tower, Suite 1700, San Francisco, CA 94104, June 1990.

EXHIBIT 4.5   **Service Measurement/Monitoring and Recovery Process**

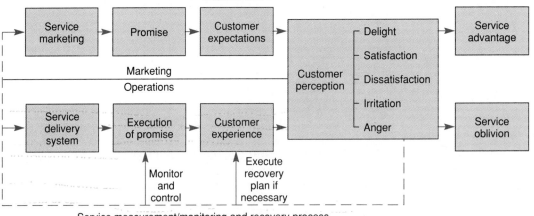

Service measurement/monitoring and recovery process

Source: The MAC Group: Building Value through Creating a Service Advantage, 1 Montgomery St., Telesis Tower, Suite 1700, San Francisco, CA 94104, June 1990.

the customer experience. The feedback loop indicates that if outcomes are not satisfactory or do not create service advantage, management may alter either the service marketing strategy or the delivery system. The need to monitor and control the execution phase and have a recovery plan to diffuse negative reactions before the customer leaves the system is also indicated.

Monitoring and controlling involves the standard managerial actions of reassigning workers to deal with short-run demand variations (e.g., Lucky Supermarkets opening up another checkout stand when there are more than three people in line); checking with customers and employees as to how things are going; and for many services, simply being visible to customers.

Recovery planning involves training frontline workers to respond to such situations as overbooking, lost luggage, or a bad meal. (See the Insert for a classic recovery experienced by one of the authors.)

INSERT   Mouse as Amenity

While eating in the basement of a rustic Mexican restaurant in Boston, my wife and I observed a mouse run out from behind a stack of Carta Blanca beer cartons, nibble something, and scurry back along a wall baseboard. It so happened that one of the ovens was out of order that night, and though we had been informed of a likely delay for our meal, the manager came over to us and offered us a free drink to make amends. We told him that wasn't necessary and mentioned that we had just seen a mouse! His response: "A mouse? Oh, you mean Harry . . . . Everybody knows Harry. And you know what the good news is? . . . Mice and rats don't coexist." He then walked away, leaving us to appreciate the benefits of being under Harry's protection against the dreaded rats that roam the streets of Boston.

Moral: A quick-thinking manager invoked a recovery action that converted visible evidence of vermin infestation into a service amenity!

A company that can't achieve competitive advantage in its service delivery must at least achieve parity with its competitors. In this regard, Kevin Coyne has made the following observations about investing in improved service:

> Investments to reach minimum standards cannot be "traded off" against other investments; they are a cost of doing business and should be considered required investments. However, achieving effective parity often requires less investment than managers might expect, for three reasons: First, most service encounters and attributes do not matter to customers except in extreme situations. Second, most customers are indifferent to a fairly wide variation in the level of service provided for most encounters, once the lower threshold of service is reached. Finally, customers have imprecise impressions as to the actual level of service being provided, and it is often difficult for customers to compare one provider's service offerings to those of competitors. Thus, two providers may offer significantly different levels of service in a particular encounter, yet be at effective parity.[3]

---

[3] Kevin Coyne, "Beyond Service Fads—Meaningful Strategies for the Real World," *Sloan Management Review,* Summer 1989, p. 74.

4.4 STRUCTURING THE SERVICE ENCOUNTER: SERVICE-SYSTEM DESIGN MATRIX

Service encounters can be configured in a number of different ways. The **service-system design matrix** in Exhibit 4.6 identifies six common alternatives.

The top of the matrix shows the degree of customer/server contact: the *buffered core,* which is physically separated from the customer; the *permeable system,* which is penetrable by the customer via phone or face-to-face contact; and the *reactive system,* which is both penetrable and reactive to the customer's requirements. The left side of the matrix shows what we believe to be a logical marketing proposition, namely, that the greater the amount of contact, the greater the sales opportunity; the right side shows the impact on production efficiency as the customer exerts more influence on the operation.

The entries within the matrix list the ways in which service can be delivered. At one extreme, service contact is by mail; customers have little interaction with the system. At the other extreme, customers "have it their way," through face-to-face contact. The remaining four entries in the exhibit contain varying degrees of interaction.

As one would guess, production efficiency decreases as the customer has more contact (and therefore more influence) on the system. To offset this, however, the face-to-face contact provides high sales opportunity to sell additional products. Conversely, low contact, such as mail, allows the system to work more efficiently because the customer is unable to significantly affect (or disrupt) the system. However, there is relatively little sales opportunity for additional product sales.

There can be some shifting in the positioning of each entry. Consider the Exhibit 4.6 entry "face-to-face tight specs." This refers to those situations where there is little variation in the service process—neither customer nor server has much discretion in creating the service. Fast-food restaurants and Disneyland come to mind. Face-to-face loose specs refers to situations where the service process is generally understood but there are options in the way it will be performed or the physical goods that are a part of it. A full-service restaurant or a car sales agency are examples. Face-to-face total customization refers to service encounters whose specifications must be developed through some interaction between the customer and server. Legal and medical services are of this type, and the degree to which the resources of the system are mustered for the service determines whether the system is reactive or merely permeable. Examples would be the mobilization of an advertising firm's resources in preparation for an office visit by a major client, or an operating team scrambling to prepare for emergency surgery.

Exhibit 4.7 extends the design matrix. It shows the changes in workers, operations, and types of technical innovations as the degree of customer/ service system contact changes. For worker requirements, the relationships between mail contact and clerical skills, on-site technology and helping skills, and phone contact and verbal skills, are self-evident. Face-to-face tight specs

EXHIBIT 4.6   Service-System Design Matrix

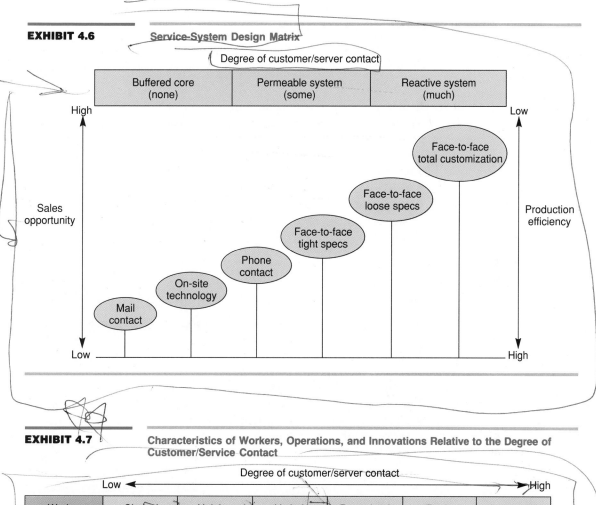

EXHIBIT 4.7   Characteristics of Workers, Operations, and Innovations Relative to the Degree of Customer/Service Contact

	Low ◄——— Degree of customer/server contact ———► High					
Worker requirements	Clerical skills	Helping skills	Verbal skills	Procedural skills	Trade skills	Diagnostic skills
Focus of operations	Paper handling	Demand management	Scripting calls	Flow control	Capacity management	Client mix
Technological innovations	Office automation	Routing methods	Computer databases	Electronic aids	Self-serve	Client/worker teams

requires procedural skills in particular, because the worker must follow the routine in conducting a generally standardized, high-volume process. Face-to-face loose specs frequently calls for trade skills (shoemaker, draftsperson, maitre d', dental hygienist) to finalize the design for the service. Face-to-face total customization tends to call for diagnostic skills of the professional to ascertain the needs or desires of the client.

Strategic Uses of the Matrix

The matrix has both operational and strategic uses. Its operational uses are reflected in its identification of worker requirements, focus of operations, and innovations previously discussed. Some of its strategic uses are

1. Enabling systematic integration of operations and marketing strategy. Trade-offs become more clear-cut, and, more important, at least some of the major design variables are crystalized for analysis purposes. For example, the matrix indicates that it would make little sense relative to sales for a service firm to invest in high-skilled workers if it plans to operate using tight specs.

2. Clarifying exactly which combination of service delivery the firm is in fact providing. As the company incorporates the delivery options listed on the diagonal, it is becoming diversified in its production process.

3. Permitting comparison with other firms in the way specific services are delivered. This helps to pinpoint a firm's competitive advantage.

4. Indicating evolutionary or life cycle changes that might be in order as the firm grows. Unlike the product-process matrix for manufacturing, however, where natural growth moves in one direction (from the job shop to flow shop as a volume increases), evolution of service delivery can move in either direction along the diagonal as a function of a sales-efficiency trade-off.

5. Providing flexibility. The user of the matrix can go into depth, placing particular service products of a small firm or individual department on it, or cover a large service organization at a more aggregated level.

4.5 SERVICE BLUEPRINTING

Just as is the case with manufacturing process design, the standard tool for service process design is the flowchart. In 1978, Lynn Shostack added the concept of the *line of visability* and emphasized the identification of potential fail points in her version of the flowchart called a **service blueprint.**[4] She has also made a compelling case for having blueprints on every aspect of a service, and having the "keeper of the blueprint" as a specific job function in any large service organization. Current practice in some companies is to have blueprints available on computers for senior managers so when problems arise, they can home in on any portion of a service process and thereby make more informed decisions about how to resolve them. One example is the elaborate service

---

[4] G. Lynn Shostack, "Designing Services That Deliver," *Harvard Business Review* 62, no. 1 (January–February 1984), p. 135.

blueprint for a discount brokerage in Exhibit 4.8. The steps involved in developing a blueprint for a simple shoeshine process, including a profitablity analysis, are as follows:

1. *Identify processes.*   The first step in creating such a blueprint is mapping the processes that constitute the service. Exhibit 4.9 maps a shoeshine parlor. As the service is simple and clear-cut, the map is straightforward. It might be useful to specify how the proprietor will perform the step called *buff.*

2. *Isolate fail points.*   Having diagrammed the processes involved, the designer can now see where the system might go awry. The shoeshiner may pick up and apply the wrong color wax. So the designer must build in a subprocess to correct this possible error. The identification of fail points and the design of fail-safe processes are critical. The consequences of service failures can be greatly reduced by analyzing fail points at the design stage.

3. *Establish a time frame.*   Since all services depend on time, which is usually the major cost determinant, the designer should establish a standard execution time.

4. *Analyze profitability.*   The customer can spend the three minutes between standard and acceptable execution time at the corner parlor waiting in line or during service, if an error occurs or if the shoeshiner does certain things too slowly. Whatever its source, a delay can affect profits dramatically. Exhibit 4.10 quantifies the cost of delay; after four minutes the proprietor loses money. A service designer must establish a time-of-service-execution standard to assure a profitable business.

In the shoeshine example, the standard execution time is two minutes. Research showed that the customer would tolerate up to five minutes of performance before lowering his or her assessment of quality. Acceptable execution time for a shoeshine is then five minutes.

4.6 THREE CONTRASTING SERVICE DESIGNS

The three general approaches to delivering on-site services are the production line approach made famous by McDonald's Corporation, the customer involvement approach made famous by ATMs and gas stations, and the personal attention approach made famous by Nordstrom's department stores.

The Production Line Approach

The production line approach pioneered by McDonald's refers to more than just the steps required to assemble a Big Mac. Rather, as Theodore Levitt notes, it is treating the delivery of fast food as a manufacturing process rather than a service process.[5] The value of this philosophy is that it overcomes many

---

[5] Theodore Levitt, "Production-Line Approach to Service," *Harvard Business Review* 50, no. 5 (September–October 1972), pp. 41–52.

EXHIBIT 4.8 Service Blueprint for a Discount Brokerage

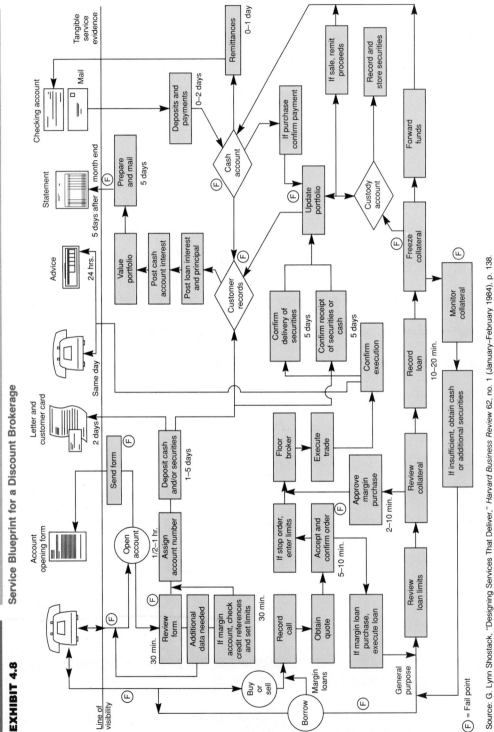

Source: G. Lynn Shostack, "Designing Services That Deliver," *Harvard Business Review* 62, no. 1 (January–February 1984), p. 138.

EXHIBIT 4.9   **Blueprint for a Corner Shoeshine**

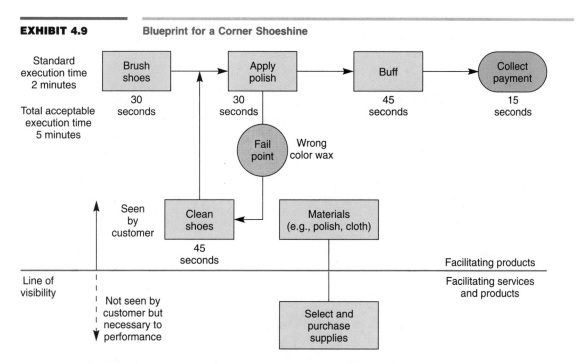

Standard execution time 2 minutes

Total acceptable execution time 5 minutes

| Brush shoes | Apply polish | Buff | Collect payment |
| 30 seconds | 30 seconds | 45 seconds | 15 seconds |

Fail point   Wrong color wax

Seen by customer

Clean shoes
45 seconds

Materials (e.g., polish, cloth)

Facilitating products

Line of visibility

Facilitating services and products

Not seen by customer but necessary to performance

Select and purchase supplies

Source: G. Lynn Shostack, "Designing Services That Deliver," *Harvard Business Review* 62, no. 1 (January–February 1984), p. 134.

EXHIBIT 4.10

Shoeshine Profitability Analysis

| | EXECUTION TIME | | |
	2 Minutes	3 Minutes	4 Minutes
Price	$.50	$.50	$.50
Costs			
Time @ $.10 per minute	.20	.30	.40
Wax	.03	.03	.03
Other operating expenses	.09	.09	.09
Total costs	$.32	$.42	$.52
Pretax profit	$.18	$.08	($.02)

Source: G. Lynn Shostack, "Designing Services That Deliver," *Harvard Business Review* 62, no. 1 (January–February 1984), p. 135.

of the problems inherent in the concept of service itself. That is, service implies subordination or subjugation of the server to the served; manufacturing, on the other hand, avoids this connotation because it focuses on things rather than people. Thus in manufacturing and at McDonald's, "the orientation is toward the efficient production of results not on the attendance on others." Levitt notes that besides McDonald's marketing and financial skills, the company carefully controls "the execution of each outlet's central function—the rapid delivery of a uniform, a high-quality mix of prepared foods in an environment of obvious cleanliness, order, and cheerful courtesy. The systematic substitution of equipment for people, combined with the carefully planned use and positioning of technology, enables McDonald's to attract and hold patronage in proportions no predecessor or imitator has managed to duplicate."

Levitt cites several aspects of McDonald's operations to illustrate the concepts:

- The McDonald's french fryer allows cooking of the optimum number of french fries at one time.
- A wide-mouthed scoop is used to pick up the precise amount of french fries for each order size. (The employee never touches the product.)
- Storage space is expressly designed for a predetermined mix of pre-packaged and premeasured products.
- Cleanliness is pursued by providing ample trash cans in and outside each facility (and the larger outlets have motorized sweepers for the parking area).
- Hamburgers are wrapped in color-coded paper.
- Through painstaking attention to total design and facilities planning, everything is built integrally into the (McDonald's) machine itself—into the technology of the system. The only choice available to the attendant is to operate it exactly as the designers intended.

The Customer Involvement Approach

In contrast to the production line approach, C. H. Lovelock and R. F. Young propose that the service process can be enhanced by having the customer take a greater role in the production of the service.[6] Automatic teller machines, self-service gas stations, salad bars, and in-room coffee-making equipment in motels are approaches by which the service burden is shifted to the consumer. Obviously, this philosophy requires some selling on the part of the service organization to convince customers that this is beneficial to them. To this end, Lovelock and Young propose a number of steps, including developing customer trust, promoting the benefits of cost, speed, and convenience, and following up to make sure that the procedures are being effectively used. In

---

[6] C. H. Lovelock and R. F. Young, "Look to Customers to Increase Productivity," *Harvard Business Review* 57, no. 2, pp. 168–78.

essence, this turns customers into "partial employees" who must be trained in what to do and be compensated primarily through low prices charged for the service.

The Personal Attention Approach

The following example by Tom Peters describes how Nordstrom's department store operationalizes its personal attention philosophy.[7]

> After several visits to a store's men's clothing department, a customer's suit still did not fit. He wrote the company president, who sent a tailor to the customer's office with a new suit for fitting. When the alterations were completed, the suit was delivered to the customer—free of charge.
>
> This incident involved the $1.3 billion, Seattle-based Nordstrom, a specialty clothing retailer. Its sales per square foot are about five times that of a typical department store. Who received the customer's letter and urged the extreme (by others' standards) response? Co-chairman John Nordstrom.
>
> The frontline providers of this good service are well paid. Nordstrom's salespersons earn a couple of bucks an hour more than competitors, plus a 6.75 percent commission. Its top salesperson moves over $1 million a year in merchandise. Nordstrom lives for its customers and salespeople. Its only official organization chart puts the customer at the top, followed by sales and sales support people. Next come department managers, then store managers, and the board of directors at the very bottom.
>
> Salespersons religiously carry a "personal book," where they record voluminous information about each of their customers; senior, successful salespeople often have three or four bulging books, which they carry everywhere, according to Betsy Sanders, the vice president who orchestrated the firm's wildly successful penetration of the tough southern California market. "My objective is to get one new personal customer a day," says a budding Nordstrom star. The system helps him do just that. He has a virtually unlimited budget to send cards, flowers, and thank-you notes to customers. He also is encouraged to shepherd his customer to any department in the store to assist in a successful shopping trip.
>
> He also is abetted by what may be the most liberal returns policy in this or any other business: Return *anything,* no questions asked. Sanders says that "trusting customers," or "our bosses" as she repeatedly calls them, is vital to the Nordstrom philosophy. President Jim Nordstrom told the *Los Angeles Times,* "I don't care if they roll a Goodyear tire into the store. If they say they paid $200, give them $200 (in cash) for it." Sanders acknowledges that a few customers rip the store off—"rent hose from us," to use a common insider's line. But this is more than offset by goodwill from the 99 percent-plus who benefit from the "No Problem at Nordstrom" logo that the company lives up to with unmatched zeal.
>
> No bureaucracy gets in the way of serving the customer. Policy? Sanders explains to a dumbfounded group of Silicon Valley executives, "I know this drives the lawyers nuts, but our whole 'policy manual' is just one sentence, 'Use your own

---

[7] Tom Peters, *Quality!* (Palo Alto, Calif.: TPG Communications, 1986), pp. 10–12.

best judgment at all times.'" One store manager offers a translation, "Don't chew gum. Don't steal from us."

No matter what approach is taken to design a service, the need for the service characteristics shown in the Insert should be evident.

INSERT   Seven Characteristics of a Well-Designed Service System

1. *Each element of the service system is consistent with the operating focus of the firm.* For example, when the focus is on speed of delivery, each step in the process should help to foster speed.

2. *It is user-friendly.* This means that the customer can interact with it easily— that is, it has good signage, understandable forms, logical steps in the process, and service workers available to answer questions.

3. *It is robust.* That is, it can cope effectively with variations in demand and re- source availability. For example, if the computer goes down, effective backup systems are in place to permit service to continue.

4. *It is structured so that consistent performance by its people and systems is easily main- tained.* This means the tasks required of the workers are doable, and the supporting technologies are truly supportive and reliable.

5. *It provides effective links between the back office and the front office so that nothing falls between the cracks.*

6. *It manages the evidence of service quality in such a way that customers see the value of the service provided.* Many services do a great job behind the scenes but fail to make this visible to the customer. This is particularly true where a service improvement is made. Unless customers are made aware of the improvement through explicit communication about it, the improved performance is un- likely to gain maximum impact.

7. *It is cost-effective.* There is minimum waste of time and resources in delivering the service.

4.7 SERVICE GUARANTEES AS DESIGN DRIVERS

The phrases, "Positively, absolutely, overnight," and "Thirty minutes or $3.00 off your pizza," are examples of service guarantees most of us know by heart. Hiding behind such marketing promises of service satisfaction are a set of actions that must be taken by the operations organization to fulfill these promises.

Thousands of companies have launched **service guarantees** as a marketing tool designed to provide peace of mind for customers unsure about trying their service. From an operations perspective, a service guarantee can be used not only as an improvement tool but also at the design stage to focus the firm's

EXHIBIT 4.11

Sample Service
Guarantee

GOOF-PROOF BANKING

...OR WE PAY.

Great service should be a lot more than just being greeted with a warm hello and a pleasant smile.

Great service requires professionals who are also dedicated to going out of their way to satisfy your banking needs.

At First Interstate Bank of California, we are committed to going the extra mile for you. Day in and day out.

Perhaps that's why, according to a statewide survey of major banks and savings and loans, First Interstate ranked #1 in overall service. And we intend to remain #1. Because you deserve nothing less.

So, to insure that we continue to provide you with the best banking service in California, we are introducing a comprehensive Service Guarantee. Here's what it means for you:

WE GOOF...WE PAY. If you find any error on your account statement—we'll pay you $5.

YOU WAIT...WE PAY. If you have to wait more than 5 minutes in the main teller line—we'll pay you $5.

WE BREAK...WE PAY. If our Day & Night Teller® ATM isn't working when it should be—we'll pay you $5.

WE DAWDLE...WE PAY. If you have a question or problem and one of our Customer Assistance Representatives doesn't respond to you within 24 hours—we'll pay you $5.

WE DELAY...WE PAY. If you apply for a loan and don't get an answer within 24 hours—we'll pay you $5.

Now that's service. The best in California. Our customers know it. Let us prove it to you, too.

Come to First Interstate Bank of California. We go the extra mile for you. Contact any branch for details regarding program qualifications and limitations.

First Interstate Bank

We go the extra mile for you.

delivery system squarely on the things it must do so well to satisfy the customer. Consider First Interstate Bank of California's service guarantee in Exhibit 4.11. It requires operations to have its back office working well, preventive maintenance for its ATMs, its branch office personnel on their toes, and its loan department working quickly.

4.8 DESIGNING INTERNAL SERVICES

As we discussed earlier, every person and department within an organization has a customer or customers. Many times, the customer is not external, it is someone at the next desk or in the next office. Usually when we talk about **internal service** in manufacturing, we are referring to service departments such as MIS, personnel, or maintenance. In services, labels get blurred. In a hospital, radiology and anesthesiology are, in effect, service departments even though they may not have a service designation. Likewise, in insurance companies it is very common for home office personnel to have field office personnel as their customers. From a service design standpoint, current practice is to have field office personnel identify what their service needs are and then work with their suppliers in the home office to translate their service needs into operating specifications. Frequently, this requires the aid of MIS specialists and methods analysts to develop the technical details. While the general concepts of service design for external customers usually pertain to internal service, the actual process of providing good internal service may be much more difficult. For example, in a hotel chain, setting up a new computer system or selecting appropriate personnel to fill job vacancies are internal services that are more uncertain in execution than are those services required to rent rooms. There are additional problems of management as well: Whose budget does this system go on? Who has first priority on getting a computer fixed? Nevertheless, we repeat that the same approach used to develop services for the external customer—Identifying the target market, service concept, service strategy, and service delivery system—can and should be used for all internal service activities as well.

4.9 CONCLUSION

Service design is still pretty much of an art, requiring an understanding of marketing, human relations, and technology, as well as operations. The future development of services appears to lie in information technology, since information exchange of one sort or another is the common thread that binds virtually all services. There is also a blurring between what we think of as manufacturing firms and what we think of as service firms. Indeed, companies such as Bally Manufacturing, RCA, Turner Construction, and Exxon Pipeline, which started out manufacturing products, are now listed among the Fortune 500 service companies.

If we reflect on the manufacturing side of such businesses, we find that the new technologies (FMS, CIM) permit the factory to compete very directly on fast, customized service. In fact, we predict that the next hot topic among manufacturers will be service, supplanting even quality.

4.10 REVIEW AND DISCUSSION QUESTIONS

1. Who is the "customer" in a jail? A cemetery? A summer camp for children?

2. How has price competition changed McDonald's basic formula for success?

3. Is it possible for a service firm to use a production line approach or use a self-serve design and still keep a high customer focus (personal attention)? Explain and support your answer with examples.

4. Explain why a manager of a bank home office should be evaluated differently than a manager of a bank branch.

5. Identify the high-contact and low-contact operations of the following services:
    a. A dental office.
    b. An airline.
    c. An accounting office.
    d. An automobile agency.

6. Some suggest that customer expectation is the key to service success. Give an example from your own experience to support or refute this assertion.

7. Where would you place a drive-in church, a campus food vending machine, and a bar's automatic mixed drink machine on the service-system design matrix?

8. What do customer expectations have to do with service quality?

9. What elements would you like to see guaranteed in addition to those given in First Interstate's guarantee?

10. What are the risks associated with the following guarantee offered by one of the authors of this book for his advanced MBA Service Operations class?

    My Service Guarantee: If you are not satisfied with the quality of the class, I will refund the cost of books and cases and $250 of your course fees.

4.11 PROBLEMS

1. Place the following functions of a department store on the service-system design matrix: Mail order (i.e., catalog), phone order, hardware, stationery, apparel, cosmetics, customer service (i.e., complaints).

2. Do the same as in the previous problem for a hospital with the following activities and relationships: Physician/patient, nurse/patient, billing, medical records, lab tests, admissions, diagnostic tests (e.g., X-rays).

3. The service designer for the shoeshine shop of Exhibit 4.9 and 4.10 has decided to study the following changes:

    ■ Add a premium two-coat service, which will repeat Steps 2 and 3 (Apply polish and Buff). The price of the premium service will be set at $.70.

    ■ Provide each customer (both regular and premium) with a receipt and a sample of shoe polish imprinted with the shop's name. This will add $.01 to operating expenses and 0.5 minutes to the execution time but will provide the customer with some tangible evidence of the service.

Both of these changes are to be made simultaneously. Do the following:

a. Draw the blueprint for the premium service.

b. Provide a profitability analysis for the premium service.

c. Provide an updated profitability analysis for the regular service.

4. SYSTEM DESCRIPTION EXERCISE

The beginning step in studying a productive system is to develop a description of that system. Once a system is described, we are better able to determine why the system works well or poorly and to recommend production-related improvements. Since we are all familiar with fast-food restaurants, try your hand at describing the production system employed at, say, a McDonald's. In doing so, answer the following questions:

a. What are the important aspects of the service package?

b. Which skills and attitudes are needed by the service personnel?

c. How can customer demand be altered?

d. Provide a rough-cut blueprint of the delivery system. (It is not necessary to provide execution times, just diagram the basic flow through the system.) Critique the blueprint. Are there any unnecessary steps or can fail points be eliminated?

e. Can the customer/provider interface be changed to include more technology? More self-serve?

f. Which measures are being used to evaluate and measure the service? Which could be used?

g. How does it measure up on the seven characteristics of a well-designed service?

4.12 CASE: KINKO'S COPIER STORES*

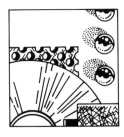

"We're not your average printer," says Annie Odell, Kinko's regional manager for Louisiana. She's right. She may have the only printshops in town where customers come as much for the company as for the copies. It's a free-wheeling, hi-tech operation that marches to the beat of a different drum machine. It looks chaotic; it is chaotic. Yet it produces profit as well as fun.

Odell's copy shop empire has grown from one to seven in six years, including five in the greater New Orleans area.

Kinko's keeps its sales figures a secret, but Odell estimates her New Orleans stores make about 40 million copies a year. At the firm's advertised 4½ cents-per copy price, that would mean around $1.8 million a year in sales, or an average of over $300,000 per shop. The New Orleans operations rank among Kinko's top 25 percent nationally, reports Becky Barieau of Kinko's of Georgia.

Sales in New Orleans have climbed even while the marketplace has been sinking. At the Carrollton store, revenues increased 10 percent over last year, an excellent showing considering the 4½ cents-per copy rate has not budged since 1980.

---

* Source: Mark Ballard, "Working in a Fishbowl," *Quick Printing,* May 1987, pp. 30–32. Reprinted by permission.

"Depression seems to generate more need for copies," says Wallis Windsor, manager of the Carrollton store, "There are bankruptcies, legal documents and resumes—hundreds of people who want 50 copies of their resumes on specialty paper."

Printers Sneer

Kinko's is unique. For one thing, it doesn't do a lick of offset printing. It makes copies, copies, and almost nothing but copies. On the side it binds, folds, staples, collates, makes pads, and takes passport photos.

Kinko's is also unique among quick printing chains in that it doesn't franchise. All 300 or so Kinko's stores are divided among a few closely held corporations, and founder Paul Orfalea holds a piece of virtually all of them. Odell explains that the company avoids franchising to ensure tight control over quality at its outlets.

Others attribute the structure to a desire to avoid the legal restrictions and paperwork demanded by setting up franchises in different states. How it's been kept together is a management feat in itself.

Even the name sticks out. The Yellow Pages list dozens of quick printers with some reference to speed in their names, often intentionally misspelled. "Kinko's" denotes a place that's . . . well, a little kinky. For the record, Orfalea, who plugged in his first photocopier when he was in college, was nicknamed by classmates as "Kinko" for his curly head of hair.

Broadway and Benihana

Kinko's management style draws on both the restaurant business and the stage. Fast copies are like fast food, say the managers. It's not just that every Big Mac is a copy of every other one. Images of eating come up again and again as they try to explain what keeps their customers coming back.

"Making copies is addictive," says Windsor, and points to her clientele of "regulars," who "have made this their office. They will spend four or five hours here although they don't spend more than $5 or $6. People have suggested we open a bar in here."

"Instant gratification is what Kinko's is offering," says another manager.

The last time managers from around the country huddled in Santa Barbara for the company "picnic," they studied looseleaf binders crammed full of floor plans for McDonald's and Benihana of Tokyo—a variation on the acclaimed art of Japanese management.

"You'd find it hard to believe," says Odell, "but Benihana is a lot like Kinko's. They're masters of efficiency. We'll try to set up the floor to get one person operating two copiers, just like Benihana puts one cook between two tables. Our paper is centrally located, just as they have all the chopping prepared ahead of time. Then there's the floater, who floats around and pops in wherever he's needed."

Both Kinko's and Benihana's use theater to attract clients, charging their employees with putting on a good show as well as putting out good service. At the Japanese restaurant, the show is the cook, who sizzles a sukiyaki right in front of your table. At Kinko's, it's the clatter of copy machines and the Charlie Chaplinlike spectacle of operators running back and forth between them.

"They do it right in front of you and you get instant quality control," says Odell, "There's no way you're going to drop that document with the customer watching you."

She deliberately displays all her machines and personnel in one big room. "We work out with the public. That's why it's fun," says Odell, "The other guys are behind closed doors.

Windsor enjoys working in a fishbowl. "My personality changes," she says. "I'll be a little more dramatic and louder than I would be in a closed group. I walk quickly. I'll wad up and throw papers a lot."

She believes customers unconsciously get into the act. "Some of the mildest-mannered people get aggressive in here. I've seen a little old lady elbow her way in ahead of people, where if she were in a bank she'd stand in line neatly."

Kinko's does no broadcast and little print advertising, counting on price and word-of-mouth to draw customers, and ambience doesn't hurt. Each Kinko's has its "regulars," who get friendly with particular operators and who favor particular machines. The area in front of the counter is strewn with typewriters, lettering machines and light tables, all the better to hook people into making themselves comfortable and coming back.

A recent addition to that melange is the customer comment form. The customer mails the postage-paid form straight to headquarters in Santa Barbara, where senior management review it and send a thank-you note to the author before routing it back to the shop manager for action. Odell has several inches of forms on file, along with notes on the follow-up calls she made to the customers.

"We don't choose our market so much as our market chooses us," she says. Each shop keeps a different mix of machines, depending on the needs of its patrons. An operator learns quickly that the Xerox 1000 series picks up blue but not yellow, while the 9000 series picks up yellow and black but not blue. Thus, the store adjoining the Tulane campus does not have a 9000 because students tend to bring in notes and books highlighted with yellow markers.

Another adaptation to the market is "Professor Publishing," a service which lets professors excerpt chapters from several books and print them up together as a single textbook. During the first two weeks of every semester, the Broadway office works virtually around-the-clock on this specialty.

Odell maintains that her managers clear all material with publishers before printing a professor's anthology. Indeed, Kinko's says it is one of the most scrupulous of the copy chains about observing copyright laws.

* * * * *

Printing in a Fishbowl

If working at the Kinko's shops in New Orleans is like working in a fishbowl, it's a two-way fishbowl where the fish are always peering back at their audience. The crazy-quilt mix of customers provides endless entertainment and a fund of oddball stories to exchange over beers. A sampling:

- One woman insisted that the manager throw away the ribbon on the self-service typewriter she'd just used, fearing that someone might try to use it to recreate her document. Another customer wanted several confidential pages typed, and asked, "Can you get me a typist who won't read them?"

- Some artists enjoy using the photocopiers for the oddest things. One woman brings in stuffed dead birds for reproduction. Another brought in a box of pecans purported to be from the backyard of a house where Tennessee Williams once lived.

- A tipsy woman, about 25 years of age, meandered in from a Mardi Gras parade, curled up next to a window, and fell asleep. There she remained for four hours, while the copiers and binding machines pounded and rattled. Manager Raynell Murphy called the home office. "What should I do?" she asked.

    "Get a picture," came the word from California, "We can use it as a promotion, you know, to show what a relaxed atmosphere we have at Kinko's."

    Finally, a hulking woman who had just bought some copies walked over to the sleeper, kicked her a couple of times, and asked, "Are you ready yet?" The sleeper arose and groggily headed out the door.

QUESTIONS

1. Can general operational standards be developed and implemented in all or a majority of Kinko's shops?

2. Discuss the idea of grouping copiers in machine centers so that certain copiers are available for specific tasks.

3. How do the different services offered (private copying versus copying services provided) present separate types of problems for management?

4. Kinko's Professor Publishing apparently did not pan out. What do you think might have been the cause?

4.13 SELECTED BIBLIOGRAPHY

Bitran, Gabriel R., and Johannes Hoech. "The Humanization of Service: Respect at the Moment of Truth." *Sloan Management Review,* Winter 1990, pp. 89–96.

Chase, R. B. "The Customer Contact Approach to Services: Theoretical Bases and Practical Extensions." *Operations Research* 21, no. 4 (1981), pp. 698–705.

Cohen, Morris A., and Hau L. Lee. "Out of Touch with Customer Needs?" *Sloan Management Review,* Winter 1990, pp. 55–66.

Collier, D. A. *Service Management: The Automation of Services.* Reston, Va.: Reston Publishing, 1986.

Farsad, Behshid, and Ahmad K. Elshennawy. "Defining Service Quality Is Difficult for Service and Manufacturing Firms." *Industrial Engineering,* March 1989, pp. 17–20.

Firnstahl, Timothy W. "My Employees Are My Service Guarantee." *Harvard Business Review,* July–August 1989, pp. 28–33.

Fitzsimmons, J. A., and R. S. Sullivan. *Service Operations Management.* New York: McGraw-Hill, 1983.

Flint, Jerry, and William Heuslein. "An Urge to Service." *Forbes,* September 18, 1989, pp. 172–74.

Hackett, Gregory P. "Investment in Technology: The Service Sector Sinkhole? *Sloan Management Review,* Winter 1990, pp. 97–103.

Heskett, J. L. *Managing in the Service Economy.* Cambridge, Mass.: Harvard University Press, 1986.

Peavey, Dennis E. "It's Time for a Change." *Management Accounting,* February 1990, pp. 31–35.

Shapiro, Benson P.; V. Kasturi Rangan; Rowland T. Moriarty; and Elliot B. Ross. "Manage Customers for Profits, Not Just Sales." *Harvard Business Review,* September–October 1987, pp. 101–8.

Sonnenberg, Frank K. "Service Quality: Forethought, Not Afterthought." *Journal of Business Strategy,* September–October 1989, pp. 54–57.

Supplement

Waiting Line Theory

EPIGRAPH

No matter which line you get in, the other line will move faster.

That the other lines move faster is known as Ettore's observation (*Harpers,* August 1974). The full version is: "The Other Line Moves Faster. This applies to all lines—bank, supermarket, toll booth, and so on. And don't try to change lines. If you do, the other line—the one you were in originally—will then move faster."

KEY TERMS

Queue

Arrival Rate

Exponential Distribution

Poisson Distribution

Erlang Distribution

Single Channel, Single Phase

MultiChannel, MultiPhase

Service Rate

*U*nderstanding waiting lines and learning how to manage them is one of the most important areas in operations management. It is basic to creating schedules, job design, inventory levels, and so on. In our service economy we wait in line every day, from driving to work to checking out at the supermarket. We also encounter waiting lines at factories—jobs wait in lines to be worked on at different machines, and machines themselves wait their turn to be overhauled. In short, waiting lines are pervasive.

What causes waiting lines in the first place? Whenever there is more than one user of a limited resource, a waiting line or **queue** takes form. This delay phenomenon occurs in a wide range of activities affecting many types of users and resources. When the waiting line consists of inanimate objects (such as materials, components, electrical impulses) waiting for some sort of processing (say, on a machine), this is primarily an economic problem: how long should the line be, how much in-process inventory is acceptable, how much equipment should be purchased, and similar questions. When the line consists of people waiting for a service, the problem has psychological as well as economic aspects.

In this supplement we discuss the basic elements of waiting line problems and provide standard steady-state formulas for solving them. These formulas, arrived at in the course of developing queuing theory, enable planners to analyze service requirements and establish service facilities appropriate to stated conditions. Queuing theory is broad enough to cover such dissimilar delays as those encountered by customers in a shopping mall or aircraft in a holding pattern awaiting landing slots.

We present some of the statistical aspects of the subject; however, the mathematics used to derive the formulas is somewhat involved and is covered in many statistics and operations research textbooks.

Modern queuing theory is based on studies performed during the early part of the 20th century by A. K. Erlang, a Danish telephone engineer. Erlang was concerned with capacities and applications of automatic telephone switching. Queuing theory is used extensively in industry and is a standard tool of operations management in such areas as scheduling, machine loading, and others.

S4.1 ECONOMICS OF THE WAITING LINE PROBLEM

The central problem in virtually every waiting line situation is a trade-off decision. The planner must weigh the added cost of providing more rapid service (more traffic lanes, additional landing strips, more checkout stands) against the inherent cost of waiting. But the waiting line condition can arise even when there are more than enough servers to handle the influx, when the facilities are *under*loaded.

Consider, for example, a serve-yourself four-island gas station with enough pumps (servers) to accommodate an average of 220 cars per hour. Even if the average number of cars is only 160 per hour at this particular station, the system can still be saturated at times. In a gas station, as in many other facilities, service capabilities are based on the *average* number of arrivals in a given time and the *average* time needed per customer. But in practice, customers arrive at a random rate subject to local traffic patterns, and the time needed per customer varies with the quantity of gas pumped, the dexterity of the customer, and so on. This variability in arrival rates and serving times may also cause periods where there are neither waiting lines nor customers at the pumps.

Frequently the cost trade-off decision is straightforward. For example, if we find that the total time our employees spend in line waiting to use a copying machine would otherwise be spent in productive activities, we could compare the cost of installing one additional machine to the value of employee time saved. The decision could then be reduced to dollar terms and the choice easily made.

On the other hand, suppose that our waiting line problem centers on demand for beds in a hospital. We can compute the cost of additional beds by summing the costs for building construction, additional equipment required, and increased maintenance. But what is on the other side of the scale? Here we are confronted with the problem of trying to place a dollar figure on a patient's need for a hospital bed that is unavailable. While we can arrive at an estimate of lost hospital income, what about the human cost arising from this lack of adequate hospital care?

Cost Effectiveness Balance

The ultimate objective of waiting line analysis is to achieve acceptable (minimal) levels in service capacity and in costs of customer waiting time. Exhibit S4.1 illustrates the essential trade-off relationship under typical (steady-state) customer traffic conditions. Initially, with minimal service capacity, the waiting line cost is at a maximum. As service capacity is increased, there is a reduction in the number of customers in the line and in their waiting times, resulting in a decreased waiting line cost. The variation in this function is often represented by the negative exponential curve. The cost of installing service capacity is shown simplistically as a linear rather than step function. The aggregate or total cost is shown as a U-shaped curve, a common approximation in such equilibrium problems. The idealized optimal cost is found at the crossover point between the service capacity and waiting line curves.

The Practical View of Waiting Lines

Before we precede with a traditional presentation of waiting line theory, we need to look at the intuitive side of the issue and what it means. Exhibit S4.2 shows arrivals at a service facility (e.g., a bank) and service requirements at

EXHIBIT S4.1

Service Capacity versus Waiting Line Trade-Off

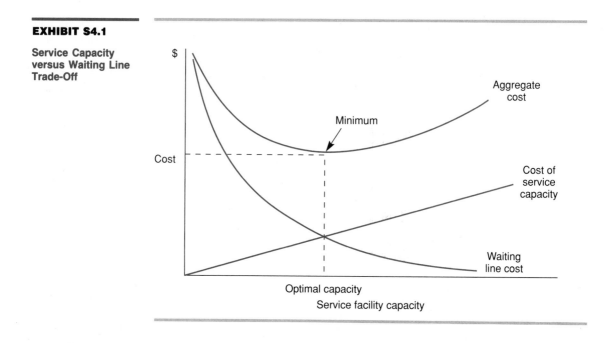

EXHIBIT S4.2   **Arrival and Service Profiles**

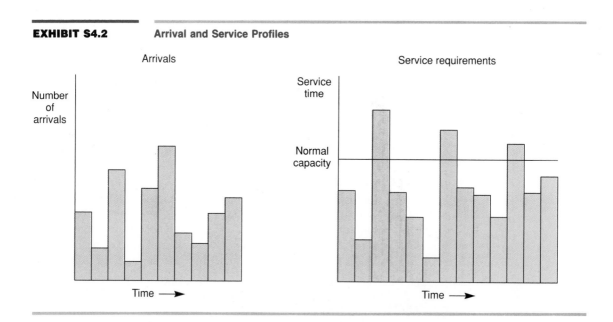

that facility (e.g., tellers, loan officer, etc.) One important thing is the number of arrivals over the course of the hours that the service system is open. From the service delivery viewpoint, customers demand varying amounts of service, often exceeding normal capacity.

We can have some control over arrivals in a variety of ways. For example, we can have a short line (such as a drive-in at a fast-food restaurant with only several spaces), we can establish specific hours for specific customers, we can run specials, and so forth. For the server, we can affect service time by using faster or slower servers, faster or slower machines, different tooling, different material, different layout, faster setup time, and so on.

We have interrupted the traditional waiting line treatment at this point to specifically point out that waiting lines are *not* a fixed condition of a productive system but are to a very large extent within the control of the system management and design.

S4.2 WAITING LINE CHARACTERISTICS

The waiting line (or queuing) phenomenon consists essentially of six major components: the source population, the way customers arrive at the service facility, the physical line itself, the way customers are selected from the line, the characteristics of the service facility itself (such as how the customers flow through the system and how much time it takes to serve each customer), and the condition of the customer exiting the system (back to the source population or not?). We discuss these six areas in Exhibit S4.3 separately in following sections.

Population Source

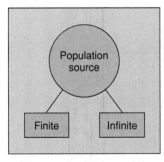

Arrivals at a service system may be drawn from a *finite* or an *infinite* population. The distinction is important because the analyses are based on different premises and require different equations for their solution.

Finite population.   A *finite population* refers to the limited size customer pool which is the source that will use the service, and at times form a line. The

EXHIBIT S4.3　　　　**Framework for Viewing Waiting Line Situations**

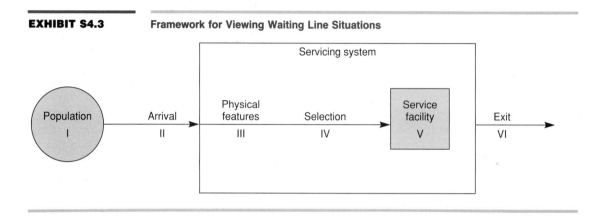

reason this finite classification is important is because when a customer leaves its position as a member of the population of users (by breaking down and requiring service, for example), the size of the user group is therefore reduced by one, which reduces the probability of the next breakdown. Conversely, when a customer is serviced and returns to the user group, the population increases and the probability of a user requiring service also increases. This finite class of problems requires a separate set of formulas from that of the infinite population case.

As an example, consider a group of six machines maintained by one repairperson. When one machine breaks down, the source population reduces to five, and the chances of one of the five breaking down and needing repair is certainly different than the chances of one out of six, as in the original size. If two machines are down with only four operating, the probability of another breakdown is again changed. Conversely, when a machine is repaired and returned to service, the machine population increases and therefore increases the probability of the next breakdown.

Infinite population.　　An infinite population is one large enough in relation to the service system so that the changes in the population size caused by subtractions or additions to the population (a customer needing service or a serviced customer returning to the population) does not significantly affect the system probabilities. If, in the preceding finite explanation, there were one hundred machines instead of six, then if one or two machines broke down, the probabilities for the next breakdowns would not be very different and the assumption could be made without a great deal of error that the population (for all practical purposes) was infinite. Nor would the formulas for "infinite" queuing problems cause much error if applied to a physician who has 1,000 patients, or a department store which has 10,000 customers.

EXHIBIT S4.4

Arrival
Characteristics
in Queues

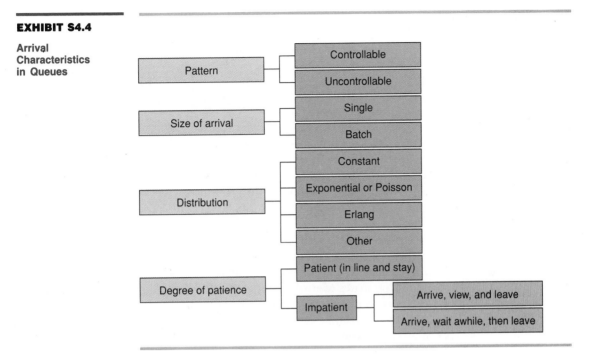

Arrival Characteristics

Another determinant in the analysis of waiting line problems is the *arrival characteristics* of the queue members. As shown in Exhibit S4.4, there are four main descriptors of arrivals: the *pattern of arrivals* (whether arrivals are controllable or uncontrollable); the *size of arrival units* (whether they arrive one at a time or in batches); the *distribution pattern* (whether the time between arrivals is constant or follows a statistical distribution such as a Poisson, exponential, or Erlang); and the *degree of patience* (whether the arrival stays in line or leaves). We describe each of these in more detail.

Arrival patterns

The arrivals at a system are far more *controllable* than is generally recognized. Barbers may decrease their Saturday arrival rate (and supposedly shift it to other days of the week) by charging an extra $1 for adult haircuts or charging adult prices for children's haircuts. Department stores run sales during the off season or one-day-only sales in part for purposes of control. Airlines offer excursion and off-season rates for similar reasons. The simplest of all arrival-control devices is the posting of business hours.

Some service demands are clearly *uncontrollable,* such as emergency medical demands on a city's hospital facilities. However, even in these situations, the

EXHIBIT S4.5

Constant Arrival
Pattern with Time
Interval = *t* and
Variance = 0

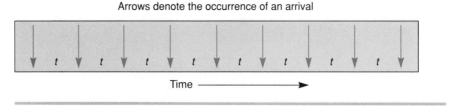

Arrows denote the occurrence of an arrival

Time ⟶

arrivals at emergency rooms in specific hospitals are controllable to some extent by, say, keeping ambulance drivers in the service region informed of the status of their respective host hospitals.

Size of arrival units

A *single arrival* may be thought of as one unit (a unit is the smallest number handled). A single arrival on the floor of the New York Stock Exchange (NYSE) is 100 shares of stock; a single arrival at an egg-processing plant might be a dozen eggs or a flat of two and a half dozen.

A *batch arrival* is some multiple of the unit, as a block of 1,000 shares on the NYSE, a case of eggs at the processing plant, or a party of five at a restaurant.

Distribution of arrivals

Waiting line formulas generally require an **arrival rate,** or the number of units per period (such as 10 units per hour). The time between arrivals is the interarrival time (such as an average of one every 6 minutes). A *constant* arrival distribution is periodic, with exactly the same time period between successive arrivals (see Exhibit S4.5). In productive systems, about the only arrivals that truly approach a constant interarrival period are those that are subject to machine control. Much more common are *variable* (random) arrival distributions.

In observing arrivals at a service facility, we can look at them from two viewpoints: We can analyze the time between successive arrivals to see if the times follow some statistical distribution, or we can set some time length (T) and try to determine how many arrivals might enter the system within T. (See Exhibit S4.6.) Patterns that occur most frequently in system models are described by the *negative exponential, Poisson,* or *Erlang* distributions.

Exponential distribution.   In the first case, when arrivals at a service facility occur on a purely random fashion, a plot of the interarrival times yields an **exponential distribution** such as that shown in Exhibit S4.7. The probability function is

$$f(t) = \lambda e^{-\lambda t} \tag{1}$$

The cumulative area underneath the curve in Exhibit S4.7 is the summation of Equation (1) over its positive range, which is $e^{-\lambda t}$. This integral allows us to

EXHIBIT S4.6

Variable Arrival
Pattern

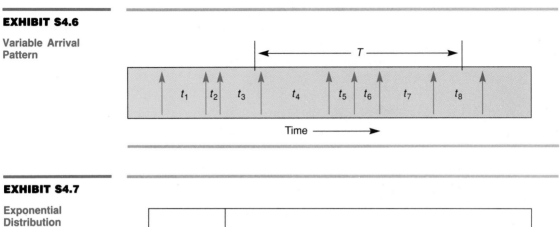

EXHIBIT S4.7

Exponential
Distribution

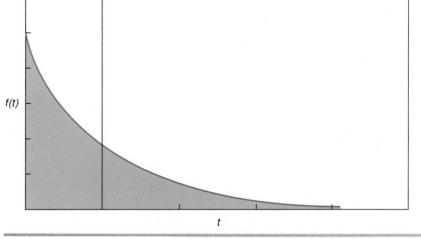

compute the probabilities of arrivals within a specified time. For example, for the case of single arrivals to a waiting line ($\lambda = 1$), the following table can be derived either by solving $e^{-\lambda t}$, or using Appendix F. Column 2 shows the probability that it will be more than t minutes until the next arrival. Column 3 shows the probability of the next arrival within t minutes (computed as 1 minus Column 2).

(1) t (minutes)	(2) Probability that the Next Arrival Will Occur in t Minutes or More (from Appendix F or solving e^{-t})	(3) Probability that the Next Arrival Will Occur in t Minutes or Less [1 − Column (2)]
0	1.00	0
0.5	0.61	0.39
1.0	0.37	0.63
1.5	0.22	0.78
2.0	0.14	0.86

Poisson distribution. In the second case, where one is interested in the number of arrivals during some time period T, the distribution appears as in Exhibit S4.8 and is obtained by finding the probability of n arrivals during T. If the arrival process is random, the distribution is the **Poisson,** and the formula is

$$P_T(n) = \frac{(\lambda T)^n e^{-\lambda T}}{n!} \qquad (2)$$

Equation (2) shows the probability of exactly n arrivals in time T. For example, if the mean arrival rate of units into a system is three per minute ($\lambda = 3$) and we want to find the probability that exactly five units will arrive within a one-minute period ($n = 5$, $T = 1$), we have

$$P_1(5) = \frac{(3 \times 1)^5 e^{-3 \times 1}}{5!} = \frac{3^5 e^{-3}}{120} = 2.025 e^{-3} = 0.101$$

That is, there is a 10.1 percent chance that there will be five arrivals in any one-minute interval.

Although often shown as a smoothed curve, as in Exhibit S4.8, the Poisson is a discrete distribution (the curve becomes smoother as n becomes larger). The distribution is discrete because n refers, in our example, to the number of arrivals in a system, and this must be an integer (for example, there cannot be 1.5 arrivals).

Parameters of the exponential and Poisson distributions. The exponential and Poisson distributions can be derived from one another. The mean and variance of the Poisson are equal and denoted by λ. The mean of the exponential is $1/\lambda$ and its variance is $1/\lambda^2$. (Remember: the time between arrivals is exponentially distributed and the number of arrivals per unit of time is Poisson distributed.)

Negative exponential. Appendix F provides tables for the negative exponential distribution (or natural logarithms). You might wish to see if you can obtain the same values from these tables that we obtained from solving the formula for $f(t)$. Note that the tables can be used in exactly the same way for analyzing service times and service rates as they are for arrivals. However, by convention, the term μ is used instead of λ when referring to service.

Erlang distribution. The term **Erlang** applies to a class of density functions that are useful in representing a variety of interarrival time distributions. The generic function for any Erlang distribution is

$$f(t) = \frac{K\lambda(K\lambda t)^{K-1} e^{-K\lambda t}}{(K - 1)!} \qquad (3)$$

All such distributions have a mean of $1/\lambda$ and a variance of $1/K\lambda^2$. In this formula, K is any positive integer and is used to distinguish one Erlang distribution from another; that is, if $K = 1$, we would be referring to a first-

EXHIBIT S4.8   Poisson Distribution for $\lambda T = 3$

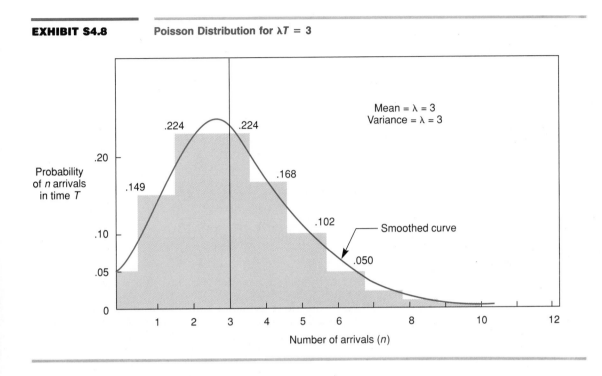

order Erlang distribution, if $K = 2$, to a second-order Erlang distribution, and so forth.

Depending on which value of K is selected, a distribution may be shaped to approximate the actual observed data. Examining the extremes of this equation, we note that when $K = 1$, the time to observe one arrival reduces to $\lambda e^{-\lambda t}$, which is in fact the exponential distribution. When K becomes very large, the variance becomes zero, which means that the time between arrivals becomes constant. Exhibit S4.9 shows several Erlang distributions with $\lambda = 1$.

Goodness of fit.   We can use several methods to determine whether or not the observed pattern of arrivals (or services) matches one of the preceding distributions. In many instances, a graph of the data may be sufficient. However, if more certainty is deemed necessary, then statistical tests for goodness of fit (for example, chi-square) should be applied. If the distributions clearly do not fit the Poisson-exponential model, then the simulation techniques in the Supplement to Chapter 15 are probably necessary to solve the queuing problem at hand.

Degree of patience

A *patient* arrival is one who waits as long as necessary until the service facility is ready to serve him or her. (Even if arrivals grumble and behave impatiently,

EXHIBIT S4.9   Erlang Distributions with $\lambda = 1$

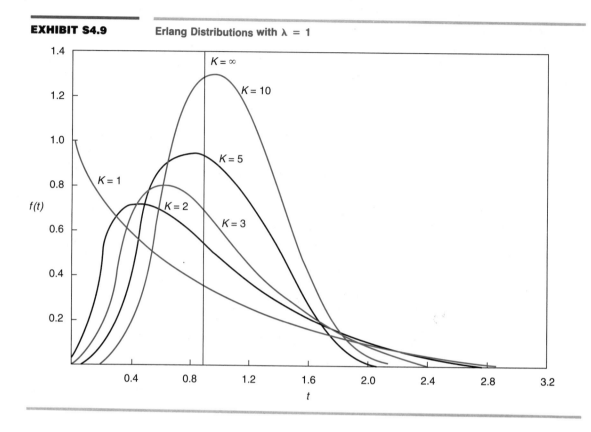

the fact that they wait is sufficient to label them as patient arrivals for purposes of waiting line theory.)

There are two classes of *impatient* arrivals. Members of the first class arrive, survey both the service facility and the length of the line, and then decide to leave. Those in the second class arrive, view the situation, and join the waiting line, and then, after some period of time, depart. The behavior of the first type is termed *balking,* and the second is termed *reneging.*

Physical Features of Lines

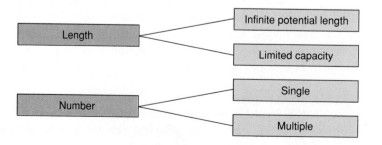

Length

In a practical sense, an infinite line is very long in terms of the capacity of the service system. Examples of *infinite potential length* are a line of vehicles backed up for miles at a bridge crossing and customers who must form a line around the block as they wait to purchase tickets at a theater.

Gas stations, loading docks, and parking lots have *limited line capacity* caused by legal restrictions or physical space characteristics. This complicates the waiting line problem not only in service system utilization and waiting line computations but also in the shape of the actual arrival distribution as well. The arrival denied entry into the line because of lack of space may rejoin the population for a later try or may seek service elsewhere. Either action makes an obvious difference in the finite population case.

Number of lines

A *single line* or single file is, of course, one line only. The term *multiple lines* refers either to the single lines that form in front of two or more servers or to single lines that converge at some central redistribution point. The disadvantage of multiple lines in a busy facility is that arrivals often shift lines if several previous services have been of short duration or if those customers currently in other lines appear to require a short service time.

Selection from the Waiting Line

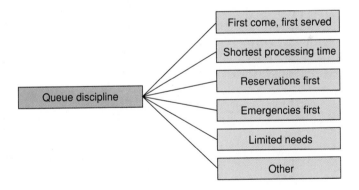

Queue discipline

A queue discipline is a priority rule, or set of rules, for determining the order of service to customers in a waiting line. The rules selected can have a dramatic effect on the system's overall performance. The number of customers in line, the average waiting time, the range of variability in waiting time, and the efficiency of the service facility are just a few of the factors affected by the choice of priority rules.

Probably the most common priority rule is *first come, first served* (FCFS). This rule states that the customers in line are served on the basis of their chronological arrival; no other characteristics have any bearing on the selection process. This is popularly accepted as the fairest rule, even though in practice, it discriminates against the arrival requiring a short service time.

Reservations first, emergencies first, highest-profit customer first, largest orders first, best customers first, longest waiting time in line, and soonest promised date are other examples of priority rules. Each has attractive features as well as shortcomings.

Line structuring rules.   Directives such as "single transactions only" (as in a bank) or "cash only" express lane (such as a quick checkout in a market) seem similar to priority rules, but in reality they are methodologies for structuring the line itself. Such lines are formed of a specific class of customers with similar characteristics. Within each line, however, priority rules still apply (as before) to the method of selecting the next customer to be served. A classic case of line structuring is the fast checkout line for customers with 12 items or less in a busy supermarket.

Service Facility

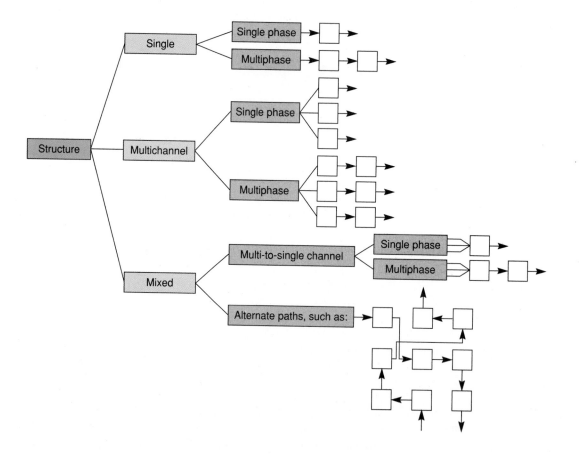

Structure

The physical flow of items to be serviced may go through a single line, multiple lines, or some mixtures of the two. The choice of format depends partly on the volume of customers served and partly on the restrictions imposed by sequential requirements governing the order in which service must be performed.

Single channel, single phase.   This is the simplest type of waiting line structure, and straightforward formulas are available to solve the problem for standard distribution patterns of arrival and service. When the distributions are nonstandard, the problem is easily solved by computer simulation. A typical example of a single-channel, single-phase situation is the one-person barbershop.

Single channel, multiphase.   A car wash is an illustration, for a series of services—vacuuming, wetting, washing, rinsing, drying, window cleaning, and parking—is performed in a fairly uniform sequence. A critical factor in the single-channel case with service in series is the amount of buildup of items allowed in front of each service, which in turn constitutes separate waiting lines.

Because of the inherent variability in service times, the optimal situation in maximizing the use of the service station is to allow an infinite waiting line to build in front of each station. The worst situation is that in which no line is permitted and only one customer at a time is allowed. When no sublines are allowed to build up in front of each station, as in a car wash, the use of the overall service facility is governed by the probability that a long service time will be required by any one of the servers in the system. This problem is common in most product-oriented systems, such as assembly lines. In process-oriented systems, such as job shops, the processing of orders in lots, rather than singly, permits maximum use of the server by allowing the inventory of available items to absorb the variation in performance time.

Multichannel, single phase.   Tellers' windows in a bank and checkout counters in high-volume department stores exemplify this type of structure. The difficulty with this format is that the uneven service time given each customer results in unequal speed or flow among the lines. This results in some customers' being served before others who arrived earlier as well as in some degree of line shifting. Varying this structure to assure the servicing of arrivals in chronological order would require forming a single line, from which, as a server becomes available, the next customer in the queue is assigned.

The major problem of this structure is that it requires rigid control of the line to maintain order and to direct customers to available servers. In some instances, assigning numbers to customers in order of their arrival helps alleviate this problem.

Multichannel, multiphase.   This case is similar to the preceding one except that two or more services are performed in sequence. The admission of patients in a hospital follows this pattern because a specific sequence of steps is usually followed: initial contact at the admissions desk, filling out forms, making identification tags, obtaining a room assignment, escorting the patient to the room, and so forth. Since several servers are usually available for this procedure, more than one patient at a time may be processed.

Mixed.   Under this general heading, we may consider two subcategories: (*a*) *multiple-to-single channel structures* and (*b*) *alternate path structures*. Under (*a*), we find either lines that merge into one for single-phase service, as at a bridge crossing where two lanes merge into one, or lines that merge into one for multiphase service, such as subassembly lines feeding into a main line. Under (*b*), we encounter two structures that differ in directional flow requirements. The first is similar to the multichannel-multiphase case, except that (1) there may be switching from one channel to the next after the first service has been rendered and (2) the number of channels and phases may vary—again—after performance of the first service.

The second structure has no flow restrictions, and customers arriving at this facility may obtain whatever services are required and in any sequence. This is the job shop format, and here we encounter a very complex scheduling problem. To date, there are no known methods for obtaining an optimal solution for such problems. Most progress has been through computer simulation that uses a variety of configurations and priority rules (see Chapter 15).

Service rate

The rationale underlying these distributions is similar to that described under the heading Distribution of arrivals. Waiting line formulas generally require **service rate** as the capacity of the server in number of units per time period (such as 12 completions per hour) and *not* as service time, which might average five minutes each. A *constant* service time rule states that each service takes exactly the same time. As in constant arrivals, this characteristic is generally limited to machine-controlled operations. As with arrival rates, Erlang and hyperexponential distributions represent variable service times.

A frequently used illustration of the *Erlang* distribution employs a single-channel, multiservice situation. However, the conditions that must be met for the Erlang approximation are so severe that practical application is rare. The distribution applies only when each service in the series is exponentially distributed with the same mean and no time delay is allowed between them. An example illustrates the restrictions in one application. Suppose that, in rebuilding machines, one repairperson has a sequence of five operations to perform. If the service time for *each* operation is exponentially distributed, with *each* having the same average completion time, the Erlang equations may be used to solve the problem (with K equal to the number of services, or five in this example). Such conditions, however, are seldom found in practice.

The *exponential* distribution is frequently used to approximate the actual service distribution. This practice, however, may lead to incorrect results; few service situations are exactly represented by the exponential function since the service facility must be able to perform services much shorter than the average time of service. Telephone usage (the original subject of queuing theory) is one of the few systems that embodies this feature, and therefore, it is well approximated by the exponential. Telephone usage may range from a few seconds—where the user picks up the receiver and replaces it, having changed his or her mind about making the call, or where the user dialed the first number wrong and starts over again—to a conversation of an hour or more.

Even in telephone service, however, this distribution has its peculiarities. For example, there is a noticeable variation between the actual service time and the exponential approximation of between 20 and 30 seconds. This happens in the case of a caller who, having dialed a number, waits for an answer to determine whether the call is to the correct destination and whether the party he or she is calling is available. Another deviation from the exponential approximation occurs with toll calls when a minimum charge is made for a specific number of minutes. If the caller is charged for three minutes' usage, there is an observed tendency to approach that minimum rather than complete the call in one or two minutes.

Most other services also have some practical minimum time. A clerk in a checkout line may have a three-minute average service time but a one-minute minimum time. This is particularly true where another checkout aisle provides a quick service. Likewise in a barbershop, while the average service time may be 20 minutes, a barber rarely cuts hair or gives a shave in less than 10 or more than 45 minutes.

Hence, these and similar types of services that have strong time dependency are poorly characterized by the exponential curve. Unfortunately, data collectors on a given problem frequently group their data in increments so that, when they are plotted as a histogram, the exponential approximation seems valid. If smaller time increments were taken, however, the inapplicability of the distribution would be obvious at the lower time values.

Exit

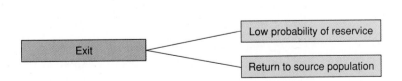

Once a customer is served, two exit fates are possible: (1) the customer may return to the source population and immediately become a competing candidate for service again or (2) there may be a low probability of reservice. The first case can be illustrated by a machine that has been routinely repaired and returned to duty but may break down again; the second can be illustrated by a machine that has been overhauled or modified and has a low probability of reservice over the near future. In a lighter vein, we might refer to the first as the "recurring-common-cold case" and to the second as the "appendectomy-only-once case."

It should be apparent that when the population source is finite, any change in the service performed on customers who return to the population modifies the arrival rate at the service facility. This, of course, alters the characteristics of the waiting line under study and necessitates reanalysis of the problem.

S4.3 WAITING LINE EQUATIONS

To underscore the importance and wide range of application of waiting line analysis, in this section we present seven sample problems followed by their solutions. Each has a slightly different structure (see Exhibit S4.10) and solution equation (see Exhibit S4.11). There are more types of models than these seven, but the formulas and solutions become quite complicated and those problems are generally solved using computer simulation. Also, in using these formulas, keep in mind that they are steady-state formulas derived on the assumption that the process under study is ongoing. Thus, they may provide inaccurate results when applied to initial operations such as the manufacture of a new product or the start of a new business day by a service firm until the system settles down to the steady state.

Most students and practitioners are reasonably proficient in (or at least have been exposed to) computer spreadsheets. There are a number of good ones, including Lotus, Excel, Quattro, and Supercalc. The equations in Exhibit S4.11 for Models 1 through 5 are shown in Exhibit S4.13 as formulae on a Lotus spreadsheet. Lotus seems to be the most common spreadsheet used both in the academia and industry, so we elected to use that format as an alternate way to present the waiting line formulas.

We did not write Model 6 because at this time Lotus has not included a simple way to include factorials such as n!, nor summations such as

$$\sum_{n=0}^{M-1} \left(\frac{\lambda}{\mu}\right)^n$$

The cells where the values for arrival rate, service rate, and maximum Q, are input into the spreadsheet such as those shown as 15, 20, and 4. These cells were specifically named in Lotus in the following way: Placing the highlighted cell where the value of the quantity will be input (in the first case, 15 for the arrival rate), the cell for the arrival rate was named: /Range/Name/Create LAMBDA and hit return to place the name LAMBDA only for that cell. In

EXHIBIT S4.10 Properties of Some Specific Waiting Line Models

Model	Layout	Service Phase	Source Population	Arrival Pattern	Queue Discipline	Service Pattern	Permissible Queue Length	Typical Example
1	Single channel	Single	Infinite	Poisson	FCFS	Exponential	Unlimited	Drive-in teller at bank, one-lane toll bridge.
2	Single channel	Single	Infinite	Poisson	FCFS	Constant	Unlimited	Automatic car wash, roller coaster rides in amusement park
3	Single channel	Single	Infinite	Poisson	FCFS	Exponential	Limited	Ice cream stand, cashier in a restaurant
4	Single channel	Single	Infinite	Poisson	FCFS	Discrete distribution	Unlimited	Empirically derived distribution of flight time for a transcontinental flight
5	Single channel	Single	Infinite	Poisson	FCFS	Erlang	Unlimited	One-person barbershop
6	Multichannel	Single	Infinite	Poisson	FCFS	Exponential	Unlimited	Parts counter in auto agency, two-lane toll bridge
7	Single channel	Single	Finite	Poisson	FCFS	Exponential	Unlimited	Machine breakdown and repair in a factory

EXHIBIT S4.11

Equations for Solving
Seven Model
Problems

Model 1

$$\bar{n}_l = \frac{\lambda^2}{\mu(\mu - \lambda)} \qquad \bar{t}_l = \frac{\lambda}{\mu(\mu - \lambda)} \qquad P_n = \left(1 - \frac{\lambda}{\mu}\right)\left(\frac{\lambda}{\mu}\right)^n$$

$$\bar{n}_s = \frac{\lambda}{\mu - \lambda} \qquad \bar{t}_s = \frac{1}{\mu - \lambda} \qquad \rho = \frac{\lambda}{\mu}$$

Model 2

$$\bar{n}_l = \frac{\lambda^2}{2\mu(\mu - \lambda)} \qquad \bar{t}_l = \frac{\lambda}{2\mu(\mu - \lambda)}$$

$$\bar{n}_s = \bar{n}_l + \frac{\lambda}{\mu} \qquad \bar{t}_s = \bar{t}_l + \frac{1}{\mu}$$

Model 3

$$\bar{n}_l = \left(\frac{\lambda}{\mu}\right)^2 \left[\frac{1 - Q\left(\frac{\lambda}{\mu}\right)^{Q-1} + (Q - 1)\left(\frac{\lambda}{\mu}\right)^Q}{\left(1 - \frac{\lambda}{\mu}\right)\left(1 - \left(\frac{\lambda}{\mu}\right)^Q\right)} \right]$$

$$\bar{n}_s = \frac{\lambda}{\mu} \left[\frac{1 - (Q + 1)\left(\frac{\lambda}{\mu}\right)^Q + Q\left(\frac{\lambda}{\mu}\right)^{Q+1}}{\left(1 - \frac{\lambda}{\mu}\right)\left(1 - \left(\frac{\lambda}{\mu}\right)^{Q+1}\right)} \right] \qquad P_n = \left[\frac{1 - \frac{\lambda}{\mu}}{1 - \left(\frac{\lambda}{\mu}\right)^{Q+1}} \right]\left(\frac{\lambda}{\mu}\right)^n$$

Model 4

$$\bar{n}_l = \frac{\left(\frac{\lambda}{\mu}\right)^2 + \lambda^2\sigma^2}{2\left(1 - \frac{\lambda}{\mu}\right)} \qquad \bar{t}_l = \frac{\frac{\lambda}{\mu^2} + \lambda\sigma^2}{2\left(1 - \frac{\lambda}{\mu}\right)}$$

$$\bar{n}_s = \bar{n}_i + \frac{\lambda}{\mu} \qquad \bar{t}_s = \bar{t}_l + \frac{1}{\mu}$$

Model 5

$$\bar{n}_l = \frac{K + 1}{2K} \cdot \frac{\lambda^2}{\mu(\mu - \lambda)} \qquad \bar{t}_l = \frac{K + 1}{2K} \cdot \frac{\lambda}{\mu(\mu - \lambda)}$$

$$\bar{n}_s = \bar{n}_l + \frac{\lambda}{\mu} \qquad \bar{t}_s = t_l + \frac{1}{\mu}$$

Model 6

$$\bar{n}_l = \frac{\lambda\mu\left(\frac{\lambda}{\mu}\right)^M}{(M - 1)!(M\mu - \lambda)^2} P_0 \qquad \bar{t}_l = \frac{P_0}{\mu M M!\left(1 - \frac{\lambda}{\mu M}\right)^2}\left(\frac{\lambda}{\mu}\right)^M$$

$$\bar{n}_s = \bar{n}_l + \frac{\lambda}{\mu} \qquad \bar{t}_s = \bar{t}_l + \frac{1}{\mu}$$

$$P_0 = \frac{1}{\sum_{n=0}^{M-1}\frac{\left(\frac{\lambda}{\mu}\right)^n}{n!} + \frac{\left(\frac{\lambda}{\mu}\right)^M}{M!\left(1 - \frac{\lambda}{\mu M}\right)}} \qquad P_w = \left(\frac{\lambda}{\mu}\right)^M \frac{P_0}{M!\left(1 - \frac{\lambda}{\mu M}\right)}$$

This is a finite queuing situation that is most easily solved by using finite tables. These tables, in turn, require the manipulation of specific terms.

Model 7

$$X = \frac{T}{T + U} \qquad H = FNX \qquad L = N(1 - F) \qquad n = L + H$$

$$P_n = \frac{N!}{(N - n)!} X^n P_0 \qquad J = NF(1 - X)$$

$$W = \frac{L(T + U)}{N - L} = \frac{LT}{H} \qquad F = \frac{T + U}{T + U + W}$$

this way, any use of the word *lambda* throughout the spreadsheet takes on the value entered in this cell.

Service rate *mu* was created for the service rate cell value (in this case 20) as /Range/Name/Create MU [return]. Any spreadsheet use of the word *mu* takes on this value. The remaining cell names were created as Q, n, SIGMA SQUARED, K and M in successive order.

The reason for creating the formulas this way is so that they can then be used to try various values to see the effects on the waiting line performance.

S4.4 SEVEN TYPICAL WAITING LINE SITUATIONS

Here is a quick preview of the seven problems we have used to illustrate each of the seven waiting line models in Exhibits 4.10 and 4.11:

Problem 1: Customers in line.   A bank wants to know how many customers are waiting for a drive-in teller, how long they have to wait, the utilization of the teller, what the service rate would have to be so that 95 percent of the time there will not be more than three cars in the system at any one time.

Problem 2: Equipment selection.   A franchisee for Robot Car Wash must decide which equipment to purchase out of a choice of three. Larger units cost more, but wash cars faster. To make the decision, costs are related to revenue.

Problem 3: Limited parking space.   A drive-through ice cream stand has limited space but can rent more spaces if it is economically justified. Based on costs and profits, the correct number of spaces to rent is derived.

Problem 4: Estimating completion time.   A small home building contractor is offering to build your house. However, before you sign a contract, you want to estimate how long it will take to build.

Problem 5: Estimating completion time.   You need a haircut and wonder if you have time now to do it, since you have another appointment soon. This differs from Problem 4 in that the nature of the service distribution time is different.

Problem 6: Determining the number of servers.   An auto agency parts department must decide how many clerks to employ at the counter. More clerks cost more money, but there is a savings because mechanics wait less time.

Problem 7: Finite population source.   Whereas the previous models assume a large population, finite queuing employs a separate set of equations for those cases where the calling customer population is small. In this last problem, there are just four weaving machines that mechanics must service to keep them operating. Based on the costs associated with machines being idle and the costs of mechanics to service them, the problem is to decide how many mechanics to use.

The seven problems are solved using the equations in Exhibit S4.11 with the notations defined in Exhibit S4.12. The first five can also be solved using the Lotus equations in Exhibit S4.13.

EXHIBIT S4.12   Notations for Equations (Exhibit S4.11)

Infinite Queuing Notation: Models 1–6	Finite Queuing Notation: Model 7

Infinite Queuing Notation: Models 1–6

σ = Standard deviation
λ = Arrival rate
μ = Service rate
$\dfrac{1}{\mu}$ = Average service time
$\dfrac{1}{\lambda}$ = Average time between arrivals
ρ = Potential utilization of the service facility (defined as λ/μ)
$\bar{n}_l$ = Average number waiting in line
$\bar{n}_s$ = Average number in system (including any being served)
$\bar{t}_l$ = Average time waiting in line
$\bar{t}_s$ = Average total time in system (including time to be served)
K = Kth distribution in the Erlang family of curves
n = Number of units in the system
M = Number of identical service channels
Q = Maximum queue length (sum of waiting space and service space)
P_n = Probability of exactly n units in system
P_w = Probability of waiting in line

Finite Queuing Notation: Model 7

D = Probability that an arrival must wait in line
F = Efficiency factor, a measure of the effect of having to wait in line
H = Average number of units being serviced
J = Population source less those in queuing system $(N - n)$
L = Average number of units in line
M = Number of service channels
n = Average number of units in queuing system (including the one being served)
N = Number of units in population source
P_n = Probability of exactly n units in queuing system
T = Average time to perform the service
U = Average time between customer service requirements
W = Average waiting time in line
X = Service factor, or proportion of service time required

Problem 1: Customers in Line

Western National Bank is considering opening a drive-in window for customer service. Management estimates that customers will arrive at the rate of 15 per hour. The teller who will staff the window can service customers at the rate of one every three minutes.

Assuming Poisson arrivals and exponential service, find

1. Utilization of the teller.
2. Average number in the waiting line.
3. Average number in the system.
4. Average waiting time in line.
5. Average waiting time in the system, including service.

Solution

1. The average utilization of the teller is

$$\rho = \frac{\lambda}{\mu} = \frac{15}{20} = 75 \text{ percent}$$

2. The average number in the waiting line is

$$\bar{n}_l = \frac{\lambda^2}{\mu(\mu - \lambda)} = \frac{(15)^2}{20(20 - 15)} = 2.25 \text{ customers}$$

EXHIBIT S4.13   Waiting Line Formulae in a Lotus Spreadsheet Format

```
Value of variables
  Arrival rate (LAMBDA) =                    15.000   ┌              ┐
  Service rate (MU) =                        20.000   │
  Maximum queue length (Q) =                  4.000   │  Insert
  Maximum number of units in system (N) =     3.000   │  appropriate
  Variance (SIGMA SQUARED) =                  0.011   │  numbers
  Kth distribution in Erlang (K)              2.000   │
  Number if identical svc channels (M)        3.000   └              ┘
```

Model 1
```
        Ave no in line                +LAMBDA^2/(MU*(MU-LAMBDA))
        Ave no in system              +LAMBDA/(MU-LAMBDA)
        Ave time in line              +LAMBDA/(MU*(MU-LAMBDA))
        Ave time in system            1/(MU-LAMBDA)
        Prob of exactly n in system   (1-(LAMBDA/MU))*(LAMBDA/MU)^$N
        Utilization                   +LAMBDA/MU
```
Model 2
```
        Ave no in line                +LAMBDA^2/(2*MU*(MU-LAMBDA))
        Ave no in system              +LAMBDA^2/(2*MU*(MU-LAMBDA))+LAMBDA/MU
        Ave time in line              +LAMBDA/(2*MU*(MU-LAMBDA))
        Ave time in system            +LAMBDA/(2*MU*(MU-LAMBDA))+1/MU
        Utilization                   +LAMBDA/MU
```
Model 3
```
        Ave no in line                (LAMBDA/MU)^2*(1-$Q*(LAMBDA/MU)^($Q-1)+($Q-1)*
                                      (LAMBDA/MU)^$Q)/(1 -LAMBDA/MU)*
                                      (1-(LAMBDA/MU)^$Q)
        Ave no in system              +LAMBDA/MU*(1-($Q+1)*(LAMBDA/MU)^$Q+$Q*
                                      (LAMBDA/MU)^($Q+1))/((1 -LAMBDA/MU)*
                                      (1-(LAMBDA/MU)^($Q+1)))
        Prob of exactly n in system   ((1-LAMBDA/MU)/(1-(LAMBDA/MU)^($Q+1)))*
                                      (LAMBDA/MU)^$N
```
Model 4
```
        Ave no in line                ((LAMBDA/MU)^2+LAMBDA^2*SIGMA SQUARED)/
                                      (2*(1-(LAMBDA/MU)))
        Ave no in system              ((LAMBDA/MU)^2+LAMBDA^2*SIGMA SQUARED)/
                                      (2*(1-(LAMBDA/MU)))+LAMBDA/MU
        Ave time in line              (LAMBDA/MU^2+LAMBDA*SIGMA SQUARED)/
                                      (2*(1-LAMBDA/MU))
        Ave time in system            (LAMBDA/MU^2+LAMBDA*SIGMA SQUARED)/
                                      (2*(1-LAMBDA/MU))+1/MU
        Utilization                   +LAMBDA/MU
```
Model 5
```
        Ave no in line                (K+1)/(2*K)*LAMBDA^2/(MU*(MU-LAMBDA))
        Ave no in system              (K+1)/(2*K)*LAMBDA^2/(MU*(MU-LAMBDA))+LAMBDA/MU
        Ave time in line              ((K+1)/(2*K))*LAMBDA/(MU*(MU-LAMBDA))
        Ave time in system            ((K+1)/(2*K))*LAMBDA/(MU*(MU-LAMBDA))+1/MU
        Utilization                   +LAMBDA/MU
```

3. The average number in the system is

$$\bar{n}_s = \frac{\lambda}{\mu - \lambda} = \frac{15}{20 - 15} = 3 \text{ customers}$$

4. Average waiting time in line is

$$\bar{t}_l = \frac{\lambda}{\mu(\mu - \lambda)} = \frac{15}{20(20 - 15)} = 0.15 \text{ hour, or 9 minutes}$$

5. Average waiting time in the system is

$$\bar{t}_s = \frac{1}{\mu - \lambda} = \frac{1}{20 - 15} = 0.2 \text{ hour, or 12 minutes}$$

Because of limited space availability and a desire to provide an acceptable level of service, the bank manager would like to ensure, with 95 percent confidence, that not more than three cars will be in the system at any one time. What is the present level of service for the three-car limit? What level of teller use must be attained and what must be the service rate of the teller to assure the 95 percent level of service?

Solution
The present level of service for three cars or less is the probability that there are 0, 1, 2, or 3 cars in the system.
From Model 1, Exhibit S4.11:

$$P_n = \left(1 - \frac{\lambda}{\mu}\right)\left(\frac{\lambda}{\mu}\right)^n$$

at $n = 0$ $P_0 = (1 - 15/20)$ $(15/20)^0 = 0.250$
at $n = 1$ $P_1 = (1/4)$ $(15/20)^1 = 0.188$
at $n = 2$ $P_2 = (1/4)$ $(15/20)^2 = 0.141$
at $n = 3$ $P_3 = (1/4)$ $(15/20)^3 = \underline{0.106}$
                                          0.685, or 68.5 percent

The probability of having more than three cars in the system is 1.0 minus the probability of three cars or less ($1.0 - 0.685 = 31.5$ percent).
For a 95 percent service level to three cars or less, this states that $P_0 + P_1 + P_2 + P_3 = 95$ percent.

$$0.95 = \left(1 - \frac{\lambda}{\mu}\right)\left(\frac{\lambda}{\mu}\right)^0 + \left(1 - \frac{\lambda}{\mu}\right)\left(\frac{\lambda}{\mu}\right)^1 + \left(1 - \frac{\lambda}{\mu}\right)\left(\frac{\lambda}{\mu}\right)^2 + \left(1 - \frac{\lambda}{\mu}\right)\left(\frac{\lambda}{\mu}\right)^3$$

$$0.95 = \left(1 - \frac{\lambda}{\mu}\right)\left[1 + \frac{\lambda}{\mu} + \left(\frac{\lambda}{\mu}\right)^2 + \left(\frac{\lambda}{\mu}\right)^3\right]$$

We can solve this by trial and error for values of λ/μ. If $\lambda/\mu = 0.50$:

$0.95 \stackrel{?}{=} 0.5(1 + 0.05 + 0.25 + 0.125)$
$0.95 \neq 0.9375$

With $\lambda/\mu = 0.45$,

$0.95 \stackrel{?}{=} (1 - 0.45)(1 + 0.45 + 0.203 + 0.091)$
$0.95 \neq 0.96$

With $\lambda/\mu = 0.47$,

$0.95 \stackrel{?}{=} (1 - 0.47)(1 + 0.47 + 0.221 + 0.104) = 0.95135$
$0.95 \approx 0.95135$

Therefore, with the utilization $\rho = \lambda/\mu$ of 47 percent, the probability of three cars or less in the system is 95 percent.

To find the rate of service required to attain this 95 percent service level, we simply solve the equation $\lambda/\mu = 0.47$, where λ = number of arrivals per hour. This gives $\mu = 32$ per hour.

That is, the teller must serve approximately 32 people per hour—a 60 percent increase over the original 20-per-hour capability—for 95 percent confidence that not more than three cars will be in the system. Perhaps service may be speeded up by modifying the method of service, adding another teller, or limiting the types of transactions available at the drive-in window. Note that with the condition of 95 percent confidence that three or fewer cars will be in the system, the teller will be idle 53 percent of the time.

Problem 2: Equipment Selection

The Robot Company franchises combination gas and car wash stations throughout the United States. Robot gives a free car wash for a gasoline fill-up or, for a wash alone, charges $0.50. Past experience shows that the number of customers that have car washes following fill-ups is about the same as for a wash alone. The average profit on a gasoline fill-up is about $0.70, and the cost of the car wash to Robot is $0.10. Robot stays open 14 hours per day.

Robot has three power units and drive assemblies, and a franchisee must select the unit preferred. Unit I can wash cars at the rate of one every five minutes and is leased for $12 per day. Unit II, a larger unit, can wash cars at the rate of one every four minutes but costs $16 per day. Unit III, the largest, costs $22 per day and can wash a car in three minutes.

The franchisee estimates that customers will not wait in line more than five minutes for a car wash. A longer time will cause Robot to lose the gasoline sales as well as the car wash sale.

If the estimate of customer arrivals resulting in washes is 10 per hour, which wash unit should be selected?

Solution

Using Unit I, calculate the average waiting time of customers in the wash line (μ for Unit I = 12 per hour). From the Model 2 equations (Exhibit S4.11),

$$\bar{t}_l = \frac{\lambda}{2\mu(\mu - \lambda)} = \frac{10}{2(12)(12 - 10)} = 0.208 \text{ hour, or } 12\frac{1}{2} \text{ minutes}$$

For Unit II at 15 per hour,

$$\bar{t}_l = \frac{10}{2(15)(15 - 10)} = 0.067 \text{ hour, or 4 minutes}$$

If waiting time is the only criterion, Unit II should be purchased. However, before we make the final decision, we must look at the profit differential between both units.

With Unit I, some customers would balk and renege because of the 12½-minute wait. And although this greatly complicates the mathematical analysis, we can gain some estimate of lost sales with Unit I by inserting $i = 5$ minutes or $\frac{1}{12}$ hour (the average length of time customers will wait) and solving for λ. This would be the effective arrival rate of customers:

$$\bar{t}_l = \frac{\lambda}{2\mu(\mu - \lambda)}$$

$$\lambda = \frac{2\bar{t}_l\mu^2}{1 + 2\bar{t}_l\mu}$$

$$\lambda = \frac{2(\frac{1}{12})(12)^2}{1 + 2(\frac{1}{12})(12)} = 8 \text{ per hour}$$

Therefore, since the original estimate of λ was 10 per hour, an estimated 2 customers per hour will be lost. Lost profit of 2 customers per hour $\times$ 14 hours $\times$ ½ ($0.70 fill-up profit + $0.40 wash profit) = $15.40 per day.

Because the additional cost of Unit II over Unit I is only $4 per day, the loss of $15.40 profit obviously warrants the installation of Unit II.

The original constraint of a five-minute maximum wait is satisfied by Unit II. Therefore Unit III is not considered unless the arrival rate is expected to increase in the future.

Problem 3: Limited Parking Space

A drive-through ice cream stand has space for a four-car line, including the car being served (the stand is on a main thoroughfare and the line cannot extend onto the street). The average arrival rate of potential customers is 40 cars per hour, and the service rate in filling the ice cream orders is 50 cars per hour. Average profit on ice cream purchased per car is $0.50. Additional driveway space is available from the owner of the lot next door at a leased rate of $5 per day. The stand is open 14 hours per day.

Assuming Poisson arrivals and exponential service, should space be rented in the adjacent lot? if so, how many spaces?

Solution
This is a limited queue-length problem and the Model 3 formulas are applicable. The easiest approach to solving this problem is to assume an increasing number of auto spaces and compare the additional profit generated by each

space. Additional spaces will be rented until the profit becomes less than the $5 cost of rental.

Ice cream will be served to customers at the rate of 50 cars per hour any time there are cars in the system. To find the amount of time there are customers, we can solve for the probability of zero in the system and subtract this from one. This will give us the percent of time ice cream is served.

From Model 3, (Exhibit S4.11):

$$P_n = \left[\frac{1 - \frac{\lambda}{\mu}}{1 - \left(\frac{\lambda}{\mu}\right)^{Q+1}} \right] \left(\frac{\lambda}{\mu}\right)^n$$

For the probability of zero cars in the system, with four spaces on the premises ($Q = 4$):

$$P_0 = \left[\frac{1 - \frac{\lambda}{\mu}}{1 - \left(\frac{\lambda}{\mu}\right)^{Q+1}} \right] \left(\frac{\lambda}{\mu}\right)^0 = \left[\frac{1 - \frac{40}{50}}{1 - \left(\frac{40}{50}\right)^5} \right] 1 = \frac{0.2}{1 - 0.328} = 0.298$$

And ice cream is being served 70.2 percent of the time ($1 - 0.298 = 0.702$).

When one space is rented ($Q = 4 + 1 = 5$),

$$P_0 = \left[\frac{0.2}{1 - \left(\frac{40}{50}\right)^6} \right] = 0.271$$

Service is then being carried out ($1 - 0.271$) = 0.729, or 72.9 percent of the time, or an increase of 2.8 percent ($72.9 - 70.2$). In profit, this is worth

$$0.028 \ (50 \text{ cars per hour} \times 14 \text{ hours per day} \times \$0.50 \text{ per car}) = \$9.80$$

When a second space is rented ($Q = 4 + 2 = 6$),

$$P_0 = \left[\frac{0.2}{1 - \left(\frac{40}{50}\right)^7} \right] = 0.253$$

and the facility is busy $1 - 0.253 = 0.747$, or 74.7 percent of the time.

Thus, the additional space increases the use of the stand by 1.8 percent (74.7 percent $-$ 72.9 percent) and increases profit by $6.30 (0.018) ($50 \times 14 \times$ $0.50). Because this amount is greater than the $5 rental charge, the space should be rented.

A third rented space, with $Q = 4 + 3 = 7$, gives

$$P_0 = \left[\frac{0.2}{1 - \left(\frac{40}{50}\right)^8} \right] = 0.241$$

and $1 - 0.241 = 0.759$.

Increased service is 1.2 percent (75.9 percent − 74.7 percent) and added profit is (50 × 0.012 × 14 × $0.50) or $4.20. The third space should not be rented since it would incur an $.80 loss ($5 − $4.20).

The optimal solution, then, is to rent just two spaces. The profit will be $261.45 per day (0.747) (50 × 14 × $0.50)—quite reasonable for a good location.

We can also obtain some other useful information about the ice cream stand. The average number of cars in the system, both in line and being served, when two rented spaces are added, is

$$\bar{n}_s = \frac{\lambda}{\mu} \left[\frac{1 - (Q + 1)\left(\frac{\lambda}{\mu}\right)^Q + Q\left(\frac{\lambda}{\mu}\right)^{Q+1}}{\left(1 - \frac{\lambda}{\mu}\right)\left[1 - \left(\frac{\lambda}{\mu}\right)^{Q+1}\right]} \right]$$

$$\bar{n}_s = \frac{40}{50} \left[\frac{1 - (6 + 1)\left(\frac{40}{50}\right)^6 + 6\left(\frac{40}{50}\right)^7}{\left(1 - \frac{40}{50}\right)\left[1 - \left(\frac{40}{50}\right)^7\right]} \right]$$

$$\bar{n}_s = 2.15 \text{ cars}$$

It is interesting to note that if an unlimited waiting line were possible, the increase in the efficiency (working time) of the ice cream stand would be increased by only 5.3 percent (the efficiency for an infinite line is $p = \lambda/\mu = 4/5 = 0.80$, or 80 percent). The average number of cars in the system, on the other hand, would amost double since $\lambda/(\mu − \lambda) = 4$ for the infinite case, as opposed to 2.15, for a maximum of six cars.

Problem 4: Estimating Completion Time

The C. J. Ballard Company is entering its second year in building residential homes. You are transferring to this city and are considering contracting with Ballard to build a home, but first you would like some idea of the completion time so that you can plan the sale of your old home and time the cross-country move.

From your discussions, you found that Ballard completed 10 homes last year. To speed the time span, Ballard uses one basic floor plan so that it can prepour the concrete floor slabs on selected lots. This saves not only the time of excavating, form building, laying the service lines (plumbing, electrical conduit, and air conditioning return ducts), and pouring concrete, but also the time necessary for concrete curing. Ballard has only a small crew and builds only one house at a time, carrying it to completion before starting the next one.

Once a customer has picked the lot and signed the contract, Ballard is able to build a house in about a month. Actual figures for completion time per home last year were 30, 32, 29, 34, 27, 29, 29, 33, 30, and 31 calendar days.

Although Ballard built just 10 homes last year, it has the capability of building 12 ($\mu = 12$). Further investigation shows that of the various people who discuss home building with Ballard, nine actually contract with the firm. These contracts appear to be randomly distributed (Poisson) through the year ($\lambda = 9$).

Estimate the completion time of your home if you should sign a contract.

Solution

Without any justification for assuming a common frequency distribution curve for the building time (such as exponential, normal, or Erlang), we can use the equation from basic statistics to estimate the mean and variance of service times.

$$\overline{X} = \frac{\sum\limits_{i=1}^{N} X_i}{N} \tag{1}$$

where

$\overline{X}$ = Average time
X = Actual time data point
i = Identification of each time element
N = Number of time elements

$$\sigma^2 = \frac{\sum\limits_{i=1}^{N} (X_i - \overline{X})^2}{N} \tag{2}$$

σ^2 = Variance of the distribution

Using the data given in the problem and equation 1, we get:

$$\overline{X} = \frac{30 + 32 + 29 + 34 + 27 + 29 + 29 + 33 + 30 + 31}{10} = 30.4 \text{ days}$$

From equation 2, we get:

$$\sigma^2 = (30 - 30.4)^2 + (32 - 30.4)^2 + (29 - 30.4)^2 + (34 - 30.4)^2$$
$$+ (27 - 30.4)^2 + (29 - 30.4)^2 + (29 - 30.4)^2 + (33 - 30.4)^2$$
$$\frac{+ (30 - 30.4)^2 + (31 - 30.4)^2}{10}$$

$$\sigma^2 = \frac{0.16 + 2.56 + 1.96 + 12.96 + 11.6 + 1.96 + 1.96 + 6.76 + 0.16 + 0.36}{10}$$

$$\sigma^2 = \frac{40.44}{10} = 4.044 \text{ days}$$

Keeping everything on the basis of days,

λ = 9 contracts per 365 days or λ = .0246/day

μ = 1 house per month, or μ = $\frac{1}{30}$ or .0333/day

From Exhibit S4.11 Model 4,

$$\bar{t}_s = \frac{\frac{\lambda}{\mu^2} + \lambda\sigma^2}{2\left(1 - \frac{\lambda}{\mu}\right)} + \frac{1}{\mu}$$

$$t_s = \frac{\frac{.0246}{(.0333)^2} + .0246(4.044)}{2\left(1 - \frac{.0246}{.0333}\right)} + \frac{1}{.0333}$$

$$t_s = \frac{22.2 + .1}{.5} + 30 \text{ or about 75 days}$$

Under the assumption of the problem—that homes are built in the order of their contract signing (first come, first served)—you will have to wait 75 days for your home to be built.

Ballard's average number of active contracts (homes waiting to be started plus any being built) is

$$\bar{n}_s = \frac{\left(\frac{\lambda}{\mu}\right)^2 + \lambda^2\sigma^2}{2\left(1 - \frac{\lambda}{\mu}\right)} + \frac{\lambda}{\mu}$$

$$\bar{n}_s = \frac{\left(\frac{.0246}{.0333}\right)^2 + (.0246)^2(4.044)}{2\left(1 - \frac{.0246}{.0333}\right)} + \frac{.0246}{.0333}$$

$$\bar{n}_s = \frac{.546 + .00245}{.5} + .75$$

$$\bar{n}_s = 1.10 + .75$$

$$\bar{n}_s = 1.85 \text{ contracts}$$

Problem 5: Estimating Completion Time

The barber at the one-person Speedway Barbershop averages 15 minutes per haircut. Customers arrive at the shop in Poisson fashion with a mean arrival rate of two per hour. Suppose you want a haircut and you have an appointment with your tax accountant 30 minutes after you arrive at the shop.

Assuming that it is a three-minute walk to your appointment location from the shop and that haircutting time is Erlang distributed with $K = 3$, would you expect to be on time to meet your accountant?

Solution
Given that $\lambda = 2$ arrivals per hour and $\mu = 4$ haircuts per hour, the problem is simply to determine the expected time in the system, $\bar{t}_s$. Using the $\bar{t}_s$ formula from Exhibit S4.11, Model 5, we have

$$\bar{t}_s = \frac{K + 1}{2K} \cdot \frac{\lambda}{\mu(\mu - \lambda)} + \frac{1}{\mu}$$

Substituting

$$\bar{t}_s = \frac{3 + 1}{2(3)} \cdot \frac{2}{4(4 - 2)} + \frac{1}{4}$$

we get

$$\bar{t}_s = \frac{1}{6} + \frac{1}{4} = \frac{5}{12} \text{ of an hour, or 25 minutes}$$

Thus, you should be able to make your appointment (if you don't dawdle along the way).

Problem 6: Determining the Number of Servers

In the service department of the Glenn–Mark Auto Agency, mechanics requiring parts for auto repair or service present their request forms at the parts department counter. The parts clerk fills a request while the mechanic waits. Mechanics arrive in a random (Poisson) fashion at the rate of 40 per hour, and a clerk can fill requests at the rate of 20 per hour (exponential). If the cost for a parts clerk is $6 per hour and the cost for a mechanic is $12 per hour, determine the optimum number of clerks to staff the counter. (Because of the high arrival rate, an infinite source may be assumed.)

Solution
First, assume that three clerks will be used because only one or two clerks would create long lines (since $\lambda = 40$ and $\mu = 20$). From Exhibit S4.11, Model 6

$$P_0 = \cfrac{1}{\displaystyle\sum_{n=0}^{M-1} \frac{\left(\frac{\lambda}{\mu}\right)^n}{n!} + \cfrac{\left(\frac{\lambda}{\mu}\right)^M}{M!\left(1 - \frac{\lambda}{\mu M}\right)}}$$

with $M = 3$

$$P_0 = \cfrac{1}{\displaystyle\sum_{n=0}^{2} \cfrac{\left(\cfrac{40}{20}\right)^n}{n!} + \cfrac{\left(\cfrac{40}{20}\right)^3}{3!\left(1 - \cfrac{40}{20(3)}\right)}}$$

$$P_0 = \cfrac{1}{\cfrac{(2)^0}{0!} + \cfrac{(2)^1}{1!} + \cfrac{(2)^2}{2!} + \cfrac{(2)^3}{3!\left(1 - \cfrac{2}{3}\right)}} = \cfrac{1}{1 + 2 + 2 + 4} = 0.111$$

The average number in line is

$$\bar{n}_l = \cfrac{\lambda\mu\left(\cfrac{\lambda}{\mu}\right)^M}{(M - 1)!(M\mu - \lambda)^2}P_0$$

$$\bar{n}_l = \cfrac{40(20)\left(\cfrac{40}{20}\right)^3}{(3 - 1)![3(20) - 40]^2}(0.111) = \cfrac{800(8)}{2(60 - 40)^2}(0.111)$$

$$\bar{n}_l = \cfrac{6400}{800}(0.111) = 0.888 \text{ mechanic}$$

At this point, we see that we have an average of 0.888 mechanic waiting all day. For an eight-hour day at \$12 per hour, there is a loss of mechanic's time worth 0.888 mechanic × \$12 per hour × 8 hours = \$85.25.

Our next step is to recalculate the waiting time if we add another parts clerk. We will then compare the added cost of the additional employee with the time saved by the mechanics. Using our P_0 equation when $M = 4$;

$$P_0 = \cfrac{1}{\displaystyle\sum_{n=0}^{3} \cfrac{(2)^n}{n!} + \cfrac{(2)^4}{4!\left(1 - \cfrac{4}{2(4)}\right)}}$$

$$P_0 = \cfrac{1}{\cfrac{(2)^0}{0!} + \cfrac{(2)^1}{1!} + \cfrac{(2)^2}{2!} + \cfrac{(2)^3}{3!} + \cfrac{16}{24\left(1 - \cfrac{1}{2}\right)}}$$

$$P_0 = \cfrac{1}{1 + 2 + 2 + \cfrac{8}{6} + \cfrac{8}{6}} = 0.130$$

$$\bar{n}_l = \cfrac{40(20)(2)^4}{(4 - 1)![4(20) - 40]^2}(0.130)$$

$$\bar{n}_l = \cfrac{800(16)}{6(80 - 40)^2}(0.130)$$

$\bar{n}_l = 1.333 \times 0.130 = 0.173$ mechanic in line

$0.173 \times \$12 \times 8$ hours $= \$16.61$ cost of mechanic's waiting in line

Value of mechanics' time saved is $\$85.25 - \$16.61 = \$68.64$

Cost of additional parts clerk is 8 hour $\times$ \$6/hour $= \underline{\quad 48.00}$

Cost reduction by adding fourth clerk $\qquad\qquad = \$20.64$

This problem could be expanded to consider the addition of runners to deliver parts to mechanics; the problem then would be to determine the optimal number of runners. This, however, would have to include the added cost of lost time caused by errors in parts receipts. For example, a mechanic would recognize a wrong part at the counter and obtain immediate correction, whereas the parts runner may not.

Problem 7: Finite Population Source

Studies of a bank of four weaving machines at the Loose Knit textile mill have shown that, on average, each machine needs adjusting every hour and that the current serviceperson averages 7½ minutes per adjustment. Assuming Poisson arrivals, exponential service, and a machine idle time cost of $40 per hour, determine if a second serviceperson (who also averages 7½ minutes per adjustment) should be hired at a rate of $7 per hour.

Solution
This is a finite queuing problem that can be solved by using finite queuing tables (see Exhibit S4.14). The approach in this problem is to compare the costs of machine downtime (either waiting in line or being serviced) and the cost of one repairperson, to the cost of machine downtime and two repairpeople. We do this by finding the average number of machines that are in the service system and multiply this number by the downtime cost per hour. To this we add the repairpeople's cost.

Before we proceed, we first define some terms:

N = Number of machines in the population

M = Number of repairpeople

T = Time required to service a machine

U = Average time a machine runs before requiring service

X = Service factor, or proportion of service time required for each machine $(X = T/(T + U))$

L = Average number of machines waiting in line to be serviced

H = Average number of machines being serviced

The values to be determined from the finite tables are

D = Probability that a machine needing service will have to wait

EXHIBIT S4.14

Finite Queuing Tables

POPULATION 4

X	M	D	F	X	M	D	F	X	M	D	F
.015	1	.045	.999		1	.479	.899	.400	3	.064	.992
.022	1	.066	.998	.180	2	.088	.991		2	.372	.915
.030	1	.090	.997		1	.503	.887		1	.866	.595
.034	1	.102	.996	.190	2	.098	.990	.420	3	.074	.990
.038	1	.114	.995		1	.526	.874		2	.403	.903
.042	1	.126	.994	.200	3	.008	.999		1	.884	.572
.046	1	.137	.993		2	.108	.988	.440	3	.085	.986
.048	1	.143	.992	.200	1	.549	.862		2	.435	.891
.052	1	.155	.991	.210	3	.009	.999		1	.900	.551
.054	1	.161	.990		2	.118	.986	.460	3	.097	.985
.058	1	.173	.989		1	.572	.849		2	.466	.878
.060	1	.179	.988	.220	3	.011	.999		1	.914	.530
.062	1	.184	.987		2	.129	.984	.480	3	.111	.983
.064	1	.190	.986		1	.593	.835		2	.498	.864
.066	1	.196	.985	.230	3	.012	.999	.480	1	.926	.511
.070	2	.014	.999		2	.140	.982	.500	3	.125	.980
	1	.208	.984		1	.614	.822		2	.529	.850
.075	2	.016	.999	.240	3	.014	.999		1	.937	.492
	1	.222	.981		2	.151	.980	.520	3	.141	.976
.080	2	.018	.999		1	.634	.808		2	.561	.835
	1	.237	.978	.250	3	.016	.999		1	.947	.475
.085	2	.021	.999		2	.163	.977	.540	3	.157	.972
	1	.251	.975		1	.654	.794		2	.592	.820
.090	2	.023	.999	.260	3	.018	.998		1	.956	.459
	1	.265	.972		2	.175	.975	.560	3	.176	.968
.095	2	.026	.999		1	.673	.780		2	.623	.805
	1	.280	.969	.270	3	.020	.998		1	.963	.443
.100	2	.028	.999		2	.187	.972	.580	3	.195	.964
	1	.294	.965		1	.691	.766		2	.653	.789
.105	2	.031	.998	.280	3	.022	.998		1	.969	.429
	1	.308	.962		2	.200	.968	.600	3	.216	.959
.110	2	.034	.998		1	.708	.752		2	.682	.774
	1	.321	.958	.290	3	.024	.998		1	.975	.415
.115	2	.037	.998		2	.213	.965	.650	3	.275	.944
	1	.335	.954		1	.725	.738		2	.752	.734
.120	2	.041	.997	.300	3	.027	.997		1	.985	.384
	1	.349	.950		2	.226	.962	.700	3	.343	.926
.125	2	.044	.997		1	.741	.724		2	.816	.695
	1	.362	.945	.310	3	.030	.997		1	.991	.357
.130	2	.047	.997		2	.240	.958	.750	3	.422	.905
	1	.376	.941		1	.756	.710		2	.871	.657
.135	2	.051	.996	.320	3	.033	.997		1	.996	.333
	1	.389	.936		2	.254	.954	.800	3	.512	.880
.140	2	.055	.996		1	.771	.696		2	.917	.621
	1	.402	.931	.330	3	.036	.996		1	.998	.312
.145	2	.058	.995		2	.268	.950	.850	3	.614	.852
	1	.415	.926		1	.785	.683		2	.954	.587
.150	2	.062	.995	.340	3	.039	.996		1	.999	.294
	1	.428	.921		2	.282	.945	.900	3	.729	.821
.155	2	.066	.994		1	.798	.670		2	.979	.555
	1	.441	.916	.360	3	.047	.994	.950	3	.857	.786
.160	2	.071	.994		2	.312	.936		2	.995	.526
	1	.454	.910		1	.823	.644				
.165	2	.075	.993	.380	3	.055	.993				
	1	.466	.904		2	.342	.926				
.170	2	.079	.993		1	.846	.619				

EXHIBIT S4.14

Concluded

POPULATION 5

X	M	D	F
.012	1	.048	.999
.019	1	.076	.998
.025	1	.100	.997
.030	1	.120	.996
.034	1	.135	.995
.036	1	.143	.994
.040	1	.159	.993
.042	1	.167	.992
.044	1	.175	.991
.046	1	.183	.990
.050	1	.198	.989
.052	1	.206	.988
.054	1	.214	.987
.056	2	.018	.999
	1	.222	.985
.058	2	.019	.999
	1	.229	.984
.060	2	.020	.999
	1	.237	.983
.062	2	.022	.999
	1	.245	.982
.064	2	.023	.999
	1	.253	.981
.066	2	.024	.999
	1	.260	.979
.068	2	.026	.999
	1	.268	.978
.070	2	.027	.999
	1	.275	.977
.075	2	.031	.999
	1	.294	.973
.080	2	.035	.998
	1	.313	.969
.085	2	.040	.998
	1	.332	.965
.090	2	.044	.998
	1	.350	.960
.095	2	.049	.997
	1	.368	.955
.100	2	.054	.997
	1	.386	.950
.105	2	.059	.997
	1	.404	.945
.110	2	.065	.996
	1	.421	.939
.115	2	.071	.995
	1	.439	.933
.120	2	.076	.995
	1	.456	.927
.125	2	.082	.994
	1	.473	.920
.130	2	.089	.993
	1	.489	.914
.135	2	.095	.993
	1	.505	.907
.140	2	.102	.992
	1	.521	.900
.145	3	.011	.999
	2	.109	.991
	1	.537	.892
.150	3	.012	.999
	2	.115	.990
	1	.553	.885
.155	3	.013	.999
	2	.123	.989
	1	.568	.877
.160	3	.015	.999
	2	.130	.988
	1	.582	.869
.165	3	.016	.999
	2	.137	.987
	1	.597	.861
.170	3	.017	.999
	2	.145	.985
	1	.611	.853
.180	3	.021	.999
	2	.161	.983
	1	.638	.836
.190	3	.024	.998
	2	.177	.980
	1	.665	.819
.200	3	.028	.998
	2	.194	.976
	1	.689	.801
.210	3	.032	.998
	2	.211	.973
	1	.713	.783
.220	3	.036	.997
	2	.229	.969
	1	.735	.765
.230	3	.041	.997
	2	.247	.965
	1	.756	.747
.240	3	.046	.996
	2	.265	.960
	1	.775	.730
.250	3	.052	.995
	2	.284	.955
	1	.794	.712
.260	3	.058	.994
	2	.303	.950
	1	.811	.695
.270	3	.064	.994
	2	.323	.944
	1	.827	.677
.280	3	.071	.993
	2	.342	.938
	1	.842	.661
.290	4	.007	.999
	3	.079	.992
	2	.362	.932
	1	.856	.644
.300	4	.008	.999
	3	.086	.990
	2	.382	.926
	1	.869	.628
.310	4	.009	.999
	3	.094	.989
	2	.402	.919
	1	.881	.613
.320	4	.010	.999
	3	.103	.988
	2	.422	.912
	1	.892	.597
.330	4	.012	.999
	3	.112	.986
	2	.442	.904
	1	.902	.583
.340	4	.013	.999
	3	.121	.985
	2	.462	.896
	1	.911	.569
.360	4	.017	.998
	3	.141	.981
	2	.501	.880
	1	.927	.542
.380	4	.021	.998
	3	.163	.976
	2	.540	.863
	1	.941	.516
.400	4	.026	.997
	3	.186	.972
	2	.579	.845
	1	.952	.493
.420	4	.031	.997
	3	.211	.966
	2	.616	.826
	1	.961	.471
.440	4	.037	.996
	3	.238	.960
	2	.652	.807
	1	.969	.451
.460	4	.045	.995
	3	.266	.953
	2	.686	.787
	1	.975	.432
.480	4	.053	.994
	3	.296	.945
	2	.719	.767
	1	.980	.415
.500	4	.063	.992
	3	.327	.936
	2	.750	.748
	1	.985	.399
.520	4	.073	.991
	3	.359	.927
	2	.779	.728
	1	.988	.384
.540	4	.085	.989
	3	.392	.917
	2	.806	.708
	1	.991	.370
.560	4	.098	.986
	3	.426	.906
	2	.831	.689
	1	.993	.357
.580	4	.113	.984
	3	.461	.895
	2	.854	.670
	1	.994	.345
.600	4	.130	.981
	3	.497	.883
	2	.875	.652
	1	.996	.333
.650	4	.179	.972
	3	.588	.850
	2	.918	.608
	1	.998	.308
.700	4	.240	.960
	3	.678	.815
	2	.950	.568
	1	.999	.286
.750	4	.316	.944
	3	.763	.777
	2	.972	.532
.800	4	.410	.924
	3	.841	.739
	2	.987	.500
.850	4	.522	.900
	3	.907	.702
	2	.995	.470
.900	4	.656	.871
	3	.957	.666
	2	.998	.444
.950	4	.815	.838
	3	.989	.631

Source: L. G. Peck and R. N. Hazelwood, *Finite Queueing Tables* (New York: John Wiley & Sons, 1958), pp. 3–4.

F = Efficiency factor, which is a measure of the effect of having to wait in line to be serviced

The tables are arranged according to three variables: N, population size; X, service factor; and M, the number of service channels (repairpeople in this problem). To look up a value, first find the table for the correct N size, then search the first column for the appropriate X, and finally find the line for M. Then read off D and F. (In addition to these values, other characteristics about a finite queuing system can be found by using the finite formulas.)

To solve the problem, consider Case I with one repairperson, and Case II with two repairpeople.

Case I: One repairperson.   From the problem statement,

$N = 4$

$M = 1$

$T = 7\frac{1}{2}$ minutes

$U = 60$ minutes

$$X = \frac{T}{T + U} = \frac{7.5}{7.5 + 60} = 0.111$$

From Exhibit S4.14, which displays the table for $N = 4$, F is interpolated as being approximately 0.957 at $X = 0.111$ and $M = 1$.

The number of machines waiting in line to be serviced is L, where

$$L = N(1 - F) = 4(1 - 0.957) = 0.172 \text{ machines}$$

The number of machines being serviced is H, where

$$H = FNX = 0.957(4)(0.111) = 0.425 \text{ machines}$$

Exhibit S4.15 shows the cost resulting from unproductive machine time and the cost of the repairperson.

Case II: Two repairpeople.   From Exhibit S4.14, at $X = 0.111$ and $M = 2$, $F = 0.998$.

The number of machines waiting in line, L, is

$$L = N(1 - F) = 4(1 - 0.998) = 0.008 \text{ machines}$$

The number of machines being serviced, H, is

$$H = FNX = 0.998(4)(0.111) = 0.443 \text{ machines}$$

The costs for the machines being idle and for the two repairpeople are shown in Exhibit S4.15. The final column of that exhibit indicates that retaining just one repairperson is the best choice.

S4.5   COMPUTER SIMULATION OF WAITING LINES

Some waiting line problems that seem very simple on first impression turn out to be extremely difficult or impossible to solve. Throughout this chapter we

EXHIBIT S4.15

A Comparison of
Downtime Costs for
Service and Repair of
Four Machines

Number of Repairpeople	Number of Machines Down ($H + L$)	Cost per Hour for Machines Down ($H + L$) × \$40/hour	Cost of Repairpeople \$7/hour each	Total Cost per Hour
1	0.597	\$23.88	\$ 7.00	\$30.88
2	0.451	18.04	14.00	32.04

have been treating waiting line situations that are independent; that is, either the entire system consists of a single phase, or else each service that is performed in a series is independent (this could happen if the output of one service location is allowed to build up in front of the next one so that this, in essence, becomes a calling population for the next service). When a series of services is performed in sequence where the output rate of one becomes the input rate of the next, we can no longer use the simple formulas. This is also true for any problem where conditions do not meet the conditions of the equations, as specified in Exhibit S4.12. The technique best suited to solving this type of problem is computer simulation. We treat the topic of modeling and simulation in the Supplement to Chapter 15, and we also include a waiting line problem that can only be solved on a computer.

S4.6 CONCLUSION

Waiting line problems present both a challenge and frustration to those who try to solve them. The basic objective is to balance the cost of waiting with the cost of adding more resources. For a service system this means that the utilization of a server may be quite low to provide a short waiting time to the customer. One of the main concerns in dealing with waiting line problems is what procedure or priority rule to use in selecting the next product or customer to be served.

Many queuing problems appear simple until an attempt is made to solve them. This supplement has dealt with the simpler problems. When the situation becomes more complex, when there are multiple phases or where services are performed only in a particular sequence, computer simulation is necessary to obtain the optimal solution.

S4.7 REVIEW AND DISCUSSION QUESTIONS

1. How many waiting lines did you encounter during your last airline flight?
2. Distinguish between a *channel* and a *phase*.
3. What is the major cost trade-off that must be made in managing waiting line situations?
4. Which assumptions are necessary to employ the formulas given for Model 1?

5. In what way might the first-come, first-served rule be unfair to the customers waiting for service in a bank or hospital?

6. Define, in a practical sense, what is meant by an *exponential service time*.

7. Would you expect the exponential distribution to be a good approximation of service times for
   a. Buying an airline ticket at the airport?
   b. Riding a merry-go-round at a carnival?
   c. Checking out of a hotel?
   d. Completing a midterm exam in your OM class?

8. Would you expect the Poisson distribution to be a good approximation of
   a. Runners crossing the finish line in the Boston Marathon?
   b. Arrival times of the students in your OM class?
   c. Arrival times of the bus to your stop at school?

S4.8 PROBLEMS

*1. Quick Lube Inc. operates a fast lube and oil change garage. On a typical day, customers arrive at the rate of three per hour, and lube jobs are performed at an average rate of one every 15 minutes. The mechanics operate as a team on one car at a time.

   Assuming Poisson arrivals and exponential service, find
   a. Utilization of the lube team.
   b. The average number of cars in line.
   c. The average time a car waits before it is lubed.
   d. The total time it takes to go through the system (i.e., waiting in line plus lube time.)

*2. American Vending Inc. (AVI) supplies vended food to a large university. Because students kick the machines at every opportunity out of anger and frustration, management has a constant repair problem. The machines break down on an average of three per hour, and the breakdowns are distributed in a Poisson manner. Downtime costs the company $25/hour per machine, and each maintenance worker gets $4 per hour. One worker can service machines at an average rate of five per hour, distributed exponentially; two workers, working together, can service seven per hour, distributed exponentially; and a team of three workers can do eight per hour, distributed exponentially.

   What is the optimum maintenance crew size for servicing the machines?

3. Burrito King is a new fast-food franchise that is opening up nationwide. Burrito King has been successful in automating burrito production for its drive-up fast-food establishments. The Burro-Master 9000 requires a constant 45 seconds to produce a burrito (with any of the standard fillings). It has been estimated that customers will arrive at the drive-up window according to a Poisson distribution at an average of 1 every 50 seconds.

   Several issues must be addressed by management. What is the expected average time in the system?

   To help determine the amount of space needed for the line at the drive-up

---

* Problems 1 and 2 are completely solved in Appendix H.

window, Burrito King would like to know the average line length (in cars) and the average number of cars in the system (both in line and at the window).

4. Big Jack's drive-through hamburger service is planning to build another stand at a new location and must decide how much land to lease to optimize returns. Leased space for cars will cost $1,000 per year per space. Big Jack is aware of the highly competitive nature of the quick-food service industry and knows that if his drive-in is full, customers will go elsewhere. The location under consideration has a potential customer arrival rate of 30 per hour (Poisson). Customers' orders are filled at the rate of 40 per hour (exponential) since Big Jack prepares food ahead of time. The average profit on each arrival is $0.60, and the stand is open from noon to midnight every day. How many spaces for cars should be leased?

5. To support National Heart Week, the Heart Association plans to install a free blood pressure testing booth in El Con Mall for the week. Previous experience indicates that, on the average, 10 persons per hour request a test. Assume arrivals are Poisson from an infinite population. Blood pressure measurements can be made at a constant time of five minutes each. Assume the queue length can be infinite with FCFS discipline.
   a. What average number in line can be expected?
   b. What average number of persons can be expected to be in the system?
   c. What is the average amount of time that a person can expect to spend in line?
   d. On the average, how much time will it take to measure a person's blood pressure, including waiting time?
   e. On weekends, the arrival rate can be expected to increase to nearly 12 per hour. What effect will this have on the number in the waiting line?

6. A cafeteria serving line has a coffee urn from which customers serve themselves. Arrivals at the urn follow a Poisson distribution at the rate of three per minute. In serving themselves, customers take about 15 seconds, exponentially distributed.
   a. How many customers would you expect to see on the average at the coffee urn? *(Total no. in system)*
   b. How long would you expect it to take to get a cup of coffee?
   c. What percentage of time is the urn being used?
   d. What is the probability that there would be three or more people in the cafeteria?
   If the cafeteria installs an automatic vendor that dispenses a cup of coffee at a constant time of 15 seconds, how does this change your answers to *a* and *b?*

7. An engineering firm retains a technical specialist to assist five design engineers working on a project. The help that the specialist gives engineers ranges widely in time consumption. The specialist has some answers available in memory, others require computation, and still others require significant search time. On the average, each request for assistance takes the specialist one hour.
   The engineers require help from the specialist on the average of once each day. Since each assistance takes about an hour, each engineer can work for seven hours, on the average, without assistance. One further point: engineers needing help do not interrupt if the specialist is already involved with another problem.
   Treat this as a finite queuing problem and answer the following questions:
   a. How many engineers, on the average, are waiting for the technical specialist for help?
   b. What is the average time that an engineer has to wait for the specialist?

c. What is the probability that an engineer will have to wait in line for the specialist?

8. L. Winston Martin is an allergist in Tucson who has an excellent system for handling his regular patients who come in just for allergy injections. Patients arrive for an injection and fill out a name slip, which is then placed in an open slot that passes into another room staffed by one or two nurses. The specific injections for a patient are prepared and the patient is called through a speaker system into the room to receive the injection. At certain times during the day, patient load drops and only one nurse is needed to administer the injections.

Let's focus on the simpler case of the two—i.e., when there is one nurse. Also assume that patients arrive in a Poisson fashion and the service rate of the nurse is exponentially distributed. During this slower period, patients arrive with an interarrival time of approximately three minutes. It takes the nurse an average of two minutes to prepare the patients' serum and administer the injection.

a. What is the average number you would expect to see in Dr. Martin's facilities?

b. How long would it take for a patient to arrive, get an injection, and leave?

c. What is the probability that there will be three or more patients on the premises?

d. What is the utilization of the nurse?

9. The NOL Income Tax Service is analyzing its customer service operations during the month prior to the April filing deadline. On the basis of past data it has been estimated that customers arrive according to a Poisson process with an average interarrival time of 12 minutes. The time to complete a return for a customer is exponentially distributed with a mean of 10 minutes. Based on this information, answer the following questions.

a. If you went to NOL, how much time would you allow for getting your return done?

b. On average, how much room should be allowed for the waiting area?

c. If the NOL service were operating 12 hours per day, how many hours on average, per day, would the office be busy?

d. What is the probability that the system is idle?

e. If the arrival rate remained unchanged but the average time in system must be 45 minutes or less, what would need to be changed?

f. A robotic replacement has been developed for preparing the new "simplified" tax forms. If the service time became a constant nine minutes, what would total time in the system become?

10. Raul's Reptile Emporium is considering adding an express lane for "feeder" mammal service. The special lane will only stock standard small rodents. The population of customers is assumed to be infinite and will arrive according to a Poisson process. The arrival rate has been estimated to be 20 per hour. The service time follows an Erlang distribution with a mean of two minutes and a K = 2. Answer the following questions.

a. What is the average number of customers in line?

b. What is the average time to wait and purchase a small mammal?

c. If Raul's will be open from 9 A.M. to 5 P.M. daily, how many hours, on average, will the drive-up window be busy?

11. The law firm of Larry, Darryl and Darryl (L,D & D) specialize in the practice of waste disposal law. They are interested in analyzing their caseload. Data was

collected on the number of cases they received in a year and the times to complete each case. They consider themselves a dedicated firm and will only take on one case at a time. Calls for their services apparently follow a Poisson process with a mean of one case every 30 days. Given the fact that L,D & D are outstanding in their field, clients will wait for their turn and are served on a first come, first served basis. The data on the time to complete each case for the last 10 cases are 27, 26, 26, 25, 27, 24, 27, 23, 22, and 23.

Determine the average time for L,D & D to complete a case, the average number of clients waiting, and the average wait for each client.

12.   A graphics reproduction firm has four units of equipment that are automatic, but occasionally become inoperative because of the need for supplies, maintenance, or repair. Each unit requires service roughly twice each hour, or more precisely, each unit of equipment runs an average of 30 minutes before needing service. Service times vary widely, ranging from a simple service (such as hitting a restart switch or repositioning paper) to more involved equipment disassembly. The average service time, however, is five minutes.

Equipment downtime results in a loss of $20 per hour. The one equipment attendant is paid $6 per hour.

Using finite queuing analysis, answer the following questions:
   a.   What is the average number of units in line?
   b.   What is the average number of units still in operation?
   c.   What is the average number of units being serviced?
   d.   The firm is considering adding another attendant at the same $6 rate. Should the firm do it?

13.   Trucks carrying produce for sale in Arizona arrive at the Nogales, Sonora, inspection station at the rate of one every four minutes. Inspectors have the capacity to inspect about 18 trucks per hour. For simplicity, assume that this is a simple queuing situation and therefore the models assuming Poisson arrivals and exponential service times can apply.
   a.   How many trucks would you expect to see in the system?
   b.   How long would it take for a truck that just arrived to get through the system?
   c.   What is the utilization of the person staffing the checkin point?
   d.   What is the probability that there are more than three trucks in the system?

14.   Benny the Barber owns a one-chair shop. At barber college, they told Benny that his customers would exhibit a Poisson arrival distribution and that he would provide an exponential service distribution. His market survey data indicate that customers arrive at a rate of two per hour. It will take Benny an average of 20 minutes to give a haircut. Based on these figures, find the following:
   a.   The average number of customers waiting.
   b.   The average time a customer waits.
   c.   The average time a customer is in the shop.
   d.   The average utilization of Benny's time.

15.   Customers enter the camera department of a department store at the average rate of six per hour. The department is staffed by one employee, who takes an average of six minutes to serve each arrival. Assume this is a simple Poisson arrival exponentially distributed service time situation.
   a.   As a casual observer, how many people would you expect to see in the camera department (excluding the clerk)?

    b.   How long would a customer expect to spend in the camera department (total time)?

    c.   What is the utilization of the clerk?

    d.   What is the probability that there are *more than* two people in the camera department (excluding the clerk)?

16.   Arrivals at a free beer dispensing station at an after finals party come at the rate of one thirsty student or faculty member every 15 seconds. The bartender can pour one beer every 10 seconds.

    a.   How many thirsty beer drinkers would you expect to see in the line?

    b.   What is the probability that there will be two or more people in line?

    c.   How long would you expect to wait to get a beer?

17.   Kenny Livingston, bartender at the Tucson Racquet Club, can serve drinks at the rate of one every 50 seconds. During a hot evening recently, the bar was particularly busy and every 55 seconds someone was at the bar asking for a drink.

    a.   Assuming that everyone in the bar drank at the same rate and that Kenny served people on a first-come, first-served basis, how long would you expect to have to wait for a drink?

    b.   How many people would you expect to be waiting for drinks?

    c.   What is the probability that three or more people are waiting for drinks?

    d.   What is the utilization of the bartender; how busy is he?

    e.   If the bartender is replaced with an automatic drink dispensing machine, how would this change *a* above?

18.   An office employs several clerks who originate documents and one operator who enters the document information in a word processor. The group originates documents at a rate of 25 per hour. The operator can enter the information with average exponentially distributed time of two minutes. Assume the population is infinite, arrivals are Poisson, queue length is infinite with FCFS discipline. Calculate:

    a.   The percent of utilization of the operator.

    b.   The average number of documents in the system.

    c.   The average time in the system.

    d.   The probability of four or more documents being in the system.

    e.   If another clerk were added, the document origination rate would increase to 30 per hour. What would this do to the word processor workload? Show why.

19.   A study-aid desk manned by a graduate student has been established to answer students' questions and help in working problems in your OM course. The desk is staffed eight hours per day. The dean wants to know how the facility is working. Statistics indicate that students arrive at a rate of four per hour, and the distribution is approximately Poisson. Assistance time averages 10 minutes, distributed exponentially. Assume population and line length can be infinite and queue discipline is FCFS. For the report to the dean, calculate:

    a.   The percent of utilization of the graduate student.

    b.   The average number of students in the system.

    c.   The average time in the system.

    d.   The probability of four or more students being in line or being served.

    e.   Before a test, the arrival of students increases to six per hour on the average. What does this do to the average length of the line?

20. A beverage store has determined that it is economically feasible to add a drive-in window, with space for two cars: one at the window and one waiting. The owner wants to know whether more waiting space should be obtained.

Cars are expected to arrive (with a Poisson distribution) at a rate of eight per hour. Transactions average 10 per hour, and the times are exponentially distributed. Each transaction makes $1 profit. The owner plans to be open 12 hours per day, 6 days per week, 52 weeks per year. Additional spaces cost $2,000 each. How many spaces is it worthwhile to purchase?

(Hint: Begin your analysis with $Q = 2$. Assume infinite population, finite queue with FCFS discipline.)

21. At the California border inspection station, vehicles arrive at the rate of 10 per minute in a Poisson distribution. For simplicity in this problem, assume that there is only one lane and one inspector, who can inspect vehicles at the rate of 12 per minute in an exponentially distributed fashion.
   a. What is the average length of the waiting line?
   b. What is the average time that a vehicle must wait to get through the system?
   c. What is the utilization of the inspector?
   d. What is the probability that when you arrive there will be three or more vehicles ahead of you?

22. Consider a service system staffed by a person who takes 10 minutes to satisfy a customer's needs. Customers arrive at this system at the rate of five per hour.
   a. How many customers would you expect to find in *line* waiting?
   b. What total time would you expect a customer to spend in the *system?*
   c. What is the probability that there are three or more customers in the system?

23. During the campus Spring Fling, the bumper car amusement attraction has a problem of cars becoming disabled and in need of repair. Repair personnel can be hired at the rate of $5 per hour, but they only work as one team. Thus if one person is hired he or she works alone; two or three people only work together on the same repair.

One repairperson can repair cars in an average time of 30 minutes. Two repairpeople take 20 minutes, and three take 15 minutes each. While these cars are down, lost income is $20 per hour. Cars tend to break down at the rate of two per hour.

How many repairpeople should be hired?

24. The Holland Tunnel under the Hudson River in New York collects tolls for its use. For a portion of a particular day, only one toll booth was open. Automobiles were arriving at this gate at the rate of 750 per hour. The toll collector took an average of four seconds to collect the fee.
   a. What was the utilization of the toll booth operator?
   b. How much time would you expect to take to arrive, pay your toll, and move on?
   c. How many cars would you expect to see in the system?
   d. What is the probability that there will be more than four cars in the system?

25. A typist in an office can, on the average, type a letter in eight minutes. This typist works for a large number of people, and they tend to send letters to be typed on the average of one every 10 minutes.
   a. What is the utilization of the typist?

    b. If your letter was just sent to the typist's desk, how long would you expect it to take from that point to the completed typed letter?

    c. How many letters would you expect to see in line?

    d. What is the probability that there will be more than three letters in the system?

26. Because it is getting close to flu season, the university is considering setting up a station to dispense flu shots free to all students, staff, and faculty. There is a question of staffing for a variety of possible demands. One option is to hire just one nurse. Assume that the nurse can give 120 shots per hour, exponentially distributed. People arrive about every 36 seconds, on the average.

    a. What is the utilization of the nurse?

    b. How many people would you expect to find in the system (excluding the nurse)?

    c. How long would it take if you just joined the line to get completely through the system (with shot)?

    d. What is the probability that there will be more than three people in the system (excluding the nurse)?

27. The Erlang distribution can have the same effect as an exponential distribution, or it can be close to a Poisson, normal, or in the extreme case, a single value, depending on the value of K chosen. Note Exhibit S4.9 while working the following problem and use the Model 5 Lotus equations in Exhibit S4.13.

    A worker in a service system has arrivals to the workstation of one every 12 minutes, on the average (LAMBDA = 5/hour). The server, on the average, can perform the required work in an average time of 10 minutes (MU = 6/hour).

    Use a spreadsheet and test the effects on the waiting line system (number in line, in the system, time in the system, etc.) as K changes from 1 (exponential service) to infinity (constant service). Use small increments in the low range of K (e.g., 1, 2, 4, 6, 8, 10, 20, 50, 100 etc.).

    What general statements can you make about the service time distribution on the waiting line performance?

S4.9 SELECTED BIBLIOGRAPHY

Bartfai, P., and J. Tomko. *Point Processes Queuing Problems.* New York: Elsevier-North Holland Publishing, 1981.

Bruell, Steven C. *Computational Algorithms for Closed Queuing Networks.* New York: Elsevier-North Holland Publishing, 1980.

Cooper, Robert B. *Introduction to Queuing Theory.* 2nd ed. New York: Elsevier-North Holland Publishing, 1980.

Gorney, Leonard. *Queuing Theory: A Solving Approach.* Princeton, N.J.: Petrocelli, 1981.

Griffin, Walter C. *Queuing: Basic Theory and Application.* Columbus, Ohio: Grid, 1978.

Hillier, Frederick S., et al. *Queuing Tables and Graphs.* New York: Elsevier-North Holland Publishing, 1981.

Newell, Gordon F. *Applications of Queuing Theory.* New York: Chapman and Hall, 1982.

————. *Approximate Behavior of Tandem Queues.* New York: Springer-Verlag, 1980.

Solomon, Susan L. *Simulation of Waiting Lines.* Englewood Cliffs, N. J.: Prentice Hall, 1983.

Srivastava, H. M., and B. R. Kashyap. *Special Functions in Queuing Theory: And Related Stochastic Processes.* New York: Academic Press, 1982.

Vinrod, B., and T. Altiok. "Approximating Unreliable Queuing Networks under the Assumption of Exponentiality." *Journal of the Operational Research Society,* March 1986, pp. 309–16.

Chapter 5

Design for Total Quality Management

EPIGRAPH

The reason for poor quality is what I would call "Cliff Claven (of the "Cheers" TV show) Management"—all talk and no follow-through. The result is Norm Peterson-type employees.

System + Passion + Persistence = Quality Revolution

> Tom Peters, *Quality* (Palo Alto, Calif.: The Tom Peters Group, 1986), p. 28.

KEY TERMS

Total Quality Management (TQM)

Design Quality

Conformance Quality

Dimensions of Quality

Quality Function Deployment (QFD)

House of Quality

Prevention

Zero Defects

Cost of Quality

Quality at the Source

Continuous Process Improvement

Statistical Process Control (SPC)

Statistical Quality Control (SQC)

Acceptance Sampling

Process Control

Acceptable Quality Level (AQL)

Operating Characteristic (OC)

Taguchi Methods

Once in a generation, perhaps, something happens that profoundly changes the world and how we look at it. Business is no different. From time to time, someone develops a new way of operation that spreads from industry to industry. Those who adopt and adapt, prosper; those who do not, disappear. Well-known examples of such processes include the adoption of the factory system in the 18th century and the assembly line in the 20th century. Without question, total quality management (TQM) is an innovation on this scale. The automotive industry best illustrates this point. The impact on North American manufacturers of high-quality competition from Honda, Toyota, and others has been enormous. Between 1978 and 1988, Honda tripled its share of the North American market from 2.4 percent to 7.2 percent while Toyota increased its share from 3.9 percent to 6.5 percent. The Japanese inroads were made through reliability and high resale value based on product quality. Now we are seeing the emergence of the Acura Legend, the Toyota Lexus, and the Nissan Infiniti models that embody the same high-quality standards in designs competitive with domestic and European luxury cars selling for much more. American manufacturers have certainly not been standing still on the quality front. However, despite Ford's successes in regaining some of its market share through quality efforts and Cadillac winning the 1990 Malcolm Baldrige National Quality Award, the fact remains that Japanese cars are the symbols of quality in the U.S. marketplace.[1]

The Japanese success at quality derives from their top executives and their industry-government organization—the Japanese Union of Scientists and Engineers (JUSE)—implementing the ideas of U.S. quality experts W. Edwards Deming and Joseph Juran.[2] In the years following World War II, these individuals preached a very simple message: That controlling the process, rather than inspecting items that come from the process is the key to quality; that process control depends on a knowledge of process control statistical concepts; and that total quality management requires participation and training of all members of the organization.

In this chapter we develop some of the basic ideas of TQM which underlie the successful quality programs not only of the Japanese but also of quality leaders in Europe and North America. In addition, we discuss some of the standard and emerging technical topics of quality control (QC) of which all managers should be aware.

5.1 THE ELEMENTS OF TQM

Total quality management (TQM) may be defined as managing the entire organization so that it excels in all dimensions of products and services that are

---

[1] This introductory section is based on John F. Gilks, "Total Quality: Wave of the Future," *Canadian Business Review,* Spring 1990, pp. 17–20.

[2] See Exhibit 5.18 at the end of chapter for a summary of the views of the quality gurus.

EXHIBIT 5.1   **Elements of Total Quality Management**

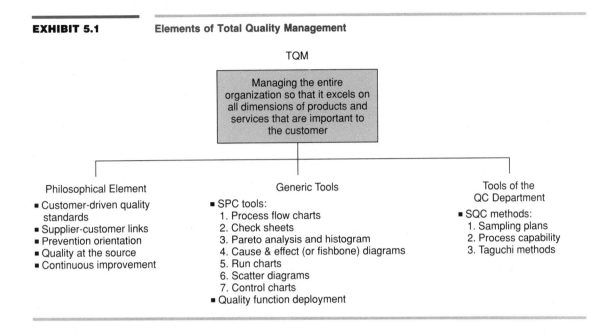

TQM

Managing the entire organization so that it excels on all dimensions of products and services that are important to the customer

Philosophical Element
- Customer-driven quality standards
- Supplier-customer links
- Prevention orientation
- Quality at the source
- Continuous improvement

Generic Tools
- SPC tools:
  1. Process flow charts
  2. Check sheets
  3. Pareto analysis and histogram
  4. Cause & effect (or fishbone) diagrams
  5. Run charts
  6. Scatter diagrams
  7. Control charts
- Quality function deployment

Tools of the QC Department
- SQC methods:
  1. Sampling plans
  2. Process capability
  3. Taguchi methods

important to the customer. The key notions in this definition are that quality extends throughout the organization in everything it does and that quality is ultimately defined by the customer.

Exhibit 5.1 presents a framework summarizing the important elements of TQM. Most of the fuss in the quality movement is about the first two categories. That is, the major philosophical precepts and generic quality improvement tools which have been made popular by the quality gurus— Deming, Juran, and Crosby. The third category consists of statistical tools commonly used by QC professionals working in QC departments.

5.2 PHILOSOPHICAL ELEMENTS

Customer-Driven Quality Standards

What this says is that "your product isn't reliable unless the customer says it's reliable," and "your service isn't fast unless the customer says it's fast." What this means is that the customer's perception of quality must be taken into account in setting acceptable quality levels. Translating customer quality demands into specifications requires marketing (or product development) to accurately assess what the customer wants, and requires product designers to develop a product (or service) that can be produced to consistently achieve that quality level. This in turn, requires that we have an operational definition of quality, an understanding of its dimensions, and methodologies for including

**The Dimensions of
Design Quality**

Dimension	Meaning
Performance	Primary product or service characteristics
Features	Added touches, bells and whistles, secondary characteristics
Reliability	Consistency of performance over time
Durability	Useful life
Serviceability	Resolution of problems and complaints
Response	Characteristics of the human-to-human interface (timeliness, courtesy, professionalism, etc.)
Esthetics	Sensory characteristics (sound, feel, look, etc.)
Reputation	Past performance and other intangibles

Source: Modified from Paul E. Plsek, "Defining Quality at the Marketing/Development Interface," *Quality Progress*, June 1987, pp. 28–36.

the voice of the customer in those specifications. The quality of a product or service may be defined in the quality of its design and the quality of its conformance to that design. **Design quality** refers to the inherent value of the product in the marketplace and is thus a strategic decision for the firm. The common dimensions of design quality are listed in Exhibit 5.2.

Conformance quality refers to the degree to which the product or service design specifications are met. It, too, has strategic implications, but the execution of the activities involved in achieving conformance are of a tactical day-to-day nature. It should be evident that a product or service can have high design quality but low conformance quality, and vice versa.

The operations function and the quality organization within the firm are primarily concerned with quality of conformance. Achieving all the quality specifications is typically the responsibility of manufacturing management, where a product is involved, and branch operations management in a service industry. Exhibit 5.3 shows two examples of the **dimensions of quality:** one is a stereo amplifier that meets the signal-to-noise ratio standard, and the second a checking account transaction in a bank.

Both quality of design and quality of conformance should provide products that meet the customer's objectives for those products. This is often termed the product's *fitness for use,* and it entails identifying the dimensions of the product (or service) that the customer wants and developing a quality control program to ensure these dimensions are met.

Quality function deployment.   One approach to getting the voice of the customer into the design specifications of a product is **quality function deployment** (QFD).[3] This approach, which uses interfunctional teams from

---

[3] The term *quality* is actually a mistranslation of the Japanese word for *qualities*. Because QFD is widely used in the context of quality management, however, we elected to put it in this chapter rather than in Chapter 3 on product design.

EXHIBIT 5.3

Examples of Dimensions of Quality

	MEASURES	
Dimension	Product Example: Stereo Amplifier	Service Example: Checking Account at Bank
Performance	Signal-to-noise ratio, power	Time to process customer requests
Features	Remote control	Automatic bill paying
Reliability	Mean time to failure	Variability of time to process requests
Durability	Useful life (with repair)	Keeping pace with industry trends
Serviceability	Ease of repair	Resolution of errors
Response	Courtesy of dealer	Courtesy of teller
Esthetics	Oak-finished cabinet	Appearance of bank lobby
Reputation	*Consumer Reports* ranking	Advice of friends, years in business

Source: Modified from Paul E. Plsek, "Defining Quality at the Marketing/Development Interface," *Quality Progress*, June 1987, pp. 28–36.

marketing, design engineering, and manufacturing, has been credited by Toyota Motor Corporation for reducing the costs on its cars by more than 60 percent by significantly shortening design times.

The QFD process begins with studying and listening to customers to determine the characteristics of a superior product. Through market research, the consumers' product needs and preferences are defined and broken down into categories called *customer attributes*. For example, an automobile manufacturer would like to improve the design of a car door. Through customer surveys and interviews, it determines that two important customer attributes desired in a car door are that it "stays open on a hill" and is "easy to close from the outside." After the customer attributes are defined, they are weighted based on their relative importance to the customer. Next, the consumer is asked to compare and rate the company's products with the products of competitors. This process helps the company to determine the product characteristics that are important to the consumer and to evaluate its product in relation to others. The end result is a better understanding and focus on product characteristics that require improvement.

Customer attribute information forms the basis for a matrix called the **house of quality** (see Exhibit 5.4). By building a house of quality matrix, the cross-functional QFD team can use customer feedback to make engineering, marketing, and design decisions. The matrix helps the team to translate customer attribute information into concrete operating or engineering goals. The important product characteristics and goals for improvement are jointly agreed on and detailed in the house. This process encourages the different departments to work closely together and results in a better understanding of one another's goals and issues. However, the most important benefit of the house of quality is that it helps the team to focus on building a product that satisfies customers.

EXHIBIT 5.4

Completed House of
Quality Matrix for a
Car Door

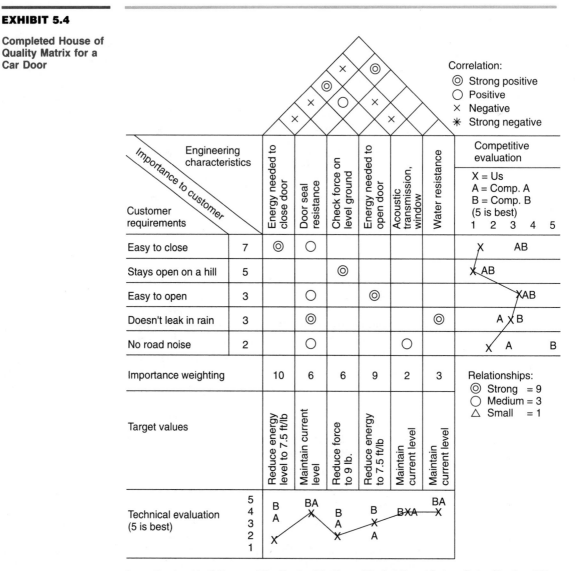

Source: Based on John R. Hauser and Don Clausing, "The House of Quality," *Harvard Business Review*, May–June 1988, pp. 62–73.

Although the house of quality appears complicated, it is not difficult to understand once the house is analyzed in sections. The customer attributes are found on the left side of the house with their relative importances to the customer specified. The customer perceptions of how the product compares to the competition on each characteristic is located on the far right side of the house. The second story of the house lists the engineering or operating characteristics of the product that are likely to affect the customer attributes. The interfunctional team completes the matrix in the middle of the house by indicating how much each engineering or operating characteristic affects each customer attribute. The strength and direction of the relationship is indicated by coded symbols. The roof of the house is also completed by QFD team, and it indicates the correlations the various engineering or operating characteristics have with one another.

The importance weighting section specifies the significance of the engineering or operating characteristics listed in the matrix. The weight is based on the symbols in the middle of the matrix showing the relationship between the characteristic and the customer attributes. "Target values" for the engineering or operating characteristics are then defined by the QFD team. These are specific goals (often numeric) that the team believes enable them to fulfill the desired customer attributes. Finally, the team compares the technical characteristics of its product to those of the competition.

Supplier–Customer Links

Supplier-customer links refer to the fact that everybody in an organization has a customer. Such customers may be internal (e.g., the next worker or next department in the production process) as well as external (distributors, retailers, or end users). Each of these customers have quality requirements with respect to one or more of the dimensions shown in Exhibit 5.3. Some have argued that the only customer that really matters is the person who buys the product or service. We agree with this view up to a point: It is important to keep your eye on the ball with respect to whom the organization serves. On the other hand, an organization is a network of relationships among people each of whom is dependent on his or her co-workers to create the product or service. Thinking of co-workers downstream in the production process as customers is simply a way of creating a cooperative and focused network to achieve the results required by the end customer.

Prevention Orientation

"An ounce of prevention is worth a pound of cure." This ancient homily captures the essence of the prevention orientation, and indeed, the contemporary philosophy of TQM. Later mantras include: DIRTFT (Do It Right The First Time) and "You can't inspect-in quality."

A classic example of the success of a **prevention** orientation is recounted by David Garvin, in his discussion of zero defects, another prevention call to arms.

Zero defects had its genesis at the Martin Company in 1961–62. At the time, Martin was building Pershing missiles for the U.S. Army. Their quality, though generally good, was achieved only through massive inspection. Incentives were offered to workers to lower the defect rate still further; together with even more intensive inspection and testing, these efforts led, on December 13, 1961, to the delivery of a Pershing missile to Cape Canaveral with zero discrepancies.

A defect-free missile could therefore be made, although it was likely to require extensive debugging before shipment. A month later, Martin's general manager in Orlando, Florida, accepted a request from the U.S. Army's missile command to deliver the first field Pershing one month ahead of schedule. He went even further—he promised that the missile would be perfect, with no hardware problems, no document errors, and all equipment set up and fully operational 10 days after delivery (the norm was 90 days or more). Two months of feverish activity followed. Since little time was available for the usual inspection and after-the-fact correction of errors, all employees were asked to contribute to building the missile exactly right the first time. The result was still a surprise: In February 1962 a perfect missile was delivered. It arrived on time and was fully operational in less than 24 hours.

This experience was an eye-opener for Martin. After careful review, management concluded that the project's success was primarily a reflection of its own changed attitude: "The reason behind the lack of perfection was simply that perfection had not been expected. The one time management demanded perfection, it happened!" Similar reasoning suggested a need to focus on workers' motivation and awareness. Of the three most common causes of worker errors—lack of knowledge, lack of proper facilities, and lack of attention—management concluded that the last had been least often addressed. It set out to design a program whose overriding goal was to "promote a constant, conscious desire to do a job (any job) right the first time." The resulting program was called zero defects.[4]

Cost of quality.   While few can quarrel with the notion of prevention, management often needs hard numbers to determine how much prevention activities will cost. This issue was recognized by Joseph Juran, who wrote about it in 1951 in his *Quality Control Handbook*. Today, **cost of quality** (COQ) analyses are common in industry and constitute one of the primary functions of QC departments.

There are a number of definitions and interpretations of the term *cost of quality*. From the purist's point of view, it means all the costs attributable to the production of quality that is not 100 percent perfect. A less stringent definition considers only those costs that are the difference between what can be expected from excellent performance and the current costs that exist.

How significant is the cost of quality? It has been estimated at between 15 and 20 percent of every sales dollar—the cost of reworking, scrapping, repeated service, inspections, tests, warranties, and other quality-related items. Philip Crosby states that the correct cost for a well-run quality management

---

[4] David A. Garvin, *Managing Quality, The Strategic and Competitive Edge* (New York: Free Press, 1988), pp. 16–17.

program should be under 2.5 percent.[5] In China, the cost of poor quality can be extremely high! (See Insert.)

INSERT   Talk about the Cost of Quality!

MANAGERS EXECUTED FOR SHODDY QUALITY
(Beijing)—Eighteen factory managers were executed for poor product quality at Chien Bien Refrigerator Factory on the outskirts of the Chinese capital. The managers—12 men and 6 women—were taken to a rice paddy outside the factory and unceremoniously shot to death as 500 plant workers looked on.

Minister of Economic Reform spokesman, Xi Ten Haun, said the action was required for committing unpardonable crimes against the people of China. He blamed the managers for ignoring quality and forcing shoddy work, saying the factory's output of refrigerators had a reputation for failure. For years, factory workers complained that many component parts did not meet specification and the end product did not function as required. Complaining workers quoted the plant manager as saying, "Ship it." Refrigerators are among the most sought-after consumer items in China. Customers, who waited up to five years for their appliances, were outraged.

"It is understandable our citizens would express shock and outrage when managers are careless in their attitudes toward the welfare of others," Haun says. "Our soldiers are justified in wishing to bring proper justice to these errant managers."

The executed included the plant manager, the quality control manager, the engineering managers and their top staff.

Source: Excerpted from *The Wall Street Journal*, October 17, 1989.

Three basic assumptions justify an analysis of the costs of quality:[6]

1. That failures are caused.
2. That prevention is cheaper.
3. That performance can be measured.

The *costs of quality* are generally classified into four types:

1. Appraisal costs: the costs of the inspection, testing, and other tasks to ensure that the product or process is acceptable.
2. Prevention costs: the sum of all the costs to prevent defects, such as the costs to identify the *cause* of the defect, to implement corrective action to eliminate the cause, to train personnel, to redesign the product or system, and for new equipment or modifications.

---

[5] Philip B. Crosby, *Quality Is Free* (New York: New American Library, 1979), p. 15.

[6] Frank Scanlon, "Quality Costs in a Non-Manufacturing Environment," *ASQC Quality Congress Transactions*, 1983, pp. 296–300.

EXHIBIT 5.5

Quality Cost Report

	Current Month's Cost	Percent of Total
Prevention costs		
Quality training	$ 2,000	1.3%
Reliability engineering	10,000	6.5
Pilot studies	5,000	3.3
Systems development	8,000	5.2
Total prevention	25,000	16.3
Appraisal costs		
Materials inspection	6,000	3.9
Supplies inspection	3,000	2.0
Reliability testing	5,000	3.3
Laboratory	25,000	16.3
Total appraisal	39,000	25.5
Internal failure costs		
Scrap	15,000	9.8
Repair	18,000	11.8
Rework	12,000	7.8
Downtime	6,000	3.9
Total internal failure	51,000	33.3
External failure costs		
Warranty costs	14,000	9.2
Out-of-warranty repairs and replacement	6,000	3.9
Customer complaints	3,000	2.0
Product liability	10,000	6.5
Transportation losses	5,000	3.3
Total external failure	38,000	24.9
Total quality costs	$153,000	100.0

Source: Harold P. Roth and Wayne J. Morse, "Let's Help Measure and Report Quality Costs," *Management Accounting*, August 1983, p. 53.

3. Failure costs.
   a. Internal. The costs incurred within the system: scrap, rework, repair.
   b. External. The costs for defects that pass through the system: customer warranty replacements, loss of customer or goodwill, handling complaints, and product repair.[7]

Exhibit 5.5 illustrates the type of report that might be submitted to show the various costs by categories. Exhibit 5.6 conveys the message: Spend more money on prevention and you should be able to reduce appraisal and failure

---

[7] For a description of reports that Honeywell created to state these four costs by department, see Vyasaraj V. Murthy, "Managing Cost of Quality at Honeywell," *ASQC Quality Congress Transactions*, 1983, pp. 463–65.

EXHIBIT 5.6   Prevention Costs Reduce Total Costs

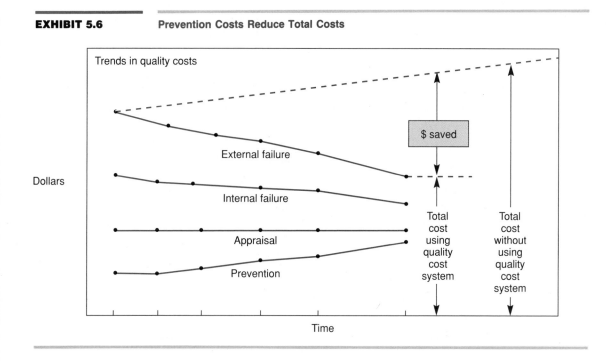

costs. The rule of thumb says that for every dollar you spend in prevention, you can save $10 in failure and appraisal costs.

Often, increases in productivity occur as a by-product of efforts to reduce the cost of quality. A bank, for example, set out to improve quality and reduce the cost of quality and found that it had also boosted productivity. The bank developed this productivity measure for the loan processing area: the number of tickets processed divided by the resources required (labor cost, computer time, ticket forms). Before the quality improvement program, the productivity index was 0.2660 [2,080/($11.23 × 640 hours + $0.05 × 2,600 forms + $500 for systems costs)]. After the quality improvement project was completed, labor time fell to 546 hours and the number of forms to 2,100 for a change in the index to 0.3088, or an increase in productivity of 16 percent.

Quality at the Source

Quality at the source means that each worker is a quality inspector for his or her own work. This view changes the often adversarial practice of having a QC inspector, typically from the QC department, making decisions about good or bad quality. This philosophy, as currently practiced, extends beyond the worker to include the work group, all departments, and to the suppliers of parts and services to the organization.

To make quality at the source effective requires a host of philosophical changes and actions on the part of all members of the organization. As usual, it starts with top management's commitment to empower workers to make quality decisions. This commitment must be backed up by training in the tools to both prevent defects and to fix them when they occur. It also requires a change in role of the quality control department from that of being a police officer to that of being a provider of technical assistance in designing the methods and tools to prevent defects. Relative to the latter point, imbedding inspections within the process itself can be used not only to identify defects but also to correct them before the product goes to the next stage of production. The development of simple methods used by the operator to accomplish this is a major feature of the continuous improvement approach developed by Japanese quality expert, Shigeo Shingo. These simple methods are called *poka-yoke* (Japanese for "fail-safe") which Shingo developed as part of the Toyota just-in-time system. (See Chapter 17 for a detailed discussion of poka-yoke.)

Continuous Improvement

Continuous improvement has a general meaning and a specific TQM meaning. Its general meaning is an ongoing effort to simply make improvements in every part of the organization relative to all of its deliverables to its customers. Its more specific meaning focuses on continual improvement in the quality of the processes by which work is accomplished. Thus, the phrase **continuous process improvement** often defines its purpose in the context of TQM. Chapter 17 deals with continuous process improvement in depth.

5.3 GENERIC TOOLS

The generic tools of TQM are those developed for **statistical process control** (SPC); as used by nonspecialists, they are also the main tools of continuous process improvement.[8] With the exception of control charts, SPC tools are really just ways of organizing and analyzing numerical data for problem solving, not heavy-duty statistics. Exhibit 5.7 provides a brief discription of the basic tools. Please note, however, that a variety of other tools are associated with the so-called PDCA (Plan, Do, Check, Act) Cycle of continuous improvement. We have included six of the seven tools of QC used by the Japanese, with run charts substituted for stratification. Stratification uses several of the other tools to break down aggregated data into related categories. For example, rather than graph defects per month for the entire company, it would graph defects per month by department. (Incidentally, the "Seven Basic Tools of QC" correspond to the "Seven Weapons of the Samurai Warrior.")

---

[8] Quality Function Deployment (discussed earlier) is also a tool that is used by non-QC specialists.

EXHIBIT 5.7   SPC Tools Commonly Used for Problem Solving and Continuous Improvement

These tools do not substitute for judgment and process knowledge. They help deal with complexity and turn raw data into information that can be used to take action.

Process Flow Chart

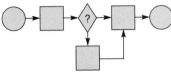

A picture which describes the main steps, branches and eventual outputs of a process.

Pareto Analysis

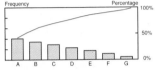

A coordinated approach for identifying, ranking, and working to permanently eliminate defects. Focuses on important error sources. 80/20 rule: 80 percent of the problems are due to 20 percent of the causes.

Run Chart

A time sequence chart showing plotted values of a characteristic.

Data Collection

Always have an agreed upon and clear reason for any data you collect. Prepare in advance your strategy for both collecting and analyzing the data. Questions that might be asked of data collection: Why? What? Where? How much? When? How? Who? How long?

Histogram

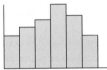

A distribution showing the frequency of occurrences between the high and low range of data.

Scatter Diagram

Also known as a correlation chart. A graph of the value of one characteristic versus another characteristic.

Checksheet

An organized method for recording data.

Causes and Effect Diagram

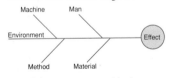

A tool that uses a graphical description of the process elements to analyze potential sources of process variation.

Control Charts

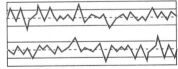

A time sequence chart showing plotted values of a statistic, including a central line and one or more statistically derived control limits.

Source: Coopers and Lybrand, *Quality Practices* brochure, 1989.

5.4 TOOLS OF THE QC DEPARTMENT

The typical manufacturing QC department has a variety of functions to perform. These include testing designs for their reliability in the lab and the field; gathering performance data on products in the field and resolving quality problems in the field; planning and budgeting the QC program in the plant; and, finally, designing and overseeing quality control systems and inspection procedures, and actually carrying out inspection activities requiring special technical knowledge to perform. The tools of the QC department fall under the heading of statistical quality control (SQC).

Statistical Quality Control

The subject of **statistical quality control** can be divided into *acceptance sampling* and *process control*. **Acceptance sampling** involves testing a random sample of existing goods and deciding whether to accept an entire lot based on the quality of the random sample. **Process control** involves testing a random sample of output from a process to determine whether the process is producing items within a preselected range. When the tested output exceeds that range, it is a signal to adjust the production process to force the output back into the acceptable range. This is accomplished by adjusting the process itself. Acceptance sampling is frequently used in a purchasing or receiving situation, while process control is used in a production situation of any type.

Quality control for both acceptance sampling and process control measures either attributes or variables. Goods or services may be observed to be either good or bad, or functioning or malfunctioning. For example, a lawnmower either runs or it doesn't; it attains a certain level of torque and horsepower or it doesn't. This type of measurement is known as sampling by attributes. Alternatively, a lawnmower's torque and horsepower can be measured as an amount of deviation from a set standard. This type of measurement is known as sampling by variables. The following sections describe some standard approaches to developing acceptance sampling plans and process control procedures.

5.5 ACCEPTANCE SAMPLING

Design of a Single Sampling Plan for Attributes

Acceptance sampling is performed on goods that already exist to determine what percentage of products conform to specifications. These products may be items received from another company and evaluated by the receiving department or they may be components that have passed through a processing step and are evaluated by company personnel either in production or later in the warehousing function. Whether inspection should be done at all is addressed in the Insert entitled "Costs to Justify Inspection."

Acceptance sampling is executed through a sampling plan. In this section, we illustrate the planning procedures for a single sampling plan—that is, a plan in which the quality is determined from the evaluation of one sample. (Other plans may be developed using two or more samples. See J. M. Juran and F. M. Gryna's *Quality Planning and Analysis* for a discussion of these plans.

INSERT   Costs to Justify Inspection

Total (100 percent) inspection is justified when the cost of a loss incurred by not inspecting is greater than the cost of inspection. For example, suppose a faulty item results in a $10 loss. If the average percentage of defective items in a lot is 3 percent, the expected cost of faulty items is 0.03 × $10, or $0.30 each. Therefore, if the cost of inspecting each item is less than $0.30, the economic decision is to perform 100 percent inspection. Not all defective items will be removed, however, since inspectors will pass some bad items and reject some good ones.

The purposes of a sampling plan are to test the lot to either (1) find its quality or (2) ensure that the quality is what it is supposed to be. Thus, if a quality control supervisor already knows the quality (such as the 0.03 given in the example), he or she does not sample for defects. Either all of them must be inspected to remove the defects or none of them should be inspected, and the rejects pass into the process. The choice simply depends on the cost to inspect and the cost incurred by passing a reject.

A single sampling plan is defined by n and c, where n is the number of units in the sample and c is the acceptance number. The size of n may vary from one up to all the items in the lot (usually denoted as N) from which it is drawn. The acceptance number c denotes the maximum number of defective items that can be found in the sample before the lot is rejected. Values for n and c are determined by the interaction of four factors that quantify the objectives of the product's producer and its consumer. The objective of the producer is to ensure that the sampling plan has a low probability of rejecting good lots. Lots are defined as good if they contain no more than a specified level of defectives, termed the **acceptable quality level** (AQL).[9] The objective of the consumer is to ensure that the sampling plan has a low probability of accepting bad lots. Lots are defined as bad if the percentage of defectives is greater than a specified amount, termed *lot tolerance percent defective* (LTPD). The probability associated with rejecting a good lot is denoted by the Greek letter alpha (α) and is termed the *producer's risk*. The probability associated with accepting a bad lot is denoted by the letter beta (β) and is termed the *consumer's risk*. The selection of particular values for AQL, α, LTPD, and β is an economic decision based on a cost trade-off or, more typically, on company policy or contractual requirements.

---

[9] There is some controversy surrounding AQLs. This is based on the argument that specifying some acceptable percent of defectives is inconsistent with the philosophical goal of zero defects. In practice, even in the best QC companies, there is an acceptable quality level. The difference is that it may be stated in parts per million rather than in parts per hundred. This is the case in Motorola's Six Sigma Quality standard which holds that no more than 3.4 defects per million parts are acceptable.

There is a humorous story supposedly about Hewlett-Packard during its first dealings with Japanese vendors, who place a great deal of emphasis on high-quality production. HP had insisted on 2 percent AQL in a purchase of 100 cables. During the purchase agreement some heated discussion took place wherein the Japanese vendor did not want this AQL specification; HP insisted that they would not budge from the 2 percent AQL. The Japanese vendor finally agreed. Later, when the box arrived, there were two packages inside. One contained 100 good cables. The other package had 2 cables with a note stating: "We have sent you 100 good cables. Since you insisted on 2 percent AQL, we have enclosed 2 defective cables in this package, though we do not understand why you want them."

The following example, using an excerpt from a standard acceptance sampling table, illustrates how the four parameters—AQL, α, LTPD, and β—are used in developing a sampling plan.

Example

Hi-Tech Industries manufactures Z-Band radar scanners used to detect speed traps. The printed circuit boards in the scanners are purchased from an outside vendor. The vendor produces the boards to an acceptable quality level (AQL) of 2 percent defectives and is willing to run a 5 percent risk (α) of having lots of this level or fewer defectives rejected. Hi-Tech considers lots of 8 percent or more defectives (LTPD) unacceptable and wants to ensure that it will accept such poor-quality lots no more than 10 percent of the time (β). A large shipment has just been delivered. What values of n and c should be selected to determine the quality of this lot?

Solution

The parameters of the problem are: AQL $= 0.02$, $\alpha = 0.05$, LTPD $= 0.08$, and $\beta = 0.10$. We can use Exhibit 5.8 to find c and then n.

First divide LTPD by AQL ($0.08 \div 0.02 = 4$). Then find the ratio in column 2 that is equal to or just greater than that amount (i.e., 4). This value is 4.057, which is associated with $c = 4$.

Finally, find the value in column 3 that is in the same row as $c = 4$, and divide that quantity by AQL to obtain n ($1.970 \div 0.02 = 98.5$).

The appropriate sampling plan is: $c = 4$, $n = 99$.

Operating Characteristic Curves

While a sampling plan such as the one just described meets our requirements for the extreme values of good and bad quality, we cannot readily determine how well the plan discriminates between good and bad lots at intermediate values. For this reason, sampling plans are generally displayed graphically through the use of **operating characteristic** (OC) curves. These curves, which are unique for each combination of n and c, simply illustrate the probability of accepting lots with varying percent defectives. The procedure we have followed in developing the plan, in fact, specifies two points on an OC curve—one point defined by AQL and $1 - \alpha$, and the other point defined

EXHIBIT 5.8

Excerpt from a
Sampling Plan Table
for $\alpha = 0.05$,
$\beta = 0.10$

c	LTPD ÷ AQL	n · AQL
0	44.890	0.052
1	10.946	0.355
2	6.509	0.818
3	4.890	1.366
4	4.057	1.970
5	3.549	2.613
6	3.206	3.286
7	2.957	3.981
8	2.768	4.695
9	2.618	5.426

by LTPD and β. Curves for common values of n and c can be computed or obtained from available tables.[10]

Shaping the OC Curve

A sampling plan discriminating perfectly between good and bad lots has an infinite slope (vertical) at the selected value of AQL. In Exhibit 5.9, percent defectives to the left of 2 percent would always be accepted and to the right, always rejected. However, such a curve is possible only with complete inspection of all units and thus not a possibility with a true sampling plan.

An OC curve should be steep in the region of most interest (between the AQL and the LTPD), which is accomplished by varying n and c. If c remains constant, increasing the sample size n causes the OC curve to be more vertical. While holding n constant, decreasing c (the maximum number of defective units) also makes the slope more vertical, moving closer to the origin.

The Effects of Lot Size

The size of the lot the sample is taken from has relatively little effect on the quality of protection. Consider, for example, that samples—all of the same size of 20 units—are taken from different lots ranging from a lot size of 200 units to a lot size of infinity. If each lot is known to have 5 percent defectives, the probability of accepting the lot based on the sample of 20 units ranges from about 0.34 to about 0.36. What this means is that so long as the lot size is several times the sample size, it makes very little difference how large the lot is. It seems a bit difficult to accept, but statistically (on the average in the long run) whether we have a carload or box full, we'll get about the same answer. It just seems that a carload should have a larger sample size.

---

[10] See, for example, H. F. Dodge and H. G. Romig, *Sampling Inspection Tables—Single and Double Sampling* (New York: John Wiley & Sons, 1959), and *Military Standard Sampling Procedures and Tables for Inspection by Attributes* (MIL-STD-105D) (Washington, D.C.: U.S. Government Printing Office, 1963).

EXHIBIT 5.9   Operating Characteristic Curve for AQL = 0.02, α = 0.05, LTPD = 0.08, β = 0.10

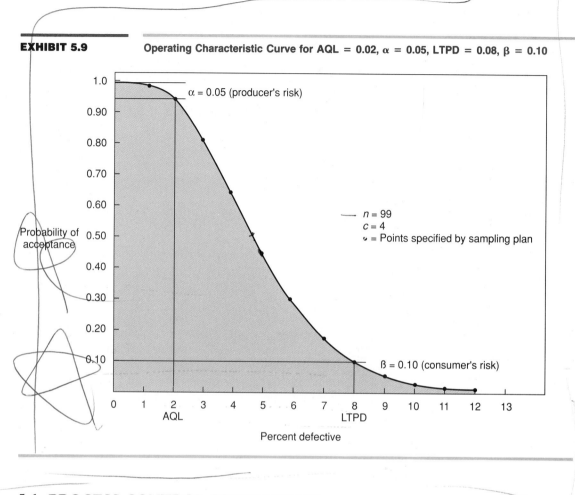

5.6 PROCESS CONTROL PROCEDURES

Process control is concerned with monitoring quality *while the product or service is being produced*. Typical objectives of process control plans are to provide timely information on whether currently produced items are meeting design specifications and to detect shifts in the process that signal that future products may not meet specifications. The actual control phase of process control occurs when corrective action is taken, such as a worn part replaced, a machine overhauled, or a new supplier found. Process control concepts, especially statistically based control charts, are being used in services as well as in manufacturing.

Process Control Using Attribute Measurements

Measurements by attributes means taking samples and using a single decision—the item is good, or it is bad. Because it is a yes-no decision, we can use simple statistics to create an upper control limit (UCL) and a lower control limit (LCL). We can draw these control limits on a graph and then plot the fraction defective of each individual sample tested. The process is assumed to be working correctly when the samples, which are taken periodically during the day, continue to stay between the control limits.

$$\bar{p} = \frac{\text{Total number of defects from all samples}}{\text{Number of samples} \times \text{Sample size}}$$

$$s_p = \sqrt{\frac{\bar{p}(1 - \bar{p})}{n}}$$

$$\text{UCL} = \bar{p} + zs_p$$

$$\text{LCL} = \bar{p} - zs_p$$

where p is the fraction defective, s is the standard deviation, and z is the number of standard deviations for a specific confidence. Typically, $z = 3$(99.7 percent confidence) or $z = 2.58$ (99 percent confidence) are used.

Exhibit 5.10 shows information that can be gained from control charts. We do not give an example of attribute process control here so that in the next section we can demonstrate $\overline{X}$ and R charts, which tend to have wider application in process control.

Process Control with Variable Measurements Using $\overline{X}$ and R Charts

$\overline{X}$ and R (range) charts are widely used in statistical process control.

In attributes sampling, we determine whether something is good or bad, fit or didn't fit—it was a go/no-go situation. In variables sampling, we measure the weight, volume, number of inches, or other variable measurements, and we develop control charts to determine the acceptability or rejection of the process based on those measurements.

There are four main issues to address in creating a control chart: the size of the samples, the number of samples, frequency of samples, and the control limits.

Size of samples

For industrial applications in process control, it is preferable to keep the sample size small. There are two main reasons: first, the sample needs to be taken within a reasonable length of time, otherwise the process might change while the samples are taken. Second, the larger the sample, the more it costs to take.

Sample sizes of four or five units seem to be the preferred numbers. The *means* of samples of this size have an approximately normal distribution, no matter what the distribution of the parent population looks like. Sample sizes greater than five give narrower control limits and thus more sensitivity. For detecting finer variations of a process it may be necessary, in fact, to use larger sample sizes. However, when sample sizes exceed 15 or so, it would be better to use the standard deviation σ and $\overline{X}$ charts rather than R and $\overline{X}$ charts.

EXHIBIT 5.10   **Control Chart Evidence for Investigation**

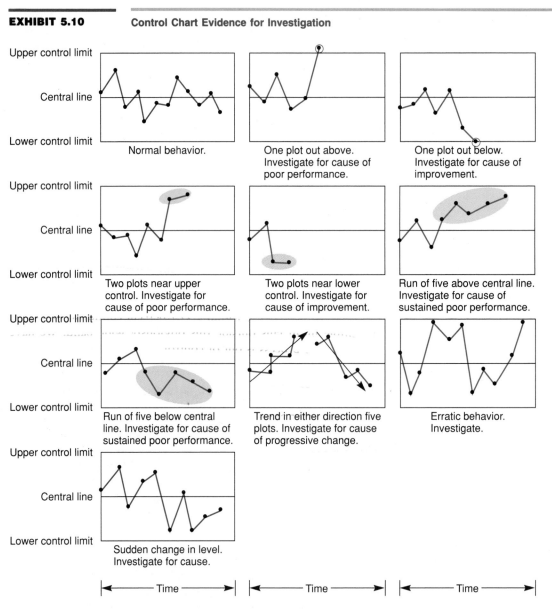

Upper control limit

Central line

Lower control limit

Normal behavior.

One plot out above.
Investigate for cause of
poor performance.

One plot out below.
Investigate for cause of
improvement.

Upper control limit

Central line

Lower control limit

Two plots near upper
control. Investigate for
cause of poor performance.

Two plots near lower
control. Investigate for
cause of improvement.

Run of five above central line.
Investigate for cause of
sustained poor performance.

Upper control limit

Central line

Lower control limit

Run of five below central
line. Investigate for cause of
sustained poor performance.

Trend in either direction five
plots. Investigate for cause
of progressive change.

Erratic behavior.
Investigate.

Upper control limit

Central line

Lower control limit

Sudden change in level.
Investigate for cause.

|← ———— Time ————→| |← ———— Time ————→| |← ———— Time ————→|

Source: Bertrand L. Hansen, *Quality Control: Theory and Applications,* © 1963, p. 65. Reprinted by permission of Prentice Hall, Inc., Englewood Cliffs, N.J.

Number of samples

Once the chart has been set up, each sample taken can be compared to the chart and a decision made about whether the process is acceptable. To set up the charts, however, prudence (and statistics) suggests that 25 or so samples be taken.

Frequency of samples

How often to take a sample is a trade-off between the cost of sampling (along with the cost of the unit if it is destroyed as part of the test), and the benefit of adjusting the system. Usually, it is best to start off with frequent sampling of a process and taper off as confidence in the process builds. For example, one might start with a sample of five units every half hour and end up feeling that one sample per day is adequate.

Control limits

Standard practice in statistical process control for variables is to set control limits three standard deviations above the mean and three standard deviations below. This means that 99.7 percent of the sample means are expected to fall within these control limits (that is, within a 99.7 percent confidence interval). Thus, if one sample mean falls outside this obviously wide band, we have strong evidence that the process is out of control.

How to Construct $\overline{X}$ and R Charts

An $\overline{X}$ chart is simply a plot of the means of the samples that were taken from a process. An $\overline{X}$ is the average of the means.

An R chart is a plot of the range within each sample. The range is the difference between the highest and the lowest number in that sample. R values provide an easily calculated measure of variation used like a standard deviation. An $\overline{R}$ chart is the average of the range of each sample. More specifically defined, these are

$$\overline{X} = \frac{\sum_{i=1}^{n} X_i}{n}$$

where

$\overline{X}$ = Mean of the sample

i = Item number

n = Total number of items in the sample

$$\overline{\overline{X}} = \frac{\sum_{j=1}^{m} \overline{X}_j}{m}$$

where

$\overline{\overline{X}}$ = The average of the means of the samples

j = Sample number

m = Total number of samples

R_j = Difference between the highest and lowest measurement in the sample

$\overline{R}$ = Average of the measurement differences R for all samples, or

$$\overline{R} = \frac{\sum\limits_{j=1}^{m} R_j}{m}$$

EXHIBIT 5.11

Factors for Determining from $\overline{R}$ the 3-Sigma Control Limits for $\overline{X}$ and R Charts

Number of Observations in Subgroup n	Factor for $\overline{X}$ Chart A_2	FACTORS FOR R CHART	
		Lower Control Limit D_3	Upper Control Limit D_4
2	1.88	0	3.27
3	1.02	0	2.57
4	0.73	0	2.28
5	0.58	0	2.11
6	0.48	0	2.00
7	0.42	0.08	1.92
8	0.37	0.14	1.86
9	0.34	0.18	1.82
10	0.31	0.22	1.78
11	0.29	0.26	1.74
12	0.27	0.28	1.72
13	0.25	0.31	1.69
14	0.24	0.33	1.67
15	0.22	0.35	1.65
16	0.21	0.36	1.64
17	0.20	0.38	1.62
18	0.19	0.39	1.61
19	0.19	0.40	1.60
20	0.18	0.41	1.59

Upper control limit for $\overline{X}$ = $UCL_{\overline{X}}$ = $\overline{\overline{X}} + A_2\overline{R}$
Lower control limit for $\overline{X}$ = $LCL_{\overline{X}}$ = $\overline{\overline{X}} - A_2\overline{R}$

Upper control limit for R = UCL_R = $D_4\overline{R}$
Lower control limit for R = LCL_R = $D_3\overline{R}$

Note: All factors are based on the normal distribution.

Source: E. L. Grant, *Statistical Quality Control*, 6th ed. (New York: McGraw-Hill, 1988). Reprinted by permission of McGraw-Hill, Inc.

E. L. Grant and R. Leavenworth computed a table that allows us to easily compute the upper and lower control limits for both the $\overline{X}$ chart and the R chart.[11] These are defined as:

Upper control limit for $\overline{X} = \overline{\overline{X}} + A_2\overline{R}$
Lower control limit for $\overline{X} = \overline{\overline{X}} - A_2\overline{R}$
Upper control limit for $R = D_4\overline{R}$
Lower control limit for $R = D_3\overline{R}$

Example

We would like to create an $\overline{X}$ and an R chart for a process. Exhibit 5.12 shows the measurements that were taken of all 25 samples. The last two columns show the average of the sample $\overline{X}$ and the range R.

Values for A_2, D_3, and D_4 were obtained from Exhibit 5.11.

EXHIBIT 5.12

Measurements in Samples of Five from a Process

Sample Number	Each Unit in Sample					Average $\overline{X}$	Range R
1	10.60	10.40	10.30	9.90	10.20	10.28	.70
2	9.98	10.25	10.05	10.23	10.33	10.17	.35
3	9.85	9.90	10.20	10.25	10.15	10.07	.40
4	10.20	10.10	10.30	9.90	9.95	10.09	.40
5	10.30	10.20	10.24	10.50	10.30	10.31	.30
6	10.10	10.30	10.20	10.30	9.90	10.16	.40
7	9.98	9.90	10.20	10.40	10.10	10.12	.50
8	10.10	10.30	10.40	10.24	10.30	10.27	.30
9	10.30	10.20	10.60	10.50	10.10	10.34	.50
10	10.30	10.40	10.50	10.10	10.20	10.30	.40
11	9.90	9.50	10.20	10.30	10.35	10.05	.85
12	10.10	10.36	10.50	9.80	9.95	10.14	.70
13	10.20	10.50	10.70	10.10	9.90	10.28	.80
14	10.20	10.60	10.50	10.30	10.40	10.40	.40
15	10.54	10.30	10.40	10.55	10.00	10.36	.55
16	10.20	10.60	10.15	10.00	10.50	10.29	.60
17	10.20	10.40	10.60	10.80	10.10	10.42	.70
18	9.90	9.50	9.90	10.50	10.00	9.96	1.00
19	10.60	10.30	10.50	9.90	9.80	10.22	.80
20	10.60	10.40	10.30	10.40	10.20	10.38	.40
21	9.90	9.60	10.50	10.10	10.60	10.14	1.00
22	9.95	10.20	10.50	10.30	10.20	10.23	.55
23	10.20	9.50	9.60	9.80	10.30	9.88	.80
24	10.30	10.60	10.30	9.90	9.80	10.18	.80
25	9.90	10.30	10.60	9.90	10.10	10.16	.70

$$\overline{\overline{X}} = 10.21$$

$$\overline{R} = .60$$

[11] E. L. Grant and R. Leavenworth, *Statistical Quality Control* (New York: McGraw-Hill, 1964), p. 562. Reprinted by permission.

$$\text{Upper control limit for } \overline{X} = \overline{\overline{X}} + A_2\overline{R}$$
$$= 10.21 + .58(.60) = 10.56$$
$$\text{Lower control limit for } \overline{X} = \overline{\overline{X}} - A_2\overline{R}$$
$$= 10.21 - .58(.60) = 9.86$$
$$\text{Upper control limit for } R = D_4\overline{R}$$
$$= 2.11(.60) = 1.26$$
$$\text{Lower control limit for } R = D_3\overline{R}$$
$$= 0(1.27) = 0$$

EXHIBIT 5.13

$\overline{X}$ **Chart and** R **Chart**

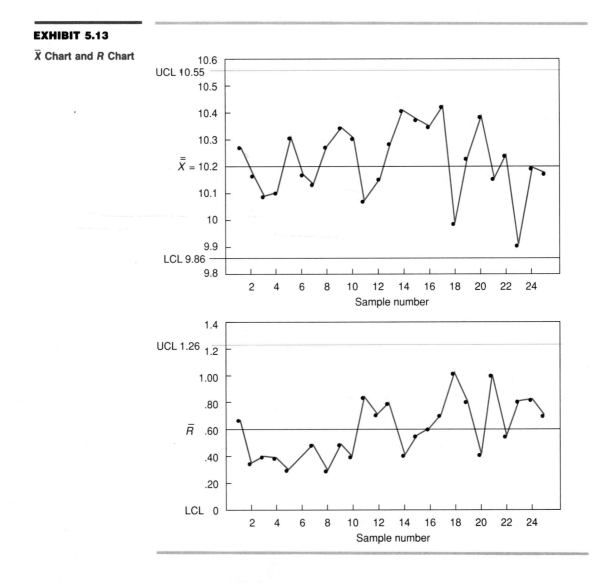

Exhibit 5.13 shows the $\overline{X}$ chart and R chart with a plot of all the sample means and ranges of the samples. All the points are well within the control limits, although sample 23 is close to the $\overline{X}$ lower control limit.

Process Capability

Control charts are of little value if the process itself is not capable of making products within design specification (or tolerance) limits. In section A of Exhibit 5.14, we see a process that on average is producing items within the control limits but its variation is such that it can't meet specifications for all items. Exhibit 5.14 (B) shows reduction in this variability, but the process is still deficient. Finally, in Exhibit 5.14 (C), we see that the process variability has been brought under control. How is this accomplished? By working to improve the performance of each source of variance: workers, machine, tooling, setup, material, and the environment.

Process capability ratio.   In order for a process to be both in control and within tolerance, the part tolerance limits must be equal to or wider than the upper and lower limits of the process control chart. Since these control limits

---

EXHIBIT 5.14   Reducing Process Variance So That All Parts Are in Tolerance

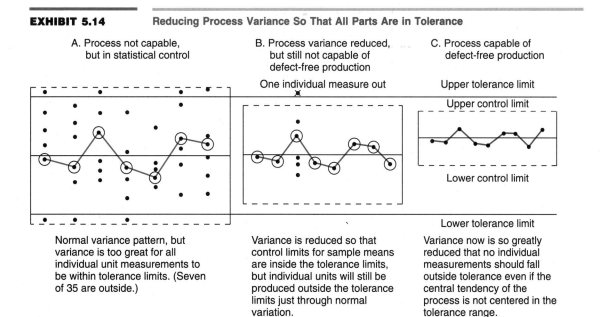

A. Process not capable, but in statistical control

B. Process variance reduced, but still not capable of defect-free production

C. Process capable of defect-free production

Normal variance pattern, but variance is too great for all individual unit measurements to be within tolerance limits. (Seven of 35 are outside.)

Variance is reduced so that control limits for sample means are inside the tolerance limits, but individual units will still be produced outside the tolerance limits just through normal variation.

Variance now is so greatly reduced that no individual measurements should fall outside tolerance even if the central tendency of the process is not centered in the tolerance range.

Tolerance: The range within which all individual measurements of units produced is desired to fall.

Source: Robert W. Hall, *Attaining Manufacturing Excellence: Just-in-Time Manufacturing, Total Quality, Total People Involvement* (Homewood, Ill.: Dow Jones–Irwin, 1987), p. 66.

are at plus or minus three standard deviations (3 sigma), the tolerance limits must exceed 6 sigma. A quick way of making this determination is through the use of a process capability ratio. This ratio is calculated by dividing the tolerance width by 6 sigma (the process capability), as shown in the following formula in which s, the sample standard deviation, is substituted for sigma, the population standard deviation.

$$\text{Process capability ratio} = \frac{\text{Upper tolerance limit} - \text{Lower tolerance limit}}{6s}$$

The larger the ratio, the greater the potential for producing parts within tolerance from the specified process. A ratio that is greater than 1 indicates that the tolerance limit range is wider than the actual range of measurements. If the ratio is less than 1, then some parts will be out of tolerance. The minimum capability index is frequently established at 1.33. Below this value, design engineers have to seek approval from manufacturing before the product can be released for production.

Capability index (C_{pk}).   The just defined capability ratio does not specifically indicate how well the process is performing relative to the target dimension. Thus, a second performance index, called C_{pk}, must be employed to determine whether the process mean is closer to the upper tolerance limit, UTL, or the lower tolerance limit, LTL.

$$C_{pk} = \min\left[\frac{\overline{X} - \text{LTL}}{3s}, \frac{\text{UTL} - \overline{X}}{3s}\right]$$

When C_{pk} equals the capability ratio, then the process mean is centered between the two tolerance limits. Otherwise, the process mean is closest to the tolerance limit corresponding to the minimum of the two C_{pk} ratios. Consider the following example.

Example

A manufacturing process produces a certain part with a mean diameter of 2 inches and a standard deviation of .03 inches. The upper tolerance limit equals 2.05 inches and the lower tolerance limit equals 1.9 inches. From this information, a process capability ratio and C_{pk} were calculated.

$$\text{Process capability ratio} = \frac{2.05 - 1.90}{6(.03)} = .833$$

$$C_{pk} \text{ for LTL} = \frac{2 - 1.90}{3(.03)} = 1.11$$

$$C_{pk} \text{ for UTL} = \frac{2.05 - 2}{3(.03)} = .55$$

From the process capability ratio, we can conclude that the process is capable of producing parts within tolerance. The C_{pk} analysis points out that the process mean is closer to the upper tolerance limit. Given this information, work can be done on the manufacturing process to center the mean between the two tolerance limits. This may involve, for example, a simple adjustment of a machine tool setting.

5.7 TAGUCHI METHODS

Throughout the chapter we have discussed quality control from the point of view of process adjustments. In what many have termed a revolution in quality thinking, Genichi Taguchi of Japan has suggested the following: Instead of constantly fiddling with production equipment to ensure consistent quality, design the product to be robust enough to achieve high quality despite fluctuations on the production line. This simple idea has been employed by such companies as Ford Motor Company, ITT, and IBM; as a result, they have saved millions of dollars in manufacturing.

Taguchi methods are basically statistical techniques for conducting experiments to determine the best combinations of product and process variables to make a product. *Best* means lowest cost with highest uniformity. This can be a complicated, time-consuming process. For example, in designing the process for a new product, one might find that a single processing step with only eight process variables (machine speed, cutting angle, and so on) could be combined in up to 5,000 different ways. Thus, finding the combination that makes the product with the highest uniformity at the lowest cost can't be done by trial and error. Taguchi has found a way around this problem by focusing on only a few combinations that represent the spectrum of product/process outcomes.

Taguchi is also known for the development of the concept of a quality loss function (QLF) to tie cost of quality directly to variation in a process. The following discussion from an article by Joseph Turner develops this concept in detail.[12]

IS AN OUT-OF-SPEC PRODUCT REALLY OUT OF SPEC?

VARIATION AROUND US

It is generally accepted that, as variation is reduced, quality is improved. Sometimes that knowledge is intuitive. If a train is always on time, schedules can be planned more precisely. If clothing sizes are consistent, time can be saved by ordering from a catalog. But rarely are such things thought about in terms of the value of low variability. With engineers, the knowledge is better defined. Pistons must fit cylinders, doors must fit openings, electrical components must be compatible, and boxes of cereal must have the

---

[12] Adapted from Joseph Turner, "Is an Out-of-Spec Product Really Out of Spec?," *Quality Progress,* December 1990, pp. 57–59.

right amount of raisins—otherwise quality will be unacceptable and customers will be dissatisfied.

However, engineers also know that it is impossible to have zero variability. For this reason, designers establish specifications that define not only the target value of something, but also acceptable limits about the target. For example, if the aim value of a dimension is 10 in., the design specifications might then be 10.00 in. ±0.02 in. This would tell the manufacturing department that, while it should aim for exactly 10 in., anything between 9.98 in. and 10.02 in. is OK.

A traditional way of interpreting such a specification is that any part that falls within the allowed range is equally good, while any part falling outside the range is totally bad. This is illustrated in Exhibit 5.15. (Note that the cost is zero over the entire specification range, and then there is a quantum leap in cost once the limit is violated.)

Taguchi has pointed out that such a view is nonsense for two reasons:

1. From the customer's view, there is often practically no difference between a product just inside specifications and a product just outside. Conversely, there is a far greater difference in the quality of a product that is at the target and the quality of one that is near a limit.

2. As customers get more demanding, there is pressure to reduce variability. An Exhibit 5.15 outlook does not recognize this pressure.

Taguchi suggests that a more correct picture of the loss is shown in Exhibit 5.16. Notice that in this graph the cost is represented by a smooth curve. There are dozens of illustrations of this notion: the meshing of gears in a transmission, the speed of photographic film, the temperature in a workplace or department store. In nearly anything that can be measured, the customer sees not a sharp line, but a gradation of acceptability. Customers see the loss function as Exhibit 5.16 rather than Exhibit 5.15.

What are the elements of loss to society? While different authorities suggest different things, it seems reasonable to think of both internal and external costs. Internally, the more variable the manufacturing process, the more scrap generated and the more a company will have to spend on testing and inspecting for conformance. Externally, customers will find that the product does not last as long or work as well if it is not close to aim. Perhaps, when used in adverse situations, the product will not perform at all, even though it meets specifications that were developed based on normal usage.

While the actual shape of the loss curve might vary considerably, a simple parabolic curve, as shown in Exhibit 5.16, has a lot of intuitive appeal, especially when specification limits are symmetrical about the target value. With a parabola, the loss is relatively small when we are close to aim and grows at an increasing rate the farther we move from the target.

Of course, if products are consistently scrapped when they are outside specifications, the loss curve flattens out in most cases at a value equivalent to scrap cost in the ranges outside specifications. This is because such products, theoretically at least, will never be sold, so there is no external cost to society. However, in many practical situations, either the process is capable of producing a very high percentage of product within specifications and/or 100 percent checking is not done and/or out-of-spec products can be reworked to bring them to within specs. In any of these situations, the parabolic loss function is usually a reasonable assumption.

EXHIBIT 5.15

A Traditional View of the Cost of Variability

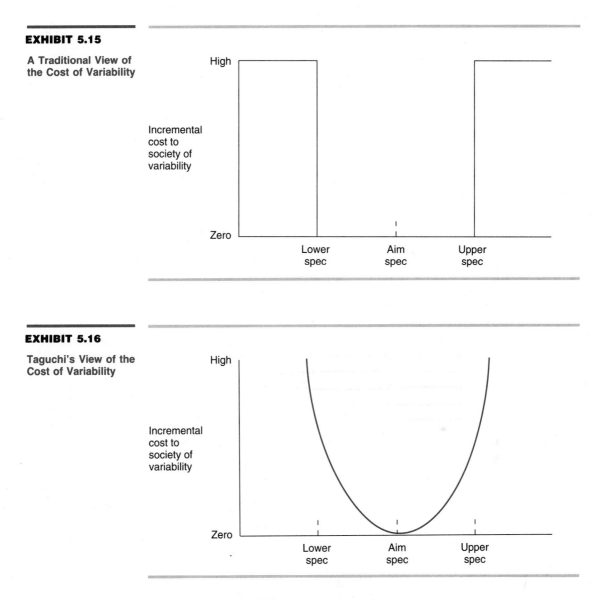

EXHIBIT 5.16

Taguchi's View of the Cost of Variability

In such cases, the following formula applies:

(1) $L = K(x - a)^2$

where

L = Loss to society associated with a unit of product produced at a value x

a = Aim or target; assume that at a, $L = 0$

K = A constant

Then, adding the following variables, and solving for K:

c = The loss associated with a unit of product produced at a specification limit, assuming that the loss for a unit at target is zero

d = Distance from the target to the spec limit

(2) $K = c/d^2$

With n units of product, the average loss per unit becomes:

(3) $\overline{L} = K[\Sigma(x - a)^2/n]$

While this formula assesses average loss, it is somewhat cumbersome because data are not usually collected in a way that makes the computation of $\Sigma(x - a)$ convenient. However, data are often available on the historical mean and standard deviation for the item of interest. When these are known, the average loss is closely approximated by:

(4) $\overline{L} = K [s^2 + (\overline{x} - a)^2]$

where

$\overline{x}$ = Process average

s = Process standard deviation

The only difficulty in applying the preceding formula to a practical situation is coming up with a valid estimate of c, the incremental loss to society associated with a unit of product produced at the limit, compared to the loss associated with a unit produced at target. While this is, at best, a guesstimate, it is possible for knowledgeable people to suggest a value that represents educated thinking. One group of engineers suggested the value should be one tenth of the selling price of a particular item. This means that if a unit were right at the limit, there is a reasonable chance that, because of test variability, the unit might fail final inspection. Furthermore, there is a reasonable chance the customer would encounter greater problems with a unit at the limit than with a unit made at target, and this would result in loss to the customer and possible warranty returns. While this estimate was admittedly a bit arbitrary, it seemed a reasonable starting point as a minimum estimate and resulted in a surprisingly high estimated loss value.

The approach is illustrated in the following example: The specification for a key dimension on an automotive part is 8.5 in. ±0.05 in. Historical data indicate that over the past several months, the mean value has been 8.492 in. and the standard deviation, 0.016 in. The part sells for $20, and engineers have estimated the loss to society as $2 for a part that is exactly at the upper or lower limit. Production is 250,000 parts per year. The situation is pictured in Exhibit 5.17.

Applying equation (4), the average loss per part is

$\overline{L} = [2/(.05)^2] [(.016)^2 + (.008)^2] = 25.6$ cents

Applying this to the volume of 250,000 units produces a total annual loss of $64,000. If engineers want to reduce this loss, they can pursue three avenues:

1.   Shift the mean value so it is on aim (i.e., 8.5 in.).

EXHIBIT 5.17

**Example of
Automotive Part**

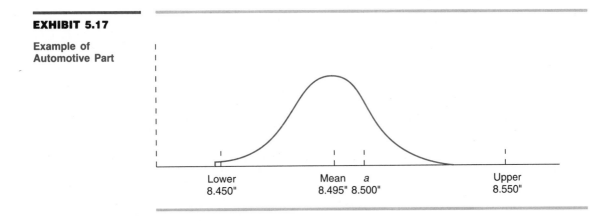

Lower	Mean	a	Upper
8.450"	8.495"	8.500"	8.550"

2. Reduce the variability (for example, make $s = 0.01$ in.).
3. Accomplish both 1 and 2.

Applying equation (4) to the three situations produces the following results:

1. By moving the mean value to aim, $\overline{L} = 20.5$ cents; total annual loss = \$51,250.
2. By reducing the variability to $s = 0.01$ in., $\overline{L} = 13.1$ cents; total annual loss = \$32,750.
3. By accomplishing both 1 and 2, $\overline{L} = 8$ cents; total annual loss = \$20,000.

Note that if higher or lower estimates were used for c, the resulting numbers would be affected proportionately. Thus, it is possible to easily perform a sensitivity analysis assuming a range of values for c. For example, if c were estimated at \$4 rather than \$2, all of the results would be exactly double those shown.

5.8 CONCLUSION

Exhibit 5.18 gives a summary of the various views of the quality gurus. Although each of these approaches has a proven track record, the key to long–term success is converting a Crosby, Deming, or Juran philosophy to "our philosophy." Quality management is a strategic issue and hence should not be approached as an off-the-shelf program devised by others. Quality must be integrated internally and externally (see Exhibit 5.19). Managers are paid to use new concepts, but more importantly, to lead customization and integration of these concepts into their organizations. The supplement to this chapter dealing with the Malcolm Baldrige National Quality Award gives numerous examples of how award-winning companies have accomplished this customization and integration.

EXHIBIT 5.18 The Quality Gurus Compared

	Crosby	Deming	Juran
Definition of quality	Conformance to requirements	A predictable degree of uniformity and dependability at low cost and suited to the market	Fitness for use
Degree of senior management responsibility	Responsible for quality	Responsible for 94% of quality problems	Less than 20% of quality problems are due to workers
Performance standard/motivation	Zero defects	Quality has many 'scales': use statistics to measure performance in all areas; critical of zero defects	Avoid campaigns to do perfect work
General approach	Prevention, not inspection	Reduce variability by continuous improvement; cease mass inspection	General management approach to quality, especially human elements
Structure	14 steps to quality improvement	14 points for management	10 steps to quality improvement
Statistical process control (SPC)	Rejects statistically acceptable levels of quality	Statistical methods of quality control must be used	Recommends SPC but warns that it can lead to tool-driven approach
Improvement basis	A process, not a program; improvement goals	Continuous to reduce variation; eliminate goals without methods	Project-by-project team approach; set goals
Teamwork	Quality improvement teams; quality councils	Employee participation in decision making; break down barriers between departments	Team and quality circle approach
Costs of quality	Cost of nonconformance; quality is free	No optimum, continuous improvement	Quality is not free, there is an optimum
Purchasing and goods received	State requirements; supplier is extension of business; most faults due to purchasers themselves	Inspection too late; allows defects to enter system through AQLs; statistical evidence and control charts required	Problems are complex; carry out formal surveys
Vendor rating	Yes and buyers; quality audits useless	No, critical of most systems	Yes, but help supplier improve
Single sourcing of supply		Yes	No, can neglect to sharpen competitive edge

Source: Modified from John S. Oakland, *Total Quality Management* (London: Heinemann Professional Publishing Ltd., 1989), pp. 291–92.

5.9 REVIEW AND DISCUSSION QUESTIONS

1. Is quality free? Debate!
2. What are the quality characteristics, as defined in Exhibit 5.2, for each of the following:
   a. IBM personal computer.

EXHIBIT 5.19	**Three Schools of Total Quality Management Programs**		
	Total Quality Harangue	Total Quality Tools	Total Quality Integration
Noticeable characteristics	Exhortation, lots of talk about quality; generally a marketing campaign intended to create buying signals without incurring the expense of fundamental changes	Introduction of specific tools; viz, Statistical Process Control, Employee Involvement Programs, and/or Quality Circles	Serious review of all elements of the organization; efforts to involve suppliers and customers
Rationale	Management may believe that quality is better than generally known or may be creating a smoke screen; viz, "everybody's doing it," "it's the thing to do these days"	Valued customers insist on implementation of a team program; or competitors have introduced successful programs creating a "bandwagon" effect	Systematic effort to improve earnings through differentiation based on quality
Responsibility for quality	Unchanged; specific function within organization assigned responsibility for quality	Lower-level members of organization regardless of function	Shared responsibility, senior management accepts responsibility to create an environment encouraging quality
Structural changes	None; the organization remains unchanged	Incremental changes within functional areas or processes	Dramatic changes integrating functions within the organization and involving customers and suppliers in the total production process
Representative employee attitudes and behaviors	Total quality is just a fad, "this too shall pass"; smart employees learn to keep their heads down, they talk about quality when expected to but know that business continues as usual	"It's a nice idea, too bad management isn't really serious about quality"; clever employees participate in seminars and use appropriate tools to fix obvious flaws in their areas of responsibility, but are careful not to rock the boat	"At last, we've got a chance to do it right"; committed employees study the total quality vision, actively search for opportunities to improve performance across the organization, challenge conventional assumptions, and seek to involve customers and suppliers
Role of the quality professional	Policeman, watchdog	Resident expert, advisor	Strategic leader, change agent

Source: Eric W. Skopec, Strategic Visions Inc. (used by permission).

    b.   School registration process.

    c.   Steakhouse.

3. An agreement is made between a supplier and a customer such that the supplier must ensure that all parts are within tolerance before shipment to the customer. What is the effect on the cost of quality to the customer?

4. In the situation described in Question 3, what would be the effect on the cost of quality to the supplier?

5. What are the limitations of QFD for designing a service encounter?

6. If line employees are required to assume the quality control function, their productivity will decrease. Discuss this.

7. "You don't inspect quality into a product; you have to build it in." Discuss the implications of this statement.

8. "Before you build quality in, you must think it in." How do the implications of this statement differ from those of Question 7?

9. Discuss the trade-off between achieving a zero AQL (acceptable quantity level) and a positive AQL, e.g., an AQL of two percent.

5.10 PROBLEMS

*1. Completed forms from a particular department of an insurance company were sampled on a daily basis as a check against the quality of performance of that department. In order to establish a tentative norm for the department, one sample of 100 units was collected each day for 15 days, with these results:

Sample	Sample Size	Number of Forms with Errors
1	100	4
2	100	3
3	100	5
4	100	0
5	100	2
6	100	8
7	100	1
8	100	3
9	100	4
10	100	2
11	100	7
12	100	2
13	100	1
14	100	3
15	100	1

a. Develop a p-chart using a 95 percent confidence interval ($1.96\ S_p$).
b. Plot the 15 samples collected.
c. What comments can you make about the process?

*2. Management is trying to decide whether Part A, which is produced with a consistent 3 percent defective, should be inspected. If it is not inspected, the 3 percent defectives will go through a product assembly phase and have to be replaced later. If all Part A's are inspected, one third of the defectives will be found, thus raising the quality to 2 percent defectives.
a. Should the inspection be done if the cost of inspecting is $0.01 per unit and the cost of replacing a defective in the final assembly is $4.00?
b. Suppose the cost of inspecting is $0.05 per unit rather than $0.01. Would this change your answer in a?

3. The following is a partial house of quality for a golf club. Provide an importance weighting from your perspective (or that of a golfing friend) in the unshaded areas. If you can, compare it to a club where you or your friend plays using the QFD approach.

---

* Problems 1 and 2 are solved in Appendix H.

WHATs versus HOWs Strong Relationship: • Medium Relationship: o Weak Relationship: △	Physical Aspects	Course location	Ground maintainance	Landscaping	Pin placement	Course tuning	Tee placement	Service Facilities	Customer-trained attendants	Top quality food	Highly rated chefs	Attractive restaurant	Tournament Activities	Calloway handicapping	Exciting door prizes	Perception Issues	Invitation only	Types of guests	Income level	Celebrity
Physical Aspects																				
Manicured grounds																				
Easy access																				
Challenging																				
Service Facilities																				
Restaurant Facilities																				
Good food																				
Good service																				
Good layout																				
Plush locker room																				
Helpful service attend																				
Tournament Facilities																				
Good tournament prize																				
Types of players																				
Fair handicapping sys																				
Perception Issues																				
Prestigious																				

4. A company currently using an inspection process in its material receiving department is trying to install an overall cost reduction program. One possible reduction is the elimination of one of the inspection positions. This position tests material that has a defective content on the average of 0.04. By inspecting all items, the inspector is able to remove all defects. The inspector can inspect 50 units per hour. Hourly rate including fringe benefits for this position is $9. If the inspection position is eliminated, defects will go into product assembly and will have to be replaced later at a cost of $10 each when they are detected in final product testing.

    a. Should this inspection position be eliminated?

    b. What is the cost to inspect each unit?

    c. Is there benefit (or loss) from the current inspection process? How much?

5. A metal fabricator produces connecting rods with an outer diameter that has a $1 +/- .01$ inch specification. A machine operator takes several sample measurements over time and determines the sample mean outer diameter to be 1.002 inches with a standard deviation of .003 inches.

    a. Calculate the process capability ratio for this example.

    b. What does this figure tell you about the process?

6. Ten samples of 15 parts each were taken from an ongoing process to establish a *p*-chart for control. The samples and the number of defectives in each are shown here.

Sample	*n*	Number of Defects in Sample
1	15	3
2	15	1
3	15	0
4	15	0
5	15	0
6	15	2
7	15	0
8	15	3
9	15	1
10	15	0

a. Develop a *p*-chart for 95 percent confidence (1.96 standard deviations).
b. Based on the plotted data points, what comments can you make?

7. Output from a process contains 0.02 defective units. Defective units that go undetected into final assemblies cost $25 each to replace. An inspection process, which would detect and remove all defectives, can be established to test these units. However, the inspector, who can test 20 units per hour, is paid a rate of $8 per hour, including fringe benefits. Should an inspection station be established to test all units?
a. What is the cost to inspect each unit?
b. What is the benefit (or loss) from the inspection process?

8. There is a 3 percent error rate at a specific point in a production process. If an inspector is placed at this point, all the errors can be detected and eliminated. However, the inspector is paid $8 per hour and can inspect units in the process at the rate of 30 per hour.

    If no inspector is used and defects are allowed to pass this point, there is a cost of $10 per unit to correct the defect later on.

    Should an inspector be hired?

9. Resistors for electronic circuits are being manufactured on a high-speed automated machine. The machine is being set up to produce a large run of resistors of 1,000 ohms each.

    To set up the machine and to create a control chart to be used throughout the run, 15 samples were taken with 4 resistors in each sample. The complete list of samples and their measured values are as follows:

Sample Number	Readings (in ohms)			
1	1010	991	985	986
2	995	996	1009	994
3	990	1003	1015	1008
4	1015	1020	1009	998
5	1013	1019	1005	993
6	994	1001	994	1005
7	989	992	982	1020
8	1001	986	996	996
9	1006	989	1005	1007

Sample Number	Readings (in ohms)			
10	992	1007	1006	979
11	996	1006	997	989
12	1019	996	991	1011
13	981	991	989	1003
14	999	993	988	984
15	1013	1002	1005	992

Develop an $\overline{X}$ chart and an R chart and plot the values. From the charts, what comments can you make about the process? (Use 3-sigma control limits as in Appendix C.)

10. In the past, Alpha Corporation has not performed incoming quality control inspections but has taken the word of its vendors. However, Alpha has been having some unsatisfactory experience recently with the quality of purchased items and wants to set up sampling plans for the receiving department to use.

For a particular component, X, Alpha has a lot tolerance percent defective of 10 percent. Zenon Corporation, from whom Alpha purchases this component, has an acceptable quality level in its production facility of 3 percent for component X. Alpha has a consumer's risk of 10 percent and Zenon has a producer's risk of 5 percent.

a. When a shipment of X is received from Zenon Corporation, what is the sample size that the receiving department should test?

b. What is the allowable number of defects in order to accept the shipment?

11. You are the newly appointed assistant administrator at a local hospital, and your first project is to investigate the quality of the patient meals put out by the food-service department. You conducted a 10-day survey by submitting a simple questionnaire to the 400 patients with each meal, asking that they simply check off either that the meal was satisfactory or unsatisfactory. For simplicity in this problem, assume that the response was 1,000 returned questionnaires from the 1,200 meals each day. The results ran as follows:

	Number of Unsatisfactory Meals	Sample Size
December 1	74	1,000
December 2	42	1,000
December 3	64	1,000
December 4	80	1,000
December 5	40	1,000
December 6	50	1,000
December 7	65	1,000
December 8	70	1,000
December 9	40	1,000
December 10	75	1,000
	600	10,000

a. Construct a p-chart based on the questionnaire results, using a confidence interval of 95.5 percent, which is two standard deviations.

b. What comments can you make about the results of the survey?

12. Large scale integrated (LSI) circuit chips are made in one department of an electronics firm. These chips are incorporated into analog devices that are then

encased in epoxy. The yield is not particularly good for LSI manufacture, so the AQL specified by that department is 0.15 while the LTPD acceptable by the assembly department is 0.40.

a.   Develop a sampling plan.

b.   Explain what the sampling plan means; that is, how would you tell someone to do the test?

13.   The state and local police departments are trying to analyze crime rate areas so that they can shift their patrols from decreasing-rate areas to areas when rates are increasing. The city and county have been geographically segmented into areas containing 5,000 residences. The police recognize that all crimes and offenses are not reported; people either do not want to become involved, consider the offenses too small to report, are too embarrassed to make a police report, or do not take the time, among other reasons. Every month, because of this, the police are contacting by phone a random sample of 1,000 of the 5,000 residences for data on crime (the respondents are guaranteed anonymity). The data collected for the past 12 months for one area are as follows.

Month	Crime Incidence	Sample Size	Crime Rate
January	7	1,000	0.007
February	9	1,000	0.009
March	7	1,000	0.007
April	7	1,000	0.007
May	7	1,000	0.007
June	9	1,000	0.009
July	7	1,000	0.007
August	10	1,000	0.010
September	8	1,000	0.008
October	11	1,000	0.011
November	10	1,000	0.010
December	8	1,000	0.008

Construct a p-chart for 95 percent confidence (1.96) and plot each of the months. If the next three months show crime incidences in this area as

January   = 10 (out of 1,000 sampled)

February = 12 (out of 1,000 sampled)

March   = 11 (out of 1,000 sampled)

what comments can you make regarding the crime rate?

14.   Some of the citizens complained to city council members that there should be equal protection under the law against the occurrence of crimes. The citizens argued that this equal protection should be interpreted as indicating that high-crime areas should have more police protection than low-crime areas. Therefore, police patrols and other methods for preventing crime (such as street lighting or cleaning up abandoned areas and buildings) should be used proportionately to crime occurrence.

In a fashion similar to Problem 13, the city has been broken down into 20 geographical areas, each containing 5,000 residences. The 1,000 sampled from each area showed the following incidence of crime during the past month.

Area	Number of Crimes	Sample Size	Crime Rate
1	14	1,000	0.014
2	3	1,000	0.003
3	19	1,000	0.019
4	18	1,000	0.018
5	14	1,000	0.014
6	28	1,000	0.028
7	10	1,000	0.010
8	18	1,000	0.018
9	12	1,000	0.012
10	3	1,000	0.003
11	20	1,000	0.020
12	15	1,000	0.015
13	12	1,000	0.012
14	14	1,000	0.014
15	10	1,000	0.010
16	30	1,000	0.030
17	4	1,000	0.004
18	20	1,000	0.020
19	6	1,000	0.006
20	30	1,000	0.030
	300		

Suggest a reallocation of crime protection effort, if indicated, based on a p-chart analysis. In order to be reasonably certain in your recommendation, select a 95 percent confidence level (i.e., $Z = 1.96$).

15. AmalgoTech engineers are trying to improve the design of a gear that has an outer diameter of 13 inches with a tolerance of plus or minus .003 inches. Available inspection data from the past year indicates that the mean value of the diameter has been 13.001 with a standard deviation of .0025 inches. The gear sells for $125. The estimated loss to society is $20 for any gear that has a diameter at the upper or lower tolerance limit. Annual sales of the gear amount to 40,000 units.

   a. Calculate the average loss per unit of production.
   b. What is the expected loss per year?
   c. What happens to the average loss per unit and the expected loss per year if the mean is shifted to the target value of 13 inches?

16. The operations manager of a small metal fabricating company is concerned about the variability of a milling process. Although the average width of a metal connector is identical to the target of .25 inches, the standard deviation of the process is .01 inches. The tolerance limits for the part are plus or minus .008 inches. The expected loss to society for any metal connector that is produced with widths at the limits of tolerance is $1.75 per unit. The specialized connectors sell for $18.00 each.

   a. Calculate the average loss per unit of production.
   b. If the average width shifts from the target value of .25 inches but stays within tolerance, what will happen to value of the average loss per unit of production?
   c. What is the value of the average loss per unit if the standard deviation can be reduced from .01 to .0075?

5.11 CASE: VAPORTECH PRESSURE TRANSDUCERS*

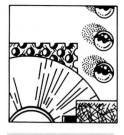

Vaportech is a small company in the business of producing pressure transducers, devices used to sense changes in pressure in jet engines. The production process involves 16 steps of intricate assembly, followed by test and final inspection. Any transducers that fail test or inspection are sent to a separate rework area. Three types of pressure transducers are built on the same assembly line. The only difference in the transducers is the spring; each model uses a different spring tension. The pressure transducers are pressure-tested in batches of 25 common units for 16 hours. One-hundred-percent final inspection is conducted after the test to check the torque applied to several connecting devices and to look for any material blemishes.

Fully 35 percent of the cost of producing parts is consumed by the rework and final inspection processes. The yield of acceptable products from the test area is 80 percent. Of the units that pass test, 12 percent fail final inspection. The company employs 16 full-time assemblers, 3 full-time technicians, 6 full-time final inspectors, and 5 rework technicians.

Jim Gladstone, the production manager, is frustrated by the failure in promoting the importance of quality. In front of each assembler, signs promoting "Customer is Number 1" and "Quality Is Everyone's Responsibility" are covered with pictures of husbands and children. Each employee received a full day of training on the importance of quality, yet yield is low and rework costs are on the rise.

The assemblers blame the quality of vendor-supplied parts for the test and inspection failures. The vendors claim that all parts are 100-percent inspected prior to being shipped to Vaportech. The test technicians blame problems on the poor workmanship of the assemblers. Production morale is low and turnover of employees is becoming a pressing problem. One thing is certain. Jim Gladstone desperately needs to do something to improve quality and lower costs. What action should Jim take to achieve this?

5.12 SELECTED BIBLIOGRAPHY

Crosby, Philip B. *Quality Is Free.* New York: McGraw-Hill, 1979.

——. *Quality without Tears.* New York: McGraw-Hill, 1984.

——. *Running Things.* New York: McGraw-Hill, 1986.

Deming, Walter E. *Quality, Productivity, and Competitive Position.* Cambridge, Mass.: MIT Center for Advanced Engineering Study, 1982.

——. *Out of the Crisis.* Cambridge, Mass.: MIT Center for Advanced Engineering Study, 1986.

Feigenbaum, A. V. *Total Quality Control.* 3rd ed. New York: McGraw-Hill, 1983.

Gitlow, Howard S., and Shelly J. Gitlow. *The Deming Guide to Quality and Competitive Position.* Englewood Cliffs, N.J.: Prentice Hall, 1987.

---

* Another case dealing with quality issues is "Hank Kolb" given at the end of Chapter 17.

Ishikawa, Kaoru. (translated by David J. Lu). *What Is Total Quality Control?—the Japanese Way*. Englewood Cliffs, N.J.: Prentice Hall, 1985.

Juran, Joseph M. *Quality Control Handbook*. 3rd ed. New York: McGraw-Hill, 1979.

Juran, Joseph M., and F. M. Gryna. *Quality Planning and Analysis*. 2nd ed. New York: McGraw-Hill, 1980.

Mann, N. R. *The Keys to Excellence: The Story of the Deming Philosophy*. Los Angeles, Calif.: Prestwick Books, 1985.

Oakland, John S. *Total Quality Control*. London: Heinemann, 1989.

Peters, Thomas J., and Robert H. Waterman, Jr. *In Search of Excellence*. New York: Harper and Row, 1982.

Scherkenbach, W. W. *The Deming Route to Quality and Productivity: Road Maps and Road Blocks*. Rockville, Md.: Mercury Press/Fairchild Publications, 1986.

Shingo, Shigeo. *Zero Quality Control: Source Inspection and the Poka-yoke System*. Stamford, Conn.: Productivity Press, 1986.

Taguchi, G. *Introduction to Off-line Quality Control*. Magaya: Central Japan Quality Control Association, 1979.

————. *On-line Quality Control during Production*. Tokyo: Japanese Standards Association, 1987.

Townsend, Patrick L., and Joan E. Gebhart. *Commit to Quality*. New York: John Wiley and Sons, 1986.

Supplement

The Malcolm Baldrige National Quality Award

EPIGRAPH

A decision to apply for the Baldrige is a marketing/public relations issue. A decision to adopt the criteria may be a matter of survival.

KEY TERMS

Public Law 100–107

Deming Prize

Baldridge Criteria

1. Leadership
2. Information and Analysis
3. Strategic Quality Planning
4. Human Resource Utilization
5. Quality Assurance of Products and Services
6. Quality Results
7. Customer Satisfaction

*A*t the annual awards ceremony for the Malcolm Baldrige National Quality Award, the Commerce Department of the United States displays all the pomp and drama of the Miss America pageant.[1] On a stage bedecked by blue, white, and gold bunting, following fanfare from a military band, the president of the United States presents the government's most prestigious business award to four winners from corporate America. The suspense is a little less riveting than a beauty pageant as the winners are preannounced. Also, the executives of the winning companies aren't expected to embrace each other and shed tears of joy.

Like beauty queens, many of the contenders have put in grueling months of preparation behind the scenes. Winning the award is considered valuable public relations and is just as eagerly sought by companies as the Miss America crown is by beauty queens.

In 1987, Congress created what has since become the template for quality management for thousands of U.S. companies, the Malcolm Baldrige Award. In this supplement, we provide an updated version of the outstanding Harvard Business School Case Note by W. L. Hart, C. Bogen, and L. Harper, and present portions of the 1991 application guidelines describing the award's philosophies and evaluation system.[2] We also include some material from the Baldrige preparation course taken by Baldrige examiners, an excerpt from Xerox's winning application, summaries of the quality programs and results of some other Baldrige winners, and some suggestions on what it takes to win the award. At the end of the supplement, we provide a description of the First National Bank of Chicago's quality program which can be used as vehicle for readers to consider the broad features of the Baldrige Award.

S5.1 BACKGROUND

On August 20, 1987, President Ronald Reagan affixed his signature to **Public Law 100–107**. This groundbreaking legislation, known commonly as the Malcolm Baldrige National Quality Improvement Act, established the nation's annual award to recognize total quality management in American industry. The Malcolm Baldrige National Quality Award represents the United States government's endorsement of quality as an essential part of successful business strategy in the 1980s and beyond.

By establishing a national quality improvement act, the Congress sought to encourage and incite greater U.S. competitiveness through the recognition and commendation of exceptional quality in American business. As an instrument of government, the Baldrige Award seeks to improve quality and productivity by:

---

[1] Stephen Kreider Yoder et al., "All That's Lacking Is Bert Parks Singing, Cadillac, Cadillac," *The Wall Street Journal,* December 13, 1990, p. 1.

[2] W. L. Hart, C. Bogen, and L. Harper, "The Malcolm Baldrige National Quality Award," Harvard Business School, 1989.

1. Helping to stimulate American companies to improve quality and productivity for the pride of recognition while obtaining a competitive edge through decreased costs and increased profits.
2. Establishing guidelines and criteria that can be used by business, industrial, governmental, and other organizations in evaluating their quality improvement efforts.
3. Recognizing the achievements of those companies that improve the quality of their goods and services and thereby provide an example to others.
4. Providing specific guidance for other American organizations that wish to learn how to manage for high quality by making available detailed information on how winning organizations were able to change their cultures and achieve quality eminence.

Without question, the Baldrige Award and its comprehensive criteria for evaluating total quality in an organization have had considerable impact. Some observers have begun referring to the award as the Nobel Prize for business. (See the table below for past winners.) In the first four months of 1989, the National Institute of Standards and Technology (NIST), which helps administer the award, sent out approximately 25,000 application forms, each containing the 192-point Baldrige criteria for assessing overall organization quality. In 1990, they were deluged with requests for more than 180,000 applications.

Applications are reviewed without funding from the United States government. Review expenses are paid primarily through application fees and partial support for the reviews is provided by the Baldrige Foundation. Through extensive volunteer efforts by members of the Board of Examiners, application review fees are kept to a minimum.

Indeed, quality has become a business imperative for a growing number of American corporations. Market competition, from auto and semiconductor sales to package delivery and financial services, is increasingly taking place in a world arena. Confronted by foreign competitors that often enjoy lower labor costs and their home government's active policy support, American firms are turning to companywide total quality management as a strategy to reduce their costs, improve productivity, and increase customer satisfaction and customer loyalty—all of which tend to translate into increased market share, higher profits, and greater overall competitiveness. "Quality," observes a senior vice president at Federal Express, "is to economic success as the nuclear reaction process is to energy production: the output is wildly disproportionate to the input once it builds to a chain reaction."

Though many of the analytical techniques most commonly associated with quality control were developed in the United States, the Japanese transformed quality from arcane statistical analysis used primarily to control variability in manufacturing processes to a system of values that have broad-reaching implications for nearly all business activities. Quality was a linchpin in Japan's post–World War II reconstruction strategy. Doggedly pursuing this strategy, the tiny island nation has risen phoenixlike from econimic ruin to what sometimes seems to be near hegemony in many industries.

For nearly 40 years Japan has recognized its corporate quality leaders by bestowing on them the prestigious **Deming Prize** (see Exhibit S5.1), named after the American statistician, Dr. W. Edwards Deming, who championed many of the analytical techniques employed in formal quality control. The Deming Prize has become so esteemed in Japan that each year, much like America's Academy Awards, millions of Japanese watch the Deming Prize ceremony aired live on television.

BALDRIGE AWARD WINNERS BY CATEGORY

Manufacturing	Service	Small Business
Motorola Inc. (1988)	Federal Express (1990)	Globe Metallurgical Inc. (1988)
Westinghouse Commercial Nuclear Fuel Division (1989)		Wallace Co. (1990)
Milliken & Co. (1989)		Marlow Industries (1991)
Xerox Business Products (1989)		
Cadillac (1990)		
IBM Rochester (1990)		
Solectron (1991)		
Zytec Corp. (1991)		

EXHIBIT S5.1

Comparison of the Deming Prize and Baldrige Award

Japan's highly coveted Deming Prize recognizes successful efforts in instituting companywide quality control (CWQC) principles. The Deming Prize is awarded to all companies that meet a standard. based on the evaluation process. For those that do not qualify, the examination process is automatically extended (up to two times over three years). Although both the Deming Prize and the Baldrige Award are designed to recognize outstanding business accomplishments, some notable differences follow:

Topic	Baldrige Award	Deming Prize
Primary focus	Customer satisfaction and quality	Statistical quality control
Grading criteria	Leadership Information and analysis Strategic quality planning Human resource utilization Quality assurance Quality results Customer satisfaction	Policy and objectives Organization and operation Education and extension Data gathering/reporting Analysis Standardization Control Quality assurance Effects Future plans
Winners	Maximum of two per category	All firms meeting standard
Scope	United States firms only	Firms from any country
Grading time	Six months	One year
First award	1987	1951
Sponsor	National Institute of Standards and Technology	Union of Japanese Scientists and Engineers

Source: David Bush and Kevin Dooley, "The Deming Prize and Baldrige Award: How They Compare," *Quality Progress*, January 1989, pp. 28–30.

S5.2 THE BALDRIGE AWARD AND QUALITY CRITERIA

Named after Malcolm Baldrige, who served as United States secretary of commerce from 1981 until his death in July of 1987, the Baldrige National Quality Award focuses on an organization's total quality management system and the improvements that system generates. To evaluate and recognize effective quality systems, Baldrige administrators at NIST created a comprehensive process (see Exhibit S5.2) and set of quality criteria based on the comments and observations of experts from throughout the country. The **Baldrige criteria** consequently reflects the combined experience and wisdom of many people. As a set of principles, it is nondenominational in the sense that it does not favor any one system or dogma (see Exhibit S5.3). Instead, the Baldrige criteria are designed to be flexible, evaluating quality on three broad dimensions: (1) the soundness of the approach or systems; (2) the deployment or integration of those systems throughout the entire organization; and (3) the results generated by those systems (see Exhibit S5.4).

The Baldrige quality criteria focuses on seven broad topical areas that are integrally and dynamically related (see Exhibit S5.5). Leadership is the starting point and a key measure of an organization's total quality program. Leadership drives the entire quality system, which in the Baldrige vernacular consists of four areas: Information and Analysis, Planning, Human Resource Utilization, and Quality Assurance. Actual quantitative and anecdotal results tracked over time provide a way to measure progress and to judge the effectiveness of the system. Customer satisfaction is the ultimate goal or touchstone of an organization's combined quality programs.

In short, the Baldrige criteria creates an integrated set of indicators of excellence and continuity that describes total quality. In the Baldrige view, total quality is a value system. It is a way of life, an approach to doing business that affects every corporate decision and permeates the entire organization.

When a company applies for the Baldrige Award or uses the Baldrige criteria internally to evaluate its quality program, the organization must address 32 subcategories and 99 individual items that fall under the seven broad topical areas. Each topical area and subcategory are weighted according to general importance (see Exhibit S5.6).

For evaluation purposes, a maximum 1,000 points are allocated for the seven Baldrige quality categories. Just as the Japanese stress the importance of both the means and ends when considering quality, the Baldrige criteria tie approximately half their points to the quality process (methods and means) and half to the results (ends and trends). The means or process is a leading indicator of the ends that will be attained. In turn, the results verify that the appropriate process is in place and being used effectively.

Leadership, to which 10 percent of the applicant's total score is assigned, examines how senior executives create and sustain clear and visible quality values in the organization. This section also focuses on top management's involvement in and commitment to creating and championing quality both inside and outside the company.

EXHIBIT S5.2

Baldrige Examination Process

The mechanics of the examination are as follows:

1. Submission of eligibility determination form (March).
2. Submission of application package (April), 75 pages plus 50-page supplemental section(s) if applicant comprises units of a company that are in essentially different businesses (with a $3,000 fee for large companies and $1,500 for small businesses; $1,500 per supplemental section).
3. Written application review—Stage 1 (April–June): Conducted by at least four members of the board of examiners. At the end of this review, the panel of judges determines which applications should be referred for consensus review. Stage 2 (June–August): Consensus review by at least four examiners led by a senior examiner. (Note that there are about 200 members of the examining board drawn from thousands of quality professionals who apply each year.)
4. Five-day site visit by at least five examiners and a senior examiner (September). A report is provided to the panel of judges.
5. Final review by panel of judges (October).
6. Award ceremony (October or November). Feedback reports distributed to all applicants in November or December.

EXHIBIT S5.3

Key Concepts in the Award Examination Criteria

The Award Examination is built on a number of key concepts that together underlie all requirements included in the examination items.

- Quality is defined by the customer.
- The senior leadership of business needs to create clear quality values and build the values into the way the company operates.
- Quality excellence derives from well-designed and well-executed systems and processes.
- Continuous improvement must be part of the management of all systems and processes.
- Companies need to develop goals, as well as strategic and operational plans to achieve quality leadership.
- Shortening the response time of all operations and processes of the company needs to be part of the quality improvement effort.
- Operations and decisions of the company need to be based on facts and data.
- All employees must be suitably trained and developed and involved in quality activities.
- Design quality and defect and error prevention should be major elements of the quality system.
- Companies need to communicate quality requirements to suppliers and work to elevate supplier quality performance.

Source: Taken from the 1991 Baldrige Award application.

EXHIBIT S5.4

Baldrige Criteria— Scoring Guidelines

Score	Approach	Deployment	Results
0%	No systems evident	Limited to examples	Anecdotal
10–40%	Beginnings of sound, systematic, prevention-based approach	Major areas Extension plans	Positive trends in major areas with evidence that results are caused by approach
50%	Sound, systematic, effective, approach refined through evaluation/improvement cycles World-class approach Excellent integration	Full deployment Excellent integration	Excellent (world-class) results in major areas Good to excellent results in support areas Sustained results Results clearly caused by approach

EXHIBIT S5.5   **Examination Categories** (Dynamic relationships)

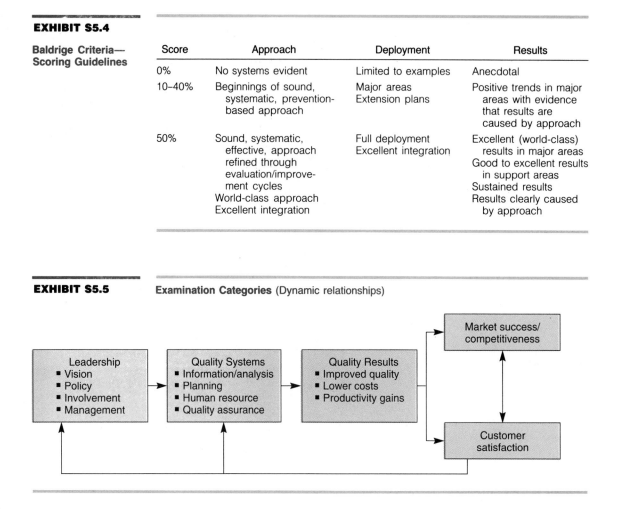

At the heart of the Baldrige criteria is the belief that quality permeates every nook and cranny, including the executive suite, of preeminent companies. In these organizations, senior management plays a constant, direct, and active role in quality improvement. "I will tell you that today, as an operating general manager, one of the highest priorities I have every day is quality," observes a Motorola executive. "It governs every single decision I make. I never ask a question about how much did we ship; I only ask the question of how much improvement did we get in quality."

From leadership, the Baldrige criteria direct focus at **Information and Analysis,** which accounts for 7 percent of the overall application score. This section examines the scope, validity, and use of the data underlying a company's total quality system. Next comes **Strategic Quality Planning,** which

EXHIBIT S5.6

Examination
Categories and Items

Categories/Items	Maximum Points
1.0 Leadership	**100**
1.1 Senior executive leadership	40
1.2 Quality values	15
1.3 Management for quality	25
1.4 Public responsibility	20
2.0 Information and analysis	**70**
2.1 Scope and management of quality data and information	20
2.2 Competitive comparisons and benchmarks	30
2.3 Analysis of quality data and information	20
3.0 Strategic quality planning	**60**
3.1 Strategic quality planning process	35
3.2 Quality goals and plans	25
4.0 Human resource utilization	**150**
4.1 Human resource management	20
4.2 Employee involvement	40
4.3 Quality education and training	40
4.4 Employee recognition and performance management	25
4.5 Employee well-being and morale	25
5.0 Quality assurance of products and services	**140**
5.1 Design and introduction of quality products and services	35
5.2 Process quality control	20
5.3 Continuous improvement of process	20
5.4 Quality assessment	15
5.5 Documentation	10
5.6 Business process and support service quality	20
5.7 Supplier quality	20
6.0 Quality results	**180**
6.1 Product and service quality results	90
6.2 Business process, operational, and support service quality results	50
6.3 Supplier quality results	40
7.0 Customer satisfaction	**300**
7.1 Determining customer requirements and expectations	30
7.2 Customer relationship management	50
7.3 Customer service standards	20
7.4 Commitment to customers	15
7.5 Complaint resolution for quality improvement	25
7.6 Determining customer satisfaction	20
7.7 Customer satisfaction results	70
7.8 Customer satisfaction comparison	70
Total points	**1,000**

accounts for 6 percent of the Baldrige application score (see Exhibit S5.7). This section examines how a company integrates quality planning into its overall business planning and then explores strategies for achieving and retaining short-term and long-term quality leadership. In its efforts to internalize quality, for instance, Globe Metallurgical Inc. has created a five-year quality plan tied directly to its five-year strategic plan. The company's long-term quality

EXHIBIT S5.7

Grading Criteria for the Strategic Planning Category

3.0   Strategic quality planning (60 pts.)

The Strategic Quality Planning category examines the company's planning process for achieving or retaining quality leadership and how the company integrates quality improvement planning into overall business planning. Also examined are the company's short-term and longer-term plans to achieve and/or sustain a quality leadership position.

3.1   Strategic quality planning process (35 pts.)

Describe the company's strategic quality planning process for short-term (1–2 years) and longer-term (3 years or more) quality leadership and customer satisfaction.

Areas to Address
a. How goals for quality leadership are set using: (1) current and future quality requirements for leadership in the company's target markets; and (2) company's current quality levels and trends versus competitors' in these markets.
b. Principal types of data, information, and analysis used in developing plans and evaluating feasibility based on goals: (1) customer requirements; (2) process capabilities; (3) competitive and benchmark data; and (4) supplier capabilities; outline how these data are used in developing plans.
c. How strategic plans and goals are implemented and reviewed: (1) how specific plans, goals, and performance indicators are deployed to all work units and suppliers; and (2) how resources are committed for key requirements such as capital expenditures and training; and (3) how performance relative to plans and goals is reviewed and acted on.
d. How the goal-setting and strategic planning processes are evaluated and improved.

Notes:
1. Strategic quality plans address in detail how the company will pursue market leadership through providing superior quality products and services and through improving the effectiveness of all operations of the company.
2. Item 3.1 focuses on the processes of goal setting and strategic planning. Item 3.2 focuses on actual goals and plans.

3.2   Quality goals and plans (25 pts.)

Summarize the company's goals and strategies. Outline principal quality plans for the short term (1–2 years) and longer term (3 years or more).

Areas to Address
a. Major quality goals and principal strategies for achieving these goals.
b. Principal short-term plans: (1) summary of key requirements and performance indicators deployed to work units and suppliers; and (2) resources committed to accomplish the key requirements.
c. Principal longer-term plans: brief summary of major requirements, and how they will be met.
d. Two-to-five-year projection of significant changes in the company's most important quality levels. Describe how these levels may be expected to compare with those of key competitors over this time period.

Note: The company's most important quality levels are those for the key product and service quality features. Projections are estimates of future quality levels based on implementation of the plans described in Item 3.2.

plan covers 96 items in 20 pages, including projects, goals, responsibility assignments, and target dates. Moreover, employees throughout the company keep two-year quality calendars on their walls with dates and deadlines for all important quality assignments.

Human Resource Utilization, which represents 15 percent of the overall Baldrige application score, examines an organization's effectiveness in developing and using the full potential of its work force for quality improvement. Worker participation, education and training, recognition of achievements, and workplace environment are a few of the areas covered.

How important is human resource development in quality-driven companies? At an organization such as Westinghouse's CNFD, nearly 90 percent of the work force has received quality-related training in the past three years. Indeed, Motorola spends $45 million annually to support one million hours of training of which at least 40 percent "is devoted to quality improvement processes, principles, technology, and objectives."

The **Quality Assurance of Products and Services,** to which 14 percent of the application's total score is assigned, scrutinizes a company's overall quality control systems. First, it closely examines the ways an organization attempts to design quality into its goods and services, and then it evaluates the manner in which the company integrates quality control with continuous quality improvement. The Baldrige criteria views quality assurance in far-reaching terms, asking companies to demonstrate that their control systems actively involve suppliers, dealers, distributors, and all other external providers of the organization's goods and services.

The Baldrige criteria's sixth area of focus is **Quality Results.** Curt Reimann, director of the Baldrige Award, explains the importance of this category, which accounts for 18 percent of the application's total score, by observing that "if it doesn't get measured, it doesn't get improved." Quantitative results, tracked over time, provide verification that appropriate quality control systems are in place and function well. This sixth category evaluates current quality levels and improvement trends over a three- to five-year time horizon. Both product and process quality trends are examined, comparing an organization's results to industry averages and to the performance of competitors. This concept of benchmarking an organization's performance against its own hisorical performance and the performance of other companies is central to the Baldrige criteria. By tracking their own and competitors' performances over time, organizations become involved in continuous evaluation to effect continuous improvement and learning. It's not surprising that Baldrige winners excel in collecting, analyzing, and using their results to drive continuous quality improvement. Globe Metallurgical, for example, calculates daily cost of nonconformance figures for its operations. Motorola states that the organization has saved $250 million from quality improvements over the past two years. Richard Buetow, Motorola's director of quality, estimates his company has received a 20 to 1 return for every dollar invested in its quality improvement programs. This kind of quantification and continual improvement has helped Globe, Motorola, and Westinghouse's CNFD set new world standards for their products.

Customer Satisfaction is the last Baldrige category and the final arbiter of the merit and effectiveness of an organization's quality system. In the Baldrige view, customer satisfaction is the ultimate goal of quality; accordingly this section accounts for 30 percent of the application's total score. Companies are asked to examine extensively their knowledge of their customers, their customer service systems, and their ability to meet their customers' requirements.

All Baldrige winners carry to extremes their commitment to customer satisfaction. Motorola managers, for instance, wear pagers so that customers can reach them at any time, any place. Globe responds to all customer queries and complaints—no matter from where the complaint emanates—within 24 hours, and CNFD, which has had 100 percent on-time delivery for the past three years and a product reliability record that approaches perfection, creates quality teams comprised of CNFD employees and customers.

The award examination is designed to permit evaluation of the widest range of quality systems for manufacturing and service companies of any size, type of business, or scope of market.[3] The 32 items and 99 areas to address have been selected because of their importance to virtually all businesses. Nevertheless, the importance of the items and areas to address may not be equally applicable to all businesses, even to businesses of comparable size in the same industry. Specific business factors that may bear upon the evaluation are considered at every stage of preparation for evaluations as well as in the evaluations themselves. An outline of the key business factors and how they are considered in the award examination follows:

- Size and resources of the applicant.
- Number and types of employees.
- Nature of the applicant's business: products, services, and technologies; special requirements of customers or markets.
- Scope of the applicant's market: local, regional, national, or international regulatory environment within which the applicant operates.
- Importance of suppliers, dealers, and other external businesses to the applicant and the degree of influence the applicant has over its suppliers.

S5.3   APPLICATIONS OF THE BALDRIGE QUALITY CRITERIA

For companies using them, the Baldrige criteria serve many purposes. Indeed, part of the Baldrige criteria's power lies in the fact that they can be applied in many different ways to organizations whose quality improvement programs are of all different maturities.

As a practical tool for assessing operations, the Baldrige guidelines can be used:

1. To help define and design a total quality system.
2. To evaluate ongoing internal relationships among departments, divisions, and functional units within an organization.

---

[3] 1991 Baldrige application instructions.

3. To assess and assist outside suppliers of goods and services to a company.

4. To assess customer satisfaction.

Early-stage companies can literally use the Baldrige guidelines as a checklist or blueprint to help them design their overall quality programs. Middle-stage companies can use them as a road map to guide them down the road to continued quality improvement; and advanced-stage companies can use them as an evaluative tool to help fine-tune their quality programs and benchmark them against other industry and world leaders.

"The (Baldrige) feedback has shaken us awake," admits Bob Lea, a vice president of human resources at the Paul Revere Insurance Company, one of two service firms to receive final site visits by senior award examiners during the 1988 Baldrige competition. "We see we still have a long way to go." Though Paul Revere did not formally apply for the 1989 Baldrige Award, the company continues to focus on the Baldrige criteria. "If you want greater market share, more new business and more repeat business, then you do what it takes to get the Baldrige Award," says Jane Gallagher, Paul Revere's quality manager. "These things go hand in hand."

The Baldrige guidelines also provide a common language for discussing quality across companies, functional areas, industries, and disciplines. The field of quality traditionally has been a babel of ideas, jargon, and philosophy, much of which does not translate easily from one setting to another. By providing a broad, flexible approach to assessing total quality, the Baldrige system fosters improved information sharing and overall communications. These activities, in turn, lead employees and management to develop a shared meaning of total quality that can be built into the organization's goals and policies. From such shared meaning develops an organizational value system that is customer-focused, quality-driven, and central to the culture of the company. So deeply does Motorola believe in the value of total quality control that the company has ordered all 3,500 of its suppliers to apply for the Baldrige Award, as tangible evidence of their commitment to total quality management, or lose Motorola's business.

The role of the Baldrige Award as an instructor of quality is also rapidly growing. The application process compels management and employees:

1. To recognize the far-reaching importance of quality.

2. To examine the organization's total quality progress and current standing.

3. To exchange information between departments, divisions, and organizational levels.

One service company, for instance, has designated seven-person teams from each of its 11 divisions to prepare individual Baldrige applications. A companywide application is then consolidated from the group efforts. Through this process, the company exposes many employees to the Baldrige criteria. Moreover, as these divisional teams discover weaknesses within their operating areas, they flag these weaknesses for immediate corrective action.

Assimilating the Baldrige view of total quality can also lead to actions with profound long-term consequences. At Globe, Motorola, and Westinghouse's CNFD, quality planning has been elevated to the same level as strategic planning and integrated with it. Indeed, all these organizations have wrought significant cultural and organizational changes to support companywide total quality.

S5.4   AWARD PROCESS

Thousands of companies have requested the Baldrige guidelines for internal use. However, a much smaller number of companies actually submit the 50- to 75-page written applications in May, formally seeking the award. In 1988, the Baldrige Award's first year, 66 companies applied. In 1989, 40 companies applied, and in 1990, 97 applied. Ultimately, no more than two companies in each of the three categories—manufacturing, service, and small business—are named Baldrige winners. In 1988, the judges deemed only three companies—Motorola and Westinghouse's CNFD in Manufacturing and Globe in small business—worthy of Baldrige Awards. Although nine service companies applied that first year, none received an award. The judges were sending out a signal: Only the absolute best companies receive Baldrige Awards; being good is not enough.

The Baldrige applications are scored by quality experts from business, consulting, and academia (see Exhibit S5.8 for an example of examiner's score sheet). Of the 1,000 points that can possibly be awarded on the overall application, only 11 of 66 applicants received more than 751 points in 1988. A good company usually falls in the 500 range on the Baldrige scoring (see Exhibit S5.9).

Only about 10 percent of the applicants become Baldrige finalists and receive site visits from a team of examiners (i.e., 13 in 1988, 10 in 1989, and 12 in 1990 received site visits). From this group of finalists, the Baldrige winners are chosen. All companies applying for the award receive from the examiners written feedback reports summarizing the examiners' findings of the company's organizational strengths and weaknesses.

Many companies speculate about the best way to prepare a winning application. The preparation course taken by the Baldrige examiners discusses general observations about winners and losers (see Exhibit S5.10), however, there is no right approach. Curt W. Reimann, director of the Baldrige Award, lists eight critical factors for which the judges and examiners look:

1. A plan to keep improving all operations continuously.
2. A system for measuring these improvements accurately.

EXHIBIT S5.8

Examiner's Score Sheet, Quality Results Section

6.0 Quality results (180 points possible)
6.1   Quality of products and services

6.1.1	40 _____ % _____
6.1.2	50 _____ % _____

6.2   Operational and business process
     Quality improvement

6.2.1	30 _____ % _____
6.2.2	29 _____ % _____
6.3.1 Quality improvement applications	40 _____ % _____
Category total	180 _____ _____
	Sum A Sum C

ITEM	AREAS TO ADDRESS	PERCENT SCORE

■ **6.0 Quality results** (90 points)
The Quality Results category examines quality levels and quality improvement based on objective measures derived from analysis of customers' requirements and expectations and from analysis of business operations. Also examined are current quality levels in relation to those of competing firms.

6.1   Quality of products and services
6.1.1 (40 points) Based on key product service quality measures derived from customers' needs and expectations, summarize trends in improvement. Site Visit Issues:

    a. trends in key product and service quality measures
    b. other objective measures of improved quality
    c. connections between quality improvement results and improvement projects or initiatives

6.1.1 (+) Strengths and (−) Areas for Improvement

Check one:
☐ All Areas Addressed
☐ Areas Not Addressed _____

3. A strategic plan based on benchmarks that compare the company's performance with the world's best.

4. A close partnership with suppliers and customers that feeds improvements back into the operation.

5. A deep understanding of the customers so that their wants can be translated into products.

6. A long-lasting relationship with customers, going beyond the delivery of the product to include sales, service, and ease of maintenance.

EXHIBIT S5.9

Distribution of Written Application Scores (1988)

Range of Scores	Range Number	Percent of Applicants in Range	Comments
0–125	1	0	No evidence of effort in any category. Virtually no attention to quality.
126–250	2	0	Only slight evidence of effort in any category. Quality issues of low priority.
251–400	3	1.6	Some evidence of effort in a few categories, but not outstanding in any. Poor integration of efforts. Largely based on reaction to problems with little preventative efforts.
401–600	4	47.5	Evidence of effective efforts in many categories, and outstanding in some. A good prevention-based process. Many areas lack maturity. Further deployment and results needed to demonstrate continuity.
601–750	5	34.4	Evidence of effective efforts in most categories, and outstanding in several. Deployment and results show strength, but some efforts may lack maturity. Clear areas for further attention.
751–875	6	16.4	Effective efforts in all categories, and outstanding in many. Good integration and good to excellent results in all areas. Full deployment. Many industry leaders.
876–1,000	7	0	Outstanding efforts and results in all categories. Effective integration and sustained results. National and world leaders.

EXHIBIT S5.10

Observations of Higher and Lower Scores

Higher Scores	Lower Scores

More quantitative
  Benchmarking
  Problem solving
  Analysis
External orientation
  "Missionary"
  Knowledge of world quality scene
  Suppliers, dealers, customers
Full deployment/integration/involvement
Proactive customer systems
	Passive leadership
	Reactive customer systems
	Limited benchmarking
	"Plateau effects"
	Weak integration
	Absence of evaluation-change cycles
	Partial deployment/involvement

7. A focus on preventing mistakes rather than merely correcting them.

8. A commitment to improving quality that runs from the top of the organization to the bottom.[4]

One Fortune 500 company acknowledged that over several weeks, it deployed more than 80 people and spent more than $250,000 in its unsuccessful efforts to write, edit, and professionally publish a winning application in 1988. In contrast, one person wrote Globe Metallurgical's application over a three-day weekend.

For those companies that actually win Baldrige Awards, sudden celebrity is assured. The three 1988 winners report receiving between 10 to 15 calls daily from organizations wishing to learn about their winning strategies. Even a small company such as Globe, which employs less than 150 people, has seen inquiries come pouring in from throughout the world, including invitations to speak on quality in Moscow, Beijing, and London. (In fact, one of its owners resigned from the company to devote full time to consulting on the Baldrige.)

S5.5 CONCLUSION

Four years after the establishment of the Malcolm Baldrige National Quality Award, the award's vital signs are strong. In that time, it has grown from a fragile infant into a healthy toddler. Will the Baldrige Award incite the broad-based revolution in American productivity and competitiveness that the members of Congress hoped to foment when drafting the Malcolm Baldrige Quality Improvement Act of 1987? That remains to be seen.

The initial response to the Baldrige criteria for evaluating total quality has been overwhelmingly positive. The Baldrige guidelines are proving to be useful and inspirational to scores of companies at all different stages of developing and deploying total quality systems. Moreover, the award itself has brought international attention and prestige to a handful of American companies that have clearly demonstrated their preeminent leadership in total quality management.

The experience of the award's winners suggests that companies throughout the country—indeed, around the world—are deeply interested and concerned about quality.[5] Starting in 1992, companies in the integrated European Community (EC) have required their suppliers to be audited and registered under a set of quality standards called ISO 9000. The purpose is to establish a mechanism whereby a purchaser in one country can be assured of the quality system

---

[4] Jeremy Main, "How to Win the Baldrige Award," *Fortune,* April 23, 1990, pp. 101–16.

[5] John J. Kendrick, "U.S. Companies Bone Up on EC/ISO 9000 Series Standards," *Quality,* May 1990, p. 13.

of a supplier in another country without having to complete an audit. Many of the leading companies in the United States that plan to do business in the EC are adopting the Baldrige Award criteria as their vision to be followed beyond the basic requirements of the ISO 9000 standards.

The United States is also considering adopting a set of quality standards for suppliers to U.S. companies. Perhaps the Baldrige criteria will become the U.S. quality standard in the future. The Baldrige Award and quality guidelines have the potential of becoming much more than a mere prize and grading system. They may even become the global standard by which organizational quality is judged.

S5.6 REVIEW AND DISCUSSION QUESTIONS

1. What are the commonalities among the Baldrige Award winning companies profiled in this chapter?
2. How could you apply the Baldrige Award criteria to your university?
3. "Baldrige criteria are more appropriate for evaluating manufacturing firms than service firms." Comment.
4. How is the award process beneficial to companies who do not win?
5. Discuss the implications of Motorola's requirement that its suppliers must apply for the award to continue to supply to Motorola.
6. Discuss the ways that the winning companies in sections 5.8 and 5.9 provide superior service to their customers.
7. Although over 60 percent of the Baldrige Award criteria are based on quality and customer satisfaction, universities tend to focus their courses on the other categories. Discuss the reasons for and the implications of this emphasis.

S5.7 READING: EXCERPT FROM 1990 XEROX APPLICATION*

Xerox fulfills many complex requirements to meet all the diverse needs of our customers. The true measure of our product and service quality is the total value we provide our customers—the degree to which we enable them to make their offices more productive and achieve a competitive advantage in their marketplaces.

Xerox customers range from small businesses to major corporations to all aspects of government. Users range from expert operators, who look upon the product as production equipment, to casual users, who may use it only two or three times during the work day. A general purpose copier in an office environment may average 100 users, which means it must withstand rugged treatment.

Our customers tell us that their basic requirements are product quality, copy quality, reliability, operability, and productivity. The value of these product attributes in relation to the total cost of ownership is the final determinant of customer satisfaction

---

* Source: 1991 Xerox Baldrige Award application.

with the product. Satisfaction with Xerox as a business partner extends beyond the product to include the competence and professionalism of our sales, service and administrative people.

The results of Xerox quality improvement efforts follow, in the order of importance to our customers.

The primary measure of product quality is defects per machine. Reading Exhibit 1A shows the continuous improvement in manufacturing quality we have achieved despite our increasingly severe criteria over this time span. A defect is defined as any variance from customer requirements. In the early 1980s, manufacturing tracked only those defects attributable to internal operations. However, with the beginning of the total quality approach, defects arising from all causes were given equal focus. Beginning in 1985, Xerox manufacturing quality measurements became a mirror image of customer requirements. This includes not only the specifications for product and packaging, but

**READING
EXHIBIT 1**

Xerox Product Quality and Performance

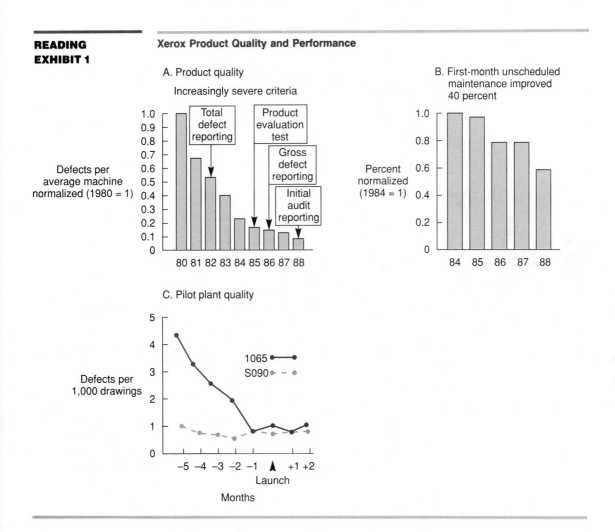

A. Product quality

Increasingly severe criteria

Defects per average machine normalized (1980 = 1)

Total defect reporting

Product evaluation test

Gross defect reporting

Initial audit reporting

80 81 82 83 84 85 86 87 88

B. First-month unscheduled maintenance improved 40 percent

Percent normalized (1984 = 1)

84 85 86 87 88

C. Pilot plant quality

Defects per 1,000 drawings

1065
S090

−5 −4 −3 −2 −1 Launch +1 +2

Months

simulations of field install procedures and customer use. Two further refinements were instituted in 1986 and 1988 as this process reached full TQC maturity: gross defect reporting and initial audit reporting. These changes disallowed waivers for any reason, effectively focusing management action on achieving zero defects. Based on our examination of other copier manufacturers, these are the most stringent requirements in the industry.

After a new machine is installed, quality results for reliability are monitored via customer reports. In order to verify internal results, we use early unscheduled maintenance calls as a key indicator. Reading Exhibit 1B shows the performance of Xerox products during the first 30 days of use. A 40 percent improvement has been achieved in the last four years, coinciding with manufacturing improvements.

Xerox manufacturing people are continuously working to systematically eliminate defect causes in order to fail-safe the process. Using statistical tools and guided by Cost of Quality (COQ) analysis, each product team targets and tracks quality improvement. In the Webster assembly plant, the 1090 product team, working with their suppliers in the Webster components plant, reduced electrical connector defects by 70 percent. The 1025 product team reduced their largest defect problem, photoreceptor damage, by 40 percent using problem-solving tools; and the 1065 team improved settings on pre-transfer transports by 85 percent. Improvements such as these are reviewed daily in the plant manager's quality meeting.

This quality management process begins in advance of manufacturing. In 1985 for instance, a 1065-copier QIT calling themselves "Organizing for Quality" led the way for marked improvement in pilot-plant quality when the 50 Series entered that Phase in 1987. Reading Exhibit 1C shows the improved performance of the 5090, which utilized the process, over the 1065. All products currently under development use this process.

S5.8   READING: MOTOROLA INC.*

In 1981, Motorola launched an ambitious drive for a tenfold improvement in the quality of its products and services. Motorola succeeded. Now, the company has evidence that many of its products are the best in their class. Looking ahead, Motorola intends to top its achievements—further gains in quality for 1989, yet another leap in 1991, and near perfection a year later. The company's quality goal is simply stated: "Zero defects in everything we do."

Motorola's managers literally carry with them the corporate objective of "total customer satisfaction." It's on a printed card in their pockets. Corporate officials and business managers wear pagers to make themselves available to customers, and they regularly visit customers' businesses to find out their likes and dislikes about Motorola products and services. This information, along with data gathered through an extensive network of customer surveys, complaint hotlines, field audits, and other customer feedback measures, guides planning for quality improvement and product development.

* Source: Motorola Inc., 1990.

Company at a Glance

Employing 99,000 workers at 53 major facilities worldwide and based in Schaumburg, Illinois, 60-year-old Motorola is an integrated company that produces an array of products, distributing most through direct sales and service operations. Communication systems—primarily two-way radios and pagers—account for 36 percent of annual sales, and semiconductors account for 32 percent. The remaining revenues come from sales of cellular telephones and equipment for defense and aerospace applications, data communications, information processing, and automotive and industrial uses. Sales in 1987 totalled $6.7 billion.

Responding to the rapid rise of Japanese firms in world markets for electronics, Motorola's management began an almost evangelical crusade for quality improvement; addressing it as a company issue and, through speeches and full-page ads in major publications, as a national issue.

The company's most persuasive messages, however, are the results of its quest for quality. Most products have increased their market share, here and abroad. In Japan, for example, Motorola pagers, supplied to Nippon Telegraph and Telephone, were introduced in 1982 and now claim a major share of that market. Over the past two years alone, Motorola has received nearly 50 quality awards and certified supplier citations, tops among the 600 electronics firms responding to a survey published in March 1987.

Key Quality Initiatives

To accomplish its quality and total customer satisfaction goals, Motorola concentrates on several key operational initiatives. At the top of the list is "Six Sigma Quality," a statistical measure of variation from a desired result. In concrete terms, Six Sigma translates into a target of no more than 3.4 defects per million products, customer services included. At the manufacturing end, this requires designs that accommodate reasonable variation in component parts but production processes that yield consistently uniform final products. Motorola employees record the defects found in every function of the business, and statistical technologies are increasingly made a part of each and every employee's job.

Reducing the "total cycle time"—the time from when a Motorola customer places an order until it is delivered—is another vital part of the company's quality initiatives. In fact, in the case of new products, Motorola's cycle-time reduction is even more ambitious; the clock starts ticking the moment the product is conceived. This calls for an examination of the total system, including design, manufacturing, marketing, and administration.

Motorola management demonstrates its quality leadership in a variety of ways, including top-level meetings to review quality programs with results passed on through the organization. But all levels of the company are involved. Nonexecutive employees contribute directly through Motorola's Participative Management Program (PMP). Composed of employees who work in the same area or are assigned to achieve a specific aim, PMP teams meet often to assess progress toward meeting quality goals, identify new initiatives, and work on problems. To reward high-quality work, savings that stem from team recommendations are shared. PMP bonuses over the past four years have averaged about 3 percent of Motorola's payroll.

To ensure that employees have the skills necessary to achieve company objectives, Motorola has set up its own training center and spent in excess of $170 million on worker education between 1983 and 1987. About 40 percent of the worker training the company provided last year was devoted to quality matters, ranging from general principles of quality improvement to designing for manufacturability.

Motorola knows what levels of quality its products must achieve to top its competitors. Each of the firm's six major groups and sectors have "benchmarking" programs that analyze all aspects of a competitor's products to assess their manufacturability, realiability, manufacturing cost, and performance. Motorola has measured the products of some 125 companies against its own standards, verifying that many Motorola products rank as best in their class.

S5.9 READING: 1990 AWARD RECIPIENTS*

CADILLAC MOTOR CAR COMPANY

During the 1980s, able foreign and domestic competitors gained market share at Cadillac's expense. By effectively integrating quality into all endeavors—from product planning to personnel practices—Cadillac has reversed its decline in market share, attracting new buyers while boasting the highest percentage of repeat buyers in the car industry. Its partnerships with the United Auto Workers have been a catalyst in this transformation. Cadillac employs about 10,000 people at its Detroit area headquarters, four Michigan-based manufacturing plants, and 10 sales and service zone offices in the United States.

Cadillac's turnaround began in 1985 with implementation of simultaneous engineering (SE), the first of several major changes designed to ensure that the division's products and services would be first to meet or exceed the expectations of potential buyers. More than 700 employees and supplier representatives now participate on SE teams responsible for defining, engineering, marketing, and continuously improving all Cadillac products. Alongside customers and employees, suppliers and dealers are fully integrated into Cadillac's customer-focused quality improvement efforts. Three-fourths of the division's 55 Product Development and Improvement Teams have suppliers as members. External suppliers must demonstrate continuous improvement in meeting "targets for excellence" in five key areas: quality, cost, delivery, technology, and management. Virtually all measures of performance indicate that continuous quality improvement is paying off for Cadillac.

IBM ROCHESTER

The concept of quality at IBM Rochester is linked directly to the customer. Detailed features are crafted from analysis of needs and expectations of existing and potential owners of computer hardware and software manufactured by IBM Rochester. Customers are directly involved in every aspect of the product from design to delivery.

---

* Source: 1991 Baldrige Application Guidelines.

Managers and non-managers alike have clearly defined quality improvement goals. Often working in teams that erase departmental boundaries, they have the authority to determine how best to accomplish those goals.

IBM Rochester, which employees more than 8,100 people, recently strengthened its strategic quality initiatives by formulating improvement plans based on six critical success factors: improved product and service requirements definition, enhanced product strategy, six sigma defect elimination strategy, further cycle time reductions, improved education, and increased employee involvement and ownership.

The IBM Rochester quality culture has been transformed from reliance on technology-driven processes to market-driven processes directly involving suppliers, business partners, and customers, delivering solutions. A 30-percent productivity improvement occurred between 1986 and 1989. Product-development time for new mid-range computer systems has been reduced by more than half, while the manufacturing cycle has been trimmed 60 percent since 1983. Customers benefited from a threefold increase in product reliability and a reduced cost. IBM Rochester's share of the world market for intermediate computers increased one full percentage point in both 1988 and 1989, and revenue growth in 1989 was double the industry rate.

FEDERAL EXPRESS CORPORATION

Federal Express's "People-Service-Profit" philosophy guides management policies and actions. Employees are encouraged to innovate and make decisions that advance quality goals. Federal Express provides employees with the information and technology needed to continuously improve their performance. Consistently included in listings of the best U.S. companies to work for, Federal Express has a "no lay-off" philosophy, and its "guaranteed fair treatment procedure" for handling employee grievances is used as a model by firms in many industries.

Seventeen years ago Federal Express launched the air-express industry. The company achieved high levels of customer satisfaction and experienced rapid sales growth. Today, approximately 90,000 Federal Express employees, at over 1,650 sites process 1.5 million shipments daily. Domestic overnight and second-day deliveries account for nearly three-fourths of the total, with the remainder being international deliveries. The firm's air cargo fleet is now the world's largest. Federal Express revenues totaled $7 billion in fiscal year 1990.

Customer satisfaction is high, but past accomplishments do not ensure future success. Through a quality improvement program focusing on 12 Service Quality Indicators (SQIs) tied to customer expectations, the Memphis-based firm sets higher standards for service and customer satisfaction. The company has set up cross-functional teams for each service component in the SQI. Two of these corporate-wide teams have over 1,000 employees working on improvements. Measuring themselves against a 100 percent service standard, managers and employees strive to improve all aspects of Federal Express.

WALLACE CO., INC.

Founded in 1942, Wallace is a family-owned distribution company headquartered in Houston that primarily serves the chemical and petrochemical industries. Its 10 offices, located in Texas, Louisiana, and Alabama, distribute pipe, valves, and fittings, as well as value-added specialty products such as actuated valves and plastic-lined pipe. Wallace distributes directly in the Gulf Coast area but serves international markets as well. In 1989, sales totaled $79 million. The company employs 280 associates, all of whom have been trained in quality improvement concepts and methods.

The Wallace quality initiatives have paid numerous dividends. Since 1987, Wallace's market share has increased from 10.4 percent to 18 percent. In 1985, Wallace adopted a long-term strategy of Continuous Quality Improvement. In only a few years, the company distinguished itself from its competitors by setting new standards for service. Wallace effectively merged business and quality goals, built new partnerships with customers and suppliers, and instilled associates with a commitment to one overriding aim: total customer satisfaction. Nearly everyone at Wallace is a member of a quality team.

Wallace established a Total Customer Response Network that must respond to all inquiries and complaints within 60 minutes. Its customer base has expanded. As a result, since 1987 its sales volume has grown 69 percent and, because of greater efficiency, operating profits through 1989 increased 7.4 times.

S5.10   CASE: THE FIRST NATIONAL BANK OF CHICAGO'S QUALITY PROGRAM*

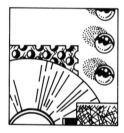

Skeptics say it is impossible to measure quality in service industries like banking, air travel and insurance. The First National Bank of Chicago believes it has proven the skeptics wrong.

In 1981, the bank set out to increase its market share by positioning itself as the quality provider of corporate cash management services. (Cash management services are non-credit services like checking, funds transfer and shareholder services.) Management at First Chicago believes that a strategy focused on quality is the best way any company can respond to competition.

First Chicago was pleasantly surprised to find that an emphasis on quality also helps control costs: The quality program has resulted in savings of $7 million to $10 million annually, the bank claims.

Founded in 1863, First Chicago reportedly is the 11th largest bank holding company and the 10th largest bank in the United States. It also is the largest bank in the Midwest. It is the oldest and largest national bank operating under its original name and charter. First Chicago has the second highest ratio of primary capital to indebtedness among major money center bank holding companies. The bank also is the third largest issuer of bank credit cards in the United States.

The company has 13,000 employees working worldwide. Its common stock is listed on the New York, Midwest, Pacific, London and Tokyo exchanges, and it has about 11,700 shareholders. The 57 offices worldwide are organized into three business areas: global corporate banking, consumer banking, and middle-market banking.

---

* Source: This article is adapted from Case Study 61, written by Steve R. Stewart, staff writer at the Houston-based American Productivity and Quality Center.

Traditionally, the non-credit services of the banking industry were set up as cost centers, and their products were viewed as "giveaway" services. The non-credit services were usually located in the bowels of a bank. They often were referred to as the "back office."

Today, outside influences have dramatically affected banks' "front offices." The financial services aspect of banking—for instance, the corporate loan area and trade services—has been affected by U.S. and foreign regulations and substitute products like commercial paper and money market funds. Banks also are being pushed by new competitors, including foreign banks, non-banks, investment banks and data processing companies.

Since 1971, the required return on equity of the banking industry has been on the decline. If a bank wants to stay alive, First Chicago believes, it must change its business mix, its pricing, and/or its costs.

The focus on providing high-quality services stemmed from research indicating that quality is the key controllable buying determinant in non-credit services. First Chicago was determined to become the best in the non-credit services business.

"Satisfying customer needs and expectations is the number-one reason for being in any business," says Aleta Holub, vice president for quality assurance at First Chicago. "Customers' standards are constantly rising. A company's failure to respond to raised expectations is like denying the force of the tide. It can leave you high and dry on the beach, while customers sail off to competitors' ports."

The bank began the quality process by altering its organizational framework. Separate strategic business units were created—each based on an individual product family. For instance, the money transfer unit's product family includes all domestic and international payment services. The corporate trust business unit deals with the trustee and shareholder services family of products. The documentary products unit is comprised of all import, export and standby letters of credit, as well as international documentary collections.

The strategic business unit manager suddenly became an entrepreneur. The manager was vested with the power to control not only expenses, but also product features, pricing, promotion and quality. The new structure provides all the essential elements for a manager to meet customer requirements. "The strategic business unit framework brought our managers closer to our customer and made them more directly accountable for the quality of our products," says Holub.

Each business unit has its own customer-service representatives to handle inquiries and problems. They act as conduits, communicating customer concerns to the business unit. Through this decentralized customer-service approach, the customer talks to a service representative trained as a product specialist. Because the customer-service function and production area are in the same location, the representatives can respond more efficiently to problems.

The non-credit services area of First Chicago designed a quality program to insure "that we were doing the right things right the first time," says Holub.

"By asking and listening to our customers, we learned that what they wanted and expected most from us was timeliness, accuracy and responsive service. These are issues not unlike those faced by other service industries . . . surely on-time, accurate and responsive service are quality elements that customers want and expect from airlines, insurance companies, doctors and so on," she says.

The next step was to make certain that customer priorities were being met by the bank. An extensive performance measurement system using nearly 700 charts was developed to track on a weekly basis every business unit's performance in relation to its products and the corresponding customer concerns. For example, the accurate processing of money transfers and the turnaround time for letters of credit are measured. By concentrating on the attributes of each major product and service, the bank learns how to fix a quality problem or sustain a quality advantage.

"A customer-based assessment of quality allows a company to recognize if its customers are satisfied with the current attributes of its products," says Holub. The bank's reporting system includes a series of different customer surveys conducted throughout the year.

Using the customer's perspective and industry standards, a management team established minimum acceptable performance (MAP) levels for each indicator, as well as goals for exceptional performance. "These goals are a point of pride and a source of competition among the business unit managers," Holub claims.

The minimum acceptable performance and goal lines for each chart are set by the strategic business unit manager and approved by senior management. To encourage performance improvement, the minimum acceptable and goal lines are continually adjusted upward, "so that the carrot is always just in front of the rabbit," Holub says.

To help increase management's commitment to the performance measurement program, a management bonus system was put in place, with bonuses tied to attainment of minimum acceptable performances and goals for each business unit.

Each unit's performance charts are reviewed weekly with senior department management. All this measuring is not done simply to encourage in-house competition. The measuring provides early warning when something is wrong so that corrective action can be taken.

"For example, when the chart showing the time taken to answer the telephone-initiated money transfers started to reflect a downward trend, the business unit manager analyzed the operation," says Holub. "The manager discovered that calls were backing up during peek periods and slowing down the average. So personnel were shifted around to accommodate peak times. Soon after, performance improved."

Bank customers and suppliers are invited to weekly performance measurement meetings. "A twofold benefit is gained by inviting both customers and suppliers to attend these meetings," says Holub. "First, the bank has an additional forum in which to learn about customers' expectations and concerns involving their products and services. We regularly use that knowledge to refine and improve both. More important, we are sending a loud and clear message that the customer is our central interest.

"The second benefit is that service levels from our vendors also have improved. Vendors are invited to see how well they are doing in relation to the bank's performance objectives," she says.

At the weekly performance meetings, competing vendors sit next to each other. For instance, the IBM Corporation representative may sit beside the competitor from Tandem Computers Inc. Each vendor has the chance to view the other's performance and to prepare ways to do better. The bank believes that it receives its "fair share plus" of vendors attention and service.

The bank's quality efforts do not stop with the performance measurement system. First Chicago currently has more than 30 active quality circles. These small groups are brought together to identify problems or opportunities and to recommend actions to improve performance.

For example, a quality circle in the money transfer group spotted a potential improvement in the processing of money transfers initiated by telephone. This group discovered that 67 percent of the authorization cards used to verify money transfer requests were being returned by customers with incomplete or inaccurate information. This caused additional checking and confirmation, which resulted in delays in processing time.

The group analyzed the problem and presented the following recommendations:

- Send a sample card with instructions to customers.
- Transfer card-update responsibility to the customer-service unit.
- Develop a method to provide confirmation personnel with more information on the verification screen.

All three recommendations were approved and implemented, and cards are now being returned with more complete and accurate information. The combination of properly completed cards and improved information flow has improved processing time in the unit by more than one-third.

Yet another element of the First Chicago quality process is a program that the bank refers to as its behavioral engineering systems training (BEST) program. This program evaluates individual employee performance. It permits a manager to look at how each staff member is performing, so he can identify the source of a problem and work with that person to fix the problem.

"This is not a 'big brother is watching' kind of thing." Holub stresses. "We measure for improvement, not perfection. The training program sets employee performance goals, measuring timeliness, accuracy rate and completeness. The baseline performance is identified by the manager, who then sets a goal 10 to 15 percent above that for each employee. Employees record their performance each day so they can see how they rank in relation to the base and to the standard. The system offers immediate feedback and positive reinforcement when progress is made."

To supplement the BEST program, the company's business units havaed added individual performance programs. The "Walk an Extra Mile" program recognizes customer-service employees who go out of their way to help an external or internal customer. Customer surveys are part of the evaluation process for service employees. Recognition awards vary according to the desires of employees in each business unit but include cash and tickets to sporting events.

Positive strokes such as "most improved," "best sustained superior performance," and "most effective in improving quality in a changing environment" were all given to work "teams" at First Chicago's 1986 non-credit services performance awards banquet. The bank realizes the importance of recognizing the accomplishments of employee groups within the business units. These "teams," however, vary in structure.

Some employees form a team from their normal work group and address problems affecting their department's productivity. Then there are employee teams based on larger issues. These team members might not normally work together.

A team also can be a form of recognition for accurate performance by a number of employees. For instance, if an employee consistently makes no errors over a specified time period, he is honored by being made part of a team. This type of team is an honor group, not a problem-solving group.

A dozen employee teams—one for each month—receive recognition and attend a banquet each year.

Each month's winning team receives a plaque and a paid group outing of its choice. The outing usually is dinner, theater or a sports event. There is a maximum of $100 per person, with a ceiling of $1,000 per group. Each team member also receives a certificate and an entry in a grand-prize drawing held during the annual banquet. The grand prize is round-trip air fare for two in the United States, plus $500 spending money. Several weekend trips also are awarded.

One of the winning teams was the crossed-account project team. This team handled the problem of deposits credited to the wrong account. When deposits are credited incorrectly, one account has too high a balance and the other, too low. This calls for float (uncollected funds) adjustments in both accounts. In this situation, customers may make incorrect cash management choices if they access balance information before adjustment can be made.

"Our customers were not pleased, and the problems caused our customer-service area hours of unnecessary research to rectify the accounts," says Elverage Allen of check collection/production, who nominated the winning team.

The crossed-account project team identified the causes of crossed account, established procedures to eliminate them, and reduced these accounts and the corresponding float adjustments from 649 in May 1985 to 37 during the following March. By the year's end, the team had cut the number of crossed accounts to eight.

Another monthly performance award went to the disbursement services error-free team, which was an honor team. "They did it right every time," Holub says of the team. To be eligible for the team, employees in the production area of disbursement services had to be error-free for at least 12 months. Employees were graded on their accuracy in corporate check handling, corporate/official reconcilement, information services, shipping and sorting. Twenty-four of the 64 employees, or 38 percent, received the award. One person met the standard of 12 months, while 21 employees were error-free for 13 to 24 months, and two for 25 to 35 months.

A controlled disbursement team, comprised of 13 employees in disbursement service and four in check collection, won a performance award by beating the check-clearing information delivery times of other major Chicago banks.

First Chicago believes the quality emphasis has had a measurable effect on performance. In 1982, one of the bank's operations experienced an average of one error in every 4,000 transactions. Today, the figure is one in 10,000.

"The success of the quality program within the non-credit services area alone is telling proof that providing excellent products and services, and containing costs, can be mutually compatible efforts," says president Richard L. Thomas. "In fact, we have learned firsthand that an emphasis on quality is one of the most effective ways to control costs."

For example, Thomas says, it generally costs First Chicago just under $10 to perform a money transfer. But that is a transfer done right the first time. If the money goes to the wrong place or does not make it on schedule, the cost of fixing an error can quickly rocket to $400 or more, depending on the amount of money involved, the complexity of the case and so on. Thus, reduction in the error rate has saved millions of dollars.

First Chicago realized the importance of communicating the quality commitment to its customers. So annually, the bank puts together a comprehensive booklet of key performance measurement charts for customers to see what the bank monitors and how it performs in those areas. The company's advertising theme, "Performance has always been a Chicago tradition," also reflects the quality emphasis.

QUESTION

Evaluate the approach, deployment, and results of First Chicago's Quality Program. Based on your analysis, do they have Baldrige potential?

S5.11 SELECTED BIBLIOGRAPHY

Bush, D., and K. Dooley. "The Deming Prize and Baldrige Award: How They Compare." *Quality Progress,* January 1989, pp. 28–30.

Hart, C. W. L.; Christopher Bogan; and Lee Harper. Harvard University Case Note, 1989.

Kendrick, J. J. "U.S. Companies Bone Up on EC/ISO 9000 Series Standards." *Quality,* May 1990, p. 13.

Main, J. "How to Win the Baldrige Award." *Fortune,* April 23, 1990, pp. 101–16.

1991 Baldrige application instructions.

1991 Xerox Baldrige Award application.

Yoder, S. K., et al. "All That's Lacking Is Bert Parks Singing, Cadillac, Cadillac." *The Wall Street Journal,* December 13, 1990, p. 1.

SECTION III

DESIGN OF FACILITIES AND JOBS

Once a firm decides what it is to make and how it is to make it, the focus shifts to putting a production system into place. This section addresses this issue, beginning with an integrated approach to production management—Just-in-Time systems. We then examine such basic questions as: what is the forecasted product demand, where is the plant to be located, how much capacity should it have, how should it be laid out, and how should its jobs be designed. In addition to covering some quantitative techniques for solving specific OM problems, this section introduces four powerful analytical tools—decision trees, linear programming, simulation modeling, and time series techniques—that find application in virtually all areas of business administration.

Chapter 6

Just-in-Time Production Systems

EPIGRAPH

I need it now! Not yesterday, and not tomorrow!

Inventory reduction is not something that management specifically decides in a JIT system, but rather it is a result of effective JIT implementation.

KEY TERMS

Eliminate Waste

Respect for People

Focused Factory Networks

Jidoka

Kanban Pull System

Bottom Round Management

Quality Circles

Total Quality Control

JIT Themes

Focused Improvement Groups

*J*ust-in-Time production is based on the logic that nothing will be produced until it is needed. Need is created by the product being pulled away or used. In theory, when an item is sold, the market pulls a replacement from the last position in the production system. In the case of a production line product, a worker then pulls another unit from an upstream station to replace the unit taken. This upstream station then pulls from the next station further upstream, and so on all the way back to the original release of materials. The objective in Just-in-Time production is to reduce inventory as much as possible by meeting demand only as it is needed.

Just-in-Time (JIT), sometimes called "lean production," has become the dominant design approach in modern manufacturing. JIT began in Japan and the person credited with the idea is Taiichi Ohno who was vice president of manufacturing in Japan's Toyota Motor Company plant. Ohno, incidentally, stated that he got the idea from U.S. supermarkets.[1]

Most Americans have heard the term *Just-in-Time* by now, even though they may not be fully aware of how it works. Just-in-Time production can be viewed in a colloquial fashion as consisting of "Big JIT" and "Little JIT." Big JIT is really a philosophy of operations management that encompasses all aspects of a firm's production activities—human relations, vendor relations, and technology, as well as the management of materials per se. Little JIT, from our perspective, is limited in scope to production-control methods—specifically, Just-in-Time deliveries and inventory management. In this chapter, our interest is in both aspects but our emphasis is on Big JIT since to make Little JIT maximally effective, we need an appreciation of the big (JIT) picture.

The first part of this chapter presents an edited paper written by Kenneth A. Wantuck describing the Japanese approach to productivity.[2] This paper has become a classic overview of the techniques and philosophy of the major developers and users of the JIT approach, the Japanese. The second part of the chapter develops some of these issues in more detail and presents an approach to JIT implementation.

6.1 THE JAPANESE APPROACH TO PRODUCTIVITY

Everyone is aware of the inroads the Japanese have made in world markets. Many product areas, such as televisions, video recorders, cameras, watches, motorcycles, and even shipbuilding, have become dominated by Japanese companies. Of particular concern today are machine tools and automotive products, but an impact is also being felt in the aerospace-electronics field. In all areas, we know that not only do the Japanese compete with us at

---

[1] Paul H. Zipkin, "Does Manufacturing Need a JIT Revolution?" *Harvard Business Review*, January–February 1991, p. 41.

[2] Kenneth A. Wantuck, "The Japanese Approach to Productivity," Southfield, Mich.: Bendix Corporation, 1983.

competitive prices, as discussed in the previous chapter, but in the area of quality as well. See Exhibits 6.1 and 6.2.

Many people believe these accomplishments are attributable to cultural differences. They envision the Japanese dedicating their lives to their companies and working long hours for substandard wages, which would be unthinkable in America. The evidence, however, is contrary to these distorted

---

EXHIBIT 6.1

1977 Hertz Repair Study

This study, undertaken by Hertz, was the first widely publicized evidence of the Japanese quality superiority in automobiles.

Model	Repairs per 100 Vehicles
Ford	326
Chevrolet	425
Pinto	306
Toyota	55

EXHIBIT 6.2

Comparative U.S. and Japanese Inventory Turnover Rates for 15 Industries

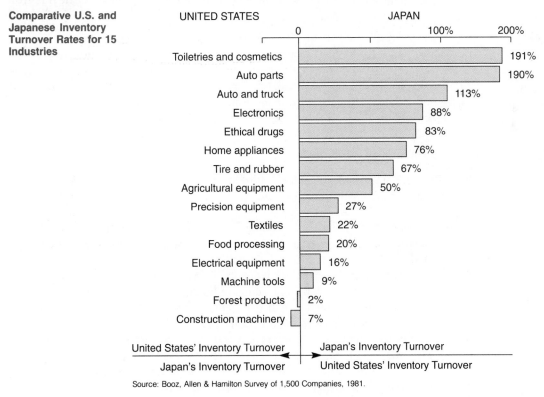

Source: Booz, Allen & Hamilton Survey of 1,500 Companies, 1981.

EXHIBIT 6.3

Quasar Plant
Productivity

	Under Motorola	Under Matsushita*
Direct labor employees	1,000	1,000†
Indirect employees	600	300
Total employees	1,600	1,300
Daily production	1,000	2,000
Assembly repairs	130%	6%
Annual warranty cost ($ millions)	$16	$2

* 2 years later.
† Same people

notions. Consider the following: In 1977, a Japanese company named Matsushita purchased a television plant in Chicago from a U.S. company. In the purchase contract, Matsushita agreed that all the hourly personnel would be retained. Two years later, they still had essentially the same 1,000 hourly employees and had managed to reduce the indirect staff by 50 percent (see Exhibit 6.3). Yet, during that period, daily production had doubled. The quality, as measured by the number of repairs done in-house, improved more than 20-fold. Outside quality indicators also improved. Where the U.S. company (Motorola) had spent an average amount of $16 million a year on warranty costs, Matsushita's expenditures were $2 million. (That's for twice as many TV sets, so it's really a 16 to 1 ratio.) These are big differences, achieved in the United States with American workers. The issue is, How do the Japanese do this and what can we learn from them?

Isolating the Elements

First, it's important to understand that the Japanese, as a nation, have had one fundamental economic goal since 1945: full employment through industrialization. The strategy employed to achieve it called for obtaining market dominance in very select product areas. They very carefully chose those industries in which they believed they could become dominant and concentrated on them, rather than diluting their efforts over a broad spectrum.

The tactics of the Japanese were threefold: (1) They imported their technology. (The entire Japanese semiconductor industry was built around a $25,000 purchase from Texas Instruments for the rights to the basic semiconductor process.) Instead of reinventing the wheel, they avoided major R&D expenditures, with the attendant risks, then negotiated license agreements to make the successful, workable new products. (2) They concentrated their ingenuity on the factory to achieve high productivity and low unit cost. The best engineering talent available was directed to the shop floor, instead of the product design department. (3) Finally, they embarked on a drive to improve product quality and reliability to the highest possible levels, to give their customers product reliability that competitors were not able to supply.

Implementation of these tactics was governed by two fundamental concepts (most of us agree with these things in principle, but the difference is the degree to which the Japanese practice them):

1. They are firm believers that in every way, shape, and form you must **eliminate waste.**
2. They practice a great **respect for people.**

Elimination of waste

When the Japanese talk about waste, the definition given by Fujio Cho, from the Toyota Motor Company, probably states it as well as anything. He calls it "anything other than the *minimum* amount of equipment, materials, parts, and workers (working time) which are *absolutely essential* to production." That means no surplus, no safety stock. That means nothing is banked. If you can't use it now you don't make it now because it's waste. There are seven basic elements under this concept.

1. Focused factory networks.
2. Group technology.
3. *Jidoka*—quality at the source.
4. Just-in-Time production.
5. Uniform plant loading.
6. Kanban production control system.
7. Minimized setup times.

Focused factory networks.   The first element is **focused factory networks.** Instead of building a large manufacturing facility that does everything (highly vertically integrated), the Japanese build small plants that are specialized. There are several reasons for doing this. First, it's very difficult to manage a large installation; the bigger it gets, the more bureaucratic it gets. Their management style does not lend itself to this kind of environment.

Second, when a plant is specifically designed for one purpose it can be constructed and operated more economically than its universal counterpart. It's comparable to buying a special machine tool to do a critical job instead of trying to adapt a universal tool. Fewer than 750 plants in Japan have as many as 1,000 employees. The bulk of them, some 60,000 plants, have between 30 and 1,000 workers and over 180,000 have fewer than 30 employees. When we talk about the Japanese approach to productivity and the impressive things they're doing, we're talking primarily about the middle group, where most of their model manufacturing plants fit.

Two illustrative examples have been cited by the Ford Motor Company: The Escort automobile needed a transaxle, which was going to require a $300 million expansion at the Ford plant in Batavia, Ohio. Ford asked the Japanese for an equivalent quotation and Toyo-Kogyo offered to construct a brand-new plant with the same rate of output at a competitive unit price for $100 million, a one-third ratio. A second example relates to Ford's Valencia engine plant, which produces two engines per employee per day, and requires 900,000 square feet of floor space. An almost identical engine is produced by the Toyota Motor Company in Japan, where they make nine engines per employee per day in a plant that has only 300,000 square feet of space. The issue is not only productivity per person but also a much lower capital investment to achieve this manufacturing capability.

Group technology.   Inside the plant the Japanese employ a technique called *group technology*. Incidentally, group technology is nothing new to America; it was invented here, like so many of the techniques the Japanese successfully employ, but only recently has been practiced widely in the United States. A simplified diagram of the technique is shown in Exhibit 6.4. The lower portion shows the way we operate our plants today. Most companies process a job and send it from department to department because that's the way our plants are organized (saw department, grinders, lathes). Each machine in those departments is usually staffed by a worker who specializes in that function. Getting a job through a shop can be a long and complicated process because there's a lot of waiting time and moving time involved (usually between 90 percent and 95 percent of the total processing time).

The Japanese, on the other hand, consider all the operations required to make a part and try to group those machines together. The upper part of Exhibit 6.4 shows clusters of dissimilar machines designed to be work centers for given parts or families of parts. One operator runs all three machines shown in the upper left corner, increasing the utility of the individual operator and eliminating the move and queue time between operations in a given cluster. Thus, not only does productivity go up but the work-in-process inventory also comes down dramatically.

To achieve this, people have to be flexible; to be flexible, people must identify with their companies and have a high degree of job security.

Jidoka—quality at the source.   When management demonstrates a high degree of confidence in people, it is possible to implement a quality concept that the Japanese call **Jidoka.** The word means "Stop everything when something goes wrong." It can be thought of as controlling quality at the source. Instead of using inspectors to find the problems that somebody else may have created, the worker in a Japanese factory becomes his or her own inspector. This concept was developed by Taiichi Ohno, who, as mentioned earlier, was vice president of manufacturing for Toyota Motor Company, in the early 1950s.

Ohno was convinced that one of the big problems faced by Toyota was bringing quality levels up to the necessary standards to penetrate the world automotive market. He felt that there was too much looking over each other's shoulders; he wanted every individual to be responsible personally for the quality of the product or component that he or she produced.

EXHIBIT 6.4

Group Technology versus Departmental Specialty

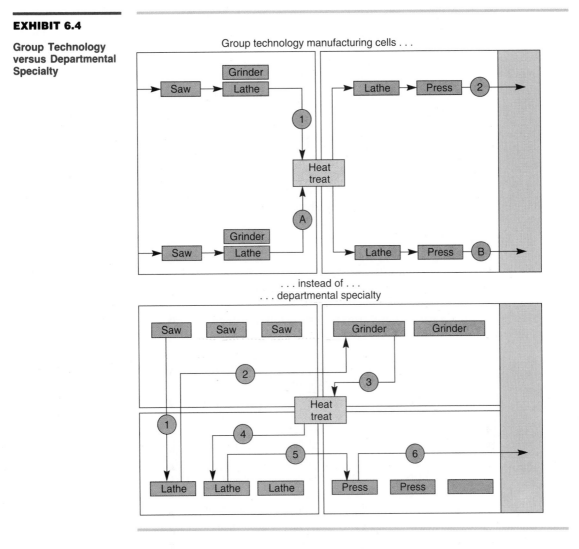

Group technology manufacturing cells . . .

. . . instead of . . .
. . . departmental specialty

Ohno determined that the best thing to do was to give each person only one part to work on at a time so that under no circumstances would he or she be able to bury problems by working on alternate parts. Jidoka push buttons were installed on the assembly lines. If anything went wrong—if a worker found a defective part, if he or she could not keep up with production, if production was going too fast according to the pace that was set for the day, or if he or she found a safety hazard—that worker was obligated to push the button. When the button was pushed, a light flashed, a bell rang, and the entire assembly line came to a grinding halt. People descended on the spot where the light was flashing. It was something like a volunteer fire department: people were coming from the industrial engineering department, from management, from everywhere to respond to that particular alarm, and they fixed the problem on the spot. Meanwhile, the workers polished their machines, swept the floor, or did whatever else they could to keep busy, but the line didn't move until the problem was fixed.

Jidoka also encompasses automated inspection, sometimes called *autonomation*. Just like automation and robotics, the Japanese believe that if inspection can be done by a machine, because it's faster, easier, more repeatable, or redundant, then a person shouldn't have to do it. However, the inspection step is a part of the production process, does not involve a separate location or person to perform it, and automatically shuts off a machine when a problem arises. This prevents the mass production of defective parts.

Now contrast that with our operations. How long does it take us to find a problem, to convince somebody it's real, to get it solved, and to get the fix implemented? How much do we produce in the meantime that isn't any good? Line shutdowns in Japan are encouraged to protect quality and because management has confidence in the individual worker. No one likes to see a line stopped, but Ohno suggests that a day without a single Jidoka drill can mean people aren't being careful enough.

Just-in-Time production.   The Japanese system is based on a fundamental concept called Just-in-Time production. It requires the production of precisely the necessary units in the necessary quantities at the necessary time, with the objective of achieving plus or minus *zero* performance to schedule. It means that producing one extra piece is just as bad as being one piece short. In fact, anything over the minimum amount necessary is viewed as waste, since effort and material expended for something not needed now cannot be utilized now. (Later requirements are handled later.) That's another different idea for us, since our measure of good performance has always been to meet or exceed the schedule. It is a most difficult concept for American manufacturing management to accept because it is contrary to our current practice, which is to stock extra material just in case something goes wrong. Exhibit 6.5 highlights what Just-in-Time is, what it does, what is required, and what it assumes.

The Just-in-Time concept applies primarily to a repetitive manufacturing process. It does not necessarily require large volumes, but is restricted to those operations that produce the same parts over and over again. Ideally, the finished product would be repetitive in nature. However, as a Westinghouse team learned during a visit to Mitsubishi Inazawa, a Japanese elevator manufacturer, the repetitive segments of the business may only appear several levels down the product structure. Even so, applying Just-in-Time concepts to a portion of the business produced significant improvements for them.

Under Just-in-Time, the ideal lot size is *one piece*. The Japanese view the manufacturing process as a giant network of interconnected work centers, where the perfect arrangement would be to have each worker complete his or her task on a part and pass it directly to the next worker just as that person was ready for another piece. The idea is to drive all queues toward zero in order to:

EXHIBIT 6.5

Just-in-Time

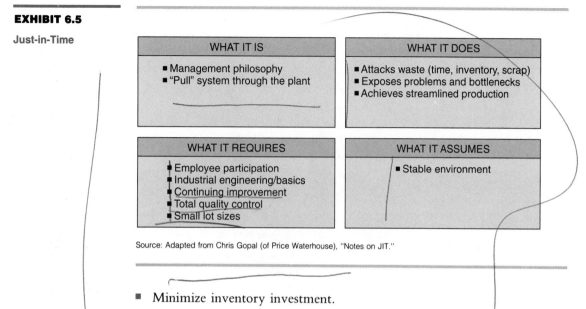

WHAT IT IS	WHAT IT DOES
■ Management philosophy ■ "Pull" system through the plant	■ Attacks waste (time, inventory, scrap) ■ Exposes problems and bottlenecks ■ Achieves streamlined production

WHAT IT REQUIRES	WHAT IT ASSUMES
■ Employee participation ■ Industrial engineering/basics ■ Continuing improvement ■ Total quality control ■ Small lot sizes	■ Stable environment

Source: Adapted from Chris Gopal (of Price Waterhouse), "Notes on JIT."

- Minimize inventory investment.
- Shorten production lead times.
- React faster to demand changes.
- Uncover any quality problems.

Exhibit 6.6 is a graphic that the Japanese use to depict the last idea. They look on the water level in a pond as inventory and the rocks as problems that might occur in a shop. A lot of water in the pond hides the problems. Management assumes everything is fine. Invariably, the water level drops at the worst possible time, such as during an economic downturn. Management must then address the problems without the necessary resources to solve them. The Japanese say it is better to force the water level down on purpose (especially in good times), expose the problems, and fix them now, before they cause trouble.

The zeal with which the Japanese hammer at inventories is incredible. To begin with, inventory is viewed as a negative, not an asset. According to Toyota, "The value of inventory is disavowed." Auto air conditioner manufacturer Nippondenso's attitude is even more severe: inventory is "the root of all evil." Almost universally, the Japanese see inventory as a deterrent to product quality. Finally, since the shop floor is programmed to have very little inventory, the slightest aberration in the process that results in extra parts is readily visible and serves as a red flag to which immediate response is required.

Because it is impossible to have every worker in a complex manufacturing process adjacent to one another, and since the network also includes outside suppliers, the Japanese recognize that the system must allow for transit time between centers. However, transfer quantities are kept as small as possible. Typical internal lot sizes are one tenth of a day's production, vendors ship

EXHIBIT 6.6

Inventory Hides
Problems

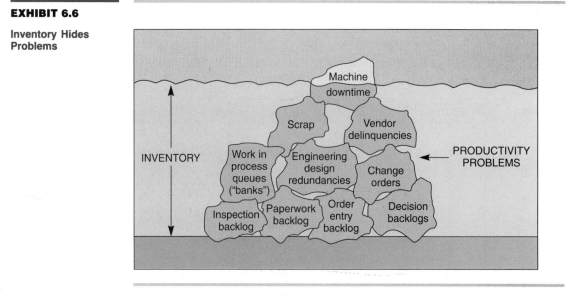

several times a day to their customers, and constant pressure is exercised to reduce the number of lots in the system.

Just-in-Time production makes no allowances for contingencies. Every piece is expected to be correct when received. Every machine is expected to be available when needed to produce parts. Every delivery commitment is expected to be honored at the precise time it is scheduled. Consequently, the Japanese heavily emphasize quality, preventive maintenance, and a high degree of mutual trust among all participants in the manufacturing enterprise. The process is gospel and everyone conscientiously adheres to it.

Uniform plant loading.   To use the Just-in-Time production concept, it is necessary that production flow as smoothly as possible in the shop. The starting point is what the Japanese call *uniform plant loading.* Its objective is to dampen the reaction waves that normally occur in response to schedule variations. For example, when a significant change is made in final assembly, it creates changed requirements in feeder operations that are usually amplified because of lot sizing rules, setups, queues, and waiting time. By the time the impact is felt at the start of the supply chain, a 10 percent change at assembly could easily result in a 100 percent change at the front end.

The Japanese tell us the only way to eliminate that problem is to make the perturbations at the end as small as possible so that we get ripples going through the shop, not shock waves. Japanese companies accomplish it by setting up a firm monthly production plan for which the output rate is frozen. Most U.S manufacturing people have been trying to achieve that for years, without success, because they've tried to freeze a specific, sequential configuration. The Japanese circumvent this issue by planning to build the same mix

EXHIBIT 6.7

Toyota Example of Mixed-Model Production Cycle in a Japanese Assembly Plant

Model	Monthly Quantity	Daily Quantity	Cycle Time (minutes)
Sedan	5,000	250	2
Hardtop	2,500	125	4
Wagon	2,500	125	4

Sequence: Sedan, hardtop, sedan, wagon, sedan, hardtop, sedan; wagon, etc.

of products every day, even if the total quantities are small. For example if they're only building a hundred pieces a month, they'll build five each day. Because they expect to build some quantity of everything that's on the schedule daily, they always have a total mix available to respond to variations in demand.

Going even further, they'll take those five units and intermix them on the assembly line. An example of how Toyota would do this is shown in Exhibit 6.7. Presume three kinds of vehicles being made in an assembly plant: sedans, hardtops, and station wagons. The monthly rates shown are then reduced to daily quantities (presuming a 20-day month) of 250, 125, and 125, respectively. From this, the Japanese compute the necessary cycle times. *Cycle time* in Japan is the period of time between two identical units coming off the production line. The Japanese use this figure to adjust their resources to produce precisely the quantity that's needed, no more, no less.

The Japanese do not concern themselves with achieving the rated speeds of their equipment. In American shops, a given machine is rated at 1,000 pieces per hour so if we need 5,000 pieces we run it five hours to obtain this month's requirement. The Japanese produce only the needed quantity each day, as required. To them, cycle time is an indicator that defines how to assemble their resources to meet this month's production. If the rate for next month changes, the resources are reconfigured.

Kanban production control system. The Kanban approach calls for a control system that is simple and self-regulating and provides good management visibility.[3] The shop floor/vendor release and control system is called *Kanban* (kahn-bahn), from the Japanese word meaning *card*. It is a paperless system, using dedicated containers and recycling traveling requisitions/cards, which is quite different from our old, manual shop-packet systems. This is referred to as a **Kanban pull system,** since the authority to produce or supply comes from downstream operations. While work centers and vendors plan their

---

[3] The majority of factories in Japan don't use Kanban. Kanban is a Toyota Motor Company system, not a generic Japanese one. However, many companies in both the United States and Japan use pull systems with other types of signaling devices.

work based on schedules, they execute based on Kanbans, which are completely manual.

There are two types of Kanban cards. The production Kanban authorizes the manufacturing of a container of material. The withdrawal Kanban authorizes the withdrawal and movement of that container. The number of pieces in a container never varies for a given part number.

When production rates change, containers are added to or deleted from the system, according to a simple formula. The idea of safety stock is included in the basic calculation but is limited to 10 percent of a single day's demand. This gives the theoretical number of Kanban/containers required. In practice, efforts are made to reduce the number in circulation to keep inventories to a minimum.

The flow of Kanban cards between two work centers is shown in Exhibit 6.8. The machining center shown is making two parts, A and B, which are stored in standard containers next to the work center. When the assembly line starts to use Part A from a full container, a worker takes the withdrawal Kanban from the container and travels to the machining center storage area. He or she finds a container of Part A, removes the production Kanban, and replaces it with the withdrawal Kanban card, which authorizes him or her to move the container. The freed production Kanban is then placed in a rack by the machining center as a work authorization for another lot of material. Parts are manufactured in the order in which cards are placed on the rack (the Japanese call this the Kanban hanging), which makes the set of cards in the rack a dispatch list.[4]

If it turns out that the demand for Part A is greater than planned and less than planned for Part B, the system self-regulates to these changes because there can be no more parts built than called for by the Kanban cards in circulation. Mix changes of 10 to 20 percent can easily be accommodated because the shifts are gradual and the increments are small. The ripple effect upstream is similarly dampened.

The same approach is used to authorize vendor shipments. When both the customer and the vendor are using the Kanban system, the withdrawal Kanban serves as the vendor release/shipping document while the production Kanban at the vendor's plant regulates production there.

The whole system hinges on everyone doing exactly what is authorized and following procedures explicitly. In fact, the Japanese use no production coordinators on the shop floor, relying solely on supervisors to ensure compliance. Cooperative worker attitudes are essential to its success.

---

[4] Many firms use withdrawal cards only. Under the simplest form of one-card system, the worker at the assembly line (or more likely a material handler) walks to the machine center with an empty container and a withdrawal Kanban. He or she would then place the empty container at a designated spot, attach the withdrawal card to a filled container, and carry it back to the assembly line. The worker at the machining center would know that a refill is required. This type of system is appropriate where the same part is made by the same people every day.

EXHIBIT 6.8

Flow of Two Kanbans

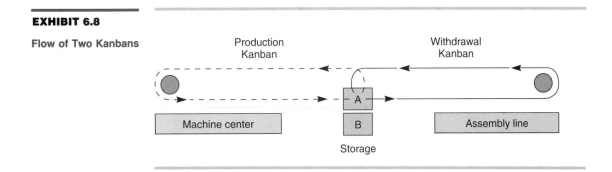

Results can be impressive. Jidosha Kiki, a Bendix braking components affiliate in Japan, installed the Kanban/Just-in-Time system in 1977 with the help of its customer, Toyota. Within two years they had doubled productivity, tripled inventory turnover, and substantially reduced overtime and space requirements. Jidosha Kiki stated that this was a slow and difficult learning process for its employees, even considering the Japanese culture, because all the old rules of thumb had to be tossed out the window and deep-rooted ideas had to be changed.

Minimized setup times. The Japanese approach to productivity demands that small lots be run in production. This is impossible to do if machine setups take hours to accomplish. In fact, we use the economic order quantity (EOQ) formula in the United States to determine what quantity we should run to absorb a long and costly setup time. (EOQ is discussed in Chapter 13.)

The Japanese have the same formula, but they've turned it around. Instead of accepting setup times as fixed numbers, they fixed the lot sizes (very small) and went to work to reduce setup time.

That is a crucial factor in the Japanese approach. Their success in this area has received widespread acclaim. Many Americans have been to Japan and witnessed a team of press operators change an 800-ton press in 10 minutes. Compare those data with ours as shown in Exhibit 6.9. The Japanese aim for single-digit setup times (i.e., less than 10 minutes) for every machine in their factories. They've addressed not only big things, like presses, but small molding machines and standard machine tools as well.

Successful setup reduction is easily achieved when approached from a methods engineering perspective. The Japanese separate setup time into two segments: *internal*—that part that must be done while a machine is stopped, and *external*—that part that can be done while the machine is operating. Simple things, such as the staging of replacement dies, fall into the external category, which, on the average, represents half of the usual setup time.

Another 50 percent reduction can be achieved by the application of time and motion studies and practice. (It is not unusual for a Japanese setup team to spend a full Saturday practicing changeovers.) Time-saving devices like

EXHIBIT 6.9

Minimizing Setup
Time—Hood and
Fender Press
Comparison
(800-ton press)

	Toyota	USA	Sweden	W. Germany
Setup time	10 minutes	6 hours	4 hours	4 hours
Setups/day	3	1	—	½
Lot size	1 day*	10 days	1 month	—

*For low-demand items (less than 1,000 month), as large as seven days.

EXHIBIT 6.10

Setup Reduction
Results at JKC

	PERCENT REDUCTION		
Setup Time	1976	1977	1980
>60 minutes	30%	0%	0%
30–60 minutes	19	0	0
20–30 minutes	26	10	3
10–20 minutes	20	12	7
5–10 minutes	5	20	12
100 second-5 minutes	0	17	16
<100 seconds	0	41	62

hinged bolts, roller platforms, and folding brackets for temporary die staging are commonly seen, all of which are low-cost items.

Only then is it necessary to spend larger sums, to reduce the last 15 percent or so, on things such as automatic positioning of dies, rolling bolsters, and duplicate tool holders. The result is that 90 percent or *more* of percent setup times can be eliminated if we have a desire to do so.

Referring again to Jidosha Kiki Corporation, Exhibit 6.10 shows the remarkable progress the company made in just four years. These data relate to all the machines in the factory. It's interesting that while we are quite impressed that two thirds of their equipment can be changed over in less than 2 minutes, the company is embarrassed that 10 percent still takes more than 10 minutes!

The savings in setup time are used to increase the number of lots produced, with a corollary reduction in lot sizes. This makes the use of Just-in-Time production principles feasible, which in turn makes the Kanban control system practical. All the pieces fit together.

Respect for people

The second guiding principle for the Japanese, along with elimination of waste, is respect for people. This principle, too, has seven basic elements:

1. Lifetime employment.
2. Company unions.
3. Attitude toward workers.

4. Automation/robotics.
5. Bottom-round management
6. Subcontractor networks.
7. Quality circles.

Lifetime employment.   Much has been written about the Japanese concept of lifetime employment. When Japanese workers are hired for permanent positions with a major industrial firm, they have jobs with that company for life (or until retirement age) provided they work diligently. If economic conditions deteriorate, the company maintains the payroll almost to the point of going out of business. We should understand, though, that these kinds of benefits apply only to permanent workers, who constitute about one third of the work force in Japan. What's important is that the concept is pervasive. When people can identify with the company as the place they're going to spend their working life, not just an interim place to get a paycheck, then they have a tendency to be more flexible and to want to do all they can do to help achieve the company's goals.

Company unions.   When General Douglas MacArthur introduced the union concept to Japan during the post–World War II reconstruction period, he undoubtedly had in mind trade unions, but the Japanese didn't think that way. Japanese workers at Toyota were concerned about Toyota. They really didn't identify with the other automobile manufacturing employees in the rest of the country. They identified not with the kind of work they were doing but rather with the company for which they were working. So Toyota formed a union that included everybody who worked for Toyota, no matter what their skills were. The objective of both the union and management was to make the company as healthy as possible so there would be benefits accruing to the people in a secure and shared method. The resulting relationship was cooperative, not adversarial.

The Japanese system of compensation reinforces these goals because it is based on company performance bonuses. Everybody in a Japanese company, from the lowest employee to the highest, gets a bonus twice a year. In good times the bonus is high (up to 50 percent of their salaries), while in bad times there may be no bonus. As a result, the employees have an attitude that says, "If the company does well, I do well," which is important from the standpoint of soliciting the workers' help to improve productivity.

Attitude toward workers.   The attitude of management toward the workers is also critical. The Japanese do not look at people as human machines. As a matter of fact, they believe that if a machine can do a job, then a person *shouldn't* do it because it's below his or her dignity. In the United States, we all believe in the value of human worth, but when it comes to the shop floor we don't necessarily practice it. A corollary concept says that if workers are really as important as people you must also believe that they can do much more than you are now giving them the opportunity to do. We normally have to see people in a job for some time before we accept their competence.

The Japanese say, "What workers are doing today is only tapping their capability. We must give them an opportunity to do more." Thus, a third and most significant attitude requires that the management system provide every worker with an opportunity to display his or her maximum capabilities. These concepts are practiced, not just discussed, and the Japanese spend more for employee training and education—at all levels—than any other industrial nation.

Automation/robotics.   When people feel secure, identify with the company, and believe that they are being given an opportunity to fully display their talents, the introduction of automation and robotics is not considered as a staff-cutting move. The Japanese feel that this is a way to eliminate dull jobs so people can do more important things, and they have been making major capital investments in these areas. Interestingly enough, Japan has invested one third of its gross national product in capital improvements for the last 20 years, compared to about 19 percent for the United States during the same period.

In automation, the Japanese have invested first in low-cost enhancements to existing or standard equipment, using some clever approaches. In the capital area they have been concentrating on programmable robots. A recent survey showed that Japan had approximately five times the number of programmable robots (some of them quite simple) as the United States. Most of those robots were built here. Again, we shipped our technology to Japan, where it was used to build products to compete with us. Today, Japan is building its own robots at a rapid pace and has become both the leading robot producer and robot user in the world. (A survey in the June 19, 1984, *Japan Economic Journal* gave the 1984 planned sales of the top 20 Japanese robot producers as around 100,000 units.)

Because the Japanese honestly believe that robots free people for more important tasks, there is little worker resistance to the robotics implementation. In fact, workers go out of their way to figure out how to eliminate their jobs, if they find them dull, because they know the company will find something better and more interesting for them to do.

Bottom-round management.   This kind of mutual reliance is a manifestation of the management style the Japanese call **bottom-round management.** It's also been identified as *consensus management* or *committee management.* It is innate to the Japanese culture because they have grown up with the concept that the importance of the group supercedes that of the individual. Consider that in Japan more than 124 million people are crowded on a tiny island group about the size of California, 80 percent of which is mountainous. In those circumstances, citizens must have considerable respect for their neighbors, or social survival would be impossible. This cultural concept is ideal in a manufacturing facility because the process requires that people work together in a group to make a product. The individual cannot function independently, without concern for others, because he or she would only get out of synchronization with the rest of the group and disrupt the process.

Bottom-round management is a slow decision-making process. In attempting to arrive at a true consensus, not a compromise, the Japanese involve all potentially interested parties, talk over a problem at great length, often interrupt the process, seek out more information, and retalk the problem until everyone finally agrees. While we have often criticized the slowness of this method, the Japanese have an interesting response.

They say, "You Americans will make an instant decision and then you'll take a very long time to implement it. The decision is made so quickly, without consulting many of the people it's going to affect, that as you try to implement it you begin to encounter all sorts of unforeseen obstacles. Now, in our system, we take a long time to make a decision, but it only takes a short time to implement it because by the time we've finally reached a conclusion, everybody involved has had their say."

A key to bottom-round management is that decisions are made at the lowest possible level. In essence, the employees recognize a problem, work out a potential solution with their peers, and make recommendations to the next level of management. They, in turn, do the same thing and make the next recommendation up the line And so it goes, with everyone participating. As a result, top management in Japanese companies makes very few operating decisions, being almost totally devoted to strategic planning. Note, though, that the use of bottom-round management makes it extremely difficult to manage a large, complex manufacturing organization. That's another reason why the Japanese build focused factories, which were discussed earlier.

Subcontractor networks.   The specialized nature of Japanese factories has fostered the development of an enormous subcontractor network; most subcontractors have fewer than 30 employees. More than 90 percent of all Japanese companies are part of the supplier network, which is many tiers deep, because there is so little vertical integration in Japanese factories.

There are two kinds of suppliers: specialists in a narrow field who serve multiple customers (very much like U.S. suppliers), and captives, who usually make a small variety of parts for a single customer. The second kind is more predominant in Japan. Of course, the idea of sole-source suppliers is diametrically opposed to the U.S. multisource concept. Sole-source arrangements work in Japan because the relationships are based on a tremendous amount of mutual trust. They seek long-term partnerships between customer and supplier. Americans who do business with Japanese companies know that the very first stages of negotiation involve an elaborate ceremony of getting to know one another to determine whether there is a potential long-term relationship in the picture. Japanese businesspeople are rarely interested in a one-time buy, so it's a different way of doing business for us.

Suppliers in Japan consider themselves part of their customers' families. Very often key suppliers are invited to company functions such as picnics or parties. In return, suppliers deliver high-quality parts many times per day, often directly to the customer's assembly line, bypassing receiving and inspection. A typical scenario would have the supplier's truck arriving at a precise time of day, the driver unloading the truck, transporting the parts into the factory and delivering them to the assembly line at a given station, depositing the parts, picking up the empty containers, loading them in the truck, and leaving, without any interference. No receiving, no incoming inspection, no paper, no delays. It's an almost paper-free system, all built on mutual trust.

Trust is a two-way street. Because so many of the suppliers are small and undercapitalized, Japanese customers advance money to finance them, if necessary. Customer process engineers and quality personnel help vendors improve their manufacturing systems to meet the rigid quality and delivery standards imposed. Efforts are also made to help vendors reduce their production process cost to help ensure their profitability. When there is an economic downturn, however, the customers do more of the work in-house which they were previously buying from vendors. They do this to protect their own work forces. Vendors are small and do not have the permanent, lifetime employment guarantees that the major companies do. However, this is known in advance and is an accepted risk to the suppliers.

Quality circles.   Another interesting technique, with which many Americans are already familiar, is **quality circles.** The Japanese call them *small group improvement activities* (SGIA). A quality circle is a group of volunteer employees who meet once a week on a scheduled basis to discuss their function and the problems they're encountering, to try to devise solutions to those problems, and to propose those solutions to their management. The group may be led by a supervisor or a production worker. It usually includes people from a given discipline or a given production area, like Assembly Line A or the turning department. It can also be multidisciplined, for instance all material handlers who deliver materials to a department and the industrial engineers who work in that department. It does have to be led, though, by someone who is trained as a group leader. The trainers are facilitators, and each one may coordinate the activities of a number of quality circles. Westinghouse Electric Corporation, for example, has 275 quality circles and about 25 facilitators.

It really works because it's an open forum. It takes some skill to prevent it from becoming a gripe session, but that's where the trained group leaders keep the members on target. Interestingly enough, only about one third of the proposals generated turn out to be quality related. More than half are productivity oriented. It's really amazing how many good ideas these motivated employees can contribute toward the profitability and the improved productivity of their companies. Quality circles are actually a manifestation of the consensus, bottom-round management approach but are limited to these small groups.

Authors' Postscript: Applicability of Japanese Concepts to U.S. Manufacturers

Of the 14 techniques and concepts just described in Wantuck's paper, the following are particularly difficult to implement in the American environment:

- Lifetime employment, company unions, and subcontractor networks. These rely on the Japanese culture or economic relationships not prevalent in the United States.

- Attitude toward workers and bottom-round management. These are characteristics of Japanese management style, which will be appropriate only for some U.S. companies.

- Focused factory networks and automation/robotics. These are most definitely applicable to U.S. companies, but currently they are major strategic and investment decisions performed by top management. In short, few operations managers can influence these decisions in the short run.

What do we have left to import? According to Edward J. Hay, a consultant in Just-in-Time production,

> We have left a group of six elements in which, in my opinion, are the most important elements of all. In addition to being most important they are the most appropriate and practical for the American environment and are well within our ability to implement. One of the main reasons why these techniques are so transferable is because, in one form or another, most of them had their origins in the United States. As a group, they make up a powerful set of manufacturing and quality control techniques, increasingly being referred to under the collective term, Just-in-Time production. For purposes of perspective, I have sorted these six elements under three labels:
>
> 1. Attitude.
>   Just-in-Time (philosophy).
>   Quality at the source.
> 2. Manufacturing engineering.
>   Minimized setup times.
>   Uniform plant load.
>   Group technology.
> 3. Production control.
>   Kanban system.
>
> The philosophy of Just-in-Time is the framework that gives organization and meaning to the other five elements. It requires:
>
> —Production of only the minimum necessary units in the smallest possible quantities at the latest possible time.
> —Elimination of inventories.[5]

---

[5] Edward J. Hay, *Just-in-Time Production: A Winning Combination of Neglected American Ideas* (East Greenwich, R.I.: Edward J. Hay Associates, 1983), p. 2.

Pragmatic JIT versus Romantic JIT

In the opening paragraphs of this chapter we referred to "Big JIT" and "Little JIT" as two views of Just-in-Time production. Paul Zipkin has two categories of his own, which he calls "pragmatic" JIT and "romantic" JIT. The pragmatic view focuses on the practical problems of factory management.[6] This requires reaching into the engineering or production manager's toolbox and pulling out techniques to help reduce setups, to improve layouts, to better quality control, and to create simpler designs. This pragmatic approach can be slow. The process of continuous improvement can take many years. Ohno, president of Toyota and the person credited for the creation of JIT, gives an example of reducing the changing of a die in the production process from several hours to several minutes—this change took 25 years to accomplish! Ohno was a pragmatist. So was Shigeo Shingo.[7] Shingo developed ways to reduce setup times, and created devices such as jigs and fixtures to improve quality. Many of these were simple devices to prevent errors such as parts being installed backwards.

Romantic JIT calls for revolutionary action: "We must adopt JIT if we are to survive" and so on. JIT is proclaimed to be natural and simple without complexity. One visualizes an ideal factory without obstacles and where materials and components move in perfect harmony.

Zipkin questions the universality of JIT, however, stating "If the need for JIT is so urgent, if its many benefits are so manifest, who has prevented us all from reaping the bountiful fruits? Like other revolutionary movements, this one casts the blame for problems, pitfalls, and shortcomings on assorted villains." Who are these villains? Are they staff experts with self-serving objectives? Or are there any villains at all? The problem is that simple JIT doesn't mean that JIT is easy to implement.

6.2 ELIMINATION OF WASTE

At the cost of being somewhat repetitive with material earlier in this chapter. Kiyoshi Suzaki gives an excellent summarization of wasteful items.[8] He quotes Fujio Cho of Toyota in his definition of waste and a list of seven types of waste. Waste is defined as "Anything other than the minimum amount of equipment, materials, parts, space, and worker's time, which are absolutely essential to add value to the product." The seven most prominent types of waste are

[6] Paul H. Zipkin, "Does Manufacturing Need a JIT Revolution?" *Harvard Business Review,* January–February 1991, pp. 40–43.

[7] Shigeo Shingo, *A Study of the Toyoto Production System from an Industrial Engineering Viewpoint* (Cambridge: Productivity Press, 1989).

[8] Kiyoshi Suzaki, *The New Manufacturing Challenge: Techniques for Continuous Improvement* (New York: Free Press, 1987), pp. 7–24.

1. Waste from overproduction.
2. Waste of waiting time.
3. Transportation waste.
4. Inventory waste.
5. Processing waste.
6. Waste of motion.
7. Waste from product defects.

Waste from Overproduction

While overproduction is not as big a problem during market upswings, it becomes unsold goods during downswings. This happens by getting ahead of production. It is one of the worst wastes. In overproduction, more raw materials are consumed than are necessary; this also requires additional materials handling, additional space, and so on. Overproduction also confuses the environment by distracting workers, adding confusion as to what needs to be done first, and so on.

Waste of Waiting Time

While overproduction causes excess inventory, it also tends to hide idle worker time. If workers only produce the required amount and are not allowed to work ahead, their idleness is obvious. Some appropriate actions or other use of their time may, therefore, be possible.

Time is also wasted if the worker's task is simply to watch a machine run. Rather than having a worker watch the machine, a machine may be equipped with an alarm or automatic stop switch that activates when the need to stop arises.

Transportation Waste

Moving material is expensive and time consuming. Opportunities may exist to have incoming materials delivered directly to the production location, for example; rather than storing them somewhere and then moving them a second time. Distances between production processes should also be considered. Transportation waste can be eliminated through improvement in layout, coordination of processes, methods of transportation, housekeeping, and workplace organization.

Processing Waste

The production method used may be wasteful if it can be improved. For example, a die-casting operation may need another worker to file and finish surfaces. If the die were redesigned or the product were modified, there may not be a need for the finish work. It may also be possible to change or modify tools and fixtures to save operator time.

Inventory Waste

Excess inventory may be caused by the first item on the list—over production. This results in extra handling, extra space, extra interest costs, extra workers, extra paperwork, and so forth. There should be a conscious effort to discard obsolete inventory, to use smaller lots in manufacturing and purchasing, and to refrain from producing ahead of schedule.

Waste of Motion

Motions should be efficient and workplaces well designed. Spending time looking for tools is a waste. Walking around may also be a waste that may be corrected by rearranging the work environment.

Waste from Product Defects

Waste occurs from the rework required, from the inspection which may be necessary, from the disassembly of the products, from the time wasted by subsequent workstations waiting for the corrected product, from the product if it is scrapped, and, most importantly, from the customer (through warranty, lost future business, etc.).

6.3 HOW TO ACCOMPLISH JIT PRODUCTION

In this section, our objective is to explain how to accomplish JIT production. To structure our discussion we follow the steps given in Exhibit 6.11, expanding on some ideas given in the Wantuck paper and explaining selected features not previously discussed. In going through these steps, keep in mind that we are talking about *repetitive* production systems—those that make the same basic product over and over again. Also keep in mind that we are talking about features of a *total system,* which means that actions taken regarding any one of these features have some impact on other features of the system. Finally, note that different companies use different terms to describe their JIT systems. IBM uses *continuous flow manufacture,* Hewlett-Packard Company uses *stockless production* at one plant and *repetitive manufacturing system* at another, while many other companies use *lean production.*

JIT Layouts/Design Flow Process

JIT requires that the plant layout be designed to ensure balanced work flow with a minimum of work in process. This means that we must conceive of each workstation as part of a production line, whether or not a physical line

EXHIBIT 6.11   **How to Accomplish Just-in-Time Production**

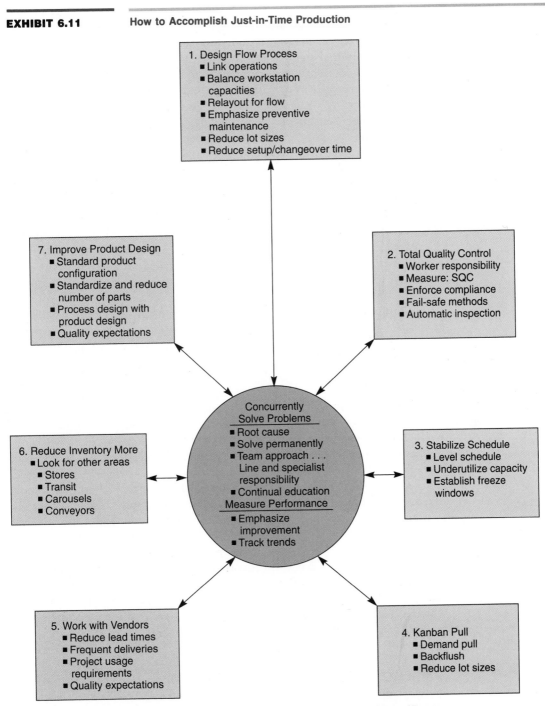

1. Design Flow Process
   - Link operations
   - Balance workstation capacities
   - Relayout for flow
   - Emphasize preventive maintenance
   - Reduce lot sizes
   - Reduce setup/changeover time

7. Improve Product Design
   - Standard product configuration
   - Standardize and reduce number of parts
   - Process design with product design
   - Quality expectations

2. Total Quality Control
   - Worker responsibility
   - Measure: SQC
   - Enforce compliance
   - Fail-safe methods
   - Automatic inspection

Concurrently Solve Problems
- Root cause
- Solve permanently
- Team approach . . . Line and specialist responsibility
- Continual education

Measure Performance
- Emphasize improvement
- Track trends

6. Reduce Inventory More
   - Look for other areas
   - Stores
   - Transit
   - Carousels
   - Conveyors

3. Stabilize Schedule
   - Level schedule
   - Underutilize capacity
   - Establish freeze windows

5. Work with Vendors
   - Reduce lead times
   - Frequent deliveries
   - Project usage requirements
   - Quality expectations

4. Kanban Pull
   - Demand pull
   - Backflush
   - Reduce lot sizes

This diagram is modeled after the one used by Hewlett-Packard's Boise plant to accomplish its JIT program.

actually exists. Capacity balancing is done using the same logic as for an assembly line, and operations are linked through a pull system (described later). This also means that the system designer must have a vision of how all aspects of the internal and external logistics system tie to the layout.

Preventive maintenance is emphasized to ensure that a continuous work flow is not interrupted by machine downtime or as a result of poor quality from malfunctioning equipment. Much of this maintenance is carried out by the operators because they are responsible for the quality of products coming off the machines, and also because of their sensitivity to the idiosyncrasies of the machines as a result of working on them day in and day out. Finally, the fact that the JIT philosophy favors many simple machines rather than a few complex ones enables operators to handle routine maintenance activities.

Reduction in setup/changeover time and lot sizes are interrelated and are key to achieving a smooth flow (and JIT success in general). Exhibit 6.12 illustrates the fundamental relationship between lot size and setup cost. Under the traditional approach, setup cost is treated as a constant, and the optimal order quantity is shown as six. Under the Kanban approach of JIT, setup cost is treated as a variable and the optimal order quantity, in this case, was reduced to two. This type of reduction can be achieved by employing setup time-saving procedures such as those described earlier in the chapter. *The ultimate goal of JIT from an inventory standpoint is to achieve an economic lot size of one.*

Even though we go into considerable detail about layout types in Chapter 9, we will briefly describe a line flow operation and a job-shop layout to show how JIT can be applied.

Most people think of high volume assembly lines when they think of JIT. This is because most literature and discussion of this topic has been about line layouts. However, job-shop environments, where functions are grouped together, offer perhaps the greatest benefits for JIT application.

In assembly or fabrication lines, the focus is on product flow. Volume may be high enough or tasks simple enough or costs low enough so that the required resources (people, machines, materials, etc.) can be arranged close together in a simple flow. "Put stuff in at one end, add some more stuff as you go along, and out the other end comes a completed product."

The majority of manufacturing plants are organized by function or process (similar machines are grouped together, paint departments, heat treating, etc.) Many service facilities are also organized by function or process: hospitals, universities, department stores, and so forth. The main reason for this organization is because these machines or processes serve a variety of needs, none of which is large enough to justify a machine of its own. In this environment, the product or person requiring service must move longer distances.

JIT in a line flow layout

Exhibit 6.13 shows a pull system in a simple line flow. In theory, no one does any work until the product has been pulled from the end of the line. This item could have been sold or used somewhere else. To fill this void created by the

EXHIBIT 6.12

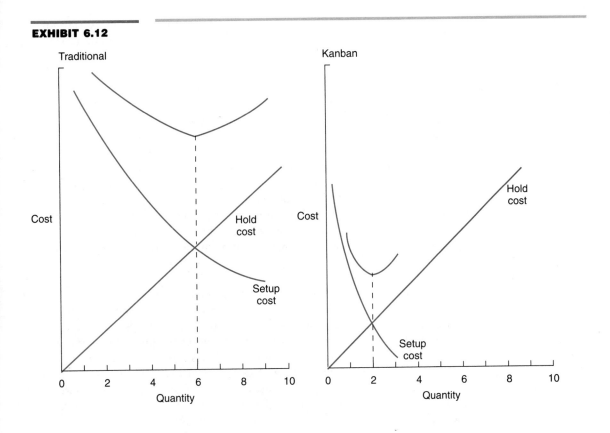

EXHIBIT 6.13

JIT in a Line Flow Layout

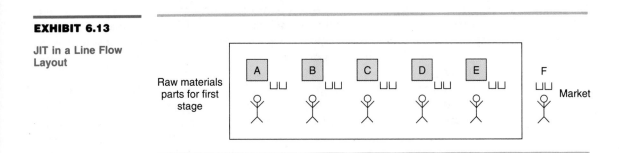

pulled item, a replenishment unit is pulled from upstream. In theory, supposing, in Exhibit 6.13, an item of finished goods is pulled from the finished goods inventory (F). The inventory clerk then goes to processing (E) and takes replacement product to fill the void. Because operator E has an operating policy of keeping a specific number of completed units at the workstation, the operator goes upstream to process D to get replacement units which will then be processed. This pattern continues up to worker A who pulls material from raw material inventory or from whatever process precedes this line. In practice, however, a schedule would be created for the completion of items based on the demand, rather than using inventory clerk F to initiate the chain of events. Operating rules are straightforward: Always keep products which have been completed at your workstation. If someone takes your completed work away, go upstream and get some more to work on. Completed work stays on the "completed" side of the machine. For clarity, we haven't shown it in the exhibit, but materials and parts may be supplied from side lines feeding each workstation as the product progresses.

JIT in a functional (job shop) layout

To justify considering JIT as a valid way to produce goods, the basic requirement is that there is a continual need for the product. This doesn't mean that the product has to be produced continuously in every phase of its creation. Product can be produced intermittently in batches throughout the majority of the sequence except for the final processing or final assembly, which is continuous. Consider a firm that produces several products in constant demand. To simplify it a bit further, assume that the demands are relatively constant throughout the entire year. Let's say that management decides to try to match the production rate with the demand rate, letting demand control production by only producing when goods are pulled from the system—that is, Just-in-Time.

Some of the products require a final assembly—that is, several parts and components produced in various parts of the firm are assembled together and then sold. Other parts require some types of finish machining at a work center and then are sold. In both cases, work on the products is continuous. If there is a demand pull—finished goods are pulled from the system—these steps are truly Just-in-Time.

The rest of the system preceding this final stage area may not be Just-in-Time. Consider the machine centers, paint shops, foundries, heat treating areas, and the countless other locations that these parts and components go through before they reach the final stages. Can we operate these locations in the same Kanban and container logic as we normally use for Just-in-Time? Yes, we can and we should. (See Exhibit 6.14.)

Parts and components produced in various work centers are used in a variety of final products; therefore, these work centers should have completed containers of the entire variety of output that is designated for Just-in-Time production. Supposing a work center produces 10 different parts used by

EXHIBIT 6.14

JIT in a Job-Shop
Layout Showing the
Materials Handling
Vehicle Route
Connecting Machine
Centers and Line
Operations

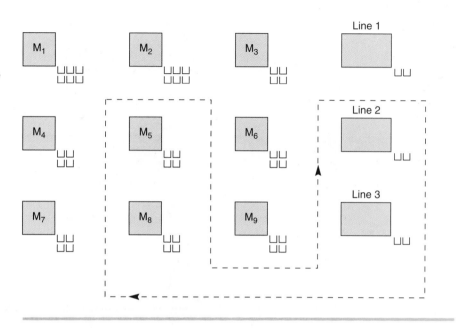

several products which are produced Just-in-Time. This work center must maintain containers of completed output of all 10 parts at the work center to be picked up by those users who need them. If a large part of the facility is organized this way, it would be convenient to have a materials handling vehicle make periodic rounds throughout the facility, such as hourly. This vehicle and operator would stop at the Just-in-Time assembly stations and machine centers and pick up empty containers (and their production move cards if cards are used). These would be dropped off at the corresponding upstream work centers and full containers picked up. By using periodic material handling routes, the system operates in a Just-in-Time mode with its production Kanbans and withdrawal or move Kanbans.

Total Quality Control

JIT and total quality control have become linked in the minds of many managers—and for good reason. Consistent with the previous chapter, **total quality control** refers to "building in" quality and *not* "inspecting it in." It also refers to all plant personnel taking responsibility for maintaining quality, not just "leaving it to the quality control department." When employees assume this responsibility, JIT is permitted to work at its optimal level, since only good products are pulled through the system. What results is having your cake and eating it too—high quality and high productivity. Exhibit 6.15 illustrates this subtle relationship.

EXHIBIT 6.15

**Relationship between
JIT and Quality**

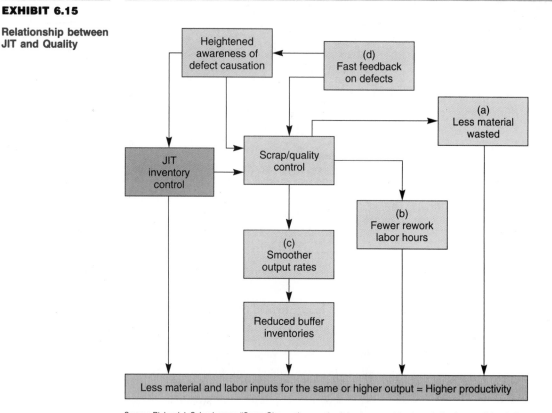

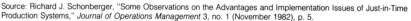

Source: Richard J. Schonberger, "Some Observations on the Advantages and Implementation Issues of Just-in-Time Production Systems," *Journal of Operations Management* 3, no. 1 (November 1982), p. 5.

Statistical quality control uses simple control methods (control charts, primarily) to monitor *all* aspects of a production system. If all aspects of a production process (raw materials, machine variability, etc.) are in control, one can assume that the product coming out of that process is good. When items are produced in small lots, such as in the Kanban system, the inspection may be reduced to just two items—the first and the last. If they are perfect, assume that those produced in between are perfect as well.

Stabilize Schedule

Efficient repetitive manufacture requires a level schedule over a fairly long time horizon. (The actual length depends on many factors, but primarily two: whether the firm makes to order or makes to stock, and the range of product options it offers.) As Robert Hall notes,

A level schedule is one that requires material to be pulled into final assembly in a pattern uniform enough to allow the various elements of production to respond to pull signals. It does not necessarily mean that the usage of every part on an assembly line is identical hour by hour for days on end; it does mean that a given production system equipped with flexible setups and a fixed amount of material in the pipelines can respond.[9]

The term *freeze window* refers to that period of time during which the schedule can't be changed.

Underutilization of capacity is probably the most controversial feature of JIT. Underutilized (or excess) capacity is really the cost incurred by eliminating inventories as a buffer in the system. In traditional manufacturing, safety stocks and early deliveries are used as a hedge against shortfalls in production from such things as poor quality, machine failures, and unanticipated bottlenecks. Under JIT, excess labor and machines provide the hedge. However, excess capacity in the form of labor and equipment is generally far less expensive than carrying excess inventory. Moreover, excess labor can be put to work on other activities during those periods when it is not needed for direct production. Further, the low idle-time cost incurred by the relatively inexpensive machines favored by JIT producers makes machine utilization a secondary issue for many firms. Finally, much of the excess capacity is by design—workers are expected to have time at the end of their shifts to meet with their work groups, clean up their workstations, and ponder potential improvements.

Kanban Pull

Most people view JIT systems as pull systems, where the material is drawn or sent for by the users of the material as needed.[10] Production Kanbans are just one of many devices to signal the need for more parts. Note that the signal sent is for a standard lot size conveyed in a standardized container, not just for a "bunch of parts."

Some typical Kanban-type signals used to initiate production are

"Hey Joe, make me another widget."

A flashing light over a work center, indicating need for more parts.

A signal marker hanging on a post by the using workstations. (See Exhibit 6.16.)

Pull systems typically start with the master schedule specifying the final assembly schedule. By referring to the final assembly schedule, materials

---

[9] Robert H. Hall, *Zero Inventories* (Homewood, Ill.: Dow Jones-Irwin, 1983), p. 64.

[10] As Hall notes, citing a no-nonsense plant supervisor, "You don't never make nothin' and *send* it no place. Somebody has to come and get it." Ibid., p. 41.

EXHIBIT 6.16

Diagram of Outbound
Stockpoint with
Warning Signal
Marker

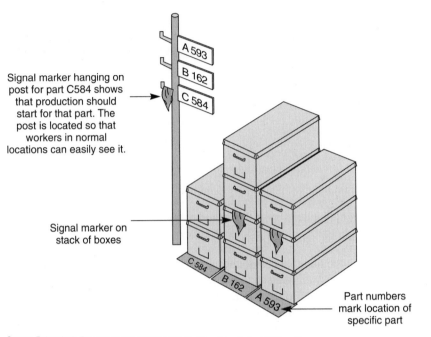

Signal marker hanging on
post for part C584 shows
that production should
start for that part. The
post is located so that
workers in normal
locations can easily see it.

Signal marker on
stack of boxes

Part numbers
mark location of
specific part

Source: Robert Hall, *Zero Inventories* (Homewood, Ill.: Dow Jones-Irwin, 1983), p. 51.

schedulers and supervisors can see the days during the month when each part will be needed. They determine when to schedule supplier deliveries or internal parts manufacture by offsetting lead times from final assembly dates. Basically, then, the final assembly schedule exerts the initial pull on the system, with Kanbans controlling the flow.

How many Kanban cards should be used? There can be a two-card system, a one-card system, or no cards at all. We list the rules for the two-card and one-card systems which Hall has described so well.[11]

Rules for the two-card system are simple but strict:

One card, whether a [withdrawal or] move card or a production card, represents only one standard container for one type of part, and exactly the same number of that part that goes into each.

As soon as parts start to be taken from a standard container at its point of use, the move card is detached from the container. It is returned to the supplying operation as authorization to bring another standard container of the same part.

Containers filled with parts should await pick up at clearly designated locations next to the supplying operations. When a full container is taken, the production card

[11] Robert W. Hall, *Attaining Manufacturing Excellence* (Homewood, Ill: Dow Jones-Irwin, 1987), pp. 91–94.

is detached and left at the supply point. The move card is attached to the full container and taken to the point of use.

The production card left behind is authorization to the supply operation to make another standard container of the same part and leave it with the production card attached at the same outboard location, ready for pick up.

This system of material control replaces exactly what has been consumed and no more. The two-card system is actually one of the more complex ways of controlling this. Between two operations within sight of each other, no cards are needed at all—only a strict restriction on the inventory between. This can be done by marking a space between operations called a *Kanban square*. If squares are empty, workers fill them up, but leave no extras.

A one-card system uses only the move card. Space restrictions or visible limits sufficiently restrict the quantity of each part in its location specified for pick up. If the move cards are permanently attached to the containers, the returning empty containers serve as signals to be filled up.

Replenishment signals can be sent electronically back to the supplying operation to save time. However, care needs to be observed since a large amount of the value of the Kanban system is its simplicity.

Backflush is a term used to designate how component parts are accounted for in a pull system. Rather than keeping track of each individual part on a daily basis by job, JIT systems typically explode the bill of materials periodically, such as once a month, and calculate how many of each part must have gone into the final product(s). This eliminates a major shop-floor data collection activity, and thereby further simplifies the production management job.

Reducing lot sizes in a pull system means removing interstage inventory. This is accomplished in a variety of ways—by better balance of operations so that only two Kanban containers are used between two workstations rather than three, by moving workstations closer together to cut transit time, by automating processes that have high variability, and of course by Just-in-Time deliveries.

Work with Vendors

All the items in this category in Exhibit 6.11 except "project usage requirements" have been discussed earlier. *Project usage requirements* means that the vendors are given a long-run picture of the demands that will be placed on their production and distribution systems. This permits them to develop level production schedules.

Reduce Inventory More

Stores, transit systems, carousels, and conveyors are places where inventory is held; thus, they are targets for inventory reduction efforts. Often there is heated debate when it comes to doing away with them. One reason is that such inventory locations are frequently the focus or result of a previous inventory improvement effort that has shown good results compared to the system used before that. The people involved in such an effort are unlikely to rush to support doing away with something that has been working.

Improve Product Design

Standard product configurations and fewer, standardized parts are important elements in good product design for JIT. When the objective is to establish a simple routine process, anything that reduces variability in the end item or the materials that go into it is worth careful consideration.

Process design with product design refers to the early involvement activities among product designers, process designers, and manufacturing discussed in Chapter 3. Besides improving the producibility of the product, such interaction facilitates the processing of engineering changes. Engineering changes (ECs) to a product can be extremely disruptive to the production process. They alter the specifications of the product, which in turn may call for new materials, new methods, and even new schedules. To minimize such disruptions, many JIT producers introduce their ECs in batches, properly sequenced with the production schedule, rather than one by one, as is common in traditional manufacturing. While batching sounds obvious and simple, it requires a great deal of coordination and a willingness to delay what may be significant changes in a product design in exchange for maintaining production stability.

Concurrently Solve Problems and Measure Performance

A JIT application is not an overnight, turnkey installation. Rather, it is an evolutionary system that is continually seeking ways of improving production. Improvement comes through looking at problems as challenges rather than threats—problems that can be solved with common sense and detailed, rigorous analysis.

The techniques for problem solving are primarily continuous improvement methods, described in detail in Chapter 17. Effective problem solving means that the problem is solved permanently. Because JIT requires a team effort, problems are treated in a team context. Staff personnel are expected to be seen frequently on the shop floor, and in some companies are expected to arrive a half hour before production workers to ensure that things are in order, thus avoiding problems.

Continual education is absolutely essential if the system is to avoid stagnation. While JIT may cost little in the way of hardware, it requires a substantial investment in training people at all levels of the organization in what the system demands and how they fit into it.

Many performance measures emphasize the number of processes and practices changed to improve materials flow and reduce labor content, and the degree to which they do so. If the processes physically improve over time, lower costs follow. According to Hall, a department head in a Japanese JIT system is likely to be evaluated on the following factors:

1. Improvement trends, including number of improvement projects undertaken, trends in costs, and productivity. Productivity is measured as:

$$P = \frac{\text{Measurement of department output}}{\text{Total employees (direct + indirect)}}$$

2. Quality trends, including reduction in defect rates, improvement in process capability, and improvement in quality procedures.
3. Running to a level schedule and providing parts when others need them.
4. Trends in departmental inventory levels, e.g., speed of flow.
5. Staying within budget for expenses.
6. Developing work force skills, versatility, participation in changes, and morale.[12]

6.4 SOME TECHNICAL ISSUES ABOUT KANBAN

Kanban as a Fixed-Order Quantity/Reorder Point Inventory System

Both Kanban and the simple fixed-order quantity/reorder point system are reactive systems. Both systems are designed to replenish inventory, not in anticipation of future orders, but as soon as the inventory is depleted. Also, both assume continuous review, predetermined reorder points, and fixed replenishment quantities. The inventory behavior under the two systems is identical with the one exception that Kanban displays a lumpy usage pattern. The reason for this is that unlike the fixed-order quantity system where parts are withdrawn one at a time, Kanban withdraws a fixed number of them in standard-sized containers. Such standardized containers, in turn, define the lot size, so each time one is withdrawn, a reorder point is reached.

In light of the basic similarity of the two systems, why has Kanban performed so well, while the fixed-order quantity system has generally failed? The answer is that Japanese management has been able to structure a manufacturing environment conducive to Kanban operation. The major contribution of Japanese management (relative to inventory control) lies in demand management and lead-time management, two features that are implicit in our discussion of JIT.

---

[12] Ibid., pp. 254–55.

JIT and Cost Accounting

Cost accounting systems have focused on direct labor since the Industrial Revolution. However, under JIT (and computer-integrated management) overhead costs are dominant, often 20 times as high as direct labor. Moreover, with permanent employment, workers maintaining their own equipment, and other measures, the distinction between direct and indirect labor has become blurred for cost-allocation purposes. Hewlett-Packard has recognized this and has eliminated the cost category of direct labor, now using simply "labor" instead.

It appears at this time that the primary difference between traditional and JIT cost accounting is the application of overhead on the basis of product time in the system (cycle time) rather than direct labor or machine hours.[13]

6.5 COMPANY EXPERIENCES WITH JIT

Exhibit 6.17 summarizes the experiences of five major U.S. companies that have installed JIT (and TQC, total quality control). As can be seen, the impact on these companies' performance measures is overwhelmingly positive. Similar results have been reported in European and British firms. One study of 80 plants in Europe, for example, listed the following benefits from JIT:

1. An average reduction in inventory of about 50 percent.
2. A reduction in throughput time of 50 to 70 percent.
3. Reduction in setup times of as much as 50 percent without major investment in plant and equipment.
4. An increase in productivity of between 20 and 50 percent.
5. Payback time for investment in JIT averaged less than nine months.[14]

Additional success stories abound in the production-control journals. This is not to say that the implementation of JIT is trouble free, however. Exhibit 6.18 indicates that some problems just won't go away quickly.

6.6 JIT IN SERVICES

Service organizations and service operations within manufacturing firms present interesting opportunities for applications of JIT concepts. Here is an edited version of a paper by Randall J. Benson, a consultant for Coopers &

---

[13] Mohan V. Tatikonda, "Just-in-Time and Modern Manufacturing Environments: Implications for Cost Accounting," *Production and Inventory Management Journal* 28, no. 1 (1988), pp. 1–5.

[14] Amrik Sohal and Keith Howard, "Trends in Materials Management," *International Journal of Production Distribution and Materials Management* 17, no. 5 (1987), pp. 3–41.

EXHIBIT 6.17   Summary of JIT/TQC Activities for Five U.S. Companies

Company Name (Division)	Product Category	Production Characteristics	Start/ Reporting Period	Who Initiated Action?	Why Started?	Where Started?	How Implemented	Problems Observed
Deere & Company	Heavy machinery Farm equipment Lawn-care equipment	Repetitive manufacturing	1980 1982–1984	CEO/ manufacturing managers (trip to Japan) Steering committee	Survival Foreign competition	Four plants	Visit to Japan Task force in plant Education Pilot projects Work-flow analysis	Initially, worker doubts Underestimated educational needs
Black & Decker (Consumer Power Tools)	Electrical products	Repetitive manufacturing Floor space 385,000 sq. ft. Employees: 1,010	1982 1982–1984	Staff Production control committee	Large expenses in inventory carrying costs (high interest rates)	Assembly Purchasing	Education Balanced flow Rewrote work procedures Started to produce in weekly quantity	Vendor resistance Resistance to change
Omark Industries	Forestry equipment and sporting goods	Mostly repetitive 18 plants	1980 1981–1983	CEO (trip to Japan) Corporate task force Plant study terms	Corporate task force found JIT/ TQC/employee involvement as reason for success	Five pilot plants	Steering committee Plant study team Presentation by corporate staff Pilot projects	Middle management resistance Underestimated training needs Slowdown after first projects
Hewlett-Packard (Computer Systems)	Computer and test systems	Forming/assembly/testing Many options	TQC: 3 years JIT: 1 year (1983–1984)	Steering committee	Questioned why overseas suppliers produced quality products	Assembly flow rearrangement	TQC first Employee training/ involvement Leveled schedule Process simplification	Cut WIP levels too quickly Major changes faster than could assimilate
FMC	Industrial equipment Defense Automotive Electrical	Multiple divisions with variety of products 50 manufacturing and mining operations	1982 1982–1984	Operations support staff Manufacturing vice president Controller	Survival Absence of patent protection Keen cost competition	Pilot projects Automotive and electrical: well-managed first operation	Seminars Pilot project Pilot plants Setup time Inventory target Positive reinforcement	Fine tuning Not enough manpower to implement ideas Occasional line stop from parts shortage

EXHIBIT 6.17 (concluded)

Company Name (Division)	Start/ Reporting Period	Labor Productivity Improvement	Setup Time (improvement)	Inventory Reductions	Quality Improvements	Space Savings	Production Lead Times	Effect on Corporate Culture	Comments
Deere & Company	1980 1982–1984	Subassembly: 19–35% Welding: 7–38% Manufacturing cost: 10–20% Materials handling: 40%	Presses: 38–80% Drills: 24–33% Shears: 45% Grinders: 44% Average: 45%	Raw steel: 40% Purchased parts: 7% Crane shafts: 30 days → 3 days Average: 31%	Implemented process control charting in 40% of operations	Significant	Significant	Unexpected enthusiasm More responsive to all Increased employee participation	Japan's Yanmar Diesel's support Did not introduce TQC in the beginning
Black & Decker (Consumer Power Tools)	1982 1982–1984	Assembly: 24 operators → 6 operators Support: 7 → 5	Punch press: 1 hr. → 1 min. Drastic in many areas	Turns: 16 → 30	Reduced complaints in packaging 98% 100% customer service level	Significant	Products made in weekly lots 50% → 95%		Number of suppliers reduced by 40% Quality audit of suppliers
Omark Industries	1981/Jan. 1981–1983	Plant A: 30% Plant B: 30% Plant C: 20%	A: 165 → 5 min. B: 43 → 17 min. C: 360 → 17 min. D: 45 → 6 min.	Product A: 92% Product B: 29% Product C: 50%	Product A scrap and rework: 20% Product E Customer service cost: 50%	Parts travel distance: Product C: 24% Product E: 68%	A: 3 weeks → 3 days E: 21 days → 3 days	Hourly workers making decisions High employee involvement	JIT/TQC at the same time
Hewlett-Packard (Computer Systems)	TQC: 3 yrs. JIT: 1 yr. (1983–1984)	Standard hours: 87 hrs. → 39 hrs.	Not available	PC Assembly inventory: $675,000 (100) → $190,000 (28)	Solder defects: 5000 PPM → 100 Scrap: $80,000/ mo. → $5,000	PC Assembly: 8,500 → 5,750 sq.ft.	PC Assembly: 15 days → 1.5 days	Corporate culture (H-P way) helped JIT Proud to be among first to implement JIT/TQC	Adopted TQC/ JIT separately MRP did not support JIT
FMC	1982 1982–1984	Direct labor productivity: 13% (Automotive service equipment division)	Defense equipment group: 60%–75% Automotive/electrical: 80%	Turns: 1.9 → 4.0 (Automotive service equipment division)	Customer service: 88% → 98% Cost of quality: 3.5% → 2.1% (Auto. Svc. Eq. Div.)	Automotive/ electrical: 25% Eliminated stockroom	Automotive/ electrical: 1 mo. → 1 wk Suppliers: months → days	Grass-roots movement toward manufacturing excellence	Reduced suppliers by 50% Corporate plan to implement TQC/JIT at all plants by 1986

Source: From Kiyoshi Suzaki, "Comparative Study of JIT/TQC Activities in Japanese and Western Companies," First World Congress of Production and Inventory Control, Vienna, Austria, 1985, pp. 63–66.

EXHIBIT 6.18

Implementation
Problems

Problem Area	Was a Problem	Still a Problem	Now Under Control
Customer schedule changes	62.0%	57.4%	4.6%
Poor supplier quality	59.3	49.1	10.2
Poor production quality (internal)	57.4	43.5	13.9
Inability to change paperwork systems	57.4	46.3	11.1
Shortage of critical parts	57.4	44.4	13.0
Supplier inability to deliver JIT	56.5	49.1	7.4
Lack of employee commitment	49.0	30.5	18.5
Inability to reduce setup time	48.1	36.1	12.0
Inadequate equipment and tooling	45.4	30.6	14.8
Surplus of noncritical parts	43.5	33.3	10.2
Lack of top-management commitment	42.6	27.8	14.8
Labor contract problems	35.2	25.9	9.3

Source: Albert F. Celley, W. H. Gregg, A. W. Smith, and Ann A. Vondermbsc, "Implementation of JIT in the United States," *Journal of Purchasing and Materials Management* 22, no. 4 (Winter 1986), pp. 9–15.

Lybrand; it explains why JIT is not just for the factory.[15] The last part of this section describes the successful use of JIT techniques at a Japanese sushi house.

Despite the many differences between service and manufacturing, they share the most basic attributes of production. Both manufacturing and services employ processes that add value to the basic inputs to create the end product or service.

JIT focuses on processes, not products. We can apply it to any group of processes, from manufacturing to service production. The JIT goal is approached by testing each step in the production process to determine if it adds value to the product or service. If the steps do not add value, then the process is a candidate for re-engineering. In this way, the production of processes gradually and continually improves.

Both manufacturing and service production can be improved with JIT because both are systems of production processes and because JIT is essentially a process-oriented waste-elimination philosophy. The themes for JIT process improvement should apply equally in a service environment.

How Do the JIT Themes Fit Service?

The following eight **JIT themes** make no reference to manufactured products. These themes are applicable to all areas of JIT manufacturing, regardless of the specific technique being applied. Because they are process as opposed to product oriented, they should apply equally well to service production. Indeed, they lead to some interesting insights into service operations management.

---

[15] Randall J. Benson, "JIT: Not Just for the Factory," *Proceedings from the 29th Annual International Conference for the American Production and Inventory Control Society*, St. Louis, Missouri, October 20–24, 1986, pp. 370–74.

1. Total visibility.   Total visibility means that the equipment, people, material, processes, process status, and process flows are visible to those participating in the production process. Visibility has a special marketing importance to service producers because the customer participates in the process. The service process is often the key tangible evidence of the value and quality of the service.

2. Synchronization and balance.   This is the concept that "If you don't need it now, don't make it now." A balanced operation runs at the same rate at every production stage because the processes are synchronized and extra inventory is eliminated.

Service producers are typically required to synchronize sales and production almost perfectly because customers do not wait for service if they have other alternatives.

3. Respect for people.   Each time a service employee interacts with a customer, a moment of truth takes place. It determines the customer's perception of the quality and value of the service. A negative moment of truth carries a much heavier weight in the customer's perception than a positive one. Service employees are often personally responsible for the quality, consistency, and value of the service.

4. Flexibility.   Flexibility refers to the ability to rapidly adapt the process to produce what the customers want when they want it, without wasting production resources. Service producers must be especially flexible because they must produce a service instantaneously and tailor the service to the customer's expectations.

5. Continuous improvement.   Continuous improvement involves moving always closer to the ideal by making many small improvements in the processes.

Because services tend to be labor intense, most of the improvements change the employees' activities. Many service firms have successfully used employee-centered improvement groups to improve the quality and value of the service.

6. Responsibility for the environment.   Service operations have no more room for errors than manufacturing. In labor-intensive service industries, the employees have even more impact on the performance of the production process. Every service employee must take full responsibility for each moment of truth that takes place during the customer contact and for improving the production processes.

7. Holistic approach.   JIT works best when it is implemented as a company philosophy to eliminate waste, not just a technique to reduce inventory. All departments and all levels of operations get involved in eliminating waste.

In service firms the holistic approach is essential, because production and marketing cannot be separated. Service firms must approach production process changes as marketing needs change because the customers are influenced by the production process itself. A customer's perception of the quality and value of the service is largely determined by the production process.

8. Simplicity.   The simplicity of the process allows people who run the process to identify opportunities for process improvements and to plan the process changes themselves.

Simplicity is no less important in the service sector. It may be even more important due to the worker-intensive nature of the service delivery system. Furthermore, customer participation is more successful if the process is simple. Simple processes, systems, and controls allow customers to easily engage, participate in, and disengage from the service delivery process.

The JIT themes just described are entirely appropriate for service firms. In fact, one could argue that the JIT improvements in manufacturing actually allow the manufacturer to operate more like a successful service firm. Isn't stockless production based on synchronization of fast-flow processes an excellent description of a service process?

JIT has already been applied successfully in diverse service industries. This is a significant step for service firms because the service sector presently lacks a general and comprehensive approach to service operation improvements. A service version of JIT holds the promise to rationalize service operations across very dissimilar industries.

Which JIT Techniques Are Appropriate for Services?

Many of the JIT techniques have been successfully applied by service firms. Just as in manufacturing, the suitability of each technique and the corresponding work steps depends on the characteristics of the firm's markets, production and equipment technology, skill sets, and corporate culture. Service firms are not different in this respect. Following are some of the more successful applications:

Organize problem-solving groups.   **Focused improvement groups** and quality circles improve the quality and cost performance of manufacturing processes. The groups use methods such as group dynamics, brainstorming, Pareto analysis, and root-cause analysis to rethink manufacturing processes.

Honeywell is extending its quality circles from manufacturing into its service operations. Other corporations as diverse as First Bank/Dallas, Standard Meat Company, and Miller Brewing Company are using similar approaches to improve service. British Airways used quality circles as a fundamental part of its strategy to implement new service practices.

Upgrade housekeeping.   Good housekeeping means more than winning the clean broom award. It means that only the necessary items are kept in a work area, that there is a place for everything, that everything is clean and in a constant state of readiness. The employees clean their own areas.

Service organizations such as McDonald's, Disneyland, and Speedi-Lube have recognized the critical nature of housekeeping. Their dedication to housekeeping has meant that service processes work better, the attitude of the continuous improvement is easier to develop, and customers perceive that they are receiving better service.

Upgrade quality.   The only cost-effective way to improve quality is to develop reliable process capabilities. Process quality is quality at the source—it guarantees first-time production of consistent and uniform products and services.

McDonald's is famous for building quality into its service delivery process. It literally "industrialized" the service delivery system so that part-time, casual workers could provide the same eating experience anywhere in the world. Quality doesn't mean producing the best, it means consistently producing products and services that meet the "fitness for use" criteria.

Clarify process flows.   Clarification of the flows, based on the JIT themes, can dramatically improve the process performance.

For example, Federal Express Corporation changed air flight patterns from origin-to-destination to origin-to-hub where the freight is transferred to an outbound plane heading for the destination. This revolutionized the air transport industry. The order entry department of a manufacturing firm converted from functional departments to customer-centered work groups and reduced the order processing lead time from eight to two days. A county government used the JIT approach to cut the time to record a deed transfer by 50 percent. Supermaids sends in a team of house cleaners, each with a specific responsibility, to clean each house quickly with parallel processes. Changes in process flows can literally revolutionize service industries.

Revise equipment and process technologies.   Revising technologies involves evaluation of the equipment and processes for their ability to meet the process requirements, process consistently within tolerance, and to fit the scale and capacity of the work group.

Speedi-Lube converted the standard service-station concept to a specialized lubrication and inspection center by changing the service bays from drive-in to drive-through and by eliminating the hoists and building pits under the cars where the employees have full access to the lubrication areas on the vehicle.

A hospital reduced the operating-room setup time so that it had the flexibility to perform a wider range of operations without reducing the operation room availability.

Level the facility load.   Service firms synchronize production with demand. They have developed unique approaches to leveling demand so they can avoid making customers wait for service. The Source sells time for less during the evening. McDonald's offers a special breakfast menu in the morning. Retail stores use take-a-number systems. The post office charges more for next-day delivery. These are all examples of the service approach for creating uniform facility loads.

Eliminate unnecessary activities.   A step that does not add value is a candidate for elimination. A step that does add value may be a candidate for re-engineering to improve the process consistency or to reduce the time to perform the tasks.

A hospital discovered that a significant amount of time during an operation was spent waiting for an instrument that was not available when the operation began. It developed a checklist of instruments required for each category of operation. Speedi-Lube eliminated steps, but it also added steps that didn't improve the lubrication process but did make customers feel more assured about the work that was being performed.

Reorganize physical configuration.   The work-area configurations frequently require reorganization during a JIT implementation. Often manufacturers accomplish this by setting up manufacturing cells to produce items in small lots, synchronous to demand. These cells amount to "micro-factories" inside the plant.

Most service firms are far behind manufacturers in this area. However, a few interesting examples do come out of the service sector. Some hospitals, instead of routing patients all over the building for tests, exams, X-rays, and injections are reorganizing their services into work groups based on the type of problem. Teams that treat only trauma are common, but other work groups have been formed to treat less immediate conditions like hernias. These amount to micro-clinics within the hospital facility.

Introduce demand-pull scheduling.   Due to the nature of service production and consumption, demand-pull (customer-driven) scheduling is necessary for operating a service business. Moreover, many service firms are separating their operations into "back room" and "customer contact" facilities. This approach creates new problems in coordinating the schedules between the facilities. The original Wendy's restaurants were set up so the cooks could see the cars enter the parking lot. They put a pre-established number of hamburger patties onto the grill for each car. This pull system was designed to have a fresh patty on the grill before the customer even placed an order.

Develop supplier networks.   Supplier networks in the JIT context refer to the cooperative association of suppliers and customers working over the long term for mutual benefit. Service firms have not emphasized supplier networks for materials because the service costs are often predominantly labor. Notable exceptions must include service organizations like McDonald's, one of the biggest food products purchasers in the world. A contract manufacturer recognized that it needed a cooperative relationships for temporary employees as well as for parts. It is considering a campaign to establish JIT-type relationships with a temporary employment service and a trade school to develop a reliable source of trained assemblers.

Theodore Levitt eloquently summarized the need to apply manufacturing thinking to service:

> Until we think of service in more positive and encompassing terms, until it is enthusiastically viewed as manufacturing in the field, receptive to the same kinds of technological approaches that are used in the factory, the results are likely to be just as costly and idiosyncratic as the results of the lonely journeyman carving things laboriously by hand at home.[16]

Once we start thinking of services as an organized system of production processes, we can consider the use of JIT-type concepts to re-engineer service delivery operations. The result will be consistent services of high quality and excellent value, produced with high productivity.

Japanese Management and the 100 Yen Sushi House

The 100 Yen Sushi House is no ordinary sushi restaurant.[17] It is the ultimate showcase of Japanese productivity. As we entered the shop, there was a chorus of *"iratsai,"* a welcome from everyone working in the shop—cooks, waitresses, the owner, and the owner's children. The house features an ellipsoid-shaped serving area in the middle of the room, where three or four cooks were busily preparing sushi. Perhaps 30 stools surrounded the serving area. We took seats at the counters and were promptly served with a cup of "misoshiru," which is a bean paste soup, a pair of chopsticks, a cup of green tea, a tiny plate to make our own sauce, and a small china piece to hold the chopsticks. So far, the service was average for any sushi house. Then, I noticed something special. There was a conveyor belt going around the ellipsoid service area, like a toy train track. On it I saw a train of plates of sushi. You can find any kind of sushi that you can think of—from the cheapest seaweed or octopus kind to the expensive raw salmon or shrimp dishes. The price is uniform, however, 100 yen per plate. On closer examination, while my eyes were racing to keep up with the speed of the traveling plates, I found that a cheap seaweed plate had four pieces, while the more expensive raw salmon dish had only two pieces. I sat down and looked around at the other customers at the counters. They were all enjoying their sushi and slurping their soup while reading newspapers or magazines.

---

[16] Theodore Leavitt, "Production Line Approach to Service," *Harvard Business Review* 50, no. 5 (September–October 1972), p. 52.

[17] Sang M. Lee, "Japanese Management and the 100 Yen Sushi House," *Operations Management Review* 1, no. 2 (Winter 1983), pp. 45–48.

I saw a man with eight plates all stacked up neatly. As he got up to leave, the cashier looked over and said, "800 yen, please." The cashier had no cash register, since she can simply count the number of plates and then multiply by 100 yen. As the customer was leaving, once again we heard a chorus of *"Arigato Gosaimas"* (thank you), from all the workers.

The owner's daily operation is based on a careful analysis of information. The owner has a complete summary of demand information about different types of sushi plates, and thus he knows exactly how many of each type of sushi plates he should prepare and when. Furthermore, the whole operation is based on the repetitive manufacturing principle with appropriate Just-in-Time and quality control systems. For example, the store has a very limited refrigerator capacity (we could see several whole fish or octopus in the glassed chambers right in front of our counter). Thus, the store uses the Just-in-Time inventory control system. Instead of increasing the refrigeration capacity by purchasing new refrigeration systems, the company has an agreement with the fish vendor to deliver fresh fish several times a day so that materials arrive just in time to be used for sushi making. Therefore, the inventory cost is minimum.

In the Just-in-Time operation system, the safety stock principle is turned upside down. In other words, the safety stock is deliberately removed gradually, to uncover problems and their possible solutions. The available floor space is for workers and their necessary equipment but not for holding inventory. In the 100 Yen Sushi House, workers and their equipment are positioned so close that sushi making is passed on hand to hand rather than as independent operations. The absence of walls of inventory allows the owner and workers to be involved in the total operation, from greeting the customer to serving what is ordered. Their tasks are tightly interrelated and everyone rushes to a problem spot to prevent the cascading effect of the problem throughout the work process.

The 100 Yen Sushi House is a labor-intensive operation, which is based mostly on simplicity and common sense rather than high technology, contrary to American perceptions. I was very impressed. As I finished my fifth plate, I saw the same octopus sushi plate going around for about the thirtieth time. Perhaps I had discovered the pitfall of the system. So I asked the owner how he takes care of the sanitary problems when a sushi plate goes around all day long, until an unfortunate customer eats it and perhaps gets food poisoning. He bowed with an apologetic smile and said, "Well, sir, we never let our sushi plates go unsold longer than about 30 minutes." Then he scratched his head and said, "Whenever one of our employees takes a break, he or she can take off unsold plates of sushi and either eat them or throw them away. We are very serious about our sushi quality." As we laughed, he laughed, along with a 90-degree bow. As we were walking out of the sushi house, while *"arigato gosaimas"* was ringing in my ears, I was contemplating how to introduce the 100 Yen Sushi House concept to the States. Perhaps I can suggest the concept to the student union at the university for an experiment. Maybe McDonald's, Pizza Hut, Wendy's . . .

6.7 CONCLUSION

We have listed many of the potential benefits of Just-in-Time systems. In our concluding remarks, however, we need to caution that JIT applications are not universal. There are specific requirements for successful implementaiton and we need to be careful not to be caught up in the excitement and promises.

In 1983, Hewlett-Packard created a videotape at its Boulder, Colorado, plant. It was an excellent video and fun to watch. Its purpose was to convince viewers that a JIT pull system would produce significant benefits for most manufacturing plants. Although instructors still use this video in their classrooms, many of us caution against the message conveyed.

The video does not carry through a numerical analysis of the performance times, number of defects, work in process, and so on. This can lead to the wrong conclusions—that is, that the JIT pull system was responsible for improved conditions.

In a recent article, Jerry Bowman presented the data.[18] After analyzing the data he commented that the most significant benefits did not result from the pull system but from reducing lot sizes. The HP video showed that the best performance occurred when items were processed using a pull system in lots of one unit. Bowman commented, "If you manufacture in lot sizes of one in a 'flow' environment, you probably couldn't tell whether you were "pushing" or "pulling", nor would it matter."

This is also consistent with students' difficulties in distinguishing between an American automobile assembly line and a Japanese automobile assembly line. JIT is becoming a principal manufacturing management concept and undoubtedly will continue to be so throughout the 1990s. But again, we caution you to be careful in its use.

6.8 REVIEW AND DISCUSSION QUESTIONS

1. What is meant by "pragmatic" JIT versus "romantic" JIT?
2. Stopping waste is one of the most important parts of JIT. Identify some of the sources of waste and discuss how they may be eliminated.
3. Discuss JIT in a job-shop layout and in a line layout.
4. Why is it important for JIT to have a stable schedule?
5. Are there any aspects of the Japanese approach that you could apply to your own current school activities? Explain.
6. Do you believe that Fredrick W. Taylor, the father of scientific management, would be for or against the Japanese approach?
7. Which objections might a marketing manager have against uniform plant loading?

---

[18] D. Jerry Bowman, "If You Don't Understand JIT, How Can You Implement It?" *Industrial Engineering*, February 1991, pp. 38–39.

8. What are the implications for cost accounting of JIT production?

9. Which questions would you want to ask the president of Toyota about his operations management?

10. Explain how cards are used in a Kanban system.

11. In which ways, if any, are the following systems analogous to Kanban: returning empty bottles to the supermarket and picking up filled ones; running a hot dog stand at lunchtime; withdrawing money from a checking account; collecting eggs at a chicken ranch?

12. How does the old saying, "There's no such thing as a free lunch," pertain to the Japanese elimination of inventory?

13. Why do ECs cause so much trouble under JIT systems? How do the Japanese handle them?

14. Explain the relationship between quality and productivity under the JIT philosophy.

6.9 CASE: XYZ PRODUCTS COMPANY

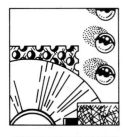

XYZ Products Company is a supplier of gizmos for a large computer manufacturer located a few miles away. The company produces three different models of gizmos in production runs ranging from 100 to 300 units.

The production flow of Models X and Y is shown in Case Exhibit 1. Model Z requires milling as its first step, but otherwise follows the same flow pattern as X and Y. Skids can hold up to 20 gizmos at a time. Approximate processing times per unit by operation number and equipment setup times are shown in the following table.

Operation Number and Name		Operation Times (minutes)	Setup Times (minutes)
—	Milling for Z	20	60
1	Lathe	50	30
2	Mod. 14 drill	15	5
3	Mod. 14 drill	40	5
4	Assembly step 1	50	
	Assembly step 2	45	
	Assembly step 3	50	
5	Inspection	30	
6	Paint	30	20
7	Oven	50	
8	Packing	5	

The demand for gizmos from the computer company ranges between 125 and 175 per month, equally divided among X, Y, and Z. Subassembly builds up inventory early in the month to make certain that a buffer stock is always available. Raw materials and purchased parts for subassemblies each constitute 40 percent of manufacturing cost of a gizmo. Both categories of parts are multiple sourced from about 80 vendors and are delivered at random times. (Gizmos have 40 different part numbers.)

CASE EXHIBIT 1

Gizmo Production Flow

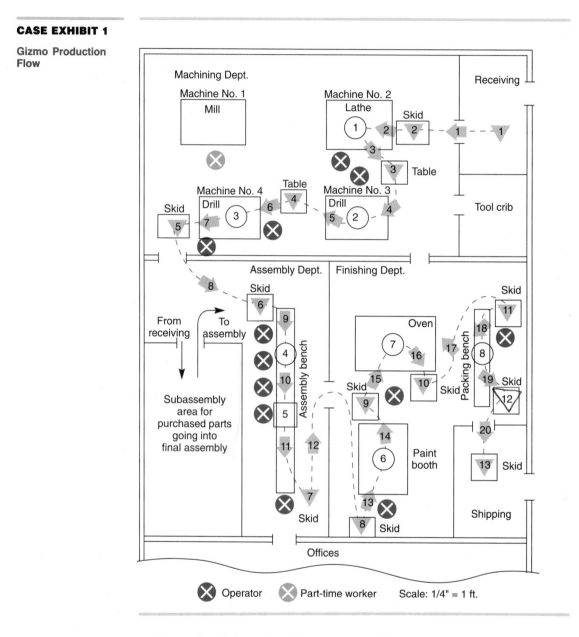

Some other information: Scrap rates are about 10 percent at each operation, inventory turns twice yearly, employees are paid on day rate, employee turnover is 25 percent per year, and net profit from operations is steady at 5 percent per year. Maintenance is performed as needed.

The manager of XYZ has been contemplating installing an MRP system to help control inventories and to "keep the skids filled." (It is his view that two days of work in front of a workstation motivates the worker to produce at top speed.) He is also planning to add three inspectors to clean up the quality problem. Further, he is thinking about setting up a rework line to speed up repairs. While he is pleased with the high utilization of most of his equipment and labor, he is concerned about the idle time of his milling machine. Finally, he has asked his industrial engineering department to look into high-rise shelving to store parts coming off Machine 4.

QUESTIONS

1. Which of the changes being considered by the manager of XYZ go counter to the JIT philosophy?
2. Make recommendations for JIT improvements in such areas as scheduling, layout, Kanban, task groupings, and inventory. Use quantitative data as much as possible; state necessary assumptions.
3. Sketch the operation of a pull system for XYZ's current system.
4. Outline a plan for the introduction of JIT at XYZ.

6.10 SELECTED BIBLIOGRAPHY

Davidson, William H. *The Amazing Race: Winning the Technorivalry with Japan.* New York: John Wiley & Sons, 1984.

Fucini, Joseph J., and Suzy Fucini. *Working for the Japanese.* New York: Free Press, 1990.

Garvin, David A. "Quality on the Line." *Harvard Business Review* 61, no. 5 (September–October 1983), pp. 65–75.

Hall, Robert. *Zero Inventories.* Homewood, Ill.: Dow Jones-Irwin, 1983.

————. *Attaining Manufacturing Excellence.* Homewood, Ill.: Dow Jones-Irwin, 1987.

Inman, R. Anthony, and Satish Mehra. "The Transferability of Just-in-Time Concepts to American Small Business." *Interfaces* 20, no. 2 (March–April 1990), pp. 30–37.

Klein, Janice. "A Re-examination of Autonomy in Light of New Manufacturing Practices." *Human Relations* 43, 1990.

Monden, Yasuhiro. *Toyota Production System, Practical Approach to Production Management.* Atlanta, Ga.: Industrial Engineering and Management Press, 1983.

————. "What Makes the Toyota Production System Really Tick?" *Industrial Engineering* 13, no. 1 (January 1981), pp. 36–46.

Ohno, Taiichi. *Toyota Production System: Beyond Large-Scale Production.* Cambridge, Mass.: Productivity Press, 1988.

Ohno, Taiichi, and Setsuo Mito. *Just-in-Time for Today and Tomorrow.* Cambridge, Mass.: Productivity Press, 1988.

Schonberger, Richard J. *Japanese Productivity Techniques.* New York: Free Press, 1982.

————. *World-Class Manufacturing: The Lessons of Simplicity Applied.* New York: Free Press, 1986.

————. *Building a Chain of Customers: Linking Business Functions to Create a World-Class Company.* New York: Free Press, 1989.

Sewell, G. "Management Information Systems for JIT Production." *Omega* 18, no. 5 (1990), pp. 481–503.

Shingo, Shigeo. *A Study of the Toyota Production System from an Industrial Engineering Viewpoint.* Cambridge, Mass.: Productivity Press, 1989.

Weiss, Andrew. "Simple Truths of Japanese Manufacturing." *Harvard Business Review* 62, no. 4 (July–August 1984), pp. 119–25.

Zipkin, Paul H. "Does Manufacturing Need a JIT Revolution?" *Harvard Business Review,* January–February 1991, pp. 40–50.

Chapter 7

Forecasting

If I had only known that would happen, I would have . . .

KEY TERMS

Time Series Analysis

Moving Averages

Exponential Smoothing

Smoothing Constants Alpha and Delta

Mean Absolute Deviation (MAD)

Tracking Signal

Linear Regression Forecasting

Trend Effects

Seasonal Factors

Deseasonalization of Demand

Causal Relationship

Focus Forecasting

Often times people confuse forecasting with precision. They say, "You can't forecast!" And, we answer "Sure we can. But you have to understand what the forecast means."

Critics of forecasting techniques make erroneous frequently heard comments such as, "Forecasts are always wrong," and so on.[1] Those who criticize forecasting the stock market cite studies based on dart throwing, random walk theories, and comparisons of experts on Wall Street.

We could force a forecast of the stock market quite easily. Consider the following exchange:

Them: "It's impossible to forecast the stock market."

Us: "OK, then. Do you think that the Dow Jones Industrial Average will go to 10,000 by next month?"

Them: "Of course not. Don't be absurd."

Us: "OK, then. Do you think that the Dow Jones Industrial Average will fall to 100 by next month?"

Them: "That's also a ridiculous question."

Us: "You don't realize it, but you just created a stock market forecast. Your forecast is that you expect the stock market DJIA to be between 100 and 10,000 next month!"

Someone trying to use this forecast to invest money may not find the forecast range useful, but that is because the limits are wide, not because the forecast is wrong.

The preceding scenario is a useful approach when trying to force estimates from people who distrust forecasts or who find the forecasting procedure difficult. In using the questionnaire procedure, the extremes can be brought closer and closer together until the person being questioned stops the process. Although making guesses or forcing extreme boundaries seems crude, nonetheless they provide a learning opportunity. Once convinced forecasting is possible and valuable, better techniques than guessing can be employed, though we never want to underestimate guessing.

We've just illustrated a forecast range. What about the average, or the single number most people believe is the forecast? If the weather reporter forecasts 78 degrees tomorrow and it only reaches 75 degrees, was the forecast wrong?

There are two parts of a forecast—the number itself (often the mean) and the range. If the weather reporter said that the forecast for tomorrow was 78 degrees with a range of 76 to 80 degrees, the 75 degrees is outside that range. If the weather reporter is often outside the range, we can say that the forecasting technique is probably wrong. We discuss the issue of forecast errors in this chapter under "Forecast Errors" and also under "Linear Regression Analysis."

---

[1] We make these comments ourselves sometimes, but we do it to make an issue, not state a fact.

Most businesses use a standard forecasting technique of the type discussed in this chapter.

Forecasts are very important to every business organization and for every significant management decision. Forecasting is the basis of corporate long-run planning. In the functional areas of finance and accounting, forecasts provide the basis for budgetary planning and cost control. Marketing relies on sales forecasting to plan new products, compensate sales personnel, and make other key decisions. Production and operations personnel use forecasts to make periodic decisions involving process selection, capacity planning, facility layout; and for continual decisions about production planning, scheduling, and inventory.

Bear in mind that a perfect forecast is usually an impossibility. There are simply too many factors in the business environment that cannot be predicted with certainty. Therefore, rather than search for the perfect forecast, what is far more important is to establish the practice of continual review of forecasts and to learn to live with inaccurate forecasts. This is not to say that we should not try to improve the forecasting model or methodology, but that we should try to find and use the best forecasting method available, *within reason.*

When forecasting, a good strategy is to use two or three methods and look at them for the commonsense view. Are there expected changes in the general economy that will affect the forecast? Are there changes in industrial and private consumer behaviors? Will there be a shortage of essential complementary items? Continual review and updating in light of new data are basic to successful forecasting. Learning to live with forecast inaccuracy is an unavoidable requirement of most production systems and is accomplished by having a flexible production planning system and competent production managers.   In this chapter we look at *qualitative* and *quantitative* forecasting and concentrate primarily on several quantitative time series techniques. We cover in some depth: moving averages, linear regression, trends, seasonal ratios (including deseasonalization), and focused forecasting. We also discuss sources and measurements of errors.

7.1 DEMAND MANAGEMENT

The purpose of demand management is to coordinate and control all of the sources of demand so that the productive system can be used efficiently and the product delivered on time.

Where does the demand for a firm's product or service come from, and what can a firm do about it? There are two basic sources of demand—dependent demand and independent demand. *Dependent demand* is the demand for a product or service that is caused by the demand for other products or services. For example, if a firm sells 1,000 tricycles, there is no question that 1,000 front wheels and 2,000 rear wheels are needed. This type of internal demand does not need a forecast, simply a tabulation. As to how many tricycles the firm might sell, this is called *independent demand* because its demand is independent or does not depend on the demand for other products.[2] We discuss dependence and independence more fully in Chapters 13 and 14.

There isn't too much a firm can do about dependent demand. It must be met (although the product or service can be purchased rather than produced internally). There's a lot that a firm can do about independent demand, if it wants to. The firm can

1. *Take an active role to influence demand.* The firm can apply pressure on its sales force, it can offer incentives both to customers and to its own personnel, it can wage campaigns to sell products, and it can cut prices. These actions can increase demand. Conversely, demand can be decreased through price increases or reduced sales efforts.

2. *Take a passive role and simply respond to demand.* There are several reasons a firm may not try to change demand but simply accept what happens. If a firm is running at full capacity it may not want to do anything about demand. Other reasons are a firm may be powerless to change demand because of the expense to advertise; the market may be fixed in size and static; or that demand is beyond their control (e.g, sole supplier). There are other competitive reasons, legal reasons, environmental reasons, and ethical and moral reasons why market demand is passively accepted.

A great deal of coordination is required to manage these dependent and independent, and active and passive demands. These demands originate both internally and externally in the form of new product sales from marketing, repair parts for previously sold products from product service, restocking from the factory warehouses, and supply items for manufacturing. In this chapter, our primary interest is in forecasting for independent items.

7.2 TYPES OF FORECASTING

Forecasting can be classified into four basic types—*qualitative, time series analysis, causal relationships, and simulation.*

Qualitative techniques are subjective or judgmental and are based on estimates and opinions. **Time series analysis,** the primary focus of this chapter, is based on the idea that data relating to past demand can be used to predict future demand. Past data may include several components, such as trend, seasonal, or cyclical influences, and is described in the following section. Causal forecasting, which we discuss using the linear regression technique, assumes that demand is related to some underlying factor or factors in the environment. Simulation models allow the forecaster to run through a range of assumptions about the condition of the forecast. Exhibit 7.1 briefly

---

[2] There are obviously other product relationships such as complimentary products, causal relationships, and so forth.

EXHIBIT 7.1   Forecasting Techniques and Common Models

I. Qualitative   Subjective; judgmental. Based on estimates and opinions.

Delphi method   Group of experts responds to questionnaire. A moderator compiles results and formulates new questionnaire again submitted to the group. Thus, there is a learning process for the group as they receive new information and there is no influence of group pressure or dominating individual.

Market research   Sets out to collect data in a variety of ways (surveys, interviews, etc.) to test hypotheses about the market. This is typically used to forecast long-range and new-product sales.

Panel consensus   Free open exchange at meetings. The idea is that discussion by the group will produce better forecasts than any one individual. Participants may be executives, salespeople, or customers.

Historical analogy   Ties what is being forecast to a similar item. Important in planning new products where a forecast may be derived by using the history of a similar product.

Grass roots   Derives a forecast by compiling input from those at the end of the hierarchy who deal with what is being forecast. For example, an overall sales forecast may be derived by combining inputs from each salesperson, who is closest to his or her own territory.

II. Time series analysis   Based on the idea that the history of occurrences over time can be used to predict the future.

Simple moving average   A time period containing a number of data points is averaged by dividing the sum of the point values by the number of points. Each, therefore, has equal influence.

Weighted moving average   Specific points may be weighted more or less than the others, as seen fit by experience.

Exponential smoothing   Recent data points are weighted more with weighting declining exponentially as data becomes older.

Regression analysis   Fits a straight line to past data generally relating the data value to time. Most common fitting technique is least squares.

Box Jenkins technique   Very complicated but apparently the most accurate statistical technique available. Relates a class of statistical models to data and fits the model to the time series by using Bayesian posterior distributions.

Shiskin time series   (Also called X-11). Developed by Julius Shiskin of the Census Bureau. An effective method to decompose a time series into seasonals, trends, and irregular. It needs at least three years of history. Very good in identifying turning points, for example, in company sales.

Trend projections   Fits a mathematical trend line to the data points and projects it into the future.

III. Causal   Tries to understand the system underlying and surrounding the item being forecast. For example, sales may be affected by advertising, quality, and competitors.

Regression analysis   Similar to least squares method in time series but may contain multiple variables. Basis is that forecast is caused by the occurrence of other events.

Econometric models   Attempts to describe some sector of the economy by a series of interdependent equations.

Input/output models   Focuses on sales of each industry to other firms and governments. Indicates the changes in sales that a producer industry might expect because of purchasing changes by another industry.

Leading indicators   Statistics that move in the same direction as the series being forecast but move before the series, such as an increase in the price of gasoline indicating a future drop in the sale of large cars.

IV. Simulation models   Dynamic models, usually computer based, that allow the forecaster to make assumptions about the internal variables and external environment in the model. Depending on the variables in the model, the forecaster may ask such questions as: What would happen to my forecast if price increased by 10 percent? What effect would a mild national recession have on my forecast?

describes a variety of the four basic types of forecasting models. In this chapter we discuss the four time series analysis methods in the exhibit and the first of the causal techniques.

7.3 COMPONENTS OF DEMAND

In most cases, the demand for products or services can be broken down into six components: average demand for the period, a trend, seasonal influence, cyclical elements, random variation, and autocorrelation. Exhibit 7.2 illustrates a demand over a four-year period, showing the average, trend, and seasonal components, and randomness around the smoothed demand curve.

Cyclical factors are more difficult to determine since the time span may be unknown or the cause of the cycle may not be considered. Cyclical influence on demand may come from such occurrences as political elections, war, economic conditions, or sociological pressures.

Random variations are caused by chance events. Statistically, when all the known causes for demand (average, trend, seasonal, cyclical, and autocorrelative) are subtracted from the total demand, what remains is the unexplained portion of demand. If one is unable to identify the cause of this remainder, it is assumed to be purely random chance.

Autocorrelation denotes the persistence of occurrence. More specifically, the value expected at any point is highly correlated with its own past values. In waiting line theory, the length of a waiting line is highly autocorrelated. That is, if a line is relatively long at one time, then shortly after that time one would expect the line still to be long.

EXHIBIT 7.2   Historical Product Demand Consisting of a Growth Trend and Seasonal Demand

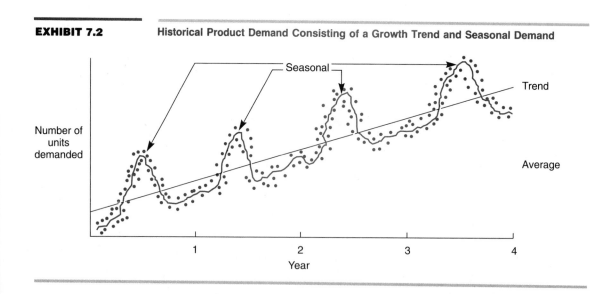

When the demand is random, the demand from one week to another may vary widely. Where high autocorrelation exists, the demand is not expected to change very much from one week to the next.

Trend lines are the usual starting point in developing a forecast. These trend lines are then adjusted for seasonal effects, cyclical, and any other expected events that may influence the final forecast. Exhibit 7.3 shows four of the most common types of trends. A linear trend is obviously a straight continuous relationship. An S-curve is typical of a product growth and maturity cycle.

EXHIBIT 7.3   **Common Types of Trends**

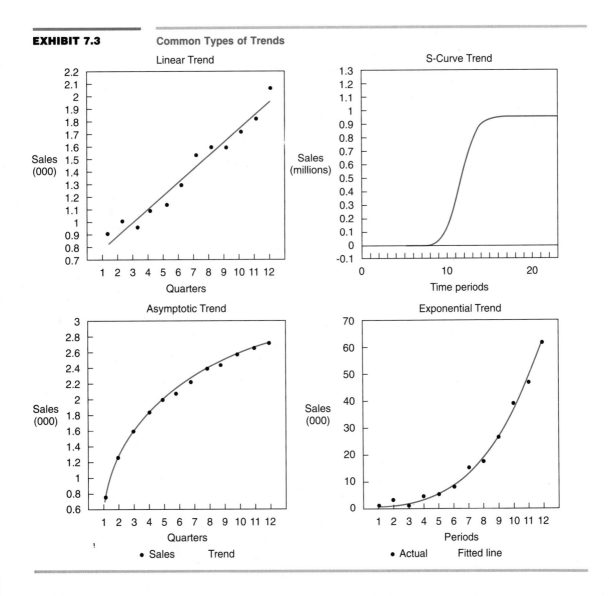

The most important point in the S-curve is where the trend changes from a slow growth to a fast growth, or from fast to slow. An asymptotic trend starts with the highest demand growth at the beginning which then tapers off. Such a curve could happen when a firm enters an existing market with the objective of saturating and capturing a large share of the market. An exponential curve is common in products with explosive growth. The exponential trend suggests that sales will continue to increase—an assumption that may not be safe to make.

7.4 TIME SERIES ANALYSIS

Time series forecasting models try to predict the future based on past data. For example, sales figures collected for each of the past six weeks can be used to forecast sales for the seventh week. Quarterly sales figures collected for the past several years can be used to forecast future quarters. Even though both examples contain sales, different forecasting time series models would likely be used for forecasting.

Exhibit 7.4 shows the time series models and some of their characteristics. For comparison we've also included one qualitative and one causal model. Note that the moving averages and exponential smoothing are the best and easiest to use for short-term forecasting with little data required and provide average results. The long-term models are more complex, requiring much more data input, and provide high accuracy. While recognizing that terms such as *short, medium,* and *long* are relative to the context in which they are used, in business forecasting short term usually refers to under three months, medium term to three months to two years, and long term to greater than two years. In general, the short-term models compensate for random variation and adjust for short-term changes (such as consumers' responses to a new product). Medium-term forecasts are useful for seasonal effects, and long-term models detect general trends and are especially useful in identifying major turning points.

Which forecasting model a firm should choose depends on:

1. Time horizon to forecast.
2. Data availability.
3. Accuracy required.
4. Size of forecasting budget.
5. Availability of qualified personnel.

In selecting a forecasting model, there are other issues such as the firm's degree of flexibility (the greater the ability to react quickly to changes, the less accurate the forecast needs to be). Another item is the consequence of a bad forecast. If a large capital investment decision is to be based on a forecast, it should be a good forecast.

EXHIBIT 7.4

Comparison of
Forecasting
Techniques

Technique	Time Horizon	Model Complexity	Model Accuracy	Data Requirements
I. Qualitative forecasts	Long	High	Varies	High
II. Time series				
Moving averages	Short	Very low	Medium	Low
Exponential smoothing	Short	Low	Fair	Very low
Box Jenkins	Short	Very high	High	High
Linear regression	Long	Medium high	Medium high	High
III. Causal				
Regression analysis	Long	Fairly high	High	High

Simple Moving Average

When demand for a product is neither growing nor declining rapidly, and if it does not have seasonal characteristics, a moving average can be useful in removing the random fluctuations for forecasting. Although **moving averages** are frequently centered, it is more convenient to use past data to predict the following period directly. To illustrate, a centered five-month average of January, February, March, April, and May gives an average centered on March. However, all five months of data must already exist. If our objective is to forecast for June, we must project our moving average—by some means—from March to June. If the average is not centered but is at the forward end, we can forecast more easily, though perhaps we lose some accuracy. Thus if we want to forecast June with a five-month moving average, we can take the average of January, February, March, April, and May. When June passes, the forecast for July would be the average of February, March, April, May, and June. This is the way Exhibits 7.5 and 7.6 were computed.

Although it is important to select the best period for the moving average, there are several conflicting effects of different period lengths: the longer the moving-average period, the greater the random elements are smoothed (which may be desirable in many cases). However, if there is a trend in the data—either increasing or decreasing—the moving average has the adverse characteristic of lagging the trend. Therefore, while a shorter time span produces more oscillation, there is a closer following of the trend. Conversely, a longer time span gives a smoother response but lags the trend.

Exhibit 7.6, a plot of the data in Exhibit 7.5, illustrates the effects of various lengths of the period of a moving average. We see that the growth trend levels off at about the 23rd week. The three-week moving average responds better in following this change than the nine-week, although overall, the nine-week average is smoother.

The main disadvantage in calculating a moving average is that all individual elements must be carried as data since a new forecast period involves adding new data and dropping the earliest data. For a three- or six-period moving

EXHIBIT 7.5

Forecast Demand
Based on a Three-
and a Nine-Week
Simple Moving
Average

Week	Demand	3 Week	9 Week	Week	Demand	3 Week	9 Week
1	800			16	1,700	2,200	1,811
2	1,400			17	1,800	2,000	1,800
3	1,000			18	2,200	1,833	1,811
4	1,500	1,067		19	1,900	1,900	1,911
5	1,500	1,300		20	2,400	1,967	1,933
6	1,300	1,333		21	2,400	2,167	2,011
7	1,800	1,433		22	2,600	2,233	2,111
8	1,700	1,533		23	2,000	2,467	2,144
9	1,300	1,600		24	2,500	2,333	2,111
10	1,700	1,600	1,367	25	2,600	2,367	2,167
11	1,700	1,567	1,467	26	2,200	2,367	2,267
12	1,500	1,567	1,500	27	2,200	2,433	2,311
13	2,300	1,633	1,556	28	2,500	2,333	2,311
14	2,300	1,833	1,644	29	2,400	2,300	2,378
15	2,000	2,033	1,733	30	2,100	2,367	2,378

EXHIBIT 7.6   **Moving Average Forecast of Three- and Nine-Week Periods versus Actual Demand**

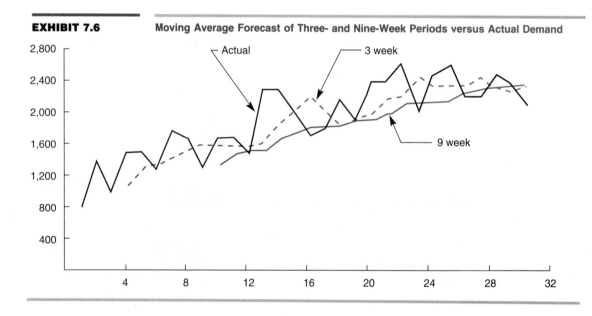

average, this is not too severe; however, plotting a 60-day moving average for the usage of each of 20,000 items in inventory would involve a significant amount of data.

Weighted Moving Average

Whereas the simple moving average gives equal weight to each component of the moving-average database, a weighted moving average allows any weights to be placed on each element, providing, of course, that the sum of all weights equals one. For example, a department store may find that in a four-month period the best forecast is derived by using 40 percent of the actual sales for the most recent month, 30 percent of two months ago, 20 percent of three months ago, and 10 percent of four months ago. If actual sales experience was as follows,

Month 1	Month 2	Month 3	Month 4	Month 5
100	90	105	95	?

the forecast for month 5 would be:

$$F_5 = 0.40(95) + 0.30(105) + 0.20(90) + 0.10(100)$$
$$= 38 + 31.5 + 18 + 10$$
$$= 97.5$$

Suppose sales for month 5 actually turned out to be 110; then the forecast for month 6 would be:

$$F_6 = 0.40(110) + 0.30(95) + 0.20(105) + 0.10(90)$$
$$= 44 + 28.5 + 21 + 9$$
$$= 102.5$$

The weighted moving average has a definite advantage over the simple moving average in being able to vary the effects of past data. However, it is more inconvenient and costly to use.

Exponential Smoothing

In the previous methods of forecasting (simple and weighted moving average), the major drawback is the need to continually carry a large amount of historical data. (This is also true for regression analysis techniques, covered in the next section.) As each new piece of data is added in these methods, the oldest observation is dropped, and the new forecast is calculated. In many applications (perhaps in most), the most recent occurrences are more indicative of the future than those in the more distant past. If this premise is valid—that the importance of data diminishes as the past becomes more distant—then **exponential smoothing** may be the most logical and easiest method to use.

The reason this is called "exponential smoothing" is because each increment in the past is decreased by $(1 - \alpha)$, or

		Weighting at $\alpha = 0.05$
Most recent weighting	$= \alpha(1 - \alpha)^0$	0.0500
Data 1 time period older	$= \alpha(1 - \alpha)^1$	0.0475
Data 2 time periods older	$= \alpha(1 - \alpha)^2$	0.0451
Data 3 time periods older	$= \alpha(1 - \alpha)^3$	0.0429

Therefore, the exponents $0,1,2,3 \ldots$, etc. give it its name.

Exponential smoothing is the most used of all forecasting techniques. It is an integral part of virtually all computerized forecasting programs, and is widely used in ordering inventory in retail firms, wholesale companies, and service agencies.

The most comprehensive coverage of exponential smoothing is presented in a paper by Everette Gardner.[3] Not only does he trace the history of the development of exponential smoothing from its development somewhere during the time of World War II, but he also critically comments on the merits of various models and challenges or discredits some models based on his own and others' work.

The major reasons that exponential smoothing techniques have become so well accepted are

1. Exponential models are surprisingly accurate.
2. Formulating an exponential model is relatively easy.
3. The user can understand how the model works.
4. There is very little computation required to use the model.
5. Computer storage requirements are small because of the limited use of historical data.
6. Tests for accuracy as to how well the model is performing are easy to compute.

In the exponential smoothing method, only three pieces of data are needed to forecast the future: the most recent forecast, the actual demand that occurred for that forecast period, and a **smoothing constant alpha** (α). This smoothing constant determines the level of smoothing and the speed of reaction to differences between forecasts and actual occurrences. The value for the constant is arbitrary and is determined both by the nature of the product and the manager's sense of what constitutes a good response rate. For example, if a firm produced a standard item with relatively stable demand, the reaction rate to differences between actual and forecast demand would tend to be small, perhaps just a few percentage points. However, if the firm were experiencing growth, it would be desirable to have a higher reaction rate, to

---

[3] Everette S. Gardner, Jr., "Exponential Smoothing: The State of the Art," *Journal of Forecasting* 4, no. 1 (March 1985).

give greater importance to recent growth experience. The more rapid the growth, the higher the reaction rate should be. Sometimes, users of the simple moving average switch to exponential smoothing but like to keep the forecasts about the same as the simple moving average. In this case, α is approximated by $2 \div (n + 1)$ where n was the number of time periods.

The equation for a single exponential smoothing forecast is simply

$$F_t = F_{t-1} + \alpha(A_{t-1} - F_{t-1})$$

where

F_t = The exponentially smoothed forecast for period t

F_{t-1} = The exponentially smoothed forecast made for the prior period

A_{t-1} = The actual demand in the prior period

α = The desired response rate, or smoothing constant

This equation states that the new forecast is equal to the old forecast plus a portion of the error (the difference between the previous forecast and what actually occurred).[4]

To demonstrate the method, assume that the long-run demand for the product under study is relatively stable and a smoothing constant (α) of 0.05 is considered appropriate. If the exponential method were used as a continuing policy, a forecast would have been made for last month.[5] Assume that last month's forecast (F_{t-1}) was 1,050 units. If 1,000 actually were demanded, rather than 1,050, the forecast for this month would be:

$$
\begin{aligned}
F_t &= F_{t-1} + \alpha(A_{t-1} - F_{t-1}) \\
&= 1,050 + 0.05(1,000 - 1,050) \\
&= 1,050 + 0.05(-50) \\
&= 1,047.5 \text{ units}
\end{aligned}
$$

Because the smoothing coefficient is small, the reaction of the new forecast to an error of 50 units is to decrease the next month's forecast by only 2½ units.

Single exponential smoothing has the shortcoming of lagging changes in demand. Exhibit 7.7 shows actual data plotted as a smooth curve to show the lagging effects of the exponential forecasts. The forecast lags during an increase or decrease, but overshoots when a change in the direction occurs. Note that the higher the value of alpha, the more closely the forecast follows the actual. To help in closer tracking of actual demand, a trend factor may be added. What also helps is to adjust the value of alpha. This is termed *adaptive forecasting*. Both trend effects and adaptive forecasting are briefly explained in following sections.

---

[4] Some writers prefer to call F_t a smoothed average.

[5] When exponential smoothing is first introduced, the initial forecast or starting point may be obtained by using a simple estimate or an average of preceding periods.

EXHIBIT 7.7

Exponential Forecasts versus Actual Demands for Units of a Product over Time Showing the Forecast Lag

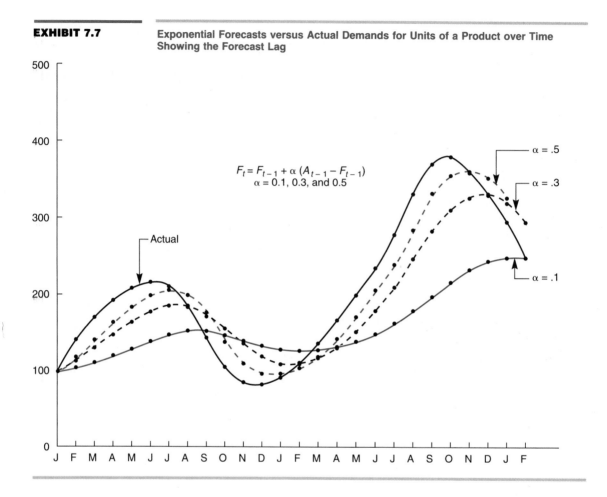

$$F_t = F_{t-1} + \alpha (A_{t-1} - F_{t-1})$$
$$\alpha = 0.1, 0.3, \text{ and } 0.5$$

The simple exponential smoothing model has many applications in OM in addition to inventory control. William Berry, Vincent Mabert, and Myles Marcus have shown that simple exponential smoothing can be valuable in scheduling services, such as bank tellers.[6] Their study showed that the causes of customer demand can be identified and used to improve forecasting (such as by banks located near large employers using known payday schedules). Although this is often done intuitively, the study shows how such forecasting can be routinely used as an ongoing, continually updated planning tool.

[6] William L. Berry, Vincent A. Mabert, and Myles Marcus, "Forecasting Teller Window Demand with Exponential Smoothing," *Journal of the Academy of Management* 22, no. 1 (March 1979), pp. 129–37.

Trend effects in exponential smoothing

Remember that an upward or downward trend in data collected over a sequence of time periods causes the exponential forecast to always lag behind (be above or below) the actual occurrence. Exponentially smoothed forecasts can be corrected somewhat by adding in a trend adjustment. To correct the trend, we need two smoothing constants. In addition to the smoothing constant α, the trend equation also uses a **smoothing constant delta** (δ). The delta reduces the impact of the error which occurs between the actual and the forecast. If both alpha and delta are not included, the trend would overreact to errors.

To get the trend equation going, the first time it is used the trend value must be entered manually. This initial trend value can be an educated guess or a computation based on observed past data.

The equation to compute the forecast including trend (FIT) is

$$FIT_t = F_t + T_t$$

where

$$F_t = FIT_{t-1} + \alpha(A_{t-1} - FIT_{t-1})$$
$$T_t = T_{t-1} + \alpha\delta(A_{t-1} - FIT_{t-1})$$

Example 7.1

Assume an initial starting F_t of 100 units, a trend of 10 units, an alpha of .20, and a delta of .30. If actual demand turned out to be 115 rather than the forecast 100, calculate the forecast for the next period.

Adding the starting forecast and the trend, we have

$$FIT_{t-1} = F_{t-1} + T_{t-1} = 100 + 10 = 110$$

The actual A_{t-1} is given as 115. Therefore,

$$F_t = FIT_{t-1} + \alpha(A_{t-1} - FIT_{t-1})$$
$$= 110 + .2(115 - 110) = 111.0$$
$$T_t = T_{t-1} + \alpha\delta(A_{t-1} - FIT_{t-1})$$
$$= 10 + (.2)(.3)(115 - 110) = 10.3$$
$$FIT_t = F_t + T_t = 111.0 + 10.3 = 121.3$$

If, instead of 121.3, the actual turned out to be 120, the sequence would be repeated and the forecast for the next period would be:

$$F_{t+1} = 121.3 + .2(120 - 121.3) = 121.04$$
$$T_{t+1} = 10.3 + (.2)(.3)(120 - 121.3) = 10.22$$
$$FIT_{t+1} = 121.04 + 10.22 = 131.26$$

Choosing the appropriate value for alpha

Exponential smoothing requires that the smoothing constant alpha (α) be given a value between 0 and 1. If the real demand is stable (such as demand for electricity or food), we would like a small alpha to lessen the effects of short-term or random changes. If the real demand is rapidly increasing or decreasing (such as in fashion items or new small appliances), we would like a large alpha to try to keep up with the change. It would be ideal if we were able to predict which alpha we should use. Unfortunately, two things are going against us; first, it would take some passage of time to determine the best alpha that would fit our actual data. This would be tedious to follow and revise. Second, because demands do change, the alpha we pick this week may need to be revised in the near future. Therefore, we need some automatic method to track and change our alpha values.

Adaptive forecasting.   There are two approaches to controlling the value of alpha. One uses various values of alpha and the other uses a tracking signal.

1. *Two or more predetermined values of alpha.*   Clay Whybark measures the amount of error between the forecast and the actual demand.[7] Depending on the degree of error, different values of alpha are used. Alpha values are not computed but are discrete values selected by Whybark. For example, if the error is large, alpha is 0.8; if the error is small, alpha is 0.2.

2. *Computed values for alpha.*   D. W. Trigg and D. H. Leach use a tracking signal that computes whether the forecast is keeping pace with genuine upward or downward changes in demand (as opposed to random changes).[8] The tracking signal is defined as the exponentially smoothed actual error divided by the exponentially smoothed absolute error. Alpha is set equal to this tracking signal and therefore changes from period to period within the possible range of 0 to 1.

In logic, computing alpha seems simple. In practice, however, it is quite prone to error. There are three exponential equations—one for the single exponentially smoothed forecast as done in the previous section of this chapter, one to compute an exponentially smoothed actual error, and the third to compute the exponentially smoothed absolute error. Thus, the user must keep three equations running in sequence for each period. Further, assumptions must be made during the early periods until the technique has a chance to start computing values. For example, alpha must be given a value for the first two periods until actual data are available. Also, the user must select a smoothing constant in addition to alpha, which is used in the actual and absolute error equations. Clearly, anyone using adaptive forecasting on a regular basis would be wise to use a programmable calculator or a computer.

---

[7] D. Clay Whybark "A Comparison of Adaptive Forecasting Techniques," *The Logistics Transportation Review* 9, no. 1 (1973), pp. 13–26.

[8] D. W. Trigg and D. H. Leach, "Exponential Smoothing with an Adaptive Response Rate," *Operational Research Quarterly* 18 (1967), pp. 53–59.

Forecast Errors

When we use the word *error,* we are referring to the difference between the forecast value and what actually occurred. So long as the forecast value is within the confidence limits, as we discuss later in "Measurement of Error," this is not really an error. However, common usage refers to the difference as an error.

Demand for a product is generated through the interaction of a number of factors too complex to describe accurately in a model. Therefore, all forecasts certainly contain some error. In discussing forecast errors, it is convenient to distinguish between *sources of error* and the *measurement of error.*

Sources of Error

Errors can come from a variety of sources. One common source that many forecasters are unaware of is caused by projecting past trends into the future. For example, when we talk about statistical errors in regression analysis, we are referring to the deviations of observations from our regression line. It is common to attach a confidence band (i.e., statistical control limits, described in Chapter 5), to the regression line to reduce the unexplained error. However, when we then use this regression line as a forecasting device by projecting it into the future, the error may not be correctly defined by the projected confidence band. This is because the confidence interval is based on past data; it may or may not hold for projected data points and therefore cannot be used with the same confidence. In fact, experience has shown that the actual errors tend to be greater than those predicted from forecast models.

Errors can be classified as bias or random. *Bias errors* occur when a consistent mistake is made. Sources of bias are failing to include the right variables; using the wrong relationships among variables; employing the wrong trend line; mistakenly shifting the seasonal demand from where it normally occurs; and the existence of some undetected secular trend.

Random errors can be defined as those that cannot be explained by the forecast model being used. There is a bit of irony in this statement, though, since, if one desires to minimize the error in explaining past data, a sophisticated model can be used, such as a Fourier series with a large number of terms. While this can reduce the forecasting model's error on the data to almost zero, it may do no better in forecasting future demand than a simpler model with a higher error.

Measurement of Error

Several of the common terms used to describe the degree of error are *standard error, mean squared error* (or *variance*), and *mean absolute deviation.* In addition, tracking signals may be used to indicate the existence of any positive or negative bias in the forecast.

Standard error is discussed in the section on linear regression in this chapter. Since the standard error is the square root of a function, it is often more convenient to use the function itself. This is called the mean square error, or variance.

The **mean absolute deviation (MAD)** was in vogue in the past but subsequently was ignored in favor of standard deviation and standard error measures. In recent years, MAD has made a comeback because of its simplicity and usefulness in obtaining tracking signals. MAD is the average error in the forecasts, using absolute values. It is valuable because MAD, like the standard deviation, measures the dispersion of some observed value from some expected value.

MAD is computed using the differences between the actual demand and the forecast demand without regard to sign. It is equal to the sum of the absolute deviations divided by the number of data points, or, stated in equation form,

$$\text{MAD} = \frac{\sum\limits_{t=1}^{n} \left| A_t - F_t \right|}{n}$$

where

t = Period number
A = Actual demand for the period
F = Forecast demand for the period
n = Total number of periods
$|\ |$ = A symbol used to indicate the absolute value disregarding positive and negative signs

When the errors that occur in the forecast are normally distributed (the usual case), the mean absolute deviation relates to the standard deviation as

1 standard deviation = $\sqrt{\dfrac{\pi}{2}} \times$ MAD, or approximately 1.25 MAD.

Conversely,

1 MAD = 0.8 standard deviation

The standard deviation is the larger measure. If the MAD of a set of points was found to be 60 units, then the standard deviation would be 75 units. And, in the usual statistical manner, if control limits were set at plus or minus 3 standard deviations (or ± 3.75 MADs), then 99.7 percent of the points would fall within these limits.

A **tracking signal** is a measurement that indicates whether the forecast average is keeping pace with any genuine upward or downward changes in demand. As used in forecasting, the tracking signal is the *number* of mean

EXHIBIT 7.8

A Normal Distribution with a Mean = 0 and a MAD = 1

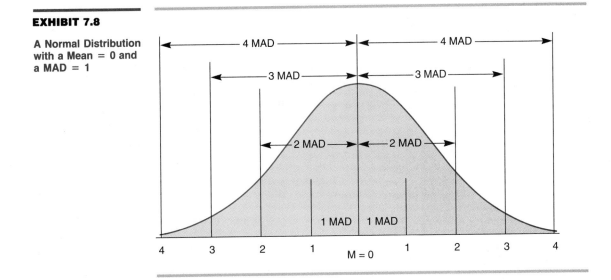

EXHIBIT 7.9

Computing the Mean Absolute Deviation (MAD), the Running Sum of Forecast Errors (RSFE), and the Tracking Signal from Forecast and Actual Data

Month	Demand Forecast	Actual	Deviation	(RSFE)	Abs Dev	Sum of Abs Dev	MAD*	TS = $\frac{RSFE†}{MAD}$
1	1,000	950	−50	−50	50	50	50	−1
2	1,000	1,070	+70	+20	70	120	60	.33
3	1,000	1,100	+100	+120	100	220	73.3	1.64
4	1,000	960	−40	+80	40	260	65	1.2
5	1,000	1,090	+90	+170	90	350	70	2.4
6	1,000	1,050	+50	+220	50	400	66.7	3.3

*Mean absolute deviation (MAD). For Month 6, MAD = 400 ÷ 6 = 66.7.
†Tracking signal = $\frac{RSFE}{MAD}$. For Month 6, TS = $\frac{RSFE}{MAD} = \frac{220}{66.7} = 3.3$ MADs.

absolute deviations that the forecast value is above or below the actual occurrence. Exhibit 7.8 shows a normal distribution with a mean of zero and a MAD equal to one. Thus, if computing the tracking signal and finding it equal to minus 2, we can notice that the forecast model is providing forecasts that are quite a bit above the mean of the actual occurrences.

A tracking signal can be calculated using the arithmetic sum of forecast deviations divided by the mean absolute deviation. Exhibit 7.9 illustrates the procedure for computing MAD and the tracking signal for a six-month period where the forecast had been set at a constant 1,000 and the actual demands that occurred are as shown. In this example, the forecast, on the average, was off

EXHIBIT 7.10

A Plot of the
Tracking Signals
Calculated in
Exhibit 7.9

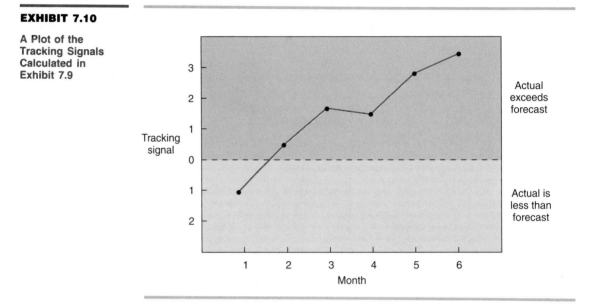

by 66.7 units and the tracking signal was equal to 3.3 mean absolute deviations.

We can get a better feel for what the MAD and tracking signal mean by plotting the points on a graph. While not completely legitimate from a sample size standpoint, we plotted each month in Exhibit 7.10 to show the drifting of the tracking signal. Note that it drifted from minus 1 MAD to plus 3.3 MADs. This happened because actual demand was greater than the forecast in four of the six periods. If the actual demand doesn't fall below the forecast to offset the continual positive RSFE, the tracking signal would continue to rise and we would conclude that assuming a demand of 1,000 is a bad forecast.

Acceptable limits for the tracking signal depend on the size of the demand being forecast (high-volume or high-revenue items should be monitored frequently) and the amount of personnel time available (narrower acceptable limits cause more forecasts to be out of limits and therefore require more time to investigate). Exhibit 7.11 shows the area within the control limits for a range of zero to four MADs.

In a perfect forecasting model, the sum of the actual forecast errors would be zero; that is, the errors that result in overestimates should be offset by errors that are underestimates. The tracking signal would then also be zero, indicating an unbiased model, neither leading nor lagging the actual demands.

Often, MAD is used to forecast errors. It might then be desirable to make the MAD more sensitive to recent data. A useful technique to do this is to compute an exponentially smoothed MAD as a forecast for the next period's error range. The procedure is similar to single exponential smoothing covered

EXHIBIT 7.11

The Percentages of Points Included within the Control Limits for a Range of 0 to 4 MADs

CONTROL LIMITS

Number of MADs	Related Number of Standard Deviations	Percentage of Points Lying within Control Limits
±1	0.798	57.048
±2	1.596	88.946
±3	2.394	98.334
±4	3.192	99.856

earlier in this chapter. The value of the MAD forecast is to provide a range of error; in the case of inventory control, this is useful in setting safety stock levels.

$$\text{MAD}_t = \alpha \, | \, A_{t-1} - F_{t-1} \, | + (1 - \alpha)\text{MAD}_{t-1}$$

where

MAD_t = Forecast MAD for the tth period

α = Smoothing constant (normally in the range of 0.05 to 0.20)

A_{t-1} = Actual demand in the period t-1

F_{t-1} = Forecast demand for period t-1

Linear Regression Analysis

Regression can be defined as a functional relationship between two or more correlated variables and is used to predict one variable given the other. The relationship is usually developed from observed data. Linear regression refers to the special class of regression where the relationship between variables forms a straight line.

The linear regression line is of the form $Y = a + bX$, where Y is the value of the dependent variable that we are solving for, a is the Y intercept, b is the slope, and X is the independent variable (in time series analysis, X is units of time).

Linear regression is useful for long-term forecasting of major occurrences and aggregate planning. For example, linear regression would be very useful to forecast demands for product families. Even though demand for individual products within a family may vary widely during a time period, demand for the total product family is surprisingly smooth.

The major restriction in using **linear regression forecasting** is, as the name implies, that past data and future projections are assumed to fall about a straight line. While this does limit its application, sometimes, if we use a shorter period of time, linear regression analysis can still be used. For example, if a growth trend is present, if we use a 10- or 20-year period, the trend is lost in all that data and the next year's projection will be low. If we use only the past several years however, the forecast will be more accurate. Part of the linear regression procedure develops an estimate of how well the line fits the data.

Linear regression is used for both time series forecasting and for causal relationship forecasting. When the dependent variable (usually the vertical axis on a graph) changes as a result of time (plotted as the horizontal axis) it is time series analysis. If one variable changes because of the change in another variable, this is a causal relationship (such as the number of deaths from lung cancer increasing with the number of people who smoke).

We use the following example several times in this chapter to compare forecasting models and types of analysis. We use it for hand fitting a line, for the least squares analysis, and for a decomposition example.

Hand fitting a trend line

A firm's sales for a product line during the 12 quarters of the past three years were as follows:

Quarter	Sales
1	600
2	1,550
3	1,500
4	1,500
5	2,400
6	3,100
7	2,600
8	2,900
9	3,800
10	4,500
11	4,000
12	4,900

The firm wants to forecast each quarter of the fourth year, that is, quarters 13, 14, 15, and 16. In hand fitting a curve, we plot the data and use simple eyeballing or OHA (Ocular Heuristic Approximation). The procedure is quite simple: lay a straightedge (clear plastic rulers are nice) across the data points until the line seems to fit well, and draw the line. This is the regression line. The next step is to determine the intercept a and the slope b.

Exhibit 7.12 shows a plot of the data and the straight line which we drew through the points. The intercept a, where the line cuts the vertical axis appears to be about 400. The slope b is the "rise" divided by the "run," or the change in the height of some portion of the line divided by the number of units in the horizontal axis. Any two points can be used, but two points some distance apart give the best accuracy because of the errors in reading values from the graph. We use values for the 1st and 12th quarters.

In Exhibit 7.12, by reading from the points on the line the Y values for quarter 1 and quarter 12 are about 750 and 4,950. Therefore,

$$b = (4{,}950 - 750) / (12 - 1) = 382$$

EXHIBIT 7.12

A Hand Fitting Regression

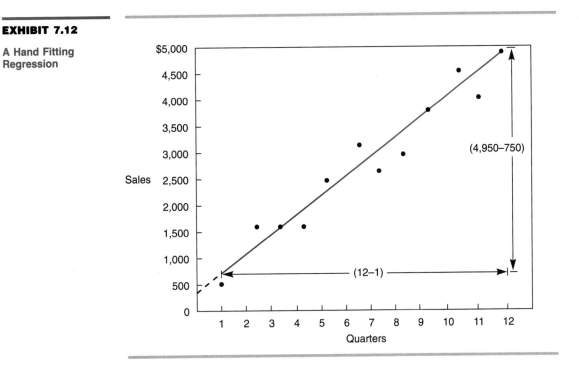

The hand fitted regression equation is therefore,

$$Y = 400 + 382 X$$

The forecasts for quarters 13 through 16 are

Quarter	Forecast
13	400 + 382(13) = 5,366
14	400 + 382(14) = 5,748
15	400 + 382(15) = 6,130
16	400 + 382(16) = 6,512

These forecasts are based on the line only and do not identify nor adjust for elements such as seasonal or cyclical elements.

Least squares method

The equation in the least squares equation for linear regression is the same as we used in our hand fitted example; that is,

$$Y = a + bX$$

where

Y = Dependent variable computed by the equation
y = Dependent variable data point

a = Y intercept

b = Slope of the line

X = Time period

The least squares method tries to fit the line to the data *which minimizes the sum of the squares of the vertical distance* between each data point and its corresponding point on the line. Exhibit 7.12 showed the 12 data points. If a straight line is drawn through the general area of the points, the difference between the point and the line is $y - Y$. Exhibit 7.13 shows these differences. The sum of the squares of the differences between the plotted data points and the line points is

$$(y_1 - Y_1)^2 + (y_2 - Y_2)^2 + \ldots + (y_{12} - Y_{12})^2$$

The best line to use is the one that minimizes this total.

As before, the straight line equation is

$$Y = a + bX$$

Previously we determined a and b from the graph. In the least squares method, the equations for a and b are

EXHIBIT 7.13

Least Squares Regression Line

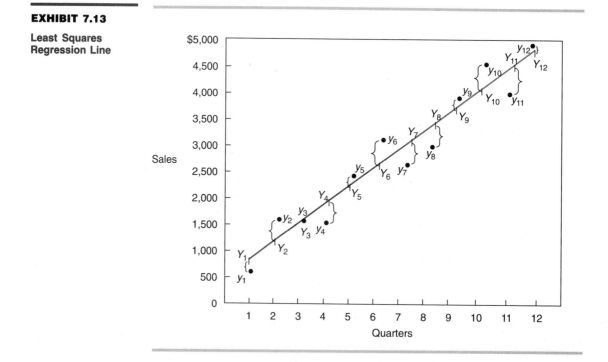

$$a = \overline{Y} - b\overline{X}$$

$$b = \frac{\Sigma XY - n\overline{X} \cdot \overline{Y}}{\Sigma X^2 - n\overline{X}^2}$$

where

a = Y intercept

b = Slope of the line

$\overline{Y}$ = Average of all Ys

$\overline{X}$ = Average of all Xs

X = X value at each data point

y = Y value at each data point

n = Number of data points

Y = Value of the dependent variable computed with the regression equation

Exhibit 7.14 shows these computations carried out for the 12 data points in Exhibit 7.12. Note that the final equation for Y shows an intercept of 441.6 and a slope of 359.6. The slope shows that for every unit change in X, that Y changes by 359.6.

EXHIBIT 7.14

Least Squares Regression Analysis

(1) X	(2) Y	(3) XY	(4) X²	(5) Y²	(6) Y New
1	600	600	1	360,000	801.3
2	1,550	3,100	4	2,402,500	1,160.9
3	1,500	4,500	9	2,250,000	1,520.5
4	1,500	6,000	16	2,250,000	1,880.1
5	2,400	12,000	25	5,760,000	2,239.7
6	3,100	18,600	36	9,610,000	2,599.4
7	2,600	18,200	49	6,760,000	2,959.0
8	2,900	23,200	64	8,410,000	3,318.6
9	3,800	34,200	81	14,440,000	3,678.2
10	4,500	45,000	100	20,250,000	4,037.8
11	4,000	44,000	121	16,000,000	4,397.4
12	4,900	58,800	144	24,010,000	4,757.1
78	33,350	268,200	650	112,502,500	

$\overline{X}$ = 6.5

$\overline{Y}$ = 2,779.17

b = 359.6153

a = 441.6666

Therefore: $Y = 441.66 + 359.6 X$

S_{YX} = 363.9

Strictly based on the equation, forecasts for periods 13 through 16 would be

$$Y_{13} = 441.6 + 359.6 \, (13) = 5,116.4$$
$$Y_{14} = 441.6 + 359.6 \, (14) = 5,476.0$$
$$Y_{15} = 441.6 + 359.6 \, (15) = 5,835.6$$
$$Y_{16} = 441.6 + 359.6 \, (16) = 6,195.2$$

The standard error of estimate, or how well the line fits the data, is[9]

$$S_{YX} = \sqrt{\frac{\sum\limits_{i=1}^{n} (y_i - Y_i)^2}{n - 2}}$$

The standard error of estimate is computed from the first and last columns of Exhibit 7.14:

$$S_{YX} = \sqrt{\frac{(600 - 801.3)^2 + (1.550 - 1160.9)^2 + (1,500 - 1520.5)^2 + \ldots + (4,900 - 4,757.1)^2}{10}}$$

$$S_{YX} = 363.9$$

We discuss the possible existence of seasonal components in the next section on decomposition of a time series.

Decomposition of a Time Series

A *time series* can be defined as chronologically ordered data that may contain one or more components of demand—trend, seasonal, cyclical, autocorrelation, and random. *Decomposition* of a time series means identifying and separating the time series data into these components. In practice, it is relatively easy to identify the trend (even without mathematical analysis, it is usually easy to plot and see the direction of movement) and the seasonal component (by comparing the same period year to year.) It is considerably more difficult to identify the cycles (these may be many months or years long), autocorrelation, and random components (the forecaster usually calls random anything left over that cannot be identified as another component).

When demand contains both seasonal and **trend effects** at the same time, the question is how they relate to each other. In this description, we examine two types of seasonal variation: *additive* and *multiplicative*.

Additive seasonal variation
Additive seasonal variation simply assumes that the seasonal amount is a constant no matter what the trend or average amount is.

---

[9] An equation for the standard error that is often easier to compute is

$$S_{YX} = \sqrt{\frac{\Sigma Y^2 - a\Sigma Y - b\Sigma XY}{n - 2}}$$

EXHIBIT 7.15

Additive and Multiplicative Seasonal Variation Superimposed on Changing Trend

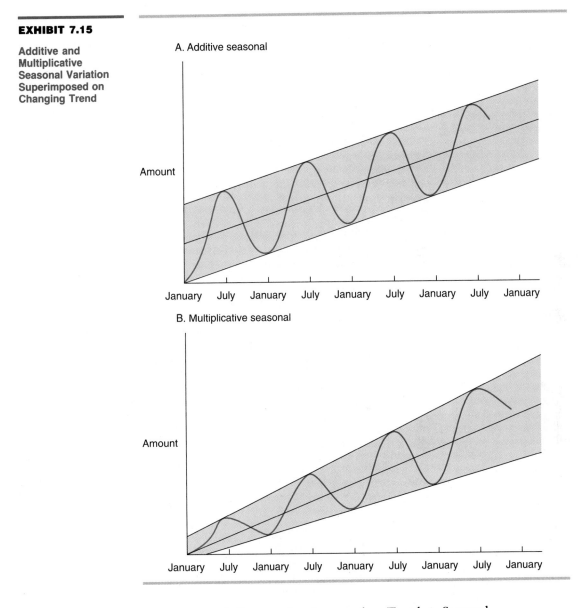

A. Additive seasonal

Amount

January   July   January   July   January   July   January   July   January

B. Multiplicative seasonal

Amount

January   July   January   July   January   July   January   July   January

Forecast including trend and seasonal = Trend + Seasonal

Exhibit 7.15A shows an example of increasing trend with constant seasonal amounts.

Multiplicative seasonal variation
In multiplicative seasonal variation, the trend is multiplied by the seasonal factors.

Forecast including trend and seasonal = Trend × Seasonal factor

Exhibit 7.15B shows the seasonal variation increasing as the trend increases since its size depends on the trend.

The multiplicative seasonal variation is the more useful relationship and is explained in more detail later.

Seasonal factor (or index)

A **seasonal factor** is the amount of correction needed in a time series to adjust for the season of the year.

We usually associate *seasonal* with a period of the year characterized by some particular activity. We use the word *cyclical* to indicate other than annual recurrent periods of repetitive activity.

We show examples where seasonal indexes are determined and used to forecast (1) a simple calculation based on past seasonal data, and (2) the trend and seasonal index from a hand fitted regression line. We follow this with a more formal procedure for the decomposition of data and forecasting using least squares regression.

Example 7.2 Simple proportion

Assume that a firm in past years sold an average 1,000 units of a particular product line each year. On the average, 200 units were sold in the spring, 350 in the summer, 300 in the fall, and 150 in the winter. The seasonal factor (or index) is the ratio of the amount sold during each season divided by the average for all seasons. In this example, the yearly amount divided equally over all seasons is 1,000 ÷ 4 = 250. The seasonal factors therefore are

	Past Sales	Average Sales for Each Season (1,000/4)	Seasonal Factor
Spring	200	250	200/250 = 0.8
Summer	350	250	350/250 = 1.4
Fall	300	250	300/250 = 1.2
Winter	150	250	150/250 = 0.6
Total	1,000		

Using these factors, if we expected the demand for next year to be 1,100 units, we would forecast the demand to occur as:

	Expected Demand for Next Year	Average Sales for Each Season (1,100/4)	Seasonal Factor	Next Year's Seasonal Forecast
Spring		275	× 0.8 =	220
Summer		275	× 1.4 =	385
Fall		275	× 1.2 =	330
Winter		275	× 0.6 =	165
Total	1,100			

The seasonal factor may be periodically updated as new data are available. To illustrate the seasonal factor and the multiplicative seasonal variation, consider the following example:

Example 7.3 Computing trend and seasonal factor from a hand fit straight line

In this example, the problem requires that the trend be computed as well as the seasonal factors. We solve this problem by simply hand fitting a straight line through the data points and measuring the trend and intercept from the graph.

Hand fitting data.   Assume the history of data is as follows:

Quarter	Amount	Quarter	Amount
I—1990	300	I—1991	520
II—1990	200	II—1991	420
III—1990	220	III—1991	400
IV—1990	530	IV—1991	700

First we plot as in Exhibit 7.16 and then fit a straight line through the data simply by eyeballing. The equation for the line is:

$$\text{Trend}_t = 170 + 55t$$

This was derived from the intercept 170 plus a rise of $(610 - 170) \div 8$ periods. Next we can derive a seasonal index by comparing the actual data with the trend line as in Exhibit 7.17. The seasonal factor was developed by averaging the same quarters in each year.

We can compute the 1992 forecast including trend and seasonal factors (FITS) as follows:

$$FITS_t = \text{Trend} \times \text{Seasonal}$$

I—1992	$FITS_9 = [170 + 55(9)]1.25 = 831$
II—1992	$FITS_{10} = [170 + 55(10)]0.78 = 562$
III—1992	$FITS_{11} = [170 + 55(11)]0.69 = 535$
IV—1992	$FITS_{12} = [170 + 55(12)]1.25 = 1{,}038$

Decomposition using least squares regression

Decomposition of a time series means to find the series' basic components of trend, seasonal, and cyclical. Indexes are calculated for seasons and cycles. The forecasting procedure then reverses the process by projecting the trend and adjusting it by the seasonal and cyclical indices, which were determined in the decomposition process. More formally the process is

1. Decompose the time series into its components.
   a. Find seasonal component.
   b. Deseasonalize the demand.
   c. Find trend component.

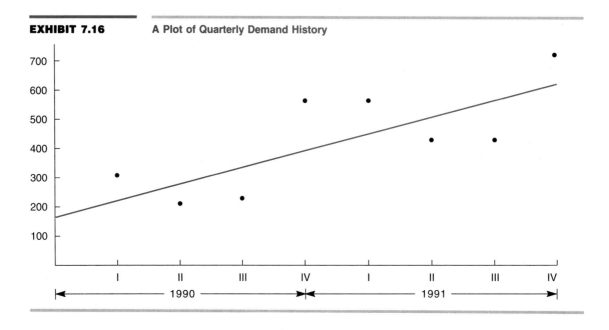

EXHIBIT 7.16

A Plot of Quarterly Demand History

EXHIBIT 7.17

Computing a
Seasonal Factor from
the Actual Data and
Trend Line

Quarter	Actual Amount	From Trend Equation $T_t = 170 + 55t$	Ratio of Actual ÷ Trend	Seasonal Factor (average of same quarters in both years)
1990				
I	300	225	1.33	
II	200	280	.71	I—1.25
III	220	335	.66	II—0.78
IV	530	390	1.36	III—0.69
1991				IV—1.25
I	520	445	1.17	
II	420	500	.84	
III	400	555	.72	
IV	700	610	1.15	

2. Forecast future values of each component.
   a. Project trend component into the future.
   b. Multiply trend component by seasonal component.

Note that the random component is not included in this list. We implicitly remove the random component from the time series when we average as in Step 1. It is pointless to attempt a projection of the random component in Step 2, unless we have information about some unusual event, such as a major labor

EXHIBIT 7.18   Deseasonalized Demand

(1) Period (X)	(2) Quarter	(3) Actual Demand (Y)	(4) Average of the Same Quarters of Each Year	(5) Seasonal Factor	(6) Deseasonalized Demand	(7) X^2 (Col 1)^2	(8) X × Y Col (1) × Col (3)
1	I	600	(600 + 2,400 + 3,800)/3 = 2,266.7	0.82	735.7	1	735.7
2	II	1,550	(1,550 + 3,100 + 4,500)/3 = 3,050	1.10	1,412.4	4	2,824.7
3	III	1,500	(1,500 + 2,600 + 4,000)/3 = 2,700	0.97	1,554.0	9	4,631.9
4	IV	1,500	(1,500 + 2,900 + 4,900)/3 = 3,100	1.12	1,344.8	16	5,379.0
5	I	2,400		0.82	2,942.6	25	14,713.2
6	II	3,100		1.10	2,824.7	36	16,948.4
7	III	2,600		0.97	2,676.2	49	18,733.6
8	IV	2,900		1.12	2,599.9	64	20,798.9
9	I	3,800		0.82	4,659.2	81	41,932.7
10	II	4,500		1.12	4,100.4	100	41,004.1
11	III	4,000		0.97	4,117.3	121	45,290.1
12	IV	4,900		1.12	4,392.9	144	52,714.5
78		33,350		12	33,360.1*	650	265,706.9

$$\bar{X} = \frac{78}{12} = 6.5$$

$$\bar{Y} = 33,350/12 = 2,779.2$$

$$b = \frac{\Sigma XY - n\bar{X}\bar{Y}}{\Sigma X^2 - n\bar{X}^2} = \frac{265,706.9 - 12(6.5)2,779.2}{650 - 12\,(6.5)^2} = 342.2$$

$$a = \bar{Y} - b\bar{X} = 2,779.2 - 342.2(6.5) = 554.9$$

Therefore: $Y = a + bX$
$$Y = 554.9 + 342.2X$$

* Column 3 and Column 6 totals should be equal at 33,350. Differences are due to rounding.

dispute, that could adversely affect product demand (and this would not really be random).

In Exhibit 7.18 we show the decomposition of a time series using least squares regression and the same basic data we used in our previous examples. Each data point corresponds to using a single three-month quarter of the three-year (12-quarter) period. Our objective is to forecast demand for the four quarters of the fourth year.

Step 1.   *Determine the seasonal factor (or index).* Exhibit 7.18 summarizes all of the calculations needed. Column 4 develops an average for the same quarters in the three-year period. For example, the first quarters of the three years are added together and divided by three. A seasonal factor is then derived by dividing that average by the general average for all 12 quarters $\left(\frac{33,350}{12}, \text{ or } 2,779\right)$. These are entered in column 5. Note that the seasonal factors are identical for similar quarters in each year.

Step 2.   *Deseasonalize the original data.* To remove the seasonal effect on the data, we divide the original data by the seasonal factor. This step is called the **deseasonalization of demand** and is shown in Exhibit 7.18 in column 6.

Step 3.   *Develop a least squares regression line for the deseasonalized data.* The purpose here is to develop an equation for the trend line Y, which we then modify with the seasonal factor. The procedure is the same as we used before, that is,

$$Y = a + bX$$

where

$Y =$ Deseasonalized demand
$X =$ Quarter
$a =$ Y intercept
$b =$ Slope of the line

The least squares calculations using Exhibit 7.18 columns 1, 7, and 8 are shown in the lower section of the exhibit. The final deseasonalized equation for our data is $Y = 554.9 + 342.2X$. This straight line is shown on Exhibit 7.19.

EXHIBIT 7.19

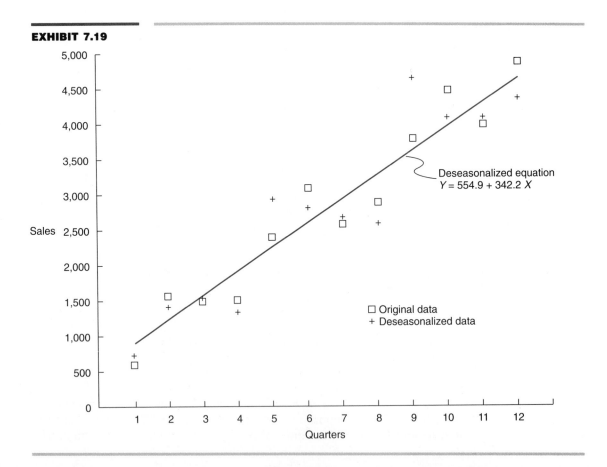

Deseasonalized equation
$Y = 554.9 + 342.2 X$

□ Original data
+ Deseasonalized data

Step 4.   *Project the regression line through the period to be forecast.* Our purpose is to forecast periods 13 through 16. We start by solving the equation for Y at each of these periods (shown in step 5, column 3).

Step 5.   *Create the final forecast by adjusting the regression line by the seasonal factor.* Recall that the Y equation has been deseasonalized. We now reverse the procedure by multiplying the quarterly data we derived by the seasonal factor for that quarter. This is done as follows:

Period	Quarter	Y from Regression Line	Seasonal Factor	Forecast (Y × Seasonal Factor)
13	1	5,003.3	0.82	4,080.7
14	2	5,345.5	1.10	5,866.5
15	3	5,687.7	0.97	5,525.7
16	4	6,029.9	1.12	6,726.0

Our forecast is now complete. The procedure is generally the same as what we did in the hand fit previous example. In the present example, however, we followed a more formal procedure and computed the least squares regression line as well.

Error range

When a straight line is fitted through data points and then used for forecasting, errors can come from two sources: first, there are the usual errors similar to the standard deviation of any set of data; second, there are errors which arise because the line is wrong. Exhibit 7.20 shows this error range. We do not develop the statistics here. To briefly explain why the range broadens, visualize that one line is drawn which has some error in that it slants too steeply upward. Standard errors are then calculated for this line. Now visualize another line that slants too steeply downward. It also has a standard error. The total error range, for this analysis, consists of errors resulting from both lines as well as all other possible lines. We included this exhibit to show how the error range widens as we go further into the future.

7.5 CAUSAL RELATIONSHIP FORECASTING

To be of value for the purpose of forecasting, any independent variable must be a leading indicator. For example, we can expect that an extended period of rainy days will increase the sales of umbrellas and raincoats. The rain causes the sale of rain gear. This is a **causal relationship** where one occurrence causes another. If the causing element is far enough in advance, it can be used as a basis for forecasting. Several days of rain (or even rainy weather forecasts) can form a useful basis to forecast sales of rain gear. Running out of gas while driving down a highway, however, does not provide useful data to forecast that the car will stop. The car will stop, of course, but we would like to know enough in advance in order to do something about it. A "low gas level" warning light, for example, is a good forecasting device.

EXHIBIT 7.20

**Prediction Intervals
for Linear Trend**

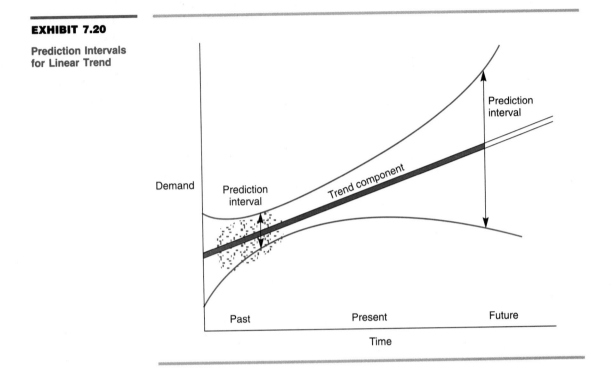

The first step in causal relationship forecasting is to find those occurrences that are really the causes. Often leading indicators are not causal relationships but in some indirect way may suggest that some other things might happen. Other noncausal relationships just seem to exist as a coincidence. One study some years ago showed that the amount of alcohol sold in Sweden was directly proportional to teachers' salaries. Presumably this was a spurious, or false, relationship.

We show just one example of a forecast using a causal relationship.

Example 7.4

The Carpet City Store in Carpenteria has kept records of its sales (in square yards) each year, along with the number of permits for new houses in its area.

Year	Number of Housing Start Permits	Sales (in sq. yds.)
1983	18	13,000
1984	15	12,000
1985	12	11,000
1986	10	10,000
1987	20	14,000
1988	28	16,000
1989	35	19,000
1990	30	17,000
1991	20	13,000

EXHIBIT 7.21

**Causal Relationship:
Sales to Housing
Starts**

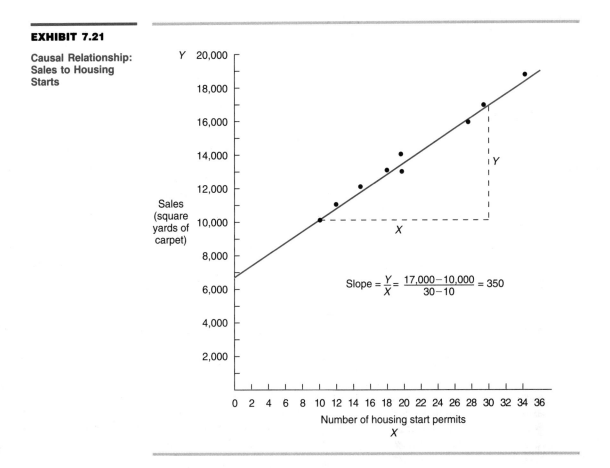

Carpet City's operations manager believes forecasting sales is possible if housing starts are known for that year. First, the data are plotted on Exhibit 7.21, with

X = Number of housing start permits

Y = Sales of carpeting

Since the points appear to be in a straight line, the manager decides to use the linear relationship $Y = a + bX$. We solve this problem by hand fitting a line. However, we could solve for this equation using least squares regression as we did earlier.

Projecting the hand fit line causes it to intercept the Y axis at about 7,000 yards. This could be interpreted as the demand when no new houses are built; that is, probably as replacement for old carpeting. To estimate the slope, two points are selected, such as:

Year	X	Y
1986	10	10,000
1990	30	17,000

From algebra the slope is calculated as:

$$b = \frac{Y(90) - Y(86)}{X(90) - X(86)} = \frac{17,000 - 10,000}{30 - 10} = \frac{7,000}{20} = 350$$

The manager interprets the slope as the average number of square yards of carpet sold for each new house built in the area. The forecasting equation is therefore:

$$Y = 7,000 + 350X$$

Now suppose that there are 25 permits for houses to be built in 1992. The 1992 sales forecast would therefore be:

$$7,000 + 350(25) = 15,750 \text{ square yards}$$

In this problem, the lag between filing the permit with the appropriate agency and the new homeowner coming to Carpet City to buy carpet makes a causal relationship feasible for forecasting.

Multiple Regression Analysis

Another forecasting method is multiple regression analysis, in which a number of variables are considered, together with the effects of each on the item of interest. For example, in the home furnishings field, the effects of the number of marriages, housing starts, disposable income, and the trend can be expressed in a multiple regression equation, as

$$S = B + B_m(M) + B_h(H) + B_i(I) + B_t(T)$$

where

$S =$ Gross sales for year
$B =$ Base sales, a starting point from which other factors have influence
$M =$ Marriages during the year
$H =$ Housing starts during the year
$I =$ Annual disposable personal income
$T =$ Time trend (first year $= 1$, second $= 2$, third $= 3$, and so forth)

B_m, B_h, B_i, and B_t represent the influence on expected sales of the number of marriages and housing starts, income, and trend.

Forecasting by multiple regression is very appropriate when a number of factors influence a variable of interest—in this case, sales. Its difficulty lies with the data gathering, and particularly with the mathematical computation. Fortunately, standard programs for multiple regression analysis are available for most computers, relieving the need for tedious manual calculation.

7.6 FOCUS FORECASTING

Focus forecasting is the creation of Bernie Smith, who claims that this method of forecasting is a revolutionary concept.[10] He uses it primarily in finished-goods inventory management, and he has laid such significant claims to its success that we feel obligated to include a coverage of the topic here. Smith makes a strong and substantiated argument that statistical approaches used in forecasting do not give the best results. He states that simple techniques that work well on past data also prove the best in forecasting the future.

Methodology of Focus Forecasting

Focus forecasting simply tries several rules that seem logical and easy to understand to project the past data into the future. Each of these rules is used in a computer simulation program to actually project demand and then measure how well or how badly that rule performed when compared to what actually happened. Therefore, the two components of the focus forecasting system are (1) several simple forecasting strategies and (2) computer simulation of these strategies on past data.

These are simple, commonsense rules made up and then tested to see whether they should be kept. Examples of simple forecasting strategies could include the following:

1. Whatever we sold in the past three months is what we will probably sell in the next three months.
2. What we sold in the same three-month period last year, we will probably sell in that three-month period this year. (This would account for seasonal effects.)
3. We will probably sell 10 percent more in the next three months than we sold in the last three months.
4. We will probably sell 50 percent more over the next three months than we did for the same three months of last year.
5. Whatever percentage change we had for the past three months this year compared to the same three months last year, will probably be the same percentage change that we will have for the next three months of this year.

These forecasting rules are not hard and fast. If a new rule seems to work well, it is added. If one has not been working well, it is deleted.

The second part of the process is computer simulation. To use the system, a data history should be available; for example, 18 to 24 months of data. The simulation process then uses each of the forecasting strategies to predict some

---

[10] Bernard T. Smith, *Focus Forecasting: Computer Techniques for Inventory Control* (Boston: CBI Publishing, 1984).

recent past data. The strategy that did best in predicting the past is the strategy used to predict the future. Example 7.5 is an exercise used by Smith.[11]

Example 7.5

Exhibit 7.22 shows demands for an 18-month period. (Try to guess what the demand might be for July, August, and September, and compare your guess to the actual data presented later.)

For brevity, we will use only two strategies to demonstrate the method: 1 and 5. In practice, they would all be used.

Using focus forecasting, we first try forecasting strategy 1—whatever we sold in the last three months is what we will probably sell in the next three months. (We are using the terms *demand* and *sales* interchangeably, assuming that demands culminated in actual sales.) We first test this strategy on the past three months; that is,

$$\text{Forecast (April, May, June)} = \text{Demand (January + February + March)}$$
$$= 72 + 90 + 108 = 270$$

Since what actually occurred was 363 (134 + 92 + 137), the forecast was 270/363 = 74 percent; or, in other words, it was 26 percent low.

Let's try another, say strategy 5—whatever percentage change we had over last year in the past three months will probably be the same percentage change we will have over last year in the next three months.

Forecast (April + May + June)

$$= \frac{\text{Demand (January + February + March) this year}}{\text{Demand (January + February + March) last year}} \times$$
$$\text{Demand (April + May + June) last year}$$

$$= \frac{72 + 90 + 108}{6 + 212 + 378} \times (129 + 163 + 96)$$

$$= \frac{270}{596}(388) = 175.77$$

What actually occurred during April, May, and June this year was 363 so the forecast was 175/363, or only 48 percent of the actual demand.

Since strategy 1 was better in predicting the past three months, we use that strategy in predicting July, August, and September of this year. Strategy 1 says that whatever we sold in the last three months is what we will probably sell in the next three months.

$$\text{Forecast (July + August + September)} = \text{Demand (April + May + June)}$$
$$= 134 + 92 + 137$$
$$= 363$$

---

[11] We chose to use this exercise because it is real data from the records of American Hardware Supply Company where Smith was inventory manager. This forecasting exercise has been played by many people: buyers for American Hardware, inventory consultants, and many participants at the national meeting of the American Production and Inventory Control Society. Further, data for the remainder of the year exist that allow for checking the results.

EXHIBIT 7.22

Demand in Units for a Broiler Pan

	Last Year	This Year
January	6	72
February	212	90
March	378	108
April	129	134
May	163	92
June	96	137
July	167	
August	159	
September	201	
October	153	
November	76	
December	30	

EXHIBIT 7.23

Demand in Units for a Broiler Pan

	Last Year	This Year
January	6	72
February	212	90
March	378	108
April	129	134
May	163	92
June	96	137
July	167	120
August	159	151
September	201	86
October	153	113
November	76	97
December	30	40

The actual demand for the period was 357. Exhibit 7.23 shows the completed demand history for this year and serves as a basis for comparison.

Forecasts made using focus forcasting logic are then reviewed and modified (if necessary) by buyers or inventory control personnel who have responsibility over these items. When they see the forecasts made by the computer, they know which method was used and can either accept it or change the forecast if they do not agree. Smith says that about 8 percent of the forecasts are changed by the buyers because they know something that the computer doesn't (such as the cause of a previous large demand, or that the next forecast is too high because a competitor is introducing a competing product).

Smith states that in all the forecast simulations he has run using variations of exponential smoothing, including adaptive smoothing, focus forecasting gave significantly better results.

Developing a Focus Forecasting System

Here are suggestions for developing a focus forecasting system:

1. Don't try to add a seasonality index. Let the forecasting system find that out by itself because, especially with new items, seasonality may not apply until the pipeline is filled and the system is stable. The forecasting strategies can handle it.

2. When a forecast is unusually high or low (such as two or three times the previous period, or the previous year if there is seasonality) print out an indicator such as the letter R telling the person affected by this demand to review it. Don't just disregard unusual demands since they may, in fact, be valid changes in the demand pattern.

3. Let the people who will be using the forecasts (such as buyers or inventory planners) participate in creating the strategies. Smith plays his "can you outguess focus forecasting" game with all the company's buyers. Using two years' data and 2,000 items, focus forecasting makes forecasts for the past six months. Buyers are asked to forecast the past six months using any strategy they prefer. If they are consistently better than the existing forecasting strategies, their strategies are added to the list.

4. Keep the strategies simple. In that way they will be easily understood and trusted by users of the forecast.

In summary, it appears that focus forecasting has significant merit when demand is generated outside the system, such as in forecasting end-item demand, spare parts, and materials and suppliers used in a variety of products.

Computer time apparently is not very large since Smith forecasts 100,000 items every month using his focus forecasting strategies.

7.7 COMPUTER PROGRAMS

Many commercial forecasting programs are available. Some exist as library routines within a mainframe computer system, some may be purchased separately from a vendor, and some are part of larger programs. Many programs are available for microcomputers. Most computer manufacturers either produce their own, team up with a software company, or entice software companies to write programs for their computers.

All but the most sophisticated forecasting formulas are quite easy to understand. Anyone who can use a spreadsheet such as Lotus® 1-2-3®, SuperCalc®, Quattro®, or Excel®, can create a forecasting program on a PC. Depending on one's knowledge of the spreadsheet, a program can be written in anywhere from a few minutes to a couple of hours. How this forecast is to be used by the firm could be the bigger challenge. If the demand for many items is to be forecast, this becomes a data-handling problem, not a problem in the forecasting logic.

7.8 CONCLUSION

Forecasting is fundamental to any planning effort. In the short run, a forecast is needed to predict the requirements for materials, products, services, or other resources to respond to changes in demand. Forecasts permit adjusting schedules and varying labor and materials. In the long run, forecasting is required as a basis for strategic changes, such as developing new markets, developing new products or services, and expanding or creating new facilities.

For long-term forecasts that lead to heavy financial commitments, great care should be taken to derive the forecast. Several approaches should be used. Causal methods such as regression analysis or multiple regression analysis are beneficial. These provide a basis for discussion. Economic factors, product trends, growth factors, and competition, as well as a myriad of other possible variables, need to be considered and the forecast adjusted to reflect the influence of each.

Short- and intermediate-term forecasting, such as required for inventory control, and staffing and material scheduling, may be satisfied with simpler models, such as exponential smoothing with perhaps an adaptive feature or a seasonal index. In these applications, thousands of items are usually being forecast. The forecasting routine should therefore be simple and run quickly on a computer. The routines should also detect and respond rapidly to definite short-term changes in demand while at the same time ignoring the occasional spurious demands. Exponential smoothing, when monitored by management to control the value of alpha, is an effective technique.

Focus forecasting appears to offer a reasonable approach to short-term forecasting, say, monthly or quarterly but certainly less than a year. If there is one thing focus forecasting offers, it is close monitoring and rapid response. Quick detection and response would be assured if one of the strategies used were "Demand for the next period is equal to the demand for the last period."

In summary, forecasting is tough. A perfect forecast is like a hole-in-one in golf: great to get but we should be satisfied just to get close to the cup—or, to push the metaphor, just to land on the green. The ideal philosophy is to create the best forecast that you reasonably can and then hedge by maintaining flexibility in the system to account for the inevitable forecast error.

7.9 REVIEW AND DISCUSSION QUESTIONS

1. What is the difference between dependent and independent demand?
2. Examine Exhibit 7.4 and suggest which model you might use for: (1) bathing suits; (2) demand for new houses; (3) electrical power usage; (4) new plant expansion plans.
3. What is the logic in the least squares method of linear regression analysis?
4. Explain the procedure to create a forecast using the decomposition method of least squares regression.

5. Give some very simple rules you might use to manage demand for a firm's product. (An example is "limited to stock on hand.")

6. What strategies are used by supermarkets, airlines, hospitals, banks, and cereal manufacturers to influence demand?

7. All forecasting methods using exponential smoothing, adaptive smoothing, and exponential smoothing including trend require starting values to get the equations going. How would you select the starting value for, say, F_{t-1}?

8. From the choice of simple moving average, weighted moving average, exponential smoothing, and single regression analysis, which forecasting technique would you consider the most accurate? Why?

9. Give some examples that you can think of that have a multiplicative seasonal trend relationship.

10. What is the main disadvantage of daily forecasting using regression analysis?

11. What are the main problems with using adaptive exponential smoothing in forecasting?

12. How is a seasonal index computed from a regression line analysis?

13. Discuss the basic differences between the mean absolute deviation (MAD) and the standard deviation.

14. What implications do the existence of forecast errors have for the search for ultrasophisticated statistical forecasting models?

15. What are focused forecasting's strongest selling points?

16. Causal relationships are potentially useful for which component of a time series?

7.10 PROBLEMS

*1. Sunrise Baking Company markets doughnuts through a chain of food stores and has been experiencing over- and underproduction because of forecasting errors. The following data are their demands in dozens of doughnuts for the past four weeks. The bakery is closed Saturday, so Friday's production must satisfy demand for both Saturday and Sunday.

	4 Weeks Ago	3 Weeks Ago	2 Weeks Ago	Last Week
Monday	2,200	2,400	2,300	2,400
Tuesday	2,000	2,100	2,200	2,200
Wednesday	2,300	2,400	2,300	2,500
Thursday	1,800	1,900	1,800	2,000
Friday	1,900	1,800	2,100	2,000
Saturday } Sunday	2,800	2,700	3,000	2,900

Make a forecast for this week on the following basis:

a. Daily, using a simple four-week moving average.

b. Daily, using a weighted average of 0.40, 0.30, 0.20, and 0.10 for the past four weeks.

___
* Problems 1 through 4 are completely solved in Appendix H.

c.   Sunrise is also planning its purchases of ingredients for bread production. If bread demand had been forecast for last week at 22,000 loaves and only 21,000 loaves were actually demanded, what would Sunrise's forecast be for this week using exponential smoothing with $\alpha = 0.10$?

d.   Supposing, with the forecast made in (c), this week's demand actually turns out to be 22,500. What would the new forecast be for the next week?

*2.   Following are the actual demands for a product for the past six quarters. Using forecasting strategies 1 to 5, find the best strategy to use in predicting the seventh quarter.

| | QUARTER | | | |
	I	II	III	IV
Last year	1,200	700	900	1,100
This year	1,400	1,000		

*3.   A specific forecasting model was used to forecast demands for a product. The forecasts and the corresponding demands that subsequently occurred are shown below.

Use the MAD and tracking signal technique to evaluate the accuracy of the forecasting model.

Month	Actual	Forecast
October	700	660
November	760	840
December	780	750
January	790	835
February	850	910
March	950	890

*4.   Quarterly data for the last two years are given below. From this data prepare a forecast for the upcoming year using decomposition.

Period	Actual
1	300
2	540
3	885
4	580
5	416
6	760
7	1191
8	760

5.   Demand for stereo headphones and CD players for joggers has caused Nina Industries to experience a growth of almost 50 percent over the past year. The number of joggers is continuing to expand, so Nina expects demand for headsets to also expand, since there have, as yet, been no safety laws passed to prevent joggers from wearing them.

Demands for the stereo units for last year were as follows:

Month	Demand (units)	Month	Demand (units)
January	4,200	July	5,300
February	4,300	August	4,900
March	4,000	September	5,400
April	4,400	October	5,700
May	5,000	November	6,300
June	4,700	December	6,000

a. Using least squares regression analysis, what would you estimate demand to be for each month next year? Follow the general format in Exhibit 7.14.

b. To be reasonably confident of meeting demand, Nina decides to use three standard errors of estimate for safety. How many additional units should be held to meet this level of confidence?

6. The historical demand for a product is:

Month	Demand
January	12
February	11
March	15
April	12
May	16
June	15

a. Using a weighted moving average with weights of 0.60, 0.30, and 0.10, find the July forecast.

b. Using a simple three-month moving average, find the July forecast.

c. Using single exponential smoothing with $\alpha = 0.2$ and a June forecast $= 13$, find the July forecast. Make whatever assumptions you wish.

d. Using simple linear regression analysis, calculate the regression equation for the preceding demand data.

e. Using the regression equation in *(d)*, calculate the forecast for July.

7. The following tabulations are actual sales of units for six months and a starting forecast in January.

a. Calculate forecasts for the remaining five months using simple exponential smoothing with alpha $= 0.2$.

b. Calculate MAD for the forecasts.

	Actual	Forecast
January	100	80
February	94	
March	106	
April	80	
May	68	
June	94	

8. Zeus Computer Chips, Inc. used to have major contracts to produce 8088, 8086, and 286 type chips. The market has been declining during the past three years because of the 386 and 486 type chips which they are unable to produce, so Zeus has the unpleasant task of forecasting next year. The task is unpleasant because

they have not been able to find replacement chips for their product lines. Below are the demands for the past 12 quarters:

1989		1990		1991	
I	4,800	I	3,500	I	3,200
II	3,500	II	2,700	II	2,100
III	4,300	III	3,500	III	2,700
IV	3,000	IV	2,400	IV	1,700

Use the decomposition technique to forecast the four quarters of 1992.

9. Sales data for two years is given below. The data is aggregated with two months of sales in each "period."

Period	Sales
January–February	109
March–April	104
May–June	150
July–August	170
September–October	120
November–December	100
January–February	115
March–April	112
May–June	159
July–August	182
September–October	126
November–December	106

a. Plot the data.
b. Fit a simple linear regression model to the sales data.
c. In addition to the regression model, determine multiplicative seasonal index factors. A full cycle is assumed to be a full year.
d. Using the results from parts (b) and (c) prepare a forecast for the next year.

10. The tracking signals that were computed using the past demand history for three different products are shown below. Each product used the same forecasting technique.

	TS 1	TS 2	TS 3
1	−2.70	1.54	0.10
2	−2.32	−0.64	0.43
3	−1.70	2.05	1.08
4	−1.1	2.58	1.74
5	−0.87	−0.95	1.94
6	−0.05	−1.23	2.24
7	0.10	0.75	2.96
8	0.40	−1.59	3.02
9	1.50	0.47	3.54
10	2.20	2.74	3.75

Discuss the tracking signals for each product and what the implications are.

11. Prepare a forecast for each quarter of the next year from the following past two years' quarterly sales information. Assume that there are both trend and seasonal factors and that the season cycle is one year. Use time series decompositon.

Quarter	Sales
1	160
2	195
3	150
4	140
5	215
6	240
7	205
8	190

12. Tucson Machinery, Inc., manufactures numerically controlled machines, which sell for an average price of $0.5 million each. Sales for these NCMs for the past two years were as follows:

Quarter	Quantity (units)
1990	
I	12
II	18
III	26
IV	16
1991	
I	16
II	24
III	28
IV	18

   a. Hand fit a line (or do a regression if you have that feature on your calculator).
   b. Find the trend and seasonal factors.
   c. Forecast sales for 1992.

13. Not all the items in your office supply store are evenly distributed as far as demand is concerned, so you decide to forecast demand to help you plan your stock. Past data for lined tablets for the month of August are as follows:

Week 1	300
Week 2	400
Week 3	600
Week 4	700

   a. Using a three-week moving average, what would you forecast the next week to be?
   b. Using exponential smoothing with alpha equal to 0.20, if the exponential forecast for week 3 was estimated as the average of the first two weeks [(300 + 400)/2 = 350)], what would you forecast week 5 to be?

14. Given the following history, use focus forecasting to forecast the third quarter of this year. Use three focus forecasting strategies.

Last year	100	125	135	175	185	200	150	140	130	200	225	250
This year	125	135	135	190	200	190						

15. Following are the actual tabulated demands for an item for a nine-month period, from January through September. Your supervisor wants to test two forecasting methods to see which method was better over this period.

	Actual
January	110
February	130
March	150
April	170
May	160
June	180
July	140
August	130
September	140

a. Forecast April through September using a three-month moving average.
b. Using simple exponential smoothing to estimate April through September.
c. Use MAD to decide which method produced the better forecast over the six-month period.

16. A particular forecasting model was used to forecast a six-month period. The forecasts and the actual demands that resulted are shown:

	Forecast	Actual
April	250	200
May	325	250
June	400	325
July	350	300
Aug	375	325
Sept	450	400

Find the tracking signal and state whether you think the model being used is giving acceptable answers.

17. Harlen Industries has a very simple forecasting model: take the actual demand for the same month last year and divide that by the number of fractional weeks in that month, producing the average weekly demand for that month. This weekly average is used as the weekly forecast this year.

The following eight weeks shows the forecast (based on last year) and the demand that actually occurred.

Week	Forecast Demand	Actual Demand
1	140	137
2	140	133
3	140	150
4	140	160
5	140	180
6	150	170
7	150	185
8	150	205

a. Compute the MAD of forecast errors.
b. Using the RSFE, compute the tracking signal.
c. Based on your answers to (a) and (b) what comments can you make about Harlen's method of forecasting?

18. The historical demand for a product is: January, 80; February, 100; March, 60; April, 80; and May, 90.
    a. Using a simple four-month moving average, what is the forecast for June? If June experienced a demand of 100, what would your forecast be for July?
    b. Using single exponential smoothing with $\alpha = 0.20$, if the forecast for January had been 70, compute what the exponentially smoothed forecast would have been for the remaining months through June.
    c. Using least squares regression analysis, compute a forecast for June, July, and August.
    d. Using a weighted moving average with weights of 0.30, 0.25, 0.20, 0.15, and 0.10, what is June's forecast?

19. In this problem, you are to test the validity of your forecasting model. Following are the forecasts for a model you have been using and the actual demands that occurred.

Week	Forecast	Actual
1	800	900
2	850	1,000
3	950	1,050
4	950	900
5	1,000	900
6	975	1,100

Use the method stated in the text to compute the MAD and the tracking signal and draw a conclusion as to whether the forecasting model you have been using is giving reasonable results.

20. Assume that your stock of sales merchandise is maintained based on the forecast demand. If the distributor's sales personnel call on the first day of each month, compute your forecast sales by each of the three methods requested here.

	Actual
June	140
July	180
August	170

    a. Using a simple three-month moving average, what is the forecast for September?
    b. Using a weighted moving average, what is the forecast for September with weights of .20, .30, and .50 for June, July, and August, respectively?
    c. Using single exponential smoothing and assuming that the forecast for June had been 130, calculate the forecasts for September with a smoothing constant alpha of .30.

21. The historical demand for a product is:

Month	Demand
April	60
May	55
June	75
July	60
August	80
September	75

    a.   Using a simple four-month moving average, calculate a forecast for October.

    b.   Using single exponential smoothing with $\alpha = 0.2$ and a September forecast $= 65$, calculate a forecast for October.

    c.   Using simple linear regression, calculate the trend line for the historical data. To help in your calculations, the following data are given: The X axis is April $= 1$, May $= 2$, and so on. The Y axis is demand.

$$n = 6$$
$$\Sigma X = 21$$
$$\Sigma Y = 405$$
$$\Sigma X^2 = 91$$
$$\Sigma Y^2 = 27,875$$
$$\Sigma XY = 1,485$$

    d.   Calculate a forecast for October.

22.   Sales by quarter for last year and the first three quarters of this year were as follows:

	|	||	|||	IV
		QUARTER		
Last year	23,000	27,000	18,000	9,000
This year	19,000	24,000	15,000	

    Using the focus forecasting procedure described in the text, forecast the expected sales for the fourth quarter of this year.

23.   A forecasting method you have been using to predict product demand is shown in the following table along with the actual demand that occurred.

Forecast	Actual
1,500	1,550
1,400	1,500
1,700	1,600
1,750	1,650
1,800	1,700

    a.   Compute the tracking signal using the mean absolute deviation and running sum of forecast errors.

    b.   Comment on whether you feel the forecasting method is giving good predictions.

24.   Sales during the past six months have been as follows:

January	115
February	123
March	132
April	134
May	140
June	147

    a.   Using a simple three-month moving average, make forecasts for April through July. What is the main weakness of using a simple moving average with data that is patterned like this?

b. Using single exponential smoothing with alpha = 0.70, if the forecast for January had been 110, compute the exponentially smoothed forecasts for each month through July. Is this method more accurate for this data? Why or why not?

c. Using least squares regression analysis, compute the forecasts for the rest of the year. Does your regression line seem to fit the January through June data well? If so, briefly describe a pattern of data with which linear regression would not work well.

d. Calculate the mean absolute deviation for January through June using the trend equation from (*c*).

25. Use regression analysis on deseasonalized demand to forecast demand in summer 1992, given the following historical demand data:

Year	Season	Actual Demand
1990	Spring	205
	Summer	140
	Fall	375
	Winter	575
1991	Spring	475
	Summer	275
	Fall	685
	Winter	965

26. Following are the data for the past 21 months for actual sales of a particular product.

	1990	1991
January	300	275
February	400	375
March	425	350
April	450	425
May	400	400
June	460	350
July	400	350
August	300	275
September	375	350
October	500	
November	550	
December	500	

Develop a forecast for the fourth quarter using three different focus forecasting strategies. (Note that to correctly use this procedure, the strategies are first tested on the third quarter and the best performing one is used to forecast the fourth quarter.) Do the problem using quarters, as opposed to forecasting separate months.

27. Actual demand for a product for the past three months was:

Three months ago	400 units
Two months ago	350 units
Last month	325 units

a. Using a simple three-month moving average, what would the forecast be for this month?

b. If 300 units actually occurred this month, what would your forecast be for next month?

c. Using simple exponential smoothing, what would your forecast be for this month if the exponentially smoothed forecast for three months ago was 450 units and the smoothing constant was 0.20?

28. After using your forecasting model for a period of six months, you decide to test it using MAD and a tracking signal. Following are the forecasted and actual demands for the six-month period:

Period	Forecast	Actual
May	450	500
June	500	550
July	550	400
August	600	500
September	650	675
October	700	600

a. Find the tracking signal.

b. Decide whether your forecasting routine is acceptable.

29. Goodyear Tire and Rubber Company is the world's largest rubber manufacturer, with automotive products accounting for 82 percent of sales. Cooper Tire and Rubber Company is the ninth largest tire manufacturer in the world, with tires accounting for about 80 percent of sales.

Shown below are the earnings per share for each company by quarter for the period from the first quarter of 1988 through the second quarter of 1991. Forecast the earnings per share for the remainder of 1991 and 1992. Use exponential smoothing to forecast the third period of 1991, and the time series decomposition method to forecast the last two quarters of 1991 and all four quarters of 1992. (It's much easier to solve this problem on a computer spreadsheet so that you can see what's going on.)

EARNINGS PER SHARE ($)

Year	Quarter	Goodyear Tire	Cooper Tire
1988	I	1.67	0.17
	II	2.35	0.24
	III	1.11	0.26
	IV	1.15	0.34
1989	I	1.56	0.25
	II	2.04	0.37
	III	1.14	0.36
	IV	0.38	0.44
1990	I	0.29	0.33
	II	d0.18 (loss)	0.40
	III	d0.97 (loss)	0.41
	IV	0.20	0.47
1991	I	d1.54 (loss)	0.30
	II	0.38	0.47

a. For the exponential smoothing method, choose the first quarter of 1988 as the beginning forecast. Make two forecasts: one with an alpha of 0.10 and one with an alpha of 0.30.

  b. Using the MAD method of testing the forecasting model's performance, and the actual data from 1988 through the second quarter of 1991, how well did the model perform?

  c. Using the decomposition of a time series method of forecasting, forecast the earnings per share for the last two quarters of 1991 and all four quarters of 1992. Is there a seasonal factor in the earnings?

  d. From your forecasts, what comments would you make about each company—Cooper Tire and Goodyear Tire?

30. Consolidated Edison Company of New York, Inc., sells electricity, gas, and steam to New York City and Westchester County. Sales revenue for the years 1981 to 1991 are shown below. (The last four months of 1991 are estimated.) Forecast the revenues for 1992 through 1995. Use your own judgment, intuition, or common sense concerning which model or method to use, as well as the period of data to include.

Year	Revenue (millions)
1981	$4,865.9
1982	5,067.4
1983	5,515.6
1984	5,728.8
1985	5,497.9
1986	5,197.7
1987	5,094.4
1988	5,108.8
1989	5,550.6
1990	5,738.9
1991	5,860.0

7.11 SELECTED BIBLIOGRAPHY

Abraham, B., and J. Ledolter. *Statistical Methods for Forecasting.* New York: John Wiley & Sons, 1983.

Armstrong, J. Scott. "Forecasting by Extrapolation: Conclusions from 25 Years of Research." *Interfaces* 14, no. 6 (November 1984), pp. 52–66.

Bails, Dale G., and Larry C. Peppers. *Business Fluctuations: Forecasting Techniques and Applications.* Englewood Cliffs, N.J.: Prentice Hall, 1982.

Bowerman, B. L., and R. T. O'Connell. *Time Series Forecasting.* Boston: Duxbury, 1986.

Box, G. E. P., and G. M. Jenkins. *Time Series Analysis: Forecasting and Control.* 2nd ed. Oakland, Calif.: Holden-Day, 1976.

Brown, Robert G. *Decision Rules for Inventory Management.* New York: Holt, Rinehart & Winston, 1967.

Cryer, J. *Time Series Analysis.* Boston: Duxbury, 1986.

Ekern, S. "Adaptive Exponential Smoothing Revisited." *Journal of the Operations Research Society* 32 (1981), pp. 775–82.

A VIEW OF
MANUFACTURING

Then and Now

Labor intensive duties on the manufacturing lines of yesterday have been replaced with computer-integrated manufacturing methods.
Courtesy of Maytag Company

Today, Maytag's newest manufacturing line machines and assembles a completely redesigned transmission used in all Maytag washing machines. This transmission has fewer parts and much higher quality, resulting in better reliability and a 10-year warranty.
Courtesy of Maytag Company

Then and Now

Before shipping, every appliance is tested on a unique "merry-go-round" test station—a quality control test procedure designed to take each appliance through a full-cycle test.
Courtesy of Maytag Company

In the 1930s, workers at a Nabisco plant manually packaged trays of Shredded Wheat into boxes.
Courtesy of Baker Library, Harvard Business School

Today, Spoon Size Shredded Wheat biscuits are automatically weighed and packaged.
Photo © 1990 Harvard Business Review

Boxes of cereal had to be hand-packed from a conveyor belt.
Courtesy of Baker Library, Harvard Business School

Today, sealed packages are automatically stacked and then packed into shipping cartons.
Photo © 1990 Harvard Business Review

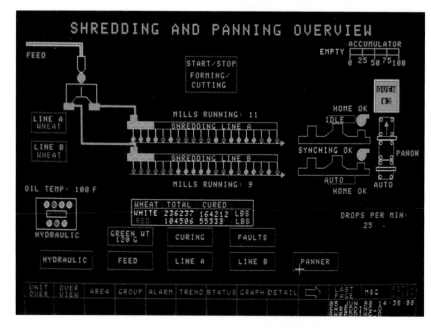

Modern technology allows for computer control over the process of cereal shredding.
Photo © 1990 Harvard Business Review

Quality Control

At Hewlett-Packard, quality circles are employed to involve managers and engineers in improving the quality capabilities of the system.
Courtesy of Hewlett-Packard

Workers are also actively involved in quality circles, as well as in cooperating with co-workers during production.
Courtesy of Hewlett-Packard

Line operators check production quality. At this stage, the operator is sampling items to be sure products are up to specifications.
Courtesy of Hershey Foods Corporation

Quality Control

Operating employees inspect the manufacture of Reese's peanut butter cups. This is the last stage of full quality control where defectives are removed.
Courtesy of Hershey Foods Corporation

Ford Motor Company uses lasers to verify dimensions within 1/1,000th of an inch. Computer-operated mechanical prods perform the function, reducing variation in the system. This quality control procedure, which used to take two hours, can now be completed in 30 minutes.
Courtesy of Ford Motor Company

Malcolm Baldrige National Quality Award

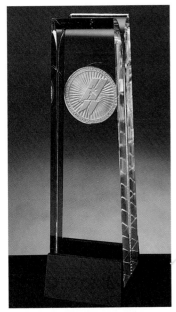

In 1987, President Ronald Reagan passed the Malcolm Baldrige National Quality Improvement Act. This act established the prestigious award that is presented annually to those select companies that have exhibited superior total quality management.
Stueben Glass/Courtesy of Malcolm Baldrige National Quality Award Office

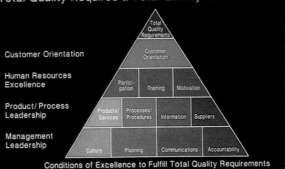

We Have Learned That . . .
Total Quality Requires a Total Quality Culture

Customer Orientation

Human Resources Excellence

Product/Process Leadership

Management Leadership

Conditions of Excellence to Fulfill Total Quality Requirements

Westinghouse Electric's Commercial Nuclear Fuel Division has achieved a 100% on-time delivery record for its fuel-rod assemblies. This can be credited to the division's total quality approach.
Courtesy of Westinghouse Electric Corporation/Commercial Nuclear Fuel Division

Milliken & Company employees work in self-managed teams and are responsible for everything from training to halting a production process if a quality or safety problem is detected.
Courtesy of Milliken & Company

Motorola Inc.'s quality goal is simply "Zero defects in everything we do." Being a major manufacturer of communication systems, primarily two-way radios and pagers, customer feedback guides all planning for quality improvement and product development. In addition, Motorola employees are responsible for locating and recording defects found in every function of the business. Employees are trained in all quality matters.
Courtesy of Motorola Inc.

Just-in-Time

JIT is important at Federal Express, a service operation. Here at the superhub in Memphis, more than 650,000 packages are sorted and dispatched each night.
Courtesy of Federal Express

Here at Hewlett-Packard's Cupertino facility, employees assemble computers using the Just-in-Time procedures— keeping enough parts on hand to complete an order—to reduce costs and increase productivity.
Courtesy of Hewlett-Packard

An empty Kanban square signals the need to be filled by a disk drive unit.
Courtesy of McDonnell-Douglas

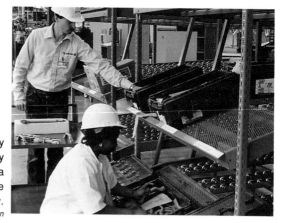

At Saturn, a vacancy on a subassembly shelf generates a purchase order to the vendor to resupply.
Courtesy of Saturn Corporation

Gardner, E. S. "Exponential Smoothing: The State of the Art." *Journal of Forecasting* 4, no. 1 (March 1985).

Hank, J. E., and A. Reitsch. *Business Forecasting*. 2nd ed. Boston: Allyn & Bacon, 1986.

Makridakis, Spyros; Steven C. Wheelwright; and Victor E. McGee. *Forecasting: Methods and Applications*. 2nd ed. New York: John Wiley & Sons, 1983.

————. "The Accuracy of Extrapolation (Time Series) Methods: Results of a Forecasting Competition." *Journal of Forecasting* 1 (1982), pp. 111–15.

Smith, Bernard T. *Focus Forecasting: Computer Techniques for Inventory Control*. Boston: CBI Publishing, 1984.

Sweet, A. L. "Adaptive Smoothing for Forecasting Seasonal Series." *AIIE Transactions* 13 (1981), pp. 243–48.

Taylor, S. G. "Initialization of Exponential Smoothing Forecasts." *AIIE Transactions* 13 (1981), pp. 199–205.

Chapter 8

Capacity Planning and Location

EPIGRAPH

The response to new technologies should not be building large plants with huge bureaucracies that ultimately result in diseconomies of scale. Rather, firms should attempt to have facilities that have a focused product line and no more than 500 employees.

Ulf Hoglund
Chief Executive, GKN Automotive
(Germany) Speech at the Designing and
Sustaining World-Class Organizations
Conference, Carnegie Mellon University,
May 31, 1991.

KEY TERMS

Capacity

Design Capacity

Maximum Capacity

Capacity Flexibility

Capacity Focus

Complexity

Capacity Planning

Decision Tree

Center of Gravity Method

*H*ow much should a plant or service facility be able to produce? Where should it be located? These questions top the strategic agendas of contemporary manufacturing and service firms, particularly in this age of global markets and global production. Answering the "how much" question entails capacity planning, which is the focus of the first part of the chapter; answering the "where" question involves facility location analysis, the focus of the second part. In practice, however, the questions are very much linked together as evidenced by two competitive imperatives:

1. The need to produce close to the customer due to time-based competition, trade agreements, and shipping costs.
2. The need to locate near the appropriate labor pool to take advantage of low wage costs and/or high technical skills.

We discuss elements of both imperatives in the Insert about Volkswagen's reasons to produce in Czechoslovakia.

INSERT   VW's Reasons to Produce in Czechoslovakia

Volkswagen (VW) bought a 31 percent stake in Skoda, an auto plant, when it was turned into a joint-stock company in 1991. The shareholding will increase to a controlling 70 percent by 1995; VW also plans to invest $6.4 billion in Skoda over the next 10 years.

This expansion bolsters VW's position as Europe's biggest car manufacturer, just ahead of Fiat. VW aims to more than double Skoda's annual production to 400,000 cars a year by 1997. VW believes that Skoda will be able to produce vehicles for about 30 percent less than their German factories because of low Czechoslovakian wages. Moreover, owning a company producing less expensive cars under a different brand name will make VW more competitive at the lower end of the market.

The main reason VW is investing heavily in Skoda is to expand its manufacturing capacity to meet an expected boom in car sales with the opening markets of Eastern Europe. The huge pent-up demand for cars in East Europe just as the West European new-car market turns down is a mouthwatering prospect for VW and other competitors.

Source: "The People's Car Heads East," *The Economist*, December 15, 1990, p. 74.

8.1 IMPORTANCE OF CAPACITY DECISIONS

The capacity of the production system defines the firm's competitive boundaries. Specifically, it sets the firm's response rate to the market, its cost structure, its work-force composition, its level of technology, its management and staff support requirements, and its general inventory strategy. If capacity is inadequate, a company may lose customers through slow service or by allowing competitors to enter the market. If capacity is excessive, a company may have to reduce its prices to stimulate demand, underutilize its work force, carry excess inventory, or seek additional, less profitable products to stay in business.

Definition of Capacity

Capacity is the rate of output that can be achieved from a process. This characteristic is measured in units of output per unit of time: an electronics plant can produce some number of computers per year, or a credit card company can process so many bills per hour. **Design capacity** is the rate at which a firm would like to produce under normal circumstances and for which the system was designed. **Maximum capacity** is used to describe the maximum output rate that could be achieved when productive resources are used to their maximum. However, at this maximum level, utilization of resources may be inefficient (for example, increasing energy costs, the need for overtime, higher maintenance costs, etc.).

Factors Affecting Capacity

Capacity is affected by both external and internal factors. The external factors include government regulations (working hours, safety, pollution), union agreements, and supplier capabilities. The internal factors include product and service design, personnel and jobs (worker training, motivation, learning, job content, and methods), plant layout and process flow, equipment capabilities and maintenance, materials management, quality control systems, and management capabilities.

8.2 IMPORTANT CAPACITY CONCEPTS

Best Operating Level

The *best operating level* is the level of capacity for which the average unit cost is at a minimum. This is depicted in Exhibit 8.1. Note that as we move down the curve, we achieve economies of scale until we reach the best operating level, and we encounter diseconomies of scale as we exceed this point.

Economies of Scale

The basic notion is well known: as a plant gets larger and volume increases, the average cost per unit of output drops because each succeeding unit absorbs part of the fixed costs. This reduction in average unit cost continues until the plant gets so big that coordination of material flows and staffing becomes so expensive that new sources of capacity must be found. This concept can be related to

EXHIBIT 8.1

Best Operating Level

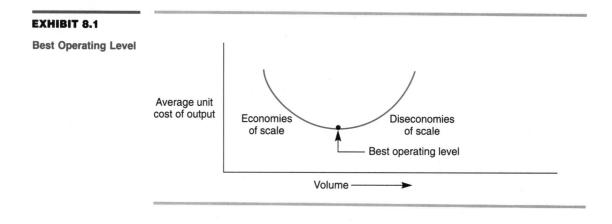

EXHIBIT 8.2

Economies of Scale

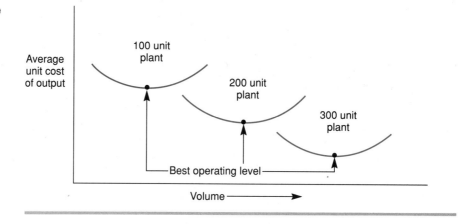

best operating levels by comparing the average unit cost of different sized plants. Exhibit 8.2 shows the best operating levels for 100-, 200-, and 300-unit (per year) plants. The average unit cost is shown as dropping from best operating level to best operating level as we move from 100 to 300 units. Diseconomies of scale would be evidenced if we had, say, a 400-unit plant where cost was higher than for the 300-unit plant. However, moving to the right along any of the three average cost curves would not be evidence of diseconomy of scale because the plant size has not increased. Rather, it would indicate that management has tried to get more from the plant than it can most efficiently provide. Exhibit 8.2 also shows that there is a second dimension to the concept. Not only is there an optimal size for a facility but also an optimal operating level for a facility of a given size. Economies (as well as diseconomies) of scale are found not just between cost curves, but also within each one.

As the output approaches a facility's best operating level, economies of scale are realized. Beyond that level, diseconomies set in.

Although finding the best size and operating level is illusive, managers often set policies regarding the maximum size for any one facility. As a result, the real challenge is predicting how costs will change for different output rates and facility sizes. This assessment requires careful attention to the different causes of economies of scale for each situation.

In the past several years, we have begun to see that diseconomies of scale come much sooner than we once supposed. This recognition, along with technological capability to do more in a plant, has resulted in a shift toward small facilities. The steel industry, with its declining number of big, integrated plants and its corresponding shift toward minimills, is a well-known case in point.

Capacity Utilization Rate

The extent to which a firm uses its capacity is defined by its *capacity utilization rate*, which is calculated as follows:

Capacity used ÷ Design capacity

The capacity utilization rate is expressed as a percentage and requires that both the numerator and the denominator be measured in similar units and time periods (machine hours/day, barrels of oil/day, patients/day, dollar of output/month).

Capacity Cushions

A capacity cushion is an amount of capacity in excess of expected demand. For example, if the expected monthly demand on a facility is $1 million worth of products per month and the design capacity is $1.2 million per month, it has a 20 percent capacity cushion. A 20 percent capacity cushion equates to an 83 percent utilization rate (100% ÷ 120%).

When a firm's design capacity is less than the capacity required to meet its demand, it is said to have a *negative capacity cushion*. If, for example, a firm has a demand for $1.2 million of products per month but can produce only $1 million per month, it has a negative capacity cushion of 20 percent.

Capacity Flexibility

Capacity flexibility essentially means having the capability to deliver what the customer wants within a lead time shorter than competitors'. Such flexibility is achieved through flexible plants, processes, workers, and through strategies that use the capacity of other organizations.

Flexible plants

Perhaps the ultimate in plant flexibility is the *zero-changeover-time* plant. Using movable equipment, knockdown walls, easily accessible and reroutable utilities, such a plant can adapt to change in real time. An analogy to a familiar service business captures the flavor quite well—a plant with equipment "that is easy to install and easy to tear down and move—like the Ringling Bros.– Barnum and Bailey Circus in the old tent-circus days."[1]

Flexible processes

Flexible processes are epitomized by flexible manufacturing systems on the one hand, and simple, easily set-up equipment on the other. Both of these technological approaches permit rapid low-cost switching from one product line to another, enabling what is sometimes referred to as *economies of scope*. (By definition, economies of scope exist when multiple products can be produced at a lower cost in combination than they can separately.)

Flexible workers

Flexible workers have multiple skills and the ability to switch easily from one kind of task to another. They require broader training than specialized workers and need managers and staff support to facilitate quick changes in their work assignments.

Using external capacity

Two common strategies for creating flexibility by using the capacity of other organizations are subcontracting and sharing capacity. An example of subcontracting is Japanese banks in California subcontracting check-clearing operations to the First Interstate Bank of California's check clearinghouse. An example of sharing capacity is two domestic airlines flying different routes with different seasonal demands exchanging aircraft (suitably repainted) when one's routes are heavily used and the other's are not.

Capacity Balance

In a perfectly balanced plant, the output of Stage 1 provides the exact input requirement for Stage 2, Stage 2's output provides the exact input requirement for Stage 3, and so on. In practice, however, achieving such a "perfect" design is usually both impossible and undesirable. One reason is that the best operating levels for each stage generally differ. For instance, Department 1 may operate most efficiently over a range of 90 to 110 units per month while Department 2, the next stage in the process, is most efficient at 75 to 85 units per month, and Department 3, the third stage, works best over a range of 150 to 200 units per month. Another reason is that variability in product demand

---

[1] See R. J. Schonberger, "The Rationalization of Production," *Proceedings of the 50th Anniversary of the Academy of Management* (Chicago: Academy of Management, 1986), pp. 64–70.

and the processes themselves generally lead to imbalance except in automated production lines which, in essence, are just one big machine. There are various ways of dealing with imbalance. One is to add capacity to those stages that are the bottlenecks. This can be done by temporary measures such as scheduling overtime, leasing equipment, or going outside the system and purchasing additional capacity through subcontracting. A second way is through the use of buffer inventories in front of the bottleneck stage to assure that it always has something to work on. (This is a central feature of Synchronous Production approach discussed in detail in Chapter 18). A third approach involves duplicating the facilities of one department on which another is dependent.

Capacity Focus

In 1974, Wickham Skinner introduced the concept of the focused factory, which holds that a production facility works best when it focuses on a fairly limited set of production objectives.[2] This means, for example, that a firm should not expect to excel in every aspect of manufacturing performance—cost, quality, flexibility, new-product introductions, reliability, short lead times, and low investment. Rather, it should select a limited set of tasks that contribute the most to corporate objectives. However, given the breakthroughs in manufacturing technology, there is an evolution in factory objectives toward trying to do everything well. How do we deal with these apparent contradictions? One way is to say that if the firm does not have the technology to master multiple objectives, then a narrow focus is the logical choice. Another way is to recognize the practical reality that not all firms are in industries that require them to use their full range of capabilities to compete.

The **capacity focus** concept can also be operationalized through the mechanism of plants within plants—*PWPs* in Skinner's terms. A focused plant may have several PWPs, each of which may have separate suborganizations, equipment and process policies, work-force management policies, production control methods, and so forth for different products—even if they are made under the same roof. This, in effect, permits finding the best operating level for each component of the organization and thereby carries the focus concept down to the operating level.

Capacity and Complexity

One of the main factors that must be considered in capacity planning is how much **complexity** is added to the manager's job as a result of how that capacity is deployed. This is especially true in multisite services where the locations of capacity are, by definition, widely disbursed and inherently difficult to coordinate.

---

[2] Wickham Skinner, "The Focused Factory," *Harvard Business Review* (May–June 1974), pp. 113–21.

EXHIBIT 8.3

**The Contributors
to Managing and
Planning Complexity
in Multisite Services**

Capacity Dependent Choices	MANAGERIAL COMPLEXITY	
	Low	High
Number of facilities	Few	Many
Diversity of facility types	Standardized	Nonstandardized
Dispersion of facilities	Concentrated	Scattered
Breadth of service offering	Narrow	Broad
Number of employees	Few	Many
Degree of backward integration	Little	Much
Volume of transactions	Few	Many

Source: W. E. Sasser, R. Paul Olsen, and D. D. Wyckoff, *Management of Service Operations* (New York: Allyn & Bacon, 1978), p. 562.

Exhibit 8.3 provides a summary of how choices among various capacity and design features affect managerial complexity. Obviously, the higher the complexity of the operations, the more difficult the capacity planning process.

8.3 CAPACITY PLANNING

The objective of **capacity planning** is to specify which level of capacity will meet market demands in a cost-efficient way. Capacity planning can be viewed in three time durations: long range (greater than one year), intermediate range (the next 6 to 18 months), and short range (less than six months).

Our focus in this chapter is on long-range capacity planning, where the firm makes its major investment decisions. In addition to planning large chunks of capacity (such as a new factory, as illustrated in Exhibit 8.4), typical long-range capacity planning efforts must also address the demands for individual product lines, individual plant capabilities, and allocation of production throughout the plant network. Typically, these are carried out according to the following steps:

1. Forecast sales for each product line.
2. Forecast sales for individual products within each product line.
3. Calculate labor and equipment requirements to meet product line forecasts.
4. Project labor and equipment availabilities over the planning horizon.

Long-Range Capacity Planning at a Pharmaceutical Company

The following example describes the procedures used by a major pharmaceutical producer in developing its Five Year National Resource Plan (NRP).[3] Note

---

[3] Mark Louis Smith, "Production Planning Simplicity," in *Strategic Manufacturing: Dynamic New Directions for the 1990s,* edited by Patricia E. Moody (Homewood, Ill.: BUSINESS ONE IRWIN, 1990), pp. 242–46.

EXHIBIT 8.4

One Company's Approach to a Major Capacity and Facilities Planning Project

Assignment

In-depth analysis of all major options for meeting the division's capacity requirements for next five or more years, followed by preparation of capital request for management-selected option.

Timing

Project team to complete analysis of alternatives in four months and preparation of capital request for selected option by the end of fifth month.

Project Team Staff

Senior division industrial engineer (team leader)
Staff analyst from corporate planning
Division industrial engineers (up to four, as needed)

Plan Outline

A. Determine manufacturing requirements.
  1. Obtain sales forecasts from marketing—pessimistic, most likely, optimistic—covering five years.
  2. Obtain from marketing a prediction of business conditions for subsequent 10-year period.
  3. Establish whether or not it is likely we will attempt to build domestically the small end of the product line.
B. Measure requirements.
  1. Convert forecasts into direct labor hours and adjust for performance.
  2. Separate above into requirements for:
    a. Product line A.
    b. Product line B.
    c. Product line C.
    d. Product line D.
  3. Group requirements for various alternative plans.
C. Prepare alternative plans.
  1. Product line as is at Plant 1 and product line as is at Plant 2.
  2. Provide new facility for Product C.
  3. Transfer manufacturing of Product line C to Plant 2; transfer Product line B to Plant 1.
  4. Provide a new facility for Product line D.
  Note: Analysis of each alternate plan is to include:
    1. Floor space requirements.
    2. Direct labor requirements.
    3. Assessment of learning curves.
    4. Capital equipment requirements.
    5. Schedule for transfer of work (if required).
    6. Provisions for future expansion.
    7. Profitability index.
D. Decision making.
  1. Evaluate alternatives.
  2. Decide on best alternative(s).
  3. Make recommendation(s) to management.
  4. Obtain management approval.
E. Prepare capital authorization request(s).

Source: Robert Hayes and Steven Wheelwright, *Restoring Our Competitive Edge: Competing through Manufacturing* (New York: John Wiley & Sons, 1984), pp. 132–33.

that while this example assumes an existing set of factories, the procedure could easily be applied to determining the capacity requirements of planned or potential facilities as well.

The Five-Year National Resource Plan provides aggregate roughcut capacities for both capital and skilled labor resources by manufacturing location. It is prepared and reviewed with each manufacturing location twice annually. Local plant management uses the NRP as a template to develop their business and operating plans. The NRP has evolved from a document hand-calculated annually with no simulation capability to today's computer-driven model with the ability to regenerate simulations every six to eight minutes. The model uses simple planning concepts and can be set up on a mainframe using a database language (FOCUS® or QUERY UPDATE®) or on a personal computer using either a database (dBASE® or PFS®) or spreadsheet language (Lotus 1-2-3® or Excel®).

From the NRP, the following strategic operational decisions are made:

- To change a plant's focus, for example, from manufacturing high-volume, single-ingredient products with few stockkeeping units (SKUs), to manufacturing low-volume, multi-ingredient products with many SKUs.

- To change the manufacturing location for a product line to eliminate a capacity constraint or to take advantage of a cost differential.

- To make appropriation requests for capital funds to support new products, line extensions, and sales growth and to upgrade or replace aged capital.

- To request approval or justifications for additional skilled-labor sources.

Calculation of the NRP starts with two pieces of information:

1. The current annual sales forecast in SKU detail.
2. The five-year forecasted growth for each product family (see Exhibit 8.5).

In Exhibit 8.5, for example, the term *Product Family A* represents a group of common SKUs (e.g., 20-, 50-, and 100-count packages) of cough medication.

The next step in the planning process is to develop five years of SKU detail. Each SKU is extended by the forecasted growth for its product family. For instance, in Exhibit 8.5, SKU 1 in Year 2 for Product Family A is calculated by extending the current year value of 1,000 by the year 2 forecasted growth of 5 percent, to yield a value of 1,050 (1,000 × 1.05 = 1,050). In year 3, the value of SKU 1 for Product Family A is calculated from the year 2 (1,050) value, extended by the forecasted growth of 4 percent, yielding a value of 1,092 (1,050 × 1.04 = 1,092). This process continues for all SKUs and all product families. Exhibit 8.6 shows the completed forecast extensions.

If, however, marketing or sales has unique plans for a given SKU, such as a promotional campaign, the extension by growth may be manually overridden.

EXHIBIT 8.5

Five-Year Growth
Forecast for Two
Product Families

	SKU	Current Year	Year 2	Year 3	Year 4	Year 5
Product Family A						
Forecasts	1	1,000				
	2	5,000				
	3	3,000				
Total		9,000				
Forecasted growth			5%	4%	4%	4%
Product Family B						
Forecasts	1	6,000				
	2	4,000				
	3	2,000				
Total		12,000				
Forecasted growth			7%	8%	8%	9%

EXHIBIT 8.6

Five-Year Growth
Forecast with SKU
Detail

	SKU	Current Year	Year 2	Year 3	Year 4	Year 5
Product Family A						
Forecasts	1	1,000	1,050	1,092	1,136	1,181
	2	5,000	5,250	5,460	5,678	5,906
	3	3,000	3,150	3,276	3,407	3,543
Total		9,000	9,450	9,828	10,221	10,630
Forecasted growth			5%	4%	4%	4%
Product Family B						
Forecasts	1	6,000	6,420	6,934	7,488	8,162
	2	4,000	4,280	4,622	4,992	5,441
	3	2,000	2,140	2,311	2,496	2,721
Total		12,000	12,840	13,867	14,977	16,324
Forecasted growth			7%	8%	8%	9%

Explosion of forecasts: Once the forecasts have been developed, they are
exploded through the bills of material[4] and extended, using standard–machine
and labor-planning values in the workflow routings, into machine and labor
requirements (see Exhibit 8.7).

- *Equipment planning value:* the expected annual output for a specific SKU
  on a specific production center. Example: Product Family A, SKU 1:
  Planned or assigned annual output = 2,000 units.

- *Equipment demand:* the amount of equipment needed to support the forecast for a specific SKU (also expressed as machine shifts, machine hours,
  etc.). Example: Product Family A, SKU 1: Forecast = 1,000, equipment

---

[4] A bill of material is the listing of the ingredients and containers needed to produce and
ship the pharmaceuticals. See Chapter 14 for a detailed discussion of bills of material.

EXHIBIT 8.7

Five-Year Growth
Forecast's
Implications for
Production

	SKU	Current Year	Year 2	Year 3	Year 4	Year 5	Planning Values
Product Family A							
Forecasts	1	1,000	1,050	1,092	1,136	1,181	
	2	5,000	5,250	5,460	5,678	5,906	
	3	3,000	3,150	3,276	3,407	3,543	
Equipment demand	1	0.5	0.5	0.5	0.6	0.6	2,000
	2	0.6	0.7	0.7	0.7	0.7	8,000
	3	0.8	0.8	0.8	0.9	0.9	4,000
Total		1.9	2.0	2.0	2.1	2.2	
Labor demand	1	3	3	3	3	4	6
	2	4	4	4	4	4	6
	3	7	7	7	8	8	9
Total		14	14	14	15	16	
Product Family B							
Forecasts	1	6,000	6,420	6,934	7,488	8,162	
	2	4,000	4,280	4,622	4,992	5,441	
	3	2,000	2,140	2,311	2,496	2,721	
Equipment demand	1	0.5	0.6	0.6	0.7	0.7	11,000
	2	0.8	0.9	0.9	1.0	1.1	5,000
	3	0.7	0.7	0.8	0.8	0.9	3,000
Total		2.0	2.2	2.3	2.5	2.7	
Labor demand	1	3	4	4	4	4	6
	2	5	5	6	6	7	6
	3	6	6	7	7	8	9
Total		14	15	17	17	19	
Equipment and Labor Totals							
Equipment demand		3.9	4.1	4.4	4.6	5.0	
Equipment supply		5	5	5	5	5	
Loading		78%	82%	87%	93%	99%	
Labor demand		28	29	31	33	35	
Labor supply		86	86	86	86	86	
Variance		58	57	55	53	51	

planning value = 2,000, equipment demand = 1,000/2,000 = 0.5 machines or lines.

- *Labor planning value:* the amount of labor required to run the equipment. Example: Product Family A, SKU 1: crew size or labor planning value = 6.
- *Labor demand:* the average amount of labor required to support the forecast for a specific SKU. Example: Product Family A, SKU 1: Equipment demand = 0.5 machines/annually, labor planning value = 6, average annual demand = (0.5)(6) = 3.
- *Equipment and labor supply* are assumed values for the example and would represent the actual resources available.

Following the template provided by the NRP, the Corporate Planning Department and the Plant Production and Inventory Control Departments begin development of the intermediate range, or aggregate plan. (See Chapter 12 for a discussion of aggregate planning.)

Capacity Planning Using Decision Trees

A convenient way to lay out the steps of a problem is called a *decision tree*. The tree format helps not only in understanding the problem but also in finding a solution. A **decision tree** is a schematic model of the sequence of steps in a problem and the conditions and consequences of each step.

Decision trees are composed of decision nodes with branches to and from them. By convention, squares represent decision points and circles represent chance events. Branches from decision points show the choices available to the decision maker; branches from chance events show the probabilities for their occurrence.

In solving decision tree problems, we work from the end of the tree backward to the start of the tree. As we work back, we calculate the expected values at each step.

Once the calculations are made, we prune the tree by eliminating from each decision point all branches except for the one with the highest payoff. This process continues to the first decision problem, and the decision problem is thereby solved.

We now demonstrate an application to capacity planning for Hackers Computer Store.

The owner of Hackers Computer Store is considering what to do with his business over the next five years. Sales growth over the last couple of years has been good, but sales could grow substantially if a major electronics firm is built in his area as proposed. Hackers' owner sees three options: the first is to enlarge his current store, the second is to locate at a new site, and the third is to simply wait and do nothing. The decision to expand or move would take little time and, therefore, the store would not lose revenue. If nothing were done the first year and strong growth occurred, then the decision to expand would be reconsidered. Waiting longer than one year would allow competition to move in and make expansion no longer feasible.

The assumptions and conditions are:

1. Strong growth as a result of the increased population of computer fanatics from the electronics firm has a 55 percent probability.
2. Strong growth with a new site would give annual returns of $195,000 per year. Weak growth with a new site would mean annual returns of $115,000.
3. Strong growth with an expansion would give annual returns of $190,000 per year. Weak growth with an expansion would mean annual returns of $100,000.

4. At the existing store with no changes, there would be returns of $170,000 per year if there is strong growth and $105,000 per year if growth is weak.

5. Expansion at the current site would cost $87,000.

6. The move to the new site would cost $210,000.

7. If growth is strong and the existing site is enlarged for the second year, the cost would still be $87,000.

8. Operating costs for all options are equal.

We construct a decision tree to advise Hackers' owner on the best action.

Exhibit 8.8 shows the decision tree for this problem. There are two decision points (square nodes), and three chance occurrences (round nodes). The value of the nodes and decision points are as follows:

Node A. Move to new location.

Return with strong growth	$195,000/yr. × 5 yrs. = $975,000
Return with weak growth	$115,000/yr. × 5 yrs. = $575,000
Expected return at A =	($975,000 × .55) + ($575,000 × .45)
	$ 795,000
Less new site costs =	−210,000
New site net return	$ 585,000

Node B. Enlarge the existing store.

Return with strong growth	$190,000/yr. × 5 yrs. = $950,000
Return with weak growth	$100,000/yr. × 5 yrs. = $500,000
Expected return at B =	($950,000 × .55) + ($500,000 × .45)
	$747,500
Less costs of expansion =	−87,000
Expansion net return	$660,500

Decision point 2. After one year, reconsider:

Enlarging existing store:

Return with strong growth	$190,000/yr. × 4 yrs. =	$760,000
Less expansion costs		−87,000
Net return		$673,000

Keeping existing store the same:

Return with strong growth	$170,000/yr. × 4 yrs. = $680,000

Decision point 2 shows the choice of $673,000 if the existing store is enlarged versus $680,000 if the existing store is kept the same. Therefore, we would prune the expansion branch because it is less.

Node C. Do nothing.

Strong growth in first year =	$170,000/yr. × 1 yr. =	$170,000
Value of best decision of not to expand	=	680,000
		$850,000
Weak growth in first year	=	$105,000
Keep store the same next four years (4 × $105,000) =		420,000
		$525,000

Expected return at Node C = (.55 × $850,000) + (.45 × $525,000)
= $703,750

EXHIBIT 8.8   **Decision Tree for Hackers Computer Store**

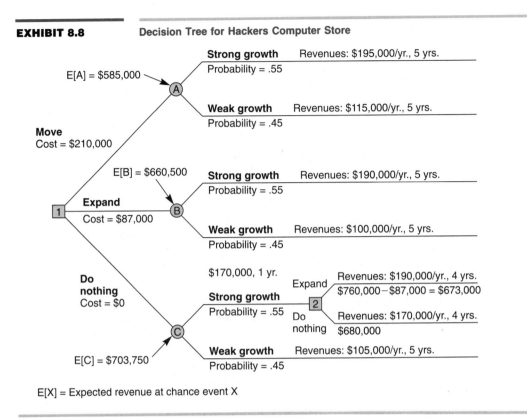

E[X] = Expected revenue at chance event X

The best choice is to do nothing with a value of $703,750 compared to $585,000 for the new site and $660,500 for the expansion.

8.4 FACILITY LOCATION

For manufacturers, the facility location problem is broadly categorized into factory location and warehouse location. Within this categorization, we may be interested in locating the firm's first factory or warehouse, or locating a new factory or warehouse relative to existing facilities.

The general objective in choosing a location is to select that site or combination of sites that minimizes three classes of costs: regional costs, outbound distribution costs, and inbound distribution costs. Regional costs are those associated with a given locale and include land, construction, labor, taxes, and energy costs. Outbound distribution costs are those costs incurred in shipping products to retailers, wholesalers, and other plants in the network. Inbound distribution costs refer to the availability and costs of raw materials and supplies, as well as the lead time to acquire these inputs. Because the location of the initial plant is usually determined by the historical context of the firm, economic analysis of facility location has focused on the problem of adding warehouses or factories to the existing production–distribution network.

Plant Location Methods

"If the boss likes Bakersfield, I like Bakersfield." The set of decisions that a company must make in choosing a plant location are summarized in Exhibit 8.9. While the exhibit implies a step-by-step process, virtually all activities listed take place simultaneously. As suggested by the preceding vote for Bakersfield, political decisions may occasionally override systematic analysis.

The evaluation of alternative regions, subregions, and communities is commonly termed *macro analysis,* and the evaluation of specific sites in the selected community is termed *micro analysis.* Some of the techniques used for macro analyses are factor-rating systems, linear programming, and center of gravity. A detailed cost analysis would accompany each of these methods, of course.

Factor-rating systems

Factor-rating systems are perhaps the most widely used of the general location techniques because they provide a mechanism to combine diverse factors in an easy-to-understand format.

By way of example, a refinery assigned the following range of point values to major factors affecting a set of possible sites.

	Range
Fuels in region	0 to 330
Power availability and reliability	0 to 200
Labor climate	0 to 100
Living conditions	0 to 100
Transportation	0 to 50
Water supply	0 to 10
Climate	0 to 50
Supplies	0 to 60
Tax policies and laws	0 to 20

Each site was then rated against each factor and a point value selected from its assigned range. The sums of assigned points for each site were then compared and the site with the maximum number of points was selected.

One of the major problems with simple point-rating schemes is that they do not account for the wide range of costs that may occur within each factor. For example, there may be only a few hundred dollars' difference between the best and worst locations on one factor and several thousands of dollars' difference between the best and the worst on another. The first factor may have the most points available to it but provide little help in making the location decision; the latter may have few points available but potentially show a real difference in the value of locations. To deal with this problem, Phillip Hicks and Areen

EXHIBIT 8.9

**Plant Search:
Company XYZ**

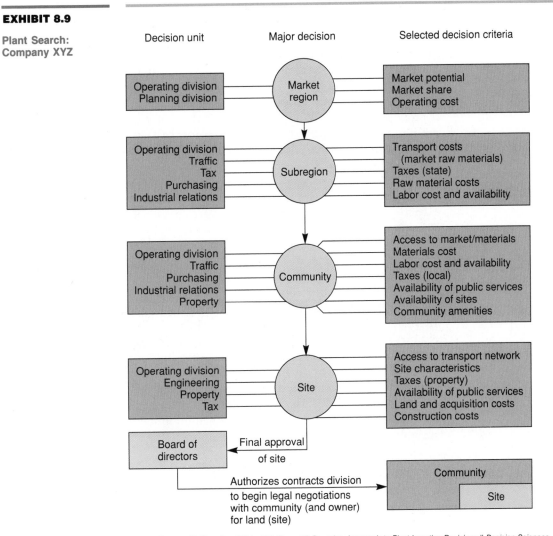

Source: Thomas M. Carroll and Robert D. Dean, "A Bayesian Approach to Plant-Location Decisions," *Decision Sciences* 11, no. 1 (January 1980), p. 87.

Kumtha suggest that points possible for each factor be derived using a weighting scale based on standard deviations of costs rather than simply total cost amounts.[5] This method is useful and the interested reader should consult the original publication for details of calculation.

---

[5] Phillip E. Hicks and Areen M. Kumtha, "One Way to Tighten Up Plant Location Decisions," *Industrial Engineering* 9 (April 1971), pp. 19–23.

Linear programming

The transportation method of linear programming (discussed in the supplement to this chapter) can be used to test the cost impact of different candidate locations on the entire production-distribution network. The way it works can be seen by reference to the Puck and Pawn Company example in the supplement. Here, we might add a new row which contains the unit shipping costs from a factory in a new location, X, to warehouses E, F, G, and H, along with the total amount it could supply. We could then solve this particular matrix for minimum total cost. Next we would replace the factory located in X in the same row of the matrix with a factory at a different location, say Y, and again solve for minimum total cost. Assuming factories in X and Y would be identical in other important respects, the location resulting in the lowest total cost for the network would be selected. As can be seen, this method is quite easy to use but it does require that at least subregional locations be identified before a solution can be found.

Center of gravity method

The **center of gravity method** is a technique for locating single facilities that considers the existing facilities, the distances between them, and the volumes of goods that need to be shipped. The technique is often used to locate intermediate or distribution warehouses. In its simplest form, this method assumes that inbound and outbound transportation costs are equal, and it does not include special shipping costs for less than full loads.

The center of gravity method begins by placing the existing locations on a coordinate grid system. The choice of coordinate systems is entirely arbitrary. The purpose is to establish relative distances between locations. Using longitude and latitude coordinates might be helpful in international decisions. An example of a grid layout is shown in Exhibit 8.10.

The center of gravity is found by calculating the X and Y coordinates that result in the minimal transportation cost. The following formulas are used:

$$C_x = \frac{\Sigma d_{ix} V_i}{\Sigma V_i}$$

$$C_y = \frac{\Sigma d_{iy} V_i}{\Sigma V_i}$$

where

C_x = X coordinate of the center of gravity
C_y = Y coordinate of the center of gravity
d_{ix} = X coordinate of the ith location
d_{iy} = Y coordinate of the ith location
V_i = Volume of goods moved to or from the ith location

EXHIBIT 8.10

Grid Map for Center
of Gravity Example

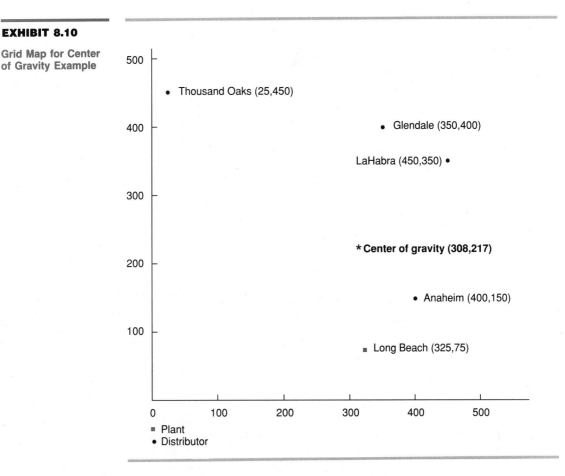

Example

The HiOctane Refining Company needs to locate an intermediate holding facility between its refining plant in Long Beach and its major distributors. The coordinate map is shown in Exhibit 8.10. The amount of gasoline shipped to or from the plant and distributors is shown in Exhibit 8.11.

In this example, the data for the Long Beach location (the first location) are

$$d_{1x} = 325$$
$$d_{1y} = 75$$
$$V_1 = 1,500$$

Using the information in Exhibits 8.10 and 8.11, we are able to calculate the coordinates of the center of gravity as follows:

EXHIBIT 8.11

Shipping Volumes,
Center of Gravity
Example

Locations	Gallons of Gasoline per Month (000,000)
Long Beach	1,500
Anaheim	250
LaHabra	450
Glendale	350
Thousand Oaks	450

$$C_x = \frac{(325 \times 1,500) + (400 \times 250) + (450 \times 450) + (350 \times 350) + (25 \times 450)}{1,500 + 450 + 250 + 350 + 450}$$

$$= \frac{923,750}{3,000}$$

$$= 307.9$$

$$C_y = \frac{(75 \times 1,500) + (150 \times 250) + (350 \times 450) + (400 \times 350) + (450 \times 450)}{1,500 + 450 + 250 + 350 + 450}$$

$$= \frac{650,000}{3,000}$$

$$= 216.7$$

This gives management the X and Y coordinates of approximately 308 and 217 respectively, and provides an initial starting point to search for a new site. By examining the location of the calculated center of gravity on the grid map, we can see that it might be more cost efficient to ship directly between the Long Beach plant and the Anaheim distributor than to ship via a warehouse near the center of gravity. Before a location decision is made, management would probably recalculate the center of gravity, changing the data to reflect this (i.e., decrease the gallons shipped from Long Beach by the amount Anaheim needs and remove Anaheim from the formula).

Detailed cost analyses
A detailed cost analysis must be done before a location decision is finalized. Exhibit 8.12, taken from *Factory* magazine, presents an actual cost analysis used by a company contemplating the relocation of its plant. Note that present-value calculations are also commonly used to augment cost calculations shown in this exhibit.

8.5 LOCATING SERVICE FACILITIES

In service organizations, the facility location decision is also major; as a rule, the choice of locale is based on nearness to the customer rather than on resource considerations. Because of the variety of service firms and the relatively low cost

EXHIBIT 8.12   Cost Analysis Example (Present location versus recommended communities)

Operating Expenses	Present Location	Community A	Community B	Community C
Transportation				
Inbound	$ 202,942	$ 212,209	$ 207,467	$ 220,009
Outbound	480,605	361,268	393,402	365,198
Labor				
Hourly direct and indirect	1,520,943	1,339,790	1,146,087	1,223,416
Fringe benefits	304,189	187,571	126,070	159,044
Plant overhead				
Rent or carrying costs	271,436	290,000	280,000	295,000
Real estate taxes	43,345	39,000	34,000	39,000
Personal property and other locally assessed				
taxes	16,899	—	—	8,500
Fuel for heating	19,260	11,000	9,500	13,000
Utilities				
Power	56,580	61,304	41,712	49,007
Gas	18,460	19,812	13,767	16,633
Water	12,474	8,200	4,500	4,500
Treatment of effluent	6,376	—	2,300	—
State factors				
State taxes	67,811	73,400	44,920	71,000
Workers' compensation insurance	30,499	24,000	14,000	17,000
Total	$3,051,819	$ 2,627,554	$ 2,317,725	$ 2,481,337
Savings through construction of new plant				
New plant layout		$(210,000)	$(210,000)	$(210,000)
Reduced materials handling		(38,000)	(38,000)	(38,000)
Elimination of present local interplant				
movements		(60,000)	(60,000)	(60,000)
Reduced public warehousing		(30,000)	(30,000)	(30,000)
Reduced supervisory personnel		(27,000)	(27,000)	(27,000)
Savings through new construction		$(365,000)	$(365,000)	$(365,000)
Annual operating costs	$3,051,819	$ 2,262,554	$ 1,952,725	$ 2,116,337
Potential annual savings over present location		$ 789,265	$ 1,099,094	$ 935,482
Percentage of savings		25.9%	36.0%	30.7%

Source: "New Plants and Expansions, End of Tunnel May Be in Sight," *Factory* (September 1975), p. 57.

of establishing a service facility compared to one for manufacturing, new service facilities are far more common than new factories and warehouses. Indeed, there are few communities in which rapid population growth has not been paralleled by a concurrent rapid growth in retail outlets, restaurants, municipal services, and entertainment facilities.

Services typically have multiple sites to maintain close contact with customers. The location decision is closely tied to the market selection decision. If the target market is college-age groups, locations in retirement communities, despite desirability in terms of cost, resource availability, and so forth, are not viable alternatives. Market needs also affect the number of sites to be built, the size, and the characteristics of the sites. Whereas manufacturing location decisions are often made by minimizing costs, many of the service location decision techniques maximize the profit potential of various sites.

Screening Location Sites at La Quinta Motor Inns

Selecting good sites plays a crucial role in the success of a hotel chain. Of the four major marketing considerations: price, product, promotion, and location, location and product have been shown to be the most important for multisite

---

EXHIBIT 8.13

Independent Variables Collected for the Initial Model Building Stage

Category	Name	Description
Competitive	INNRATE	Inn price
	PRICE	Room rate for the inn
	RATE	Average competitive room rate
	RMS1	Hotel rooms within 1 mile
	RMSTOTAL	Hotel rooms within 3 miles
	ROOMSINN	Inn rooms
Demand generators	CIVILIAN	Civilian personnel on base
	COLLEGE	College enrollment
	HOSP1	Hospital beds within 1 mile
	HOSPTOTL	Hospital beds within 4 miles
	HVYIND	Heavy industrial employment
	LGTIND	Light industrial acreage
	MALLS	Shopping mall square footage
	MILBLKD	Military base blocked
	MILITARY	Military personnel
	MILTOT	MILITARY + CIVILIAN
	OFCI	Office space within 1 mile
	OFCTOTAL	Office space within 4 miles
	OFCCBD	Office space in CBD
	PASSENGR	Airport passengers enplaned
	RETAIL	Scale ranking of retail activity
	TOURISTS	Annual tourists
	TRAFFIC	Traffic count
	VAN	Airport van
Demographic	EMPLYPCT	Unemployment percentage
	INCOME	Average family income
	POPULACE	Residential population
Market awareness	AGE	Years inn has been open
	NEAREST	Distance to nearest inn
	STATE	State population per inn
	URBAN	Urban population per inn
Physical	ACCESS	Accessibility
	ARTERY	Major traffic artery
	DISTCBD	Distance to downtown
	SIGNVIS	Sign visibility

Source: Reprinted by permission of Sheryl E. Kimes and James A. Fitzsimmons, "Selecting Profitable Hotel Sites at La Quinta Motor Inns," *Interfaces* 20 (March–April 1990). Copyright 1990 The Institute of Management Sciences, 290 Westminster Street, Providence, Rhode Island 02903 USA.

firms. As a result, hotel chain owners who can pick good sites quickly have a distinct competitive advantage.

Exhibit 8.13 shows the initial list of variables included in a study to assist La Quinta Motor Inns in screening potential locations for its new hotels.[6] Data were collected on 57 existing La Quinta Inns. Analysis of the data identified the variables that correlated with operating profit in 1983 and 1986 (see Exhibit 8.14).

A regression model was then constructed and in its final form appears as follows:

$$
\begin{aligned}
\text{Profitability} = 39.05 &- 5.41 \times \text{State population per inn (1,000)} \\
&+ 5.86 \times \text{Price of the inn} \\
&- 3.91 \times \text{Square root of the median income of the area (1,000)} \\
&+ 1.75 \times \text{College students within four miles.}
\end{aligned}
$$

The model shows that profitability is affected by market penetration, positively affected by price, negatively affected by higher incomes (the inns do better in lower median income areas), and positively affected by colleges nearby.

La Quinta implemented the model on a Lotus 1-2-3 spreadsheet and routinely uses the spreadsheet to screen potential real estate acquisitions. The

EXHIBIT 8.14

A Summary of the Variables that Correlated with Operating Margin in 1983 and 1986

Variable	1983	1986
ACCESS	.20	
AGE	.29	.49
COLLEGE		.25
DISTCBD		−.22
EMPLYPCT	−.22	−.22
INCOME		−.23
MILTOT		.22
NEAREST	−.51	
OFCCBD	.30	
POPULACE	.30	.35
PRICE	.38	.58
RATE		.27
STATE	−.32	−.33
SIGNVIS	.25	
TRAFFIC	.32	
URBAN	−.22	−.26

Source: Reprinted by permission of Sheryl E. Kimes and James A. Fitzsimmons, "Selecting Profitable Hotel Sites at La Quinta Motor Inns," *Interfaces* 20 (March–April 1990). Copyright 1990 The Institute of Management Sciences, 290 Westminster Street, Providence, Rhode Island 02903 USA.

---

[6] Sheryl E. Kimes and James A. Fitzsimmons, "Selecting Profitable Hotel Sites at La Quinta Motor Inns," *Interfaces* 20 (March–April 1990), pp. 12–20.

founder and president of La Quinta has accepted the model's validity and no longer feels obligated to personally select the sites.

This example shows that a specific model can be obtained from the requirements of service organizations and used to identify those features that are most important in making the right site selection. The Insert discusses the expansion criteria and strategies of AM/PM International.

INSERT   **How AM/PM International Selects Its Sites**

AM/PM convenience stores are a subsidiary of the ARCO Corporation. These stores are usually connected with service stations. The goals of AM/PM International are to leverage the existing AM/PM program through brand licensing agreements in foreign countries and joint-venture participation. Furthermore, ARCO wants to participate aggressively in emerging international markets and leverage its international presence. ARCO also wants to generate additional long-term profits.

To select a new potential country, AM/PM International looks at four main criteria:

1. The population should be over 1 million in a targeted city.
2. Annual per-capita income should be over $2,000.
3. The political system should be fairly stable.
4. The host country should have minimal restrictions on hard currency repatriation.

Once AM/PM has selected a potential country for its business, it evaluates further, the country's

1. Stage of industrial development.
2. People/car ratio. (This is important because the AM/PM stores are located in service stations.)
3. Population density in rural and urban areas.
4. Availability and cost of labor.
5. Infrastructure (supply and distribution, equipment availability, real estate cost, and reliability of utilities).
6. Tax regulations.
7. Legal issues.

AM/PM International uses franchising as a rapid and convenient way to expand in the Pacific Rim, Europe, and North America. The company's prospect list for the next expansion includes Italy, France, Denmark, Mexico, Brazil, Malysia, and Canada.

AM/PM's international expansion strategy is based on three points:

First, using the existing service station staff to run the convenience store.

Second, for the first year an American-trained manager works closely with the new licensee.

Third, to develop new stores in selected countries as quickly as possible.

Source: ARCO presentation to U.S.C. MBA students, June 5, 1991.

A common problem encountered by service-providing organizations is decid-ing how many service outlets to establish within a geographical area, and where. The problem is complicated by the fact that there are usually many possible locations and several options in the absolute number of service cen-ters. Thus, attempting to find a good solution, much less an optimal one, can be extremely time consuming, even for a relatively small problem. For exam-ple, there would be 243 possible solutions for a problem involving choosing among one, two, or three retail outlets to serve four geographically dispersed customer populations, even where there are only three possible locations for the outlets. To illustrate one approach to searching for feasible solutions to such problems, we apply to a sample problem a heuristic method based on one described by Alireza Ardalan.[7]

Example

Suppose that a medical consortium wishes to establish two clinics to provide medical care for people living in four communities in Off Tackle County, Ohio. Assume that the sites under study are in each community and that the population of each community is evenly distributed within the community's boundaries. Further, assume that the potential use of the clinics by members of the various communities has been determined and weighting factors reflecting the relative importance of serving members of the population of each commu-nity have been developed. (This information is given in Exhibit 8.15.) The objective of the problem: find the two clinics that can serve all communities at the lowest weighted travel-distance cost.

Procedure
Step 1. Construct a weighted population-distance table from initial data table, multiplying distance times weighting factor (Exhibit 8.16). For exam-ple, Community A to Clinic B is $11 \times 1.1 \times 10 = 121$.

EXHIBIT 8.15

Distances,
Population, and
Relative Weights

From Community	MILES TO CLINIC				Population of Community (thousands)	Relative Weighting of Population
	A	B	C	D		
A	0	11	8	12	10	1.1
B	11	0	10	7	8	1.4
C	8	10	0	9	20	0.7
D	9.5	7	9	0	12	1.0

---

[7] Alireza Ardalan, "An Efficient Heuristic for Service Facility Location," *Proceedings, North-east Decision Sciences Institute Conference,* 1984, pp. 181–82.

EXHIBIT 8.16

Weighted Population
Distances

From Community	TO CLINIC			
	A	B	C	D
A	0	121	88	132
B	123.2	0	112	78.4
C	112	140	0	126
D	114	84	108	0

Step 2. Add the amounts in each column. Choose the community with the lowest cost and locate a facility there (Community C, in our example). (Recall that costs are expressed in weighted population–distance units.)

From Community	TO CLINIC LOCATED IN COMMUNITY			
	A	B	C	D
A	0	121	88	132
B	123.2	0	112	78.4
C	112	140	0	126
D	114	84	108	0
	349.2	345	308	336.4

Step 3. For each row, compare the cost of each column entry to the community clinics already located. If the cost is less, do not change them. If the cost is greater, reduce the cost to the lowest of the sites already selected.

From Community	TO CLINIC LOCATED IN COMMUNITY			
	A	B	C	D
A	0	88	88	88
B	112	0	112	78.4
C	0	0	0	0
D	108	84	108	0
	220	172	308	166.4

Step 4. If additional locations are desired, choose the community with the lowest cost from those not already selected (Community D in our example).

Step 5. Repeat step 3, reducing each row entry that exceeds the entry in the column just selected.

From Community	TO CLINIC LOCATED IN COMMUNITY		
	A	B	D
A	0	88	88
B	78.4	0	78.4
C	0	0	0
D	0	0	0
	78.4	88	166.4

Continue repeating Steps 4 and 5 until the desired number of locations is selected. If we wished to compute the complete list, it would be as follows:

	TO CLINIC LOCATED IN COMMUNITY	
From Community	A	B
A	0	0
B	78.4	0
C	0	0
D	0	0
	78.4	0

The problem has now been solved for all four possible locations. Choose C first, then D, then A, then B.

The logic in this procedure is as follows:

1. Selecting the least total cost column is obvious, since this column location represents the lowest travel cost of all communities traveling to that location.

2. Once a location is chosen, no rational member of a community would travel to any other community that was more costly. In Step 2, for example, residents in Community A would certainly prefer going to a clinic located in Community C (88), which has already been decided on, than to B (121) or D (132). Therefore, the maximum number of weighted population-distance units that residents of A would be willing to pay is 88, and we can use this amount as our top limit. If a clinic is located in A, however, residents of A would patronize their own community clinic (at a cost of 0). Residents in Community B would prefer C (112) to A (123.2) but not to B (0) or D (78.4). Therefore, the cost 123.2 is reduced to 112, but 0 and 78.4 remain unchanged.

3. Once a community location is selected and the matrix costs adjusted, that community can be dropped from the matrix, since the column costs are no longer relevant.

8.6 CONCLUSION

Like so many topics in operations management, capacity planning and location decisions are becoming heavily affected by the information revolution and globalization of production. The emergence of the network firm (or *hollow corporation* that coordinates production of multiple suppliers rather than producing them in house) has changed the way management views its available capacity, and the growth of international markets has altered its location strategies. It is already clear that the operations executives of many companies must catch a plane to see the multiple shop floors that constitute the capacity of their organizations.

8.7 REVIEW AND DISCUSSION QUESTIONS

1. Does it make sense to say that a particular plant is working at 110 percent of capacity?

2. List some practical limits to economies of scale; that is, when should a plant stop growing?

3. What are some capacity balance problems faced by the following organizations or facilities?
   a. An airline terminal.
   b. A university computing center.
   c. A clothing manufacturer.

4. What are the primary capacity planning considerations for foreign companies locating their facilities in the United States?

5. What are some major capacity considerations in a hospital? How do they differ from those of a factory?

6. Develop a list of five major reasons why a new electronics firm should move into your city or town.

7. How do facilities planning decisions differ for service facilities and manufacturing plants?

8. Management may choose to build up capacity in anticipation of demand or in response to developing demand. Cite the advantages and disadvantges of both approaches.

9. Which motivations typically cause firms to initiate major capacity/facilities planning projects, such as the one described in Exhibit 8.4?

10. What is capacity balance? Why is this condition difficult to achieve? What methods are used to deal with capacity imbalances?

11. How does the emergence of the network firm (hollow corporation) change the way management plans for capacity?

8.8 PROBLEMS

*1. The managers of Banana Computers Inc., manufacturer of computer peripheral equipment, after having read this chapter, decide to develop a Six-Year National Resource Plan for the three existing plants. Two product lines will be considered. The first product line (Product Family A) involves the production of hard disks of similar access time (28ms), but different memory sizes (20, 40, and 80 megabytes). The second line (Product Family B) involves the production of laser printers with capacities of 8 pages per minute, 15 pages per minute, and 30 pages per minute. The current annual sales forecast in stockkeeping units detail is

	SKU	Product Family A	Product Family B
Forecasts	1	5,700	1,200
	2	4,200	5,400
	3	2,900	2,800

---

* Solutions to Problems 1a, 1b, and 2 are provided in Appendix H.

The forecasted growth for Product Family A, for years 2 through 6 is 6, 5, 5, 6, and 7 percent, respectively. The forecasted growth for Product Family B, for years 2 through 6 is 8, 8, 9, 9, and 7 percent, respectively.

The equipment and labor planning values for the two product families are

	SKU	Product Family A	Product Family B
Equipment planning values	1	10,000	3,000
	2	7,000	10,000
	3	6,000	7,000
Labor planning values	1	12	12
	2	12	12
	3	10	10

a. Develop a six-year growth forecast with SKU detail for Banana Computers Inc.

b. Calculate the equipment demand, as well as the labor demand for both product families.

c. The Banana marketing department has just finished preparing a large scale promotional campaign for Product Family B, the results of which will have a tremendous impact on the Product Family B sales, for the next two years. The following table shows the forecast extensions for Product Family B according to the Banana marketing department. Modify your answer in *a* and *b* to include the effects of the campaign. Forecasts for years 4 through 6 will be the same as those calculated in part *a*.

		PRODUCT FAMILY B		
	SKU	Current Year	Year 2	Year 3
Forecasts	1	1,200	2,000	2,500
	2	5,400	8,000	10,000
	3	2,800	4,000	5,000

*2. Sam Malone, owner of Cheers is moving to Los Angeles and trying to decide whether to lease a bar at a site near the Ventura Freeway in Hollywood or build a new bar near a fork in the Slauson Freeway in Inglewood. The bar will be built on state-leased land that will be part of a new expanded intersection in 10 years. Thus, there is no salvage value at the termination of the 10-year period.

The initial lease will run for a period of two years. If the owner is satisfied at that time, he will extend the lease for an additional eight years. Sam attaches a 50-50 probability to this renewal. If the lease is canceled, Sam knows of another cafe-bar nearby that will be available for leasing, but the lease will be 30 percent more than the present site. Given this information and the following information, develop a decision tree to help Sam choose between these sites. (Use a 10-year planning horizon.) Disregard the cost of capital.

Decision Variables	Hollywood Site	Probability	Inglewood Site	Probability
Cost to lease per year	$250,000			
Cost to build			$1,000,000	.
Gross revenue per year				
High sales	700,000	0.5	400,000	0.5
Medium sales	500,000	0.3	300,000	0.3
Low sales	300,000	0.2	200,000	0.2
Operating costs per year	200,000		200,000	

EXHIBIT 8.17

Plant Location Matrix

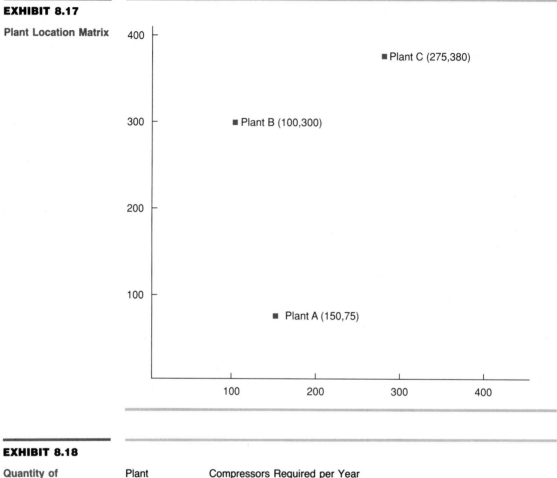

EXHIBIT 8.18

Quantity of Compressors Required by Each Plant

Plant	Compressors Required per Year
A	6,000
B	8,200
C	7,000

3. Cool Air, a manufacturer of automotive air conditioners, currently produces its XB-300 line at three different locations, Plant A, Plant B, and Plant C. Recently, management decided to build all compressors, a major product component, in a separate dedicated facility, Plant D.

   Using the center of gravity method and the information displayed in Exhibits 8.17 and 8.18, determine the best location for Plant D. Assume a linear relationship between volumes shipped and shipping costs (no premium charges).

4. Refer to the information given in Problem 3. Suppose management decides to shift 2,000 units of production from Plant B to Plant A. Does this change the

proposed location of Plant D, the compressor production facility? If so, where should Plant D be located?

5. A drugstore chain plans to open four stores in a medium-sized city. However, funds are limited, so only two can be opened this year.

   a. Given the following matrix showing the weighted population distance costs for each of the four areas and four store sites, select the two to be opened up first.

   b. If additional funds become available, which store should be the third to open?

		Store			
		1	2	3	4
Geographic Area	1	0	20	160	60
	2	80	0	40	80
	3	120	80	0	100
	4	80	100	60	0

6. A firm is considering four possible office locations within a particular city. Eventually, the firm would like to have an office in each location, but at the present time the firm's managers would like to open just one; however, they would like to know the sequence in which they should open all four offices. Following is a matrix that shows the costs for opening each office in each area. Determine the order in which they should be opened.

		Office			
		A	B	C	D
Geographic Area	A	0	34	40	30
	B	24	0	36	54
	C	60	20	0	36
	D	50	40	60	0

7. A builder has located a piece of property that he would like to buy and eventually build on. What he does not yet know is exactly what he will build. The land is currently zoned for four homes per acre, but he is planning to request new zoning. What he builds depends on approval of zoning requests and your analysis of this problem to advise him. With his input and your help, the decision process has been reduced to the following costs, alternatives, and probabilities:

Cost of land: $2 million.

Probability of rezoning: .60.

If the land is rezoned, there will be additional costs for new roads, lighting, and so on, of $1 million.

If the land is rezoned, the contractor must decide whether to build a shopping center or 1,500 apartments that the tentative plan shows would be possible. If he builds a shopping center, there is a 70 percent chance that he can sell the shopping center to a large department chain for $4 million over his construction cost which excludes the land, and there is a 30 percent chance that he may be able to sell it to an insurance company for $5 million over his construction cost (also excluding the land). If, instead of the shopping center, he decides to build the 1,500 apartments, he places probabilities on the profits as follows: There is a 60 percent chance that he can sell the apartments to a real estate investment corporation for $3,000 each over his construction cost and a 40 percent chance that he may be able to get only $2,000 each over his construction cost (both exclude his land cost).

If the land is not rezoned, he will comply with the existing zoning restrictions and simply build 600 homes on which he expects to make $4,000 over his construction cost on each one (excluding his cost of land).

Draw a decision tree of the problem and determine the best solution and the expected net profit.

8.9 CASE: COMMUNITY HOSPITAL*

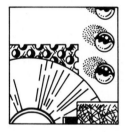

In 1983, Community Hospital, which had served the downtown area of a large West Coast city for over a quarter century, closed and then built a new hospital in a thinly populated area about 30 miles west of the city. The new hospital, also named Community Hospital, was located on a parcel of land owned by the original hospital for many years.

This new hospital, which opened October 1, 1983, is a four-story structure that includes all the latest innovations in health-care technology. The first floor houses the emergency department; intensive care unit; operating room; radiology, laboratory, and therapy departments; pharmacy; and housekeeping and maintenance facilities and supplies, as well as other supportive operations. All administrative offices, such as the business office, medical records department, special services, and so forth, are located on the second floor, as are the cafeteria and food service facilities. The two upper floors contain patient rooms divided into surgical, medical, pediatric, and obstetric units.

Community Hospital has a total capacity of 177 beds assigned as follows:

Unit	Number of Beds
Surgical	45
Medical	65
Pediatrics	35
Obstetrics	20
Intensive care	12

For the first six months of the hospital's operation, things were rather chaotic for the administrator, Sam Jones. All his time was occupied with the multitude of activities that go along with starting a new facility, seeing that malfunctioning equipment is repaired, arranging for new staff to be hired and trained, establishing procedures and schedules, making necessary purchasing decisions, and attending endless conferences and meetings.

All during this period, Mr. Jones had been getting some rather disturbing reports from his controller, Bob Cash, regarding Community Hospital's financial situation.

---

* Reprinted with permission from *Hospital Cost Containment through Operations Management,* published by the American Hospital Association. Copyright 1984.

But he decided that these financial matters would simply have to wait until things had settled down.

Finally, in April, Mr. Jones asked Mr. Cash to prepare a comprehensive report on the hospital's financial position and to make a presentation to himself and his new assistant administrator, Tim Newman, who had recently received a degree in hospital administration.

In his report, Mr. Cash stated: "As you both know, we have been running at an operating cash deficit since we opened last October. We expected, of course, to be losing money at the start until we were able to establish ourselves in the community and draw in patients. We certainly were right. During our first month, we lost almost $221,000. Last month, in March, we lost $58,000.

"The reason, of course, is pretty straightforward. Our income is directly related to our patient load. On the other hand, our expenses are fixed and are running at about $235,000 a month for salaries and wages, $75,000 a month for supplies and equipment, and another $10,000 a month in interest charges. Our accumulated operating deficit for the six months we've been here totals $715,000, which we've covered with our bank line of credit. I suppose we can continue to borrow for another couple of months, but after that I don't know what we're going to do."

Mr. Jones replied, "As you said, Bob, we did expect to be losing money in the beginning, but I never expected the loss to go on for six months or to accumulate to almost three quarters of a million dollars. Well, at least last month was a lot better than the first month. Do you have any figures showing the month-to-month trend?"

Bob Cash laid the following worksheet on the table:

COMMUNITY HOSPITAL'S
Six-Month Operating Statement,
October 1983–March 1984
(in thousands of dollars)

	1983			1984			
	October	November	December	January	February	March	Total
Income	$ 101	$ 163	$ 199	$ 235	$ 245	$ 262	$ 1,205
Expenses (excluding interest)							
Salaries, wages	232	233	239	235	236	236	1,410
Supplies, other	80	73	74	75	73	75	450
Total	312	306	313	310	309	310	1,860
Interest	10	10	10	10	10	10	60
Operating loss	$(221)	$(153)	$(124)	$(85)	$(74)	$(58)	$(715)
Average daily census	42	68	83	98	102	109	
Occupancy	24%	38%	47%	55%	58%	62%	

QUESTIONS

1. Evaluate the situation at Community Hospital with respect to trends in daily census, occupancy rate, and income.

2. Has there been any change in revenue per patient-day over the six-month period (assuming a 30-day month)?

3. At what capacity level will the hospital achieve breakeven?

4. What questions might we raise about the constant level of salaries and supplies relative to past and future operations?

8.10 SELECTED BIBLIOGRAPHY

Blackburn, Joseph, D. *Time-Based Competition: The Next Battle Ground in American Manufacturing.* Homewood, Ill.: Richard D. Irwin, 1991.

Coyle, John J., and Edward J. Bardi. *The Management of Logistics,* 2nd ed. St. Paul: West Publishing, 1980, pp. 294–98.

Francis, R. L., and J. A. White. *Facilities Layout and Location: An Analytical Approach.* Englewood Cliffs, N.J.: Prentice Hall, 1987.

Graziano, Vincent J. "Production Capacity Planning—Long Term." *Production and Inventory Management* 15, no. 2 (Second Quarter 1974), pp. 66–80.

Heskett, J. L.; W. E. Sasser, Jr.; and C. W. L. Hart. *Service Breakthroughs: Changing the Rules of the Game.* New York: Free Press, 1990.

Shycon, Harvey N. "Site Location Analysis, Cost and Customer Service Consideration." *Proceedings of the Seventeenth Annual International Conference,* American Production and Inventory Control Society, 1974, pp. 335–47.

Skinner, Wickham. "The Focused Factory." *Harvard Business Review,* May–June 1974, pp. 113–21.

Tompkins, James A., and John A. White. *Facilities Planning.* New York: John Wiley & Sons, 1984.

Wheelwright, Steven C., ed. *Capacity Planning and Facilities Choice: Course Module.* Boston: Harvard Business School, 1979.

Supplement

Linear Programming

EPIGRAPH

Unquestionably, linear optimization models are among the most commercially successful applications of operations research; in fact, there is considerable evidence that they rate highest in economic impact.

Harvey Wagner

KEY TERMS

Graphical Linear Programming

Objective Functions

Constraint Equations

Convex Polygon

Simplex Method

Slack Variables

Maximization and Minimization

Shadow Prices

Sensitivity Analysis

Integer Programming

Transportation Method

Assignment Method

Karmarkar's Algorithm

General Algebraic Modeling System (GAMS)

*T*he term *linear programming,* as used in this supplement, refers to a mathematical technique which can allocate limited resources. A given sum of money in your pocket, for example, can be used to buy food, drink, entertainment, and so forth.

In addition to money, you may have a watch which you could pawn, and perhaps other items of jewelry. The programming problem that you could be faced with is, "How do I get the most value from the products and services that I purchase given the resources that I have?" If the ratios are all linear (e.g., two units are twice as good or cost twice as much as one), the linear programming technique can be used to solve the problem.

Linear programming (LP) is a mathematical optimization approach which finds wide use in such areas as airline routing, fuel blending, and distribution planning. In this supplement we discuss various LP models, including the simplex method (which can solve any reasonable-size linear programming problem) and the special application methods of graphical, transportation, and assignment methods. We also discuss shadow prices, ranging, and sensitivity analysis. Additionally, we included an illustration of the General Algebraic Modeling System (GAMS) and a discussion of Karmarkar's algorithm.

There are essentially four major conditions in a problem situation for linear programming to pertain. First, there must be limited resources (e.g., a limited number of workers, equipment, finances, material); otherwise there would be no problem. Second, there must be an explicit objective (such as maximize profit or minimize cost). Third, there must be linearity (two is twice as good as one; if it takes three hours to make a part, then two parts would take six hours, three parts would take nine hours). Last, there must be homogeneity (the products produced on a machine are identical, or all the hours available from a worker are equally productive). Another condition concerns the question of divisibility: normal linear programming assumes that products and resources can be subdivided into fractions. If this subdivision is not possible (such as flying half an airplane or hiring one fourth of a person), a modification of linear programming, called *integer programming,* can be used.

When a single objective is to be maximized (e.g., profit) or minimized (e.g., costs), we can use *linear programming.* When multiple objectives exist, *goal programming* is used. If a problem is best solved in stages or time frames, this is *dynamic programming.* Other restrictions on the nature of the problem may require that it be solved by other variations of the technique, such as *nonlinear programming* or *quadratic programming.*

Solving a linear programming problem of even several equations is almost impossible to do by hand. Any practical problem must be solved on a computer. The greatest boon to making linear programming a common choice to solve problems is the tremendous increase in the speed of computers in recent years. From the original PC marketed in 1980 with an 8088 chip, we have progressed through the 286, 386, 486, and other higher architectures such as the IBM RS6000. Furthermore, several linear programming software programs now either incorporate or are adaptable to spreadsheet programs. This has made them much more understandable and easy to use. In this supplement, we include a list of available linear programming software programs, prices, capacities, and so on. These were selected to represent a range from the simple to the complex.

S8.1 THE LINEAR PROGRAMMING MODEL

Stated formally, the linear programming problem entails an optimizing process in which nonnegative values for a set of decision variables $X_1, X_2 \ldots X_n$ are selected so as to maximize (or minimize) an objective function in the form

Maximize (minimize) $Z = C_1 X_1 + C_2 X_2 + \ldots + C_n X_n$

subject to resource constraints in the form

$$A_{11} X_1 + A_{12} X_2 + \ldots + A_{1n} X_n \leq B_1$$
$$A_{21} X_1 + A_{22} X_2 + \ldots + A_{2n} X_n \leq B_2$$

$$.$$
$$.$$
$$.$$

$$A_{m1} X_1 + A_{m2} X_2 + \ldots + A_{mn} X_n \leq B_m$$

where C_j, A_{ij}, and B_i are given constants.

Depending on the problem, the constraints may also be stated with equal-to signs ($=$) or greater-than-or-equal-to signs ($\geq$).

To repeat from the fourth paragraph of this chapter, the conditions for linear programming are

1. Resources must be limited.
2. There must be an objective function.
3. There must be linearity in the constraint equations and in the objective function.
4. Resources and products must be homogeneous.
5. For normal linear programming, variables must be divisible and non-negative.

S8.2 GRAPHICAL LINEAR PROGRAMMING

Though limited in application to problems involving two decision variables (or three variables for three-dimensional graphing), **graphical linear programming** provides a quick insight into the nature of linear programming and illustrates what takes place in the general simplex method described later.

We describe the steps involved in the graphical method in the context of a sample problem, that of the Puck and Pawn Company, which manufactures hockey sticks and chess sets. Each hockey stick yields an incremental profit of $2 and each chess set, $4. A hockey stick requires four hours of processing at Machine center A and two hours at Machine center B. A chess set requires six hours at Machine center A, six hours at Machine center B, and one hour at Machine center C. Machine center A has a maximum of 120 hours of available capacity per day, Machine center B has 72 hours, and Machine center C has 10 hours.

If the company wishes to maximize profit, how many hockey sticks and chess sets should be produced per day?

1. Formulate the problem in mathematical terms.   If H is the number of hockey sticks and C is the number of chess sets, to maximize profit the **objective function** may be stated as:

Maximize $Z = \$2H + \$4C$

The maximization will be subject to the following constraints:
   (1) $4H + 6C \leq 120$ (Machine center A)
   (2) $2H + 6C \leq 72$ (Machine center B)
   (3) $1C \leq 10$ (Machine center C)
         $H, C \geq 0$

2. Plot constraint equations.   The **constraint equations** are easily plotted by letting one variable equal zero and solving for the axis intercept of the other. (The inequality portions of the restrictions are disregarded for this step.) For the Machine center A constraint equation when $H = 0$, $C = 20$, and when $C = 0$, $H = 30$. For the Machine center B constraint equation, when $H = 0$, $C = 12$, and when $C = 0$, $H = 36$. For the Machine center C constraint equation, $C = 10$ for all values of H. These lines are graphed in Exhibit S8.1.

3. Determine the area of feasibility.   The direction of inequality signs in each constraint determines the area where a feasible solution is found. In this case, all inequalities are of the less-than-or-equal-to variety, which means that it would be impossible to produce any combination of products that would lie to the right of any constraint line on the graph. The region of feasible solutions is unshaded on the graph and forms a convex polygon. A **convex polygon** exists when a line drawn between any two points in the polygon stays within the boundaries of that polygon. If this condition of convexity does not exist, the problem is either incorrectly set up or not amenable to linear programming.

4. Plot the objective function.   The objective function may be plotted by assuming some arbitrary total profit figure and then solving for the axis

EXHIBIT S8.1   Graph of Hockey Stick and Chess Set Problem

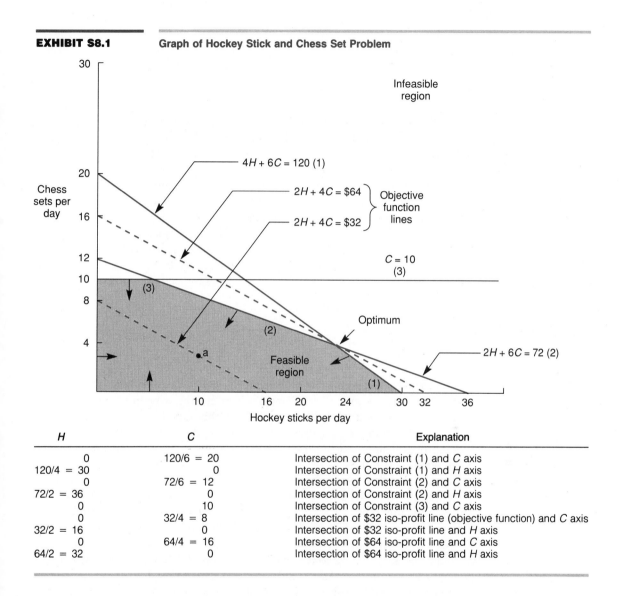

H	C	Explanation
0	120/6 = 20	Intersection of Constraint (1) and C axis
120/4 = 30	0	Intersection of Constraint (1) and H axis
0	72/6 = 12	Intersection of Constraint (2) and C axis
72/2 = 36	0	Intersection of Constraint (2) and H axis
0	10	Intersection of Constraint (3) and C axis
0	32/4 = 8	Intersection of $32 iso-profit line (objective function) and C axis
32/2 = 16	0	Intersection of $32 iso-profit line and H axis
0	64/4 = 16	Intersection of $64 iso-profit line and C axis
64/2 = 32	0	Intersection of $64 iso-profit line and H axis

coordinates, as was done for the constraint equations. Other terms for the objective function, when used in this context, are the *iso-profit* or *equal contribution line,* because it shows all possible production combinations for any given profit figure. For example, from the dotted line closest to the origin on the graph, we can determine all possible combinations of hockey sticks and chess sets that yield $32 by picking a point on the line and reading the number of each product that can be made at that point. The combination yielding $32 at point *a* would be 10 hockey sticks and 3 chess sets. This can be verified by substituting $H = 10$ and $C = 3$ in the objective function:

$2(10) + $4(3) = $20 + $12 = $32

5. Find the optimum point.   It can be shown mathematically that the optimal combination of decision variables is always found at an extreme point (corner point) of the convex polygon. In Exhibit S8.1 there are four corner points (excluding the origin), and we can determine which one is the optimum by either of two approaches. The first approach is to find the values of the various corner solutions algebraically. This entails simultaneously solving the equations of various pairs of intersecting lines and substituting the quantities of the resultant variables in the objective function. For example, the calculations for the intersection of $2H + 6C = 72$ and $C = 10$ would be as follows:

Substituting $C = 10$ in $2H + 6C = 72$ gives $2H + 6(10) = 72$, $2H = 12$, or $H = 6$. Substituting $H = 6$ and $C = 10$ in the objective function, we get:

$$\begin{aligned}
\text{Profit} &= \$2H + \$4C \\
&= \$2(6) + \$4(10) \\
&= \$12 + \$40 \\
&= \$52
\end{aligned}$$

A variation of this approach is to read the H and C quantities directly from the graph and substitute these quantities into the objective function, as shown in the previous calculation. The drawback in this approach is that in problems with a large number of constraint equations, there will be many possible points to evaluate, and the procedure of testing each one mathematically is somewhat inefficient.

The second and generally preferred approach entails using the objective function or iso-profit line directly to find the optimum point. The procedure involves simply drawing a straight line *parallel* to any arbitrarily selected initial iso-profit line so that the iso-profit line is farthest from the origin of the graph. (In cost minimization problems, the objective would be to draw the line through the point closest to the origin.) In Exhibit S8.1, the dashed line labeled $2H + \$4C = \$64$ intersects the most extreme point. Note that the initial arbitrarily selected iso-profit line is necessary to display the slope of the objective function for the particular problem.[1] This is important since a different objective function (try profit $= 3H + 3C$) might indicate that some other point is farthest from the origin. Given that $2H + \$4C = \$64$ is optimal, the amount of each variable to produce can be read from the graph: 24 hockey sticks and 4 chess sets. No other combination of the products yields a greater profit.

---

[1] The slope of the objective function is -2. If $P = $ profit, $P = \$2H + \$4C$; $2H = P - \$4C$; $H = p/2 - 2C$. Thus the slope is -2.

S8.3 THE SIMPLEX METHOD

The **simplex method** is an algebraic procedure that, through a series of repetitive operations, progressively approaches an optimal solution.[2] Theoretically, the simplex method can solve a problem consisting of any number of variables and constraints, although for problems containing more than, say, four variables or four constraint equations, the actual calculations are best left to the computer. There are many linear programming computer software packages available, and we would not expect anyone to try to solve even modest-sized problems by hand.

However, to fully understand linear programming, to know how to construct equations that would be put into a program, and to be able to use the output from the computer program, it is well worth the effort to go through the simplex method manually a few times.

Six-Step Solution Procedure

There are a number of technical steps in the simplex method, and each one is described in detail and summarized at the end of the section. We use the hockey stick and chess set problem to demonstrate the procedure involved.

Step 1: Problem formulation
Recall that to maximize profit we had

Maximize $Z = \$2H + \$4C$

subject to
    (1) $4H + 6C \leq 120$ (Machine center A constraint)
    (2) $2H + 6C \leq 72$ (Machine center B constraint)
    (3) $1C \leq 10$ (Machine center C constraint)
          $H, C \geq 0$ (nonnegativity requirement)

Step 2: Set up initial tableau with slack variables in solution
To use the simplex method requires two major adjustments to the problem as stated: (1) the introduction of slack variables and (2) the establishment of a solution table or tableau.

Introduce slack variables.   Each constraint equation is expanded to include a slack variable. A **slack variable,** which may be thought of as an idle resource in a practical sense, computationally represents the amount required to make one side of a constraint equation equal to the other—in other words, to convert the inequalities to equalities. For our problem, we need three slack variables: S_1 for the first constraint equation, S_2 for the second, and S_3 for the third.

---

[2] Simplex does not mean "simple"; it is a term used in n-space geometry.

The constraint equations appear as follows.

$$4H + 6C + 1S_1 = 120$$
$$2H + 6C + 1S_2 = 72$$
$$1C + 1S_3 = 10$$

So that all variables are represented in each equation, each slack variable not originally associated with a constraint equation is given a zero coefficient and added to that equation. Adjusting the system of equations in this way gives

$$4H + 6C + 1S_1 + 0S_2 + 0S_3 = 120$$
$$2H + 6C + 0S_1 + 1S_2 + 0S_3 = 72$$
$$0H + 1C + 0S_1 + 0S_2 + 1S_3 = 10$$

Note that the variable H, with a zero coefficient, is entered in the third equation to ensure that it also will be represented in all equations. Likewise, the objective function reflects the addition of slack variables, but since they yield no profit, their coefficient is $0:

$$Z = \$2H + \$4C + \$0S_1 + \$0S_2 + \$0S_3$$

Construct initial tableau.   A tableau (see Exhibit S8.2) is a convenient way of setting up the problem for simplex computation. A tableau provides the following information:

1. The variables that are in the solution at that point.
2. The profit associated with the solution.
3. The variable (if any) that adds most to profit if brought into the solution.
4. The amount of reduction in the variables in the solution that results from introducing one unit of each variable. This amount is termed the *substitution rate*.
5. The worth of an additional unit (e.g., hour) of resource capacity. This is referred to as a *shadow price*.

EXHIBIT S8.2

Initial Tableau of the Hockey Stick and Chess Set Problem

C_j	C_j Row	$2	$4	$0	$0	$0	
Column	Solution Mix	H	C	S_1	S_2	S_3	Quantity
$0	S_1	4	6	1	0	0	120
$0	S_2	2	6	0	1	0	72
$0	S_3	0	1	0	0	1	10 ←
	Z_j	$0	$0	$0	$0	$0	$0
	$C_j - Z_j$	$2	$4	$0	$0	$0	
		↑					

The first four features are discussed in reference to the first tableau; the last one is considered later.

The top row of Exhibit S8.2 contains the C_j's, or the contribution to total profit associated with the production of one unit of each alternative product. This row is a direct restatement of the coefficients of the variables in the objective function, and therefore remains the same for all subsequent tableaus. The first column, headed by C_j, merely lists, for convenience, the profit per unit of the variables included in the solution at any stage of the problem.

The variables chosen for the first tableau are listed under Solution Mix. As you can see, only slack variables are considered in the initial solution, and their profit coefficients are zero, which is indicated by the C_j column.

The constraint variables are listed to the right of Solution Mix, and under each one is the particular variable's coefficient in each constraint equation. That is, 4, 6, 1, 0, and 0 are the coefficients of the Machine center A constraint; 2, 6, 0, 1, and 0 for Machine center B; and 0, 1, 0, 0, and 1 for Machine center C.

Substitution rates can be ascertained from the numbers as well. For example, consider 4, 2, and 0, listed under H in the third column. For every unit of product H introduced into the solution, four units of S_1, two units of S_2, and zero units of S_3 must be withdrawn from the quantities available. The entries in the Quantity column refer to how many units of each resource are available in each machine center. In the initial tableau, this is a restatement of the right side of each constraint equation. With the exception of the value in the quantity column, the Z_j values in the second row from the bottom refer to the amount of *gross* profit that is given up by introducing one unit of that variable into the solution. The subscript j refers to the specific variable being considered. The Z_j value under the quantity column is the total profit for the solution. In the initial solution of a simplex problem, all values of Z_j are zero because no real product is being produced (all machines are idle), and hence there is no gross profit to be lost if they are replaced.

The bottom row of the tableau contains the *net* profit per unit, obtained by introducing one unit of a given variable into the solution. This row is designated the $C_j - Z_j$ row. The procedure for calculating Z_j and each $C_j - Z_j$ is demonstrated in Exhibit S8.3.

The initial solution to the problem is read directly from Exhibit S8.2: the company produces 120 units of S_1, 72 units of S_2, and 10 units of S_3. The total profit from this solution is \$0. Thus, no capacity has yet been allocated and no real product produced.

Step 3: Determine which variable to bring into solution

An improved solution is possible if there is a positive value in the $C_j - Z_j$ row. Recall that this row provides the net profit obtained by adding one unit of its associated column variable in the solution. In this example, there are two positive values to choose from: \$2, associated with H, and \$4, associated with C. Since our objective is to maximize profit, the logical choice is to pick the variable with the largest payoff to enter the solution, so variable C will be

---

EXHIBIT S8.3   Calculations of Z_j and $C_j - Z_j$

C_j H	C_j C	C_j S_1	C_j S_2	C_j S_3	C_j Quantity
\$0 × 4 = 0	\$0 × 6 = 0	\$0 × 1 = 0	\$0 × 0 = 0	\$0 × 0 = 0	\$0 × 120 = 0
+	+	+	+	+	+
\$0 × 2 = 0	\$0 × 6 = 0	\$0 × 0 = 0	\$0 × 1 = 0	\$0 × 0 = 0	\$0 × 72 = 0
+	+	+	+	+	+
\$0 × 0 = 0	\$0 × 1 = 0	\$0 × 0 = 0	\$0 × 0 = 0	\$0 × 1 = 0	\$0 × 10 = 0
Z_H = \$0	Z_C = \$0	Z_{S_1} = \$0	Z_{S_2} = \$0	Z_{S_3} = \$0	Z_Q = \$0

$C_j - Z_j$ calculations:
$$C_H - Z_H = \$2 - 0 = \$2$$
$$C_C - Z_C = \$4 - 0 = \$4$$
$$C_{S_1} - Z_{S_1} = \$0 - 0 = \$0$$
$$C_{S_2} - Z_{S_2} = \$0 - 0 = \$0$$
$$C_{S_3} - Z_{S_3} = \$0 - 0 = \$0$$

---

introduced. The column associated with this variable is designated by the small arrow beneath column C in Exhibit S8.2. (Only one variable at a time can be added in developing each improved solution.)

Step 4: Determine which variable to replace
Given that it is desirable to introduce C into the solution, the next question is to determine which variable it will replace. To make this determination, we divide each amount in the Quantity column by the amount in the comparable row of the C column and choose the variable associated with the smallest positive quotient as the one to be replaced:

For the S_1 row: 120/6 = 20
For the S_2 row: 72/6 = 12
For the S_3 row: 10/1 = 10

Since the smallest quotient is 10, S_3 will be replaced, and its row is identified by the small arrow to the right of the tableau in Exhibit S8.2. This is the maximum amount of C that can be brought into the solution; that is, production of more than 10 units of C would exceed the available capacity of Machine C. This can be verified mathematically by considering the constraint $C \leq 10$ and visually by examining the graphical representation of the problem in Exhibit S8.1. The graph also shows that the 20 and 12 are the C intercepts of the other two constraints, and if $C \leq 10$ were removed, the amount of C introduced could be increased by 2 units.

Step 5: Calculate new row values for entering variable
The introduction of C into the solution requires that the entire S_3 row be replaced. The values for C, the replacing row, are obtained by dividing each value presently in the S_3 row by the value in column C in the same row. This

EXHIBIT S8.4

Calculation of New
Row Values for
Entering Variable

$$C$$
$$6$$
$$6$$

S_3 0 ① 0 0 1 10   0 / 1 = 0, 1 / 1 = 1, 0 / 1 = 0, 0 / 1 = 0, 1 / 1 = 1, 10 / 1 = 10

$4

EXHIBIT S8.5   Pivot Method

Old S_1 Row	−	Intersectional Element of Old S_1 Row	×	Corresponding Element of New C Row	=	Updated S_1 Row	Old S_2 Row	−	Intersectional Element of Old S_2 Row	×	Corresponding Element of New C Row	=	Updated S_2 Row
4	−	(6	×	0)	=	4	2	−	(6	×	0)	=	2
6	−	(6	×	1)	=	0	6	−	(6	×	1)	=	0
1	−	(6	×	0)	=	1	0	−	(6	×	0)	=	0
0	−	(6	×	0)	=	0	1	−	(6	×	0)	=	1
0	−	(6	×	1)	=	−6	0	−	(6	×	1)	=	−6
120	−	(6	×	10)	=	60	72	−	(6	×	10)	=	12

value is termed the *intersectional element* since it occurs at the intersection of a row and column. This intersectional relationship is abstracted from the rest of the tableau and the necessary divisions are shown in Exhibit S8.4.

Step 6: Revise remaining rows
The new third-row values (now associated with C) are 0, 1, 0, 0, 1, and 10, which in this case are identical to those of the old third row.

Introducing a new variable into the problem affects the values of the remaining variables, and a second set of calculations must be performed to update the tableau. Specifically, we want to determine the effect of introducing C on the S_1 and S_2 rows. These calculations can be carried out by using what is termed the *pivot method* or by algebraic substitution. The pivot method is a more mechanical procedure and is generally used in practice, while algebraic substitution is more useful in explaining the logic of the updating process. The procedure using the pivot method to arrive at new values for S_1 and S_2 is shown in Exhibit S8.5. (In essence, the method subtracts six times row 3 from both the S_1 and S_2 rows.)

Updating by algebraic substitution entails substituting the entire equation for the entering row into each of the remaining rows and solving for the revised values for each row's variable. The procedure, summarized in Exhibit S8.6, illustrates the fact that linear programming via the simplex method is essentially the solving of a number of simultaneous equations.

EXHIBIT S8.6

**Algebraic
Substitution**

To find new values for S_1,
1. Reconstruct old S_1 row as a constraint with slack variables added (from first tableau):

$$4H + 6C + 1S_1 + 0S_2 + 0S_3 = 120$$

2. Write entering row as a constraint with slack variables added (these are the values computed in Exhibit T2.4):

$$0H + C + 0S_1 + 0S_2 + 1S_3 = 10$$

3. Rearrange entering row in terms of C, the entering variable:

$$10 - S_3$$

4. Substitute $10 - S_3$ for C in the first equation (the old S_1 row) and solve for each variable coefficient:

$$4H + 6(10 - S_3) + 1S_1 = 120$$
$$4H + 60 - 6S_3 + 1S_1 = 120$$
$$4H + 1S_1 - 6S_3 = 120 - 60$$
$$4H + 1S_1 - 6S_3 = 60$$

or

$$4H + 0C + 1S_1 + 0S_2 - 6S_3 = 60$$

EXHIBIT S8.7

**Second Tableau of
the Hockey Stick and
Chess Problem**

C_j		$2	$4	$0	$0	$0	
	Solution Mix	H	C	S_1	S_2	S_3	Quantity
$0	S_1	4	0	1	0	-6	60
$0	S_2	2	0	0	1	-6	12 ←
$4	C	0	1	0	0	1	10
	Z_j	$0	$4	$0	$0	$ 4	$40
	$C_j - Z_j$	$2	$0	$0	$0	$-4	
		↑					

Isolating the variable coefficients yields the same values for the new S_1 row as did the pivot method: 4, 0, 1, 0, -6, 60.

The results of the computations carried out in Steps 3 through 6, along with the calculations of Z_j and $C_j - Z_j$ are shown in the revised tableau, Exhibit S8.7. In mathematical programming terminology, we have completed one *iteration* of the problem.

In evaluating this solution, we note two things: the profit is $40, but, more important, further improvement is possible since there is a positive value in the $C_j - Z_j$ row.

EXHIBIT S8.8   Updating S_1 and C rows

Old S_1 Row	−	⎛Inter-sectional Element of Old S_1 Row	×	Corre-sponding Element of New H Row⎞	=	New S_1 Row	Old C Row	−	⎛Inter-sectional Element of Old C Row	×	Corre-sponding Element of New H Row⎞	=	New C Row
4	−	(4	×	1)	=	0	0	−	(0	×	1)	=	0
0	−	(4	×	0)	=	0	1	−	(0	×	0)	=	1
1	−	(4	×	0)	=	1	0	−	(0	×	0)	=	0
0	−	(4	×	½)	=	−2	0	−	(0	×	½)	=	0
−6	−	(4	×	−3)	=	6	1	−	(0	×	−3)	=	1
60	−	(4	×	6)	=	36	10	−	(0	×	6)	=	10

Second iteration.   The entering variable is H because it has the largest $C_j - Z_j$ amount (2). The replaced variable is S_2 since it has the smallest quotient when the Quantity column values are divided by their comparable amounts in the H column:

$$S_1 = 60/4 = 15, \ S_2 = 12/2 = 6, \ C_3 = 10/0 = \infty$$

Values of entering (H) row are

$$2/2 = 1, \ 0/2 = 0, \ 0/2 = 0, \ 1/2 = 1/2, \ -6/2 = -3, \ 12/2 = 6$$

Updated S_1 row from Exhibit S8.8: 0, 0, 1, −2, 6, 36.
Updated C row from Exhibit S8.8: 0, 1, 0, 0, 1, 10.

Using the result from Exhibit S8.8, we obtain the third tableau: Exhibit S8.9.

Examination of the third tableau indicates that further improvement is possible by introducing the maximum amount of S_3 that is technically feasible. From the computation at the bottom of Exhibit S8.9, the maximum amount of S_3 that can be brought into the solution is six units because of the limited supply of S_1. Replacing S_1 by S_3 and performing the updating operations yields the tableau shown in Exhibit S8.10. Since the $C_j - Z_j$ row contains only negative numbers, no further improvement is possible, and an optimal solution ($H = 24, C = 4$) has been achieved in three iterations.

Summary of Steps in the Simplex Method: Maximization Problems

1. Formulate problem in terms of an objective function and a set of constraints.
2. Set up initial tableau with slack variables in the solution mix and calculate the Z_j and $C_j - Z_j$ rows.
3. Determine which variable to bring into solution (largest $C_j - Z_j$ value).

EXHIBIT S8.9

Third Tableau of the Hockey Stick and Chess Set Problem

C_j		$2	$4	$0	$0	$0	
	Solution Mix	H	C	S_1	S_2	S_3	Quantity
$0	S_1	0	0	1	-2	6	36 ←
$2	H	1	0	0	½	-3	6
$4	C	0	1	0	0	1	10
	Z_j	$2	$4	$0	$ 1	$-2	$52
	$C_j - Z_j$	$0	$0	$0	$-1	$ 2	
						↑	

36/6 = 6
6/−3 = −2 (negative)*
10/1 = 10

* Since there are three constraint equations, there must be three variables with nonnegative values in the solution. Therefore a negative amount cannot be considered for introduction into the solution.

EXHIBIT S8.10

Fourth Tableau of the Hockey Stick and Chess Set Problem (Optimal solution)

C_j		$2	$4	$0	$0	$0	
	Solution Mix	H	C	S_1	S_2	S_3	Quantity
$0	S_3	0	0	⅙	−⅓	1	6
$2	H	1	0	½	−½	0	24
$4	C	0	1	−⅙	⅓	0	4
	Z_j	$2	$4	$ ⅓	$ ⅓	$0	$64
	$C_j - Z_j$	$0	$0	$−⅓	$−⅓	$0	

4. Determine which variable to replace (smallest positive ratio of quantity column to its comparable value in the column selected in Step 3).

5. Calculate new row values for entering variable and insert into new tableau (row to be replaced plus intersectional element).

6. Update remaining rows and enter into new tableau; compute new Z_j and $C_j - Z_j$ rows (old row minus intersectional element of old row times corresponding element in new row). If no positive $C_j - Z_j$ value is found, solution is optimal. If there is a positive value of $C_j - Z_j$, repeat Steps 3 to 6.

Minimization problems

Both **maximization and minimization** problems use identical procedures. When the objective is to minimize rather than maximize, however, a negative $C_j - Z_j$ value indicates potential improvement; therefore the variable associated with the largest negative $C_j - Z_j$ value would be brought into solution first. Also, additional variables must be brought in to set up such problems. Since minimization problems include greater-than-or-equal-to constraints, which must be treated differently from less-than-or-equal-to constraints, which typify maximization problems. (See the section dealing with greater-than-or-equal-to and equal-to constraints in the simplex method, later in this chapter.)

Search Path Followed by the Simplex Method

As mentioned earlier, the optimal solution to linear programming problems is obtained by finding the extreme corner point. The simplex procedure starts with an initial solution, searches for the most profitable direction to follow, and hops from point to point of intersecting lines (or planes in multidimensional space). The evaluation of a corner point takes one iteration, and when the furthermost point is reached (in the case of profit maximization problems as shown by the next point's decreasing profit), the solution is complete.

Consider the graph of the example problem shown in Exhibit S8.11, where the simplex method began at point a (profit = \$0). In the first iteration, 10 units of C were introduced at point b (profit = \$40). In the second iteration, 6 units of H were introduced at point c (profit = \$52). The third iteration left the problem at point d (profit = \$64), which is optimal. Note that the solution procedure did not calculate profit for all corners of this problem. It did, however, *look ahead*—by virtue of the $C_j - Z_j$ calculations—to see if further improvement was possible by moving to another point (point e), but no improvement was indicated by such a change. These two characteristics—evaluating corner points and looking ahead for improvements—are the essential features of the simplex method.

Another feature that is also characteristic of the basic simplex method is that it does not necessarily converge on the optimum point by the shortest route around the feasible area. Reference to the graph shows that if the solution procedure had proceeded along the path $a \longrightarrow e \longrightarrow d$, an optimum would have been reached in two iterations rather than three.

The reason why this route was not followed was that the profit per chess set was higher than for a hockey stick, and therefore, the simplex method indicated that C, rather than H, be introduced in the first iteration. This, in turn, set the pattern for subsequent iterations to points c and d. Note that since the solution space forms a convex polygon (as previously defined), profit cannot increase, decrease, and then again increase.

Shadow Prices, Ranging, and Sensitivity

By examining the final (optimal) simplex tableau, we can learn a great deal. In addition to showing the solution, the final tableau provides valuable information about the resources used, the range where the optimal decision remains unchanged, and the range where the coefficients in the objective function do not change the optimal solution. Specifically, it enables us to answer such

EXHIBIT S8.11

Graph of Hockey
Stick and Chess Set
Problem Showing
Successive Corner
Evaluations

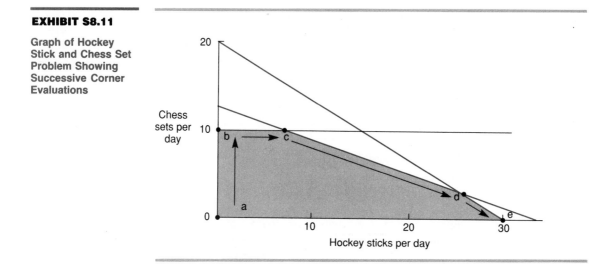

questions as: Would you like to buy any more of a resource? If so, what price should you pay? How many units should you buy at that price? Similar questions can be answered about selling resources; even though a resource may be currently used in making products, at some price it is worthwhile to forgo production and sell it. These considerations are of interest because they lead to decisions that can increase profit or reduce cost. These profit increases or cost decreases are *in addition* to the optimal solution calculated in the final tableau objective function.

Other questions are of the sort: If we change the profit per unit (by changing the coefficient in the objective function) will this change the optimal solution? This is **sensitivity analysis,** and refers to how much the solution changes for a small change in the objective function or, conversely, for a small change in the solution, the change that occurs in the objective function.

Referring to Exhibit S8.10, the $C_j - Z_j$ values associated with the slack variables are termed **shadow prices,** *marginal values, incremental values,* or *break-even prices.* Note that the shadow prices for S_1 and S_2 were $\$\frac{1}{3}$ (or 33 cents) each, and the shadow price for S_3 was $\$0$. Above each price, management would be willing to sell resources, and below each price, it would be willing to buy. Let's take another look at this problem and all the information available in a computer printout.

Computer Program Output

Exhibit S8.12 shows the output from a computer program for the same hockey stick and chess set problem. This output differs somewhat from the hand-solved simplex solution in that the rows and columns are rotated as well

EXHIBIT S8.12

Computer Output for the Hockey Stick and Chess Set Problem

OBJECTIVE FUNCTION VALUE = 64

ROW	EQUATION	SLACK	RIGHT HAND SIDE	SHADOW PRICE
1	MACHINE A	0	120	.33
2	MACHINE B	0	72	.33
3	MACHINE C	6	10	0

COL	VARIABLE	VALUE	RELATIVE PROFIT
1	HOCKEY	24	0
2	CHESS	4	0

RIGHT HAND SENSITIVITY

ROW	EQUATION	RANGE	LEAVE	RATE
1	MACHINE A	144	CHESS	.33
1	MACHINE A	84	MACHINE C	-.33
2	MACHINE B	90	MACHINE C	.33
2	MACHINE B	60	CHESS	-.33
3	MACHINE C	INF		
3	MACHINE C	4	MACHINE C	0

OBJECTIVE SENSITIVITY

COL	VARIABLE	RANGE	ENTER	RATE
1	HOCKEY	2.67	MACHINE B	24
1	HOCKEY	1.33	MACHINE A	-24
2	CHESS	6.0	MACHINE A	4
2	CHESS	3.0	MACHINE B	-4

as some other minor differences in the way it is displayed. The top line shows the objective function value of $64. Row 1 has Machine A with no slack and therefore all 120 units being used up. The shadow price is $.33 per unit. Row 2 shows no slack also and all 72 units used up and a shadow price of $.33. Row 3 shows Machine 3 has 6 of the 10 units slack (and therefore only 4 units being used). Since there are excess units, it has zero shadow price.

In the next section of Exhibit S8.12, column 1 shows that there are 24 hockey sticks in solution (the zero relative profit indicates that it is in solution; if it were not in solution the relative profit would show as $2—the value shown in the objective function). Column 2 shows that there are four chess sets in solution.

The Right-Hand Sensitivity section shows that as resources are added or subtracted, there is a point where the problem changes. For example, row 1 shows that additional Machine A time can be purchased at a rate less than $.33 per hour up to a total of 144 hours. As we add more Machine A time, however, we make more hockey sticks and fewer chess sets (shown as Chess leaving the solution). To see this pictorially, look at Exhibit S8.1, which shows that as the $4H + 6C = 120$ equation shifts to the right the optimum point goes up with more hockey sticks and fewer chess sets. If we decide to sell Machine A time at a price greater than $.33, we can sell up to the point where we have 84 left. In this case we would make fewer hockey sticks and more chess sets. If all 36 resource units of A were sold, all resource units of C would be used and Machine center C slack would become zero.

The purpose of buying or selling resources is to try to obtain profit (in this case) greater than the $64 currently given by the objective function. To be optimal, the changes are constrained to lie on the boundary of the bounded area of feasibility. In this example, the optimal solution lies on a segment of the line $4H + 6C = K$, where K is the number of resource units for Machine center A within the range 84 to 144. (The value of doing the analysis the way we have in this section is that we can obtain optimal solutions for changes in the equations without re-solving the simplex algorithm.)

Using the same logic, Machine B hours can be sold or purchased so long as the total remains within the range of 60 to 90. If we buy units of B, we make fewer hockey sticks but more chess sets. In the limit, slack for Machine center C becomes zero. If we sell units of B, we would make more hockey sticks and fewer chess sets. The limit would be where we would use 60 units of resource B and would make 30 hockey sticks and zero chess sets.

Recall that Machine C had excess capacity; we can therefore add an infinite supply if it is offered at a price of less than zero (someone pays us to take it), but we can only sell up to four units at a price of greater than zero.

The objective sensitivity shows the effect of changing the profit of each hockey stick and chess set as stated in the objective equation. If hockey sticks are increased in price, the slope becomes less steep (in Exhibit S8.1). Above $2.67, the optimal solution shifts, producing 30 hockey sticks and no chess sets and Machine B is used less. When the profit drops below $1.33 each, the solution shifts to 10 chess sets and 6 hockey sticks and Machine A has idle time. The same logic exists for the chess set profit. So long as the profit of the chess set stays within the range of $3 to $6, the optimum point does not change. The Rate column in this section simply refers to the change in the value of the objective function per unit. Since there are 24 hockey sticks in solution, for example, an increase in the profit of $1 increases the value of the profit equation (objective function) by $24.

Let's look at the final simplex tableau in Exhibit S8.13. S_1 has a shadow price of $⅓ per unit. If the price is less than $⅓, we would be willing to buy 24 units. (See Exhibit S8.13A.) The S_1 column shows that for every S_1 produced, ⅙ of a chess set must be given up. Therefore, since 4 exist, giving up ⅙ at a time means we can add 24 units.

If we sell S_1 (at a price greater than $⅓) we would have to give up ⅙ of an S_2 and ½ of an H for each S_1 sold. Therefore, our limit would be the smallest of 36 or 48, which would limit our selling to just 36 units.

The same analysis of S_2 (not shown in the exhibit) would show that $18S_2$ could be purchased or $12S_2$ sold. This corresponds to the Right-Hand Sensitivity section of Exhibit S8.12 where there would be a total of 90 Machine B hours as the upper range (the original 72 plus the 18 purchased), and 60 as the lower range (the original 72 less 12 sold).

EXHIBIT S8.13

Final Tableau for
Hockey Stick and
Chess Set Buy and
Sell Questions

H	C	S_1	S_2	S_3	Quantity
0	0	⅙	−⅓	1	6
1	0	½	−½	0	24
0	1	−⅙	⅓	0	4
		−⅓	−⅓		

A. For the S_1 decisions to buy if the price is less than $ ⅓.

S_1	Quantity	Limit
⅙	6	no limit
½	24	no limit
−⅙	4	24 (4 divided by ⅙)

B. For the S_1 decisions to sell if the price is more than $ ⅓.

S_1	Quantity	Limit
⅙	6	36 (6 divided by ⅙)
½	24	48 (24 divided by ½)
−⅙	4	no limit

*Dealing with greater-than-or-equal-to and equal-to constraints
in the simplex*

Greater-than-or-equal-to constraints ($\geq$) and equal-to constraints ($=$) must be handled somewhat differently from the less-than-or-equal-to constraints ($\leq$) in setting up and solving simplex problems.

Recall that with $\leq$ constraints, we added a slack variable to convert the inequality to an equality. For example, in converting the inequality $4H + 6C \leq 120$ to an equality, we added S_1, giving us $4H + 6C + S_1 = 120$. Now suppose that the sign was changed to a greater-than-or-equal-to sign, yielding $4H + 6C \geq 120$. Initially, we would surmise that subtracting a slack variable would convert this to an equality and it would be written as $4H + 6C - 1S_1 = 120$.

Unfortunately, this adjustment would lead to difficulties in the simplex method, because the initial simplex solution starts with fictitious variables and hence a negative value ($-1S_1$) would be in the solution—a condition not permitted in linear programming. To overcome this problem, the simplex procedure requires that a different type of variable—an artificial variable—be added to each equal-to-or-greater-than equation. An artificial variable may be thought of as representing a fictitious product having a very high cost, which, though permitted in the initial solution to a simplex problem, would never appear in the final solution. Defining A as the artificial variable, the constraint given above would now appear as

$$4H + 6C - 1S_1 + 1A_1 = 120$$

And, assuming that we were minimizing cost rather than maximizing profit, the objective function would appear as

$$\$2H + \$4C + \$0S_1 + \$MA_1$$

where $\$M$ is assumed to be a very large cost, for example, a million or a billion dollars.[3] (Note also that S_1 is added to the objective function even though it is negative in the constraint equation.)

An artificial variable must also be included in constraints with equality signs. For example, if $4H + 6C = 120$, this must be changed to $4H + 6C + 1A_1 = 120$ to satisfy the simplex requirement that each constraint equation have a nonnegative variable in the initial solution. It would be reflected in the objective function, again as $\$MA_1$, but would have no slack variable accompanying it in the constraint equation.

Procedurally, where such constraints exist, the simplex method starts with artificial variables in the initial solution but otherwise treats them the same as it would real or slack variables.

Integer Programming

As we pointed out in the opening paragraphs of this chapter, linear programming assumes divisibility. Divisibility means that a variable can take on fractional values such as halves, quarters, eighths, or any fraction whatsoever.

Often, the solution to a problem must be in whole numbers—whole airplanes scheduled in airline routing, employees' times assigned in entirety to a project, products packaged in units only (tons, gross, barrels, etc.), capacity added or assigned in increments (buying another machine, adding another server in a restaurant, subcontracting a job lot). Requiring that the solution to a linear programming problem be in terms of whole numbers changes the problem to **integer programming.** If every variable must have an integer (nonfractional) value, the procedure is called *pure* integer programming. If some variables may be integers and some fractional, the procedure is called *mixed* integer programming.

The solution to an integer programming problem is considerably more complex than the solution to a linear programming problem. This is because a linear programming problem converges at its optimal solution, which is usually a single point. When the variables must be in whole numbers, many points may have to be examined to find the optimal. Even then, there may be no guarantee that the solution found really is the optimal.

Two approaches to solving an integer programming problem are the *cutting plane* method and the *backtrack* method. The cutting plane method starts with

---

[3] When a $\geq$ or $=$ constraint is encountered in a maximization problem, an artificial variable is assumed to have a large negative profit coefficient in the objective function to assure that it would not appear in the final solution.

an optimal linear programming solution but adds additional constraints for the integer requirement. This can be quite time consuming because of the additional equations to ensure that answers are in whole numbers. The backtrack method also starts with an optimal linear programming solution, but differs in that it generates a family of separate linear programming problems to include the integer requirements. Algorithms are used to converge on a solution. The most popular method for the solution to this problem is called the *branch and bound technique*. Coverage is beyond the intent of this text; the interested reader can find detailed discussion in most operations research textbooks.

S8.4 COMMERCIAL LINEAR PROGRAMMING SOFTWARE

Linear programming software has been available for computers since digital computers first became commercially available 35 years ago. These were large mainframe computers, however. With the recent tremendous growth in personal computer power, linear programs with high capabilities are now available to individuals for use on personal computers independent of any mainframe tie-in.

Exhibit S8.14 shows 10 of the many linear programs available. Eight of these programs can be run on personal computers. Prices range from $495 to $45,000. Several of the programs under $2,000 can solve very large problems.

In comparing speeds of operation of various personal computers, a personal computer using a 286 chip can solve problems about twice as fast as a computer with an 8088 chip.[4] A 16MHz 386 personal computer can solve the problems about five times faster than the 286 (or 15 times faster than the 8088). Many of the computers and programs have been refined in their problem-solving techniques, so these increases in speed can double or triple. Though not incorporated yet into a personal computer, the new IBM RS/6000 computer architecture can solve problems about 15 times faster than a 386 computer (or more than 200 times faster than an 8088 computer).[5]

As stated in the introduction to this supplement, one of the great improvements in linear programming is its user-friendliness. Several spreadsheet programs either have LP built into them, or they allow external LP programs to be accessed. This simplifies the use of the programs and makes them much more understandable and user-friendly.

Incidentally, the output of the hockey stick and chess set problem shown in Exhibit S8.12 was solved using XMP Software's OB1.

---

[4] R. Sharda, "Mathematical Programming on Microcomputers: Directions in Performance and User Interfaces," in *Mathematical Models for Decision Support*, ed. G. Mitra (New York: Springer-Verlag, 1988), pp. 279–93.

[5] R. Sharda, "Linear Programming Software for the Microcomputer: Recent Advances," in *Decision-Aiding Software and Decision Analysis*, ed. S. Nagel (Cambridge: Cambridge University Press, 1990).

EXHIBIT S8.14   Commercially Available Linear Programming Software

Software	Publisher and Address	Platforms It Runs On	Size of Problems It Can Solve M = # of rows N = # of columns NZ = # of nonzeros	Minimum Hardware Required to Run a Problem of Specified Capacity	
LP88-Linear Programming	Eastern Software Products P.O. Box 15328 Alexandria, VA 22309 Tel. 703-360-7600	IBM compatible PCs	M = 3,000 N = 15,000 NZ = 64,000	640 K RAM, co-processor RAM disk or hard disk.	
GAMS—General Algebraic Modelling System	GAMS-General 651 Gateway Blvd San Francisco, CA 94080-7014 Tel. 415-583-8840	386/486 PCs Mainframe	M = 32,000 N = 32,000 NZ = 32,000	512K RAM; DOS-2.0 or higher Math coprocessor for PC.	
MIMI/LP	Chesapeake Decision Sciences Inc. 200 South Street New Providence, NJ 07974 Tel. 201-464-8300	IBM-PS/2, RS/6000, RT PC, 9370, 43xx, mainframes; DEC-VAX, VAX Station, DEC Station; HP–386/486 Vectra	—	1 MB RAM–small applic. 32 MB RAM–lg. applic. with graphic capabilities.	
OB1	XMP Software Inc. P.O. Box 58119 Tucson, AZ 85732 Tel. 602-298-7873	Workstations, e.g. IBM, RISC 6000, DEC, and SUN	M = 100,000 N & NZ = unlimited	16MB memory	
Optimization Subroutine Library (OSL)	IBM 41U/276 Neighborhood Road Kingston, NY 12401 Tel. 914-385-6744	PS/2 M70, M80 AIX RS/6000 AIX	M = 16 million N = 2 billion	PS/2 Model 70 with math coprocessor	

Spreadsheet Compatibility	INTEGER PROGRAMMING			INPUT FILES SUPPORTED			Cost Information	Comments
	Avail-able?	Binary	General Integer	MPS format	Spread-sheet	Propri-etary		
Can read any Lotus compatible. Can import and export text files	No	—	—	Yes	Yes	—	$1,500; $50,000 site lic.; DOS: $795; $50-educational; $25,000-site lic.	The company will help you convert or develop your model or package at competitive consult-ing rates. They offer resources to support continued growth and flexible business ar-rangements with large end-users and devel-opers.
Add on–VINO Separate Lindo pck.	Yes	Yes	Yes	—	—	Yes	$1,600-mod-ule; $320-educational	Provides high-level language for easy rep-resentation of large complex problems. Three modules: Base GAMS' BDMLP Linear solver; GAMS, MINOS—non-linear solver; GAMS zoom—mixed integer solver.
Provides its own data-base for data, model mgmt., matrix gen-eration, and solution re-porting. Can be accessed from other spread-sheets, etc.	Yes	Yes	Yes	Yes	—	Yes	Available upon request	Chesapeake provides solutions for production planning and schedul-ing. Products combine database, operations research and expert system capabilities to provide an integrated package. A graphics-based user interface is under development using X Window and OSF Motif.
Can import and export text files	No	—	—	Yes	—	—	$20,000	Intended for any large or difficult problems, particularly multiperiod models.
—	Yes	Yes	Yes	Yes	—	Yes	$2,000	Provides capability to solve problems with convex quadratic ob-jective functions (QP); runs on all system/370 systems with and with-out vector facility.

(continued)

EXHIBIT S8.14   *concluded*

Software	Publisher and Address	Platforms It Runs On	Size of Problems It Can Solve M = # of rows N = # of columns NZ = # of nonzeros	Minimum Hardware Required to Run a Problem of Specified Capacity	
PIMS	Bechtel 3000 Post Oak Boulevard Houston, TX 77056 Tel. 713-235-2741	IBM compatible PCs IBM PS/2	M = 6,000 N = 6,000 NZ = 50,000	—	
Quattro Pro	Borland International 1800 Green Hills Road Scotts Valley, CA 95067-0001 408-438-8400	286/386/486 PCs	—	512K RAM	
VIG—A Visual Interactive Goal Program	NumPlan Ltd. PL128 03101 Nummela, Finland Tel. 358-0-2271900	IBM compatible PCs	M = 100 N = 96 NZ = 9,600	256K RAM	
What's Best! 386 Version	Lindo Systems Box 148231 Chicago, IL 60614 Tel. 312-871-2524	386 PCs Mac	M = 8,000 N = 16,000 NZ = 128,000	80287 or 80387 coprocessor and 1 MB RAM	
Workstation Lindo	Lindo Systems Inc. P.O. Box 148231 Chicago, IL 60614 Tel. 312-871-2524	Micro VAX, Sun SPARC most others by request	M = 6,000 N = 20,000 NZ = 300,000	8 MB required 16 MB recommended	

Source: John Llewellyn and Ramesh Sharda, "Linear Programming Software for Personal Computers: 1990 Survey," *OR/MS Today,* October 1990, pp. 35–47.

Spreadsheet Compatibility	INTEGER PROGRAMMING			INPUT FILES SUPPORTED			Cost Information	Comments
	Avail-able?	Binary	General Integer	MPS format	Spread-sheet	Propri-etary		
Add on—Lotus, Excel, Symphony, Quattro Pro, Lotus V3.0	No	—	—	Yes	Yes	—	$45,000; $45,000 site license	The PIMS family of products includes multiplant and multiperiod systems.
Can read and write to spreadsheet files Can import and export text files	No	—	—	—	Yes	—	$495; $69.95–educational prices; site license negotiable	Quattro Pro is a high-end PC-based spreadsheet with linear programming tools built-in. Quattro Pro is fully compatible with Lotus 1-2-3, 2.01, files & macros.
Add on—fully based on spread-sheets	No	—	—	—	Yes	—	$974; $470 educational prices	VIG is a dynamic, visual and interactive system for structuring and solving multiple objective linear programming problems.
Add on—Lotus 1-2-3 2.X, 3, Symphony	Yes	Yes	No	—	Yes	—	$2,995; $1,495 educational prices	What'sBest!, a true Lotus add-in for 1-2-3 release 2.X, 3 or Symphony, allows modeling in a natural spreadsheet fashion. Makes modeling easy enough for the LP novice, yet it's powerful enough for the professional.
Can import and export text files	Yes	Yes	Yes	Yes	—	Yes	$3,000; $1,280–educ. prices; $200 site license ($100 educ. price)	Lindo is a general purpose LP, QP and IP optimizer. Most people familiar with LP can use it immediately without instruction. Recognizes free variables and bounded variables.

Linear Programming on a Spreadsheet—Quattro Pro®

As we previously mentioned, spreadsheets can be used to solve linear programming problems. Both Borland's Quattro Pro and Lotus 1-2-3/G® have optimization routines built in. Most other spreadsheets can access add-on routines so that they can solve linear programming problems. Linear programming on a spreadsheet is very easy to use and understand. To demonstrate, we use Quattro Pro to solve the hockey stick and chess set problem completed earlier in the chapter.

Exhibit S8.15 shows a pull down menu with the cell locations already defined. For the first "Linear constraint coefficients" we entered B15..C17. This meant that we had three equations (rows 15, 16, and 17) and two variables (columns B and C). This menu is accessed in Quattro Pro from Tools, Advanced Math, Optimization. Going down the list in the menu, we are prompted to enter the cell locations. For our hockey stick and chess set problem we proceeded as follows working from the top of the menu:

1. Define the coefficients for the constraints in cells B15 through C17.
2. Define the relationships from the < symbols next to each constraint in column E.

EXHIBIT S8.15   Quattro Pro Spreadsheet Linear Programming Menu

```
 2     Linear Programm│ Linear constraint coefficients        B15..C17
 3                     │ Inequality/equality relations         E15..E17
 4                     │ Constant constraint terms             F15..F17
 5                     │ Bounds for variables
 6                     │ Formula constraints                   D15..D17
 7                     │ Objective function                    B10..C10
 8     Number Produce│ Extremum                                 Largest
 9
10       Profit/Unit │ Solution                                G8..G8
11                   │ Variables                               B8..C8
12                   │ Dual values                             G15..G17
13   Constraints     │ Additional dual values
14
15   Mach. Center A│ Go
16   Mach. Center B│ Reset
17   Mach. Center C│ Quit
18
19
20
21
```

3. State the right side of the constraints in column F.

4. Define the constraint formulas in column D.

5. Enter the objective function coefficients in row 10.

6. Choose "Largest" for maximizing. (Someone in the software firm must like Latin having used *Extremum* meaning to maximize (largest) or minimize (smallest).

7. Select an area to output the solution.

8. Define the cells B8 and C8 as the variables.

9. Select a column next to the constraint right sides for dual values (shadow prices).

10. Hit "Go" to solve.

Exhibit S8.16 shows the data that we entered: profits per unit for hockey sticks ($2) and chess sets ($4), required hours per unit on the three machines, and available capacities on each machine. We established the initial starting point as the origin by putting zeros in cells B8 and C8 (the numbers of hockey sticks and chess sets produced). The formula for the profit is placed in cell E8 ($2*B8 + $4*C8).

Exhibit S8.17 shows the final template after the solution has been generated. The maximum profit of $64 comes from producing 24 hockey sticks and 4

EXHIBIT S8.16   Quattro Pro Spreadsheet LP Program for Hockey Stick and Chess Set Problem—Initial Setup

```
 2   Linear Programming Example - Chess Sets and Hockey Sticks
 3
 4
 5                     Hockey  Chess        Total        Optimal
 6                     Sticks  Sets         Profit       Profit
 7
 8   Number Produced     0       0         $0.00
 9
10     Profit/Unit    $2.00   $4.00
11                                                Max.
12                                   Cap.         Cap.   Shadow
13   Constraints     Hours per Unit Used         Avail. Prices
14
15   Mach. Center A      4       6       0    <    120
16   Mach. Center B      2       6       0    <     72
17   Mach. Center C      0       1       0    <     10
18
19
20
21
```

EXHIBIT S8.17   Quattro Pro Spreadsheet Linear Programming for Hockey Stick and Chess Set Problem—Final Solution

```
 2   Linear Programming Example - Chess Sets and Hockey Sticks
 3
 4
 5                     Hockey  Chess         Total              Optimal
 6                     Sticks  Sets          Profit             Profit
 7
 8   Number Produced    24      4           $64.00                 64
 9
10     Profit/Unit    $2.00  $4.00
11                                                  Max.
12                                    Cap.          Cap.    Shadow
13   Constraints    Hours per Unit Used           Avail.   Prices
14
15   Mach. Center A      4      6     120     <     120    0.3333
16   Mach. Center B      2      6      72     <      72    0.3333
17   Mach. Center C      0      1       4     <      10    0.0000
18                                                            0
19                                                            0
20                                                            0
21
```

chess sets. In addition, the shadow prices for Machine centers A and B are $0.333 per unit.

Once a spreadsheet has been defined in this way, running the program is straightforward. What-if questions are easily answered, such as "What if the price for chess sets changes to $5? How many would we then produce?" and so on.

S8.5   TRANSPORTATION METHOD

The **transportation method** is a simplified special case of the simplex method. It gets its name from its application to problems involving transporting products from several sources to several destinations.[6] The two common objectives of such problems are either (1) minimize the cost of shipping n units to m destinations or (2) maximize the profit of shipping n units to m destinations. There are three general steps in solving transportation problems, and we discuss each one in the context of a simple example.

---

[6] For other applications, see Exhibit S8.24.

EXHIBIT S8.18

Data for Chess Set
Transportation
Problem

Factory	Supply	Warehouse	Demand	From	SHIPPING COSTS PER CASE (IN DOLLARS)			
					To E	To F	To G	To H
A	15	E	10	A	$25	$35	$36	$60
B	6	F	12	B	55	30	45	38
C	14	G	15	C	40	50	26	65
D	11	H	9	D	60	40	66	27

Suppose the Puck and Pawn Company has four factories supplying four
warehouses and its management wants to determine the minimum-cost shipping schedule for its monthly output of chess sets. Factory supply, warehouse
demands, and shipping costs per case of chess sets are as shown in Exhibit
S8.18.

Step 1: Set Up Transportation Matrix

The transportation matrix for this example appears in Exhibit S8.19, where
supply availability at each factory is shown in the far right column and the
warehouse demands are shown in the bottom row. The unit shipping costs are
shown in the small boxes within the cells. It is important at this step to make
sure that the total supply availabilities and total demand requirements are
equal. In this case they are both the same, 46 units, but quite often there is an
excess supply or demand. In such situations, for the transportation method to
work, a dummy warehouse or factory must be added. Procedurally, this
involves inserting an extra row (for an additional factory) or an extra column
(for an additional warehouse). The amount of supply or demand required by
the dummy is equal to the difference between the row and column totals.

For example, the following problem might be restated to indicate a total
demand of 36 cases, and therefore, a new column would be inserted with a
demand of 10 cases to bring the total up to 46 cases. The cost figures in each
cell of the dummy row would be set at zero, and therefore, any units sent there
would not incur a transportation cost. Theoretically, this adjustment is equivalent to the simplex procedure of inserting a slack variable in a constraint
inequality to convert it to an equation, and, as in the simplex, the cost of the
dummy would be zero in the objective function.

Step 2: Make Initial Allocations

Initial allocation entails assigning numbers to cells to satisfy supply and demand constraints. There are several methods for carrying this out, but we
describe only one, the northwest-corner method.

EXHIBIT S8.19

Transportation Matrix
for Chess Set
Problem

From \ To	E	F	G	H	Factory supply
A	25	35	36	60	15
B	55	30	45	38	6
C	40	50	26	65	14
D	60	40	66	27	11
Destination requirements	10	12	15	9	46 / 46

Northwest-corner method of allocation

The northwest-corner method, as the name implies, begins allocation by starting at the northwest corner of the matrix and assigning as much as possible to each cell in the first row.[7] The procedure is then repeated for the second row, third row, and so on, until all row and column requirements are met. Exhibit S8.20 shows a northwest-corner assignment (Cell *A-E* was assigned first, *A-F* second, *B-F* third, and so forth.)

Inspection of Exhibit S8.20 indicates some high–cost cells were assigned and some low–cost cells bypassed by using the northwest-corner method. Indeed, this is to be expected since this method ignores costs in favor of following an easily programmable allocation algorithm.[8]

---

[7] Assign as many units as possible to each cell to meet the requirements of having no more than $m + n - 1$ filled cells, where m = number of rows and n = number of columns.

[8] Vogel's Approximation Method (VAM) does take account of costs. Its rules are take the difference between the two lowest cost cells in all rows and columns, including dummies, and allocate as much as possible to the lowest cost cell in the row or column with the largest difference. The process is repeated until all cells are assigned. One study found that VAM yields an optimum solution in 80 percent of the sample problems tested. Our students have observed that the remaining 20 percent are found on examinations.

EXHIBIT S8.20

Northwest-Corner
Assignment

From \ To	E		F		G		H		Factory supply
A		25		35		36		60	15
	10		5						
B		55		30		45		38	6
			6						
C		40		50		26		65	14
			1		13				
D		60		40		66		27	11
					2		9		
Destination requirements	10		12		15		9		46 / 46

Total cost = 10($25) + 5($35) + 6($30) + 1($50) + 13($26) + 2($66) + 9($27) = $1,368

Step 3: Develop Optimal Solution

To develop an optimal solution in a transportation problem means evaluating each unused cell to determine whether a shift into it is advantageous from a total-cost standpoint. If it is, the shift is made, and the process is repeated. When all cells have been evaluated and appropriate shifts made, the problem is solved.

Stepping stone method of evaluation
One approach to making this evaluation is the stepping stone method. The term *stepping stone* appeared in early descriptions of the method, in which unused cells were referred to as "water" and used cells as "stones"—from the analogy of walking on a path of stones half-submerged in water. We now apply the method to the northwest-corner solution to the sample problem, as shown in Exhibit S8.20.

Step 1: Pick any empty cell.
Step 2: Identify the closed path leading to the cell. A closed path consists of horizontal and vertical lines leading from an empty cell back to itself.[9] In the

---

[9] If assignments have been made correctly, the matrix has only one closed path for each empty cell.

EXHIBIT S8.21

Stepping Stone
Method—
Identification of
Closed Paths

From \ To	E	F	G	H	Factory supply
A	25 10 a	35 5	36 b	60	15
B	55 6	30	45	38	6
C	40 1	50	26 13	65	14
D	60	40 2	66	27 9	11
Destination requirements	10	12	15	9	46 46

closed path there can only be one empty cell that we are examining. The 90-degree turns must therefore occur at those places that meet this requirement. Two closed paths are identified in Exhibit S8.21. Closed path *a* is required to evaluate empty cell *B-E;* closed path *b* is required to evaluate empty cell *A-H.*

Step 3: Move one unit into the empty cell from a filled cell at a corner of the closed path and modify the remaining filled cells at the other corners of the closed path to reflect this move.[10] Modifying entails adding to and subtracting from filled cells in such a way that supply and demand constraints are not violated. This requires that one unit always be subtracted in a given row or column for each unit added to that row or column. Thus, the following additions and subtractions would be required for path *a.*

Add one unit to *B-E* (the empty cell).

Subtract one unit from *B-F.*

Add one unit to *A-F.*

Subtract one unit from *A-E.*

---

[10] More than one unit could be used to test the desirability of a shift. However, since the problem is linear, if it is desirable to shift one unit, it is desirable to shift more than one, and vice versa.

And, for the longer path *b*,

> Add one unit to *A-H* (the empty cell).
> Subtract one unit from *D-H*.
> Add one unit to *D-G*.
> Subtract one unit from *C-G*.
> Add one unit to *C-F*.
> Subtract one unit from *A-F*.

Step 4: Determine desirability of the move. This is easily done by (1) summing the cost values for the cell to which a unit has been added, (2) summing the cost values of the cells from which a unit has been subtracted, and (3) taking the difference between the two sums to determine if there is a cost reduction. If the cost is reduced by making the move, as many units as possible should be shifted out of the evaluated filled cells into the empty cell. If the cost is increased, no move should be made and the empty cell should be crossed out or otherwise marked to show that it has been evaluated. (A large plus sign is typically used to denote a cell that has been evaluated and found undesirable in cost-minimizing problems. A large minus sign is used for this purpose in profit–maximizing problems.) For cell *B-E*, the pluses and minuses are as follows:

+		−	
$55	(*B-E*)	$30	(*B-F*)
35	(*A-F*)	25	(*A-E*)
$90		$55	

For cell *A-H*:

+		−	
$ 60	(*A-H*)	$27	(*D-H*)
66	(*D-G*)	26	(*C-G*)
50	(*C-F*)	35	(*A-F*)
$176		$88	

Thus in both cases it is apparent that no move into either of the empty cells should be made.

Step 5: Repeat steps 1 through 4 until all empty cells have been evaluated. To illustrate the mechanics of carrying out a move, consider cell *D-F* and the closed path leading to it, which is a short one: *C-F*, *C-G*, and *D-G*. The pluses and minuses are

+		−	
$40	(*D-F*)	$ 50	(*C-F*)
26	(*C-G*)	66	(*D-G*)
$66		$116	

EXHIBIT S8.22

Revised
Transportation Matrix

From \ To	E	F	G	H	Factory supply
A	25 / 10	35 / 5	36 /	60 / +	15
B	55 / +	30 / 6	45 /	38 /	6
C	40 /	50 / +	26 / 14	65 /	14
D	60 /	40 / 1	66 / 1	27 / 9	11
Destination requirements	10	12	15	9	46 / 46

Total cost = 10($25) + 5($35) + 6($30) + 14($26) + 1($40)
    + 1($66) + 9($27) = $1,318

Since there is a savings of $50 per unit from shipping via *D-F,* as many units as possible should be moved into this cell. In this case, however, the maximum amount that can be shifted is one unit—because the maximum amount added to any cell may not exceed the quantity found in the lowest-amount cell from which a subtraction is to be made. To do otherwise would violate the supply and demand constraints of the problem. Here we see that the limiting cell is *C-F,* since it contains only one unit.

The revised matrix, showing the effects of this move and the previous evaluations, is presented in Exhibit S8.22. Applying the stepping stone method to the remaining unfilled cells and making shifts where indicated yields an optimal solution.

In particular, the empty cell *A-G* in Exhibit S8.22 has closed path *D-G, D-F,* and *A-F.* The pluses and minuses are

+		−	
36	(*A-G*)	35	(*A-F*)
40	(*D-F*)	66	(*D-G*)
76		101	

Since savings = 101 − 76 = $25, we shift 1 unit to *A-G.* Exhibit S8.23 shows the optimal matrix, with minimum transportation cost = $1,293.

EXHIBIT S8.23

Optimal Solution to
Transportation
Problem

From \ To	E	F	G	H	Factory supply
A	25 10	35 5−4=1	36 0+1=1	60	15
B	55	30 6	45	38	6
C	40	50	26 14	65	14
D	60	40 1+1=2	66 1−1=0	27 9	11
Destination requirements	10	12	15	9	46 46

Total cost = 10($25) + 4($35) + 1($36) + 6($30) + 14($26)
+ 2($40) + 9($27) = $1,293

To verify that we have the optimum, we should evaluate each empty cell to
see if it is desirable to bring in that cell. If we did this, we would have a plus
sign in each of these cells.

Degeneracy

Degeneracy exists in a transportation problem when the number of filled cells
is less than the number of rows plus the number of columns minus one (i.e.,
$m + n - 1$). Degeneracy may be observed during the initial allocation when
the first entry in a row or column satisfies *both* the row and column requirements. Degeneracy requires some adjustment in the matrix to evaluate the
solution achieved. The form of this adjustment involves inserting some value
in an empty cell so a closed path can be developed to evaluate other empty
cells. This value may be thought of as an infinitely small amount, having no
direct bearing on the cost of the solution.

Procedurally, the value (often denoted by the Greek letter theta, θ) is used in
exactly the same manner as a real number except that it may initially be placed
in any empty cell, even though row and column requirements have been met
by real numbers. A degenerate transportation problem showing an optimal
minimum cost allocation is presented in Exhibit S8.24, where we can see that
if θ were not assigned to the matrix, it would be impossible to evaluate several

From \ To	W	X	Y	Factory supply
T	8 / 3	6 / 8	4 / θ	11
U	9	8	0 / 9	9
V	5 / 3	3	10	3
Destination requirements	6	8	9	23 / 23

$m + n - 1 =$
5 filled cells

Actual allocation =
4 filled cells

cells (including the one where it is added). Once a θ has been inserted into the solution, it remains there until it is removed by subtraction or until a final solution is reached.

While the choice of where to put a θ is arbitrary, it saves time if it is placed where it may be used to evaluate as many cells as possible without being shifted. In this regard, verify for yourself that θ is optimally allocated in Exhibit S8.24.

Alternate optimal solutions
When the evaluation of an empty cell yields the same cost as the existing allocation, an alternate optimal solution exists.[11] In such cases, management has additional flexibility and can invoke nontransportation cost factors in deciding on a final shipping schedule. (A large zero is commonly placed in an empty cell that has been identified as an alternate optimal route.)

S8.6 ASSIGNMENT METHOD

The **assignment method** is a special case of the transportation method of linear programming to apply to situations where there are n supply sources and n demand uses (e.g., five jobs on five machines) and the objective is to minimize or maximize some measure of effectiveness. Assignment problems are quite similar to transportation problems, but the fact that each allocation in

---

[11] Assuming that all other cells are optimally assigned.

EXHIBIT S8.25

Assignment Matrix
Showing Machine
Processing Costs for
Each Job

Job	MACHINE				
	A	B	C	D	E
I	$5	$6	$4	$8	$3
II	6	4	9	8	5
III	4	3	2	5	4
IV	7	2	4	5	3
V	3	6	4	5	5

an assignment problem simultaneously satisfies both a row and column requirement makes all such problems multidegenerate. This technique is convenient in applications such as in job shop scheduling to allocate people to jobs, jobs to machines, and so forth. The assignment method is appropriate in solving problems that have the following characteristics.

1. There are n "things" to be distributed to n "destinations."
2. Each "thing" must be assigned to one and only one "destination."
3. Only one criterion can be used—minimum cost, maximum profit, minimum completion time.

For example, suppose that a scheduler has five jobs that can be performed on any of five machines ($n = 5$) and that the cost of completing each job-machine combination is shown in Exhibit S8.25. The scheduler would like to devise a minimum-cost assignment. (There are 5!, or 120, possible assignments.) This problem may be solved by the assignment method, which consists of the following four steps:

1. Subtract the smallest number in each *row* from itself and all other numbers in that row. (There will then be at least one zero in each row.)
2. Subtract the smallest number in each *column* from all other numbers in that column.
3. Determine if the *minimum* number of lines required to cover each zero is equal to n. If so, an optimum solution has been found, since job machine assignments must be made at the zero entries and this test proves that this is possible. If the minimum number of lines required is less than n, go to Step 4.
4. Draw the least possible number of lines through all the zeros (these may be the same lines used in Step 3). Subtract the smallest number not covered by lines from itself and all other uncovered numbers and add it to the number at each intersection of lines. Repeat Step 3.

For the example problem, the steps listed in Exhibit S8.26 would be followed.

EXHIBIT S8.26   Procedure to Solve an Assignment Matrix

Step 1: Row reduction—the smallest number is subtracted from each row.

MACHINE

Job	A	B	C	D	E
I	2	3	1	5	0
II	2	0	5	4	1
III	2	1	0	3	2
IV	5	0	2	3	1
V	0	3	1	2	2

Step 2: Column reduction—the smallest number is subtracted from each column.

MACHINE

Job	A	B	C	D	E
I	2	3	1	3	0
II	2	0	5	2	1
III	2	1	0	1	2
IV	5	0	2	1	1
V	0	3	1	0	2

Step 3: Apply line test—the number of lines to cover all zeros is 4; since 5 are required, go to step 4.

MACHINE

Job	A	B	C	D	E
I	2	3	1	3	0
II	2	0	5	2	1
III	2	1	0	1	2
IV	5	0	2	1	1
V	0	3	1	0	2

Step 4: Subtract smallest uncovered number and add to intersection of lines—using lines drawn in step 3, smallest uncovered number is 1.

MACHINE

Job	A	B	C	D	E
I	1	3	0	2	0
II	1	0	4	1	1
III	2	2	0	1	3
IV	4	0	1	0	1
V	0	4	1	0	3

Optimum solution—by "line test."

MACHINE

Job	A	B	C	D	E
I	1	3	0	2	0
II	1	0	4	1	1
III	2	2	0	1	3
IV	4	0	1	0	1
V	0	4	1	0	3

Optimum assignments and their costs.

Job I to Machine E	$3
Job II to Machine B	$4
Job III to Machine C	$2
Job IV to Machine D	$5
Job V to Machine A	$3
Total cost	$17

Note that even though there are two zeros in three rows and three columns, the solution shown in Exhibit S8.26 is the only one possible for this problem since Job III must be assigned to Machine C to meet the "assign to zero" requirement. Other problems may have more than one optimum solution, depending, of course, on the costs involved. The nonmathematical rationale of the assignment method is one of minimizing opportunity costs.[12] For

---

[12] The underlying rationale of the procedure of adding and subtracting the smallest cell values is as follows: Additional zeros are entered into the matrix by subtracting an amount equal to one of the cells from all cells. Negative numbers, which are not permissible, occur in the matrix. To get rid of the negative numbers, an amount equal to the maximum negative number must be added to each element of the row or column in which it occurs. This results in adding this amount twice to any cell that lies at the intersection of a row and a column that were both changed. The net result is that the lined rows and columns revert to their original amounts, and the intersections increase by the amount subtracted from the uncovered cells. (The reader may wish to prove this by solving the example without using lines.)

EXHIBIT S8.27

Typical Operations
Management
Applications of
Linear Programming*

Simplex*

Aggregate production planning: Finding the minimum-cost production schedule, including rate change costs, given constraints on size of work force and inventory levels.

Product planning: Finding the optimal product mix where several products have different costs and resource requirements (e.g., finding the optimal blend of constituents for gasolines, paints, human diets, animal feeds).

Product routing: Finding the optimal routing for a product that must be processed sequentially through several machine centers, with each machine in a center having its own cost and output characteristics.

Process control: Minimizing the amount of scrap material generated by cutting steel, leather, or fabric from a roll or sheet of stock material.

Inventory control: Finding the optimal combination of products to stock in a warehouse or store.

Transportation

Aggregate production planning: Finding the minimum-cost production schedule, taking into account inventory carrying costs, overtime costs, and subcontracting costs.

Distribution scheduling: Finding the optimal shipping schedule for distributing products between factories and warehouses or warehouses and retailers.

Plant location studies: Finding the optimal location of a new plant by evaluating shipping costs between alternative locations and supply and demand sources.

Materials handling: Finding the minimum cost routings of material handling devices (e.g., forklift trucks) between departments in a plant and of hauling materials from a supply yard to work sites by trucks, with each truck having different capacity and performance capabilities.

Assignment

Scheduling: Minimum cost assignment of trucks to pickup points and ships to berths.

Worker assignments: Minimum cost assignment of workers to machines and to jobs.

*The graphical method is not included since it may be applied in the same situations as simplex if the problem has fewer than three variables.

example, if we decided to assign Job I to Machine A instead of to Machine E, we would be sacrificing the opportunity to save $2 ($5 − $3). The assignment algorithm in effect performs such comparisons for the entire set of alternative assignments by means of row and column reduction, as described in Steps 1 and 2. It makes similar comparisons in Step 4. Obviously, if assignments are made to zero cells, no opportunity cost, with respect to the entire matrix, is incurred.

Typical Operations Management Applications of Linear Programming

Exhibit S8.27 summarizes some typical operations management applications of linear programming according to the particular technique by which the application is usually carried out.

Even though the simplex method can be applied to any of the situations presented in the table, it is generally more expedient to employ the transportation or the assignment method if the problem lends itself to these forms.

S8.7 KARMARKAR'S ALGORITHM FOR SOLVING LINEAR PROGRAMMING PROBLEMS

If you've gotten this far in following the simplex method of linear programming, it is worthwhile to see how Karmarkar's method works to simplify the solution of very large problems. This material is very difficult, and the intention here is merely to give a very brief introduction to the logic.

We have seen how the simplex algorithm can be used to solve linear programming problems, but many real-world linear programming problems are very large—their formulation would require 40,000 variables or more. Such large problems arise in many areas of business, including airline scheduling, oil refining, and the design of large telephone networks. Problems with 40,000 variables are not solvable on the computer using the simplex method because they would take too long. In 1984, Narendra Karmarkar of AT&T's Bell Laboratories proposed a faster algorithm for such large-scale problems. Its greater speed has made previously unsolvable problems solvable.

EXHIBIT S8.28

How the Simplex Method (dots) and Projective Scaling Method (circles) Approach the Optimal Solution of a Small Problem

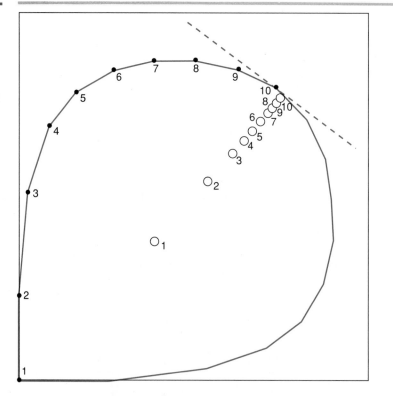

Here the projective scaling method requires at least as many iterations as the simplex method, but in large problems it requires only a fraction as many.

Source: J. N. Hooker, "Karmarkar's Linear Programming Algorithm," *Interfaces* 16, no. 4 (July–August 1986), p. 76.

Karmarkar's algorithm is difficult to understand because it requires understanding the "close enough ideas" of the ellipsoidal algorithm, the auxiliary functions, and the interior point search. It is difficult to explain what is going on since the simplest example requires multidimensional space. Finally, a computer is necessary to solve a problem of any size. A two-variable example in simplex requires a six-by-six matrix in Karmarkar's algorithm, and the numbers get worse with each iteration.[13]

In spite of these complications we can convey an idea of how it works. Exhibit S8.28 shows an enclosed area created by the intersections of 20 linear equations. The top half of the area has 10 numbered intersections and shows the path that the simplex method would take—from point to point around the exterior of the area, continuing as long as the objective function improves. Karmarkar's algorithm, however, travels internally.

We can further illustrate how it works by graphic illustrations for a simple linear programming problem that maximizes profit, subject to just one constraint. Suppose we are trying to solve the following one-constraint LP problem:

Maximize $Z = 5X + 4Y = $ Profit

subject to $3X + 2Y \leq 6$

Exhibit S8.29 reviews the steps in the simplex method, starting at the origin and gradually moving to the optimum by way of corner points.

EXHIBIT S8.29

Graph of Simplex Approach to One-Constraint Problem

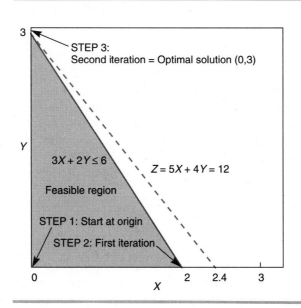

STEP 3:
Second iteration = Optimal solution (0,3)

$3X + 2Y \leq 6$

$Z = 5X + 4Y = 12$

Feasible region

STEP 1: Start at origin

STEP 2: First iteration

[13] Craig Tovey, "Teaching Karmarkar's Algorithm," *OR/MS Today* 15, no. 2 (April 1988), pp. 18–19.

EXHIBIT S8.30   Graphs of First Two Iterations of Karmarkar Solution to One-Constraint Problem

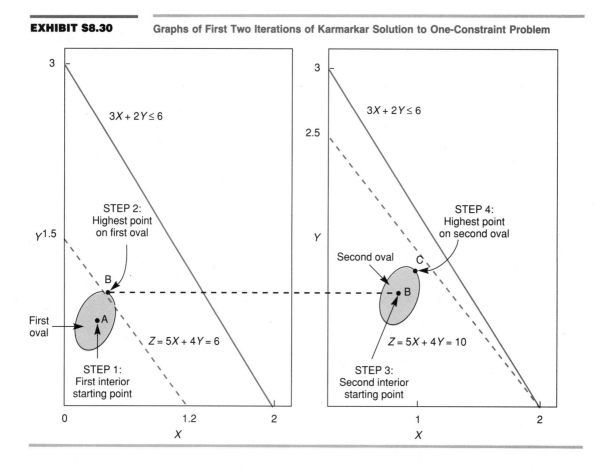

By contrast, Karmarkar does not start at the origin, but rather at a point in the *interior* of the feasible region, such as point A in Exhibit S8.30. Step 1 includes constructing an oval region around point A, so that the oval lies entirely within the feasible region. Step 2 finds the maximum profit point on that oval, point B in Exhibit S8.30. Point B lies on the highest reachable iso-profit line for that oval, namely a profit = 6, just as the maximum profit point on the feasible region in simplex lies on the highest reachable iso-profit line.

Now point B becomes a new starting point in Step 3, as shown on the right graph of Exhibit S8.30. A new oval is drawn around point B, and a new maximum profit point C is found in Step 4. This process is repeated until it becomes very close to the optimal solution. Notice that corner points do not play an important role as they did in the simplex method.

How does Karmarkar locate the maximum profit point for each oval when there are 40,000 variables? It turns out that the best approach is to use a circle, which is a special oval. Then each starting point should be the center of the circle. To find the maximum profit point for each circle, we move from the center of the circle in the direction of the *profit direction arrow*, which is the long

EXHIBIT S8.31

Karmarkar's Profit
Direction Arrow

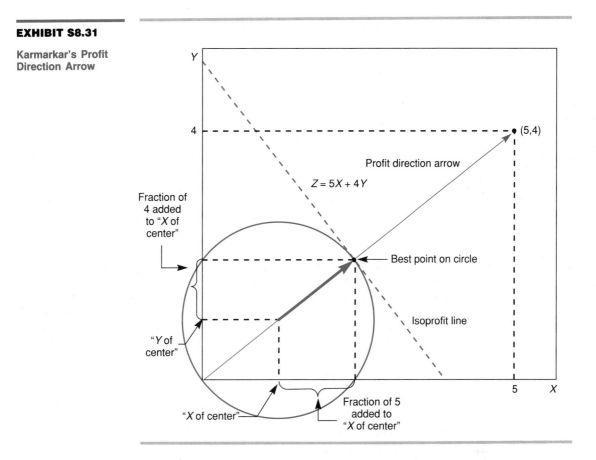

arrow in Exhibit S8.31. The long arrow ends at the point (5, 4) in Exhibit S8.31, but that far from the origin would take us out of the feasible region. Instead, we travel only part of the distance, which is illustrated by the bold arrow in the same graph. The wide arrow starts at the center of the circle and stops at the edge of the circle, where it meets an iso-profit line at a right angle. The distance traveled along the wide arrow must be some *fraction* of the distance from the origin to (5, 4).

Returning now to Exhibit S8.30, when we moved from point A to B to C, profits were increasing, but we were not headed toward the optimum at (0, 3), which we already knew from the simplex in Exhibit S8.29, Step 3. In fact, this problem was the hardest to solve, and Karmarkar's solution—projective transformation—is equally hard to explain. Before each circle is drawn, the whole feasible region is distorted (or warped) to bring the starting point to the middle of the feasible region. One analogy is the projection of a spherical globe onto a flat sheet of paper—a world map. Greenland is distorted on the world map, but you can still use this map to sail from New York to Greenland.

The main difference between the simplex method and Karmarkar's algorithm is in processing-time requirements. While Karmarkar's algorithm has a polynomial increase in processing time as the size of the problem increases, the simplex method increases exponentially as 2^N.

Many researchers are continuing to improve on Karmarkar's procedure by developing different algorithms. At this point, however it appears that both the simplex method and Karmarkar's method will continue to be used for awhile. It had been believed that small- to medium-sized problems were best solved by using simplex and very large problems with Karmarkar's algorithm. However, the most recent research with variations of Karmarkar's algorithm have shown it to be equally appropriate for medium-sized problems. Computer processing times have become surprisingly similar.

S8.8 GENERAL ALGEBRAIC MODELING SYSTEM (GAMS)

One of the difficulties with any computer model is that it tends to be unique to the person or persons who created it. If that person leaves, it can take a very long time for the successor to understand what is taking place within the model. Also, when several people work on different portions of a model, the testing, debugging, and interfacing problems often are enormous. Therefore, there is a need to simplify the process.

The **General Algebraic Modeling System (GAMS)** simplifies the construction of models that are easily understood by the modeler and the computer.[14] Such a modeling system:

1. Provides a high-level language for the easy representation of large and complex models.
2. Simplifies making changes in the model.
3. Allows clear algebraic relationships to be made.
4. Separates the creation of a model from the solution technique or method used on the model.

To illustrate the simplicity of using GAMS, David Kedrick and Alexander Meeraus use a very simplified example of determining the best shipping schedule to minimize the costs of shipping from two plants of a canning company to three markets.

The canning company has two plants: one in Seattle with a capacity of 350 cases per week, and the other in San Diego with a capacity of 600 cases per week. The three markets, New York, Chicago, and Topeka, require 325, 300, and 275 cases per week respectively.

Distances from the two plants to the three markets are from Seattle to New York—2,500 miles, to Chicago—1,700 miles, and to Topeka—1,800 miles;

---

[14] David Kedrick and Alexander Meeraus, *GAMS, an Introduction* (draft) (The World Bank: Development and Research Department, 1985). Also see the listing on Exhibit S8.14.

from San Diego to New York—2,500 miles, to Chicago—1,800 miles, and to Topeka—1,400 miles. Transportation costs are 90 cents per case per thousand miles.

Inputs to GAMS (what they are in this canning problem are shown in parenthesis) are called sets (plants and markets), data (plant capacities, market requirements, distances, and shipping costs), variables (total transportation cost and cases shipped), and equations (equations for the total cost, the total supply available, and the total amount required).

Given this input information, GAMS is directed to solve the problem using linear programming and minimizing the transportation cost T. The input to GAMS and the output are shown in Exhibit S8.32. The optimal solution which resulted from the LP run is shown as Seattle to New York and Chicago (50 and 300 cases), and San Diego to New York and Topeka (275 cases each). The total cost for these shipments is $1,536.80.

The advantage of GAMS is that the person trying to solve the problem does not have to write all of the equations. All that is necessary is to specify what goes into the equations and the general form that they should take. The program does the actual equation writing. Certainly for this small program we could have written the equations ourselves probably faster than we could have used GAMS. It's obvious, however, that the number of equations can increase very rapidly even for problems of modest size. GAMS can be a big help in the equation writing. For example, to learn GAMS, several of the students of one of the authors of this text used it to solve the Nichols Case in Chapter 14. GAMS generated the more than 1,000 equations required (much more time than our students would be willing to spend writing each of these equations themselves).

S8.9   CONCLUSION

This supplement has dealt mainly with the mechanics of solution procedures for linear programming problems. It would be a rare instance when a linear programming problem would actually be solved by hand. There are too many computers around and too many LP software programs to justify spending time for manual solution. We firmly believe, though, that to truly understand the computer output, it is necessary to take the time to solve some simple problems, as we have done here.

Formulating the linear programming problem, with its constraints and objective function, is the usual stumbling block in using linear programming methods. We could also easily devote equal length on how to abstract data from a real-world situation and translate it into a form suitable for linear programming. Many recent variants of linear programming overcome some of the inherent limitations of the simplex model. In particular, we expect to see

EXHIBIT S8.32

Input and Output of an LP Problem, using GAMS

```
SETS
        I  PLANTS
           / SEATTLE, SAN-DIEGO /

        J  MARKETS
           / NEW-YORK, CHICAGO, TOPEKA /

DATA
                K(I)  CAPACITY OF PLANTS IN CASES
              SEATTLE      350
              SAN-DIEGO    600  /

                R(J)  REQUIREMENTS AT MARKETS IN CASES
           /  NEW-YORK    325
              CHICAGO     300
              TOPEKA      275  /

              D(I,J)  DISTANCES IN THOUSANDS OF MILES
                          NEW-YORK      CHICAGO      TOPEKA
              SEATTLE        2.5          1.7         1.8
              SAN-DIEGO      2.5          1.8         1.4

        F  FREIGHT RATE IN DOLLARS PER THOUSAND MILES  /.90/;

              C(I,J)  TRANSPORTATION COST IN DOLLARS PER CASE;
              C(I,J) = F * D(I,J);

VARIABLES
        T          TOTAL TRANSPORTATION COST
        X(I,J)  SHIPMENTS

EQUATIONS
        COST    OBJECTIVE FUNCTION
        SUPPLY  AVAILABILITY CONSTRAINT
        DEMAND  REQUIREMENTS CONSTRAINT;

COST..      T = SUM((I,J), C(I,J)*X(I,J));
SUPPLY(I)..  K = SUM(J, X(I,J))
DEMAND(J)..  R = SUM(I, X(I,J))

SOLVE CANNERY USING LP MINIMIZING T;

DISPLAY X,L;

SOLUTION REPORT
        1  OPTIMAL SOLUTION

                  NEW-YORK      CHICAGO      TOPEKA
        SEATTLE     50.000      300.000
        SAN-DIEGO  275.000                   275.000

VALUE OF OBJECTIVE FUNCTION =    1536.8
```

much more development and application of time-saving and simplifying techniques such as the General Algebraic Modeling System (GAMS) and greater application of Karmarkar's algorithm.

S8.10 REVIEW AND DISCUSSION QUESTIONS

1. What structural requirements of a problem are needed to solve it by linear programming?
2. What type of information is provided in a solved simplex tableau?
3. What type of information is provided by shadow prices?
4. What are slack variables? Why are they necessary in the simplex method? When are they used in the transportation method?
5. It has been stated in this chapter that an optimal solution for a simplex problem always lies at a corner point. Under what conditions might an equally desirable solution be found anywhere along a constraint line?
6. What is a convex polygon? How is it identified?
7. How do you know if a transportation problem is degenerate? What must be done if a degenerate problem is to be tested for optimality?
8. Why is an assignment problem multidegenerate?
9. Why is Karmarkar's algorithm so important?

S8.11 PROBLEMS

*1. Two products, X and Y, both require processing time on Machines I and II. Machine I has 200 hours available, and Machine II has 400 hours available. Product X requires one hour on Machine I and four hours on Machine II. Product Y requires one hour on Machine I and one hour on Machine II. Each unit of product X yields $10 profit and each unit of Y yields $5 profit. These statements reduce to the following set of equations:

$$X + Y \leq 200$$
$$4X + Y \leq 400$$

Maximize $10X + 5Y$

Solve the problem graphically showing the optimal utilization of machine time.

*2. Solve Problem 1 using the simplex method.

3. Following is a set of linear equations. Solve *graphically* for the optimum point.

$$4A + 6B \geq 120$$
$$2A + 6B \geq 72$$
$$B \geq 10$$

Minimize $2A + 4B$

---

* The complete solution to Problems 1 and 2 are in Appendix H.

4. Solve the following problem using the graphical method of linear programming.

$$5X + 4Y \leq 40$$
$$3X + 2Y \geq 12$$
$$5X + 12Y \geq 60$$

Minimize $3X + Y$

5. Following is the partially completed simplex tableau of a linear programming product mix problem involving three products (X_1, X_2, and X_3) and three departments. All costs and profits are in dollars per unit. Department restrictions are expressed in hours.

C_j Row	2	5	3	0	0	0	
Solution Mix	X_1	X_2	X_3	S_1	S_2	S_3	Quantity
	0	0	2	-2	1	1	20
	1	0	$-\frac{1}{4}$	$\frac{1}{2}$	$-\frac{1}{4}$	0	100
	0	1	$\frac{3}{2}$	0	$\frac{1}{2}$	0	230
Z_j	2	5	7	1	2	0	
$(C_j - Z)$	0	0	-4	-1	-2	0	

a. What is the optimal product mix?
b. If a customer offers you a net $2 per hour, would you lease time in Department 3? How many hours would you lease?

6. The following equations define a linear programming problem. Solve the problem using the graphical method of linear programming.

$$16X + 10Y \leq 160$$
$$12X + 14Y \leq 168$$
$$Y \geq 2$$

Maximize $2X + 10Y$

Draw the graph, show the objective line, and point out the optimal answer.

7. A manufacturing firm has discontinued production of a certain unprofitable product line. Considerable excess production capacity was created as a result. Management is considering devoting this excess capacity to one or more of three products, X_1, X_2, and X_3.

Machine hours required per unit are as follows:

	PRODUCT		
Machine Type	X_1	X_2	X_3
Milling machine	8	2	3
Lathe	4	3	0
Grinder	2	0	1

The available time in machine hours per week are

Machine Hours per Week	
Milling machines	800
Lathes	480
Grinders	320

The salespeople estimate that they can sell all the units of X_1 and X_2 that can be made. But the sales potential of X_3 is 80 units per week maximum.

Unit profits for the three products are

Unit Profits	
X_1	$20
X_2	6
X_3	8

a. Set up the equations that can be solved to maximize the profit per week.
b. Solve these equations using the simplex method.
c. What is the optimal solution? How many of each product should be made and what should the resultant profit be?
d. What is the situation with respect to the machine groups? Would they work at capacity, or would there be unused available time? Will X_3 be at maximum sales capacity?
e. Suppose that an additional 200 hours per week can be obtained from the milling machines by working overtime. The incremental cost would be $1.50 per hour. Would you recommend doing this? Explain how you arrived at your answer.

8. A diet is being prepared for the University of Arizona dorms. The objective is to feed the students at the least possible cost, but the diet must have between 1,800 and 3,600 calories. No more than 1,400 calories can be starch, and no fewer than 400 can be protein. The varied diet is to be made of two foods, A and B. Food A costs $0.75 per pound and contains 600 calories, 400 of which are protein and 200 starch. No more than two pounds of Food A can be used per resident. Food B costs $0.15 per pound and contains 900 calories, of which 700 are starch, 100 are protein, and 100 are fat.
    a. Write out the equations representing this information.
    b. Solve the problem graphically for the amounts of each food that should be used.

9. Do Problem 8 with the added constraint that not more than 150 calories shall be fat, and that the price of food has escalated to $1.75 per pound for Food A and $2.50 per pound for Food B.

10. Logan Manufacturing wants to mix two fuels (A and B) for its trucks to minimize cost. It needs no fewer than 3,000 gallons to run its trucks during the next month. It has a maximum fuel storage capacity of 4,000 gallons. There are 2,000 gallons of Fuel A and 4,000 gallons of Fuel B available. The mixed fuel must have an octane rating of no less than 80.

     When mixing fuels, the amount of fuel obtained is just equal to the sum of the amounts put in. The octane rating is the weighted average of the individual octanes, weighted in proportion to the respective volumes.

The following is known: Fuel A has an octane of 90 and costs $1.20 per gallon; Fuel B has an octane of 75 and costs $0.90 per gallon.

a. Write out the equations expressing this information.

b. Solve the problem graphically, giving the amount of each fuel to be used. State any assumptions necessary to solve the problem.

11. Shown here is a solved simplex tableau.

X	Y	Z	S_1	S_2	S_3	
0	5	0	-2	1	1	40
0	-3	1	3	-2	0	90
1	4	0	-4	3	0	60
0	-7	0	-2	-3	0	

a. What are the values of X, Y, Z, S_1, S_2, and S_3?

b.

	Would you buy?	At what price?	How many?
S_1			
S_2			
S_3			

	Would you sell?	At what price?	How many?
S_1			
S_2			
S_3			

12. The following tableau is the final optimal iteration in a simplex linear programming problem.

A	B	C	S_1	S_2	S_3	
-4	0	1	-3	4	0	400
2	0	0	1	-2	1	300
-3	1	0	-2	6	0	100
-2.00	0	0	-4.00	-6.00	0	

a. What are the values of A, B, C, S_1, S_2, and S_3?

b. Answer the following questions about S_1, S_2, and S_3.

	Would you buy?	At what price?	How many?
S_1			
S_2			
S_3			

	Would you sell?	At what price?	How many?
S_1			
S_2			
S_3			

13. Find the optimal solution for the following transportation-type linear programming problem.

Sources	Availability	Destinations	Required
A	200	D	300
B	300	E	125
C	150	F	140

Transportation costs

AD = $10	BD = $4	CD = $9
AE = $12	BE = $13	CE = $14
AF = $4	BF = $15	CF = $2

14. You are trying to create a budget to optimize the use of a portion of your disposable income. You have a maximum of $700 per month to be allocated to food, shelter, and entertainment. The amount spent on food and shelter combined must not exceed $500. The amount spent on shelter alone must not exceed $100. Entertainment cannot exceed $300 per month. Each dollar spent on food has a satisfaction value of 2, each dollar spent on shelter has a satisfaction value of 3, and each dollar spent on entertainment has a satisfaction value of 5.

   Assuming a linear relationship, use the simplex method of linear programming to determine the optimal allocation of your funds.

15. A landscaping firm has asked you to help set up a method to schedule its jobs. You decide on the transportation method of linear programming, because you understand that the company will be getting in a PC for the office and will be able to use this same format to get the optimum schedule when they get the computer and an LP program.

   This information and data were supplied to you:

   There are nine workers sent out on jobs. The normal work week is 40 hours, and overtime, if necessary, is limited to an additional 8 hours per week. The hourly rate is $15, which includes tools and overhead. If the work is not completed on time, there is an additional cost to the landscaping firm (by contract) of $5 per hour per week late. If the work is done early, there is an additional cost of $3 per hour per week because certain preparations have not been made that make the job more difficult.

   Develop a transportation matrix showing your schedule for the next four weeks. Demands from customers (in hours) for the next four weeks are: 375, 400, 500, 400. Do not try to find the optimum, just develop a feasible (and reasonable) schedule.

16. Bindley Corporation has a one-year contract to supply motors for all washing machines produced by Rinso Ltd. Rinso manufactures the washers at four locations around the country: New York, Fort Worth, San Diego, and Minneapolis. Plans call for the following numbers of washing machines to be produced at each location.

New York	50,000
Ft. Worth	70,000
San Diego	60,000
Minneapolis	80,000

Bindley has three plants that are capable of producing the motors. The plants and production capacities are

Boulder   100,000
Macon   100,000
Gary   150,000

Due to varying production and transportation costs, the profit Bindley earns on each 1,000 units depends on where it was produced and where it was shipped to. The following table gives the accounting department estimates of the profit per unit. (Shipment will be made in lots of 1,000.)

Produced at	SHIPPED TO			
	New York	Fort Worth	San Diego	Minneapolis
Boulder	7	11	8	13
Macon	20	17	12	10
Gary	8	18	13	16

Given profit *maximization* as a criterion, Bindley would like to determine how many motors should be produced at each plant and how many motors should be shipped from each plant to each destination.

a. Develop a transportation tableau for this problem.

b. Find the optimal solution.

17. Given the following transportation problem:

From \ To	A	B	C	D	Supply
1	$120	$100	$ 90	$150	360
2	100	80	20	100	250
3	90	50	130	80	300
Demand	260	400	250	300	

a. Find an initial solution by the northwest-corner method.

b. Solve the problem by the stepping stone method.

18. Minimize the following transportation problem.

From \ To	D	E	F	G	H	Supply
A	1	4	10	4	10	52
B	8	2	8	2	1	20
C	10	1	8	8	2	20
Demand	16	22	4	19	31	92 / 92

19. Maximize the following transportation problem.

From \ To	D	E	F	G	Supply
A	17	12	32	4	300
B	9	18	7	11	700
C	3	21	14	9	400
Demand	200	500	350	350	1400 / 1400

20. PORTFOLIO SELECTION

National Insurance Associates carries an investment portfolio on a variety of stocks, bonds, and other investment alternatives. Currently $200,000 of funds has become available and must be considered for new investment opportunities. The four stock options National is considering and the relevant financial data are as follows:

	INVESTMENT ALTERNATIVE			
	A	B	C	D
Price per share	$100	$50	$80	$40
Annual rate of return	0.12	0.08	0.06	0.10
Risk measure per dollar invested (higher values indicate greater risk)	0.10	0.07	0.05	0.08

The risk measure indicates the relative uncertainty associated with the stock in terms of its realizing the projected annual return. The risk measures are provided by the firm's top financial advisor.

National's top management has stipulated the following investment guidelines:

1. All of the $200,000 is to be invested.
2. The weighted average risk measure (weighted by the dollar amount invested) for the entire portfolio should not exceed 0.08.
3. No one stock can account for more than 50 percent of the total funds available of $200,000.

Management's problem is to determine the number of shares to be bought of each of the four investment alternatives to maximize the total dollar return at the end of the year. Set up the problem as a linear program to assist management. Use these decision variables:

A = Number of shares of Stock A to be bought
B = Number of shares of Stock B to be bought
C = Number of shares of Stock C to be bought
D = Number of shares of Stock D to be bought

a. Write the objective equation and the constraint equations.

After setting up the linear program and running it on a computer, the following output was obtained. Based on this computer output, answer the following questions.

RESULTS

VARIABLE		VARIABLE VALUE	ORIGINAL COEFFICIENT	COEFFICIENT SENSITIVITY
A	STOCK A	600	12	0
B	STOCK B	0	4	.2
C	STOCK C	500	4.8	0
D	STOCK D	2500	4	0

CONSTRAINT NUMBER	ORIGINAL RIGHT-HAND VALUE	SLACK OR SURPLUS	SHADOW PRICE
1 UPPER LIMIT A	100000	39999.996	0
2 UPPER LIMIT B	100000	100000	0
3 UPPER LIMIT C	100000	60000	0
4 UPPER LIMIT D	100000	0	.004
5 LIMIT ON RISK	200000	0	.096
6 TOTAL AVAILABLE FOR INVESTMENT	0	0	1.2

OBJECTIVE FUNCTION VALUE: 19600

OBJECTIVE FUNCTION COEFFICIENTS

VARIABLE	LOWER LIMIT	ORIGINAL COEFFICIENT	UPPER LIMIT
A	11	12	12.667
B	NO LIMIT	4	4.2
C	4.267	4.8	5.6
D	3.84	4	NO LIMIT

RIGHT-HAND-SIDE VALUES

CONSTRAINT NUMBER	LOWER LIMIT	ORIGINAL VALUE	UPPER LIMIT
1	60000.004	100000	NO LIMIT
2	0	100000	NO LIMIT
3	40000	100000	NO LIMIT
4	33333.336	100000	200000.016
5	99999.984	200000	266666.656
6	-- 2000	0	3000

b. Suppose the annual rate of return for Stock C is actually 0.05 (and not 0.06). What is the impact on total dollar return at the end of the year?

c. Suppose the investment guideline is changed so that the upper limit on investment in Stock A is decreased to 25 percent of total funds available. What will be the impact on annual dollar return?

d. Suppose the investment guideline is changed so that the upper limit on investment in Stock B is increased to 60 percent. What will be the impact on annual dollar return?

e. If we can invest a dollar in Stock D for a return of 0.10 and it has the same risk measure of 0.08 that is required of the portfolio, why is the return from an additional dollar invested only 0.096 (shadow price of constraint 5)?

21. RajMark Inc., a small company based in Southern California, manufactures two products—RUM and GIN. In the middle of March, the president, marketing manager, and operations manager were finalizing the product mix decisions for April 1992. The marketing manager estimated that, in April, they could sell up to 4,000 gallons of RUM and up to 7,000 gallons of GIN without any difficulty. The net profit per gallon for both RUM and GIN was estimated to be $120. The operations manager indicated that they had 200 employees and there were 150 work hours in April per employee. It took five hours per employee to produce a gallon of RUM and four hours per employee to produce a gallon of GIN.

The production process also releases a pollutant by-product, TOX, that is partially treated and dumped in the ocean. Every gallon of RUM results in the production of 0.1 pounds of TOX, and every gallon of GIN results in the production of 0.2 pounds of TOX. With all the concern about environmental issues in Southern California, a few years ago the state government regulated that the company cannot release more than 1,200 pounds of TOX into the ocean each month. Please help the management team make up the product mix decision so as to maximize profits by setting up their problem as a linear program.

a. Write the objective equation and the constraint equations.

b. After solving the problem using a computer program, the following output was obtained. Based on the computer output provided below, answer the questions that follow.

RESULTS

VARIABLE	VARIABLE VALUE	ORIGINAL COEFFICIENT	COEFFICIENT SENSITIVITY
RUM	2000	120	0
GIN	5000	120	0

CONSTRAINT NUMBER	ORIGINAL RIGHT-HAND VALUE	SLACK OR SURPLUS	SHADOW PRICE
1 (RUM)	4000	2000	0
2 (GIN)	7000	2000	0
3 (LABOR)	30000	0	20
4 (TOX)	1200	0	200

OBJECTIVE FUNCTION VALUE: 840000

SENSITIVITY ANALYSIS

OBJECTIVE FUNCTION COEFFICIENTS

VARIABLE	LOWER LIMIT	ORIGINAL COEFFICIENT	UPPER LIMIT
RUM	60	120	150
GIN	96	120	240

RIGHT-HAND-SIDE VALUES

CONSTRAINT NUMBER	LOWER LIMIT	ORIGINAL VALUE	UPPER LIMIT
1 (RUM)	2000	4000	NO LIMIT
2 (GIN)	5000	7000	NO LIMIT
3 (LABOR)	24000	30000	36000
4 (TOX)	900	1200	1440

c. What is the amount of TOX produced in the optimal solution?

d. The marketing manager plans to raise the price of RUM by $2.00 per gallon that would lead to a $2.00 increase in the net profit per gallon. What would be the impact on overall net profits?

e. The marketing manager is disappointed that they are planning to produce only 5,000 gallons of GIN. He proposes that overtime be scheduled to produce an additional 1,000 gallons of GIN. The cost of an hour of overtime is $15.00. Would you accept the marketing manager's proposal? Provide reasons. What would be the net impact of the marketing manager's proposal on profits?

f. The president is planning to lobby the state government to increase the upper limit on TOX released to 1,300 pounds. What is the maximum amount he would be willing to pay for such a lobbying effort, assuming the increase is allowed only for April?

g. A local firm has offered a treatment facility that converts TOX to a harmless product that has no government regulations. The firm has made a proposal to RajMark to treat up to 200 pounds of TOX on a contract basis. The proposal involves a monthly fixed cost of $30,000 that is independent of the volume of TOX treated and a variable cost of $100 per pound of TOX treated.

Would you accept their proposal? How many pounds of TOX would you send to the firm for treatment and what would be the net impact on profits?

h. While the president is mulling over such issues, the state government has a surprise (not a pleasant one!) in store for him. They have overwhelmingly lowered the upper limit on the amount of TOX that can be released by small companies such as RajMark to 1,000 pounds. Also, this takes effect in April 1992. The government, realizing that firms may not be able to change their equipment immediately, has indicated that the companies can *instead* pay a penalty of $200 per pound of TOX released in excess of the *new* upper limit. Should RajMark

   (1) Stick to the product mix decided above and pay the penalty to the state government

      or

(2) Change the product mix to satisfy the new limits imposed by the government?

or

(3) Get their TOX treated by the local firm based on their proposal in question *e*?

What would you recommend to the president and why? Access the impact on profits of your recommendation.

i. The marketing manager argues that the company should actually produce more GIN using overtime (since they are currently at labor capacity) even if the cost per hour of overtime is $25. He argues that since four labor hours are required to make a gallon of GIN, the incremental cost would be $100. Since they make a profit of $120 per gallon of GIN, they would be better off producing additional amounts. What is the fallacy in the argument?

S8.12 SELECTED BIBLIOGRAPHY

Barnes, Earl R. "A Variable of Karmarkar's Algorithm for Solving Linear Programming Problems." *Mathematical Programming* 36 (1986).

Bierman, H.; Charles Bonini; and W. Hausman. *Quantitative Analysis for Business Decisions.* 6th ed. Homewood, Ill.: Richard D. Irwin, 1981.

Eppen, G. D., and F. J. Gould. *Introductory Management Science.* 2nd ed. Englewood Cliffs, N.J.: Prentice Hall, 1987.

Hooker, J. N. "Karmarkar's Linear Programming Algorithm." *Interfaces* 16, no. 4 (July–August 1986), pp. 75–90.

Karmarkar, N. "A New Polynomial Time Algorithm for Linear Programming." *Combinatorica* 4 (1984), pp. 373–95.

Llewellyn, John, and Ramesh Sharda. "Linear Programming Software for Personal Computers: 1990 Survey." *OR/MS Today,* October 1990, pp. 35–47.

Luenberger, D. G. *Linear and Nonlinear Programming.* 2nd ed. Reading, Mass.: Addison-Wesley, 1985.

Murty, K. *Linear Programming.* 2nd ed. New York: John Wiley & Sons, 1983.

Rockett, A. M., and J. C. Stevenson. "Karmarkar's Algorithm." *Byte* (September 1987), pp. 146–60.

Sharda, R. "Mathematical Programming on Microcomputers: Directions in Performance and User Interfaces." In *Mathematical Models for Decision Support.* ed. G. Mitra. New York: Springer-Verlag, 1988, pp. 279–93.

————. "Linear Programming Software for the Microcomputer: Recent Advances." In *Decision-Aiding Software and Decision Analysis.* ed. S. Nagel. Cambridge: Cambridge University Press, 1990.

Thierauf, Robert J.; Robert C. Klenkamp; and Marcia L. Ruwe. *Management Science: A Model Formulation Approach with Computer Applications.* Columbus, Ohio: Charles E. Merrill, 1985.

Tovey, Craig. "Teaching Karmarkar's Algorithm." *OR/MS Today* 15, no. 2 (April 1988), pp. 18–19.

Winston, Wayne. *Operations Research.* Boston: Duxbury, 1987.

Chapter 9

Facility Layout

Layout is where "the rubber meets the road"
in every production system.

Anonymous

KEY TERMS

Product Layout

Process Layout

Group Technology (GT) Layout

Just-in-Time Layout

Fixed-Position Layout

Cycle Time

Assembly Line Balancing

Precedence Relationship

Mixed-Model Lines

T he layout decision entails determining the placement of departments, workstations, machines, and stock-holding points within a productive facility. Its general objective is to arrange these elements in a way that ensures a smooth work flow (in a factory) or a particular traffic pattern (in a service organization). The inputs to the layout decision are:

1. Specification of objectives of the system in output and flexibility.
2. Estimation of product or service demand on the system.
3. Processing requirements in number of operations and amount of flow between departments and work centers.
4. Space availability within the facility itself.

All these inputs are, in fact, outputs of process selection and capacity planning discussed in previous chapters. In our treatment of layout in this chapter, we examine how layouts are developed under various formats (or work-flow) structures. Our emphasis is on quantitative techniques used in locating departments within a facility and on workstation arrangements and balance in the important area of assembly lines. Before embarking on this discussion, however, it is useful to note the marks of a good layout listed in Exhibit 9.1.

EXHIBIT 9.1

Marks of a Good Layout

Manufacturing and Back-Office Operations
1. Straight-line flow pattern (or adaptation).
2. Backtracking kept to a minimum.
3. Production time predictable.
4. Little interstage storage of materials.
5. Open plant floors so everyone can see what's going on.
6. Bottleneck operations under control.
7. Workstations close together.
8. Orderly handling and storage of materials.
9. No unnecessary rehandling of materials.
10. Easily adjustable to changing conditions.

Face-to-Face Services
1. Easily understood service flow pattern.
2. Adequate waiting facilities.
3. Easy communication with customers.
4. Customer surveillance easily maintained.
5. Clear exit and entry points with adequate checkout capabilities.
6. Departments and processes arranged so that customers see only what you want them to see.
7. Balance between waiting areas and service areas.
8. Minimum walking and material movement.
9. Lack of clutter.
10. High sales volume per square foot of facility.

9.1 BASIC LAYOUT FORMATS

The formats by which departments are arranged in a facility are defined by the general pattern of work flow and are of three basic types—product layout, process layout, and fixed-position layout—and one hybrid type, group technology or cellular layout. We also refer to JIT as a layout type. In this chapter we consider all but the fixed-position layout.

A **product layout** (also called a *flow-shop layout*) is one in which equipment or work processes are arranged according to the progressive steps by which the product is made. If equipment is dedicated to continual production of a narrow product line, this is usually called a *production line* or *assembly line*. Examples are the manufacture of small appliances (toasters, irons, beaters), large appliances (dishwashers, refrigerators, washing machines), electronics (computers, CD players), and automobiles.

A *flow shop* refers to a production system that has been rearranged to make the dominant products flow easier. The product range is wider than on production lines, and equipment is less specialized. Production tends to be in batches of each item rather than as a mixed continual sequence.

In a **process layout** (also called a *job-shop layout* or *layout by function*), similar equipment or functions are grouped together, such as all lathes in one area and all stamping machines in another. A part being worked on then travels, according to the established sequence of operations, from area to area, where the proper machines are located for each operation. This type of layout is typical of hospitals, for example, where we find areas dedicated to particular types of medical care, such as maternity, pediatrics, and intensive care units.

A **group technology (GT) layout** groups dissimilar machines into work centers (or cells) to work on products that have similar shapes and processing requirements. A GT layout is similar to process layout, in that cells are designed to perform a specific set of processes, and it is similar to product layout in that the cells are dedicated to a limited range of products. (*Group technology* also refers to the parts classification and coding system used to specify machine types that go into a GT cell.)

Just-in-Time layouts can be of two types: a flow line similar to an assembly line and a job shop process layout. In a line layout, equipment and workstations are arranged in sequence. In a job shop or process layout, focus is on simplifying material handling and creating standard routes linking the system with very frequent materials movement.

In a **fixed-position layout,** by virtue of its bulk or weight, the product remains at one location. The manufacturing equipment is moved to the product rather than vice versa. Shipyards, construction sites, and professors' offices are examples of this format.

Many manufacturing facilities present a combination of two layout types. For example, a given floor may be laid out by process, while another floor may be laid out by product. It is also common to find an entire plant arranged according to general product flow (fabrication, subassembly, and final assembly), coupled with process layout within fabrication and product layout within the assembly department. Likewise, group technology is frequently found within a department that itself is located according to a plantwide product-oriented layout.

Production layout continually changes because the internal and external environment of production is dynamic. As demands change, so can layout. As technology changes, so can layout. In Chapter 3 we discussed a product/process matrix indicating that as products and volumes change, the most efficient layout is also likely to change. Therefore, the decision on a specific layout type may be a temporary one.

9.2 PRODUCT LAYOUT

A product layout focuses attention on making the product flow easier. When product demand is high enough and continuous over a period of time, it is usually cost effective to rearrange resources close together in the sequence required by the product. We often call these *assembly* lines, although the ratio of direct manual labor to machine work can vary widely. Assembly lines can vary from virtually 100 percent parts assembly by workers, to the other extreme, a *transfer* line, where all direct work is done by machine. In between are all types: Automobile lines have tools ranging from simple hammers and wrenches to automatic welding and painting. Assembly lines in electronics can also range widely from manual parts assembly to equipment for automatic parts insertion, automatic soldering, and automatic testing.

Assembly Lines

Assembly lines are a special case of product layout. In a general sense, the term *assembly line* refers to progressive assembly linked by some material handling device. The usual assumption is that some form of pacing is present and the allowable processing time is equivalent for all workstations. Within this broad definition, there are important differences among line types. A few of these are: material handling devices (belt or roller conveyor, overhead crane); line configuration (U-shape, straight, branching); pacing (mechanical, human); product mix (one product or multiple products); workstation characteristics (workers may sit, stand, walk with the line, or ride the line); and length of the line (few or many workers).

The range of products partially or completely assembled on lines includes toys, appliances, autos, planes, guns, garden equipment, clothing, and a wide variety of electronic components. In fact, it is probably safe to say that virtually any product with multiple parts and produced in large volume uses assembly lines to some degree. Clearly, lines are an important technology, and to really understand their managerial requirements one must have some familiarity with how a line is balanced.

Assembly line balancing

The most common assembly line is a moving conveyor that passes a series of workstations in a uniform time interval called the **cycle time** (which is also the time between successive units coming off the end of the line). At each workstation, work is performed on a product either by adding parts or by completing assembly operations. The work performed at each station is made up of many bits of work, termed *tasks, elements,* and *work units.* Such tasks are described by motion-time analysis. Generally, they are groupings that cannot be subdivided on the assembly line without paying a penalty in extra motions.

The total work to be performed at a workstation is equal to the sum of the tasks assigned to that workstation. The **assembly line balancing** problem is one of assigning all tasks to a series of workstations so that each workstation has no more than can be done in the cycle time, and so that the unassigned (i.e., idle) time across all workstations is minimized. The problem is complicated by the relationships among tasks imposed by product design and process technologies. This is called the **precedence relationship,** which specifies the order in which the tasks must be performed in the assembly process.

Steps in assembly line balancing.   The steps in balancing an assembly line are straightforward:

1. Specify the sequential relationships among tasks using a precedence diagram. The diagram consists of circles and arrows. Circles represent individual tasks, arrows indicate the order of task performance.

2. Determine the required cycle time (*C*), using the following formula:

$$C = \frac{\text{Production time per day}}{\text{Output per day (in units)}}$$

3. Determine the theoretical minimum number of workstations (N_t) required to satisfy the cycle time constraint, using the following formula:

$$N_t = \frac{\text{Sum of task times } (T)}{\text{Cycle time } (C)}$$

4. Select a primary rule by which tasks are to be assigned to workstations, and a secondary rule to break ties.

5. Assign tasks, one at a time, to the first workstation until the sum of the task times is equal to the cycle time, or no other tasks are feasible because of time or sequence restrictions. Repeat the process for Workstation 2, Workstation 3, etc., until all tasks are assigned.

6. Evaluate the efficiency of the balance derived using the formula:

$$\text{Efficiency} = \frac{\text{Sum of task times } (T)}{\text{Actual number of workstations } (N_a) \times \text{Cycle time } (C)}$$

7. If efficiency is unsatisfactory, rebalance using a different decision rule.

Example problem.   The Model J Wagon is to be assembled on a conveyor belt. Five hundred wagons are required per day. Production time per day is 420 minutes, and the assembly steps and times for the wagon are given in Exhibit 9.2. Assignment: Find the balance that minimizes the number of workstations, subject to cycle time and precedence constraints.

1. Draw a precedence diagram. Exhibit 9.3 illustrates the sequential relationships identified in Exhibit 9.2. (The length of the arrows has no meaning.)

2. Cycle time determination. Here we have to convert to seconds since our task times are in seconds.

$$C = \frac{\text{Production time per day}}{\text{Output per day}} = \frac{60 \text{ sec.} \times 420 \text{ min.}}{500 \text{ wagons}} = \frac{25,200}{500} = 50.4$$

3. Theoretical minimum number of workstations required (the actual number may be greater):

$$N_t = \frac{T}{C} = \frac{195 \text{ seconds}}{50.4 \text{ seconds}} = 3.86$$

EXHIBIT 9.2

Assembly Steps and Times for Model J Wagon

Task	Performance Time (in seconds)	Description	Tasks that Must Precede
A	45	Position rear axle support and hand fasten four screws to nuts	—
B	11	Insert rear axle	A
C	9	Tighten rear axle support screws to nuts	B
D	50	Position front axle assembly and hand fasten with four screws to nuts	—
E	15	Tighten front axle assembly screws	D
F	12	Position rear wheel #1 and fasten hub cab	C
G	12	Position rear wheel #2 and fasten hub cab	C
H	12	Position front wheel #1 and fasten hub cap	E
I	12	Position front wheel #2 and fasten hub cap	E
J	8	Position wagon handle shaft on front axle assembly and hand fasten bolt and nut	F, G, H, I
K	9	Tighten bolt and nut	J
	195		

4. Select assignment rules. Research has demonstrated that some rules are better than others for certain problem structures. In general, the strategy is to use a rule assigning tasks that either have many followers or are of long duration since they effectively limit the balance achievable. In this case, we use as our primary rule:

   a. Assign tasks in order of the largest number of following tasks. Our secondary rule, to be invoked where ties exist from our primary rule, is

   b. Assign tasks in order of longest operating time.

Task	Number of Following Tasks
A	6
B or D	5
C or E	4
F, G, H, or I	2
J	1
K	0

5. Make task assignments to form Workstation 1, Workstation 2, and so forth, until all tasks are assigned. The actual assignment is given in Exhibit 9.4A and is shown graphically in Exhibit 9.4B.

6. Do the efficiency calculation. This is shown in Exhibit 9.4C.

7. Evaluate solution. An efficiency of 77 percent indicates an imbalance or idle time of 23 percent $(1.0 - .77)$ across the entire line. From Exhibit 9.4A we can see that there are 57 total seconds of idle time, and the "choice" job is at Workstation 5.

Is a better balance possible? In this case, yes. Try balancing the line with rule *b* and breaking ties with rule *a*. (This will give you a feasible four-station balance.)

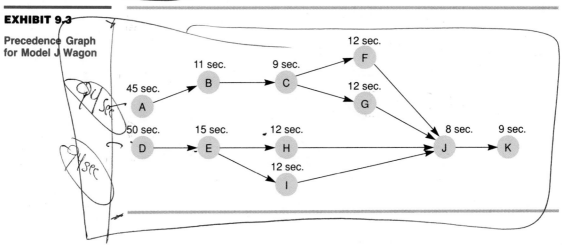

EXHIBIT 9.3

Precedence Graph for Model J Wagon

EXHIBIT 9.4

A. Balance Made According to Largest Number of Following Tasks Rule

	Task	Task Time (in seconds)	Remaining Unassigned Time (in seconds)	Feasible Remaining Tasks	Task with Most Followers	Task with Longest Operation Time
Station 1	A	45	5.4 idle	None		
Station 2	D	50	0.4 idle	None		
Station 3	B	11	39.4	C, E	C, E	E
	E	15	24.4	C, H, I	C	
	C	9	15.4	F, G, H, I	F, G, H, I	F, G, H, I
	F*	12	3.4 idle	None		
Station 4	G	12	38.4	H, I	H, I	H, I
	H*	12	26.4	I		
	I	12	14.4	J		
	J	8	6.4 idle	None		
Station 5	K	9	41.4 idle	None		

* Denotes task arbitrarily selected where there is a tie between longest operation times.

B. Precedence Graph for Model J. Wagon

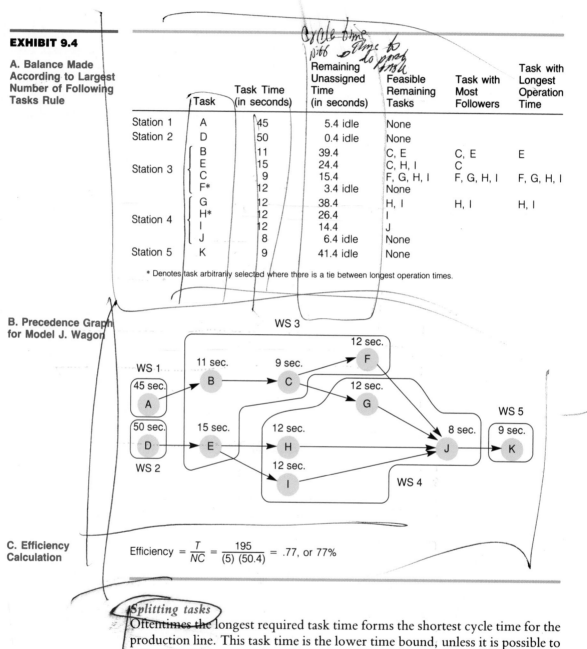

C. Efficiency Calculation

$$\text{Efficiency} = \frac{T}{NC} = \frac{195}{(5)(50.4)} = .77, \text{ or } 77\%$$

Splitting tasks

Oftentimes the longest required task time forms the shortest cycle time for the production line. This task time is the lower time bound, unless it is possible to split the task into two or more workstations.

Consider the following illustration: Supposing that an assembly line contains the following task times in seconds: 40, 30, 15, 25, 20, 18, 15. The line runs for 7½ hours per day and demand for output is 750 per day.

The cycle time required to produce 750 per day is 36 seconds ([7½ hours × 60 minutes × 60 seconds]/[750]). How do we deal with the task that is 40 seconds long?

There are several ways that we may be able to accommodate the 40-second task in a 36-second cycle. Possibilities are

1. *Split the task*. Can we split the task so that complete units are processed in two workstations?

2. *Share the task*. Can the task somehow be shared so an adjacent workstation does part of the work? This differs from the split task in the first option because the adjacent station acts to assist, not to do some units containing the entire task.

3. *Use a more skilled worker*. Since this task exceeds the cycle time by just 11 percent, a faster worker may be able to meet the 36-second time.

4. *Work overtime*. Producing at a rate of one every 40 seconds would produce 675 per day, 75 short of the needed 750. The amount of overtime required to do the additional 75 is 50 minutes (75 × 40 seconds/60 seconds).

5. *Redesign*. It may be possible to redesign the product to reduce the task time slightly.

Other possibilities to reduce the task time include equipment upgrading, a roaming helper to support the line, a change of materials, and multiskilled workers to operate the line as a team rather than as independent workers.

Flexible line layouts

As we saw in the preceding example, assembly line balances frequently result in unequal workstation times. Flexible line layouts such as shown in Exhibit 9.5 are a common way of dealing with this problem. In our toy company example, the U-shaped line with work sharing at the bottom of the figure could help resolve the imbalance.

Computerized line balancing

Companies engaged in assembly methods commonly employ a computer for line balancing. Most develop their own computer programs, but commercial package programs are also widely applied. One of these is General Electric Company's *Assembly-Line Configuration (ASYBL$)*, which uses the "ranked positional weight" rule in selecting tasks for workstations. Specifically, this rule states that tasks are assigned according to their positional weights, which is the time for a given task plus the task times of all those that follow it. Thus, the task with the highest positional weight would be assigned to the first workstation (subject to time, precedence, and zoning constraints). As is typical with such software, the user has several options for how the problem is to be

EXHIBIT 9.5

Flexible Line Layouts

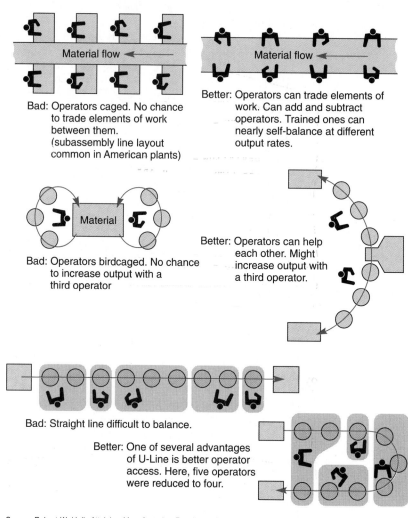

Bad: Operators caged. No chance
to trade elements of work
between them.
(subassembly line layout
common in American plants)

Better: Operators can trade elements of
work. Can add and subtract
operators. Trained ones can
nearly self-balance at different
output rates.

Bad: Operators birdcaged. No chance
to increase output with a
third operator

Better: Operators can help
each other. Might
increase output with
a third operator.

Bad: Straight line difficult to balance.

Better: One of several advantages
of U-Line is better operator
access. Here, five operators
were reduced to four.

Source: Robert W. Hall, *Attaining Manufacturing Excellence* (Homewood, Ill.: Dow Jones-Irwin, 1987), p. 125.

solved. Exhibit 9.6 illustrates a portion of program output when a target level of efficiency is used as a basis for deriving and comparing different balances for a 35-task assembly line. (The program can handle up to 450 tasks.) Note the trade-offs that take place as the number of workstations changes. In this case, the larger number of workstations allows for a better balance and, therefore, a higher efficiency.

One of the earlier computerized line balancing is the MUST algorithm, which can generate about 100 different balance solutions of equal quality for

EXHIBIT 9.6

Sample Computer Output

```
ENTER OPTION NUMBER?3

ENTER TARGET EFFICIENCY?.85

TOTAL EFFICIENCY   =    82%
STANDARD DEVIATION =      0.0153
TARGET CYCLE TIME  =      0.347
MINIM. CYCLE TIME  =      0.343
NO. OF STATIONS =    19

TOTAL EFFICIENCY   =    80%
STANDARD DEVIATION =      0.0175
TARGET CYCLE TIME  =      0.368
MINIM. CYCLE TIME  =      0.368
NO. OF STATIONS =    18

TOTAL EFFICIENCY   =    75%
STANDARD DEVIATION =      0.0214
TARGET CYCLE TIME  =      0.417
MINIM. CYCLE TIME  =      0.415
NO. OF STATIONS =    17
```

Source: General Electric Company, *Assembly-Line Configuration, ASYBL$ User's Guide* (1975), p. 28.

single product lines. The big advantage is that it eliminates the time-consuming process of making manual adjustments to workstation assignments, which are often necessary when there is only one solution to work from. The article by E. M. Dar-El and Y. Rubinovitch (see Selected Bibliography) explains how the program works.

Roger Johnson developed an algorithm to balance much larger assembly lines on the order of 1,000 tasks.[1] A branch and bound procedure is used to find optimal solutions. To find the solution the problem has been simplified somewhat by defining workstations to have an average of six tasks and few between task precedence requirements. We also comment a bit more on computerized line balancing in the next section about mixed model line balancing.

Mixed-model line balancing

To meet the demand for a variety of products and to avoid building high inventories of one product model, many manufacturers schedule several different models to be produced over a given day or week on the same line. To illustrate how this is done, suppose our toy company has a fabrication line to bore holes in its Model J Wagon frame and its Model K Wagon frame. The time required to bore the holes is different for each wagon type.

Assume that the final assembly line downstream requires equal numbers of model J and model K wagon frames. Assume also that we want to develop a

---

[1] Roger Johnson, "Optimally Balancing Large Assembly Lines with FABLE," *Management Science* 34, no. 2 (February 1988), pp. 240–53.

cycle time for the fabrication line which is balanced for the production of equal numbers of J and K frames. Of course, we could produce model J frames for several days and then produce model K frames until an equal number of frames has been produced. However, this would build up unnecessary work in process inventory.

If we want to reduce the amount of in process inventory, we could develop a cycle mix which greatly reduces inventory buildup while keeping within the restrictions of equal numbers of J and K wagon frames.

Process times: 6 minutes per J and 4 minutes per K.

The day consists of 480 minutes (8 hours × 60 minutes).

$6J + 4K = 480$

Since equal numbers of J and K are to be produced (or J = K), produce 48J and 48K per day, or 6J and 6K per hour.

The following shows one balance of J and K frames.

Balanced Mixed-Model Sequence

Model sequence	J J	K K K	J J	J J	K K K	
Operation time	6 6	4 4 4	6 6	6 6	4 4 4	Repeats 8 times per day
Minicycle time	12	12	12	12	12	
Total cycle time			60			

This line is balanced at six frames of each type per hour with a minicycle time of 12 minutes.

Another balance is J K K J K J, with times of 6, 4, 4, 6, 4, 6. This balance produces three J and three K every 30 minutes with a minicycle time of 10 minutes (JK, KJ, KJ).

The simplicity of mixed-model balancing (under conditions of a level production schedule) is seen in Yasuhiro Mondon's description of Toyota Motor Corporation's operations:

1. Final assembly lines of Toyota are mixed product lines. The production per day is averaged by taking the number of vehicles in the monthly production schedule classified by specifications, and dividing by the number of working days.

2. In regard to the production sequence during each day, the cycle time of each different specification vehicle is calculated and in order to have all specification vehicles appear at their own cycle time, different specification vehicles are ordered to follow each other.[2]

---

[2] Yasuhiro Mondon, *Toyota Production System, Practical Approach to Production Management* (Atlanta, Ga.: Industrial Engineering and Management Press, Institute of Industrial Engineers, 1983), p. 208.

As we have shown and discussed, the **mixed model line** appears to be a relatively straightforward sequencing problem. This is because in our example the two models fit nicely into a common time period that also matched demand. From a mathematical standpoint, designing a mixed model line is very difficult and no technique exists to provide the optimum assignment of tasks to workstations. This is because the mixed model line involves multiple lot sizes, lot sequencing, setup times for each lot, differing workstation sizes along the line, and task variations. The problem is to design the assembly line and workstations and specify exactly which tasks are to be done in each.

The objectives of a mixed model line design are to minimize idle time and minimize the inefficiencies caused by changing from model to model. Researchers have used integer programming, branch and bound techniques, and simulation. They still are not able to find the optimal solution for a realistic-sized real-world problem.

An excellent review of mixed model lines (and assembly lines in general) was done by Soumen Ghosh and Roger Gagnon.[3] These authors state that the best methods for finding reasonable balances are still the heuristic-based programs such as COMSOAL, which was done in the 1960s. Heuristic programs use general rules—most of which seem logical. Examples of heuristic rules for an automobile assembly line would be: (1) assign additional tasks to a workstation which use the same tool as the previous task (to save changing tools); and (2) assign the next task to the workstation which is on the same side of the car (to save moving to the other side of the line).

Current Thoughts on Assembly Lines

It is true that the widespread use of assembly-line methods in manufacturing has dramatically increased output rates. Historically, the focus has almost always been on full utilization of human labor; that is, to design assembly lines minimizing human idle time. Equipment and facility utilization stood in the background as much less important. Past research has tried to find optimal solutions as if the problem stood in a never-changing world.

Newer views of assembly lines take a broader perspective. Intentions are to incorporate greater flexibility in products produced on the line, more variability in workstations (such as size, number of workers), improved reliability (through routine preventive maintenance), and high-quality output (through improved tooling and training). Exhibit 9.7 compares some old and new ideas about production lines.

---

[3] Soumen Ghosh, and Roger Gagnon, "A Comprehensive Literature Review and Analysis of the Design, Balancing, and Scheduling of Assembly Systems," *International Journal of Production Research* 27, no. 4 (1989), pp. 637–70.

EXHIBIT 9.7

Assembly Lines: Traditional versus New Focus

Traditional	New Focus
1. Top priority: line balance	Top priority: flexibility
2. Strategy: stability—long production runs so that the need to rebalance seldom occurs	Strategy: flexibility—expect to rebalance often to match output to changing demand
3. Assume fixed labor assignments	Flexible labor: move to the problems or to where the current workload is
4. Use inventory buffers to cushion effects of equipment failure	Employ maximal preventive maintenance to keep equipment from breaking down
5. Need sophisticated analysis (e.g., using computers) to evaluate and cull the many options	Need human ingenuity to provide flexibility and ways around bottlenecks
6. Planned by staff	Supervisor may lead design effort and will adjust plan as needed
7. Plan to run at fixed rate; send quality problems off line	Slow for quality problems; speed up when quality is right
8. Linear or L-shaped lines	U-shaped or parallel lines
9. Conveyorized material movement is desirable	Put stations close together and avoid conveyors
10. Buy "supermachines" and keep them busy	Make (or buy) small machines; add more copies as needed
11. Applied in labor-intensive final assembly	Applied even to capital-intensive subassembly and fabrication work
12. Run mixed models where labor content is similar from model to model	Strive for mixed-model production, even in subassembly and fabrication

Source: Richard J. Schonberger, *Japanese Manufacturing Techniques: Nine Hidden Lessons in Simplicity* (New York: Free Press, 1982), p. 133.

9.3 PROCESS LAYOUT

The most common approach in developing a process layout is to arrange departments consisting of like processes in a way that optimizes their relative placement. In many installations, optimal placement often means placing departments with large amounts of interdepartment traffic adjacent to one another.

Minimizing Interdependent Movement Costs

Consider the following example: Suppose that we want to arrange the eight departments of a toy factory to minimize the interdepartmental material handling cost. Initially, let us make the simplifying assumption that all departments have the same amount of space, say, 40 feet by 40 feet and that the building is 80 feet wide and 160 feet long (and thus compatible with the department dimensions). The first thing we would want to know is the nature of the flow between departments and the way the material is transported. If the

EXHIBIT 9.8

Interdepartmental Flow

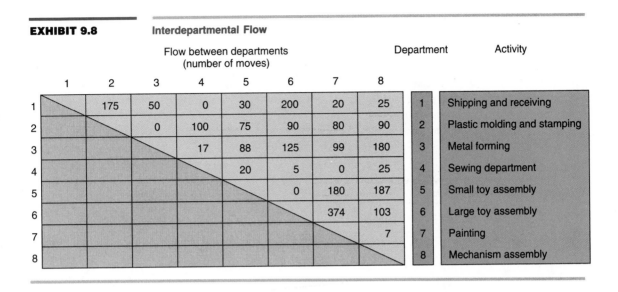

Flow between departments
(number of moves)

	1	2	3	4	5	6	7	8	Department	Activity
1		175	50	0	30	200	20	25	1	Shipping and receiving
2			0	100	75	90	80	90	2	Plastic molding and stamping
3				17	88	125	99	180	3	Metal forming
4					20	5	0	25	4	Sewing department
5						0	180	187	5	Small toy assembly
6							374	103	6	Large toy assembly
7								7	7	Painting
8									8	Mechanism assembly

EXHIBIT 9.9

Building Dimensions and Departments

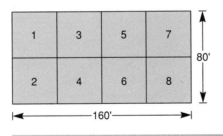

company has another factory that makes similar products, information about flow patterns might be abstracted from the records. On the other hand, if this is a new product line, such information would have to come from routing sheets (see Chapter 3) or from estimates by knowledgeable personnel such as process or industrial engineers. Of course these data, regardless of their source, have to be modified to reflect the nature of future orders over the projected life at the proposed layout.

Let us assume that this information is available. We find that all material is transported in a standard-size crate by forklift truck, one crate to a truck (which constitutes one "load"). Now suppose that transportation costs are $1 to move a load between adjacent departments and $1 extra for each department in between. The expected loads between departments for the first year of operation are tabulated in Exhibit 9.8; the available plant space is depicted in Exhibit 9.9.

Given this information, our first step is to illustrate the interdepartmental flow by a model, such as Exhibit 9.10, which is Exhibit 9.8 displayed in the building layout in Exhibit 9.9. This provides the basic layout pattern, which we try to improve.

The second step is to determine the cost of this layout by multiplying the material handling cost by the number of loads moved between each department. Exhibit 9.11 presents this information, which is derived as follows: The annual material handling cost between Departments 1 and 2 is $175 ($1 × 175 moves), $60 between Departments 1 and 5 ($2 × 30 moves), $60 between

EXHIBIT 9.10

Interdepartmental Flow Graph with Number of Annual Movements

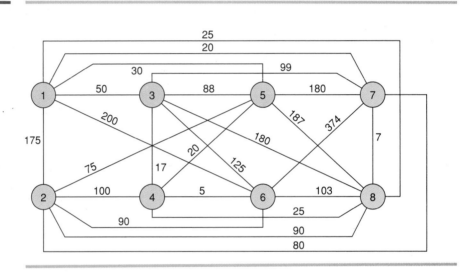

EXHIBIT 9.11

Cost Matrix—First Solution

	1	2	3	4	5	6	7	8
1		175	50	0	60	400	60	75
2			0	100	150	180	240	270
3				17	88	125	198	360
4					20	5	0	50
5						0	180	187
6							374	103
7								7
8								

Total cost: $3,474

Departments 1 and 7 (\$3 × 20 moves), and so forth. (The distances are taken from Exhibit 9.9 or 9.10, not Exhibit 9.8.)

The third step is a search for departmental changes that reduces costs. On the basis of the graph and the cost matrix, it seems desirable to place Departments 1 and 6 closer together to reduce their high move-distance costs. However, this requires shifting several other departments, thereby affecting their move-distance costs and the total cost of the second solution. Exhibit 9.12 shows the revised layout resulting from relocating Department 6 and an adjacent department (Department 4 is arbitrarily selected for this purpose). The revised cost matrix for the exchange, with the cost changes circled, is given in Exhibit 9.13. Note the total cost is \$262 *greater* than in the initial

EXHIBIT 9.12

Revised Interdepartmental Flow chart (Only interdepartmental flow with effect on cost is depicted)

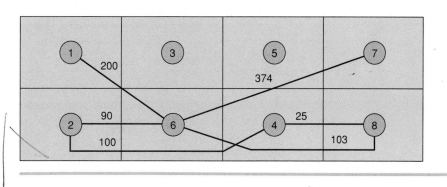

EXHIBIT 9.13   Cost Matrix—Second Solution

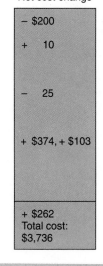

	1	2	3	4	5	6	7	8	Net cost change
1		175	50	0	60	(200)	60	75	− \$200
2			0	(200)	150	(90)	240	270	+ 10
3				17	88	125	198	360	
4					20	5	0	(25)	− 25
5						0	180	187	
6							(748)	(206)	+ \$374, + \$103
7								7	
8									
									+ \$262 Total cost: \$3,736

Small toy assembly 5	Mechanism assembly 8	Shipping and receiving 1	Large toy assembly 6
Metal forming 3	Plastic molding and stamping 2	Sewing 4	Painting 7

solution. Clearly, doubling the distance between Departments 6 and 7 accounted for the major part of the cost increase. This points out the fact that, even in a small problem, it is rarely easy to decide the correct "obvious move" on the basis of casual inspection.

Thus far, we have shown only one exchange among a large number of potential exchanges; in fact, for an eight-department problem there are 8! (or 40,320) possible arrangements. Therefore, the procedure we have employed would have only a remote possibility of achieving an optimal combination in a "reasonable" number of tries. Nor does our problem stop here.

Suppose that we *do* arrive at a good cut-and-try solution solely on the basis of material handling cost, such as that shown in Exhibit 9.14 (whose total cost is $3,244). We would note, first of all, that our shipping and receiving department is near the center of the factory—an arrangement that probably would not be acceptable. The sewing department is next to the painting department, introducing the hazard that lint, thread, and cloth particles might drift onto painted items. Further, small-toy assembly and large-toy assembly are located at opposite ends of the plant, which would increase travel time for assemblers, who very likely would be needed in both departments at various times of the day, and for supervisors, who might otherwise supervise both departments simultaneously.

Systematic Layout Planning

In certain layout problems, numerical flow of items between departments either is impractical to obtain or does not reveal the qualitative factors that may be crucial to the placement decision. In these situations, the technique known as *systematic layout planning* (SLP) is commonly used.[4] It involves developing a relationship chart showing the degree of importance of having each department located adjacent to every other department. From this chart is developed

4 See Richard Muther and John D. Wheeler, "Simplified Systematic Layout Planning," *Factory* 120, nos. 8, 9, 10 (August, September, October 1962), pp. 68–77, 111–19, 101–103.

an activity relationship diagram similar to the flow graph used for illustrating material handling between departments. The activity relationship diagram is then adjusted by trial and error until a satisficing adjacency pattern is obtained. This pattern, in turn, is modified department by department to meet building space limitations. Exhibit 9.15 illustrates the technique with a simple five-department problem involving laying out a floor of a department store.

Note that the letters in Exhibit 9.15A represent the importance for departments to be close together and the numbers give the reason. For example, the first cell shows that it is important (I) for the credit department to be close to the toy department because of psychology (6). We also see in cell 3,5 that it is undesirable (X) to have the wine department next to the candy department because of the type of customer. SLP points out the importance of considering other factors besides costs in creating a layout.

Computerized Layout Techniques—CRAFT

A number of computerized layout programs have been developed over the past 25 years to help devise good process layouts. Of these, the orginal and still useful program is the Computerized Relative Allocation of Facilities Technique (CRAFT).[5]

The CRAFT method follows the same basic idea we developed in the layout of the toy factory but with some significant operational differences. Like the toy factory example, it requires a load matrix and a distance matrix as initial inputs, but in addition requires a cost-per-unit distance traveled, say $.10 per foot moved. (Remember, we made the simplifying assumption that cost doubled when material had to jump one department, tripled when it had to jump two departments, and so forth.) With these inputs and an initial layout in the program, CRAFT then tries to improve the relative placement of the departments as measured by total material handling cost for the layout. (Material handling cost between departments = Number of loads × Rectilinear distance between department centroids × Cost-per-unit distance.) It makes improvements by exchanging pairs of departments in an iterative manner until no further cost reductions are possible. That is, the program calculates the effect on total cost of exchanging departments; if this yields a reduction the exchange is made, which constitutes an iteration. As we saw in the manual method, the departments are part of a material flow network, so even a simple pairwise exchange generally affects flow patterns among many other departments.

Each iteration is displayed in block layout form with the total cost for that layout, the cost reduction just made, and the departments just exchanged listed on the bottom of the printout. An example printout of CRAFT showing a final layout is given in Exhibit 9.16. (Letters designate and define the shape of

[5] For a discussion of CRAFT and other methods, see R. L. Francis and J. A. White, *Facility Layout and Location: An Analytical Approach* (Englewood Cliffs, N.J.: Prentice Hall, 1974).

EXHIBIT 9.15   Systematic Layout Planning for a Floor of a Department Store

A. Relationship chart (based upon Tables B and C)

From	To				Area (sq. ft.)
	2	3	4	5	
1. Credit department	I 6	U —	A 4	U —	100
2. Toy department		U —	I 1	A 1,6	400
3. Wine department			U —	X 1	300
4. Camera department				X 1	100
5. Candy department					100

Letter	← Closeness rating
Number	← Reason for rating

B.

Code	Reason*
1	Type of customer
2	Ease of supervision
3	Common personnel
4	Contact necessary
5	Share same space
6	Psychology

*Others may be used.

C.

Value	Closeness	Line code*	Color code†
A	Absolutely necessary	≡	Red
E	Especially important	=	Orange
I	Important	—	Green
O	Ordinary closeness OK	—	Blue
U	Unimportant		None
X	Undesirable	∧∧∨	Brown

*Used for example purposes only.
†Used in practice.

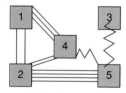

Initial relationship
diagram (based upon
Tables A and C)

Initial layout based upon
relationship diagram
(ignoring space and
building constraints)

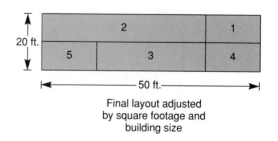

Final layout adjusted
by square footage and
building size

EXHIBIT 9.16

Sample CRAFT Printout

Location pattern

	1	2	3	4	5	6	7	8	9	10	11	12	13	14	15	16
1	A	A	A	A	A	A	A	A	L	L	L	J	J	I	I	I
2	A					A	A	L		L	J		J	I		I
3	A					A	L	L		L	J	J	J	I		I
4	A					A	L	L	L	L	L	L	L	I		I
5	A					A	G	G	G	L			L	I		I
6	A	A	A	A	A	A	G	G	G	L			L	I	I	I
7	B	B	B	B	B	B	G	G	L	L			L	K	K	K
8	B					B	B	C	C	L		L	L	L	K	K
9	B					B	C	C	C	L		L	H	H	H	H
10	B					B	C		C	L	L	L	L	H		H
11	B	B	B	B	B	C	C	C	L	F	F	F	H			H
12	D	D	D	D	E	C	C	C	F	F	F	F	H	H	H	H
13	D		D	E	E	E	F	F	F	F	M	M	M	M	M	M
14	D		D	E		E	M	M	M	M	M					M
15	D		D	E		E	M									
16	D	D	D	E	E	E	M	M	M	M	M	M	M	M	M	M

Total cost 87963.81   Estimated cost reduction 1410.00

each department. Lines would be drawn around each department to provide a more finished depiction of the layout.)

Distinguishing features of CRAFT and issues relating to it are

1. It is a heuristic program; it uses a simple rule of thumb in making evaluations: "compare two departments at a time and exchange them if it reduces the total cost of the layout." This type of rule is obviously necessary to analyze even a modest-sized layout.

2. It doesn't guarantee an optimal solution.

3. CRAFT is "biased" by its starting conditions: where you start (i.e., the initial layout) determines the final layout.

4. Starting with a reasonably good solution is more likely to yield a lower-cost final solution, but not always. This means that a good strategy for using CRAFT is to generate a variety of different starting layouts to expose the program to different pairwise exchanges.

5. It can handle up to 40 departments and rarely exceeds 10 iterations in arriving at a solution.

6. CRAFT departments consist of combinations of square modules (typically representing floor areas 10 feet by 10 feet). This permits

multiple departmental configurations, but often results in strange departmental shapes that have to be modified manually to obtain a realistic layout. (Take a look at Department L, for example, in Exhibit 9.16.)

7. A modified version has been created to use SLP closeness rating objectives when unit material handling costs are not important.[6]

8. CRAFT assumes the existence of variable path material handling equipment such as forklift trucks. Therefore, when computerized fixed-path equipment applications grow (as discussed later), the applicability of CRAFT becomes greatly reduced.

9.4 GROUP TECHNOLOGY (CELLULAR) LAYOUT

Group technology (or cellular) layout allocates dissimilar machines into cells to work on products that have similar shapes and processing requirements. Group technology (GT) layouts are now widely used in metal fabricating, computer chip manufacture, and assembly work. The overall objective is to gain the benefits of product layout in job-shop kinds of production. These benefits include:

1. Better human relations. Cells consist of a few workers who form a small work team; a team turns out complete units of work.

2. Improved operator expertise. Workers see only a limited number of different pairs in a finite production cycle, so repetition means quick learning.

3. Less in-process inventory and material handling. A cell combines several production stages, so fewer parts travel through the shop.

4. Faster production setup. Fewer jobs mean reduced tooling and hence faster tooling changes.

Developing a GT Layout

Shifting from process layout to a GT cellular layout entails three steps:

1. Grouping parts into families that follow a common sequence of steps. This step requires developing and maintaining a computerized parts classification and coding system. This is often a major expense with such systems, although many companies have developed short-cut procedures for identifying parts families.

---

[6] S. Manivannan and Dipak Chudhuri, "Computer-Aided Facility Layout Algorithm Generates Alternatives to Increase Firm's Productivity," *Industrial Engineering,* May 1984, pp. 81–84.

2. Identifying dominant flow patterns of parts families as a basis for location or relocation of processes.

3. Physically grouping machines and processes into cells. Often some parts cannot be associated with a family and specialized machinery cannot be placed in any one cell because of its general use. These unattached parts and machinery are placed in a "remainder cell."

Exhibit 9.17 illustrates the cell development process followed by Rockwell's Telecommunication Division, maker of wave-guide parts. Part A shows the original process-oriented layout; part B the planned relocation of process based on parts-family production requirements; and part C an enlarged layout of the cell designed to perform all but the finishing operation. According to Richard Schonberger, cellular organization was practical here because (1) distinct parts families existed; (2) there were several of each type of machine, and taking a machine out of a cluster therefore did not rob the cluster of all its capacity, leaving no way to produce other products; (3) the work centers were easily movable stand-alone machine tools—heavy, but anchored to the floor rather simply. He adds that these three features represent general guidelines for deciding where a cellular layout or group technology make sense.[7]

The group technology (GT) problem consists of three phases:

1. Develop a classification and coding scheme for items (shape, size, materials, etc.).

2. From processing requirements and routings, group parts into families to form cell groups.

3. Create the physical layout positioning cells relative to each other.

The first phase is more of an engineering problem of describing work pieces or parts. The third phase is essentially solvable using a layout evaluation such as CRAFT (discussed earlier in this chapter) to minimize the material flow among cells. The second phase is what is generally thought of as the GT problem—how to form cells.

To form cells, the first thing to do is create a flow matrix showing which components flow to each machine. Exhibit 9.18, which is the final grouping, started with a list of 24 components (rows 1 to 24) and 14 machines (columns 1 to 14). To force these rows and columns into groups, the method used here was a binary weighting scheme. This weighted the lowest row as 2^0; second lowest, 2^1; third lowest, 2^2; and so on up to the first row.[8] Columns are

[7] Richard J. Schonberger, *World Class Manufacturing: The Lessons of Simplicity Applied* (New York: Free Press, 1986), p. 112.

[8] J. L. King, "Machine Component Group Formation for Group Technology" (*Proceedings of the Fifth International Conference on Production Research*), p. 193.

EXHIBIT 9.17

Developing a Cell to
Produce Wave-Guide
Parts

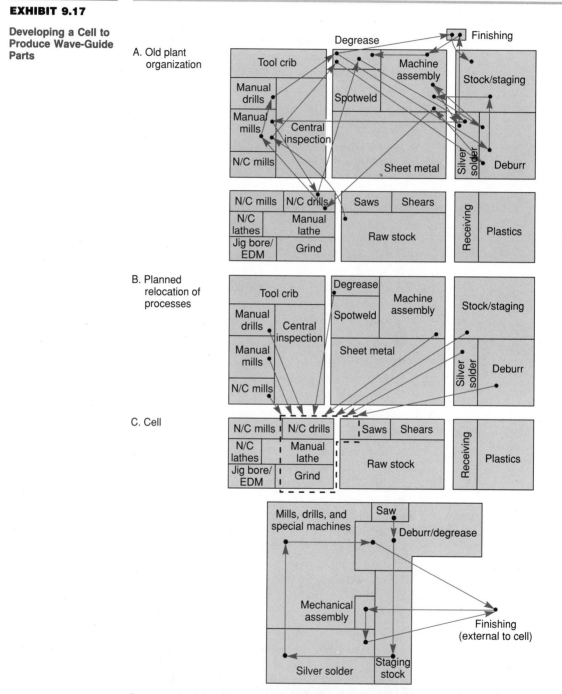

A. Old plant organization

B. Planned relocation of processes

C. Cell

EXHIBIT 9.18   Component/Machine Grouping by Weighting Rows and Columns

MACHINE

Component	7	4	5	13	1	12	11	3	2	10	8	9	6	14
2	1	1	1											
17	1	1	1											
20	1	1	1											
3	1	1	1											
8	1			1	1	1								
23		1	1	1										
19		1												
7				1	1									
9				1		1								
18				1										
4							1	1	1	1				
5							1	1	1					
21							1	1						
24										1				
15											1	1	1	1
10											1	1	1	1
12											1	1	1	
6											1	1		
1											1		1	
14											1		1	
16											1		1	
13												1		1
11													1	1

weighted the same way with the rightmost column 2^0; second from the right, 2^1; third from the right, 2^2; and so on back to the first column. The matrix contains only ones and blanks; a 1 means that part is processed on that machine. Each row is multiplied by each column. For example, the 4th column from the right and 3rd row from the bottom would have a value of $2^3 \times 2^2$, or 32. The matrix is reorganized with the highest weights from top to bottom and from left to right. This weighting forces the common parts and machines to group together. The multiplication and rearranging is repeated more times until the matrix stays unchanged. This forms the basis for GT cells.

Another way to create GT cells is based on cost. Ronald Askin and S. P. Subramanian use the following costs:

1. Setup costs.
2. Variable production costs.
3. Production cycle inventory costs.
4. Work-in-process (WIP) inventory costs.
5. Material handling costs.
6. Fixed machine costs.

They also assume the following conditions:

1. Each part has a predetermined desired processing sequence with associated setup and run times.
2. Planning horizon is infinite and mean demand is constant.
3. Shortages are not allowed.
4. An entire batch of parts must be at the workstation prior to starting production (i.e., no lot splitting).
5. Each part belongs to an initial coding family—intrafamily setups are inexpensive as compared to interfamily setups.[9]

Groups were created by considering combinations of parts and machines and the resulting costs. The starting point is to arrange the groups in order of machine similarity. Initially, each part is called a group, and a total cost is computed based on the preceding cost list. Then, evaluations are made in sequence to test the benefits of combining adjacent groups. For example, during the first pass each group contains only one part. The cost for Group 1 and Group 2 together is compared to the cost of Group 1 and Group 2 separately. If the combined cost is less, then we combine. If not, we compare the combined cost of Group 2 and Group 3 to their separate costs. Again, if the combined cost is less, we combine; otherwise we continue testing successive pairs.

If the combined cost for a pair is less, the combination is made and the procedure continues. For example, suppose Groups 3 and 4 were combined because their total costs were less than their separate costs; next the cost would be computed for adding Group 5 to Group 3–4, creating a group of 3 parts. If the cost were less, this group would expand to include parts 3, 4, and 5. Exhibit 9.19 shows the flow and the logic of the combining procedure.

Conceptual GT Layout

When equipment is not easily movable, many companies dedicate a given machine out of a set of identical machines in a process layout. A conceptual GT cell for, say, a two-month production run for the job might consist of Drill 1 in the drills area, Mill 3 in the mill area, and Assembly Area 1 in the machine assembly area. To approximate a GT flow, all work on the particular part family would be done only on these specific machines.

9.5   JUST-IN-TIME LAYOUT

In Chapter 6 we discuss the logic of Just-in-Time (JIT) and its influence on layout. When demand is continuous and tasks in each job sequence are relatively balanced, workstations may be located adjacent to each other. In theory,

---

[9] Ronald G. Askin and S. P. Subramanian, "A Cost-Based Heuristic for Group Technology Configuration," *International Journal of Production Research* 25, no. 1 (1987), pp. 101–13.

EXHIBIT 9.19   Flowchart to Form GT Cells Based on Total Costs

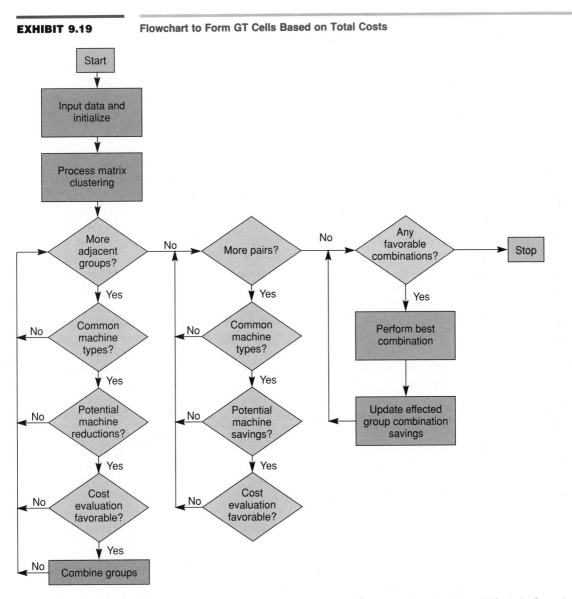

Source: Ronald G. Askin and S. P. Subramanian. "A Cost-Based Heuristic for Group Technology Configuration." *International Journal of Production Research* 25, no. 1 (1987), p. 109.

when some amount of product is pulled from the end of the line, the system operates by pulling from up the line to replace the units removed. In practice, it means the production and movement of parts are approximately at a fixed scheduled pace, but not until each worker has finished and released it. See Exhibit 6.13 in Chapter 6. When demand is not continuous, JIT can be arranged in other ways, such as grouping by function as well as lines, as shown in Exhibit 6.14 in Chapter 6. The pull in this case is provided through a materials handling procedure.

9.6   CONCLUSION

The big question affecting layout decisions in manufacturing is: How flexible should the layout be to deal with changes in product demand and product mix? Some have argued that the best strategy is to have movable equipment that can be shifted easily from place to place to reduce material flow time for near-term contracts. However, while this is appealing in general, the limitations of existing buildings and firmly anchored equipment, and the general plant disruption that is created make this a very costly strategy.

A major trend in layout is to envision the plant as an assembly line, whether it is physically so or not. One way to think of this in a more concrete fashion is to view departments as workstations whose work load is balanced in the same general way as workstations on a line. The just-in-time methods and some of the newer computer scheduling approaches discussed in later chapters implicitly follow this conceptualization.

In service systems, particularly franchises, the study of layout has become extremely important because the selected layout may become replicated at hundreds or even thousands of facilities. Indeed, a layout error in a fast-food chain has a more immediate, and generally a more far-reaching, effect on profits than a layout error in a factory.

The simulation supplement to Chapter 15 provides procedures that can be used for analyzing alternative layout formats. Simulation, coupled with computer graphics, constitutes the state of the art in quantitative layout approaches.

9.7   REVIEW AND DISCUSSION QUESTIONS

1. What kind of layout is used in a physical fitness center?
2. What is the key difference between SLP and CRAFT?
3. What is the objective of assembly line balancing? How would you deal with the situation where one worker, although trying hard, is 20 percent slower than the other 10 people on a line?
4. How do you determine the idle-time percentage from a given assembly line balance?

5. What information of particular importance do route sheets and process charts (discussed in Chapter 3) provide to the layout planner?

6. What is the essential requirement for mixed-model lines to be practical?

7. Why might it be difficult to develop a GT layout?

8. In what respects is facility layout a marketing problem in services? Give an example of a service system layout designed to maximize the amount of time the customer is in the system.

9.8 PROBLEMS

*1. A university advising office has four rooms, each dedicated to specific problems: petitions (Room A), schedule advising (Room B), grade complaints (Room C), and student counseling (Room D). The office is 80 feet long and 20 feet wide. Each room is 20 feet by 20 feet. The present location of rooms is A, B, C, D; that is, a straight line. The load summary shows the number of contacts that each advisor in a room has with other advisors in the other rooms. Assume that all advisors are equal in this value.

Load summary: $AB = 10$, $AC = 20$, $AD = 30$,

$BC = 15$, $BD = 10$, $CD = 20$..

  a. Evaluate this layout according to one of the methods in the chapter.
  b. Improve the layout by exchanging functions within rooms. Show your amount of improvement using the same method as in (a).

*2. The following tasks must be performed on an assembly line in the sequence and times specified.

Task	Task Time (seconds)	Tasks That Must Precede
A	50	—
B	40	—
C	20	A
D	45	C
E	20	C
F	25	D
G	10	E
H	35	B, F, G

  a. Draw the schematic diagram.
  b. What is the theoretical minimum number of stations required to meet a forecasted demand of 400 units per eight-hour day?
  c. Use the longest operating time rule and balance the line in the minimum number of stations to produce 400 units per day.

3. An assembly line makes two models of trucks—a Buster and a Duster. Busters take 12 minutes each and Dusters take 8 minutes each. The daily output requirement is 24 of each per day. Develop a perfectly balanced mixed-model sequence to satsify demand.

---

* Solutions to Problems 1 and 2 are given in Appendix H.

4. The following tasks and the order in which they must be performed according to their assembly requirements are shown in the following table. These are to be combined into workstations to create an assembly line.

The assembly line operates 7½ hours per day. The output requirement is 1,000 units per day.

Task	Preceding Tasks	Time (seconds)
A	—	15
B	A	24
C	A	6
D	B	12
E	B	18
F	C	7
G	C	11
H	D	9
I	E	14
J	F, G	7
K	H, I	15
L	J, K	10

a. What is the cycle time?
b. Balance the line based on the 1,000 unit forecast, stating which tasks would be done in each workstation.
c. For b above, what is the efficiency of your line balance?
d. After production was started, Marketing realized that they understated demand and will need to increase output to 1,100 units. What action would you take? Be specific in quantitative terms, if appropriate.

5. An assembly line is operated seven hours per day and produces 420 units per day. Following are the tasks that are performed with their performance time and preceding tasks.

Task	Time (seconds)	Preceding Tasks
A	15	None
B	15	None
C	45	A, B
D	45	C

Compute the cycle time and the theoretical minimum number of workstations, and prepare an initial line configuration. Determine the efficiency of your layout.

6. An initial solution has been given to the following process layout problem. Given the flows described and a cost of $2.00 per unit per foot, compute the total cost for the layout. Each location is 100 feet long and 50 feet wide as shown on the figure below. Use the centers of departments for distances.

		Department			
		A	B	C	D
	A	0	10	25	55
Department	B		0	10	5
	C			0	15
	D				0

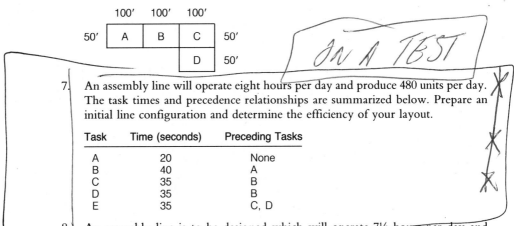

7. An assembly line will operate eight hours per day and produce 480 units per day. The task times and precedence relationships are summarized below. Prepare an initial line configuration and determine the efficiency of your layout.

Task	Time (seconds)	Preceding Tasks
A	20	None
B	40	A
C	35	B
D	35	B
E	35	C, D

8. An assembly line is to be designed which will operate 7½ hours per day and supply a steady demand of 300 units per day. Following are the tasks and their task performance times.

Task	Preceding Tasks	Performance Time (Seconds)
a	—	70
b	—	40
c	—	45
d	a	10
e	b	30
f	c	20
g	d	60
h	e	50
i	f	15
j	g	25
k	h, i	20
l	j, k	25

a. Draw the precedence diagram.
b. What is the cycle time?
c. What is the theoretical minimum number of workstations?
d. Assign tasks to workstations stating what your logical rules are.
e. What is the efficiency of your line balance?
f. Suppose demand increases by 10 percent. How would you react to this?

9. The Royal University of Dorton was created for the purpose of providing higher education for the aristocracy of the kingdom, the sons and daughters of resident foreign dignitaries, and other loyal and influential subjects. The regent of the country and university (Queen Harriet) has allocated a rectangular (40 by 80 feet) portion of the first floor of the south wing of the Imperial Palace for the purpose of constructing lecture halls, laboratories, and so forth. The interior layout was designed by S. L. P. Craft, and is one of the first examples of flexible layout by means of modular partitions in Dorton. The basic module is 10 feet square, and the tentative design is shown in Exhibit 9.20.

Unlike most American universities, Dorton has only six categories of students. The members of each category are assigned the same classes and schedules during their years at the university. Each class meets for 50 minutes each day, and the students are required to proceed directly to their next class. The schedule for the current semester is indicated in Exhibit 9.21.

The architect is interested in gaining the favor of the queen and has contracted for you to verify his layout and suggest improvements. He has asked you to:

a. Prepare a flow matrix for the class sequence similar to the load summary shown in Exhibit 9.8.

EXHIBIT 9.20

Current Layout of the Royal University of Dorton

Number	Activity	Number	Activity
1	Entrance	9	Accounting
2	Meditation	10	Electrical engineering
3	Basket weaving*	11	Psychology
4	Calculus	12	Assertiveness training
5	Arithmetic	13	Humanities
6	Finance	14	Art
7	Production management	15	Philosophy
8	Economics	16	Exit

* Location must remain fixed due to its proximity to the fountain for soaking the weaving material.

EXHIBIT 9.21   Dorton University's Semester Schedule

			CLASS MEETING TIME										
		8	9	10	11	12	1	2	3	4	5	6	
Category	Number of Students					Classroom Number							
1. Queen's children	8	15	4	7	11	6	10	12	13	2	9	8	
2. Queen's children (by a previous marriage)	4	3	14	5									
3. Merchants' children	32	5	9	6	8	11	7						
4. Nobles' children	25	12	3	13	7	4							
5. Children of idle rich	42	7	12	14	13	3							
6. Children of foreign officials	17	2	7	4	10	15	6	14					

b. Determine the cost of the existing layout in terms of walking. (Since the architect wishes to gain favor with the queen, he values each foot walked by the recent children of the queen as equivalent to two feet walked by the children from a previous marriage and to four feet walked by all others.)

c. Create a better layout, keeping room areas the same and fitting into a 40 by 80-foot rectangular space. *Note:* The entrance and exit must remain in the same position.

10. Given the following data on the task precedence relationships for an assembled product and assuming the tasks cannot be split, what is the theoretical minimum cycle time? Assume a cycle time of seven minutes.

Task	Performance Time (minutes)	Tasks That Must Precede
A	3	
B	6	A
C	7	A
D	5	A
E	2	A
F	4	B, C
G	5	C
H	5	D, E, F, G

a. Determine the number of workstations needed to achieve this cycle time using the "ranked positional weight" rule.

b. Determine the minimium number of stations needed to meet a cycle time of 10 minutes according to the "largest number of following tasks" rule.

c. Compute the efficiency of the balances achieved.

11. S. L. P. Craft would like your help in developing a layout for a new outpatient clinic to be built in Dorton. Based on analysis of another recently built clinic, he obtains the following data for the number of trips made by patients between departments on a typical day (shown above diagonal line), and the closeness ratings (defined in Exhibit 9.15C) between departments as specified by the new clinic's physicians (below diagonal). The new building will be 60 feet by 20 feet.

a. Develop an interdepartmental flow graph that minimizes patient travel.

b. Develop a "good" relationship diagram using systematic layout planning.

Departments	2	3	4	5	6	Area requirement (sq. ft.)
1 Reception	A — 2	O — 5	E — 200	U — 0	O — 10	100
2 X-ray		E — 10	I — 300	U — 0	O — 8	100
3 Surgery			I — 100	U — 0	A — 4	200
4 Examining rooms (5)				U — 0	I — 15	500
5 Lab					O — 3	100
6 Nurses' station						100

c. Choose either of the layouts obtained in *a* or *b* and sketch the departments to scale within the building.

d. Will this layout be satisfactory to the nursing staff? Explain.

12. Simon's Mattress Factory is planning to introduce a new line of "pillow-top" mattresses. Current plans are to produce the mattresses on an assembly line. Mattresses will be built on individual platforms pulled by a chain in a track in the floor. This will allow workers to completely walk around the mattress. Tools will be suspended from the ceiling, so that there will not be a problem with tangling cords or wrapping them around the platform.

The assembly-line process starts with the basic spring foundation and builds the mattress as it progresses down the line. There are 12 operations required and their times and process sequence are as follows:

Operation	Time (minutes)	Tasks That Must Precede
A	1	—
B	3	A
C	4	B
D	1	B
E	5	C
F	4	D
G	1	E, F
H	2	G
I	5	G
J	3	H
K	2	I
L	3	J, K

Tentative plans are to operate the line 7½ hours per day. Demand for the mattresses is expected to be 70 per day.

a. Draw the schematic diagram.

b. What is the cycle time?

c. What is the theoretical minimum number of workstations.

d. Create a reasonable layout.

e. Supposing the plan was to produce these in a job shop layout. Discuss and compare the characteristics, pros, cons, etc. of job shop versus assembly line for this mattress production.

13. XYZ Manufacturing Company received a contract for 20,000 units of a product to be delivered in equal weekly quantities over a six-month period. XYZ works 250 days per year on a single-shift 40-hour work week.

The table below states the tasks required and their precedence sequence and task times in seconds.

Task	Task That Must Precede	Task Time (seconds)
A	—	150
B	A	120
C	B	150
D	A	30
E	D	100
F	C, E	40
G	E	30
H	F, G	100

a. Develop an assembly line meeting the requirements.

b. State the cycle time.

c. What is the "efficiency" of the line.

d. Supposing the vendor asked you to increase output by 10 percent. State specifically how you would respond to this.

14. The following tasks are to be performed on an assembly line:

Task	Seconds	Tasks That Must Precede
A	20	—
B	7	A
C	20	B
D	22	B
E	15	C
F	10	D
G	16	EF
H	8	G

Given:
The workday is 7 hours long.
Demand for completed product is 750 per day.

a. Find the cycle time.

b. What is the theoretical number of workstations?

c. Draw the precedence diagram.

d. Balance the line using sequential restrictions and the longest operating time rule.

e. What is the efficiency of the line balanced as in *d?*

f. Suppose that demand rose from 750 per day to 800 units per day. What would you do? Show any amounts or calculations.

g. Suppose that demand rose from 750 per day to 1,000 units per day. What would you do? Show any amounts or calculations.

15. Assembly lines have definite advantages over job shop layouts in certain applications. Discuss where assembly line layouts are best used and what the objectives, balancing techniques, performance measurements, cycle times, capitalization requirements, worker skill levels, etc., are.

16. The Dorton University president has asked the OM department to assign eight biology professors (A, B, C, D, E, F, G, and H) to eight offices (numbered 1 to 8 in the diagram) in the new Biology Building.

North Wing

1	2	3	4

Courtyard

New Biology Building

5	6	7	8

South Wing

The following distances and two-way flows are given:

DISTANCES BETWEEN OFFICES (FEET)										TWO-WAY FLOWS (UNITS PER PERIOD)							
	1	2	3	4	5	6	7	8		A	B	C	D	E	F	G	H
1	—	10	20	30	15	18	25	34	A	—	2	0	0	5	0	0	0
2		—	10	20	18	15	18	25	B		—	0	0	0	3	0	2
3			—	10	25	18	15	18	C			—	0	0	0	0	3
4				—	34	25	18	15	D				—	4	0	0	0
5					—	10	20	30	E					—	1	0	0
6						—	10	20	F						—	1	0
7							—	10	G							—	4
8								—	H								—

a. If there are no restrictions (constraints) on the assignment of professors to offices, how many alternative assignments are there to evaluate?

b. The biology department has sent the following information and requests to the OM department:

> Offices 1, 4, 5, and 8 are the only offices with windows.
> A must be assigned Office 1.
> D and E, the biology department co-chairpeople, must have windows.
> H must be directly across the courtyard from D.
> A, G, and H must be in the same wing.
> F must *not* be next to D or G or directly across from G.

Find the optimal assignment of professors to offices that meets all the requests of the biology department and minimizes total material handling cost. You may use the path flow list as a computational aid.

Path	Flow	Path	Flow	Path	Flow	Path	Flow	Path	Flow	Path	Flow
A–B	2	B–C	0	C–D	0	D–E	4	E–F	1		
A–C	0	B–D	0	C–E	0	D–F	0	E–G	0		
A–D	0	B–E	0	C–F	0	D–G	0	E–H	0		
A–E	5	B–F	3	C–G	0	D–H	0	F–G	1		
A–F	0	B–G	0	C–H	3			F–H	0		
A–G	0	B–H	2					G–H	4		
A–H	0										

9.9 SELECTED BIBLIOGRAPHY

Askin, Ronald G., and S. P. Subramanian. "A Cost-Based Heuristic for Group Technology Configuration." *International Journal of Production Research* 25, no. 1 (1987), pp. 101–13.

Choobineh, F. "A Framework for the Design of Cellular Manufacturing Systems." *International Journal of Production Research* 26, no. 7 (1988), pp. 1161–72.

Dar-El, E. M., and Y. Rubinovitch. "MUST—A Multiple Solutions Technique for Balancing Single Model Assembly Lines." *Management Science* 25, no. 11 (November 1979), pp. 1, 105–14.

Francis, R. L., and J. A. White. *Facility Layout and Location: An Analytical Approach.* Englewood Cliffs, N.J.: Prentice Hall, 1987.

Ghosh, Soumen, and Roger Gagnon. "A Comprehensive Literature Review and Analysis of the Design, Balancing and Scheduling of Assembly Systems." *International Journal of Production Research* 27, no. 4 (1989), pp. 637–70.

Green, Timothy J., and Randall P. Sadowski. "A Review of Cellular Manufacturing Assumptions, Advantages and Design Techniques." *Journal of Operations Management* 4, no. 2 (February 1984), pp. 85–97.

Gunther, R. E.; G. D. Johnson; and R. S. Peterson. "Currently Practiced Formulations for the Assembly Line Balance Problem." *Journal of Operations Management* 3, no. 4 (August 1983), pp. 209–21.

Hyer, Nancy Lea. "The Potential of Group Technology for U.S. Manufacturing." *Journal of Operations Management* 4, no. 3 (May 1984), pp. 183–202.

Johnson, Roger. "Optimally Balancing Large Assembly Lines with FABLE." *Management Science* 34, no. 2 (February 1988), pp. 240–53.

Mondon, Yasuhiro. *Toyota Production System, Practical Approach to Production Management.* Atlanta, Ga.: Industrial Engineering and Management Press, 1983.

Schonberger, Richard J. *Japanese Manufacturing Techniques.* New York: Free Press, 1982.

Thompkins, James A., and James M. Moore. *Computer Aided Layout: A User's Guide.* Publication no. 1, Facilities Planning and Design Division, American Institute of Industrial Engineers, Inc., Atlanta: AIIE, Inc., 1978.

Vannelli, Anthony, and K. Ravi Kumar. "A Method for Finding Minimal Bottleneck Cells for Grouping Part-Machine Families." *International Journal of Production Research* 24, no. 2 (1986), pp. 387–400.

Chapter 10

Job Design and Work Measurement

Strange things happen at the best plants. Workers complain about machines being idle for too long and then fix them on their own to reduce the downtime. A plant manager smiles approvingly when he encounters the head of the janitorial crew dictating a letter to the manager's own secretary. The fanciest conference rooms are sometimes found not in the administration building, but inside the plant for workers to use when meeting with foremen.

Gene Bylinsky, "America's Best Managed Factories," *Fortune*, May 28, 1984, p. 16.

KEY TERMS

Job Design

Specialization of Labor

Sociotechnical Systems

Work Measurement

Financial Incentive Plans

The quote that opens this chapter captures the flavor of how many of our better-run companies are now relating to their work forces, and how the work forces are relating to them. In the first part of this chapter we touch on some of the job-design concepts that are giving rise to and support these relationships. In the remainder of the chapter we discuss the technical concepts required to standardize and measure work and compensate the work force.

10.1 JOB DESIGN

Perhaps the most challenging (and perplexing) design activity encountered by the productive system is the development of the jobs that each worker and work group are to perform. This is so for at least three reasons:

1. There is often an inherent conflict between the needs and goals of the worker and work group, and the requirements of the production process.
2. The unique nature of each individual results in a wide range of attitudinal, physiological, and productivity responses in performing any given task.
3. The character of the work force and the work itself are changing, which lays open to question the traditional models of worker behavior and the efficacy of standard approaches to work development.

In this section, we explore these and other issues in job design and present some guidelines for carrying out the job-design function. We begin by noting some trends in job design:

1. *Quality control as part of the worker's job.* Now often referred to as "quality at the source" (see Chapter 5), quality control is linked with the concept of *empowerment.* Empowerment, in turn refers to workers being given authority to stop a production line if there is a quality problem, or to give a customer an on-the-spot refund if service was not satisfactory.

2. *Cross-training workers to perform multiskilled jobs.* This is more often seen in the factory than in the office despite pressures on the clerical work force as described in the Insert. Indeed, bank check processing centers and the majority of high-volume clerical jobs are far more factorylike than many factories.

3. *Employee involvement and team approaches to designing and organizing work.* This is a central feature in total quality management (TQM) and continuous improvement efforts. In fact, it is safe to say that virtually all TQM programs are team based.

4. *"Informating" ordinary workers through telecommunication networks and computers thereby expanding the nature of their work and their ability to do it.* In this context, informating is more than just automating work, it is revising work's fundamental structure. Northeast Utilities' computer system, for example,

EXHIBIT 10.1

People-Related Objectives of Hewlett-Packard

1. **Belief in our people**
   - Confidence in, and respect for, ⟨ r people as opposed to depending upon extensive rules, procedures, and so forth.
   - Depend upon people to do their job right (individual freedom) without constant directives.
   - Opportunity for meaningful participation (job dignity).

2. **Emphasis on working together and sharing rewards (teamwork and partnership)**
   - Share responsibilities; help each other; learn from each other; chance to make mistakes.
   - Recognition based on contribution to results—sense of achievement and self-esteem.
   - Profit sharing, stock purchase plan, retirement program, and so on are aimed at employees and company sharing in each other's successes.
   - Company financial management emphasis on protecting employee's job security.

3. **A superior working environment which other companies seek but few achieve**
   - Informality—open, honest communications; no artificial distinctions between employees (first-name basis); management by walking around; and open-door communication policy.
   - Develop and promote from within—lifetime training, education, career counseling to help employees get maximum opportunity to grow and develop with the company.
   - Decentralization—emphasis on keeping work groups as small as possible for maximum employee identification with our businesses and customers.

can pinpoint a problem in a service area before the customer service representative answers the phone. The rep uses the computer to troubleshoot serious problems, to weigh probabilities that other customers in the area have been affected, and to dispatch repair crews before other calls are even received.

5. Any time, any place production. The ability to do work away from the factory or office, again due primarily to information technology, is a growing trend throughout the world. (See the Insert.)

6. Automation of heavy manual work. Examples abound in both services (one-person trash pickup trucks) and manufacturing (robot spray painting on auto lines). These changes are driven by safety regulations as well as economics and personnel reasons. (See the Insert.)

7. Most important of all, organizational commitment to providing meaningful and rewarding jobs for all employees. (See Exhibit 10.1).

INSERT   The New World of Work

- London firms are now sending typing to Taipei. To survive, London typists must realize they are competing with Taipei typists. They must learn to "add value" (e.g., know more software programs, more languages than their Taiwanese counterparts) or else they'd better learn to love pounding the pavement.

- The FI Group, one of Britain's largest software systems houses, employs about 1,100, most of whom are part-time free-lancers who need toil no more than 20 hours per week. More than two-thirds of the firm's work is done at home: All told, employees live in 800 sites and serve 400 clients at any time. Life at FI is captured in the November 1988 issue of *Business:* "Chris Eyles, project manager, sat down in her office in Esher, Surrey, and called up the electronic 'chit chat' mailbox. . . . The printer began to churn out messages. 'Help!' said [a message] from her secretary, based a few miles away in Weybridge. Somewhere in the Esher area, a computer analyst was in trouble. . . . Eyles checked the team diary and her wall plan, located the analyst and the problem and set up a meeting at FI's work center in Horley, 25 miles away."

- So who's left to sweep the floor? A visit to a 3M facility in Austin, Texas, suggests that floor sweeping, food handling, and security guarding are fast becoming almost as sophisticated as engineering. Computer-based floor sweepers and new security systems call for a sophisticated worker in virtually every job. A new, highly automated facility belonging to the huge drug distributor, Bergen Brunswig, is illustrative: Most manual work is done by machine. Work teams that dot the facility are not so much in the business of "doing" (by old standards), but in the business of improving the system. They are brain-involved, improvement-project creators, not muscle-driven lump shifters. There is no room on the staff for anyone who sees himself or herself as a pair of hands, punching a time clock.

Source: Tom Peters, "Prometheus Barely Unbound," *The Executive* IV, no. 4 (November 1990), pp. 79–80, 83.

Job Design Defined

Job design may be defined as the function of specifying the work activities of an individual or group in an organizational setting. Its objective is to develop work assignments that meet the requirements of the organization and the technology and that satisfy the personal and individual requirements of the jobholder. The term *job* (in the context of nonsupervisory work) and the activities subsumed under it are defined here:

1. *Micromotion:* the smallest work activities, involving such elementary movements as reaching, grasping, positioning, or releasing an object.
2. *Element:* an aggregation of two or more micromotions, usually thought of as a more or less complete entity, such as picking up, transporting, and positioning an item.
3. *Task:* an aggregation of two or more elements into a complete activity, such as wiring a circuit board, sweeping a floor, or cutting a tree.
4. *Job:* the set of all tasks that must be performed by a given worker. A job may consist of several tasks, such as typing, filing, and taking dictation (in secretarial work), or it may consist of a single task, such as attaching a wheel to a car (as in automobile assembly).

EXHIBIT 10.2   Factors in Job Design

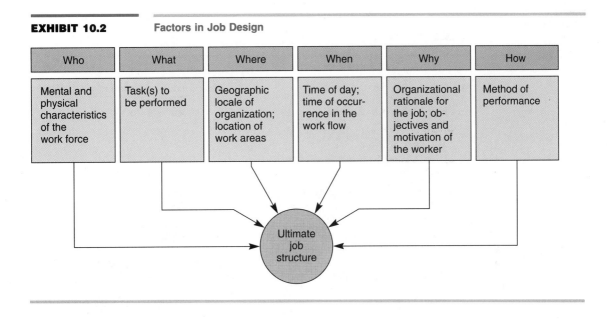

Job design is a complex function because of the variety of factors that enter into arriving at the ultimate job structure. Decisions must be made about who is to perform the job, where it is to be performed, and how. And, as we can see in Exhibit 10.2, each of these factors may have additional considerations.

10.2 BEHAVIORAL CONSIDERATIONS IN JOB DESIGN

Degree of Labor Specialization

Specialization of labor is the two-edged sword of job design. On one hand, specialization has made possible high-speed, low-cost production, and, from a materialistic standpoint, has greatly enhanced our standard of living. On the other hand, it is well known that extreme specialization, such as that encountered in mass-production industries, often has serious adverse effects on workers, which in turn are passed on to the production systems. In essence, the problem is to determine how much specialization is enough: at what point do the disadvantages outweigh the advantages? (See Exhibit 10.3.)

Recent research suggests that the disadvantages dominate the advantages much more commonly than was thought in the past. However, simply stating that, for purely humanitarian reasons, specialization should be avoided is risky. The reason, of course, is that people differ in what they want from their work and what they are willing to put into it. Some workers prefer not to make decisions about their work, some like to daydream on the job, and

EXHIBIT 10.3

Advantages and Disadvantages of Specialization of Labor

ADVANTAGES OF SPECIALIZATION

To Management	To Labor
1. Rapid training of the work force	1. Little or no education required to obtain work
2. Ease in recruiting new workers	
3. High output due to simple and repetitive work	2. Ease in learning job
4. Low wages due to ease of sub-stitutability of labor	
5. Close control over work flow and work-loads	

DISADVANTAGES OF SPECIALIZATION

To Management	To Labor
1. Difficulty in controlling quality since no one person has responsibility for entire product	1. Boredom stemming from repetitive nature of work
2. "Hidden" costs of worker dissatisfaction, arising from	2. Little gratification from work itself because of small contribution to each item
a. turnover	3. Little or no control over the work pace, leading to frustration and fatigue (in assembly-line situations)
b. absenteeism	
c. tardiness	
d. grievances	4. Little opportunity to progress to a better job since significant learning is rarely possible on fractionated work
e. intentional disruption of production process	
3. Reduced likelihood of obtaining im-provement in the process because of worker's limited perspective	5. Little opportunity to show initiative through developing better methods or tools
	6. Local muscular fatigue caused by use of the same muscles in performing the task
	7. Little opportunity for communication with fellow workers because of layout of the work area

others are simply not capable of performing more complex work.[1] Still, there is a good deal of worker frustration with the way many jobs are structured, leading organizations to try different approaches to job design. Two popular contemporary approaches are job enrichment and sociotechnical systems. The philosophical objective underlying these approaches is to improve the quality of work life of the employee, and so they are often applied as central features of what is termed a quality of work life (QWL) program.

---

[1] Indeed, the widely discussed problems with our educational system have resulted in creating job designs that don't require the ability to read.

Job Enrichment

Job enlargement generally entails making adjustments to a specialized job to make it more interesting to the jobholder. A job is said to be enlarged *horizontally* if the worker performs a greater number or variety of tasks, and it is said to be enlarged *vertically* if the worker is involved in planning, organizing, and inspecting his or her own work. Horizontal job enlargement is intended to counteract oversimplification and to permit the worker to perform a "whole unit of work." Vertical enlargement (traditionally termed *job enrichment*) attempts to broaden the workers' influence in the transformation process by giving them certain managerial powers over their own activities. Today, common practice is to apply both horizontal and vertical enlargement to a given job and refer to the total approach as *job enrichment*.

Sociotechnical Systems

Consistent with the job-enrichment philosophy but focusing more on the interaction between technology and the work group is the **sociotechnical systems** approach. It attempts to develop jobs that adjust the needs of the production process technology to the needs of the worker and work group. The term was developed from studies of weaving mills in India and coal mines in England in the early 1950s. In these studies, it was discovered that work groups could effectively handle many production problems better than management if they wre permitted to make their own decisions on scheduling, work allocation among members, bonus sharing, and so forth. This was particularly true when there were variations in the production process requiring quick reactions by the group or when the work of one shift overlapped with the work of other shifts.

Since these pioneering studies, the sociotechnical approach has been applied in many countries, though often under the heading of "autonomous work groups", or "Japanese-style work groups," or employee involvement (EI) teams in the United States.

One of the major conclusions from these studies is that the individual or the work group requires a logically integrated pattern of work activities that incorporates the following job design principles:

Task variety.   An attempt must be made to provide an optimal variety of tasks within each job. Too much variety can be inefficient for training and frustrating for the employee. Too little can lead to boredom and fatigue. The optimal level is one that allows the employee to take a rest from a high level of attention or effort while working on another task or, conversely, to stretch after periods of routine activity.

Skill variety.   Research suggests that employees derive satisfaction from using a number of different kinds of skill levels.

Feedback.   There should be some means for informing employees quickly when they have achieved their targets. Fast feedback aids the learning process. Ideally, employees should have some responsibility for setting their own standards of quantity and quality.

Task identity.   Sets of tasks should be separated from other sets of tasks by some clear boundary. Whenever possible, a group or individual employee should have responsibility for a set of tasks that is clearly defined, visible, and meaningful. In this way, work is seen as important by the group or individual undertaking it, and others understand and respect its significance.

Task autonomy.   Employees should be able to exercise some control over their work. Areas of discretion and decision making should be available to them.[2]

Classic Examples of Sociotechnical Systems in Three Countries

Holland: Phillips N.V.

The truck chassis assembly groups have real decision-making power. Production groups of 5 to 12 workers with related job duties decide among themselves how they will do their jobs, within the quality and production standards defined by higher management; they can rotate job assignments—do a smaller or larger part of the overall task. At the same time, jobs of all production group members were enlarged, making them jointly responsible for simple service and maintenance activities, housekeeping, and quality control in their work area, duties formerly performed by staff personnel.[3]

United States: Travelers Insurance Company

The objective was to enrich the keypunching job itself, starting with a training program for the supervisors. At the time of the initial implementation, work output was deemed inadequate, the error rate was excessive, and absenteeism too high. The keypunch job lacked skill variety, task identity, task significance, and autonomy. The changes introduced were:

1. *Natural units of work.* The random batch assignment of work was replaced by assigning to each operator continuing responsibility for cer-

---

[2] This summary is taken from Enid Mumford and Mary Weir, *Computer Systems in Work Design—the ETHICS Method* (New York: Halstead, 1979), p. 42.

[3] William F. Dawling, "Farewell to the Blue-Collar Blues," *Organizational Dynamics,* Autumn 1973.

tain accounts—either particular departments or particular recurring jobs.

2. *Task combination.* Some planning and control functions were combined with the central task of keypunching.

3. *Client relationships.* Each operator was given several channels of direct contact with clients. The operators, not their assignment clerks, now inspect their documents for correctness and legibility. When problems arise, the operator, not the supervisor, takes them up with the client.

4. *Feedback.* In addition to feedback from client contact . . . the computer department now returns incorrect cards to the operator who punched them, and the operators correct their own errors. . . . Each operator receives weekly a computer printout of her errors and productivity that is sent to her directly, rather than given to her supervisor.

5. *Vertical loading.* Operators now have the authority to correct obvious coding errors on their own. Operators may set their own schedules and plan their daily work. Some competent operators have been given the option of not verifying their work.

The results of the study: A reduction in keypunch operators needed, reduction in absenteeism, improved job attitudes, and less need for controls. Actual first-year savings totaled over $64,000. Potential annual savings from potential expanded application was given as $92,000.[4]

Japan: Automobile Manufacturers

An American Motors Company study team observed Japanese workers at five automobile manufacturers and noted these characteristics of Japanese production style:

- The work force is dedicated. The workers believe they are better, and consequently they strive to demonstrate their capabilities and loyalty to the company. They have tremendous pride.

- The pace of work varies between 110 and 140 percent. Employees help each other.

- Workers do not eat or smoke on the job. There is almost no talking on the line.

- Worker support includes low absenteeism (1–2 percent), high morale, and strong support of management plans for further automation.

- Worker recognition is evident in the plants. Pictures of employees, with listings of their skills, are posted on numerous department bulletin boards.

---

[4] John Miner, *Theories of Organizational Behavior* (Hinsdale, Ill.: Dryden Press, 1980), pp. 256–57.

- All plants operated on a mass relief plan (two 10-minute break periods) for which employees are not paid.
- Time-card racks were installed in each department, accessible to work areas, rather than at an entrance to the plant, thus avoiding long lines for checking in and checking out.
- In addition to Ping-Pong tables and basketball courts, skip ropes were provided for employees to use at their leisure.
- Not only is the plant clean, every worker is clean. Each plant was orderly—there was a place for everything and everything was in its place. Little or no cardboard was visible in the plants.
- Most of the plants had only a few work classifications—one for direct labor and two or three for indirect labor.
- Employees, including production management, change shifts weekly. Also, the company rotates a portion of the work force to different jobs every six months, with no interference from the union.
- The goal of job rotation is practiced. There are no job jurisdiction problems in the Japanese automotive industry.
- Techniques of statistical quality control are taught to all workers. Job training is actually on-the-job training offered on a one-to-one basis.
- Technical training and education are provided, either through off-the-job, on-site training, or through basic education.
- Quality is an obsession with Japanese workers. They perform their jobs while thinking of ways to upgrade it. Workers are authorized to stop the line any time they deem is necessary to maintain quality.
- A system of colored lights, bells, or music is used by employees to alert supervisors when there is a problem on the line that requires assistance. If there is no response, the employee is empowered to stop the line. The essence of this concept is to build the job correctly on the line, not in the garage. At Mitsubishi, where this practice was not followed, there were numerous vehicles in the garage area in need of repair.
- Departments are distinguished by color-coded hard hats (skilled trades, quality control, etc.). Color-coded rings around hard hats identify foremen, group leaders, and so forth.
- There is a broad range of indirect participation in management through the union in the form of union-management joint consultation councils. These councils meet once every three months, or when necessary, to promote understanding and to exchange views and information on all matters directly or indirectly concerning the workers.
- As a whole, computer applications were limited. Many manual applications were noted.
- Rather than stopwatch studies, Work Factor Systems of Elemental Motion Times was used for developing work assignments. (Elemental

standard-time data systems are discussed in the work measurement section of this chapter.)

- People can work wonders when they:
  - are treated like intelligent human beings.
  - are never placed in a position where their dignity is compromised.
  - are always treated with respect.
  - are allowed to be involved in the pursuit of the company's goals.
  - are well trained for their jobs.
  - have a clear and common goal.
  - feel secure and confident.
  - are allowed to make a significant contribution to the organization.
  - are assured of sharing some of the gains of a successful enterprise.
- This great team spirit—everyone pulling together for the good of the organization, everyone dedicated and committed to achieving the company's goals—is the most important key to success and an absolute necessity for producing products of perfect quality.[5]

INSERT   Sanyo Electric Company's Experiences in the United States

Today, Japanese-owned factories are commonplace in America, and their success is presumed. But as Japanese plants and ventures in the United States multiply—tripling since 1981—one thing is becoming clear: Some of the problems that have bedeviled domestic manufacturers can vex newly arrived Japanese companies, too.

Sanyo took charge of a Warwick Electronics Inc. plant in 1977. Employment had been skidding, and the television sets being made for Sears, Roebuck & Co. were suffering both from Japanese competition and from their own quality problems.

Here came Sanyo, pouring in capital and engineering talent. It rehired hundreds of cast-off workers. It set high quality standards, yet embraced the local union and sponsored outings for employees and townspeople.

For a while, things were great. Production jumped fifteen-fold. Sanyo heaped praise on the teamwork and spirit of its workers, and the born-again plant came to symbolize the superiority of Japanese management.

The miracle was a mirage. Initial productivity and sales gains were real enough but mostly reflected use of high-grade Japanese-made components that were easy to assembly and reduced rejects.

The plant location is in a half-black, half-white community of 13,803, situated 90 miles east of Little Rock. Its first integrated high school prom made headlines just last month. The arrival of a clutch of Japanese executives—and some alien management concepts—was a shock.

---

[5] Reprinted from Irwin Otis, "Observations on the Japanese Automotive Industry: A Lesson for American Managers," *Industrial Management,* May–June 1987, pp. 8–9. Copyright Institute of Industrial Engineers, 25 Technology Park/Atlanta, Norcross, Georgia 30092.

Sanyo initially wanted to import quality circles, calisthenics, and company uniforms, but it backed off. Tanemichi Sohma, a retired Sanyo vice president, recalls, "The union would have just thought we were trying to brainwash them." Sanyo tried consensus management with an operating committee of three Americans and three Japanese. But only one Sanyo executive spoke fluent English, so every meeting required an interpreter.

Tensions exploded in 1985, with the second strike in six years. Sanyo, fearing an industry shakeout, was on a tough tack. It demanded medical-insurance cuts, seniority-system changes, and the right to shift workers from job to job. The strike left the Japanese bitter and disillusioned. "How could we survive if the workers wouldn't help us?" asks Sohma. "With the union, no matter what we do, it was not enough for them. It got to be so difficult, the attitude was to heck with them."

Only 350 employees work at the plant now; more than 2,000 used to. It will roll up something like a $28 million loss this fiscal year, on top of $40 million in losses over the past three years. In March 1988 a microwave oven production line was shut down, and only two of the nine television lines now operate.

Source: Excerpted from J. Ernest Beazley, "In Spite of Mystique, Japanese Plants in U.S. Find Problems Abound," *The Wall Street Journal*, June 22, 1988. Reprinted with permission.

10.3 PHYSICAL CONSIDERATIONS IN JOB DESIGN

Beyond the behavioral components of job design, another aspect warrants consideration: the physical side. Indeed, while motivation and work-group structure strongly influence worker performance, they may be of secondary importance if the job is too demanding or is otherwise ill designed from a physical standpoint.

Work Task Continuum

One way of viewing the general nature of the physical requirements inherent in work is through the work task continuum in Exhibit 10.4. In this typology, *manual tasks* put stress on large muscle groups in the body and lead to overall fatigue, as measured by increases in the vital functions. In this context, the body is viewed as a heat engine that is supplied by fuel—food and liquids—and uses oxygen to transform fuel into energy (calories are a common measure of energy used in a job; see Exhibit 10.5). *Motor tasks* are controlled by the central nervous system, and their measure of effectiveness is the speed and precision of movements. While these tasks lead to fatigue, the effect is localized in the smaller muscle groups, such as the fingers, hands, and arms and, hence, cannot be adequately measured by indices of *general* fatigue. (In measuring the physiological stress of motor tasks, researchers are investigating the use of electromyography, which records the changes in electrical potential in the involved muscular extremity; that is, the hands, arms, and fingers.) *Mental tasks* involve rapid decision making based on certain types of stimuli, such as

EXHIBIT 10.4   **Work Task Continuum** (Human work)

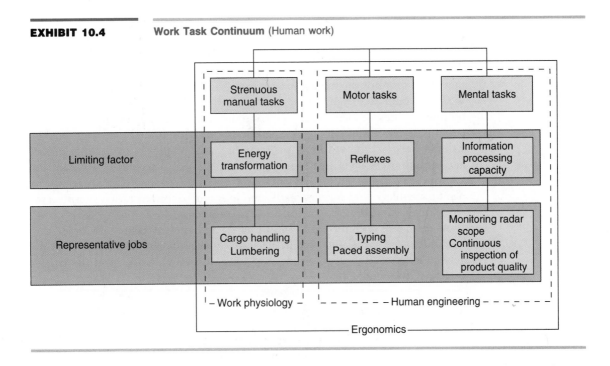

EXHIBIT 10.5

Calorie Requirements for Various Activities

Type of Activity	Typical Energy Cost in Calories per Minute*
Sitting at rest	1.7
Writing	2.0
Typing on a computer	2.0
Medium assembly work	2.9
Shoe repair	3.0
Machining	3.3
Ironing	4.4
Heavy assembly work	5.1
Chopping wood	7.5
Digging	8.9
Tending furnace	12.0
Walking upstairs	12.0

* Five calories per minute is generally considered the maximum sustainable level throughout the workday.

blips on a radar screen or defects in a product. Here the measure of effectiveness is generally some combination of time to respond and number and kind of error. Research into this type of work is usually predicated on concepts from the discipline of information theory, and as might be expected by the nature of the tasks, much of the source work has been provided by military agencies.

In the private sector, Westinghouse's Human Science Laboratory has been exploring the use of brain waves as a means of determining an individual's level of attention and cognitive processing. The laboratory manager predicts that within the next decade Westinghouse could market a complete system that could monitor the mental processing efforts of employees as they work. A worker would wear something like a baseball cap fitted with an electronic monitoring device that would pick up and send relevant brain waves to a computer. The computer would then flash a warning if the brain-wave analysis indicated that the worker's attention had wandered too far, or that his or her mental stress level had climbed too high. Such a technology would be appropriate for such life-dependent jobs as air traffic controller, nuclear power plant controllers, and surgery staffs, and jobs where concentration is critical to work quality, such as inspection and accounting work.[6]

As noted in Exhibit 10.4, motor tasks and mental tasks fall under the heading *human engineering,* while the study of the physical aspects of work in general is called *ergonomics* (from the Greek noun for "work" and the Greek verb for "to manage").

The Work Environment

Several factors in the work environment may affect job performance—lighting, noise, temperature and humidity, and air quality. Though each is worthy of discussion, space does not permit thorough treatment of these topics, and interested readers are referred to E. J. McCormick's work listed in the bibliography at the end of the chapter. Note also that these factors have a strong bearing on the safety and general health of workers and therefore have been subjected to legal regulation through the Occupational Safety and Health Act of 1970.

10.4   METHODS, MEASUREMENT, AND PAYMENT

In this section, our focus shifts from delineating the boundaries and general character of the job to the specifics of job performance. In particular, we wish to consider:

1. How the work should be accomplished (work methods).
2. How performance may be evaluated (work measurement).
3. How workers should be compensated (wage payment plans).

The first two constitute the basis for setting work standards, which in turn are the basis for capacity and production-planning decisions.

---

[6] Michael Schrage, " Big Brother Time May Be Coming to the Workplace," *Washington Post,* June 9, 1984.

Work Methods

In our development of the productive system, we have defined the tasks that must be done by workers. But how should they be done? Years ago, production workers were craftspeople who had their own (sometimes secret) methods for doing work. However, as products became more complicated, as mechanization of a higher order was introduced, and as output rates increased, the responsibilities for work methods were necessarily transferred to management. It was no longer logical or economically feasible to allow individual workers to produce the same product by different methods. Work specialization brought much of the concept of craftwork to an end, as less-skilled workers were employed to do the simpler tasks.

In contemporary industry, the responsibility for developing work methods in large firms is typically assigned either to a staff department designated *methods analysis* or to an industrial engineering department. In small firms, this activity is often performed by consulting firms that specialize in work methods design.

The principal approach to the study of work methods is the construction of charts, such as operations charts, worker-machine charts, simo (simultaneous motion) charts, and activity charts, in conjunction with time study or standard time data. The choice of which charting method to use depends on the activity level of the task; that is, whether the focus is on (1) the overall productive system, (2) the worker at a fixed workplace, (3) a worker interacting with equipment, or (4) a worker interacting with other workers (see Exhibit 10.6). (Several of these charting techniques were introduced in Chapter 3, where they were used to aid in manufacturing process design. Chapter 4 introduced the service blueprint that accounts for customer interactions.)

EXHIBIT 10.6

Work Methods Design Aids

Activity	Objective of Study	Study Techniques
Overall productive system	Eliminate or combine steps; shorten transport distance; identify delays	Flow diagram, service blueprint, process chart
Worker at fixed workplace	Simplify method; minimize motions	Operations charts, simo charts; apply principles of motion economy
Worker interacts with equipment	Minimize idle time; find number or combination of machines to balance cost of worker and machine idle time	Activity chart, worker-machine charts
Worker interacts with other workers	Maximize productivity; minimize interference	Activity charts, gang process charts

Overall productive system

The objective in studying the overall productive system is to identify delays, transport distances, processes, and processing time requirements, to simplify the entire operation. The underlying philosophy is to eliminate any step in the process that does not add value to the product. The approach is to flow chart the process and then ask the following questions:

What is done? Must it be done? What would happen if it were not done?

Where is the task done? Must it be done at that location or could it be done somewhere else?

When is the task done? Is it critical that it be done then or is there flexibility in time and sequence? Could it be done in combination with some other step in the process?

How is the task done? Why is it done this way? Is there another way?

Who does the task? Can someone else do it? Should the worker be of a higher or lower skill level?

These thought-provoking questions usually help to eliminate much unnecessary work, as well as to simplify the remaining work, by combining a number of processing steps and changing the order of performance.

Use of the process chart is valuable in studying an overall system, though care must be taken to follow the same item throughout the process. The subject may be a product being manufactured, a service being created, or a person performing a sequence of activities. An example of a process chart (and flow diagram) for a clerical operation is shown in Exhibit 10.7. Common notation in process charting is given in Exhibit 10.8.

Worker at a fixed workplace

Many jobs require the worker to remain at a specified workstation. When the nature of the work is primarily manual (such as sorting, inspecting, making entries, or assembly operations), the focus of work design is on simplifying the work method and making the required operator motions as few and as easy as possible.

There are two basic ways to determine the best method when a method analyst studies a single worker performing an essentially manual task. The first is to search among the workers and find the one who performs the job best. That person's method is then accepted as the standard, and others are trained to perform it in the same way. This was basically F. W. Taylor's approach, though after determining the best method, he searched for "first-class men" to perform according to the method. (A first-class man possessed the natural ability to do much more productive work in a particular task than the average. Men who were not first class were transferred to other jobs.) The second way is to observe the performance of a number of workers, analyze in detail each step of their work, and pick out the superior features of each worker's performance. This results in a composite method that combines the best

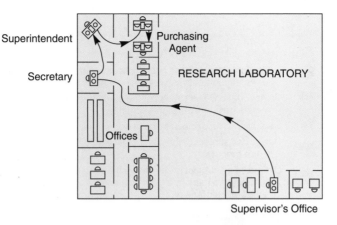

<table>
<tr><td colspan="4">Present Method ☒
Proposed Method ☐</td><td colspan="2" align="center">PROCESS CHART</td></tr>
</table>

Present Method ☒   PROCESS CHART
Proposed Method ☐

SUBJECT CHARTED Requisition for small tools   DATE _____

Chart begins at supervisor's desk and ends at   CHART BY J.C.H.

typist's desk in purchasing department   CHART NO. R136

DEPARTMENT Research laboratory   SHEET NO. 1 OF 1

DIST. IN FEET	TIME IN MINS.	CHART SYMBOLS	PROCESS DESCRIPTION
		●⇨□D▽	Requisitions written by supervisor (one copy)
		○⇨□D▽	On supervisor's desk (awaiting messenger)
65		○⇨□D▽	By messenger to superintendent's secretary
		○⇨□D▽	On secretary's desk (awaiting typing)
		●⇨□D▽	Requisition typed (original requisition copied)
15		○⇨□D▽	By secretary to superintendent
		○⇨□D▽	On superintendent's desk (awaiting messenger)
		○⇨■D▽	Examined and approved
		○⇨□D▽	On superintendent's desk (awaiting messenger)
20		○⇨□D▽	To purchasing department
		○⇨□D▽	On purchasing agent's desk (awaiting approval)
		○⇨■D▽	Examined and approved
		○⇨□D▽	On purchasing agent's desk (awaiting messenger)
5		○⇨□D▽	To typist's desk
		○⇨□D▽	On typist's desk (awaiting typing of purchase order)
		●⇨□D▽	Purchase order typed
		○⇨□D▽	On typist's desk (awaiting transfer to main office)
		○⇨□D▽	
105		3 4 2 8	Total

* Requisition is written by supervisor, typed by secretary, approved by superintendent, and approved by purchasing agent; then a purchase order is prepared by a stenographer.

Source: Ralph M. Barnes, *Motion and Time Study* (New York: Wiley & Sons, 1980, pp. 76–79).

EXHIBIT 10.8

**Common Notation in
Process Charting**

● **Operation.** Something is actually being done. This may be work on a product, some support activity or anything that is directly productive in nature.

➡ **Transportation.** The subject of the study (product, service, or person) moves from one location to another.

■ **Inspection.** The subject is observed for quality and correctness.

◗ **Delay.** The subject of the study must wait before starting the next step in the process.

▼ **Storage.** The subject is stored, such as finished products in inventory or completed papers in a file. Frequently, a distinction is made between temporary storage and permanent storage by inserting a T or P in the triangle.

elements of the group studied. This was the procedure used by Frank Gilbreth, the father of motion study, to determine the "one best way" to perform a work task.

Taylor observed actual performance to find the best method; Frank Gilbreth and his wife Lillian relied on movie film. Through micromotion analysis— observing the filmed work performance frame by frame—the Gilbreths studied work very closely and defined its basic elements, which were termed *therbligs* ("Gilbreth" spelled backward, with the *t* and *h* transposed). Their study led to the rules or principles of motion economy listed in Exhibit 10.9.

Once the motions for performing the task have been identified, an *operations chart* may be made, listing the operations and their sequence of performance. For greater detail, a *simo* (simultaneous motion) *chart* may be constructed, listing not only the operations but also the times for both left and right hands. This chart may be assembled from the data collected with a stopwatch, from analysis of a film of the operation, or from predetermined motion-time data (discussed later in the chapter). Many aspects of poor design are immediately obvious: a hand being used as a holding device (rather than a jig or fixture), an idle hand, or an exceptionally long time for positioning.

Worker interaction with equipment

When a person and equipment operate together to perform the productive process, interest focuses on the efficient use of the person's time and equipment time. When the working time of the operator is less than the equipment run time, a worker-machine chart is a useful device in analysis. If the operator can operate several pieces of equipment, the problem is to find the most economical combination of operator and equipment, when the combined cost of the idle time of a particular combination of equipment and the idle time for the worker is at a minimum.

Worker-machine charts are always drawn to scale, the scale being time as measured by length. Exhibit 10.10 gives an example of a worker-machine chart in a service setting. The question here is, Whose use is most important?

EXHIBIT 10.9

Principles of Motion Economy

Using the human body the way it works best

1. The work should be arranged to provide a natural rhythm that can become automatic.
2. The symmetrical nature of the body should be considered:
   a. The motions of the arms should be simultaneous, beginning and completing their motions at the same time.
   b. Motions of the arms should be opposite and symmetrical.
3. The human body is an ultimate machine and its full capabilities should be employed:
   a. Neither hand should ever be idle.
   b. Work should be distributed to other parts of the body in line with their ability.
   c. The safe design limits of the body should be observed.
   d. The human should be employed at its highest use.
4. The arms and hands as weights are subject to the physical laws, and energy should be conserved:
   a. Momentum should work for the person and not against him or her.
   b. The smooth, continuous arc of the ballistic is more efficient.
   c. The distance of movements should be minimized.
   d. Tasks should be turned over to machines.
5. The tasks should be simplified:
   a. Eye contacts should be few and grouped together.
   b. Unnecessary actions, delays, and idle time should be eliminated.
   c. The degree of required precision and control should be reduced.
   d. The number of individual motions should be minimized along with the number of muscle groups involved.

Arranging the workplace to assist performance

1. There should be a definite place for all tools and materials.
2. Tools, materials, and controls should be located close to the point of use.
3. Tools, materials, and controls should be located to permit the best sequence and path of motions.

Using mechanical devices to reduce human effort

1. Vises and clamps can hold the work precisely where needed.
2. Guides can assist in positioning the work without close operator attention.
3. Controls and foot-operated devices can relieve the hands of work.
4. Mechanical devices can multiply human abilities.
5. Mechanical systems should be fitted to human use.

Source: Frank C. Barnes, "Principles of Motion Economy: Revisited, Reviewed, and Restored," *Proceedings of the Southern Management Association Annual Meeting*, Atlanta, 1983, p. 298.

Workers interacting with other workers

A great amount of our productive output in manufacturing and service industries is performed by teams. The degree of interaction may be as simple as one operator handing a part to another, or as complex as a cardiovascular surgical team of doctors, nurses, anesthesiologist, operator of an artificial heart machine, X-ray technician, standby blood donors, and pathologist (and perhaps a minister to pray a little).

An activity or a gang process chart is useful in plotting the activities of each individual on a time scale similar to that of the worker-machine chart. A gang process chart is usually employed to trace the interaction of a number of workers with machines of a specified operating cycle, to find the best combination of workers and machines. An activity chart is less restrictive and may

EXHIBIT 10.10   Worker-Machine Chart for a Gourmet Coffee Store

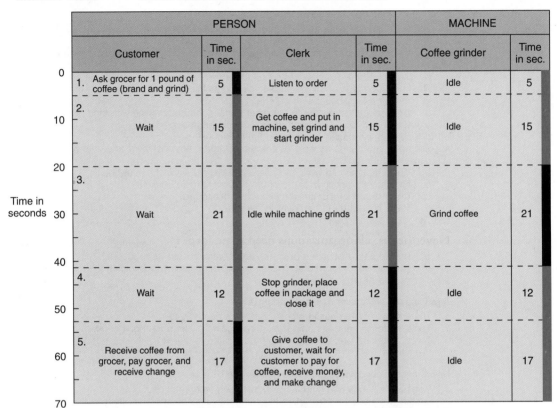

	PERSON				MACHINE	
Time in seconds	Customer	Time in sec.	Clerk	Time in sec.	Coffee grinder	Time in sec.
0	1. Ask grocer for 1 pound of coffee (brand and grind)	5	Listen to order	5	Idle	5
10	2. Wait	15	Get coffee and put in machine, set grind and start grinder	15	Idle	15
20 30	3. Wait	21	Idle while machine grinds	21	Grind coffee	21
40	4. Wait	12	Stop grinder, place coffee in package and close it	12	Idle	12
50 60 70	5. Receive coffee from grocer, pay grocer, and receive change	17	Give coffee to customer, wait for customer to pay for coffee, receive money, and make change	17	Idle	17

Summary

	Customer	Clerk	Coffee grinder
Idle time	48 sec.	21 sec.	49 sec.
Working time	22	49	21
Total cycle time	70	70	70
Utilization in percent	Customer utilization = $\frac{22}{70}$ = 31%	Clerk utilization = $\frac{49}{70}$ = 70%	Machine utilization = $\frac{21}{70}$ = 30%

The customer, the clerk, and the coffee grinder (machine) are involved in this operation. It required 1 minute and 10 seconds for the customer to purchase a pound of coffee in this particular store. During this time the customer spent 22 seconds, or 31 percent of the time, giving the clerk his order, receiving the ground coffee, and paying the clerk for it. He was idle during the remaining 69 percent of the time. The clerk worked 49 seconds, or 70 percent of the time, and was idle 21 seconds, or 30 percent of the time. The coffee grinder was in operation 21 seconds, or 30 percent of the time, and was idle 70 percent of the time.

be used to follow the interaction of any group of operators, with or without equipment being involved. Such charts are often used to study and define each operator in an ongoing repetitive process, and they are extremely valuable in developing a standardized procedure for a specific task. Exhibit 10.11, for example, shows an activity chart for a hospital's emergency routine in performing a tracheotomy (opening a patient's throat surgically to allow him or her to breathe), where detailed activity analysis is of major importance and any delay could be fatal.

Work Measurement

The subject of work measurement for establishing time standards has been controversial since the days of Taylor. With the widespread adoption of W. Edwards Deming's ideas, it has become the subject of renewed bashing. (Deming has argued that work standards and quotas inhibit process improvement and tend to focus the worker's efforts on speed rather than quality.) Nevertheless, all organizations need some form of standard time estimates to do planning and budgeting, and many companies use them with success in work design, as demonstrated in the UPS case at end of chapter. In any event, it is important to understand the basic industrial engineering methods used to set standards. They are as follows:

1. Time study (stopwatch and micromotion analysis).
2. Elemental standard time data.
3. Predetermined motion–time data.
4. Work sampling.

Each method has some advantages over the others and has particular areas of application. Exhibit 10.12 lists these methods and relates them to a general class of jobs.

Time study

A time study is generally made with a stopwatch, either on the spot or by analyzing a videotape of the job. Procedurally, the job or task to be studied is separated into measurable parts or elements, and each element is timed individually. After a number of repetitions, the collected times are averaged. (The standard deviation may be computed to give a measure of variance in the performance times.) The averaged times for each element are added, and the result is the performance time for the operator. However, to make this operator's time usable for all workers, a measure of speed or *performance rating* must be included to "normalize" the job. The application of a rating factor gives what is called *normal time*. For example, if an operator performs a task in two minutes and the time study analyst estimates him or her to be performing

EXHIBIT 10.11   Activity Chart of Emergency Tracheotomy

Time	Nurse	First doctor	Orderly	Second doctor	Nurse supervisor	Scrub nurse	Time
0	Detects problem Notifies doctor						0
1							1
2	Gets mobile cart						2
3		Makes diagnosis					3
4							4
5	Notifies nurse supervisor						5
6	Notifies second doctor	Assists patient to breathe			Opens OR Calls scrub nurse		6
7	Notifies orderly			Assures availability of laryngoscope and endotracheal tube			7
8	Moves patient to OR	Moves to OR	Moves patient to OR			Moves to OR Sets up equipment	8
9		Scrubs					9
10		Dons gown and gloves		Operates laryngoscope and inserts endotracheal tube			10
11							11
12		Performs tracheotomy		Calls for IPPB machine			12
13							13
14							14
15							15
16							16

Source: Data taken from Harold E. Smalley and John Freeman, *Hospital Industrial Engineering* (New York: Reinhold, 1966), p. 409.

EXHIBIT 10.12

**Types of Work
Measurement Applied
to Differing Tasks**

Type of Work	Major Methods of Determining Task Time
Very short interval, highly repetitive	Videotape analysis
Short interval, repetitive	Stopwatch time study: predetermined motion-time data
Task in conjunction with machinery or other fixed-processing-time equipment	Elemental data
Infrequent work or work of a long cycle time	Work sampling

about 20 percent faster than normal, the normal time would be computed as 2 minutes + 0.20(2 minutes), or 2.4 minutes. In equation form,

Normal time = Observed performance time per unit × Performance rating

In this example, denoting normal time by *NT*,

$$NT = 2(1.2) = 2.4 \text{ minutes}$$

When an operator is observed for a period of time, the number of units produced during this time, along with the performance rating, gives the normal time as

$$NT = \frac{\text{Time worked}}{\text{Number of units produced}} \times \text{Performance rating}$$

Standard time is derived by adding to normal time allowances for personal needs (washroom and coffee breaks, and so forth), unavoidable work delays (equipment breakdown, lack of materials, and so forth), and worker fatigue (physical or mental). Two such equations are

Standard time = Normal Time + (Allowances × Normal time)

or

$$ST = NT(1 + \text{Allowances}) \tag{1}$$

and

$$ST = \frac{NT}{1 - \text{Allowances}} \tag{2}$$

Equation (1) is most often used in practice. If one presumes that allowances should be applied to the total work period, then equation (2) is the correct one. To illustrate, suppose that the normal time to perform a task is 1 minute and that allowances for personal needs, delays, and fatigue total 15 percent; then, by equation (1),

$$ST = 1(1 + 0.15) = 1.15 \text{ minutes}$$

In an eight-hour day, a worker would produce $8 \times 60/1.15$, or 417 units. This implies 417 minutes working and $480 - 417$ (or 63) minutes for allowances.

With equation (2),

$$ST = \frac{1}{1 - 0.15} = 1.18 \text{ minutes}$$

In the same eight-hour day, $8 \times 60/1.18$ (or 408) units are produced with 408 working minutes and 72 minutes for allowances. Depending on which equation is used, there is a difference of 9 minutes in the daily allowance time.

Before a time study is made, the task is broken down into elements or parts. Some general rules for this breakdown are

1. Define each work element short in duration but long enough so each can be timed with a stopwatch and the time can be written down.
2. If the operator works with equipment that runs separately—the operator performs a task and the equipment runs independently—separate the actions of the operator and of the equipment into different elements.
3. Define any delays by the operator or equipment into separate elements.

Exhibit 10.13 shows a time study of 10 cycles of a four-element job. For each element, there is a space for the watch reading in 100ths of a minute (R) and each element subtracted time (T). The value for T is obtained after the time study observations are completed, since in this case the watch is read continuously.[7] PR denotes the performance rating and T the average time for each element. The standard time, calculated according to equation (1), is given at the bottom of the time study sheet.

How many observations are enough? Time study is really a sampling process, that is, we take relatively few observations as being representative of many subsequent cycles to be performed by the worker. Based on a great deal of analysis and experience, Benjamin Niebel's table shown in Exhibit 10.14 indicates that enough is a function of cycle length and number of repetitions of the job over a one-year planning period.

Elemental standard-time data

Elemental standard-time data is obtained from previous time studies and codified in tables in a handbook or computer data bank. Such data are used to develop time standards for new jobs or to make time adjustments to reflect changes in existing jobs. They are more correctly viewed as *normal-time data,* because tabled values have been modified by an average performance rating, and allowances must be added to obtain a standard time.

---

[7] Not surprisingly, this is called the *continuous method* of timing. When the watch is reset after each element is recorded, it is called the *snapback method.*

EXHIBIT 10.13

Time-Study Observation Sheet

Time Study Observation Sheet																

Identification of operation	Assemble 24" x 36" chart blanks					Date 10/9										
Began timing: *9:26* Ended timing: *9:32*	Operator 109		Approval *BgR*			Observer *fD.f.*										

Element description and breakpoint			Cycles										Summary			
			1 0.00	2	3	4	5	6	7	8	9	10	ΣT	T̄	PR	NT
1	Fold over end (grasp stapler)	T	.07	.07	.05	.07	.09	.06	.05	.08	.08	.06	.68	.07	.90	.06
		R	.07	.61	.14	.67	.24	.78	.33	.88	.47	.09				
2	Staple five times (drop stapler)	T	.16	.14	.14	.15	.16	.16	.14	.17	.14	.15	1.51	.15	1.05	.16
		R	.23	.75	.28	.82	.40	.94	.47	.05	.61	.24				
3	Bend and insert wire (drop pliers)	T	.22	.25	.22	.25	.23	.23	.21	.26	.25	.24	2.36	.24	1.00	.24
		R	.45	.00	.50	.07	.63	.17	.68	.31	.86	.48				
4	Dispose of finished chart (touch next sheet)	T	.09	.09	.10	.08	.09	.11	.12	.08	.17	.08	1.01	.10	.90	.09
		R	.54	.09	.60	.15	.72	.28	.80	.39	.03	.56				
5		T														
		R												0.55 normal minute for cycle		
6		T														
10		T														
		R														

Normal cycle time ___0.55___ + Allowance $\dfrac{(0.55 \times 0.143)}{\text{or } 0.08}$ = Std. time 0.63 min./pc.

Calculating a **time standard** for a new job using elemental standard-time data tables entails the following steps:

1. Break down the new job into its basic elements (such as shown on the time study sheet in Exhibit 10.13).

2. Match these elements to the time for similar elements in the table.

3. Adjust element times for special characteristics of the new job. (In metal cutting, for instance, this is often done by a formula that modifies the time required as a function of type of metal, size of the cutting tool, depth of the cut, and so forth.)

4. Add element times together and add delay and fatigue allowances as specified by company policy for the given class of work.

EXHIBIT 10.14

Guide to Number
of Cycles to Be
Observed in a
Time Study

When Time per Cycle Is More than		MINIMUM NUMBER OF CYCLES OF STUDY (ACTIVITY)		
		Over 10,000 per Year	1,000– 10,000	Under 1,000
8	hours	2	1	1
3		3	2	1
2		4	2	1
1		5	3	2
48	minutes	6	3	2
30		8	4	3
20		10	5	4
12		12	6	5
8		15	8	6
5		20	10	8
3		25	12	10
2		30	15	12
1		40	20	15
.7		50	25	20
.5		60	30	25
.3		80	40	30
.2		100	50	40
.1		120	60	50
Under .1		140	80	60

Source: Benjamin W. Niebel, *Motion and Time Study*, 7th ed. (Homewood, Ill.: Richard D. Irwin, 1982), p. 337.

The obvious benefit of elemental standard data is cost savings: it eliminates the need for a new time study for each new job. This saves staff time and avoids disruption of the work force. The main practical requirements of the approach is that the elemental data must be kept up to date and easily accessible.

Predetermined motion-time data systems

Predetermined motion-time data systems (PMTS) also use existing tabled data to artificially create a time standard. These systems differ from elemental standard data systems in several respects. First, they provide times for basic motions rather than job-specific work elements. Second, they are generic to a wide range of manual work; elemental standard data is company or industry specific. Finally, since they typically require the use of many basic motions to describe even a short-duration job, they require far more analyst time to develop a standard. For this reason, the systems discussed next are being simplified as much as possible to facilitate their use, and new, faster versions with computer support are being marketed.

The three predetermined motion-time data systems that are most often used are *methods time measurement* (MTM), *basic motion time study* (BMT), and *work factor*. Each was developed in the laboratory, and all are proprietary. MTM even has its own journal, user certification program, and an association of MTM organizations (the International MTM Directorate).

EXHIBIT 10.15   MTM Predetermined Motion-Time Data for the Hand and Arm Movement "Reach" (1 TMU = .0006 minutes)

REACH—R

Distance Moved Inches	Time TMU				Hand in motion		CASE AND DESCRIPTION	
	A	B	C or D	E	A	B		
3/4 or less	2.0	2.0	2.0	2.0	1.6	1.6	A	Reach to object in fixed location, or to object in other hand or on which other hand rests.
1	2.5	2.5	3.6	2.4	2.3	2.3		
2	4.0	4.0	5.9	3.8	3.5	2.7		
3	5.3	5.3	7.3	5.3	4.5	3.6	B	Reach to single object in location which may vary slightly from cycle to cycle.
4	6.1	6.4	8.4	6.8	4.9	4.3		
5	6.5	7.8	9.4	7.4	5.3	5.0		
6	7.0	8.6	10.1	8.0	5.7	5.7		
7	7.4	9.3	10.8	8.7	6.1	6.5	C	Reach to object jumbled with other objects in a group so that search and select occur.
8	7.9	10.1	11.5	9.3	6.5	7.2		
9	8.3	10.8	12.2	9.9	6.9	7.9		
10	8.7	11.5	12.9	10.5	7.3	8.6		
12	9.6	12.9	14.2	11.8	8.1	10.1	D	Reach to a very small object or where accurate grasp is required.
14	10.5	14.4	15.6	13.0	8.9	11.5		
16	11.4	15.8	17.0	14.2	9.7	12.9		
18	12.3	17.2	18.4	15.5	10.5	14.4		
20	13.1	18.6	19.8	16.7	11.3	15.8		
22	14.0	20.1	21.2	18.0	12.1	17.3	E	Reach to indefinite location to get hand in position for body balance or next motion or out of way.
24	14.9	21.5	22.5	19.2	12.9	18.8		
26	15.8	22.9	23.9	20.4	13.7	20.2		
28	16.7	24.4	25.3	21.7	14.5	21.7		
30	17.5	25.8	26.7	22.9	15.3	23.2		

Source: Copyright by the MTM Association for Standards and Research. Reprinted with permission from the MTM Association, 9–10 Saddle River Road, Fair Lawn, New Jersey 07410.

Exhibit 10.15 presents a sample MTM table. This table describes the movement designated as Reach, stipulating the different times allowed for varying conditions. (Other standard movement categories in the basic version of the system, MTM-1, are Grasp, Move, Position, and Release.) Note that times are measured in *time measurement units* (TMUs) of .0006 minutes. To derive an MTM standard time for a job, you would list all the movements that go into it, find the appropriate TMU value for each, sum the times, and add allowances.

PMTS have been used successfully for more than 40 years. Among their advantages are

1. They enable development of standards before the job is done.
2. They have been tested extensively in the laboratory and the field.

3. They include performance rating in the times given in the tables, so the user need not calculate them.

4. They can be used to audit time studies for accuracy.

5. They are accepted as part of many union contracts.

Work sampling

As the name suggests, work sampling involves observing a portion or sample of the work activity. Then, based on the findings in this sample, some statements can be made about the activity. For example, if we were to observe a fire department rescue squad 100 random times during the day and found it was involved in a rescue mission for 30 of the 100 times (en route, on site, or returning from a call), we would estimate that the rescue squad spends 30 percent of its time directly on rescue mission calls. (The time it takes to make an observation depends on what is being observed. Many times only a glance is needed to determine the activity, and the majority of studies require only several seconds' observation.)

Observing an activity even 100 times may not, however, provide the accuracy desired in the estimate. To refine this estimate, three main issues must be decided (these points are discussed later in this section, along with an example):

1. What level of statistical confidence is desired in the results?

2. How many observations are necessary?

3. Precisely when should the observations be made?

The three primary applications for work sampling are:

1. *Ratio delay:* to determine the activity-time percentage for personnel or equipment. For example, management may be interested in the amount of time a machine is running or idle.

2. *Performance measurement:* to develop a performance index for workers. When the amount of work time is related to the quantity of output, a measure of performance is developed. This is useful for periodic performance evaluation.

3. *Time standards:* to obtain the standard time for a task. When work sampling is used for this purpose, however, the observer must be experienced since he or she must attach a performance rating to the observations.

The number of observations required in a work sampling study can be fairly large, ranging from several hundred to several thousand, depending on the activity and the desired degree of accuracy. Although the number can be computed from formulas, the easiest way is to refer to a table such as Exhibit 10.16, which gives the number of observations needed for a 95 percent confidence level in terms of absolute error. Absolute error is the actual range of

EXHIBIT 10.16   **Determining Number of Observations Required for a Given Absolute Error at Various Values of p, with 95 Percent Confidence Level**

Percentage of Total Time Occupied by Activity or Delay, p	ABSOLUTE ERROR					
	±1.0%	±1.5%	±2.0%	±2.5%	±3.0%	±3.5%
1 or 99	396	176	99	63	44	32
2 or 98	784	348	196	125	87	64
3 or 97	1,164	517	291	186	129	95
4 or 96	1,536	683	384	246	171	125
5 or 95	1,900	844	475	304	211	155
6 or 94	2,256	1,003	564	361	251	184
7 or 93	2,604	1,157	651	417	289	213
8 or 92	2,944	1,308	736	471	327	240
9 or 91	3,276	1,456	819	524	364	267
10 or 90	3,600	1,600	900	576	400	294
11 or 89	3,916	1,740	979	627	435	320
12 or 88	4,224	1,877	1,056	676	469	344
13 or 87	4,524	2,011	1,131	724	503	369
14 or 86	4,816	2,140	1,204	771	535	393
15 or 85	5,100	2,267	1,275	816	567	416
16 or 84	5,376	2,389	1,344	860	597	439
17 or 83	5,644	2,508	1,411	903	627	461
18 or 82	5,904	2,624	1,476	945	656	482
19 or 81	6,156	2,736	1,539	985	684	502
20 or 80	6,400	2,844	1,600	1,024	711	522
21 or 79	6,636	2,949	1,659	1,062	737	542
22 or 78	6,864	3,050	1,716	1,098	763	560
23 or 77	7,084	3,148	1,771	1,133	787	578
24 or 76	7,296	3,243	1,824	1,167	811	596
25 or 75	7,500	3,333	1,875	1,200	833	612
26 or 74	7,696	3,420	1,924	1,231	855	628
27 or 73	7,884	3,504	1,971	1,261	876	644
28 or 72	8,064	3,584	2,016	1,290	896	658
29 or 71	8,236	3,660	2,059	1,318	915	672
30 or 70	8,400	3,733	2,100	1,344	933	686
31 or 69	8,556	3,803	2,139	1,369	951	698
32 or 68	8,704	3,868	2,176	1,393	967	710
33 or 67	8,844	3,931	2,211	1,415	983	722
34 or 66	8,976	3,989	2,244	1,436	997	733
35 or 65	9,100	4,044	2,275	1,456	1,011	743
36 or 64	9,216	4,096	2,304	1,475	1,024	753
37 or 63	9,324	4,144	2,331	1,492	1,036	761
38 or 62	9,424	4,188	2,356	1,508	1,047	769
39 or 61	9,516	4,229	2,379	1,523	1,057	777
40 or 60	9,600	4,266	2,400	1,536	1,067	784
41 or 59	9,676	4,300	2,419	1,548	1,075	790
42 or 58	9,744	4,330	2,436	1,559	1,083	795
43 or 57	9,804	4,357	2,451	1,569	1,089	800
44 or 56	9,856	4,380	2,464	1,577	1,095	804
45 or 55	9,900	4,400	2,475	1,584	1,099	808
46 or 54	9,936	4,416	2,484	1,590	1,104	811
47 or 53	9,964	4,428	2,491	1,594	1,107	813
48 or 52	9,984	4,437	2,496	1,597	1,109	815
49 or 51	9,996	4,442	2,499	1,599	1,110	816
50	10,000	4,444	2,500	1,600	1,111	816

Note: Number of observations is obtained from the formula $E = Z \sqrt{\dfrac{p(1-p)}{N}}$; the required sample (N) is $N = \dfrac{Z^2 p(1-p)}{E^2}$

where E = Absolute error

p = Percentage occurrence of activity or delay being measured

N = Number of random observations (sample size)

Z = Number of standard deviations to give desired confidence level (e.g., for 90 percent confidence, $Z = 1.65$; 95 percent, $Z = 1.96$; 99 percent, $Z = 2.23$). In this table $Z = 2$.

the observations. For example, if a clerk is idle 10 percent of the time and the designer of the study is satisfied with a 2.5 percent range (meaning that the true percentage lies within 7.5 and 12.5 percent), the number of observations required for the work sampling is 576. A 2 percent error (or an interval of 8 to 12 percent) would require 900 observations.

The steps involved in making a work sampling study are

1. Identify the specific activity or activities that are the main purpose for the study. For example, determine the percentage of time equipment is working, idle, or under repair.

2. Estimate the proportion of time of the activity of interest to the total time (e.g., that the equipment is working 80 percent of the time). These estimates can be made from the analyst's knowledge, past data, reliable guesses from others, or a pilot work-sampling study.

3. State the desired accuracy in the study results.

4. Determine the specific times when each observation is to be made.

5. At two or three intervals during the study period, recompute the required sample size by using the data collected thus far. Adjust the number of observations if appropriate.

The number of observations to be taken in a work sampling study is usually divided equally over the study period. Thus, if 500 observations are to be made over a 10-day period, the observations are usually scheduled at 500/10, or 50 per day. Each day's observations are then assigned a specific time by using a random number table.

Work sampling applied to nursing.   There has been a long-standing argument that a large amount of nurses' hospital time is spent on nonnursing activities. This, the argument goes, creates an apparent shortage of well-trained nursing personnel, a significant waste of talent, a corresponding loss of efficiency, and increased hospital costs, because nurses' wages are the highest single cost in the operation of a hospital. Further, pressure is growing for hospitals and hospital administrators to contain costs. With that in mind, let us use work sampling to test the hypothesis that a large portion of nurses' time is spent on nonnursing duties.

Assume at the outset that we have made a list of all the activities that are part of nursing and will make our observations in only two categories: nursing and nonnursing activities.[8] (An expanded study could list all nursing activities to determine the portion of time spent in each.) Therefore, when we observe a nurse during the study and find her performing one of the duties on the nursing list, we simply place a tally mark in the nursing column. If we observe

---

[8] Actually, there is much debate on what constitutes nursing activity. For instance, is talking to a patient a nursing duty?

her doing anything besides nursing, we place a tally mark in the nonnursing column.

We can now proceed to plan the study. Assume that we (or the nursing supervisor) estimate that nurses spend 60 percent of their time in nursing activities. Assume that we would like to be 95 percent confident that the findings of our study are within the absolute error range of plus or minus 3 percent; that is, that if our study shows nurses spend 60 percent of their time on nursing duties, we are 95 percent confident that the true percentage lies between 57 and 63 percent. From Exhibit 10.16, we find that 1,067 observations are required for 60 percent activity time and ±3 percent error. If our study is to take place over 10 days, we start with 107 observations per day.

To determine when each day's observations are to be made, we assign specific numbers to each minute and a random number table to set up a schedule. If the study extends over an eight-hour shift, we can assign numbers to correspond to each consecutive minute.[9] The list in Exhibit 10.17 shows the assignment of numbers to corresponding minutes. For simplicity, because each number corresponds to one minute, a three-number scheme is used, with the second and third number corresponding to the minute of the hour. A number of other schemes would also be appropriate.[10]

If we refer to a random number table and list three-digit numbers, we can assign each number to a time. The random numbers shown in Exhibit 10.18 demonstrate the procedure for seven observations.

This procedure is followed to generate 107 observation times, and the times are rearranged chronologically for ease in planning. Rearranging the times determined in Exhibit 10.18 gives the total observations per day shown in Exhibit 10.19 (for our sample of seven).

To be perfectly random in this study, we should also "randomize" the nurse we observe each time (the use of various nurses minimizes the effect of bias). In the study, our first observation is made at 7:13 A.M. for Nurse X. We walk into her area and, on seeing her, check either a nursing or a nonnursing activity. Each observation need be only long enough to determine the class of activity—in most cases only a glance. At 8:04 A.M. we observe Nurse Y. We continue in this way to the end of the day and the 107 observations. At the end of the second day (and 214 observations), we decide to check for the adequacy of our sample size.

Let's say we made 150 observations of nurses working and 64 of them not working, which gives 70.1 percent working. From Exhibit 10.16, this corresponds to 933 observations. Since we have already taken 214 observations, we need take only 719 over the next eight days, or 90 per day.

---

[9] For this study, it is likely that the night shift (11:00 P.M. to 7:00 A.M.) would be run separately, since the nature of nighttime nursing duties is considerably different from that of daytime duties.

[10] If a number of studies are planned, a computer program may be used to generate a randomized schedule for the observation times.

EXHIBIT 10.17

Assignment of Numbers to Corresponding Minutes

Time	Assigned Numbers
7:00– 7:59 A.M.	100–159
8:00– 8:59 A.M.	200–259
9:00– 9:59 A.M.	300–359
10:00–10:59 A.M.	400–459
11:00–11:59 A.M.	500–559
12:00–12:59 P.M.	600–659
1:00– 1:59 P.M.	700–759
2:00– 2:59 P.M.	800–859

EXHIBIT 10.18

Determination of Observation Times

Random Number	Corresponding Time from the Preceding List
669	Nonexistent
831	2:31 P.M.
555	11:55 A.M.
470	Nonexistent
113	7:13 A.M.
080	Nonexistent
520	11:20 A.M.
204	8:04 A.M.
732	1:32 P.M.
420	10:20 A.M.

EXHIBIT 10.19

Observation Schedule

Observation	Scheduled Time	Nursing Activity (✔)	Nonnursing Activity (✔)
1	7:13 A.M.		
2	8:04 A.M.		
3	10:20 A.M.		
4	11:20 A.M.		
5	11:55 A.M.		
6	1:32 P.M.		
7	2:31 P.M.		

When the study is half over, another check should be made. For instance, if Days 3, 4, and 5 showed 55, 59, and 64 working observations, the cumulative data would give 328 working observations of a total 484, or a 67.8 percent working activity. Exhibit 10.16 shows the sample size to be about 967, leaving 483 to be made—at 97 per day—for the following five days. Another computation should be made before the last day to see if another adjustment is required. If after the tenth day several more observations are indicated, these can be made on Day 11.

If at the end of the study we find that 66 percent of nurses' time is involved with what has been defined as nursing activity, there should be an analysis to identify the remaining 34 percent. Approximately 12 to 15 percent is justifiable for coffee breaks and personal needs, which leaves 20 to 22 percent of the time that must be justified and compared to what the industry considers ideal levels of nursing activity. To identify the nonnursing activities, a more detailed breakdown could have been originally built into the sampling plan. Otherwise, a follow-up study may be in order.

Setting time standards using work sampling.   As mentioned earlier, work sampling can be used to set time standards. To do this, the analyst must record the subject's performance rate (or index) along with working observations. The additional data required and the formula for calculating standard time are given in Exhibit 10.20.

Work sampling compared to time study.   Work sampling offers several advantages:

1. Several work sampling studies may be conducted simultaneously by one observer.

EXHIBIT 10.20

Deriving a Time Standard Using Work Sampling

Information	Source of Data	Data for One Day
Total time expended by operator (working time and idle time)	Time cards	480 min.
Number of parts produced	Inspection Department	420 pieces
Working time in percent	Work sampling	85%
Idle time in percent	Work sampling	15%
Average performance index	Work sampling	110%
Total allowances	Company time-study manual	15%

$$\text{Standard time per piece} = \frac{\left(\begin{array}{c}\text{Total time} \\ \text{in minutes}\end{array}\right) \times \left(\begin{array}{c}\text{Working time} \\ \text{proportion}\end{array}\right) \times (\text{Performance index})}{\text{Total number of pieces produced}} \times \frac{1}{1 - \text{Allowances}}$$

$$= \left(\frac{480 \times 0.85 \times 1.10}{420}\right) \times \left(\frac{1}{1 - 0.15}\right) = 1.26 \text{ minutes}$$

Source: R. M. Barnes, *Working Sampling,* 2nd ed. (New York: John Wiley & Sons, 1966), p. 81

2. The observer need not be a trained analyst unless the purpose of the study is to determine a time standard.

3. No timing devices are required.

4. Work of a long cycle time may be studied with fewer observer hours.

5. The duration of the study is longer, so that the effects of short-period variations are minimized.

6. The study may be temporarily delayed at any time with little effect.

7. Since work sampling needs only instantaneous observations (made over a longer period), the operator has less chance to influence the findings by changing his or her work method.

When the cycle time is short, time study (or PMTS) rather than work sampling is more appropriate. One drawback of work sampling is that it does not provide as complete a breakdown of elements as time study. Another difficulty with work sampling is that observers, rather than following a random sequence of observations, tend to develop a repetitive route of travel. This may allow the time of the observations to be predictable and thus invalidate the findings. A third factor—a potential drawback—is that the basic assumption in work sampling is that all observations pertain to the same static system. If the system is in the process of change, work sampling may give misleading results.

Financial Incentive Plans

The third piece of the job design equation is the paycheck. In this section we briefly review common methods for setting financial incentives.

Basic compensation systems

The main forms of basic compensation are hourly pay, straight salary, piece rate, and commissions. The first two are based on time spent on the job, with individual performance rewarded by an increase in the base rate. Piece-rate plans reward on the basis of direct daily output (a worker is paid $5 a unit and if he produces 10 units per day, he earns $50). Sometimes, a guaranteed base is included in a piece-rate plan; a worker would receive this base amount regardless of output, plus his piece-rate bonus. (For example, the worker's hourly base pay is $8, so this coupled with $50 piece-rate earnings would give him $114 for an eight-hour day.) Commissions may be thought of as sales-based piece rates and are calculated in the same general way.

The two broad categories of **financial incentive plans** are individual or small group incentive plans and organizationwide plans.

Individual or small group incentive plans

Individual and work-group plans traditionally have rewarded performance by using output (often defined by piece rates) and quality measures. Quality is accounted for by a quality adjustment factor, say percent of rework.[11] (For example: Incentive pay = Total output × [1 − Percent deduction for rework].) In recent years skill development has also been rewarded. Sometimes called *pay for knowledge,* this means a worker is compensated for learning new tasks. This is particularly important in job shops using group technology, and in banking, where supervisors' jobs require knowledge of new types of financial instruments and selling approaches.

AT&T, for example, instituted incentive programs for its managers—an Individual Incentive Award (IIA) and a Management Team Incentive Award (MTIA). The IIA provides lump-sum bonuses to outstanding performers. These outstanding performers were determined by individual performance ratings accompanied by extensive documentation. The lump-sum bonus could range between 15 and 30 percent of base pay.

MTIAs are granted to members of specific divisions or units. Appropriate division or unit goals are established at the beginning of the year. The goals include department service objectives and interdepartmental goals. A typical MTIA could call for a standard amount equivalent to 1.5 percent of wages plus overtime for the next three years based on the performance in the current year.

Organizationwide plans

Profit sharing and gain sharing are the major types of organizationwide plans. *Profit sharing* is simply distributing a percentage of corporate profits across the work force. In the United States, at least one third of all organizations have profit sharing. In Japan, most major companies give profit-based bonuses twice a year to all employees. Such bonuses may go as high as 50 percent of salaries in good years, to nothing in bad years.

Gain sharing also involves giving organizationwide bonuses, but differs from profit sharing in two important respects: First, it typically measures controllable costs or units of output, not profits, in calculating a bonus. Second, gain sharing is always combined with a participative approach to management. The original and best-known gainsharing plan is the Scanlon Plan (discussed next).

Scanlon Plan.   In the late 1930s, the Lapointe Machine and Tool Company was on the verge of bankruptcy, but through the efforts of union president Joseph Scanlon and company management, a plan was devised to save the company by reducing labor costs. In essence, this plan started with the normal labor cost within the firm. Workers as a group were rewarded for any reductions in labor cost below this base cost. The plan's success depended on committees of workers throughout the firm whose purpose was to search out

---

[11] For a complete discussion of incentive plans including quality measures, see S. Globerson and R. Parsons, "Multi-factor Incentive Systems: Current Practices," *Operations Management Review* 3, no. 2 (Winter 1985).

areas for cost saving and to devise ways of improvement. There were many improvements, and the plan did, in fact, save the company.

The basic elements of the Scanlon Plan are

1. *The ratio.* The ratio is the standard that serves as a measure for judging business performance. It can be expressed as:

$$\text{Ratio} = \frac{\text{Total labor cost}}{\text{Sales value of production}}$$

2. *The bonus.* The amount of bonus depends on the reduction in costs below the preset ratio.

3. *The production committee.* The production committee is formed to encourage employee suggestions to increase productivity, improve quality, reduce waste, and so forth. The purpose of a production committee is similar to that of a QC circle.

4. *The screening committee.* The screening committee consists of top management and worker representatives who review monthly bonuses, discuss production problems, and consider improvement suggestions.

Gain-sharing plans are now used by more than a thousand firms in the United States and Europe, and are growing in popularity. One recent survey in the United States indicated that about 13 percent of all firms have them, and that more than 70 percent were started after 1982.[12] Though originally established in small companies such as Lapointe, Lincoln Electric Company, and Herman Miller, gain sharing is now being installed by large firms such as TRW, General Electric Company, Motorola, and Firestone. These companies apply gain sharing to organizational units; Motorola, for example, has virtually all its plant employees covered by gain sharing. These plans are increasing because "they are more than just pay incentive plans; they are a participative approach to management and are often used as a way to install participative management."[13]

10.5 CONCLUSION

Most readers of this book will encounter questions of job design and work methods and measurement in the service sector. It appears that in services, as well as in manufacturing, the new performance metric will be speed, achieved through improved work methods and teamwork. ServiceMaster, for example, has been able to dominate the institutional custodial business (hospitals,

---

[12] C. O'Dell, *People, Performance, and Pay* (Houston: American Productivity Center, 1987).

[13] E. E. Lawler III, "Paying for Organizational Performance," Report G 87–1 (92), Center for Effective Organizations, University of Southern California, 1987.

schools, and offices) by applying fast cleaning methods to such tasks as mopping floors and washing windows. (Rather than using cumbersome ladders to wash windows, they employ specially designed, light-weight, long-handled squeegies using easy-to-remove velcro-backed washable cleaning cloths. Between uses, the clothes are soaked in fluids developed in ServiceMaster's laboratory.) Southwest Airlines uses teamwork (involving its ground crew, baggage handlers, and flight attendants) to achieve a 15-minute turnaround of its flights. (See the Insert: "Anatomy of a 15-Minute Turnaround.") Interestingly enough, these examples epitomize the ideas that Fredrick W. Taylor advocated almost a century ago.

INSERT   Anatomy of a 15-Minute Turnaround

On a recent weekday a Southwest Airlines flight arrived at New Orleans from Houston. The scheduled arrival time was 8:00 A.M., and departure for Birmingham, Alabama was 8:15 A.M. *Forbes* clocked the turnaround, half-minute by half-minute.

7:55	Ground crew chat around gate position.
8:03:30	Ground crew alerted, move to their vehicles.
8:04	Plane begins to pull into gate; crew move toward plane.
8:04:30	Plane stops; jetway telescopes out; baggage door opens.
8:06:30	Baggage unloaded; refueling and other servicing under way.
8:07	Passengers off plane.
8:08	Boarding call; baggage loading, refueling complete.
8:10	Boarding complete; most of ground crew leave.
8:15	Jetway retracts.
8:15:30	Pushback from gate.
8:18	Pushback tractor disengages; plane leaves for runway.

Source: Subrata N. Chakravarty, "Hit 'em Hardest with the Mostest," *Forbes*, September 16, 1991, p. 51.

10.6 REVIEW AND DISCUSSION QUESTIONS

1. What does the chapter opening quotation imply to you about good management? Is there a loser in such free-wheeling plants?

2. A management consultant, Roy Walters, occasionally publishes a list of the "Ten Worst Jobs." On one such list, he included the following (in no special order): highway toll collector, car watcher in a tunnel, pool typist, copy-machine operator, bogus-type setter (i.e., type that is not to be used), computer-tape librarian, housewife (not to be confused with mother), and automatic-elevator operator.

   a. With reference to the sociotechnical systems discussion, what characteristics of good job design are absent from each of these jobs?

   b. Do you have any contemporary job you might suggest for inclusion in Walters' list? What makes this job undesirable?

3. Why might the job enrichment and sociotechnical approaches to job design be looked at with skepticism by practicing managers and industrial engineers?

4. Comment on the statement, "Heavy manual work is really such a small component of modern American industry that further study of it is not really necessary."

5. Chase and Aquilano commonly complain to their families that book writing is hard work and that they should be excused from helping out with the housework so that they can rest. Which exhibit in this chapter should they never let their families see?

6. Is there an inconsistency when a company requires precise time standards and encourages job enlargement?

7. Match the following techniques to their most appropriate application:

MTM	Washing clothes at laundromat
SIMO chart	Tracing your steps in getting a parking permit
Man–machine chart	Faculty office hours kept
Process chart	Development of a new word processor keyboard
Work sampling	Planning the assembly process for a new electronic device

8. You have timed your friend, Lefty, assembling widgets. His time averages 12 minutes for the two cycles you timed. He was working very hard, and you believe that none of the nine other operators doing the same job would beat his time. Are you ready to put this time forth as the standard for making an order of 5,000 widgets? If not, what else should you do?

9. Comment on the following:
   a. "Work measurement is old hat. We have automated our office, and now we run every bill through our computer (after our 25 clerks have typed the data into our computer database)."
   b. "It's best that our workers don't know that they are being time studied. That way, they can't complain about us getting in the way when we set time standards."
   c. "Once we get everybody on an incentive plan, then we will start our work measurement program."
   d. "Rhythm is fine for dancing, but it has no place on the shop floor."

10. The American Motors study team observed that the Japanese used techniques such as job rotation, making line workers responsible for quality control, minimal work classifications, and indirect employee participation in management. What gains could be made with this approach, contrasted with the job specialization approach? If this approach is applied in a specialized job environment, what changes would be necessary?

11. Organizationwide financial incentive plans cover all the workers. Some units or individuals may have contributed more to corporate profits than others. Does this detract from the effectiveness of the incentive plan system? How would your incentive scheme for a small software development firm compare to an established automobile manufacturing firm?

12. The conclusion of this chapter describes Southwest Airlines' fast flight turnarounds. What has to be done inside the terminal to attain this performance?

10.7 PROBLEMS

*1. Felix Unger is a very organized person and wants to plan his day perfectly. To do this, he has his friend Oscar time his daily activities. Following are the results of Oscar timing Felix on polishing two pairs of black shoes using the snapback method of timing. What is the standard time for polishing two pair? (Assume a 5 percent allowance factor for Felix to get Oscar an ashtray for his cigar. Account for noncyclically recurring elements by dividing their observed times by the total number of cycles observed.)

| | | | OBSERVED TIMES | | | | | |
	Element	1	2	3	4	ΣT	T	Performance Rating	NT
	Get shoeshine kit	0.50						125%	
	Polish shoes	0.94	0.85	0.80	0.81			110	
	Put away kit				0.75			80	

*2. A total of 15 observations have been taken on a head baker for a school district. The numerical breakdown of her activities is

Make Ready	Do	Clean Up	Idle
2	6	3	4

Based on this information, how many work sampling observations are required to determine how much of the baker's time is spent in "doing"? Assume a 5 percent desired absolute accuracy and 95 percent confidence level.

3. Use the following form to evaluate a job you have held relative to the five principles of job design given in the chapter. Develop a numerical score by summing the numbers in parentheses.

	Poor (0)	Adequate (1)	Good (2)	Outstanding (3)
Task variety				
Skill variety				
Feeback				
Task identity				
Task autonomy				

a. Compute the score for your job. Does the score match your subjective feelings about the job as a whole? Explain.

b. Compare your score with the scores generated by your classmates. Is there one kind of job that everybody likes and one kind that everybody dislikes?

4. Examine the process chart in Exhibit 10.7. Can you recommend some improvements to cut down on delays and transportation? (Hint: The research laboratory can suggest changes in the requisition form.)

5. As time-study analyst, you have observed that a worker has produced 40 parts in a one-hour period. From your experience, you rate the worker as performing

---

* Problems 1 and 2 are completely solved in Appendix H.

slightly faster than 100 percent—so you estimate performance as 110 percent. The company allows 15 percent for fatigue and delay.

   a.   What is the normal time?

   b.   What is the standard time?

   c.   If a worker produces 300 units per day and has a base rate of $6 per hour, what would the day's wages be for this worker if payment was on a 100 percent wage incentive payment plan?

6.   A time study was made of an existing job to develop new time standards. A worker was observed for a period of 45 minutes. During that period, 30 units were produced. The analyst rated the worker as performing at a 90 percent performance rate. Allowances in the firm for rest and personal time are 12 percent.

   a.   What is the normal time for the task?

   b.   What is the standard time for the task?

   c.   If the worker produced 300 units in an eight-hour day, what would the day's pay be if the basic rate was $6 per hour and the premium payment system paid on a 100 percent basis?

7.   The Bullington Company wants a time standard established on the painting operation of souvenir horseshoes for the local Pioneer Village. Work sampling is to be used. It is estimated that working time averages 95 percent of total time (working time plus idle time). A co-op student is available to do the work sampling between the hours of 8:00 A.M. and 12:00 noon. Sixty working days are to be used for the study. Use Exhibit 10.16 and an absolute error of 2.5 percent. Use the table of random numbers (Appendix B) to calculate the sampling schedule for the first day; i.e., show the times of day that an observation of working/idle should be made. Hint: Start random number selection with the first row

8.   The final result of the study in Problem 7 estimated working time at 91.0 percent. In a 480-minute shift the best operator painted 1,000 horseshoes. The student's performance index was estimated to be 115 percent. Total allowances per company standard are 10 percent. Calculate the standard time per piece.

9.   A time-study analyst has obtained the following performance times by observing a worker over 15 operating cycles:

Performance Number	Time (seconds)	Performance Number	Time (seconds)
1	15	9	14
2	12	10	18
3	16	11	13
4	11	12	15
5	13	13	16
6	14	14	15
7	16	15	11
8	12		

The worker was rated as performing at 115 percent. Allowances for personal time and fatigue in the company are 10 percent. The base rate for the worker is $5 per hour and the company operates on a 100 percent premium plan.

   a.   What is the normal time?

   b.   What is the standard time?

   c.   If the worker produced 2,500 in a day, what would the gross pay for the day be if the premium rate was 100 percent?

10. A work-sampling study is to be conducted over the next 30 consecutive days of an activity in the city fire department. Washing trucks, which is the subject of the study, is to be observed, and it is estimated that this occurs 10 percent of the time. A 3.5 percent accuracy with 95 percent confidence is acceptable. State specifically when observations should be made on one day. Use a 10-hour day from 8:00 A.M. to 6:00 P.M.

11. Suppose you want to set a time standard for the baker making her specialty, square donuts. A work-sampling study of her on "donut day" yielded the following results:

Time spent (working and idle)	320 minutes
Number of donuts produced	5,000
Working time	280 minutes
Performance rating	125%
Allowances	10%

What is the standard time per donut?

12. In an attempt to increase productivity and reduce costs, Rho Sigma Corporation is planning to install an incentive pay plan in its manufacturing plant.

   In developing standards for one operation, time-study analysts observed a worker for a 30-minute period. During that time the worker completed 42 parts. The analysts rated the worker as producing at 130 percent. The base wage rate of the worker is $5 per hour. The firm has established 15 percent as a fatigue and personal time allowance.

   a. What is the normal time for the task?
   b. What is the standard time for the task?
   c. If the worker produced 500 units during an eight-hour day, what wages would the worker have earned?

13. Since new regulations will greatly change the products and services offered by savings and loan associations, time studies must be performed on tellers and other personnel to determine the number and types of personnel needed and incentive wage payment plans that might be installed.

   As an example of the studies that the various tasks will undergo, consider the following problem and come up with the appropriate answers:

   A hypothetical case was set up in which the teller (to be retitled later as an *account adviser*) was required to examine a customer's portfolio and determine whether it was more beneficial for the customer to consolidate various CDs into a single issue currently offered, or to leave the portfolio unaltered. A time study was made of the teller, with the following findings:

Time of study	90 minutes
Number of portfolios examined	10 portfolios
Performance rating	130 percent
Rest for personal time	15 percent
Teller's proposed new pay rate	$12 per hour

   a. What is the normal time for the teller to do a portfolio analysis for the CDs?
   b. What is the standard time for the analysis?
   c. If the S&L decides to pay the new tellers on a 100 percent premium payment plan, how much would a teller earn for a day in which he or she analyzed 50 customer portfolios?

14. A work-sampling study was made of an order clerk to estimate the percentage of the total week that she spent on each activity (results follow). In addition to classifying the order clerk's activity, the observer rated her performance level whenever a sampling observation found her doing one of the productive activities. Since all order forms carried consecutive preprinted numbers, it was an easy matter to determine how many orders the order clerk wrote.

Assume that such a check revealed that the order clerk under study wrote 583 orders during the week of the sampling study. Further assume that on the basis of the sampling study, it is determined that the averages of the performance ratings made of her working pace for the four productive activities are those given here. The company policy is to give a personal allowance of 10 percent of the normal time for all office work. From the results of the sampling study, the assumptions just given, and the fact that the order clerk worked a total of 40 hours during the week covered by the sampling study, determine the standard time (minutes per order) for the order-writing operation.

Activity	Actual Percentage of Week	Average Performance Rating (normal = 100%)
Order writing	52.5%	80%
Filing	12.5	90
Walking	15.0	75
Receiving instructions	9.6	100
Idle	10.4	
	100.0%	

15. It is estimated that a bank teller spends about 10 percent of his time in a particular type of transaction. The bank manager would like a work-sampling study that shows, within plus or minus 3 percent, whether the clerk's time is really 10 percent (i.e., from 7 to 13 percent). The manager is well satisfied with a 95 percent confidence level.

From Exhibit 10.16 you observe that, for the first "cut" at the problem, a sample size of 400 is indicated for the 10 percent activity time and ±3 percent absolute error.

State how you would perform the work-sampling study. If the study were to be made over a five-week period with five days per week from the hours of 9:00 to 5:00, specify the exact time (in minute increments) that you would make Monday's observations.

10.8 CASE: UP TO SPEED: UNITED PARCEL SERVICE GETS DELIVERIES DONE BY DRIVING ITS WORKERS*

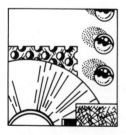

Grabbing a package under his arm, Joseph Polise, a driver for United Parcel Service (UPS), bounds from his brown delivery truck and toward an office building here. A few paces behind him, Marjorie Cusack, a UPS industrial engineer, clutches a digital timer.

Her eyes fixed on Mr. Polise, she counts his steps and times his contact with

---

* Daniel Machalaba, "Up to Speed: United Parcel Service Gets Deliveries Done by Driving Its Workers," *The Wall Street Journal,* April 22, 1986, p. 1.

customers. Scribbling on a clipboard, Mrs. Cusack records every second taken up by stoplights, traffic, detours, doorbells, walkways, stairways, and coffee breaks. "If he goes to the bathroom, we time him," she says.

Such attention to detail is nothing new at UPS, the nation's largest deliverer of packages. Through meticulous human-engineering and close scrutiny of its 152,000 employees, the privately held company, which is based in Greenwich, Connecticut, has grown highly profitable despite stiff competition. In fact, UPS is one of the most efficient companies anywhere, productivity experts say.

"You never see anybody sitting on his duff at UPS," says Bernard La Londe, a transportation professor at The Ohio State University. "The only other place you see the same commitment to productivity is at Japanese companies."

Getting Up to Speed

At UPS, more than 1,000 industrial engineers use time study to set standards for a myriad of closely supervised tasks. Drivers are instructed to walk to a customer's door at the brisk pace of three feet per second and to knock first lest seconds be lost searching for the doorbell. Supervisors then ride with the "least best drivers" until they learn to finish on time. "It's human nature to get away with as much as possible," says Michael Kamienski, a UPS district manager. "But we bring workers up to our level of acceptance. We don't go down to their level."

If UPS isn't quite a throwback to old-time work measurement, it nevertheless runs counter to the drift of many U.S. companies. To increase productivity, others are turning more often to employee-involvement techniques that stress consultation and reject the rigid monitoring of workers.

"Workers are better educated and want more to say about what happens to them," says Roger Weiss, a vice president of H. B. Maynard & Co., a consulting concern. "Time study is a dark-ages technique, and it's dehumanizing to track someone around with a stopwatch."

UPS dismisses the criticism. "We don't use the standards as hammers, but they do give accountability," says Larry P. Breakiron, the company's senior vice president for engineering. "Our ability to manage labor and hold it accountable is the key to our success."

New Competition

Those techniques are about to be tested. Long engaged in a battle for parcels with the Postal Service, UPS recently has charged into overnight delivery against Federal Express Corporation, Purolator Courier, Airborne Freight, Emery Air Freight and others. What's more, it now is being challenged on its own turf by Roadway Services Inc., which last March started a parcel delivery company called Roadway Package System that is implementing management ideas of its own.

The upstart competitor boasts that its owner-operator drivers, unlike UPS's closely scrutinized, but highly paid and unionized, drivers, are motivated by the challenge of running their own business. "Our people don't drive brown trucks; they own their trucks," says Ivan Hoffman, a vice president of Roadway.

Roadway also is trying to gain the edge in productivity by eliminating people as much as possible through automation. Its package hubs use bar codes, laser scanners, computers, and special mechanical devices to sort packages, a task still handled at UPS by armies of workers. UPS calls its rival's methods unreliable, inflexible, and expensive. Those are the same epithets that Roadway hurls at UPS's human sorters.

The outcome of this budding competition interests package shippers. "UPS has taken the engineering of people as far as it can be taken," says Michael Birkholm, the director of transportation for American Greetings Corporation. "But the question is whether technologically sophisticated Roadway can dent the big brown UPS machine."

Burgeoning Competition

If the competition intensifies, productivity improvements will be at the heart of UPS's counterattack. Indeed, UPS long has used efficiency to overcome rivals. Founded in Seattle in 1907 as a messenger service, UPS over the years won parcel deliveries from department stores and captured package business once handled by the Postal Service because of its lower rates and superior service.

UPS's founder, James E. Casey, put a premium on efficiency. In the 1920s, he turned to Frank B. Gilbreth and other pioneers of time study to develop techniques to measure the time consumed each day by each UPS driver. Later, UPS engineers cut away the sides of a UPS delivery truck, or "package car" as the company calls the vehicle, to study a driver at work. Resultant changes in package loading techniques increased efficiency 30 percent.

Mr. Casey also shaped the company culture, which stresses achievement and teamwork in addition to efficiency. Copies of his tract, "Determined Men," and of "Pursuit of Excellence," a pamphlet written by one-time UPS Chairman George Smith, are handed out to the company's managers. "We still use Jim's and George's quotes in everything we do," says George Lamb, Jr., a UPS director and past chairman.

Another guiding principle: a fair day's work for a fair day's pay. The company's drivers, all of them Teamsters, earn wages of $15 an hour, about $1 more than the best-paid drivers at other trucking companies earn. With overtime, many UPS drivers gross $35,000 to $40,000 a year.

In return, UPS seeks maximum output from its drivers, as is shown by the time study Mrs. Cusack is conducting. On this day in suburban Whippany, she determines time allowances for each of Polise's 120 stops while watching for inefficiency in his methods. "What are you doing, Joe?" she asks as Mr. Polise wastes precious seconds handling packages more than once. She says that a mere 30 seconds wasted at each stop can snowball into big delays by day's end.

Some UPS drivers with nicknames like Ace, Hammer Slick, and Rocket Shoes take pride in meeting the standards day after day. "We used to joke that a good driver could get to his stop and back to the car before the seat belt stopped swaying," Mrs. Cusack says. (UPS has since redesigned its seat belts to eliminate sway.)

But not all UPS drivers enjoy the pace. For example, Michael Kipila, a driver in East Brunswick, New Jersey, says, "They squeeze every ounce out of you. You're always in a hurry, and you can't work relaxed." Some drivers say they cut their breaks in order to finish on time.

UPS officials maintain that the company's work standards are not just a matter of increasing output, but of making the job easier. "If you do it our way, you'll be less tired at the end of the day," says a UPS spokesman.

Had Enough

The pressures cause some UPS employees—supervisors and drivers alike—to quit. Jose Vega, a former UPS supervisor, says he would ride with one New York driver, noting each time "pace too slow, customer contact too long." Vega says he tried to embarrass the driver so as to speed him up: "Are you falling asleep? Do you want a sleeping bag?" After a while, "it's like you're abusing this person," says Vega, who now drives for Roadway.

"There's a fine line between motivation and harassment, and many times UPS crosses that line," says Mario Perrucci, the secretary-treasurer of Teamsters Local 177 in Hillside, New Jersey. Mr. Perrucci has battled UPS for years over a requirement that drivers tap their horns when they approach a stop in the hopes that the customer will hurry to the door seconds sooner.

UPS's efforts to increase productivity get mixed reactions from the Teamsters union. While some local Teamsters officials such as Perrucci say that UPS is driving its workers "beyond endurance," the union's national executives are grateful that the company is successful. "I'd rather see UPS pushing the men too hard," says a Teamsters official in Washington, "than see UPS in bankruptcy court."

Many trucking companies employing Teamsters are shutting down or, like Roadway Package System, turning to nonunion workers. But, UPS continues to be the largest single employer of Teamsters members, with more than 100,000 unionized workers, a 33 percent rise since 1980.

A Game of Inches

To sustain growth, UPS executives are looking for new efficiencies. For example, they are seeking to make work standards for truck mechanics more exact. And at UPS's Parsippany, New Jersey, package sorting hub, 1 of more than 100 that the company operates, officials are making the most of space by parking delivery trucks just five inches apart. But productivity has its price. New York City says that UPS drivers have received more than $1 million in unpaid parking tickets since March 1985 while making local deliveries. A company attorney says the amount is "much too high." UPS has contested the fines.

The new competition from Roadway Package System also looms large. Roadway is cutting labor expenses 20 percent to 30 percent by using independent drivers. Because Roadway drivers buy their own trucks, uniforms, and insurance, Roadway is saving money that it is using to automate package sorting. "We'll use technology to be the low-cost producer," says Bram Johnson, a Roadway vice president.

Roadway says it reduced personnel 25 percent at its five sorting hubs through automation. At its York, Pennsylvania, hub, for example, a moving belt of tilt trays following instructions from a computer drops packages down a series of chutes.

QUESTIONS

1. What are the advantages and disadvantages of the UPS approach to job design and work measurement?
2. Compare the UPS approach to people with that of Japanese auto manufacturers as listed on page 501.

10.9 CASE: AT&T CREDIT CORP.*

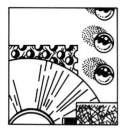

Millions of clerical employees toil in the back offices of financial companies, processing applications, claims, and customer accounts on what amounts to electronic assembly lines. The jobs are dull and repetitive and efficiency gains minuscule—when they come at all.

That was the case with AT&T Credit Corp. (ATTCC) when it opened shop in 1985 as a newly created subsidiary of American Telephone & Telegraph Co. Based in Morristown, New Jersey, ATTCC provides financing for customers who lease equipment from AT&T and other companies. A bank initially retained by ATTCC to process lease applications couldn't keep up with the volume of new business.

ATTCC President Thomas C. Wajnert saw that the fault lay in the bank's method of dividing labor into narrow tasks and organizing work by function. One department handled applications and checked the customer's credit standing, a second drew up contracts, and a third collected payments. So no one person or group had responsibility for providing full service to a customer. "The employees had no sense of how their jobs contributed to the final solution for the customer," Wajnert says.

Unexpected Bonus

Wajnert decided to hire his own employees and give them "ownership and accountability." His first concern was to increase efficiency, not to provide more rewarding jobs. But in the end, he did both.

In 1986, ATTCC set up 11 teams of 10 to 15 newly hired workers in a high-volume division serving small businesses. The three major lease-processing functions were combined in each team. No longer were calls from customers shunted from department to department. The company also divided its national staff of field agents into seven regions and assigned two or three teams to handle business from each region. That way, the same teams always worked with the same sales staff, establishing a personal relationship with them and their customers. Above all, team members took responsibility for solving customers' problems. ATTCC's new slogan: "Whoever gets the call owns the problem."

The teams largely manage themselves. Members make most decisions on how to deal with customers, schedule their own time off, reassign work when people are absent, and interview prospective new employees. The only supervisors are seven regional managers who advise the team members, rather than give orders. The result: The teams process up to 800 lease applications a day versus 400 under the old system. Instead of taking several days to give a final yes or no, the teams do it in 24 to 48 hours. As a result, ATTCC is growing at a 40-percent to 50-percent compound annual rate, Wajnert says.

Extra Cash

The teams also have economic incentives for providing good service. A bonus plan tied to each team's costs and profits can produce extra cash. The employees, most of whom

---

* Source: John Hoerr, "The Payoff from Teamwork," *Business Week*, July 10, 1989, p. 59.

are young college graduates, can add $1,500 a year to average salaries of $28,000, and pay rises as employees learn new skills. "It's a phenomenal learning opportunity," says 24-year-old team member Michael LoCastro.

But LoCastro and others complain that promotions are rare because there are few managerial positions. And everyone comes under intense pressure from co-workers to produce more. The annual turnover rate is high: Some 20 percent of ATTCC employees either quit or transfer to other parts of AT&T. Still, the team experiment has been so successful that ATTCC is involving employees in planning to extend the concept throughout the company. "They will probably come up with as good an organizational design as management could," Wajnert says, "and it will work a lot better because the employees will take ownership for it."

QUESTION
What would you do to reduce the turnover rate at ATTCC?

10.10 SELECTED BIBLIOGRAPHY

Barnes, Ralph M. *Motion and Time Study: Design and Measurement of Work.* 8th ed. New York: John Wiley & Sons, 1980.

Carlisle, Brian. "Job Design Implications for Operations Managers." *International Journal of Operations and Production Management* 3, no. 3 (1983), pp. 40–48.

Cusumano, Michael. *Japan's Software Factories: A Challenge to U.S. Management.* New York: Oxford University Press, 1991.

Davis, L. E., and J. C. Taylor. *Design of Jobs.* 2nd ed. Santa Monica, Calif.: Goodyear Publishing, 1979.

Kirkman, Frank. "Who Cares About Job Design? Some Reflections on Its Present and Future." *International Journal of Operations and Production Management* 2, no. 1 (1981), pp. 3–13.

Konz, Stephan. *Work Design: Industrial Ergonomics.* 2nd ed. New York: John Wiley & Sons, 1983.

McCormick, E. J. *Human Factors in Engineering and Design.* 4th ed. New York: McGraw-Hill, 1976.

Niebel, Benjamin W. *Motion and Time Study.* 7th ed. Homewood, Ill.: Richard D. Irwin, 1982.

Niles, John L. "To Increase Productivity, Audit the Old Incentive Plan." *Industrial Engineering* (January 1980), pp. 20–23.

Sasser, W. Earl, and William E. Fulmer. "Creating Personalized Service Delivery Systems," in *Service Management Effectiveness,* eds. D. Bowen, R. Chase, and T. Cummings. San Francisco: Josey-Bass, 1990, pp. 213–33.

Zuboff, Shoshana. *In the Age of the Smart Machine: The Future of Work and Power.* New York: Basic Books, 1984.

SECTION IV

STARTUP OF THE SYSTEM

Once designed, it is no easy task to bring a production system up to full operation. Numerous problems are experienced in this phase of the production system cycle. One discovers that tasks and activities were not well defined, some aspects of the system were overlooked, and unexpected incidents occur.

Perhaps the most appropriate way to guide this transitional period between the design of the system and its steady-state operation is through the techniques of project management. Within this section, we discuss project management and how it differs from traditional management—in purpose, structure, and operation. We also discuss the scheduling techniques of PERT and CPM, which provide a logical analysis of activity performance times and help in estimating the time for project completion.

Chapter 11

Project Planning and Control

Ninety-Ninety Rule of Project Schedules: the first 90 percent of the task takes 90 percent of the time, the last 10 percent takes the other 90 percent.

CHAPTER OUTLINE

KEY TERMS

Project

Program

Milestones

Work Breakdown Structure

PERT

CPM

Gantt Chart

Early Start/Late Start Schedules

Time-Cost Models

We seem to be on an exponential curve as to the pace in which technology, products, and markets are changing. Rapid changes are also occurring throughout all phases of production: from technology as the basis of design and manufacturing, through methods of operation and control of production, to delivery to the marketplace. Whereas two or three decades ago a product may have had a life cycle of several years, today's products in many areas (particularly in electronics) may have an existence of only several months.

If firms are to survive in such an environment where forecasting is very difficult and the time span from product design to full production just a matter of months, they must focus on the management of change. We believe that project management offers the best available technique to plan, operate, and control operations.

Project management techniques are also very appropriate for exactly the opposite type of environment: one where product lead time may be long. The key factor in this case is that where frequency of production is low, each item produced tends to be a separate project. Examples are shipbuilding, airplane manufacture, and production of large turbines and generators.

What distinguishes project management from other techniques is that it is goal oriented. It focuses on achieving an objective, which can be almost anything that can be defined within the project management criteria—constructing a house, opening a new facility, controlling research and development effort, managing a campaign (whether it is someone running for a public office or raising funds), or introducing a new product.

There are two main thrusts in project management: one heavily emphasizes the organization and the behavior of *people,* and the other focuses on technology of the *method* (computing start and completion times, critical paths, etc.). In this chapter we lean far more toward describing the method of project management and leave the balance to a course on management and organizational behavior. We describe the work breakdown structure, review basic forms of traditional functional management, and contrast this to project management and matrix organization. Most of the chapter concentrates on project scheduling techniques, primarily CPM and PERT. Since project management software has become readily available for microcomputers, we also compare four project management programs and show the sample output from one of them.

11.1 DEFINITION OF PROJECT MANAGEMENT

A project is simply a statement or proposal of something to be done. In a broader sense, a **project** could be defined as a series of related jobs usually directed toward some major output and requiring a significant period of time to perform. *Project management* can be defined as planning, directing, and controlling resources (people, equipment, material) to meet the technical, cost, and time constraints of the project.

While projects are often thought to be one-time occurrences, the fact is that many projects can be repeated or transferred to other settings or products. The result will be another project output. A contractor building houses or a firm producing low-volume products such as supercomputers, locomotives, or linear accelerators can effectively consider these as projects.

A project starts out as a *statement of work* (SOW). The SOW may be a written description of the objectives to be achieved, with a brief statement of the work to be done and a proposed schedule specifying the start and completion dates. It could also contain performance measures in terms of budget and completion steps (milestones) and the written reports to be supplied.

If the proposed work is a large endeavor, it is often referred to as a **program,** although the terms *project* and *program* are often used interchangeably. A program is the highest order of complexity, may take some years to complete, and may be made up of interrelated projects completed by many organizations. As examples, the development of a missile system would be best termed a *program*. The introduction of a new statewide medical health care system is a program.

As implied earlier, a project is similar to a program, but is less complex and of shorter duration. A program may be to build a missile system; a project may be to develop the guidance control portion. In a health care system, one project is to develop a bid proposal system for health care providers.

A *task* is a further subdivision of a project. It is usually not longer than several months in duration and is performed by one group or organization.

A *subtask* may be used if needed to further subdivide the project into more meaningful pieces.

A *work package* is a group of activities combined to be assignable to a single organizational unit. It still falls into the format of all project management—that the package provides a description of what is to be done, when it is to be started and completed, the budget, measures of performance, and specific events to be reached at points in time (called **milestones**). Typical milestones might be the completion of the design, the production of a prototype, the completed testing of the prototype, and the approval of a pilot run.

Work Breakdown Structure

The **work breakdown structure** (WBDS) is the heart of project management. This subdivision of the objective into smaller and smaller pieces clearly defines the system and contributes to its understanding and success. Conventional use shows the work breakdown structure decreasing in size from top to bottom and shows this level by indentation to the right, as follows:

```
Level
  1        Program
  2            Project
  3                Task
  4                    Subtask
  5                        Work Package
```

EXHIBIT 11.1

Work Breakdown Structure, Large Optical Scanner Design

Level 1	2	3	4	5	
X					Optical simulator design
	X				Optical design
		X			Telescope design/fab
		X			Telescope/simulator optical interface
		X			Simulator zoom system design
		X			Ancillary simulator optical component specification
	X				System performance analysis
		X			Overall system firmware and software control
			X		Logic flow diagram generation and analysis
			X		Basic control algorithm design
		X			Far beam analyzer
		X			System inter- and intra-alignment method design
		X			Data recording and reduction requirements
	X				System integration
	X				Cost analysis
		X			Cost/system schedule analysis
		X			Cost/system performance analysis
	X				Management
		X			System design/engineering management
		X			Program management
	X				Long lead item procurement
		X			Large optics
		X			Target components
		X			Detectors

Exhibit 11.1 shows the work breakdown structure for a project. Note the ease in identifying activities through the level numbers. For example, telescope design (the third item down) is identified as 1.1.1 (the first item in level 1, the first item in level 2, and the first item in level 3). Data recording (the 13th item down) is 1.2.4.

The keys to a good work breakdown structure are

- Allow the elements to be worked on independently.
- Make them manageable in size.
- Give authority to carry out the program.
- Monitor and measure the program.
- Provide the required resources.

11.2 PROJECT CONTROL

Reporting Mechanisms

The Department of Defense was one of the earliest large users of project management and has published a variety of useful standard forms. Many are used directly or have been modified by firms engaged in project management. Since those early days, however, graphics programs have been written for most computers, so management, the customer, and the project manager have a wide choice of how data are presented. Exhibit 11.2 shows a sample of available presentations.

Exhibit 11.2A is a sample Gantt chart showing both the amount of time involved and the sequence in which activities can be performed. For example, "long lead time procurement" and "manufacturing schedules" are independent activities and can occur simultaneously. All of the other activities must be done in the sequence from top to bottom. Exhibit 11.2B graphically shows the proportion of money spent on labor, material, and overhead. Its value is its clarity in identifying sources and amounts of cost.

Exhibit 11.2C shows the percentage of the project's labor hours which come from the various areas of manufacturing, finance, and so on. These labor hours are related to the proportion of the project's total labor cost. For example, manufacturing is responsible for 50 percent of the project's labor hours, but this 50 percent is allocated just 40 percent of the total labor dollars charged.

The top half of Exhibit 11.2D shows the degree of completion of these projects. The dotted vertical line signifies today. Project 1, therefore, is already late since it still has work to be done. Project 2 is not being worked on temporarily and therefore the space before the projected work. Project 3 continues to be worked on without interruption. The bottom of Exhibit 11.2D shows actual total costs compared to projected costs. The exhibit shows that two cost overruns occurred.

Exhibit 11.2E is a milestone chart. The three milestones mark specific points in the project where checks can be made to see if the project is on time and where it should be. The best place to locate milestones is at the completion of a major activity. In this exhibit, the major activities completed were "purchase order release," "invoices received," and "material received."

Other standard reports can be used for a more detailed presentation comparing cost to progress (such as cost schedule status report—CSSR) or reports providing the basis for partial payment (such as "earned value" report).

11.3 CRITICAL PATH SCHEDULING

Critical path scheduling refers to a set of graphic techniques used in planning and controlling projects. In any given project, the three factors of concern are time, cost, and resource availability. Critical path techniques have been developed to deal with each of these, individually and in combination. The remainder of this chapter focuses on time-based models, time-cost models, and limited-resource models.

PERT *(program evaluation and review technique)* and **CPM** *(critical path method)*, the two best-known techniques, were both developed in the late 1950s. PERT was developed under the sponsorship of the U.S. Navy Special Projects Office in 1958 as a management tool for scheduling and controlling the Polaris missile project. CPM was developed in 1957 by J. E. Kelly of

EXHIBIT 11.2   **A Sample of Graphic Project Reports**

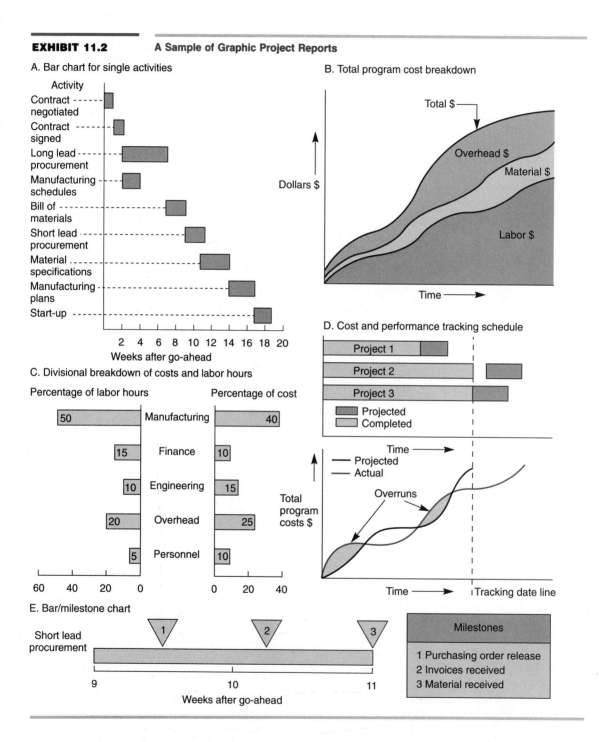

A. Bar chart for single activities

B. Total program cost breakdown

C. Divisional breakdown of costs and labor hours

D. Cost and performance tracking schedule

E. Bar/milestone chart

Remington-Rand and M. R. Walker of Du Pont to aid in scheduling maintenance shutdowns of chemical processing plants.

Critical path scheduling techniques display a project in graphic form and
relate its component tasks in a way that focuses attention on those crucial to
the project's completion. For critical path scheduling techniques to be most
applicable, a project must have the following characteristics:

1. It must have well-defined jobs or tasks whose completion marks the
   end of the project.
2. The jobs or tasks are independent; they may be started, stopped, and
   conducted separately within a given sequence.
3. The jobs or tasks are ordered; they must follow each other in a given
   sequence.

Construction, aerospace, and shipbuilding industries commonly meet these
criteria, and critical path techniques find wide application within them. We
previously noted also that the applications of project management and critical
path techniques are becoming much more common within firms in rapidly
changing industries.

11.4 TIME-ORIENTED TECHNIQUES

The basic forms of PERT and CPM focus on finding the longest time-
consuming path through a network of tasks as a basis for planning and
controlling a project. Both PERT and CPM use nodes and arrows for display.
Originally, the basic differences between PERT and CPM were that PERT
used the arrow to represent an activity and CPM used the node. The other
original difference was that PERT used three estimates—optimistic, pessimistic, and best—of an activity's required time, whereas CPM used just the
best estimate. This distinction reflects PERT's origin in scheduling advanced
projects that are characterized by uncertainty and CPM's origin in the scheduling of the fairly routine activity of plant maintenance. As years passed, these
two features no longer distinguished PERT from CPM. This is because CPM
users started to use three time estimates and PERT users often placed activities
on the nodes.

We believe the activity on the node is much easier to follow logically than
the activity on the arrow. However, the three time estimates are often very
valuable to get a measure of the probability of completion times. Therefore, in
this chapter and in this text we use the activity on the node and either a single
estimate for activity time or three time estimates depending on our objective.
We use the terms *CPM* and *PERT* interchangeably and mean the same thing,
although we tend to use the term *CPM* more frequently.

In a sense, both techniques owe their development to their widely used
predecessor, the **Gantt chart.** While the Gantt chart is able to relate activities

to time in a usable fashion for very small projects, the interrelationship of activities, when displayed in this form, becomes extremely difficult to visualize and to work with for projects with more than 25 or 30 activities. Moreover, the Gantt chart provides no direct procedure for ascertaining the critical path, which, despite its theoretical shortcomings, is of great practical value.

CPM with a Single Time Estimate

Following is an example of a project that we will develop in a normal project scheduling manner. The times for each activity have been given as a single best estimate (rather than three estimates, which will be discussed in a later example).

Many firms that have tried to enter the laptop and briefcase computer market have failed. Suppose your firm believes that there is a big demand in this market because existing products have not been designed correctly. They are either too heavy, too large, or too small to have standard-size keyboards. Your intended computer will be small enough to carry inside a jacket pocket if need be. The ideal size will be no larger than 4 inches × 9½ inches × 1 inch with a standard typewriter keyboard. It should weigh no more than 15 ounces, have a 4 to 8 line × 80 character LCD display, have a micro disk drive, and a micro printer. It should be aimed toward word processing use but have plug-in ROMs for an assortment of languages and programs. This should appeal to traveling businesspeople, but it could have a much wider market. If it can be priced to sell retail in the $175–$200 range, it should appeal to anyone who uses a typewriter. A big market is also expected to be students. College students could use this to create reports; college, high school, and elementary schoolchildren could take notes during class and during library research.

The project, then, is to design, develop, and produce a prototype of this small computer. In the rapidly changing computer industry, it is crucial to hit the market with a product of this sort in less than a year. Therefore, the project team has been allowed approximately eight months (35 weeks) to produce the prototype.

The first charge of the project team is to develop a project network chart and estimate the likelihood of completing the prototype computer within the 35 weeks. Let's follow the steps in the development of the network.

1. *Activity identification.* The project team decides that the following activities are the major components of the project: design of the computer, prototype construction, prototype testing, methods specification (summarized in a report), evaluation studies of automatic assembly equipment, an assembly equipment study report, and a final report summarizing all aspects of the design, equipment, and methods.

2. *Activity sequencing and network construction.* On the basis of discussion with his staff, the project manager develops the precedence table and sequence

EXHIBIT 11.3

CPM Network for Computer Design Project

CPM ACTIVITY DESIGNATIONS AND TIME ESTIMATES

Activity	Designation	Immediate predecessors	Time in weeks
Design	A	—	21
Build prototype	B	A	5
Evaluate equipment	C	A	7
Test prototype	D	B	2
Write equipment report	E	C, D	5
Write methods report	F	C, D	8
Write final report	G	E, F	2

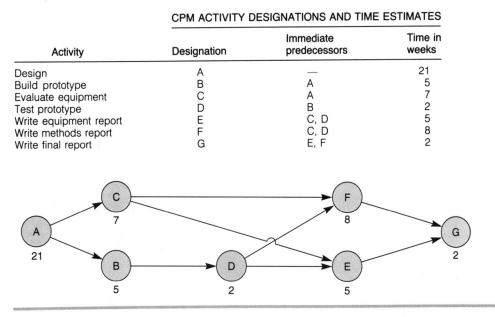

network shown in Exhibit 11.3. Activities are indicated as nodes while arrows show the sequence in which the activities must be completed.

When constructing a network, take care to ensure that the activities are in the proper order and that the logic of their relationships is maintained. For example, it would be illogical to have a situation where Event A precedes Event B, B precedes C, and C precedes A.

3. Determine the critical path. The critical path is the longest sequence of connected activities through the network and is defined as the path with zero slack time (the numbers are consecutive). *Slack time*, in turn, is calculated for each activity; it is the difference between the latest and the earliest expected completion time for an event. Slack may be thought of as the amount of time the start of a given activity may be delayed without delaying the completion of the project. To arrive at slack time requires the calculation of four time values for each activity:

- *Early start time* (ES), the earliest possible time that the activity can begin.
- *Early finish time* (EF), the early start time plus the time needed to complete the activity.
- *Late finish time* (LF), the latest time an activity can end without delaying the project.
- *Late start time* (LS), the late finish time minus the time needed to complete the activity.

EXHIBIT 11.4   **Steps to Develop and Solve a CPM Network**

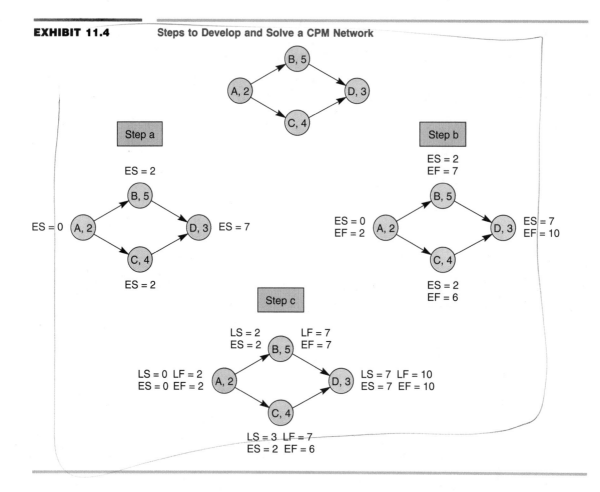

The procedure for arriving at these values and for determining slack and the critical path can best be explained by reference to the simple network shown in Exhibit 11.4. The letters denote the activities and the numbers the activity times.

a. Find ES time. Take 0 as the start of the project and set this equal to ES for Activity A. To find ES for B, we add the duration of A (which is 2) to 0 and obtain 2. Likewise, ES for C would be $0 + 2$, or 2. To find ES for D, we take the larger ES and duration time for the preceding activities: since $B = 2 + 5 = 7$ and $C = 2 + 4 = 6$, ES for $D = 7$. These values are entered on the diagram (Exhibit 11.4, Step a). The largest value is selected since activity D cannot begin until the longest time-consuming activity preceding it is completed.

b. Find EF times. The EF for A is its ES time, 0, plus its duration of 2. B's EF is its ES of 2 plus its duration of 5, or 7. C's is $2 + 4$, or 6, and D's is $7 + 3$, or 10 (Exhibit 11.4, Step b). In practice, one computes ES and EF together while proceeding through the network. Since ES plus activity time equals EF, the EF becomes the ES of the following event, and so forth.

c. Find late start and late finish times. While the procedure for making these calculations can be presented in mathematical form, the concept is much easier to explain and understand if it is presented in an intuitive way. The basic approach is to start at the end of the project with some desired or assumed completion time. Working back toward the beginning, one activity at a time, we determine how long the starting of this activity may be delayed without affecting the start of the one that follows it.

In reference to the sample network in Exhibit 11.4, Step c, let us assume that the late finish time for the project is equal to the early finish time for activity D, that is, 10. If this is the case, the latest possible starting time for D is 10 − 3, or 7. The latest time C can finish without delaying the LS of D is 7, which means that C's LS is 7 − 4, or 3. The latest time B can finish without delaying the LS of D is also 7, which means that B's LS is 7 − 5, or 2. Since A precedes two activities, the choice of LS and LF values depends on which of those activities must be started first. Clearly, B determines the LF for A since its LS is 2, whereas C can be delayed one day without extending the project. Finally, since A must be finished by Day 2, it cannot start any later than Day 0, and hence, its LS is 0.

d. Determine slack time for each activity. Slack for each activity is defined as either LS − ES or LF − EF. In this example, only activity C has slack (1 day); therefore the critical path is A, B, D.

Early start and late start schedules

An **early start schedule** is one which lists all of the activities by their early start times. For activities not on the critical path, there is slack time between the activity completion and the start of the next activity which succeeds it. The early start schedule completes the project and all of its activities as soon as possible.

A **late start schedule** lists the activities to start as late as possible without delaying the completion date of the project. One of the motivations for using a late start schedule is that savings are realized by postponing purchases of materials, the use of labor, and other costs until necessary.

Applying CPM to the computer design project

Following through the steps just described, we find the critical path and early and late start times as shown in Exhibit 11.5.

CPM with Three Activity Time Estimates

If a single estimate of the time required to complete an activity is not reliable, the best procedure is to use three time estimates. These three times not only give us the opportunity to estimate the activity time but also to obtain a probability estimate for completion time for the entire network. Briefly, the

EXHIBIT 11.5   **CPM Network for Computer Design Project**

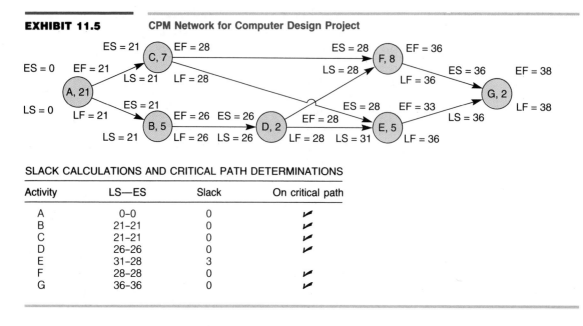

SLACK CALCULATIONS AND CRITICAL PATH DETERMINATIONS

Activity	LS—ES	Slack	On critical path
A	0–0	0	✔
B	21–21	0	✔
C	21–21	0	✔
D	26–26	0	✔
E	31–28	3	
F	28–28	0	✔
G	36–36	0	✔

procedure is as follows: The estimated activity time is a weighted average, with more weight given to the best estimate and less to the maximum and minimum times. The ratio generally used is 4, 1, 1 as shown later. The estimated completion time of the network is computed using basic statistics which states that the standard deviation of a sequence of events is the square root of the sum of the variances of each event. This is the logic of Z shown in Step 7 below. Then, simply by locating Z (the number of standard deviations) in a probability table (as in Appendix E) we obtain the probability of completion. We use the same example as previously, with the exception that activities have three time estimates.

1. *Identify each activity to be done in the project.*

2. *Determine the sequence of activities and construct a network reflecting the precedence relationships.*

3. *The three estimates for an activity time are*

a = Optimistic time: the minimum reasonable period of time in which the activity can be completed. (There is only a small probability, typically assumed to be 1 percent, that the activity can be completed in a shorter period of time.)

m = Most likely time: the best guess of the time required. Since m would be the time thought most likely to appear, it is also the mode of the beta distribution discussed in Step 4.

b = Pessimistic time: the maximum reasonable period of time the activity would take to be completed. (There is only a small probability, typically assumed to be 1 percent, that it would take longer).

Typically, this information is gathered from those people who are to perform the activity.

4. *Calculate the expected time (ET) for each activity.* The formula for this calculation is as follows:

$$ET = \frac{a + 4m + b}{6}$$

This is based on the beta statistical distribution and weights the most likely time (m) four times more than either the optimistic time (a) or the pessimistic time (b). The beta distribution is extremely flexible; it can take on the variety of forms that typically arise, it has finite end points, which limit the possible activity times to the area between a and b (see Exhibit 11.6), and, in the simplified version permits straightforward computation of the activity mean and standard deviation. Four typical beta curves are illustrated in Exhibit 11.6.

5. *Determine the critical path.* Using the estimated times a critical path is calculated in the same way as the single time case.

6. *Calculate the variances (σ^2) of the activity times.* Specifically, this is the variance, σ^2, associated with each ET, and is computed as follows:

$$\sigma^2 = \left(\frac{b - a}{6}\right)^2$$

As you can see, the variance is the square of one sixth the difference between the two extreme time estimates, and of course, the greater this difference, the larger the variance.

7. *Determine the probability of completing the project on a given date.* A valuable feature of using three time estimates is that it enables the analyst to assess the effect of uncertainty on project completion time. The mechanics of deriving this probability are as follows:

a. Sum the variance values associated with each activity on the critical path.

b. Substitute this figure, along with the project due date and the project expected completion time, into the Z transformation formula. This formula is:

$$Z = \frac{D - T_E}{\sqrt{\Sigma\sigma_{cp}^2}}$$

where

D = Desired completion date for project

T_E = Earliest expected completion time for the project

$\Sigma\sigma_{cp}^2$ = Sum of the variances along the critical path

c. Calculate the value of Z, which is the number of standard deviations the project due date is from the expected completion time.

d. Using the value for Z, find the probability of meeting the project due date (using a table of normal probabilities such as Appendix E). The *earliest expected completion time* is the starting time plus the sum of the activity times on the critical path.

EXHIBIT 11.6   **Typical Beta Curves**

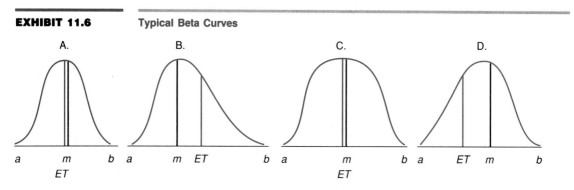

Curve A indicates very little uncertainty about the activity time, and since it is symmetrical, the expected time (*ET*) and the most likely or modal time (*m*) fall along the same point.

Curve B indicates a high probability of finishing the activity early, but if something goes wrong, the activity time could be greatly extended.

Curve C is almost a rectangular distribution, which suggests that the estimator sees the probability of finishing the activity early or late as equally likely, and $m \cong ET$.

Curve D indicates that there is a small chance of finishing the activity early, but it is more probable that it will take an extended period of time.

EXHIBIT 11.7

Activity Expected Times and Variances

Activity	Activity Designation	TIME ESTIMATES a	m	b	Expected Times (*ET*) $\dfrac{a + 4m + b}{6}$	Activity Variances (σ^2) $\left(\dfrac{b - a}{6}\right)^2$
Design	A	10	22	28	21	9
Build prototype	B	4	4	10	5	1
Evaluate equipment	C	4	6	14	7	2⅞
Test prototype	D	1	2	3	2	⅑
Write report	E	1	5	9	5	1⅞
Write methods report	F	7	8	9	8	⅑
Write final report	G	2	2	2	2	0

Following the steps just outlined, we developed Exhibit 11.7 showing expected times and variances. The project network was created the same as we did previously. The only difference is that the activity times are weighted averages. We determine the critical path as before, using these values as if they were single numbers. The difference between the single time estimate and range of three times is in computing probabilities of completion. Exhibit 11.8 shows the network and critical path.

Since there are two critical paths in the network, a decision must be made as to which variances to use in arriving at the probability of meeting the project due date. A conservative approach dictates that the path with the largest total variance be used since this would focus management's attention on the activities most likely to exhibit broad variations. On this basis, the variances

EXHIBIT 11.8   **Computer Design Project with Three Time Estimates**

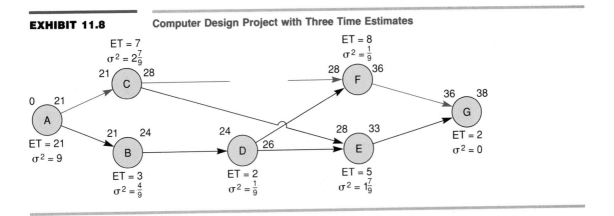

associated with activities A, C, E, and G would be used to find the probability of completion. Thus $\Sigma\sigma_{cp}^2 = 9 + 2\frac{7}{9} + \frac{1}{9} + 0 = 11.89$. Suppose management asks for the probability of completing the project in 35 weeks. D, then, is 35. The earliest expected completion time was found to be 38. Substituting into the Z equation and solving, we obtain

$$ Z = \frac{D - T_E}{\sqrt{\Sigma\sigma_{cp}^2}} = \frac{35 - 38}{\sqrt{11.89}} = -0.87 $$

Looking at Appendix E we see that a Z value -0.87 yields a probability of 0.19, which means that the project manager has only about a 19 percent chance of completing the project in 35 weeks.

Maintaining Ongoing Project Schedules

It is important to keep a project schedule accurate and current. The schedule tracks progress and identifies problems as they occur while corrective time may still be available. It also monitors the progress of cost and is often the basis for partial payments. Yet, schedules are often sloppily kept, or even totally abandoned.

Excuses for failing to maintain project schedules are several:

"The project schedule was required by the contractor for us to get the contract, but we don't really need it to operate."

"I don't have the time to send in a report every week and neither do my personnel."

"The time and cost estimates we gave you were only wild guesses anyway, and what do you get when you revise and report on guesses?"

Perhaps the most important reasons are that managers are not committed enough to the technique to insist that schedules be kept up, with the resulting poor schedules giving project scheduling a bad name. Experience in project scheduling techniques is important and this job should not be carelessly relegated to the closest warm body. The project manager must support the schedule and see to it that it is maintained

Standardized Networks

When projects are repeated (another building built, another golf course designed) logic seems to imply that some part of the experience on the last project should be reusable. Clifford Gray et al. suggest the use of standardized networks.[1] Often project managers have been reluctant to use network techniques because of the high cost to analyze project components, determine resource levels, develop networks, and collect data. The clearest case for standard networks would be the contractor who uses the same activity network in a high-rise apartment, office, or hotel because each floor is typically similar. How about a home builder who builds standard models?

The advantages of standardized networks are:

1. Preparation effort for the network is greatly reduced.
2. Data are more reliable since they resulted from a prior application.
3. The entire project planning process can be performed by lower-level personnel.
4. Planning time is greatly reduced.
5. Through close replication of the same or similar projects, communication and coordination are greatly improved.

The procedure that we used earlier to calculate expected completion times, early start and early finish times, and so forth is also used in standardized networks. The network is retained either in a computer program or as an accessible file; whenever that project is to be repeated, the network is brought up and modified to suit the present application, if necessary. Any one of the project management computer programs in Exhibit 11.13 can be used for this purpose.

11.5   TIME-COST MODELS

In practice, project managers are as much concerned with the cost to complete a project as with the time to complete the project. For this reason, **time-cost models** have been devised. These models—extensions of PERT and CPM—attempt to develop a minimum-cost schedule for an entire project and to control budgetary expenditures during the project.

---

[1] Clifford F. Gray, Bruce Woodworth, and Sean Shanahan, "Standardized Networks: An Extension for Further Reducing Input Requirements," *Project Management Quarterly* 13, no. 3 (September 1982), pp. 32–34.

Minimum-Cost Scheduling (Time—Cost Trade-Off)

The basic assumption in minimum-cost scheduling is that there is a relationship between activity completion time and the cost of a project. On one hand, it costs money to expedite an activity; on the other, it costs money to sustain (or lengthen) the project. The costs associated with expediting activities are termed *activity direct costs* and add to the project direct cost. Some of these may be worker related, such as overtime work, hiring more workers, and transferring workers from other jobs, while others are resource related, such as buying or leasing additional or more efficient equipment and drawing on additional support facilities.

The costs associated with sustaining the project are termed *project indirect costs:* overhead, facilities, and resource opportunity costs, and, under certain contractual situations, penalty costs or lost incentive payments. Since *activity direct costs* and *project indirect costs* are opposing costs dependent on time, the scheduling problem is essentially one of finding the project duration that minimizes their sum or, in other words, finding the optimum point in a time—cost trade-off.

The procedure for finding this point consists of the following five steps; it is explained by using the simple four-activity network that we expanded from Exhibit 11.4 and it is shown in Exhibit 11.9. Assume in this example that the indirect costs remain constant for eight days and then increase at the rate of $5 per day.

1. *Prepare a CPM-type network diagram.*   For each activity this diagram should list:

   a. Normal cost (NC): The lowest expected activity cost (these are the lesser of the cost figures shown under each node in Exhibit 11.9).

   b. Normal time (NT): The time associated with each normal cost.

   c. Crash time (CT): The shortest possible activity time.

   d. Crash cost (CC): The cost associated with each crash time.

2. *Determine the cost per unit of time (assume days) to expedite each activity.* The relationship between activity time and cost may be shown graphically by plotting CC and CT coordinates and connecting them to the NC and NT coordinates by a concave, convex, or straight line—or some other form, depending on the actual cost structure of activity performance, as in Exhibit 11.9. For Activity A, we assume a linear relationship between time and cost. This assumption is common in practice and facilitates the derivation of the cost per day to expedite since this value may be found directly by taking the slope of the line using the formula Slope = $(CC - NC) \div (NT - CT)$. (When the assumption of linearity cannot be made, the cost of expediting must be determined graphically for each of the days the activity may be shortened.)

The calculations needed to obtain the cost of expediting the remaining activities are shown in Exhibit 11.10.

3. *Compute the critical path.*   For the simple network we have been using, this schedule would take 10 days. The critical path is A, B, D.

EXHIBIT 11.9   **Example of Time–Cost Trade-Off Procedure**

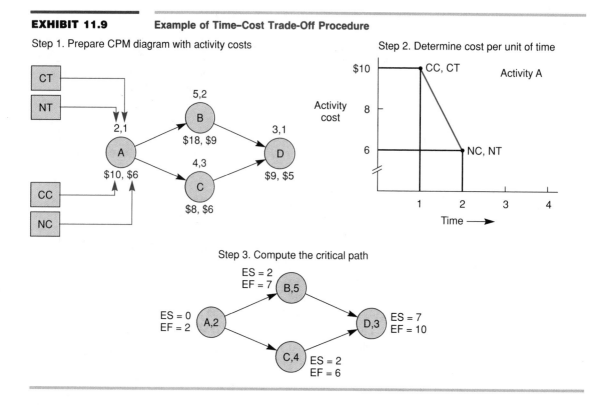

Step 1. Prepare CPM diagram with activity costs

Step 2. Determine cost per unit of time

Step 3. Compute the critical path

EXHIBIT 11.10

Calculation of Cost per Day to Expedite Each Activity

Activity	CC − NC	NT − CT	$\dfrac{CC - NC}{NT - CT}$	Cost per Day to Expedite	Number of Days Activity May Be Shortened
A	$10 − $6	2 − 1	$\dfrac{\$10 - \$6}{2 - 1}$	$4	1
B	$18 − $9	5 − 2	$\dfrac{\$18 - \$9}{5 - 2}$	$3	3
C	$ 8 − $6	4 − 3	$\dfrac{\$8 - \$6}{4 - 3}$	$2	1
D	$ 9 − $5	3 − 1	$\dfrac{\$9 - \$5}{3 - 1}$	$2	2

4. Shorten the critical path at the least cost. The easiest way to proceed is to start with the normal schedule, find the critical path, and reduce the path time by one day using the lowest-cost activity. Then recompute and find the new critical path and reduce it by one day also. Repeat this procedure until the time of completion is satisfactory, or until there can be no further reduction in the

EXHIBIT 11.11

Reducing the Project Completion Time One Day at a Time

Current Critical Path	Remaining Number of Days Activity May Be Shortened	Cost per Day to Expedite Each Activity	Least Cost Activity to Expedite	Total Cost of All Activities in Network	Project Completion Time
ABD	All activity times and costs are normal			$26	10
ABD	A-1, B-3, D-2	A-4, B-3, D-2	D	28	9
ABD	A-1, B-3, D-1	A-4, B-3, D-2	D	30	8
ABD	A-1, B-3	A-4, B-3	B	33	7
ABCD	A-1, B-2, C-1	A-4, B-3, C-2	A*	37	6
ABCD	B-2, C-1	B-3, C-2	B&C†	42	5
ABCD	B-1	B-3	B	45	5

* To reduce the critical path by one day, reduce either A alone, or B and C together at the same time (since either B or C by itself just modifies the critical path without shortening it).

† B&C must be crashed together to reduce the path by one day.

EXHIBIT 11.12   Plot of Costs and Minimum Cost Schedule

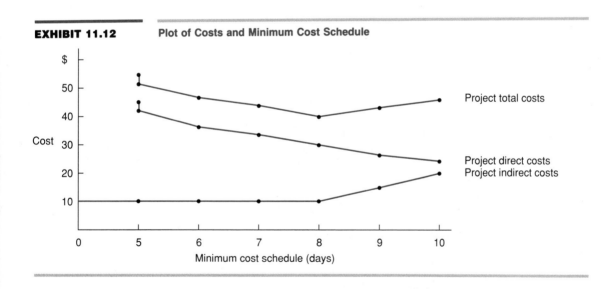

EXHIBIT 11.12

project completion time. Exhibit 11.11 shows the reduction of the network one day at a time.

5. Plot project direct, indirect, and total-cost curves and find minimum-cost schedule.   Exhibit 11.12 shows the indirect cost plotted as a constant $10 per day for eight days and increasing $5 per day thereafter. The direct costs are plotted from Exhibit 11.11 and the total project cost is shown as the total of the two costs.

Summing the values for direct and indirect costs for each day yields the project total cost curve. As you can see, this curve is at its minimum for an eight-day schedule, which costs $40 ($30 direct + $10 indirect).

11.6 COMPUTER PROGRAMS FOR PROJECT SCHEDULING

Many project scheduling programs are available for microcomputers as well as mainframe computers. Kim O'Neal presents data on software produced by 55 companies, organized by price, which ranges from under $100 to $46,000.[2] Exhibit 11.13 compares the features of four microcomputer programs; realize, however, that software programs are continuously being revised and updated.

Exhibits 11.14 to 11.17 show some sample reports available from Microsoft's Project 4.0 program. A very useful report is Exhibit 11.16, which compares cash flow requirements for early start and late start schedules. Exhibit 11.17, the final output from Microsoft's Project 4.0, shows the classic Gantt chart.

11.7 CRITICISMS OF PERT AND CPM

There are several assumptions that need to be made to use project networks and CPM or PERT analysis. This section summarizes some of the more significant assumptions and their criticisms. One point of particular difficulty for the operating personnel is understanding the statistics when three time estimates are used. The beta distribution of activity times, the three time estimates, the activity variances, and the use of normal distribution to arrive at project completion probabilities are all potential sources of misunderstandings, and with misunderstanding comes distrust and obstruction. Thus, management must be sure that the people charged with monitoring and controlling activity performance have a general understanding of the statistics.

1. *Assumption:* Project activities can be identified as entities (that is, there is a clear beginning and ending point for each activity).
   Criticism: Projects, especially complex ones, change in content over time, and therefore a network made at the beginning may be highly inaccurate later on. Also, the very fact that activities are specified and a network formalized tends to limit the flexibility that is required to handle changing situations as the project progresses.

2. *Assumption:* Project activity sequence relationships can be specified and networked.
   Criticism: Sequence relationships cannot always be specified beforehand. In some projects, in fact, ordering certain activities is conditional on previous activities. (PERT and CPM, in their basic form, have no provision for treating this problem, although some other techniques have been proposed that present the project manager with several contingency paths, given different outcomes from each activity.)

---

[2] Kim O'Neal, "Project Management Computer Software Buyer's Guide," *Industrial Engineering* 19, no. 1 (January 1987).

EXHIBIT 11.13   Four Project Management Computer Programs

Vendor name / Product name and version number	Primavera Systems, Inc. Primavera Project Planner 3.0	Breakthrough Software Corp. Time Line 2.0	Software Publishing Corp. Harvard Total Project Manager II	Microsoft Corp. Project 4.0
System requirements				
Operating systems	MS-/PC-DOS 2.0 and higher, VMS 4.4 and higher	MS-/PC-DOS 2.0 and higher	MS-/PC-DOS 2.0 and higher	MS-/PC-DOS 2.0 and higher
Minimum memory	512K	256K	512K	256K
Program characteristics				
Number of tasks per project	10,000	Limited by disk space	280	999
Number of resources per project	Unlimited	Limited by disk space	100	255
Number of resources per task	Unlimited	12	2,000	8
Permits linking of projects	Yes	Yes	Yes	Yes
Permits subprojects	Yes	Yes	Yes	Yes
Permits overlapping tasks	Yes	Yes	Yes	Yes
Permits gaps between tasks	Yes	Yes	Yes	Yes
Permits project sorting	Yes	Yes	Yes	Yes
Dynamic scheduling	No			Yes
Calendar modifications	Workdays, nonworkdays, holidays	Hours, workdays, nonworkdays, holidays	Hours, workdays, nonworkdays, holidays	Hours, workdays, nonworkdays, holidays, by resource
Activity durations supported	Days	Minutes, hours, days, weeks, months	Minutes, hours, days, weeks, months, years	Minutes, hours, days, weeks, months
Costs supported	Fixed costs, variable costs, earned value analysis, proration of costs	Fixed costs, variable costs, earned value analysis, proration of costs, unit costs	Fixed costs, variable costs, earned value analysis, proration of costs	Fixed costs, variable costs
Graphics/report generation				
Chart types supported	Gantt, PERT, resource histogram, calendar, cost	Gantt, PERT, resource histogram, act.-vs.-planned, time-scaled PERT	Gantt, PERT, resource histogram, calendar, cost, Work Breakdown Structure	Gantt, PERT, resource histogram, calendar
Total number standard reports	38	17	24	21
Management-exception reports	Yes	Yes	Yes	Yes
File compatibility				
Formats supported	ASCII, DBF, Lotus WKS, Microsoft Project	ASCII, Sylk, DIF, DBF, Lotus WKS/WRK	ASCII, DIF, DBF, Lotus WKS	ASCII, DIF, DBF, Lotus WKS, Microsoft Chart
Pricing/installed data				
Onetime/Retail purchase price ($)	2,500.00	495.00	595.00	495.00
Number installed (all versions)	4,200	33,000	—	80,000
Comments	Primavision—$1,500; control proj. in I–J & preced. networks using critical path sched. resource level., resource/cost control for proj. to 10,000 activities	Time Line Graphics: presentation quality graphics in time-scaled PERT, actual-vs.-plan Gantt, std. Gantt - $195		Plotter support, resource leveling, links to Primavera Project Planner and Primavision, custom formatting of reports

EXHIBIT 11.14   **Sample Reports Available from MicroSoft Corp's Project 4.0 Software Program**

Activity List

Date: Jun 16, 1987   3:09 PM

Activity Description	Early Start Date	Late Start Date	Total Duration	Slack
Software Selection Plan	Jul 9, 1986 8:00 AM	Jul 9, 1986 8:00 AM	4 Days	None
Define Technical Capabilities	Jul 15, 1986 8:00 AM	Jul 21, 1986 8:00 AM	3 Days	4 Days
Prescreen Vendor Software	Jul 18, 1986 8:00 AM	Jul 24, 1986 8:00 AM	10 Days	4 Days
Define Labor Info Requirements	Jul 15, 1986 8:00 AM	Aug 19, 1986 8:00 AM	4 Days	25 Days

Resource Responsibilities

Date: Jun 16, 1987   4:15 PM

Resource Name	Activity Description	Activity Duration
System Manager	Software Selection Plan	4 Days
	Define Technical Capabilities	3 Days
	Prescreen Vendor Software	10 Days
	Prepare Requirements Report	5 Days

Resource Profile
Period Demand Report
Hours/Month

Date: Jun 20, 1987   11:12 AM

Period ending	Aug 1, 1987	Sep 1, 1987	Oct 1, 1987
1 Draftsmen	736.0	352.0	568.0
2 Asst Facil Mgr	20.0	48.8	130.4
3 Supervsng Engr	161.6	95.2	133.6

Activity Report

Date: Aug 6, 1987   12:00 AM

Activity Number	Activity Description	Scheduled Start Date	Scheduled Finish Date	Total Cost
* 1	Gen mktg plans	Jun 3, 1987 1:00 PM	Jun 24, 1987 12:00 PM	$2492.30
* 2	Assign responsibilities	Jun 24, 1987 1:00 PM	Jul 1, 1987 12:00 PM	$1131.92
3	Consolidate plans	Jun 24, 1987 1:00 PM	Jul 1, 1987 12:00 PM	$1546.34
4	Review product lines	Jun 3, 1987 1:00 PM	Jun 24, 1987 12:00 PM	$4326.92

Resource Cost
Date: Jun 16, 1987 2:58 PM

Resource Number	Resource Name	Resource Unit Cost	Total Cost
1	Junior Analyst	$2200.00 / Month	$924.00
2	System Supvsr	$2800.00 / Month	$3553.84
3	System Manager	$3300.00 / Month	$1644.92
4	Financl Analyst	$2750.00 / Month	$2601.92

Earned Value
Date: Aug 6, 1987 12:00 AM

Activity Number	Activity Description	Total Cost (F)	% Complete	Cost to Date (A)	Cost to Date (F)	Cost to Date Variance
* 1	Gen mktg plans	$2492.30	100%	$2492.30	$2492.30	$0.00
* 2	Assign responsibilities	$452.76	100%	$1131.92	$452.76	$679.15
3	Consolidate plans	$3092.69	100%	$1546.34	$3092.69	-$1546.34
4	Review product lines	$4326.92	100%	$4326.92	$4326.92	$0.00

Duration Variance Report
Date: Jun 20, 1987 11:42 AM

Activity Number	Activity Description	Total Duration (F)	Total Duration (A)	Duration Variance	% Duration Variance
* 1	Reinforced Shop Drawings	24 Days	35 Days	11 Days	+45.83%
* 2	Approve Reinforced Shop Drawings	9 Days	9 Days	None	0%
3	Metal Wall Panel Shop Drawings	13 Days	9 Days	-4 Days	-30.77%
4	Approve Wall Panel Shop Drawings	9 Days	9 Days	None	0%

* Activity on critical path.

EXHIBIT 11.15

Resource Utilization Sample Output from Project 4.0

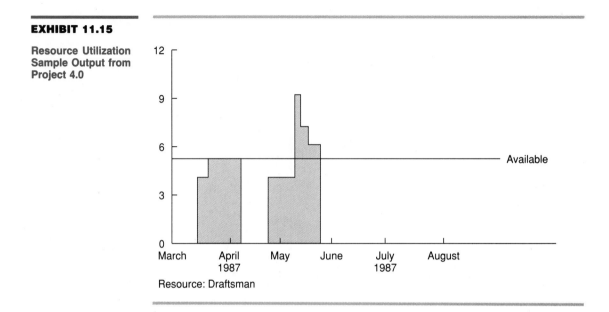

Resource: Draftsman

EXHIBIT 11.16   **Cost Accumulations for Early Start and Late Start Schedules Using Project 4.0 Software**

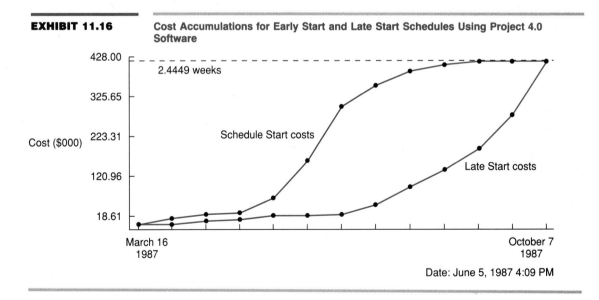

EXHIBIT 11.17   Microsoft Project 4.0 Sample Plotter Output

		Start Date	1987 Sep	Oct	Nov	Dec	1988 Jan	Feb
1	Gen mktg plans	9/ 9/87 9/ 9/87						
2	Assign responsibilities	9/30/87 10/ 7/87						
3	Consolidate plans	9/30/87 10/ 7/87						
4	Hire prototype artist	10/ 7/87 10/14/87						
5	Hire layout artist	10/ 7/87 10/14/87						
6	Review product lines	10/ 7/87 10/21/87						
7	Hire new production crew	10/23/87 10/30/87						
8	Design prototypes	10/28/87 11/11/87						
9	Train new production crew	11/ 6/87 11/20/87						
10	Review prototypes	12/ 9/87 12/23/87						
11	Final selection	12/15/87 12/29/87						
12	Prepare national ads	12/16/87 12/30/87						
13	Draft press releases	12/16/87 12/30/87						
14	Approve press releases	12/30/87 1/20/88						
15	Approve advertising	1/13/88 1/27/88						
16	Produce advertising	1/20/88 2/ 3/88						
17	Press ready	2/ 9/88 2/23/88						

Planned Noncritical ▮ Planned Critical ▮	Microsoft Project 4.0
Actual Noncritical ▯ Actual Critical ▮	Sample Plotter output
Slack Milestone ▭	Hewlett Packard 7475A
Project: DEVELOP Date: Oct 7, 1987 12:00 AM	

3. *Assumption:* Project control should focus on the critical path.
Criticism: It is not necessarily true that the longest time-consuming path (or the path with zero slack) obtained from summing activity expected time values ultimately determines project completion time. What often happens as the project progresses is that some activity not on the critical path becomes delayed to such a degree that it extends the entire project. For this reason it has been suggested that a "critical activity" concept replace the critical path concept as focus of managerial control. Under this approach, attention would center on those activities that have a high potential variation and lie on a "near-

critical path." A near-critical path is one that does not share any activities with the critical path and, though it has slack, could become critical if one or a few activities along it become delayed. Obviously, the more parallelism in a network, the more likely that one or more near-critical paths exist. Conversely, the more a network approximates a single series of activities, the less likely it is to have near-critical paths.

4. *Assumption:* The activity times in PERT follow the beta distribution, with the variance of the project assumed to be equal to the sum of the variances along the critical path.

   Criticism: Although originally the beta distribution was selected for a variety of good reasons, each component of the statistical treatment has been brought into question. First, the formulas are in reality a modification of the beta distribution mean and variance, which, when compared to the basic formulas, could be expected to lead to absolute errors on the order of 10 percent for ET and 5 percent for the individual variances. Second, given that the activity-time distributions have the properties of unimodality, continuity, and finite positive end points, other distributions with the same properties would yield different means and variances. Third, obtaining three "valid" time estimates to put into the formulas presents operational problems—it is often difficult to arrive at one activity time estimate, let alone three, and the subjective definitions of *a* and *b* do not help the matter. (How optimistic and pessimistic should one be?)

A second problem, investigated by Robert R. Britney, relates to the cost of over- and underestimating activity duration times. "Underestimates precipitate reallocations of resources and, in many cases, cause costly project delays. Overestimates, on the other hand, result in inactivity and tend to misdirect management's attention to relatively unfruitful areas causing planning losses." Britney recommends a modification of PERT called BPERT (which employs concepts from Bayesian decision theory) to explicitly consider these two categories of cost in deriving a project network plan.[3]

Another problem that sometimes arises, especially when CPM or PERT is used by subcontractors working with the government, is the attempt to "beat" the network to get on or off the critical path. Many government contracts provide cost incentives for finishing a project early or on a "cost-plus-fixed-fee" basis. Contractors on the critical path generally have more leverage in obtaining additional funds since they have a major influence on the project duration. On the other hand—for political reasons we will not go into here—some contractors deem it desirable to be less visible and therefore adjust their time estimates and activity descriptions to ensure they *won't* be on the critical path.

---

[3] Robert R. Britney, "Bayesian Point Estimation and the PERT Scheduling of Stochastic Activities," *Management Science* 22, no. 9 (May 1976), pp. 938–48.

Finally, the cost of applying critical path methods to a project is sometimes used as a basis for criticism. However, the cost of applying PERT or CPM rarely exceeds 2 percent of total project cost. When used with added features of a work breakdown structure and various reports it is more expensive but rarely exceeds 5 percent of total project costs. Thus, this added cost is generally outweighed by the savings from improved scheduling and reduced project time.

The critical path techniques of PERT and CPM have proved themselves for more than three decades and promise to be of continued value in the future. With the rapidly changing business environment and high costs, management needs to be able to plan and control the activities of the firm. The inherent values of a tool that allows management to structure complex projects in an understandable way, to pick out possible sources of delay before they occur, to isolate areas of responsibility, and, of course, to save time in costly projects virtually ensure that the use of project management will expand. The availability of inexpensive computer programs for project scheduling encourages the expanded use.

11.8 CONCLUSION

Although much of this chapter has dealt with networking techniques used in project management, effective project management involves much more than simply setting up a CPM or PERT schedule. It requires, in addition, clearly identified project responsibilities, a simple and timely progress reporting system, and good people-management practices.

Projects fail for a number of reasons. The most important reason is that those involved do not take project scheduling seriously. Often, personnel who have been newly exposed and those who have had unsatisfactory experiences, do not comply with the procedure. They may neither spend the time to develop their parts of the network, nor to even submit good time and cost estimates. This attitude usually continues throughout the project with a reluctance to revise schedules. Exhibit 11.18 shows that as time passes on the project and new data are entered into the network, the errors become less and less.

We've included Exhibit 11.19 showing the genetic tree for various project scheduling techniques. As we pointed out earlier though, the tree is no longer clear since there have been adaptations and adoptions of features by many of the techniques.

11.9 REVIEW AND DISCUSSION QUESTIONS

1. Define project management.
2. Describe or define work breakdown structure, program, project, task, subtask, and work package.
3. What are some of the reasons project scheduling is not done well?

EXHIBIT 11.18

Reduction in Estimate Error as New Data Occur

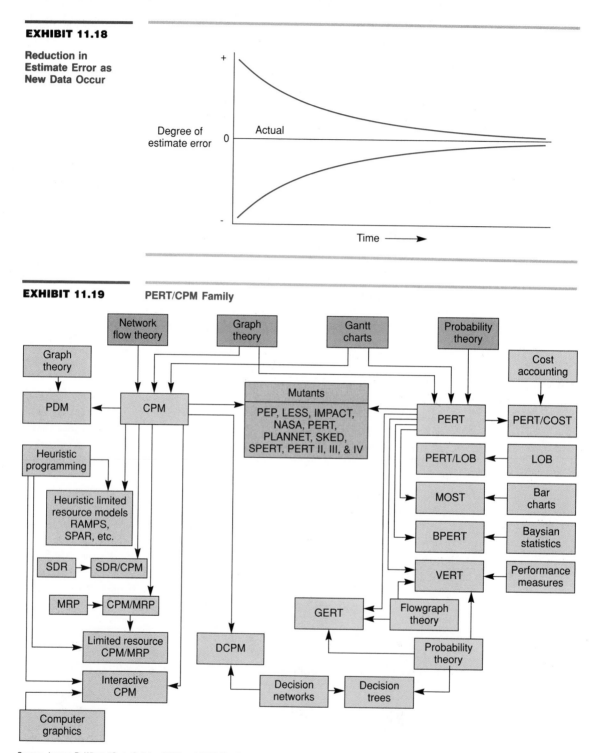

EXHIBIT 11.19   **PERT/CPM Family**

Source: Jerome D. Wiest, "Gene Splicing PERT and CPM: The Engineering of Project Network Models," *Conference Proceedings of the Institute of Industrial Engineers*, 1982, p. 226.

568

4. Discuss the graphic presentations in Exhibit 11.2. Are there any other graphic outputs you would like to see if you were the project manager?

5. Which characteristics must a project have for critical path scheduling to be applicable? What types of projects have been subjected to critical path analysis?

6. What are the underlying assumptions of minimum-cost scheduling? Are they equally realistic?

7. "Project control should always focus on the critical path." Comment.

8. Why would subcontractors for a government project want their activities on the critical path? Under which conditions would they try to avoid being on the critical path?

11.10 PROBLEMS

*1. A project has been defined to contain the following list of activities, along with their required times for completion:

Activity	Time (days)	Immediate Predecessors
A	1	—
B	4	A
C	3	A
D	7	A
E	6	B
F	2	C, D
G	7	E, F
H	9	D
I	4	G, H

a. Draw the critical path diagram.
b. Show the early start and early finish times.
c. Show the critical path.
d. What would happen if Activity F was revised to take four days instead of two?

*2. Following are the precedence requirements, normal and crash activity times, and normal and crash costs for a construction project.

Activity	Preceding Activities	REQUIRED TIME (WEEKS)		COST	
		Normal	Crash	Normal	Crash
A	—	4	3	$10,000	$11,000
B	A	3	2	6,000	9,000
C	A	2	1	4,000	6,000
D	B	5	3	14,000	18,000
E	B, C	1	1	9,000	9,000
F	C	3	2	7,000	8,000
G	E, F	4	2	13,000	25,000
H	D, E	4	1	11,000	18,000
I	H, G	6	5	20,000	29,000

*Complete solutions for Problems 1 and 2 are in Appendix H.

    a. What is the critical path and the estimated completion time?

    b. To shorten the project by three weeks, which tasks would be shortened and what would the final total project cost be?

3. The following activities are part of a project to be scheduled using CPM:

Activity	Intermediate Predecessor	Time (weeks)
A	—	6
B	A	3
C	A	7
D	C	2
E	B, D	4
F	D	3
G	E, F	7

    a. Draw the network.

    b. What is the critical path?

    c. How many weeks will it take to complete the project?

    d. How much slack does Activity B have?

4. American Steam Turbine and Generator Company manufactures electric power generating systems for the major electric power companies. Turbine/generator sets are made to specific order and generally require a three-to-five year lead time. Costs range from $8 to $15 million per set.

    Management has been planning their production using traditional planning techniques such as planning charts, gantt charts, and other shop floor control methods. However, management would now like to introduce CPM project planning and control methods where each turbine/generator set is considered a separate project.

    Following is a segment of the total activities involved in the turbine/generator production:

Activity	Time (weeks)	Immediate Predecessors
a	8	—
b	16	a
c	12	a
d	7	a
e	22	b, c
f	40	c, d
g	15	e, f
h	14	—
i	9	h
j	13	i
k	7	i
l	36	j
m	40	k
n	9	l, m
o	10	g, n

    a. Draw the network.

    b. Find the critical path.

c. If the project is to be cut by two weeks, show which activities would be on the list to be investigated for cutting performance time.

d. If the project is to be cut by 10 weeks, show which activities would be on the list to be investigated for cutting performance time.

5. The R&D Department is planning to bid on a large project for the development of a new communication system for commercial planes. The table below shows the activities, times, and sequences required.

Activity	Immediate Predecessor	Time (weeks)
A	—	3
B	A	2
C	A	4
D	A	4
E	B	6
F	C, D	6
G	D, F	2
H	D	3
I	E, G, H	3

a. Draw the network diagram.

b. What is the critical path?

c. Supposing you wanted to shorten the completion time as much as possible, and had the option of shortening any or all of B, C, D, and G each two weeks. Which would you shorten?

d. What is the new path and earliest completion time?

6. A construction project is broken down into the 10 activities listed below.

Activity	Preceding Activity	Time (weeks)
1	—	4
2	1	2
3	1	4
4	1	3
5	2, 3	5
6	3	6
7	4	2
8	5	3
9	6, 7	5
10	8, 9	7

a. Draw the precedence diagram.

b. Find the critical path.

c. If activities 1 and 10 cannot be shortened, but activities 2 through 9 can be shortened to a minimum of 1 week each at a cost of $10,000 per week, which activities would you shorten to shorten the project by four weeks?

7. A manufacturing concern has received a special order for a number of units of a special product that consists of two component parts, X and Y. The product is a nonstandard item that the firm has never produced before, and scheduling personnel have decided that the application of CPM is warranted. A team of manufacturing engineers has prepared the following table:

Activity	Description	Immediate Predecessors	Expected Time (days)
A	Plan production	—	5
B	Procure materials for Part X	A	14
C	Manufacture Part X	B	9
D	Procure materials for Part Y	A	15
E	Manufacture Part Y	D	10
F	Assemble Parts X and Y	C, E	4
G	Inspect assemblies	F	2
H	Completed	G	0

   a. Construct a graphic representation of the CPM network.
   b. Identify the critical path.
   c. What is the length of time to complete the project?
   d. Which activities have slack, and how much?

8. Following is a CPM network with activity times in weeks:

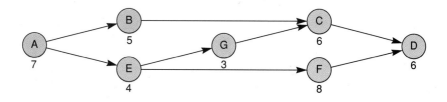

   a. Determine the critical path.
   b. How many weeks will the project take to complete?
   c. Supposing F could be shortened by two weeks and B by one week. What effect would this have on the completion date?

9. The following represents a plan for a project:

Job No.	Predecessor Job(s)	a	m	b
1	—	2	3	4
2	1	1	2	3
3	1	4	5	12
4	1	3	4	11
5	2	1	3	5
6	3	1	2	3
7	4	1	8	9
8	5, 6	2	4	6
9	8	2	4	12
10	7	3	4	5
11	9, 10	5	7	8

   a. Construct the appropriate network diagram.
   b. Indicate the critical path.
   c. What is the expected completion time for the project?
   d. You can accomplish any one of the following at an additional cost of $1,500:
       (1) Reduce Job 5 by two days.

(2) Reduce Job 3 by two days.

(3) Reduce Job 7 by two days.

  If you will save $1,000 for each day that the earliest completion time is reduced, which action, if any, would you choose?

e. What is the probability that the project will take more than 30 days to complete?

10. Following is a network with the activity times shown under the nodes in days:

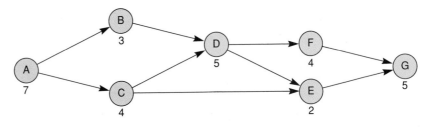

a. Find the critical path.

b. The following table shows the normal times and the crash times, along with the associated costs for each of the activities.

Activity	Normal Time	Crash Time	Normal Cost	Crash Cost
A	7	6	$7,000	$ 8,000
B	3	2	5,000	7,000
C	4	3	9,000	10,200
D	5	4	3,000	4,500
E	2	1	2,000	3,000
F	4	2	4,000	7,000
G	5	4	5,000	8,000

  If the project is to be shortened by four days, show which activities in order of reduction would be shortened and the resulting cost.

11. The home office billing department of a chain of department stores prepares monthly inventory reports for use by the stores' purchasing agents. Given the following information, use the critical path method to determine:

a. How long the total process will take.

b. Which jobs can be delayed without delaying the early start of any subsequent activity.

	Job and Description	Immediate Predecessors	Time (hours)
a	Start	—	0
b	Get computer printouts of customer purchases	a	10
c	Get stock records for the month	a	20
d	Reconcile purchase printouts and stock records	b, c	30
e	Total stock records by department	b, c	20
f	Determine reorder quantities for coming period	e	40
g	Prepare stock reports for purchasing agents	d, f	20
h	Finish	g	0

12.   For the network shown:

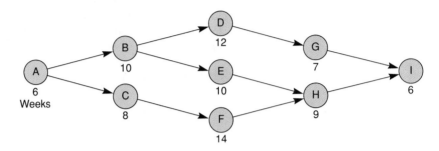

a.   Determine the critical path and the early completion time for the project.

Activity*	Normal Time (weeks)	Normal Cost	Crash Time (weeks)	Crash Cost
A	6	$ 6,000	4	$12,000
B	10	10,000	9	11,000
C	8	8,000	7	10,000
D	12	12,000	10	14,000
E	10	10,000	7	12,000
F	14	14,000	12	19,000
G	7	7,000	5	10,000
H	9	9,000	6	15,000
I	6	6,000	5	8,000

* An activity cannot be shortened to less than its crash time.

b.   Using the data shown, reduce the project completion time by four weeks. Assume a linear cost per day shortened and show, step by step, how you arrived at your schedule. Also indicate the critical path.

13.   The following CPM network has estimates of the *normal time* listed for the activities:

a.   Identify the critical path.

b.   What is the length of time to complete the project?

c.   Which activities have slack, and how much?

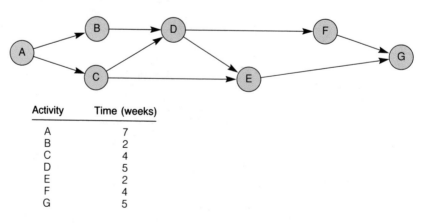

Activity	Time (weeks)
A	7
B	2
C	4
D	5
E	2
F	4
G	5

d. Following is a table of normal and crash times and costs. Which activities would you shorten to cut two weeks from the schedule in a rational fashion? What would be the incremental cost? Is the critical path changed?

Activity	Normal Time	Crash Time	Normal Cost	Crash Cost	Possible Number of Weeks Decrease	Cost/ Week to Expedite
A	7	6	$7,000	$ 8,000		
B	2	1	5,000	7,000		
C	4	3	9,000	10,200		
D	5	4	3,000	4,500		
E	2	1	2,000	3,000		
F	4	2	4,000	7,000		
G	5	4	5,000	8,000		

11.11 SELECTED BIBLIOGRAPHY

Cleland, David I., and William R. King. *Project Management Handbook*. New York: Van Nostrand Reinhold, 1983.

Goodman, Louis J., and Ralph N. Love. *Project Planning and Management: An Integrated Approach*. New York: Pergamon Press, 1980.

Hughes, Michael William. "Why Projects Fail: The Effects of Ignoring the Obvious." *Industrial Engineering* 18, no. 4 (April 1986), pp. 14–18.

Kerzner, Harold. *Project Management for Executives*. New York: Van Nostrand Reinhold, 1984.

O'Neal, Kim. "Project Management Computer Software Buyer's Guide." *Industrial Engineering* 19, no. 1 (January 1987).

Peterson, P. "Project Control Systems." *Datamation*, June 1979, pp. 147–63.

Smith-Daniels, Dwight E., and Nicholas J. Aquilano. "Constrained Resource Project Scheduling." *Journal of Operations Management* 4, no. 4 (1984), pp. 369–87.

————. "Using a Late-Start Resource-Constrained Project Schedule to Improve Project Net Present Value." *Decision Sciences* 18, no. 4 (Fall 1987), pp. 617–30.

Smith-Daniels, Dwight E., and Vikki L. Smith-Daniels. "Optimal Project Scheduling with Materials Ordering." *IIE Transactions* 19, no. 2 (June 1987), pp. 122–29.

Supplement

Learning Curves

EPIGRAPH

Every day in every way I get better and better.

Recollection of Mothers' teachings.

How did we do it the last time?

SUPPLEMENT OUTLINE

KEY TERMS

Learning Curve

Exponential Curve

Time-Constant Model

Forgetting Factor

Learning Percentages

Industry Learning Curves

Progress Curves

Organizational Learning

L earning (or experience) curve theory has a wide range of application. In manufacturing, it can be used to estimate the time for product design and production, as well as costs. Experience curves are important and sometimes overlooked as one of the trade-offs in Just-in-Time systems, where sequencing and short runs achieve lower inventories by forfeiting some advantages of experience benefits from long product runs. Learning curves are also an integral part in planning corporate strategy, such as decisions concerning pricing, capital investment, and operating costs based on experience curves.

In this supplement, we present the simple exponential model which is useful in predicting times and rates based on specific assumptions. We then discuss learning percentages, the duration of learning, management's use of learning curves, and the range of applications of experience curve models.

S11.1 PREDICTING STARTUP PROGRESS: LEARNING CURVES

A **learning curve,** in its basic form, is simply a line displaying the relationship between unit production time and the number of consecutive units of production. Learning curves may be viewed as "internal forecasts" of production output and, as such, are particularly useful in developing bids for new projects. Learning curves are also called *experience curves, improvement curves,* and *progress functions.*

Learning curves can be applied to individuals or organizations. Individual learning is improvement that results when people repeat a process and gain skill or efficiency from their own experience. That is, "practice makes perfect." Organizational learning results from practice as well but also comes from changes in administration, equipment, and product design. In organizational settings, we expect to see both kinds of learning occurring simultaneously and often describe the combined effect with a single learning curve.

Learning curve theory is based on three assumptions:

1. The amount of time required to complete a given task or unit of a product will be less each time the task is undertaken.
2. The unit time will decrease at a decreasing rate.
3. The reduction in time will follow a predictable pattern.

Each of these assumptions was found to hold true in the airframe industry, where learning curves were first applied. Specifically, it was observed that, as output doubled, there was a 20 percent reduction in direct production worker-hours per unit between doubled units. Thus, if it took 100,000 hours for Plane 1, it would take 80,000 hours for Plane 2, 64,000 hours for Plane 4, and so forth. Since the 20 percent reduction meant that, say, Unit 4 took only 80 percent of the production time required for Unit 2, the line connecting the coordinates of output and time was referred to as an "80 percent learning curve." (By convention, the percentage learning rate is used to denote any given exponential learning curve.)

A learning curve may be developed from an arithmetic tabulation, by logarithms or by some other curve-fitting method, depending on the amount and form of the available data.

There are two ways to think about the improved performance that comes with learning curves; that is time per unit (as in Exhibit S11.1A) or as units of output per time period (as in S11.1B and C). *Time per unit* shows the decrease in time required for each successive unit. *Cumulative average time* shows the cumulative average performance times as the total number of units increases. Time per unit and cumulative average times are also called *progress curves* or *product learning,* and are useful for complex products or products with a longer cycle time. *Units of output per time period* is also called *industry learning* and is generally applied to high-volume production (short cycle time).

Note in Exhibit S11.1A that the cumulative average curve does not decrease as fast as the time per unit because the time is being averaged. For example, if the time for Units 1, 2, 3, and 4 were 100, 80, 70, and 64, they would be plotted that way on the time per unit graph, but would be plotted as 100, 90, 83.3, and 78.5 on the cumulative average time graph.

There are, of course, many ways to analyze past data to fit a useful trend line; this supplement focuses on the simple **exponential curve**. We present the simple exponential curve first as an arithmetic procedure and then by a logarithmic analysis.

S11.2 SIMPLE EXPONENTIAL CURVE

Arithmetical Tabulation

In an arithmetical tabulation approach, a column for units is created by doubling, row by row, as: 1, 2, 4, 8, 16. . . . The time for the first unit is multiplied by the learning percent to obtain the time for the second unit. The second unit is multiplied by the learning percent for the fourth unit, and so on. Thus, if we are developing an 80 percent learning curve, we would arrive at the figures listed in column 2 of Exhibit S11.2. Since it is often desirable for planning purposes to know the cumulative direct labor hours, column 4, which lists this information, is also provided. The calculation of these figures is straightforward; for example, for Unit 4, cumulative average direct labor hours would be found by dividing cumulative direct labor hours by 4, yielding the figure given in column 4.

Exhibit S11.3 shows three curves with different learning rates: 90 percent, 80 percent, and 70 percent. Note that if the cost of the 1st unit was $100, the 30th unit would cost $59.63 at the 90 percent rate and $17.37 at the 70 percent rate. Differences in learning rates can have dramatic effects.

In practice, learning curves are plotted on log-log paper, with the results that the unit curves become linear throughout their entire range and the cumulative curve becomes linear after the first few units. The property of linearity is desirable because it facilitates extrapolation and permits a more

EXHIBIT S11.1

Learning Curves
Plotted as Times and
Numbers of Units

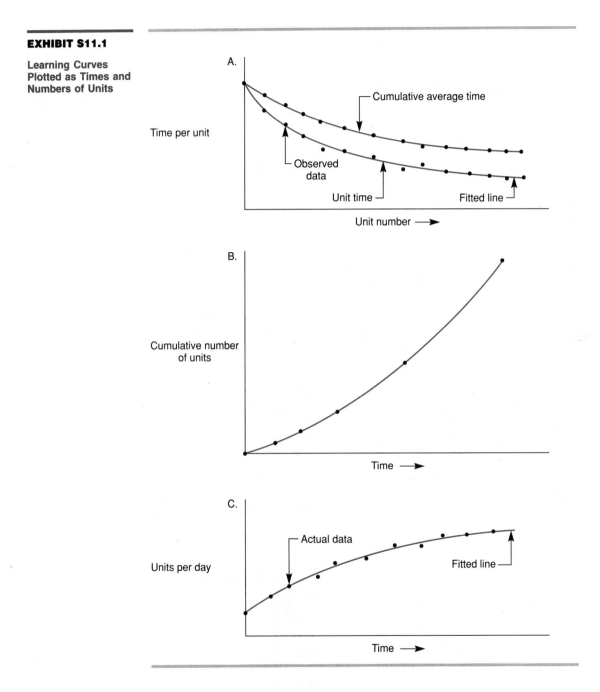

A.

Time per unit

Cumulative average time

Observed
data

Unit time

Fitted line

Unit number →

B.

Cumulative number
of units

Time →

C.

Units per day

Actual data

Fitted line

Time →

EXHIBIT S11.2

Unit, Cumulative, and Cumulative Average Direct Labor Worker-Hours Required for an 80 Percent Learning Curve

(1) Unit Number	(2) Unit Direct Labor Hours	(3) Cumulative Direct Labor Hours	(4) Cumulative Average Direct Labor Hours
1	100,000	100,000	100,000
2	80,000	180,000	90,000
4	64,000	314,210	78,553
8	51,200	534,591	66,824
16	40,960	892,014	55,751
32	32,768	1,467,862	45,871
64	26,214	2,392,453	37,382
128	20,972	3,874,395	30,269
256	16,777	6,247,318	24,404

EXHIBIT S11.3   Arithmetic Plot of 70, 80, and 90 Percent Learning Curves

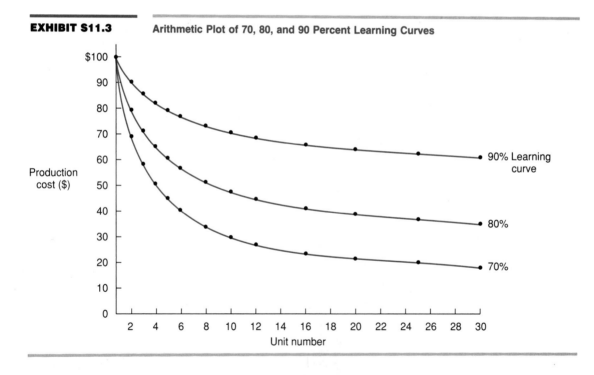

accurate reading of the cumulative curve. Exhibit S11.4 shows the 80 percent unit cost curve and average cost curve on logarithmic paper. Note that the cumulative average cost is essentially linear after the eighth unit.

While the arithmetic tabulation approach is useful, direct logarithmic analysis of learning curve problems is generally more efficient since it does not

EXHIBIT S11.4   **Logarithmic Plot of an 80 Percent Learning Curve**

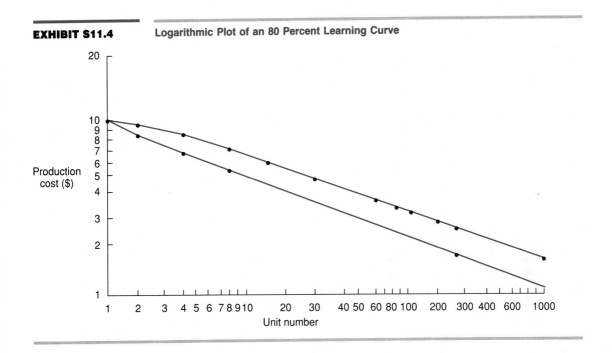

require a complete enumeration of successive time-output combinations. Moreover, where such data are not available, an analytical model that uses logarithms may be the most convenient way of obtaining output estimates.

Logarithmic Analysis

The normal form of the learning curve equation is[1]:

$$Y_x = Kx^n \tag{1}$$

where

x = Unit number
Y_x = Number of direct labor hours required to produce the xth unit
K = Number of direct labor hours required to produce the first unit
n = Log b/log 2 where b = Learning percentage

Thus to find the labor-hour requirement for the eighth unit in our example (Exhibit S11.2), we would substitute as follows:

$$Y_8 = (100,000) (8)^n$$

---

[1] This equation says that the number of direct labor hours required for any given unit is reduced exponentially as more units are produced.

This may be solved by using logarithms:

$$Y_8 = 100,000 \ (8)^{\log 0.8/\log 2}$$
$$= 100,000(8)^{-0.322}$$
$$= \frac{100,000}{(8)^{0.322}}$$
$$= \frac{100,000}{1.9535}$$
$$= 51,900$$

Therefore, it would take 51,900 hours to make the eighth unit.

Learning Curve Tables

When the learning percentage is known, Exhibits S11.5 and S11.6 can be easily used to calculate estimated labor hours for a specific unit or for cumulative groups of units. We need only multiply the initial unit labor hour figure by appropriate tabled value.

To illustrate, suppose we want to double check the figures in Exhibit S11.2 for unit and cumulative labor hours for Unit 16. From Exhibit S11.5, the improvement factor for Unit 16 at 80 percent is .4096. This multiplied by 100,000 (the hours for Unit 1) gives 40,960, the same as in Exhibit S11.2. From Exhibit S11.6, the improvement factor for cumulative hours for the first 16 units is 8.920. When multiplied by 100,000, this gives 892,000, which is reasonably close to the exact value of 892,014 shown on Exhibit S11.2.

A more involved example of the application of a learning curve to a production problem is given in the Insert.

INSERT   Sample Learning Curve Problem

Captain Nemo, owner of the Suboptimum Underwater Boat Company (SUB), is puzzled. He has a contract for 11 boats and has completed 4 of them. He has observed that his production manager, young Mr. Overick, has been reassigning more and more people to torpedo assembly after the construction of the first four boats. The first boat, for example, required 225 workers, each working a 40-hour week, while 45 fewer workers were required for the second boat. Overick has told them that "this is just the beginning" and that he will complete the last boat in the current contract with only 100 workers!

Overick is banking on the learning curve, but has he gone overboard?

Answer: Since the second boat required 180 workers and using a simple exponential curve, then the learning percentage is 80 percent (180 ÷ 225). To find out how many workers are required for the 11th boat, we look up unit 11 for an 80 percent improvement ratio in Exhibit S11.5 and multiply this value by the number required for the first sub. By interpolating between Unit 10 and Unit 12 we find the

EXHIBIT S11.5

**Improvement Curves:
Table of Unit Values**

IMPROVEMENT RATIOS

Unit	60%	65%	70%	75%	80%	85%	90%	95%
1	1.0000	1.0000	1.0000	1.0000	1.0000	1.0000	1.0000	1.0000
2	.6000	.6500	.7000	.7500	.8000	.8500	.9000	.9500
3	.4450	.5052	.5682	.6338	.7021	.7729	.8462	.9219
4	.3600	.4225	.4900	.5625	.6400	.7225	.8100	.9025
5	.3054	.3678	.4368	.5127	.5956	.6857	.7830	.8877
6	.2670	.3284	.3977	.4754	.5617	.6570	.7616	.8758
7	.2383	.2984	.3674	.4459	.5345	.6337	.7439	.8659
8	.2160	.2746	.3430	.4219	.5120	.6141	.7290	.8574
9	.1980	.2552	.3228	.4017	.4930	.5974	.7161	.8499
10	.1832	.2391	.3058	.3846	.4765	.5828	.7047	.8433
12	.1602	.2135	.2784	.3565	.4493	.5584	.6854	.8320
14	.1430	.1940	.2572	.3344	.4276	.5386	.6696	.8226
16	.1296	.1785	.2401	.3164	.4096	.5220	.6561	.8145
18	.1188	.1659	.2260	.3013	.3944	.5078	.6445	.8074
20	.1099	.1554	.2141	.2884	.3812	.4954	.6342	.8012
22	.1025	.1465	.2038	.2772	.3697	.4844	.6251	.7955
24	.0961	.1387	.1949	.2674	.3595	.4747	.6169	.7904
25	.0933	.1353	.1908	.2629	.3548	.4701	.6131	.7880
30	.0815	.1208	.1737	.2437	.3346	.4505	.5963	.7775
35	.0728	.1097	.1605	.2286	.3184	.4345	.5825	.7687
40	.0660	.1010	.1498	.2163	.3050	.4211	.5708	.7611
45	.0605	.0939	.1410	.2060	.2936	.4096	.5607	.7545
50	.0560	.0879	.1336	.1972	.2838	.3996	.5518	.7486
60	.0489	.0785	.1216	.1828	.2676	.3829	.5367	.7386
70	.0437	.0713	.1123	.1715	.2547	.3693	.5243	.7302
80	.0396	.0657	.1049	.1622	.2440	.3579	.5137	.7231
90	.0363	.0610	.0987	.1545	.2349	.3482	.5046	.7168
100	.0336	.0572	.0935	.1479	.2271	.3397	.4966	.7112
120	.0294	.0510	.0851	.1371	.2141	.3255	.4830	.7017
140	.0262	.0464	.0786	.1287	.2038	.3139	.4718	.6937
160	.0237	.0427	.0734	.1217	.1952	.3042	.4623	.6869
180	.0218	.0397	.0691	.1159	.1879	.2959	.4541	.6809
200	.0201	.0371	.0655	.1109	.1816	.2887	.4469	.6757
250	.0171	.0323	.0584	.1011	.1691	.2740	.4320	.6646
300	.0149	.0289	.0531	.0937	.1594	.2625	.4202	.6557
350	.0133	.0262	.0491	.0879	.1517	.2532	.4105	.6482
400	.0121	.0241	.0458	.0832	.1453	.2454	.4022	.6419
450	.0111	.0224	.0431	.0792	.1399	.2387	.3951	.6363
500	.0103	.0210	.0408	.0758	.1352	.2329	.3888	.6314
600	.0090	.0188	.0372	.0703	.1275	.2232	.3782	.6229
700	.0080	.0171	.0344	.0659	.1214	.2152	.3694	.6158
800	.0073	.0157	.0321	.0624	.1163	.2086	.3620	.6098
900	.0067	.0146	.0302	.0594	.1119	.2029	.3556	.6045
1,000	.0062	.0137	.0286	.0569	.1082	.1980	.3499	.5998
1,200	.0054	.0122	.0260	.0527	.1020	.1897	.3404	.5918
1,400	.0048	.0111	.0240	.0495	.0971	.1830	.3325	.5850
1,600	.0044	.0102	.0225	.0468	.0930	.1773	.3258	.5793
1,800	.0040	.0095	.0211	.0446	.0895	.1725	.3200	.5743
2,000	.0037	.0089	.0200	.0427	.0866	.1683	.3149	.5698
2,500	.0031	.0077	.0178	.0389	.0806	.1597	.3044	.5605
3,000	.0027	.0069	.0162	.0360	.0760	.1530	.2961	.5530

Source: R. C. Meier, *Cases in Production and Operations Management* (New York: McGraw-Hill), pp. 310–14.

EXHIBIT S11.6

Improvement Curves: Table of Cumulative Values

IMPROVEMENT RATIOS

Unit	60%	65%	70%	75%	80%	85%	90%	95%
1	1.000	1.000	1.000	1.000	1.000	1.000	1.000	1.000
2	1.600	1.650	1.700	1.750	1.800	1.850	1.900	1.950
3	2.045	2.155	2.268	2.384	2.502	2.623	2.746	2.872
4	2.405	2.578	2.758	2.946	3.142	3.345	3.556	3.774
5	2.710	2.946	3.195	3.459	3.738	4.031	4.339	4.662
6	2.977	3.274	3.593	3.934	4.299	4.688	5.101	5.538
7	3.216	3.572	3.960	4.380	4.834	5.322	5.845	6.404
8	3.432	3.847	4.303	4.802	5.346	5.936	6.574	7.261
9	3.630	4.102	4.626	5.204	5.839	6.533	7.290	8.111
10	3.813	4.341	4.931	5.589	6.315	7.116	7.994	8.955
12	4.144	4.780	5.501	6.315	7.227	8.244	9.374	10.62
14	4.438	5.177	6.026	6.994	8.092	9.331	10.72	12.27
16	4.704	5.541	6.514	7.635	8.920	10.38	12.04	13.91
18	4.946	5.879	6.972	8.245	9.716	11.41	13.33	15.52
20	5.171	6.195	7.407	8.828	10.48	12.40	14.61	17.13
22	5.379	6.492	7.819	9.388	11.23	13.38	15.86	18.72
24	5.574	6.773	8.213	9.928	11.95	14.33	17.10	20.31
25	5.668	6.909	8.404	10.19	12.31	14.80	17.71	21.10
30	6.097	7.540	9.305	11.45	14.02	17.09	20.73	25.00
35	6.478	8.109	10.13	12.72	15.64	19.29	23.67	28.86
40	6.821	8.631	10.90	13.72	17.19	21.43	26.54	32.68
45	7.134	9.114	11.62	14.77	18.68	23.50	29.37	36.47
50	7.422	9.565	12.31	15.78	20.12	25.51	32.14	40.22
60	7.941	10.39	13.57	17.67	22.87	29.41	37.57	47.65
70	8.401	11.13	14.74	19.43	25.47	33.17	42.87	54.99
80	8.814	11.82	15.82	21.09	27.96	36.80	48.05	62.25
90	9.191	12.45	16.83	22.67	30.35	40.32	53.14	69.45
100	9.539	13.03	17.79	24.18	32.65	43.75	58.14	76.59
120	10.16	14.11	19.57	27.02	37.05	50.39	67.93	90.71
140	10.72	15.08	21.20	29.67	41.22	56.78	77.46	104.7
160	11.21	15.97	22.72	32.17	45.20	62.95	86.80	118.5
180	11.67	16.79	24.14	34.54	49.03	68.95	95.96	132.1
200	12.09	17.55	25.48	36.80	52.72	74.79	105.0	145.7
250	13.01	19.28	28.56	42.08	61.47	88.83	126.9	179.2
300	13.81	20.81	31.34	46.94	69.66	102.2	148.2	212.2
350	14.51	22.18	33.89	51.48	77.43	115.1	169.0	244.8
400	15.14	23.44	36.26	55.75	84.85	127.6	189.3	277.0
450	15.72	24.60	38.48	59.80	91.97	139.7	209.2	309.0
500	16.26	25.68	40.58	63.68	98.85	151.5	228.8	340.6
600	17.21	27.67	44.47	70.97	112.0	174.2	267.1	403.3
700	18.06	29.45	48.04	77.77	124.4	196.1	304.5	465.3
800	18.82	31.09	51.36	84.18	136.3	217.3	341.0	526.5
900	19.51	32.60	54.46	90.26	147.7	237.9	376.9	587.2
1,000	20.15	34.01	57.40	96.07	158.7	257.9	412.2	647.4
1,200	21.30	36.59	62.85	107.0	179.7	296.6	481.2	766.6
1,400	22.32	38.92	67.85	117.2	199.6	333.9	548.4	884.2
1,600	23.23	41.04	72.49	126.8	218.6	369.9	614.2	1001.
1,800	24.06	43.00	76.85	135.9	236.8	404.9	678.8	1116.
2,000	24.83	44.84	80.96	144.7	254.4	438.9	742.3	1230.
2,500	26.53	48.97	90.39	165.0	296.1	520.8	897.0	1513.
3,000	27.99	52.62	98.90	183.7	335.2	598.9	1047.	1791.

improvement ratio equal to 0.4629. This yields 104.15 workers (.4629 interpolated from table × 225). Thus, Overick's estimate missed the boat by 4 people.

SUB has produced the first unit of a new line of minisubs at a cost of $500,000—$200,000 for materials and $300,000 for labor. It has agreed to accept a 10 percent profit, based on cost, and it is willing to contract on the basis of a 70 percent learning curve. What will be the contract price for three minisubs?

Cost of first sub		$ 500,000
Cost of second sub		
Materials	$200,000	
Labor: $300,000 × .70	210,000	410,000
Cost of third sub		
Materials	200,000	
Labor: $300,000 × .5682	170,460	370,460
Total cost		1,280,460
Markup: $1,280,460 × .10		128,046
Selling price		$1,408,506

If the operation is interrupted, then some relearning must occur. How far to go back up the learning curve can be estimated in some cases; we discuss this later in the supplement.

Estimating the Learning Percentage

If production has been underway for some time, the learning percentage is easily obtained from production records. Generally speaking, the longer the production history, the more accurate the estimate. Since a variety of other problems can occur during the early stages of production, most companies do not begin to collect data for learning curve analysis until some units have been completed.

Statistical analysis should also be used. For example, in an exponential learning curve to find out how well the curve fits past data, it can be converted to a straight-line logarithmic (data plotted on log-log graph paper). If the data are questionable because they do not fit a line well, a correlation analysis is performed. A good correlation would be about .90. A correlation of .70 or less when the number of data points is 20 or more would be considered a poor fit.

If production has not started, estimating the learning percentage becomes enlightened guesswork. In these cases the analyst has these options:

1. Assume that the learning percentage will be the same as it has been for previous applications within the same industry.
2. Assume that it will be the same as it has been for the same or similar products.
3. Analyze the similarities and differences between the proposed startup and previous startups and develop a revised learning percentage that appears best to fit the situation.

In selecting the option, the decision turns to how closely the startup under consideration approximates previous startups in the same industry or with the same or similar products. In any case, while a number of industries have used learning curves extensively, acceptance of the industry norm (such as the 80 percent figure for the airframe industry) is risky. An analysis of the company's own data should be undertaken even though it may ultimately lead to the industry improvement percentage.

There are two reasons for disparities between a firm's learning rate and that of its industry. First, there are the inevitable differences in operating characteristics between any two firms, stemming from the equipment, methods, product design, plant organization, and so forth. Second, procedural differences are manifested in the development of the learning percentage itself, such as whether the industry rate is based on a single product or on a product line, and the manner in which the data were aggregated.

How Long Does Learning Go On?

Does output stabilize, or is there continual improvement? Some areas can be shown to improve continually even over decades—radios, computers, and other electronic devices; and, if we allow for the effects of inflation, also automobiles, washing machines, refrigerators, and most other manufactured goods. If the learning curve has been valid for several hundreds or thousands of units, it will probably be valid for several hundreds or thousands more. On the other hand, highly automated systems may have a near zero learning curve since, after installation, they quickly reach a constant volume.

S11.3 GENERAL GUIDELINES FOR LEARNING

In this supplement we presented learning curve theory without focusing on any specific subject of learning. That is, "who or what is doing the learning?" Helpful guidelines could be developed for learners whether they are individuals, machines, computers, organizations, or animals. We summarize some guidelines which can improve individual learning and organizational learning.

Individual Learning

A number of factors affect an individual's performance and rate of learning. We should not forget the two elements involved: the rate of learning and the initial starting levels. To explain this more clearly, compare the two learning curves in Exhibit S11.7. Suppose these were the times for two individuals who performed a simple mechanical test administered by the personnel department as part of their application for employment in the assembly area of manufacturing.

EXHIBIT S11.7

**Test Results of Two
Job Applicants**

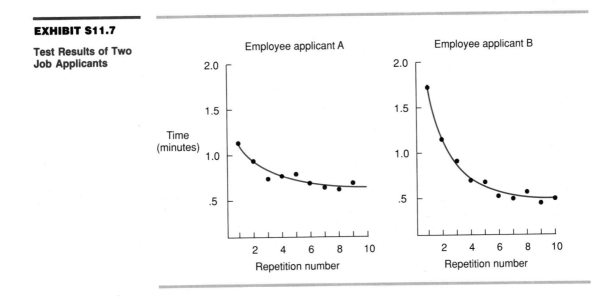

Which applicant would you hire? Applicant A had a much lower starting point but a slower learning rate. Applicant B, although starting at a much higher rate, is clearly the better choice. This points out that performance times are important—not just the learning rate by itself.

Some general guidelines to improve individual performance based on learning curves:

1. *Proper selection of workers.* A test should be administered to help choose the workers. These tests should be representative of the planned work: A dexterity test for assembly work, a mental ability test for mental work, tests for interaction with customers for front office work, and so on.

2. *Proper training.* The more effective the training, the faster the learning rate.

3. *Motivation.* Productivity gains based on learning curves are not achieved unless there is a reward. Rewards can be money (individual or group incentive plans) or nonmonetary (such as employee of the month, etc.).

4. *Work specialization.* As a general rule, the simpler the task, the faster the learning. Be careful that boredom doesn't interfere; if it does, redesign the task.

5. *Do one or very few jobs at a time.* Learning is faster on each job if completed one at a time, rather than working on all jobs simultaneously.

6. *Use tools or equipment that assist or support performance.*

7. *Provide quick and easy access for help.* The benefits from training are realized and continue when assistance is available.

8. *Allow workers to help redesign their tasks.* Taking more performance factors into the scope of the learning curve can, in effect, shift the curve downward.

Organizational Learning

When referring to learning curves, most people tend to think of individual performance, that is, the increase in output as the individual gains experience. Organizations learn as well. For example, in a manufacturing unit the learning curve would include technology, equipment, engineering, and training.

Learning rates differ among firms and across industries. These differences are due to the peculiarities and opportunities in various industries, as well as individual firms' performances. Exhibit S11.8 depicts the learning rates in 108 firms in various industries. While the majority of firms had learning rates of 70 to 80 percent, several were lower and higher. One firm had very rapid learning rate of 55 to 56 percent. At the other extreme, one firm had a learning rate of 107 to 108 percent. (We wonder if this firm is still in business.) Any learning rate greater than 100 percent means dislearning; or, the more times a task is done, the longer it takes.

Learning curves are widely used by major firms in developing corporate strategy.

Learning curves reflect the cost-volume relationship that exists for a company's product line. This means that a firm has at its disposal a tool to predict its manufacturing costs and, hence, to set cost-based sales prices. For setting corporate strategy then, a firm with a good understanding of its own learning curve might choose the following approach for a new product: Price the product low to establish its market share and then sustain this share by continuing to reduce its price to reflect the cost reduction gained from experience. Alternatively, a firm facing an existing market may use the learning curve idea to see if it is logical to enter with a similar product. This company may examine its own facilities management and worker skills and conclude that it can take advantage of the learning it has achieved from similar products and be competitive sooner (e.g., at a lower volume).

Entering an existing market requires recognition of competitors' learning curves as well. Assume that an existing firm entered the market two years ago, producing 1,000 units per year with an 80 percent learning curve and an initial product cost of $100. If a new firm decides to enter the market now, the existing firm already has its price down to $8.66 for that 2,000th unit. To compete, the new firm must either have a faster learning rate or start at a much lower initial cost. In fact, successful newcomers that enter existing product markets often do so using a high degree of mechanization or even complete automation.

EXHIBIT S11.8

Learning Curve Rates Observed in 22 Field Studies in Different Industries (n = 108)

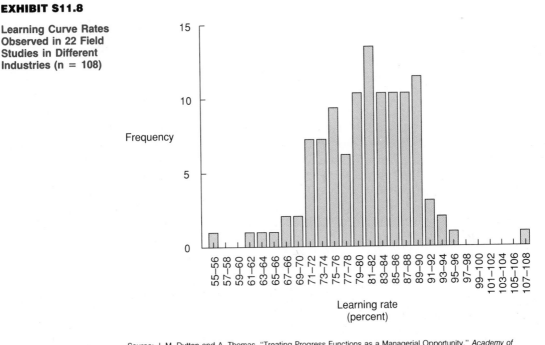

Source: J. M. Dutton and A. Thomas, "Treating Progress Functions as a Managerial Opportunity," *Academy of Management Review* 9 (1984), p. 235.

In contract negotiations for delivery of product in several spaced lots, or in follow-on contracts, a great deal of care must be taken concerning learning rates. The spacing of contracts for identical items can lead to problems between buyer and seller. While the buyer may expect that subsequent contracts are simply continuations of previous contracts, the seller may have significant relearning efforts. The longer the spacing between contracts, the greater the opportunity for forgetting and for other changes such as shifting of personnel to other areas, equipment changes, and so forth. For example, new studies are coming out showing organizational learning rates in quality defects and productivity gains. These types of studies should have widespread benefits.

Why do organizations differ in their performance, even when they produce the same product or service? There are a number of reasons, some of these are:

1. *Position on the learning curve.* All other things being equal, the firm that has the higher cumulative output should have the lower cost.

2. *Rate of output.* Studies have shown that recent experience has much more effect in reducing cost than more distant experience. Therefore, if we compare two firms with the same cumulative output, the

firm with the higher rate should have a lower cost curve because its experience is more recent.

3. *Employee participation in productivity and cost reduction.* Programs such as employee stock purchases, profit sharing, and group incentive plans can significantly improve the rate of learning. As in the case of individual performance, groups also need motivation to improve.

4. *Existence of standards.* Without a comparison base, performance cannot be measured. Standards can be historically based (what has been done before); however, it would be better to establish standards using more formal methods. For example, these could be engineering specifications for equipment speeds or stopwatch time studies for assembly operations.

5. *Presence of similar experiences.* A firm can take advantage of its existing experience by choosing complimentary products. Much of the knowledge may be transferrable resulting in a more rapid learning rate as well as starting at a lower initial point. If two organizations produce the same product, the one with a related product has a higher learning rate.

6. *Ability to learn from other firms.* Much can be learned from industry or other data about competitor's performances. However, it is interesting that this knowledge only helps during the initial starting phase. Once underway, a firm's learning is dominated by its own experiences.

7. *Simplification of work tasks.* The simpler the task, the easier it is to learn. Training is a major factor in learning rates. Therefore, simpler tasks normally require less training.

8. *Avoiding discontinuity.* Interruptions require relearning even if it only involves a simple restart of an operation. More lengthy interruptions, such as plant shutdown, or strikes, or those involving employee turnover can take a long time to regain the previous learning curve rate.

9. *Avoid employee turnover.* Organizational learning is a composite of many factors. New employees require training and thereby affect the learning rate.

10. *Maintain demand.* Regressing in learning-curve-based output occurs not only from interruptions in the production process but also from decreased production rates. Rather than reducing production rates to meet reduced demand, make a conscious effort to find alternative markets simply to maintain demand.

11. *Standard design of work tasks for an entire industry.* There are numerous rewards when firms in an industry develop standard designs and procedures. A simple example is when a company can hire a worker

with prior experience from another firm and benefit from that employee's experience. A warning is also evident here and should be heeded: Don't change the design significantly unless it is justified.

12. *Attending meetings, conferences, and professional associations, results in a transfer of knowledge across organizations.*

13. *Hire experienced personnel (especially from the competition).* The value of outside experience is very important during the early stages of a learning curve. Similar to "learning from other firms," after just a short time, progression down the learning curve becomes diluted with the existing firm.

14. *Effects of calendar time.* It is interesting that calendar time is not as good a predictor of performance as cumulative output. Spending some time learning from others at the beginning is important (calendar time to learn from others); however, shortly after productivity begins, the firm's own experience is more important.

15. *Separate the work when operating two or more shifts.* Rather than having two or three shifts with duplicate learning rates for the same jobs, assign different jobs to each of them. Each shift achieves higher productivity by producing more units and moving further down the learning curve.

16. *Economies of scale.* Recognize the benefits of increasing output through economies of scale in equipment, personnel, and operations. Increases in productivity through economies of scale are added to the productivity gains from learning. This double benefit can be reversed, however, if rates or methods are changed and diseconomies of scale occur.

Heart transplants and learning curves

The idea of the same learning rate applying to all parts of a unit's performance is simply not true. As we state elsewhere in this supplement, there are different learning rates for each aspect of performance; for example, one learning rate for labor, another for materials, another for cost, and so on.

Learning curves provide an excellent means to examine performance. The best comparison for one's performance would be the learning rates for competitor's in the industry. Even when a standard or expected level is unknown, a lot can still be learned by simply using and plotting data in a learning curve fashion. As an illustration of this ability to learn about one's performance, we present the experience of a heart transplant facility in a hospital.[2] Do not draw the wrong conclusions from the heart transplant exhibits when you see the

---

[2] David B. Smith, and Jan L. Larsson, "The Impact of Learning on Cost: The Case of Heart Transplantation," *Hospital and Health Sciences Administration* 34, no. 1 (Spring 1989), pp. 85–97.

vertical scale. With the exception of the death rates exhibit, the others are truncated, that is, the starting point is not zero.

In addition to the simple exponential learning curve presented earlier, there are other forms. Some standard models can be fitted to data. The model in the heart transplant analysis was of the form

$$Y_i = B_0 + B_1^{-xB_2}$$

Y_i is the cumulative average resource consumption (the total number of deaths, costs, etc. divided by the number of transplants), B_0 is the lower bound (the minimum), B_1 is the maximum possible reduction (the difference between the first unit and minimum B_0), x is the total number of units produced, and B_2 is the rate of change for each successive unit as it moves toward the lower bound.

Exhibit S11.9 shows the coefficients which were obtained for the model. Exhibit S11.10 shows the cumulative death rate. This seems to follow an industrial learning curve with a rate just over 80 percent. Seven of the first 23 transplant patients died within a year after transplant surgery. Only 4 of next 39 patients died within a year. For the cumulative average length of stay, however, the death reduction rate is approximately 9 percent. Note in Exhibit S11.11 the vertical axis extends from 55 to 15, not 55 to 0.

The least sloping curve (the lowest learning rate) is the cost of heart transplants. Exhibit S11.12 shows that the initial costs were in the vicinity of $150,000. After 51 surviving patients (62 procedures, 11 died), the average cost was still close to $100,000.

Why are learning rates high in death rate reduction and low in average length of stay and the lowest rate in cost reduction? David Smith and Jan Larsson question whether the low learning rates may be related to conservatism in dealing with human lives. Or could it be due to the power and insulation of the heart transplant team from pressure to reduce cost? The importance and purpose of this study on learning curves was to make institutions and administrators aware of learning. Institutions need to behave in a learning curve logic—that is, in pricing as well as a motivation for continuous improvement.

EXHIBIT S11.9

Consumption Coefficients for Heart Transplant Learning Model

	B_0 (asymptote)	B_1 (range)	B_2 (rate)	Percent Decrease
Death rate	.2329	.8815	.2362	21.04%
Length of stay	28.26	23.76	.0943	9.00
Units of service	1,282.84	592.311	.0763	7.35
Adjusted charges	$96,465.90	$53,015.80	.0667	6.45

EXHIBIT S11.10   Cumulative Death Rates, Less than One Year Survival

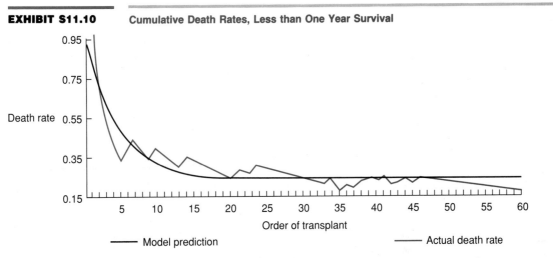

Source: David B. Smith and Jan L. Larsson, "The Impact of Learning on Cost: The Case of Heart Transplantation," *Hospital and Health Services Administration* 34, no. 1 (Spring 1989), p. 92.

EXHIBIT S11.11   Cumulative Average Length of Stay (ALOS) for Heart Transplant Survivors

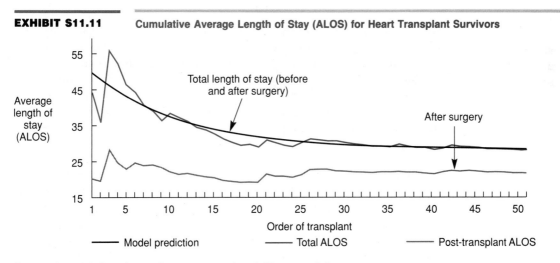

For transplant admission only, actual costs are approximately 50 percent of charges.

Source: David B. Smith and Jan L. Larsson, "The Impact of Learning on Cost: The Case of Heart Transplantation," *Hospital and Health Services Administration* 34, no. 1 (Spring 1989), p. 93.

EXHIBIT S11.12 **Cumulative Average Charges for Heart Transplant Survivors**

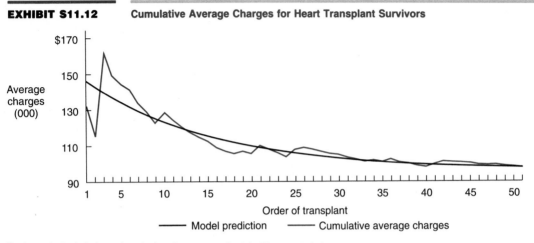

For transplant admission only, actual costs are approximately 50 percent of charges.

Source: David B. Smith and Jan L. Larsson, "The Impact of Learning on Cost: The Case of Heart Implantation," *Hospital and Health Services Administration* 34, no. 1 (Spring 1989), p. 95.

S11.4 THE FORGETTING FACTOR

Forgetting is a function of the amount learned and the length of interruption. Short-term interruptions in production occur when jobs are split and when an expedited job interrupts an existing job. Long-term interruptions require regaining lost knowledge (mental), dexterity (physical), rhythm, work conditions (e.g., building a new workplace), and support services (equipment maintenance, etc.). During long interruptions there may also be changes in personnel and transfer of equipment and facilities to other uses. Long-term interruptions are the most serious because of the degree of changes that may occur.

In this section we cover some of the logic of forgetting and its effects on learning. We show an example where a production order is performed in partial lots and forgetting occurs.

Example

LCM Inc. is negotiating an order for 400 units of product X. Product X carries an initial production time of four hours and an 80 percent learning rate. The order is not particularly large (normally this size order would have manufacturing cost of just under $100,000), but a major question is how to deal with the conditions for delivery. LCM would like to produce the entire lot at one time; however, the customer insists on delivery in four equal batches spread over a two-year period. Focusing on production time per unit, we look at the effects of three levels of forgetting: (1) no forgetting; (2) 50 percent forgetting; and (3) complete or 100 percent forgetting.

If all 400 items are produced consecutively, production rates would start at 2 per day and end at 13.76 per day. The starting rate of two per day is based on an eight-hour work day. Because the first unit was produced in four hours, the rate is 8/4 or two per day for that unit. The second unit has a higher rate. Referring to Exhibit S11.5 under the 80 percent learning rate column, the required time for the second unit 0.8 times the first unit. The rate is therefore 8 hours/(0.8 × 4) or 2.5 per day. The 400th unit in the column takes 0.1453 times the first unit or 0.5812. The daily rate is therefore 8/.5812 or 13.76.

Next we consider the 400 units split as four batches interrupted by significant periods of time. In Exhibit S11.13A there is no forgetting. Production rates are identical to the previous exhibit and would look the same if the segments were pushed together. Exhibit S11.13B has a 50 percent forgetting factor. In this example 50 percent forgetting is taken as one half the distance between the starting rate and the stopping rate of the previous segment. Exhibit S11.13C shows complete forgetting, or where each segment is the same as the first segment. There are no learning curve effects carried over. Production rates for all four segments start at two per day and end at 8.81 per day (from Exhibit S11.5, at 100 units; 8 hours/0.2271 × 4).

With no forgetting, the total amount of time to produce all 400 units is 84.85 × 4 or 339.4 hours (using Exhibit S11.6 and the 80 percent cumulative column, or summing equation (1) for 400 units). With complete forgetting between segments, the total time is 130.6 hours (32.65 × 4) for first segment times 4 segments, or 522.4 hours (Exhibit S11.6 at 100 units × 4).

Finding the total time for the 50 percent forgetting factor is a bit more involved so we are not solving it here.[3] If each batch of 100 units has to be treated as a new separate order (100 percent forgetting), production time increases by 54 percent (183 hours/339.4 hours = 54 percent). A single batch of 400 units takes 339.4 hours while 4 batches of 100 units take 522.4 hours.

LCM's problem, therefore, is to compute the trade-offs of producing in four lots or producing in one lot and carrying that lot forward with periodic deliveries. The final decision would be influenced by the forgetting factor and carrying costs.

Relearning Curves

The so-called classical view of forgetting and relearning is that relearning involves retracking back up the original learning curve. We are not aware of any studies that have uncovered a relearning curve logic. Such logic could form the basis to forecast a relearning curve, though. Nonetheless, the classical view assumption has been challenged.[4]

---

[3] It's necessary to find the equivalent starting unit for each batch. For example, the second batch of 100 takes approximately the time to produce the 5th unit to the 105th unit.

[4] Charles D. Bailey, "Forgetting and the Learning Curve: A Laboratory Study," *Management Science* 35, no. 3 (March 1989), pp. 340–52.

EXHIBIT S11.13   Output Rate per Day with Significant Time Periods between Each of the Four Lots

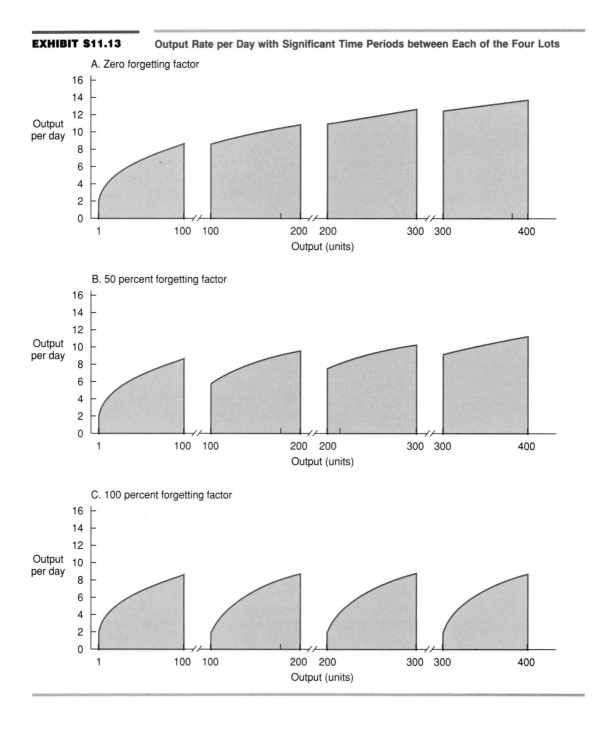

In Exhibit S11.14 we've shown the classical regression back up the learning curve. This was the assumption we used in the previous example in this section. Each batch involved a retracing back up the curve halfway between the start of the last batch and the last unit of the last batch.

In Exhibit S11.15 we've created some other possible learning rates. Learning curve A is a good possibility because it shows a more rapid learning during the early part of relearning, but then declines to the same original learning curve. Learning curve B has a learning rate that shows more improvement than the original rate. This curve surpassing the original could happen through other enhancements, such as changes in performance capability of equipment, technology, design, and personnel during the interruption period.

EXHIBIT S11.14   **Production in Four Lots with Interruptions** (Relearning rate is one half of the improvement of the previous lot)

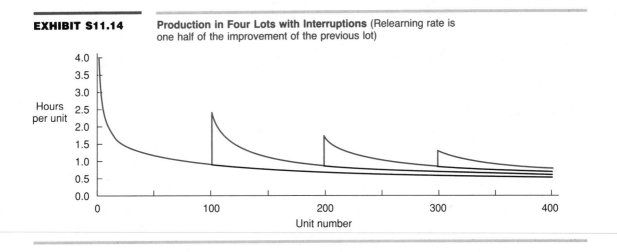

EXHIBIT S11.15   **Producing a Second Lot of 200 Units after an Interruption** (Three possible relearning curves)

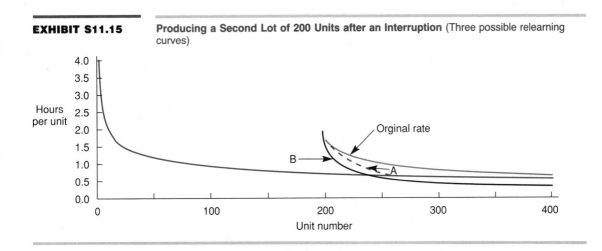

At this point we don't know that much about forgetting and relearning and their effects on output rates. The best guidance that can be offered is that these phenomena do occur—accept them and consider their effects, even though crudely.

S11.5 CONCLUSION

Learning curve theory is of great value. The curves themselves are measures of continuing performance and allow for forecasting future needs. Based on these curves, estimates can be made for such items as production costs, lead times, likelihood of success in entering an existing product market, and so on. Although new technology may have an impact on existing performance, to estimate its impact one can examine learning curves for that type of technology. This prepares the firm not only to expect new innovation but also tells when to expect it.

Forgetting and relearning are two areas of importance. Both the rate of forgetting and the rate to relearn are unclear. Forgetting results from both total interruptions where productivity ceases and decreased rate where output continues but at a slower pace. When operations resume or the pace increases, the actual rate of relearning is unknown. Adequate research does not exist to provide clear insight into forgetting rates and relearning rates. At this point, all we can do is caution that both are difficult to estimate with no clear guidelines.

S11.6 REVIEW AND DISCUSSION QUESTIONS

1. If you kept any of your old exam grades from last semester, get them out and write down the grades. Use Exhibit S11.5 or use log-log graph paper to find whether the exponential curve fits showing that you experienced learning over the semester (insofar as your exam performance is concerned). If not, can you give some reasons why not?

2. How might the following business specialists use learning curves: accountants, marketers, financial analysts, personnel managers, and computer programmers?

3. As a manager, which learning percentage would you prefer (other things being equal), 110 percent or 60 percent? Explain.

4. Discuss the influence of the learning curve forgetting factor on a company's contract bidding.

5. What difference does it make if a customer wants a 10,000 unit order produced and delivered all at one time or in 2,500 unit batches?

S11.7 PROBLEMS

*1. After completing a total of 10 minisubs, SUB (see the Insert in Section S11.2) receives an order for two subs from a Loch Ness Monster search team. Given the

---

* Answers for Problems 1 and 2 are contained in Appendix H.

fact that a 70 percent learning curve prevailed for the previous order, what price should SUB quote the search team, assuming that SUB wishes to make the same percentage profit as before?

*2. A job applicant is being tested for an assembly line position. Management feels that steady-state times have been approximately reached after 1,000 performances. Regular assembly line workers are expected to perform the task within four minutes.

    a. If the job applicant performed the first test operation in 10 minutes and the second one in 9 minutes, should this applicant be hired?

    b. What is the expected time that the job applicant would finish the 10th unit?

3. A time standard was set as .20 hours per unit after observing 50 cycles. If the task has a 90 percent learning curve, what would be the average time per unit after 100, 200, and 400 cycles?

4. You have just received 10 units of a special subassembly from an electronics manufacturer at a price of $250 per unit. A new order has also just come in for your company's product that uses these subassemblies, and you wish to purchase 40 more to be shipped in lots of 10 units each. (The subassemblies are bulky, and you need only 10 a month to fill your new order.)

    a. Assuming a 70 percent learning curve by your supplier on a similar product last year, how much should you pay for each lot? What would be your justification for your bid to the supplier? (Hint: Treat each lot of 10 as your basis for pricing.)

    b. Suppose you are the supplier and can produce 20 units now but cannot start production on the second 20 units for two months. What price would you try to negotiate?

    c. The same as b, but assuming that there is a 50 percent forgetting factor.

5. As a result of the Persian Gulf War, the government's stock of Patriot missiles has been depleted. Rather than replenish existing stock, an order for a new generation antimissile missile will be awarded. The pilot run of these new missiles was already in production during the Persian Gulf War. The first run of 10 missiles had the following times and costs:

Missile Number	Production Hours	Total Cost
1	3,000	$800,000
2	2,300	700,000
3	2,200	690,000
4	1,900	630,000
5	1,800	610,000
6	1,600	620,000
7	1,600	600,000
8	1,500	570,000
9	1,500	570,000
10	1,400	560,000

An order for another 50 missiles is to be awarded. The Department of Defense allows a 10 percent profit on the total contract.

    a. What would you expect the contract price to be?

    b. How long will the *last missile* take to produce?

6. Johnson Industries received a contract to develop and produce four high-intensity long-distance receiver/transmitters for cellular telephones. The first

took 2,000 labor hours and $39,000 worth of purchased and manufactured parts, the second took 1,500 labor hours and $37,000 in parts, the third took 1,450 labor hours and $31,000 in parts, and the fourth took 1,270 labor hours and $31,000 in parts.

Johnson was asked to bid on a follow-on contract for another dozen receiver/transmitter units. Ignoring any forgetting factor effects, what should Johnson estimate their time and parts costs to be for the dozen units? Estimate the learning curve using log-log paper. (Hint: There are two learning curves—one for labor and one for parts.)

7. Lambda Computer Products competed for and won a contract to produce two prototype units of a new type of computer, based on optics using lasers rather than electronic binary bits.

The first unit produced by Lambda took 5,000 hours to produce and required $250,000 worth of material, equipment usage and supplies. The second unit took 3,500 hours and used $200,000 worth of materials, equipment usage and supplies. Labor is $30 per hour.

a. You were asked by your customer to present a bid for 10 additional units as soon as the second unit was completed. Production would start immediately. What would your bid be?

b. Suppose there was a significant delay between both contracts. During this time, personnel and equipment were reassigned to other projects. Explain how this would affect your subsequent bid.

8. You've just completed a pilot run of 10 units of a major product and found the processing time for each unit was as follows:

Unit Number	Time (hours)
1	970
2	640
3	420
4	380
5	320
6	250
7	220
8	240
9	190
10	190

a. According to the pilot run, what would you estimate the learning rate to be?

b. Based on a, how much time would it take for the next 190 units, assuming no loss of learning?

c. How much time would it take to make the 1,000th unit?

9. Lazer Technologies, Inc., (LTI) has produced a total of 20 high-power laser systems that could be used to disable surveillance satellites or disarm and destroy any approaching enemy missiles or aircraft. The 20 units have been produced, funded in part as private research within the research and development arm of LTI, but the bulk of the funding came from a contract with the U.S. Department of Defense (DOD).

Testing of the laser units has shown that they are effective defense weapons, and, through redesign to add portability and easier field maintenance, the units could be truck-mounted.

DOD has asked LTI to submit a bid for 100 units, which DOD intends to deploy throughout all American military bases.

The 20 units that LTI built so far cost the following amounts and are listed in the order in which they were produced:

Unit Number	Cost ($ millions)	Unit Number	Cost ($ millions)	Unit Number	Cost ($ millions)	Unit Number	Cost ($ millions)
1	$12	6	$6	11	$3.9	16	$2.6
2	10	7	5	12	3.5	17	2.3
3	6	8	3.6	13	3.0	18	3.0
4	6.5	9	3.6	14	2.8	19	2.9
5	5.8	10	4.1	15	2.7	20	2.6

   a. Based on past experience, what is the learning rate? (Hint: You may use log-log paper to plot the values and make estimates.)

   b. What bid should LTI submit for the total order of 100 units, assuming that learning continues?

   c. What is the cost expected to be for the last unit, under the learning rate you estimated?

10. Jack Simpson, contract negotiator for Nebula Airframe Company, is currently involved in bidding on a follow-up government contract. In gathering cost data from the first three units, which Nebula produced under a research and development contract, he found that the first unit took 2,000 labor hours, the second took 1,800 labor hours, and the third took 1,692 hours.

In a contract for three more units, how many labor hours should Simpson plan for?

11. Honda Motor Company has discovered a problem in the exhaust system of one of its automobile lines and has voluntarily agreed to make the necessary modifications to conform with government safety requirements. Standard procedure is for the firm to pay a flat fee to dealers for each modification completed.

Honda is trying to establish a fair amount of compensation to pay dealers and has decided to choose a number of randomly selected mechanics and observe their performance and learning rate. Analysis demonstrated that the average learning rate was 90 percent, and Honda then decided to pay a $60 fee for each repair (3 hours × $20 per flat-rate hour).

Southwest Honda, Inc., has complained to Honda Motor Company about the fee. Six mechanics, working independently, have completed two modifications each. All took 9 hours on the average to do the first unit and 6.3 hours to do the second. Southwest refuses to do any more unless Honda allows at least 4½ hours.

What is your opinion of Honda's allowed rate and the mechanics' performance?

12. United Research Associates (URA) had received a contract to produce two units of a new cruise missile guidance control. The first unit took 4,000 hours to complete and cost $30,000 in materials and equipment usage. The second took 3,200 hours and cost $21,000 in materials and equipment usage. Labor cost is charged at $18 per hour.

The prime contractor has now approached URA and asked to submit a bid for the cost of producing *another* 20 guidance controls.

   a. What will the last unit cost to build?

   b. What will be the average time for the 20 missile guidance controls?

   c. What will the average cost be per guidance control for the 20 in the contract?

13. A contract currently in negotiation for two units of a multimillion–dollar product has a major point of disagreement between the parties. One schedule calls for production of both items to be consecutive with the first and second deliveries, and payments taking place at each separate completion. The second schedule calls for a significant production delay between the two units. The accepted bid price on the first unit was $10 million. The disagreement is with the price of the second unit. Since the learning rate in the industry is 80 percent for this type of product, the buyer wants to pay only $8 million for the second unit. The product's manufacturer, however, estimates that there will be a 40 percent forgetting factor (to replan, assign equipment, personnel, facilities, etc).

What price would be fair? Assume that the forgetting factor is linear; i.e., retracing back toward the previous unit the same percent as the forgetting factor. Use Exhibit S11.6.

14. United Assembly Products (UAP) has a personnel screening process for job applicants to test their ability to perform at the department's long-term average rate. UAP has asked you to modify the test by incorporating learning theory. From the company's data, you discovered that if people can perform a given task in 30 minutes or less on the 20th unit, they achieve the group long-run average. Obviously, all job applicants cannot be subjected to 20 performances of such a task, so you are to determine whether they will likely achieve the desired rate based only on two performances.

a. Suppose a person took 100 minutes on the first unit and 80 minutes on the second. Should this person be hired?

b. What procedure might you establish for hiring (i.e., how to evaluate the job applicant for his or her two performances)?

15. A potentially large customer offered to subcontract assembly work which is profitable only if you can perform the operations at an average time of less than 20 hours each. The contract is for 1,000 units.

You run a test and do the first one in 50 hours and the second one in 40 hours.

a. How long would you expect it to take to do the third one?

b. Would you take the contract? Explain.

16. Western Turbine, Inc., has just completed the production of the 10th unit of a new high-efficiency turbine/generator. Its analysis showed that a learning rate of 84 percent existed over the production of the 10 units. If the 10th unit contained labor costs of $2.5 million, what price should Western Turbine charge for labor on the 11th and 12th units to make a profit of 10 percent of the selling price?

S11.8 SELECTED BIBLIOGRAPHY

Argote, Linda, and Dennis Epple. "Learning Curves in Manufacturing." *Science* 247 (February 1990), pp. 920–24.

Bailey, Charles D. "Forgetting and the Learning Curve: A Laboratory Study." *Management Science* 35, no. 3 (March 1989), pp. 340–52.

Camm, Jeffrey D. "A Note on Learning Curve Parameters." *Decision Sciences* 16, no. 3 (Summer 1985), pp. 325–27.

Dutton, J. M., and A. Thomas. "Treating Progress Functions as a Managerial Opportunity." *Academy of Management Review* 9 (1984), p. 235.

Globerson, Shlomo. "The Influence of Job-Related Variables on the Predictability Power of Three Learning Curve Models." *AIIE Transactions* 12, no. 1 (March 1980), pp. 64–69.

Irving, Robert. "A Convenient Method for Computing the Learning Curve." *Industrial Engineering* 14, no. 5 (May 1982), pp. 52–54.

Kopsco, David P., and William C. Nemitz. "Learning Curves and Lot Sizing for Independent and Dependent Demand." *Journal of Operations Management* 4, no. 1 (November 1983), pp. 73–83.

Smith, David B., and Jan L. Larsson. "The Impact of Learning on Cost: The Case of Heart Transplantation." *Hospital and Health Services Administration* 34, no. 1 (Spring 1989), pp. 85–97.

Smunt, Timothy L. "A Comparison of Learning Curve Analysis and Moving Average Ratio Analysis for Detailed Operational Planning." *Decision Sciences* 17, no. 4 (Fall 1986), pp. 475–95.

Towill, D. R. "The Use of Learning Curve Models for Prediction of Batch Production Performance." *International Journal of Operations and Production Management* 5, no. 2 (1985), pp. 13–24.

Yelle, Louie E. "The Learning Curves: Historical Review and Comprehensive Survey." *Decision Sciences* 10, no. 2 (April 1979), pp. 302–28.

SECTION V

THE SYSTEM IN STEADY STATE

The steady-state period is the longest phase of the typical system's life cycle, and managing it constitutes the heart of the operations manager's job. The focus of this period is on production planning and control activities: aggregate planning, inventory control, and scheduling.

For most manufacturers, the steady-state period consists of recurring manufacturing cycles: material acquisition, fabrication, assembly, testing, and distribution of the end product to the field.

For most service firms, the steady-state period consists of daily cycles in which system capacity is made available to the public.

Chapter 12

Aggregate Planning

EPIGRAPH

Harry, I just got the word from marketing. They want us to rough out a plan to make 50,000 Bart Simpson dolls. We're going head to head with an Indonesian producer, and I need your estimates fast!

KEY TERMS

Long-, Medium-, and Short-Range Planning

Aggregate Production Planning

Master Production Schedule

Rough-Cut Capacity Planning

Capacity Requirements Planning

Final Assembly Scheduling

Input/Output Planning and Control

Production Activity Control

Purchase Planning and Control

Production Rate

Work-Force Level

Inventory on Hand

Production Planning Strategies

Pure Strategy

Mixed Strategy

A ny business organization—public or private, manufacturing, services, or agriculture—must start with a plan. Aggregate planning means translating annual and quarterly business plans into broad labor and output categories. Aggregate plans do not specify details but rather groupings; for example, planning for product lines rather than specific products in the line; planning for general numbers of workers needed, rather than how many of each type of skilled worker.

In this chapter, we focus on quantitative techniques for aggregate planning in both manufacturing and service settings. In later chapters, we discuss how the aggregate plan becomes converted into short-term plans for materials ordering and later scheduling.

12.1 OVERVIEW OF MANUFACTURING PLANNING ACTIVITIES

The firm must plan its manufacturing activities at a variety of levels and operate these as a system. Exhibit 12.1 presents an overall view of planning and shows how aggregate production planning relates to other activities of a manufacturing firm. The time dimension is shown as long, medium, and short range.

Long-range planning is generally done annually, focusing on a horizon greater than one year. **Medium-range planning** usually covers the period from 6 to 18 months, with time increments that are monthly or sometimes quarterly. **Short-range planning** covers the period from one day to six months, with the time increment usually weekly.

Long-Range Planning

Long-range planning begins with a statement of organizational objectives and goals for the next two to ten years. *Corporate strategic planning* articulates how these objectives and goals are to be achieved in light of the company's capabilities and its economic and political environment as projected by its *business forecasting*. Elements of the strategic plan include product-line delineation, quality and pricing levels, and market penetration goals. *Product and market planning* translates these into individual market and product-line objectives, and includes a long-range production plan (basically a forecast of items to be manufactured for two years or more into the future). *Financial planning* analyzes the financial feasibility of these objectives relative to capital requirements and return on investment goals. *Resource planning* identifies the facilities, equipment, and personnel needed to accomplish the long-range production plan, and thus is frequently referred to as *long-run capacity planning*. (See Chapter 8 for a discussion of how this is done.)

EXHIBIT 12.1

Overview of Manufacturing Planning Activities

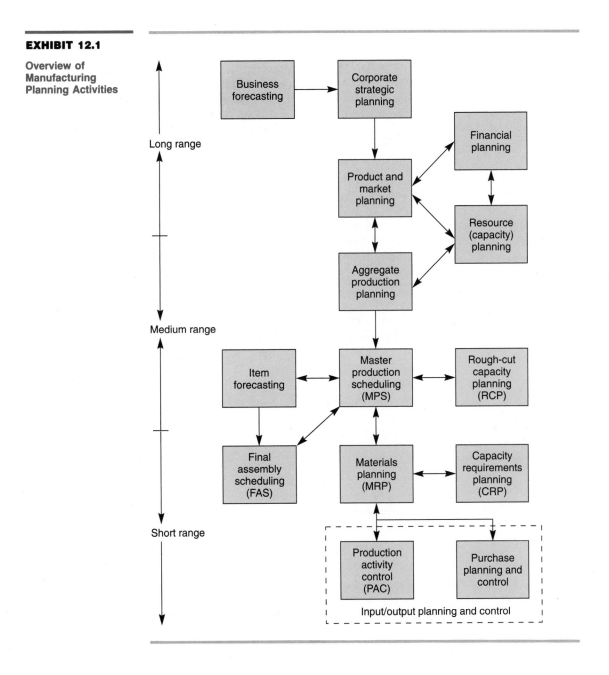

Medium-Range Planning

Aggregate production planning
This activity specifies output requirements by major product groups either in labor hours required or in units of production for monthly periods up to 18 months into the future. Its main inputs are the product and market plans and the resource plan. **Aggregate production planning** seeks to find that combination of monthly work force levels and inventory levels that minimizes total production-related costs over the planning period.

Item forecasting
This provides an estimate of specific products (and replacement parts), which, when integrated with the aggregate production plan, becomes the output requirement for the master production schedule. The process of monitoring and integrating this information is termed *demand management* (as discussed in Chapter 7).

Master production scheduling (MPS)
The MPS generates the amounts and dates for the manufacture of specific end products. The **master production schedule** is usually fixed over the short run (six to eight weeks). Beyond six to eight weeks, various changes can be made, with essentially complete revisions possible after six months (see Chapter 14). As shown in Exhibit 12.1, the MPS depends on the product and market plans and resource plans outlined in the aggregate production plan.

Rough-cut capacity planning
This reviews the MPS to make sure that no obvious capacity constraints would require changing the schedule. **Rough-cut capacity planning** includes verifying that production and warehouse facilities, equipment, and labor are available and that key vendors have allocated sufficient capacity to provide materials when needed.

Short-Range Planning

Materials planning
Also known as *material requirements planning* (MRP), this system takes the end product requirements from the MPS and breaks them down into their component parts and subassemblies. The materials plan specifies when production and purchase orders must be placed for each part and subassembly to complete the products on schedule (see Chapter 14).

Capacity requirements planning
Capacity requirements planning (CRP) should really be referred to as capacity requirements *scheduling*, since it provides a detailed schedule of when

each operation is to be run on each work center and how long it will take to process. The information it uses comes from planned and open orders from the materials plan. The CRP itself helps to validate the rough cut capacity plan.

Final assembly scheduling

Final assembly scheduling provides the operations required to put the product in its final form. It is here that customized or final features of the product are scheduled. For example, a printer manufacturer would typically specify from various options a control panel configuration at this scheduling stage.

Input/output planning and control

Input/output planning and control refers to a variety of reports and procedures focusing on scheduled demands and capacity constraints deriving from the materials plan (see Chapter 15).

Production activity control

Production activity control (PAC) is a relatively new term used to describe scheduling and shop-floor control activities. PAC involves the scheduling and controlling of day-to-day activities on the shop floor. At this point, the master production schedule is translated into the immediate priorities of daily work schedules.

Purchase planning and control

Purchase planning and control deals with the acquisition and control of purchased items, again as specified by the materials plan. Input/output planning and control are necessary to make sure that purchasing not only is obtaining materials in time to meet the schedule, but is also aware of those orders that, for various reasons, call for rescheduling purchases.

In summary, all the planning approaches attempt to balance capacity required with capacity available, and then schedule and control production in light of changes in the capacity balance. A good planning system is complete without being overwhelming, and has the confidence of its users up and down the organization structure.

12.2 HIERARCHICAL PRODUCTION PLANNING

So far, we have looked at manufacturing planning activities within a framework of long range, medium range, and short range. If we were to overlay the organization chart of a firm onto Exhibit 12.1, we would note that higher levels within the organization deal with long-range and lower levels with short-range planning. In a more formal way, Harlan Meal uses the term *hierarchical production planning* (HPP) to tailor the planning structure to the

EXHIBIT 12.2

Hierarchical Planning Process

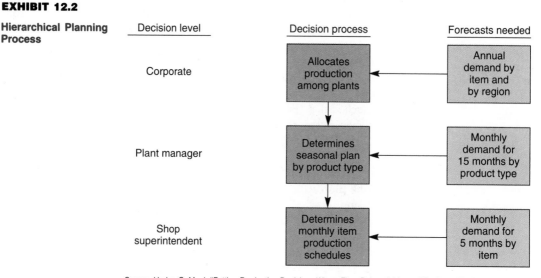

Decision level	Decision process	Forecasts needed
Corporate	Allocates production among plants	Annual demand by item and by region
Plant manager	Determines seasonal plan by product type	Monthly demand for 15 months by product type
Shop superintendent	Determines monthly item production schedules	Monthly demand for 5 months by item

Source: Harlan C. Meal, "Putting Production Decisions Where They Belong," *Harvard Business Review* 62, no. 2 (March–April 1984), p. 101.

organization.[1] As noted in Exhibit 12.2, higher levels of management would use aggregate data for top-level decisions and shop-floor decisions would be made using detailed data. In the extreme case HPP logically states that top management should not become involved in determining the production lot size at a machine center. By the same token, the production line supervisor should not become involved in planning new product lines. Exhibit 12.3 shows some additional decisions and characteristics of HPP.

Meal cites as an example a tire manufacturer with several plants. With a *conventional* approach, each plant would tend to build a stock of tires it was confident of selling. An unsatisfactory consequence was that slow-moving items were produced in small quantities during peak season when capacity was scarce.

By centralizing the decision, top managers expected that they would be able to somehow decide which plants would produce which tires in what quantities. This became impossible; not only were the number of detailed variables much too large to review but also it took the decision-making power away from plant management where it rightly belonged.

The hierarchical procedure divided the decision making, with top management allocating tire production among the plants on an annual basis. Plant management in each of the plants would decide on seasonal effects, buildup of

---

[1] Harlan C. Meal, "Putting Production Decisions Where They Belong," *Harvard Business Review* 62, no. 2 (March–April 1984), pp. 102–11.

EXHIBIT 12.3

Production Planning Decision Hierarchy

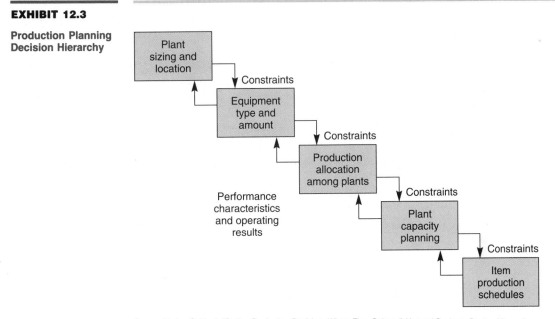

Source: Harlan C. Meal, "Putting Production Decisions Where They Belong," *Harvard Business Review* 62, no. 2 (March–April 1984), p. 106.

inventory, hiring, and so on. Shop management would perform the detailed scheduling of individual items. Shop supervisors, knowing the proportion of time they needed to spend on each product group, could then fill up available capacity.

An advantage of hierarchical planning is that each successive level has a smaller database and a simpler structure.

12.3 AGGREGATE PRODUCTION PLANNING

Again, aggregate production planning is concerned with setting production rates by product group or other broad categories for the intermediate term (6 to 18 months). Note again from our first exhibit that the aggregate plan precedes the master schedule. *The main purpose of the aggregate plan is to specify the optimal combination of production rate, the work-force level, and inventory on hand.* **Production rate** refers to the number of units completed per unit of time (such as per hour or per day). **Work-force level** is the number of workers needed for production. **Inventory on hand** is the balance of unused inventory carried over from the previous period.

A formal statement of the aggregate planning problem is: Given the demand forecast F_t for each period t in the planning horizon that extends over T

periods, determine the production level P_t, inventory level I_t, and work-force level W_t for periods $t = 1, 2, \ldots, T$ that minimize the relevant costs over the planning horizon.[2]

The form of the aggregate plan varies from company to company. In some firms, it is a formalized report containing planning objectives and the planning premises on which it is based. In other companies, particularly smaller ones, "it may take shape in verbal directives or writings on the back of matchbook covers."[3]

The process by which the plan itself is derived also varies. One common approach is to derive it from the corporate annual plan, as was shown in Exhibit 12.1. A typical corporate plan contains a section on manufacturing that specifies how many units in each major product line need to be produced over the next 12 months to meet the sales forecast. The planner takes this information and attempts to determine how best to meet these requirements with available resources. Alternatively, some organizations combine output requirements into equivalent units and use this as the basis for aggregate planning. For example, a division of General Motors may be asked to produce a certain number of cars of all types at a particular facility. The production planner would then take the average labor hours required for all models as a basis for the overall aggregate plan. Refinements to this plan, specifically model types to be produced, would be reflected in shorter-term production plans.

Another approach is to develop the aggregate plan by simulating various master production schedules and calculating corresponding capacity requirements to see if adequate labor and equipment exist at each work center. If capacity is inadequate, additional requirements for overtime, subcontracting, extra workers, and so forth are specified for each product line and combined into a rough-cut plan. This plan is then modified by cut-and-try or mathematical methods to derive a final and, one hopes, lower-cost plan.

Production Planning Environment

Exhibit 12.4 illustrates the internal and external factors that constitute the production planning environment. In general, the external environment is outside the production planner's direct control. In some firms, demand for the product can be managed, as noted in Chapter 7, but even so, the production planner must live with the sales projections and orders promised by the marketing function. This leaves the internal factors as the variables that can be manipulated in deriving a production plan.

---

[2] J. M. Mellichamp and R. M. Love, "Production Switching Heuristics for the Aggregate Planning Problem," *Management Science* 24, no. 12 (1978), p. 1242.

[3] M. Nelson, "I Read the Book: The Master Scheduler Did It" (21st Annual American Production and Inventory Control Society Conference proceedings, 1978), p. 666.

EXHIBIT 12.4   **Required Inputs to the Production Planning System**

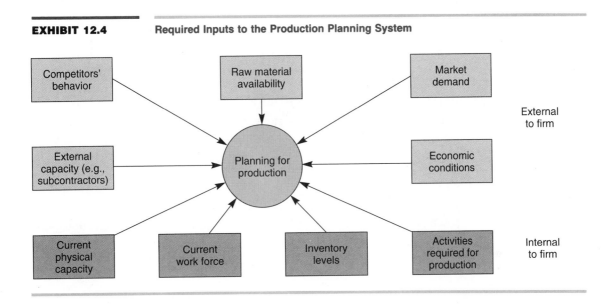

The internal factors themselves differ in their controllability. Current physical capacity (plant and equipment) is usually pretty nearly fixed in the short run; union agreements often constrain what can be done in changing the work force; physical capacity cannot always be increased; and top management may set limits on the amount of money that can be tied up in inventories. Still, there is always some flexibility in managing these factors, and production planners can implement one or a combination of the **production planning strategies** discussed here.

Production planning strategies

There are essentially three production planning strategies. These strategies involve trade-offs among the work force size, work hours, inventory, and backlogs.

1. *Chase strategy.*[4] Match the production rate to the order rate by hiring and laying off employees as the order rate varies. The success of this strategy depends on having a pool of easily trained applicants to draw on as order volumes increase. There are obvious motivational impacts. When order backlogs are low, employees may feel compelled to slow down out of fear of being laid off as soon existing orders are completed.

------

[4] No relation to one of the authors of this text.

2. *Stable work force—variable work hours.* Vary the output by varying the number of hours worked through flexible work schedules or overtime. By varying the number of work hours, production quantities can be matched to orders. This strategy provides workforce continuity and avoids many of the emotional and tangible costs of hiring and firing associated with the chase strategy.

3. *Level strategy.* Maintain a stable work force working at a constant output rate. Shortages and surpluses are absorbed by fluctuating inventory levels, order backlogs, and lost sales. Employees benefit from stable work hours at the costs of potentially decreased customer service levels and increased inventory costs. Another concern is the possibility of inventoried products becoming obsolete.

When just one of these variables is used to absorb demand fluctuations, it is termed a **pure strategy;** one or more used in combination is a **mixed strategy.** As you might suspect, mixed strategies are more widely applied in industry.

Subcontracting

In addition to these strategies, managers may also choose to subcontract some portion of production. This strategy is similar to the chase strategy, but hiring and laying off is translated into subcontracting and not subcontracting. Some level of subcontracting can be desirable to accommodate demand fluctuations. However, unless the relationship with the supplier is particularly strong, a manufacturer can lose some control over schedule and quality. For this reason, extensive subcontracting may be viewed as a high-risk strategy.

Relevant Costs

There are four costs relevant to aggregate production planning. These relate to the production cost itself, as well as the cost to hold inventory and to have unfilled orders. More specifically, these are

1. *Basic production costs.* These are the fixed and variable costs incurred in producing a given product type in a given time period. Included are direct and indirect labor costs and regular as well as overtime compensation.

2. *Costs associated with changes in the production rate.* Typical costs in this category are those involved in hiring, training, and laying off personnel.

3. *Inventory holding costs.* A major component is the cost of capital tied up in inventory. Other components are storing, insurance, taxes, spoilage, and obsolescence.

4. *Backlogging costs.* Usually these are very hard to measure and include

costs of expediting, loss of customer goodwill, and loss of sales revenues resulting from backlogging.

Budgets

To receive funding, operations managers are generally required to submit annual, and sometimes quarterly, budget requests. Aggregate planning activities are key to the success of the budgeting process. Recall that the goal of aggregate planning is to minimize the total production-related costs over the planning horizon by determining the optimal combination of work force levels and inventory levels. Thus, aggregate planning provides justification for the requested budget amount. Accurate medium-range planning increases both the likelihood of receiving the requested budget and operating within the limits of the budget.

In the next section, we provide examples of medium-range planning in both a manufacturing and a service setting. These examples illustrate the trade-offs associated with different production planning strategies.

12.4 AGGREGATE PLANNING TECHNIQUES

Companies still use simple cut-and-try charting and graphic methods in developing their aggregate plans. A cut-and-try approach involves costing out various production planning alternatives and selecting the one with the lowest cost. In addition, there are more sophisticated approaches, including linear programming, the Linear Decision Rule, and various heuristic methods. Of these, only linear programming has seen broad application; we discuss it later.

A Cut-and-Try Example: The C&A Company

A firm with pronounced seasonal variation normally plans production for a full year to capture the extremes in demand during the busiest and slowest months. However, it is possible to illustrate the general principles involved with a shorter horizon. Suppose we wish to set up a production plan for the C&A Company for the next six months. We are given the following information:

Month	Demand Forecast	Number of Working Days
January	1,800	22
February	1,500	19
March	1,100	21
April	900	21
May	1,100	22
June	1,600	20
	8,000 units	125 days

Costs	
Materials	$100/unit
Inventory holding cost	$1.50/unit-month
Marginal cost of stockout	$5/unit/month
Marginal cost of subcontracting	$20/unit ($120 subcontracting cost less $100 material savings)
Hiring and training cost	$200/worker
Layoff cost	$250/worker
Labor hours required	5/unit
Straight line cost (first 8 hours each day)	$4/hour
Overtime cost (time and a half)	$6/hour

Inventory	
Beginning inventory	400 units

In solving this problem, we can exclude the material costs. We could have included this $100 cost in all our calculations, but if we assume that a $100 cost is common to each demanded unit, then we need only to concern ourselves with the marginal costs. Since the subcontracting cost is $120, our true cost for subcontracting is just $20 because we save the materials.

Note that many costs are expressed in a different form than typically found in the accounting records of a firm. Therefore, do not expect to obtain all these costs directly from such records, but indirectly from management personnel, who can help interpret the data.

Inventory at the beginning of the first period is 400 units. Because the demand forecast is imperfect, the C&A Company has determined that a *safety stock,* or buffer inventory, should be established to reduce the likelihood of stockouts. For this example, assume the safety stock should be one-quarter of the demand forecast (Chapter 13 covers this topic in more depth).

Before investigating alternative production plans, it is often quite useful to convert demand forecasts into *production requirements,* which take into account the safety stock estimates. In Exhibit 12.5, note that these requirements

EXHIBIT 12.5

Aggregate Production Planning Requirements

Month	(1) Beginning Inventory	(2) Demand Forecast	(3) = .25 × (2) Safety Stock	(4) = (2) + (3) − (1) Production Requirement	(5) = (1) + (4) − (2) Ending Inventory
January	400	1,800	450	1,850	450
February	450	1,500	375	1,425	375
March	375	1,100	275	1,000	275
April	275	900	225	850	225
May	225	1,100	275	1,150	275
June	275	1,600	400	1,725	400
				8,000	

implicitly assume that the safety stock is never actually used, so that the ending inventory each month equals the safety stock for that month. For example, the January safety stock of 450 (25 percent of January demand of 1,800) becomes the inventory at the end of January. The production requirement for January is demand plus safety stock minus beginning inventory (1,800 + 450 − 400 = 1,850).

Now we must formulate alternative production plans for the C&A Company. We investigate four different plans with the objective of finding the one with the lowest total cost.

Plan 1. Produce to exact monthly production requirements using a regular eight-hour day by varying work-force size.

Plan 2. Produce to meet expected average demand over the next six months by maintaining a constant work force. This constant number of workers is calculated by *averaging* the demand forecast over the horizon. Take the total production requirements for all six months and determine how many workers would be needed if each month's requirements were the same [(8,000 units × 5 hours per unit) ÷ (125 days × 8 hours per day) = 40 workers]. Inventory is allowed to accumulate, with shortages filled from next month's production by back ordering.

Plan 3. Produce to meet the minimum expected demand (April) using a constant work force on regular time. Subcontract to meet additional output requirements. The number of workers is calculated by locating the minimum monthly production requirement and determining how many workers would be needed for that month [(850 units × 6 months × 5 hours per unit) ÷ (125 days × 8 hours per day) = 25 workers] and subcontracting any monthly difference between requirements and production.

Plan 4. Produce to meet expected demand for all but the first two months using a constant work force on regular time. Use overtime to meet additional output requirements. The number of workers is more difficult to compute for this plan, but the goal is to finish June with an ending inventory as close as possible to the June safety stock. By trial and error it can be shown that constant work force of 38 workers is the closest approximation.

The next step is to calculate the cost of each plan. This requires the series of simple calculations shown in Exhibit 12.6. Note that the headings in each column are different for each plan because each is a different problem requiring its own data and calculations.

The final step is to tabulate and graph each plan and make a comparison of their costs. From Exhibit 12.7, we can see that making use of subcontracting resulted in the lowest cost (Plan 3). Exhibit 12.8 shows the effects of the four plans. This is a cumulative graph illustrating the expected results on the total production requirement.

Note that we have made one other assumption in this example: the plan can start with any number of workers with no hiring or layoff cost. This usually is the case since an aggregate plan draws on existing personnel, and we can start

EXHIBIT 12.6 Costs of Four Production Plans

PRODUCTION PLAN 1: EXACT PRODUCTION; VARY WORK FORCE

Month	(1) = (4) in Exhibit 12.5 Production Requirement	(2) = (1) × 5 Hr/Unit Production Hours Required	(3) Working Days per Month	(4) = (3) × 8 Hr/Day Hours per Month per Worker	(5) = (2) ÷ (4) Workers Required	(6) New Workers Hired	(7) = (6) × $200 Hiring Cost	(8) Workers Laid Off	(9) = (8) × $250 Layoff Cost	(10) = (2) × $4 Straight-Time Cost
Jan.	1,850	9,250	22	176	53	0*	—	—	—	$ 37,000
Feb.	1,425	7,125	19	152	47	0	0	6	$1,500	28,500
Mar.	1,000	5,000	21	168	30	0	0	17	4,250	20,000
Apr.	850	4,250	21	168	25	0	0	5	1,250	17,000
May	1,150	5,750	22	176	33	8	$1,600	0	0	23,000
June	1,725	8,625	20	160	54	21	4,200	0	0	34,500
							$5,800		$7,000	$160,000

* Assuming opening work force equal to first month's requirement of 53 workers.

PRODUCTION PLAN 2: CONSTANT WORK FORCE; VARY INVENTORY AND STOCKOUT

Month	(1) Beginning Inventory	(2) Working Days per Month	(3) = (2) × 8 Hr/Day × 40 Workers* Production Hours Available	(4) = (3) ÷ 5 Hr/Unit Actual Production	(5) = (2) in Exhibit 12.5 Demand Forecast	(6) = (1) + (4) − (5) Ending Inventory	(7) Units Short	(8) = (7) × $5 Shortage Cost	(9) = (3) in Exhibit 12.5 Safety Stock	(10) = (6) − (9) Units Excess	(11) = (10) × $1.50 Inventory Cost	(12) = (3) × $4 Straight-Time Cost
Jan.	400	22	7,040	1,408	1,800	8	0	0	450	0	0	$ 28,160
Feb.	8	19	6,080	1,216	1,500	−276	276	$1,380	375	0	0	24,320
Mar.	−276	21	6,720	1,344	1,100	−32	32	160	275	0	0	26,880
Apr.	−32	21	6,720	1,344	900	412	0	0	225	187	$281	26,880
May	412	22	7,040	1,408	1,100	720	0	0	275	445	667	28,160
June	720	20	6,400	1,280	1,600	400	0	0	400	0	0	25,600
		125						$1,540			$948	$160,000

* (Sum of Col. 4 in Exhibit 12.5 × 5 hr/unit) ÷ (Sum of Col. (2) × 8 hr/day) = (8,000 × 5) ÷ (125 × 8) = 40.

620

PRODUCTION PLAN 3: CONSTANT LOW WORK FORCE; SUBCONTRACT

Month	(1) = (4) in Exhibit 12.5 Production Requirement	(2) Working Days per Month	(3) = (2) × 8 Hr/Day × 25 Workers* Production Hours Available	(4) = (3) ÷ 5 Hr/Unit Actual Production	(5) = (1) − (4) Units Subcontracted	(6) = (5) × $20 Subcontracting Cost	(7) = (3) × $4 Straight-Time Cost
Jan.	1,850	22	4,400	880	970	$19,400	$ 17,600
Feb.	1,425	19	3,800	760	665	13,300	15,200
Mar.	1,000	21	4,200	840	160	3,200	16,800
Apr.	850	21	4,200	840	10	200	16,800
May	1,150	22	4,400	880	270	5,400	17,600
June	1,725	20	4,000	800	925	18,500	16,000
						$60,000	$100,000

* Minimum production requirement. For example, (Col 1 for April × 6 months × 5 hr/unit) ÷ (Sum of Col 2 × 8 hr/day) = (850 × 6 × 5) ÷ (125 × 8) = 25 workers.

PRODUCTION PLAN 4: CONSTANT WORK FORCE; OVERTIME

Month	(1) Beginning Inventory	(2) Working Days per Month	(3) = (2) × 8 Hr/Day × 38 Workers Production Hours Available	(4) = (3) ÷ 5 Hr/Unit Regular Shift Production	(5) = (2) in Exhibit 12.5 Demand Forecast	(6) = (1) + (4) − (5) Units Available before Overtime	(7) From (6) Units Overtime	(8) = (7) × 5 Hr/Unit × $6/Hr Overtime Cost	(9) = (3) in Exhibit 12.5 Safety Stock	(10) = (6) − (9) Units Excess	(11) = (10) × $1.50 Inventory Cost	(12) = (3) × $4 Straight-Time Cost
Jan.	400	22	6,688	1,338	1,800	−62	62	$ 1,860	450	0	0	$ 26,752
Feb.	0	19	5,776	1,155	1,500	−345	345	10,350	375	0	0	23,104
Mar.	0	21	6,384	1,277	1,100	177	0	0	275	0	0	25,536
Apr.	177	21	6,384	1,277	900	554	0	0	225	329	$ 493	25,536
May	554	22	6,688	1,338	1,100	792	0	0	275	517	776	26,752
June	792	20	6,080	1,216	1,600	408	0	0	400	8	12	24,320
								$12,210			$1281	$152,000

EXHIBIT 12.7

Comparison of Four Plans

Cost	Plan 1: Exact Production; Vary Work Force	Plan 2: Constant Work Force; Vary Inventory and Stockout	Plan 3: Constant Low Work Force; Subcontract	Plan 4: Constant Work Force; Overtime
Hiring	$ 5,800	$ 0	$ 0	$ 0
Layoff	7,000	0	0	0
Excess inventory	0	948	0	1,281
Shortage	0	1,540	0	0
Subcontract	0	0	60,000	0
Overtime	0	0	0	12,210
Straight time	160,000	160,000	100,000	152,000
	$172,800	$162,488	$160,000	$165,491

the plan that way. However, in an actual application, the availability of existing personnel transferable from other areas of the firm changes the assumptions in this example.

Each of these four plans focused on one particular cost, and the first three were simple pure strategies. Obviously, there are many other feasible plans, some of which would use a combination of work-force changes, overtime, and some subcontracting. The problem set at the end of this chapter includes examples of such mixed strategies. In practice, the final plan chosen would come from searching a variety of alternatives and future projections beyond the six-month planning horizon we have used.

Keep in mind that the cut-and-try approach does not guarantee finding the minimum-cost solution. However, recent advances in computer hardware and software have elevated this kind of what-if analysis to a fine art. Spreadsheet programs, such as Lotus or Excel, can perform cut-and-try cost estimates in seconds on a personal computer. More sophisticated programs can generate much better solutions without the user having to intercede, as in the cut-and-try method.

Aggregate Planning Applied to Services: Tucson Parks and Recreation Department

Charting and graphic techniques are also very useful for aggregate planning in service applications. The following example shows how a city's parks and recreation department could use the alternatives of full-time employees, part-time employees, and subcontracting to meet its commitment to provide a service to the city.

Tucson Parks and Recreation Department has an operation and maintenance budget of $9,760,000. The department is responsible for developing and maintaining open space, all public recreational programs, adult sports leagues,

EXHIBIT 12.8

Four Plans for Satisfying a Production Requirement over the Number of Production Days Available

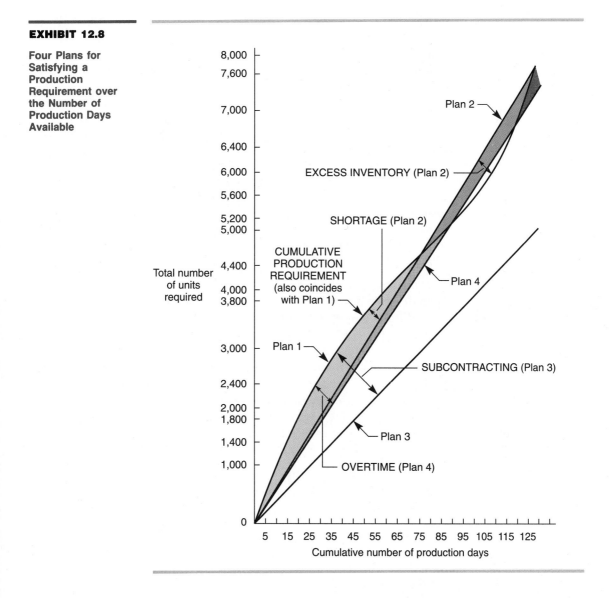

golf courses, tennis courts, pools, and so forth. There are 336 full-time-equivalent employees (FTEs). Of these, 216 are full-time permanent personnel who provide the administration and year-round maintenance to all areas. The remaining 120 year-long FTE positions are part time; about three-quarters of them are used during the summer and the remaining quarter in the fall, winter, and spring seasons. The three-fourths (or 90 FTE positions) show up as approximately 800 part-time summer jobs: lifeguards, baseball umpires, and instructors in summer programs for children. Eight hundred part-time jobs came from 90 FTEs because many last only for a month or two while the FTEs are a year long.

Currently, the only parks and recreation work subcontracted amounts to less than $100,000. This is for the golf and tennis pros and for grounds maintenance at the libraries and veterans cemetery.

Because of the nature of city employment, the probable bad public image, and civil service rules, the option to hire and fire full-time help daily or weekly to meet seasonal demand is pretty much out of the question. However, temporary part-time help is authorized and traditional. Also, it is virtually impossible to have regular (full-time) staff for all the summer jobs. During the summer months, the approximately 800 part-time employees are staffing many programs that occur simultaneously, prohibiting level scheduling over a normal 40-hour week. Also, a wider variety of skills is required than can be expected from full-time employees (e.g., umpires; coaches; lifeguards; teachers of ceramics, guitar, karate, belly dancing, and yoga).

Three options are open to the department in its aggregate planning.

1. The present method, which is to maintain a medium-level full-time staff and schedule work during off seasons (such as rebuilding baseball fields during the winter months) and to use part-time help during peak demands.
2. Maintain a lower level of staff over the year and subcontract all additional work presently done by full-time staff (still using part-time help).
3. Maintain an administrative staff only and subcontract all work, including part-time help. (This would entail contracts to landscaping firms, pool-maintenance companies, and to newly created private firms to employ and supply part-time help.)

The common unit of measure of work across all areas is full-time equivalent jobs or employees (or FTEs). For example, assume in the same week that 30 lifeguards worked 20 hours each, 40 instructors worked 15 hours each, and 35 baseball umpires worked 10 hours each. This is equivalent to $(30 \times 20) + (40 \times 15) + (35 \times 10) = 1,550 \div 40 = 38.75$ FTE positions for that week. Although a considerable amount of workload can be shifted to off season, most of the work must be done when required.

Full-time employees consist of three groups: (1) the skeleton group of key department personnel coordinating with the city, setting policy, determining budgets, measuring performance, and so forth; (2) the administrative group of supervisory and office personnel who are responsible for or whose jobs are directly linked to the direct-labor workers; and (3) the direct-labor work force of 116 full-time positions. These workers physically maintain the department's areas of responsibility, such as cleaning up, mowing golf greens and ballfields, trimming trees, and watering grass.

EXHIBIT 12.9 — Actual Demand Requirement for Full-Time Direct Employees and Full-Time-Equivalent (FTE) Part-Time Employees

	January	February	March	April	May	June	July	August	September	October	November	December	Total
Days	22	20	21	22	21	20	21	21	21	23	18	22	252
Full-time employees	66	28	130	90	195	290	325	92	45	32	29	60	
Full-time days*	1,452	560	2,730	1,980	4,095	5,800	6,825	1,932	945	736	522	1,320	28,897
Full-time-equivalent part-time employees	41	75	72	68	72	302	576	72	0	68	84	27	
FTE days	902	1,500	1,512	1,496	1,512	6,040	12,096	1,512	0	1,564	1,512	594	30,240

Note: Some work weeks are staggered to include weekdays, but this does not affect the number of work days per employee.
* Full-time days derived by multiplying the number of days in each month by the number of workers.

Cost information needed to determine the best alternative strategy is

Full-time direct-labor employees
    Average wage rate $4.45 per hour
    Fringe benefits   17% of wage rate
    Administrative costs   20% of wage rate
Part-time employees
    Average wage rate $4.03 per hour
    Fringe benefits   11% of wage rate
    Administrative costs   25% of wage rate
Subcontracting all full-time jobs $1.6 million
Subcontracting all part-time jobs $1.85 million

June and July are the peak demand seasons in Tucson. Exhibits 12.9 and 12.10 show the high requirements for June and July personnel. The part-time

EXHIBIT 12.10   **Monthly Requirement for Full-Time Direct-Labor Employees (other than key personnel) and Full-Time-Equivalent Part-Time Employees**

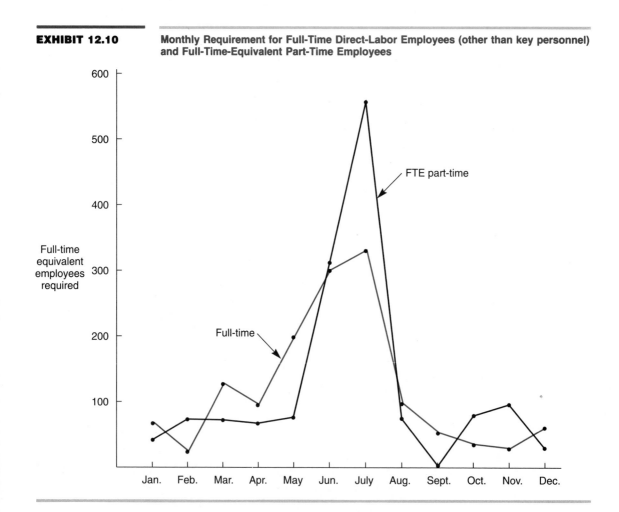

EXHIBIT 12.11 Three Possible Plans for the Parks and Recreation Department

Alternative 1: Maintain 116 full-time regular direct workers. Schedule work during off seasons to level workload throughout the year. Continue to use 120 full-time-equivalent (FTE) part-time employees to meet high demand periods.

Costs	Days per Year (Exhibit 12.9)	Hours (employees × days × 8 hours)	Wages (full-time, $4.45; part-time, $4.03)	Fringe Benefits (full-time, 17%; part-time, 11%)	Administrative Cost (full-time, 20%; part-time, 25%)
116 full-time regular employees	252	233,856	$1,040,659	$176,912	$208,132
120 part-time employees	252	241,920	974,938	107,243	243,735
Total cost = $2,751,619			$2,015,597	$284,155	$451,867

Alternative 2: Maintain 50 full-time regular direct workers and the present 120 FTE part-time employees. Subcontract jobs releasing 66 full-time regular employees. Subcontract cost, $1,100,000.

Cost	Days per Year (Exhibit 12.9)	Hours (employees × days × 8 hours)	Wages (full-time, $4.45; part-time, $4.03)	Fringe Benefits (full-time, 17%; part-time, 11%)	Administrative Cost (full-time, 20%; part-time, 25%)	Subcontract Cost
50 full-time employees	252	100,800	$ 448,560	$ 76,255	$ 89,712	
120 FTE part-time employees subcontracting cost	252	241,920	974,938	107,243	243,735	$1,100,000
Total cost = $3,040,443			$1,423,498	$183,498	$333,447	$1,100,000

Alternative 3: Subcontract all jobs previously performed by 116 full-time regular employees. Subcontract cost $1,600,000. Subcontract all jobs previously performed by 120 full-time-equivalent part-time employees. Subcontract cost $1,850,000.

Cost	Subcontract Cost
0 Full-time employees	
0 Part-time employees	
Subcontract full-time jobs	$1,600,000
Subcontract part-time jobs	1,850,000
Total cost	$3,450,000

EXHIBIT 12.12   Comparison of Costs for All Three Alternatives

	Alternative 1: 116 Full-Time Direct Labor Employees, 120 Full-Time Equivalent Part-Time Employees	Alternative 2: 50 Full-Time Direct Labor Employees, 120 Full-Time Equivalent Part-Time Employees, Subcontracting	Alternative 3: Subcontracting Jobs Formerly Performed by 116 Direct Labor Full-Time Employees and 120 FTE Part-Time Employees
Wages	$2,015,597	$1,423,498	—
Fringe benefits	284,155	183,498	—
Administrative costs	451,867	333,447	—
Subcontracting, full-time jobs		1,100,000	$1,600,000
Subcontracting, part-time jobs			1,850,000
Total	$2,751,619	$3,040,443	$3,450,000

help reaches 575 full-time-equivalent positions (although in actual numbers, this is approximately 800 different employees). After a low fall and winter staffing level, the demand shown as "full-time direct" reaches 130 in March when grounds are reseeded and fertilized and then increases to a high of 325 in July. The present method levels this uneven demand over the year to an average of 116 full-time year-round employees by early scheduling of work. As previously mentioned, no attempt is made to hire and lay off full-time workers to meet this uneven demand.

Exhibit 12.11 shows the cost calculations for all three alternatives. Exhibit 12.12 compares the total costs for each alternative. From this analysis, it appears that the department is already using the lowest-cost alternative (Alternative 1).

Level Scheduling

In this chapter we looked at four primary strategies for production planning: vary work-force size to meet demand, work overtime and undertime, vary inventory through excesses and shortages, and subcontract.

The Just-in-Time approach concentrates on keeping a *level production schedule*. A level schedule holds production constant over a period of time. It is something of a combination of the strategies we have mentioned here: for that period it keeps the work force constant and inventory low, and depends on demand to pull products through. Level production has a number of advantages:

1. The entire system can be planned to minimize inventory and work in process.

2. Product modifications are up-to-date because of the low amount of work in process.

3. There is a smooth flow throughout the production system.
4. Purchased items from vendors can be delivered when needed, and, in fact, often directly to the production line.

Toyota Motor Corporation, for example, creates a yearly production plan that shows the total number of cars to be made and sold. The aggregate production plan creates the system requirements to produce this total number with a level schedule. The secret to success in the Japanese level schedule is *production smoothing*. The aggregate plan is translated into monthly and daily schedules that *sequence* products through the production system. The procedure is essentially this: Two months in advance, the car types and quantities needed are established. This is converted to a detailed plan one month ahead. These quantities are given to subcontractors and vendors so that they can plan on meeting Toyota's needs. The monthly needs of various car types are then translated into daily schedules. For example, if 8,000 units of car type A are needed in one month, along with 6,000 type B, 4,000 type C, and 2,000 type D, and if we assume the line operates 20 days per month, then this would be translated to a daily output of 400, 300, 200, and 100, respectively. Further, this would be sequenced as four units of A, three of B, two of C, and one of D each 9.6 minutes of a two-shift day (960 minutes).

Each worker operates a number of machines, producing a sequence of products. To use this level scheduling technique:

1. Production should be repetitive (assembly-line format).
2. The system must contain excess capacity.
3. Output of the system must be fixed for a period of time (preferably a month).
4. There must be a smooth relationship among purchasing, marketing, and production.
5. The cost of carrying inventory must be high.
6. Equipment costs must be low.
7. Work force must be multiskilled.

For more about level scheduling, see uniform plant loading in Chapter 6 on Just-in-Time production systems.

Mathematical Techniques

Linear programming

Linear programming (LP) is appropriate to aggregate planning if the cost and variable relationships are linear and demand can be treated as deterministic. For the general case, the simplex method can be used. For the special case where hiring and firing are not considerations, the more easily formulated transportation method can be applied.

EXHIBIT 12.13   Aggregate Planning by the Transportation Method of Linear Programming

Production periods (sources)		1	Sales periods 2	3	4	Ending inventory	Unused capacity	Total capacity
Beginning inventory		[0] 50	[5]	[10]	[15]	[20]	[0]	50
1	Regular time	[50] 700	[55]	[60]	[65]	[70]	[0]	700
	Overtime	[75] 50	[80]	[85]	[90]	[95] 50	[0] 250	350
2	Regular time	X	[50] 700	[55]	[60]	[65]	[0]	700
	Overtime	X	[75] 100	[80]	[85]	[90] 150	[0]	250
3	Regular time	X	X	[50] 700	[55]	[60]	[0]	700
	Overtime	X	X	[75] 100	[80]	[85] 150	[0]	250
4	Regular time	X	X	X	[50] 700	[55]	[0]	700
	Overtime	X	X	X	[75] 100	[80] 150	[0]	250
Total requirements		800	800	800	800	500	250	3,950

The application of an LP transportation matrix to aggregate planning is illustrated by the solved problem in Exhibit 12.13. This formulation is termed a *period model* since it relates production demand to production capacity by periods.[5] In this case, there are four subperiods with demand forecast as 800 units in each. The total capacity available is 3,950 or an excess capacity of 750 (3,950 − 3,200). However, the bottom row of the matrix indicates a desire for 500 units in inventory at the end of the planning period, so unused capacity is reduced to 250. The left side of the matrix indicates the means by which production is made available over the planning period: that is, beginning inventory and regular and overtime work during each period. The X indicate those periods where production cannot be backlogged. That is, you can't produce in, say, Period 3 to meet demand in Period 2 (this is feasible if the situation allows back orders). Finally, the costs in each cell are incremented by a holding cost of $5 for each period. Thus, if one produces on regular time in Period 1 to satisfy demand for Period 4, there will be a $15 holding cost. Overtime is, of course, more expensive to start with, but holding costs in this

---

[5] The analogy used here to the standard transportation problem is that production periods are factories and sales periods are warehouses, wages and holding costs are the transportation costs, and ending inventory and unused capacity are dummy warehouses.

EXHIBIT 12.14

Additional Factors That Can Be Included in the Transportation Method for Aggregate Planning

1. **Multiproduct production.** When more than one product shares common facilities, additional columns are included corresponding to each product. For each month, the number of columns will be equal to the number of products, and the cost entry in each cell will be equal to the cost for the corresponding product.

2. **Backlogging.** The backlog time and the cost of backlogging can be included by treating the shaded assignments in Exhibit 12.13 as feasible. If a product demanded in period 1 is delivered in period 2, this is equivalent to meeting period 1's demand with production in period 2. For, say, a $10 unit cost associated with such a backlog, the cost entry in the cell corresponding to period 2 regular time row and period 1 column will be $60 ($10 plus the $50 cost of regular-time production in period 2).

3. **Lost sales.** When stockouts are allowed and a part of the demand is not met, the firm incurs opportunity cost equal to the lost revenue. This can be included in the matrix by adding a "lost-sales" row for each period. The cost entry in the cell will be equal to lost revenue per unit.

4. **Perishability.** When perishability does not permit the sale of a product after it has been in stock for a certain period, the corresponding cells in the matrix are treated as infeasible. If the product in Exhibit 12.13 cannot be sold after it has been in stock for two periods, the cells occupying the intersection of period 1 rows and columns beyond period 3 will be infeasible.

5. **Subcontracting.** This can be included by adding a "subcontracting" row for each period. Cost values in each cell would be the unit cost to subcontract plus any inventory holding cost (incremented in the same fashion as regular time and overtime costs).

6. **Learning effects.** Learning effects result in increased capacity and lower cost per unit. These changes are incorporated by making corresponding adjustments in capacity (total amount available from source) column and cost entry in the cells.

Source: K. Singhal, "A Generalized Model for Production Scheduling by Transportation Method of LP," *Industrial Management* 19, no. 5 (September–October 1977), pp. 1–6.

example are not affected by whether production is on regular time or overtime. The solution shown is an optimal one. The same allocation and evaluation methods (e.g., the stepping stone method) applied to the transportation problems shown in the Supplement to Chapter 8 can be applied to the period model.

The transportation matrix is remarkably versatile and can incorporate a variety of aggregate planning factors as described in Exhibit 12.14.

Observations on linear programming and mathematical techniques
Linear programming is appropriate when the cost and variable relationships are linear or can be cut into approximately linear segments. Regarding current application of several aggregate planning techniques in industry (see Exhibit 12.15), only linear programming has seen wide usage. Commenting on this issue, R. Peterson and E. A. Silver suggest that the answer lies in the decision-making style of management.[6] The basic issue, in their view, is management's

_____
[6] R. Peterson and E. A. Silver, *Decision Systems for Inventory Management and Production Planning* (New York: John Wiley & Sons, 1979), p. 662.

EXHIBIT 12.15   Summary Data on Aggregate Planning Methods

Methods	Assumptions	Technique
1. Graphic and charting	None	Tests alternative plans through trial and error. Non-optimal, but simple to develop and easy to understand.
2. Simulation of master schedule	Existence of a computer-based production system	Tests aggregate plans developed by other methods.
3. Linear programming—transportation method	Linearity, constant work force	Useful for the special case where hiring and firing costs are not a consideration. Gives optimal solution.
4. Linear programming—simplex method	Linearity	Can handle any number of variables but often difficult to formulate. Gives optimal solution.
5. Linear decision rules*	Quadratic cost functions	Uses mathematically derived coefficients to specify production rates and work-force levels in a series of equations.
6. Management coefficients†	Managers are basically good decision makers	Uses statistical analysis of past decisions to make future decisions. Applies, therefore, to just one group of managers; nonoptimal.
7. Search decision rules‡	Any type of cost structure	Uses pattern search procedure to find minimum points on total cost curves. Complicated to develop, nonoptimal.

* Charles C. Holt et al., *Planning Production, Inventories, and Work Force* (Englewood Cliffs, N.J.: Prentice Hall, 1960).
† Edward H. Bowman and Robert B. Fetter, *Analysis for Production and Operations Management*, 3rd ed. (Homewood, Ill.: Richard D. Irwin, 1957).
‡ William H. Taubert, "A Search Decision Rule for the Aggregate Scheduling Problem," *Management Science*, February 1978, pp. B343–59.

attitude toward models in general. Those companies where modeling is a way of life are likely to try the more sophisticated methods; in those where it is not, one would suspect that graphic and charting approaches would be used. Somewhere in the middle ground lie companies that have substantial experience in data processing and use the computer primarily for detailed scheduling. In these firms, we would expect to see experimentation with alternative cut-and-try plans in developing master schedules.

12.5 CONCLUSION

Remember that aggregate planning translates the corporate strategic and capacity plans into broad categories of work-force size, inventory quantity, and production levels. It does not do detailed planning. It is also useful to point out some practical considerations in aggregate planning.

First, demand variations are a fact of life, so the planning system must include sufficient flexibility to cope with such variations. Flexibility can be achieved by developing alternative sources of supply, cross-training workers to handle a wide variety of orders, and engaging in more frequent replanning during high demand periods.

Second, decision rules for production planning should be adhered to once they have been selected. However, they should be carefully analyzed prior to implementation by such checks as simulation of historical data to see what really would have happened if they had been in operation in the past.

12.6 REVIEW AND DISCUSSION QUESTIONS

1. What are the basic controllable variables of a production planning problem? What are the four major costs?
2. Distinguish between pure and mixed strategies in production planning.
3. Define level scheduling. How does it differ from the pure strategies in production planning?
4. Compare the best plans in the C&A Company and the Tucson Parks and Recreation Department. What do they have in common?
5. Under which conditions would you have to use the general simplex method rather than the period model in aggregate planning?
6. How does forecast accuracy relate, in general, to the practical application of the aggregate planning models discussed in the chapter?
7. In which way does the time horizon chosen for an aggregate plan determine whether or not it is the best plan for the firm?

12.7 PROBLEMS

*1. Jason Enterprises (JE) is producing video telephones for the home market. Quality is not quite as good as it could be at this point, but the selling price is low and Jason has the opportunity to study market response while spending more time in additional R&D work.

At this stage, however, JE needs to develop an aggregate production plan for the six months from January through June. As you can guess, you have been commissioned to create the plan. The following information is available to help you:

	January	February	March	April	May	June
Demand data						
Beginning inventory	200					
Forecast demand	500	600	650	800	900	800
Cost data						
Holding cost		$10/unit/month				
Stockout cost		$20/unit/month				
Subcontracting cost/unit		$100				
Hiring cost/worker		$50				
Layoff cost/worker		$100				
Labor cost/hour—straight time		$12.50				
Labor cost/hour—overtime		$18.75				
Production data						
Labor hours/unit	4					
Workdays/month	22					
Current work force	10					

---

* Solution to Problem 1 is given in Appendix H.

What is the cost of each of the following production strategies?

a.   Exact production; vary work force (assuming a starting work force of 10).

b.   Constant work force; vary inventory and stockout only (assuming a starting work force of 10).

c.   Constant work force of 10; vary overtime only.

2.   For Problem 1, devise the least costly plan you can. You may choose your starting work force level.

3.   Assume that Alan Industries has purchased Jason Enterprises and has instituted Japanese-style management in which workers are guaranteed a job for life (with no layoffs). Based on the data in Problem 1 (and additional information provided here), develop a production plan using the transportation method of linear programming. To keep things simple, plan for the first three months only and convert costs from hours to units in your model. Additional information: overtime is limited to 11 units per month per worker and up to 5 units per month may be subcontracted at a cost of $100 per unit.

4.   Develop a production plan and calculate the annual cost for a firm whose demand forecast is fall, 10,000; winter, 8,000; spring, 7,000; summer, 12,000. Inventory at the beginning of fall is 500 units. At the beginning of fall you currently have 30 workers, but you plan to hire temporary workers at the beginning of summer and lay them off at the end of summer. In addition, you have negotiated with the union an option to use the regular work force on overtime during winter or spring if overtime is necessary to prevent stockouts at the end of those quarters. Overtime is *not* available during the fall. Relevant costs are: hiring, $100 for each temp; layoff, $200 for each worker laid off; inventory holding, $5 per unit-quarter; back order, $10 per unit; straight time, $5 per hour; overtime, $8 per hour. Assume that the productivity is two worker hours per unit, with eight hours per day and 60 days per season.

5.   Plan production for a four-month period: February through May. For February and March, you should produce to exact demand forecast. For April and May, you should use overtime and inventory with a stable work force; *stable* means that the number of workers needed for March will be held constant through May. However, government constraints put a maximum of 5,000 hours of overtime labor per month in April and May (zero overtime in February and March). If demand exceeds supply, then back orders occur. There are 100 workers on January 1. You are given the following demand forecast: February, 80,000; March, 64,000; April, 100,000; May, 40,000. Productivity is four units per worker hour, eight hours per day, 20 days per month. Assume zero inventory on February 1. Costs are: hiring, $50 per new worker; layoff, $70 per worker laid off; inventory holding, $10 per unit-month; straight-time labor, $10 per hour; overtime, $15 per hour; back order, $20 per unit. Find the total cost of this plan.

6.   Plan production for the next year. The demand forecast is spring, 20,000; summer, 10,000; fall, 15,000; winter, 18,000. At the beginning of spring you have 70 workers and 1,000 units in inventory. The union contract specifies that you may lay off workers only once a year, at the beginning of summer. Also, you may hire new workers only at the end of summer to begin regular work in the fall. The number of workers laid off at the beginning of summer and the number hired at the end of summer should result in planned production levels for summer and fall

that equal the demand forecasts for summer and fall respectively. If demand exceeds supply, use overtime in spring only, which means that back orders could occur in winter. You are given these costs: hiring, $100 per new worker; layoff, $200 per worker laid off; holding, $20 per unit-quarter; back-order cost, $8 per unit; straight-time labor, $10 per hour; overtime, $15 per hour. Productivity is two worker hours per unit, eight hours per day, 50 days per quarter. Find the total cost.

7. DAT, Inc. needs to develop an aggregate plan for its product line. Relevant data are

Production time	1 hour per unit
Average labor cost	$10 per hour
Work week	5 days, 8 hours each day
Days per month	Assume 20 work days per month
Beginning inventory	500 units
Safety stock	One half month
Shortage cost	$20 per unit per month
Carry cost	$5 per unit per month

The forecast for January to December 1988 is

January	February	March	April	May	June	July	August	September	October	November	December
2,500	3,000	4,000	3,500	3,500	3,000	3,000	4,000	4,000	4,000	3,000	3,000

Management prefers to keep a constant work force and production level, absorbing variations in demand through inventory excesses and shortages. Demand not met is carried over to the following month.

Develop an aggregate plan that will meet the demand and other conditions of the problem. Do not try to find the optimum; just find a good solution and state the procedure you might use to test for a better solution. Make any necessary assumptions.

8. Old Pueblo Engineering Contractors creates six-month "rolling" schedules, which are recomputed monthly. For competitive reasons (they would need to divulge proprietary design criteria, methods, etc.), Old Pueblo does not subcontract. Therefore, its only options to meet customer requirements are (1) work on regular time; (2) work on overtime, which is limited to 30 percent of regular time; (3) do customers' work early, which would cost an additional $5 per hour per month; (4) perform customers' work late, which would cost an additional $10 per hour per month penalty, as provided by their contract.

Old Pueblo has 25 engineers on its staff at an hourly rate of $30. Customers' hourly requirements for the six months from January to June are

January	February	March	April	May	June
5,000	4,000	6,000	6,000	5,000	4,000

Develop an aggregate plan using the transportation method of linear programming. Assume 20 working days in each month.

9. Alan Industries is expanding its product line to include new models: Model A, Model B, and Model C. These are to be produced on the same productive equipment and the objective is to meet the demands for the three products using

overtime where necessary. The demand forecast for the next four months, in required hours, is

Product	April	May	June	July
Model A	800	600	800	1,200
Model B	600	700	900	1,100
Model C	700	500	700	850

Because the products deteriorate rapidly, there is a high loss in quality and, consequently, a high carryover cost into subsequent periods. Each hour's production carried into future months costs $3 per productive hour of Model A, $4 for Model B, and $5 for Model C.

Production can take place either during regular working hours or during overtime. Regular time is paid at $4 when working on Model A, $5 for Model B, and $6 for Model C. Overtime premium is 50 percent.

The available production capacity for regular time and overtime is

	April	May	June	July
Regular time	1,500	1,300	1,800	1,700
Overtime	700	650	900	850

a. Set the problem up in matrix form and show appropriate costs.

b. Show a feasible solution.

10. Shoney Video Concepts produces a line of video disc players to be linked to personal computers for video games. Video discs have much faster access time than tape. With such a computer/video link, the game becomes a very realistic experience. In a simple driving game where the joystick steers the vehicle, for example, rather than seeing computer graphics on the screen, the player is actually viewing a segment of a video disc shot from a real moving vehicle. Depending on the action of the player (hitting a guard rail, for example) the disc moves virtually instantaneously to that segment and the player becomes part of an actual accident of real vehicles (staged, of course).

Shoney is trying to determine a production plan for the next 12 months. The main criterion for this plan is that the employment level is to be held constant over the period. Shoney is continuing in its R&D efforts to develop new applications and prefers not to cause any adverse feeling with the local work force. For the same reasons, all employees should put in full work weeks, even if this is not the lowest-cost alternative. The forecast for the next 12 months is:

Month	Forecast Demand	Month	Forecast Demand
January	600	July	200
February	800	August	200
March	900	September	300
April	600	October	700
May	400	November	800
June	300	December	900

Manufacturing cost is $200 per set, equally divided between materials and labor. Inventory storage costs are $5 per month. A shortage of sets results in lost sales and is estimated to cost an overall $20 per unit short.

The inventory on hand at the beginning of the planning period is 200 units. Ten labor hours are required per video disc player. The work day is eight hours.

Develop an aggregate production schedule for the year using a constant work force. For simplicity, assume 22 working days each month except July, when the plant closes down for three weeks' vacation (leaving seven working days). Make any assumptions you need.

11. Develop a production schedule to produce the exact production requirements by varying the work-force size for the following problem. Use the example in the chapter as a guide (Plan 1).

The monthly forecast for Product X for January, February, and March is 1,000, 1,500, and 1,200, respectively. Safety stock policy recommends that one half of the forecast for that month be defined as safety stock. There are 22 working days in January, 19 in February, and 21 in March. Beginning inventory is 500 units.

Following are additional data: Manufacturing cost is $200 per unit, storage costs are $3 per unit per month, standard pay rate is $6 per hour, overtime rate is $9 per hour, cost of stockout is $10 per unit per month, marginal cost of subcontracting is $10 per unit, hiring and training cost is $200 per worker, layoff costs are $300 per worker, and production worker hours required per unit are 10. Make whatever assumptions are necessary.

12.8 CASE: XYZ BROKERAGE FIRM*

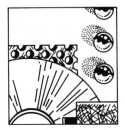

Consider the national operations group of the XYZ brokerage firm. The group, housed in an office building located in the Wall Street area, handles the transactions generated by registered representatives in more than 100 branch offices throughout the United States. As with all firms in the brokerage industry, XYZ's transactions must be settled within five trading days. This five-day period allows operations managers to smooth out the daily volume fluctuations.

Fundamental shifts in the stock market's volume and mix can occur overnight, so the operations manager must be prepared to handle extremely wide swings in volume. For example, on the strength of an international peace rumor, the number of transactions for XYZ rose from 5,600 one day to 12,200 the next.

Managers of XYZ, not unlike their counterparts in other firms, have trouble predicting volume. In fact, a random number generator can predict volume a month or even a week into the future almost as well as the managers can.

How do the operations managers in XYZ manage capacity when there are such wide swings? The answer differs according to the tasks and constraints facing each manager. Here's what two managers in the same firm might say:

---

* W. E. Sasser, R. P. Olsen, and D. D. Wyckoff, *Management of Service Operations,* (Boston: Allyn & Bacon, 1978), pp. 303–4.

Manager A: The capacity in our operation is currently 12,000 transactions per day. Of course, what we should gear up for is always a problem. For example, our volume this year ranged from 4,000 to 15,000 transactions per day. It's a good thing we have a turnover rate, because in periods of low volume it helps us reduce our personnel without the morale problems caused by layoffs. [The labor turnover rate in this department is over 100 percent per year.]

Manager B: For any valid budgeting procedure, one needs to estimate volume within 15 percent. Correlations between actual and expected volume in the brokerage industry have been so poor that I question the value of budgeting at all. I maintain our capacity at a level of 17,000 transactions per day.

Why the big difference in capacity management in the same firm? Manager A is in charge of the cashiering operation—the handling of certificates, checks, and cash. The personnel in cashiering are messengers, clerks, and supervisors. The equipment—file cabinets, vaults, calculators—is uncomplicated.

Manager B, however, is in charge of handling orders, an information-processing function. The personnel are keypunch operators, EDP specialists, and systems analysts. The equipment is complex—computers, LANs, file servers, and communication devices that link national operations with the branches. The employees under B's control had performed their tasks manually until decreased volume and a standardization of the information needs made it worthwhile to install computers.

Because the lead times required to increase the capacity of the information-processing operation are long, however, and the incremental cost of the capacity to handle the last 5,000 transactions is low (only some extra peripheral equipment is needed), Manager B maintains the capacity to handle 17,000 transactions per day. He holds to this level even though the average number of daily transactions for any month has never been higher than 11,000 and the number of transactions for any one day has never been higher than 16,000.

Because a great deal of uncertainty about the future status of the stock certificate exists, the situation is completely different in cashiering. Attempts to automate the cashiering function to the degree reached by the order-processing group have been thwarted because the high risk of selecting a system not compatible with the future format of the stock certificate.

In other words, Manager A is tied to the "chase demand" strategy, and his counterpart, Manager B in the adjacent office, is locked into the "level capacity" strategy. However, each desires to incorporate more of the other's strategy into his own. A is developing a computerized system to handle the information-processing requirements of cashiering; B is searching for some variable costs in the order-processing operation that can be deleted in periods of low volume.

QUESTIONS

1. What appear to be the primary differences between each department?
2. Do these differences eliminate certain strategy choices for either manager?
3. Which factors cause the current strategy to be desirable for each manager?

4. What are the mixed or subcontracting possibilities?

5. What are the problems associated with low standardization?

12.9 SELECTED BIBLIOGRAPHY

Buffa, Elwood S., and Jeffrey G. Miller. *Production-Inventory Systems: Planning and Control.* 3rd ed. Homewood, Ill.: Richard D. Irwin, 1979.

Fisk, J. C., and J. P. Seagle. "Integration of Aggregate Planning with Resource Requirements Planning." *Production and Inventory Management,* Third Quarter 1978, p. 87.

McLeavy, D., and S. Narasimhan. *Production Planning and Inventory Control.* Boston: Allyn & Bacon, 1985.

Monden, Yasuhiro. *Toyota Production System.* Atlanta, Ga.: Industrial Engineering and Management Press, 1983.

Plossl, G. W. *Production and Inventory Control: Principles and Techniques.* 2nd ed. Englewood Cliffs, N.J.: Prentice Hall, 1985.

Silver, E. A., and R. Peterson. *Decision Systems for Inventory Management and Production Planning.* 2nd ed. New York: John Wiley & Sons, 1985.

Vollmann, T. E.; W. L. Berry; and D. C. Whybark. *Manufacturing Planning and Control Systems.* 2nd ed. Homewood, Ill.: Richard D. Irwin, 1988.

Wight, Oliver W. *Production and Inventory Management in the Computer Age.* Boston: Cahners Publishing, 1974.

Chapter 13

Inventory Systems for Independent Demand

When the bottle gets down to four, that's the time to buy some more.

Alka-Seltzer jingle from the 1950s.

KEY TERMS

Raw Materials, Finished Goods, Work-in-Process Inventory

Independent and Dependent Demand

Fixed–Order Quantity Model

Fixed–Time Period Model

Service Level

Safety Stock

Price–Break Order Quantities

ABC Analysis

Inventory Accuracy

Cycle Counting

*I*nventory is expensive to have; the average cost of inventory across all manufacturing in the United States is 30 to 35 percent of its value. For example, if a firm carries an inventory of $20 million, it costs the firm more than $6 million per year. These costs are due to obsolescence, insurance, opportunity costs, and so forth. If the amount of inventory could be reduced to $10 million, for instance, the firm would save over $3 million which goes directly to the bottom line. That is, the savings from reduced inventory shows as increased profit.

Probably no topic in manufacturing today is more often discussed or perceived to be more important than inventory. The name of the game is to reduce inventory quantities on hand at all levels: in raw materials and purchased parts through direct delivery by the vendor (often directly to the production line); in work in process by techniques such as Just-in-Time production or scheduling with small batch sizes; and finally, in finished goods through a close matching of output to market requirements, and shipments to those markets as soon as possible. There is a spreading effort to reduce all inventory inspired by new measurements and performance evaluation based not on the percentage of resource utilization, but rather on inventory turns and product quality.

There are changing views concerning the teaching of classical inventory models. On one side, articles claim that economic order quantity (EOQ) models are invalid. The other side defends their use. We believe both sides are correct—from within their own arenas. While one must be careful in their application, there certainly are situations in manufacturing, where EOQ models can be successfully used. It is definitely worth understanding these models. Just-in-Time manufacturing (JIT), for example, is based on the classical production-consumption model. Classical models still appear to be valid for the many thousands of companies engaged in product and parts distribution.

In this chapter, we present fixed-order and fixed-time period models, including those with protective inventory to assure specific service levels. Also included are special purpose models, such as price-break, as well as the ABC technique. In addition, we discuss the questions of inventory accuracy and show simple applications of the models in the real-world environment.

13.1 DEFINITION OF INVENTORY

Inventory is the stock of any item or resource used in an organization. An *inventory system* is the set of policies and controls that monitors levels of inventory and determines what levels should be maintained, when stock should be replenished, and how large orders should be.

In its complete scope, inventory includes inputs such as human, financial, energy, equipment, and **raw materials;** outputs such as parts, components, and **finished goods;** and interim stages of the process, such as partially finished goods or **work in process.** The choice of which items to include in inventory depends on the organization. A manufacturing operation can have an inventory of personnel, machines, and working capital, as well as raw materials and finished goods. An airline can have an inventory of seats; a modern drugstore, an inventory of medicines, batteries, and toys; and an engineering firm, an inventory of engineering talent.

By convention, manufacturing inventory generally refers to materials entities that contribute to or become part of a firm's product output. Manufacturing inventory is typically classified into segments:

Raw materials.

Finished products.

Component parts.

Supplies.

Work in process.

In services, inventory generally refers to the tangible goods to be sold and the supplies necessary to administer the service.

The basic purpose of inventory analysis in manufacturing and stockkeeping services is to specify (1) when items should be ordered and (2) how large the order should be. Recent trends in industry have modified the simple questions of "when" and "how many." Many firms are tending to enter into longer-term relationships with vendors to supply their needs for perhaps the entire year. This changes the "when" and "how many to order" to "when" and "how many to deliver."

13.2 PURPOSES OF INVENTORY

In goods production, a stock of inventory is kept to satisfy the following needs:

1. To maintain independence of operations.   A supply of materials at a work center allows that center flexibility in operations. For example, because there are costs for making each new production setup, this inventory allows management to reduce the number of setups.

Workplaces on an assembly line usually are not independent because raw materials and products to work on are fed at the line speed. There may be none or only a few extra products to work on in the event the worker performs either faster or slower than line speed, or if the workstation upstream slows down output. The unit completed at a workstation passes to the next person.

2. To meet variation in product demand.   If the demand for the product is known precisely, it may be possible (though not necessarily economical) to produce the product to exactly meet the demand. Usually, however, demand is not completely known, and a safety or buffer stock must be maintained to absorb variation.

3. To allow flexibility in production scheduling.   A stock of inventory relieves the pressure on the production system to get the goods out. This causes longer lead times, which permit production planning for smoother flow and lower-cost operation through larger lot-size production. High setup costs, for example, favor the production of a larger number of units once the setup has been made.

4. To provide a safeguard for variation in raw material delivery time.   When material is ordered from a vendor, delays can occur for a variety of reasons: a normal variation in shipping time, a shortage of material at the vendor's plant causing backlogs, an unexpected strike at the vendor's plant or at one of the shipping companies, a lost order, or a shipment of incorrect or defective material.

5. To take advantage of economic purchase-order size.   Obviously, there are costs to place an order: labor, phone calls, typing, postage, and so on. Therefore, the larger the size of each order, the fewer the number of orders that need be written. Also, the nonlinearity of shipping costs favors larger orders: the larger the shipment, the lower the per-unit cost.

13.3 INVENTORY COSTS

In making any decision that affects inventory size, the following costs must be considered.

1. Holding (or carrying) costs.   This broad category includes the costs for storage facilities, handling, insurance, pilferage, breakage, obsolescence, depreciation, taxes, and the opportunity cost of capital. Obviously, high holding costs tend to favor low inventory levels and frequent replenishment.

2. Setup (or production change) costs.   To make each different product involves obtaining the necessary materials, arranging specific equipment setups, filling out the required papers, appropriately charging time and materials, and moving out the previous stock of material. In addition, other costs may be involved in hiring, training, or layoff of workers, and in idle time or overtime.

If there were no costs or loss of time in changing from one product to another, many small lots would be produced. This would reduce inventory levels, with a resulting savings in cost. However, changeover costs usually exist, and one of the challenges today is to try to reduce these setup costs to permit smaller lot sizes.

3. Ordering costs.   These costs refer to the managerial and clerical costs to prepare the purchase or production order. Common terminology subdivides these into two categories: (1) header cost, which is the cost of identifying and issuing an order to a single vendor and (2) line cost, which is the cost for computing each separate item ordered from the same vendor. Thus, ordering three items from a vendor entails one header cost and three line costs.

4. Shortage costs.   When the stock of an item is depleted, an order for that item must either wait until the stock is replenished or be canceled. There is a trade-off between carrying stock to satisfy demand and the costs resulting from stockout. This balance is sometimes difficult to obtain, since it may not be possible to estimate lost profits, the effects of lost customers, or lateness penalties. Frequently, the assumed shortage cost is little more than a guess, although it is usually possible to specify a range of such costs.

Establishing the correct quantity to order from vendors or the size of lots submitted to the firm's productive facilities involves a search for the minimum total cost resulting from the combined effects of four individual costs: holding costs, setup or ordering costs, and shortage costs.

13.4 INDEPENDENT VERSUS DEPENDENT DEMAND

Briefly, the distinction between **independent and dependent demand** is this: In independent demand, the demand for various items is unrelated to each other and therefore needed quantities of each must be determined separately. In dependent demand, the need for any one item is a direct result of the need for some other item, usually a higher-level item of which it is part.

In concept, dependent demand is a relatively straightforward computational problem. Needed quantities of a dependent-demand item are simply computed, based on the number needed in each higher-level item where it is used. For example, if an automobile company plans on producing 500 automobiles per day, then obviously it will need 2,000 wheels and tires (plus spares). The number of wheels and tires needed is *dependent* on the production levels and not derived separately. The demand for automobiles, on the other hand, is *independent*—it comes from many sources external to the automobile firm and is not a part of other products and so is unrelated to the demand for other products.

To determine the quantities of independent items that must be produced, firms usually turn to their sales and market research departments. They use a variety of techniques, including customer surveys, forecasting techniques, and economic and sociological trends. Because independent demand is uncertain, extra units must be carried in inventory. This chapter presents models to determine how many extra units should be carried to provide a specified *service level* (percentage of independent demand) that the firm would like to satisfy.

13.5 INVENTORY SYSTEMS

An inventory system provides the organizational structure and the operating policies for maintaining and controlling goods to be stocked. The system is responsible for ordering and receipt of goods: timing the order placement and keeping track of what has been ordered, how much, and from whom. The system must also follow up to provide answers to such questions as: Has the vendor received the order? Has it been shipped? Are the dates correct? Are the procedures established for reordering or returning undesirable merchandise?

Classifying Models by Fixed-Order Quantity or Fixed-Time Period

There are two general types of inventory systems: **fixed-order quantity models** (also called the *economic order quantity,* or EOQ) and **fixed-time period models** (also referred to variously as the *periodic* system, the *periodic review* system, and the *fixed-order interval* system).

The basic distinction is that fixed-order quantity models are "event triggered" and fixed-time period models are "time triggered." That is, a fixed-order quantity model initiates an order when the event of reaching a specified reorder level occurs. This event may take place at any time, depending on the demand for the items considered. In contrast, the fixed-time period model is limited to placing orders at the end of a predetermined time period; only the passage of time triggers the model.

To use the fixed-order quantity model, which places an order when the remaining inventory drops to a predetermined order point, *R,* the inventory remaining must be continually monitored. Thus, the fixed-order quantity model is a *perpetual* system, which requires that every time a withdrawal from inventory or an addition to inventory is made, records must be updated to assure that the reorder point has or has not been reached. The review period for the fixed-time period model is only at the review period. No counting takes place in the interim (although some firms have created variations of systems that combine features of both).

Some additional differences that tend to influence the choice of systems are (also see Exhibit 13.1):

- The fixed-time period model has a larger average inventory since it must also protect against stockout during the review period, *T;* the fixed-quantity model has no review period.

EXHIBIT 13.1

Fixed-Order Quantity and Fixed-Time Period Differences

Feature	Fixed-Order Quantity Model	Fixed-Time Period Model
Order quantity	Q—constant (the same amount ordered each time)	Q—variable (varies each time order is placed)
When to place order	R—when quantity on hand drops to the reorder level	T—when the review period arrives
Recordkeeping	Each time a withdrawal or addition is made	Counted only at review period
Size of inventory	Less than fixed time-period model	Larger than fixed order-quantity model
Time to maintain	Higher due to perpetual recordkeeping	
Type of items	Higher-priced, critical, or important items	

- The fixed-order quantity model favors more expensive items since average inventory is lower.
- The fixed-order quantity model is more appropriate for important items such as critical repair parts since there is closer monitoring and therefore quicker response to potential stockout.
- The fixed-order quantity model requires more time to maintain since every addition or withdrawal is logged.

Exhibit 13.2 depicts what occurs when each of the two models is put into use and becomes an operating system. As we can see, the fixed-order quantity system focuses on order quantities and reorder points. Procedurally, each time a unit is taken out of stock, the withdrawal is logged and the amount remain-

EXHIBIT 13.2   Comparison of Fixed-Order Quantity and Fixed-Time Period Reordering Inventory Systems

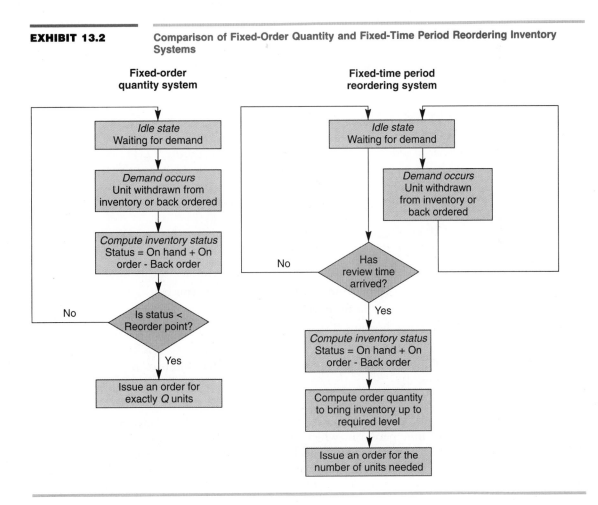

ing in inventory is immediately compared to the reorder point. If it has dropped to this point, an order for Q items is placed. If it has not, the system remains in an idle state until the next withdrawal.

In the fixed-time period system, a decision to place an order is made after the stock has been counted or reviewed. Whether an order is actually placed depends on the inventory status at that time.

13.6 BASIC MODEL TYPES

Basic Sawtooth Model

The simplest models in this category occur when all aspects of the situation are known with certainty. If the annual demand for a product is 1,000 units, it is precisely 1,000—not 1,000 plus or minus 10 percent. The same is true for setup costs and holding costs. Although the assumption of complete certainty is rarely valid, it provides a good starting point for our coverage of inventory models.

Fixed-order quantity models

Fixed-order quantity models attempt to determine the specific point, R, at which an order will be placed and the size of that order, Q. The order point, R, is always a specified number of units actually in inventory. The solution to a fixed-order quantity model may stipulate something like this: When the number of units of inventory on hand drops to 36, place an order for 57 more units.

Exhibit 13.3 and the discussion about deriving the optimal order quantity are based on the following characteristics of the model:

- Demand for the product is constant and uniform throughout the period.
- Lead time (time from ordering to receipt) is constant.
- Price per unit of product is constant.
- Inventory holding cost is based on average inventory.
- Ordering or setup costs are constant.
- All demands for the product will be satisfied (no back orders are allowed).

The "sawtooth effect" relating Q and R in Exhibit 13.3 shows that when inventory drops to point R, a reorder is placed. This order is received at the end of time period L, which does not vary in this model.

In constructing any inventory model, the first step is to develop a functional relationship between the variables of interest and the measure of effectiveness. In this case, since we are concerned with cost, the following equation would

EXHIBIT 13.3

**Basic Fixed-Order
Quantity Model**

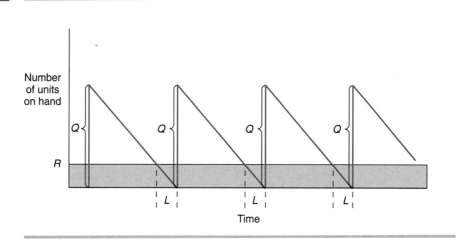

pertain:

Total	Annual	Annual	Annual
annual	= purchase	+ ordering	+ holding
cost	cost	cost	cost

or

$$TC = DC + \frac{D}{Q}S + \frac{Q}{2}H \qquad (1)$$

where

TC = Total annual cost

D = Demand (annual)

C = Cost per unit

Q = Quantity to be ordered (the optimum amount is termed the *economic order quantity*—EOQ, or Q_{opt})

S = Setup cost or cost of placing an order

R = Reorder point

L = Lead time

H = Annual holding and storage cost per unit of average inventory. (Often, holding cost is taken as a percent of the cost of the item, such as $H = iC$ where i is the percent carrying cost.)

On the right side of the equation, DC is the annual purchase cost for the units, $(D/Q)S$ is the annual ordering cost (the actual number of orders placed, D/Q, times the cost of each order, S), and $(Q/2)H$ is the annual holding cost

EXHIBIT 13.4   **Annual Product Costs, Based on Size of the Order**

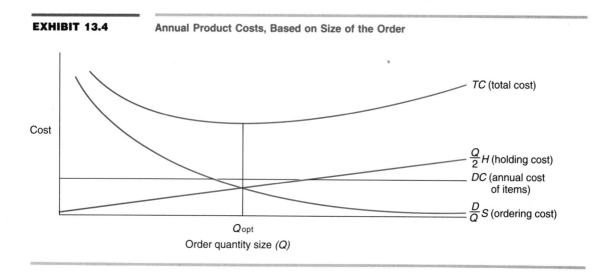

(the average inventory, $Q/2$, times the cost per unit for holding and storage, H). These cost relationships are shown graphically in Exhibit 13.4.

The second step in model development is to find that order quantity, Q, for which total cost is a minimum. In Exhibit 13.4, the total cost is minimum at the point where the slope of the curve is zero. Using calculus, the appropriate procedure involves taking the derivative of total cost with respect to Q and setting this equal to zero. For the basic model considered here, the calculations would be as follows:

$$TC = DC + \frac{D}{Q}S + \frac{Q}{2}H$$

$$\frac{dTC}{dQ} = 0 + \left(\frac{-DS}{Q^2}\right) + \frac{H}{2} = 0 \tag{2}$$

$$Q_{opt} = \sqrt{\frac{2DS}{H}}$$

Since this simple model assumes constant demand and lead time, no safety stock is necessary, and the reorder point, R, is simply

$$R = \bar{d}\,L \tag{3}$$

where

$\bar{d}$ = Average daily demand [constant]

L = Lead time in days [constant]

Example 13.1   Find the economic order quantity and the reorder point, given the following data:

Annual demand (D) = 1,000 units
Average daily demand $(\bar{d})$ = 1,000/365
Ordering cost (S) = \$5 per order
Holding cost (H) = \$1.25 per unit per year
Lead time (L) = 5 days
Cost per unit (C) = \$12.50

What quantity should be ordered?

Solution

The optimal order quantity is

$$Q_{opt} = \sqrt{\frac{2DS}{H}} = \sqrt{\frac{2(1,000)5}{1.25}} = \sqrt{8,000} = 89.4 \text{ units}$$

The reorder point is

$$R = \bar{d}L = \frac{1,000}{365}(5) = 13.7 \text{ units}$$

Rounding to the nearest unit, the inventory policy is as follows: When the number of units in inventory drops to 14, place an order for 89 more.

The total annual cost will be

$$TC = DC + \frac{D}{Q}S + \frac{Q}{2}H$$

$$= 1,000(12.50) + \frac{1,000}{89}(5) + \frac{89}{2}(1.25)$$

$$= \$12,611.81$$

Note that in this example, the purchase cost of the units was not required to determine the order quantity and the reorder point.

Customizing Economic Order Quantity Formula

The EOQ or Q_{opt} formula can be modified to fit many situations. It simply involves creating the correct total cost equation and then, with calculus, deriving the order quantity. We illustrate just one variation to show how easy the procedure is.

Differences in process batch and transfer batch size

Typically, the order quantity Q refers to the production or the purchase lot size. In a production environment, for example, suppose that management prefers to transfer the lot size of Q in several parts, rather than waiting for the entire lot to be completed. How does this change the equation?

Assume that the process lot size of Q will be transferred in n lots. Therefore, the average transfer batch size is Q/n. Staying with the previous conditions that cost is based on the average lot size, the inventory holding cost then becomes $(Q/2n)H$. The derivation is as follows:

$$TC = DC + \frac{D}{Q}S + \frac{Q}{2n}H$$

$$\frac{dTC}{dQ} = 0 - \frac{DS}{Q^2} + \frac{H}{2n} \tag{4}$$

$$HQ^2 = 2nDS$$

$$\therefore Q = \sqrt{\frac{2nDS}{H}}$$

Note that there is only a slight difference in the equation for Q, as you probably guessed. The effect is to increase the process batch size Q by the square root of the number of transfer batches. Consider the following problem:

$$D = 10,000$$
$$S = \$20$$
$$H = \$1.50$$

Case 1. Solve for Q when the transfer batch equals the process batch ($n = 1$).

$$Q = \sqrt{\frac{2nDS}{H}} = \sqrt{\frac{2(1)10,000(20)}{1.50}}$$

$$Q = 516 \text{ units}$$

Case 2. Solve for Q when the transfer batch is one fourth of the process batch ($n = 4$).

$$Q = \sqrt{\frac{2nDS}{H}} = \sqrt{\frac{2(4)10,000(20)}{1.50}}$$

$$Q = 1,032 \text{ units}$$

Case 3. Solve for Q when the transfer batch is one tenth of the process batch ($n = 10$).

$$Q = \sqrt{\frac{2nDS}{H}} = \sqrt{\frac{2(10)10,000(20)}{1.50}}$$

$$Q = 1,632 \text{ units}$$

This presentation of a transfer batch model is premised on a valid application of transfer batches. That is, the nature of the production system is such that products can be processed downstream as they are being produced in the process batch quantity. If items were not being used downstream, then the problem hasn't been correctly defined since the transfer batches might simply accumulate somewhere else, instead of at the resource producing the process batch. This would then be more like the order quantity model with usage, which is covered in the next section.

Also note that material handling costs have not been included. When items are transferred in less than process batch size, one of the considerations which determines transfer batch size is the cost to handle and move the material, not just holding costs.

Fixed-Order Quantity Model with Usage

Example 13.1 assumed that the quantity ordered would be received in one lot, but frequently this is not the case. In many situations, in fact, production of an inventory item and usage of that item take place simultaneously. This is particularly true where one part of a production system acts as a supplier to another part. For example, while aluminum extrusions are being made to fill an order for aluminum windows, the extrusions are cut and assembled before the entire extrusion order is completed. Also, companies are beginning to enter longer-term arrangements with vendors. Under such contracts, a single order may cover product or material needs over a six-month or year period, with the vendor making deliveries weekly or sometimes even more frequently. This model differs from our previous discussion of process and transfer batch sizes since this model has a continual usage rate d. If we let d denote a constant demand rate for some item going into production and p the production rate of that process that uses the item, we may develop the following total cost equation:[1]

$$TC = DC + \frac{D}{Q}S + \frac{(p - d)QH}{2p}$$

Again differentiating with respect to Q and setting the equation equal to zero, we obtain

$$Q_{opt} = \sqrt{\frac{2DS}{H} \cdot \frac{p}{(p - d)}} \tag{5}$$

This model is shown in Exhibit 13.5. We can see that the number of units on hand is always less than the order quantity, Q.

Example 13.2   Product X is a standard item in a firm's inventory. Final assembly of the product is performed on an assembly line that is in operation every day. One of the components of product X (call it component X_1) is produced in another department. This department, when it produces X_1, does so at the rate of 100 units per day. The assembly line uses component X_1 at the rate of 40 units per day.

Given the following data, what is the optimal lot size for production of component X_1?

---

[1] Obviously, the production rate must exceed the rate of usage; otherwise Q would be infinite, resulting in continual production.

EXHIBIT 13.5

Fixed-Order Quantity Model with Usage during Production Time

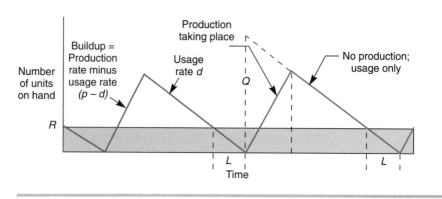

Daily usage rate (d) = 40 units

Annual demand (D) = 10,000 (40 units × 250 working days)

Daily production (p) = 100 units

Cost for production setup (S) = $50

Annual holding cost (H) = $0.50 per unit

Cost of component X_1 (C) = $7 each

Lead time (L) = 7 days

Solution

The optimal order quantity and the reorder point are calculated as follows:

$$Q_{opt} = \sqrt{\frac{2DS}{H} \cdot \frac{p}{p-d}} = \sqrt{\frac{2(10,000)50}{0.50} \cdot \frac{100}{100-40}} = 1,826 \text{ units}$$

$$R = dL = 40(7) = 280 \text{ units}$$

This states that an order for 1,826 units of component X_1 should be placed when the stock drops to 280 units.

At 100 units per day, this run would take 18.26 days and provide a 45.65-day supply for the assembly line (1,826/40). Theoretically, the department would be occupied with other work for the 27.39 days when component X_1 is not being produced.

Establishing Safety Stock Using Service Levels

The previous model assumed that demand was constant and known. In the majority of cases, though, demand is not constant but varies from day to day. Safety stock must therefore be maintained to provide some level of protection against stockouts. The general literature on the subject of safety stocks contains two approaches relating to the demand for the inventory that is to be protected: First, the *probability* that demand will exceed some specified amount. For example, an objective may be something like: "Set the safety stock level so that there will only be a 5 percent chance that demand will exceed 300 units."

The second approach deals with the *expected number* of units that will be out of stock. For example, an objective might be to set the inventory level so that we will be able to meet 95 percent of the demands for that unit (or out of stock 5 percent of the time). Note that the first approach deals with the *probability* of exceeding a value and the second approach is concerned with *how many* units were short.

In this chapter on inventory, we deal primarily with the second question, since it is far more interesting and the more realistic one to be answered. To clarify the two measures, we briefly discuss them in a later section titled "Comparing the Probability of a Stockout versus the Expected Number Short."

Service level refers to the number of units that can be supplied from stock currently on hand. For example, if the annual demand for an item is 1,000 units, a 95 percent service level means that 950 can be supplied immediately from stock and 50 units are short. (This concept assumes that orders are small and randomly distributed—one or several at a time; this model would not apply, for example, where the entire annual demand might be sold to a dozen customers.)

Safety stock can be defined as inventory carried to assure that the desired service level is met.

The discussion in this section on service levels is based on a statistical concept known as Expected z, or $E(z)$. $E(z)$ is the expected number of units short during each lead time. This entire discussion assumes, as previously stated, that demands (withdrawals from the inventory stock) are in very small quantities—in comparison to the total stock—and are normally distributed.

To compute service level, we need to know *how many* units are short. For example, assume that the average weekly demand for an item is 100 units with a standard deviation of 10 units. If we stock 110 units, how many will we expect to be short? To do this we need to summarize the probability that 111 is demanded (1 short), the probability that 112 is demanded (2 short), plus the probability that 113 is demanded (3 short), and so on. This summary would give us the number of units we would expect to be short by stocking 110 units.

While the concept is simple, the equations are impractical to solve by hand. Fortunately, Robert Brown has provided tables of expected values that we have included as Exhibit 13.6.[2]

We'll carry the explanations further within the context of our two basic model types: the fixed-order quantity and fixed-time period. We'll also discuss the important questions to be answered, such as: How do we control our inventory to provide a customer service level of 95 percent?

---

[2] Robert G. Brown, *Decision Rules for Inventory Management* (New York: Holt, Rinehart & Winston, 1967).

EXHIBIT 13.6

Expected Number Out of Stock versus the Standard Deviation (This table is normalized to a mean of zero and a standard deviation of 1)

μ = 0
σ = 1

E(z)	z	E(z)	z
4.500	−4.50	0.399	0.00
4.400	−4.40	0.351	0.10
4.300	−4.30	0.307	0.20
4.200	−4.20	0.267	0.30
4.100	−4.10	0.230	0.40
4.000	−4.00	0.198	0.50
3.900	−3.90	0.169	0.60
3.800	−3.80	0.143	0.70
3.700	−3.70	0.120	0.80
3.600	−3.60	0.100	0.90
3.500	−3.50	0.083	1.00
3.400	−3.40	0.069	1.10
3.300	−3.30	0.056	1.20
3.200	−3.20	0.046	1.30
3.100	−3.10	0.037	1.40
3.000	−3.00	0.029	1.50
2.901	−2.90	0.023	1.60
2.801	−2.80	0.018	1.70
2.701	−2.70	0.014	1.80
2.601	−2.60	0.011	1.90
2.502	−2.50	0.008	2.00
2.403	−2.40	0.006	2.10
2.303	−2.30	0.005	2.20
2.205	−2.20	0.004	2.30
2.106	−2.10	0.003	2.40
2.008	−2.00	0.002	2.50
1.911	−1.90	0.001	2.60
1.814	−1.80	0.001	2.70
1.718	−1.70	0.001	2.80
1.623	−1.60	0.001	2.90
1.529	−1.50	0.000	3.00
1.437	−1.40	0.000	3.10
1.346	−1.30	0.000	3.20
1.256	−1.20	0.000	3.30
1.169	−1.10	0.000	3.40
1.083	−1.00	0.000	3.50
1.000	−0.90	0.000	3.60
0.920	−0.80	0.000	3.70
0.843	−0.70	0.000	3.80
0.769	−0.60	0.000	3.90
0.698	−0.50	0.000	4.00
0.630	−0.40	0.000	4.10
0.567	−0.30	0.000	4.20
0.507	−0.20	0.000	4.30
0.451	−0.10	0.000	4.40
0.399	0.00	0.000	4.50

z = Number of standard deviations of safety stock
$E(z)$ = Expected number of units short

Source: Revised from Robert G. Brown, *Decision Rules for Inventory Management* (New York: Holt, Rinehart & Winston,1967), pp. 95–103.

Fixed-Order Quantity Model with Specified Service Level

A fixed-order quantity system perpetually monitors the inventory level and places a new order when stock reaches some level, R. The danger of stockout in this model occurs only during the lead time, between the time an order is placed and the time it is received. As shown in Exhibit 13.7, an order is placed when the inventory level drops to the reorder point, R. During this lead time (L), a range of demands is possible. This range is determined either from an analysis of past demand data or from an estimate (if past data are not available).

The amount of safety stock depends on the service level desired, as previously discussed. The quantity to be ordered, Q, is calculated in the usual way considering the demand, shortage cost, ordering cost, holding cost, and so forth. A fixed-order quantity model can be used to compute Q such as the simple Q_{opt} model previously discussed. The reorder point is then set to cover the expected demand during the lead time plus a safety stock determined by the desired service level. Thus, *the key difference between a fixed-order quantity model under certainty in demand and uncertainty in demand is not in computing the order quantity (both will be the same) but in computing the reorder point, which includes safety stock.*

The reorder point is

$$R = \overline{d}L + z\sigma_L \tag{6}$$

where

R = Reorder point in units

$\overline{d}$ = Average daily demand

L = Lead time in days (time between placing an order and receiving the items)

EXHIBIT 13.7

Fixed-Order Quantity Model

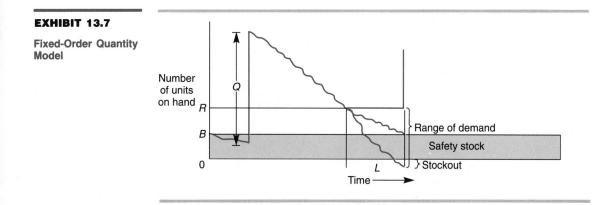

z = Number of standard deviations for a specified service level

σ_L = Standard deviation of usage during lead time.

The term $z\sigma_L$ is the amount of safety stock. Note that if safety stock is positive, the effect is to place a reorder sooner. That is, R without safety stock is simply the average demand during the lead time. If lead time usage was expected to be 20, for example, and safety stock was computed to be 5 units, then the order would be placed sooner, when 25 units remained. The greater the safety stock, the sooner the order is placed.

Computing $\bar{d}$, σ_L and z.   Demand during the lead time to receive a replenishment order is really an estimate or forecast of what is expected. It may be a single number (for example if the lead time is a month, the demand may be taken as the previous year's demand divided by 12), or it may be a summation of expected demands over the lead time (such as the sum of daily demands over a 30-day lead time). For the daily demand situation, d can be a forecasted demand using any of the models in Chapter 7 on forecasting. For example, if a 30-day period was used to calculate $\bar{d}$, then

$$\bar{d} = \frac{\sum\limits_{i=1}^{30} d_i}{30} \tag{7}$$

The error in using $\bar{d}$ to forecast the future is measured by the standard deviation of errors, which is

$$\sigma_d = \frac{\sqrt{\sum\limits_{i=1}^{30} (d_i - \bar{d})^2}}{30} \tag{8}$$

Since σ_d refers to one day, if lead time extends over several days we can use the statistical premise that the standard deviation of a series of independent occurrences is equal to the square root of the sum of the variances. That is, in general,

$$\sigma_s = \sqrt{\sigma_1^2 + \sigma_2^2 + \ldots + \sigma_i^2} \tag{9}$$

For example, suppose we computed the standard deviation of demand to be 10 units per day. If our lead time to get an order is five days, the standard deviation for the five-day period, since each day can be considered independent, would be

$$\sigma_L = \sqrt{(10)^2 + (10)^2 + (10)^2 + (10)^2 + (10)^2} = 22.36$$

Next we need to compute z. We do this by computing $E(z)$, the number of units short that meets our desired service level, and then looking this up in Exhibit 13.6 for the appropriate z.

Suppose we wanted a service level of P (for example, P might be 95 percent). In the course of a year we would be short $(1 - P) D$ units, or $0.05D$, where D is the annual demand. If we ordered Q units each time, we would be placing D/Q orders per year. Exhibit 13.6 is based on $\sigma_L = 1$. Therefore, any $E(z)$ that we read from the table needs to be multiplied by σ_L if it is other than 1. The number of units short per order, therefore, is $E(z)\sigma_L$. For the year, the number of units short is $E(z)\sigma_L D/Q$. Stated again, we have,

$$\begin{array}{ccccc} \begin{array}{c}\text{Percentage} \\ \text{short}\end{array} & \times & \begin{array}{c}\text{Annual} \\ \text{demand}\end{array} & = & \begin{array}{c}\text{Number short} \\ \text{per order}\end{array} & \times & \begin{array}{c}\text{Number of} \\ \text{orders per year}\end{array} \end{array}$$

$$(1 - P) \quad \times \quad D \quad = \quad E(z)\sigma_L \quad \times \quad \frac{D}{Q}$$

which simplifies to

$$E(z) = \frac{(1 - P)Q}{\sigma_L} \tag{10}$$

where

$\quad\quad P =$ Service level desired (such as satisfying 95 percent of demand from items in stock)

$(1 - P) =$ Unsatisfied demand

$\quad\quad D =$ Annual demand

$\quad\quad \sigma_L =$ Standard deviation of demand during lead time

$\quad\quad Q =$ Economic order quantity calculated in the usual way (such as $Q = \sqrt{2DS/H}$)

$\quad\quad E(z) =$ Expected number of units short from a normalized table where the mean $= 0$ and $\sigma = 1$

We now compare two examples. The difference between them is that in the first, the variation in demand is stated in terms of standard deviation over the entire lead time, and in the second, it is stated in terms of standard deviation per day (or other unit of time).

Example 13.3

Consider an economic order quantity case where annual demand $D = 1,000$ units, economic order quantity $Q = 200$ units, the desired service level $P = .95$, the standard deviation of demand during lead time $\sigma_L = 50$ units, and lead time $L = 15$ days. Determine the reorder point.

Solution

In our example, $\bar{d} = 4$ (1,000 over a 250-workday year), and lead time is 15 days. Therefore, from the equation

$$R = \bar{d}L + z\sigma_L$$
$$= 4(15) + z(50)$$

To find z, we use the equation for $E(z)$ and look this value up in the table. Our problem data gave us $Q = 200$, service level $P = .95$, and standard deviation of demand during lead time $= 50$. Therefore,

$$E(z) = \frac{(1 - P)Q}{\sigma_L} = \frac{(1 - .95)200}{50} = .2$$

From Exhibit 13.6, and through interpolation at $E(z) = .2$, we find $z = 49$. Completing the solution for R, we find

$$R = 4(15) + z(50) = 60 + .49(50) = 84.5 \text{ units}$$

This says when the stock on hand gets down to 85 units, order 200 more.

Just to satisfy any skepticism, we can calculate the number served per year to see if it really is 95 percent. $E(z)$ is the expected number short on each order based on a standard deviation of 1. The number short on each order for our problem is $E(z)\sigma_L = .2(50) = 10$. Since there are five orders per year (1,000/200), this results in 50 units short. This verifies our achievement of a 95 percent service level, since 950 out of 1,000 demand were filled from stock.

Example 13.4

The daily demand for a certain product is normally distributed with a mean of 60 and a standard deviation of 7. The source of supply is reliable and maintains a constant lead time of six days. The cost of placing the order is $10 and annual holding costs are $0.50 per unit. There are no stockout costs, and unfilled orders are filled as soon as the order arrives. Assume sales occur over the entire year. Find the order quantity and reorder point to satisfy 95 percent of the customers.

Solution

In this problem we need to calculate the order quantity Q, as well as the reorder point R.

$$\bar{d} = 60$$
$$\sigma_d = 7$$
$$D = 60(365)$$
$$S = \$10$$
$$H = \$0.50$$
$$L = 6$$

The optimal order quantity is

$$Q_{\text{opt}} = \sqrt{\frac{2DS}{H}} = \sqrt{\frac{2(60)365(10)}{0.50}} = \sqrt{876,000} = 936 \text{ units}$$

To compute the reorder point, we need to calculate the amount of product used during the lead time and add this to the safety stock.

The standard deviation of demand during the lead time of six days is calculated from the variance of the individual days. Since each day's demand is independent[3]

$$\sigma_L = \sqrt{\sum_{i=1}^{L} \sigma_{d_i^2}} = \sqrt{6(7)^2} = 17.2$$

Next we need to know how many standard deviations are needed for a specified service level. As previously defined,

$$E(z) = \frac{Q(1 - P)}{\sigma_L}$$

Therefore

$$E(z) = \frac{936(1 - .95)}{17.2} = 2.721$$

From Exhibit 13.6, interpolating at $E(z) = 2.721$, $z = -2.72$. The reorder point is

$$R = \bar{d}L + z\sigma_L$$
$$= 60(6) + -2.72(17.2)$$
$$= 313.2 \text{ units}$$

To summarize the policy derived in this example, an order for 936 units is placed whenever the number of units remaining in inventory drops to 313.

Note that in this case the safety stock $(z\sigma_L)$ turns out to be negative. This means that if we had ordered the average demand of 360 units during the lead time (60×6), we would have had a higher service level than we wanted. To get down to 95 percent service, we need to create more shortages by ordering less. While this may seem strange, nevertheless it's true. Our service is too good and we need to run out of stock more often!

We can verify our service level in this example by noting that we would place 23.4 orders per year $[60(365)/936]$. Each period would experience 46.8 units out of stock (2.72×17.2). Thus we would be out of stock 1,095 units per year (46.8×23.4). Service level, therefore, is 0.95 as we intended $[(21,900 - 1,095)/21,900]$.

As shown in these two examples, this technique of determining safety stock levels is relatively simple and straightforward. It allows us to control inventory to meet our desired service levels.

---

[3] As previously discussed, the standard deviation of a sum of independent variables is equal to the square root of the sum of the variances.

Comparing the Probability of a Stockout versus the Expected Number Short

Earlier in this chapter we described the two views of being out of stock for an inventory item. Some authors still define service level as the probability of a stockout occurring, whereas we defined service level as the percentage of units that can be supplied directly from stock on hand.

As you may recall from statistics, in a two tail distribution, plus or minus 3 standard deviations includes 99.7 percent of the population. For inventory, however, we are dealing with only a single tail distribution because our concern is with demand above or below a single point—not the demand between two points. Therefore, in a single tail distribution, 3 standard deviations is 99.85 percent. (You can check Appendix E.)

Visualize, for a moment, that we have an average demand for a product of 100 units with a standard deviation of 1 unit. If we stock 97 units and 100 people demand the product, then 97 percent of them get a product. This is a 97 percent service level. The second definition of service level (which we do not use) equates it to the probability of a stockout. In our example of stocking 97 units, then, we have a 99.85 percent chance of a stockout. It doesn't make much sense in many respects, does it? There is a 99.85 percent chance that we will run out of stock, but 97 percent of the customers' demands are satisfied! It's important to recognize the differences between the two measures.

Also worthwhile is to compare the differences in Example 13.4 which we would obtain by solving the equations both ways. Using the equation,

$$R = \bar{d}L + z\sigma_L$$

At a 95 percent service level we obtained $R = 313$ in Example 13.4. Now we will compare this reorder point with one computed using a probability of stockout of 95 percent. From Appendix E at 95 percent, $z = 1.65$. Therefore,

$$R = \bar{d}L + z\sigma_L$$
$$R = 60(6) + 1.65\,(17.2) \text{ or } 388 \text{ units.}$$

Using the probability of stockout results in a 24 percent increase over the service level definition (388 versus 313). The next question is: "What was the actual service level provided under the probability of stockout method?" Working backwards in the equation,

$$E(z) = \frac{Q\,(1 - P)}{\sigma_L}$$

From Exhibit 13.6 at $z = 1.65$ from our comparing case, $E(z) = .021$. Solving for P,

$$.021 = \frac{388 \ (1 - P)}{17.2}$$

$$P = .999 \text{ or } 99.9 \text{ percent}$$

With an order quantity of 388 rather than 313, virtually all demands were met; the service level was 99.9 percent. While this sounds nice, observe that the extra 4.9 percent service gained (from 95 percent to 99.9 percent) required a 25 percent increase in inventory.

Fixed-Time Period Model with Service Level

In a fixed-time period system, inventory is counted only at particular times, such as every week or every month. Counting inventory and placing orders on a periodic basis is desirable in situations such as when vendors make routine visits to customers and take orders for their complete line of products, or when buyers want to combine orders to save transportation costs. Other firms operate on a fixed time period to facilitate planning their inventory count; for example, Distributor X calls every two weeks and employees know that all Distributor X's product must be counted.

Fixed-time period models generate order quantities that vary from period to period, depending on the usage rates. These generally require a higher level of safety stock than a fixed-order quantity system. The fixed-order quantity system assumes continual counting of inventory on hand, with an order immediately placed when the reorder point is reached. In contrast, the standard fixed-time period models assume that inventory is counted only at the time specified for review. It is possible that some large demand will draw the stock down to zero right after an order is placed. This condition could go unnoticed until the next review period. Then the new order, when placed, still takes time to arrive. Thus, it is possible to be out of stock throughout the entire review period, T, and the order lead time, L. Safety stock, therefore, must provide protection against stockouts during the review period itself, as well as during the lead time from order placement to order receipt.

In a fixed-time period system, reorders are placed at the time of review (T), and the safety stock that must be reordered is

Safety stock $= z\sigma_{T+L}$

Exhibit 13.8 shows a fixed-time period system with a review cycle of T and a constant lead time L. In this case, demand is randomly distributed about a mean $\overline{d}$. The quantity to order, q, is

$$\begin{array}{ccc}
\text{Order} & = & \text{Average demand} \\
\text{quantity} & & \text{over the vulner-} \\
& & \text{able period}
\end{array} + \begin{array}{c} \text{Safety} \\ \text{stock} \end{array} - \begin{array}{c} \text{Inventory currently} \\ \text{on hand (plus on} \\ \text{order, if any)} \end{array}$$

$$q = \overline{d}(T + L) + z\sigma_{T+L} - I \tag{11}$$

EXHIBIT 13.8

Fixed-Time Period Inventory Model

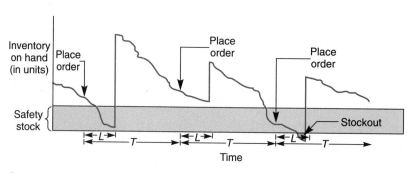

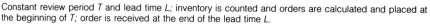

Constant review period T and lead time L; inventory is counted and orders are calculated and placed at the beginning of T; order is received at the end of the lead time L.

where

$q =$ Quantity to be ordered

$T =$ The number of days between reviews

$L =$ Lead time in days (time between placing an order and receiving it)

$\bar{d} =$ Forecasted average daily demand

$z =$ Number of standard deviations for a specified service level

$\sigma_{T+L} =$ Standard deviation of demand over the review and lead time

$I =$ Current inventory level (includes items on order)

Note: The demand, lead time, review period, and so forth can be any time units such as days, weeks, or years, so long as it is consistent throughout the equation.

In this model, demand ($\bar{d}$) can be forecast and revised each review period, if desired, or the yearly average may be used if appropriate.

The value of z can be obtained by solving the following equation for $E(z)$ and reading the corresponding z value from Exhibit 13.6.

$$E(z) = \frac{\bar{d}\,T(1 - P)}{\sigma_{T+L}} \tag{12}$$

where

$E(z) =$ Expected number units short from a formalized table where the mean $= 0$ and $\sigma = 1$

$P =$ Service level desired

$\bar{d}\,T =$ Demand during the review period where $\bar{d}$ is daily demand and T is the number of days

$\sigma_{T+L} =$ Standard deviation over the review period and lead time

Example 13.5   Daily demand for a product is 10 units with a standard deviation of 3 units. The review period is 30 days, and lead time is 14 days. Management has set a policy of satisfying 98 percent of demand from items in stock. At the beginning of this review period, there are 150 units in inventory.

How many units should be ordered?

Solution   The quantity to order is

$$q = \bar{d}(T + L) + z\sigma_{T+L} - I$$
$$= 10(30 + 14) + z\sigma_{T+L} - 150$$

Before we can complete the solution, we need to find σ_{T+L} and z. To find σ_{T+L}, we use the notion, as before, that the standard deviation of a sequence of independent random variables is equal to the square root of the sum of the variances. Therefore, the standard deviation during the period $T + L$ is the square root of the sum of the variances for each day, or

$$\sigma_{T+L} = \sqrt{\sum_{i=1}^{T+L} \sigma_{d_i}^2} \qquad (13)$$

Since each day is independent and σ_d is constant,

$$\sigma_{T+L} = \sqrt{(T + L)\,\sigma_d^2} = \sqrt{(30 + 14)(3)^2} = 19.90$$

Now to find z, we first need to find $E(z)$ and look this value up in the table. In this case, demand during the review period is $\bar{d}\,T$. Therefore,

$$E(z) = \frac{\bar{d}\,T(1 - P)}{\sigma_{T+L}} = \frac{10(30)(1 - .98)}{19.90} = 0.30151$$

From Exhibit 13.6 at $E(z) = 0.30151$, by interpolation $z = .21$.

The quantity to order, then, is

$$q = \bar{d}(T + L) + z\sigma_{T+L} - I$$
$$= 10(30 + 14) + .21(19.90) - 150$$
$$= 294 \text{ units}$$

To satisfy 98 percent of the demand for units, order 294 at this review period.

Special-Purpose Models

The fixed-order quantity and the fixed-time period models presented thus far differed in their assumptions but had two characteristics in common: (1) the cost of units remained constant for any order size and (2) the reordering process was continuous; that is, the items were ordered and stocked with the expectation that the need would continue. This section presents two new models: the first illustrates the effect on order quantity when unit price changes with order size; the second is a single period model (sometimes called a *static model*) in which ordering and stocking require a cost trade-off each time. This type of model is amenable to solution by marginal analysis.

Price-break models

Price-break models deal with the fact that generally, the selling price of an item varies with the order size. This is a discrete or step change rather than a per-unit change. For example, wood screws may cost $0.02 each for 1 to 99 screws, $1.60 per 100, and $13.50 per 1,000. To determine the optimal quantity of any item to order, we simply solve for the economic order quantity for each price and at the point of price change. However, not all the economic order quantities determined by the formula are feasible. In the wood-screw example, the Q_{opt} formula might tell us that the optimal decision at the price of 1.6 cents is to order 75 screws. This would be impossible, however, because 75 screws would cost 2 cents each.

The total cost for each feasible economic order quantity and **price-break order quantity** is tabulated, and the Q that leads to the minimum cost is the optimal order size. If holding cost is based on a percentage of unit price, it may not be necessary to compute economic order quantities at each price. Procedurally, the largest order quantity (lowest unit price) is solved first; if the resulting Q is valid, that is the answer. If not, the next largest order quantity (second lowest price) is derived. If that is feasible, the cost of this Q is compared to the cost of using the order quantity at the price break above, and the lowest cost determines the optimal Q.

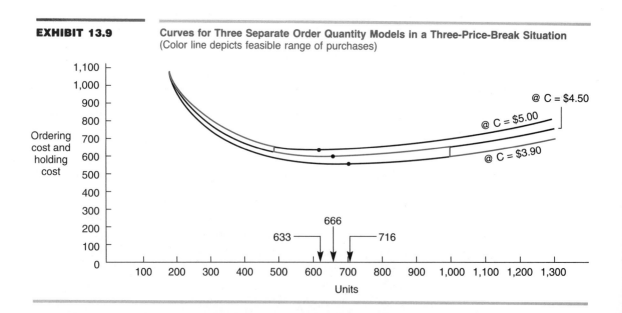

EXHIBIT 13.9   Curves for Three Separate Order Quantity Models in a Three-Price-Break Situation
(Color line depicts feasible range of purchases)

Looking at Exhibit 13.9, we see that order quantities are solved from right to left, or from the lowest unit price to the highest, until a valid Q is obtained. Then the order quantity at each *price break* above this Q is used to find which order quantity has the least cost—the computed Q or the Q at one of the price breaks.

Example 13.6   Consider the following case, where

D = 10,000 units (annual demand)

S = \$20 to place each order

i = 20 percent of cost (annual carrying cost, storage, interest, obsolescence, etc.)

C = Cost per unit (according to the order size; orders of 0 to 499 units, \$5.00 per unit; 500 to 999, \$4.50 per unit; 1,000 and up, \$3.90 per unit)

What quantity should be ordered?

Solution   The appropriate equations from the basic fixed-quantity case are

$$TC = DC + \frac{D}{Q}S + \frac{Q}{2}iC$$

and

$$Q = \sqrt{\frac{2DS}{iC}} \qquad (14)$$

Solving for the economic order size at each price, we obtain

@ C = \$5.00, Q = 633
@ C = \$4.50, Q = 666
@ C = \$3.90, Q = 716

In Exhibit 13.9, which displays the cost relationship and order quantity range, note that most of the order quantity–cost relationships lie outside the feasible range and that only a single, continuous range results. This should be readily apparent since, for example, the first order quantity specifies buying 633 units at \$5.00 per unit. However, if 633 units are ordered, the price is \$4.50—not \$5.00. The same holds true for the third order quantity, which specifies an order of 716 units at \$3.90 each. This \$3.90 price is not available on orders of less than 1,000 units.

Exhibit 13.10 itemizes the total costs at the economic order quantities and at the price breaks. The optimal order quantity is shown to be 1,000 units.

One practical consideration in price-break problems is that the price reduction from volume purchases frequently makes it seemingly economical to order amounts larger than the Q_{opt}. Thus, when applying the model we must

---

EXHIBIT 13.10   **Relevant Costs in a Three-Price-Break Model**

	Q = 633 where C = $5	Q = 666 where C = $4.50	Q = 716 where C = $3.90	Price Break 1,000
Holding cost $\left(\frac{Q}{2}iC\right)$		$\frac{666}{2}(0.20)4.50$ $= \$299.70$		$\frac{1,000}{2}(0.20)3.90$ $= \$390$
Ordering cost $\left(\frac{D}{Q}S\right)$	Not feasible	$\frac{10,000(20)}{666}$ $= \$300$	Not feasible	$\frac{10,000(20)}{1,000}$ $= \$200$
Holding and ordering cost		$600		$590
Item cost (DC)		10,000(4.50)		10,000(3.90)
Total cost		$45,599.70		$39,590

---

be particularly careful to obtain a valid estimate of product obsolescence and warehousing costs.

Single-period models

Some inventory situations involve placing orders to cover only one demand period or to cover short-lived items at frequent intervals. Sometimes called single-period or "newsboy" problems (for example, how many papers should a newsboy order each day), they are amenable to solution through the classic economic approach of marginal analysis. The optimal stocking decision, using marginal analysis, occurs at the point where the benefits derived from carrying the next unit are less than the costs for that unit. Of course, the selection of the specific benefits and costs depends on the problem; for example, we may be looking at costs of holding versus shortage costs, or (as we develop further) marginal profit versus marginal loss.

When stocked items are sold, the optimal decision—using marginal analysis—is to stock that quantity where the profit from the sale or use of the last unit is equal to or greater than the losses if the last unit remains unsold. In symbolic terms, this is the condition where $MP \geq ML$, where

MP = Profit resulting from the nth unit if it is sold

ML = Loss resulting from the nth unit if it is not sold

Marginal analysis is also valid when we are dealing with probabilities of occurrence. In these situations we are looking at expected profits and expected losses. By introducing probabilities, the marginal profit–marginal loss equation becomes

$$P(MP) \geq (1 - P)ML$$

EXHIBIT 13.11

Demand and
Cumulative
Probabilities

Number of Units Demanded	(p) Probability of This Demand	(P) Probability of Selling This Unit Is	
35	0.10	1 to 35	1.00
36	0.15	36	0.90
37	0.25	37	0.75
38	0.25	38	0.50
39	0.15	39	0.25
40	0.10	40	0.10
41	0	41 or more	0

where P is the probability of the unit's being sold and $1 - P$ is the probability of it not being sold, since one or the other must occur (the unit is sold or is not sold).[4]

Then, solving for P, we obtain

$$P \geq \frac{ML}{MP + ML} \tag{15}$$

This equation states that we should continue to increase the size of the inventory so long as the probability of selling the last unit added is equal to or greater than the ratio $ML/(MP + ML)$.

Salvage value.   Salvage value, or any other benefits derived from unsold goods, can easily be included in the problem. This simply reduces the marginal loss, as demonstrated in the following example.

Example 13.7   A product is priced to sell at $100 per unit, and its cost is constant at $70 per unit. Each unsold unit has a salvage value of $30. Demand is expected to range between 35 and 40 units for the period: 35 units definitely can be sold and no units over 40 will be sold. The demand probabilities and the associated cumulative probability distribution (P) for this situation are shown in Exhibit 13.11.

The marginal profit if a unit is sold is the selling price less the cost, or $MP = \$100 - \$70 = \$30$.

The marginal loss incurred if the unit is not sold is the cost of the unit less the salvage value, or $ML = \$70 - \$30 = \$40$.

How many units should be ordered?

---

[4] P is actually a cumulative probability since the sale of the nth unit depends not only on exactly n being demanded but also on the demand for any number greater than n.

EXHIBIT 13.12   Marginal Inventory Analysis for Units Having Salvage Value

(N) Units of Demand	(p) Probability of Demand	(P) Probability of Selling nth Unit	(MP) Expected Marginal Profit of nth Unit P(100 − 70)	(ML) Expected Marginal Unit of nth Unit (1 − P)(70 − 30)	(Net) (MP) − (ML)
35	0.10	1.00	$30	$ 0	$30.00
36	0.15	0.90	27	4	23.00
37	0.25	0.75	22.50	10	12.50
38	0.25	0.50	15	20	(5.00)
39	0.15	0.25	7.50	30	(22.50)
40	0.10	0.10	3	36	(33.00)
41	0	0			(40.00)

Note: Expected marginal profit is the selling price of $100 less the unit cost of $70 times the probability the unit will be sold. Expected marginal loss is the unit cost of $70 less the salvage value of $30 times the probability the unit will not be sold.

Solution

The optimal probability of the last unit being sold is

$$P \geq \frac{ML}{MP + ML} = \frac{40}{30 + 40} = 0.57$$

According to the cumulative probability table (the last column in Exhibit 13.11), the probability of selling the unit must be equal to or greater than 0.57; therefore, 37 units should be stocked. The probability of selling the 37th unit is 0.75. The net benefit from stocking the 37th unit is the expected marginal profit minus the expected marginal loss.

$$\begin{aligned} \text{Net} &= P(MP) - (1 - P)(ML) \\ &= 0.75(\$100 - \$70) - (1 - 0.75)(\$70 - \$30) \\ &= \$22.50 - \$10.00 = \$12.50 \end{aligned}$$

For the sake of illustration, Exhibit 13.12 shows all possible decisions. From the last column, we can confirm that the optimum decision is 37 units.

13.7 ECONOMIC ORDER QUANTITY MODELS IN RELATION TO THE REAL WORLD

There are several issues concerning the appropriate use of economic order quantity models. We make two brief points with illustrations concerning correct applications and understanding and using the correct logic.

An Application of the Economic Order Quantity Model

We have already suggested that economic lot size models would be useful in a distribution environment. This is because there is no fabrication or assembly, and end items are usually stocked to be sold. This is also an independent inventory situation where an order for one product does not trigger an order for others. In such applications, economic order quantity models are appropriate. C. A. Ntuen gives an example of the application of classical EOQ models in a warehouse at Kayser-Roth Corporation.[5] An economic distribution quantity (EDQ) was developed that has the same sense as an EOQ and is also based on minimizing total cost. Total cost is the sum of shipping cost (called CD by the author) and storage cost (CS). In the same way as the classical EOQ derivation, he uses calculus to derive the optimum shipment size. The equation is the same form as our equation for Q, where the right side is the square root of distribution and storage costs. In his application, Ntuen was also selecting one of four types of storage racks to hold the inventory. Storage costs were based on the rack chosen.

Ntuen used his model in an example of the distribution and storage of pantyhose. Costs are $7 per case for shipping and $12 per case for storage. There are 25 dozen per case. Storage space is 25 compartments per rack (n), 5 rows per compartment (R), and 10 bins per row (B). By solving the problem, he learned that the economic distribution quantity is 13 cases of pantyhose with 31 dozen pantyhose per bin. The total cost is $2,300.

Economic Order Quantity Logic (or Philosophy)

The recent bashing of classical inventory models seems fashionable to some members of industry and consulting groups. Proportionally, there is much less open criticism from academia. In a manufacturing environment, the major criticisms of classical EOQ models focus on the numbers. These numbers are the values of setup costs, holding costs, and demands used in the equations. These types of costs are very difficult to measure and, therefore, error prone. Also, demand is not a constant but a fluctuating number. One cannot argue that the EOQ equations are wrong. The equations are correct!

Elliott Weiss states the problem nicely by explaining that many users of the equations focus on optimizing a set of numbers which often are taken as a given fact.[6] Rather, he states, we should be managing lot sizing and inventory control. The current moves toward reduced inventory costs and quantities, such as Just-in-Time systems, stress the importance in reducing lot sizes. The means to reducing lot sizes is to reduce setup time and cost. When smaller lots are run, holding cost is reduced. The point is to understand the logic and know where to apply it.

In Chapter 18, we cover the idea of a bottleneck resource (whose capacity is fully used) and nonbottlenecks (which have excess capacity). In a bottleneck, it

[5] C. A. Ntuen, "Physical Resource Availability Figured into EOQ Formulation Cuts Warehouse Logistics Cost," *Industrial Engineering*, May 1990, pp. 20–22.

[6] Elliot N. Weiss, "Lot Sizing Is Dead: Long Live Lot Sizing," *Production and Inventory Management Journal*, First Quarter 1990, pp. 76–78.

is very important to reduce setup time. Not only does this reduce total costs but it also increases the production throughout for the system. For nonbottlenecks, setup time need not necessarily be reduced. This is because idle time exists for those operations and, if the workers are assigned to those operations, they have available time to make more setups until no more idle time exists. The important point here is that the total cost might take the following general form:

Total cost = Sum of all setup costs + Sum of all holding costs

or

$$TC = \sum_{i=1}^{n} \sum_{j=1}^{n} \sum_{K=1}^{n} \frac{D_i}{Q_j} S_K + \sum_{j=1}^{n} \sum_{m=1}^{n} Q_j H_m$$

Subscripts $i, j, k,$ and m refer to the various demands, lot sizes, holding, and setup costs throughout the system. The major caution in this equation is to understand that it consists of more than just a set of numbers to be inserted. It requires that the user understand bottlenecks, nonbottlenecks, idle time, which labor hours are fixed and which are variable, and so forth. The intent of current industry practice to minimize inventory is not inconsistent with this logic.

A second caution in using formulas such as this is not to try to minimize costs as the objective criterion. While minimizing costs might help, a better objective would be something like maximizing profit. Because cost minimization is often a local measurement, it can even interfere with the major objective of the firm, which might be "making money."

13.8 A MAJOR PROBLEM: DETERMINING REALISTIC COSTS

Most inventory models give optimal solutions so long as conditions of the system meet the constraints of the model. While this is easy to state, it is difficult to meet. Obtaining actual order, setup, carrying, and shortage costs is difficult—sometimes impossible. Part of the problem occurs because accounting data are usually averages, whereas we need the marginal costs. Exhibit 13.13 compares the assumed smoothly ascending cost to the more realistic actual cost. For example, a buyer is a salaried person. The marginal cost for the buyer's labor to place additional orders up to a full workload is zero. When another buyer is hired, it is a step function. (In theory, the marginal cost of the order that caused hiring the new buyer is the cost for the additional buyer.)

The same problem occurs in determining carrying costs. Warehouse cost, for example, may be close to zero if empty storage areas are still available. Also, most companies can only estimate true carrying costs, since they include obsolescence (a guess, at best), cost of capital (depends on internal money available, alternate investment opportunities, and sources of new capital), and

EXHIBIT 13.13

Cost to Place Orders
versus the Number of
Orders Placed: Linear
Assumption and
Normal Reality

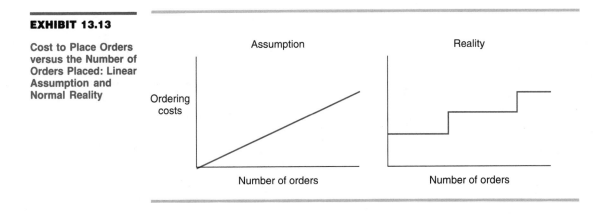

insurance costs (which may range from zero if current insurance premiums cover more than the assets on hand, to the cost of a new policy).

We can take two approaches to deal with this data inaccuracy. First, we can analyze the effects of error. That is, we can do a sensitivity analysis of our inventory model to errors in ordering, setup, and carrying costs and the effect on total annual cost. Second, we can conduct our inventory analysis in terms of inventory investment and workload, rather than in terms of order costs and carrying costs.

Errors in Costs

Inventory models generally involve quadratic equations. Therefore, even significant errors often have less effect than one might expect. The point here is that a high degree of accuracy is not necessary to receive the major part of the potential benefit. These comments are not meant to suggest you should reduce emphasis on computing order quantities, but rather to recognize where inventory costs come from and where emphasis must be placed to reduce costs significantly.

Exhibit 13.14 shows the computed order quantity for an item with an annual demand of 1,000 units, unit cost of $25, an inventory carrying cost of 25 percent of the cost (or $6.25), and various setup costs. The model used for the computation was the simple sawtooth model without safety stock. Note the effects on variable and total cost. If we assume that the true setup cost was $10, the optimal order quantity is 56.57 units. If a setup cost of $5 is used instead (half as much), the variable cost would be computed 29 percent low. If a setup cost of $20 (twice as much) is used, the variable cost would be computed as 41 percent higher. (The total variable cost at $S = \$10$ is $353.55; at $S = \$5$, total variable cost is $250; at $S = \$20$, total variable cost is $500.) The total range of error in using S—from half as much to double the true value—made a total annual difference of $250. The total cost, however, varies

EXHIBIT 13.14   Cost Effects of Changing Setup Cost *S*

(1)	(2)	(3)	(4)	(5)	(6)	(7)	(8)	(9)	(10)	(11)	(12)
	Setup							Total	Total	Change in	Change in
	Cost			$\frac{H}{i \times C}$				Variable	Annual	Variable	Total
D	*S*	*C*	*i*		*Q*	*D/Q* × *S*	*Q/2* × *H*	(7 + 8)	Cost	Cost	Cost
1,000	5	25	.25	6.25	40.00	125.00	125.00	250.00	25,250	−.29	−.0041
1,000	6	25	.25	6.25	43.82	136.93	136.93	273.86	25,274	−.23	−.0031
1,000	7	25	.25	6.25	47.33	147.90	147.90	295.00	25,296	−.16	−.0023
1,000	8	25	.25	6.25	50.60	158.11	158.11	316.22	25,316	−.11	−.0015
1,000	9	25	.25	6.25	53.67	167.71	167.71	335.41	25,335	−.05	−.0007
1,000	10	25	.25	6.25	56.57	176.78	176.78	353.55	25,354	.00	.0000
1,000	12	25	.25	6.25	61.97	193.65	193.65	387.30	25,387	.10	.0013
1,000	14	25	.25	6.25	66.93	209.17	209.17	418.33	25,418	.18	.0026
1,000	16	25	.25	6.25	71.55	223.61	223.61	447.21	25,447	.26	.0037
1,000	18	25	.25	6.25	75.89	237.17	237.17	474.34	25,474	.34	.0048
1,000	20	25	.25	6.25	80.00	250.00	250.00	500.00	25,500	.41	.0058

EXHIBIT 13.15

Order Quantity versus Setup Cost

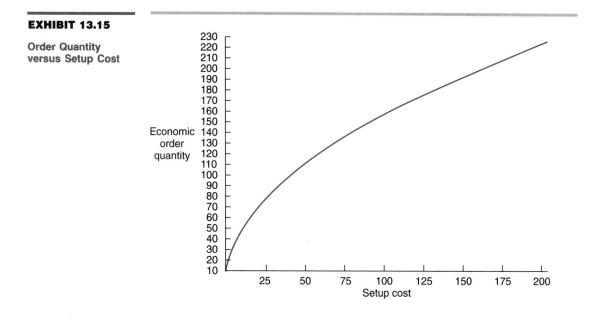

less than 1 percent—ranging from 0.4 percent low to 0.6 percent high. Exhibit 13.15 shows an expanded plot of Exhibit 13.14. Order quantity versus setup costs are shown for a range up to 230 units for *Q*, and $200 setup cost. Because *Q* is proportional to the square root of *S*, we note that the order quantity therefore increases exponentially.

All inventory systems are plagued by two major problems: maintaining adequate control over each inventory item and ensuring that accurate records of stock on hand are kept. In this section, we present **ABC analysis**—an inventory system offering a control technique and inventory cycle counting that can improve record accuracy.

ABC Inventory Planning

Maintaining inventory through counting, placing orders, receiving stock, and so on takes personnel time and costs money. When there are limits on these resources, the logical move is to try to use the available resources to control inventory in the best way. In other words, focus on the most important items in inventory.

In the 18th century, Villefredo Pareto, in a study of the distribution of wealth in Milan, found that 20 percent of the people controlled 80 percent of the wealth. This logic of the few having the greatest importance and the many having little importance has been broadened to include many situations and is termed the *Pareto Principle*. This is true in our everyday lives (most of the decisions we make are relatively unimportant but a few shape our future) and is certainly true in inventory systems (where a few items account for the bulk of our investment).

Any inventory system must specify when an order is to be placed for an item and how many units to order. In most situations involving inventory control, there are so many items involved, it is not practical to model and give thorough treatment to each item. To get around this problem, the ABC classification scheme divides inventory items into three groupings: high dollar volume (A), moderate dollar volume (B), and low dollar volume (C). Dollar volume is a measure of importance; an item low in cost but high in volume can be more important than a high-cost item with low volume.

ABC classification

If the annual usage of items in inventory is listed according to dollar volume, generally the list shows that a small number of items account for a large dollar volume and that a large number of items account for a small dollar volume. Exhibit 13.16 illustrates the relationship.

The ABC approach divides this list into three groupings by value: A items constitute roughly the top 15 percent of the items, B items the next 35 percent, and C items the last 50 percent. From observation, it appears that the list in Exhibit 13.16 may be meaningfully grouped with A including 20 percent (2 of the 10), B including 30 percent, and C including 50 percent. These points show clear delineations between sections. The result of this segmentation is shown in Exhibit 13.17 and is plotted in Exhibit 13.18.

Segmentation may not always occur so neatly. The objective, though, is to try to separate the important from the unimportant. Where the lines actually break depends on the particular inventory under question and on how much

EXHIBIT 13.16

Annual Usage of Inventory by Value

Item Number	Annual Dollar Usage	Percent of Total Value
22	$ 95,000	40.8%
68	75,000	32.1
27	25,000	10.7
03	15,000	6.4
82	13,000	5.6
54	7,500	3.2
36	1,500	0.6
19	800	0.3
23	425	0.2
41	225	0.1
	$233,450	100.0%

EXHIBIT 13.17

ABC Grouping of Inventory Items

Classification	Item Number	Annual Dollar Usage	Percent of Total
A	22, 68	$170,000	72.9%
B	27, 03, 82	53,000	22.7
C	54, 36, 19, 23, 41	10,450	4.4
		$233,450	100.0%

EXHIBIT 13.18

ABC Inventory Classification (Inventory value for each group versus the group's portion of the total list)

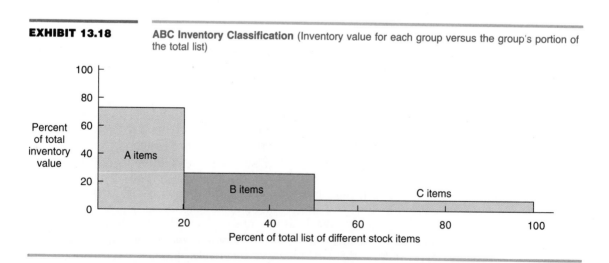

personnel time is available (with more time a firm could define larger A or B categories).

The purpose of classifying items into groups is to establish the appropriate degree of control over each item. On a periodic basis, for example, Class A items may be more clearly controlled with weekly ordering, B items may be ordered biweekly, and C items may be ordered monthly or bimonthly. Note that the unit cost of items is not related to their classification. An A item may have a high dollar volume through a combination of either low cost and high usage or high cost and low usage. Similarly, C items may have a low dollar volume either because of low demand or low cost. In an automobile service station, gasoline would be an A item with daily tabulation; tires, batteries, oil, grease, and transmission fluid may be B items and ordered every two to four weeks; and C items would consist of valve stems, windshield wiper blades, radiator caps, hoses, fan belts, oil and gas additives, car wax, and so forth. C items may be ordered every two or three months or even be allowed to run out before reordering since the penalty for stockout is not serious.

Sometimes, an item may be critical to a system if its absence creates a sizable loss. In this case, regardless of the item's classification, sufficiently large stocks should be kept on hand to prevent runout. One way to ensure closer control is to designate this item an A or a B, forcing it into the category even if its dollar volume does not warrant such inclusion.

Inventory Accuracy and Cycle Counting

Inventory records usually differ from the actual physical count and **inventory accuracy** refers to how well the two agree. The question is, How much error is acceptable? If the record shows a balance of 683 of Part X and an actual count shows 652, is this within reason? Suppose the actual count shows 750, an excess of 67 over the record; is this any better?

Every production system must have agreement, within some specified range, between what the record says is in inventory and what actually is in inventory. There are many reasons records and inventory may not agree. For example, an open stockroom area allows items to be removed for both legitimate and unauthorized purposes. The legitimate removal may have been done in a hurry and simply not recorded. Sometimes parts are misplaced, turning up months later. Parts are often stored in several locations, but records may be lost or the location recorded incorrectly. Sometimes stock replenishment orders are recorded as received, when in fact they never were. Occasionally, a group of parts are recorded as removed from inventory, but the customer order is canceled and the parts are replaced in inventory without canceling the record. To keep the production system flowing smoothly without parts shortages and efficiently without excess balances, it is important that records are accurate.

How can a firm keep accurate, up-to-date records? The first general rule is to keep the storeroom locked. If only storeroom personnel have access, and one of their measures of performance when it comes time for personnel evaluation and merit increases is record accuracy, there is a strong motivation to comply. Every location of inventory storage, whether in a locked storeroom or on the production floor, should have a recordkeeping mechanism. A second way is to convey the importance of accurate records to all personnel and depend on them to assist in this effort. (What this all boils down to is: Put a fence that goes all the way to the ceiling around the storage area so that workers can't climb over to get parts; put a lock on the gate and give one person the key. Nobody, but nobody, can pull parts without having the transaction authorized and recorded.)

Another way to ensure accuracy is to count inventory frequently and match this against records. A widely used method is called *cycle counting*.

Cycle counting is a physical inventory-taking technique in which inventory is counted on a frequent basis rather than once or twice a year. The key to effective cycle counting and, therefore, to accurate records lies in deciding which items are to be counted, when, and by whom.

Virtually all inventory systems these days are computerized; the computer can be programmed to produce a cycle count notice in the following cases:

1. When the record shows a low or zero balance on hand. (Obviously it is easier to count fewer items.)
2. When the record shows a positive balance but a backorder was written (indicating a discrepancy).
3. After some specified level of activity.
4. To signal a review based on the importance of the item (as in the ABC system) such as in the following example.

Annual Dollar Usage	Review Period
$10,000 or more	30 days or less
$3,000–$10,000	45 days or less
$250–3,000	90 days or less
Less than $250	180 days or less

Obviously, the easiest time for stock to be counted is when there is no activity in the stockroom or on the production floor. This means on the weekends or during the second or third shift, when the facility is less busy. If this is not possible, more careful logging and separation of items are required to do an inventory count while production is going on and transactions are occurring.

The counting cycle depends on the available personnel. Some firms schedule regular stockroom personnel to do the counting during the lull times of the regular working day. Other companies contract out to private firms who come in and count inventory. Still other firms use full-time cycle counters who do nothing but count inventory and resolve differences with the records. While this last method sounds expensive, many firms believe that it is actually less costly than the usual hectic annual inventory count generally performed during the two- or three-week annual vacation shutdown.

The question of how much error is tolerable between physical inventory and records has been much debated. While some firms strive for 100 percent accuracy, others accept 1, 2, or 3 percent error. The accuracy level recommended by the American Production and Inventory Control Society (APICS) is: ± 0.2 percent for A items, ± 1 percent for B items, and ± 5 percent for C items. Regardless of the specific accuracy decided on, the important point is that the level be dependable so that safety stocks may be provided as a cushion. Accuracy is important for a smooth production process so that customer orders can be processed as scheduled and not held up because of the unavailability of parts.

Inventory Control in Services

To demonstrate how inventory control is conducted in service organizations, we have selected two areas to describe: a department store and an automobile service agency.

Department store inventory policy

The common term used to identify an inventory item in a department store is *stock-keeping unit* or SKU. The SKU identifies each item, its manufacturer, and its cost. The number of SKUs becomes large even for small departments. For example, if towels carried in a domestic items department are obtained from three manufacturers in three quality levels, three sizes (hand towel, face towel, and bath towel), and four colors, there are 108 different items ($3 \times 3 \times 3 \times 4$). Even if towels are sold only in sets of three pieces (hand towel, face towel, and bath towel), the number of SKUs needed to identify the towel sets is $3 \times 3 \times 1 \times 4$, or 36. Depending on the store, a housewares department may carry 3,000 to 4,000 SKUs, and a linen and domestic items department may carry 5,000 to 6,000.

Obviously, such large numbers mean that individual economic order quantities cannot be calculated for each item by hand. How, then, does a department keep tabs on its stock and place orders for replenishment? We answer this question in the context of an example dealing with a housewares department.

Housewares department.

Generally, housewares are divided into staple and promotional items. Within these major divisions, further classifications are used, such as cookware and tableware. Also, items are frequently classified by price, as $5 items, $4, $3, and so forth.

The housewares department usually purchases from a distributor rather than directly from a manufacturer. The use of a distributor, who handles products from many manufacturers, has the advantage of fewer orders and faster shipping time (shorter lead time). Further, the distributor's sales personnel may visit the housewares department weekly and count all the items they supply to this department. Then, in line with the replenishment level that has been established by the buyer, the distributor's salesperson places orders for the buyer. This saves the department time in counting inventory and placing orders. The typical lead time for receipt of stock from a housewares distributor is two or three days. The safety stock, therefore, is quite low, and the buyer establishes the replenishment level so as to supply only enough items for the two- to three-day lead time, plus expected demand during the period until the distributor's salesperson's next visit.

Note that a formal method of estimating stockout and establishing safety-stock levels is usually not followed because the number of items is too great. Instead, the total value of items in the department is monitored. Thus, replenishment levels are set by dollar allocation.

Through planning, each department has an established monthly value for inventory. By tabulating inventory balance, monthly sales, and items on order, an "open-to-buy" figure is determined. ("Open-to-buy" is the unspent portion of the budget.) This dollar amount is the sum available to the buyer for the following month. When an increase in demand is expected (Christmas, Mother's Day, and so forth), the allocation of funds to the department is increased, resulting in a larger open-to-buy position. Then the replenishment levels are raised in line with the class of goods, responding to the demand increase, thereby creating a higher stock of goods on hand.

In practice, the open-to-buy funds are largely spent during the first days of the month. However, the buyer tries to reserve some funds for special purchases or to restock fast-moving items. Promotional items in housewares are controlled individually (or by class) by the buyer.

Maintaining an auto replacement-parts inventory
A firm in the automobile service business purchases most of its parts supplies from a small number of distributors. Franchised new-car dealers purchase the great bulk of their supplies from the automobile manufacturer. A dealer's demand for auto parts originates primarily from the general public and other departments of the agency, such as the service department or body shop. The problem, in this case, is to determine the order quantities for the several thousand items carried.

A franchised automobile agency of medium size may carry a parts inventory valued in the area of $500,000. Because of the nature of this industry, alternate uses of funds are plentiful, and therefore, opportunity costs are high. For example, dealers may lease cars, carry their own contracts, stock a larger new-car inventory, or open sidelines such as tire shops, trailer sales, or recreational vehicle sales—all with potentially high returns. This creates pressure to try to carry a low inventory level of parts and supplies while still meeting an acceptable service level.

While many dealers still perform their inventory ordering by hand, there is a definite trend in the industry to use computers. For both manual and computerized systems, an ABC classification works well. Expensive and high-turnover supplies are counted and ordered frequently; low-cost items are ordered in large quantities at infrequent intervals. A common drawback of frequent order placement is the extensive amount of time needed to physically put the items on the shelves and log them in. (However, this restocking procedure does not greatly add to an auto agency's cost because parts department personnel generally do this during slow periods.)

A great variety of computerized systems is currently in use. One program gives a choice of using either a simple weighted average or exponential smoothing to forecast the next period's demand. In a monthly reordering system, for example, the items to be ordered are counted and the number on hand is entered into the computer. By subtracting the number on hand from the previous month's inventory and adding the orders received during the month, the usage rate is determined. Some programs use exponential smoothing forecasts while others use a weighted-average method. For the weighted-average method the computer program stores the usage rate for, say, four previous months. Then, with the application of a set of weighting factors, a forecast is made in the same manner as described in Chapter 7. This works as follows: Suppose usage of a part during January, February, March, and April was 17, 19, 11, and 23, respectively, and the set of corresponding weights was 0.10, 0.20, 0.30, and 0.40. Thus, the forecast for May is $0.10(17) + 0.20(19) + 0.30(11) + 0.40(23)$, or 18 units. If safety stock were included and equal to one-month demand, then 36 units would be ordered (one-month demand plus one-month safety stock) less whatever is on hand at the time of order placement. This simple two-month rule allows for forecasted usage during the lead time plus the review period, with the balance providing the safety stock.

The computer output provides a useful reference file, identifying the item, cost, order size, and number of units on hand. The output itself constitutes the purchase order and is sent to the distributor or factory supply house. The simplicity in this is attractive since, once the forecast weighting is selected, all that needs to be done is to input the number of units of each item on hand. Thus, negligible computation is involved, and very little preparation is needed to send the order out.

13.9 CONCLUSION

This chapter introduced the two main classes of demand: independent demand referring to the external demand for a firm's end product, and dependent demand, usually referring—within the firm—to the demand for items created because of the demand for more complex items of which they are a part. Most industries have items in both classes. In manufacturing, for example, independent demand is common for finished products, service and repair parts, and operating supplies; and dependent demand is common for those parts and materials needed to produce the end product. In wholesale and retail sales of consumer goods, most demand is independent—each item is an end item, with the wholesaler or retailer doing no further assembly or fabrication.

Independent demand, the focus of this chapter, is based on statistics. In the fixed-order quantity and fixed-time period models, the influence of service level was shown on safety stock and reorder point determinations. Two special-purpose models—price break and single-period—were also presented.

To distinguish among item categories for analysis and control, the ABC method was offered. The importance of inventory accuracy was also noted, and cycle counting was described. Finally, brief descriptions of inventory procedures in a department store and an auto parts shop were given to illustrate some of the simpler ways nonmanufacturing firms carry out their inventory control functions.

In this chapter we also pointed out that inventory reduction requires a knowledge of the operating system. It is not simply a case of selecting a model off the shelf and plugging in some numbers. In the first place, a model might not even be appropriate. In the second case, the numbers might be full of errors or even based on erroneous data. It is vital to understand that this is also not a trade-off compromise. Very often determining order quantities is referred to as a trade-off problem; that is, trading off holding costs for setup costs. Note that companies really want to reduce both.

The simple fact is that firms have very large investments in inventory, and the cost to carry this inventory runs from 25 to 35 percent of the inventory's worth annually. Therefore, a major goal of most firms today is to reduce inventory; they expect this to also lead to improved quality and performance and to greatly reduce cost.

13.10 REVIEW AND DISCUSSION QUESTIONS

1. Distinguish between dependent and independent demand in a McDonald's, in an integrated manufacturer of personal copiers, and in a pharmaceutical supply house.

2. Distinguish between in-process inventory, safety stock inventory, and seasonal inventory.

3. Discuss the nature of the costs that affect inventory size.

4. Under which conditions would a plant manager elect to use a fixed-order quantity model as opposed to a fixed-time period model? What are the disadvantages of using a fixed-time period ordering system?

5. Define the term *service level* as used in this text. How does it differ from the concept of probability of stockout?

6. Discuss the general procedure for determining the order quantity when price breaks are involved. Would there be any differences in the procedure if holding cost were a fixed percentage of price rather than a constant amount?

7. What two basic questions must be answered by an inventory-control decision rule?

8. Discuss the assumptions that are inherent in production setup cost, ordering cost, and carrying costs. How valid are they?

9. "The nice thing about inventory models is that you can pull one off the shelf and apply it so long as your cost estimates are accurate." Comment.

10. Which type of inventory system would you use in the following situations?
    a. Supplying your kitchen with fresh food.
    b. Obtaining a daily newspaper.
    c. Buying gasoline for your car.
    To which of these items do you impute the highest stockout cost?

11. Why is it desirable to classify items into groups, as the ABC classification does?

12. What kind of policy or procedure would you recommend to improve the inventory operation in a department store? What advantages and disadvantages does your system have vis-à-vis the department store inventory operation described in this chapter?

13.11 PROBLEMS

*1. Items purchased from a vendor cost $20 each, and the forecast for next year's demand is 1,000 units. If it costs $5 every time an order is placed for more units and the storage cost is $4 per unit per year, what quantity should be ordered each time?
    a. What is the total ordering cost for a year?
    b. What is the total storage cost for a year?

*2. Daily demand for a product is 120 units, with a standard deviation of 30 units. The review period is 14 days and the lead time is 7 days. At the time of review there are 130 units in stock. If 99 percent of all demand is to be satisfied from items in stock, how many units should be ordered?

*3. A company currently has 200 units of a product on hand which it orders every two weeks when the salesperson visits the premises. Demand for the product averages 20 units per day with a standard deviation of five units. Lead time for the product to arrive is seven days. Management has a goal of providing a 99 percent service level for this product.

    The salesperson is due to come in late this afternoon when there are 180 units left in stock (assuming that 20 are sold today). How many units should be ordered?

4. Annual demand for an item is 2,500 units. The cost to place an order is $5, and holding cost is 20 percent of the cost of the item. Items have the following cost schedule:

1 to 99	$10.00 each
100 to 199	$ 9.80 each
over 200	$ 9.60 each

    What is the optimal number to order each time?

5. Electronic Memos, Inc., (EMI) produces pocket-size microcassette recorders for business and professional people to record notes and for transcribing. These recorders are sold through retailers nationally.

    EMI would like to provide its retailers with guidelines to help them determine what size orders they should place, what safety stocks to carry, the reorder points,

---

* Problems 1, 2, and 3 are completely solved in Appendix H.

and so forth. EMI has just hired you to develop a set of charts that would be distributed to its retailers and would be useful to them during their reordering periods.

Because technology in the entire electronics area is changing so rapidly (recorders included), EMI is recommending that its dealers review their inventory on hand and place orders monthly.

During an interview for a job with EMI, the recruiter has explained this reordering situation to you and has asked you to demonstrate that you are qualified to take on this task as your first assignment with the company. You happen to have a copy of your operations management text with you and he is allowing you to use the equations and tables.

The tables cover a wide variety of possibilities. The problem you are to solve has the following features:

Demand for the coming 30-day month is 40 units.

Standard deviation of daily demand is 4 units.

The firm is open every day.

It takes 10 calendar days to receive an order.

The firm would like to satisfy 95 percent of the customers.

There are currently 30 units in stock.

How many units should be ordered?

6. Dunstreet's Department Store would like to develop an inventory ordering policy to satisfy 95 percent of its customers' demands for products directly from inventory stock on hand. To illustrate your recommended procedure, use as an example the ordering policy for white percale sheets.

Demand for white percale sheets is 5,000 per year. The store is open 365 days per year. Every two weeks (14 days) an inventory count is made and a new order is placed. It takes 10 days for the sheets to be delivered. Standard deviation of demand for the sheets is 5 per day. There are currently 150 sheets on hand.

How many sheets should you order?

7. Charlie's Pizza orders all of its pepperoni, olives, anchovies, and mozzarella cheese to be shipped directly from Italy. An American distributor stops by every four weeks to take orders. Since the orders are shipped directly from Italy, it takes three weeks to arrive.

Charlie's Pizza uses an average of 150 pounds of pepperoni each week, with a standard deviation of 30 pounds. Since Charlie's prides itself on offering only the best quality ingredients and a high level of service, they want to assure that they will be able to satisfy 99 percent of the customers who demand pepperoni on their pizza.

Assume that the sales representative just walked in the door and there is currently 500 pounds of pepperoni in the walk-in cooler. How many pounds of pepperoni would you order?

8. Given the information below, formulate an inventory management system. The item is demanded 50 weeks a year.

Item cost	$10.00
Order cost	$250.00
Holding cost (%)	33% of item cost

Annual demand	25,750
Average demand	515 per week
Standard deviation of demand	25 per week
Lead time	1 week
Service level	95%

    a.   State the order quantity and the reorder point.

    b.   Determine the annual holding and order costs.

    c.   How many units per order cycle would you expect to be short?

    d.   If a price break of $50 per order was offered for purchase quantities of over 1,000 would you take advantage of it? How much would you save on an annual basis?

9.   Lieutenant Commander Data is planning to make his monthly (every 30 days) trek to Gamma Hydra City to pickup a supply of isolinear chips. The trip will take Data about two days. Before he leaves, he calls in the order to the GHC Supply Store. He uses chips at an average rate of 5 per day (seven days per week) with a standard deviation of demand of 1 per day. He needs a 99 percent service level. If he currently has 35 chips in inventory, how many should he order? What is the most he will ever have to order?

10.   Jill's Job Shop buys two parts (Tegdiws and Widgets) which they use in their production system from two different suppliers. The parts are needed throughout the entire 52-week year. Tegdiws are used at a relatively constant rate and are ordered whenever the remaining quantity drops to the reorder level. Widgets are ordered from a supplier who stops by every three weeks.

    Data for both products are as follows:

Item	Tegdiw	Widget
Annual demand	10,000	5,000
Holding cost (% of item cost)	20%	20%
Setup or order cost	$150.00	$25.00
Lead time	4 weeks	1 week
Safety stock	55 units	5 units
Item cost	$10.00	$2.00

    Management would like to stock these items with a 95 percent service level.

    a.   What is the inventory control system for Tegdiws; that is, what is the reorder quantity and what is the reorder point?

    b.   What is the inventory control system for Widgets?

11.   Demand for an item is 1,000 units per year. Each order placed costs $10; the annual cost to carry items in inventory is $2 each.

    a.   In what quantities should the item be ordered?

    b.   Supposing a $100 discount on each order is given if orders are placed in quantities of 500 or more. Should orders be placed in quantities of 500, or should you stick to the decision you made in *a*?

12.   The annual demand for a product is 15,600 units. The weekly demand is 300 units with a standard deviation of 90 units. The cost to place an order is $31.20, and the time from ordering to receipt is four weeks. The annual inventory carrying cost is $0.10 per unit. Find the reorder point necessary to provide a 99 percent service level.

    Suppose the production manager is ordered to reduce the safety stock of this item by 50 percent. If he does so, what will the new service level be?

13. Daily demand for a product is 100 units, with a standard deviation of 25 units. The review period is 10 days and the lead time is 6 days. At the time of review there are 50 units in stock. If 98 percent of all demand is to be satisfied from items in stock, how many units should be ordered?

14. Item X is a standard item stocked in a company's inventory of component parts. Each year, the firm, on a random basis, uses about 2,000 of Item X, which costs $25 each. Storage costs, which include insurance and cost of capital, amount to $5 per unit of average inventory. Every time an order is placed for more Item X, it costs $10.
   a. Whenever Item X is ordered, what should the order size be?
   b. What is the annual cost for ordering Item X?
   c. What is the annual cost for storing Item X?

15. The annual demand for a product is 13,000 units; the weekly demand is 250 units with a standard deviation of 40 units. The cost of placing an order is $100, and the time from ordering to receipt is four weeks. The annual inventory carrying cost is $0.65 per unit. To provide a 99 percent service level, what must the reorder point be?

   Suppose the production manager is told to reduce the safety stock of this item by 10 units. If this is done, what will the new service level be?

16. A particular raw material is available to a company at three different prices, depending on the size of the orders, as follows:

Less than 100 pounds	$20 per pound
100 pounds to 999 pounds	$19 per pound
more than 1,000 pounds	$18 per pound

   The cost to place an order is $40. Annual demand is 3,000 units. Holding (or carrying) cost is 25 percent of the material price.
   What is the economic order quantity to buy each time?

17. In the past, Taylor Industries has used a fixed-time inventory system that involved taking a complete inventory count of all items each month. However, increasing labor costs are forcing Taylor Industries to examine alternate ways to reduce the amount of labor involved in inventory stockrooms, yet without increasing other costs, such as shortage costs.
   Following is a random sample of 20 of Taylor's items.

Item Number	Annual Usage	Item Number	Annual Usage
1	$ 1,500	11	$13,000
2	12,000	12	600
3	2,200	13	42,000
4	50,000	14	9,900
5	9,600	15	1,200
6	750	16	10,200
7	2,000	17	4,000
8	11,000	18	61,000
9	800	19	3,500
10	15,000	20	2,900

   a. What would you recommend Taylor do to cut back its labor cost? (Illustrate using an ABC plan.)

     b.   Item 15 is critical to continued operations. How would you recommend it be classified?

18.   Gentle Ben's Bar and Restaurant uses 5,000 quart bottles of an imported wine each year. The effervescent wine costs $3 per bottle and is served in whole bottles only since it loses its bubbles quickly. Ben figures that it costs $10 each time an order is placed, and holding costs are 20 percent of the purchase price. It takes three weeks for an order to arrive. Weekly demand is 100 bottles (closed two weeks per year) with a standard deviation of 30 bottles.

    Ben would like to use an inventory system that minimizes inventory cost and will satisfy 95 percent of his customers who order this wine.

    a.   What is the economic order quantity for Ben to order?

    b.   At what inventory level should he place an order?

    c.   How many bottles of wine will be short during each order cycle?

19.   Retailers Warehouse (RW) is an independent supplier of household items to department stores. RW attempts to stock enough items to satisfy 98 percent of the requests from its customers.

    A stainless steel knife set is one of the items stocked by RW. Demand is 2,400 sets per year, relatively stable over the entire year. Whenever new stock is ordered, a buyer must ensure that numbers are correct for stock on hand and phone in a new order. The total cost involved to place an order is about $5. RW figures that to hold inventory in stock and to pay for interest on borrowed capital, insurance, and so on adds up to about $4 holding cost per unit per year.

    Analysis of the past data shows that the standard deviation of demand from retailers is about four units per day for a 365-day year. Lead time to get the order once placed is seven days.

    a.   What is the economic order quantity?

    b.   What is the reorder point?

20.   Daily demand for a product is 60 units with a standard deviation of 10 units. The review period is 10 days, and the lead time is 2 days. At the time of review there are 100 units in stock. If 98 percent of all demand is to be satisfied from items in stock, how many units should be ordered?

21.   University Drug Pharmaceuticals orders its antibiotics every two weeks (14 days) when a salesperson visits from one of the pharmaceutical companies. Tetracycline is one of its most prescribed antibiotics, with an average daily demand of 2,000 capsules. The standard deviation of daily demand was derived from examining prescriptions filled over the past three months and was found to be 800 capsules. It takes five days for the order to arrive. University Drug would like to satisfy 99 percent of the prescriptions. The salesperson just arrived, and there are currently 25,000 capsules in stock.

    How many capsules should be ordered?

22.   SJM Manufacturing, Inc., is planning to change its scheduling and materials handling procedures. Several of their machine centers produce a number of parts on each machine; these parts are then used internally elsewhere in the production process. SJM would like to study and understand the interaction between process batch sizes and transfer batch sizes and their effect on total cost. Currently the process batch is transferred after it is totally completed.

    One of their operations management staff noticed that some of the machines produce batches of different parts that are then used on other machines; these machines also produce batches of different products. The question arose as to whether there could be some coordination between these processes so that items could be transferred in batches smaller than the total process batch. Also, what potential benefits might there be?

One item was selected to use for a quick calculation of costs. This item has an annual demand of 24,000 units and a manufacturing cost of $8 each. Carrying cost is 25 percent of manufacturing cost, and setup cost is estimated to be $40.

a.   While ignoring materials handling costs, what would the process batch size be if parts could be tranferred in two batches, five batches, and ten batches, rather than in one batch containing the entire process batch?

b.   What would the total costs due to setup and holding be for each batch size? (Ignore materials handling and other costs.)

c.   Discuss the results.

23.   Magnetron, Inc., manufactures microwave ovens for the commercial market. Currently, Magnetron is producing part 2104 in its fabrication shop for use in the adjacent unit assembly area. Next year's requirement for part 2104 is estimated at 20,000 units. Part 2104 is valued at $50 per unit, and the combined storage and handling cost is $8 per unit per year. The cost of preparing the order and making the production setup is $200. The plant operates 250 days per year. The assembly area operates every working day, completing 80 units, and the fabrication shop produces 160 units per day when it is producing part 2104.

a.   Compute the economic order quantity.

b.   How many orders will be placed each year?

c.   If part 2104 could be purchased from another firm with the same costs as described, what would the order quantity be? (The order is received all at once.)

d.   If the average lead time to order from another firm is 10 working days and a safety stock level is set at 500 units, what is the reorder point?

24.   Garrett Corporation, a turbine manufacturer, works an 18-hour day, 300 days a year. Titanium blades can be produced on its turbine blade machine number 1, TBM1, at a rate of 500 per hour, and the average usage rate is 5,000 per day. The blades cost $15 apiece, and storage costs $0.10 per day per blade because of insurance, interest on investments, and space allocation. TBM1 costs $250 to set up for each run. Lead time requires production to begin after stock drops to 500 blades. What is the optimal production run for TBM1?

25.   Famous Albert prides himself on being the Cookie King of the West. Small, freshly baked cookies are the specialty of his shops; day-old cookies are sold at reduced prices.

Famous Albert has asked for help to determine the number of cookies he should make each day. From an analysis of its past demands, Famous Albert estimates the demand for cookies as

Demand	Probability of Demand
1,800 dozen	0.05
2,000	0.10
2,200	0.20
2,400	0.30
2,600	0.20
2,800	0.10
3,000	0.05

Each dozen sells for $.69 and costs $.49, which includes handling and transportation. Cookies that are not sold at the end of the day are reduced to $0.29 and sold the following day as day-old merchandise.

a. Construct a table showing the profits or losses for each possible quantity.

b. What is the optimal number of cookies to make?

c. Solve this problem by using marginal analysis.

26. The text described how one department store conducted its inventory ordering for a housewares department. How would you apply the theory and models in this chapter to enhance the operation of that store's system?

27. Alpha Products, Inc. is having a problem trying to control inventory. There is insufficient time to devote to all its items equally. Following is a sample of some items stocked, along with the annual usage of each item expressed in dollar volume.

Item	Annual Dollar Usage	Item	Annual Dollar Usage
a	$ 7,000	k	$80,000
b	1,000	l	400
c	14,000	m	1,100
d	2,000	n	30,000
e	24,000	o	1,900
f	68,000	p	800
g	17,000	q	90,000
h	900	r	12,000
i	1,700	s	3,000
j	2,300	t	32,000

Can you suggest a system for allocating control time? Specify where each item from the list would be placed.

28. After graduation you decide to go into a partnership in an office supply store. The store has existed for a number of years and, walking through the store and stockrooms, you find a great discrepancy in service levels. Some spaces and bins for items are completely empty; others have supplies covered with dust and have obviously been there a long time. You decide to take on the project of establishing consistent levels of inventory to meet customer demands. Most of your supplies are purchased from just a few distributors, and these distributors call on your store once every two weeks.

You choose, as your first item for study, computer printer paper. You examine the sales records and purchase orders and find that demand for the past 12 months was 5,000 boxes. Using your calculator you sample some days' demands and estimate that the standard deviation of daily demand is 10 boxes. You also searched out these figures:

Cost per box of paper: $11.

Desired service level: 98 percent.

Store is open every day.

Salesperson visits every 2 weeks.

Delivery time following visit: 3 days.

Using your procedure, how many boxes of paper would be ordered if, on the day the salesperson calls, there are 60 boxes on hand?

29. A distributor of large appliances needs to determine the order quantities and reorder points for the various products it carries. The following data refers to a specific refrigerator in its product line:

Cost to place an order	$30
Holding cost	20 percent of product cost per year
Cost of refrigerator	$300 each
Annual demand	500 refrigerators
Standard deviation during lead time	10 refrigerators
Lead time	7 days

Consider an even daily demand and a 365-day year.

a. What is the economic order quantity?

b. If the distributor wants to satisfy 97 percent of its demand, what reorder point, R, should be used?

30. It is your responsibility, as the new head of the automotive section of Nichols Department Store, to assure that reorder quantities for the various items have been correctly established. You decide to test one of the items and choose Michelin tires, XW size 185 × 14 BSW.

A perpetual inventory system has been used so you examine this as well as other records and come up with the following data:

Cost per tire	$35 each
Holding cost	20 percent of tire cost per year
Demand	1,000 per year
Ordering cost	$20 per order
Standard deviation of daily demand	3 tires
Delivery lead time	4 days

Because customers generally do not wait for tires but go elsewhere, you decide on a service level of 98 percent.

a. Determine the order quantity.

b. Determine the reorder point.

31. UA Hamburger Hamlet places an order for its high-volume items daily (hamburger patties, buns, milk, etc.). UAHH counts its current inventory on hand once per day and phones in its order for delivery 24 hours later.

Your problem here is to determine the number of hamburgers UAHH should order for the following conditions:

Average daily demand	600
Standard deviation of demand	100
Desired service level	99%

On the particular day for this problem, the inventory count shows 800 hamburgers on hand. How many hamburgers should be ordered?

32. CU, Incorporated, (CUI), produces copper contacts that it uses in switches and relays. CUI needs to determine the order quantity, Q, to meet the annual demand at the lowest cost.

The price of copper depends on the quantity ordered. Following are the price-break data and the other data for the problem:

Price of copper	$0.82 per pound up to 2,499 pounds
	$0.81 per pound for orders between 2,500 to 4,999 pounds
	$0.80 per pound for orders greater than 5,000 pounds

Annual demand	50,000 pounds per year
Holding cost	20 percent per unit per year of the price of the copper
Ordering cost	$30

Which quantity should be ordered?

33. DAT, Inc. produces digital audiotapes to be used in the consumer audio division. DAT doesn't have sufficient personnel in its inventory supply section to closely control each item stocked, so others asked you to determine an ABC classification. The following shows a sample from the inventory records:

Item	Average Monthly Demand	Price per Unit
1	700	$ 6.00
2	200	4.00
3	2,000	12.00
4	1,100	20.00
5	4,000	21.00
6	100	10.00
7	3,000	2.00
8	2,500	1.00
9	500	10.00
10	1,000	2.00

Develop an ABC classification for these 10 items.

34. A local service station is open 7 days per week, 365 days per year. Sales of 10W40 grade premium oil average 20 cans per day. Inventory holding costs are $0.50 per can per year. Ordering costs are $10 per order and the lead time is two weeks. Back orders are not practical—the motorist drives away.

   a. Based on this data, choose the appropriate inventory model and calculate the economic order quantity and the reorder point. Describe in a sentence how the plan would work. Hint: Assume demand is deterministic.

   b. The boss is concerned about this model because demand really varies. The standard deviation of demand was determined from a data sample to be 6.15 cans per day. The manager wants to satisfy 99.5 percent of his customers (practically all) when they ask for oil. Determine a new inventory plan based on this new information and the data in (a). Use Q_{opt} from (a).

13.12 SELECTED BIBLIOGRAPHY

Anderson, Edward J. "Testing Feasibility in a Lot Scheduling Problem." *Operations Research,* November–December 1990, pp. 1079–89.

Bernhard, Paul. "The Carrying Cost Paradox: How Do You Manage It?" *Industrial Engineering,* November 1989, pp. 40–46.

Davis, Samuel G. "Scheduling Economic Lot Size Production Runs." *Management Science,* August 1990, pp. 985–99.

Fogarty, Donald W.; John H. Blackstone; and Thomas R. Hoffmann. *Production and Inventory Management.* 2nd ed. Cincinnati, Ohio: South-Western Publishing, 1991.

Freeland, James R.; John P. Leschke; and Elliott N. Weiss. "Guidelines for Setup Reduction Programs to Achieve Zero Inventory." *Journal of Operations Management,* January 1990, pp. 75–80.

Greene, James H. *Production and Inventory Control Handbook.* 2nd ed. New York: McGraw-Hill, 1987.

Harris, Ford Whitman. "How Many Parts to Make at Once." *Operations Research,* November–December 1990, pp. 947–51.

Tersine, Richard J. *Principles of Inventory and Materials Management.* 3rd ed. New York: North-Holland, 1988.

Trigeiro, William W. "A Simple Heuristic for Lot Sizing with Setup Times." *Decision Sciences,* Spring 1989, pp. 294–303.

Vollmann, T. E.; W. L. Berry; and D. C. Whybark. *Manufacturing Planning and Control Systems.* 2nd ed. Homewood, Ill.: Richard D. Irwin, 1988.

Young, Jan B. *Modern Inventory Operations: Methods for Accuracy and Productivity.* New York: Van Nostrand Reinhold, 1991.

Chapter 14

Inventory Systems for Dependent Demand: Materials Requirements Planning

EPIGRAPH

To make Grandma's Chocolate Cake, take 1 cup shortening, 2 cups sugar, 1 teaspoon salt, 1 teaspoon vanilla, 2 eggs, 2¼ cups flour, 1 cup buttermilk, ½ cup cocoa, 2 teaspoons soda, and 1 cup hot water. . . .

Material requirements planning (MRP) systems have been installed almost universally, in manufacturing firms, even those considered small. The reason is that MRP is a logical and easily understandable approach to the problem of determining the number of parts, components, and materials needed to produce each end item. MRP also provides the time schedule specifying when each of these materials, parts, and components should be ordered or produced.

The original MRP planned only materials. However, as computer power grew in the past 20 or so years and applications expanded, so did the breadth of MRP. Soon it considered resources as well as materials; now MRP stands for **manufacturing resource planning.** A complete MRP program includes 20 or so modules controlling the entire system from order entry through scheduling, inventory control, finance, accounting, accounts payable, and so on. Today MRP impacts the entire system.

Manufacturing firms (all firms for that matter) maintain a bill of materials file (BOM) which is simply the sequence of everything that goes into the final product. It can be called a *schematic* or *flow diagram,* which shows the order of creating the item. Also maintained by all firms, is an inventory file. This database contains specifications about each item, where it is purchased or produced, and how long it takes. MRP, then, is a computer program determining how much of each item is needed and when it is needed to complete a specified number of units in a specific time period. MRP does this by reaching into the bill of materials file and inventory records file to create a time schedule and the number of units needed at each step in the process.

MRP is based on dependent demand. Dependent demand is that demand caused by the demand for a higher-level item. Tires, wheels, and engines are dependent demand items that depend on the demand for automobiles.

Determining the number of dependent demand items needed is essentially a straightforward multiplication process. If one Part A takes five parts of B to make, then five parts of A requires twenty-five parts of B. The basic difference in independent demand covered in the previous chapter and dependent demand covered in this chapter, is as follows: If Part A is sold outside of the firm, the amount of Part A that we sell is uncertain. We need to create a forecast using past data or to do something like a market analysis. Part A is an independent item. However, Part B is a dependent part and its use depends on Part A. The number of B needed is simply the number of A times five. As a result of this type of multiplication, the requirements of other dependent demand items tends to become more and more lumpy as we go farther down into the product creation sequence. Lumpiness means that the requirements tend to bunch or lump rather than having an even disbursement. This is also caused by the way manufacturing is done. Generally manufacturing occurs in lots; items needed to produce the lot are withdrawn from inventory in quantities (perhaps all at once) rather than one at a time.

The main purpose of this chapter is to explain MRP more thoroughly and to demonstrate its use through several illustrations. We also discuss samples of existing MRP programs currently in use in industry. Finally, we show that Just-in-Time (JIT) systems and MRP are not necessarily competing ways for production but can work effectively together.

14.1 A SIMPLE MRP EXAMPLE

Before discussing details of an MRP system, we very briefly explain how quantities are calculated, lead times are offset, and order releases and receipts are established.

Suppose that we are to produce Product T, which is made of two parts U and three parts V. Part U, in turn, is made of one part W and two parts X. Part V is made of two parts W and two parts Y. Exhibit 14.1 shows the product structure tree of Product T. By simple computation, we calculate that if 100 units of T are required, we need:

$$
\begin{array}{llll}
\text{Part U:} & 2 \times \text{number of Ts} = & 2 \times 100 & = 200 \\
\text{Part V:} & 3 \times \text{number of Ts} = & 3 \times 100 & = 300 \\
\text{Part W:} \left\{ \begin{array}{l} 1 \times \text{number of Us} = \\ +2 \times \text{number of Vs} = \end{array} \right. & \left\{ \begin{array}{l} 1 \times 200 \\ +2 \times 300 \end{array} \right\} & = 800 \\
\text{Part X:} & 2 \times \text{number of Us} = & 2 \times 200 & = 400 \\
\text{Part Y:} & 2 \times \text{number of Vs} = & 2 \times 300 & = 600
\end{array}
$$

Now, consider the time needed to obtain these items, either to produce the part internally or to obtain it from an outside vendor. Assume, now, that T takes one week to make; U, 2 weeks; V, 2 weeks; W, 3 weeks; X, 1 week; and Y, 1 week. If we know when Product T is required, we can create a time schedule chart specifying when all materials must be ordered and received to meet the demand for T. Exhibit 14.2 shows which items are needed and when.

EXHIBIT 14.1

Product Structure Tree for Product T

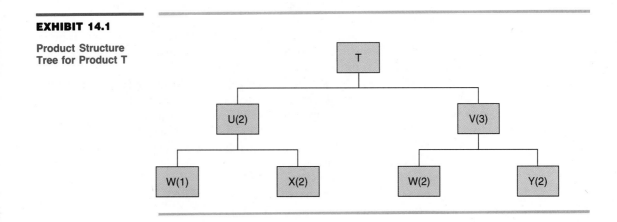

		\multicolumn{8}{c}{Week}	
		1	2	3	4	5	6	7	
T	Required date							100	T Lead time = 1 week
	Order placement						100		
U	Required date						200		U Lead time = 2 weeks
	Order placement			200					
V	Required date						300		V Lead time = 2 weeks
	Order placement				300				
W	Required date				800				W lead time = 3 weeks
	Order placement	800							
X	Required date				400				X Lead time = 1 week
	Order placement			400					
Y	Required date				600				Y Lead time = 1 week
	Order placement			600					

We have thus created a material requirements plan based on the demand for Product T and the knowledge of how T is made and the time needed to obtain each part.

From this simple illustration, it is apparent that developing a material requirements plan manually for thousands or even hundreds of items would be impractical—a great deal of computation is needed, and a tremendous amount of data must be available about the inventory status (number of units on hand, on order, and so forth) and about the product structure (how the product is made and how many units of each material are required). Because we are compelled to use a computer, our emphasis from here on in this chapter is to discuss the files needed for a computer program and the general makeup of the system. However, the basic logic of the program is essentially the same as that for our simple example.

Generally, the master schedule deals with end items. If the end item is quite large or quite expensive, however, the master schedule may schedule major subassemblies or components instead.

All production systems have limited capacity and limited resources. This presents a challenging job for the master scheduler. Exhibit 14.3 shows the environment in which the master scheduler works. While the aggregate plan provides the general range of operation, the master scheduler must specify exactly what is to be produced. These decisions are made while responding to pressures from various functional areas.

To determine an acceptable feasible schedule to be released to the shop, trial master production schedules are run through the MRP program. The resulting

EXHIBIT 14.3

The Environment of the Master Scheduler

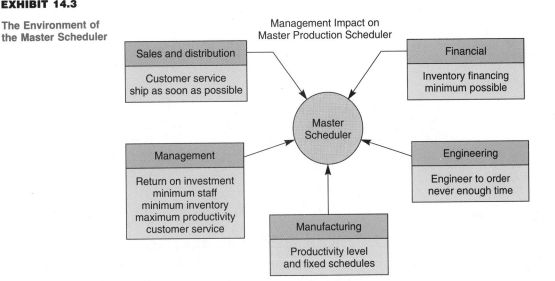

Source: Romeyn C. Everdell and Woodrow W. Chamberlain, "Master Scheduling in a Multi-Plant Environment," *Proceedings of the American Production and Inventory Control Society*, 1980, p. 421.

planned order releases (the detailed production schedules) are checked to make sure that resources are available and the completion times are reasonable. What appears to be a feasible master schedule may turn out to require excessive resources once the product explosion has taken place and materials, parts, and components from lower levels are determined. If this does happen (the usual case), the master production schedule is then modified with these limitations and the MRP program is run again. To ensure good master scheduling, the master schedul*er* (the human being) must:

Include all demands from product sales, warehouse replenishment, spares, and interplant requirements.

Never lose sight of the aggregate plan.

Be involved with customer order promising.

Be visible to all levels of management.

Objectively trade off manufacturing, marketing, and engineering conflicts.

Identify and communicate all problems.

The upper portion of Exhibit 14.4 shows an aggregate plan for the total number of mattresses planned per month, without regard for mattress type. The lower portion shows a master production schedule specifying the exact

EXHIBIT 14.4

The Aggregate Plan and the Master Production Schedule for Mattresses

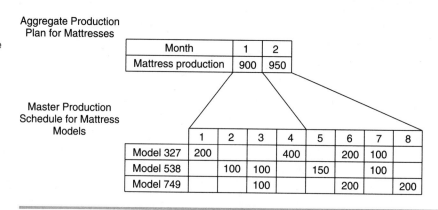

Aggregate Production Plan for Mattresses

Month	1	2
Mattress production	900	950

Master Production Schedule for Mattress Models

	1	2	3	4	5	6	7	8
Model 327	200			400		200	100	
Model 538		100	100		150		100	
Model 749			100			200		200

type of mattress and the quantity planned for production by week. The next level down (not shown) would be the MRP program that develops detailed schedules showing when cotton batting, springs, and hardwood are needed to make the mattresses. If carried further, this mattress example would look like Exhibit 14.16 which shows parts and subassemblies for electrical meters.

14.2 MASTER PRODUCTION SCHEDULE

The aggregate production plan, discussed in Chapter 12, specifies product groups. It does not specify exact items. The next level down in the planning process is the master production schedule. The **master production schedule (MPS)** is the time-phased plan specifying how many and when the firm plans to build each end item. For example, the aggregate plan for a furniture company may specify the total volume of mattresses it plans to produce over the next month or next quarter. The MPS goes the next step down and identifies the exact size mattresses and their qualities and styles. All the mattresses sold by the company would be specified by the MPS. The MPS also states period by period (usually weekly) how many and when each of these mattress types is needed.

Still further down the disaggregation process is the MRP program, which calculates and schedules all of the raw materials, parts, and supplies needed to make the mattress specified by the MPS.

Time Fences

The question of flexibility within a master production schedule depends on several factors: production lead time, commitment of parts and components to a specific end item, relationship between the customer and vendor, amount of

EXHIBIT 14.5

Master Production
Schedule Time
Fences

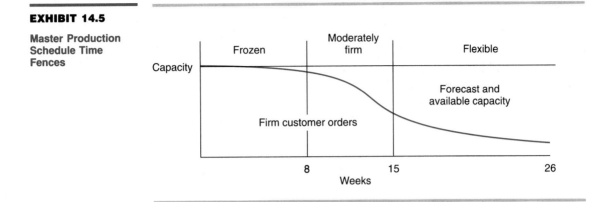

excess capacity, and the reluctance or willingness of management to make changes.

Exhibit 14.5 shows an example of a master production schedule time fence. Management defines *time fences* as periods of time having some specified level of opportunity for the customer to make changes. (The customer may be the firm's own marketing department which may be considering product promotions, broadening variety, etc.) Note in the exhibit that for the next eight weeks this particular master schedule is frozen. Each firm has its own time fences and operating rules. Under these rules, *frozen* could be defined as anything from absolutely no changes in one firm to only the most minor of changes in another. *Moderately firm* may allow changes in specific products within a product group, so long as parts are available. *Flexible* may allow almost any variations in products, with the provision that capacity remains about the same and that there are no long lead time items involved.

The purpose of time fences is to maintain a reasonably controlled flow through the production system. Unless some operating rules are established and adhered to, the system could be chaotic and filled with overdue orders and constant expediting.

14.3 MATERIAL REQUIREMENTS PLANNING (MRP) SYSTEMS

Based on a *master schedule* derived from a *production plan,* a *material requirements planning* (MRP) system creates schedules identifying the specific parts and materials required to produce end items, the exact numbers needed, and the dates when orders for these materials should be released and be received or completed within the production cycle. Today's MRP systems use a computer program to carry out these operations. Most firms have used computerized inventory systems for years, but they were independent of the scheduling system; MRP links them together.

Material requirements planning is not new in concept. Logic dictates that the Romans probably used it in their construction projects, the Venetians in their shipbuilding, and the Chinese in building the Great Wall. Building contractors have always been forced into planning for material to be delivered when needed and not before, because of space limitations. What is new is the larger scale and the more rapid changes that can be made by the use of computers. Now firms that produce many products involving thousands of parts and materials can take advantage of MRP.

Purposes, Objectives, and Philosophy of MRP

The main purposes of a basic MRP system are to control inventory levels, assign operating priorities for items, and plan capacity to load the production system. These may be briefly expanded as follows:

Inventory
   Order the right part.
   Order in the right quantity.
   Order at the right time.

Priorities
   Order with the right due date.
   Keep the due date valid.

Capacity
   Plan for a complete load.
   Plan an accurate load.
   Plan for an adequate time to view future load.

The *theme* of MRP is "getting the right materials to the right place at the right time."

The *objectives* of inventory management under an MRP system are to improve customer service, minimize inventory investment, and maximize production operating efficiency.

The *philosophy* of material requirements planning is that materials should be expedited (hurried) when their lack would delay the overall production schedule and de-expedited (delayed) when the schedule falls behind and postpones their need. Traditionally, and perhaps still typically, when an order is behind schedule, significant effort is spent trying to get it back on schedule. However, the opposite is not always true; when an order, for whatever reason, has its completion date delayed, the appropriate adjustments are not made in the schedule. This results in a one-sided effort—later orders are hurried, but early orders are not rescheduled for later. Aside from perhaps using scarce capacity, it is preferable not to have raw materials and work in process before the actual need since inventories tie up finances, clutter up stockrooms, prohibit design changes, and prevent the cancellation or delay of orders.

Benefits of an MRP System

Manufacturing companies with more than $10 million in annual sales likely have computerized MRP systems. A computerized system is necessary because of the sheer volume of materials, supplies, and components that are part of expanding product lines, and the speed that firms need to react to constant changes in the system. In past years, when firms switched from existing manual or computerized systems to an MRP system, they realized many benefits as:

Ability to price more competitively.

Reduced sales price.

Reduced inventory.

Better customer service.

Better response to market demands.

Ability to change the master schedule.

Reduced setup and tear-down costs.

Reduced idle time.

In addition, the MRP system:

Gives advance notice so managers can see the planned schedule before actual release orders.

Tells when to de-expedite as well as expedite.

Delays or cancels orders.

Changes order quantities.

Advances or delays order due dates.

Aids capacity planning.

During their conversions to MRP systems many firms claimed as much as 40 percent reductions in inventory investment.

14.4 MATERIAL REQUIREMENTS PLANNING SYSTEM STRUCTURE

The material requirements planning portion of manufacturing activities most closely interacts with the master schedule, bill of materials file, inventory records file, and the output reports. Exhibit 14.6 shows a portion of Exhibit 12.1 in Chapter 12 with several additions. Note that capacity is not considered in this exhibit, nor are there any feedback loops to higher levels. We discuss these elements later in this chapter under MRP II and capacity requirements planning.

Each facet of Exhibit 14.6 is explained in more detail in the following sections, but essentially the MRP system works as follows: Orders for prod-

EXHIBIT 14.6

Overall View of the
Inputs to a Standard
Material
Requirements
Planning Program
and the Reports
Generated by the
Program

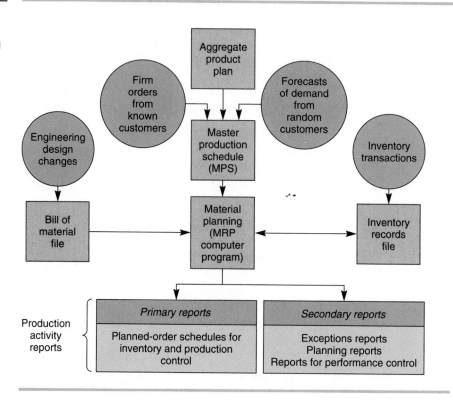

ucts are used to create a master production schedule, which states the number
of items to be produced during specific time periods. A bill of materials file
identifies the specific materials used to make each item and the correct quantities of each. The inventory records file contains data such as the number of
units on hand and on order. These three sources—master production schedule,
bill of materials file, and inventory records file—become the data sources for
the material requirements program, which expands the production schedule
into a detailed order scheduling plan for the entire production sequence.

Demand for Products

Product demand for end items stems primarily from two main sources: The
first is known customers who have placed specific orders, such as those
generated by sales personnel, or from interdepartment transactions. These
orders usually carry promised delivery dates. There is no forecasting involved
in these orders—simply add them up. The second source is forecast demand.
These are the normal independent-demand orders; the forecasting models

EXHIBIT 14.7

Product Structure
Tree for Product A

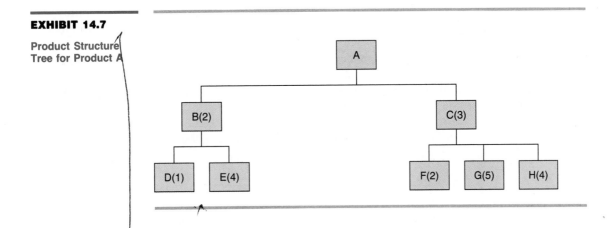

presented in Chapter 7 can be used to predict the quantities. The demand from the known customers and the forecast demand are combined and become the input for the master production schedule.

Demand for repair parts and supplies
In addition to the demand for end products, customers also order specific parts and components either as spares, or for service and repair. These demands for items less complex than the end product are not usually part of the master production schedule; instead, they are fed directly into the material requirements planning program at the appropriate levels. That is, they are added in as a gross requirement for that part or component.

Bill of Materials File

The **bill of materials (BOM)** file contains the complete product description, listing not only the materials, parts, and components but also the sequence in which the product is created. This BOM file is one of the three main inputs to the MRP program (the other two are the master schedule and the inventory records file).

The BOM file is often called the *product structure file* or *product tree* because it shows how a product is put together. It contains the information to identify each item and the quantity used per unit of the item of which it is a part. To illustrate this, consider Product A shown in Exhibit 14.7. Product A is made of two units of Part B and three units of Part C. Part B is made of one unit of Part D and four units of Part E. Part C is made of two units of Part F, five units of Part G, and four units of Part H.

In the past, bill of materials files have often listed parts as an indented file. This clearly identifies each item and the manner in which it is assembled because each indentation signifies the components of the item. A comparison of the indented parts in Exhibit 14.8 with the item structure in Exhibit 14.7 shows the ease of relating the two displays. From a computer standpoint, however, storing items in indented parts lists is very inefficient. To compute the amount of each item needed at the lower levels, each item would need to be expanded ("exploded") and summed. A more efficient procedure is to store parts data in a single-level explosion. That is, each item and component is listed showing only its parent and the number of units needed per unit of its parent. This avoids duplication because it includes each assembly only once. Exhibit 14.8 shows both the single-level parts list and the indented parts for Product A.

A data element (called a *pointer* or *locator*) is also contained in each file to identify the parent of each part and allow a retracing upward through the process.

A *modular* bill of materials is the term for a buildable item that can be produced and stocked as a subassembly. It is also a standard item with no options within the module. Many end items that are large and expensive are better scheduled and controlled as modules (or subassemblies). It is particularly advantageous to schedule subassembly modules when the same subassemblies appear in different end items. For example, a manufacturer of cranes can combine booms, transmissions, and engines in a variety of ways to meet a customer's needs. Using a modular bill of materials simplifies the scheduling and control and also makes it easier to forecast the use of different modules. Another benefit in using modular bills is that if the same item is used in a number of products, then the total inventory investment can be minimized.

A *planning* bill of materials includes items with fractional options. (A planning bill can specify, for example, 0.3 of a part. What that means is that 30 percent of the units produced contain that part and 70 percent do not.)

EXHIBIT 14.8

Parts List in an Indented Format and in a Single-Level List

Indented Parts List			Single-Level Parts List	
A			A	
	B(2)			B(2)
				C(3)
		D(1)		
		E(4)	B	
	C(3)			D(1)
				E(4)
		F(2)		
		G(5)	C	
		H(4)		
				F(2)
				G(5)
				H(4)

Low-level coding

If all identical parts occur at the same level for each end product, the total number of parts and materials needed for a product can be computed easily. Consider Product L shown in Exhibit 14.9a. Notice that Item N, for example, occurs both as an input to L and as an input to M. Item N therefore needs to be lowered to level 2 (Exhibit 14.9b) to bring all Ns to the same level. If all identical items are placed at the same level, it becomes a simple matter for the computer to scan across each level and summarize the number of units of each item required.

Inventory Records File

The **inventory records file** under a computerized system can be quite lengthy. Each item in inventory is carried as a separate file and the range of details carried about an item is almost limitless. Though Exhibit 14.10 is from the earlier versions of the MRP, it shows the variety of information contained in the inventory records files. The MRP program accesses the *status* segment of the file according to specific time periods (called *time buckets* in MRP slang). These files are accessed as needed during the program run.

The MRP program performs its analysis from the top of the product structure downward, exploding requirements level by level. There are times, however, when it is desirable to identify the parent item that caused the material requirement. The MRP program allows the creation of a *peg record* file either separately or as part of the inventory record file. Pegging requirements allows us to retrace a material requirement upward in the product structure through each level, identifying each parent item that created the demand.

EXHIBIT 14.9   Product L Hierarchy in (a) Expanded to the Lowest Level of Each Item in (b)

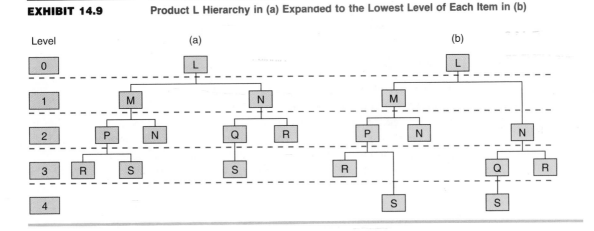

EXHIBIT 14.10

The Inventory Status
Record for an Item in
Inventory

Item master data segment	Part No.		Description			Lead time			Std. cost		Safety stock			
	Order quantity			Setup		Cycle		Last year's usage				Class		
	Scrap allowance			Cutting data			Pointers		Etc.					

					Period									
Inventory status segment	Allocated		Control balance	1	2	3	4	5	6	7	8	Totals		
	Gross requirements													
	Scheduled receipts													
	On hand													
	Planned-order releases													

Subsidiary data segment	Order details	
	Pending action	
	Counters	
	Keeping track	

Inventory transactions file

The inventory status file is kept up to date by posting inventory transactions as they occur. These changes occur because of stock receipts and disbursements, scrap losses, wrong parts, canceled orders, and so forth.

MRP Computer Program

The material requirements planning program operates on the inventory file, the master schedule, and the bill of materials file. It works in this way: A list of end items needed by time periods (as in the discussion of master scheduling in this chapter) is specified by the master schedule. A description of the materials and parts needed to make each item is specified in the bill of materials file. The number of units of each item and material currently on hand and on order are contained in the inventory file. The MRP program "works" on the inventory file (which is segmented into time periods) while continually referring to the bill of materials file to compute the quantities of each item needed. The number of units of each item required is then corrected for on-hand amounts, and the net requirement is "offset" (set back in time) to allow for the lead time needed to obtain the material.

(One obstacle that many potential users of an MRP program have found is that their current bill of materials files and inventory records files are not adequate to provide data in the format required by the program. Thus, they must modify these files before installing an MRP system.)

If the MRP program being used does not consider capacity constraints, the master scheduler must do some capacity balancing by hand. Through an iterative process, the master scheduler feeds a tentative master schedule into the MRP system (along with other items requiring the same resources) and the output is examined for production feasibility. The master schedule is adjusted to try to correct any imbalances, and the program is executed again. This process is repeated until the output is acceptable. Although it would seem to be a simple matter to have the computer simulate some schedules that consider resource limitations, in reality it is a very large and very time-consuming problem for the computer. We discuss another technique of limited resource scheduling, which has features that may relieve this problem, in Chapter 18.

To further complicate the problem today, there is not simply one master scheduler; there are a number of them. Often firms divide the scheduling work among the schedulers by assigning one master scheduler for each major product line. The result of this is competition: each master scheduler competes for limited resources for his or her own product line. As a group, however, they are trying to balance resource usage and due dates for the production system as a whole.

Output Reports

Because the MRP program has access to the bill of materials file, the master production schedule, and the inventory records file, outputs can take on an almost unlimited range of format and content. These reports are usually classified as *primary* and *secondary* reports. (With the expansion of MRP into MRP II, many additional reports are available.)

Primary reports
Primary reports are the main or normal reports used for inventory and production control. These reports consist of:

1. *Planned orders* to be released at a future time.
2. *Order release notices* to execute the planned orders.
3. *Changes in due dates* of open orders due to rescheduling.
4. *Cancellations or suspensions* of open orders due to cancellation or suspension of orders on the master production schedule.
5. *Inventory status data*.

Secondary reports

Additional reports, which are optional under the MRP system, fall into the following main categories:

1. *Planning reports* to be used, for example, in forecasting inventory and specifying requirements over some future time horizon.
2. *Performance reports* for purposes of pointing out inactive items and determining the agreement between actual and programmed item lead times and between actual and programmed quantity usage and costs.
3. *Exceptions reports* that point out serious discrepancies, such as errors, out-of-range situations, late or overdue orders, excessive scrap, or nonexistent parts.

Net Change Systems

Ordinarily an MRP system is initiated from a master schedule every week or two. This results in the complete explosion of items and the generation of the normal and exception reports. Some MRP programs, however, offer the option of generating intermediate schedules, called *net change* schedules. Net change systems are "activity" driven. Only if a transaction is processed against a particular item, would that item be reviewed in a **net change system.** However, net change systems can be modified to respond only to unplanned or exception occurrences. Rather than being buried in paperwork output from an MRP system (which is easy to do) management may elect not to have the expected occurrences reported, but only deviations that should be noted. For example, if orders are received on time, there need be no report. On the other hand, if the quantity delivered differs significantly from the order, this item is included in the net change report. Other reasons to include an item in a net change run might be to note a lost shipment, scrap losses, lead time changes, or a counting error in inventory. Based on these changes, new reports are generated.

On the surface, it appears that a daily net change program run would be highly satisfactory. In practice, however, few companies elect to use the net change option; instead most rely on their weekly or biweekly complete MRP schedule run. It seems that more frequent net change runs may not be worth the added effort required to perform them, and too-frequent runs cause overreaction or "system nervousness." However, this erratic tendency can be reduced significantly by controlling elements such as what is included in the net change, by buffering unplanned activity, and by minimizing erratic behavior. As one author noted, "Most system nervousness results from a poorly managed MRP environment. Net change systems only reflect the real world, and if the system is so nervous that one cannot respond properly, then the real world is probably chaos as well."[1]

---

[1] John M. Carlson, "The Control of Change in a Net Change MRP Environment," *Proceedings of the 23rd Annual Conference* (Falls Church, Va.: American Production and Inventory Control Society, October 1980), pp. 177–81.

14.5 AN EXAMPLE USING MRP

Ampere, Inc., produces a line of electric meters installed in residential buildings by electric utility companies to measure power consumption. Meters used on single-family homes are of two basic types for different voltage and amperage ranges. In addition to complete meters, some parts and subassemblies are sold separately for repair or for changeovers to a different voltage or power load. The problem for the MRP system is to determine a production schedule that would identify each item, the period it is needed, and the appropriate quantities. This schedule is then checked for feasibility, and the schedule is modified if necessary.

Forecasting Demand

Demand for the meters and components originates from two sources: regular customers that place firm orders, and unidentified customers that make the normal random demands for these items. The random requirements were forecast using one of the usual classical techniques described in Chapter 7 and past demand data. Exhibit 14.11 shows the requirement for Meters A and B, Subassembly D, and Part E for a six-month period.

Developing a Master Production Schedule

For the meter and component requirements specified in Exhibit 14.11, assume that the quantities to satisfy the known demands are to be delivered according to customers' delivery schedules throughout the month, but that the items to satisfy random demands must be available during the first week of the month.

Our schedule assumes that *all* items are to be available the first week of the month. This assumption trial is reasonable since management (in our example) prefers to produce meters in one single lot each month rather than a number of lots throughout the month.

Exhibit 14.12 shows the trial master schedule that we use under these conditions, with demands for months 3 and 4 shown as the first week of the month, or as weeks 9 and 13. For brevity, we work only with these two

EXHIBIT 14.11

Future Requirements for Meters A and B, Subassembly D, and Part E Stemming from Specific Customer Orders and from Random Sources

Month	METER A Known	METER A Random	METER B Known	METER B Random	SUBASSEMBLY D Known	SUBASSEMBLY D Random	PART E Known	PART E Random
3	1,000	250	400	60	200	70	300	80
4	600	250	300	60	180	70	350	80
5	300	250	500	60	250	70	300	80
6	700	250	400	60	200	70	250	80
7	600	250	300	60	150	70	200	80
8	700	250	700	60	160	70	200	80

EXHIBIT 14.12

A Master Schedule to Satisfy Demand Requirements as Specified in Exhibit 14.11

	WEEK								
	9	10	11	12	13	14	15	16	17
Meter A	1,250				850				550
Meter B	460				360				560
Subassembly D	270				250				320
Part E	380				430				380

demand periods. The schedule we develop should be examined for resource availability, capacity availability, etc., and then revised and run again. We will stop with our example at the end of this one schedule, however.

Bill of Materials (Product Structure) File

The product structure for Meters A and B is shown in Exhibit 14.13 in the typical way using low-level coding, in which each item is placed at the lowest level at which it appears in the structure hierarchy. Meters A and B consist of two subassemblies, C and D, and two parts, E and F. Quantities in parentheses indicate the number of units required per unit of the parent item.

Exhibit 14.14 shows an indented parts list for the structure of Meters A and B. As mentioned earlier in the chapter, the BOM file carries all items without indentation for computational ease, but the indented printout clearly shows the manner of product assembly.

Inventory Records (Item Master) File

The inventory records file would be similar to the one that was shown in Exhibit 14.10. The differences, as we saw earlier in this chapter, are that the inventory records file also contains much additional data, such as vendor identity, cost, and lead times. For this example, the pertinent data contained in the inventory records file are the on-hand inventory at the start of the program run and the lead times. Taken from the inventory records file, these data are shown in Exhibit 14.15.

Running the MRP Program

The correct conditions are now set to run the MRP computer program—end-item requirements have been established through the master production schedule, the status of inventory and the order lead times are contained in the

EXHIBIT 14.13   **Product Structure for Meters A and B**

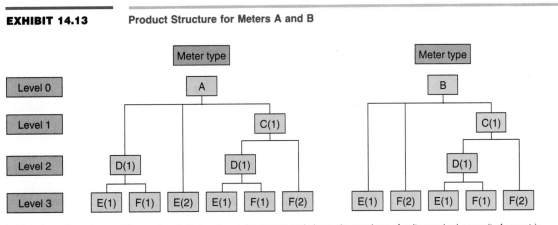

Exhibit shows the subassemblies and parts that make up the meters and shows the numbers of units required per unit of parent in parentheses.

EXHIBIT 14.14

Indented Parts List for Meter A and Meter B, with the Required Number of Items per Unit of Parent Listed in Parentheses

Meter A				Meter B		
A				B		
	D(1)				E(1)	
		E(1)			F(2)	
		F(1)			C(1)	
	E(2)					D(1)
	C(1)					E(1)
		D(1)				F(1)
			E(1)		F(2)	
			F(1)			
		F(2)				

EXHIBIT 14.15

Number of Units on Hand and Lead Time Data that Would Appear on the Inventory Record File

Item	On-Hand Inventory	Lead Time (weeks)
A	50	2
B	60	2
C	40	1
D	30	1
E	30	1
F	40	1

inventory item master file, and the bill of materials file contains the product structure data. The MRP program now explodes the item requirements according to the BOM file, level by level, in conjunction with the inventory records file. A release date for the net requirements order is offset to an earlier time period to account for the lead time. Orders for parts and subassemblies are added through the inventory file, bypassing the master production schedule, which, ordinarily, does not schedule at a low enough level to include spares and repair parts.

Exhibit 14.16 shows the planned order release dates for this particular run. The following analysis explains the program logic. (We confine our analysis to the problem of meeting the gross requirements for 1,250 units of Meter A, 460 units of Meter B, 270 units of Subassembly D and 380 units of Part E, all in Week 9.)

The 50 units of A on hand result in a net requirement of 1,200 units of A. To receive Meter A in Week 9, the order must be placed in Week 7 to account for the two-week lead time. The same procedure follows for Item B, resulting in a planned 400-unit order released in Period 7.

The rationale for these steps is that for an item to be released for processing, all its components must be available. The planned order release date for the parent item therefore becomes the same gross requirement period for the subitems.

Referring to Exhibit 14.13, level 1, one unit of C is required for each A and each B. Therefore, the gross requirements for C in Week 7 are 1,600 units (1,200 for A and 400 for B). Taking into account the 40 units on hand and the one-week lead time, 1,560 units of C must be ordered in Week 6.

Level 2 of Exhibit 14.13 shows that one unit of D is required for each A and each C. The 1,200 units of D required for A are gross requirements in Week 7, and the 1,560 units of D for item C are the gross requirements for Week 6. Using the on-hand inventory first and the one-week lead time results in the planned order releases for 1,530 units in Week 5 and 1,200 units in Week 6.

Level 3 contains Items E and F. Because E and F are each used in several places, Exhibit 14.17 is presented to identify more clearly the parent item, the number of units required for each parent item, and the week in which it is required. Two units of Item E are used in each Item A. The 1,200-unit planned order release for A in Period 7 becomes the gross requirement for 2,400 units of E in the same period. One unit of E is used in each B, so the planned order release for 400 units of B in Period 7 becomes the gross requirement for 400 units of E in Week 7. Item E is also used in Item D at the rate of one per unit. The 1,530-unit planned order release for D in Period 5 becomes the gross requirement for 1,530 units of E in Period 5 and a 1,500-unit planned order release in Period 4 after accounting for the 30 units on hand and the one-week lead time. The 1,200-unit planned order release for D in Period 6 results in gross requirements for 1,200 units of E in Week 6 and a planned order release for 1,200 units in Week 5.

EXHIBIT 14.16   Material Requirements Planning Schedule for Meters A and B, Subassemblies C and D, and Parts E and F

Item		Week										
		4	5	6	7	8	9	10	11	12	13
A	Gross requirements						1,250				850
	On hand 50						50				
	Net requirements						1,200				
(LT = 2)	Planned-order receipt						1,200				
	Planned-order release				1,200						
B	Gross requirements						460				360
	On hand 60						60				
	Net requirements						400				
(LT = 2)	Planned-order receipt						400				
	Planned-order release				400						
C	Gross requirements				400						
					1,200						
	On hand 40				40						
	Net requirements				1,560						
(LT = 1)	Planned-order receipt				1,560						
	Planned-order release			1,560							
D	Gross requirements			1,560	1,200		270				250
	On hand 30			30	0		0				
	Net requirements			1,530	1,200		270				
(LT = 1)	Planned-order receipt			1,530	1,200		270				
	Planned-order release		1,530	1,200		270					
E	Gross requirements		1,530	1,200	2,400	270	380				430
					400						
	On hand 30		30	0	0	0	0				
	Net requirements		1,500	1,200	2,800	270	380				
(LT = 1)	Planned-order receipt		1,500	1,200	2,800	270	380				
	Planned-order release	1,500	1,200	2,800	270	380					
F	Gross requirements		1,530	3,120	800	270					
				1,200							
	On hand 40		40	0	0	0					
	Net requirements		1,490	4,320	800	270					
(LT = 1)	Planned-order receipt		1,490	4,320	800	270					
	Planned-order release	1,490	4,320	800	270						

Item F is used in B, C, and D. The planned order releases for B, C, and D become the gross requirements for F for the same week, except that the planned order release for 400 units of B and 1,560 of C become gross requirements for 800 and 3,120 units of F, since the usage rate is two per unit.

EXHIBIT 14.17

The Identification of the Parent of Items C, D, E, and F and Item Gross Requirements Stated by Specific Weeks

Item	Parent	Number of Units per Parent	Resultant Gross Requirement	Gross Requirement Week
C	A	1	1,200	7
C	B	1	400	7
D	A	1	1,200	7
D	C	1	1,560	6
E	A	2	2,400	7
E	B	1	400	7
E	D	1	1,530	5
E	D	1	1,200	6
F	B	2	800	7
F	C	2	3,120	6
F	D	1	1,200	6
F	D	1	1,530	5

The independent order for 270 units of subassembly D in Week 9 is handled as an input to D's gross requirements for that week. This is then exploded into the derived requirements for 270 units of E and F. The 380-unit requirement for Part E to meet an independent repair part demand is fed directly into the gross requirements for Part E.

The independent demands for Week 13 have not been expanded as yet.

The bottom line of each item in Exhibit 14.16 is taken as a proposed load on the productive system. The final production schedule is developed manually or with the firm's computerized production package. If the schedule is infeasible or the loading unacceptable, the master production schedule is revised and the MRP package is run again with the new master schedule.

Where MRP Can Be Used

MRP is being used in a variety of industries, with a job–shop environment (meaning that a number of products are made in batches using the same productive equipment). The list in Exhibit 14.18 includes process industries, but note that the processes mentioned are confined to job runs that alternate output product and do not include continuous processes such as petroleum or steel.

As you can see in the exhibit, MRP is most valuable to companies involved in assembly operations and least valuable to those in fabrication.

One more point to note: MRP does not work well in companies that produce a low number of units annually. Especially for companies producing complex expensive products requiring advanced research and design, experience has shown that lead times tend to be too long and too uncertain, and the product configuration too complex for MRP to handle. Such companies need the control features that network scheduling techniques offer; they would

EXHIBIT 14.18

Industry Applications
and Expected
Benefits

Industry Type	Examples	Expected Benefits
Assemble-to-stock	Combines multiple component parts into a finished product, which is then stocked in inventory to satisfy customer demand. Examples: Watches, tools, appliances.	High
Fabricate-to-stock	Items are manufactured by machine rather than assembled from parts. These are standard stock items carried in anticipation of customer demand. Examples: Piston rings, electrical switches.	Low
Assemble-to-order	A final assembly is made from standard options which the customer chooses. Examples: Trucks, generators, motors.	High
Fabricate-to-order	Items manufactured by machine to customer order. These are generally industrial orders. Examples: Bearings, gears, fasteners.	Low
Manufacture-to-order	Items fabricated or assembled completely to customer specification. Examples: Turbine generators, heavy machine tools.	High
Process	Industries, such as foundries, rubber and plastics, specialty paper, chemicals, paint, drug, food processors.	Medium

be better off using project scheduling methods (covered previously in Chapter 11).

14.6 CAPACITY REQUIREMENTS PLANNING

In the sections of this chapter that concerned the master production schedule and running the MRP program, we mentioned that production capacity is usually some finite amount and obviously has limits. We also cited the interaction between the scheduler and rerunning the MRP program to obtain feasible schedules in light of this limited capacity. In this section we explicitly point out how capacity is computed and what the usual procedure is to cope with capacity constraints.

Computing Work Center Load

The place to start in computing capacity requirements is right from the routing sheets for the jobs scheduled to be processed. Exhibit 3.23 in Chapter 3 shows the routing sheet for a plug assembly. Note that the routing sheet specifies where a job is to be sent, the particular operations involved, and the standard setup time and run time per piece. These are the types of figures used to compute the total work at each work center.

While the routing sheet is a "job view" that follows a particular job around the productive facility, a work center file is the view seen from a work center. The routing sheets for each job send them to appropriate work centers for some sort of processing. Each work center is generally a functionally defined center so that jobs routed to it require the same type of work, and on the same equipment. From the work center view, if there is adequate capacity, the problem is one of priorities: which job to do first. (We discuss priority scheduling rules in Chapter 15.) If there is insufficient capacity, however, rather than a local issue at the work center, the problem must be resolved by the master scheduler.

Exhibit 14.19 shows a work center that has various jobs assigned to it. Note that the capacity per week was computed at the bottom of the exhibit at 161.5 hours. The jobs scheduled for the three weeks result in two weeks planned under work center capacity, and one week over capacity.

Exhibit 14.19 uses the terms **utilization** and **efficiency**. Both of these terms have been defined and used in a variety of ways, some conflicting. In this exhibit, utilization refers to the actual time that the machines are used. Efficiency refers to how well the machine is performing while it is being used. Efficiency is usually defined as a comparison to a defined standard output or an engineering design rate. For instance, a machine used for six hours of an eight-hour shift was utilized ⅞ or 75 percent. If the standard output for that machine is defined as 200 parts per hour and an average of 250 parts were made, then

EXHIBIT 14.19

Workload for Work Center A

Week	Job No.	Units	Setup Time	Run Time per Unit	Total Job Time	Total for Week
10	145	100	3.5	.23	26.5	
	167	160	2.4	.26	44.0	
	158	70	1.2	.13	10.3	
	193	300	6.0	.17	57.0	137.8
11	132	80	5.0	.36	33.8	
	126	150	3.0	.22	36.0	
	180	180	2.5	.30	56.5	
	178	120	4.0	.50	64.0	190.3
12	147	90	3.0	.18	19.2	
	156	200	3.5	.14	31.5	
	198	250	1.5	.16	41.5	
	172	100	2.0	.12	14.0	
	139	120	2.2	.17	22.6	128.8

Computing Work Center Capacity

The available capacity in standard hours is 161.5 hours per five-day week, calculated as:
(2 machines) (2 shifts) (10 hours/shift) (85% machine utilization) (95% efficiency).

efficiency is 125 percent. Note that in these definitions efficiency can be more than 100 percent, but utilization cannot be.

Exhibit 14.20 shows a loading representation of Work Center A for the three weeks. The scheduled work exceeds capacity for Week 11. There are several options available:

1. Work overtime.
2. Select an alternate work center that could perform the task.
3. Subcontract to an outside shop.
4. Try to schedule part of the work of Day 2 earlier into Day 1, and delay part of the work into Day 3.
5. Renegotiate the due date and reschedule.

An MRP program with a capacity requirements planning module allows rescheduling to try to level capacity. Two techniques used are backward scheduling and forward scheduling—the fourth option on the preceding list. The objective of the master scheduler is to try to spread the load in Exhibit 14.20 more evenly to remain within the available capacity.

14.7 MANUFACTURING RESOURCE PLANNING (MRP II)

In our earlier discussions of MRP in this chapter, we limited ourselves in two respects: First, we concentrated on the *material* requirements that resulted from an explosion of the master schedule, and we discussed lot sizing and safety stocks. We did not include the needs for all the other types of resources, such as staffing, facilities, or tools. Second, while we discussed *capacity requirements planning*, we did this somewhat externally to the MRP system. In this section

EXHIBIT 14.20

Scheduled Workload for Work Center A

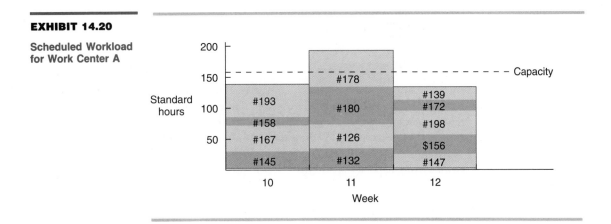

we discuss closed-loop MRP and the logic of more advanced versions of MRP that include a wider range of resources and outputs.

Closed-Loop MRP

When the material requirements planning (MRP) system has information feedback from its module outputs, this is termed **closed-loop MRP.** The American Production and Inventory Control Society defines closed-loop MRP as:

> A system built around material requirements planning and also including the additional planning functions of Production Planning, Master Production Scheduling, and Capacity Requirements Planning. Further, once the planning phase is complete and the plans have been accepted as realistic and attainable, the execution functions come into play. These include shop floor control functions of Input-Output measurement, detailed Scheduling and Dispatching, plus Anticipated Delay Reports from both the shop and vendors, Purchasing Follow-Up and Control, etc. The term "closed-loop" implies that not only is each of these elements included in the overall system but also that there is feedback from the execution functions so that the planning can be kept valid at all times.[2]

Exhibit 14.21 shows a closed loop MRP system. Note the closed loop means questions and output data are looped back up the system for verification and, if necessary, modification. Recognize that the input to the MRP system is the master production schedule, as was stated earlier in the chapter. The MRP program does an explosion of all the parts, components, and other resources needed to meet this schedule. The capacity requirements planning module then checks the MRP output to see if sufficient capacity exists. If it does not, feedback up to the MRP module indicates that the schedule needs to be modified. Continuing down the MRP system, orders are released to the production system. From that point on, it is a matter of monitoring, data collection, completing the order, and evaluating results. MRP II is not a fully automatic system. Human input and intervention must occur for control, as well as for making decisions and choices.

MRP II

An expansion of the materials requirements planning program to include other portions of the productive system was natural and to be expected. One of the first to be included was the purchasing function. At the same time, there was a more detailed inclusion of the production system itself—on the shop floor, in dispatching, and in the detailed scheduling control. MRP had already included work center capacity limitations, so it was obvious the name *material require-*

---

[2] *APICS Dictionary* (Falls Church, Va.: American Production and Inventory Control Society, 1984), p. 4.

EXHIBIT 14.21

A Closed-Loop MRP System Showing Feedback

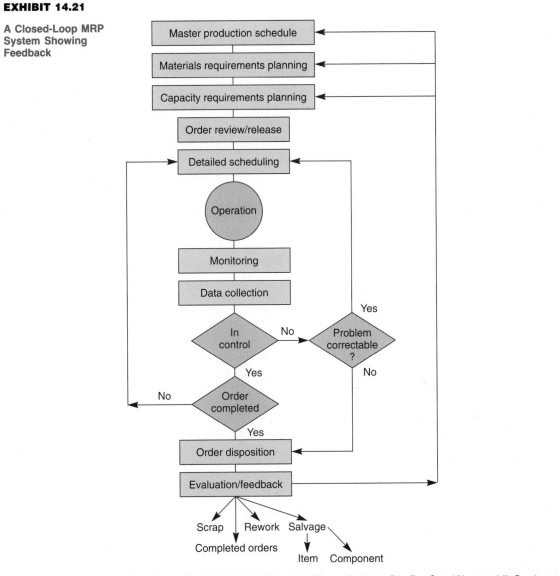

Source: Adapted from S. Melnyk, P. L. Carter, D. M. Dilts, and D. M. Lyth, *Shop Floor Control* (Homewood, Ill.: Dow Jones-Irwin, 1985), p. 40.

ments planning no longer was adequate to describe the expanded system. Someone (probably Ollie Wight) introduced the name **manufacturing resource planning (MRP II)** to reflect the idea that more and more of the firm was becoming involved in the program. To quote Wight,

The fundamental manufacturing equation is:
  What are we going to make?
  What does it take to make it?
  What do we have?
  What do we have to get?[3]

The initial intent for MRP II was to plan and monitor all the resources of a manufacturing firm—manufacturing, marketing, finance, and engineering—through a closed-loop system generating financial figures. The second important intent of the MRP II concept was that it simulate the manufacturing system. It is generally conceived now as being a total, companywide system with everyone (buyers, marketing staff, production, accounting) working with the same game plan, using the same numbers, and capable of simulation to plan and test strategies.

Cost of an MRP II System

Several software companies regularly advertise MRP systems in manufacturing-oriented journals, as well as in widely read publications such as *The Wall Street Journal*. Prices go as low as $500 and as high as $300,000 because MRP II systems can vary widely in the modules and capabilities included.

Costs for the computer hardware also have a wide range. An MRP program for a very small company can be run on a microcomputer with hard disk drives. However, most MRP II systems are run on minicomputers or mainframes because of the very large data storage requirements and the number of program modules involved. Lease costs may range from $30,000 to $500,000 per year; however, technology is changing rapidly, with a consequent drop in cost. In terms of additional personnel needed, the experiences of many companies indicate that the overall net change in personnel is close to zero. Companies simply switch people from existing areas into MRP system roles.

The typical MRP II system takes about 18 months to install. However, this can vary widely depending on the size of the application, the condition of the existing databases and how much they may have to be revised, the quality of the bills of materials, routing sheets, and inventory records, and the amount of training required. Another factor is whether the firm has been using an MRP system and is switching to an MRP II system. The entire range of time can vary from several months to three years.

Payback for an MRP installation can be quite short. When larger companies first installed MRP systems some years ago, they realized an average annual return on investment of about 300 percent.[4]

When we think of MRP II, we tend to think of large computer programs with applications confined to business giants. In fact, however, MRP II is

---

[3] Oliver Wight, *The Executive's Guide to Successful MRP II* (Williston, Vt.: Oliver Wight Limited Publications, 1982), pp. 6, 17.

[4] Wight, *Executive's Guide,* pp. 34–35.

economically feasible for manufacturing companies with annual sales of less than $1 million. Also, much of the current software is user-friendly and easy to operate.

Prices and quality of software vary widely and not necessarily in a direct relationship. Customer support is another very important factor. This is a buyer beware market, and care should be taken in choosing a program because it is a long-term commitment.

Next we will look more closely at two MRP II systems: MAPICS, from IBM, and MAX, from Micro-MRP, Inc.

Manufacturing Accounting and Production Information Control System Version 2 (MAPICS II)

MAPICS II is IBM's latest application software package for manufacturing and data collection for manufacturing and process industries. (The major difference between the two applications—manufacturing and process—is that the manufacturing applications compute in units and the process applications allow fractions. For example, you could not manufacture 12.6 cars, but you could produce 12.6 tons of a chemical.)

MAPICS II is a completely revised package; the last of the 19 interrelated modules was released in 1987. The 19 modules cover all of a firm's activities:

Accounts payable.

Accounts receivable.

Capacity requirements planning.

Cross-application support.

Data collection system support.

Financial analysis.

Forecasting.

General ledger.

Inventory management.

Inventory management for process.

Location/lot management.

Master production scheduling planning.

Material requirements planning.

Order entry and invoicing.

Payroll.

Product data management.

Production control and costing.

Purchasing.

Sales analysis.

The original **MAPICS** programs were written strictly for IBM's System 36 and 38 computer architecture. However, IBM has come out with hardware emulation cards allowing MAPICS to be run out on standard architecture. This was a significant marketing strategy; many firms willing to spend $80,000 or so for software were reluctant to commit to a new, single-purpose computer system.

One advantageous feature of the MAPICS system is that modules may be run independently. A branch or regional warehouse, for example, by purchasing a small IBM 5364 computer (about the size of a PC) for about $10,000, could install only what it would need—say order entry and invoicing, inventory management, location/lot management, accounts receivable, sales analysis, and purchasing applications. The finance department need not be committed to using the mainframe computer but could have its own PC and could run quite independently of the rest of the firm by installing the general ledger, accounts receivable, accounts payable, payroll, data collection system support, and financial analysis applications. Any of the 19 modules can be installed as a separate stand-alone application.

A very wide variety of information and options are available on this system. As an illustration, we discuss the material requirements planning portion. Orders are entered into the system through forecasts, firm planned orders, and open orders. Several choices of lot sizes are available (such as lot for lot or fixed quantity). Before an order is released, a check may be made to ensure that components are available. A check can also be made to make sure capacity is available. There are pegging reports (which show the item that generated the need for the lower-level item), purchase planning reports (showing quantities and schedules of needed purchased items), and many options to review plans, which compare forecasts to their customers' back orders, reviews of order releases, and so on. There are also order-shortage reports, item-shortage reports, and order action detail, which assist in the order release actions. This is quite a flexible system; when the system is running, accessing the data collection center and the other modules, other reports are available, including resource reports and cash-flow analysis.

Micro–MRP

High capacity quick access hard disk drives have opened the way for microcomputers to be used for MRP by smaller companies and for departments or divisions of larger companies. The most widely used of the MRP programs for microcomputers is "MAX," a product of **Micro-MRP** Inc.[5]

Exhibit 14.22 shows the positioning and applications of the various modules of MAX. We present some of the specifications, costs, and equipment requirements to gain a perspective of the application areas and then briefly describe some of the modules.

---

[5] From information provided and updated by Micro-MRP, Inc., Century Plaza I, Foster City, California, 94404, and Datapro Research Corp., Delran, New Jersey, September 1991.

EXHIBIT 14.22   **Micro-MRP Company's MAX Programs**

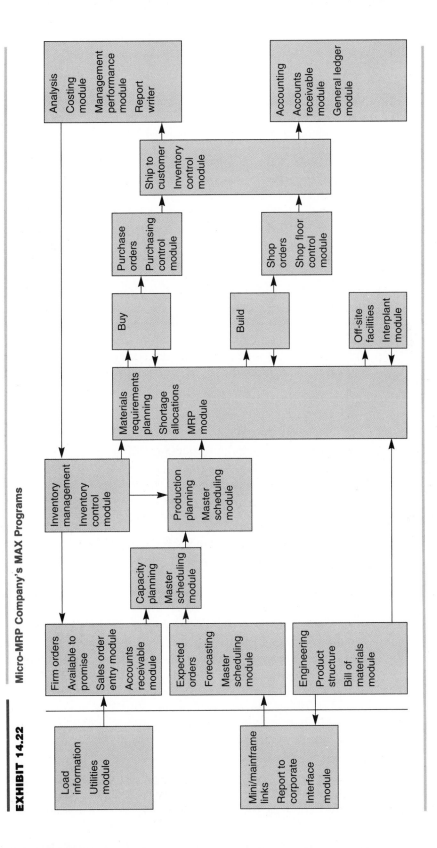

Number of MAX applications.   Marketed since 1983. Currently there are 3,400 installations. MAX is the leader in microcomputer MRP (the next closest competitor has 600 installations).

Size of using company or division.   Sales in the $0.5 to $30 million range, although larger companies are beginning to use Micro-MRP separate from the main system.

Hardware.   IBM PC/AT/XT or compatible with 640K of RAM, 30 megabyte hard disk, clock card, and 132-column printer. A 60-meg disk can store about 10,000 part numbers.

Cost of MAX software program.   An average of $8,500 for a small to medium-size manufacturer with all the manufacturing and accounting modules, but specific requirements could result in a wide range of costs as low as $495 and as high as $30,000 for a multi-user package.

Software.   MAX consists of nine basic modules and a utility module:

1. Bill of materials.
2. Interface.
3. Inventory control.
4. Master production scheduling (MPS).
5. Material requirements planning.
6. Purchasing control.
7. Shop floor control.
8. Cost performance.
9. Management performance.

A brief description of several modules follows:

Master production scheduling module—accepts customer orders and forecasts. Computes what's available-to-promise. There is also an order entry/invoicing module as part of the accounting package.

Purchasing control module—issues purchase orders, tracks costs and deliveries, maintains vendor history, and examines cash requirements.

Shop floor control module—prepares job packets, tracks the progress of orders through the shop, communicates MRP decisions to the shop floor, tracks WIP, and analyzes shortages.

Cost performance module—tracks cost variances between planned and actual costs. Also generates general ledger detail information and work-in-process analysis reports.

Management performance module—generates reports such as surplus inventory analysis, inventory cost by location and class, purchase order activity, vendor performance analysis, costed materials requirements, work order activity, production schedule analysis, posted transaction activity, and part shortage analysis.

Solomon III accounting module—Max uses the Solomon III integrated accounting package, which consists of 15 interactive modules including accounts payable, accounts receivable, general ledger, order entry/invoicing, payroll, job costing, sales analysis, and other overlapping modules.

14.8 EMBEDDING JIT INTO MRP

MRP and JIT each have benefits. The question is: Can they work together successfully, and how would one go about combining them? As stated earlier in the chapter, most major manufacturing firms use MRP. Of the firms using MRP, many in repetitive manufacturing are also implementing JIT techniques. Although JIT is best suited to repetitive manufacturing, MRP is used in everything from custom job shops to assembly-line production. Most firms that have successfully implemented MRP systems are not interested in discarding MRP to try JIT. A new challenge arises in integrating the shop floor improvement approaches of JIT with an MRP-based planning and control system. The MRP/JIT combination creates what might be considered a hybrid manufacturing system. Efforts to integrate MRP and JIT are now popular enough to justify a regular column titled "MRP/JIT Report" in *Modern Materials Handling* magazine.

MRP is a very large computerized production planning system. Trying to add JIT to this system is very difficult. Some firms are trying to create add-on modules but at present there is no standard way.

Part of the difficulty in trying to integrate both systems into a computer program is caused by their different objectives and conflicting purposes, such as:

	MRP	JIT
Based On:	MPS, BOM, and inventory records	MPS, Kanban
Objective:	Plan and control	Eliminate waste, continuous improvement
Involvement process:	Passive—no efforts toward change	Active—tries to improve and change system, and to lower inventory
Data requirements:	Detailed and strict data accuracy	Much lower and tend to be visible
Operation:	Computerized	Simple, manual shop floor controls such as Kanban

Exhibit 14.23 shows a master production schedule with a MRP system on the left. MRP systems can help create the master production schedule. From that point on, it is all MRP systems. Scheduling resources such as inventory are continuously controlled and monitored.

EXHIBIT 14.23   Controlling Production Processes with MRP Alone and MRP/JIT Combined

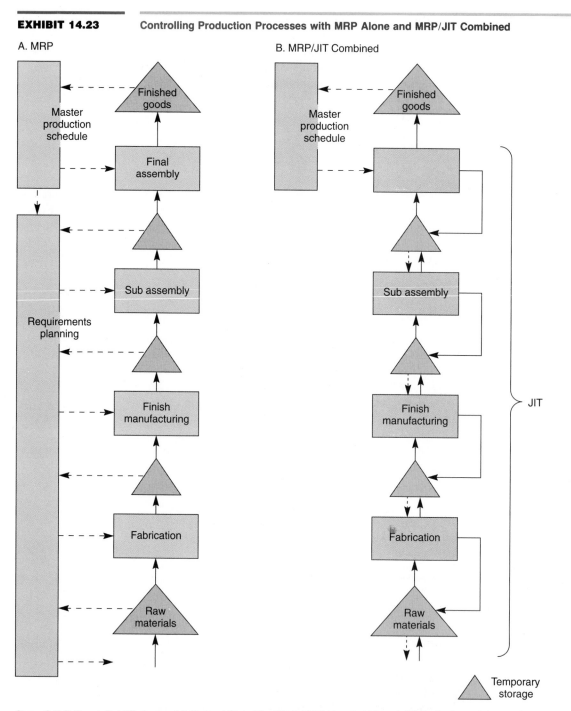

A. MRP

B. MRP/JIT Combined

Temporary storage

Source: S. D. P. Flapper, G. J. Miltenburg, and J. Wijngaard, "Embedding JIT into MRP," *International Journal of Production Research* 29, no. 2 (1991), p. 335.

The right side of Exhibit 14.23 shows a master production schedule at the top feeding a JIT system. Computer control has been severed and the JIT portion operates as its own separate pull method drawing from preceding stages. MRP may well be used to help create the master production schedule, but MRP's involvement stops there.

Phasing MRP into JIT

Assume an existing production system is currently being planned and scheduled using an MRP system. The firm's management believes JIT should be introduced because various parts of the firm produce the same products repetitively. To convert those repetitive areas into Just-in-Time manufacturing S. D. P. Flapper, G. J. Miltenburg, and J. Wijngaard propose this three-step approach:

Step 1. Create a logical flow line through rapid material handling.

Step 2. Use a pull production control system on the logical line.

Step 3. Create a physical line flow.[6]

Exhibit 14.24A shows the existing pure MRP system. It operates in its conventional fashion with work located at work centers and the main stock room. Orders are generated by the main MRP system, and all operations are continuously monitored.

Step 1—relocate inventory

The first step (Exhibit 14.24B) is to discontinue using the stock room and locate all inventory on the shop floor. A materials handling system then connects all areas of the shop floor with an automatic guided vehicle (AGV) or material handling personnel driving a vehicle. This material handling procedure replaces the discontinued method of MRP drawing inventory from main stock. The MRP system needs to be informed of the new locations of inventory, but it is still in control. Major changes need to be made in the process, such as improvements in quality, tooling, lead times, and setup times. As the system improves, inventory levels are reduced.

Step 2—introduce a pull system

A pull system is implemented (Exhibit 14.24C). Kanban cards, container sizes, and so forth are used in the conventional JIT manner. Pulling containers from work areas creates authorization to produce replacements. To be successful in this step, setup time must be greatly reduced and quality must be improved.

The MRP's position in this transition phase is to do the ordering but not the scheduling. MRP releases orders external to the firm for parts and other components that are needed. Since the internal system operates as a JIT system,

---

[6] S. D. P. Flapper, G. J. Miltenburg, and J. Wijngaard, "Embedding JIT into MRP," *International Journal of Production Research* 29, no. 2 (1991), pp. 329–41.

EXHIBIT 14.24   Embedding JIT into an MRP System

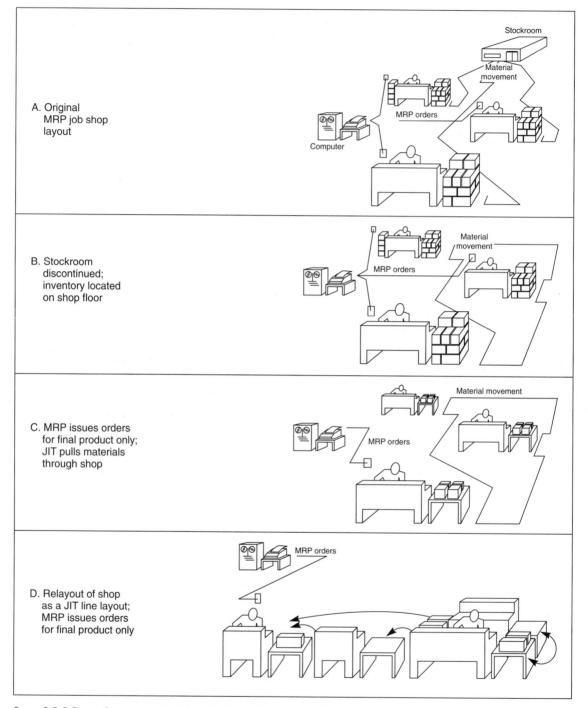

A. Original
   MRP job shop
   layout

B. Stockroom
   discontinued;
   inventory located
   on shop floor

C. MRP issues orders
   for final product only;
   JIT pulls materials
   through shop

D. Relayout of shop
   as a JIT line layout;
   MRP issues orders
   for final product only

Source: S. D. P. Flapper, G. J. Miltenburg, and J. Wijngaard, "Embedding JIT into MRP," *International Journal of Production Research* 29, no. 2 (1991), p. 331.

MRP does not do detailed scheduling. This is taken care of by the JIT system itself.

Step 3—create a new layout

When the pull system is balanced for a product group and demand is sufficient and stable, a new layout may be created. All equipment needed is arranged into a line flow as shown in Exhibit 14.24D. Efforts continue to improve the individual processes and reduce inventory. MRP's position now is (1) involvement to create the master production schedule, (2) ordering external parts and components, (3) updating inventories through backflushing, which is to compute material used based on the number of units completed.

Flapper et al. state that few companies advance beyond Step 1 (relocating stock on the shop floor) because:

1. They do not want to lose control of inventories (which happens within a JIT system).

2. They are not prepared to commit resources to training, engineering time, maintenance, and so on to make JIT improvements.

3. Management is satisfied with achievements already made in cost, lead time, quality, and inventory reduction.[7]

14.9 MISCELLANEOUS MRP ISSUES

Problems in Installing and Using MRP Systems

MRP is very well developed technically, and implementation of an MRP system should be pretty straightforward. Yet there are many problems with the MRP systems and many "failures" in trying to install them. Why do such problems and outright failures occur with a "proven" system?

The answer partially lies with organizational and behavioral factors. Three major causes have been identified: the lack of top management commitment, the failure to recognize that MRP is only a software tool that needs to be used correctly, and the integration of MRP and JIT.

Part of the blame for the lack of top management's commitment may be MRP's image. It sounds like a manufacturing system rather than a business plan. However, an MRP system is used to plan resources and develop schedules. And a well-functioning schedule can use the firm's assets effectively with the result of increased profits. MRP should be presented to top management as a planning tool with specific reference to profit results. Intensive executive education is needed, emphasizing the importance of MRP as a closed-loop, integrated, strategic planning tool.

The second cause of the problem concerns the MRP proponents that overdid themselves in selling the concept. MRP was presented and perceived as a

---

[7] Flapper et al., "Embedding JIT into MRP," p. 340.

complete and stand-alone system to run a firm, rather than part of the total system. The third issue is how MRP can be made to function with JIT as we discuss in Chapter 6. JIT and MRP can live together but there are few rules as to how they should be integrated. The system consists of the functional areas of engineering, marketing, personnel, and manufacturing, as well as techniques and concepts such as quality circles, CAD/CAM, and robotics. MRP needs to be *part* of the system, not *the* system.

In many meetings we have attended, both professional and industrial, we have heard similar installation and operational problems. They distill down to the fact that the MRP essentially runs the firm; its main objective is simply to meet the schedule. As a result, people become subservient to the MRP system. Even such simple decisions as determining a run-lot size cannot be made outside the system.

As it stands right now, MRP is a formal system requiring strict adherence to function properly. Often supervisors and workers develop an informal system for getting the job done. Their argument is that this informal system arises because the existing formal system was inadequate to deal with real inventory scheduling problems. In any event, it appears that employees at all levels must change—from the company president to the lower-level employees. Even though MRP currently does work in many installations, its good features and its shortcomings should be thoroughly understood.

Other problems encountered in using MRP include:

1. *The fallacy of static lead time.* MRP software programs treat lead time as a fixed number, while in reality lead time changes for a variety of reasons, such as normal variation in processing time, waiting for parts, delays in processing due to expedited jobs, breakdown or normal maintenance of machines, and so on.

2. *The misdefinition of lead time.* Manufacturing lead time consists of:
   a. Make-ready time—to write order, enter, prepare job packet, release order, and issue material.
   b. Queue time—time at the operation center waiting for operations to begin.
   c. Setup time—to prepare equipment for operations.
   d. Run time—to perform operations (produce product).
   e. Wait time—time waiting after operation ends.
   f. Move time—to physically move between operations.

3. *Lead time versus fabrication/production quantity.* MRP software, because it considers lead time fixed, does not account for the fact that run time (part of the lead time) varies depending on the quantity of units to be produced.

4. *Bill of materials.* MRP software programs use the bill of materials as a bottoms-up product structure representing the way firms produce products. For many firms, however, especially those producing on an assembly line, products may be produced in a very different sequence than the engineering bill of materials.

5. *Material revision control.* Many MRP systems do not easily allow changes to be made in part numbers or in the way the product is produced.

6. *Lead time versus routing.* Since many MRP programs use the bill of materials structure to schedule the shop floor, poor schedules may result. For example, there may be several routing steps at the same bill of materials level, which require more time than allowed.

7. *Fallacy of infinite capacity planning.* Few MRP programs can recognize a shop overload and reschedule.

8. *The real story of rough-cut capacity planning.* While rough-cut capacity planning was taught as the solution to overloaded work centers, in reality rough-cut capacity planning lies somewhere between the difficult and the impossible. In effect, master schedulers are expected to perform MRP and CRP explosions in their heads. Technically, the only way to really do rough-cut capacity planning is to run the MRP and CRP (capacity requirement plan) each time a change is made in the master schedule. Required computer time makes this impossible.

9. *Capacity planning versus MRP logic.* Because MRP and CRP are not run together when changes are made in the master production schedule, such changes often create "floating bottlenecks." Bottlenecks appear and disappear, depending on the master production schedule.

10. *MRP logic—a user confuser.* MRP logic differs from system to system. The user should test how the system reacts to, say, accelerating, decelerating, or canceling an order.[8]

Criticisms of the MRP Concept

In addition to the problems previously mentioned in installing and using an MRP system, there are other criticisms as well. Many critics state that MRP schedules are either impossible or are only true on the day that they were created. Too many changes take place in the system for MRP to be able to adjust to all of them.

Accuracy requirements

Because MRP uses detailed files to schedule, MRP cannot tolerate inaccuracies. In fact, for many years since MRP was introduced, companies have been rated into classes based on the accuracy of their records. Class A companies, for example, have 99-percent accuracy. MRP's failures in its scheduling performance had been blamed on inaccurate records. Now we recognize

---

[8] Adapted from Gus Berger, "Ten Ways MRP Can Defeat You," *Conference Proceedings, American Production and Inventory Control Society,* 1987, pp. 240–43.

that inaccuracy was not completely to blame; the MRP scheduling technique was also at fault.

Top management commitment

This is not so much a criticism of MRP, but of management. As in the case of many programs, MRP needs to be endorsed and continually supported by top management. An MRP system is doomed to failure if management believes its responsibilities end with authorizing purchase of the program and turning over responsibility for running the computer system to the MIS group. Continuous reinforcement and encouragement are needed; everyone must be convinced that the system is worth its time and expense. It also means spending money on training, and perhaps changing the internal measurement and reward system. If this is not done, shop floor personnel ignore MRP schedules and use their own priorities in job selection and in process batch sizes.

MRP as a database

Although MRP has been criticized for its questioned accuracy in providing workable schedules, MRP has been highly complemented for its detailed database. MRP's database extends throughout the entire facility and is linked through numerous modules. Even if a firm decides to discontinue using MRP to schedule its facilities, it would more than likely continue to maintain MRP files for their informational value.

As we discussed in Chapter 6, Just-in-Time (JIT) pull scheduling is simple, works well, and is rapidly being adopted by firms in the United States. Academicians and practitioners have discovered that JIT can be nicely linked to an MRP system.

Safety Stock

Ordinarily, adding a safety stock to required quantities is not advised in an MRP system that is based on derived demand. There is some feeling, however, that when the availability of parts could suffer from a long and inflexible lead time or is subject to strikes or cancellation, a safety stock offers protection against production delays. A safety stock is sometimes intentionally created by planning for excess. One of the main arguments against using safety stock is that the MRP system considers it a fixed quantity, and the safety stock is never actually used.

Lot Sizing in MRP Systems

The determination of lot sizes in an MRP system is a complicated and difficult problem. Lot sizes are the part quantities issued in the planned order receipt and planned order release sections of an MRP schedule. For parts produced in house, lot sizes are the production quantities or batch sizes. For purchased parts, these are the quantities ordered from the supplier. Lot sizes generally meet part requirements for one or more periods.

Most lot-sizing techniques deal with how to balance the setup or order costs and holding costs associated with meeting the net requirements generated by the MRP planning process. Many MRP systems have options for computing lot sizes based on some of the more commonly used techniques. It should be obvious, though, that the use of lot-sizing techniques increases the complexity in generating MRP schedules. When fully exploded, the numbers of parts scheduled can be enormous.

Next, we explain four lot-sizing techniques using a common example. The lot-sizing techniques presented are lot-for-lot (L4L), economic order quantity (EOQ), least total cost (LTC), and least unit cost (LUC).

Consider the following MRP lot-sizing problems; the net requirements are shown for eight scheduling periods:

Cost per item	$10.00
Order or setup cost	$47.00
Inventory carry cost/period	0.5%

Period net requirements:

1	2	3	4	5	6	7	8
50	60	70	60	95	75	60	55

Lot-for-lot

Lot-for-lot (L4L) is the most common technique; it

- Sets planned orders to exactly match the net requirements.
- Produces exactly what is needed each period with none carried over into future periods.
- Minimizes carrying cost.
- Does not take into account setup costs or capacity limitations.

Many times producing enough product to last several periods and incurring holding costs may be cheaper than producing in every period and incurring repeated setup costs. In the case of parts produced in house, the setup cost represents time that resources are not operating but getting ready to produce. This is lost capacity. Not only are setup costs higher but requiring setups in every period a part is needed also reduces the time available to produce other products.

Exhibit 14.25 shows the lot-for-lot calculations. In each period the lot size exactly matches the net requirements. A setup cost is charged for each period. The lot-for-lot technique, while minimizing holding costs, orders far too often because it places an order every time a net requirement occurs.

Economic order quantity

In Chapter 13 we already discussed the EOQ model that explicitly balances setup and holding costs. In an EOQ model, either fairly constant demand

EXHIBIT 14.25   Lot-for-Lot Run Size for an MRP Schedule

Period	Net Requirements	Production Quantity	Ending Inventory	Holding Cost	Setup Cost	Total Cost
1	50	50	0	$0.00	$47.00	$ 47.00
2	60	60	0	0.00	47.00	94.00
3	70	70	0	0.00	47.00	141.00
4	60	60	0	0.00	47.00	188.00
5	95	95	0	0.00	47.00	235.00
6	75	75	0	0.00	47.00	282.00
7	60	60	0	0.00	47.00	329.00
8	55	55	0	0.00	47.00	376.00

EXHIBIT 14.26   Economic Order Quantity Run Size for an MRP Schedule

Period	Net Requirements	Production Quantity	Ending Inventory	Holding Cost	Setup Cost	Total Cost
1	50	351	0	$15.05	$47.00	$ 62.05
2	60	0	241	12.05	0.00	74.10
3	70	0	171	8.55	0.00	82.65
4	60	0	111	5.55	0.00	88.20
5	95	0	16	0.80	0.00	89.00
6	75	351	292	14.60	47.00	150.60
7	60	0	232	11.60	0.00	162.20
8	55	0	177	8.85	0.00	171.05

EOQ assumptions:
Total requirements	525
Average requirements	65.6
Annual holding	$2.60
Annual demand	3,412.5
EOQ	351.25

must exist or safety stock must be kept to provide for demand variability. The EOQ model uses an estimate of total annual demand, the setup or order cost, and the annual holding cost. EOQ was not designed for a system with discrete time periods such as MRP. The lot-sizing techniques used for MRP assume that part requirements are satisfied at the start of the period. Holding costs are then charged only to the ending inventory for the period, not to the average inventory used in the EOQ model. EOQ assumes that parts are used on a continuous basis during the period. The lot sizes generated by EOQ do not always cover the entire number of periods. For example, the EOQ might provide the requirements for 4.6 periods.

Exhibit 14.26 shows the EOQ lot size calculated for this part. Several assumptions are made to determine the EOQ. EOQ requires an estimate of annual demand and annual holding cost. Since the holding cost per period is

EXHIBIT 14.27   Least Total Cost Run Size for an MRP Schedule

Period	Net Requirements	Production Quantity	Ending Inventory	Holding Cost	Setup Cost	Total Cost
1	50	335	285	$14.25	$47.00	$ 61.25
2	60	0	225	11.25	0.00	72.50
3	70	0	155	7.75	0.00	80.25
4	60	0	95	4.75	0.00	85.00
5	95	0	0	0.00	0.00	85.00
6	75	190	115	5.75	47.00	137.75
7	60	0	55	2.75	0.00	140.50
8	55	0	0	0.00	0.00	140.50

Periods	Quantity Ordered	Carrying Cost	Order Cost	Total Cost	
1	50	$ 0.00	$47.00	$ 47.00	
1-2	110	3.00	47.00	50.00	
1-3	180	10.00	47.00	57.00	
1-4	240	19.00	47.00	66.00	
1-5	335	38.00	47.00	85.00	← Least total cost
1-6	410	56.75	47.00	103.75	
1-7	470	74.75	47.00	121.75	
1-8	525	94.00	47.00	141.00	
6	75	0.00	47.00	47.00	
6-7	135	3.00	47.00	50.00	
6-8	190	8.50	47.00	55.50	← Least total cost

$0.05 and the MRP schedule is weekly, the annual holding cost per unit is $2.60 ($0.05 × 52 weeks). Annual demand is computed by multiplying the average weekly demand for the eight periods by 52 weeks (525/8 × 52 = 3,412.5). The resulting EOQ is 351 units. The EOQ lot size in Period 1 is enough to meet requirements for Periods 1 through 5 and a portion of Period 6. Then, in Period 6 another EOQ lot is planned to meet the requirements for Periods 6 through 8. Notice that the EOQ plan leaves some inventory at the end of Period 8 to carry forward into Period 9.

Least total cost
The least total cost method (LTC) is a dynamic lot-sizing technique that calculates the order quantity by comparing the carrying cost and the setup (or ordering) costs for various lot sizes and then selects the lot in which these are most nearly equal.

Exhibit 14.27 shows the least total cost lot size results. The procedure to compute least total cost lot sizes is to compare order costs and holding costs for various numbers of periods. For example, costs are compared for producing in Period 1 to cover the requirements for Period 1; producing in Period 1 for Periods 1 and 2; producing in Period 1 to cover Periods 1, 2, and 3, and so on. The correct selection is the lot size where the ordering costs and holding costs are approximately equal. In Exhibit 14.27 the best lot size is 335 since a $38 carrying cost and a $47 ordering cost is closer than $56.25 and $47. This lot size covers requirements for Periods 1 through 5. Unlike EOQ, the lot size covers only whole numbers of periods.

Based on the Period 1 decision to place an order to cover 5 periods, we are now located in Period 6, and our problem is to determine how many periods into the future we can provide for from here. Exhibit 14.27 shows that holding and order costs are closest in the quantity that covers requirements for Periods 6 through 8. Notice that the holding and order costs here are far apart. This is because our example extends only to Period 8. If the planning horizon were longer, the lot size planned for Period 6 would likely cover more periods into the future beyond Period 8. This brings up one of the limitations of both LTC and LUC (discussed below). Both techniques are influenced by the length of the planning horizon.

Least unit cost

The least unit cost method (LUC) is a dynamic lot-sizing technique that adds ordering and inventory carrying cost for each trial lot size and divides by the number of units in each lot size, picking the lot size with the lowest unit cost. In the example in Exhibit 14.28, the lot size of 410 covers Periods 1 through 6.

EXHIBIT 14.28   **Least Unit Cost Run Size for an MRP Schedule**

Period	Net Requirements	Production Quantity	Ending Inventory	Holding Cost	Setup Cost	Total Cost
1	50	410	360	$18.00	$47.00	$ 65.00
2	60	0	300	15.00	0.00	80.00
3	70	0	230	11.50	0.00	91.50
4	60	0	170	8.50	0.00	100.00
5	95	0	75	3.75	0.00	103.75
6	75	115	115	5.75	47.00	156.50
7	60	0	55	2.75	0.00	159.25
8	55	55	55	2.75	47.00	209.00

Periods	Quantity Ordered	Carrying Cost	Order Cost	Total Cost	Unit Cost	
1	50	$ 0.00	$47.00	$ 47.00	$0.9400	
1–2	110	3.00	47.00	50.00	0.4545	
1–3	180	10.00	47.00	57.00	0.3167	
1–4	240	19.00	47.00	66.00	0.2750	
1–5	335	38.00	47.00	85.00	0.2537	
1–6	410	56.75	47.00	103.75	0.2530	← Least unit cost
1–7	470	74.75	47.00	121.75	0.2590	
1–8	525	94.00	47.00	141.00	0.2686	
7	60	0.00	47.00	47.00	0.7833	
7–8	115	2.75	47.00	49.75	0.4326	← Least unit cost

The lot size planned for Period 7 covers through the end of the planning horizon.

Which lot size to choose

Using the lot-for-lot method, the total cost for the eight periods is $376; the EOQ total cost is $171.05; the least total cost method is $140.50; and the least unit cost is $209. The lowest cost was obtained using the least total cost method of $140.50. If there were more than eight periods, the lowest cost could differ.

The advantage of the least unit cost method is that it is a more complete analysis and would take into account ordering or setup costs that might change as the order size increases. If the ordering or setup costs remain constant, the lowest total cost method is more attractive because it is simpler and easier to compute; yet it would be just as accurate under that restriction.

14.10 INSTALLING AN MRP SYSTEM

The average time for a company to effectively install an MRP system seems to range from 18 to 24 months—not for the software, but because so much other preparation and training must take place. At the cost of being somewhat redundant, we repeat some cautions about installing an MRP system.

Preparation Steps

Bill of materials

The BOM lists all the materials required to create a product in a hierarchical form, which is usually the way in which a product is produced. The BOM is extremely important in an MRP system because it is the main driver of the system. Inaccuracies really cannot be tolerated. Without an MRP or some such computer system, BOM accuracy is not critical and firms can live with some errors. A first step before installing an MRP system is to go through the BOM for all products and ensure that they are correct.

Routing sheets and processing times

Similar to the BOM, many firms have not needed to be specific about which machine or process should be used, since adjustments could always be made on the shop floor. The same goes for processing; with the usual longer times in the shop (as opposed to MRP installations) there are opportunities to make up discrepancies (in spite of the fact that the data for accounting purposes would be in error).

Inventory stock

Most firms have errors in their inventory records. Oftentimes it is because no one wants to take the time needed to count and verify records and physical stock. Another reason is that often inventory stock is old or obsolete; bringing records up to date may mean that much inventory carried on company books as assets may have to be declared scrap. Few managers are willing to bite the bullet and do this. Reducing inventory flows directly to the bottom line and quickly catches the attention of top management. However, installing an MRP system means that errors must be removed and inventory carried must be of usable quality.

Procedures

In addition to the actual records previously mentioned, procedures must be installed to keep these records up to date. Examples are adding stock to inventory when received from vendors, and making appropriate changes when issuing stock to production. Also, ways of handling changes to the bill of materials, routing, or processing times need to be decided.

Training

Everyone—from top management through to purchasing staff, supervisors, and the workers on the shop floor—must be trained in effective use of an MRP system—how to read its reports, which leeways are allowable in quantity or schedule variations, and what results can be expected. People, by nature, are reluctant to change. Throughout MRP's history of two decades, we have blamed people whenever poor performance occurred in their MRP system (lack of understanding, lack of top management support, lack of adequate discipline, etc.). While this is now recognized as a problem caused in large part by the MRP itself (noted elsewhere in this chapter), nevertheless without support of all involved, MRP would be doomed to failure.

A complete MRP II system encompassing all phases of the firm is a major undertaking requiring years to implement. IBM's MAPICS II system, for instance, includes all phases of a firm's operation; the 9 modules cover everything from engineering, production, accounting, and finance with little left out. Needless to say, once on such a system, a firm is committed. Getting off one and onto another could take years.

14.11 CONCLUSION

In the past two decades, MRP has grown from its purpose of determining simple time schedules, to its present MRP II configuration which ties together all major functions of an organization. During its growth and its application, MRP's disadvantages as a scheduling mechanism have been well recognized. This is largely because MRP tries to do too much in light of the very dynamic and often jumpy system in which it is trying to operate.

MRP is recognized, however, for its excellent databases and linkages within the firm. MRP also does a good job in helping to produce master schedules. Because of its databases and the existence of a master production schedule, many firms in repetitive manufacturing are installing JIT systems to link with the MRP system. JIT takes the master production schedule as its pulling force and does not use MRP's generated schedule. Results indicate that this is working. To use this JIT/MRP combination, firms need not be solely in repetitive manufacturing. Portions of almost every job shop have repetitive functions. JIT can prove to be of significant benefit in these hybrid situations as well.

MRP's service applications have not fared well, even though it seems that they should have. The MRP approach would appear very valuable in producing services as service scheduling consists of identifying the final service and then tracing back to the resources needed, such as equipment, space, and personnel. Consider, for example a hospital operating room planning an open-heart surgery. The master schedule can establish a time for the surgery (or surgeries, if several are scheduled). The BOM could specify all required equipment and personnel—MDs, nurses, anesthesiologist, operating room, heart/lung machine, defibrillator, and so forth. The inventory status file would show the availability of the resources and commit them to the project. The MRP program could then produce a schedule showing when various parts of the operation are to be started, expected completion times, required materials, and so forth. Checking this schedule would allow "capacity planning" in answering such questions as: "Are all the materials and personnel available?" and "Does the system produce a feasible schedule?"

We still believe that MRP systems will eventually find their way into service applications.

14.12 REVIEW AND DISCUSSION QUESTIONS

1. Since material requirements planning appears so reasonable, discuss reasons why it did not become popular until recently.

2. Discuss the meaning of MRP teams such as *planned order release* and *scheduled order receipts*.

3. Most practitioners currently update MRP weekly or biweekly. Would it be more valuable if it were updated daily? Discuss.

4. What is the role of safety stock in an MRP system?

5. How does MRP relate to CIM? (See the supplement to Chapter 3.)

6. Contrast the significance of the term *lead time* in the traditional EOQ context and in an MRP system.

7. Discuss the importance of the master production schedule in an MRP system.

8. MRP systems are difficult to install. Discuss the problems that can occur with the system requirements (ignore behavioral problems).

9. "MRP just prepares shopping lists—it doesn't do the shopping or cook the dinner." Comment.

10. What are the sources of demand in an MRP system? Are these dependent or independent, and how are they used as inputs to the system?

11. State the types of data that would be carried in the bill of materials file and the inventory record file.

12. How does MRP II differ from MRP?

13. What is the range of costs to install an MRP system?

14.13 PROBLEMS

*1. Product X is made of two units of Y and three of Z. Y is made of one unit of A and two units of B. Z is made of two units of A and four units of C.

Lead time for X is one week; Y, two weeks; Z, three weeks; A, two weeks; B, one week; and C, three weeks.

a. Draw the product structure tree.

b. If 100 units of X are needed in week 10, develop a planning schedule showing when each item should be ordered and in what quantity.

*2. Product M is made of two units of N and three of P. N is made of two units of R and four units of S. R is made of one unit of S and three units of T. P is made of two units of T and four units of U.

a. Show the product structure tree.

b. If 100 M are required, how many units of each component are needed?

c. Show both a single-level bill of materials and an indented bill of materials.

3. In the following MRP planning scheduling for Item J, indicate the correct net requirements, planned order receipts, and planned order releases to meet the gross requirements. Lead time is one week.

Week Number

Item J	0	1	2	3	4	5
Gross requirements			75		50	70
On hand 40						
Net requirements						
Planned order receipt						
Planned order releases						

4. Repeat Problem 1 using current on-hand inventories of 20 X, 40 Y, 30 Z, 50 A, 100 B, and 900 C.

5. Assume that Product Z is made of two units of A and four units of B. A is made of three units of C and four of D. D is made of two units of E.

The lead time for purchase or fabrication of each unit to final assembly: Z takes two weeks, A, B, C, and D take one week each, and E takes three weeks.

Fifty units are required in Period 10. (Assume that there is currently no inventory on hand of any of these items.)

a. Draw a product structure tree.

---

* Problems 1 and 2 are solved in Appendix H.

    b.   Develop an MRP planning schedule showing gross and net requirements, order release and order receipt dates.

6.   *Note:* For Problems 6 through 9, to simplify data handling to include the receipt of orders that have actually been placed in previous periods, the six-level scheme shown below can be used. (There are a number of different techniques used in practice, but the important issue is to keep track of what is on hand, what is expected to arrive, what is needed, and what size orders should be placed.) One way to calculate the numbers is as follows:

				WEEK					
Gross requirements									
Scheduled receipts									
On hand from prior period									
Net requirements									
Planned order receipt									
Planned order release									

   One unit of A is made of three units of B, one unit of C, and two units of D. B is composed of two units of E and one unit of D. C is made of one unit of B and two units of E. E is made of one unit of F.

   Items B, C, E, and F have one-week lead times; A and D have lead times of two weeks.

   Assume that lot-for-lot (L4L) lot sizing is used for items A, B, and F; lots of size 50, 50, and 200 are used for items C, D, and E, respectively. Items C, E, and F have on-hand (beginning) inventories of 10, 50, and 150, respectively; all other items have zero beginning inventory. We are scheduled to receive 10 units of A in Week 5, 50 units of E in Week 4, and also 50 units of F in Week 4. There are no other scheduled receipts. If 30 units of A are required in Week 8, use the low-level-coded product structure tree to find the necessary planned order releases for all components.

7.   One unit of A is made of two units of B, three units of C, and two units of D. B is composed of one unit of E and two units of F. C is made of two units of F and one unit of D. E is made of two units of D. Items A, C, D, and F have one-week lead times; B and E have lead times of two weeks. Lot-for-lot (L4L) lot sizing is used for Items A, B, C, and D; lots of size 50 and 180 are used for items E and F, respectively. Item C has an on-hand (beginning) inventory of 15; D has an on-hand inventory of 50; all other items have zero beginning inventory. We are scheduled to receive 20 units of Item E in week 4; there are no other scheduled receipts.

   Construct simple and low-level-coded product structure trees and indented and summarized bills of material.

   If 20 units of A are required in Week 8, use the low-level-coded product structure tree to find the necessary planned order releases for all components. (See note in Problem 6.)

8. One unit of A is made of one unit of B and one unit of C. B is made of four units of C and one unit of E and F. C is made of two units of D and one unit of E. E is made of three units of F. Item C has a lead time of one week; Items A, B, E, and F have two-week lead times; and Item D has a lead time of three weeks. Lot-for-lot lot sizing is used for Items A, D, and E; lots of size 50, 100, and 50 are used for Items B, C, and F, respectively. Items A, C, D, and E have on-hand (beginning) inventories of 20, 50, 100, and 10, respectively; all other items have zero beginning inventory. We are scheduled to receive 10 units of A in week 5, 100 units of C in Week 6, and 100 units of D in Week 4; there are no other scheduled receipts. If 50 units of A are required in Week 10, use the low-level-coded product structure tree to find the necessary planned order releases for all components. (See note in Problem 6.)

9. One unit of A is made of two units of B and one unit of C. B is made of three units of D and one unit of F. C is composed of three units of B, one unit of D, and four units of E. D is made of one unit of E. Item C has a lead time of one week; Items A, B, E, and F have two-week lead times; and Item D has a lead time of 3 weeks. Lot-for-lot lot sizing is used for Items C, E, and F; lots of size 20, 40, and 160 are used for items A, B, and D, respectively. Items A, B, D, and E have on-hand (beginning) inventories of 5, 10, 100, and 100, respectively; all other items have zero beginning inventories. We are scheduled to receive 10 units of A in Week 3, 20 units of B in Week 7, 40 units of F in week 5, and 60 units of E in Week 2; there are no other scheduled receipts. If 20 units of A are required in Week 10, use the low-level-coded product structure tree to find the necessary planned order releases for all components. (See note in Problem 6.)

10. The MRP gross requirements for Item A is shown here for the next 10 weeks. Lead time for A is three weeks and setup cost is $10 per setup. There is a carrying cost of $0.01 per unit per week. Beginning inventory is 90 units.

	WEEK									
	1	2	3	4	5	6	7	8	9	10
Gross requirements	30	50	10	20	70	80	20	60	200	50

Use the least total cost or the least unit cost lot-sizing method to determine when and for what quantity the first order should be released.

11. (This problem is intended as a very simple exercise to go from the aggregate plan to the master schedule to the MRP.) Gigamemory Storage Devices, Inc. produces CD ROMs (Read Only Memory) and WORMs (Write Once Read Many) for the computer market. Aggregate demand for the WORMs for the next two quarters are 2,100 units and 2,700 units. Assume that the demand is distributed evenly for each month of the quarter.

There are two models of the WORM: an internal model, and an external model. The drive assemblies in both are the same but the electronics and housing are different. Demand is higher for the external model and currently is 70 percent of the aggregate demand.

The bill of materials and the lead times follow. One drive assembly and one electronic and housing unit go into each WORM.

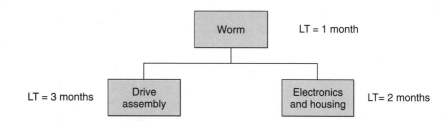

The MRP system is run monthly. Currently, 200 external WORMs are in stock and 100 internal WORMs. Also in stock are 250 drive assemblies, 50 internal electronic and housing units, and 125 external electronic and housing units.

Problem: Show the aggregate plan, the master production schedule, and the full MRP with the gross and net requirements and planned order releases.

12. Product A is an end item and is made from two units of B and four of C. B is made of three units of D and two of E. C is made of two units of F and two of E.

A has a lead time of one week. B, C, and E have lead times of two weeks, and D and F have lead times of three weeks.

a. Draw the product structure tree.

b. If 100 units of A are required in work 10, develop the MRP planning schedule, specifying when items are to be ordered and received. There are currently no units of inventory on hand.

13. Product A consists of two units of subassembly B, three units of C, and one unit of D. B is composed of four units of E and three units of F. C is made of two units and H and three units of D. H is made of five units of E and two units of G.

a. Construct a simple product structure tree.

b. Construct a product structure tree using low-level coding.

c. Construct an indented bill of materials.

d. To produce 100 units of A, determine the numbers of units of B, C, D, E, F, G, and H required.

14. The MRP gross requirements for Item X are shown here for the next 10 weeks. Lead time for A is two weeks, and setup cost is $9 per setup. There is a carrying cost of $0.02 per unit per week. Beginning inventory is 70 units.

	WEEK									
	1	2	3	4	5	6	7	8	9	10
Gross requirements	20	10	15	45	10	30	100	20	40	150

Use the least total cost or the least unit cost lot-sizing method to determine when and for what quantity the first order should be released.

15. Audio Products, Inc., produces two AM/FM cassette players for automobiles. Both radio/cassette units are identical, but the mounting hardware and finish trim differ. The standard model fits intermediate and full-size cars, and the sports model fits small sports cars.

Audio Products handles the production in the following way. The chassis (radio/cassette unit) is assembled in Mexico and has a manufacturing lead time of two weeks. The mounting hardware is purchased from a sheet steel company and has a three-week lead time. The finish trim is purchased from a Taiwan electronics company with offices in Los Angeles as prepackaged units consisting of knobs and various trim pieces. Trim packages have a two-week lead time. Final assembly time may be disregarded, since adding the trim package and mounting are performed by the customer.

Audio Products supplies wholesalers and retailers, who place specific orders for both models up to eight weeks in advance. These orders, together with enough additional units to satisfy the small number of individual sales, are summarized in the following demand schedule:

	Week							
	1	2	3	4	5	6	7	8
Standard model				300				400
Sports model					200			100

There are currently 50 radio/cassette units on hand but no trim packages or mounting hardware.

Prepare a material requirements plan to meet the demand schedule exactly. Specify the gross and net requirements, on-hand amounts, and the planned order release and receipt periods for the cassette/radio chassis, the standard trim and sports car model trim, and the standard mounting hardware and the sports car mounting hardware.

16. Brown and Brown Electronics manufactures a line of digital audiotape players. While there are differences among the various products, there are a number of common parts within each player. The product structure, showing the number of each item required, lead times, and the current inventory on hand for the parts and components, follows:

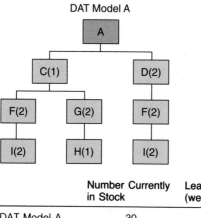

DAT Model A

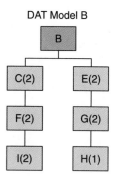

DAT Model B

	Number Currently in Stock	Lead Time (weeks)
DAT Model A	30	1
DAT Model B	50	2
Subassembly C	75	1
Subassembly D	80	2
Subassembly E	100	1
Part F	150	1
Part G	40	1
Raw material H	200	2
Raw material I	300	2

Brown and Brown created a forecast that it plans to use as its master production schedule, producing exactly to schedule. Part of the MPS shows a demand for 700 units of Model A and 1,200 units of Model B in Week 10.

Develop an MRP schedule to meet that demand.

14.14 CASE: NICHOLS COMPANY

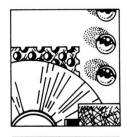

This particular December day seemed bleak to Joe Williams, president of Nichols Company (NCO). He sat in his office watching the dying embers of his fireplace, hoping to clear his mind. Suddenly there came a tapping by someone gently rapping, rapping at his office door. "Another headache," he muttered, "tapping at my office door. Only that and nothing more."[9]

The intruder was Barney Thompson, director of marketing. "A major account has just canceled a large purchase of A units because we are back ordered on tubing. This can't continue. My sales force is out beating the bushes for customers and our production manager can't provide the product."

For the past several months, operations at NCO have been unsteady. Inventory levels have been too high, while at the same time there have been stockouts. This resulted in many late deliveries, complaints, and cancellations. To compound the problem, overtime was excessive.

History

Nichols Company was started by Joe Williams and Peter Schaap, both with MBAs from the University of Arizona. Much has happened since Williams and Schaap formed the company. Schaap has left the company and is working in real estate development in Queensland, Australia. Under the direction of Williams, NCO has diversified to include a number of other products.

NCO currently has 355 full-time employees directly involved in manufacturing the three primary products, A, B, and C. Final assembly takes place in a converted warehouse adjacent to NCO's main plant.

The Meeting

Williams called a meeting the next day to get input on the problems facing NCO and to lay the groundwork for some solutions. Attending the meeting, besides himself and Barney Thompson, were Phil Bright of production and inventory control, Trevor Hansen of purchasing, and Steve Clark of accounting.

The meeting lasted all morning. Participation was vocal and intense.

Bright said, "The forecasts that marketing sends us are always way off. We are constantly having to expedite one product or another to meet current demand. This runs up our overtime."

---

[9] With apologies to E.A.P.

Thompson said, "Production tries to run too lean. We need a larger inventory of finished goods. If I had the merchandise, my salespeople could sell 20 percent more product."

Clark said, "No way! Our inventory is already uncomfortably high. We can't afford the holding costs, not to mention how fast technology changes around here causing even more inventory, much of it obsolete."

Bright said, "The only way I can meet our stringent cost requirement is to buy in volume."

At the end of the meeting, Williams had lots of input but no specific plan. What do you think he should do?

Use Case Exhibits 1–4 showing relevant data to answer the specific questions at the end of the case.

CASE EXHIBIT 1

Bills of Materials for Products A, B, and C

Product A	Product B	Product C
.A	.B	.C
.D(4)	.F(2)	.G(2)
.I(3)	.G(3)	.I(2)
.E(1)	.I(2)	.H(1)
.F(4)		

CASE EXHIBIT 2

Work Center Routings for Products and Components

Item	Work Center Number	Standard Time (hours per unit)
Product A	1	0.20
	4	0.10
Product B	2	0.30
	4	0.08
Product C	3	0.10
	4	0.05
Component D	1	0.15
	4	0.10
Component E	2	0.15
	4	0.05
Component F	2	0.15
	3	0.20
Component G	1	0.30
	2	0.10
Component H	1	0.05
	3	0.10

CASE EXHIBIT 3

Inventory Levels and Lead Times for Each Item on the Bill of Materials at the Beginning of Week 1

Product/Component	On Hand (units)	Lead Time (weeks)
Product A	100	1
Product B	200	1
Product C	175	1
Component D	200	1
Component E	195	1
Component F	120	1
Component G	200	1
Component H	200	1
I (Raw material)	300	1

CASE EXHIBIT 4

Forecasted Demand for Weeks 4–27

Week	Product A	Product B	Product C
1			
2			
3			
4	1,500	2,200	1,200
5	1,700	2,100	1,400
6	1,150	1,900	1,000
7	1,100	1,800	1,500
8	1,000	1,800	1,400
9	1,100	1,600	1,100
10	1,400	1,600	1,800
11	1,400	1,700	1,700
12	1,700	1,700	1,300
13	1,700	1,700	1,700
14	1,800	1,700	1,700
15	1,900	1,900	1,500
16	2,200	2,300	2,300
17	2,000	2,300	2,300
18	1,700	2,100	2,000
19	1,600	1,900	1,700
20	1,400	1,800	1,800
21	1,100	1,800	2,200
22	1,000	1,900	1,900
23	1,400	1,700	2,400
24	1,400	1,700	2,400
25	1,500	1,700	2,600
26	1,600	1,800	2,400
27	1,500	1,900	2,500

QUESTIONS

Use Lotus (or another spreadsheet if you prefer) to solve the Nichols Company case.

Simplifying assumption: To get the program started, some time is needed at the beginning since MRP backloads the system. For simplicity, assume that the forecasts (and therefore demands) are zero for Periods 1 through 3. Also assume that the starting inventory specified in Case Exhibit 3 is available from Week 1. For the master production schedule, use only the end Items A, B, and C.

To modify production quantities, adjust only Products A, B, and C. Do not adjust the quantities of D, E, F, G, H, and I. These should be linked so that changes in A, B, and C automatically adjust them.

1. Disregarding machine-center limitations, develop an MRP schedule and also capacity profiles for the four machine centers.

2. Work center capacities and costs follow. Repeat (1) creating a *feasible* schedule (within the capacities of the machine centers) and compute the relevant costs. Do this by adjusting the MPS only. Try to minimize the total cost of operation for the 27 weeks.

	Capacity	Cost
Work Center 1	6,000 hours available	$20 per hour
Work Center 2	4,500 hours available	$25 per hour
Work Center 3	2,400 hours available	$35 per hour
Work Center 4	1,200 hours available	$65 per hour

Inventory carrying cost	
End items A, B, and C	$2.00 per unit
Components D, E, F, G, and H	$1.50 per unit
Raw material I	$1.00 per unit
Back-order cost	
End items A, B, and C	$20 per unit
Components D, E, F, G, and H	$14 per unit
Raw material I	$ 8 per unit

3. Suppose end items had to be ordered in multiples of 100 units, components in multiples of 500 units, and raw materials in multiples of 1,000 units. How would this change your schedule?

14.15 SELECTED BIBLIOGRAPHY

Biggs, Joseph R., and Ellen J. Long. "Gaining the Competitive Edge with MRP/MRP II." *Management Accounting,* May 1988, pp. 27–32.

Flapper, S. D. P.; G. J. Miltenburg; and J. Wijngaard. "Embedding JIT into MRP." *International Journal of Production Research* 29, no. 2 (1991), pp. 329–41.

Goodrich, Thomas. "JIT & MRP Can Work Together." *Automation,* April 1989, pp. 46–47.

Journal of American Institute of Decision Science. (Articles appear discussing MRP and MRP II from a more analytical basis, examining topics such as lot sizing, safety stocks, and multiechelon inventory.)

Journal of American Production and Inventory Control Society. (Numerous articles on MRP and MRP II appear. Most of these cite the difficulties and experiences of practitioners.)

Orlicky, Joseph. *Materials Requirements Planning.* New York: McGraw-Hill, 1975. (This is the classic book on MRP.)

Proceedings of APICS and DSI. (Many papers on all aspects of MRP and MRP II are usually presented at the annual society meetings and reprinted in the proceedings.)

Rao, Ashok. "A Survey of MRP II Software Suppliers' Trends in Support of Just-In-Time." *Production and Inventory Management Journal,* 3rd Quarter 1989, pp. 14–17.

Vollmann, Thomas E.; William L. Berry; and D. Clay Whybark. *Manufacturing Planning and Control Systems.* 2nd ed. Homewood, Ill.: Richard D. Irwin, 1988.

Wallace, Thomas F. "MRP II & JIT Work Together in Plan and Practice." *Automation,* March 1990, pp. 40–42.

Chapter 15

Job Shop Scheduling and Control

Job Shops in Everyday Life:
Your house, your kitchen, your school,
your study area.

KEY TERMS

Job Shop

Flow Shop

Dispatching of Orders

Expediting

Machine-Limited and Labor-Limited Systems

Priority Rules

Critical Ratio Rule

Runout Time Method

Shop-Floor Control

Input/Output (I/O) Control

Optimized Production Technology (OPT)

YOU WANT IT WHEN ?!

Thanks to Professor Bob Parsons, Management Science Department,
Northeastern University, Boston, MA.

Despite the cartoon, attitudes that belittle scheduling and delivery due dates are no laughing matter.

In previous chapters we have addressed scheduling issues in repetitive manufacturing environments (assembly lines and JIT) and in project environments (project scheduling). In this chapter we focus on scheduling job shops[1] —the most difficult of scheduling environments—and then touch on work force scheduling in service systems.

15.1 JOB SHOP DEFINED

Even though we briefly defined the term *job shop* in an earlier chapter, this expanded definition is helpful at this point. A **job shop** is a functional organization whose departments or work centers are organized around particular types of equipment or operations, such as drilling, forging, spinning, or assembly. Products flow through departments in batches corresponding to individual orders—either stock orders or individual customer orders.[2]

As we discussed earlier, job shops are often contrasted with flow shops; they are considered as two distinctly different types of production environ-

---

[1] Scheduling in job shops is also discussed in Chapters 9 and 18.
[2] *APICS Dictionary* (Falls Church, Va.: American Production and Inventory Control Society, 1984), p. 15.

ments.[3] The scheduling literature, however, treats the flow shop as an extreme case of the general job-shop organization, and we follow that convention in this chapter. Specifically, in a **flow shop** all jobs follow the same processing sequence.

15.2 SCHEDULING AND CONTROL IN THE JOB SHOP

A schedule is a timetable for performing activities, using resources, or allocating facilities. The purpose of operations scheduling in the job shop is to disaggregate the master production schedule into time-phased weekly, daily, or hourly activities—in other words, to specify in precise terms the planned workload on the productive system in the very short run. Operations control entails monitoring job-order progress and, where necessary, expediting orders or adjusting system capacity to make sure that the master schedule is met.

In designing a scheduling and control system, provision must be made for efficient performance of the following functions:

1. Allocating orders, equipment, and personnel to work centers or other specified locations. Essentially, this is short-run capacity planning.
2. Determining the *sequence* of order performance; that is, establishing job priorities.
3. Initiating performance of the scheduled work. This is commonly termed the **dispatching of orders.**
4. Shop-floor control (or production activity control) involving:
   a. Reviewing the status and controlling the progress of orders as they are being worked on.
   b. **Expediting** late and critical orders.[4]
5. Revising the schedule in light of changes in order status.

A simple shop-scheduling process is shown in Exhibit 15.1. At the start of the day, the job dispatcher (in this case, a production control person assigned to this department) selects and sequences available jobs to be run at individual workstations. The dispatcher's decisions would be based on the operations and routing requirements of each job, status of existing jobs on the machines, the queue of work before each machine, job priorities, material availability, antici-

---

[3] For an excellent summary of these differences, see Sam G. Taylor, Samuel M. Seward, and Steven F. Bolander, "Why the Process Industries Are Different," *Production and Inventory Management,* 4th Quarter 1981, pp. 9–24.

[4] Despite the fact that expediting is frowned upon by production control specialists, it is nevertheless a reality of life. In fact, a very typical entry-level job in production control is that of expediter of "stock-chaser." In some companies, a good expediter—one who can negotiate a critical job through the system or can scrounge up materials nobody thought were available—is a prized possession.

EXHIBIT 15.1

Typical Scheduling Process

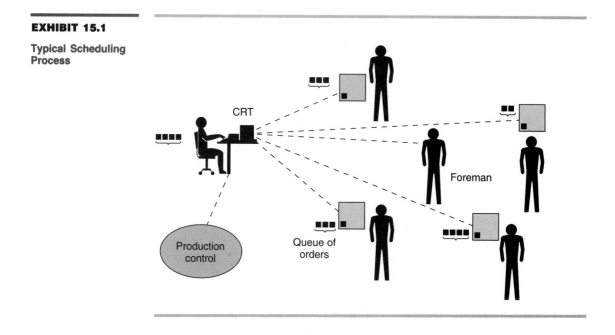

pated job orders to be released later in the day, and worker and machine capabilities. To help organize the schedule, the dispatcher would draw on shop-floor information from the previous day and external information provided by central production control, process engineering, and so on. The dispatcher would also confer with the supervisor of the department about the feasibility of the schedule, especially work-force considerations and potential bottlenecks.

15.3 ELEMENTS OF THE JOB-SHOP SCHEDULING PROBLEM

The classic approach to job-shop scheduling focuses on the following six elements, with a great deal of research invested in evaluating which priority rules are best at satisfying various performance criteria.

1. Job arrival patterns.
2. Number and variety of machines in the shop.
3. Ratio of workers to machines in the shop.
4. Flow pattern of jobs through the shop.
5. Priority rules for allocating jobs to machines.
6. Schedule evaluation criteria.

Job Arrival Patterns

Jobs can arrive at the scheduler's desk either in a batch or over a time interval according to some statistical distribution. The first arrival pattern is termed *static,* the second *dynamic*. Static arrival does not mean that orders are placed by customers at the same moment, only that they are subject to being scheduled at one time. Such a situation occurs when a production control clerk makes out a schedule, say, once a week and does not dispatch any jobs until all the previous week's incoming orders are on hand. In a dynamic arrival, jobs are dispatched as they arrive, and the overall schedule is updated to reflect their effect on the production facility.

Number and Variety of Machines in the Shop

The number of machines in the shop obviously affects the scheduling process. If there is but one machine, or if a group of machines can be treated as one, the scheduling problem is greatly simplified. On the other hand, as the number and variety of machines increase, the more complex the scheduling problem is likely to become.

Ratio of Workers to Machines in the Shop

If there are more workers than machines or an equal number of workers and machines, the shop is referred to as a **machine-limited system.** If there are more machines than workers, it is referred to as a **labor-limited system.** The machine-limited system has received a far greater amount of study, although recent investigations suggest that labor-limited systems are more pervasive in practice. In studying labor-limited systems, the primary areas of concern are the utilization of the worker on several machines and determinaion of the best way to allocate workers to machines.

Flow Patterns of Jobs through the Shop

The pattern of flow through the shop ranges from what is termed a *flow shop* (noted earlier), where all the jobs follow the same path from one machine to the next, to a *randomly routed job shop,* where there is no similar pattern of movement of jobs from one machine to the next. (Exhibit 15.2 approximates the latter situation.) Most shops fall somewhere in between. The extent to which a shop is a flow shop or a randomly routed job shop can be determined by noting the statistical probability of a job's moving from one machine to the next. Frequently such probabilities are expressed in a transitional probability matrix derived from historical data on the percentage of jobs in Machine center I going next to Machine center J, Machine center K, etc. A pure flow shop would show a probability of 1.0 for a job going from I to J; 1.0 from J to K, 1.0

EXHIBIT 15.2

Work Flow Patterns for a Hypothetical Job Shop

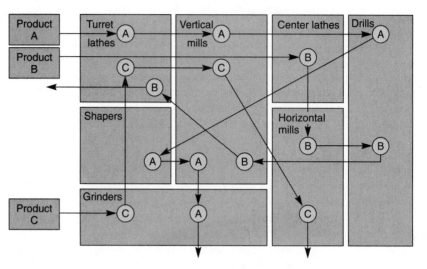

Note: First work center for each product is termed the gateway work center.

from K to L, and so on. A pure random job shop would show equal probabilities of a job going from I to J, K, or L. Likewise, if a job were in L, the pure job-shop case would show it had an equal probability of going back to either J or K. (Clearly, the pure random job shop is an unlikely configuration in the real world.)

Job Sequencing

The process of determining which job is started first on some machine or work center is known as sequencing or priority sequencing. **Priority rules** are the rules used in obtaining a job sequence. These can be very simple, requiring only that jobs be sequenced according to one piece of data, such as processing time, due date, or order of arrival. Other rules, though equally simple, may require several pieces of information, typically to derive an index number such as in the least slack rule and the **critical ratio rule** (both defined later). Still others, such as Johnson's rule (discussed later), apply to job scheduling on a sequence of machines and require a computational procedure to specify the order of performance. Ten of the more common priority rules are

1. FCFS—first-come, first-served; orders are run in the order they arrive in the department.

2. SOT—shortest operating time; run the job with the shortest completion time first, next shortest second, etc. This is identical to SPT—shortest processing time.

3. Due date—earliest due date first; run the job with the earliest due date first. DDate—when referring to the entire job; OPNDD—when referring to the next operation.

4. Start date—due date minus normal lead time. (Run the job with the earliest start date first.)

5. STR—slack time remaining; this is calculated as the difference between the time remaining before the due date minus the processing time remaining. Orders with the shortest STR are run first.

6. STR/OP—Slack time remaining per operation; orders with shortest STR/OP are run first. Calculated as follows:

$$STR/OP = \frac{\begin{array}{c} \text{Time remaining} \\ \text{before due date} \end{array} - \begin{array}{c} \text{Remaining} \\ \text{processing time} \end{array}}{\text{Number of remaining operations}}$$

7. CR—critical ratio; this is calculated as the difference between the due date and the current date divided by the work remaining. Orders with the smallest CR are run first.

8. QR—queue ratio; this is calculated as the slack time remaining in the schedule divided by the planned remaining queue time. Orders with the smallest QR are run first.

9. LCFS—last-come, first-served; this rule occurs frequently by default. As orders arrive they are placed on the top of the stack and the operator usually picks up the order on top to run first.

10. Random order—whim; the supervisors or the operators usually select whichever job they feel like running.[5]

Schedule Evaluation Criteria

The following standard measures of schedule performance are used to evaluate priority rules:

1. Meeting due dates of customers or downstream operations.
2. Minimizing flow time (the time a job spends in the shop).
3. Minimizing work in process.
4. Minimizing idle time of machines and workers.

---

[5] List modified from Donald W. Fogarty, John H. Blackstone, Jr., and Thomas R. Hoffmann, *Production and Inventory Management* (Cincinnati: South-Western Publishing, 1991), pp. 452–53.

15.4 PRIORITY RULES AND TECHNIQUES

Scheduling *n* Jobs on One Machine

Let's look at some of the 10 priority rules compared in a static scheduling situation involving four jobs on one machine. (In scheduling terminology, this class of problems is referred to as an "*n* job–one-machine problem," or simply *n*/1). The theoretical difficulty of this type of problem increases as more machines are considered rather than by the number of jobs that must be processed; therefore, the only restriction on *n* is that it be a specified, finite number.

Consider the following example: Ioannis Kyriakides is the supervisor of Legal Copy-Express, which provides copy services for L.A. law firms in the downtown Los Angeles area. Five customers submitted their orders at the beginning of the week. Specific scheduling data are as follows:

Job (in order of arrival)	Processing Time (days)	Due Date (days hence)
A	3	5
B	4	6
C	2	7
D	6	9
E	1	2

All orders require the use of the only color copy machine available; Kyriakides must decide on the processing sequence for the five orders. The evaluation criterion is minimum flow time. Suppose that Kyriakides decides to use the FCFS rule in an attempt to make Legal Copy-Express appear fair to its customers. The FCFS rule results in the following flow times:

FCFS SCHEDULE

Job	Processing Time (days)	Due Date (days)	Flow Time (days)
A	3	5	0 + 3 = 3
B	4	6	3 + 4 = 7
C	2	7	7 + 2 = 9
D	6	9	9 + 6 = 15
E	1	2	15 + 1 = 16

Total flow time = 3 + 7 + 9 + 15 + 16 = 50 days

Mean flow time = $\dfrac{50}{5}$ = 10 days

Comparing the due date of each job with its flow time, we observe that only Job A will be on time. Jobs B, C, D, and E will be late by 1, 2, 6, and 14 days, respectively. On the average, a job will be late by $(0+1+2+6+14)/5 = 4.6$ days.

Let's now consider the SOT rule. Here Kyriakides gives a highest priority to the order that has the shortest processing time. The resulting flow times are:

SOT SCHEDULE

Job	Processing Time (days)	Due Date (days)	Flow Time (days)
E	1	2	0 + 1 = 1
C	2	7	1 + 2 = 3
A	3	5	3 + 3 = 6
B	4	6	6 + 4 = 10
D	6	9	10 + 6 = 16

Total flow time = 1 + 3 + 6 + 10 + 16 = 36 days

Mean flow time = $\frac{36}{5}$ = 7.2 days

SOT results in lower average flow time. In addition, Jobs E and C will be ready before the due date, and Job A is late by only one day. On the average a job will be late by $(0+0+1+4+7)/5 = 2.4$ days.

If Kyriakides decides to use the DDate rule, the resulting schedule is:

DDATE SCHEDULE

Job	Processing Time (days)	Due Date (days)	Flow Time (days)
E	1	2	0 + 1 = 1
A	3	5	1 + 3 = 4
B	4	6	4 + 4 = 8
C	2	7	8 + 2 = 10
D	6	9	10 + 6 = 16

Total completion time = 1 + 4 + 8 + 10 + 16 = 39 days
Mean flow time = 7.8 days

In this case Jobs B, C, and D will be late. On the average, a job will be late by $(0+0+2+3+7)/5 = 2.4$ days.

Following are the resulting flow times of the LCFS, random, and STR rules:

Job	Processing Time (days)	Due Date (days)	Flow Time (days)
LCFS schedule			
E	1	2	0 + 1 = 1
D	6	9	1 + 6 = 7
C	2	7	7 + 2 = 9
B	4	6	9 + 4 = 13
A	3	5	13 + 3 = 16

Total flow time   = 46 days
Mean flow time   = 9.2 days
Average lateness = 4.0 days

Job	Processing Time (days)	Due Date (days)	Flow Time (days)
Random schedule			
D	6	9	0 + 6 = 6
C	2	7	6 + 2 = 8
A	3	5	8 + 3 = 11
E	1	2	11 + 1 = 12
B	4	6	12 + 4 = 16

Total flow time   = 53 days
Mean flow time   = 10.5 days
Average lateness = 5.4 days

Job	Processing Time (days)	Due Date (days)	Flow Time (days)
STR schedule			
E	1	2	0 + 1 = 1
A	3	5	1 + 3 = 4
B	4	6	4 + 4 = 8
D	6	9	8 + 6 = 14
C	2	7	14 + 2 = 16

Total flow time   = 43 days
Mean flow time   = 8.6 days
Average lateness = 3.2 days

Here are some of the results summarized for the rules that Kyriakides examined:

Rule	Total Completion Time (days)	Average Completion Time (days)	Average Lateness (days)
FCFS	50	10	4.6
SOT	36	7.2	2.4
DDate	39	7.8	2.4
LCFS	46	9.2	4.0
Random	53	10.6	5.4
STR	43	8.6	3.2

Obviously, here SOT is better than the rest of the rules, but is this always the case? The answer is yes. Moreover, it can be shown mathematically that the SOT rule yields an optimum solution for the $n/1$ case in such other evaluation criteria as mean waiting time and mean completion time. In fact, so powerful is this simple rule that it has been termed "the most important concept in the entire subject of sequencing."[6]

Runout method of scheduling n jobs on one machine
The **runout time method** can be used to determine production runs for a group of items that share the same production facilities or resources. Runout

---

[6] R. W. Conway, William L. Maxwell, and Louis W. Miller, *Theory of Scheduling* (Reading, Mass.: Addison-Wesley Publishing, 1967), p. 26. A classic book on the subject.

time is that period of time for which previously scheduled production, plus inventory on hand, satisfies demands for an item. The basic objective of this method is to balance the utilization of production capacity—for example, machine hours—so that all items run out at the same time. Production efforts are thereby balanced across the group of items rather than concentrated on a few items (while other items are neglected). Examples are running parts through a testing machine, sewing a unique line of dresses by a seamstress, and sequencing textbook binding through a binding machine.

This procedure is illustrated in Exhibit 15.3 for six items, where 96.5 machine hours are available to be scheduled during a week. The runout time method is to be used to develop a production schedule for the six items. First, inventory on hand and forecast weekly usage are converted into machine hours in columns 1 and 4, respectively. Next, the aggregate runout time is

EXHIBIT 15.3

Runout Time Calculations

Item	(1) Production Time (machine hours per unit)	(2) Inventory on Hand (units)	(3) Inventory on Hand (machine hours) (1) × (2)	(4) Forecast Weekly Usage (units)	(5) Forecast Weekly Usage (machine hours) (1) × (4)
A	0.2	125	25.00	60	12.00
B	0.08	250	20.00	85	6.80
C	0.5	75	37.50	30	15.00
D	0.09	300	27.00	96	8.64
E	0.15	239	35.85	78	11.70
F	0.7	98	68.60	42	29.40
Aggregate totals			213.95		83.54

$$\text{Aggregate runout time} = \frac{\text{Inventory on hand in machine hours (col. 3)} + \text{Available machine hours}}{\text{Forecast weekly usage (col. 5)}}$$

$$= \frac{213.95 + 96.5}{83.54} = 3.72 \text{ weeks}$$

Item	(6) Runout Time (computed above)	(7) Total Items Required (units) (4) × (6)	(8) Schedule (total items less beginning inventory) (7) − (2)	(9) Production Schedule (machine hours) (1) × (8)
A	3.72	223	98	19.6
B	3.72	316	66	5.3
C	3.72	112	37	18.5
D	3.72	357	57	5.1
E	3.72	290	51	7.7
F	3.72	156	58	40.6
				96.8

computed and listed in column 6. The aggregate runout time (3.72 weeks) is then used in column 7 to determine the inventories needed at the end of the week if each item is to have a runout time of 3.72 weeks. Column 8 shows the total items required after we subtract the items of the inventory on hand, shown in column 2. Finally, column 9 shows the machine hours required for each item for the production schedule developed, which uses a total of 96.8 hours. (Note that additional calculations would have to be made if there were an established production lot size for each item.)

Scheduling n Jobs on Two Machines

The next step up in complexity of job-shop types is the $n/2$ flow-shop case, where two or more jobs must be processed on two machines in a common sequence. As in the $n/1$ case, there is an approach that leads to an optimal solution according to certain criteria. The objective of this approach, termed *Johnson's rule* or *method* (after its developer), is to minimize the flow time, from the beginning of the first job until the finish of the last. Johnson's rule consists of the following steps:

1. List the operation time for each job on both machines.
2. Select the shortest operation time.
3. If the shortest time is for the first machine, do the job first; if it is for the second machine, do the job last.
4. Repeat Steps 2 and 3 for each remaining job until the schedule is complete.

We can illustrate this procedure by scheduling four jobs through two machines.

Step 1: List operation times.

Job	Operation Time on Machine 1	Operation Time on Machine 2
A	3	2
B	6	8
C	5	6
D	7	4

Steps 2 and 3: Select shortest operation time and assign. Job A is shortest on Machine 2 and is assigned first and performed last. (Job A is no longer available to be scheduled.)

Step 4: Repeat Steps 2 and 3 until completion of schedule. Select the shortest operation time among the remaining jobs. Job D is second shortest on Machine 2, thus it is performed second to last (remember Job A is last). Now, Jobs A and D are not available anymore for scheduling. Job C is the shortest on Machine 1 among the remaining jobs. Job C is performed first. Now, only Job B is left with the shortest operation time on Machine 1. Thus, according to

EXHIBIT 15.4

Optimal Schedule
of Jobs Using
Johnson's Rule

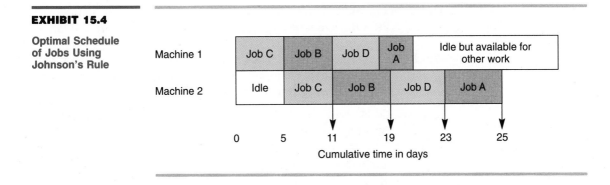

Step 3, it is performed first among the remaining, or second overall (Job C was already scheduled first).

In summary, the solution sequence is $C \rightarrow B \rightarrow D \rightarrow A$, and the flow time is 25 days, which is a minimum. Also minimized are total idle time and mean idle time. The final schedule appears in Exhibit 15.4.

These steps result in scheduling the jobs having the shortest time in the beginning and ending of the schedule. As a result, the amount of concurrent operating time for the two machines is maximized, thus minimizing the total operating time required to complete the jobs.

Johnson's method has been extended to yield an optimal solution for the $n/3$ case. When flow-shop scheduling problems larger than $n/3$ arise (and they generally do), analytical solution procedures leading to optimality are not available. The reason for this is that even though the jobs may arrive in static fashion at the first machine, the scheduling problem becomes dynamic, and series of waiting lines start to form in front of machines downstream.

Scheduling *n* Jobs on *m* Machines—Complex Job Shops

Complex job shops are characterized by multiple machine centers processing a variety of different jobs arriving at the machine centers in an intermittent fashion throughout the day. If there are n jobs to be processed on m machines and all jobs are processed on all machines, then there are $(n!)^m$ alternative schedules for this job set. Because of the large number of schedules that exist for even small job shops, Monte Carlo simulation (see the supplement to this chapter) is the only practical way to determine the relative merits of different priority rules in such situations. As in the n job on one machine case, the 10 priority rules (and more) have been compared relative to their performance on the evaluation criteria previously mentioned.

By way of example, John Kanet and Jack Hayya focused on due date-oriented priority rules to see which one was best. Their simulation of a complex job shop led to the finding that total job competition rules of

"DDATE, STR, and CR were outperformed by their 'operation' counterparts OPNDD, STR/OP, and OPCR" for all seven of the performance criteria used.[7]

Which priority rule should be used? We believe that the needs of most manufacturers are reasonably satisfied by a relatively simple priority scheme that embodies the following principles:

1. It should be dynamic, that is, computed frequently during the course of a job to reflect changing conditions.

2. It should be based in one way or another on slack (the difference between the work remaining to be done on a job and the time remaining to do it in). This embodies the due-date features suggested by Kanet and Hayya.

15.5 SHOP-FLOOR CONTROL

Scheduling job priorities is just one aspect of **shop-floor control** (now often called *production activity control*). The *APICS Dictionary* defines *shop-floor control system* as:

A system for utilizing data from the shop floor as well as data processing files to maintain and communicate status information on shop orders and work centers. The major functions of shop-floor control are:

1. Assigning priority of each shop order.
2. Maintaining work-in-process quantity information.
3. Conveying shop-order status information to the office.
4. Providing actual output data for capacity control purposes.
5. Providing quantity by location by shop order for WIP inventory and accounting purposes.
6. Providing measurement of efficiency, utilization, and productivity of manpower and machines.

Exhibit 15.5 illustrates some more of the details.

Tools of Shop-Floor Control

The basic tools of shop-floor control are

1. The *daily dispatch list,* which tells the supervisor what jobs are to be run, their priority, and how long each will take. (See Exhibit 15.6A.)

---

[7] John K. Kanet and Jack C. Hayya, "Priority Dispatching with Operation Due Dates in a Job Shop," *Journal of Operations Management* 2, no. 3 (May 1982), p. 170.

EXHIBIT 15.5

Shop-Floor Control

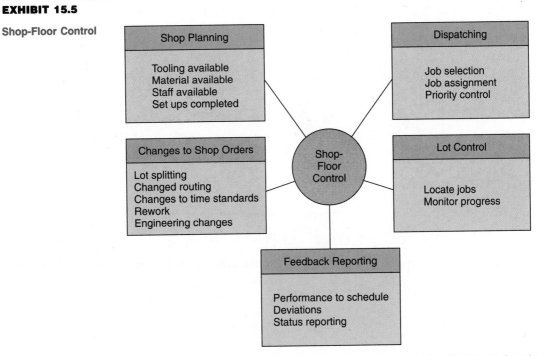

Source: "Shop Floor Control—Closing the Loop," *Inventory Management Newsletter* (Stone Mountain, Ga.: Center for Inventory Management), August 1982.

2. Various *status and exception reports,* including
   a. The anticipated delay report, made out by the shop planner once or twice a week and reviewed by the chief shop planner to see if there are any serious delays that could affect the master schedule. (See Exhibit 15.6B.)
   b. Scrap reports.
   c. Rework reports.
   d. Performance summary reports, giving the number and percentage of orders completed on schedule, lateness of unfilled orders, volume of output, and so on.
   e. Shortage list.
3. An *input/output control report,* which is used by the supervisor to monitor the workload-capacity relationship for each workstation. (See Exhibit 15.6C.)

EXHIBIT 15.6

Some Basic Tools of Shop-Floor Control

A. Dispatch list

Work center 1501—Day 205

Start date	Job #	Description	Run time
201	15131	Shaft	11.4
203	15143	Stud	20.6
205	15145	Spindle	4.3
205	15712	Spindle	8.6
207	15340	Metering rod	6.5
208	15312	Shaft	4.6

B. Anticipated delay report

Dept. 24 April 8

Part #	Sched. date	New date	Cause of delay	Action
17125	4/10	4/15	Fixture broke	Toolroom will return on 4/15
13044	4/11	5/1	Out for plating— plater on strike	New lot started
17653	4/11	4/14	New part-holes don't align	Engineering laying out new jig

C. Input/output control report (B)

Work center 0162

Week ending	505	512	519	526
Planned input	210	210	210	210
Actual input	110	150	140	130
Cumulative deviation	−100	−160	−230	−310
Planned output	210	210	210	210
Actual output	140	120	160	120
Cumulative deviation	−70	−160	−210	−300

(All figures in standard hours)

Input/Output Control

Input/output (I/O) control is a major feature of a manufacturing planning and control system. Its major precept is that the planned work input to a work center should never exceed the planned work output. When the input exceeds

EXHIBIT 15.7

Shop Capacity
Control Load Flow

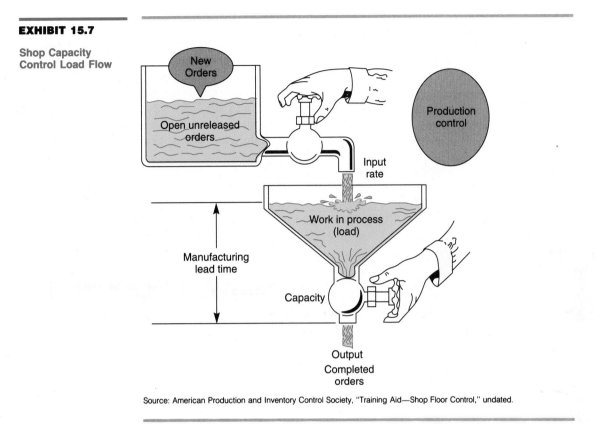

Source: American Production and Inventory Control Society, "Training Aid—Shop Floor Control," undated.

the output, backlogs build up at the work center, which in turn increases the lead-time estimates for jobs upstream. Moreover, when jobs pile up at the work center, congestion occurs, processing becomes inefficient, and the flow of work to downstream work centers becomes sporadic. (The water flow analogy to shop capacity control in Exhibit 15.7 illustrates the general phenomenon.) Exhibit 15.6C shows an I/O report for a downstream work center. Looking first at the lower or output half of the report, we see that output is far below plan. It would seem that a serious capacity problem exists for this work center. However, looking at the input part of the plan, it becomes apparent that the serious capacity problem exists at an upstream work center feeding this work center. The control process would entail finding the cause of upstream problems and adjusting capacity and inputs accordingly. The basic solution is simple: either increase capacity at the bottleneck station, or reduce the input to it. (Input reduction at bottleneck work centers, incidentally, is usually the first step recommended by production control consultants when job shops get into trouble.)

OPT Approach

A logical extension of I/O control is **optimized production technology (OPT).** One of OPT's main focuses is that the output capacity of a production system is controlled by the processes that have the least capacity.[8] A machine working continually with work to be processed still waiting would be called a *bottleneck*. Machines that have significant excess capacity are called *nonbottlenecks*. The objective is to control the flow and inventory levels in the system to always make sure the bottleneck does not stop working because its output is directly related to the output of the system. For the nonbottlenecks, the objective is to permit as little inventory as possible with the result that the flow of goods through the system is rapid, while the total inventory in the system is small. Chapter 18, Synchronous Manufacturing, discusses these concepts in more detail.

Data Integrity

Shop-floor control systems in most modern plants are now computerized, with job status information entered directly into a CRT terminal as the job enters and leaves a work center. Some plants have gone heavily into bar coding and optical scanners to speed up the reporting process and to cut down on data-entry errors.[9] As you might guess, the key problems in shop-floor control are data inaccuracy and lack of timeliness. When these occur, data fed back to the overall planning system are wrong and incorrect production decisions are made. Typical results are excess inventory or stockout problems or both, missed due dates, and inaccuracies in job costing.

Of course, maintaining data integrity requires that a sound data-gathering system be in place; but more important, it requires adherence to the system by everybody interacting with it. Most firms recognize this, but maintaining what is variously referred to as *shop discipline, data integrity,* or *data responsibility* is not always easy. And despite periodic drives to publicize the importance of careful shop-floor reporting by creating data-integrity task forces, inaccuracies can still creep into the system in many ways: A line worker drops a part under the workbench and pulls a replacement from stock without recording either transaction. An inventory clerk makes an error in a cycle count. A manufacturing engineer fails to note a change in the routing of a part. A department supervisor decides to work jobs in a different order than specified in the dispatch list.

---

[8] See the articles by R. E. Fox, "OPT—An Answer for America, Part II," *Inventories and Production Magazine* 2, no. 6 (November–December 1982); and "OPT vs. MRP: Thoughtware vs. Software," *Inventories and Production Magazine* 3, no. 6 (November–December 1983).

[9] Some companies also use "smartshelves"—inventory bins with weight sensors beneath each shelf. When an item is removed from inventory, a signal is sent to a central computer that notes the time, date, quantity, and location of the transaction.

Gantt Charts

Smaller job shops and individual departments of large ones employ the venerable Gantt chart to help plan and track jobs. As described in Chapter 12 it is a type of bar chart that plots tasks against time. Gantt charts are used for project planning, as well as to coordinate a number of scheduled activities. The example in Exhibit 15.8 indicates that Job A is behind schedule by about four hours, Job B is ahead of schedule, and Job C has been completed, after a delayed start for equipment maintenance. Note that whether the job is ahead of schedule or behind schedule is based on where it stands compared to where we are now. In Exhibit 15.8 we are at the end of Wednesday and Job A should have been completed. Job B has already had some of Thursday's work completed.

Let's consider another example; in Exhibit 15.9, a Gantt chart was efficiently used to develop a weekly schedule for the five employees of El Greco Interior Design and Decorating firm.[10] All the jobs scheduled to be completed in eight consecutive weeks are displayed with their beginning, ending, allowed, and actual progress time as explained. The current time appears to be the beginning of the third week. At this time, JoAnna is ahead of schedule in removing carpet and drapes. This is also the case with John who is ahead of schedule in scoping job with a client. Helen seems to be doing just fine, whereas Vicki and Harry are clearly behind schedule. The information presented in the Gantt chart can provide helpful guidance to the supervisor in charge of the schedule; some of her actions could be:

- Examine if JoAnna's walkthrough can take place half a week earlier, since she is ahead of schedule.
- Investigate ways of accelerating Vicki's and Harry's performance.

EXHIBIT 15.8   Gantt Chart

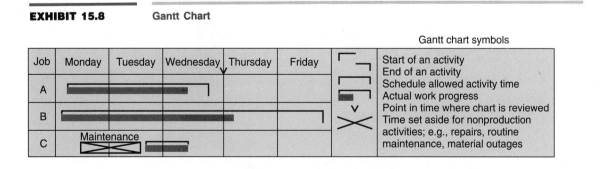

---

[10] Several example problems were provided by Andreas Soteriou, a Greek doctoral student from Cyprus at the University of Southern California.

EXHIBIT 15.9   Gantt Chart for El Greco Interior Design and Decorating Firm (Schedule for March 18–May 18)

Week

Employee	No.	1	2	3	4	5	6	7	8
JoAnna	3201	Remove drapes and carpet							
Helen	6212	Order materials					Decorate	Walk through	
						Sign contract			Order materials
John	0891	Decorate 1st floor		Scope job with client	Walk through				
Vicki	0102	Scope job with client						Decorate 2nd floor	Walk through
Harry	4013					Walk through	Decorate 3rd floor		

■ Minimize the employees' idle time. One way of achieving this is by having employees such as JoAnna who are ahead of time help the rest or provide additional work.

15.6 EXAMPLE OF A TOTAL SYSTEM: H.P.'S PRODUCTION MANAGEMENT/3000

The Hewlett-Packard *Production Management/3000* system (summarized in Exhibit 15.10) reflects and integrates many of the ideas we have been discussing thus far. Although the exhibit expresses them in somewhat different terminology, the system uses two scheduling concepts.

1. Infinite loading of work centers.   That is, the scheduling routine assumes that infinite production capacity is available at all times. Each work order is scheduled independently and requirements in excess of available capacity are identified by the capacity requirements planning (CRP) module. Modifications to the plan are made in light of capacity constraints indicated by the CRP process. (This is in contrast to *finite loading* approaches, where no work centers are initially loaded beyond their capacities.)

EXHIBIT 15.10

Hewlett-Packard Production Planning and Control System

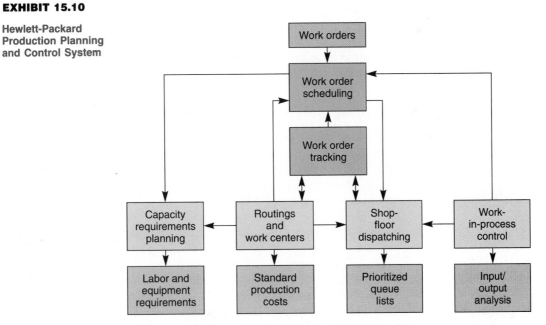

Source: HP Manufacturing System, *Production Management/3000*, 1981, p. 71.

2. Backward and forward scheduling.   Once a job's processing sequence and lead time have been established, the scheduling program permits determining ideal start dates in either of two ways: *backward scheduling* from a user-supplied order due date, or *forward scheduling* from a user-supplied order start date. The dates are established by calculating actual elapsed time required to perform any production sequence and by examining the shop calendar for each work center to determine the number of working hours scheduled for any given date and shift. In backward scheduling, the customer requests a certain delivery date and the schedule has to be worked backward from the delivery date to determine either the exact or the latest time at which the production steps have to take place. On the other hand, in forward scheduling every production step is scheduled to take place as soon as possible by considering the available capacity, as well as the necessary material required. The delivery date to be quoted to the customer is the earliest completion date with a small possible error margin. Backward scheduling is desirable because it delays investment in inventories; forward scheduling is desirable because it provides a greater likelihood of meeting the due date. (In general, companies use both of these to balance work flow and capacity.)

15.7 PERSONNEL SCHEDULING IN SERVICES

The scheduling problem in most service organizations revolves around setting staffing levels and scheduling the workweek. This is in contrast to manufacturing, where the focus of operations scheduling is on materials. In this section we present brief examples of how personnel scheduling is done in banking and nursing and provide a simple technique for scheduling days off, which can be used in a variety of settings.

Setting Staffing Levels in Banks

This example illustrates how central clearinghouses and back-office operations of large bank branches establish staffing plans. Basically, management wants to derive a staffing plan that (1) requires the least number of workers to accomplish the daily workload and (2) minimizes the variance between actual output and planned output.

In structuring the problem, bank management defines inputs (checks, statements, investment documents, and so forth), as *products,* which are routed through different processes or *functions* (receiving, sorting, encoding, and so forth).

To solve the problem, a monthly demand forecast is made by product for each function. This is converted to labor hours required per function, which in turn is converted to workers required per function. These figures are then tabled, summed, and adjusted by an absence and vacation factor to give

EXHIBIT 15.11   Daily Staff Hours Required

| | | FUNCTION | | | | | | | | |
| | | RECEIVE | | PREPROCESS | | MICROFILM | | VERIFY | | TOTALS |
Product	Daily Volume	P/H	H_{std}	P/H	H_{std}	P/H	H_{std}	P/H	H_{std}	H_{std}
Checks	2,000	1,000	2.0	600	3.3	240	8.3	640	3.1	16.7
Statements	1,000	—	—	600	1.7	250	4.0	150	6.7	12.4
Notes	200	30	6.7	15	13.3		—			20.0
Investments	400	100	4.0	50	8.0	200	2.0	150	2.7	16.7
Collections	500	300	1.7			300	1.7	60	8.4	11.8
			—		—		—		—	—
Total hours required			14.4		26.3		16.0		20.9	77.6
Times 1.25 (absences and vacations)			18.0		32.9		20.0		26.1	
			—		—		—		—	
Divided by 8 hours equals staff required			2.3		4.1		2.5		3.3	

Note: P/H indicates production rate per hour; H_{std} indicates required hours.

EXHIBIT 15.12

Staffing Plan

Function	Staff Required	Staff Available	Variance ($\pm$)	Management Actions
Receive	2.3	2.0	−0.3	Use overtime.
Preprocess	4.1	4.0	−0.1	Use overtime.
Microfilm	2.5	3.0	+0.5	Use excess to verify.
Verify	3.3	3.0	−0.3	Get 0.3 from microfilm.

planned hours. Then they are divided by the number of hours in the workday to yield the number of workers required. This yields the daily staff hours required. (See Exhibit 15.11.) This becomes the basis for a departmental staffing plan that lists the workers required, workers available, variance, and managerial action in light of variance. (See Exhibit 15.12.)

In addition to their use in day-to-day planning, the hours required and the staffing plan provide information for scheduling individual workers, controlling operations, comparing capacity utilization with other branches, and starting up new branches.

Nurse Staffing and Scheduling

W. Abernathy, N. Baloff, and J. Hershey state, "The key element of effective nurse staffing is a well-conceived procedure for achieving an overall balance

EXHIBIT 15.13

General Problems in Nurse Scheduling

Problem	Possible Solution
Accuracy of patient load forecast	Forecast frequently and rebudget monthly. Closely monitor seasonal demands, communicable diseases, and current occupancy.
Forecasting nurse availability	Develop work standards for nurses for each level of possible demand (requires systematic data collection and analysis).
Complexity and time to rebudget	Use available computer programs.
Flexibility in scheduling	Use variable staffing: Set regular staff levels slightly above minimum and absorb variation with broadskilled float nurses, part-time nurses, and overtime.

between the size of the nursing staff and the expected patient demand."[11] Their procedure, termed *aggregate budgeting,* is predicated on a variety of interrelated activities and has a short-term schedule as a primary output. A number of severe practical problems confront hospitals in deriving an effective yet low-cost aggregate budget. These difficulties, along with possible remedies, are listed in Exhibit 15.13.

Though most hospitals still use cut-and-try methods in schedule development, management scientists have applied optimizing techniques to the problem with some success. For example, a linear programming model has been developed.[12] It assumes a known, short-run (three to four days) demand for nursing care and develops a staffing pattern that:

1. Specifies the number of nurses of each skill class to be assigned among the wards and nursing shifts.

2. Satisfies total nursing personnel capacity constraints.

3. Allows for limited substitution of tasks among nurses.

4. Minimizes the cost of nursing care shortage for the scheduling period.

Scheduling Consecutive Days Off

A practical problem encountered in many organizations is setting schedules so that employees can have two consecutive days off. The importance of the problem stems from the fact that the Fair Labor Standards Act requires overtime for any work hours (by hourly workers) in excess of 40 hours per

---

[11] W. Abernathy, N. Baloff, and J. Hershey, "The Nurse Staffing Problem: Issues and Prospects," *Sloan Management Review* 13, no. 1 (Fall 1971), pp. 87–109.

[12] D. Warner and J. Prawda, "A Mathematical Programming Model for Scheduling Nursing Personnel in a Hospital," *Management Science* 19, no. 4 (December 1972), pp. 411–22.

week. Obviously, if two consecutive days off can't be scheduled each week for each employee, the likelihood of unnecessary overtime is quite high. In addition, most people probably prefer two consecutive days off per week. The following heuristic procedure was modified from that developed by James Browne and Rajen Tibrewala to deal with this problem.[13]

Objective.   Find the schedule that minimizes the number of five-day workers with two consecutive days off, subject to the demands of the daily staffing schedule.

Procedure.   Starting with the total number of workers required for each day of the week, create a schedule by adding one worker at a time. This is a two-step procedure:

Step 1.   Circle the lowest pair of consecutive days off. The lowest pair is the one where the highest number in the pair is equal to or lower than the highest number in any other pair. This ensures that the days with the highest requirements are covered by staff. (Monday and Sunday may be chosen even though they are at opposite ends of the array of days.) In case of ties choose the days-off pair with the lowest requirement on an adjacent day. This day may be before or after the pair. If a tie still remains, choose the first of the available tied pairs. (Do not bother using further tie-breaking rules, such as second lowest adjacent days.)

Step 2.   Subtract 1 from each of the remaining five days (i.e., the days not circled). This indicates that one less worker is required on these days, since the first worker has just been assigned to them.

The two steps are repeated for the second worker, the third worker, and so forth, until no more workers are required to satisfy the schedule.

Example

	M	Tu	W	Th	F	S	Su
Requirement	4	3	4	2	3	1	2
Worker 1	4	3	4	2	3	(1	2)
Worker 2	3	2	3	1	(2	1)	2
Worker 3	2	1	2	0	2	(1	1)
Worker 4	1	(0	1)	0	1	1	1
Worker 5	0	0	1	0	0	0	0

Solution

This solution consists of five workers covering 19 worker days, although slightly different assignments may be equally satisfactory.

The schedule is Worker 1 assigned S–Su off, Worker 2 F–S off, Worker 3 S–Su off, Worker 4 Tu–W off, and Worker 5 works only on Wednesday, since there are no further requirements for the other days.

---

[13] James J. Browne and Rajen K. Tibrewala, "Manpower Scheduling," *Industrial Engineering* 7, no. 8 (August 1975), pp. 22–23.

15.8 CONCLUSION

The objective of this chapter has been to provide some insight into the nature of operations planning and control, with emphasis on job-shop environments. Job-shop scheduling, like most other aspects of OM, has become computer dependent and, equally important, is now seen as being inseparable from the total manufacturing planning and control systems of which it is a part.

15.9 REVIEW AND DISCUSSION QUESTIONS

1. Distinguish between a job shop and a flow shop.
2. How would you translate the Epigraph at the start of the chapter into job shop terms?
3. What practical considerations are deterrents to using the SOT rule?
4. What priority rule do you use in scheduling your study time for midterm examinations? If you have five exams to study for, how many alternative schedules exist?
5. Data integrity is a big deal in industry. Why?
6. In the United States, we make certain assumptions about the customer-service priority rules used in banks, restaurants, and retail stores. If you have the opportunity, ask a foreigner what rules are used in his or her country. To what factors might you attribute the differences, if any?
7. What job characteristics would lead you to schedule jobs according to "longest processing time first"?
8. In what way is the scheduling problem in the home office of a bank different from that of a branch?

15.10 PROBLEMS

*1. Mr. Regan has just come across the runout method of scheduling and wonders whether he could apply this technique to allocating expense money among his three children. He would like to occasionally divide a lump sum among his children so that when added to what they currently have, it will cover each of their expenses for the same period of time. Regan's son is a freshman in high school and uses $1.95 per day ($0.50 each way bus fare plus $0.95 for lunch). His daughter is in junior high and uses $1.65 per day (bus fare $0.50 each way plus $0.65 for lunch). His youngest son is in elementary school and uses $0.55 per day (there is a free school bus). Following is the current expense money held by each child along with the scheduled expenses just mentioned.

	Expense Money in Hand	Daily Expenses
Eldest son	$3.20	$1.95
Daughter	2.40	1.65
Youngest son	1.80	0.55

---

* Solutions to Problems 1 and 2 are given in Appendix H.

Regan would like to divide $20 among his children so that each would have the same number of days of expense money. Use the runout method to find the appropriate allocation.

*2. Joe's Auto Seat Cover and Paint Shop is bidding on a contract to do all the custom work for Smiling Ed's used car dealership. One of the main requirements in obtaining this contract is rapid delivery time, since Ed—for reasons we shall not go into here—wants the cars facelifted and back on his lot in a hurry. Ed has said that if Joe can refit and repaint five cars that Ed has just received (from an unnamed source) in 24 hours or less, the contract will be his. Following is the time (in hours) required in the refitting shop and the paint shop for each of the five cars. Assuming that cars go through the refitting operations before they are repainted, can Joe meet the time requirements and get the contract?

Car	Refitting Time (hours)	Repairing Time (hours)
A	6	3
B	0	4
C	5	2
D	8	6
E	2	1

3. Joe has three cars that must be overhauled by his ace mechanic, Jim. Given the following data about the cars, use Conway's "Rule 4" (least slack per remaining operation) to determine Jim's scheduling priority for each.

Car	Customer Pick-Up Time (hours hence)	Remaining Overhaul Time (hours)	Remaining Operations
A	10	4	Painting
B	17	5	Wheel alignment, painting
C	15	1	Chrome plating, painting, seat repair

4. There are seven jobs that must be processed in two operations: A and B. All seven jobs must go through A and B in that sequence—A first, then B. Determine the optimal order in which the jobs should be sequenced through the process using these times:

Job	Process A Time	Process B Time
1	9	6
2	8	5
3	7	7
4	6	3
5	1	2
6	2	6
7	4	7

5. This problem requires use of simulation as discussed in the supplement to this chapter. Joe has the opportunity to do a big repair job for a local motorcycle club. (Their cycles were accidentally run over by a garbage truck.) The compensation for the job is good, but it is very important that the total repair time for the five cycles to be fixed be less than 40 hours. (The leader of the club has stated that he

would be very distressed if the cycles were not available for a planned rally.) Joe knows from experience that repairs of this type often entail several trips between processes for a given cycle, so estimates of time are difficult to provide. Still, Joe has the following historical data about the probability that a job will start in each process, processing time in each process, and transitional probabilities between each pair of processes:

Process	Probability of Job Starting in Process	PROCESSING TIME PROBABILITY (HOURS)			PROBABILITY OF GOING FROM PROCESS TO OTHER PROCESSES OR COMPLETION (OUT)			
		1	2	3	Frame	Engine Work	Painting	Out
Frame repair	0.5	0.2	0.4	0.4	—	0.4	0.4	0.2
Engine work	0.3	0.6	0.1	0.3	0.3	—	0.4	0.3
Painting	0.2	0.3	0.3	0.4	0.1	0.1	—	0.8

Given this information, use simulation to determine the repair times for each cycle and display your results on a Gantt chart showing an FCFS schedule. (Assume that only one cycle can be worked on at a time in each process.) Based on your simulation, what do you recommend Joe do next?

6. The following list of jobs in a critical department includes estimates of their required times:

Job	Required Time (days)	Days to Delivery Promise	Slack
A	8	12	4
B	3	9	6
C	7	8	1
D	1	11	10
E	10	−10	—
F	6	10	4
G	5	−8	—
H	4	6	2

a. Use the shortest operation time rule to schedule these jobs:

What is the schedule?

What is the mean flow time?

b. The boss doesn't like the schedule in (a). Jobs E and G must be done first, for obvious reasons (they are already late). Reschedule and do the best you can while scheduling Jobs E and G first and second, respectively.

What is the new schedule?

What is the new mean flow time?

7. John Adams is a shop supervisor for Foley and Burnham, Inc., in the component insertion area. F&B runs a fairly loose shop schedule, leaving it pretty much up to the lower managers to determine the within-week schedule for production. Because Adams produces standard items for stock and setup times are minimal, he normally tries to use up his production resources in a way that provides equal time coverages for all products.

Assume that Adams has four machine centers working 8 hours per day, five days per week, for a total of 160 production hours available per week. Adams needs to plan how to allocate his 160 total available hours over the five printed circuit board configurations for next week. Your task is to help him by using the runout method.

Item	Production Time per Unit (minutes)	Inventory on Hand (units)	Forecasted Usage for Next Week (units)
PC1	4	900	600
PC2	1	1,100	700
PC3	3	800	1,200
PC4	5	500	300
PC5	8	125	75

8. A manufacturing facility has five jobs to be scheduled into production. The following table gives the processing times plus the necessary wait times and other necessary delays for each of the jobs.

   Assume that today is April 3 and the jobs are due on the dates shown:

Job	Days of Actual Processing Time Required	Days of Necessary Delay Time	Total Time Required	Date Job Due
1	2	12	14	April 30
2	5	8	13	April 21
3	9	15	24	April 28
4	7	9	16	April 29
5	4	22	28	April 27

   Determine *two* schedules, stating the order in which the jobs are to be done. Use the critical ratio priority rule for one. You may use any other rule for the second schedule as long as you state what it is.

9. An accounting firm, Debits 'R Us, would like to keep its auditing staff to a maximum of four people yet satisfy the staffing needs and the policy of two days off per week. Given the following requirements, is this possible? What should the schedule be?

   Requirements (Monday through Sunday): 4, 3, 3, 2, 2, 4, 4.

10. Jobs A, B, C, D, and E must go through Processes I and II in that sequence (i.e., Process I first, then Process II).

    Use Johnson's rule to determine the optimal sequence to schedule the jobs to minimize the total required time.

Job	Required Processing Time on A	Required Processing Time on B
A	4	5
B	16	14
C	8	7
D	12	11
E	3	9

11. For a variety of reasons, our friend Joe now finds himself in charge of what might be called a *captive machine shop* in a government-operated establishment. The machine shop fabricates and paints metal products, including license plates, road

signs, window screens, and door frames. Joe's major responsibility is to balance the utilization of the equipment across all four products in such a way that demand for each product is satisfied. Given the following data, how might he schedule the four products to achieve this objective for the next week? How would his schedule look?

Item	Inventory	Production Time per Unit	Forecast Weekly Usage
Window screens	200	0.1 hour	100
Door frames	100	0.06	50
Road signs	70	0.3	60
License plates	150	0.7	125

Available machine hours = 90/week

12. A textile manufacturer is planning her next week's production and wants to use the runout method of scheduling. Part of her logic for using the runout method in this case is that she is running the same design on towels, washcloths, sheets, and pillowcases. She would therefore like to carry the same period amounts in the event the design is changed.

Following are the existing quantities on hand, the production times of each, and the forecast demands. There are 120 hours of capacity available on the mill in three shifts. (The same machine is used to make all the items, so the problem is to determine which will be made, how many, and how much machine time to allocate to each.)

Item	Units on Hand	Production Time for Each in Hours	Forecast Demand per Week
Washcloths	500	0.1	300
Towels	200	0.15	400
Sheets	150	0.20	200
Pillowcases	300	0.15	200

13. Joe has now been released from his government job. Based on his excellent performance, he was able to land a job as production scheduler in a brand-new custom refinishing auto service shop located near the border. Techniques have improved in the several years he was out of circulation, so processing times are considerably faster. This system is capable of handling 10 cars per day. The sequence now is customizing first, followed by repainting.

Car	Customizing Time (hours)	Painting (hours)
1	3.0	1.2
2	2.0	0.9
3	2.5	1.3
4	0.7	0.5
5	1.6	1.7
6	2.1	0.8
7	3.2	1.4
8	0.6	1.8
9	1.1	1.5
10	1.8	0.7

In what sequence should Joe schedule the cars?

15.11 CASE: McCALL DIESEL MOTOR WORKS (NEED FOR A COMPLETE SYSTEM OF PRODUCTION CONTROL)

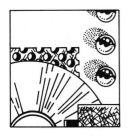

McCall Diesel Motor Works has been a pioneer in the manufacture of a particular internal combustion engine. The plant is located on tidewater in the state of New Jersey, because the company originally built engines for the marine field, chiefly fishing boats and pleasure craft. Subsequently, its activities were extended to the stationary type of engines, used primarily for the production of power in small communities, in manufacturing plants, or on farms.

During the earlier years of the company's operation, its engines were largely special-order jobs. Even at the present time about 60 percent of the output is made to order. There has been in recent years, however, a trend toward standardization of component parts and reduction in the variety of engines produced. The Engineering Department has followed the principle of simplification and standardization in the case of minor parts, such as studs, bolts, and springs, giving a degree of interchangeability of these components among the various sizes and types of engines. Sizes of marine engines have been standardized to some extent, although customer requirements still necessitate some designs. In the small engines for agricultural use there has been a genuine effort to concentrate sales on a standard line of engines of three sizes—20 HP, 40 HP, and 60 HP.

The company has always been advanced in its engineering development and design. The production phase, on the other hand, has not been progressive. The heritage of job-shop operation persists, and despite the definite trend toward standardization, manufacture continues largely on a made-to-order basis. The increasing popularity of diesel engines has brought many new producing companies into the field, with a consequent tightening of the competitive situation.

High manufacturing costs and poor service have been reflected in the loss of orders. Customer complaints, together with pressure from the Sales Department, prompted management to call in a consulting engineer to make a survey of the Manufacturing Department and recommend a plan of action.

The report of the engineer showed the following:

1. Manufacturing methods, while still largely of the job-shop character, are in the main good, and no wholesale change should be made. As production is still 60 percent special, a complete shift to line manufacture or departmentalization by product is not feasible.

2. Machinery and equipment are for the most part general purpose, in line with manufacturing requirements. Some machine tools are approaching obsolescence, and for certain operations high-production, single-purpose machines would be advisable. Extensive replacement of machine tools is not a pressing need, but an increased use of jigs and fixtures should be undertaken immediately. There are many bottlenecks existing in the plant, but contrary to your belief, as well as that of your foreman and other shop executives, there is no serious lack of productive equipment. The trouble lies in the improper utilization of the machine time available.

3. Production control is the major element of operating weakness, and improvement is imperative. The lack of proper control over production shows up in many ways:

a. High in-process inventory, as indicated by piles of partially completed parts over the entire manufacturing floor areas.

b. Absence of any record concerning the whereabouts of orders in the process from their initiation to delivery at assembly.

c. Inordinate number of rush orders, particularly in assembly but also in parts manufacture.

d. Too many parts chasers who force orders through the shops by pressure methods.

e. Piecemeal manufacture—a lot of 20 parts usually is broken up into four or five lots before it is finished. Not infrequently the last sublot remains on the shop floor for months and, in a number of instances, is lost as far as records are concerned. Subsequent orders for the same part are issued and new lots pass through to completion while the remains of the old lot lie in partially fabricated condition.

f. Excessive setup costs resulting from the piecemeal methods mentioned in *(e),* as well as failure to use proper lot sizes, even when lots are not broken up during manufacture.

g. Failure of all necessary component parts to reach assembly at approximately the same time. The floor of the assembly department is cluttered with piles of parts awaiting receipt of one or more components before engines can be assembled.

h. Lack of definite sequence of manufacturing operations for a given part. Responsibility for the exact way by which a part is to be made rests entirely on the various department foremen; these men are able machinists, but, burdened with detail, their memories cannot be relied on to ensure that parts will always be manufactured in the best, or even the same, sequence of operations. Moreover, they have the responsibility for determining the department to which a lot of parts should be sent when it has been completed in their department.

i. In the case of certain small standard parts, shop orders have been issued as many as six or eight times in a single month.

j. Information is lacking from which to estimate, with any degree of close approximation, the overall manufacturing time for an engine. The result is failure to meet delivery promises or high production cost due to rush or overtime work.

k. Parts in process or in stores, and destined for imminent assembly, are frequently taken by the Service Department to supply an emergency repair order. The question here is not the academic determination of priority between the customer whose boat may be lying idle because of a broken part and the customer who has not yet received an engine; the question is why there should be any habitual difficulty in rendering adequate repair service and at the same time meeting delivery promises.

l. Virtually all basic manufacturing data resides in the heads of the superintendent, departmental foreman, assistant foremen, and setup men.

m. Delivery dates are set by the Sales Department and generally are dates that customers arbitrarily stipulate.

n. The general superintendent shows little enthusiasm for the idea of a system of production control; in fact he is opposed to such an installation. He is of the opinion that reasonably satisfactory results are now being obtained by placing responsibility on the foremen and maintaining contact between them and the parts chasers, who in turn are held responsible for meeting delivery promises. He believes that no system can be substituted for the foremen's knowledge of the ability of the workers. He feels that operation of a production-control system requires time studies of all jobs. Time study, he points out, is difficult because of the many operations involved, the high degree of special work, the probable resistance of the workers, and the cost. He further protests that emergencies and rush orders would upset any rigid scheduling of work through the plant. Finally, he is convinced that any system of production control involves an excessive amount of clerical detail to which the foremen, who are practical shop men, object.

The state of affairs the consultant found had, he realized, two main causes:

1. The strong influence of the original job-shop character of manufacture and the very slow evolution to large-scale operation.
2. The fact that the top management of the company was essentially sales minded.

His recommendations, therefore, had to be a simple, straightforward program that would provide adequate control over production and could be instituted gradually and logically.

QUESTIONS

1. Outline the essential features of a production-control system for this company, giving sufficient detail to make clear how the system will function.
2. Indicate which part of your procedure should be centralized and which part decentralized. What functions should be handled by a central production-control office and what functions should be carried out in the various production and assembly departments?
3. What data must be compiled before your system can become fully effective?
4. Enumerate the benefits the company will derive when your production-control system is in operation.
5. Set forth in proper order the steps that should be taken and the departments that should be involved in the determination of delivery promises to customers.
6. What arguments would you advance in answer to the general superintendent's objections, as presented in paragraph *n* of the consultant's report?
7. Generally speaking, what is the foremen's place in the scheme of things when a fully developed production-control system is in operation and when a production control department has been established?

15.12 SELECTED BIBLIOGRAPHY

Baker, K. R. "The Effects of Input Control in a Simple Scheduling Model." *Journal of Operations Management* 4, no. 2 (February 1984), pp. 99–112.

Berry, W. L.; R. Penlesky; and T. E. Vollmann. "Critical Ratio Scheduling: Dynamic Due-Date Procedures under Demand Uncertainty." *IIE Transactions* 16, no. 1 (March 1984), pp. 81–89.

Conway, R. W.; William L. Maxwell; and Louis W. Miller. *Theory of Scheduling.* Reading, Mass.: Addison-Wesley Publishing, 1967.

Fox, R. E. "OPT—An Answer for America, Part II." *Inventories and Production Magazine* 2, no. 6 (November–December 1982).

————. "OPT vs. MRP: Thoughtware vs. Software." *Inventories and Production Magazine* 3, no. 6 (November–December 1983).

Gershkoff, I. "Optimizing Flight Crew Schedules." *Interfaces* 19, no. 4 (July–August 1989), pp. 29–43.

Goldratt, E. M., and J. Cox. *The Goal: A Process of Ongoing Improvement*. Croton-on-Hudson, N.Y.: North River Press, 1986.

Johnson, S. M. "Optimal Two Stage and Three Stage Production Schedules with Setup Times Included." *Naval Logistics Quarterly* 1, no. 1 (March 1954), pp. 61–68.

Moody, P. E. *Strategic Manufacturing: Dynamic New Directions for the 1990s*. Homewood, Ill.: Richard D. Irwin, 1990.

Richter, H. "Thirty Years of Airline Operations Research." *Interfaces* 19, no. 4, (July–August 1989), pp. 3–9.

Sandman, W. E., with J. P. Hayes. *How to Win Productivity in Manufacturing*. Dresher, Pa.: Yellow Book of Pennsylvania, 1980.

Wild, Ray. *International Handbook of Production and Operations Management*. London, England: Cassell Educational Ltd., 1989.

Supplement

Simulation

EPIGRAPH

The appearance of, without the reality . . .

KEY TERMS

Monte Carlo Simulation
Probability Distribution
Random Number Table
Variables and Parameters
Decision Rules
Time Incrementing
Run Length or Run Time
Computer Models

S imulation is being more widely used than ever before because of the tremendous growth in computer power. No longer is it necessary to run simulations on mainframes: for the majority of simulations, desktop computers have adequate power. The introduction of computer chips such as the Intel 80386, 80486, and especially the 80486 with 32-bit input/output (EISA) has allowed simulation programs to be run independently of mainframes.

In operations management, simulation is used to determine production schedules and material needs; to analyze waiting line systems, inventory levels, and maintenance procedures; to do capacity planning, resource requirements planning, and process planning; and the list goes on. Often, when a mathematical technique fails, we turn to simulation to save us. A survey of non-academic members of the Institute of Management Science showed that 89 percent of their firms use simulation.[1] (If the survey was repeated today, the percentage would likely be higher.) Exhibit S15.1 shows the functional areas where it is applied. Note that production heads the list, with 59 percent. Another interesting finding of the study is that 54 percent of the respondents said that simulation models are created within the functional areas themselves.

Even though simulation is one of the easiest techniques to understand, it is also one of the most misunderstood and misused. Some claim it is the ultimate technique to understand problems and systems; others say it is too expensive and too time consuming to be useful for most applications. In this supplement we define simulation, present examples of the simulation methodology, discuss simulation languages, and comment on various aspects of the techniques.

EXHIBIT S15.1

Functional Areas for Simulation in Companies

Functional Area	Percent
Production	59%
Corporate planning	53
Engineering	46
Finance	41
Research and development	37
Marketing	24
Data processing	16
Personnel	10

---

[1] David P. Christy and Hugh J. Watson, "The Application of Simulation: A Survey of Industry Practice," *Interfaces* 13, no. 5 (October 1983), pp. 47–52.

S15.1 DEFINITION OF SIMULATION

The dictionary definitions are

> *Simulation:* the imitative representation of the functioning of one system or process by means of the functioning of another (a computer simulation of an industrial process); examination of a problem often not subject to direct experimentation by means of a simulation device.
>
> *Simulator:* one that simulates; esp. a device that enables the operator to reproduce or represent under test conditions phenomena likely to occur in actual performance.[2]

These definitions are somewhat incomplete. Perhaps the best way to define and understand simulation is to consider it as two parts: First, there must be a *model* of whatever is to be simulated. There are several classifications of models but the usual types are physical (e.g., airplane model), analog (e.g., a scale where the deflection of a spring or beam represents weight), schematic (e.g., electrical circuit diagrams, organization charts), and symbolic (e.g., computer code or mathematical models representing a bank teller or a machine). In computer simulation we are primarily interested in symbolic models that we can use to represent a real system on a computer. We describe symbolic models later and show several examples, but the main point we wish to make here is that a model is created to represent *something,* and that the model is *static*—that is, it shows only a point in time and does not move.

The second part of simulation is to *pass the model through time.* Simulation gives the model life. In pilot training, for example, a trainee sits in a replica of a cockpit complete with instruments and controls (a *model* of a real airplane). This is a *physical* model of the system. The traineee then sees a variety of situations as the model is given life and is passed through time. Instruments change values and the trainee is expected to respond. Those responses are fed into a computer, which then creates new values to which the trainee must again respond. In a flight training simulator, these values are usually fed into an *analog* system as well, where the new values create electrical signals to cause physical movement. In this way, the trainee experiences the approach of a crosswind, a stall, or a tailspin. Thus the simulation is a series of actions of the model with reactions of the environment on the model.

Simulation is said to run some number of iterations or some amount of time. A model of a teller in the bank can be simulated to wait on 100 customers (i.e., 100 iterations). The trainee in the cockpit (model) can experience the same sensations as those in real flight; i.e., a half hour of simulator time equals a half hour of an actual flight. Or time can be compressed so that the trainee, during that half hour, can be fed all the situations that could be expected

---

[2] *Webster's New Collegiate Dictionary,* 9th ed. (Springfield, Mass.: Merriam-Webster, 1989).

during a six-hour transoceanic flight. This is much like the automobile manufacturer that tests the opening and closing of a car door. Whereas a car owner may open and close a car door an average of six times a day, the manufacturer can test years of usage in a short period of time by opening and closing the car door every five seconds. The basic difference is that the flight simulator is a computer-based program and the automobile manufacturer actually uses a mechanical arm to open and close the car door.

While the term *simulation* can have various meanings depending on its application, in business it generally refers to using a digital computer to perform experiments on a model of a real system. These experiments may be undertaken before the real system is operational, to aid in its design, to see how the system might react to changes in its operating rules, or to evaluate the system's response to changes in its structure. Simulation is particularly appropriate to situations in which the size or complexity of the problem makes the use of optimizing techniques difficult or impossible. Thus, job shops, which are characterized by complex queuing problems, have been studied extensively via simulation, as have certain types of inventory, layout, and maintenance problems (to name but a few). Simulation can also be used in conjunction with traditional statistical and management science techniques.

In addition, simulation is useful in training managers and workers in how the real system operates, in demonstrating the effects of changes in system variables, in real-time control, and in developing new theories about mathematical or organizational relationships. See Exhibit S15.2 for more examples.

It is commonly suggested by simulation instructors that the best way to learn about simulation is to simulate. Therefore, we turn to a simple simulation problem and develop the topic as we go along.

A Simulation Example: Al's Fish Market

Al, the owner of a small fish market, wishes to evaluate his daily ordering policy for codfish. His current rule is *order the amount demanded the previous day,* but he thinks it is time to consider another rule. Al purchases codfish at $0.20 a pound and sells it for $0.60 a pound. The fish are ordered at the end of each day and are received the following morning. Any fish not sold during the day are thrown away.

From past experience, Al has determined that his demand for codfish has ranged between 30 and 80 pounds per day. He has also kept a record of the relatively frequency of demand amounts:

Average Demand per Day	Relative Frequency
35 pounds	$1/10$
45	$3/10$
55	$2/10$
65	$3/10$
75	$1/10$

EXHIBIT S15.2

**Applications of
Simulation Methods**

Aircraft maintenance scheduling
Airport design
Air traffic control queuing
Ambulance location and dispatching
Assembly line scheduling
Bank teller scheduling
Bus (city) scheduling
Circuit design
Clerical processing system design
Communication system design
  Computer time sharing
  Telephone traffic routing
  Message system
  Mobile communications
Computer memory-fabrication test-facility
  design
Consumer behavior prediction
  Brand selection
  Promotion decisions
  Advertising allocation
  Court system resource allocation
Distribution system design
  Warehouse location
  Mail (post office)
  Soft drink bottling
  Bank courier
  Intrahospital material flow
Enterprise models
  Steel production
  Hospital
  Shipping line
  Railroad operations
  School district
Equipment scheduling
  Aircraft
Facility layout
  Pharmaceutical center
Financial forecasting
  Insurance
  Schools
  Computer leasing
Grain terminal operation
Harbor design
Industry models
  Textiles
  Petroleum (financial aspects)

Information system design
Insurance staffing decisions
Intergroup communication (sociological
  studies)
Inventory reorder rule design
  Aerospace
  Manufacturing
  Military logistics
  Hospitals
Job shop scheduling
  Aircraft parts
  Metals forming
  Work-in-process control
  Shipyard
Library operations design
Maintenance scheduling
  Airlines
  Glass furnaces
  Steel furnaces
  Computer field service
National manpower adjustment system
Natural resource (mine) scheduling
  Iron ore
  Strip mining
Numerically controlled production facility
  design
Parking facility design
Personnel scheduling
  Inspection department
  Spacecraft trips
Petrochemical process design
  Solvent recovery
Police response system design
Political voting prediction
Rail freight car dispatching
Railroad traffic scheduling
Steel mill scheduling
Taxi dispatching
Traffic light timing
Truck dispatching and loading
University financial and operational
  forecasting
Urban traffic system design
Water resources development

After some deliberation, Al settles on the following ordering rule, which he would like to compare with his current rule: *Each day order the average amount of fish that was demanded in the past* (that is, the expected value based on past daily demands), which in this case is

$$(35 \times \tfrac{1}{10}) + (45 \times \tfrac{3}{10}) + (55 \times \tfrac{2}{10}) + (65 \times \tfrac{3}{10}) + (75 \times \tfrac{1}{10}) = 55 \text{ pounds}$$

Analysis

We designate Al's current ordering rule as Rule 1 and the alternative as Rule 2. These rules can be stated mathematically, as follows:

Rule 1: $Q_n = D_{n-1}$

Rule 2: $Q_n = 55$

where

Q_n = Amount ordered on day n

D_{n-1} = Amount demanded the previous day

These ordering rules can be compared in terms of Al's daily profits, which can be stated as follows:

$$P_n = (S_n \times p) - (Q_n \times c)$$

where

P_n = Profit on day n

S_n = Amount sold on day n

p = Selling price per pound

Q_n = Amount ordered on day n (as defined above)

c = Cost per pound

To prepare the problem for simulation, we must develop some method of generating demand each day so we can compare the two decision rules. One way to do this is to treat demand generation as a game of roulette, with the slots in the roulette wheel associated with specific levels of demand. The term **Monte Carlo simulation,** taken from the name of the famous European gambling casino, is applied to simulation problems in which a chance process generates occurrences in the system. For example, if the wheel has 100 slots, we might apportion them so that 10 represent a demand for 35 pounds, 30 represent a demand for 45 pounds, 20 represent a demand for 55 pounds, and so forth. Proceeding this way and using the relative frequencies listed previously, each turn of the wheel could simulate one day of demand for Al's fish.

While a roulette wheel has a certain appeal, a more efficient way of generating demand is to use a **probability distribution** and a **random number table.** This entails converting the relative frequency values to probabilities. Then, specific numbers are attached to each probability value to reflect the proportion of numbers from 00 to 99 that corresponds to each probability entry.[3] For example, 00 to 09 represent 10 percent of the numbers from 00 to 99, 10 to 39 represent 30 percent of the numbers, 40 to 59 represent 20 percent

---

[3] A cumulative probability distribution is sometimes developed to help assure that each random number is associated with only one level of demand. It is our experience, however, that this step, as well as graphing such a distribution, is not necessary in understanding or performing a simulation.

of the numbers, and so on. The probabilities and their associated random numbers (arranged in intervals) are given in Exhibit S15.3.

With this information and a random number table (Exhibit S15.4), we are ready to carry out a hand simulation to determine the relative desirability of Rules 1 and 2. If the initial demand for Day zero is arbitrarily set at the average demand level of 55 pounds and a 20-day period is selected, each rule would be tested as follows:

1. Draw a random number from Exhibit S15.4. (The starting point on the table is immaterial, but a consistent, unvaried pattern should be

EXHIBIT S15.3

Demand Frequency Represented by Random Numbers

Demand per Day	Relative Frequency	Probability	Random Number Interval
35	1/10	0.10	00–09
45	3/10	0.30	10–39
55	2/10	0.20	40–59
65	3/10	0.30	60–89
75	1/10	0.10	90–99

EXHIBIT S15.4

Uniformly Distributed Random Numbers

06433	80674	24520	18222	10610	05794	37515	48619	02866
39208	47829	72648	37414	75755	01717	29899	78817	03500
89884	59051	67533	08123	17730	95862	08034	19473	03071
61512	32155	51906	61662	64130	16688	37275	51262	11569
99653	47635	12506	88535	36553	23757	34209	55803	96275
95913	11045	13772	76638	48423	25018	99041	77529	81360
55804	44004	13122	44115	01691	50541	00147	77685	58788
35334	82410	91601	40617	72876	33967	73830	15405	96554
59729	88646	76487	11622	96297	24160	09903	14041	22917
57383	89317	63677	70119	94739	25875	38829	68377	43918
30574	06039	07967	32422	76791	39725	53711	93385	13421
81307	13314	83580	79974	45929	85113	72208	09858	52104
02410	96385	79007	54039	21410	86980	91772	93307	34116
18969	87444	52233	62319	08598	09066	95288	04794	01534
87803	80514	66800	62297	80198	19347	73234	86265	49096
68397	10538	15438	62311	72844	60203	46412	05943	79232
28520	54247	58729	10854	99058	18260	38765	90038	94200
44285	09452	15867	70418	57012	72122	36634	97283	95943
80299	22510	33517	23309	57040	29285	07870	21913	72958
84842	05748	90894	61658	15001	94055	36308	41161	37341

followed in drawing random numbers. For example, take the first two digits in each entry in row 1, then row 2, row 3, and so forth.

2. Find the random number interval associated with the random number.

3. Read the daily demand (D_n) corresponding to the random number interval.

4. Calculate the amount sold (S_n). If $D_n \geq Q_n$, then $S_n = Q_n$; if $D_n < Q_n$, $S_n = D_n$.

5. Calculate daily profit $[P_n = (S_n \times p) - (Q_n \times c)]$.

6. Repeat Steps 1 to 5 until 20 days have been simulated.

The results of this procedure, along with the random numbers (RN) used, are summarized in Exhibit S15.5. We compare these results with those achieved by a computer simulation of the problem later in this supplement. Next we develop simulation methodology in detail.

EXHIBIT S15.5

Hand Simulation of Al's Fish Market

Day	RN	D_n	RULE 1			RULE 2		
			Q_n	S_n	P_n	Q_n	S_n	P_n
0	—	55	—	—	—	—	—	—
1	06	35	55	35	$ 10	55	35	$ 10
2	39	45	35	35	14	"	45	16
3	89	65	45	45	18	"	55	22
4	61	65	65	65	26	"	55	22
5	99	75	65	65	26	"	55	22
6	95	75	75	75	30	"	55	22
7	55	55	75	55	18	"	55	22
8	35	45	55	45	16	"	45	16
9	59	55	55	55	22	"	55	22
10	57	55	45	45	18	"	55	22
11	30	45	55	45	16	"	45	16
12	81	65	45	45	18	"	55	22
13	02	35	65	35	8	"	35	10
14	18	45	35	35	14	"	45	16
15	87	65	45	45	18	"	55	22
16	68	65	65	65	26	"	55	22
17	28	45	65	45	14	"	45	16
18	44	55	45	45	18	"	55	22
19	80	65	55	55	22	"	55	22
20	84	65	65	65	26	"	55	22
Total		1,120	1,110	1,000	$378	1,100	1,010	$386
Daily average		56	55.5	50.00	$ 18.90	55	50.5	$ 19.3

S15.2 SIMULATION METHODOLOGY

Exhibit S15.6 is a flowchart of the major phases in carrying out a simulation study. In this section, we develop each of these phases, with particular reference to the key factors noted at the right of the chart.

Problem Definition

Problem definition for purposes of simulation differs little from problem definition for any other tool of analysis. Essentially, it entails specifying the objectives and identifying the relevant controllable and uncontrollable variables of the system to be studied. The objective of a fish market owner is maximizing the profit on sales of codfish. The relevant controllable variable (i.e., under the control of the decision maker) is the ordering rule; the relevant uncontrollable variables are the daily demand levels for codfish and the amount of codfish sold. Other possible objectives could have been specified, such as to maximize profit from the sale of all fish or to maximize sales

EXHIBIT S15.6

**Major Phases in a
Simulation Study**

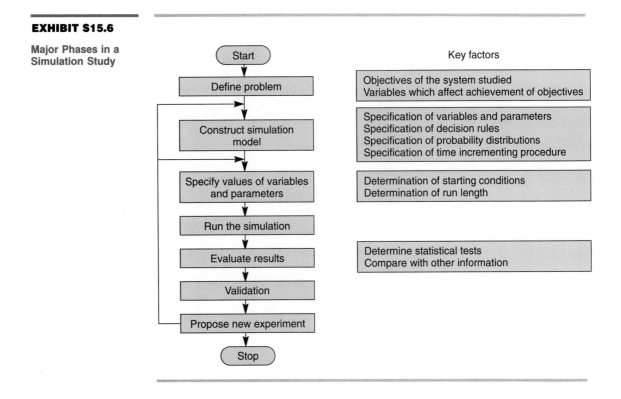

revenue. Other variables, such as the number of display cases and the use of customer priority rules, could have been identified, and demand could be controlled in part by charging a higher or lower price.

Constructing a Simulation Model

A feature that distinguishes simulation from techniques such as linear programming or queuing theory is the fact that a simulation model must be custom built for each problem situation. (A linear programming model, in contrast, can be used in a variety of situations with only a restatement of the values for the objective function and constraint equations.) There are simulation languages which make the model building easier, however. We discuss this subject later in the chapter. The unique nature of each simulation model means that the procedures discussed later for building and executing a model represent a synthesis of various approaches to simulation and are guidelines rather than rigid rules.

Specification of variables and parameters

The first step in constructing a simulation model is determining which properties of the real system should be fixed (called **parameters**) and which should be allowed to vary throughout the simulation run (called **variables**). In the fish market example, the variables were the amount of fish ordered, the amount demanded, and the amount sold; the parameters were the cost of the fish and the selling price of the fish. In most simulations, the focus is on the status of the variables at different points in time, such as the number of pounds of fish demanded and sold each day.

Specification of decision rules

Decision rules (or operating rules) are sets of conditions under which the behavior of the simulation model is observed. These rules are either directly or indirectly the focus of most simulation studies. In our example, we compared decision rules (in two separate simulations), and thus, they were the focus of the analysis. In other situations, the focus of the study may be to determine what goes on in the system as currently designed, but even here, the way the system works depends on the existing decision rules. For example, we may wish to examine the time it takes to process a claim in an insurance office after the introduction of a computerized information system. However, even though the focus of attention is on computer processing time and the manner of routing a claimant's form to and from the computer, particular assumptions about the operation must still be formalized into decision rules.

In many simulations, decision rules are priority rules (for example, which customer to serve first, which job to process first), and in certain situations can be quite involved, taking into account a large number of variables in the system. For example, an inventory ordering rule could be stated in such a way that the amount to order would depend on the amount in inventory, the amount previously ordered but not received, the amount back ordered, and the desired safety stock.

Specification of probability distributions

Two categories of distributions can be used for simulation: empirical frequency distributions and mathematical frequency distributions. In the fish market example, we used an empirical distribution—one derived from observing the relative frequency of various demands for fish. In other words, it is a custom-built demand distribution that is relevant only to our particular problem. It might have happened, however, that the demand for fish closely approximated some known distribution, such as the normal, Poisson, or gamma. If this were the case, data collection and input to the simulation would be greatly simplified.

To illustrate the procedure using a known distribution, let us suppose that, instead of using the empirical demand distribution for fish (shown in histogram form in Exhibit S15.7A), we decided that demand could be described by a normal distribution having a mean of 55 and a standard deviation of 10 (Exhibit S15.7B).[4] Under this assumption, the generation of daily demand would employ a table of randomly distributed normal numbers (or deviates) in

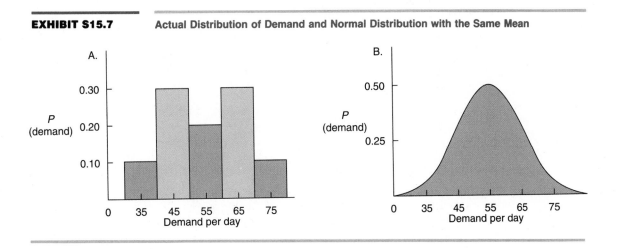

EXHIBIT S15.7   **Actual Distribution of Demand and Normal Distribution with the Same Mean**

---

[4] In practice, standard "goodness of fit" statistical tests, such as chi square, are used to determine how well a particular, known distribution approximates the empirical frequency distribution. It is rather clear in this case, however, that the normal distribution would be a very poor approximation of the empirical distribution and, therefore, should not be used.

conjunction with the statistical formula $D_n = \bar{x} + Z_n\sigma$ (terms defined later), derived from the Z transform used to enter a standard normal table.[5] The specific steps are as follows:

1. Draw a five- or six-digit figure from Exhibit S15.8. The entries in this table are randomly developed deviate values that pertain to a normal distribution having a mean of zero and a standard deviation of 1. The term *deviate* refers to the number of standard deviations some value is from the mean and, in this case, represents the number of standard deviations that any day's demand is from the mean demand. In the preceding formula for D_n, it would be the value for Z on day n. If we are simulating Day 1 and using the first entry in Exhibit S15.8, then $Z_1 = 1.23481$. A negative deviate value means simply that the particular level of demand to be found by using it will be less than the mean, not that demand will be a negative value.

2. Substitute the value of Z_1, along with the predetermined values for x and σ, into the formula

$$D_n = \bar{x} + Z_n\sigma$$

EXHIBIT S15.8

Randomly Distributed Normal Numbers

1.23481	.56176	−.23812
1.54221	1.49673	.18124
.19126	1.22318	−1.35882
−.54929	1.00826	−1.45402
1.14463	−2.75470	−.28185
−.63248	1.11241	1.16515
−.29988	−.55806	−.28278
−.32855	−.49094	1.64410
.35331	−.04187	.32468
.72576	−.98726	.34506
.04406	−.26990	.20790
−1.66161	.52304	.70691
.02629	.24826	.16760
1.18250	−1.19941	−.17022
−.87214	1.08497	2.24938
−.23153	.04496	−.95339
−.04776	−.00926	−.96893
−.31052	−.94171	.36915
−.93166	.82752	

---

[5] The basic formula is $Z = x - \mu/\sigma$, which, when restated in terms of x, appears as $x = \mu + Z\sigma$. We then substituted D_n for x and $\bar{x}$ for μ to relate the method more directly to the sample problem.

where

D_n = Demand on day n

$\bar{x}$ = Mean demand (55 in this example)

σ = Estimated standard deviation (10 in this example)

Z_n = Number of standard deviations from the mean on day n

Thus $D_n = 55 + (1.23481)(10)$.

3. Solve for D_n:

$$D_n = 55 + 12.3481$$
$$D_n = 67.3481$$

4. Repeat Steps 1 to 3, using different normal deviates from the table until the desired number of days have been simulated.

Specification of time-incrementing procedure

In a simulation model, time can be advanced by one of two methods: (1) fixed-time increments or (2) variable-time increments. Under both methods of **time incrementing,** the concept of a simulated clock is important. In the fixed-time increment method, uniform clock-time increments (e.g., minutes, hours, days) are specified and the simulation proceeds by fixed intervals from one time period to the next. At each point in clock time, the system is scanned to determine if any events are to occur. If they are, the events are simulated, and time is advanced; if they are not, time is still advanced by one unit. This was the method employed in the fish-market example, where one day was the time increment and time would have been advanced even if an event (an order) had not taken place.

In the variable-time increment method, clock time is advanced by the amount required to initiate the next event. This approach would be appropriate in the fish-market example if orders were placed when the inventory of fish reached a certain level, rather than at the end of each day.

Which method is most appropriate? Experience suggests that the fixed-time increment is desirable when events of interest occur with regularity or when the number of events is large, with several commonly occurring in the same time period. The variable-time increment method is generally desirable, taking less computer run time when there are relatively few events occurring within a considerable amount of time.[6]

---

[6] It ignores time intervals where nothing happens and immediately advances to the next point when some event does take place.

Specifying Values of Variables and Parameters

Determine starting conditions

A variable, by definition, changes in value as the simulation progresses, but must be given an initial starting value. In our example, because the amount ordered was dependent on previous orders, we assumed an average value of 55 for demand on Day zero. After Day zero, the demand for subsequent days was determined from the random numbers generated. An alternative approach would be to start on Day 1 and assume no previous demand. For Rule 1, however, this would mean that no orders would be placed, since the amount ordered under this rule would be equal to the previous day's demand.

The values for parameters in the example were $0.60 per pound for the price of the fish and $0.20 per pound for the cost of the fish. The value of a parameter, remember, stays constant; however, it may be changed as different alternatives are studied in other simulations.

Determining starting conditions for variables is a major tactical decision in simulation. This is because the model is biased by the set of initial starting values until the model has settled down to a steady state. To cope with this problem, researchers have followed various approaches, such as (1) discarding data generated during the early parts of the run, (2) selecting starting conditions that reduce the duration of the warm-up period, or (3) selecting starting conditions that eliminate bias. To employ any of these alternatives, however, the analyst must have some idea of the range of output data expected. Therefore, in one sense, the analyst biases results. On the other hand, one of the unique features of simulation is that it allows judgment to enter into the design and analysis of the simulation; so if the analyst has some information that bears on the problem, it should be included.

Determine run length

The length of the simulation run (**run length** or **run time**) depends on the purpose of the simulation. Perhaps the most common approach is to continue the simulation until it has achieved an equilibrium condition. In the context of the fish market example, this would mean that simulated demands correspond to their historical relative frequencies. Another approach is to run the simulation for a set period, such as a month, a year, or a decade, and see if the conditions at the end of the period appear reasonable. A third approach is to set run length so that a sufficiently large sample is gathered for purposes of statistical hypothesis testing. This alternative is considered further in the next section.

Evaluating Results

Determine statistical tests

The types of conclusions that can be drawn from a simulation depend, of course, on the degree to which the model reflects the real system, but they also depend on the design of the simulation in a statistical sense, Indeed, many researchers view simulation as a form of hypothesis testing, with each simulation run providing one or more pieces of sample data that are amenable to formal analysis through inferential statistical methods. For example, we might wish to test the hypothesis that the average amount of fish sold per day is 55 pounds, assuming a normal distribution of demand and a standard deviation of 10 pounds. To accept this hypothesis (or, more correctly, fail to reject it) at a particular level of statistical confidence, we would have to run the simulation for a sufficient number of days to satisfy the sample size requirements for the particular statistical test we might employ.[7] Following this approach might well alter both the length of the simulation study and the implications of the results.

In a similar vein, statistical methods could be employed to find the best alternative in a group of several competing alternatives, although in this situation, some rather sophisticated mathematical search routines are required.

Compare with other information

In most situations, the analyst has other information available with which to compare the simulation results: past operating data from the real system, operating data from the performance of similar systems, and the analyst's own intuitive understanding of the real system's operation. Admittedly, however, information obtained from these sources is probably not sufficient to validate the conclusions derived from the simulation, and thus, the only true test of a simulation is how well the real system performs after the results of the study have been implemented.

Validation

In this context, *validation* refers to testing the computer program to ensure that the simulation is correct. Specifically, it is a check to see whether the computer code is a valid translation of the flowchart model and whether the simulation adequately represents the real system. Errors may arise in the program from mistakes in the coding or from mistakes in logic. Mistakes in coding are usually easily found since the program is most likely not executed by the computer. Mistakes in logic, however, present more of a challenge. In these cases, the program runs, but it fails to yield correct results.

To deal with this problem, the analyst has three alternatives: (1) have the program print out all calculations and verify these calculations by hand, (2) simulate present conditions and compare the results with the existing system, or (3) pick some point in the simulation run and compare its output to the answer obtained from solving a relevant mathematical model of the situation

---

[7] Some of the statistical procedures commonly used in evaluating simulation results are analysis of variance, regression analysis, and *t* tests.

at that point. Even though the first two approaches have obvious drawbacks, they are more likely to be employed than the third, because if we had a relevant mathematical model in mind, we would probably be able to solve the problem without the aid of simulation.

Proposing a New Experiment

Based on the simulation results, a new simulation experiment may be in order. We might like to change many of the factors: parameters, variables, decision rules, starting conditions, and run length. As for parameters, we might be interested in replicating the simulation with several different costs or prices of a product to see what changes would occur. Trying different decision rules would obviously be in order if the initial rules led to poor results or if these runs yielded new insights into the problem. (The procedure of using the same stream of random numbers, as was done in comparing Rules 1 and 2 in the fish market example, is a good general approach in that it sharpens the differences among alternatives and permits shorter runs.) Also, the values from the previous experiment may be useful starting conditions for subsequent simulations.

Finally, whether trying different run lengths constitutes a new experiment rather than a replication of a previous experiment depends on the types of events that occur in the system operation over time. It might happen, for example, that the system has more than one stable level of operation and that reaching the second level is time dependent. Thus, while the first series of runs of, say, 100 periods shows stable conditions, doubling the length of the series may provide new and distinctly different, but equally stable, conditions. In this case, running the simulation over 200 time periods could be thought of as a new experiment.

Computerization

A computer is often the only feasible way of performing a simulation study. When using a **computer model** we reduce the system to be studied to a symbolic representation to be run on a computer. Although it is beyond the scope of this book to go into detail about the technical aspects of computer modeling, some that bear directly on simulation are

1. Computer language selection.
2. Flowcharting.
3. Coding.
4. Data generation.
5. Output reports.
6. Validation.

Computer language selection

Computer languages can be divided into general-purpose and special-purpose types. General-purpose languages are FORTRAN, COBOL, Pascal, C, PL/1, and BASIC. They have the advantage of being applicable to a wide variety of needs. Some of the simulation languages are not truly languages, however, because they simplify the simulation procedure by using standard subroutines written in another language, such as FORTRAN or APL. SIMSCRIPT, GPSS, GASP, and GERT are commonly used special-purpose simulation languages that are especially suitable for queuing and scheduling problems, because they require less programming time for these types of problems than the general-purpose languages. In addition, they have special output formats and error-checking mechanisms that add to their desirability. We discuss languages in more depth later in this supplement.

Flowcharting

Flowcharting a simulation program requires that the analyst visualize how the system responds under dynamic conditions.

Coding

Coding refers to translating the flowchart into a computer language. If the programmer is using FORTRAN or some other general-purpose language, the mechanics of writing a computer code are the same as for any mathematical or engineering problem.

Data generation

A considerable amount of theoretical study has been applied to the generation of random numbers in digital computers, dealing with such questions as true randomness, long term trends, and tendency to repeat the sequence. For most purposes, though, the built-in random number generators at most computer facilities are adequate. However, an individual planning to execute a fairly long simulation program must have some knowledge of random-number generation to decide which approach is most desirable for the particular purpose.

Output reports

General-purpose languages permit the analyst to specify any type of output report (or data) desired, providing he or she is willing to pay the price in programming effort. Special-purpose languages have standard routines that can be activated by one or two program statements to print out such data as means, variances, and standard deviations. Regardless of language, however, our experience has been that too much data from a simulation can be as dysfunctional to problem solving as too little; both situations tend to obscure important, truly meaningful information about the system under study.

S15.3 COMPUTERIZATION OF THE FISH MARKET EXAMPLE

This problem's flowchart, computer program, and comparative output reports for Rules 1 and 2 (based upon 2,000 days) are reproduced in Exhibits S15.9 through S15.12.

EXHIBIT S15.9

Simulation Flowchart for Fish Market Problem

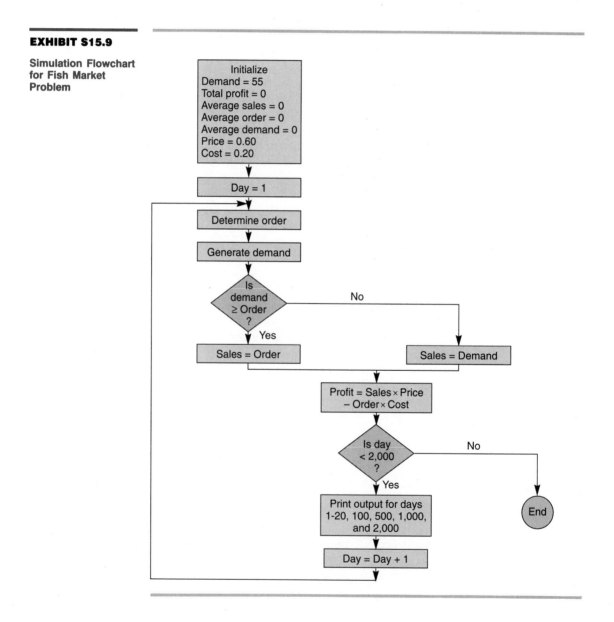

EXHIBIT S15.10   FORTRAN Program for Simulation of Al's Fish Market

```
100    PROGRAM FISHMKT (INPUT,OUTPUT)
250    DEMAND=55
260    TPROFIT=0.
265    ADD=0.
270    AOO=0.
275    ASS=0.
300    DO 100 I=1,2000
400    IDAY=I
450    ORDER=55
500    X=RANF(0)*100.
600    IF (X.GE.0.AND.X.LT.10) DEMAND=35
700    IF (X.GE.10.AND.X.LT.40) DEMAND=45
800    IF (X.GE.40.AND.X.LT.60) DEMAND=55
900    IF (X.GE.60.AND.X.LT.90) DEMAND=65
1000   IF (X.GE.90.AND.X.LT.100) DEMAND=75
1050   SALES=DEMAND
1100   IF (DEMAND.GT.ORDER) SALES = ORDER
1200   COST=.20
1300   PRICE=.60
1400   PROFIT=SALES*PRICE-ORDER*COST
1500   TPROFIT=TPROFIT+PROFIT
1550   DAY=IDAY
1560   ADD=ADD+DEMAND
1565   AD=ADD/DAY
1570   AOO=AOO+ORDER
1575   AO=AOO/DAY
1580   ASS=ASS+SALES
1585   AS=ASS/DAY
1600   AVPROF=TPROFIT/DAY
1700   IF(IDAY.GE.1.AND.IDAY.LE.20.OR.IDAY.EQ.100.OR.IDAY.EQ.500)GO TO 99
1800   IF(IDAY.EQ.1000.OR.IDAY.EQ.2000) GO TO 99
1850   GO TO 100
1900   99  PRINT 999,IDAY,DEMAND,AD,ORDER,AO,SALES,AS,PROFIT,AVPROF
2000   999  FORMAT (I5,8F8.2)
2100   100  CONTINUE
2150   PRINT 37,ADD,AOO,ASS,TPROFIT
2175   37 FORMAT(F15.2)
2200   STOP
2300   END
```

Comparing the results of this program (written in FORTRAN) with the results of the hand simulation, we observe that Rule 2 outperformed Rule 1 in both cases, For the hand simulation covering 20 days, daily profit for Rule 1 ($Q_n = D_{n-1}$) was \$18.90 and the average daily profit for Rule 2 ($Q_n = 55$) was \$19.30. For the computer simulation, average daily profit for Rule 1 was \$18.05, compared to \$19.02 for Rule 2. As we can see from the results of the 2,000-day run, although the expected profits were a bit overstated in the hand simulation, 20 days gave surprisingly good results.

EXHIBIT S15.11   Simulation of Fish Market—Rule 1 Output

```
READY.
450 ORDER=DEMAND
RUN
```

Day	Demand	Cumulative Average Demand	Order for Day	Cumulative Average Order	Sales for Day	Cumulative Average Sales	Profit for Day	Cumulative Average Profit
1	35.00	35.00	55.00	55.00	35.00	35.00	10.00	10.00
2	45.00	40.00	35.00	45.00	35.00	35.00	14.00	12.00
3	75.00	51.67	45.00	45.00	45.00	38.33	18.00	14.00
4	45.00	50.00	75.00	52.50	45.00	40.00	12.00	13.50
5	65.00	53.00	45.00	51.00	45.00	41.00	18.00	14.40
6	65.00	55.00	65.00	53.33	65.00	45.00	26.00	16.33
7	65.00	56.43	65.00	55.00	65.00	47.86	26.00	17.71
8	55.00	56.25	65.00	56.25	55.00	48.75	20.00	18.00
9	75.00	58.33	55.00	56.11	55.00	49.44	22.00	18.44
10	55.00	58.00	75.00	58.00	55.00	50.00	18.00	18.40
11	55.00	57.73	55.00	57.73	55.00	50.45	22.00	18.73
12	65.00	58.33	55.00	57.50	55.00	50.83	22.00	19.00
13	45.00	57.31	65.00	58.08	45.00	50.38	14.00	18.62
14	65.00	57.86	45.00	57.14	45.00	50.00	18.00	18.57
15	45.00	57.00	65.00	57.67	45.00	49.67	14.00	18.27
16	45.00	56.25	45.00	56.88	45.00	49.38	18.00	18.25
17	45.00	55.59	45.00	56.18	45.00	49.12	18.00	18.24
18	65.00	56.11	45.00	55.56	45.00	48.89	18.00	18.22
19	65.00	56.58	65.00	56.05	65.00	49.74	26.00	18.63
20	35.00	55.50	65.00	56.50	35.00	49.00	8.00	18.10
100	65.00	55.30	35.00	55.20	35.00	48.20	14.00	17.88
500	75.00	55.24	75.00	55.20	75.00	48.40	30.00	18.00
1000	45.00	55.22	45.00	55.23	45.00	48.52	18.00	18.07
2000	65.00	55.17	35.00	55.16	35.00	48.46	14.00	18.05

```
        Total demand  110340.00            Total sales  96930.00
        Total order   110330.00            Total profit 36092.00
```

Looking at the totals for the computer simulation, it is interesting to note that Rule 2 yielded $1,944 greater profit than Rule 1, yet the amount of fish ordered was 330 pounds less under Rule 1. This finding would tend to make Rule 2 even more attractive if the problem were enriched to include such factors as inventory holding costs and the opportunity cost of funds. Similarly, we note that Rule 2 resulted in 3,130 more orders being filled (compared to Rule 1), which would enhance the desirability of Rule 2 if a stockout penalty were included in the problem.

S15.4 SIMULATING WAITING LINES

Waiting lines that occur in series and parallel (such as in assembly lines and job shops) usually cannot be solved mathematically. However, since waiting lines

EXHIBIT S15.12   Simulation of Fish Market—Rule 2 Output

450 ORDER=55
RUN.

Day	Demand	Cumulative Average Demand	Order for Day	Cumulative Average Order	Sales for Day	Cumulative Average Sales	Profit for Day	Cumulative Average Profit
1	35.00	35.00	55.00	55.00	35.00	35.00	10.00	10.00
2	45.00	40.00	55.00	55.00	45.00	40.00	16.00	13.00
3	75.00	51.67	55.00	55.00	55.00	45.00	22.00	16.00
4	45.00	50.00	55.00	55.00	45.00	45.00	16.00	16.00
5	65.00	53.00	55.00	55.00	55.00	47.00	22.00	17.20
6	65.00	55.00	55.00	55.00	55.00	48.33	22.00	18.00
7	65.00	56.43	55.00	55.00	55.00	49.29	22.00	18.57
8	55.00	56.25	55.00	55.00	55.00	50.00	22.00	19.00
9	75.00	58.33	55.00	55.00	55.00	50.56	22.00	19.33
10	55.00	58.00	55.00	55.00	55.00	51.00	22.00	19.60
11	55.00	57.73	55.00	55.00	55.00	51.36	22.00	19.82
12	65.00	58.33	55.00	55.00	55.00	51.67	22.00	20.00
13	45.00	57.31	55.00	55.00	45.00	51.15	16.00	19.69
14	65.00	57.86	55.00	55.00	55.00	51.43	22.00	19.86
15	45.00	57.00	55.00	55.00	45.00	51.00	16.00	19.60
16	45.00	56.25	55.00	55.00	45.00	50.63	16.00	19.38
17	45.00	55.59	55.00	55.00	45.00	50.29	16.00	19.18
18	65.00	56.11	55.00	55.00	55.00	50.56	22.00	19.33
19	65.00	56.58	55.00	55.00	55.00	50.79	22.00	19.47
20	35.00	55.50	55.00	55.00	35.00	50.00	10.00	19.00
100	65.00	55.30	55.00	55.00	55.00	50.00	22.00	19.00
500	75.00	55.24	55.00	55.00	55.00	50.02	22.00	19.01
1000	45.00	55.22	55.00	55.00	45.00	50.05	16.00	19.03
2000	65.00	55.17	55.00	55.00	55.00	50.03	22.00	19.02

Total demand   110340.00   Total sales   100060.00
Total ordered 110000.00   Total profit   38036.00

are often easily simulated on a computer, we have chosen a two-stage assembly line as our second simulation example.

A Two-Stage Assembly Line

Consider manufacturing a product on an assembly line that has a significant physical size, such as for a refrigerator, stove, automobile, boat, television set, or furniture. Exhibit S15.13 shows two workstations on that line.

The size of the product is an important consideration in assembly-line analysis and design because the number of products that can exist at each workstation affects worker performance. If the product is large, then the workstations are dependent on each other. Exhibit S15.13, for example, shows Bob and Ray working on a two-stage line where Bob's output in Station 1 is fed to Ray in Station 2. If the workstations are adjacent so that there is no room

EXHIBIT S15.13

Two Workstations on an Assembly Line

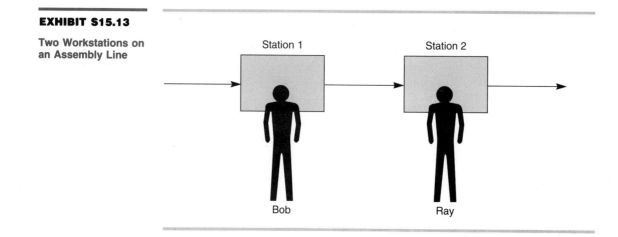

Station 1   Station 2

Bob   Ray

for items in between, then Bob, by working slowly, would cause Ray to wait. Conversely, if Bob completes a product quickly (or if Ray takes longer to finish the task) then Bob must wait for Ray.

In this simulation, assume that Bob, the first worker on the line, can pull over a new item to work on whenever needed. We concentrate our analysis on the interaction between Bob and Ray.

Objective of the study

There are a number of questions we would like to have answered about the assembly line from this study. A partial list would be:

What is the average performance time of each worker?

What is the output rate of product through this line?

How much time does Bob wait for Ray?

How much time does Ray wait for Bob?

If the space between the two stations were increased so that items could be stored there and give workers some independence, what effect would this have on output rates, wait times, etc.?

Data collection

To simulate this system, we need the performance times of Bob and Ray. One way to collect this data is to divide the range of performance times into segments, and then observe each worker. A simple check or tally mark in each of these segments results in a useful histogram of data.

Exhibit S15.14 shows the data collection form used to observe the performances of Bob and Ray. To simplify the procedure, performance time was divided into 10-second intervals. Bob was observed for 100 repetitions of the work task, and Ray was observed just 50 times. The number of observations

EXHIBIT S15.14

Data Collection Form
for Worker
Observation

Seconds	BOB	Totals	RAY	Totals
5–14.99	IIII	4	IIII	4
15–24.99	JHT I	6	JHT	5
25–34.99	JHT JHT	10	JHT I	6
35–44.99	JHT JHT JHT JHT	20	JHT II	7
45–54.99	JHT JHT JHT JHT JHT JHT JHT JHT	40	JHT JHT	10
55–64.99	JHT JHT I	11	JHT III	8
65–74.99	JHT	5	JHT I	6
75–84.99	IIII	4	IIII	4
		100		50

EXHIBIT S15.15

Random Number
Intervals for Bob
and Ray

Seconds	Time Frequencies for Bob (Operation 1)	RN Intervals	Time Frequencies for Ray (Operation 2)	RN Intervals
10	4	00–03	4	00–07
20	6	04–09	5	08–17
30	10	10–19	6	18–29
40	20	20–39	7	30–43
50	40	40–79	10	44–63
60	11	80–90	8	64–79
70	5	91–95	6	80–91
80	4	96–99	4	92–99
	100		50	

does not have to be the same, but the more there are and the smaller the size of the time segments, the more accurate the study will be. The trade-off is that more observations and smaller segments take more time and more people (as well as more time to program and run a simulation).

Exhibit S15.15 contains the random number intervals assigned that correspond to the same ratio as the actual observed data. For example, Bob had 4 out of 100 times at 10 seconds. Therefore, if we used 100 numbers, we would assign 4 of those numbers as corresponding to 10 seconds. We could have assigned any four numbers, for example, 42, 18, 12, and 93. However, these would be a nuisance to search for, so we assign consecutive numbers, such as 00, 01, 02, and 03.

There were 50 observations of Ray. There are two ways we could assign random numbers. First, we could use just 50 numbers (say 00–49) and ignore any numbers over that. However, this is wasteful, since we would discard 50 percent of all the numbers from the list. Another choice would be to double the frequency number. For example, rather than assign, say, numbers 00–03 to account for the 4 observations out of 50 that took 10 seconds, we could assign numbers 00–07 to represent 8 observations out of 100 which is double the observed number but the same frequency. Actually, for this example and the speed of computers, the savings of time by doubling is insignificant.

Exhibit S15.16 shows a hand simulation of 10 items processed by Bob and Ray. The random numbers used were from Appendix B, starting at the first column of two numbers and working downward.

Assume that we start our time at 00 and run it in continuous seconds (not bothering to convert this to hours and minutes). The first random number is 56 and corresponds to Bob's performance at 50 seconds on the first item. The item is passed to Ray, who starts at 50 seconds. Relating the next random number 83 to Exhibit S15.15, we find that Ray takes 70 seconds to complete the item. In the meantime, Bob starts on the next item at time 50 and takes 50 seconds (random number 55), finishing at time 100. However, Bob cannot start on the third item until Ray gets through with the first item at time 120. Bob, therefore, has a wait time of 20 seconds. (If there was storage space between Bob and Ray, this item could have been moved out of Bob's workstation and Bob could have started the next item at time 100.) The remainder of the exhibit was calculated following the same pattern: obtaining a random number, finding the corresponding processing time, noting the wait time, if any, and computing the finish time. Note that with no storage space between Bob and Ray, there was considerable waiting time for both workers.

EXHIBIT S15.16   Simulation of Bob and Ray—Two-Stage Assembly Line

Item Number	BOB					Storage Space	RAY				
	Random Number	Start Time	Per-formance Time	Finish Time	Wait Time		Random Number	Start Time	Per-formance Time	Finish Time	Wait Time
1	56	00	50	50		0	83	50	70	120	50
2	55	50	50	100	20	0	47	120	50	170	
3	84	120	60	180		0	08	180	20	200	10
4	36	180	40	220		0	05	220	10	230	20
5	26	220	40	260		0	42	260	40	300	30
6	95	260	70	330		0	95	330	80	410	30
7	66	330	50	380	30	0	17	410	20	430	
8	03	410	10	420	10	0	21	430	30	460	
9	57	430	50	480		0	31	480	40	520	20
10	69	480	50	530		0	90	530	70	600	10
			470		60				430		170

We can now answer some questions and make some statements about the system. For example:

The output time averages 60 seconds per unit (the complete time 600 for Ray divided by 10 units).

Utilization of Bob is $^{470}\!/_{530} = 88.7$ percent.

Utilization of Ray is $^{430}\!/_{550} = 78.2$ percent (disregarding the initial startup wait for the first item of 50 seconds).

The average performance time for Bob is $^{470}\!/_{10} = 47$ seconds.

The average performance time for Ray is $^{430}\!/_{10} = 43$ seconds.

We have demonstrated how this problem would be solved in a simple manual simulation. A sample of 10 is really too small to place much confidence in, so this problem should be run on a computer for several thousand iterations. (We extend this same problem further in the next section of this supplement).

It is also very important to study the effect of item storage space between workers. The problem would be run to see what the throughput times and worker utilization times are with no storage space between workers. A second run should increase this storage space to one unit, with the corresponding changes noted. Repeating the runs for two, three, four, and so on, offers management an opportunity to compute the additional cost of space compared with the increased use. Such increased space between workers may require a larger building, more materials and parts in the system, material handling equipment, transfer machines, added heat, light, building maintenance, and so on.

This would also be useful data for management to see what changes in the system would occur if one of the worker positions was automated. The assembly line could be simulated using data from the automated process to see if such a change would be cost justified.

S15.5 SPREADSHEET SIMULATION

As we have stated throughout this book, spreadsheets such as Lotus, Quattro, Excel, and SuperCalc are very useful for a variety of problems. Exhibit S15.17 shows Bob and Ray's two-stage assembly line on a Lotus 1-2-3 spreadsheet. The procedure follows the same pattern as our manual display in Exhibit S15.15.

The total simulation on Lotus passed through 1,200 iterations; that is, 1,200 parts were finished by Ray. Simulation, as an analytic tool, has an advantage over quantitative methods in that it is a dynamic simulation whereas analytic methods show long-run average performance. As you can see in Exhibits S15.18 and S15.19, there is an unmistakable startup (or transient) phase. We

EXHIBIT S15.17   Bob and Ray Two-Stage Assembly Line on Lotus 1-2-3

		[	--------	Bob	--------	]	[	--------	Ray	--------	]			
Item	RN	Start Time	Perf Time	Finish Time	Wait Time	RN	Start Time	Perf Time	Finish Time	Wait Time	Average Time \Unit	Total Time	Average Time in System
1	93	0	70	70	0	0	70	10	80	70	80.0	80	80.0
2	52	70	50	120	0	44	120	50	170	40	85.0	100	90.0
3	15	120	30	150	20	72	170	60	230	0	76.7	110	96.7
4	64	170	50	220	10	35	230	40	270	0	67.5	100	97.5
5	86	230	60	290	0	2	290	10	300	20	60.0	70	92.0
6	20	290	40	330	0	82	330	70	400	30	66.7	110	95.0
7	83	330	60	390	10	31	400	40	440	0	62.9	110	97.1
8	89	400	60	460	0	13	460	20	480	20	60.0	80	95.0
9	69	460	50	510	0	53	510	50	560	30	62.2	100	95.6
10	41	510	50	560	0	48	560	50	610	0	61.0	100	96.0
11	32	560	40	600	10	13	610	20	630	0	57.3	70	93.6
12	1	610	10	620	10	67	630	60	690	0	57.5	80	92.5
13	11	630	30	660	30	91	690	70	760	0	58.5	130	95.4
14	2	690	10	700	60	76	760	60	820	0	58.6	130	97.9
15	11	760	30	790	30	41	820	40	860	0	57.3	100	98.0
16	55	820	50	870	0	34	870	40	910	10	56.9	90	97.5
17	18	870	30	900	10	28	910	30	940	0	55.3	70	95.9
18	39	910	40	950	0	53	950	50	1000	10	55.6	90	95.6
19	13	950	30	980	20	41	1000	40	1040	0	54.7	90	95.3
20	7	1000	20	1020	20	21	1040	30	1070	0	53.5	70	94.0
21	29	1040	40	1080	0	54	1080	50	1130	10	53.8	90	93.8
22	58	1080	50	1130	0	39	1130	40	1170	0	53.2	90	93.6
23	95	1130	70	1200	0	70	1200	60	1260	30	54.8	130	95.2
24	27	1200	40	1240	20	60	1260	50	1310	0	54.6	110	95.8
25	59	1260	50	1310	0	93	1310	80	1390	0	55.6	130	97.2
26	85	1310	60	1370	20	51	1390	50	1440	0	55.4	130	98.5
27	12	1390	30	1420	20	35	1440	40	1480	0	54.8	90	98.1
28	34	1440	40	1480	0	51	1480	50	1530	0	54.6	90	97.9
29	60	1480	50	1530	0	87	1530	70	1600	0	55.2	120	98.6
30	97	1530	80	1610	0	29	1610	30	1640	10	54.7	110	99.0

could even raise some questions about the long-term operation of the line because it doesn't seem to have settled to a constant (steady state) value, even after the 1,200 items. Exhibit S15.18 shows 100 items that pass through the Bob and Ray two-stage system. Notice the wide variation in time for the first units completed. These figures are the average time that units take. It is a cumulative number; that is, the first unit takes the time generated by the random numbers. The average time for two units is the average time of the sum of the first and second units. The average time for three units is the average time for the sum of the first three units, and so on. This display could have almost any starting shape, not necessarily what we have shown. It all depends on the stream of random numbers. What we can be sure of is that the times do oscillate for a while until they settle down as units are finished and smooth the average.

EXHIBIT S15.18

Average Time per
Unit of Output (Finish
time/number of units)

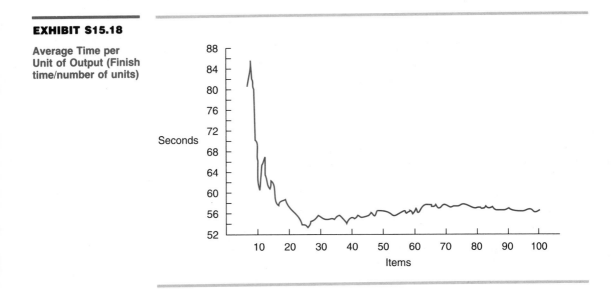

EXHIBIT S15.19

Average Time the
Product Spends in
the System

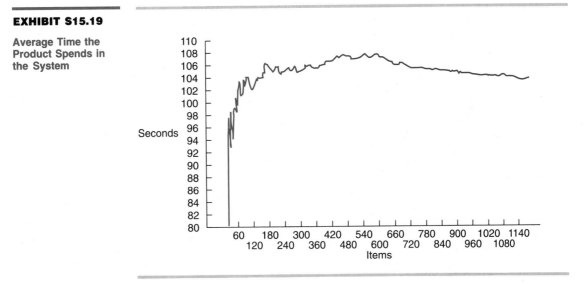

Exhibit S15.19 shows the average time that parts spend in the system. The display shows an increasing amount of time in the system. This can be expected because the system started empty and there are no interruptions for parts passing from Bob to Ray. Often parts enter the system and may have to wait between stages as work-in-process; this causes delays for subsequent parts

EXHIBIT S15.20

Results of Simulating 1,200 Units Processed by Bob and Ray

	Bob	Ray	Unit
Utilization	0.81	0.85	
Average wait time	10.02	9.63	
Average performance time	46.48	46.88	
Average time per unit			57.65
Average time in system			103.38

and adds to the waiting time. As time goes on, however, stability should occur, unless the capacity of the second stage is less than the first stage. In our present case, we did not allow space between them. Therefore, if Bob finished first, he had to wait for Ray. If Ray finished first, he had to wait for Bob.

Exhibit S15.20 shows the results of simulating Bob and Ray completing 1,200 units of product. Compare these figures to those which we obtained simulating 10 items by hand. Not too bad, is it! Considering only 10 units! The average performance time for Bob is shown as 46.48 seconds. This is close to the weighted average of what you would expect in the long run. For Bob it is $(10 \times 4 + 20 \times 6 + 30 \times 10$ etc.$)/100 = 45.9$ seconds. Ray's expected time is $(10 \times 4 + 20 \times 5 + 30 \times 6$ etc.$)/50 = 46.4$ seconds.

S15.6 SIMULATION PROGRAMS AND LANGUAGES

Simulation programs can be classified as *continuous* or *discrete*. Continuous models are based on mathematical equations and therefore are continuous, with values for all points in time. In contrast, discrete simulation occurs only at specific points. For example, customers arriving at a bank teller's window would be discrete simulation. The simulation jumps from point to point; the arrival of a customer, the state of a service, the ending of service, the arrival of the next customer, and so on. Discrete simulation can also be triggered to run by units of time (daily, hourly, minute by minute). This is called *event simulation;* points in between either have no interest or cannot be computed because of the lack of some sort of mathematical relationships to link the succeeding events. Operations management applications almost exclusively use discrete (event) simulation.

Simulation software also can be categorized as general purpose and special purpose. General-purpose software is really language that allows programmers to build their own models. Examples are SLAM II, SIMSCRIPT II.5, SIMAN, GPSS/H, GPSS/PC, PCMODEL, and RESQ. Special-purpose software simulation programs are specially built to simulate specific applications, such as MAP/1, and SIMFACTORY. In a specialized simulation for manufacturing, for example, provisions in the model allow for specifying the number of work centers, their description, arrival rates, processing time, batch sizes, quantities of work in process, available resources including labor, sequences, and so on. Additionally, the program may allow the observer to watch the animated operation and see the quantities and flows throughout the system as the simulation is running. Data is collected, analyzed, and presented in a form most suitable for that type of application.

There are many software simulation programs available to use on computers, from micros to mainframes. How, then, does one choose a program from a long list?

The first step is to understand the different types of simulation. Then it becomes a matter of reviewing programs on the market to find one that fits your specific needs. Even if a program does exist, however, sometimes it's still easier to create a special purpose one. It may be better suited and less troublesome to use.

As a last comment on simulation programs, don't rule out spreadsheets for simulation. As you noticed, we simulated Bob and Ray on a spreadsheet in the preceding section. Spreadsheets are becoming quite user-friendly and are adding many features, such as allowing random number generation and asking what-if questions. The simplicity in using a spreadsheet for simulation may well compensate for probably having to reduce the complexity of the problem somewhat in order to use the spreadsheet.

Desirable Features of Simulation Software

Simulation software takes a while to learn to use. Once a specific software is learned, the tendency is to stay with it for a long time. Therefore, care should be taken when making the choice. Simulation software should

1. Be capable of being used interactively as well as allowing complete runs.
2. Be user-friendly, easy to understand.
3. Allow modules to be built and then connected. In this way models can be worked on separately without affecting the rest of the system.
4. Allow users to write and incorporate their own routines; no simulation program can provide for all needs.
5. Have building blocks that contain built-in commands (such as statistical analysis or decision rules of where to go next).
6. Have macro capability, such as the ability to develop machining cells.
7. Have material-handling capability. In manufacturing, such a large portion of operations involves the movement of material that the program should have the ability to model trucks, cranes, conveyers, and so on.

8. Output standard statistics such as cycle times, utilizations, wait times, and so forth.

9. Allow a variety of data analysis alternatives for both input and output data.

10. Have animation capabilities to display graphically the product flow through the system.

11. Permit interactive debugging of the model so the user can trace flows through the model and more easily find errors.[8]

S15.7 ADVANTAGES AND DISADVANTAGES OF SIMULATION

The following is not intended as a comprehensive list of reasons why one should elect or not elect to use simulation as a technique. Rather, we state some of the main points usually raised.

Advantages

1. Developing the model of a system often leads to a better understanding of the real system.

2. Time can be compressed in simulation; years of experience in the real system can be compressed into seconds or minutes.

3. Simulation does not disrupt ongoing activities of the real system.

4. Simulation is far more general than mathematical models and can be used where conditions are not suitable for standard mathematical analysis.

5. Simulation can be used as a game for training experience.

6. Simulation provides a more realistic replication of a system than mathematical analysis.

7. Simulation can be used to analyze transient conditions whereas mathematical techniques usually cannot.

8. Many standard packaged models, covering a wide range of topics, are available commercially.

9. Simulation answers what-if questions.

Disadvantages

1. While a great deal of time and effort may be spent to develop a model for simulation, there is no guarantee that the model will, in fact, provide good answers.

---

[8] S. Wali Haider and Jerry Banks, "Simulation Software Products for Analyzing Manufacturing Systems," *Industrial Engineering* 18, no. 7 (July 1986), pp. 98–103.

2. The output of a simulation model cannot be proved. Simulation involves numerous repetitions of sequences that are based on randomly generated occurrences. An apparently stable system can, with the right combination of events—however unlikely—explode. There is no way to prove that a model's performance is completely reliable.

3. Depending on the system to be simulated, building a simulation model can take anywhere from an hour to 100 worker years. Complicated systems can be very costly and take a long time.

4. Simulation may be less accurate than mathematical analysis because it is randomly based. If a given system can be represented by a mathematical model, it may be better to use than simulation.

5. A significant amount of computer time may be needed to run complex models.

6. The technique of simulation, while making progress, still lacks a standardized approach. Therefore, models of the same system built by different individuals may differ widely.

S15.8 CONCLUSION

We could make the statement that anything that can be done mathematically can be done with simulation. However, simulation is not always the best choice. Mathematical analysis, when appropriate to a specific problem, is usually faster and less expensive. Also, it is usually provable as far as the technique is concerned, and the only real question is whether the system is adequately represented by the mathematical model.

Simulation, however, has nothing fixed; there are no boundaries to building a model or making assumptions about the system. Expanding computer power and memory have pushed out the limits of what can be simulated. Further, the continued development of simulation languages and programs—both general-purpose programs (SIMAN, SLAM) and special-purpose (MAP/1, SIMFACTORY)—promises to make the entire process of creating simulation models much easier.

S15.9 REVIEW AND DISCUSSION QUESTIONS

1. Why is it that simulation is often referred to as a technique of last resort?

2. Give an example of a third rule that Al (of Al's Fish Market) could use in his inventory ordering.

3. What role does statistical hypothesis testing play in simulation?

4. What determines whether a simulation model is valid?

5. Do you have to use a computer to get good information from a simulation? Explain.

6. What methods are used to increment time in a simulation model? How do they work?

7. What are the pros and cons of starting a simulation with the system empty? With the system in equilibrium?

8. Distinguish between known mathematical distribution and empirical distributions. What information is needed to simulate using a known mathematical distribution?

9. What is the importance of run length in simulation? Is a run of 100 observations twice as valid as a run of 50? Explain.

S15.10 PROBLEMS

*1. To use an old statistical example for simulation, if an urn contains 100 balls, of which 10 percent are green, 40 percent are red, and 50 percent are spotted, develop a simulation model of the process of drawing balls at random from the urn. Each time a ball is drawn and its color noted, it is replaced. Use the following random numbers as you desire.

Simulate drawing 10 balls from the urn. Show which numbers you have used.

26768	83125
42613	55503
95457	47019
95276	84828
66954	08021
17457	36458
03704	05752
56970	05752

*2. A rural clinic receives a delivery of fresh plasma once each week from a central blood bank. The supply varies according to demand from other clinics and hospitals in the region but ranges between four and nine pints of the most widely used blood type, type O. The number of patients per week requiring this blood varies from zero to four, and each patient may need from one to four pints. Given the following delivery quantities, patient distribution, and demand per patient, what would be the number of pints in excess or short for a six-week period? Use Monte Carlo simulation to derive your answer. Consider that plasma is storable and there is currently none on hand.

PATIENT DISTRIBUTION

DELIVERY QUANTITIES		Patients per Week Requiring Blood		DEMAND PER PATIENT	
Pints per Week	Frequency		Frequency	Pints	Frequency
4	0.15	0	0.25	1	0.40
5	0.20	1	0.25	2	0.30
6	0.25	2	0.30	3	0.20
7	0.15	3	0.15	4	0.10
8	0.15	4	0.05		
9	0.10				

---

* Solutions to Problems 1 and 2 are in Appendix H.

3. CLASSROOM SIMULATION: FISH FORWARDERS

This is a competitive exercise designed to test players' skills at setting inventory ordering rules over a 10-week planning horizon. Maximum profit at the end determines the winner.

Fish Forwarders supplies fresh shrimp to a variety of customers in the New Orleans area. It places orders for cases of shrimp from fleet representatives at the beginning of each week to meet a demand from its customers at the middle of the week. The shrimp are subsequently delivered to Fish Forwarders and then, at the end of the week, to its customers.

Both the supply of shrimp and the demand for shrimp are uncertain. The supply may vary as much as ± 10 percent from the amount ordered, and by contract, Fish Forwarders must purchase this supply. The probability associated with this variation is: − 10 percent, 30 percent of the time; 0 percent, 50 percent of the time, and + 10 percent, 20 percent of the time. The weekly demand for shrimp is normally distributed with a mean of 800 cases and a standard deviation of 100 cases.

A case of shrimp costs Fish Forwarders $30 and sells for $50. Any shrimp not sold at the end of the week are sold to a cat-food company at $4 per case. Fish Forwarders may, if it chooses, order the shrimp flash-frozen by the supplier at dockside, but this raises the cost of a case by $4 and, hence, costs Fish Forwarders $34 per case. Flash-freezing enables Fish Forwarders to maintain an inventory of shrimp, but it costs $2 per case per week to store the shrimp at a local icehouse. The customers are indifferent to whether they get regular or flash-frozen shrimp. Fish Forwarders figures that its shortage cost is equal to its markup; that is, each case demanded but not available costs the company $50 − $30 or $20.

Procedure for play. The game requires that each week a decision be made as to how many cases to order of regular shrimp and flash-frozen shrimp. The number ordered may be any amount. The instructor plays the role of referee and supplies the random numbers. The steps in playing the game are as follows:

a. Decide on the order amount of regular shrimp or flash-frozen shrimp and enter the figures in column 3 of the worksheet (see Exhibit S15.21). Assume that there is no opening inventory of flash-frozen shrimp.

b. Determine the amount that arrives and enter it at Orders received. To accomplish this, the referee draws a random number from a uniform random number table (such as that in Exhibit S15.4) and finds its associated level of variation from the following random number intervals: 00 to 29 = − 10 percent, 30 to 79 = 0 percent, and 80 to 99 = + 10 percent. If the random number is, say, 13, the amount of variation will be − 10 percent. Thus, if you decide to order 1,000 regular cases of shrimp and 100 flash-frozen cases, the amount you would actually receive would be 1,000 − 0.10(1,000), or 900 regular cases, and 100 − 0.10(100), or 90 flash-frozen cases. (Note that the amount of variation is the same for both regular and flash-frozen shrimp.) These amounts are then entered in column 4.

c. Add the amount of flash-frozen shrimp in inventory (if any) to the quantity of regular and flash-frozen shrimp just received and enter this amount in column 5. This would be 990, using the figures provided earlier.

d. Determine the demand for shrimp. To accomplish this, the referee draws a random normal deviate value from Exhibit S15.8 and enters it into the equation at the top of column 6. Thus, if the deviate value is −1.76, demand for the week is 800 + 100(−1.76), or 624.

EXHIBIT S15.21   Simulation Worksheet

(1)	(2)	(3) Orders placed		(4) Orders received		(5)	(6)	(7)	(8) Excess		(9)
Week	Flash-frozen inventory	Regular	Flash-frozen	Regular	Flash-frozen	Available (regular and flash-frozen)	Demand (800 + 100Z)	Sales (minimum of demand or available)	Regular	Flash	Shortages
1											
2											
3											
4											
5											
6											
7		MARDI GRAS				*					
8											
9											
10											
Total											

*Flash-frozen only.

EXHIBIT S15.22

Profit from Fish Forwarders' Operations

Revenue from sales ($50 × Col. 7)	$_____
Revenue from salvage ($4 × Col. 8 reg.)	$_____
Total revenue	$_____
Cost of regular purchases ($30 × Col. 4 reg.)	$_____
Cost of flash-frozen purchases ($34 × Col. 4 flash)	$_____
Cost of holding flash-frozen shrimp ($2 × Col. 8 flash)	$_____
Cost of shortages ($20 × Col. 9)	$_____
Total cost	$_____
Profit	$_____

e. Determine the amount sold. This will be the lesser of the amount demanded (column 6) and the amount available (column 5). Thus, if a player has received 990 and demand is 624, the quantity entered will be 624 (with 990 − 624, or 366 left over).

f. Determine the excess. The amount of excess is simply that quantity remaining after demand for a given week is filled. Always assume that regular shrimp are sold before the flash-frozen. Thus, if we use the 366 figure obtained in (e), the excess would include all the original 90 cases of flash-frozen shrimp.

g. Determine shortages. This is simply the amount of unsatisfied demand each period, and it occurs only when demand is greater than sales. (Since all customers use the shrimp within the week in which they are delivered, back orders are not relevant.) The amount of shortages (in cases of shrimp) is entered in column 9.

Profit determination. Exhibit S15.22 is provided for determining the profit achieved at the end of play. The values to be entered in the table are obtained by summing the relevant columns of Exhibit S15.21 and making the calculations.

Assignment. Simulate operations for a total of 10 weeks. It is suggested that a 10-minute break be taken at the end of Week 5 and the players attempt to evaluate how they may improve their performance. They might also wish to plan an ordering strategy for the week of Mardi Gras, when no shrimp will be supplied.

4. The manager of a small post office is concerned that her growing township is overloading the one-window service being offered. She decides to obtain sample data concerning 100 individuals who arrive for service. A data summary follows:

Time between Arrivals (minutes)	Frequency		Service Time (minutes)	Frequency
1	8		1.0	12
2	35		1.5	21
3	34		2.0	36
4	17		2.5	19
5	6		3.0	7
	100		3.5	5
				100

Using the following random number sequence, simulate six arrivals; estimate the average customer waiting time and the average idle time for clerks. RN: 08, 74, 24, 34, 45, 86, 31, 32, 45, 21, 10, 67, 60, 17, 60, 87, 74, 96

5. Thomas Magnus, a private investigator, has been contacted by a potential client in Kamalo, Molokai. The call came just in time because Magnus is down to his last $10. Employment, however, is conditional on Magnus meeting the client at Kamalo within eight hours. Magnus, presently at the Masters' residence in Kipahulu, Maui, has three alternative ways to get to Kamalo. Magnus may:

a. Drive to the native village of Honokahua and take an outrigger to Kamalo.

b. Drive to Honokahua and swim the 10 miles across Pailolo Channel to Kamalo.

c. Drive to Hana and ask his friend T. C. to fly him by helicopter to Kamalo.

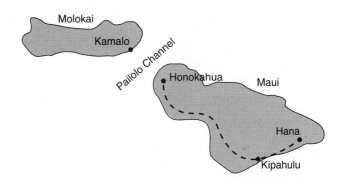

If option *a* is chosen, driving times to Honokahua are given to Distribution 1. Once at Honokahua, Magnus must negotiate with the friendly Tai natives. Negotiations always include a few Mai Tais, so if Magnus begins to negotiate, swimming becomes impossible. Negotiations center on how much each of the three outrigger crew members will be paid. Negotiation time, crew pay, and outrigger travel time are Distributions 3, 4, and 5, respectively. You may assume each crew member is paid the same amount. If crew pay totals more than $10, Magnus is out of luck—trip time may then be taken to be infinity.

If option *b* is chosen, driving times to Honokahua and swimming times are given in Distribution 1 and 6.

If option *c* is chosen, driving times to Hana are given in Distribution 2. T. C., however, is at the airport only 10 percent of the time. If T. C. is not at the airport, Magnus will wait for him to arrive. Magnus's waiting time is given by Distribution 8. T. C. may refuse to fly for the $10 Magnus has available; Magnus puts the probability of T. C. refusing to fly for $10 at 30 percent. You may assume negotiation time is zero. If T. C. refuses, Magnus will drive to Honokahua via Kipahula and swim to Kamalo. Helicopter flying times are given in Distribution 7.

Simulate each of the three alternative transportation plans *twice* and, based on your simulation results, calculate the average trip time for each plan. Use the following random numbers in the order they appear; do not skip any random numbers.

RN: 7, 3, 0, 4, 0, 5, 3, 5, 6, 1, 6, 6, 4, 8, 4, 9, 0, 7, 7, 1, 7, 0, 6, 8, 8, 7, 9, 0, 1, 2, 9, 7, 3, 2, 3, 8, 6, 0, 6, 0, 5, 9, 7, 9, 6, 4, 7, 2, 8, 7, 8, 1, 7, 0, 5

Distribution 1: Time to drive from Kipahulu to Honokahua (hours)

Time	Probability	RN
1	.2	0–1
1.5	.6	2–7
2	.2	8–9

Distribution 2: Time to drive from Kipahulu to Hana and vice versa (hours)

Time	Probability	RN
.5	.2	0–1
1	.7	2–8
1.5	.1	9

Distribution 3: Negotiation time (hours)

Time	Probability	RN
1	.2	0–1
1.5	.3	2–4
2	.3	5–7
2.5	.2	8–9

Distribution 4: Outrigger pay per crew member

Pay	Probability	RN
$2	.3	0–2
3	.3	3–5
4	.4	6–9

Distribution 5: Outrigger travel time from Honokahua to Kamolo (hours)

Time	Probability	RN
3	.1	0
4	.5	1–5
5	.4	6–9

Distribution 6: Time to swim from Honokahua to Kamalo (hours)

Time	Probability	RN
5	.2	0–1
6	.6	2–7
7	.2	8–9

Distribution 7: Time to fly from Hana to Kamalo (hours)			Distribution 8: Magnus's waiting time at airport (hours)		
Time	Probability	RN	Time	Probability	RN
1	.1	0	1	.1	0
1.5	.7	1–7	2	.2	1–2
2	.2	8–9	3	.4	3–6
			4	.3	7–9

6. A bank of machines in a manufacturing shop breaks down according to the following interarrival-time distribution. The time it takes one repairperson to complete the repair of a machine is given in the service-time distribution:

Interarrival Time (hours)	P(X)	RN		Service Time (hours)	P(X)	RN
.5	.30	0–29		.5	.25	0–24
1.0	.22	30–51		1.0	.20	25–44
1.5	.16	52–67		2.0	.25	45–69
2.0	.10	68–77		3.0	.15	70–84
3.0	.14	78–91		4.0	.10	85–94
4.0	.08	92–99		5.0	.05	95–99
	1.00				1.00	

Simulate the breakdown of five machines. Calculate the average machine downtime using two repairpersons and the following random number sequence (both repairpersons cannot work on the same machine):
RN: 30, 81, 02, 91, 51, 08, 28, 44, 86, 84, 29, 08, 37, 34, 99

7. Jennifer Jones owns a small candy store she operates herself. A study was made observing the time between customers coming into the store, and the time that Mrs. Jones took to serve them. The following data were collected from 100 customers observed:

Interarrival Time (minutes)	Number of Observations		Service Time (minutes)	Number of Observations
1	5		1	10
2	10		2	15
3	10		3	15
4	15		4	20
5	15		5	15
6	20		6	10
7	10		7	8
8	8		8	4
9	5		9	2
10	2		10	1

Simulate the system (all of the arrivals and services) until 10 customers pass through the system and are served by Mrs. Jones.

How long does the average customer spend in the system? Use Appendix B to obtain random numbers.

8. A professional football coach has six running backs on his squad. He wants to evaluate how injuries might affect his stock of running backs. A minor injury causes a player to be removed from the game and miss only the next game. A major injury puts the player out of action for the rest of the season. The probability of a major injury in a game is 0.05. There is at most one major injury per game. The probability distribution of minor injuries per game is

Number of Injuries	Probability
0	.2
1	.5
2	.22
3	.05
4	.025
5	.005
	1.000

Injuries seem to happen in a completely random manner, with no discernible pattern over the season. A season is 10 games.

Using the following random numbers, simulate the fluctuations in the coach's stock of running backs over the season. Assume that he hires no additional running backs during the season.

RN: 044, 392, 898, 615, 986, 959, 558, 353, 577, 866, 305, 813, 024, 189, 878, 023, 285, 442, 862, 848, 060, 131, 963, 874, 805, 105, 452

9. At Tucson Mills, minor breakdowns of machines occur frequently. The occurrence of breakdowns and the service time to fix the machines are randomly distributed. Management is concerned with minimizing the cost of breakdowns. The cost per hour for the machines to be down is $40. The cost of service repairpersons is $12 per hour. A preliminary study has produced the following data on times between successive breakdowns and their service times.

Relative frequency of breakdowns

Time between breakdowns (in minutes)	4	5	6	7	8	9
Relative frequency	.10	.30	.25	.20	.10	.05

Relative frequency of service times

Service time (in minutes)	4	5	6	7	8	9
Relative frequency	.10	.40	.20	.15	.10	.05

Perform a simulation of 30 breakdowns under two conditions: with one service repairperson and with two service repairpersons.

Use the following random number sequence to determine time between breakdowns:

RN: 85, 16, 65, 76, 93, 99, 65, 70, 58, 44, 02, 85, 01, 97, 63, 52, 53, 11, 62, 28, 84, 82, 27, 20, 39, 70, 26, 21, 41, 81.

Use the following random number sequence to determine service times:

RN: 68, 26, 85, 11, 16, 26, 95, 67, 97, 73, 75, 64, 26, 45, 01, 87, 20, 01, 19, 36, 69, 89, 81, 81, 02, 05, 10, 51, 24, 36.

a. Using the results of the simulations, calculate:

(1) The total idle time for the service repairpersons under each condition.

(2)   The total delay caused by waiting for a service repairperson to begin working on a breakdown.

b.   Determine the lowest-cost approach.

10.   Jethro's service station has one gasoline pump. Because everyone in Kornfield County drives big cars, there is room at the station for only three cars, including the car at the pump. Cars arriving when there are already three cars at the station drive on to another station. Use the following probability distributions to simulate the arrival of four cars to Jethro's station.

Interarrival Time (minutes)	$P(X)$	RN	Service Time (minutes)	$P(X)$	RN
10	.40	0–39	5	.45	0–44
20	.35	40–74	10	.30	45–74
30	.20	75–94	15	.20	75–94
40	.05	95–99	20	.05	95–99

Calculate the average time cars spend at the station using the following random number sequence:

RN: 99, 00, 73, 09, 38, 53, 72, 91

11.   A local motorcycle club, "The Cretins," stops at the Ranch House bar every Saturday night to sip a few brews. All Saturdays aren't peaceful, however; sometimes the guys just can't resist a good fight. Dirty Dave, the gang's leader, puts the probability of a fight at 30 percent. If a fight occurs, some of the Cretins will spend the night in jail, but the number jailed depends on how quickly the police respond. The probability distribution for number of Cretins jailed follows. Dirty Dave always pays bail for his boys Sunday morning so the club can go on its Sunday run in full force. The probability distribution for amount of bail follows (you cannot assume all riders are assigned the same bail). Because the club keeps its bail money at a local bank that does not have 24-hour teller machines, Dirty Dave must decide on Friday, before the bank closes for the weekend, how much money to withdraw. Simulate 12 Saturdays. Based on your simulation of 12 Saturdays, what is the minimum Dirty Dave must withdraw on Friday if he wants to make sure he can get everyone out?

NUMBER OF CRETINS JAILED		AMOUNT OF BAIL FOR EACH RIDER	
Number	Probability	Amount	Probability
2	.05	$ 50	.30
3	.15	100	.30
4	.40	150	.25
5	.25	200	.15
6	.15		1.00
	1.00		

RN: 92, 44, 99, 15, 97, 21, 47, 80, 28, 87, 13, 33, 42, 84, 27, 64, 59, 33, 84, 00, 10, 50, 51, 09, 31, 01, 94, 96, 77, 66, 09, 71, 69, 75, 60, 88, 54, 17, 18, 21, 04

12.   You have been hired as a consultant by a supermarket chain to provide an answer to the basic question: How many items per customer should be permitted in the fast checkout line? This is not a trivial question for the chain's management; your

findings will be the basis for corporate policy for all 2,000 stores. The vice president of operations has given you one month to do the study and two assistants to help you gather the data.

In starting this study, you have decided to avoid queuing theory as the tool for analysis (because of your concern about the reliability of its assumptions) and instead have opted for simulation. Given the following data, explain in detail how you would go about your analysis stating (1) the criteria you would use in making your recommendation; (2) what additional data you would need to set up your simulation; (3) how you would gather the preliminary data; (4) how you would set up the problem for simulation; and (5) which factors would affect the applicability of your findings to all of the stores.

Store locations:	The United States and Canada
Hours of operation:	16 per day
Average store size:	9 checkout stands including fast checkout
Available checkers:	7 to 10 (some engage in stocking activities when not at checkout stand).

S15.11 SELECTED BIBLIOGRAPHY

Bulgren, William G. *Discrete System Simulation*. Englewood Cliffs, N.J.: Prentice Hall, 1982.

Haider, S. Wali, and Jerry Banks. "Simulation Software Products for Analyzing Manufacturing Systems." *Industrial Engineering* 18, no. 7 (July 1986), pp. 98–103.

Law, Averill M. "Computer Simulation of Manufacturing Systems: Part I." *Industrial Engineering* 18, no. 5 (May 1986), pp. 46–63.

Law, Averill M., and W. David Kelton. *Simulation Modeling and Analysis*. 2nd ed. New York: McGraw-Hill, 1991.

Payne, James A. *Introduction to Simulation*. New York: McGraw-Hill, 1982.

Solomon, Susan L. *Simulation of Waiting Lines*. Englewood Cliffs, N.J.: Prentice Hall, 1983.

Watson, Hugh J. *Computer Simulation in Business*. New York: John Wiley & Sons, 1981.

Woolsey, G. "Whatever Happened to Simple Simulation? A Question and Answer." *Interfaces* 9, no. 4 (August 1979), pp. 9–11.

Chapter 16

Materials Management and Purchasing

EPIGRAPH

The lowest-cost item is not always the cheapest.

$\mathbf{G}$one are the days when a firm purchased a few raw materials and then, by adding a great deal of labor, produced a marketable product. Today, direct labor accounts for only 7 to 10 percent of the cost of goods sold. What accounts for most of the cost? Purchased materials, parts, and components account for 60 to 70 percent of the cost of goods sold. One more statistic is that materials handling adds approximately 14 percent to the cost of goods sold.

One of this text's authors was a consultant to a firm planning to phase in some aspects of Just-in-Time manufacturing. It was apparent in just walking through the plant that something was seriously wrong. There were large amounts of partially completed product sitting idle throughout. This firm, with annual sales of just over $100 million, had a purchased items cost of $67 million!

It was almost impossible to walk into the purchasing department without tripping on books and catalogs strewn all over the floor, and stacked on desks and tables. This was a five-person (including two newly hired), one-room activity. It was virtually impossible for them to keep up. They could not follow up on late orders; they did not have time to search for the best materials, lowest cost, or best vendors. To save time, they ordered in much larger quantities to try to stock up so they wouldn't be bothered with having to purchase this product again for a few months. It was a state of chaos.

The plant manager was questioned as to how he could tolerate this condition. He responded that the company was trying to cut costs; it wouldn't be acceptable to add purchasing and other materials handling personnel. After further private discussion with shop personnel to confirm the obvious, the author advised the plant manager that purchasing and materials management was in a sorry state. Purchased items sat on the loading docks and other convenient drop-off locations for as long as two to three weeks before being tested, if necessary, and logged into the plant inventory.

This plant was the dream of an operations management person. There were opportunities for improvement everywhere one turned. Materials management, from purchasing through movement, through control was handled very poorly. There seemed to be no question that just in purchasing alone, at least 1 percent of the purchasing costs could be saved just by vendor selection, order sizes, and delivery schedules. And 1 percent of $67 million is a tidy sum! The plant manager did not implement the recommendations, nor did he seem particularly concerned about the seriousness of his position. Less than a year later, the parent company closed the plant.

The many changes that have taken place in purchasing, materials handling, and distribution systems have been brought on by:

1. Competitive pressures from foreign firms.
2. Elevation of product quality to a very high level of importance.
3. International marketing and international purchasing.
4. Trends toward choosing sole-source suppliers for long-term relationships.
5. Product varieties and ranges are rapidly changing, and speed of delivery to the market is essential.

6. Product life cycles have shortened necessitating knowledge and control of inventories in the various pipelines.

7. Adoption of Just-in-Time production has changed the supplier relationships and also focused on reducing inventories.

8. Trends in the legal system hold manufacturers liable for product failures, even though causes may be outside of the production system itself.

In this chapter we examine many of these issues in discussing how materials are obtained, how they are managed through the manufacturing system, and briefly, how they are distributed. Our objective is to help you resolve or, better yet, avoid the problems observed in the plant described above.

16.1 OVERVIEW OF MATERIALS MANAGEMENT

Materials management is defined by the American Production and Inventory Control Society (APICS) as

> The grouping of management functions supporting the complete cycle of material flow, from the purchase and internal control of production materials to the planning and control of work in process to the warehousing, shipping and distribution of the finished product.[1]

The term *logistics* is often used interchangeably with materials management. APICS has defined **logistics** in two contexts.

> In an industrial context, logistics refers to the art and science of obtaining and distributing materials and product. In a military sense (where it has greater usage), its meaning can also include the movement of personnel.[2]

In this text we favor using the term *materials management*. This emphasizes the importance of the material management function, which extends from the purchase of materials from vendors through the system and out to delivery to customers. Interestingly, firms differ in how they group these functions under a single materials management manager. Some firms, for example, may leave transportation outside of the materials management activities.

Importance of Quality in Purchasing

The average manufacturer purchases two thirds of what goes into the final product—two thirds of the cost of goods sold! Therefore, through its philosophies, knowledge of processes, knowledge of materials, and vendor selection,

---

[1] *APICS Dictionary*, 6th ed. (Falls Church, Va.: American Production and Inventory Control Society, 1987).

[2] Ibid.

EXHIBIT 16.1

Cost as a Function
of Output Quality

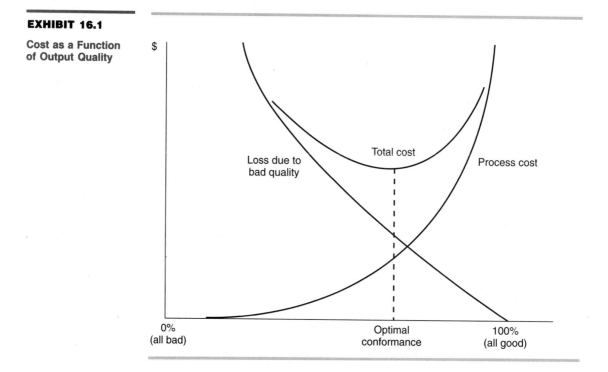

the purchasing department has twice as many opportunities to affect quality as
the production department does.

The two views of quality discussed by Wolf Reitsperger et al. are important
to compare.[3] The first, "quality is free," is the belief in a continuous quest for
perfection; the long-term payoffs include higher profits, better market share,
and so on. The second, "quality is costly," is based on the trade-off shown in
Exhibit 16.1. As quality increases, the costs for production and inspection
increase exponentially. As a general rule, each additional increment of higher
quality costs more and more to obtain. The reverse is true concerning costs of
defective product. If all product output were perfect, there would be no costs
for bad quality. Under "quality is costly" logic, the minimum point in the
total cost curve would be chosen. The "quality is costly" philosophy is said to
be the view of American management, while "quality is free" is said to be the
way Japanese managers operate.

Those who believe "quality is free" also believe in zero defects programs
that strive for perfect output. For purchasing to achieve this same high level,
there needs to be a high degree of involvement. Purchasing must closely

[3] Wolf Reitsperger, Shirley Daniel, and Abdel El-Shaieb, "Quality Is Free: A Comparative
Study of Attitudes in the U.S. and Japan," *Journal of Purchasing and Materials Management,*
Spring 1990, pp. 8–11.

EXHIBIT 16.2   **Percentage of Japanese and American Managers Adhering to Quality Is Free Concepts**

Concept	Percent 20 30 40 50 60 70 80 90 100		
1. Strategic top management involvement in managing quality	******************* 81.5% ═══════════════ 81.5%		U.S. Japan
2. Top management philosophy of working for perfection	*************** 67.8% ═══════════ 68%		U.S. Japan
3. Reject reduction does not increase long-run cost	******************** 89% ═══════ 60%		U.S.* Japan
4. AQL concept is not a superior way to manage quality	************** 63% ═════ 34%		U.S.* Japan
5. Focus on defects rather than yields	************ 62% ══════════ 71%		U.S. Japan
6. Do not accept inferior quality material even if a line stop results	***************** 78% ══════════════ 92%		U.S.* Japan
7. Do not deliver inferior quality products just to avoid an order loss	************ 57% ═══════ 50%		U.S.* Japan
8. In case of quality problem, stop the line	******************** 87% ═══════════ 63%		U.S.* Japan
9. Quality responsibility rests with production personnel rather than staff specialists	******************** 89% ═══════════ 76%		U.S.* Japan

* = Statistically significant differences.

Source: Wolf Reitsperger, Shirley Daniel, and Abdel El-Shaieb, "Quality Is Free: A Comparative Study of Attitudes in the U.S. and Japan," *Journal of Purchasing and Materials Management,* Spring 1990, p. 9.

interact with engineering, processes, quality control, and training, as well as maintain a close relationship with suppliers.

In a study of 24 Japanese electronics firms and 20 American electronics firms, the question to be answered was: "Do American managers still believe that quality is costly?" Surprisingly, Exhibit 16.2 shows that American managers have even a greater belief in the "quality is free" philosophy than the Japanese! Note from the exhibit that the American managers believe:

1. Reducing defects does not necessarily increase costs.
2. The acceptable quality level (AQL) concept is not a superior tool in managing quality.
3. The line should be stopped when a quality problem occurs.
4. Quality responsibility should be the job of production personnel rather than staff specialists.

This is a pleasant surprise and a very welcome one.

Materials Management in Various Industries

Problems encountered in materials management differ from industry to industry.[4] This is because of the types and numbers of products or services being created, the variations among suppliers and customers, the nature of the raw materials and supply inputs, and economic factors such as the values of the individual units of product or service.

Firms in the service industries are primarily concerned with procurement and material-input supplies. Their central focus is ordering, receiving, storing, and internally distributing the supplies needed to perform the service. Typical industries would be restaurants, financial institutions, distributors, government agencies, and public utilities. The output tends to be a narrow range of services or products.

In marketing firms, the output products are about the same as the input products. The marketing firm essentially performs the function of change of ownership—purchasing products, storing, selling, order picking, shipping, and so forth. Wholesalers and retailers generally carry many items purchased from many suppliers with a wide range of costs. The items are sold essentially unchanged to many customers, who tend to buy a variety of items when they shop.

Manufacturing industries tend to look like marketing firms in that there are inputs of many items from many suppliers and outputs of many items to many customers, but the input materials are changed into very different output items. The changes can be physical (such as machining parts), chemical (such as a change in molecular structure), or cumulative (created by combining parts and components, such as an assembly process). John Magee lists five activities that distinguish manufacturing materials management problems:

1. There is a major flow of materials in and out of the activity.
2. Materials physically change form in the process.
3. The change of form takes time and effort. Therefore, the conversion process occupies a great deal of the effort, capital, and managerial attention.
4. There is usually substantial internal materials management activity: flows of raw materials, parts and products within the plants themselves, and to field distribution systems.
5. Logistic activities are concerned with maintaining the flow of product in and out of the operations activity, but tend to be subordinate to the manufacturing and marketing functions. Manufacturing tends to have responsibility and a stronger control of materials flow within the manufacturing system itself, and marketing has a strong control over finished goods and distribution.

---

[4] John F. Magee, William C. Copacino, and Donald B. Rosenfield, *Modern Logistics Management, Integrating Marketing, Manufacturing and Physical Distribution* (New York: John Wiley & Sons, 1985), pp. 396–401.

16.2 MATERIALS MANAGEMENT IN MANUFACTURING

Materials management has become so important in recent years that the functions it encompasses have increased and its hierarchical position in the organization has been raised. In this section we cover the organizational placement of materials handling and some aspects of inventory control, such as bar coding and materials movement systems.

Organizational Placement of Materials Management

There is wide divergence of opinion about many aspects of materials management: where the function should be placed, what its responsibilities are, and whether it should be centralized or decentralized. While the final choice must always relate to the needs of the specific firm in question, the high cost of materials probably will support the current trend, which is to equate the materials management function with the other main functions of the organization. Such placement ensures executive-level attention to materials and gives the materials manager enough clout to be effective. A partial organization chart reflects this placement in Exhibit 16.3. Note the peculiar positioning of Production Planning and Control. This area is of utmost importance to manufacturing. As such, it may be assigned organizationally to Materials Management, but functionally to Manufacturing and physically located in the Manufacturing area.

Production planning and control is responsible for the entire manufacturing system. It schedules jobs by date, routes them through the varied resources to do the work, decides on the inventory levels, and determines process batch

EXHIBIT 16.3

Organization Chart Showing Materials Management Functions

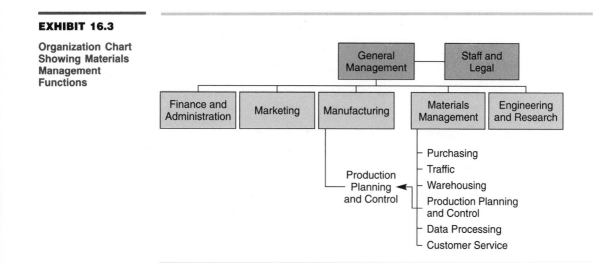

and transfer batch sizes. In other words, production planning and control sees that the manufacturing job gets done. This is why it is located within manufacturing so that personnel can closely observe the production system and respond appropriately.

Bar Coding

The term *paperless factory* refers to the flow of product through a system without the accompanying paperwork that has traditionally been part of the flow. The computer was the initial major impetus making this possible, and the next major development was the increasingly widespread use of **bar coding.**

Several bar code schedules are in use today, all involving a scanner that reads and makes sense of a series of wide and narrow lines and spaces. Exhibit 16.4 shows the characters and bar code for Code 39, and the bar code for UPC (Universal Product Code). A total of nine binary bits per symbol are used in Code 39, with wide spaces and bars representing a 1 and narrow spaces and bars representing a 0. The bar code labeled CODE 39 is reproduced wider than normal to show the lines and space corresponding to C, O, D, E, space, 3, and 9. Generally, however, the bar code uses symbols, letters, and numbers to identify an item; this scheme is then interpreted by a computer and the correct item is identified. The bar coding for #4-D silk suture thread used during operations is coded as + H206453H1A, and the UPC for purified water is 2113007446. Code 39 is widely used in manufacturing, health care, and is the system used by the Department of Defense and General Services Administration. UPC is used by retailers and wholesalers of consumer products.

Bar coding has become very important for all industries, including manufacturing and services, because it greatly simplifies inventory and production control. Using numbers to represent products allows the user to maintain a large block of information about each product—manufacturer, cost, price, order size, and weight. We've all experienced the greatly increased speed at which we can be checked out at supermarkets or department stores using bar code scanners. While the scanner identifies and prices our purchases, it is simultaneously updating inventory levels; it thus becomes part of the entire process from purchasing, receiving, stocking, moving, and distribution.

In a manufacturing environment, bar code labels attached to parts, subassemblies, and end items allow their continual monitoring. Information relayed as they pass through the process indicates where they have been and where they should go. Also, through this identification, each workstation can automatically display the processing instructions, record the processing and test results, and specify the next workstation.

In mechanized simple conveyors or more complex materials-handling systems, scanners can read the bar code and automatically route the item to its next location. The ultimate use (though expensive) can be a completely auto-

EXHIBIT 16.4   Bar Code Characters

CHARACTERS	ASCII #	CODE 39
	32	▏▊▎▊▏
✱	36	▎▎▎▎
✕	37	▌▎▎▎
✳	42	▏▊▊▎
✚	43	▏▎▎▎
—	45	▏▊▊▊
.	46	▊▏▊▊
/	47	▎▎▎▎
0	48	▌▊▊▏
1	49	▊▎▏▊
2	50	▌▊▏▊
3	51	▊▊▏▎
4	52	▌▏▊▊
5	53	▊▎▏▊
6	54	▌▊▏▊
7	55	▌▏▊▊
8	56	▊▎▏▊
9	57	▌▊▏▊
A	65	▊▌▏▊
B	66	▌▊▏▊
C	67	▊▊▏▎
D	68	▌▊▏▊
E	69	▊▌▏▎
F	70	▌▊▏▎
G	71	▎▎▊▊
H	72	▊▌▏▌
I	73	▌▊▏▌
J	74	▌▊▏▌
K	75	▊▎▎▊
L	76	▌▊▎▊
M	77	▊▊▎▎
N	78	▌▌▎▊
O	79	▊▌▎▎
P	80	▌▊▎▎
Q	81	▎▌▊▊
R	82	▊▌▏▎
S	83	▌▊▏▎
T	84	▎▎▊▏
U	85	▊▏▎▎
V	86	▏▊▎▎
W	87	▊▏▎▎
X	88	▏▎▊▎
Y	89	▊▏▎▎
Z	90	▏▊▊▎

CODE 39

Code 39

SUTURE. SILK, #4-D

+H206453H1A

UPC

Purified Water

0   21130   07446   4

Source: Reprinted from James H. Todd, "Program Constructed for On-Demand Bar Code Printing," *Industrial Engineering* 18, no. 9 (September 1986), pp. 18–24. Copyright Institute of Industrial Engineers, 25 Technology Park/Atlanta, Norcross, Georgia 30092.

mated system. Bar codes could route a job through the entire manufacturing system, such as to work centers, order the required materials and tests, and be physically moved by automatic guided vehicles or conveyers, and movement devices such as robots, mechanical diverters, or shuttle trucks—all computer controlled.

Bar code labels attached to each item can also allow automatic sorting and packaging of items flowing on a conveyer line. Even the package that then contains the sorted items can be bar coded for routing to the correct storage or shipping area.

Scanners that read bar codes can range from simple low-light-level probes to laser light-beam scanners that read the lines and spaces. Low-light-level probes using infrared or light-emitting diodes need to touch the bar code to distinguish the line and space widths. More intense light sources do not require direct contact, but still need a very short distance. The most effective scanners use laser light beams. These can be small and hand held, or they can be fixed such as positioned to read products moving along a conveyer (or products passing over it, as in a supermarket).

There are two types of laser scanners; one uses a fixed beam, which requires the operator to pass the beam over the bar code. The other type uses an oscillating or moving beam, which moves back and forth (even when the physical unit is held still) reading the bar code up to 600 times per second. In this way multiple readings of the same item increase the likelihood that the item will be read, and with a higher degree of accuracy.

Laser beam devices (a laser is a narrow beam of constant width), can read bar coding from a foot or so away. They can also read and interpret bar codes from any position—backward, forward, or sideways.

Materials Handling Systems

James Apple and Leon McGinnis are specialists in designing materials handling systems. They believe that the biggest challenge in designing materials handling systems is the development of an overall materials-flow concept, addressing the entire logistics network in both manufacturing and distribution.[5] The equipment choice is fairly straightforward, once the requirements have been established.

Apple and McGinnis state that a major problem today—especially in manufacturing—is that materials handling is an after-the-fact function, and not a "factory integrator." It should be the thread which ties the system together. They argue that materials handling is charged with moving, storing, and tracking all material, which occurs as a result of someone else doing the process planning and production scheduling. Process planning and the production scheduling and control systems should incorporate materials handling

[5] James M. Apple and Leon F. McGinnis, "Innovation in Facilities and Material Handling Systems: An Introduction," *Industrial Engineering* 19, no. 3 (March 1987), pp. 33–38.

system needs and limitations as part of their design. The final design of a materials handling system should include:

1. Handling unit and container design.
2. Micromovement (within a production workplace).
3. Macromovement (between operations).
4. Staging or storage of material.
5. Control system for directing and tracking activity.[6]

Each of these elements must also specify the level of technology, such as manual, mechanized, or fully automated.

Malcolm Sanborn describes an automated conveyer system for routing, the thermal conductor board used in IBM's top-of-the-line computer.[7] Each board weighs between 40 and 100 pounds as it passes through its processing steps. At IBM's Poughkeepsie plant, several dozen operations are performed on the board. Some are done at workstations using simple tools, others use robots, and some operations are highly technical, involving sophisticated testing. Processing times vary from 10 minutes to two hours. Several workstations could perform similar processes while others could not. Also, the complexity of the board causes the routing to change as a result of testing or the need for rework. All this causes an almost random routing that could not be controlled manually.

A conveyer system was set up under the complete control of a computer. The complex computer system included bar code readers to identify the specific boards, a main conveyer line to move the boards through the center of the plant, load/unload devices to transfer the boards from the main line to spur cars for routing to main areas, shuttle cars to transfer between spurs, and movement devices and communications between the spur and the tools, operators, and waiting work.

Trends in materials handling

Two divergent trends seem to be taking place in the United States at the present time. At one extreme is the move toward simplicity with lesser mechanization. At the other extreme is the move toward highly complex materials handling and automated manufacturing systems. While there are specific areas within which each would be more appropriate, one school of thought believes that flexibility is possible through simplicity and little capital investment, while the opposing school sees flexibility as being built into the system through elaborate machinery, controls, and materials handling devices.

The demand for large-scale automated storage systems has been decreasing for the past few years, primarily for two reasons: (1) the trend toward reducing the quantities of inventories stored, and (2) the trend toward Just-in-Time

[6] Ibid., p. 38.

[7] Malcolm A. Sanborn, "Computer Control Strategy for a Flexibility Automated System," *Industrial Engineering* 20, no. 2 (February 1988), pp. 48–52.

systems, which reduces work in process. This has, however, increased the need for smaller and more flexible systems that can be disassembled and moved easily.

Even though the trend toward Just-in-Time systems has lessened the demand for large-scale automated storage systems, demand for finished-goods warehousing systems has held constant. At the same time, new types of materials handling and storage systems have been developed.

John Hill describes some of the techniques:

1. Unit-load **automatic storage and retrieval systems** (AS/RS).   Major developments in this area include computer simulation programs that test various rules for handling materials to try to improve productivity. Also, older systems are being upgraded to enable automatic identification of items and interfacing with automatic guided vehicles (AGV).

2. Miniloads, microloads, and tote stackers.   With the trend toward maintaining small inventories, control of parts and kits is critical. Users of these devices are the automotive, airline, and electronics industries.

3. Carousels.   Vertical and horizontal carousels move the inventory storage system to the worker. Carousels have high potential because of their very low maintenance costs, as low as 0.1 percent of the original cost annually. Carousels are easily installed or, if need be, disassembled and moved to new locations.

4. Flow racks and paperless picking.   When workers pick items in conventional warehouses for orders, the potential for error is high. To increase productivity and reduce errors, some companies have assigned workers to specific inventory areas and have sent information about orders directly to them, perhaps via a CRT screen. The worker collects the needed items in the work area and presses a button to send the order on to the next inventory location, where more items are added. Results have shown error reductions of 90 percent or more, and up to 50 percent reduction in the average time to assemble the order.[8]

The demand for the materials handling systems and controls just described is expected to increase rapidly. The use of automatic guided vehicles is growing at 30 percent per year, partly because of the ease of installation. They are also being used as transporting devices to move material from one workstation to the next.

Dependency on the Production-Control System

From the standpoint of materials handling, production-control systems that rigidly specify batch production merely complicated matters. An MRP system, for example, drives the materials handling system, which can only react

---

[8] John M. Hill, "Changing Profile of Material Handling System," parts 1 and 2, *Industrial Engineering* 18, no. 11 (November 1986), pp. 68–73, and 18, no. 12 (December 1986), pp. 26–29.

to what the MRP specifies. Materials handling specialists, however, believe that much improvement can be made and would like to be part of the team that designs and controls the flow of materials and information throughout the plant. JIT systems, on the contrary, are better suited for materials handling because of the more predictable movement time and routing, and because the number of items per movement is small.

16.3 THE FIRM AS A SUPPLIER

As cartoon character Pogo might have said, "We have found a supplier, and it is us." Manufacturing firms usually view themselves as buyers; that is, they purchase components, parts, and materials, and then they produce products and services. But, who buys the components, parts, products, and services the firm produces? Manufacturing firms rarely sell directly to the consumer; some buyers are manufacturing firms who buy products and services and incorporate them into their own output. Other buyers are wholesalers, retailers, and distribution firms who buy the products and then distribute them further down the chain toward the ultimate consumers. We could probably make the statement that nature is the original supplier and the ultimate consumer is the final buyer. In between, everyone is both a buyer and a supplier. (Environmentalists, of course, would like consumers to return as much as possible to nature.)

What difference does it make whether the firm acts as the buyer from suppliers or a supplier to other buyers? Buyers talk about such things as schedules, lot sizes, costs, lead times, and Just-in-Time delivery. We often take this as a given while finding suppliers who comply with our demands. As a supplier, however, the shoe is on the other foot. Lot-size schedules sent to us by our customers may not fit our MRP schedules. Or, the Just-in-Time deliveries that we demand from our vendors may not be compatible with our job-shop production.

Some may argue that this issue—the firm as supplier—is more appropriately treated as marketing. As we look closely, though, we see the mirror image of our production planning, scheduling, and control in our customers.

Randy Myer has made some interesting points concerning the need to understand the customer, to be able to evaluate the customer's costs, and even to decide whether the customer is worth keeping.[9] He reminds us that the balance of power in some areas is changing from the supplier to the buyer. In the retail business, average net return is 1 percent of sales. Suppliers average 4 percent net return! In the United Kingdom, the reverse is true in food retailing; retailers average 4 percent and suppliers 1 percent.

---

[9] Randy Myer, "Suppliers—Manage Your Customers," *Harvard Business Review,* November–December 1989, pp. 160–68.

Revenue less:

    Cost of goods sold
    Reserves for damaged and returned merchandise
    Discounts and allowances

= Gross margin less:

    Sales cost
    Promotion cost (excluding media advertising)
    Product development cost
    Direct warehousing cost
    Customer freight cost
    Postsale service cost

= Customer contribution to overhead divided by:

    Direct asset costs
        Accounts receivable
        Inventory (finished goods)

= Customer return on assets

Source: Randy Myer, "Suppliers—Manage Your Customers," *Harvard Business Review*, November–December 1989, p. 162.

Myer suggests that firms should evaluate customers similarly to the way they calculate their own return on assets. Companies can use the customer return on assets (CRA) to measure the marketing, selling, and product development costs, as well as asset investments in inventory and receivables that they can attribute to each of their customers. Exhibit 16.5 shows the elements involved. Once the CRA has been computed for customers, further actions may be indicated; these range from promoting greater efforts to further develop high-return customers to severing relationships with others.

Exhibit 16.6 shows interesting findings by a packaged-goods company: Profitability is not a function of customer size; rather, profitability is a function of customer growth rate, though negatively. Fast-growing companies take advantage of their suppliers in relative buying, pressuring for cost reductions, taking full advantage of return allowances, or demanding Just-in-Time deliveries, payment schedules, and so on. The result of this CRA effort to evaluate customers is a better understanding of the customer, of the customer's needs, of where lines should be drawn, and of what deviations are possible.

16.4 PURCHASING

Concerning the control of costs, purchasing is by far the most important area in the firm because two thirds of the cost of goods sold are purchased items. We say elsewhere that design has the major impact on costs. But that is true

EXHIBIT 16.6

Profitability from a Customer versus Customer Size and Customer Growth Rate

As a packaged-goods company found, profitability is usually not a function of customer size

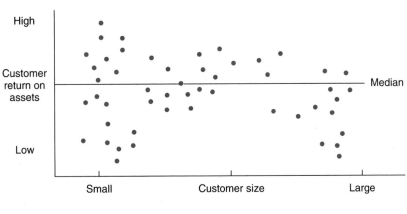

. . . but a function of customer growth rate

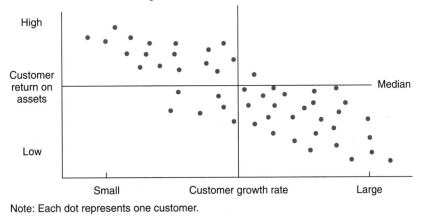

Note: Each dot represents one customer.

Source: Randy Myer, "Suppliers—Manage Your Customers," *Harvard Business Review,* November–December 1989, p. 165.

only when the design, manufacturing, and purchasing relationships are not run correctly. It is purchasing's responsibility to know what's out there. Purchasing needs to know materials, performance, availability, and suppliers. They need to know (as they should know) which features of purchased products are cosmetic and which features are functional. This directs them in their search for sources which support requirements.

In this section we discuss value analysis, the issues of single- versus multiple-sourcing, long-term manufacturer/supplier relationships, and some specific issues in Just-in-Time purchasing.

Value Analysis

An approach widely used by purchasing departments is **value analysis.** The basic idea is to compare the function performed by a purchased item with its cost in an attempt to find a lower-cost alternative. Exhibit 16.7 summarizes this approach. We must stress, though, that cost is only one issue in the broad scheme of things. Other factors that we discuss later include quality, delivery performance, technical knowledge, and compatibility.

The Purchasing Organization

Harold Fearon conducted a major purchasing organization research study of 297 large U.S. corporations in 23 industry groups, primarily in the manufac-

---

EXHIBIT 16.7

The Value Analysis Approach: Comparison of Function to Cost

I. Select a relatively high cost or high volume purchased item to value analyze. This can be a part, material, or service. Select an item you suspect is costing more than it should.

II. Find out completely how the item is used and what is expected of it—its *function*.

III. Ask questions:
  1. Does its use contribute value?
  2. Is its cost proportionate to usefulness?
  3. Does it need all its features?
  4. Is there anything better, at a more favorable purchase price, for the intended use?
  5. Can the item be eliminated?
  6. If the item is not standard, can a standard item be used?
  7. If it is a standard item, does it completely fit your application or is it a misfit?
  8. Does the item have greater capacity than required?
  9. Is there a similar item in inventory that could be used?
  10. Can the weight be reduced?
  11. Are closer tolerances specified than are necessary?
  12. Is unnecessary machining performed on the item?
  13. Are unnecessarily fine finishes specified?
  14. Is commercial quality specified?
  15. Can you make the item cheaper yourself?
  16. If you are making it now, can you buy it for less?
  17. Is the item properly classified for shipping purposes to obtain lowest transportation rates?
  18. Can cost of packaging be reduced?
  19. Are you asking your supplier for suggestions to reduce cost?
  20. Do material, reasonable labor, overhead, and profit total its cost?
  21. Will another dependable supplier provide it for less?
  22. Is anyone buying it for less?

IV. Now:
  1. Pursue those suggestions that appear practical.
  2. Get samples of the proposed item(s).
  3. Select the best possibilities and propose changes.

Source: Michael R. Leenders, Harold E. Fearon, and Wilbur B. England, *Purchasing and Materials Management*, 7th ed. (Homewood, Ill.: Richard D. Irwin, 1980), p. 516.

turing sector.[10] The study focused on the size of the professional purchasing staff, the reporting mechanisms, organizational placement, and some characteristics of the chief purchasing officer.

The findings were quite interesting and are summarized in Exhibits 16.8 and 16.9.

The first question in the study related to the number of firms that operated under a material management manager. For this study, Fearon defined the materials management concept as

> An organization in which at least three of the functions of purchasing, inventory management, production scheduling and control, inbound traffic, warehousing and stores, and incoming quality control report to a single responsible individual.[11]

In the survey, 70 percent of the firms indicated they operated under this concept. Exhibit 16.8 shows the various functions handled by materials managers. Inventory management, purchasing, and warehousing and stores were the three most common functions. Following these were inbound traffic, production and inventory control, and incoming quality control. This, incidentally, does not question the existence of materials management as we discussed in the opening paragraph to this chapter, but rather states that some functions have been combined under an organizational structure and responsibility.

Size of professional purchasing staffs. A total of 35,000 professional personnel were employed in the 297 companies in the survey. Extrapolating this to the Fortune 1000 would indicate that more than 100,000 professional purchasing personnel are employed in this group. The average number for the surveyed companies was 118.

Centralized-decentralized purchasing. Twenty-eight percent of the firms are centralized. These tend to be smaller firms. Fifty-eight percent of the firms use a combination where purchasing is done at corporate headquarters as well as major operating divisions and plants.

Reporting relationship. Purchasing reports to the president in 16 percent of the organizations and the executive VP in 18 percent. The most common reporting relationship is to the manufacturing/production/operations vice president (24 percent). Other relationships are administrative vice president (13 percent), material management vice president (7 percent) and engineering vice president (1 percent). In 33 percent of smaller firms, purchasing reports to the manufacturing/production/operations vice president.

---

[10] Harold E. Fearon, "Organizational Relationships in Purchasing," *Journal of Purchasing and Materials Management,* Winter 1988, pp. 2–12.

[11] Ibid., p. 8.

EXHIBIT 16.8   Organization of Material Management and Purchasing in Large Corporations

	Percent
Organization does use materials management concept	70%

Functions Included under the Materials Manager's Functions

Purchasing	86%
Inventory management	90
Production scheduling and control	59
Inbound traffic	67
Warehousing and stores	84
Incoming quality control	25

		PERCENT OF FIRMS BY FIRM SIZE IN SALES			
	Ave	Under $500 Million	$500 Million to $1 Billion	$1.1–5 Billion	$5.1–10 Billion	Over $10 Billion
Average number of professional purchasing personnel	118	14	42	71	366	485
Centralized, in which all, or almost all, purchasing is done at one central location for the entire firm		44%	33%	20%	16%	15%
Centralized–decentralized, in which some purchasing is done at the corporate headquarters and purchasing also is done at major operating divisions/plants		42	53	57	74	74
Decentralized, in which purchasing is done on a division/plant basis		14	13	13	10	11

To Whom Purchasing Reports	Organizations Responding
President	16%
Executive vice president	18
Financial vice president	7
Manufacturing/production/ operations vice president	24
Materials management vice president	8
Engineering vice president	1
Administrative vice president	13
Other	12
	99

Functions that Report to Purchasing	Organizations
Inbound traffic	10%
Outbound traffic	1
Both inbound and outbound traffic	31
Warehousing or stores	34
Inventory management	37
Scrap/surplus disposal	57
Receiving	26
Incoming inspection	16
Other	27

Source: Harold E. Fearon, "Organizational Relationships in Purchasing," *Journal of Purchasing and Materials Management,* Winter 1988, pp. 5–10.

EXHIBIT 16.9

Characteristics of
Chief Purchasing
Officers in Large
Corporations

Title	Percent
Purchasing agent	2%
Manager of purchasing	37
Director of purchasing	39
Vice president of purchasing	6
Materials manager	6
Director of material	2
Vice president of materials management	5
Other	2
Total	99

Education	Percent
High school	6%
Bachelor's degree	55
Bachelor's and graduate degree	39

Bachelor's Degree	Percent
Business	55%
Engineering	19
Liberal arts	13
Other	13

Experience in All Functional Areas

Purchasing	17.0 years
Operations/production	4.0
Marketing	1.6
Engineering	1.3
Traffic	1.0
Finance	.8
Accounting	.6
MIS	.5
Other	.7

Average years in present position   6

Average years with present employer   18

Source: Harold E. Fearon, "Organizational Relationships in Purchasing," *Journal of Purchasing and Materials Management,* Winter 1988, pp. 8–12.

Functions reporting to purchasing.   Scrap/surplus disposal reports to purchasing in 57 percent of the organizations because purchasing has the best information and most knowledge about market values for scrap. Inbound traffic reports to purchasing in 41 percent of the firms due to the importance of sourcing, shipment methods, and prices paid. Other groups reporting to purchasing include: warehousing, 34 percent; outbound traffic, 32 percent; receiving, 26 percent; and incoming inspection, 16 percent.

Chief purchasing officer.   Exhibit 16.9 shows some characteristics of the chief purchasing officer (CPO). The title varies widely but the two most common are also descriptive: manager of purchasing and director of purchasing. It's interesting to note that outside of purchasing, CPOs have the most experience in operations/production. CPOs have been in their positions for an average of 6 years and with their present employers 18 years. All but 6 percent are college graduates with 39 percent holding graduate degrees. Business was the most common bachelor's degree.

In summary, Fearon states, "The purchasing function has become broader in scope and responsibility and the chief PO needs to have a more varied background with a wider range of experiences to cope with the evolving increased job requirements."[12]

Multiple Suppliers versus Few Suppliers

Historically, the objective of purchasing and materials management has always been to have two or more suppliers. The thinking was that competition would drive down price and reduce the risk of supplies being cut off. JIT production, with its critical need for quality, and the new worldwide emphasis on quality products, is changing the buyer/supplier relationship.

In the early 1980s, American automobile manufacturers accepted materials, parts, and components with 1 to 3 percent defect rates. That amounts to 10,000 to 30,000 defects per million incoming parts! This defect rate is no longer acceptable.

Xerox Corporation lost half of its worldwide market share in copiers from 1976 to 1982. Xerox had over 5,000 suppliers and spent 80 percent of manufacturing cost on purchased materials. To try to turn the company around, Xerox reduced its suppliers to just 400 and trained them in statistical process control, total quality control, and Just-in-Time manufacturing. As a result, product costs were greatly reduced, reject rates were reduced by 93 percent, and production lead time was reduced from 52 weeks to 18 weeks.

Working closely with fewer suppliers has many rewards. General Electric Company, for instance, publicizes the names of its best suppliers and awards them better contracts. GE's Appliance Division invites its 100 best suppliers to its annual "Supplier Appreciation Day."

To compete effectively in world markets, a firm must have high-quality suppliers with acceptable costs and timely delivery. CPOs should compile lists of approved suppliers and then create supplier development programs to improve the suppliers' technical ability, quality, delivery, and cost. More than 70 percent of the companies in one survey had approved buyer lists.[13]

Typically and historically, subcontracting is multiple sourced and adversarial in the United States. In Japan subcontracting is single sourced and cooperative. The Western view is that single sourcing is a high risk for the buyer. Japan's single-sourcing tradition, however, may not be one of successful long-term sharing. It appears that the power is in the hands of the big buyers. John Ramsay states that so unbalanced is power in the supplier network in Japan that suppliers are more like off-site workshops of the

---

[12] Harold E. Fearon, "Organizational Relationships in Purchasing," *Journal of Purchasing and Materials Management,* Winter 1988, p. 2.

[13] Richard E. Plank and Valerie Kijewski, "The Use of Approved Supplier Lists," *International Journal of Purchasing and Materials Management,* Spring 1991, pp. 37–41.

buyer.[14] The advantage to the buyer is that during economic down periods, the subcontracted work can be brought back into the buyer's plant. The buyer's firm can maintain stable employment while the supplier has a feast-or-famine existence. There may be more differences between Japanese and Western cultures than there are similarities.

In an attempt to improve their suppliers' quality, each year Pitney Bowes (PB) sends its purchasing personnel and quality engineers to visit vendors. They take along video cameras to tape operations on each supplier's shop floor. Back at PB, design and manufacturing engineers examine the tapes to learn which equipment the supplier uses and the line operator's performance in running that equipment. They also use the videos as excuses to talk with the supplier's workers to ascertain their attitude toward quality. As a result of these visits, some suppliers were removed from the vendor list. Suppliers are also brought to PB. During vendor days suppliers see PB's operation and obtain a better understanding of their participation in PB's production process. Suppliers are also taught statistical process control if necessary. PB has found that suppliers make very useful suggestions on materials, design, and so on.

Texas Instruments perceived quality as being so important that they instituted a 13-step certification program. Results proved the program to be a very good one.

Ford Motor Company issues long-term (three to five year) contracts to vendors.[15] Practically every part is single sourced. Suppliers become involved during the design phase. Simultaneous engineering means that the design of a part depends on how it is to be made, and conversely, the process to be used to make a product influences its design. The early involvement of the supplier is very important because suppliers are experts in their areas. They certainly know more about their processes than Ford, so their knowledge influences Ford's designs.

One other interesting note on Ford's supplier relationship. In the supplement to Chapter 11 we discussed learning curves. We stated that continuous production improves performance. Since Ford's long-term contracts allow the effects of learning to really take hold and be significant, Ford attached clauses to reduce prices each year. This cost reduction was recognized to be a side benefit of the relationship and should be shared by Ford as well.

Single-Source Supplier Qualification

Choosing a company to be the **single-source supplier** to a manufacturer is a very important procedure because buyer/supplier relationships can last for years. Qualifying a supplier is a team effort directed by the buyer. Members of

---

[14] John Ramsay, "The Myth of the Cooperative Single Source," *Journal of Purchasing and Materials Management*, Winter 1990, pp. 2–5.

[15] "Suppliers Get Early Call at Ford," *Purchasing*, May 10, 1988, pp. 88–91.

the team include purchasing, quality assurance, design engineering, manufacturing engineering, operations, accounting, and industrial engineering. The buyer's team examines various areas of a supplier's operation. Richard Newman lists seven measures teams can use to evaluate a potential supplier:

1. Equipment capability. Can the supplier's equipment produce the product required by the buyer at the appropriate quality level? A process capability index (PCI) is a useful measurement. PCI is normally defined as the absolute design tolerance of the machine or process, divided by six standard deviations of the machine or process actual performance (at a PCI = 1, this includes 99.7 percent of the total output, which is $+/-3$ standard deviations).

$$PCI = \text{Absolute design tolerance}/6\ \sigma$$

For many firms, especially those operating with Just-in-Time, three defects per 1,000 would be unacceptable. Therefore, the PCI may be defined as parts per million or

$$PCI = \text{Absolute design tolerance}/12\ \sigma$$

The supplier's equipment and processes must be capable of producing to the buyer's needs. (Limits of 12 standard deviations would allow only about 4 defects per million.)

2. Quality assurance. The supplier's quality control procedures are examined to determine

a. Where and whether incoming inspection takes place.
b. The use of statistical process control by the supplier's sources.
c. The supplier's use of statistical process control.
d. Work in process inspection methods.
e. Measurement devices and calibration.
f. Procedures for handling rejected raw materials.
g. Final inspection and packaging procedures.
h. Packaging, inspecting, and testing procedures.

Because quality begins at the supplier, equipment and process and quality control are essential.

3. Financial capability. This measure is the risk of doing business, especially over the long term. Typical measures are

a. Clout ratio (Buyer's annual order value/Supplier's sales).
b. Current ratio (Current assets/Current liabilities).
c. Quick ratio [(Current assets − Inventory)/Current liabilities].
d. Inventory turnover (Sales/Inventory).
e. Collection period (Receivables/Sales per day).

These measures indicate the financial health of the firm and the clout ratio indicates the potential value of the buyer to the supplier.

4. Cost structure. A firm must know the supplier's cost structure if a long-term relationship is to be considered. This includes materials, direct labor, overhead, sales and administrative costs, and profits as well. The buyer should know that costs are reasonable and what the future costs might be. Profits or costs that are too low, for example, would create future problems.

5. Supplier value analysis effort. Because the buyer/supplier relationship is intended to be ongoing, the buyer should expect improvements in the supplier and should participate in value analysis programs. Value analysis means that the supplier must

a. Understand the need for all product specifications.

b. Know which specifications are critical to performance.

c. Know which specifications are cosmetic.

The potential supplier's past history in value analysis programs should be examined as to the type of projects attempted, degree of success, and so forth.

6. Production scheduling. The supplier's methods for production scheduling and control can affect how the buyer's orders fit into the system. Existing capacities, methods of expediting, and follow-up procedures, are important issues. Also, since production schedules are shared so that both buyer and seller can plan, compatibility of scheduling techniques is desirable.

7. Contract performance. How is performance by the supplier to be measured? While these evaluations need to be specified, they should not become a burden in the form of bulky reports. Ideally, contract performance should be on an exception basis, with only the variations creating attention.[16]

Qualifying a supplier can be time-consuming and expensive. However, the intent is to have a long-term, mutually beneficial relationship, wherein the costs and time have been well spent.

Purchasing managers believe they are on the right track in evaluating suppliers. James Morgan and Susan Zimmerman conducted the survey in Exhibit 16.10. They discovered the traits buyers look for in suppliers and the approaches buyers use to select new buyers. As shown in Exhibit 16.10, the major method, at 50 percent, was to do a technical evaluation of the supplier and then award a small amount of business as a performance test. Another survey, depicted in Exhibit 16.11, showed that quality was the most important characteristic of a supplier's performance. Delivery performance was second.

Purchasing professionals prefer having a small number of **qualified suppliers** because

1. Supplier development is costly.

2. The objective is a closer working relationship.

3. Fewer suppliers can be rewarded with substantial business.

---

[16] Richard G. Newman, "Single Source Qualification," *Journal of Purchasing and Materials Management,* Summer 1988, pp. 10–17.

EXHIBIT 16.10

Selecting and Testing Prospective New Suppliers

Traits Buyers Check First in Scanning New Suppliers

1. Quality capability.
2. Technical competence.
3. Process control.
4. Pricing/cost factors.
5. Financial stability.
6. Engineering/manufacturing support.
7. Management.
8. Delivery.
9. Service record.
10. Training programs.
11. Plant location.

How Buyers Handle Supplier Prospects

Percent	Approach
50%	Perform a technical and then give the potential supplier a limited amount of business to test out performance in a production situation.
25	Add the potential supplier to bid lists and make a technical evaluation after bids come in.
20	Add the potentially hot supplier to request for bid lists once a technical evaluation is made.
18	Perform a technical evaluation as soon as a potentially good supplier is spotted—without a specific job in mind.
6	Use all of the above approaches at one time or another.
1	Use an established rating system to measure the new prospect.

Note: Percentages do not add up to 100 percent because of use of multiple approaches.

Source: James P. Magan, and Susan Zimmerman, "Status Report: Building World-Class Supplier Relationships," *Purchasing*, August 16, 1990, pp. 62–65.

EXHIBIT 16.11

What's Important in Supplier Performance

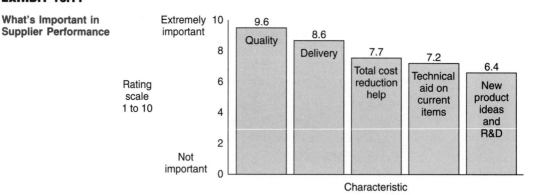

Source: Somerby Dowst, "Quality Suppliers: The Search Goes On," *Purchasing*, January 28, 1988, pp. 94A4–94A12.

Partnership Relationships: Buyer/Supplier

A **strategic partnership** between a buying firm and a supplying firm is defined as a mutual, ongoing relationship involving a commitment over an extended time period, an exchange of information, and acknowledgment of the risks and rewards of the relationship.

In addition to cost, quality, and delivery reliability, supplier selection criteria includes factors such as management compatibility, goal congruence, and strategic direction of the supplier firm. Exhibit 16.12 shows supplier selection models currently in use. The first model used by Texas Instruments weights the suppliers according to Texas Instruments' benchmarks. The second one, used by IBM, is a mathematical model that looks only at cost-based factors. The objective of the IBM model is to minimize costs.

All of the models try (1) to make the supplier selection process more objective and (2) to quantify the criteria. While these measures are qualitative, the firms need to develop some sort of scale or weighting system for each factor. The important point here is that the buyer/vendor partnership can be a very long one and therefore should be evaluated carefully.[17]

EXHIBIT 16.12

Summary of Prescriptive Research Reviewed

Study	Model
Models currently in use	
Gregory (1986)	Matrix model that weights supplier selection factors, based on predetermined, written benchmarks (Texas Instruments)
Bender et al. (1985)	Mixed integer-linear programming model, (IBM), generated by a user-friendly artificial intelligence interface
Other models	
Timmerman (1986)	1. Categorical approach that rates suppliers on a number of equally weighted factors. 2. Cost ratio method which quantifies all internal costs associated with conducting business with a supplier as a percentage of the supplier's costs, and adds these into that supplier's cost in supplier evaluation. 3. Linear averaging approach that rates suppliers on a number of factors that are weighted by their importance.
Soukup (1987)	Payoff matrix to require purchasing to evaluate potential supplier's performance under a variety of scenarios.
Thompson (1990)	Modified weighted point approach which rates suppliers on a number of factors, weighted by importance, then evaluates supplier performance under alternative scenarios by using a Monte Carlo simulation technique.

Source: Lisa M. Ellram, "The Supplier Selection-Decision in Strategic Partnerships," *Journal of Purchasing and Materials Management*, Fall 1990, p. 10.

---

[17] Lisa M. Ellram, "The Supplier Selection Decision in Strategic Partnerships," *Journal of Purchasing and Materials Management*, Fall 1990, pp. 8–14.

EXHIBIT 16.13

Supplier Partnership Selection Criteria

Financial issues
  1. Economic performance.
  2. Financial stability.
Organizational culture and strategy issues
  1. Feeling of trust.
  2. Management attitude/outlook for the future.
  3. Strategic fit.
  4. Top management compatibility.
  5. Compatibility across levels and functions of buyer and supplier firms.
  6. Supplier's organizational structure and personnel.
Technology issues
  1. Assessment of current manufacturing facilities/capabilities.
  2. Assessment of future manufacturing capabilities.
  3. Supplier's design capabilities.
  4. Supplier's speed in development.
Other factors
  1. Safety record of the supplier.
  2. Business references.
  3. Supplier's customer base.

Source: Lisa Ellram, "The Supplier Selection-Decision in Strategic Partnerships," *Journal of Purchasing and Materials Management*, Fall 1990, p. 12.

What to look for when choosing a supplier to form a partnership
Exhibit 16.13 shows four major areas of importance: First, financial issues—both firms are concerned with the financial conditions of their potential partners. Second, organizational culture and strategy. This is difficult to evaluate; much is gut feeling and personality fits among the individuals in each firm. Third, technology issues. The buying firm is looking for a supplier who has high technological capability and the ability to help in designing the buying firm's new products. The fourth area includes miscellaneous factors affecting business practices and performance.

Just-in-Time Purchasing

Just-in-Time purchasing is a major element of Just-in-Time (JIT) systems, discussed in Chapter 6. The basic idea behind Just-in-Time purchasing is to establish agreements with vendors to deliver small quantities of materials just in time for production. This can mean daily or sometimes twice-daily deliveries of purchased items. This approach contrasts with the traditional approach of bulk buying items that are delivered far in advance of production. The critical elements of JIT purchasing are

- Reduced lot sizes.
- Frequent and reliable delivery schedules.

- Reduced and highly reliable lead times.
- Consistently high quality levels for purchased materials.[18]

Each of these elements constitutes a major benefit to the purchasing firm, not the least of which is shortening the procurement cycle.

The ultimate objective should be a single reliable source for each item and the consolidation of several items from each supplier. The result is far fewer suppliers in total. U.S. companies that have implemented JIT purchasing through fewer suppliers have obtained the following benefits:

1. Consistent quality. Involving suppliers during the early stages of product design can consistently provide high-quality products.

2. Savings on resources. Minimum investment and resources, such as buyer's time, travel, and engineering are required with a limited number of suppliers.

3. Lower costs. The overall volume of items purchased is higher, which eventually leads to lower costs.

4. Special attention. The suppliers are more inclined to pay special attention to the buyer's needs, since the buyer represents a large account.

5. Saving on tooling. Buyers often provide tools to their suppliers. Concentrating on only one supplier therefore saves a great deal of tooling costs.

6. The establishment of long-term relationships with suppliers encourages loyalty and reduces the risk of an interrupted supply of parts to the buyer plant; this may be the most important benefit of all.[19]

JIT as an operating concept is a hot topic these days, but we must be careful not to become so captivated by the glamorous JIT single-source philosophy that we overlook the many occasions when multiple sourcing is justified. It is often advantageous to have suppliers compete for a firm's business. In addition to possible lower prices, during the interviewing and information in dealing with several vendors, the buyer can gain a lot of technical knowledge about the product—in many cases much more than from dealing with only one vendor. Also, many materials, parts, and supplies are critical to a firm's continued operation, and any shutdown by a vendor—some sort of labor dispute or calamity such as a major fire or accident—can significantly hurt. The Department of Defense must purchase military and critical supplies from more than one source. This is done to reduce the risk of an enemy destroying the source

---

[18] Chan K. Hahn, Peter A. Pinto, and Daniel J. Bragg, " 'Just-in-Time' Production and Purchasing," *Journal of Purchasing and Materials Management,* Fall 1983, p. 5.

[19] Sang M. Lee and A. Ansari, "Comparative Analysis of Japanese Just-in-Time Purchasing and Traditional U.S. Purchasing Systems," *International Journal of Operations and Production Management* 5, no. 4 (1985), pp. 5–14.

EXHIBIT 16.14

Characteristics of JIT Purchasing

Suppliers

Few suppliers
Nearby suppliers
Repeat business with same suppliers
Active use of analysis to enable desirable suppliers to become/stay price competitive
Clusters of remote suppliers
Competitive bidding mostly limited to new part numbers
Buyer plant resists vertical integration and subsequent wipeout of supplier business
Suppliers are encouraged to extend JIT buying to *their* suppliers

Quantities

Steady output rate (a desirable prerequisite)
Frequent deliveries in small lot quantities
Long-term contract agreements
Minimal release paperwork
Delivery quantities variable from release to release but fixed for whole contract term
Little or no permissible overage or underage of receipts
Suppliers encouraged to package in exact quantities
Suppliers encouraged to reduce their production lot sizes (or store unreleased material)

Quality

Minimal product specifications imposed on supplier
Help suppliers to meet quality requirements
Close relationships between buyers' and suppliers' quality assurance people
Suppliers encouraged to use process control charts instead of lot sampling inspection

Shipping

Scheduling of inbound freight
Gain control by use of company-owned or contract shipping, contract warehousing, and
   trailers for freight consolidation/storage where possible instead of using common carriers

Source: Richard J. Schonberger and James P. Gilbert, "Just-in-Time Purchasing: A Challenge for U.S. Industry," *California Management Review*, Fall 1983, p. 58.

of supply. Ira Horowitz notes, "Management often purchases from two or more sources to assure a source of supply, reduce the firm's uncertainty, and reduce its vulnerability to supply shortages. This accounts for the reason why obtaining the lowest cost is not the sole objective."[20]

The most critical demands placed on the purchasing department to make JIT work are (1) the need to reduce the number of suppliers and (2) locating suppliers who are nearby (see Exhibit 16.14). The strategy of single sourcing is to purchase all parts of a given kind from a single vendor. Nearby suppliers are obviously necessary to allow frequent, piece-by-piece delivery. How well purchasing handles these demands depends on the relationship the firm establishes with its suppliers. As Hahn, Pinto, and Bragg note, "Suppliers should be viewed as 'outside partners' who can contribute to the long-run welfare of the buying firm rather than as outside adversaries. The purchasing function

---

[20] Ira Horowitz, "On Two-Source Factor Purchasing," *Decision Sciences* 17, no. 2 (Spring 1986), pp. 274–79.

should look at the new system as an opportunity to reaffirm its vital role in the formation and conduct of overall corporate strategy.'[21]

JIT buyer-supplier relationship

A firm operating on a Just-in-Time basis requires that suppliers deliver very high-quality products frequently at a reasonable cost. An important significant difference between a JIT supplier and one who is not is in the ability and willingness to make frequent deliveries. As we discussed earlier in this chapter, ideal conditions suggest selecting a few high-quality suppliers with excellent design capabilities and a record of meeting delivery schedules. Thus, this long-term arrangement becomes a partnership.

Which factors are of concern for the Just-in-Time supplier? Critics of JIT state that Just-in-Time works for the buyer that sets up the JIT schedule but does not work for the supplier that must follow that schedule. This hypothesis suggests that the supplier simply delivers JIT and produces internally accord-ing to an unrelated schedule. The net result is a transfer of inventory carrying responsibilities from buyer back to supplier. In a study of 27 firms in the automobile industry, Charles O'Neal found mixed answers on this issue.[22] Twenty-two percent of the respondents perceive their suppliers to have higher inventories as a result of JIT, 30 percent about the same, and 48 percent lower. As their JIT programs continue, however, 82 percent of respondents expect their suppliers' inventories to be lower within the next five years.

In another study of 20 firms, Paul Dion, Peter Banting, and Loretta M. Hasey indicate that JIT leads to buyer's benefits of lower prices, better quality, improved service, and a reduced number of suppliers.[23] These findings are not unique to JIT environments; rather they are the result of the general trend toward preferred suppliers, single sourcing, and long-term buyer/supplier partnerships. This study did find that one of the problems was coordinating the buyer's JIT delivery with the suppliers' production schedules. One possible cause was the suppliers' commitments to other buyers.

Just-in-Time deliveries to General Motors, Ford, and Chrysler automobile plants have increased inventory turns to an averge of 40 per year compared to 8 or 9 before JIT.[24] Some Chrysler assembly plants have well over 100 turns per year. A decade ago, GM kept three months' supply of sheet steel on hand. Today, they keep three days' supply. Examples of the frequency of deliveries in the automotive industry include:

Struts arrive every four hours at Buick City.

Seats arrive every hour from a Lear Sigler plant.

---

[21] Hahn et al., " 'Just-in-Time' Production," p. 10.

[22] Charles O'Neal, "The Buyer-Seller Linkage in a Just-in-Time Environment," *Journal of Purchasing and Materials Management,* 25th anniversary issue, 1989, pp. 34–40.

[23] Paul A. Dion, Peter M. Banting, and Loretta M. Hasey, "The Impact of JIT in Indus-trial Marketers," *Industrial Marketing Management* 19, 1990, pp. 41–46.

[24] Ernest Raia, "JIT in Detroit," *Purchasing,* September 15, 1988, pp. 68–77.

Seats arrive in the exact assembly line sequence at Chrysler's Sterling Heights, Michigan; Dodge City, Montana; and St. Louis, Missouri, assembly plants.

Seats and tires arrive every hour at Honda's Marysville, Ohio, plant.

Diesel engines, axles, wheels, and tires arrive in the assembly line sequence at the Dodge plant in Warren, Michigan.[25]

Adhering to such tight delivery schedules has caused many suppliers to locate close to the buyers' plants—within 10 to 20 miles. Such moves are not absolutely necessary though. With the good roads we have in the United States and with dependable transportation, a stable schedule is more important to the supplier than the location.

16.5 PURCHASING IN THE INTERNATIONAL MARKETPLACE

Domestic suppliers cannot meet all the needs of a multinational corporation. International sourcing has become critical for meeting quality, costs, and flexibility.[26] As shown in Exhibit 16.15, the Pacific Basin countries have a labor cost advantage. For automobiles, this cost difference has been estimated to be $1,500 to $2,000 per vehicle.

Manufacturers in the United States have tried to achieve competitiveness on the labor cost issue by automating to reduce labor, buying labor-intensive components in the foreign market, and by subcontracting labor-intensive portions of production to countries with low labor costs.

EXHIBIT 16.15

Comparison of International Labor Rates, Electronics Industry, 1986

Country	Fringe Rate*	Average $ per Hour
Malaysia	25%	$ 1.44
Hong Kong	25	1.45
Taiwan	60	2.26
Singapore	35	2.59
South Korea	80	2.72
United States	46	11.90

* Percentage of hourly rate

Source: *MAPI Survey on Global Sourcing as a Corporate Strategy,* (Washington, D.C.: Machinery and Applied Products Institute, 1986).

---

[25] Ibid., pp. 68–69.

[26] Joseph R. Carter and Ram Narasimhan, "Purchasing in the International Marketplace: Implications for Operations," *Journal of Purchasing and Materials Management,* Summer 1990, pp. 2–11.

Global sourcing is a standard procedure for over half of all firms with annual sales of more than $10 million. What stands out in the list of purchased items is the small percentage of companies who purchase services. Exhibit 16.16 shows that while foreign purchases of materials, parts, and equipment range from 69 percent to 81 percent, only 16 percent of the companies surveyed purchased foreign services.

Typically, evaluating foreign suppliers is more difficult and increased costs are relevant. Exhibit 16.16 shows costs for foreign sourcing. Naturally, most of these costs differ from domestic costs because of the expenses of dealing with foreign suppliers and exchange rates.

International sourcing is a competitive weapon if used correctly. International sourcing usually requires stable production, simpler designs, reduced numbers of components, and manufactured subassemblies as well as increased quality. It also promotes greater cooperation among manufacturing, marketing, and purchasing personnel.

The top 100 industrial purchasing departments spent almost $.5 trillion on goods and services during 1989.[27] That's about 12 percent of the gross national

---

EXHIBIT 16.16

Foreign Sourcing Practices (Items purchased abroad)

Type of Purchases	Percentage of Respondents Who Partially Source Abroad
Materials	76%
Machinery and equipment	69
Component parts	81
Services	16

Cost Elements to Evaluate

1. Unit price.
2. Export taxes.
3. International transportation costs.
4. Insurance and tariffs.
5. Brokerage costs.
6. Letter of credit.
7. Cost of money.
8. Inland (domestic and foreign) freight cost.
9. Risk of obsolescence.
10. Cost of rejects.
11. Damage in transit.
12. Inventory holding costs.
13. Technical support.
14. Employee travel costs.

Source: Joseph R. Carter and Ram Narasimhan, "Purchasing in the International Marketplace: Implications for Operations," *Journal of Purchasing and Materials Management,* Summer 1990, pp. 6, 8.

---

[27] Ernest Raia, "Purchasing's Top 100," *Purchasing,* November 22, 1990, pp. 51–55.

EXHIBIT 16.17

America's
26 Largest
Purchasing
Departments

Company	$ Spent by Purchasing (millions)	% of Sales $, and % of Product Cost
General Motors	$50,566	50/60%
Ford	50,000	60/68
Chrysler	21,864	63/70
IBM	20,000	32/—
General Electric	18,500	34/—
AT&T	10,600	29/—
Du Pont	10,000	28/60
GTE	9,264	53/—
United Technologies	9,000	46/—
Boeing	8,200	41/—
Caterpillar	7,000	61/—
Xerox	7,000	40/—
Exxon	6,900	8/—
ITT	5,900	29/40
International Paper	5,800	51/—
Goodyear Tire	5,800	53/—
Union Carbide	5,600	64/75
Dow Chemical	5,400	31/60
Westinghouse	5,400	42/85
Allied-Signal	5,400	45/—
General Dynamics	5,380	54/—
Mobil	5,300	10/—
Tenneco	5,220	37/—
Shell Oil	5,064	26/—
Lockheed	5,000	51/60
Digital Equipment	4,400	34/66

Source: Ernest Raia, "Purchasing's Top 100," *Purchasing*, November 22, 1990, p. 52.

product. Exhibit 16.17 shows the top 26 of these 100 companies and the percent of purchases as compared to sales revenue and production cost. Of the 10 companies listing product cost in the last column, purchasing accounts for an average of 64.4 percent of product cost.

In the global market, service industries need logistic support as well as manufacturing industries whether it is sourcing (information or a hamburger), location (the physical distribution of products or services), or monitoring flows of material, people, information, and ideas.

For international materials management, the specific organizational form is less important than having a clear and explicit assignment of responsibility and authority. Also important is the firm's reward structure; the firm's objectives must be clearly specified and appropriately rewarded. Otherwise, individuals may establish their own objectives, such as minimizing the cost of purchasing and transportation. While important, cost minimization should not be the sought-after goal. The ultimate goal is to choose suppliers who can become strategic partners that participate from the beginning of the product design stage.

16.6 MARKETING AND DISTRIBUTION

The final phase of materials management is distribution of the finished product to the field. The distribution function, variously termed *traffic, physical distribution,* or *logistics,* is responsible for arranging the means of shipping finished goods and controlling inventory levels at various stockkeeping points in the field. Stockkeeping points are typically viewed by level or echelons, and a multiechelon system for a major manufacturer would consist of factories, a main distribution center, regional warehouses, and retail outlets.

The major concerns in managing distribution systems are deciding how much inventory is to be kept at each stock point and determining appropriate policies for inventory replenishment. The basic objective is to meet the customer's delivery requirements at a low cost. This entails a trade-off between warehousing and inventory costs and transportation costs.

One firm may follow a strategy of having many warehouses and shipping in, say, carload lots. This keeps its transportation costs low, at the expense of relatively high warehousing and inventory costs. Another firm may follow a strategy of few warehouses, low field inventory, and frequent deliveries. This keeps its warehousing and inventory costs low, at the expense of relatively high transportation costs.

The replenishment of inventory can be either as a pull system or a push system. In a pull system, warehouses order independently by pulling required items from the higher-level stocking point. The disadvantage of a pull system is that very high amplitude oscillations can occur. As the demand changes at a lower level, it becomes amplified as it passes through higher-level points and can even be doubled by the time it reaches the production facility. Production scheduling doesn't like this.

In a push system, stock levels are controlled by the production system. Forecasts are made and inventory is pushed out to the warehouse according to production's generated forecasted demand. Although this smooths out the production level, its disadvantage is that a push system is a centralized decision and not a local one. We discuss more of this under the distribution requirements planning (DRP) section in this chapter.

Warehouse Replenishment Systems

The three basic approaches to warehouse inventory replenishment are

1. The reorder point/economic order quantity system in distribution works the same way as for in-plant inventory control. The warehouse places an economic lot-size order when its inventory reaches the reorder point.

2. The base stock system works to scheduled shipment dates, and shipment size is equal to the actual usage in the previous period.

3. Distribution requirements planning (DRP) follows the logic of MRP. It converts a forecast of warehouse demand to a gross requirement, subtracts on-hand and on-order balances, and then places a replenishment order.

Of the three methods, DRP has the advantage of being based on projected demand rather than past sales. This avoids the risk of having a stockout at a central warehouse as a result of several branch warehouses reaching their reorder points simultaneously.

Distribution Requirements Planning

The American Production Inventory Control Society defines distribution requirements planning as:

> The function of determining the needs to replenish inventory at branch warehouses. A time-phased order point approach is used where the planned orders at the branch warehouse level are "exploded" via MRP logic to become gross requirements on the supplying source. In the case of multi-level distribution networks, this explosion process can continue down through the various levels of master warehouse, factory warehouse, etc., and become input to the master production schedule. Demand on the supplying source(s) is recognized as dependent, and standard MRP logic applies.[28]

DRP, from the wholesalers' and retailers' point of view pulls inventory away from the manufacturing plant. It is not necessary to go through the MPS. When items are "available to promise" in the production MRP system, they are allocated directly from MRP to DRP. If they are not available, the order is entered into the master production schedule. Using DRP, the entire distribution channel is linked together, as shown in Exhibit 16.18.

Distribution requirements planning reduces uncertainty when items are needed by summing through the channels of distribution and determining how many are available. The resemblance to MRP comes from summarizing requirements from different sources by time periods. MRP does this by summing net requirements from different product needs as gross requirements for the next lower level in the bill of materials. DRP does this summing by combining requirements from different retailers, wholesalers, local warehouses, and regional warehouses. The major difference is that DRP deals with end items only—there is no bill of materials explosion within DRP.

The advantages of DRP over forecasting are that

1. Forecasting likely comes from the manufacturer.
2. DRP comes from the distribution system. Errors—whether shortages or excesses—are caused by the distribution system itself and, therefore, are far easier to live with.

---

[28] *APICS Dictionary*, 6th ed. (Falls Church, Va.: American Production Inventory Control Society, 1987), p. 9.

EXHIBIT 16.18

Distribution Requirements Planning (DRP)

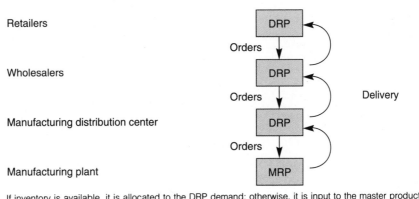

Retailers

Orders

Wholesalers

Orders   Delivery

Manufacturing distribution center

Orders

Manufacturing plant

DRP

DRP

DRP

MRP

If inventory is available, it is allocated to the DRP demand; otherwise, it is input to the master production schedule.

Demands on the production system are becoming so important to understand and to respond to that many companies are establishing a demand manager as a link between the sales department and manufacturing.

Value Density (Value per Unit Weight)

A common and extremely important purchasing decision is simply deciding whether an item should be shipped by air, or by ground transportation. While it may seem overly simplified, the value of an item per pound of weight—**value density**—is an important measure when deciding where items should be stocked geographically and how they should be shipped. In a classic Harvard case study, the Sorenson Research Company must decide whether to stock inventory for shipment at major warehouses, minor warehouses, or garage warehouses, and whether to ship by ground or air carrier.[29] Analysis shows that the time saved by shipping by air can be justified if the shipping cost is appropriate. The decision involves a trade-off: the savings of reduced transit time versus the higher cost to ship. Obviously, the solution involves a combination of methods.

We can approach the problem by examining a specific situation. Consider, for example, the cost for shipping from Boston to Tucson. Assume that the inventory cost is 30 percent per year of the product value (which includes cost of capital, insurance, decrease in warehouse costs, etc.), that regular United Parcel shipments take eight days, and that we are considering second-day air service with Federal Express. We can set up a comparison table as shown in Exhibit 16.19.

---

[29] W. Earl Sasser et al., *Cases in Operations Management* (Homewood, Ill.: Richard D. Irwin, 1982).

EXHIBIT 16.19   Sorenson Research Company Shipping Cost Comparison

Shipping Weight (pounds)	United Parcel (8 days to deliver)	Federal Express (2 days to deliver)	Cost Savings with UPS	Break-Even Product Value	Break-Even Product Value (per pound)
1	$1.91	$11.50	$ 9.59	$1,944.64	$1,944.68
2	2.37	12.50	10.13	2,054.14	1,027.07
3	2.78	13.50	10.72	2,173.78	724.59
4	3.20	14.50	11.30	2,291.39	572.85
5	3.54	15.50	11.96	2,425.22	485.04
6	3.88	16.50	12.62	2,559.06	426.51
7	4.28	17.50	13.22	2,680.72	382.96
8	4.70	18.50	13.80	2,798.33	349.79
9	5.12	19.50	14.38	2,915.94	323.99
10	5.53	20.50	14.97	3,035.58	303.56

The problem then becomes comparing the additional cost of transportation to the savings of six days. Logically we can make the general statement that expensive items can be sent by air from the factory warehouse, while lower-value items can be stocked at lower-level warehouses or shipped by a less expensive method.

Regular shipment costs − Air shipping cost = Shipping cost savings

At break-even,

$$\text{Cost savings} = \text{Inventory carrying cost}$$
$$= \frac{\text{Item value} \times 0.30 \times 6 \text{ days}}{365 \text{ days per year}}$$

Therefore,

$$\text{Item value} = \frac{365 \times \text{Cost savings}}{0.30 \times 6}$$

The last column in Exhibit 16.19 is the break-even based on the product value per pound for shipments of different weights. The exhibit indicates that any item whose value is greater than that amount should be sent by air. For example, a five-pound shipment of integrated circuits whose average value is $500 per pound should be shipped by air.

16.7 CONCLUSION

This chapter has treated materials management in the context of manufacturing, but materials management is a vitally important function in service organizations as well. Hospitals and utilities of all kinds have major materials requirements under the category of supplies. Likewise, the military has vast sums invested in materials; in fact, the Navy publishes *Naval Logistics Research Quarterly,* a major journal devoted to logistical issues. Indeed, though materials management is one of those areas that historically has received little emphasis in business schools, how well it is performed can make or break an organization.

In this chapter we looked at the importance of quality and the cost of purchased materials for the firm's products. Two thirds of the cost of goods sold are purchased materials; therefore, through its knowledge of available products the purchasing department can have a great influence on quality and cost. In qualifying suppliers, and through long-term partnerships, purchasing can enhance a firm's position and help it become a world-class business. The importance of purchasing and materials management are gaining attention and respect.

16.8 REVIEW AND DISCUSSION QUESTIONS

1. What recent changes have caused materials management and purchasing to become much more important?
2. Compare "quality is free" with "quality is costly." Which attitude would you choose?
3. When bar coding first came out, not many people took the idea seriously. What do you think about bar coding? In which areas do you think it may be used someday?
4. How are potential suppliers qualified by a firm?
5. Which characteristics of a supplier are the most important to the buyer?
6. What is meant by a *strategic partnership* between a buyer and a supplier?
7. JIT suppliers have additional pressures which other suppliers do not have. What are they?
8. Many firms have gone to other countries to buy supplies. Discuss the pros and cons of international buying.
9. What are the trade-offs in single-source versus multiple-source purchasing?
10. Which skills and training are most important for a purchasing agent?
11. The following items have been taken from the purchasing section of an MRP II audit questionnaire:

     Purchasing people believe the schedules.
     Vendor lead time is 95 percent accurate.
     Vendor delivery performance is 95 percent or better.
     Vendor scheduling is done out beyond quoted lead times.

     Explain why these items are important to MRP II success.
12. Currently you are using multiple suppliers for each purchased item. How would you go about choosing one of them to be your long-term sole source?
13. As a supplier, which factors would you consider about a buyer (your potential customer) to be important in setting up a long-term relationship?

14. What is meant by *world class* as in a world-class manufacturer and world-class supplier?"

15. "JIT purchasing is nothing more than a ploy to have vendors take over the burden of carrying inventory." Comment.

16. Distinguish between push and pull distribution systems. What are the pros and cons of each?

17. What is DRP? How does it work?

18. For the value density example given in Exhibit 16.19, what would the effect be if a competing firm offers you a similar service for 10 percent less than Federal Express's rates?

16.9 CASE: THOMAS MANUFACTURING COMPANY*

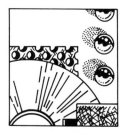

"Delivery of our 412 casting is critical. We can't just stop production for this casting every time you have a minor pattern problem," said Mr. Litt, engineer for Thomas Manufacturing.

"I'm not interested in running rejects," answered Mr. James of A&B Foundry. "I cannot overextend my time on these castings when the other jobs are waiting."

"If you can't cast them properly and on time, I'll just have to take our pattern to another foundry that can," retorted Mr. Litt.

"Go ahead! It's all yours. I have other jobs with fewer headaches," replied Mr. James.

Mr. Litt returned to Thomas Manufacturing with the 412 casting pattern. (A pattern is used in making molds in which the gray iron is formed. After cooling, the mold is broken off, leaving the desired casting.) He remembered that Mr. Dunn, vice president of manufacturing for Thomas (see Case Exhibit 1), had obtained a quote on his casting from Dawson, another gray-iron foundry, several months before. It seemed that Dawson had the necessary capabilities to handle this casting.

To Mr. Litt's surprise, Mr. Dunn was not entirely happy to find the 412 pattern back in the plant. Mr. Dunn contacted personnel at Dawson Foundry, who said that they could not accept the job because of a major facilities conversion that would take six months. Locating another supplier would be difficult. Most foundries would undertake complex casting only if a number of orders for simple casting were placed at the same time.

Mr. Dunn knew that gray-iron foundry capacity was tight. In general, foundries were specializing or closing down. Mr. Dunn had gathered some data on the gray-iron industry located within a 500-mile radius of his plant (see Case Exhibit 2), which highlighted the problems his company was facing. There were three gray-iron foundries located within 60 miles of Thomas Manufacturing. Thomas had dealt with one foundry until it suffered a 12-month strike. Thomas then moved most of its casting needs to A&B Foundry, but Mr. Dunn had given the occasional order to Dawson and requested quotes quite regularly from them. In the last four years all had gone well with

---

* From M. R. Leenders, H. E. Fearon, and W. B. England, *Purchasing and Materials Management,* 7th ed. (Homewood, Ill.: Richard D. Irwin, 1980), pp. 50–53.

CASE EXHIBIT 1

Organization Chart of
Thomas Manufac-
turing Company

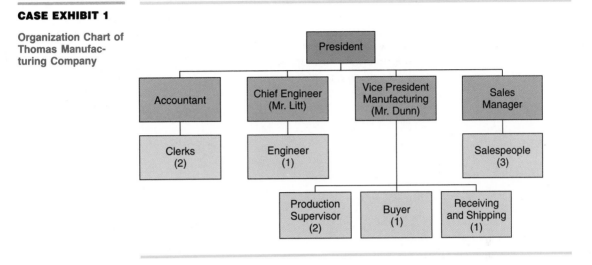

CASE EXHIBIT 2

Foundry Data for
Area within a 500-
Mile Radius of the
Thomas Plant

A. Shipments of Manufactured Goods

Gray Iron
(commerical castings)

	Quantity	Value
Previous year	280,000 tons	$65,000,000
Current year	243,000 tons	$54,000,000

B. Number of Establishments

									Current Year
140	133	131	134	137	134	134	128	126	116

Ten-Year History

A&B Foundry. Mr. Dunn had planned to share his business with both foundries. A&B was comparable to Dawson on price and had done an excellent job until now.

A telephone call back to A&B Foundry indicated to Mr. Dunn that Mr. James was adamant in his refusal to take the pattern back.

The 412 Casting

Thomas Manufacturing Company was a portable generator manufacturer with sales above the $6 million level. Thomas employed approximately 160 people in a fairly modern plant. Many of its small portable generators were sold to clients all over North America.

The 412 casting was part of the most popular middle-of-the-line generator. The casting weighed 70 pounds and cost approximately $60, and its pattern was worth $8,000. A run normally consisted of 100 castings, and Thomas usually received 100 castings every month. The 412 represented about 15 percent of Thomas's casting needs.

Normal lead time was at least eight weeks. When the supply problem arose, Thomas held six weeks' inventory.

Mr. Litt, an expert in pattern work, explained that the pattern was tricky, but once the difficulties were ironed out and the job set up, a hand molder could pour 50 castings in two days without any problems.

QUESTIONS

1. What alternatives are open to Mr. Dunn to prevent disruption of his company's most popular generator?
2. Was it appropriate for Mr. Litt to repossess the 412 pattern?
3. From the data given, does it appear that the Thomas Company has any leverage in dealing with the foundries?

16.10 CASE: OHIO TOOL COMPANY (VENDOR SELECTION)*

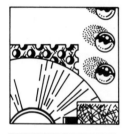

The Ohio Tool Company designed a new machine, which it considered to be superior to anything else of its type on the market. Estimated sales were about $200,000 per year. The principal advantage of this machine over competition was a unique cam arrangement enabling the operator to adjust the unit very quickly.

To achieve the advantages offered by the design, it was necessary that the cam—of which two were required per unit—be manufactured to very close tolerances (see the following sketch). Because of the difficulty of machining the several eccentric surfaces and the need for an integral locating key in the center bore, the part could not readily be made from solid bar stock.

* Source: Modified from P. E. Holden, F. E. Shallenberger, and W. E. Diehm, *Selected Case Problems in Industrial Management* (Englewood Cliffs, N.J.: Prentice Hall, 1962), pp. 123–26.

Possible methods of manufacture rapidly narrowed down to some type of casting. The materials under consideration were aluminum, zinc, and iron. Aluminum and iron sand castings were excluded because the close tolerances on the finished part would require precise and very difficult secondary machining operations. Aluminum and zinc die castings could not be used because draft or taper on the cam surfaces, required to remove the part from the die, would also necessitate secondary machining operations to render the surfaces true again.

Another possibility for producing the part seemed to be through powder metallurgy, a process by which finely divided metal particles (in this case powdered iron) were formed to the desired shape by means of high pressure in a metal die, then "sintered" at high temperature to form a solid metal piece. The Ohio Tool Company located three possible powdered-metal sources and sent parts drawings to each.

Supplier A, located about 1,000 miles away, was one of the leaders in the powder metallurgy field. The Ohio Tool Company had purchased parts for another product from this supplier within the past year, and the supplier had failed to deliver on the agreed schedule. After many delivery promises via long-distance telephone and after a special trip to the plant by the purchasing manager, the parts arrived three months late. During this delay all other parts for the project had to be set aside and some workers laid off. In addition, the delay caused the Ohio Tool Company considerable loss of face with its customers because the product had been announced to the trade.

Supplier A submitted this quotation:

Die cost—$1,968

5,000 pieces	$0.146 each	Delivery—Approximately 10 weeks, depending on the production schedule at the time order is entered.
10,000 pieces	$0.145 each	
20,000 pieces	$0.144 each	

The quotation did not include incoming freight cost of $0.012 each. Further, it was based on furnishing a cam with a slight projection on one of the surfaces, which would require a maching operation by the Ohio Tool Company at an estimated cost of $0.05 each.

Supplier B, located 300 miles away, was a relative newcomer to the powdered-metal field. The manager of the shop had been with this firm only a short time but had gained his experience from one of the old-line companies. The Ohio Tool Company's experience with this company had been very satisfactory. It had undertaken the job at the same costs as Supplier A and had produced satisfactory parts in record time.

In reply to the request for a quotation, Supplier B suggested that, since it could not manufacture to specified tolerances, they be relaxed on several dimensions. However, the engineering department at Ohio Tool insisted that the critical function of this cam necessitated the tolerances as originally specified. When this information was passed along to Supplier B, it asked to be excused from quoting.

A third supplier, with whom the Ohio Tool Company had had no previous dealings, was asked to quote on the part. Supplier C was a subsidiary of one of the large automotive concerns and had an excellent technical reputation. It was understood, however, that the parent company was considering introducing several powdered-metal parts on its line of automobiles. The quotation of Supplier C was:

5,000 pieces	$0.186 each	Die cost—$890
10,000 pieces	$0.185 each	Delivery—10 weeks
20,000 pieces	$0.183 each	

Supplier C was located 900 miles from the Ohio Tool Company plant, and incoming freight would cost $0.012 per unit. The drawing accompanying the quotation indicated a projection on one of the cam surfaces, which would have to be machined by the Ohio Tool Company for the proper functioning of the part. Although special machining techniques would be required in this case, the Ohio Tool Company estimator felt the company could machine off the projection for about $0.06 each in quantities of 5,000 or more.

Because of the past performance record of Supplier B, the purchasing manager decided that he should make an effort to obtain a quotation. He made a personal visit to the plant to discuss the problem, and learned that the plant could hold the tolerances on the center hole closer than the engineering department required, making the cumulative tolerances on the outside diameter of the cam surfaces almost within the tolerance specified. The engineering department agreed to change the drawing accordingly and grant additional latitude on the cam surfaces. On this basis, Supplier B entered the following quotation:

5,000 pieces	$0.50 each	
10,000 pieces	$0.40 each	Die cost—$1,350
20,000 pieces	$0.32 each	Delivery—10 to 12 weeks
50,000 pieces	$0.275 each	

Freight in amounted to $0.005 each. The quotation was based on a part in exact accordance with the drawing, since the cost of secondary operations had been included in the quotation and would be performed by the supplier. By the time this quotation was received, manufacture of other parts of the product was assured and final assembly was scheduled for 12 weeks from that date.

Upon reviewing all the quotations, the relatively high cost of Supplier B was readily apparent. The purchasing manager decided to call Supplier B and ask him to review his costs again. The quotation was revised:

5,000 pieces $0.45
10,000 pieces $0.37
No change in 20,000 and 50,000 price

QUESTIONS

1. Which vendor would you select for the job? Why?
2. Should a purchasing agent enter into negotiations with one vendor after bids from competitors have been examined?
3. With reference to Question 2, prepare a policy statement that would guide the future actions of the purchasing department.

16.11 SELECTED BIBLIOGRAPHY

Apple, James M., Jr., and Leon F. McGinnis, "Innovations in Facilities and Material Handling Systems: An Introduction," *Industrial Engineering* 19, no. 3 (March 1987), pp. 33–38.

A VIEW OF
MANUFACTURING

Facility Layout

The Northrop facility is a large operation broken down into small work centers.
Courtesy of Northrop Corporation

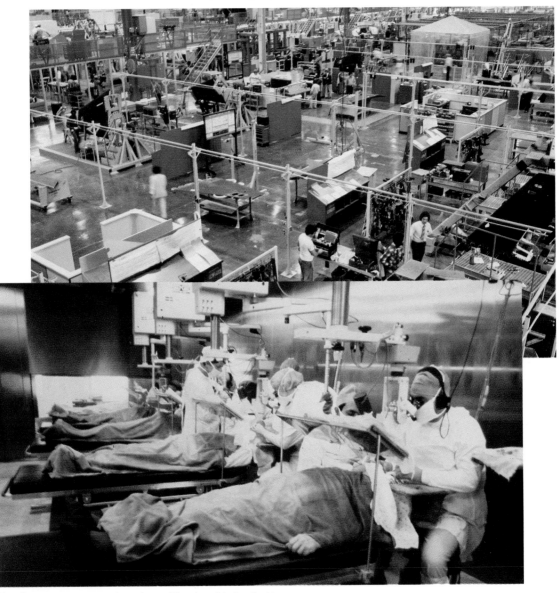

Russian cataract surgery is performed in assembly-line fashion.
Courtesy of Tass from Sovfoto

Facility Layout

As early as 1973, Volvo's Kalmar plant had done away with the traditional assembly line.
Courtesy of Volvo Cars of North America

The Human Factor

Modern manufacturing still involves people. Therefore, perhaps more than ever before, it is important to provide convenient work environments.

Compaq has tools placed hanging within easy reach of this computer assembly worker. All parts are sorted and organized in open small containers within constant view.
Reprinted with permission of Compaq Computer Corporation. All rights reserved.

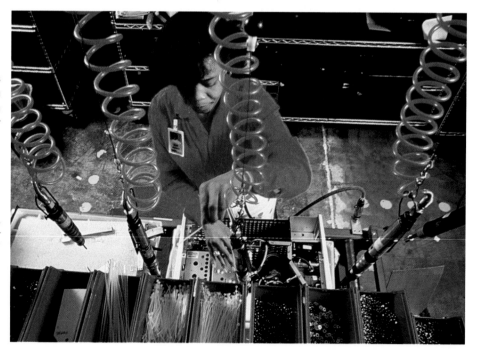

The Human Factor

Automation and Robotics

Shape Inc. has instituted a highly automated video-cassette assembly line. This operator monitors rather than does the assembly in a clean, high-speed system which enables Shape to compete effectively with rivals in Japan and Taiwan.
Courtesy of Shape Inc.

At Xerox, these automated glide vehicles are guided by wires in the floor and move around the warehouse picking and placing inventory.
Courtesy of Xerox Corporation

At the Saturn plant, this robot spot welds the frame with speed and accuracy.
Courtesy of Saturn Corporation

These modern portable car phones are assembled by high-speed robotic devices controlled by computers.
William Strode/Super Stock

Simulation

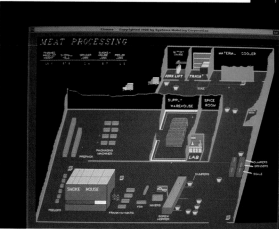

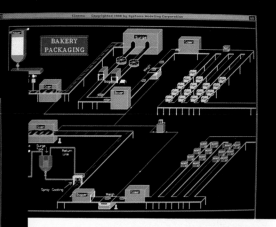

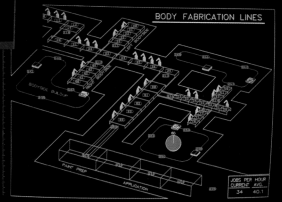

Systems Modeling Corporation makes simulation software, one of the most useful tools in designing and planning manufacturing systems. As the screen photos show, high-tech computer graphics allow their "Cinama" system to clearly picture the layout and setup of an operation. By using the underlying modeling program SIMAN, trial runs of the factory can help designers look for bugs, bottlenecks, and problems and gauge the capacity of proposed plants such as the Engine FMS system shown.

Courtesy of Peter Kauffman and Systems Modeling Corporation

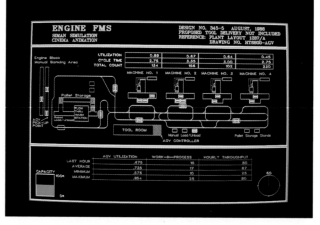

Distribution

At the Saturn Corporation, a large fleet of trucks is required to make frequent shipments of finished parts to dealers and service centers, thus avoiding the need for these retail outlets to carry unnecessarily large inventories.

Courtesy of Saturn Corporation

Albertsons, a western grocery chain, uses six full-line distribution centers, along with two "limited-line" centers. This integrated system is a major link in their high-service, forward-buying strategy.

Courtesy of Albertsons

Wal-Mart, a leading retail operation, uses its own truck fleet to resupply stores at least five times a week. This control enables them to achieve above a 99 percent reorder accuracy.

Courtesy of Wal-Mart Stores, Inc.

Ford Motor Company

Computer-aided designs (CAD) are used for accurate simulations. Here a new car idea is projected on a life-size, high-definition video screen. The image can be instantly reshaped by use of an electronic pen.
Courtesy of Ford Motor Company

An automated insertion of components on electronic engine control modules.
Courtesy of Ford Motor Company

An overhead monorail system improves the quality and efficiency of assembly operations. Here engines are being elevated into cars on a moving station.
Courtesy of Ford Motor Company

Inspectors can enter quality evaluation results into a computer via a touch pad quality control system on the plant floor.
Courtesy of Ford Motor Company

R. R. Donnelly
and Sons

This R. R. Donnelley employee is putting plates on the press roller. Such plates carry the text for the book and are printed to form 16-, 32-, or 64-page "signatures." This setup is part of the make ready phase before running hundreds to thousands of signatures.
Courtesy of R. R. Donnelley and Sons

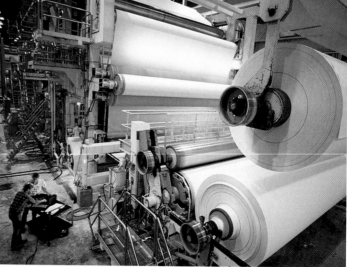

R. R. Donnelley and Sons (where this book was printed) buys paper in rolls such as those shown here.
FPG International Corporation

The signatures of text are collated, or assembled, into a book in the binding line as shown here. This photo essay, printed on a different press than the rest of the book, was inserted at this stage of assembly.
Courtesy of R. R. Donnelley and Sons

Airbus 320

Manufacturing of the Airbus 320s in France is a large-scale proposition. Here jet engines, windows, doors, and other parts are brought to the Airbus to install.

Bruno de Hogues/TSW

Bradley, Peter. "A Glimpse of Logistics of the Future." *Purchasing,* March 21, 1991, pp. 50–55.

Bragg, Daniel J., and Chan K. Hahn. "Materials Requirements Planning and Purchasing." *Journal of Purchasing and Materials Management,* 25th anniversary issue, 1989, pp. 41–46.

Burt, David N. "Managing Suppliers Up to Speed." *Harvard Business Review,* July–August 1989, pp. 127–35.

Carter, Joseph R., and Ram Narasimhan. "Purchasing in the International Marketplace: Implications for Operations." *Journal of Purchasing and Materials Management,* Summer 1990, pp. 2–11.

Dion, Paul A., Peter M. Banting, and Loretta M. Hasey. "The Impact of JIT on Industrial Marketers." *Industrial Marketing Management* 19, 1990, pp. 41–46.

Dowst, Somerby. "Quality Suppliers: The Search Goes On." *Purchasing,* January 28, 1988, pp. 94A4–94A12.

Ellram, Lisa M. "The Supplier Selection Decision in Strategic Partnerships." *Journal of Purchasing and Materials Management,* Fall 1990, pp. 8–14.

Fearon, Harold E. "Organizational Relationships in Purchasing." *Journal of Purchasing and Materials Management,* Winter 1988, pp. 2–12.

Guinipero, Larry C. "Motivating and Monitoring JIT Supplier Performance." *Journal of Purchasing and Materials Management,* Summer 1990, pp. 19–24.

Hahn, Chan K.; Charles A. Watts; and Kee Young Kim. "The Supplier Development Program." *Journal of Purchasing and Materials Management,* Spring 1990, pp. 2–7.

Jackson, Ralph W. "How Multidimensional Is the Purchasing Job?" *Journal of Purchasing and Materials Management,* Fall 1990, pp. 27–32.

Lee, Sang M., and A. Ansari, "Comparative Analysis of Japanese Just-in-Time Purchasing and Traditional U.S. Purchasing Systems." *International Journal of Operations and Production Management* 5, no. 4 (1985), pp. 5–14.

Lyons, Thomas F.; A. Richard Krachenberg; and John W. Henke, Jr. "Mixed Motive Marriages: What's Next for Buyer Supplier Relations?" *Sloan Management Review,* Spring 1990, pp. 29–36.

Millen, Anne. "How Effective Is Purchasing?" *Purchasing,* October 25, 1990, pp. 58–62.

Monczka, Robert M., and Steven J. Trecha. "Cost-Based Supplier Performance Evaluation." *Journal of Purchasing and Materials Management,* Spring 1988, pp. 2–7.

Morgan, James P., and Susan Zimmerman. "Building World-Class Supplier Relationships." *Purchasing,* August 16, 1990, pp. 62–65.

Morgan, James P., and Somerby Dowst. "Partnering for World-Class Suppliers." *Purchasing,* November 10, 1988, pp. 49–62.

Myer, Randy. "Suppliers—Manage Your Customers." *Harvard Business Review,* November–December 1989, pp. 160–68.

Newman, Richard G. "Single-Source Qualification." *Journal of Purchasing and Materials Management,* Summer 1989, pp. 10–17.

O'Neal, Charles R. "The Buyer-Seller Linkage in a Just-in-Time Environment." *Journal of Purchasing and Materials Management,* 25th anniversary issue, 1989, pp. 34–40.

Plank, Richard E., and Valerie Kijewski. "The Use of Approved Supplier Lists." *International Journal of Purchasing and Materials Management,* Spring 1991, pp. 3–41.

Presutti, William D. "Technology Management: An Important Element in the Supplier Capability Survey." *International Journal of Purchasing and Materials Management,* Winter 1991, pp. 11–15.

Raia, Ernest. "JIT in Detroit." *Purchasing,* September 15, 1988, pp. 68–77.

————. "Purchasing's Top 100." *Purchasing,* November 22, 1990, pp. 51–55.

Ramsay, John. "The Myth of the Cooperative Single Source." *Journal of Purchasing and Materials Management,* Winter 1990, pp. 2–5.

Reitsperger, Wolf; Shirley Daniel; and Abdel El-Shaieb. " 'Quality Is Free': A Comparative Study of Attitudes in the U.S. and Japan." *Journal of Purchasing and Materials Management,* Spring 1990, pp. 8–11.

St. John, Carol H., and Scott T. Young. "The Strategic Consistency between Purchasing and Production." *International Journal of Purchasing and Materials Management,* Spring 1991, pp. 15–20.

Thompson, Kenneth N. "Scaling Evaluative Criteria and Supplier Performance Estimates in Weighted Point Prepurchase Decision Models." *International Journal of Purchasing and Materials Management,* Winter 1991, pp. 27–36.

Whybark, D. Clay. "Education and Global Logistics." *Logistics and Transportation Review* 26, no. 3, pp. 261–70.

SECTION VI

IMPROVING THE SYSTEM

"If it ain't broke, don't fix it" is an obsolete maxim in the business world of today. If a company isn't improving its production systems, its managers aren't doing their jobs. In this section we describe two major approaches to improvement—one focusing on quality, *continuous improvement,* and the other focusing on the next generation of production planning concepts, *synchronized manufacturing.*

Section VI (and the book) conclude with the broader issue of revising operations strategy and the means for improving the competitiveness of the firm as a whole.

Chapter 17

Continuous Improvement

EPIGRAPH

Ask any manager at a successful Japanese company what top management is pressing for, and the answer will be, "KAIZEN" (improvement). . . . the concept of KAIZEN is so deeply ingrained in the minds of both managers and workers that they often do not even realize that they are thinking KAIZEN.

Masaaki Imai, *Kaizen, The Key to Japan's Competitive Success*, Random House, 1986, p. 6.

KAIZEN, SCHMIZEN! . . . They took it from us! We just have to get back to doing it ourselves."

The Cynical Historian

KEY TERMS

Continuous Improvement Systems

Kaizen

Standard Maintaining Systems

Tools of CI

Poka-yoke

Benchmarking

Activity-Based Costing

Continuous improvement (CI) is a management philosophy that approaches the challenge of product and process improvement as a never-ending process of achieving small wins. Specifically, **continuous improvement** seeks *continual improvement of machinery, materials, labor utilization, and production methods through application of suggestions and ideas of team members.*[1] Though pioneered by U.S. firms, this philosophy has become the cornerstone of the Japanese approach to operations and is often contrasted with the traditional Western approach of relying on major technological or theoretical innovations to achieve "big win" improvements. As can be seen in Exhibit 17.1 in a recent survey of 872 North American manufacturing executives, the majority of world-class manufacturers favored continuous improvement over 11 other management enhancement programs. Clearly, continuous improvement is a subject that warrants a careful look.

In this chapter we discuss the key managerial elements of continuous improvement and apply some of the basic tools associated with the CI process. We also present two breakthrough concepts impacting quality improvement and performance measurement in manufacturing: the Shingo system and activity-based costing.

EXHIBIT 17.1

Manufacturing Enhancement Programs

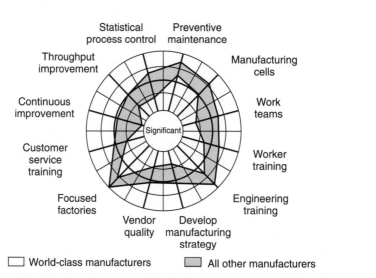

☐ World-class manufacturers   ▨ All other manufacturers

Note: Closer to center equates to better performance.

Source: Craig Giffi and Aleda V. Roth, "Taking Aim at World-Class Manufacturing: Annual Survey of North American Manufacturing Technology," Deloitte & Touche Manufacturing Consulting Services, 1991, p. 20.

---

[1] Paul R. Thompson, "The Nummi Production System," *Proceedings of the 1985 American Society of Inventory and Production Control Society Conference* (Washington D.C.: APICS, 1985), p. 399.

17.1 BRIEF HISTORY OF CONTINUOUS IMPROVEMENT

Although continuous improvement is usually associated with Japanese management, in fact CI programs were conceived, developed, and brought to maturation in the United States.[2]

In 1894, just before the end of the last century, the National Cash Register Company (NCR) established a program to solve quality problems which arose from poor working conditions and low morale. The need for improvement was identified as critical when buyers returned a shipment of defective cash registers from England to the Dayton, Ohio, plant. Managers discovered that NCR employees had poured acid into the mechanisms. After the founder/president of the company moved his desk onto the shop floor to find out what was going on, he launched a program to improve the factory (e.g., making it a well-lit and pleasant facility whose walls were 80 percent glass). Other changes included adding doctors and nurses to the staff, improving safety practices, and even instituting a mandatory daily exercise period to foster a team spirit. At the same time, the company established an extensive suggestion system, with awards reaching $500 in gold by 1897. NCR also provided night classes for the education and development of employees, to help qualify them for advancement.

Even in 1915, continuous improvement was evident in the Lincoln Electric Company, currently the world's largest manufacturer of arc-welding supplies and equipment. To harness the problem-solving abilities of his employees, the founder set piece-rate contracts that would not be changed if employees found a better method. (That is, no "rate cutting.") In 1929, the company remunerated the employees with half the savings resulting from the first year's implementation of their improvement ideas. This 1929 plan later became part of a profit-based bonus system that included ideas generated in calculating individual bonuses. Ironically, during World War II, Lincoln's success at using CI created concerns that the company was competing unfairly because it could produce for less than government-set prices. Thus, even though Lincoln was willing to share its practices with other companies, it received a good deal of hassling from the government.

In the 1960s, Procter & Gamble instituted what they termed *deliberate change* as a team-based approach to cut production costs.[3] It is predicated on the belief that significant cost savings result from methods improvements, not from exhorting workers to work harder. Currently embedded in P&G's CI program, the approach has as its key tenet the philosophy that "perfection is no barrier to change." This implies that where further improvement to an exist-

---

[2] This section is based on Dean M. Schroeder and Alan G. Robinson, "America's Most Successful Export to Japan: Continuous Improvement Programs," *Sloan Management Review,* Spring 1991, pp. 67–78.

[3] Arthur Spinanger, "Increasing Profits through Deliberate Methods Change," *Proceedings of Seventeenth Annual Industrial Engineering Institute* (Berkeley: University of California Press, 1965), pp. 33–37.

ing work method is nearly impossible, a different and superior method may be feasible.

In Japan, the continuous improvement philosophy was adopted in full measure beginning in the early 1950s. This came about for two reasons: One is that it was an inexpensive means to improve production and reduce costs during a period of severe resource shortages. As the CEO of Toyota Motor Corporation explained after his 1950 visit to the United States:

> Soon after my return to Japan, payment for the procurements had not come in yet, so management got together and discussed what internal changes the company should be making that didn't require an input of cash. We decided then and there that we could streamline operations and cut transportation costs. Both could be accomplished without further expenditures. All we had to do was use our know-how. While at Ford, I had seen how considerable savings in manpower could be had in materials handling by judiciously making even minor changes, so we decided to begin there. That's how Toyota's suggestion system got started."[4]

The second reason was pressure from the occupation authorities to use CI methods to help speed rebuilding after World War II. In 1949, the U.S. military contracted with TWI (Training Within Industries) Inc., a company that had played a major role in training supervisors, to develop training programs to be used by Japanese companies. The basic idea behind these programs was to train people in standard methods, who would then train others, that is, train the trainers.[5]

Even though the Japanese were using quality circles and suggestion systems. as part of everyday management, CI (*kaizen*) became especially attractive during the 1973 oil crisis as a way of cutting costs without major investment. Toyota, for example, received six times the number of suggestions in that year than it did in 1970. In the mid-70s, Canon, Inc. embarked on its campaign to become a world-class company and saved an estimated $200 million in direct costs through CI.

In the 1980s, U.S. companies began to introduce, or reintroduce CI. Xerox, for example, did its homework on Canon, and embarked on its own Leadership through Quality Program with a heavy CI orientation.

Perhaps the leading exponent of CI in the United States at this time is New United Motor Manufacturing, Inc. (NUMMI). NUMMI is a joint-venture company established by General Motors and Toyota to manufacture subcompact cars. The plant was established in 1984 at the site of an old GM plant in Fremont, California. The old plant had been closed down, primarily because of labor-management conflict, poor-quality production, and low productivity. To address these problems Nummi (1) installed JIT practices (such as those

---

[4] E. Toyoda, *Fifty Years in Motion,* cited in Schroeder and Robinson, "America's Most Successful Export to Japan," p. 71.

[5] Some Japanese companies (e.g., Toshiba), had already started CI programs as early as 1946 after visits by Japanese executives to U.S. firms.

described in Chapter 6) and (2) set forth in their contract with the United Auto Workers Union that both parties would constantly seek improvement in quality, efficiency, and the work environment through *kaizen,* QC circles, and suggestion programs. To make this work, the union agreed to reduce the number of job classifications from 64 to 4, and NUMMI guaranteed that workers (known as *team members*) would never be laid off due to productivity increases.

Although management in both Japan and the West historically have implemented CI in manufacturing plants, interest is growing about using it in services, as part of the TQM movement. Consider the following *Fortune* excerpt about Federal Express:

> At lunch with one team [of back-office employees], this reporter sat impressed as entry-level workers, most with only high school educations, ate their chicken and dropped sophisticated management terms like *kaisen,* the Japanese art of continuous improvement, and *pareto,* a form of problem solving that requires workers to take a logical step-by-step approach. The team described how one day during a weekly meeting, a clerk from quality control pointed out a billing problem. The bigger a package, he explained, the more Fedex charges to deliver it. But the company's wildly busy delivery people sometimes forgot to check whether customers had properly marked the weight of packages on the air bill. That meant that Fedex, whose policy in such cases is to charge customers the lowest rate, was losing money. The team switched on its turbochargers. An employee in billing services found out which field offices in Fedex's labyrinthine 30,000-person courier network were forgetting to check the packages, and then explained the problem to the delivery people. Another worker in billing set up a system to examine the invoices and made sure the solution was working. Last year alone the team's ideas saved the company $2.1 million.[6]

INSERT   Pros and Cons of Continuous Improvement in Achieving Productivity Increases (Relative to Advanced Automation)

Pros:

1. Automation has frequently failed to live up to expectations due to difficulties in implementation and the complexity associated with the design and management of automated systems.
2. Automation or other major technological advances can be purchased by competitors. Continuous improvement is proprietary to the company that uses it.
3. Relative to automation, CI is a low-cost strategy. Moreover, the investment made in training people in its methods pays back in improvement savings year after year.

---

[6] Brian Dumaine, "Who Needs a Boss?" *Fortune,* May 7, 1990, p. 54.

Cons:

1. CI takes time, so in the short run, for some companies, automation may be the only way to meet volume requirements.
2. CI requires great effort to maintain it, whereas automation requires little effort.

17.2 DISTINGUISHING FEATURES OF CI

Based on a review of CI programs by Arlyn Melcher et al., two essential features distinguish continuous improvement systems from the traditional, or what has been termed **standard maintaining systems** (SMS):[7]

1. Management's view of performance standards of the organization. Under continuous improvement, management views the performance level of the firm as something to be "continuously challenged and incrementally upgraded." Under the standard-maintaining systems management sees performance standards as essentially fixed by the constraints of technology and the existing organization. These constraints appear unbreakable without a major innovation in technology or production theory. (In fact, Masaaki Imai, in *Kaizen, the Key to Japan's Competitive Success,* calls the SMS approach "innovation".) Exhibit 17.2 contrasts CIS and SMS views relative to organizational processes. The Insert above gives the pros and cons of using CI for increasing productivity relative to advanced automation.

2. The way management views the contribution and role of its work force. The real potency of CI comes from the people management side of the approach. CEOs and operations executives of successful firms believe employee involvement and team efforts are the key to improvement. Such is not always the case with executives who adhere to the standard maintaining approach. Although they certainly say that people are important, they are more likely to get dewy eyed over the new generation of automated equipment they contemplate installing. This is not meant to suggest that CI executives don't employ some advanced technology in their plants; indeed, they often do. Rather, it's to point out that the philosophy of continuous improvement makes them think first of how such technology can be used to leverage the work and growth of the work force. (Some specific work force management differences between the SMS approach and the CIS approach are that the latter is characterized by multifunctional work teams, participative management, a group orientation, and decentralized decision making.)

---

[7] Arlyn Melcher, William Acar, Paul Dumont, and Moutaz Khouja, "Standard-Maintaining and Continuous-Improvement Systems: Experiences and Comparisons," *Interfaces* 20, no. 3 (May–June 1990), pp. 24–40.

EXHIBIT 17.2   **Standard Maintaining Versus Continuous Improvement Systems**

	Standard-Maintaining Systems	Continuous-Improvement Systems
Method for discovering problems	Breakdown from natural stressors such as: ▪ variations in demand ▪ defective raw materials ▪ tool wearout	Planned intervention in addition to natural stressors: ▪ labor reduction ▪ work-in-progress reduction
Scope of analysis	Localized: Problems are segmented and solved where they occur	Holistic: Problem classifications move from the subsystem toward the whole system
Time frame of solutions	Short term: Treat the symptoms of the problem	Long term: Address the root causes of problems
Types of solutions	▪ add resource buffers (inventory or labor) ▪ punish to motivate ▪ establish tighter control	System improvement: ▪ change layout ▪ change product design ▪ modify machines ▪ train and educate employees
Generality of solutions	Solutions considered unique to problem area	Solutions evaluated for deployment in other areas
Direction of information flow	Mostly downward: ▪ communicate standards and the means to achieving them ▪ how to handle deviation	Upward and horizontal: ▪ suggestions flow upward for evaluation ▪ solutions are communicated horizontally for deployment
Frequency of information flow	Low, exceptional: ▪ when deviations from the standard occur ▪ when changes are implemented	High, regular: ▪ the suggestion system and its evaluations
Role of operational level management	Close supervision: ▪ monitors the workers ▪ provides instruction to individuals	Arm's-length supervision: ▪ acts as a consultant to workers individually ▪ directs instructions generally to groups of workers engaged in problem solving
Role of middle management	Monitors and solves problems: ▪ monitors performance ▪ intervenes if performance is substandard	Supports and trains: ▪ trains workers to solve problems ▪ evaluates and helps implement suggestions
Role of top management	Traditional: ▪ short-term control ▪ watches the bottom line ▪ presses for immediate relief to present crises	Futuristic: ▪ long-term vision ▪ watches the environment ▪ provides the leadership for interactive planning
Environmental scanning and benchmarking	Minimal: ▪ No such function is formally acknowledged	Extensive: ▪ Either through a formal function or by means of shared responsibility

Organizational processes. The left column profiles the organizational processes of SMS (standard-maintaining systems) in contrast to those of CIS (continuous-improvement systems) profiled in the right column.

Source: Arlyn Melcher, William Acar, Paul Dumont, and Moutaz Khouja, "Standard-Maintaining and Continuous-Improvement Systems–Experiences and Comparisons," *Interfaces*, 20, no. 3 (May–June 1990), p. 27.

17.3 MANAGEMENT REQUIREMENTS FOR SUCCESSFUL CI SYSTEMS

1. Improvements require a learning period before they yield benefits. Though CI focuses on quickly implemented small improvements, even small improvements cause dislocations in work patterns and hence reductions in output in the short run. (See the Supplement following Chapter 11 to learn the impact of changes in production methods on output.)

2. Labor and management must trust each other to generate the free flow of ideas that drive a CI effort. Such trust can be broken in several ways: One is by inequitable compensation systems for salaries or improvement awards. A second way is by reducing the budgets of units that have reduced their costs. A third is by not guaranteeing employment for individuals who have made productivity improvements that could eliminate their jobs.

3. A reward system must promote interdepartmental cooperation. Process improvements initiated in one department often impact other departments. One sure way to destroy CI is to set up a reward system that penalizes either department. If, for example, an improvement suggested by an assembly team requires additional work by a plastic molding team, neither group's budget should be affected as a result. Indeed, there should be appropriate recognition and rewards for both as a result of their cooperation.

4. Continuous improvement equals continuous training. Continuous training is of two types: training in problem-solving methods that lead to improvements, and training in new procedures necessary to operationalize the improvements themselves. Training is the big cost in continuous improvement. Costs mount due to employees taking time away from their work activities to engage in group problem solving, temporary assignment to other functions to gain understanding of problems outside their own work groups, and of course, formal CI training programs.

5. CI requires an efficient system to handle improvement ideas and administer the reward process. "Without a well-planned means to gather, evaluate, implement, and reward improvement ideas, no continuous improvement program will succeed."[8] This means that ideas must be reviewed quickly, judged quickly, implemented quickly, and rewarded equitably. Feedback on ideas that aren't accepted should explain why in a way that expands the contributor's knowledge of the operation. In other words, the improvement suggestion system should itself be a model of CI.[9]

17.4 TOOLS AND PROCEDURES OF CONTINUOUS IMPROVEMENT

The approaches companies take to CI as a process range from very structured programs utilizing SPC tools (the Japanese model) to simple suggestion sys-

---

[8] Schroeder and Robinson, "America's Most Successful Export to Japan," p. 78.

[9] Most of these suggestions are taken from Schroeder and Robinson, "America's Most Successful Export to Japan," pp. 75–78.

tems relying on brainstorming and "back-of-an-envelope" analyses. Here we describe the **tools of CI** and procedures of a structured approach.

These fundamental concepts underlie the typical structured approach to CI process:

The plan-do-check-act (PDCA) cycle

Detailed problem structuring and analysis of the facts

Standardization of the improvement

The PDCA cycle, sometimes called the Deming Wheel (see Exhibit 17.3) conveys the sequential and continual nature of the CI process. The *plan* phase of the cycle is where an improvement area (sometimes called a *theme*) and a specific problem with it are identified. It is also where the analysis is done, using one or more of the SPC problem-solving tools mentioned in Chapter 5. (See the Insert for a summary of these tools.) Workers use these tools in conjunction with brainstorming approaches such as the 5W2H method shown in Exhibit 17.4 to arrive at an improvement. Typical of many CI applications is the identification of countermeasures directed toward eliminating the cause of a problem, or the barrier to a solution.

The *do* phase of the PDCA cycle deals with implementing the change. Experts usually recommend that the plan be done on a small scale first, and that any changes in the plan be documented. (Check sheets are useful here, too.) The *check* phase deals with evaluating data collected during the implementation. The objective is to see if there is a good fit between the original goal and the actual results. The *act* phase is where the improvement is codified as the new standard procedure and replicated in similar processes throughout the organization.

The group level CI process is frequently represented as if one were developing a storyboard for a movie. Exhibit 17.5 for example, summarizes the steps just discussed as the "QI (quality improvement) Story."

EXHIBIT 17.3

PDCA Cycle (Deming wheel)

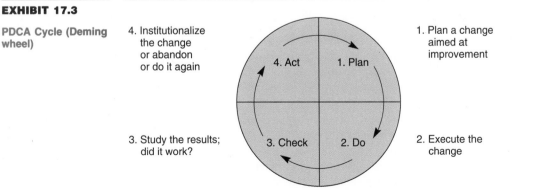

4. Institutionalize the change or abandon or do it again

3. Study the results; did it work?

4. Act

1. Plan

3. Check

2. Do

1. Plan a change aimed at improvement

2. Execute the change

Source: Ernest C. Huge, "Quality of Conformance to Design," in Ernst & Young Quality Consulting Group, *Total Quality: An Executive's Guide for the 1990s* (Homewood, Ill.: BUSINESS ONE IRWIN, 1990), p. 144.

EXHIBIT 17.4

The 5W2H Method

Type	5W2H	Description	Countermeasure
Subject matter	What?	What is being done? Can this task be eliminated?	Eliminate unnecessary tasks
Purpose	Why?	Why is this task necessary? Clarify the purpose.	
Location	Where?	Where is it being done? Does it have to be done there?	
Sequence	When?	When is the best time to do it? Does it have to be done then?	Change the sequence or combination
People	Who?	Who is doing it? Should someone else do it? Why am I doing it?	
Method	How?	How is it being done? Is this the best method? Is there some other way?	Simplify the task
Cost	How much?	How much does it cost now? What will the cost be after improvement?	Select an improvement method

A number of simple guidelines have been developed to help people or groups generate new ideas. In general, these guidelines urge you to question everything, from every conceivable angle. The figure outlines the 5W2H Method, which stands for the five "w's"—what, why, where, when, and who—and the two "h's"—how and how much.

Source: Alan Robinson, *Continuous Improvement in Operations: A Systematic Approach to Waste Reduction* (Cambridge, Mass.: Productivity Press, 1991), p. 245.

INSERT   Basic Seven SPC Tools*

1. *Pareto analysis* applies the 80/20 rule to identify the significant few causes that account for most of the problems. It separates the "vital few" from the "trivial many." All potential causes or variation problems are ranked according to their contribution to cost, variation, or other measure.

2. *Process flow chart* depicts the relevant steps in a process and aids understanding of a process.

3. *Check sheet* provides quantitative evidence of the frequency of events. For example, it can be used to verify that what people believe is a problem really is a problem.

4. *Cause-and-effect diagram* depicts and organizes by major category the potential causes of the undesired or desired effect.

5. *Histogram* displays the distribution of a number of real variables, such as weight, in frequency form. This is a way to evaluate the data visually.

6. *Scatter diagram* helps to study the relationship between data.

7. *Control chart* is used to determine the nature of the cause of variation (i.e., common causes or special causes).

* The Basic Seven sometime combine histograms with pareto and add run charts or stratification of data diagrams.

Source: Ernst & Young Quality Improvement Consulting Group, *Total Quality: An Executive's Guide for the 1990s* (Homewood, Ill.: BUSINESS ONE IRWIN, 1990).

EXHIBIT 17.5

The QI Story

	QI Story Step	Function	Tools
	1. Select theme	▪ Decide theme for improvement ▪ Make clear why the theme is selected	"Next processes are our customers" ▪ Standardization ▪ Education ▪ Immediate remedy versus recurrence prevention
	2. Grasp the current situation	▪ Collect data ▪ Find the key characteristics of the theme ▪ Narrow down the problem area ▪ Establish priorities: serious problems first	▪ Check sheet ▪ Histogram ▪ Pareto
Plan	3. Analysis	▪ List all the possible causes of the most serious problem ▪ Study the relations between possible causes and between causes and problem ▪ Select some causes and establish hypotheses about possible relations ▪ Collect data and study cause-effect relation	▪ Fishbone ▪ Check sheet ▪ Scatter diagram ▪ Stratification
	4. Countermeasures	▪ Devise countermeasures to eliminate the cause(s) of a problem	▪ Intrinsic technology ▪ Experience
Do		▪ Implement countermeasures (experiment)	
Check	5. Confirm the effect of countermeasure	▪ Collect data on the effects of the countermeasure ▪ Before–after comparison	▪ All seven tools
Act	6. Standardize the countermeasure	▪ Amend the existing standards according to the countermeasures whose effects are confirmed	
	7. Identify the remaining problems and evaluate the whole procedure		

Source: Paul Lillrank and Noriak Kano, *Continuous Improvement: Quality Control Circles in Japanese Industry* (Ann Arbor: University of Michigan, Center for Japanese Studies, 1989), p. 27.

The new seven tools of CI: These tools are the management analogue of the seven SPC tools cited in the Insert. The new seven are oriented toward those management situations where all the data is not available. In essence, they focus on clarifying complex situations, such as figuring out what has to be done in a marketing program or what kind of design is necessary for a new process. They consist of tree diagrams, various forms of relationship diagrams, matrices, and the familiar CPM chart. (See the Gitlow reference in the chapter bibliography for details of these techniques relative to CI.)

17.5 TWO CI CASE EXAMPLES

The following cases illustrate the how a bank and an airline applied some of the basic seven SPC tools and storyboard concepts to improve customer service.

17.6 CASE: SHORTENING CUSTOMERS' TELEPHONE WAITING TIME*

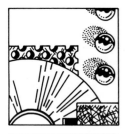

This is the story of a QC program that was implemented in the main office of a large bank. An average of 500 customers call this office every day. Surveys indicated that the callers tended to become irritated if the phone rang more than five times before it was answered, and often would not call the company again. In contrast, a prompt answer after just two rings reassured the customers and made them feel more comfortable doing business by phone.

1. Selection of a theme.   Telephone reception was chosen as a QC theme for the following reasons: (1) Telephone reception is the first impression a customer receives from the company, (2) this theme coincided with the company's telephone reception slogan, "Don't make customers wait, and avoid needless switching from extension to extension," and (3) it also coincided with a companywide campaign being promoted at that time which advocated being friendly to everyone one met.

First, the staff discussed why the present method of answering calls made callers wait. Case Exhibit 1 illustrates a frequent situation, where a call from customer B comes in while the operator is talking with customer A. Let's see why the customer has to wait.

At (1), the operator receives a call from the customer but, due to lack of experience, does not know where to connect the call. At (2), the receiving party cannot answer the phone quickly, perhaps because he or she is unavailable, and no one else can take the call. The result is that the operator must transfer the call to another extension while apologizing for the delay.

---

* From "The Quest for Higher Quality—the Deming Prize and Quality Control," Ricoh Company, Ltd. in Masaaki Imai, *Kaizen, the Key to Japan's Competitive Success* (Random House, 1986), pp. 54–58.

2. Cause-and-effect diagram and situation analysis.   In order to fully understand the situation, the circle members decided to conduct a survey regarding the callers who waited for more than five rings. Circle members itemized factors at a brainstorming discussion and arranged them in a cause-and-effect diagram (see Case Exhibit 2). Operators then kept checksheets on several points to tally the results spanning 12 days from June 4 to 16. (See Case Exhibit 3A.)

CASE EXHIBIT 1

Why Customers Had to Wait

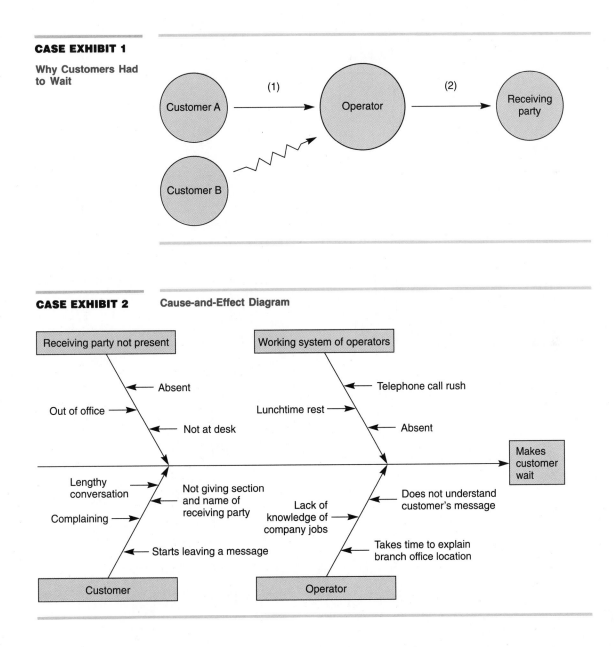

CASE EXHIBIT 2   Cause-and-Effect Diagram

CASE EXHIBIT 3

A. Checksheet—designed to identify the problems

Reason Date	No one present in the section receiving the call	Receiving party not present	Only one operator (partner out of the office)	Total
June 4	/////	/////	/////	24
June 5	/////	/////	/////	32
June 6	/////	/////	/////	28
June 15	/////	/////	/////	25

B. Reasons why callers had to wait

		Daily average	Total number
A	One operator (partner out of the office)	14.3	172
B	Receiving party not present	6.1	73
C	No one present in the section receiving the call	5.1	61
D	Section and name of receiving party not given	1.6	19
E	Inquiry about branch office locations	1.3	16
F	Other reasons	0.8	10
	Total	29.2	351

Period: 12 days from June 4 to 16, 1980

C. Reasons why callers had to wait (Pareto diagram)

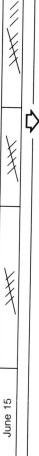

100%
87.1%
71.2%
49.0%

300
200
100
0

A B C D E F

888

3. Results of the checksheet situation analysis.   The data recorded on the checksheets unexpectedly revealed that "one operator (partner out of the office)" topped the list by a big margin, occurring a total of 172 times. In this case, the operator on duty had to deal with large numbers of calls when the phones were busy. Customers who had to wait a long time averaged 29.2 daily, which accounted for 6 percent of the calls received every day. (See Case Exhibits 3B and 3C.)

4. Setting the target.   After an intense but productive discussion, the staff decided to set a QC program goal of reducing these waiting callers to zero. That is to say that all incoming calls would be handled promptly, without inconveniencing the customer.

CASE EXHIBIT 4

A. Effects of QC (Comparison of before and after QC)

	Reasons why callers had to wait	TOTAL NUMBER		DAILY AVERAGE	
		Before	After	Before	After
A	One operator (partner out of the office)	172	15	14.5	1.2
B	Receiving party not present	73	17	6.1	1.4
C	No one present in the section receiving the call	61	20	5.1	1.7
D	Section and name of receiving party not given	19	4	1.6	0.3
E	Inquiry about branch office locations	16	3	1.3	0.2
F	Others	10	0	0.8	0
	Total	351	59	29.2	4.8

Period: 12 days from Aug. 17 to 30.

Problems are classified according to cause and presented in order of the amount of time consumed. They are illustrated in a bar graph. 100% indicates the total number of time-consuming calls.

B. Effects of QC (Pareto diagram)

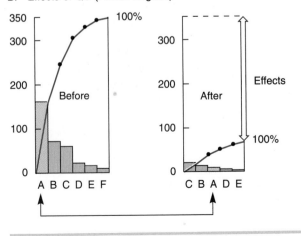

5. *Measures and execution.*   (a) Taking lunches on three different shifts, leaving at least two operators on the job at all times.

Up until this resolution was made, a two-shift lunch system had been employed, leaving only one operator on the job while the other was taking her lunch break. However, since the survey revealed that this was a major cause of customers waiting on the line, the company brought in a helper operator from the clerical section.

(b) Asking all employees to leave messages when leaving their desks.

The objective of this rule was to simplify the operator's chores when the receiving party was not at his or her desk. The new program was explained at the employees' regular morning meetings, and companywide support was requested. To help implement this practice, posters were placed around the office to publicize the new measures.

(c) Compiling a directory listing the personnel and their respective jobs.

The notebook was specially designed to aid the operators, who could not be expected to know the details of every employee's job or where to connect his incoming calls.

6. *Confirming the results.*   Although the waiting calls could not be reduced to zero, all items presented showed a marked improvement as shown in Case Exhibits 4A and 4B. The major cause of delays, "one operator (partner out of the office)," plummeted from 172 incidents during the control period to 15 in the follow-up survey.

17.7 MIDWAY AIRLINES PROBLEM-SOLVING GROUPS APPLY ANALYTICAL TOOLS TO DEPARTURE DELAYS

Midway Airlines is a small airline specializing in the frequent-traveler market.[10] Based on a customer survey, it was determined that a reduction in departure delays was critical to the airline's service.

Midway's front-line employees developed a fishbone diagram to determine the cause of the delays (Exhibit 17.6). They then did a pareto analysis, which revealed that nearly 90 percent of the departure delays for all airports other than the hub were accounted for by only four of the causes shown on the diagram. The actual causes of the late departures for one month of operation are displayed on the histogram in Exhibit 17.7. Obviously, accommodating late passengers was a major cause of flight delays. These passengers were not late from connecting flights; they were simply casual about getting to the airport. Individual gate agents had been making their own decisions about what was best for Midway in these circumstances. Most agents were anxious that Midway not lose the fares of the latecomers, and most agents were also

---

[10] This example is taken from D. Daryl Wyckoff, "New Tools for Achieving Service Quality," *Managing Services: Marketing, Operations, and Human Resources,* C. H. Lovelock, ed. (Englewood Cliffs, N.J.: Prentice Hall, 1988), pp. 226–39.

EXHIBIT 17.6   Midway Airlines Fishbone Analysis Causes of Flight Departure Delays

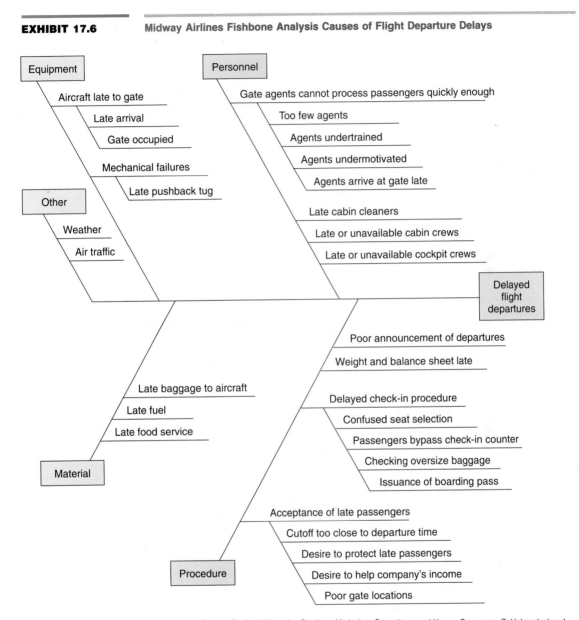

Source: D. Daryl Wyckoff, "New Tool for Achieving Service Quality," *Managing Services: Marketing, Operations, and Human Resources*, C. H. Lovelock, ed. (Englewood Cliffs, N.J.: Prentice Hall, 1988), p. 236.

EXHIBIT 17.7

Pareto Histogram of
Midway's Flight-
Departure Delays

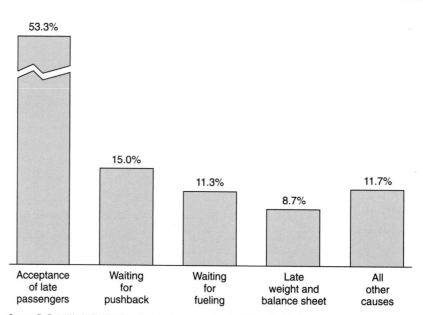

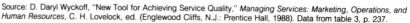

Acceptance of late passengers	Waiting for pushback	Waiting for fueling	Late weight and balance sheet	All other causes
53.3%	15.0%	11.3%	8.7%	11.7%

Source: D. Daryl Wyckoff, "New Tool for Achieving Service Quality," *Managing Services: Marketing, Operations, and Human Resources*, C. H. Lovelock, ed. (Englewood Cliffs, N.J.: Prentice Hall, 1988). Data from table 3, p. 237.

sympathetic to the late passenger (although they forgot the inconvenience to the many passengers who had made the effort to arrive on time). Midway established a policy that it would operate on time and give top service to passengers who were ready to fly on schedule. This discipline was appreciated by the passengers, and the number of late passengers soon declined.

The delays in "pushback" (moving the aircraft away from the gate with motorized tugs) were reduced by better scheduling of tugs in some locations and by working more closely with subcontractors in other locations. Similar programs were initiated with cabin-cleaning contractors and fuel suppliers, and the Midway staff placed greater priority on promptly supplying the plane's weight and balance calculations to the pilot.

In January 1983, once the flight-departure process was under control, the company set control limits. (See Exhibit 17.8.) At first, the minimum performance standard was set arbitrarily at 90 percent on-time flights. Soon there were data showing that this lower limit was too generous (but it was probably a good place to start). The company shortly decided that any month that the on-time record was more than three standard errors from the target of 95 percent, the process was out of control.

EXHIBIT 17.8

**Control Chart of
Midway Airlines
Departure Delays**

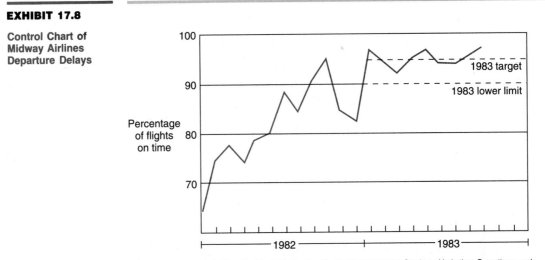

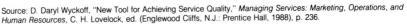

Source: D. Daryl Wyckoff, "New Tool for Achieving Service Quality," *Managing Services: Marketing, Operations, and Human Resources*, C. H. Lovelock, ed. (Englewood Cliffs, N.J.: Prentice Hall, 1988), p. 236.

17.8 VALUE ANALYSIS/VALUE ENGINEERING

The purpose of value analysis/value engineering (VA/VE) is to simplify products and processes. Its objective is to achieve equivalent or better performance at a lower cost while maintaining all functional requirements defined by the customer. VA/VE does this by identifying and eliminating unnecessary costs. Technically, VA deals with products already in production and is used to analyze product specifications and requirements as shown in production documents and purchase requests. Typically, purchasing departments use VA as a cost reduction technique. (See Chapter 16.) Performed before the production stage, value engineering is considered a cost avoidance method. In practice, however, there is a looping back and forth between the two for a given product. This occurs due to the fact that new materials, processes, and so forth, require the application of VA techniques to products that have previously undergone VE. The VA/VE analysis approach involves brainstorming such questions as:

Does the item have any design features that are not necessary?

Can two or more parts be used as one?

How can we cut down the weight?

Are there nonstandard parts that can be eliminated?

Answers to these questions are converted into ideas to be developed and then proposals for management implementation. Ted Olson et al. note some very impressive savings from VA/VE: Since 1981 Phillips Industries has saved more than $62 million in the production of parts they supply to the recreational vehicle, manufactured housing, and transportation equipment industries. Hitachi saved 5 percent, or $500 million, of the company's $10 billion operations costs in just one year.[11] They also point out that the Japanese think so highly of VA/VE that annually they give the Miles Award to companies that have demonstrated the greatest benefit from its use. (The award is named in honor of L. E. Miles of General Electric Company who originated VA in 1947).[12]

17.9 IMPROVING QUALITY PRACTICES: THE SHINGO SYSTEM

> True quality control supposedly requires the use of statistics. Although statistics is only a means, it is sometimes considered so important that the goal of quality control is forgotten.[13]

Developing in parallel and in many ways in conflict with the statistically based approach to quality control is the Shingo system. This system, or to be more precise, philosophy of production management, is named after the codeveloper of the Toyota Just-in-Time system, Shigeo Shingo. Although famous in Japan where he was known as "Mr. Improvement," Shingo's work is just now being recognized in the West. Two aspects of the Shingo system in particular have received great attention: One is how to accomplish drastic cuts in equipment setup times by single minute exchange of die (SMED) procedures. The other, and the focus of this section, is the use of source inspection and the poka-yoke system to achieve zero defects.

Shingo has argued that SQC methods do not prevent defects. Although they provide information to tell us probabilistically when a defect will occur, they are after the fact. The way to prevent defects from coming out at the end of a process is to introduce controls within the process. Central to Shingo's approach is the difference between errors and defects. Defects arise because people make errors. Even though errors are inevitable, they will not turn into defects if feedback leading to corrective action takes place at the error stage. Such feedback and action requires source inspection which should be done on

[11] Ted Olson, Craig Giffi, Aleda V. Roth, and Gregory M. Seal, *Competing in World-Class Manufacturing: America's 21st-Century Challenge* (Homewood, Ill.: Richard D. Irwin, 1990), pp. 234–36.

[12] Ibid., p. 233.

[13] Shigeo Shingo; quote cited in Alan Robinson, *Modern Approaches to Manufacturing Improvement: The Shingo System* (Cambridge, Mass.: Productivity Press, 1990), p. 204.

100 percent of the items produced. Source inspection is of two types: Self-check and successive check. *Self-check* is done by the individual worker and is appropriate by itself on all but items that require sensory judgment (e.g., existence or severity of scratches, or correct matching of shades of paint). These require the second kind of source inspection, *successive checks*. Successive check inspection is performed by the next person in the process or by an objective evaluator such as a group leader. As in the JIT approach, information on defects is immediate feedback for the worker who produced the product, who then makes the repair. Both types of source inspection rely on controls consisting of fail-safe procedures or devices (called *poka-yoke*). **Poka-yoke** include such things as check lists or special tooling that (1) prevents the worker from making an error that leads to a defect before starting a process or (2) gives rapid feedback of abnormalities in the process to the worker in time to correct it.

EXHIBIT 17.9

Poka-yoke Example: Placing Labels On Parts Coming Down A Conveyor

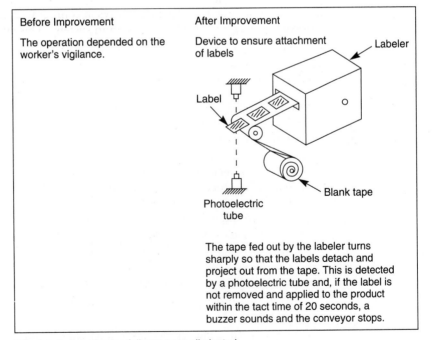

Before Improvement

The operation depended on the worker's vigilance.

After Improvement

Device to ensure attachment of labels

Labeler

Label

Photoelectric tube

Blank tape

The tape fed out by the labeler turns sharply so that the labels detach and project out from the tape. This is detected by a photoelectric tube and, if the label is not removed and applied to the product within the tact time of 20 seconds, a buzzer sounds and the conveyor stops.

Effect: Label application failures were eliminated.
Cost: ¥ 15,000 ($75)

Source: Alan Robinson, *Modern Approaches to Manufacturing Improvement: The Shingo System* (Cambridge, Mass.: Productivity Press, 1990), p. 272.

There is a wide variety of poka-yoke, ranging from checklists or kitting parts from a bin (to ensure that the right number is used in assembly) to sophisticated detection and electronic signaling devices. See an example taken from the writings of Shingo in Exhibit 17.9.

There is a good deal more to say about the work of Shingo. Blasting industry's preoccupation with control charts, Shingo states they are nothing but a mirror reflecting current conditions. When a chemical plant QC manager proudly stated that they had 200 charts in a plant of 150 people, Shingo asked him if "they had a control chart for control charts?"[14] In addition to his insights into the quality area, his work on SMED is must reading for manufacturing executives.

17.10 BENCHMARKING

The CI approaches described so far are more or less inward looking: they seek to make improvements by analyzing in detail the current practices of the company itself. **Benchmarking,** however, goes outside the organization to examine what industry competitors and excellent performers outside the industry are doing. Its basic objective is simple: Find the best practices that lead to superior performance and see how you can use them. The practice of benchmarking is a hallmark of Malcolm Baldrige National Quality Award winners and is widely used throughout industry in general. Benchmarking typically involves the following steps:

1. *Identify those processes needing improvement.* This is equivalent to selecting a theme in CI.

2. *Identify a firm that is the world leader in performing the process.* For many processes, this may be a company that is not in the same industry. Examples include Xerox using L. L. Bean as the benchmark in evaluating its order entry system, or ICL, a major British computer maker benchmarking Marks and Spenser, a large U.K. clothing retailer, to improve its distribution system. A McKinsey study cited a firm that measured pit-stops on a motor racing circuit as a benchmark for worker changes on their assembly line.[15]

3. *Contact the managers of that company and make a personal visit interviewing managers and workers.* Many companies select a team of workers from that process to be on a benchmarking team as part of a CI program.

4. *Analyze data.* This entails looking at gaps between what your company is doing and what the benchmark company is doing. There are

---

[14] Robinson, *Modern Approaches to Manufacturing Improvement,* p. 234.

[15] Steven Walleck, David O'Halloran, and Charles Leader, "Benchmarking World-Class Performance," *McKinsey Quarterly,* 1991, no. 1, p. 7.

two aspects of the study: One is comparing the actual processes, and the other is comparing the performance of those processes according to some set of measures. The processes are often described using flow charts, or simply written descriptions. (In some cases, companies permit videotaping although there is a tendency now for benchmarked companies to keep things under wraps in fear of giving away process secrets.)

Typical performance measures for process comparisons are breakouts of cost, quality, and service, such as cost per order, percent defectives, and service response time. The Insert gives a discussion of Xerox's benchmarking process.

INSERT   Benchmarking the Benchmarker

Xerox proudly proclaims that "the world comes to us to understand our benchmarking process. In 1988 over 200 visitors from Japanese and American companies came to Xerox for the purpose of studying our benchmarking process and its practice."

The benchmarking terms Xerox uses include:

Industry average: The mean performance of companies in our industry.
Competitive or industry benchmark: The best performance in our industry.
World-class benchmark: The best performance in any industry.

Benchmarking plans are periodically assessed, with four questions being asked:

1. *What are we accomplishing as a result of our plan?*
   Daily schedule attainment improved to 75 percent in 1988, compared to 50 percent in 1984. (*Example relates to scheduling practices.*)
2. *What are the benchmark company's current and projected strengths?*
   Consistent improvement in cycle time reduction.
   Use of statistical process control.
3. *What parts of our plan need to be readjusted?*
   Material replenishment to be Just-in-Time.
4. *Is a recalibration process in place?*
   Yes: Each year performance measures are studied and recalibrated.

Source: Xerox Malcolm Baldrige National Quality Award Application, 1988, Section 3.1.

17.11 ACTIVITY-BASED COSTING

One of the ways of measuring the effects of improvement is to examine costs of activities before and after the quality improvement effort. In most cases, the desirable outcome is a reduction in costs. In some cases, certain activities may increase in cost to improve the overall quality from a systemwide perspective.

Regardless of the intended cost effect, accurate measurement of the costs of production is essential to knowing whether improvement goals have been achieved.

In a broad sense, costs can be divided into two categories: The first category is direct costs. These variable costs are directly traceable to the labor and materials used in the hands-on production and service-delivery activities. The second cost category, overhead, includes indirect materials, indirect labor such as management, depreciation of plant and equipment, and utilities. These costs do not tend to greatly fluctuate over time because fixed costs make up the majority of overhead.

To know how much it costs to make a certain product or deliver a service, some method of allocating overhead costs to production activities must be applied. The traditional approach is to allocate overhead costs to products on the basis of direct labor dollars or hours. By dividing the total estimated overhead costs by total budgeted direct labor hours, an overhead rate can be established. The problem with this approach is that direct labor, as a percentage of total costs, has reduced dramatically over the past decade. For example, introduction of advanced manufacturing technology and other productivity improvements has driven direct labor to as low as 7 to 10 percent of total manufacturing costs in many industries (as stated in Chapter 16). As a result, overhead rates of 600 percent or even 1,000 percent are found in some highly automated plants.[16]

This traditional accounting practice of allocating overhead to direct labor can lead to questionable investment decisions, e.g., automated processes may be chosen over labor-intensive processes based on a comparison of projected costs. Unfortunately, overhead does not disappear when the equipment is installed and overall costs may actually be lower with the labor-intensive process. It can also lead to wasted effort since an inordinate amount of time is spent tracking direct labor hours. For example, one plant spent 65 percent of computer costs tracking information about direct labor transactions even though direct labor accounted for only 4 percent of total production costs.[17]

Activity-based costing techniques have been developed to alleviate these problems by refining the overhead allocation process to more directly reflect actual proportions of overhead consumed by the production activity. Causal factors, known as cost drivers, are identified and used as the means for allocating overhead. These factors might include machine hours, beds occupied, computer time, flight hours, or miles driven. The accuracy of overhead allocation, of course, depends on the selection of appropriate cost drivers.

[16] Matthew J. Libertore, *Selection and Evaluation of Advanced Manufacturing Technologies* (New York: Springer-Verlag, 1990), pp. 231–56.

[17] Thomas Johnson and Robert Kaplan, *Relevance Lost: The Rise and Fall of Management Accounting* (Boston: Harvard Business School Press, 1987), p. 188.

Activity-based costing involves a two-stage allocation process with the first stage assigning overhead costs to cost activity pools. These pools represent activities such as performing machine setups, issuing purchase orders, and inspecting parts. In the second stage, costs are assigned from these pools to activities based on the number or amount of pool-related activity required in their completion. Exhibit 17.10 shows a comparison of traditional cost accounting and activity-based costing.

Consider the example of activity-based costing presented in Exhibit 17.11. Two products, A and B, are produced using the same number of labor hours. Applying traditional costing, identical overhead costs would be charged to each product. By applying activity-based costing, traceable costs are assigned to specific activities. Because each product required a different amount of transactions, different overhead amounts are allocated to these products from the pools.

As stated earlier, activity-based costing overcomes the problem of cost distortion by creating a cost pool for each activity or transaction that can be identified as a cost driver, and by assigning overhead cost to products or jobs on a basis of the number of separate activities required for their completion. Thus, in the previous situation, the low-volume product would be assigned the bulk of the costs for machine setup, purchase orders, and quality inspections, thereby showing it to have high unit costs compared to the other product.

Finally, activity-based costing is sometimes referred to as *transactions costing*. This transactions focus gives rise to another major advantage over other costing methods: that is, that it improves the traceability of overhead costs and thus results in more accurate *unit* cost data for management.

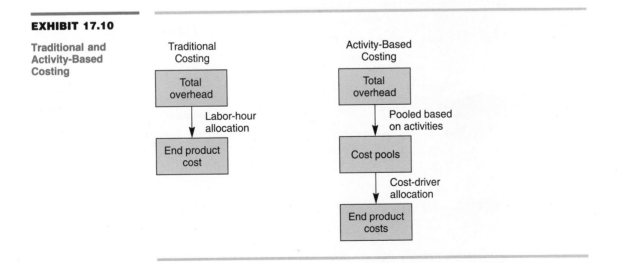

EXHIBIT 17.10

Traditional and Activity-Based Costing

EXHIBIT 17.11

Overhead Allocations
by an Activity
Approach

Basic Data

Activity	Traceable Costs	EVENTS OF TRANSACTIONS		
		Total	Product A	Product B
Machine setups	$230,000	5,000	3,000	2,000
Quality inspections	160,000	8,000	5,000	3,000
Production orders	81,000	600	200	400
Machine-hours worked	314,000	40,000	12,000	28,000
Material receipts	90,000	750	150	600
	$875,000			

Overhead Rates by Activity

Activity	(a) Traceable Costs	(b) Total Events or Transactions	(a) ÷ (b) Rate per Event or Transaction
Machine setups	$230,000	5,000	$46/setup
Quality inspections	160,000	8,000	$20/inspection
Production orders	81,000	600	$135/order
Machine-hours worked	314,000	40,000	$7.85/hour
Material receipts	90,000	750	$120/receipt

Overhead Cost per Unit of Product

	PRODUCT A		PRODUCT B	
	Events or Transactions	Amount	Events or Transactions	Amount
Machine setups, at $46/setup	3,000	$138,000	2,000	$ 92,000
Quality inspections, at $20/inspection	5,000	100,000	3,000	60,000
Production orders, at $135/order	200	27,000	400	54,000
Machine-hours worked, at $7.85/hour	12,000	94,200	28,000	219,800
Material receipts, at $120/receipt	150	18,000	600	72,000
Total overhead cost assigned (a)		$377,200		$497,800
Number of units produced (b)		5,000		20,000
Overhead cost per unit, (a) ÷ (b)		$75.44		$24.89

Source: Ray Garrison, *Managerial Accounting* (Homewood, Ill.: Richard D. Irwin, 1991), p. 94.

17.12 CONCLUSION: THIS IS NOT ROCKET SCIENCE

Examination of the concepts and case studies in this chapter should convey the
fact that CI is not rocket science. Theoretically, it is an inherently simple
process that any organization can use with success. Where we appear to need

rocket-scientist-level thinking is in finding ways to break down the organizational barriers of departmental enclaves and conflicting reward systems that inhibit work groups from getting on with the task.

17.13 REVIEW AND DISCUSSION QUESTIONS

1. Business writer Tom Peters has suggested that in making process changes, we should "Try it, test it, and get on with it." How does this philosophy square with the continuous improvement philosophy?

2. Midway Airlines went into bankruptcy in 1991 despite their success in operations problem solving. What does this imply regarding the use of the CI?

3. Think about a job you have held. Was the organization you worked for more like a standard maintaining system or a CI system? (Use Exhibit 17.2 as a guide to the details.)

4. How valuable to customers is the improvement developed in the bank case study in the chapter about shortening customers' waiting time on the phone?

5. Are there any poka-yoke that could be applied to the bank study referred to in question 4?

6. Conduct a quick value analysis on a recent purchase you have made. Are you a "happy camper" or do you have buyer's regret?

7. You are the VE person for the company that made the product you analyzed in question 6. What design changes would you make?

8. Shingo tells a story of a poka-yoke he developed to make sure that operators avoided the mistake of putting less than the required four springs in a push button device. The existing method involved assemblers taking individual springs from a box containing several hundred, and then placing two of them behind an on button and two more behind an off button. What was the poka-yoke Shingo came up with?

9. The typical computerized word processing package is loaded with poka-yokes. List three. Are there any others you wish the packages had?

10. How can activity-based costing be used as a continuous improvement tool? Are there any limitations in using it for this purpose?

17.14 PROBLEMS

1. Professor Chase is frustrated by his inability to make a good cup of coffee in the morning. Show how you would use a fishbone diagram to analyze the process he uses to make a cup of his evil brew.

2. Use the benchmarking process and as many CI tools as you can to improve your performance in your weakest course in school.

3. ACME Mirror produces two types of rearview mirrors for a major automobile manufacturer. The company produces 120,000 standard mirrors and 80,000 deluxe mirrors per year. Direct labor requirements are 10 minutes per deluxe unit and 5 minutes per standard unit. Unit costs for materials and direct labor are as follows:

	Standard Mirror	Deluxe Mirror
Direct materials	$18	$25
Direct labor	3	6

The company also collected information on traceable costs by activity for each product.

Activity	Traceable Costs	EVENTS OR TRANSACTIONS	
		Standard	Deluxe
Machine setups required	$290,000	1,100	350
Purchase orders issued	75,000	650	125
Machine hours required	195,000	300	700
	$560,000		

a. For the current year, the company estimated that it would incur $560,000 in overhead costs. Using a labor-hour overhead allocation method, determine the unit cost to manufacture each product.

b. Applying activity-based costing, determine the unit cost to manufacture each product.

c. What information did activity-based costing provide to management that was not provided by the traditional labor-based costing method?

17.15 CASE: HANK KOLB, DIRECTOR QUALITY ASSURANCE*

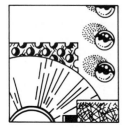

Hank Kolb was whistling as he walked toward his office, still feeling a bit like a stranger since he had been hired four weeks before as director, quality assurance. All that week he had been away from the plant at an interesting seminar, entitled "Quality in the 90's," given for quality managers of manufacturing plants by the corporate training department. He was now looking forward to digging into the quality problems at this industrial products plant employing 1,200 people.

Kolb poked his head into Mark Hamler's office, his immediate subordinate as the quality control manager, and asked him how things had gone during the past week. Hamler's muted smile and an "Oh, fine," stopped Kolb in his tracks. He didn't know Hamler very well and was unsure about pursuing this reply any further. Kolb was still uncertain of how to start building a relationship with him since Hamler had been passed over for the promotion to Kolb's job—Hamler's evaluation form had stated "superb technical knowledge; managerial skills lacking." Kolb decided to inquire a little further and asked Hamler what had happened; he replied: "Oh, just another typical quality snafu. We had a little problem on the Greasex line last week [a specialized degreasing solvent packed in a spray can for the high technology sector]. A little high pressure was found in some cans on the second shift, but a supervisor vented them so that we could

     * Copyright © 1981 by the President and Fellows of Harvard College, Harvard Business School.

ship them out. We met our delivery schedule!" Since Kolb was still relatively unfamiliar with the plant and its products, he asked Hamler to elaborate; painfully, Hamler continued:

> We've been having some trouble with the new filling equipment and some of the cans were pressurized beyond our AQL [acceptable quality level] on a psi rating scale. The production rate is still 50 percent of standard, about 14 cases per shift, and we caught it halfway into the shift. Mac Evans [the inspector for that line] picked it up, tagged the cases "hold," and went on about his duties. When he returned at the end of the shift to write up the rejects, Wayne Simmons, first-line supervisor, was by a pallet of finished goods finishing sealing up a carton of the rejected Greasex; the reject "hold" tags had been removed. He told Mac that he had heard about the high pressure from another inspector at coffee break, had come back, taken off the tags, individually turned the cans upside down and vented every one of them in the eight rejected cartons. He told Mac that production planning was really pushing for the stuff and they couldn't delay by having it sent through the rework area. He told Mac that he would get on the operator to run the equipment right next time. Mac didn't write it up but came in about three days ago to tell me about it. Oh, it happens every once in a while and I told him to make sure to check with maintenance to make sure the filling machine was adjusted; and I saw Wayne in the hall and told him that he ought to send the stuff through rework next time.

Kolb was a bit dumbfounded at this and didn't say much—he didn't know if this was a big deal or not. When he got to his office he thought again what Morganthal, general manager, had said when he had hired him. He warned Kolb about the "lack of quality attitude" in the plant, and said that Kolb "should try and do something about this." Morganthal further emphasized the quality problems in the plant: "We have to improve our quality, it's costing us a lot of money, I'm sure of it, but I can't prove it! Hank, you have my full support in this matter; you're in charge of these quality problems. This downward quality-productivity-turnover spiral has to end!"

The incident had happened a week before; the goods were probably out in the customer's hands by now, and everyone had forgotten about it (or wanted to). There seemed to be more pressing problems than this for Kolb to spend his time on, but this continued to nag him. He felt that the quality department was being treated as a joke, and he also felt that this was a personal slap from manufacturing. He didn't want to start a war with the production people, but what could he do? Kolb was troubled enough to cancel his appointments and spend the morning talking to a few people. After a long and very tactful morning, he learned the following information:

1. *From personnel.*   The operator for the filling equipment had just been transferred from shipping two weeks ago. He had had no formal training in this job but was being trained by Wayne, on-the-job, to run the equipment. When Mac had tested the high pressure cans the operator was nowhere to be found and had only learned of the rejected material from Wayne after the shift was over.

2. *From plant maintenance.*   This particular piece of automated filling equipment had been purchased two years ago for use on another product. It had been switched to the Greasex line six months ago and maintenance had had 12 work orders during the last month for repairs or adjustments on it. The equipment had been adapted by plant maintenance for handling the lower viscosity of Greasex, which it had not originally been designed for. This included designing a special filling head. There was no scheduled preventive maintenance for this equipment and the parts for the sensitive filling head, replaced three times in the last six months, had to be made at a nearby machine shop. Nonstandard downtime was running at 15 percent of actual running time.

3. From purchasing.   The plastic nozzle heads for the Greasex can, designed by a vendor for this new product on a rush order, were often found with slight burrs on the inside rim, and this caused some trouble in fitting the top to the can. An increase in application pressure at the filling head by maintenance adjustment had solved the burr application problem or had at least forced the nozzle heads on despite burrs. Purchasing agents said that they were going to talk to the sales representative of the nozzle head supplier about this the next time he came in.

4. From product design and packaging.   The can, designed especially for Greasex, had been contoured to allow better gripping by the user. This change, instigated by marketing research, set Greasex apart from the appearance of its competitors and was seen as significant by the designers. There had been no test of the effects of the contoured can on filling speed or filling hydrodynamics from a high-pressured filling head. Kolb had a hunch that the new design was acting as a venturi (carrier creating suction) when being filled, but the packaging designer thought that was unlikely.

5. From manufacturing manager.   He had heard about the problem; in fact, Simmons had made a joke about it, bragging about how he beat his production quota to the other foremen and shift supervisors. The manufacturing manager thought Simmons was one of the "best foremen we have . . . he always gets his production out." His promotion papers were actually on the manufacturing manager's desk when Kolb dropped by. Simmons was being strongly considered for promotion to shift supervisor. The manufacturing manager, under pressure from Morganthal for cost improvements and reduced delivery times, sympathized with Kolb but said that the rework area would have vented with their pressure gauges what Wayne had done by hand. "But, I'll speak with Wayne about the incident," he said.

6. From marketing.   The introduction of Greasex had been rushed to market to beat competitors and a major promotional-advertising campaign was underway to increase consumer awareness. A deluge of orders was swamping the order-taking department and putting Greasex high on the back-order list. Production had to turn the stuff out; even being a little off spec was tolerable because "it would be better to have it on the shelf than not there at all. Who cares if the label is a little crooked or the stuff comes out with a little too much pressure? We need market share now in that high-tech segment."

What bothered Kolb most was the safety issue of the high pressure in the cans. He had no way of knowing how much of a hazard the high pressure was or if Simmons had vented them enough to effectively reduce the hazard. The data from the can manufacturer, which Hamler had showed him, indicated that the high pressure found by the inspector was not in the danger area. But, again, the inspector had only used a sample testing procedure to reject the eight cases. Even if he could morally accept that there was no product safety hazard, could Kolb make sure that this would never happen again?

Skipping lunch, Kolb sat in his office and thought about the morning's events. The past week's seminar had talked about the role of quality, productivity and quality, creating a new attitude, and the quality challenge, but where had they told him what to do when this happened? He had left a very good job to come here because he thought the company was serious about the importance of quality, and he wanted a challenge. Kolb had demanded and received a salary equal to the manufacturing, marketing, and R&D directors, and he was one of the direct reports to the general manager. Yet he still didn't know exactly what he should or shouldn't do, or even what he could or couldn't do under these circumstances.

QUESTIONS

1. What are the causes of the quality problems on the Greasex line? Display your answer on a fishbone diagram.

2. What general steps should Hank follow in setting up a CI program for the company? What problems will he have to overcome to make it work?

17.16 SELECTED BIBLIOGRAPHY

Ernst & Young Quality Improvement Consulting Group. *Total Quality: An Executive's Guide for the 1990s.* Homewood, Ill.: BUSINESS ONE IRWIN, 1990.

Gitlow, Howard S., and Shelly J. Gitlow. *The Deming Guide to Quality and Competitive Position.* Englewood Cliffs, N.J.: Prentice Hall, 1987.

Hayes, Robert H.; Steven C. Wheelwright; and Kim B. Clark. *Dynamic Manufacturing: Creating the Learning Organization.* New York: Free Press, 1988.

Imai, Masaaki. *Kaizen: The Key to Japan's Competitive Success.* New York: Random House, 1986.

Olson, Ted; Craig Giffi; Aleda V. Roth; and Gregory M. Seal. *Competing in World-Class Manufacturing: America's 21st-Century Challenge.* Homewood, Ill.: Richard D. Irwin, 1990.

Robinson, Alan. *Modern Approaches to Manufacturing Improvement: The Shingo System.* Cambridge, Mass.: Productivity Press, 1990.

Tatsuno, Sheridan M. "Hitting for Singles." *Across the Board,* April 1990, pp. 30–35.

Chapter 18

Synchronous Production

EPIGRAPH

The action you're proposing:
  Will it increase throughput?
  Will it decrease inventory?
  Will it decrease operating expense?

Dr. Eliyahu M. Goldratt

CHAPTER OUTLINE

KEY TERMS

Synchronous Production

Hockey-Stick Phenomenon

Throughput

Inventory

Operating Expense

Productivity

Unbalanced Capacity

Bottleneck

Nonbottleneck

Capacity-Constrained Resource

Drum

Buffer

Rope

Time Buffer

Process Batch

Transfer Batches

Dollar Days

Backward/Forward Scheduling

VAT Classification

*F*rom about 1970 through about 1985 MRP (including both *material requirements planning* and *manufacturing resource planning*) was touted as *the* way to run a manufacturing firm. If companies did not receive the promised benefits, we concluded it was because they had problems within their own organizations. It was *their* fault for being unable to reap the benefits of MRP, *not* the problems of the technique itself. As we progressed through this period, rather than overtaking the Japanese in their tremendous success in capturing world markets, American industries continued to slip farther and farther behind. More and more effort was put into making MRP successful, but eventually companies began to realize that the technique would not solve all their problems and that the system itself had some inherent shortcomings.

Everyone in the United States who was analyzing possible reasons for Japan's success in manufacturing cited a variety of causes: cultural differences, quality control circles, government participation, and life-long employment. All these explanations, we now know, ignore one simple truth—Japan's JIT (Just-in-Time) manufacturing scheduling and control system was doing an excellent job in repetitive manufacturing areas. Finally, in the mid-1980s, firms in the United States began to copy the Japanese and were running full bore to install JIT in every plant possible. What U.S. manufacturing firms fail to realize, however, is that installing JIT is a slow process, derived essentially by trial and error. It is not an effective technique to use if the goal is to catch up to and pass Japan and thereby recapture lost market share.

About 1980, Dr. Eliyahu Goldratt developed software that scheduled jobs through manufacturing processes, taking into account limited facilities, machines, personnel, tools, materials, and any other constraints that would affect a firm's ability to adhere to a schedule. The schedules were feasible and accurate, and could be run on a computer in a fraction of the time that an MRP system took. This was because the scheduling logic was based on the separation of bottleneck and nonbottleneck operations. After approximately 100 large firms had installed this software, Goldratt and Robert Fox went on to promote the logic of the approach rather than the software. Goldratt has since developed his "General Theory of Constraints," and, in fact, is no longer associated with the software company.

We believe in the logic of Goldratt's approach to manufacturing and his focus: dealing with constraints. Therefore, we are devoting this chapter to Goldratt's teachings and applications. To correctly treat the topic, we decided to approach it in the same way that Goldratt did; that is, first defining some basic issues about firms—purposes, goals, performance measurements, etc.—

Note: Most of this chapter is based on the writings and teachings of Dr. Eliyahu M. Goldratt and Robert E. Fox; see the bibliography at the end of this chapter for a list of their publications. One of the authors of this text was a participant in several of their week-long seminars and courses. We express our thanks to Dr. Goldratt for his permission to freely use his concepts, definitions, and other material.

then dealing with scheduling, providing buffer inventories, the influences of quality, and the interactions with marketing, and accounting.

In this chapter we discuss synchronous production. **Synchronous production** refers to the entire production process working together in harmony to achieve the goals of the firm. Any production system consists of a wide variety of cycles with varying time lengths. Synchronous production logic attempts to coordinate all of the cycles so that they work together and are in harmony, or "synchronized." In such a synchronous state, emphasis is on the total system performance and not on localized performance measures such as labor or machine utilization.

18.1 HOCKEY-STICK PHENOMENON

Just about every company faces a problem called the **hockey-stick phenomenon**—rushing to meet quotas at the *end* of the time period. If the time period is a month, then this is an end-of-the-month-syndrome; if the period is a quarter, it is an end-of-the-quarter syndrome (see Exhibit 18.1). It's called a

EXHIBIT 18.1

Hockey-Stick Phenomenon—The End-of-the-Period Rush

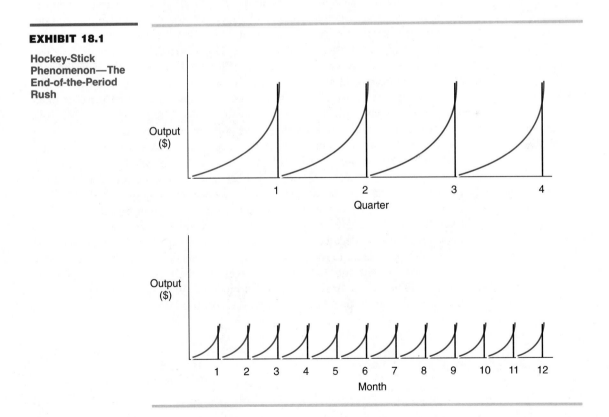

hockey stick because it looks like a hockey stick—with a relatively flat bottom and a long rapid rise like a handle. The reason that this is a problem is primarily because of the chaos that occurs at the end of the month. The system never runs smoothly; everyone works under pressure during the early flat part of the cycle as well as during the end of the cycle. The cause of the problem is that two sets of measurements are being employed: At the beginning of the period, cost-accounting *efficiency* measurements are used for utilizations and variances from standards. These are local measurements. This encourages minimizing setups through large batches and minimizing variances. As the end of the month approaches, however, pressure mounts to meet a different set of measurements, ones that relate to financial *performance*. These global measurements vary at different points within a plant. They are stated in terms such as dollars of output shipped. On the financial statements these measurements are expressed as net profit, return on investment, and cash flow. As soon as the end of the month passes (with its frantic overtime and weekend work along with constant expediting and frequent setups aimed toward getting the product out), pressure decreases and everyone again looks at the cost-accounting measurements of variances and utilization. And so the cycle repeats.

To emphasize the value of techniques such as synchronous production, Goldratt tells two stories of what can happen. One is about a firm that did not need the third shift because of a slump in the market. The workers were highly skilled and, because the company expected the market to rebound in three months, it decided to keep the workers. With a weekly payroll of $25,000, the company allocated $300,000 to carry the workers for three months, within which time they expected renewed market demand. To the surprise of management, however, these workers consumed $400,000 worth of inventory during the first week and another $400,000 during the second week, so the workers were laid off. There was so much pressure to keep the workers busy that they were not allowed to just be idle (nor would the workers feel right just sitting around waiting). Two months later market demand increased, but not for the products that the workers had been working on.

The second story is about a plant whose demand went down because the overall market had deteriorated. Because the company was having some cash flow problems, it decided to cut expenses. Noticing that the setup workers were the highest paid in the plant, management decided to double all the batch sizes (which meant only half the setups were needed) and lay off half the setup workers. The result put the plant out of business! With double batch sizes, the increase in work in process drained all the company's cash so that it could no longer operate.

18.2 GOAL OF THE FIRM

Although many people disagree with him. Goldratt has a very straightforward idea of the goal of a firm.

THE GOAL OF A FIRM IS TO MAKE MONEY

Goldratt argues that while an organization may have many purposes—providing jobs, consuming raw materials, increasing sales, increasing share of the market, developing technology, or producing high-quality products—these do not guarantee long-term survival of the firm. They are means to achieve the goal, not the goal itself. If the firm makes money—and only then—it will prosper. When a firm has money, then it can place more emphasis on other objectives.

18.3 PERFORMANCE MEASUREMENTS

To adequately measure a firm's performance, two sets of measurements must be used: one from the financial point of view, and the other from the operations point of view.

Financial Measurements

How do we measure the firm's ability to make money? In financial terms, we keep track of:

1. **Net profit,** which is an absolute measurement in dollars.
2. **Return on investment,** which is a relative measure based on investment.
3. **Cash flow,** which is a survival measurement.

To accurately evaluate a firm's performance in financial terms, all three measurements must be used together. For example, a *net profit* of $10 million is important as one measurement, but it has no real meaning until we know how much investment it took to generate that $10 million. If the investment was $100 million, then this is a 10 percent *return on investment. Cash flow* is important since cash is necessary to pay bills for day-to-day operations; without cash, a firm can go bankrupt even though it is very sound in normal accounting terms. A firm can have a high profit and a high return on investment, but can still be short on cash if, for example, the profit is invested in new equipment or tied up in inventory.

Operational Measurements

While financial measurements work well at the higher level, they cannot be used at the operational level. Here we need another set of measurements that will give us guidance. There are three:

1. **Throughput**—the rate at which money is generated by the system through sales.

2. **Inventory**—all the money that the system has invested in purchasing things it intends to sell.

3. **Operating expenses**—all the money that the system spends to turn inventory into throughput.

Throughput is specifically defined as goods *sold*. An inventory of finished goods is not throughput, but inventory. Actual sales must occur. It is specifically defined this way to prevent the system from continuing to produce under the illusion that the goods *might* be sold. Such action simply increases costs, builds inventory, and consumes cash. Inventory that is carried—regardless of the stage (work in process or finished goods)—is valued only at the cost of the materials it contains. Money spent to convert the raw materials into throughput is ignored. (In traditional accounting terms, money spent is called *value added*.)

While this is often an arguable point, using only the raw-material cost is a conservative view. When using the value-added method (which includes all costs of production), inventory is inflated and presents some serious income and balance sheet problems. Consider, for example, work-in-process or finished-goods inventory that has become obsolete, or for which a contract was canceled. It is a difficult management decision to declare large amounts of inventory as scrap since it is often carried on the books as assets, even though it may really have no value. Using just raw-material cost also avoids the problem of determining which costs are direct and which are indirect.

Operating expenses include production costs, such as direct labor, indirect labor, inventory carrying costs, equipment depreciation, materials and supplies used in production, and administrative costs. The key difference here is that there is no need to separate direct and indirect labor.

As shown in Exhibit 18.2, the objective of a firm is to treat all three measurements simultaneously, and continually; this achieves the goal of making money.

EXHIBIT 18.2

Operational Goal

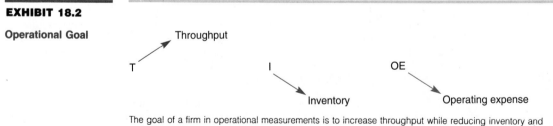

The goal of a firm in operational measurements is to increase throughput while reducing inventory and operating expense.

In these operational measurements, the goal of the firm is to

INCREASE THROUGHPUT WHILE SIMULTANEOUSLY
REDUCING INVENTORY AND REDUCING OPERATING
EXPENSE.

Productivity

Typically, **productivity** is measured in terms of output per labor hour. However, this measurement does not ensure that the firm will make money (for example, when extra output is not sold but accumulates as inventory). To test whether or not productivity has increased, we should ask these questions: Has the action taken increased throughput? Has it decreased inventory? Has it decreased operational expense? This leads us to a new definition:

PRODUCTIVITY IS ALL THE ACTIONS THAT BRING A
COMPANY CLOSER TO ITS GOALS.

18.4 UNBALANCED CAPACITY

Historically (and still typically in most firms), manufacturers have tried to balance capacity across a sequence of processes, in an attempt to match capacity with market demand. Using systems manufacturing logic, however, this is the wrong thing to do—**unbalanced capacity** is better. Consider a simple process line with several stations, for example. Once the cycle time (or average output rate) of the line has been established, production people try to make the capacities of all stations the same. This is done by adjusting machines or equipment used, work loads, skill and type of labor assigned, tools used, overtime budgeted, and so on.

In synchronous production thinking, however, making all capacities the same is viewed as a bad decision. Such a balance would be possible only if the output times of all stations were constant or had a very narrow distribution. A normal variation in output times causes downstream stations to have idle time when upstream stations take longer to process. Conversely, when upstream stations process in a shorter time, inventory builds up between the stations. The effect of the statistical variation is cumulative. The only way that this variation can be smoothed is by increasing work in process to absorb the variation (a bad choice, since we should be trying to reduce work in process), or increasing capacities downstream to be able to make up for the longer upstream times. The rule here is that capacities within the process sequence should not be balanced to the same levels. Rather, attempts should be made to balance the *flow of product* through the system. When flow is balanced, capacities are unbalanced. This idea is further explained in the next section.

Dependent Events and Statistical Fluctuations

The term *dependent events* refers to a process sequence. If a process flows from A to B to C to D, and each process must be completed before passing on to the next step, then B, C, and D are dependent events. The ability to do the next process is dependent on the preceding one.

Statistical fluctuation refers to the normal variation about a mean or average. When statistical fluctuations occur in a dependent sequence without any inventory between workstations, there is no opportunity to achieve the average output. When one process takes longer than the average, the next process can not make up the time. We follow through an example of this to show what could happen. This situation exists in assembly lines, although most of them—electronic products, cars,—have shorter processing times than our example. The other extreme of longer processing times also exists: airplanes, prefab houses, and even ships are built on assembly lines.

Suppose that we wanted to process five items that could come from the two distributions in Exhibit 18.3. The processing sequence is from A to B with no space for inventory in between. Process A has a mean of 10 hours and a standard deviation of 2 hours. This means that we would expect 95.5 percent of the processing time to be between 6 hours and 14 hours (plus or minus 2 sigma). Process B has a constant processing time of 10 hours.

EXHIBIT 18.3   Processing and Completion Times, Process A to Process B

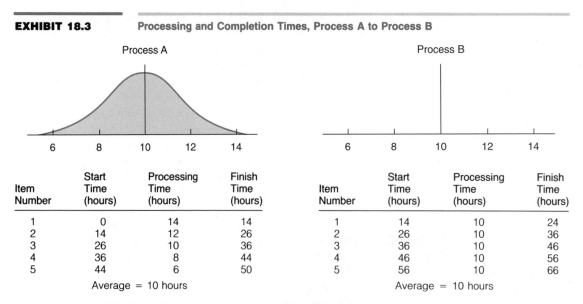

Item Number	Start Time (hours)	Processing Time (hours)	Finish Time (hours)	Item Number	Start Time (hours)	Processing Time (hours)	Finish Time (hours)
1	0	14	14	1	14	10	24
2	14	12	26	2	26	10	36
3	26	10	36	3	36	10	46
4	36	8	44	4	46	10	56
5	44	6	50	5	56	10	66
	Average = 10 hours				Average = 10 hours		

Here the flow is from Process A to Process B. Process A has a mean of 10 hours and a standard deviation of 2 hours; Process B has a constant 10-hour processing time.

We see that the last item was completed in 66 hours, for an average of 13.2 hours per item, although the expected time of completion was 60, for an average of 12 hours per item (taking into account the waiting time for the first unit by Process B).

Suppose we reverse the process—B feeds A. To illustrate the possible delays, we also reverse A's performance times (see Exhibit 18.4). Again, the completion time of the last item is greater than the average (13.2 hours rather than 12 hours). Process A and Process B have the same average performance time of 10 hours, and yet performance is late. In neither case were we able to achieve the expected output average rate. Why? Because the time lost when the second process is idle cannot be made up.

This example is intended to challenge the theory that capacities should be balanced to an average time. *Rather than balancing capacities, the flow of product through the system should be balanced.*

18.5 BOTTLENECKS, NONBOTTLENECKS, AND CAPACITY-CONSTRAINED RESOURCES

A **bottleneck** is defined as any resource whose capacity is less than the demand placed upon it. A bottleneck, in other words, is a process that limits

EXHIBIT 18.4　　Processing and Completions, Process B to Process A

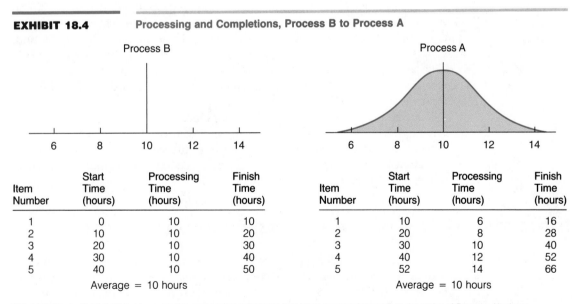

Item Number	Start Time (hours)	Processing Time (hours)	Finish Time (hours)	Item Number	Start Time (hours)	Processing Time (hours)	Finish Time (hours)
1	0	10	10	1	10	6	16
2	10	10	20	2	20	8	28
3	20	10	30	3	30	10	40
4	30	10	40	4	40	12	52
5	40	10	50	5	52	14	66
		Average = 10 hours				Average = 10 hours	

This is similar to Exhibit 18.3. However, the processing sequence has been reversed as well as the order of Process A's times.

throughput. It is that point in the manufacturing process where flow thins to a narrow stream. A bottleneck may be a machine, scarce or highly skilled labor, or a specialized tool. Observations in industry have shown that most plants have very few bottleneck operations, usually just several.

Capacity is defined as the available time for production. This excludes maintenance and other downtime. A **nonbottleneck** is a resource whose capacity is greater than the demand placed on it. A nonbottleneck, therefore, should not be working constantly since it can produce more than is needed. A nonbottleneck contains idle time.

A **capacity-constrained resource** (CCR) is one whose utilization is close to capacity and could be a bottleneck if it is not scheduled carefully. For example, a CCR may be receiving work in a job-shop environment from several sources. If these sources schedule their flow in a way that causes occasional idle time for the CCR in excess of its unused capacity time, the CCR becomes a bottleneck. This can happen if batch sizes are changed or if one of the upstream operations is not working for some reason and does not feed enough work to the CCR.

18.6 BASIC MANUFACTURING BUILDING BLOCKS

All manufacturing processes and flows can be simplified to four basic configurations, as shown in Exhibit 18.5. In Exhibit 18.5A, product that flows through Process X feeds into process Y. In section B, Y is feeding X. In section C, Process X and Process Y are creating subassemblies, which are then combined, say to feed the market demand. In section D, Process X and Process Y are independent of each other and are supplying their own markets. The last column in the exhibit shows possible sequences of nonbottleneck resources, which can be grouped and represented as Y, in order to simplify the representation.

The value in using these basic building blocks is that a production process can be greatly simplified for analysis and control. Rather than track and schedule all of the steps in a production sequence through nonbottleneck operations, for example, attention can be placed at the beginning and endpoints of the building block groupings.

18.7 METHODS FOR CONTROL IN SYNCHRONOUS PRODUCTION

In Exhibit 18.6, we illustrate the way bottlenecks and nonbottleneck resources should be managed, using the four basic building blocks in manufacturing described in Exhibit 18.5. Assume that Resource X has a market demand of 200 units of product per month and Resource Y has a market demand of 150 units per month, regardless of the building block configuration. Assume also that both X and Y have 200 hours per month available. To help understand

EXHIBIT 18.5 The Basic Building Blocks of Manufacturing Derived by Grouping Process Flows

Description	Basic Building Blocks Simplified by Grouping Nonbottlenecks	Original Representation
A. Bottleneck feeding nonbottleneck	X → Y → Market	Y over X → A → B → C → D → Market
B. Nonbottleneck feeding bottleneck	Y → X → Market	Y over A → B → C → D → X → Market
C. Output of bottleneck and nonbottleneck assembled into a product	X → Final Assembly → Market; Y → Final Assembly	X → Final Assembly → Market; A → B → C → D → Y → Final Assembly
D. Bottleneck and nonbottleneck have independent markets for their output	X → Market; Y → Market	X → Market; A → B → C → D → Market (Y over B)

X is a bottleneck.
Y is a nonbottleneck (has excess capacity).

our example, assume that each unit of product passing through X takes one hour of processing time and each unit passing through Y takes 45 minutes. With the available times, 200 hours of Resource X can produce 200 units of product and 200 hours of Resource Y can produce 267 units of product. Let's consider each of the four building blocks.

In Exhibit 18.6A, the flow of product is in a dependent sequence, that is, it must pass through both Resource X (Machine X) and Resource Y (Machine Y). Resource X is the bottleneck since it has a capacity of 200 units whereas Y has a capacity of 267 units. Resource Y can be used only 75 percent of the time, since it is starved for work (X is not feeding it enough to allow it to work longer). In this case, no extra product is produced.

Section B of the exhibit is the reverse of Section A: a nonbottleneck is feeding a bottleneck. Since X can put through only 200 units, we must be careful not to produce more than 200 on Y, or inventory will build up as work in process.

Section C of the exhibit shows that the outputs from X (a bottleneck) and Y (a nonbottleneck) are assembled into a product. As a nonbottleneck, Y has more capacity than X, so it can be used only 75 percent of the time, otherwise spare parts accumulate.

EXHIBIT 18.6

Product Flow through the Four Basic Building Blocks

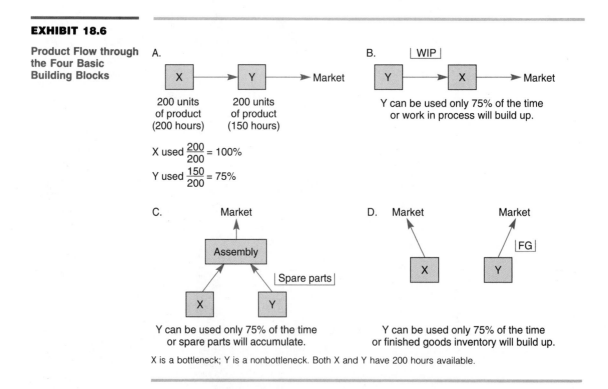

A.

X → Y → Market

200 units of product (200 hours)   200 units of product (150 hours)

X used $\frac{200}{200}$ = 100%

Y used $\frac{150}{200}$ = 75%

B. | WIP |

Y → X → Market

Y can be used only 75% of the time or work in process will build up.

C.   Market

Assembly

X   Y | Spare parts |

Y can be used only 75% of the time or spare parts will accumulate.

D.   Market   Market

| FG |

X   Y

Y can be used only 75% of the time or finished goods inventory will build up.

X is a bottleneck; Y is a nonbottleneck. Both X and Y have 200 hours available.

In Section D, market demands for X and Y are 200 units of each. Since 200 units from Y corresponds to only 75 percent of its capacity, Y can be used only 75 percent of the time or finished goods inventory will build up. The situations we have just discussed are important because current industry practice considers the percentage of resource utilization as one of the measures of performance. Such practice encourages the overuse of nonbottleneck resources, resulting in excess inventories.

Time Components

The following various kinds of time make up production cycle time:

1. *Setup time*—the time that a part spends waiting for a resource to be set up to work on this same part.
2. *Process time*—the time that the part is being processed.
3. *Queue time*—the time that a part waits for a resource while the resource is busy with something else.
4. *Wait time*—the time that a part waits not for a resource but for another part so that they can be assembled together.
5. *Idle time*—the unused time: that is, the cycle time less the sum of the setup time, processing time, queue time, and wait time.

For a part waiting to go through a bottleneck, queue time is the greatest. As we discuss later in this chapter, this is because the bottleneck has a fairly large amount of work to do in front of it (to make sure that is always working). For a nonbottleneck, wait time is the greatest. The part is just sitting there waiting for the arrival of other parts so that an assembly can take place.

Note the temptation that schedulers have to save setup times. Supposing the batch sizes are doubled to save half the setup times. What happens is that with a double batch size all of the other time would double: processing time, queue time, and wait time. Because these times are doubled while saving only half of the setup time, the net result is that the work in process is approximately doubled as is the investment in inventory.

Finding the Bottleneck

There are two ways to find the bottleneck (or bottlenecks) in a system. One is to run a capacity resource profile, and the other is to use our knowledge of the particular plant, look at the system in operation, and talk with supervisors and workers.

A *capacity resource profile* is obtained by looking at the loads placed on each resource by the products that are scheduled through them. In running a capacity profile, we assume that the data are reasonably accurate, although not necessarily perfect. As an example, consider that products have been routed through resources M1 through M5. Suppose our first computation of the resource loads on each resource caused by these products shows the following:

M1   130 percent of capacity
M2   120 percent of capacity
M3   105 percent of capacity
M4   95 percent of capacity
M5   85 percent of capacity

For this first analysis, we can disregard any resources at lower percentages since they are nonbottlenecks and should not be a problem. With the list in hand, we should physically go to the facility and check all five operations. Note that M1, M2, and M3 are overloaded, that is, scheduled above their capacities. We would expect to see large quantities of inventory in front of M1. If this is not the case, this means that errors exist somewhere—perhaps in the bill of materials or in the routing sheets. Let's say that our observations and discussions with shop personnel showed that there were errors in M1, M2, M3, and M4. We tracked them down, made the appropriate corrections, and ran the capacity profile again:

M2   115 percent of capacity
M1   110 percent of capacity
M3   105 percent of capacity
M4   90 percent of capacity
M5   85 percent of capacity

M1, M2, and M3 are still showing a lack of sufficient capacity, but M2 is the most serious. If we now have confidence in our numbers, we would use M2 as our bottleneck.

If the data contain too many errors to do a reliable data analysis, it may not be worth spending time (it could be months) making all the corrections. Instead, it would be quicker to use our knowledge about the VAT classification scheme (covered later in this chapter) to give us guidance. Defining the plant as V, A, or T helps direct us to where the bottlenecks would most likely be. To find a bottleneck, use the VAT scheme and then go and look and listen. From talking with workers and supervisors in the plant, we would expect to hear comments such as: "We're always waiting for parts from the NC machine" Or, "They're feeding me more work than I can possibly do and I can't keep up." These are clues to be followed.

Saving Time on Bottleneck and Nonbottleneck Resources

Recall that a bottleneck is a resource whose capacity is less than the demand placed on it. Since we focus on bottlenecks as restricting *throughput* (defined as *sales*), a bottleneck's capacity is less than the market demand. There are a number of ways we can save time on a bottleneck (better tooling, higher quality labor, larger batch sizes, reducing setup times, and so forth), but how valuable is this extra time? Very, very valuable!

AN HOUR SAVED AT THE BOTTLENECK ADDS AN EXTRA HOUR TO THE ENTIRE PRODUCTION SYSTEM.

How about time saved on a nonbottleneck resource?

AN HOUR SAVED AT A NONBOTTLENECK IS A MIRAGE AND ONLY ADDS AN HOUR TO ITS IDLE TIME.

Because a nonbottleneck has more capacity than the system needs for its current throughput, it already contains idle time. Implementing any measures to save more time does not increase throughput but only serves to increase its idle time.

Avoid Changing a Nonbottleneck into a Bottleneck

When nonbottleneck resources are scheduled with larger batch sizes, this action could create a bottleneck which we certainly would want to avoid. Consider the case in Exhibit 18.7, where Y_1, Y_2, Y_3, are nonbottleneck resources. Y_1 currently produces Part A, which is routed to Y_3, and Part B is routed to Y_2. To produce Part A, Y_1 has a 200-minute setup time and a processing time of 1 minute per part. Part A is currently produced in batches of 500 units; utilization is 70 percent. To produce Part B, Y_1 has a setup time of

EXHIBIT 18.7

Nonbottleneck Resources

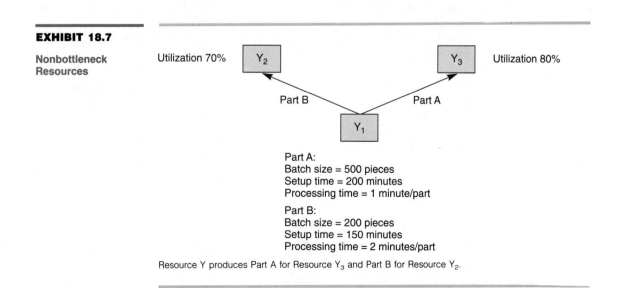

Utilization 70% Y_2 Y_3 Utilization 80%

Part B   Part A

Y_1

Part A:
Batch size = 500 pieces
Setup time = 200 minutes
Processing time = 1 minute/part

Part B:
Batch size = 200 pieces
Setup time = 150 minutes
Processing time = 2 minutes/part

Resource Y produces Part A for Resource Y_3 and Part B for Resource Y_2.

150 minutes and 2 minutes' processing time per part. Utilization is 80 percent, and Part B is currently produced in batches of 200 units.

Since setup time is 200 minutes for Y_1 on Part A, both worker and supervisor mistakenly believe that more production can be gained if fewer setups are made. Let's assume that batch size is increased to 1,500 units and see what happens. The illusion is that we have saved 400 minutes of setup. (Instead of three setups taking 600 minutes to produce three batches of 500 units each, there is just one setup with a 1,500-unit batch.)

The problem is that the 400 minutes saved serves no purpose, but this delay did interfere with the production of Part B. Y_1 also produces Part B for Y_2. The sequence before any changes were made was Part A (700 minutes), Part B (550 minutes), Part A (700 minutes), Part B (550 minutes), and so on. Now, however, when the Part A batch is increased to 1,500 units (1,700 minutes), Y_2 and Y_3 could well be starved for work and have to wait more time than they have available (30 percent idle time for Y_2 and 20 percent for Y_3). The new sequence would be: Part A (1,700 minutes), Part B (1,350 minutes), etc. Such an extended wait for Y_2 and Y_3 could be disruptive. Y_2 and Y_3 could become temporary bottlenecks and lose throughput for the system.

Drum, Buffer, Rope

Every production system needs some control point or points to control the flow of product through the system. If the system contains a bottleneck, the bottleneck is the best place for control. This control point is called the **drum,** for it strikes the beat that the rest of the system (or those parts which it influences) uses to function. Recall that a *bottleneck* is defined as a resource that does not have the capacity to meet demand. Therefore, a bottleneck is working all the time and one reason for using it as a control point is to make sure that the operations upstream do not overproduce and build up excess work-in-process inventory that the bottleneck cannot handle.

If there is no bottleneck, the next best place to set the drum would be a capacity-constrained resource (CCR). A capacity-constrained resource, remember, is one that is operating near capacity, but on the average has adequate capability as long as it is not incorrectly scheduled (for example, with too many setups, causing it to run short of capacity, or producing too large a lot size, thereby starving downstream operations).

If neither a bottleneck nor a CCR is present, the control point can be designated anywhere. The best position would generally be at some divergent point where the output of the resource is used in several downstream operations.

Dealing with the bottleneck is most critical, and our discussion focuses on assuring that the bottleneck always has work to do. Exhibit 18.8 shows a simple linear flow. Suppose that Resource D, which is a machine center, is a bottleneck. This means that the capacities are greater both upstream and downstream from it. If this sequence is not controlled, we would expect to see

EXHIBIT 18.8

Linear Flow of Product with a Bottleneck

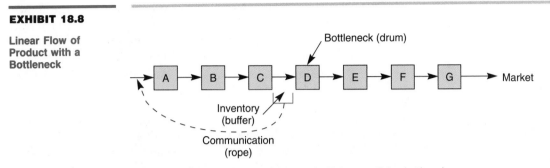

Product flows from Work centers A through G. Work center D is a bottleneck.

a large amount of inventory in front of Machine center D and very little anywhere else. There would be little finished-goods inventory because (by the definition of the term *bottleneck*) all the product produced would be taken by the market.

There are two things that we must do with this bottleneck:

1. Keep a **buffer** inventory in front of it to make sure that it always has something to work on. Because it is a bottleneck, its output determines the throughput of the system.

2. Communicate back upstream to A what D has produced so that A provides only that amount. This keeps inventory from building up. This communication is called the **rope**. It can be formal, such as a schedule, or informal, such as daily discussion.

The buffer inventory in front of a bottleneck operation is a **time buffer.** We want to make sure that Machine center D always has work to do, and it doesn't matter which of the scheduled products are worked on. We might, for example, provide 96 hours of inventory in the buffer as shown in Exhibit 18.9. Jobs A through about half of E are scheduled during the 24 hours of Day 1; Jobs E through a portion of Job I are scheduled during the second 24-hour day; Jobs I through part of L during the third 24-hour day; and Jobs L through P are scheduled during the 4th 24-hour day, for a total of 96 hours. This means that through normal variation, or if something happens upstream and the output has been temporarily stalled, D can work for another 96 hours protecting the throughput. (The 96 hours of work, incidentally, includes setups and processing times contained in the job sheets, which usually are based on engineering standard times.)

We might ask, How large should the time buffer be? The answer: As large as it needs to be to ensure that the bottleneck continues to work. By examining the variation of each operation, we can make a guess. Theoretically the size of the buffer can be computed statistically by examining past performance data, or the sequence can be simulated. In any event, precision is not critical. We could start with an estimate of the time buffer as one fourth of the total lead time of the system. Say the sequence A to G in our example (Exhibit 18.9) took a total of 16 days. We could start with a buffer of 4 days in front of D. If during the next few days or weeks the buffer runs out, we need to increase the buffer size. We do this by releasing extra material to the first operation, A. On the other hand, if we find that our buffer never drops below three days, we might want to hold back releases to A and reduce the time buffer to three days. Experience is the best determination of the final buffer size.

If the drum is not a bottleneck but a CCR (and thus it can have a small amount of idle time), we might want to create two buffer inventories—one in front of the CCR and the second at the end as finished goods. (See Exhibit 18.10.) The finished-goods inventory protects the market, and the time buffer

EXHIBIT 18.9

Capacity Profile of Machine Center D
(Showing assigned Jobs A through P over a period of four 24-hour days)

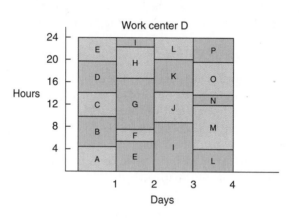

EXHIBIT 18.10

Linear Flow of Product with a Capacity-Constrained Resource

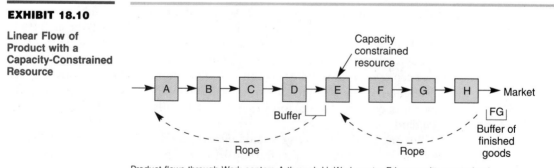

Product flows through Work centers A through H. Work center E is capacity constrained.

in front of the CCR protects throughput. For this CCR case, the market cannot take all that we can produce, so we want to ensure that finished goods are available when the market does decide to purchase.

We need two ropes in this case: (1) a rope communicating from finished-goods inventory back to the drum to increase or decrease output, and (2) a rope from the drum back to the material release point, specifying how much material is needed.

Exhibit 18.11 is a more detailed network flow showing one bottleneck. Inventory is provided not only in front of that bottleneck but also after the

EXHIBIT 18.11

Network Flow with One Bottleneck

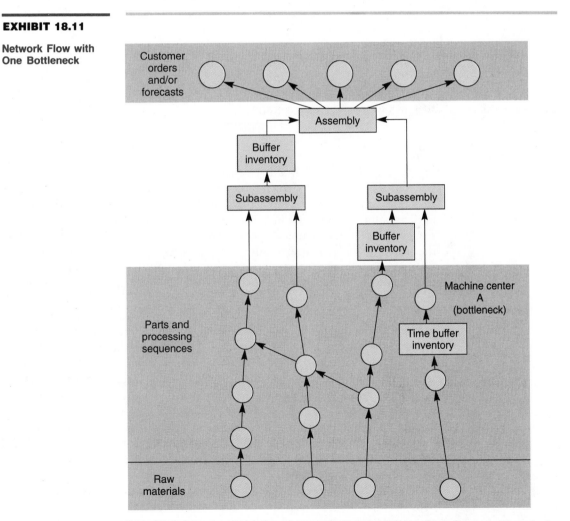

Product flows from raw materials through processing to the market. Inventory buffers protect throughput.

nonbottleneck assembly to which it is assembled. This ensures that the flow of product after it leaves the bottleneck is not slowed down by having to wait.

Importance of Quality

An MRP system allows for rejects by building a larger batch than actually needed. A JIT system cannot tolerate poor quality since JIT success is based on a balanced system. A defective part or component can cause a JIT system to shut down, thereby losing throughput of the total system. Synchronous production, however, has excess capacity throughout the system, except for the bottleneck. If a bad part is produced upstream of the bottleneck, the result is that there is a loss of material only. Because of the excess capacity, there is still time to do another operation to replace the one just scrapped. For the bottleneck, however, extra time does not exist, so that there should be a quality control inspection just prior to the bottleneck to ensure that the bottleneck works only on good product. Also, there needs to be assurance downstream from the bottleneck so that the passing product is not scrapped— that would mean lost throughput.

Batch Sizes

In an assembly line, what is the batch size? Some would say "one," because one unit is moved at a time; others would say "infinity," since the line continues to produce the same item. Both answers are correct, but they differ in their point of view. The first answer, "one," in an assembly line focuses on the *part* transferred one unit at a time. The second focuses on the *process*. From the point of view of the resource, the process batch is infinity since it is continuing to run the same units. Thus, in an assembly line, we have a **process batch** of infinity (or all the units, until we change to another process setup) and a **transfer batch** of one unit.

Setup costs and carrying costs were treated in depth in Chapter 13, Inventory Systems for Independent Demand. In the present context, setup costs relate to the process batch and carrying costs relate to the transfer batch.

A process batch is of a size large enough or small enough to be processed in a particular length of time. From the point of view of a resource, two times are involved: setup time and processing run time (ignoring downtime for maintenance or repair). Larger process batch sizes require fewer setups and therefore can generate more processing time and more output. For bottleneck resources, larger batch sizes are desirable. For nonbottleneck resources, smaller process batch sizes are desirable (by using up the existing idle time), thereby reducing work-in-process inventory.

Transfer batches refer to the movement of part of the process batch. Rather than wait for the entire batch to be finished, work that has been completed by that operation can be moved to the next downstream workstation so that it can

EXHIBIT 18.12   Effect of Changing the Process Batch Sizes on Production Lead Time for a Job Order of 1,000 Units

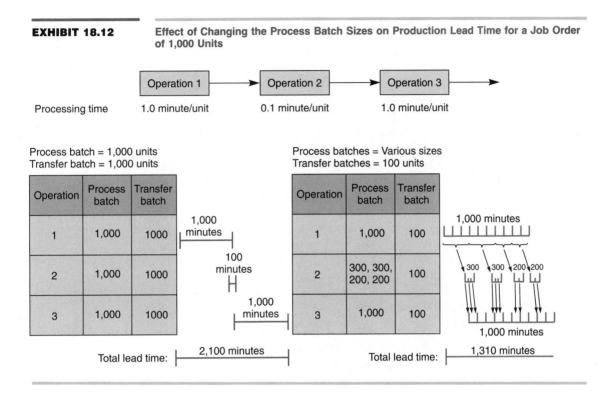

begin working on that batch. A transfer batch can be equal to a process batch but it cannot be larger.[1]

The advantage of using transfer batches that are smaller than the process batch quantity is that the total production is shorter and therefore the amount of work in process is smaller. Exhibit 18.12 shows a situation where the total production lead time was reduced from 2,100 to 1,310 minutes by using a transfer batch size of 100 rather than 1,000, and reducing the process batch sizes for Operation 2.

How to determine process batch and transfer batch sizes
Logic would suggest that the master production schedule (however it was developed) be analyzed as to its effect on various work centers. In an MRP system, this means that the master production schedule should be run through the MRP and the CRP (capacity requirements planning program) to generate a

---

[1] It would not be logical to have a transfer batch larger than the process batch. This could only occur if a completed process batch was held until sometime later when a second batch was processed. If this later time was acceptable in the beginning, then both jobs should be combined and processed together at the later time.

detailed load on each work center. Mokshagundam Srikanth states that from his experience there are too many errors in the manufacturing database to do this.[2] He suggests using the alternative procedures of first identifying the type of plant (V, A, or T, described later in this chapter) to suggest the probable CCRs and bottlenecks. There should be only one (or a few), and they should be reviewed by managers so that they understand which resources are actually controlling their plant. These resources set the drumbeat.

Rather than try to adjust the master production schedule to change resource loads, it is more practical to control the flow at each bottleneck or CCR to bring the capacities in line. The process batch sizes and transfer batch sizes are changed after comparing past performances in meeting due dates.

Smaller transfer batches give lower work-in-process inventory but faster product flow (and consequently shorter lead time). More material handling is required, however. Larger transfer batches give longer lead times and higher inventories, but there is less material handling. Therefore, the transfer batch size is determined by a trade-off of production lead times, inventory reduction benefits, and costs of material movement.

When trying to control the flow at CCRs and bottlenecks, there are four possible situations:

1. A bottleneck (no idle time) with no setup required when changing from one product to another.
2. A bottleneck with setup times required to change from one product to another.
3. A capacity constrained resource (CCR with a small amount of idle time) with no setup required to change from one product to another.
4. A CCR with setup time required when changing from one product to another.

In the first case, a bottleneck with no setup time to change products, jobs should be processed in the order of the schedule so that delivery is on time. Without setups, only the sequence is important. In the second case when setups are required, larger batch sizes combine separate similar jobs in the sequence. This means reaching ahead into future time periods. Some jobs will therefore be done early. Since this is a bottleneck resource, larger batches save setups and thereby increase throughput (the setup time saved is used for processing). The larger process batches may cause the early scheduled jobs to be late. Therefore, frequent small-sized transfer batches are necessary to try to shorten the lead time.

Situations 3 and 4 include a CCR without a setup and a CCR with setup time requirements. Handling the CCR would be similar to handling a nonbot-

---

[2] Mokshagundam L. Srikanth, "The Drum–Buffer–Rope System of Material Control" (New Haven, Conn.: Spectrum Management Group, 1987), pp. 25–37.

tleneck, though more carefully. That is, a CCR has some idle time. It would be appropriate here to cut the size of some of the process batches so that there can be more frequent changes of product. This would decrease lead time and jobs would be more likely to be done on time. In a make-to-stock situation cutting process batch sizes has a much more profound effect than increasing the number of transfer batches. This is because the resulting product mix is much greater leading to reduced WIP and production lead time.

How to Treat Inventory and Where to Charge Inventory Costs

The traditional view of inventory is that its only negative impact on a firm's performance is its carrying cost. We realize now inventory's negative impact also comes from lengthening lead times and creating problems with engineering changes. (When an engineering change on a product comes through, which is frequent, product still within the production system often must be modified to include the changes. Therefore, less work in process reduces the number of engineering changes to be made.)

Fox and Goldratt propose to treat inventory as a loan given to the manufacturing unit. The value of the loan is based only on the purchased items that are part of the inventory. As we stated earlier, inventory is treated in this chapter as material cost only, and without any accounting type value added from production. If inventory is carried as a loan to manufacturing, we need a way to measure how long the loan is carried. One measurement is dollar days.

Dollar days

A useful performance measurement is the concept of **dollar days,** which is a measurement of the value of inventory and the time it stays within an area. To use this measure, we could simply multiply the total value of inventory by the number of days.

Supposing Department X carries an average inventory of $40,000, and, on the average, the inventory stays within the department five days. In dollar days then, Department X is charged with $40,000 times five days or $200,000 dollar days of inventory. At this point one cannot say the $200,000 is high or low, but it does show where the inventory is located. Management can then see where it should focus attention and determine acceptable levels. Techniques can be instituted to try to reduce the number of dollar days while being careful that such a measure does not become a local objective (i.e., minimizing dollar days) and hurt the global objectives (such as increasing ROI, cash flow, and net profit.)

Dollar days could be beneficial in a variety of ways. Consider the current practice of using efficiencies of equipment utilization as a performance measurement. To get high utilizations, large amounts of inventory are held to keep everything working. However, high inventories would result in a high number of dollar days, which would discourage high levels of work in process. Dollar-day measurements could also be used in other areas:

- Marketing, to discourage holding large amounts of finished-goods inventory. The net result would be to encourage sale of finished products.
- Purchasing, to discourage placing large purchase orders that on the surface appear to take advantage of quantity discounts. This encourages Just-in-Time purchasing.
- Manufacturing, to discourage large work in process and producing earlier than needed. This would promote rapid flow of material within the plant.

18.8 COMPARING SYNCHRONOUS PRODUCTION TO MRP AND JIT

MRP uses **backward scheduling** after having been fed a master production schedule. MRP schedules production through a bill of materials explosion in a backward manner—working backward in time from the desired completion date. As a secondary procedure, MRP, through its capacity resource planning module, develops capacity utilization profiles of work centers. When work centers are overloaded, either the master production schedule must be adjusted or enough slack capacity must be left unscheduled in the system so that work can be smoothed at the local level (by work-center supervisors or the workers themselves). Trying to smooth capacity using MRP is so difficult and would require so many computer runs that capacity overloads and underloads are best left to local decisions, such as at the machine centers. An MRP schedule becomes invalid just days after it was created.

The synchronous manufacturing approach uses **forward scheduling** because it focuses on the critical resources. These are scheduled *forward* in time, ensuring that loads placed on them are within capacity. The noncritical (or nonbottleneck) resources are then scheduled to support the critical resources. (This can be done backward to minimize the length of time inventories are held.) This procedure ensures a feasible schedule. To help reduce lead time and work in process, in synchronous manufacturing the process batch size and transfer batch size are varied—a procedure that MRP is not able to do. (More on this later.)

Comparing JIT to synchronous manufacturing, JIT does an excellent job in reducing lead times and work in process, but it has several drawbacks:

1. JIT is limited to repetitive manufacturing.
2. JIT requires a stable production level (usually about a month long).
3. JIT does not allow very much flexibility in the products produced (products must be similar with a limited number of options).
4. JIT still requires work in process when used with Kanban so that there is "something to pull." This means that completed work must be stored on the downstream side of each workstation to be pulled by the next workstation.
5. Vendors need to be located nearby because the system depends on smaller and more frequent deliveries.

Since synchronous manufacturing uses a schedule to assign work to each workstation, there is no need for more work in process other than that being worked on. The exception is for inventory specifically placed in front of a bottleneck to ensure continual work, or at specific points downstream from a bottleneck to ensure flow of product.

Concerning continual improvements on the system, JIT is a trial-and-error procedure applied to a real system. In synchronous manufacturing, the system can be programmed and simulated on a computer, since the schedules *are* realistic (can be accomplished) and computer run time is short.

18.9 VAT CLASSIFICATION OF FIRMS

All manufacturing firms can be classified into one or a combination of three types designated V, A, and T, depending on the products and processes. Exhibit 18.13 shows all three types. The reason for using the **VAT classification** is obvious when we note the actual appearance of the product flow through the system. In a "V" plant, there are few raw materials and they are transformed through a relatively standard process into a much larger number

EXHIBIT 18.13   VAT Classification of Firms

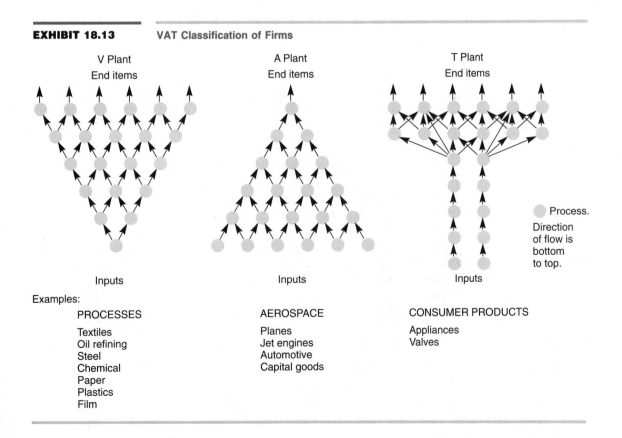

V Plant
End items

A Plant
End items

T Plant
End items

Inputs   Inputs   Inputs

Process.
Direction
of flow is
bottom
to top.

Examples:

PROCESSES   AEROSPACE   CONSUMER PRODUCTS

Textiles   Planes   Appliances
Oil refining   Jet engines   Valves
Steel   Automotive
Chemical   Capital goods
Paper
Plastics
Film

of end products. Consider a steel plant, for example: a few raw materials are converted into a large number of types of sheet steel, beams, rods, wire, and so forth.

An "A" plant is the opposite. In an "A" plant many raw materials, components, and parts are converted into few end products. Examples in aerospace would be making jet engines, airplanes, and missiles. In a "T" plant, the final product is assembled in many different ways out of similar parts and components. There are two stages in the production process: first, the basic parts and components are manufactured in a relatively straightforward way (the lower portion of the T) and are stored. Second, assembly takes place, combining these common parts into the many possible options to create the final product.

"V" Plant

Exhibit 18.14 shows the characteristics of a "V" plant. Problems that occur in a "V" plant show up as poor customer service, poor delivery, and high inventories of finished goods. The basic cause is generally a zealous effort to achieve high utilization levels, which instigates overly large process batch sizes.

"A" Plant

Exhibit 18.15 shows the characteristics of an "A" plant. In an "A" plant, management areas of concern are low equipment utilization, high unplanned overtime, parts shortages, and lack of control of the production process. When the flow is controlled correctly, there is a better utilization of resources, overtime is reduced or eliminated, and inventory levels are greatly decreased.

"T" Plant

The main characteristic of a "T" plant is that the parts and components are common to many end items. The assembly of end products in a "T" plant is a combinatorial problem, with customers placing orders for different colors, features, or sizes, thus creating many possibilities. The lead time, as far as the customer is concerned, is the height of the cross bar of the T. This means that a customer's order is assembled from the standard parts and components that are stocked. Typically, management erroneously perceives the problem as a need for better forecasting, improved inventory control in warehouses, and reduced unit cost by controlling overtime and setups and by introducing automation and simplified designs. See Exhibit 18.16 for a summary of "T" plant characteristics. The correct approach using synchronous manufacturing is to improve due-date delivery performance and to reduce operating expenses by:

1. Controlling the flow through the fabrication portion of the process.
2. Reducing batch sizes to eliminate the wavelike motion.
3. Stopping the "stealing" of parts and components at assembly.

EXHIBIT 18.14

"V" Plant

Characteristics

- There are a large number of end items, compared to the number of raw materials.
- Products use essentially the same sequence and processes.
- Equipment is generally capital intensive and specialized.
- There are a limited number of routings.
- Generally, each part crosses a resource only once.
- It tends to produce a large number of parts in a small amount of time.
- The total available space in the facility may be the only limit to inventory accumulation.
- Significant process changes require substantial resource investment.

Perceived problems

- Finished goods inventories are too large.
- Customer service/delivery is poor.
- Manufacturing managers complain that demand is constantly changing.
- Marketing managers complain that manufacturing is slow to respond.
- Interdepartmental conflicts are common.
- Production lead time becomes unpredictable.

Inventory levels

If there is a bottleneck:
- Large inventory (usually of wrong items) exists in front of the bottleneck. This inventory is caused by misallocation and overproduction prior to the bottleneck.
- Management tends to blame this wrong inventory on changing demand.
- The firm is unable to respond to market because of large inventory.
- Beyond the bottleneck there are small queues since there is excess capacity.
- Finished-goods inventories of the wrong products accumulate.

If there is no bottleneck:
There are large finished-goods inventories of the wrong products.

Causes

- Batch sizes are too large because the plant is capital intensive and the setup times are large.
- To achieve high levels of utilization, material is released to production too early.
- Supervisors are measured on utilizations.
- Jobs are combined for larger batches, and product families are grouped together.
- Considerable expediting is done at the bottleneck.

Correct course of action

- Reduce production lead times. This improves forecast accuracy and the ability to react to changes in demand.
- Increase customer service with:
  - Reliable promise dates
  - Reduced production lead times
- Reduce production costs by:
  - Selling more product
  - Reducing inventory
  - Focusing on quality improvements

EXHIBIT 18.15

"A" Plant

Characteristics

- Assembly feature is dominant.
- Machines tend to be general purpose rather than specialized.
- Assembly time tends to be long.
- Resources are shared within and across routings.
- Resource efficiencies are less than 100%, with unplanned overtime.
- Large completed-parts inventory exists but severe shortages exist for other parts.
- Process time typically is less than production lead time.
- Wandering bottlenecks occur.
- Fabrication complains that demand is changing, leading to plant chaos and poor vendor performance.
- Operating expense is a sore point (particularly the unplanned overtime).
- Problem parts are most likely not common to many assemblies.
- Relatively few parts cross the bottleneck (capacity constraint).
- Lack of control is voiced as the key problem.
- Assembly complains of shortages and mismatches.
- Production is designated early in the process (opposite of a "V" plant).
- People perceive the problem as a lack of parts.
- Routings can vary widely; one part may require 50 operations, while another for the same assembly may require only a few.
- The same machine may be used several times on the same part, during its routing.
- Parts are unique to specific end items (unlike a "V" or "T" plant); jet-engine blades, for example, are only for particular engines.
- There is little opportunity for misallocation of parts because they are peculiar to end items.

Conventional tactics for corrective-action

Reduce unit cost by

- Strict control of overtime. (Management perceives abuse of overtime; restriction of use aggravates problem.)
- Automation of processes. (This makes matters worse since flexibility is lost through the automation.)
- Better planning of labor needs. (The illusion is that there are too many workers.)

Improve control by

- Integrated production system. (The problem here is that different parts of the plant operate differently so a single system is unlikely to satisfy all needs.)

Actual causes

Too-large batch sizes and too-early release of material causing

- Moving bottlenecks
- Low utilizations
- Frequent use of overtime
- All the parts needed for assembly not there at the same time; assembly operations constantly short the parts needed to assemble the product.
- Frequent expediting to rush through missing parts.

Solution

- Reduce batch size.
- Use drum–buffer–rope for control.

EXHIBIT 18.16

"T" Plant

Characteristics

- Two distinctive processes and flows
  - Fabrication
  - Assembly
- Due-date performance is very poor; split between very early and very late (e.g., 40 percent early, 20 percent on time, 40 percent late).
- Overtime and expediting in fabrication are random and frequent.
- A very high degree of commonality of parts is dominant.
- The assignment of parts (even subassemblies) to orders occurs very late in the process.
- Fabrication is done in huge batches.
- There is a large amount of inventory at common stocking level between fabrication and assembly.

Causes of problems

- Improvement in due-date performance is attempted by heavy reliance on inventory, both finished and semifinished goods, and in volume and variety.
- The drive to attain efficiencies and dollars shipped.
  - undermines assembly activity objectives of due-date performance and assemble-to-order.
  - undermines fabrication activity objective of purchase and fabricate to forecast.
  - causes intentional misallocation of parts and cannibilization at assembly and subassembly areas.

Core problem

- Due-date performance is bad and management can't seem to be able to do anything about it.

Solution

- Reduce batch sizes in fabrication.
- Use drum–buffer–rope in fabrication to control flow.
- Stop the "stealing" of parts and components in assembly.

A Company Evolving into a "T" Plant

Motivation

- Company can expand market by offering options.

Sequence of activities occuring during the evolution

- To manage business with many options, a high number of common parts are engineered into the product.
- Common stocking levels develop.
- Business evolves to a strategy of assemble-to-order but fabricate to forecast (stock).
- Company desires to further increase responsiveness to the market.
- Customer lead times shortened by stocking subassemblies.
- Customer lead time further shortened by stocking finished goods.
- Once subassembly and fabrication are decoupled from customer demand, performance measures become key drive of these departments.
- Performance measures encourage counterproductive practices (such as stealing or misallocation of common parts).
- The original good idea has been corrupted.

EXHIBIT 18.17

Summary of VAT Plant Characteristics and Perceived Problems

Summary

"V" Plant   Capital intensive
Highly mechanized
Dedicated
Inflexible
Specialization within the flow process

"A" Plant   Less capital intensive
Versatile
Flexible machines
Can work at different levels of product flow

"T" Plant   Has fabrication and assembly areas
    Fabrication:
        Short routing
        Versatile machines
    Assembly area:
        Assembly is the predominant activity
        Short assembly lead time (days)

Management perceived problems

"V" Plant   Cost is the focus

"A" Plant   Need for control (constantly expediting, overtime, material availability, no idea of problem, wandering bottleneck)

"T" Plant   Due-date performance is usually bad and can't seem to be able to change it

Stealing parts is caused by the pressure from each supervisor in the assembly process to maintain high utilizations. When supervisors and workers are caught up on orders that are currently due, or when they cannot assemble a product because parts are missing, they reach ahead and assemble products for future orders. The result is that some other products in the assembly area are short those items and therefore late.

The second half of Exhibit 18.16 shows why a company would want to become a "T" plant and the steps it goes through as it eventually develops all the problems typical of this type plant.

In conclusion, the VAT classification can lead us quickly and directly to the source of the problem. Exhibit 18.17 shows a summary of plant characteristics and perceived problems. In a "V" plant, we would look for large inventories. In an "A" plant we would expect to find moving bottlenecks. In a "T" plant, we would suspect people are stealing parts to build ahead.

18.10 RELATIONSHIP WITH OTHER FUNCTIONAL AREAS

The production system must work closely with the other functional areas to achieve the best operating system. This section briefly discusses accounting and marketing—areas where conflicts can occur—and where cooperation and joint planning should occur.

Accounting's Influence on Equipment Investment Decisions

Sometimes we are led into making decisions to suit the measurement system rather than to follow the firm's goals. Consider the following example: Suppose that two old machines are currently being used to produce a product. The processing time for each is 20 minutes per part and, since each has the capacity of three parts per hour, they have the combined capacity of six per hour, which exactly meets the market demand of six parts per hour. Suppose that engineering finds a new machine that produces parts in 12 minutes rather than 20. However, the capacity of this one machine is only five per hour, which does not meet the market demand. Logic would seem to dictate that the supervisor should use an old machine to make up the lacking one unit per hour. However, the system does not allow this. The standard has been changed from the 20 minutes each to 12 minutes each and performance would look very bad on paper because the variance would be 67 percent high $[(20 - 12)/12]$ for units made on the old machines. The supervisor, therefore, would work the new machine on overtime.

Problems in cost-accounting measurements

Cost accounting is used for performance measurement, cost determinations, investment justification, and inventory valuation. Two sets of accounting performance measurements are used for evaluation: (1) global measurements, which are financial statements showing net profit, return on investment, and cash flow (which we agree with), and (2) local cost accounting measurements, showing efficiencies (as variances from standard) or utilization rate (hours worked/hours present).

From the cost-accounting (local measurement) viewpoint, then, performance has traditionally been based on cost and full utilization. This logic forces supervisors to activate their workers all the time, which leads to excessive inventory. The cost-accounting measurement system can also instigate other problems. For example, attempting to use the idle time to increase utilization can create a bottleneck, as we discussed earlier in this chapter. Any measurement system should support the objectives of the firm and not stand in the way. Fortunately, the cost-accounting measurement philosophy is now changing.

Marketing and Production

Marketing and production should communicate and conduct their activities in close harmony. In practice, however, they act very independently. There are many reasons for this. The difficulties range from differences in personalities and cultures to unlike systems of merits and rewards in the two functions (see Exhibit 18.18). Marketing people are judged on the growth of the company in terms of sales, market share, and new products entered. Marketing is sales oriented. Manufacturing people are evaluated on cost and utilization. Therefore, marketing wants a variety of products to increase the company's position while manufacturing is trying everything to reduce cost.

Data used for evaluating marketing and manufacturing are also quite different. Marketing data are "soft" (qualitative); manufacturing data are "hard" (quantitative). The orientation and experiences of marketing and production people also differ. Those in marketing management have likely come up through sales and a close association with customers. Top manufacturing managers have likely progressed through production operations and therefore have plant performance as a top objective.

Cultural differences can also be important in contrasting marketing and manufacturing personnel. Top managers in each can live quite differently since they have different motivations, goals, and hobbies as well. Marketing people tend to have a greater ego drive and are more outgoing. Manufacturing personnel tend to be more meticulous and perhaps more introverted (at least less extroverted than their marketing counterpart).

EXHIBIT 18.18

Marketing/ Manufacturing Areas of Necessary Cooperation but Potential Conflict

Problem Area	Typical Marketing Comment	Typical Manufacturing Comment
Capacity planning and long-range sales forecasting	"Why don't we have enough capacity?"	"Why didn't we have accurate sales forecasts?"
Production scheduling and short-range sales forecasting.	"We need faster response. Our lead times are ridiculous."	"We need realistic customer commitments and sales forecasts that don't change like wind direction."
Delivery and physical distribution	"Why don't we ever have the right merchandise in inventory?"	"We can't keep everything in inventory."
Quality assurance	"Why can't we have reasonable quality at reasonable cost?"	"Why must we always offer options that are too hard to manufacture and that offer little customer utility?"
Breadth of product line	"Our customers demand variety."	"The product line is too broad—all we get are short, uneconomical runs."
Cost control	"Our costs are so high that we are not competitive in the marketplace."	"We can't provide fast delivery, broad variety, rapid response to change, and high quality at low cost."
New-product introduction	"New products are our life blood."	"Unnecessary design changes are prohibitively expensive."
Adjunct services such as spare parts inventory support, installation, and repair	"Field-service costs are too high."	"Products are being used in ways for which they weren't designed."

Source: Reprinted by permission of the *Harvard Business Review*. An exhibit from "Can Marketing and Manufacturing Co-exist?" by Benson P. Shapiro (September/October 1977). Copyright © 1977 by the President and Fellows of Harvard College; all rights reserved.

The solution to coping with these differences is to develop an equitable set of measurements to evaluate performance in each area, and to promote strong lines of communication so that they both contribute to reaching the firm's goals.

In this section we present two examples to show that different objectives and measurement criteria can lead to the wrong decisions. These examples also show that, even though you may have all the data required, you still may not be able to solve the problem—unless you know how!

Example 18.1

In this first example, there are three products A, B and C, which are sold in the market at $50, $75 and $60 per unit respectively. The market will take all that can be supplied.

Three work centers, X, Y, and Z, process the three products in the manner shown in Exhibit 18.19. Processing times for each work center are also shown. Note that each work center works on all three products. Raw materials, parts, and components are added at each work center to produce each product. The per unit cost of these materials is shown as RM.

Which product or products should be produced?

EXHIBIT 18.19

Prices and Production Requirements for Three Products and Three Work Centers

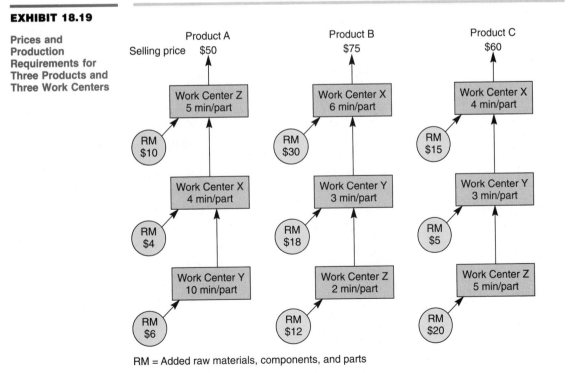

RM = Added raw materials, components, and parts

There is only one of each work center X, Y, and Z.

Solution

Three different simultaneous objectives could exist which lead to different conclusions:

1. Maximize sales revenue, since marketing personnel are paid commission based on total revenue.
2. Maximize per unit gross profit.
3. Maximize total gross profit.

In this example we use gross profit as selling price less materials. We could include other expenses as well, such as operating expenses but left them off for simplicity. (We include operating expenses in our next example.)

Objective 1: Maximize sales commission
The decision is simple. Sell only B at $75 per unit, and none of A and C.

Objective 2: Maximize per unit gross profit

(1) Product	(2) Selling Price	(3) Raw Material Cost	(4) Gross Profit per Unit (2) − (3)
A	$50	$20	$30
B	$75	$60	$15
C	$60	$40	$20

The decision would be to sell only product A which has a $30 per unit gross profit.

Objective 3: Maximize total gross profit
We can solve this problem either by finding total gross profit for the period, or the rate at which profit is generated. We use rate to solve the problem both because it is easier and because it is a more appropriate measure. We will use profit per hour as rate.

Note that each product has a different work center which limits its output. The rate at which the product is made is then based on this bottleneck work center.

(1) Product	(2) Limiting Work Center	(3) Processing Time/Unit (minutes)	(4) Product Output Rate (per hour)	(5) Selling Price	(6) Raw Material Cost	(7) Profit per Unit	(8) Profit Per Hour (4) × (7)
A	Y	10	6	$50	$20	$30	$180
B	X	6	10	75	60	15	150
C	Z	5	12	60	40	20	240

From our calculations, Product C provides the highest profit of $240 per hour.

Note that we get three different answers:

1. We choose B to maximize commission.
2. We choose A to maximize profit per unit.
3. We choose C to maximize total profit.

Choosing Product C is obviously the correct answer for the firm.

In this example, all work centers were required for each product and each product had a different work center as a constraint. We did this to simplify the problem and to assure that only one product would surface as the answer. If there were more work centers or the same work center constraint in different products, the problem can still easily be solved using linear programming (as in the Supplement to Chapter 8).

Example 2

In this example, shown in Exhibit 18.20, there are two workers on each of three shifts producing four products. The market demand is unlimited and takes all the products that the workers can produce. The only stipulation is that the ratio of products sold cannot exceed 10 to 1 between the maximum sold of any one product and the minimum of another. For example, if the maximum number sold of any one of the products is 100 units, the minimum of any other cannot be less than 10 units. Workers 1 and 2, on each shift, are not cross-trained and can only work on their own operations. The time and raw material (RM) costs are shown in the exhibit, and a summary of the costs and times involved is on the lower portion of the exhibit. Weekly operating expenses are $3,000.

The question is: What quantities of A, B, C, and D should be produced?

Solution

As in the previous example, there are three answers to this question, depending on each of the following objectives:

1. Maximum commission for sales personnel.
2. Maximizing per-unit gross profit.
3. Maximizing the utilization of the bottleneck resource (leading to maximum gross profit).

Objective 1: Maximizing sales commission on sales revenue
Sales personnel prefer to sell B and D (selling price $32) rather than A and C (selling price $30). Weekly operating expenses are $3,000.

The ratio of units sold will be: 1A : 10 B : 1 C : 10 D.

Worker 2 on each shift is the bottleneck and therefore determines the output.[3]

---

[3] Note that if this truly is a bottleneck with an unlimited market demand, this should be a seven-day-per-week operation, not just a five day work week.

EXHIBIT 18.20   Production Requirements and Selling Price for Four Products

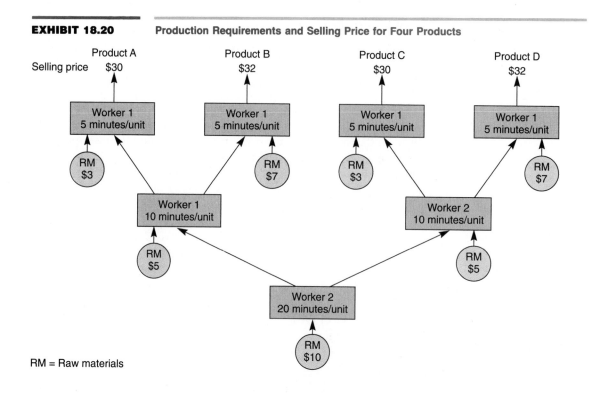

RM = Raw materials

| | | PROCESSING TIME REQUIRED PER UNIT | | |
| | Selling | | | Raw Material |
Product	Price (each)	Worker 1	Worker 2	Cost per Unit
A	$30	15 min.	20 min.	$18
B	32	15	20	22
C	30	5	30	18
D	32	5	30	22

One Worker 1 and one Worker 2 operate on each shift.
Three shifts.
Five days per week.
Eight hours per shift.
Operating expenses $3,000 per week.

5 days per week × 3 shifts × 8 hours × 60 minutes = 7,200 minutes per week available

Worker 2 spends these times on each unit:

A   20 minutes   C   30 minutes
B   20 minutes   D   30 minutes

Ratio of output units is 1 : 10 : 1 : 10. Therefore:

$$1x(20) + 10x(20) + 1x (30) + 10x(30) = 7,200$$
$$550x = 7,200$$
$$x = 13.09$$

Therefore the numbers of units produced is

A = 13
B = 131
C = 13
D = 131

Gross profit per week (selling price less raw material, less weekly expenses):

$$13(30 - 18) + 131(32 - 22) + 13(30 - 18) + 131(32 - 22) - 3,000$$
$$= 156 + 1,310 + 156 + 1,310 - 3,000$$
$$= (\$68) \text{ loss.}$$

Objective 2: Maximizing per unit gross profit

	Gross Profit	=	Selling Price	−	Raw Material Cost
A	12	=	30	−	18
B	10	=	32	−	22
C	12	=	30	−	18
D	10	=	32	−	22

A and C have the maximum gross profit so the ratio will be 10 : 1 : 10 : 1 for A, B, C, and D. Worker 2 is the constraint and has

$$5 \text{ days} \times 3 \text{ shifts} \times 8 \text{ hours} \times 60 \text{ minutes} = \frac{7,200 \text{ minutes available}}{\text{per week}}$$

As before A and B take 20 minutes, C and D take 30 minutes. Thus

$$10x(20) + 1x(20) + 10x(30) + 1x(30) = 7,200$$
$$550x = 7,200$$
$$x = 13$$

Therefore the number of units produced would be:

A = 131
B = 13
C = 131
D = 13

Gross profit (selling price less raw materials, less $3,000 weekly expense) would be:

$$131(30 - 18) + 13(32 - 22) + 131(30 - 18) + 13(32 - 22) - 3,000$$
$$= 1,572 + 130 + 1,572 + 130 - 3,000$$
$$= \$404 \text{ profit}$$

Objective 3: Maximizing the use of the bottleneck resource—Worker 2
For every hour Worker 2 works, the following number of products and gross profit result

(1) Product	(2) Production Time	(3) Units Produced per Hour	(4) Selling Price Each	(5) Raw Material Cost Each Unit	(6) Gross Profit per Hour (3) × [(4) − (5)]
A	20 minutes	3	$30	$18	$36
B	20	3	32	22	30
C	30	2	30	18	24
D	30	2	32	22	20

Product A generates the greatest gross profit per hour of Worker 2 time, so the ratio would be $10 : 1 : 1 : 1$ for A, B, C, and D.

Available time for Worker 2 is the same as before:

3 shifts × 5 days × 8 hours × 60 minutes = 7,200 minutes

Worker 2 should produce 10 A's for every 1B, 1C, and 1D, and Worker 2's average production rate will be:

$$10x(20) + 1x(20) + 1x (30) + 1x(30) = 7,200$$
$$280x = 7,200$$
$$x = 25.7$$

Therefore, the numbers of units that should be produced are:

A = 257
B = 25.7
C = 25.7
D = 25.7

And the gross profit (price less raw material, less $3,000 weekly expenses) will be:

$$257(30 - 18) + 25.7(32 - 22) + 25.7(30 - 18) + 25.7(32 - 22) - 3,000$$
$$= 3,084 + 257 + 308.4 + 257 - 3,000$$
$$= \$906.40$$

In summary, using three different objectives to decide how many of each product to make gave us three different results:

1. Maximizing sales commission resulted in a $68 loss.
2. Maximizing gross profit gave us a profit of $404.
3. Maximizing the use of the capacity-constrained worker gave us the best profit, which was $906.40.

Both examples demonstrate that production and marketing need to interact. Marketing should sell the most profitable use of available capacity. However, to plan capacity, production needs to know from marketing what products could be sold.

18.11 CONCLUSION

The measurement system within a firm should encourage the increase of net profits, return on investment, and cash flow. The firm can accomplish this if, at the operations level, it rewards performance based on the amount of throughput, inventory, and operating expense created. This is essential for the success of a firm.

To control throughput, inventory, and operating expense, the system must be analyzed to find the existence of bottlenecks and capacity-constrained resources. Only then can the company proceed to define a *drum* for control, *buffers* to assure throughput, and *ropes* for communicating the correct information to the correct locations, while minimizing work in process everywhere else. Without this focus, problems are not correctly diagnosed and solution procedures are impossible.

Goldratt defines nine rules (shown in Exhibit 18.21) to help guide the logic of an operating system and to identify the important points. These are basic to any operating system.

The underlying philosophy presented in this chapter—the vital importance of concentrating on system limitations imposed by capacity-constrained resources—has led Goldratt to broaden his view of the importance of system limitations and to develop his five-step "general theory of constraints."[4]

EXHIBIT 18.21

Goldratt's Rules of Production Scheduling

1. Do not balance capacity—balance the flow.
2. The level of utilization of a nonbottleneck resource is not determined by its own potential but by some other constraint in the system.
3. Utilization and activation of a resource are not the same.
4. An hour lost at a bottleneck is an hour lost for the entire system.
5. An hour saved at a nonbottleneck is a mirage.
6. Bottlenecks govern both throughput and inventory in the system.
7. Transfer batch may not and many times should not be equal to the process batch.
8. A process batch should be variable both along its route and in time.
9. Priorities can be set only by examining the system's constraints. Lead time is a derivative of the schedule.

---

[4] Eliyahu M. Goldratt, "Computerized Shop Floor Scheduling," *International Journal of Production Research* 26, no. 3 (1988), pp. 443–55; *The General Theory of Constraints* (New Haven, Conn.: Abraham Y. Goldratt Institute, 1989).

1. Identify the system constraints.
2. Decide how to exploit the system constraints.
3. Subordinate everything else to that decision.
4. Elevate the system constraints.
5. If, in the previous steps, the constraints have been broken, go back to Step 1, but don't let inertia become the system constraint.

In this context, Goldratt defines a constraint as "anything that limits a system from achieving higher performance versus its goal."

This general theory of constraints directs companies to find what is stopping them from moving toward their goals and finding ways to get around this limitation. If, in a manufacturing environment, the limitation is insufficient capacity, then ways to break the constraint might be overtime, specialized tools, supporting equipment, exceptionally skilled workers, subcontracting, redesigning product or process, alternate routings, and so on. Point 5 warns against letting biases in thinking prevent the search for further exploitation of constraints. For example, if a search and exploitation of a constraint has been conducted under the limitation of cost, make sure that this cost measure not be carried into the next search. Start clean each time.

One last comment in summary of this chapter: the firm should operate as a synchronized system, with all parts in harmony and supporting each other. Marketing, finance, production, and engineering (as well as all the other functional staff and administrative entities) are all necessary parts of the system and are all seeking to achieve the common goals of the firm.

18.12 REVIEW AND DISCUSSION QUESTIONS

1. State the global performance measurements and the operational performance measurements and briefly define each of them. How do these differ from the traditional accounting measurements?
2. Discuss process batch and transfer batches and how one might be able to determine what the sizes should be.
3. Compare and contrast JIT, MRP, and synchronized manufacturing stating their main features, such as, where each is or might be used, amounts of raw material and work-in-process inventories, production lead times and cycle times, methods for control, and so on.
4. Compare and contrast VAT type plants bringing in such points as where best applied, the main features of each (such as, product flow and equipment type), the major problems of each, the likely source of the problems, and the likely solutions to the problems.
5. Compare the importance and relevance of quality control in JIT, MRP, and synchronous manufacturing.
6. Discuss what is meant by forward loading and backward loading.

7. Define and explain the cause or causes of a moving bottleneck.

8. Explain how a nonbottleneck can become a bottleneck.

9. What are the functions of inventory in MRP, JIT, and synchronous production scheduling.

10. Define process batch and transfer batch and their meaning in each of these applications: MRP, JIT, and bottleneck or constrained resource logic.

11. Discuss how a production system is scheduled using MRP logic, JIT logic, and synchronous production logic.

12. Discuss the concepts of "drum, buffer, rope."

13. From the standpoint of the scheduling process, how are resource limitations treated in an MRP application and how are they treated in a synchronous production application?

14. What are the primary complaints that operations people have against the accounting procedures used in most firms? Explain how such procedures can cause poor decisions for the total company.

15. Most manufacturing firms try to balance capacity for their production sequences. Some believe that this is an invalid strategy. Explain why balancing capacity doesn't work.

16. Transfer batches and process batches many times may not and should not be equal. Discuss.

18.13 PROBLEMS

1. For the four basic configurations that follow, assume that the market is demanding product that must be processed by both Resource X and Resource Y for Cases I, II, and III. For Case IV, both resources supply separate, but dependent markets; that is, the number of units of output from both X and Y must be equal.

   Plans are being made to produce a product which requires 40 minutes for each unit on Resource X, and 30 minutes on Resource Y. Assume that there is only one unit of each of these resources, and that market demand is 1,400 units per month.

   How would you schedule X and Y? What would happen otherwise in each Case?

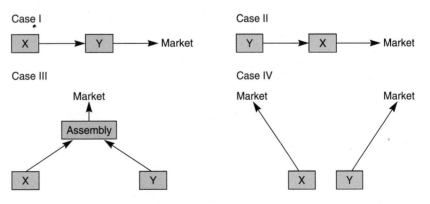

2. Following are the process flow sequences for three products: A, B, and C. There are two bottleneck operations—on the first leg and fourth leg marked with an X. Boxes represent processes, which may be either machine or manual.

    Suggest the location of the drum, buffer, and ropes.

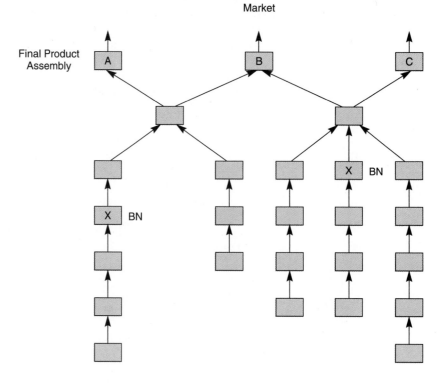

3. The following figure shows a production network model with the parts and processing sequences.

    State clearly on the figure: (1) where you would place inventory; (2) where you would perform inspection; and (3) where you would emphasize high-quality output.

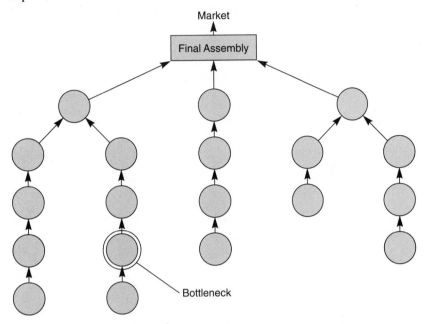

4. Following is the process flow for Products A, B, and C. Products A, B, and C sell for $20, $25, and $30, respectively. There is only one Resource X and one Resource Y which is used to produce A, B, and C for the numbers of minutes stated on the diagram. Raw materials are needed at the process steps as shown, with the costs in dollars per unit of raw material. (One unit is used for each product.)

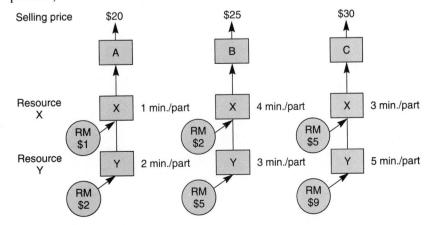

The market will take all that you can produce.

a. Which product would you produce to maximize gross margin per unit?
b. If sales personnel are paid on commission, which product or products would they sell and how many would they sell?
c. Which and how many product or products should you produce to maximize gross profit for a one-week period?
d. From (c) how much gross profit would there be for the week?

5. The following production flow shows Parts E, I, and N, Subassembly O, and final assembly for Product P.

A to B to C to D to E
F to G to H to I
J to K to L to M to N
E and I to O
N and O to P

B involves a bottleneck operation, and M involves a CCR.

a. Draw out the process flow.
b. Where would you locate buffer inventories?
c. Where would you place inspection points?
d. Where would you stress the importance of quality production?

6. Following are average process cycle times for several work centers. State which are bottlenecks, nonbottlenecks, and capacity constrained resources.

Processing time		Setup time

Processing time	Setup	Idle

Processing time	Setup	Idle

Processing time	Setup	Idle

Processing time	Setup	Idle

7. The following diagram shows the flow process, raw material costs, and machine processing time for three products: A, B, and C. There are three machines W, X, and Y, used in the production of these products and the times shown are in required minutes of production per unit. Raw material costs are shown in cost per unit of product. The market will take all that can be produced.

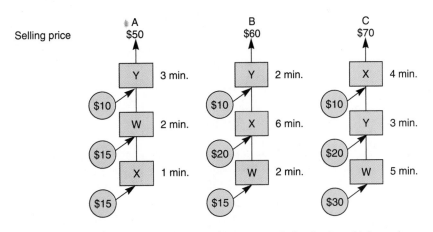

a. Assuming that sales personnel are paid on a commission basis, which product should they sell?

b. On the basis of maximizing gross profit per unit, which product should be sold?

c. To maximize total profit for the firm, which product should be sold?

8. Willard Lock Company is losing market share because of horrendous due date performance and long delivery lead times. The company's inventory level is very high and includes a good deal of finished goods that do not match the short-term orders. Material control analysis shows that purchasing has ordered on time, the vendors have delivered on time, and the scrap/rework rates have been as expected. However, the buildable mix of components and subassemblies do not generally match the short-term and past-due requirements at final assembly. End-of-month expediting and overtime is the rule, even though there is idle time early in the

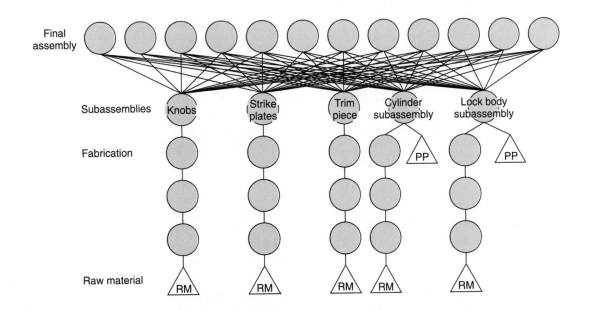

month. Overall efficiency figures are around 70 percent for the month. These figures are regarded as too low.

You have just been hired as a consultant and must come up with recommendations. Help them understand their problems and specifically state some actions that they should take.

18.14   SELECTED BIBLIOGRAPHY

Adams, Joseph; Egon Balas; and Daniel Zawack. "The Shifting Bottleneck Procedure for Job Shop Scheduling." *Management Science* 34, no 3 (March 1988), pp. 391–401.

Aggarwal, S. "MRP, JIT, OPT, FMS?" *Harvard Business Review,* September–October 1985, pp. 8–16.

Birk, Donald. "Increase Your Profits by Managing Your Constraints." *APICS, Conference Proceedings* (Falls Church, Va.: APICS, 1986), pp. 132–36.

Carrington, Gary, and David Eisenhart. "Materials Management and Finance: Partners in Systems Integration." *APICS, Conference Proceedings* (Falls Church, Va.: APICS 1983), pp. 396–99.

Connor, Susan. "Resource Costing: Reflecting the Changing Realities." *APICS, Conference Proceedings* (Falls Church, Va.: APICS, 1987), pp. 639–43.

Dunn, Alan G. "How to Determine the Real Cost of Your Product." *APICS, Conference Proceedings* (Falls Church, Va.: APICS, 1987), pp. 644–47.

Edwards, J. B., and J. A. Heard. "Is Cost Accounting the No. 1 Enemy of Productivity?" *Management Accounting,* June 1984, pp. 44–49.

Everdell, Romeyn. "MRP, JIT, and OPT: Not a Choice but a Synergy." *APICS, Readings in Zero Inventory* (Falls Church, Va.: APICS, 1985), pp. 11–16.

Fox, Robert E. "MRP, Kanban, or OPT—What's Best?" *Inventories and Production,* July–August 1982.

———. "OPT: An Answer for America, Leapfrogging the Japanese, Part IV." *Inventories and Production* 3, no. 24 (March–April 1983).

———."OPT(imizing) JIT, Leapfrogging the Japanese." *APICS, Conference Proceedings* (Falls Church, Va.: APICS, 1983), pp. 556–65.

———."OPT vs. MRP: Thoughtware vs. Software." *Inventories and Production* 3, no. 6 (November–December 1983).

Goldratt, Eliyahu M. "Computerized Shop Floor Scheduling." *International Journal of Production Research* 26, no. 3 (1988), pp. 443–55.

———. "Cost Accounting: The Number One Enemy of Productivity." *APICS, Conference Proceedings* (Falls Church, Va.: APICS, 1983), pp. 433–35.

———. "100% Data Accuracy—Need or Myth?" *APICS, Conference Proceedings* (Falls Church, Va.: APICS, 1982), pp. 64–66.

Goldratt, Eliyahu M., and Jeff Cox. *The Goal: Excellence in Manufacturing.* Croton-on-Hudson, N.Y.: North River Press, 1984.

Goldratt, Eliyahu M., and Robert E. Fox. *The Race for a Competitive Edge.* Milford, Conn.: Creative Output, 1986.

Kaplan, Robert S. "Yesterday's Accounting Undermines Production." *Harvard Business Review,* July–August 1984, pp. 95–102.

Koziol, David S. "How the Constraint Theory Improved a Job-Shop Operation." *Management Accounting,* May 1988, pp. 44–49.

LaDuke, Bettie. "Manufacturers and Accountants: Friends or Foes?" *APICS, Conference Proceedings* (Falls Church, Va.: APICS, 1987), pp. 611–13.

Main, Jeremy. "Under the Spell of Quality Gurus." *Fortune,* August 18, 1986, pp. 30–34.

Plossl, George W. "Managing by the Numbers—But Which Numbers." *APICS, Conference Proceedings* (Falls Church, Va.: APICS, 1987), pp. 499–503.

Pugliese, Richard E. "Cost Accounting in Manufacturing." *APICS, Readings in Production and Inventory Control* (Falls Church, Va.: APICS, 1985), pp. 11–16.

Shapiro, Benson. "Can Marketing and Manufacturing Coexist?" *Harvard Business Review,* September–October 1977, pp. 416–27.

Shute, David. "Standard Cost Variances: Help or Hindrance to Inventory Management." *APICS, Conference Proceedings* (Falls Church, Va.: APICS, 1987), pp. 636–38.

Srikanth, Mokshagundam L., and Harold E. Cavallaro, Jr. *Regaining Competitiveness: Putting the Goal to Work.* New Haven, Conn.: Spectrum Publishing Co., 1987.

Thompson, O., and S. J. Connor. "Manufacturing Critical Resources: A Total Manufacturing Planning System." *Production Inventory Management Review,* March 1986, pp. 24–32.

Vollmann, Thomas E. "OPT as an Enhancement to MRP II." *Production and Inventory Management,* second quarter 1986, pp. 38–47.

Wilson, Grab. "Sales and Materials: Natural Enemies or Allies." *APICS, Conference Proceedings* (Falls Church, Va.: APICS, 1986), pp. 583–87.

Chapter 19

Revising Operations Strategy

EPIGRAPH

Managers can no longer afford to view operations as a neutral apparatus for turning out goods. Every bit as much as, say, marketing, manufacturing has significant data to contribute to the broad process of strategic planning.

Alan M. Kantrow, "The Strategy-Technology Connection," *Harvard Business Review* (July–August 1980), p. 12.

KEY TERMS

Strategy

Strategic Vision

Production Capabilities

Positioning Manufacturing

Focused Factory

Manufacturing Task

Strategic Business Units

Service Strategy

Time-Based Competition

Service Factory

*W*e have titled this chapter "*Revising* Operations Strategy" to reflect the fact that the long-run success of virtually every organization depends on its ability to alter its operations strategy in light of changes in its environment. Our emphasis in this chapter is on manufacturing strategy rather than service strategy, but as we shall show, many concepts from services do pertain to manufacturing. We will begin by reviewing manufacturing's strategic role.

19.1 MANUFACTURING'S ROLE IN CORPORATE STRATEGY

The goal of any firm is to earn an acceptable return on its efforts. If the firm is a for-profit organization, the primary goal might be to maximize shareholders' wealth. Likewise, not-for-profit firms must earn some return on contributions to continue receiving funding. Whether the firm is a profit-seeking or a not-for-profit organization, the operations function must strategically add value to the chain of events required for the firm to meet its goals. Unfortunately, operations has typically been viewed as a tactical work center, rather than a strategic asset.

The development of manufacturing operations strategy has only recently been seen as worthy of the same scholarly research attention as corporate strategy, marketing strategy, and financial strategy. In the business world, manufacturing expertise was viewed as something that engineers and shop-floor people worried about, not senior executives and CEOs. In essence, manufacturing was treated as a support service, not a full partner in developing the strategy it had to implement. As a result of these attitudes, the best managers avoided manufacturing, and relatively few students studied manufacturing management. Moreover, through years of indifference to the manufacturing function (such as manufacturing executives not being invited to corporate strategy meetings), manufacturing executives failed to develop the external orientation necessary to make a positive contribution to corporate strategy. While marketing and finance executives spoke of market share and return on equity, manufacturing executives talked about machine utilization rates and inventory control practices.

The end effect of all these factors is that many U.S. manufacturing firms were less competitive than they could be, and ultimately became vulnerable in many markets to foreign competition. (See Chapter 2 on competitiveness.) The "wake-up call" has been sent, however, and manufacturing executives are now in the thick of the corporate strategy-making process.

Strategy Defined

Strategy is a set of plans and policies by which a company aims to gain advantages over its competition.[1] For the organization as a whole, strategy

---

[1] Wickham Skinner, "Manufacturing—Missing Link in Corporate Strategy," *Harvard Business Review* 47, no. 3 (May–June 1969), p. 193.

should be predicated on matching its *distinctive competence* (what it is good at) with its *primary task* (what it must do in light of competitive conditions). For the operations function (represented at the strategy level by the vice president of manufacturing or operations), operations strategy should provide clear, consistent operating policies and objectives that operations can reasonably achieve.

Robert Hayes and Steven Wheelwright list five characteristics of a strategy.[2]

1. *Time horizon.* Generally, the word *strategy* describes activities that involve an extended time horizon, both the time it takes to carry out the activities and the time it takes to observe their impact.

2. *Impact.* Although the consequences of pursuing a given strategy may not become apparent for a long time, their eventual impact can be significant.

3. *Concentration of effort.* An effective strategy usually requires concentrating activity, effort, or attention on a fairly narrow range of pursuits. Focusing on these chosen activities implicitly reduces the resources available for other activities.

4. *Pattern of decisions.* Although some companies need to make only a few major decisions to implement their chosen strategy, most strategies require that a series of certain types of decision be made over time. These decisions must be supportive of one another, in that they follow a consistent pattern.

5. *Pervasiveness.* A strategy embraces a wide spectrum of activities ranging from resource allocation processes to day-to-day operations. In addition, the need for consistency over time in these activities requires that all levels of an organization act, almost instinctively, in ways that reinforce the strategy.

A Strategic Vision for Manufacturing

An effective manufacturing strategy requires manufacturing executives to have a **strategic vision** on how all the firm's productive resources relate to one another and to the environment. Exhibit 19.1 illustrates these general relationships using the notion of world-class manufacturing (WCM) to define the overarching goal of the firm's operations. As the exhibit suggests, achievement of this goal entails continual interactions with the customer and suppliers, and integrated manufacturing through appropriate blending of total quality control (TQC), computer-integrated manufacturing (CIM), and Just-in-Time production (JIT). Central to this integration is a system perspective, for as Thomas Gunn points out, "manufacturing consists of the entire range of activities from product and process design, through manufacturing planning and control, through the production process itself, through distribution, and

---

[2] Robert H. Hayes and Steven C. Wheelwright, *Restoring Our Competitive Edge: Competing through Manufacturing* (New York: John Wiley & Sons, 1984), pp. 27–28.

EXHIBIT 19.1   Manufacturing for Competitive Advantage Framework

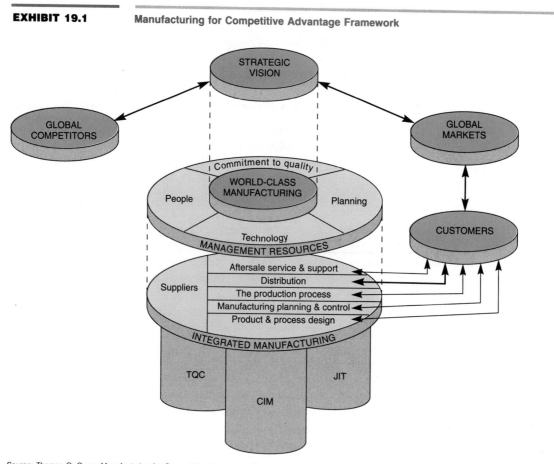

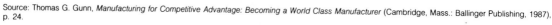

Source: Thomas G. Gunn, *Manufacturing for Competitive Advantage: Becoming a World Class Manufacturer* (Cambridge, Mass.: Ballinger Publishing, 1987), p. 24.

through after-sale services and support in the field. This is one continuous spectrum. No activity can be performed along this spectrum without affecting some other part of it either upstream or downstream."[3]

With Gunn's model, bear in mind that the WCM vision is not the only one around, nor necessarily the best one for the firm as a whole. Recall the four-stage model of Wheelwright and Hayes from Chapter 2; the important thing

---

[3] Thomas G. Gunn, *Manufacturing for Competitive Advantage: Becoming a World Class Manufacturer* (Cambridge, Mass.: Ballinger Publishing 1987), pp. 28–29.

is to select the role that best supports the corporate strategy.[4] Although it is unlikely that much support can be generated by manufacturing not being involved at all (stages 1 and 2), it is not always desirable to adopt an offensive manufacturing posture involving major capital investment to become "world class" or to "out-Japanese the Japanese." Indeed, money may be more effectively spent in better marketing, better product design, or in just shaping up current manufacturing operations through continuous improvement approaches.

Production Capabilities as Competitive Weapons

The strategic vision should recognize specific production capabilities that can be used as competitive weapons. Some sample **production capabilities** and some current concepts or tools used to enhance them or "make them go" are

Production Capabilities	Supporting Concepts or Tools
High quality	Total quality control, design for manufacturing
Adaptive production system	Flexible manufacturing systems (FMS)
Low-cost/high-volume production	Just-in-Time systems (JIT)
Speed to market	Concurrent engineering, FMS, JIT
Augmented service	Service factory concepts

The way these capabilities are used as a part of the firm's arsenal of weapons varies. Sometimes the capabilities have a particular marketing benefit. For example, E. T. Wright & Company, manufacturer of men's shoes for over 100 years, advertises its craftsmanship—as many as 17 days and 155 intricate steps, executed mostly by hand, go into making a pair of E. T. Wright shoes. In other instances, production capabilities have significant implications for corporate management in deciding what types of markets to enter. For example, Chaparral Steel of Texas uses the best production technology from around the world to produce over 350 products in its minimill. Finally, the capabilities of some companies lie in simply excelling in low-cost/high-volume manufacture. For example, the General Electric dishwasher manufacturing plant in Louisville has gone beyond manual JIT systems. The plant has adopted a "use

---

[4] Whybark summarizes this model:

The four stages reflect increasing participation of manufacturing in the strategic planning process of the firm and perceptiveness in assessing developments in manufacturing technology. They range from "internally neutral" (meaning just don't screw up), through "externally neutral" (be as good, or bad, as the competition), to "internally supportive" (make sure that manufacturing strategy is not inconsistent with company goals) and, finally, to "externally supportive" (wherein manufacturing is a full partner in the strategic planning process and looks for ways of enhancing their capability to support company goals).

From D. Clay Whybark, "Strategic Manufacturing Management," IRMIS Working Paper #W601, School of Business, Indiana University, February 1986.

a part, make a part" approach: machines produce parts right next to the assembly line.[5]

Choosing which of these capabilities to use as a company's main competitive weapon is the basic purpose of the strategy development process.

19.2 DEVELOPING AND IMPLEMENTING A MANUFACTURING STRATEGY

The cyclical process of developing and implementing a manufacturing strategy is depicted in Exhibit 19.2. Customer feedback about new product needs or desired changes are received by marketing, research and development, and manufacturing. Information is then exchanged among these groups to determine whether there is a proper balance among customers' desires, product technology, and process capabilities. This information is then fed to the corporate level to determine whether the planned product or change is consistent with the overall strategic vision of the firm.

The next step in the process is for manufacturing management to determine the proper product-process focus and define tasks and priorities. All of the strategic decisions required to implement the strategy must then be made. Finally, the actual manufacturing activity required to produce the product must be completed so the product can be delivered to the customer. By seeking feedback from the customer, a closed-loop strategy development cycle is formed in which strategy is continuously updated to meet customers' needs.

Positioning Manufacturing

Positioning manufacturing might be thought of as the matching process between the firm's distinctive competence and its primary task. This process must take account of both product and production system life cycles and survey the market environment to determine the general direction manufacturing strategy must take over the next 5 to 10 years. We can identify two extreme types of manufacturing orientations that would be considered here: process focus and product focus. *Process focus* refers to systems that produce a wide variety of customized products. These systems must be flexible; hence, management must master flexible process technologies to compete effectively. *Product focus* refers to systems that produce standardized products in relatively high volume. These systems must be highly efficient; hence, management must master the coordination required to keep inventories flowing smoothly

---

[5] The three example plants in this section have been identified as among the 10 best managed in a 1984 survey. See Gene Bylinsky, "America's Best-Managed Factories," *Fortune,* May 28, 1984, pp. 16–24.

EXHIBIT 19.2

The Manufacturing
Strategy Cycle

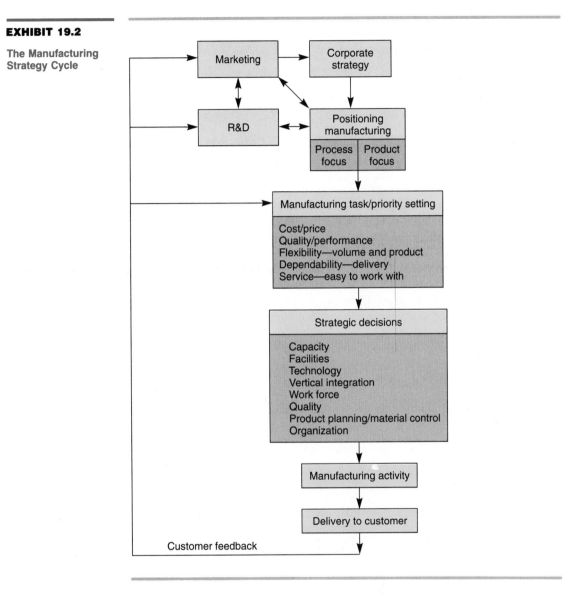

through the system. Examples of these two dimensions of positioning as they relate to finished-goods inventory policies are shown in Exhibit 19.3.

Factory Focus

Regardless of whether a firm follows a product or process positioning strategy, the factory which executes it should itself be focused. According to Wickham Skinner:

EXHIBIT 19.3

Examples of the Two
Dimensions of
Positioning

Type of System	FINISHED GOODS INVENTORY POLICY	
	Make to Stock	Make to Order
Product-focused	Office copiers TV sets Calculators Gasoline	Construction equipment Buses, trucks Experimental chemicals Textiles Wire and cable Electronic components
Process-focused	Medical instruments Test equipment Electronic components Some steel products Molded plastic parts Spare parts	Machine tools Nuclear pressure vessels Electronic components Space shuttle Ships Construction projects

Source: Elwood S. Buffa, *Meeting the Competitive Challenge* (Homewood, Ill.: Richard D. Irwin, 1984), p. 51.

A factory that focuses on a narrow product mix for a particular market niche will out-perform the conventional plant, which attempts a broader mission. Because its equipment, supporting systems, and procedures can concentrate on a limited task for one set of customers, its costs and especially its overhead are likely to be lower than those of the conventional plant. But, more importantly, such a plant can become a competitive weapon because its entire apparatus is focused to accomplish the particular manufacturing task demanded by the company's overall strategy and marketing objective.[6]

As we noted in Chapter 8 the **focused factory** concept can be applied not only to a single plant but to departments within a plant. This pertains when a company has a diversity of products, technologies, and market requirements that must be served by a single facility. Called the *plant within a plant* (PWP) concept, it divides the plant both organizationally and physically into separate units, each with its own manufacturing task, its own work force, production control system, and processing equipment. Engineering, materials handling, and so forth are specialized as needed.

An example of separating a company's total manufacturing capability into specialized units is provided by the Lynchburg Foundry, a subsidiary of the Mead Corporation. This foundry has five plants in Virginia. One plant is a job shop, making mostly one-of-a-kind products. Two plants use a decoupled batch process and make several major products. A fourth plant is a paced assembly line operation that makes only a few products, mainly for the

---

[6] Wickham Skinner, "The Focused Factory," *Harvard Business Review* (May–June 1974), p. 115.

automotive market. The fifth plant is a highly automated pipe plant, making what is largely a commodity item.

While the basic technology is somewhat different in each plant, there are many similarities. However, the production layout, the manufacturing processes, and the control systems are very different. This company chose to design its plants so that each would meet the needs of a specific segment of the market in the most competitive manner. Its success would suggest that this has been an effective way to match manufacturing capabilities with market demand.[7]

The Manufacturing Task

The output of the positioning process is the general identification of those tasks that the manufacturing function must do well. The specific formalization of these requirements is collectively referred to as the **manufacturing task,** or manufacturing priorities. These consist of the factors we've discussed throughout the book—low cost/price, high quality, high flexibility, and high dependability.

According to T. J. Hill, choosing which task is most important depends on what wins orders in the marketplace.[8] As we saw in Chapter 2, U.S. manufacturing executives saw consistent quality as the top competitive priority, so we would assume that all firms would choose to compete on quality. On the other hand, Japanese executives listed low price as their top priority so they aren't competing on quality, right? Wrong. They have *already* achieved consistent quality, so they are going after the next class of customer—the one who is price sensitive. Using another one of Hill's terms, quality has become just a *qualifying criterion* to enter the market—it lets you play but won't necessarily win orders since the other guy has high quality, too.

In one sense, this interpretation of task priorities runs counter to the generally held view that a manufacturing organization can't do everything well, and hence trade-offs among priorities must be made. A closer look, however, suggests that there is no inconsistency, providing we recognize that acceptable performance that permits qualification for a market is a given, not a priority. In our view, not excelling in everything does not always mean that a firm is doing poorly on a task priority; it simply means that it is doing better on some than on others. The key is that the firm excels on those tasks critical to supporting corporate strategy and keeps working to improve on other dimensions.

---

[7] Ibid., p. 114.

[8] T. J. Hill, "Teaching Manufacturing Strategy," *International Journal of Operations & Production Management* 6, no. 3 (1986), pp. 10–20.

Evaluating Manufacturing Task Priorities

A systematic approach to evaluating the priority of specified task elements was proposed by Wheelwright.[9] As Exhibit 19.4 shows, this approach starts by identifying **strategic business units** (SBUs), which are essentially homogenous product-market groupings within, say, a division of a company. (Such a grouping might be large home appliances for the consumer market, which is part of a general appliance division.) The next step is defining the task elements ("criteria and measurement"), which can be done through structured discussions or brainstorming. The third step is identifying, through a series of conferences, historical priorities and determining required priorities.

The results of this third step are shown in the table in Exhibit 19.5. This particular table was developed by a vice president of manufacturing to see how his peers (vice presidents) and subordinates (manufacturing managers) perceived current and required task element priorities. The task elements (cost,

EXHIBIT 19.4

Application of Manufacturing Criteria by Corporate Manufacturing Staff

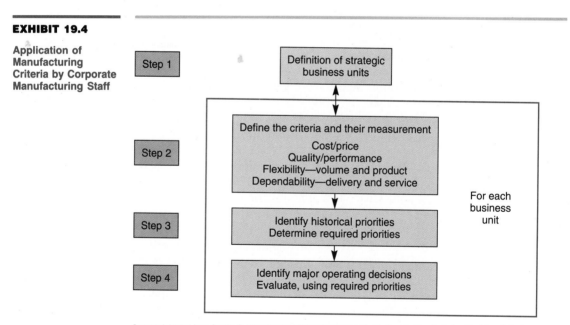

Source: Adapted from Steven C. Wheelwright, "Reflecting Corporate Strategy in Manufacturing Decisions," *Business Horizons*, February 1978, p. 63, to emphasize service.

---

[9] Steven C. Wheelwright, "Reflecting Corporate Strategy in Manufacturing Decisions," *Business Horizons*, February 1978, pp. 57–66.

quality, dependability, and flexibility) are given across the top of the table. The numerical entries in the table reflect the point totals (from 0 to 100) assigned by nonmanufacturing vice presidents (VP) and manufacturing managers (MM) to each product and task combination. "As is" refers to the current priority weighting for a task element relative to a given product; "should be" refers to what weighting should actually be applied in light of the mission of manufacturing in the corporate strategy; and "needs more (less)" refers to the numerical difference between "as is" and "should be."

The final step of the process is to make changes in operating decisions in light of the evaluation exercise.

Some of the actions indicated from an analysis of the table in Exhibit 19.5 were

Product 1 should have modest increases in quality and dependability at the expense of manufacturing cost efficiencies.

EXHIBIT 19.5

Current and Required Priorities as Assessed by Vice Presidents (VP)* and Manufacturing Managers (MM)*

	COST		QUALITY		DEPENDABILITY		FLEXIBILITY	
	VP	MM	VP	MM	VP	MM	VP	MM
Product 1								
As is	42	44	17	15	25	26	16	15
Should be	28	46	24	16	31	26	17	12
Needs more (less)	(14)	2	7	1	6	0	1	(3)
Product 2								
As is	26	20	37	43	24	22	13	15
Should be	26	30	36	38	26	20	12	12
Needs more (less)	0	10	(1)	(5)	2	(2)	(1)	(3)
Product 3								
As is	34	36	27	28	23	19	16	17
Should be	34	38	29	24	24	20	13	18
Needs more (less)	0	2	2	(4)	1	1	(3)	1
Product 4								
As is	24	34	30	22	19	17	27	27
Should be	39	44	20	25	23	15	18	16
Needs more (less)	15	10	(10)	3	4	(2)	(9)	(11)
Product 5								
As is	45	37	21	14	18	31	16	18
Should be	22	31	24	13	35	35	19	21
Needs more (less)	(23)	(6)	3	(1)	17	4	3	3

* Criteria totals for VP and MM for each priority = 100.

Source: Steven C. Wheelwright, "Reflecting Corporate Strategy in Manufacturing Decisions," *Business Horizons*, February 1978, p. 65.

Products 2 and 3 should have no significant changes in manufacturing.

Product 4 should have a significant improvement in manufacturing cost efficiencies at the expense of quality and flexibility.

Product 5 should have a significant increase in dependability at the expense of manufacturing cost efficiencies.

Developing the task statement

The following seven guidelines for specifying the production task have been recommended by Skinner.[10] An illustrative task statement is presented in the Insert.

1. The task must be written in sentences and paragraphs, not merely outlined.
2. It must explicitly state the demands and constraints on manufacturing relative to corporate strategy, marketing policy, financial policy, industry and firm economics, and industry and firm technology.
3. It must state how production can be a competitive weapon and how performance can be judged.
4. It must identify what will be especially difficult ("the name of the game").
5. It must explicitly state priorities, including what may have to suffer.
6. It must explicitly state the requirements on the production control system, quality control system, production work force, and production organization structure.
7. It should be boiled down to a symbol, slogan, or cartoon to communicate it to all members of the production organization and managers in other parts of the organization.

INSERT   Illustrative Task Statement for an Automobile Manufacturer

Our task is to be number one in the production of economy cars within the next five years. We will be judged by how quickly we can adapt our methods and technology to a competitive car design, by how our product performs under rigorous testing, and by customer satisfaction. The name of the game is quality. Cost reduction through productivity improvements will have to come later. We will structure our production organization as a product team with designers, engineers, and operations people working in unison under a "heavy duty" product manager who can

---

[10] Modified from Wickham Skinner, *Manufacturing in the Corporate Strategy* (New York: John Wiley & Sons, 1978), pp. 107–8.

maintain the integrity of the product concept throughout the design-production cycle.* Our slogan will be "80 MPG and with style".

* A "heavy-duty" product manager has a vision of the product and the clout to carry it through. See Kim B. Clark and Takahiro Fujimoto, "The Power of Product Integrity," *Harvard Business Review* 68, no. 6 (November–December 1990), pp. 107–18.

We have presented a framework that should be helpful in developing an operations strategy. In practice, there is no one best way to develop such a strategy. During a conference involving six major manufacturing firms, a summary of experiences of defining and developing manufacturing strategy was developed. This summary is displayed in Exhibit 19.6. The conference included representatives from the following industries: computer equipment, pharmaceutical, valves, telecommunications, furniture, and electrical submersible pumps. Notice that the elements of strategy involve many different decisions for operations managers.

Levels of Strategic Decisions

Strategic decisions may be generalized as being infrastructural or structural. Exhibit 19.7 lists eight common decisions that must be made when formulating manufacturing strategy. The outcomes of these decisions determine the strategic capabilities of the firm.

The first four decision categories in Exhibit 19.7 are generally viewed as structural in nature. These decisions have a long-term impact, and they are difficult to reverse once implemented due to their substantial capital investment requirements.

The last four decision categories are more tactical in nature and considered to be infrastructural. These decision categories do not typically necessitate large capital outlays. However, the outcomes of these decisions are generally difficult to change since they are tightly linked to established operating procedures. Indeed, overcoming resistance to infrastructural change can be more costly in time and other resources than replacing an expensive piece of capital equipment.

Frequent strategic decision-making obviously can be counter to maintaining consistency of strategic vision and stability of operations. However, most firms make at least one major decision that falls into one of these categories during the course of any year. The pattern of structural and infrastructural decisions constitutes the operations strategy of a business unit.

Implementation

Implementation of a revised operations strategy should be managed like any other project. That means establishing a plan of action, allocating decision

EXHIBIT 19.6

Summary of Firms' Experiences of Defining and Formulating Manufacturing Strategy

Firm	Definition of Manufacturing Strategy	Objectives of Manufacturing Strategy	Responsibility for Formulation
1	A shared vision and common vocabulary which unites the organization and determines the organizational, managerial, and measurement systems	Provide a competitive advantage and support to higher-level corporate plans	Corporate manufacturing council
2	A plan to adapt successfully to environmental changes	Match manufacturing resources to the environment	Vice president of production and engineering
3	A plan to execute strategic objectives for long-term success	Realize new opportunities for success	Corporate management with cross-functional input
4	A framework for planning	Guide the total product delivery process	Operations council
5	An overall umbrella that coordinates planning and provides consistent functional interfaces	Develop a decisive competitive edge utilizing existing resources	Executive management group
6	A focus on what is needed for survival	Provide support for marketing and customer service	Vice president of manufacturing with strategic planning unit (cross-functional)

Source: Ann Marucheck, Ronald Pannesi, and Carl Anderson, "An Exploratory Study of the Manufacturing Strategy Process in Practice," *Journal of Operations Management* 9, no. 1 (January 1990), p. 113.

EXHIBIT 19.7

Manufacturing Strategy Decision Categories

Capacity—amount, timing, type
Facilities—size, location, specialization
Technology—equipment, automation, linkages
Vertical Integration—direction, extent, balance
Work force—skill level, wage policies, employment security
Quality—defect prevention, monitoring, intervention
Production planning/materials control—sourcing policies, centralization, decision rules
Organization—structure, control/reward systems, role of staff groups

Relation to Corporate Strategy	Relation to Marketing	Elements of Strategy	Areas of Analysis
Reactive to strategic business objectives with feedback	Increasingly market oriented, plant charters change from product focus to customer/market focus	Process, capacity, technology, vertical integration, quality, mfg. planning and control, human resources, information	Identify opportunities for change. Analysis of consistency in decision-making patterns at division level and on shop floor. How can change be effected?
Reactive to corporate objectives and goals with feedback	Definitely product driven, also driven by R&D	Facility size, inventory versus service, technology, vertical integration	Communication patterns
Reactive to broad corporate objectives with continuous feedback	Supports marketing through innovation and solution of customers' problems	New product analysis, costs, delivery goals, culture development	Identify opportunities for reorganization and consolidation
Together with marketing strategy constitutes business strategy	Complements marketing strategy to determine how products will be delivered	Plant and equipment, capacity, facilities, technology, metrics, control systems, human resources, communication, plant charters	Strategy versus culture, compatibility analysis
Reactive to corporate SBU objectives, consistency checks.	Identification of logistics/service as a competitive weapon, marketing and operations share common philosophy	Product analysis, factory focus, product engineering, capacity utilization, cost structures, systems (mfg. planning and control/information)	Retailer and distributor analysis, quality analysis
Reactive with feedback to corporate strategic planning group	Reactive to marketing strategy, provides marketing support in new product development, serving new markets and maintaining showpiece manufacturing facility	Forecast versus capacity, new products, technology needs, SBU plan, culture (MRP, Quality and Human Resources)	Market attractiveness/internal strength analysis. What resources are needed to build strength in attractive markets?

responsibility, and developing the coordination and control mechanisms to ensure that the job gets done.

A particularly useful tool in clarifying who is responsible for different parts of strategy implementation is the *linear responsibility chart*. Exhibit 19.8 is an example of such a chart developed by manufacturing management personnel of a large appliance manufacturer as a basis for implementing JIT. This identifies which function has decision authority (Z), is consulted (C), or is informed (I), regarding different aspects of JIT introduction. Once the responsibilities are clearly understood, project scheduling techniques such as the critical path method can be readily employed.

EXHIBIT 19.8

Linear Responsibility Chart

Departments

Project Activities	Manufacturing	Production Control	Quality Control	Industrial Engineering	Computer Systems	Manufacturing Engineering	Design Engineering	Distribution	Training	Purchasing	Cost Accounting	Maintenance
Floor organization	Z	C		C				I		I		
Re-layout	C	C		Z		C		I				
Level schedule	C	Z			C			C		C	I	
WIP planning	C	Z			I					I	I	
Maintenance schedule	Z											C
Supplier quality				Z			C			C		
Supplier delivery	C	Z								C	I	
Pull system design	Z	C		I	C	I	C	I		I	I	I
Material handling	C	Z	C	C		C						
MRP interface	C	Z			C					I		
Equipment experiment	Z						C					
Receiving area	C	Z								I		
Costing		Z			C						C	
Supervisor training	C								Z			
Worker training	C	C							Z			

Z = Responsible for activity.
C = Consulted on activity.
I = Informed about activity.

Exhibit 19.9 lists experiences in implementing manufacturing strategy. The columns that include problems encountered and lessons learned provide particularly valuable insight gained through years of experience. Notice that lack of commitment and resistance to change seem to be recurring obstacles to strategy implementation. Key lessons learned could be summarized as the need for clear plans, employee participation, and careful performance management.

19.3 OPERATIONS STRATEGY IN SERVICES

Operations strategy development for service organizations is somewhat analogous to that for manufacturing organizations. Service organizations must also start with a strategic vision for the firm. We outlined many different aspects of this strategic vision in Chapter 4. In addition, stages of service firm competitiveness were presented in Chapter 2. One of the key distinctions between service and manufacturing strategies is that positioning of a service strategy depends on largely intangible service characteristics rather than largely tangible product characteristics of manufacturing.

Service Strategy and Leverage Points

A **service strategy** consists of these three key components: developing and positioning a service concept, formulating an operating strategy, and designing the service delivery system. If careful consideration is given to the several leverage points displayed in Exhibit 19.10, operating strategies are better matched to service concepts.

Servers are the greatest points of leverage. As the point of contact with the customer, the server represents the entire service organization. Most of us have plenty of horror and hero stories concerning servers such as salespersons, clerks, or food servers.

Networks take many forms. For example, communication and transportation networks can be critical assets or barriers to entry in travel and entertainment industries. Relationships among employees, customers, suppliers, and competitors can add value to a service organization. These relationships may be viewed as networks of information and influence. These networks help feed the information bank of the firm. Many information-intensive service firms depend heavily both formal and informal information banks.

The density of business patterns influences the productivity, thus the economics, of the firm. For example, an instant shoe repair business located in a mall relies on the density of the traffic pattern in that mall to supply a flow of prospective customers. Appropriate selection of real estate is required to take advantage of such density. Favorable lease or purchase agreements are critical to the livelihood of many retail service businesses such as the instant shoe repair business.

Technology and financial capability are also sources of strategic leverage that can make or break a service concept. Some service concepts, such as LensCrafters (eyeglass franchises), require both the technology and financial resources to implement an operations strategy.

Each of these strategic points of leverage should be considered when developing service strategies to match service concepts. A sound operations strategy also depends on many factors to match the strategy to the service delivery system. These integrating factors are also listed in Exhibit 19.10. These factors affect the success of implementing the strategy, whereas the leverage points are all factors to be considered in the development of the service strategy.

A Methodology for Service Branch Strategy Determination

R. B. Chase, G. Northcraft, and G. Wolf developed the following six-step methodology for strategy determination and implementation for branches of a

EXHIBIT 19.9

Summary of Firms'
Experiences in
Implementing
Manufacturing
Strategy

Firm	Implementation Plan	Evaluation/Feedback	Measurement Categories	Length of Strategy Experiences
1	Specific strategies for each resource. Develop tactical plans, procedures, and requirement plans	Performance measures, adherence to action plans	Quality, lead times, procurement prices, inventory reductions	7 yrs
2	Plan and performance discussed at two-day retreat. Syndicates of senior managers develop statement and objectives for specific issues	Review of operational plan, semiannual formal meetings	Inventory turns, quality costs	3 yrs
3	Manufacturing group plans developed with middle and lower levels of managers	Weekly committee reviews of group plans	Cost, vendor performance, quality, MRP/ schedule performance, inventory, accounting	4 yrs
4	Development of an operations methodology specifying communications, metrics, and management of intangibles	Quarterly meetings of operations council	Cost of quality, delivery lead time, new product introduction	15 yrs
5	Strategy sessions, task force formation, quality training, and implementation plans at cross-functional retreats	Formal monthly meeting	Cost of quality, cost reduction, manufacturing cycle time, service/ delivery goals.	5 yrs
6	Three-day meeting of cross-functional management to develop implementation plan	Monthly meetings with management, quarterly plant meetings	MRP performance, variances, cost of quality, inventory versus service, technology obsolescence	5 yrs

Source: Ann Marucheck, Ronald Pannesi, and Carl Anderson, "An Exploratory Study of the Manufacturing Strategy Process in Practice," *Journal of Operations Management* 9, no. 1 (January 1990), p. 114.

Problems Encountered	Lesson Learned	Strategy Length Reformulation	Cultural Changes	Predisposing Conditions
Focus on cost reduction, collection of data for new cost accounting system	Recognizing the difference between top-down conditions and bottom-up opportunities	—	Communications, Cost acctg system, First pass design	New CEO
Developing commitment, converting middle management, building teamwork.	Plans must be concise.	Annual/quarterly	—	New CEO
Expectations set too low, managerial inertia	Involvement, regular review, objective performance measures.	Continuous	New performance evaluation, organizational change	Several poor economic years, new president
Building new culture to match new organization and environment, sustaining successes, managerial lip service.	Must be a demonstrated need, communication, cultural change, teamwork, it takes time	3–5 yrs/quarterly	New metrics, teamwork, change agenda: education, communication, procedures, reward/evaluation	New president, flat revenue growth, revelation that certain procedures weren't adding value
Changing plant profiles, establishing new families of products, matching marketing to manufacturing capabilities, realistic service goals	Pervasiveness, participation/involvement needed, open lines of communication, integrate functions	5 yrs/quarterly	Design for manufacturing communication new vocabulary ownership of process	Poor economic year, new president
Building teamwork and trust, commitment means not changing priorities, do it right the first time.	Settle for evolutionary change, total involvement needed, consistency, breed success	1 yr/quarterly	New layout, new labor classification, decision-making style, cost acctg system, egalitarian rules	New facility, new president

EXHIBIT 19.10   **Sources of Leverage in Service Strategy**

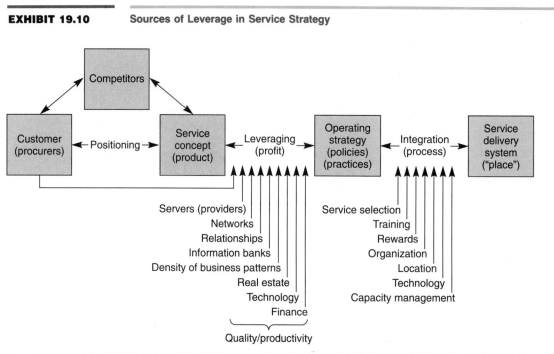

Source: James L. Heskett, "Rethinking Strategy for Service Management," in *Service Management Effectiveness,* ed. David E. Bowen, Richard B. Chase, and Thomas G. Cummings and Associates (San Francisco: Jossey-Bass Publishers, 1990), p. 30.

savings and loan.[11] Exhibit 19.11 illustrates the decision-making process involved.

1. Identify the mission of the branch of service unit.   Environmental factors (such as the presence or absence of competitors) and the overall corporate strategy combine to define a mission or optimal goal for a particular branch of the service organization. This mission should take into account the role of the service unit in the service network of the parent organization and includes both efficiency (production) and effectiveness (marketing) goals.

2. Identify the contact requirements.   A definition of the contact requirements necessary for the service unit to accomplish the goals set out in the mission is needed. The four contact features shown provide a framework for thinking about and identifying a branch's requirements. For instance, if a service unit has the goal of acquiring a reputation for personal service, contact training is the critical dimension for that service unit to consider.

---

[11] R. B. Chase, G. Northcraft, and G. Wolf, "Design of High Contact Services: Application to Branches of a Savings and Loan," *Decision Sciences* 15, no. 4 (Fall 1984), p. 551.

EXHIBIT 19.11   General Decision-Making Framework for Service System Strategy Determination

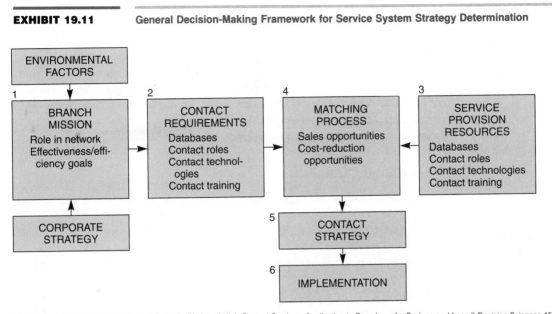

Source: R. B. Chase, G. Northcraft, and G. Wolf, "Design of High Contact Services: Application to Branches of a Savings and Loan," *Decision Sciences* 15, no. 4 (Fall 1984), p. 551.

3. Identify the service provision resources available. After identifying the contact requirements, the service unit needs to think about what resources are available to fill the needs or requirements specified in Step 2.

4. Search for a match between contact requirements and resources available. The service-provision resources and the contact requirements derived from the mission are input into a matching process. The outcomes of the matching process should pair requirements to possibilities (resources) for dealing with the requirements (e.g., sales specialists at branches that are used by higher income customers).

5. Develop a revised contact strategy. The match is turned into plans for the design of service production and delivery in the service unit. This typically boils down to deciding if a branch should focus on sales or on routine transitions.

6. Implement the revised contact strategy. For this, databases provide a means for keeping track of customer accounts and demographics to help the sales mission. *Contact roles* are the specific skills needed in interacting with the customer, and *contact technologies* are the means by which services are actually delivered.

19.4   SPEED AND SERVICE: THE NEW DIFFERENTIATORS

Recall from Chapter 2 (Exhibit 2.8) that speed and service have shown the greatest increase in importance since 1984. Product flexibility, volume flexibility, and delivery have also increased in importance. Conformance, price, and performance have decreased in importance. These factors, previously considered as differentiators, are now competitive prerequisites. Timeliness and service have emerged as new sources of distinctive competencies on which competitors can differentiate themselves in the global marketplace.

Time-Based Competition

By competing on time—developing and producing a product ahead of the competition—a firm enjoys first-mover advantages that include higher pricing, high market share, productivity improvement, and reduced risks.[12] The entire value chain that extends from conception of a new product through delivery and after-sales service must be evaluated from a time-based perspective.

Time-based competition has a goal of eliminating wasted time from all activities in the value chain. Time reduction methods include overlapping product development activities, improving communication channels, simplifying complex processes, reducing setup times, and smoothing production flow. The Japanese have excelled at these time-reducing activities.

Exhibit 19.12 illustrates the time-based advantage that a Japanese producer of marine gears has over a Western producer of equivalent products. How do the Japanese (and many progressive U.S. firms) shorten their product development cycles? Much of the answer can be seen in Exhibit 19.13. Traditional product development has occurred in distinct phases. Information was passed in one batch from one development phase to another. By overlapping product development phases and frequently transferring small batches of information among product development team members from different phases, time can be compressed.

Service-Based Competition: The Service Factory

A firm can be fast in developing and producing products but still not be user-friendly—readily accessible, easy to communicate with, and responsive to needs and complaints. In short, starting with the factory, customers want service through each stage of the production-distribution process. The *service*

---

[12] Joseph D. Blackburn, *Time-Based Competition: The Next Battleground in American Manufacturing* (Homewood, Ill.: BUSINESS ONE IRWIN, 1991), p. 95.

EXHIBIT 19.12

Improving Response Time in New Product Development (Marine Gears)

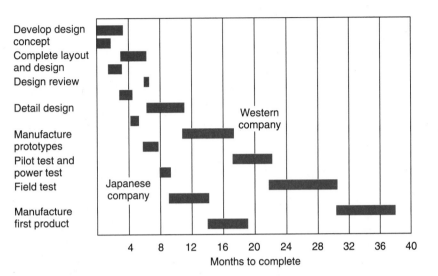

Source: Joseph D. Blackburn, *Time-Based Competition: The Next Battleground in American Manufacturing* (Homewood, Ill.: BUSINESS ONE IRWIN, 1991), p. 89.

factory concept means that a manufacturing firm, in addition to its products, produces a blend of services as well, which are integral to each of its products.[13] We believe that a manufacturing firm can become a service factory by employing the following ideas.

Redefining the factory mission as a service concept

Most contemporary manufacturers prominently feature a customer orientation in their mission statements. These statements tend to focus solely on product attributes such as functional capabilities and quality levels rather than the product's benefits to the customer. On the other hand, service businesses, because they deal with intangible processes, are usually benefit oriented. This subtle, but important, distinction is reflected in James Heskett's definition of the service concept: "What are important elements of the service to be provided in terms of results produced for the customers?" The answer to this question must be the central element of the mission statement for the service factory.

---

[13] This section has been adapted from R. B. Chase and W. J. Erikson, "The Service Factory," *The Academy of Management Executive* 2, no. 3 (1988), pp. 191–96.

EXHIBIT 19.13

Phased versus Overlapping Approach in New-Product Development

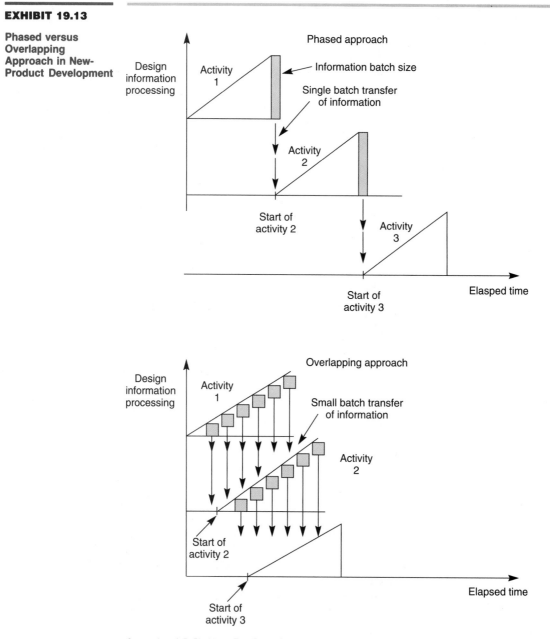

Source: Joseph D. Blackburn, *Time-Based Competition: The Next Battleground in American Manufacturing* (Homewood, Ill.: BUSINESS ONE IRWIN, 1991), p. 143.

An open systems logic

The traditional approach to manufacturing is to seal off the core production technology from outside disturbances so that production may be accomplished without disruption. Happiness for the production manager is the production of one kind of product, all of one color, with infinitely long production runs. This is done by placing organizational buffers (marketing, product design, etc.) between the customer and the production system. There are, however, fewer and fewer markets that can be effectively serviced by this closed system philosophy. What is needed today is quite the opposite—an open system that includes the customer—one that can gather and act on information from the marketplace in real time. This is more than Just-in-Time production; it is Just-in-Time service across the entire spectrum of the firm's encounters with customers.

A well-managed customer-system interface

An effective service process requires that information exchanges between the system and the customer are handled smoothly, quickly, and inexpensively. Interorganizational systems (IOS) is emerging as an approach to achieving these objectives. An IOS, in contrast to a distributed data processing system, crosses company boundaries rather than being under the control of a single organization. IOSs are common in the service industry (for example, the CIRRUS nationwide network of automated teller machines that perform banking services for a variety of banks). IOSs are just now being introduced into manufacturing, linking manufacturers with their suppliers (who should be viewed as an extension of the service factory). Where appropriate, such as in multiple sourcing situations, a firm can have its computer shop among suppliers and automatically initiate purchase orders to ensure timely and low-cost meeting of customer needs. Saturn, the newest GM division, electronically links dealers' showrooms to the factory so that orders may be made in real time.

Decoupled production facilities

The four walls of the factory no longer limit the domain of manufacturing. Manufacturing can be done at the customer's plant, in the repairshop, and even in transit. For many manufacturers, the service factory consists of multiple production units as small as one technician in the field and as large as a satellite assembly complex adjacent to a customer's plant. (This may seem like a radical notion, but companies who sell liquid oxygen and nitrogen have been installing production equipment on or next to customer sites for years.) The extension of production throughout the value-added chain call for closer coordination of field/factory operations, which may require enlarging factory management's job to include field production planning as well as internal operations. Widespread employee rotation through service positions may become a necessity as well.

Customer-oriented factory personnel

Service factory managers and supervisors should be far more inclined to interact with the customers than similar personnel of the traditional plant. This means they must be adept at communication and sensitive to customer needs, in addition to possessing technical knowledge. Like the typical service supervisor, the service factory supervisor is a visible representative of the organization, who can make or break a relationship with a customer. Of course, not all shop-floor employees should interact with customers. As a practical matter, jobs of service factory personnel can be differentiated as being high customer contact or low customer contact, as is common in service businesses.

Adoption of refined service quality measures

The typical cost of quality report used in manufacturing covers prevention costs, appraisal costs, internal failure costs, and external failure costs. The first three items are internally oriented and pertain only to tangible products. External failure costs include warranty costs, out-of-warranty repairs and replacement, customer complaints and lost future sales, product liability, and transportation costs. Of these, only customer complaints is a direct measure of service quality. We suggest that adoption of a service perspective on quality calls for a new type of report explicitly for factory management. This might be termed a *factory customer service report,* including such service measures as response time of engineering and production control to customer information requests, user's manual accuracy, completeness of the database on each customer's product needs, speed of emergency modifications and emergency repairs, perhaps even courtesy. Although many manufacturers pride themselves on responding to these service needs, few routinely measure their performance to the level of detail that service organizations do.

Goods and service marketing blended with goods production

A well-run factory is a powerful marketing tool, yet some major manufacturing firms still do not recognize this point and discourage all customers from visiting the plant. In fact, we know of a company that requires its own managers from outside the manufacturing function to go through an elaborate request and sign-off process before they are allowed to visit the shop floor! From a service perspective, this not only presents a curious image to the customer but it clearly violates a basic precept of any marketing campaign: "Gain access to the customer to show off your wares." The service factory, by recognizing its sales mission as well as its production mission, should be expressly designed to maximize the sales opportunity that exists when the customer is in the system. This is done by extending and refining the growing practice of making quality visible, highlighting workforce skills, and demonstrating the capabilities of the technology. For many companies in the production control and engineering software business as well as manufacturing, the plant should be viewed as a showroom where their own systems can be sold along with the main product. This process, however (which can be referred to as "modeling your own clothes"), has not been exploited to its full potential. Computer manufacturers, for example, sell state-of-the-art MRP systems, yet many don't use these products to run their plants. Despite the fact that there may be good reasons (software was developed by other divisions of the company, they have older systems that do the job, and so on) viewing the factory as a selling tool might well justify a change in strategy.

Applications of the Service Factory Concept

A number of manufacturers have included aspects of the service factory in their operations, although none that we know of has used the service factory notion as a unifying concept. Some examples of plants that excel in particular features follow.

Chaparral Steel and Worthington Mills are clearly adherents of an open system philosophy. They encourage customers not only to visit plants but also to work on site with factory personnel on the full range of production issues. In addition, they have production people spend time at their customers' and suppliers' facilities to gain insight into how the factory can be of service. Hewlett-Packard is well known for its customer-oriented factory personnel who, in addition to just being friendly, can spin out the technical features of HP's Just-in-Time production system at the drop of a hat.

GE's Louisville dishwasher plant was designed to show off their technologies to visitors as well as to make products. Carrying this point further, Yamazaki Machinery UK's Worcester plant was designed with two objectives: One objective is to be the most advanced CNC machine tool factory in the world. The second goal is to be "a showplace designed to impress the industrialists and engineers of Western Europe with the capabilities of the worldwide Yamazaki Corporation." An intensive publicity effort brought in 2,200 visitors during the first week of operation.

Shape Inc. of Biddeford, Maine, is beating firms from *both* Japan and Taiwan on price, quality, and service. Shape's performance is particularly surprising since they manufacture computer disks, audiocassettes, videocassettes, and similar items that most people consider to be the exclusive domain of overseas manufacturers. The key to success at Shape is the explicit recognition that the service dimension of their business is central to success. They compete not only on price and quality but also on their ability to meet customer delivery and support requirements; they do all this for small lot sizes as well as large.

The Kelly-Springfield Tire Co., another example, increased market share in an industry characterized by overcapacity and intensive price competition. Their approach was to provide better service while simultaneously reducing cost. The service issue that seemed most critical to management was shipping delays. Directly addressing this problem resulted in raising the number of units shipped within 24 hours of receipt of order from 78.8 to 85.3 percent. Costs did not rise as a result of this focus on service: they went down. The average inventory level was reduced from 94.7 days to 78.8 days sales (resulting in annual savings of $2.2 million). It seems obvious they could have reduced inventory further if they had kept service at the same 78.8 percent level instead of raising it to 85.3 percent. It is unlikely, however, they would have increased market share without a focus on *both* service and price.

Finally, Allen-Bradley's connector plant "models its own clothes," while achieving two central objectives of the service factory—flexibility and speed. The factory uses its commercially available CIM (computer integrated manufacturing) system to provide 24-hour delivery on a virtually unlimited variety of contactors and relays.

One common theme running through these examples is that service, as delivered by the service factory, is a multidimensional concept. It can refer to doing something for the customer, to doing something with the customer, or (as was the case in the new factory examples) it can refer to providing a service to another function of the business such as the marketing arm. By blending customer service needs into factory operations, these organizations found that service is not a cost factor to be controlled, but the key to increasing market share.

Suggestions for Implementation

The service factory concept implies that the service characteristics and the product characteristics be considered as a unit. The service dimension is not an "add on" feature; it must be addressed at the design stage, the manufacturing stage, and the support stage. This idea is conveyed in Exhibit 19.14, along with references to service firms that exemplify particular service actions. The dominant issue, of course, is to ensure that the service dimension is included in the mission of manufacturing. Some suggestions on how to do this follow.

Define factory output as a service package
This is a fundamental first step in changing the factory's mission. It operationalizes the service factory concept by explicitly recognizing how the intangible service must interact with the tangible product. This requires some creative thinking, of course. However, there is at least one very successful manufacturer that can be used as a role model: McDonald's. Its hamburger manufacturing process is perfectly integrated with its service process to provide a "service factory" in the field.

Specify the service goals
The service goals must be defined in as much detail as possible. It is not sufficient to say that "service comes first." It is more meaningful to state that customer orders will be shipped within 24 hours of receipt, and that response time for customer service requests will not exceed two hours. Added to this of

EXHIBIT 19.14

**Building the Factory
Service Package**

Production Steps		Service Actions
Design	Design what ←——————→ the customer wants	Bring customers on site ■ Codesign product ■ Codesign service Like Kinko's Copy Centers
Manufacturing	Build what ←——————→ they want when they want it	Design plant to facilitate ■ Fast production ■ Quality checks ■ Modifications ■ Status reporting in real time Like LensCrafters
Support	Support ←——————→ what they bought	Game plan for effective response ■ Guarantees ■ Warrantees ■ Who to contact ■ When to contact ■ How to contact Like American Express

course is TLC—which includes the usual "tender loving care," but goes on to include "thinking like a customer."

Measure service performance

Organizational performance on service goals must be measured, not just to correct deviations but to foster the further improvement mentioned earlier. Mechanisms for this include the standard service industry tools of focus groups and surveys, which here would be applied to industrial customers. Such approaches should explicitly probe service effectiveness and their findings should be given boardroom attention.

Include the customer in the service design process

Measuring customer satisfaction with service performance is but one way of involving the customer. Why not go further and have the customer help with designing the services as well? This is more than just negotiating shipment amounts and delivery times. It gets into such questions as: "What forms of contact would the customer like with the factory?" "How much service customization is necessary?" And, "How can factory operations make life easy for your customers?" Working through these questions with customers can enhance their loyalty, generate additional sales, and provide valuable public relations, which attracts new customers.

Include the employee in the service design process

The service factory requires greater participation on the part of the employees than is typical in the excessively compartmentalized factory of today. Therefore, we would suggest that manufacturing executives consider creating a permanent program to ensure that all employees are involved in the service design process.

This brief list of suggestions is a starting point. As any executive knows, it is impossible to excel in every performance measure all the time. Successful executives (and successful organizations) are aware of which performance measures are most important. We believe the service factory concept provides a framework that enhances the executive's ability to solve the right problems at the right times and to improve continuously the competitive posture of the organization.

19.5 CONCLUSION

It is appropriate to conclude this book with the topic of service in manufacturing because it is here that operations management has an expanded and critical role to play. Recently, we have seen a veritable explosion in the thinking, writing, and most important, in the actions by companies directed toward achieving excellence in manufacturing. We believe that the next step is to include the services that a company provides as an integral part of its manufactured products and operate as a service factory. This would suggest including (or augmenting) customer service within its "bill of materials," along with raw materials, parts, and subassemblies. This organization should blend the best practices of manufacturing with operating logic commonly found in effective service organizations. The net result will be a factory that excels both in producing goods and in providing the service that make the *company* the premier choice among customers.

19.6 REVIEW AND DISCUSSION QUESTIONS

1. Define the terms *structure* and *infrastructure* as they pertain to manufacturing strategy.
2. Where does McDonald's achieve its greatest profit leverage? (See Exhibit 19.10.)
3. Can a factory be fast, dependable, flexible, produce high-quality products, and still provide poor service from a customer's perspective?
4. Explain the positioning concepts of process focus and product focus. How would they pertain to services such as a gourmet restaurant and an automobile agency?
5. Using your college or university as an example, refute or support the assertion that a production system cannot excel on every measure of performance.

6. Why should a manufacturing company or a large, multisite service firm worry about being world class if it doesn't compete outside its own national borders?

7. How might a company president use the Wheelwright approach to establishing task priorities and a linear responsibility chart in strategic planning?

19.7 CASE: MEMPHIS TOY COMPANY

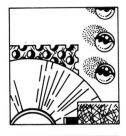

The Memphis Toy Company (MTC) views its primary task as making for stock a standardized line of high-quality, unique toys that "last from pablum to puberty." As a rule, MTC introduces one or two new toys a year. In August 1991, the owner and manufacturing manager, Dwight Smith-Daniels, has been informed by his toy inventors that they have designed an M. C. Hammer doll. This doll will stand two feet high and is capable of rapping via an electronic voice synthesizer. One of the company's three manufacturing staff departments, design engineering, states that the product can be made primarily from molded plastic using the firm's new all-purpose molders (now used for making small attachments to the firm's wooden toys). MTC, in its previous initial production of new toys, has relied heavily on its skilled work force to "debug" the product design as they make the product and to perform quality inspections on the finished product. Production runs have been short runs to fill customer orders.

If the M. C. Hammer doll is to go into production, however, the production run size will have to be large and assembly and testing procedures will have to be more refined. Currently, each toymaker performs almost all processing steps at his or her workbench. The production engineering department believes that the assembly of the new toy is well within the skill levels of the current work force but that the voice synthesizer and battery-operated movement mechanism will have to be subcontracted. MTC has always had good relations with subcontractors, primarily because the firm has placed its orders with sufficient lead time so that its vendors could optimally sequence MTC's orders with those of some larger toy producers in Memphis. Dwight Smith-Daniels has always favored long-range production planning so that he can keep his 50 toymakers busy all year. (One of the reasons he set up the factory in Memphis was so that he could draw upon the large population of toymakers from the "old country" who lived there.) Smith-Daniels believes the supervisors of the firm's three production departments—castles, puppets, and novelties—are favorable to the new product. The novelty department supervisor, Fred Avide, has stated, "My workers can make any toy—you give us an output incentive, and we'll produce around the clock."

The marketing department has forecast a demand of 50,000 M. C. Hammer dolls for the Christmas rush. The dolls should sell at retail for $29.50. A preliminary cost analysis from the process engineering department is that they will cost no more than $7 each to manufacture. The company is currently operating at 70 percent capacity. Financing is available and there is no problem with cash flow. Dwight Smith-Daniels is wondering if he should go into production of M. C. Hammer dolls.

QUESTIONS

1. How consistent is the M. C. Hammer doll order with the current capabilities and focus of MTC? Relate your answer to each of the eight manufacturing strategy decision categories listed in Exhibit 19.7

2. Should MTC (*a*) manufacture the doll itself, (*b*) subcontract the work to a Tijuana, Mexico manufacturing plant that specializes in high-volume production (at a cost of $8 per doll to MTC), or (*c*) look for another product more in line with its capabilities? The agency that holds the license to M. C. Hammer products wants a decision right away, as does the Mexican supplier.

19.8 CASE: BIG JIM'S GYM

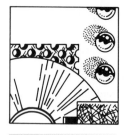

Big Jim has been in the body-building business for many years in Glendale, California. His gymnasium, originally built for men, now consists of separate facilities for men and women located beneath a pizza parlor in downtown Glendale. Jim views the primary task of his business as "providing a full range of body-building and weight-reduction services for upper- and middle-class men, women, and children in the Glendale area."

Currently, he has 20 employees who work with the customers in designing their health programs. His gym has separate weightlifting and exercise rooms for men and women, a pool, a sauna bath, and a small running track behind the building. While Jim states that every customer is different, he makes men go through his 23-step conditioning course and women follow the diet in "Big Jim's Energy Diet" pamphlet. (Customers are usually enrolled in a 10-week introductory course and then left to advance at their own pace.)

The gym is modeled after the one Jim first managed on an army base in Pennsylvania, "right down to the olive-drab walls." Jim maintains that the spartan atmosphere is necessary "to build mental and physical toughness." With some pride, Jim notes that he has all the latest barbells and slant-board apparatus. Jim has always viewed his major inventory items as liniments and bandages, which are ordered periodically from a wholesaler or purchased from a nearby drugstore if stockouts occur. (Other items are purchased from a local sporting goods store.)

Jim is very concerned about keeping all his staff busy and keeping the equipment in constant use, so he requires that customers follow a specific hour-by-hour schedule on equipment use. If the equipment is scheduled to capacity, he requests that his customers come at slow periods during the day or evening. (This procedure has met with some resistance from customers, but Jim tells them that that is the price they must pay if he is to provide the most up-to-date health center services.)

Jim has done a survey of the prices charged by the other four health centers in the area and his fees are about average.* The other health centers have about the same number of employees, although two of them use licensed beauty consultants. Jim considers this an "unnecessary frill" and tells all his customers that anybody who works for him is an expert on all aspects of body maintenance. Jim has instituted a policy of job rotation whereby each member of the staff, with the exception of the clerk-typist, changes activities each hour. Employees are paid by the hour and are primarily college graduates interested in athletics. Turnover has not been a problem, even though Jim pays only slightly more than the minimum wage.

Although Jim's capacity is fully utilized, the number of memberships has dropped off from 500 to about 300 in the last six months, and profits have dropped proportionately. His accountant is looking into the possibility of raising membership fees.

QUESTIONS

1. Relate the data in the case to each category of the decision making framework for service strategy determination shown in Exhibit 19.11.

2. Should Big Jim revise his mission and/or his service delivery system? How?

19.9 CASE: STRATEGIC ANALYSIS OF AN APPLIANCE MANUFACTURER†

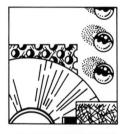

In February, the CEO of a leading major appliance company asked a consulting organization to deliver a proposal outlining how the consultants could help develop an "operations strategy for the 1990s." The following is a summary of some of the key components of the preliminary analysis performed prior to delivering the proposal.

The Major Appliance Industry

The major appliance industry was undergoing profound structural change that would likely result in one of the following scenarios—global oligopoly, global fragmentation, or national markets. Increased demand for product variety was making inflexible automated equipment obsolete. Plants set up to efficiently produce a single product type were struggling to keep up with the changes.

---

* Within this market segment, Jim is competing with, among others, Vicki's Athletic Club. VAC's facilities include 10 handball-racquetball courts, 8 tennis courts, a 50-meter pool, sauna and steam rooms, a weight room with five $5,000 Nautilus weightlifting machines, and a fully equipped health bar. VAC's staff includes a trainer, 5 masseuses, 5 instructors, and 10 other staff members.

† This case was adapted from a case supplied by The MAC Group, a Gemini Consulting Company.

Current Operations

Three large plants (X, Y, and Z) were located in the Chicago area. These plants each produced one major product line. These products were produced with many different variations such as color, trim, and components. Demand for new features and option packages was constantly increasing.

Each plant used automated, but inflexible, assembly equipment. To install some options, the equipment had to be disabled so the assembly personnel could perform the work. Most employees just kept the assembly equipment disabled at all times since the number of options and product changes was so large and unpredictable.

Due to the pressure to meet monthly quotas, management closely supervised assembly workers to make sure they were not violating any established procedures. A request to have an employee suggestion program was turned down by management since it would take too much time to respond to the suggestions. Although the plants were not unionized, there was much talk among employees of the benefits of unionization.

The quality of the products was considerably below industry average. This fact was so alarming to management that budget was allocated to double the number of inspectors at the final assembly stages. Management was confident that this extra inspection, despite its cost, would improve the quality of the products.

Manufacturing Economics

The factory burden, or overhead rates, were examined for each of the three plants. Specifically, annual production volumes were plotted against factory burdens. The resulting U-shaped plot is shown in Case Exhibit 1.

Request for Proposal

Management wanted the consultants to outline preliminary ideas about which strategic directions the company should be pursuing. Specifically, management wanted to know

CASE EXHIBIT 1   Cost-Volume Curve for Plants X, Y, and Z

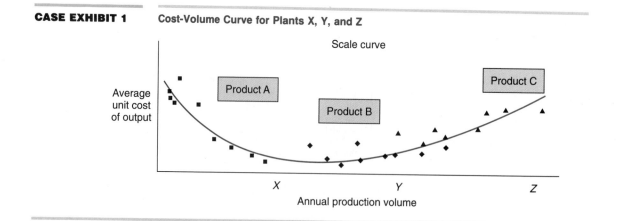

what tough strategic decisions had to be addressed in both the short-term and the long-term. Although the consultants were not expected to provide a complete solution in the proposal, management wanted to feel confident that the consultants could identify major weaknesses and outline general solution areas.

QUESTIONS

When answering the following questions, consider yourself to be one of the consultants assigned to develop the proposal.

1. What conclusions can you derive from the U-shaped plot regarding the appropriateness of the sizes of the three plants?

2. Which major weaknesses can you identify from the discussion of current operations?

3. What are some of the general solution areas you would identify in the proposal for more in-depth analysis during post-proposal stages of the project? Do these solutions involve structural or infrastructural decisions?

19.10 SELECTED BIBLIOGRAPHY

Ahmadian, A.; R. Afifi; and W. D. Chandler. *Readings in Production and Operations Management: A Productivity Perspective.* Boston: Allyn & Bacon, 1990.

Blackburn, Joseph D. *Time-Based Competition: The Next Battleground in American Manufacturing,* Homewood, Ill.: BUSINESS ONE IRWIN, 1991.

Bowen, D. E.; R. B. Chase; and T. G. Cummings. *Service Management Effectiveness.* San Francisco: Jossey-Bass, 1990.

Chase, Richard B., and David A. Garvin. "The Service Factory." *Harvard Business Review,* July–August (1989), pp. 61–69.

Chase, Richard B., and Warren J. Erikson. "The Service Factory." *The Academy of Management Executive* 2, no. 3 (1988), pp. 191–96.

Hayes, R. H., and S. C. Wheelwright. "Link Manufacturing Process and Product Life Cycles." *Harvard Business Review,* January–February 1979, pp. 133–40.

————, *Restoring Our Competitive Edge: Competing through Manufacturing.* New York: John Wiley & Sons, 1984.

Heskett, J. L. *Managing in the Service Economy.* Cambridge, Mass.: Harvard University Press, 1986.

Hill, T. J. "Manufacturing Implications in Determining Corporate Policy." *International Journal of Operations & Production Management* 1, no. 1 (1980), pp. 3–11.

Jelinek, Mariann, and Joel D. Goldhar. "Strategic Implications of the Factory of the Future." *Sloan Management Review,* Summer 1984, pp. 58–66.

Marucheck, A.; R. Pannesi; and C. Anderson. "An Exploratory Study of the Manufacturing Strategy Process in Practice." *Journal of Operations Management* 9, no. 1 (January 1990), pp. 109–18.

Peters, T. *Thriving on Chaos: Handbook for a Management Revolution.* New York: Alfred A. Knopf, 1987, pp. 158–71.

Schonberger, R. J. *World Class Manufacturing: The Lessons of Simplicity Applied.* New York: Free Press, 1986, pp. 169–71.

Skinner, W. "Manufacturing—Missing Link in Corporate Strategy." *Harvard Business Review,* May–June 1969, pp. 136–45.

————. "The Focused Factory." *Harvard Business Review,* May–June 1974, pp. 113–21.

————. *Manufacturing in the Corporate Strategy.* New York: John Wiley & Sons, 1979.

Thomas, D. R. "Strategy Is Different in a Service Business." *Harvard Business Review,* July–August 1978, pp. 158–65.

Wheelwright, S. "Reflecting Corporate Strategy in Manufacturing Decisions." *Business Horizons,* February 1978, pp. 57–66.

Wild, Ray. *International Handbook of Production and Operations Management.* London: Cassell Educational Ltd., 1989.

Appendixes

APPENDIX A: Financial Analysis in Production and Operations Management

*I*n this appendix we review basic concepts and tools of financial analysis for OM. These include: the types of cost (fixed, variable, sunk, opportunity, avoidable), risk and expected value, and depreciation (straight line, sum-of-the-years'-digits, declining balance, double-declining balance, depreciation-by-use). Our focus is on capital investment decisions.

CONCEPTS AND DEFINITIONS

We will begin this appendix with some basic definitions.

Fixed costs

A fixed cost is any expense that remains constant regardless of the level of output. Although no cost is truly fixed, many types of expense are virtually fixed over a wide range of output. Examples are rent, property taxes, most types of depreciation, insurance payments, and salaries of top management.

Variable costs

Variable costs are expenses that fluctuate directly with changes in the level of output. For example, each additional unit of sheet steel produced by USX requires a specific amount of material and labor. The incremental cost of this additional material and labor can be isolated and assigned to each unit of sheet steel produced. Many overhead expenses are also variable, since utility bills, maintenance expense, and so forth vary with the production level.

Exhibit A.1 illustrates the fixed and variable cost components of total cost. Note that total cost increases at the same rate as variable costs because fixed costs are constant.

Sunk costs

Sunk costs are past expenses or investments that have no salvage value and therefore should not be taken into account in considering investment alternatives. Sunk costs could also be current costs that are essentially fixed, such as rent on a building. For example, suppose an ice cream manufacturing firm occupies a rented building and is considering making sherbet in the same building. If the company enters sherbet production, its cost accountant will assign some of the rental expense to the sherbet operation. However, the building rent remains unchanged and therefore is not a relevant expense to be

EXHIBIT A.1

Fixed and Variable
Cost Components of
Total Cost

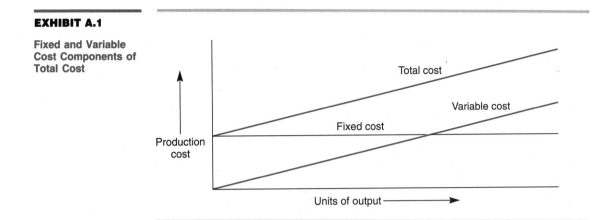

considered in making the decision. The rent is *sunk;* that is, it continues to exist and does not change in amount regardless of the decision.

Opportunity costs
Opportunity cost is the benefit *forgone,* or advantage *lost,* that results from choosing one action over the *best-known alternative* course of action.

Suppose a firm has $100,000 to invest, and two alternatives of comparable risk present themselves, each requiring a $100,000 investment. Investment A will net $25,000; Investment B will net $23,000. Investment A is clearly the better choice, with a $25,000 net return. If the decision is made to invest in B instead of A, the opportunity cost of B then is $2,000, which is the benefit foregone.

Avoidable costs
Avoidable costs include any expense that is *not* incurred if an investment is made but that *must* be incurred if the investment is *not* made. Suppose a company owns a metal lathe that is not in working condition but is needed for the firm's operations. Since the lathe must be repaired or replaced, the repair costs are avoidable if a new lathe is purchased. Avoidable costs reduce the cost of a new investment because they are not incurred if the investment is made. Avoidable costs are an example of how it is possible to "save" money by spending money.

Risk and expected value
Risk is inherent in any investment, because the future can never be predicted with absolute certainty. To deal with this uncertainty, mathematical techniques such as expected value can help. Expected value is the expected outcome multiplied by the probability of its occurrence. Recall that in the preceding example the expected outcome of Alternative A was $25,000 and B,

$23,000. Suppose the probability of A's actual outcome is 80 percent while B's probability is 90 percent. The expected values of the alternatives are determined as follows:

$$\underset{\text{outcome}}{\text{Expected}} \times \underset{\substack{\text{outcome will be the} \\ \text{expected outcome}}}{\text{Probability that actual}} = \underset{\text{value}}{\text{Expected}}$$

Investment A: $25,000 × 0.80 = $20,000
Investment B: $23,000 × 0.90 = $20,700

Investment B is now seen to be the better choice, with a net advantage over A of $700.

Economic life and obsolescence

When a firm invests in an income-producing asset, the productive life of the asset is estimated. For accounting purposes, the asset is depreciated over this period. It is assumed that the asset will perform its function during this time and then be considered obsolete or worn out, and replacement will be required. This view of asset life rarely coincides with reality.

Assume that a machine expected to have a productive life of 10 years is purchased. If at any time during the ensuing 10 years a new machine is developed that can perform the same task more efficiently or economically, the old machine has become obsolete. Whether it is "worn out" or not is irrelevant.

The *economic life* of a machine is the period over which it provides the best method for performing its task. When a superior method is developed, the machine has become obsolete. Thus, the stated *book value* of a machine can be a meaningless figure.

Depreciation

Depreciation is a method for allocating costs of capital equipment. The value of any capital asset—buildings, machinery, and so forth—decreases as its useful life is expended. *Amortization* and *depreciation* are often used interchangeably. Through convention, however, *depreciation* refers to the allocation of cost due to the physical or functional deterioration of *tangible* (physical) assets, such as buildings or equipment, while *amortization* refers to the allocation of cost over the useful life of *intangible* assets, such as patents, leases, franchises, or goodwill.

Depreciation procedures may not reflect an asset's true value at any point in its life because obsolescence may at any time cause a large difference between true value and book value. Also, since depreciation rates significantly affect taxes, a firm may choose a particular method from the several alternatives with more consideration for its effect on taxes than its ability to make the book value of an asset reflect the true resale value.

We describe five commonly used methods of depreciation next.

1. Straight-line method.   Under this method, an asset's value is reduced in uniform annual amounts over its estimated useful life. The general formula is:

$$\text{Annual amount to be depreciated} = \frac{\text{Cost} - \text{Salvage value}}{\text{Estimated useful life}}$$

A machine costing $10,000, with an estimated salvage value of $0 and an estimated life of 10 years, would be depreciated at the rate of $1,000 per year for each of the 10 years. If its estimated salvage value at the end of the 10 years is $1,000, the annual depreciation charge is:

$$\frac{\$10,000 - \$1,000}{10} = \$900$$

2. Sum-of-the-years'-digits (SYD) method.   The purpose of the SYD method is to reduce the book value of an asset rapidly in early years and at a lower rate in the later years of its life.

Supposing that the estimated useful life is 5 years. The numbers add up to 15:1 + 2 + 3 + 4 + 5 = 15. Therefore, depreciate the asset by 5 ÷ 15 after the first year, 4 ÷ 15 after the second year, and so on, down to 1 ÷ 15 in the last year.

3. Declining-balance method.   This method also achieves an accelerated depreciation. The asset's value is decreased by reducing its book value by a constant percentage each year. The percentage rate selected is often the one that just reduces book value to salvage value at the end of the asset's estimated life. In any case, the asset should never be reduced below estimated salvage value. Use of the declining-balance method and allowable rates is controlled by Internal Revenue Service regulations. As a simplified illustration, the preceding example is used in the next table with an arbitrarily selected rate of 40 percent. Note that depreciation is based on full cost, *not* cost minus salvage value.

Year	Depreciation Rate	Beginning Book Value	Depreciation Charge	Accumulated Depreciation	Ending Book Value
1	0.40	$17,000	$6,800	$ 6,800	$10,200
2	0.40	10,200	4,080	10,880	6,120
3	0.40	6,120	2,448	13,328	3,672
4	0.40	3,672	1,469	14,797	2,203
5		2,203	203	15,000	2,000

In the fifth year, reducing book value by 40 percent would have caused it to drop below salvage value. Consequently, the asset was depreciated by only $203, which decreased book value to salvage value.

4. Double-declining-balance method.   Again, for tax advantages, the double-declining-balance method offers higher depreciation early in the life span. Double-declining-balance method uses a percentage twice the straight line for the life span of the item but applies this rate to the undepreciated original cost. The method is the same as the declining-balance method, but the term *double-declining balance* means double the straight-line rate. Thus, equipment with a 10-year life span would have a straight line depreciation rate of 10 percent per year and a double-declining-balance rate (applied to the undepreciated amount) of 20 percent per year.

5. Depreciation-by-use method.   The purpose of this method is to depreciate a capital investment in proportion to its use. It is applicable, for example, to a machine that performs the same operation many times. The life of the machine is not estimated in years but rather in the total number of operations it may reasonably be expected to perform before wearing out. Suppose that a metal-stamping press has an estimated life of 1 million stamps and costs $100,000. The charge for depreciation per stamp is then $100,000 ÷ 1,000,000, or $0.10. Assuming a $0 salvage value, the depreciation charges are as shown on the next table.

Year	Total Yearly Stamps	Cost per Stamp	Yearly Depreciation Charge	Accumulated Depreciation	Ending Book Value
1	150,000	0.10	$15,000	$ 15,000	$85,000
2	300,000	0.10	30,000	45,000	55,000
3	200,000	0.10	20,000	65,000	35,000
4	200,000	0.10	20,000	85,000	15,000
5	100,000	0.10	10,000	95,000	5,000
6	50,000	0.10	5,000	100,000	0

The depreciation-by-use method is an attempt to gear depreciation charges to actual use and thereby coordinate expense charges with productive output more accurately. Also, since a machine's resale value is related to its remaining productive life, it is hoped that book value will approximate resale value. The danger, of course, is that technological improvements will render the machine obsolete, in which case book value will not reflect true value.

THE EFFECTS OF TAXES

Tax rates and the methods of applying them occasionally change. When analysts evaluate investment proposals, tax considerations often prove to be the deciding factor since depreciation expenses directly affect taxable income and therefore profit. The ability to write off depreciation in early years provides an added source of funds for investment. Before 1986, firms were able to employ an *investment tax credit,* which allowed a direct reduction in tax liability. Tax laws change; therefore, it is very important to stay on top of current tax laws and try to predict future changes that may affect current investments and accounting procedures.

For example, a one-time investment of $1,000 at 14 percent allowed to compound for 65 years could be worth $5 million. However, that 14 percent is a *nominal rate,* and nominal rates do not reflect buying power; real rates do. Real rates—that which remains after adjusting for inflation—are historically about 3 to 5 percent. If the rate of return remains 14 percent for 65 years, future inflation will erode 90 percent of the $5 million buying power!

The general formula for compound value is:

$$V_n = P_1(1 + i)^n$$

where

V = Value at the end of a specific year

n = Length of the compounding period

P_1 = Principal, or value at the beginning of a specific year

i = Interest rate

and the subscript represents the length of the compounding period.

For example, the compound value of $10 earning 10 percent interest after three years is $13.31 and is derived as follows:

$$V_3 = P_1(1 + i)^3$$
$$= \$10(1 + 0.10)^3$$
$$= \$10(1.331)$$
$$= \$13.31$$

CHOOSING AMONG SPECIFIC INVESTMENT PROPOSALS

The capital investment decision has become highly rationalized, as evidenced by the variety of techniques available for its solution. In contrast to pricing or marketing decisions, the capital investment decision can usually be made with a higher degree of confidence because the variables affecting the decision are relatively well known and can be quantified with fair accuracy.

Investment decisions may be grouped into six general categories:

1. Purchase of new equipment or facilities.
2. Replacement of existing equipment or facilities.
3. Make-or-buy decisions.

4. Lease-or-buy decisions.
5. Temporary shutdown or plant-abandonment decisions.
6. Addition or elimination of a product or product line.

Investment decisions are made with regard to the *lowest acceptable rate of return* on investment. As a starting point, the lowest acceptable rate of return may be considered to be the cost of investment capital needed to underwrite the expenditure. Certainly an investment will not be made if it does not return at least the cost of capital.

Investments are generally ranked according to the return they yield in excess of their cost of capital. In this way a business with only limited investment funds can select investment alternatives that yield the highest *net* returns. (*Net return* is the earnings an investment yields after gross earnings have been reduced by the cost of the funds used to finance the investment.) In general, investments should not be made unless the return in funds exceeds the *marginal* cost of investment capital (*marginal cost* is the incremental cost of each new acquisition of funds from outside sources).

INTEREST-RATE EFFECTS

There are two basic ways to account for the effects of interest accumulation. One is to compute the total amount created over the time period into the future as the *compound value*. The other is to remove the interest rate effect over time by reducing all future sums to present-day dollars, or the *present value*.

Compound Value of a Single Amount

Albert Einstein was once quoted as saying that compound interest is the eighth wonder of the world. After reviewing this section, with its dramatic growth effects during a longer term of years, you might wish to propose a new government regulation: on the birth of a child, the parents must put, say, $1,000 into a retirement fund for that child at age 65. This might be one way to reduce the pressure on Social Security and other state and federal pension plans. While inflation will decrease the value significantly as we showed in the previous section, there was still a lot left over. At 14 percent interest, our $1,000 increased to $500,000 after subtracting the $4.5 million for inflation. That's still 500 times.

Most calculators make such computation easy. However, many people still refer to tables for compound values. Using Appendix G, Table 1 (compound sum of $1), for example, we see that the value of $1 at 10 percent interest after three years is $1.331. Multiplying this figure by $10 gives $13.31, as computed previously. (Note: Tables 1 through 4 are in Appendix G.)

Compound Value of an Annuity

An *annuity* is the receipt of a constant sum each year for a specified number of years. Usually an annuity is received at the end of a period and does not earn interest during that period. Therefore, an annuity of $10 for three years would bring in $10 at the end of the first year (allowing the $10 to earn interest if invested for the remaining two years), $10 at the end of the second year (allowing the $10 to earn interest for the remaining one year), and $10 at the end of the third year (with no time to earn interest). If the annuity receipts were placed in a bank savings account at 5 percent interest, the total or compound value of the $10 at 5 percent for the three years would be:

Year	Receipt at End of Year	Compund Interest Factor $(1 + i)^n$	Value at End of Third Year
1	$10.00 ×	$(1 + 0.05)^2 =$	$11.02
2	10.00 ×	$(1 + 0.05)^1 =$	10.50
3	10.00 ×	$(1 + 0.05)^0 =$	10.00
			$31.52

The general formula for finding the compund value of an annuity is

$$S_n = R[(1 + i)^{n-1} + (1 + i)^{n-2} + \ldots + (1 + i)^1 + 1]$$

where

S_n = Compound value of an annuity

R = Periodic receipts in dollars

n = Length of the annuity in years

Applying this formula to the above example, we get:

$$\begin{aligned} S_n &= R[(1 + i)^2 + (1 + i) + 1] \\ &= \$10[(1 + 0.05)^2 + (1 + 0.05) + 1] \\ &= \$31.52 \end{aligned}$$

Appendix G, Table 2 lists the compound value factor of $1 for 5 percent after three years as 3.152. Multiplying this factor by $10 yields $31.52.

In a fashion similar to our previous retirement investment example, consider the beneficial effects of investing $2,000 each year, just starting at the age of 21. Assume investments in AAA-rated bonds are available today yielding 9 percent. From Table 2 in Appendix G, after 30 years (age 51) the investment is worth 136.3 times $2,000, or $272,600. Fourteen years later (age 65) this would be worth $962,993 (using a hand calculator, since the table only goes up to 30 years, and assuming the $2,000 is deposited at the end of each year)! But what 21-year-old thinks about retirement?

Present Value of a Future Single Payment

Compound values are used to determine future value after a specified period has elapsed; present-value (PV) procedures accomplish just the reverse. They are used to determine the current value of a sum or stream of receipts expected to be received in the future. Most investment decision techniques use present-value concepts rather than compound values. Since decisions affecting the future are made in the present, it is better to convert future returns into their present value at the time the decision is being made. In this way, investment alternatives are placed in better perspective in terms of current dollars.

An example makes this more apparent. If a rich uncle offers to make you a gift of $100 today or $250 after 10 years, which should you choose? You must determine whether the $250 in 10 years will be worth more than the $100 now. Suppose that you base your decision on the rate of inflation in the economy and believe that inflation averages 10 percent per year. By deflating the $250, you can compare its relative purchasing power with $100 received today. Procedurally, this is accomplished by solving the compound formula for the present sum, P, where V is the future amount of $250 in 10 years at 10 percent. The compound value formula is

$$V = P(1 + i)^n$$

Dividing both sides by $(1 + i)^n$ gives:

$$P = \frac{V}{(1 + i)^n}$$
$$= \frac{250}{(1 + 0.10)^{10}}$$
$$= \$96.39$$

This shows that, at a 10 percent inflation rate, $250 in 10 years will be worth $93.39 today. The rational choice, then, is to take the $100 now.

The use of tables is also standard practice in solving present-value problems. With reference to Appendix G, Table 3, the present-value factor for $1 received 10 years hence is 0.386. Multiplying this factor by $250 yields $96.50.

Present Value of an Annuity

The present value of an annuity is the value of an annual amount to be received over a future period expressed in terms of the present. To find the value of an annuity of $100 for three years at 10 percent, find the factor in the present-value table that applies to 10 percent in *each* of the three years in which the amount is received and multiply each receipt by this factor. Then sum the resulting figures. Remember that annuities are usually received at the end of each period.

Year	Amount Received at End of Year	Present-Value Factor at 10%	Present Value
1	$100 ×	0.909 =	$ 90.90
2	100 ×	0.826 =	82.60
3	100 ×	0.751 =	75.10
Total receipts	$300	Total Present Value =	$248.60

The general formula used to derive the present value of an annuity is

$$A_n = R\left[\frac{1}{(1 + i)} + \frac{1}{(1 + i)^2} + \ldots + \frac{1}{(1 + i)^n}\right]$$

where

A_n = Present value of an annuity of n years
R = Periodic receipts
n = Length of the annuity in years

Applying the formula to the above example gives

$$A_n = \$100\left[\frac{1}{(1 + 0.10)} + \frac{1}{(1 + 0.10)^2} + \frac{1}{(1 + 0.10)^3}\right]$$
$$= \$100\ (2.488)$$
$$= \$248.80$$

Appendix G, Table 4 contains present values of an annuity for varying maturities. The present-value factor for an annuity of $1 for three years at 10 percent (from Appendix G, Table 4) is 2.487. Since our sum is $100 rather than $1, we multiply this factor by $100 to arrive at $248.70. The slight variance from the previous answers results from rounded figures in the table.

When the stream of future receipts is uneven, the present value of each annual receipt must be calculated. The present values of the receipts for all years are then summed to arrive at total present value. This process can sometimes be tedious, but it is unavoidable.

Discounted Cash Flow

The term *discounted cash flow,* or DCF, refers to total stream of payments that an asset will generate in the future discounted to the present time. This is simply present value analysis that includes all flows: single payments, annuities, and all others.

METHODS OF RANKING INVESTMENTS

Net Present Value

The net present value method is commonly used in business. With this method, decisions are based on the amount by which the present value of a projected income stream exceeds the cost of an investment.

A firm is considering two alternative investments: the first costs $30,000 and the second, $50,000. The expected yearly cash income streams are shown in the next table.

	CASH INFLOW	
Year	Alternative A	Alternative B
1	$10,000	$15,000
2	10,000	15,000
3	10,000	15,000
4	10,000	15,000
5	10,000	15,000

To choose between Alternatives A and B, find which has the highest net present value. Assume an 8 percent cost of capital.

Alternative A

3.993 (PV factor) × $10,000 = $39,930
Less cost of investment   =   30,000
Net present value   = $ 9,930

Alternative B

3.993 (PV factor) × $15,000 = $59,895
Less cost of investment   =   50,000
Net present value   = $ 9,895

Investment A is the better alternative. Its net present value exceeds Investment B by $35 ($9,930 − $9,895 = $35).

Payback Period

The payback method ranks investments according to the time required for each investment to return earnings equal to the cost of the investment. The rationale is that the sooner the investment capital can be recovered, the sooner it can be reinvested in new revenue-producing projects. Thus, supposedly, a firm will be able to get the most benefit from its available investment funds.

Consider two alternatives requiring a $1,000 investment each. The first will earn $200 per year for six years; the second will earn $300 per year for the first three years and $100 per year for the next three years.

If the first alternative is selected, the initial investment of $1,000 will be recovered at the end of the fifth year. The income produced by the second alternative will total $1,000 after only four years. The second alternative will permit reinvestment of the full $1,000 in new revenue-producing projects one year sooner than the first.

Though the payback method is declining in popularity as the sole measure in investment decisions, it is still frequently used in conjunction with other methods to give an indication of the time commitment of funds. The major problems with payback are that it does not consider income beyond the payback period and it ignores the time value of money. A method that ignores the time value of money must be considered questionable.

Internal Rate of Return

The internal rate of return may be defined as the interest rate that equates the present value of an income stream with the cost of an investment. There is no procedure or formula that may be used directly to compute the internal rate of return—it must be found by interpolation or iterative calculation.

Suppose we wish to find the internal rate of return for an investment costing $12,000 that will yield a cash inflow of $4,000 per year for four years. We see that the present value factor sought is

$$\frac{\$12,000}{\$4,000} = 3.000 \text{ PV}$$

and we seek the interest rate that will provide this factor over a four-year period. The interest rate must lie between 12 percent and 14 percent because 3.000 lies between 3.037 and 2.914 (in the fourth row of Appendix G, Table 4). Linear interpolation between these values, according to the following equation

$$i = 12 + (14 - 12) \frac{(3.037 - 3.000)}{(3.037 - 2.914)}$$
$$= 12 + 0.602 = 12.602\%$$

gives a good approximation to the actual internal rate of return.

When the income stream is discounted at 12.6 percent, the resulting present value closely approximates the cost of investment. Thus the internal rate of return for this investment is 12.6 percent. The cost of capital can be compared with the internal rate of return to determine the net rate of return on the investment. If, in this example, the cost of capital were 8 percent, the net rate of return on the investment would be 4.6 percent.

The net present value and internal rate of return methods involve procedures that are essentially the same. They differ in that the net present value method enables investment alternatives to be compared in terms of the dollar value in excess of cost, whereas the internal rate of return method permits comparison of rates of return on alternative investments. Moreover, the internal rate of return method occasionally encounters problems in calculation, as multiple rates frequently appear in the computation.

Ranking Investments with Uneven Lives

When proposed investments have the same life expectancy, comparison among them, using the preceding methods, will give a reasonable picture of their relative value. When lives are unequal, however, there is the question of how to relate the two different time periods. Should replacements be considered the same as the original? Should productivity for the shorter-term unit that will be replaced earlier be considered to have higher productivity? How should the cost of future units be estimated?

No estimate dealing with investments unforeseen at the time of decision can be expected to reflect a high degree of accuracy. Still, the problem must be dealt with, and some assumptions must be made in order to determine a ranking.

SAMPLE PROBLEMS: INVESTMENT DECISIONS

An Expansion Decision

Problem
William J. Wilson Ceramic Products, Inc., leases plant facilities in which firebrick is manufactured. Because of rising demand, Wilson could increase sales by investing in new equipment to expand output. The selling price of $10 per brick will remain unchanged if output and sales increase. Based on engineering and cost estimates, the accounting department provides management with the following cost estimates based on an annual increased output of 100,000 bricks.

Cost of new equipment having an expected life of five years	$500,000
Equipment installation cost	20,000
Expected salvage value	0
New operation's share of annual lease expense	40,000
Annual increase in utility expenses	40,000
Annual increase in labor costs	160,000
Annual additional cost for raw materials	400,000

The sum-of-the-years'-digits method of depreciation will be used, and taxes are paid at a rate of 40 percent. Wilson's policy is not to invest capital in projects earning less than a 20 percent rate of return. Should the proposed expansion be undertaken?

Solution

Compute cost of investment:

Acquisition cost of equipment	$500,000
Equipment installation costs	20,000
Total cost of investment	$520,000

Determine yearly cash flows throughout the life of the investment.

The lease expense is a sunk cost. It will be incurred whether or not the investment is made and is therefore irrelevant to the decision and should be disregarded. Annual production expenses to be considered are utility, labor, and raw materials. These total $600,000 per year.

Annual sales revenue is $10 × 100,000 units of output, or $1,000,000. Yearly income before depreciation and taxes is thus $1,000,000 gross revenue, less $600,000 expenses, or $400,000.

Next, determine the depreciation charges to be deducted from the $400,000 income each year using the SYD method (sum-of-years' digits = 1 + 2 + 3 + 4 + 5 = 15):

Year	Proportion of $500,000 to Be Depreciated	Depreciation Charge
1	5/15 × $500,000	= $166,667
2	4/15 × 500,000	= 133,333
3	3/15 × 500,000	= 100,000
4	2/15 × 500,000	= 66,667
5	1/15 × 500,000	= 33,333
Accumulated depreciation		$500,000

Find each year's cash flow when taxes are 40 percent. Cash flow for only the first year is illustrated:

Earnings before depreciation and taxes		$400,000
Deduct: Taxes at 40%	$160,000	
Add: Tax benefit of depreciation expense (0.4 × 166,667)	66,667	93,333
Cash flow (1st year)		$306,667

Determine present value of the cash flow. Since Wilson demands at least a 20 percent rate of return on investments, multiply the cash flows by the 20 percent present-value factor for each year. The factor for each respective year must be used because the cash flows are not an annuity.

Year	Present Value Factor	Cash Flow	Present Value
1	0.833 ×	$306,667 =	$255,454
2	0.694 ×	293,333 =	203,573
3	0.579 ×	280,000 =	162,120
4	0.482 ×	266,667 =	128,533
5	0.402 ×	253,334 =	101,840
Total present value of cash flows (discounted at 20%) =			$851,520

Now find whether net present value is positive or negative:

Total present value of cash flows	$851,520
Total cost of investment	520,000
Net present value	$331,520

Decision

Net present value is positive when returns are discounted at 20 percent. Wilson will earn an amount in excess of 20 percent on the investment. The proposed expansion should be undertaken.

A Replacement Decision

Problem

For five years Bennie's Brewery has been using a machine that attaches labels to bottles. The machine was purchased for $4,000 and is being depreciated over 10 years to a $0 salvage value using straight-line depreciation. The machine can be sold now for $2,000. Bennie can buy a new labeling machine for $6,000 that will have a useful life of five years and cut labor costs by $1,200 annually. The old machine will require a major overhaul in the next few months at an estimated cost of $300. If purchased, the new machine will be depreciated over five years to a $500 salvage value using the straight-line method. The company will invest in any project earning more than the 12 percent cost of capital. The tax rate is 40 percent. Should Bennie's Brewery invest in the new machine?

Solution

Determine the cost of investment:

Price of the new machine		$6,000
Less: Sale of old machine	$2,000	
Avoidable overhaul costs	300	2,300
Effective cost of investment		$3,700

Determine the increase in cash flow resulting from investment in the new machine:

Yearly cost savings = $1,200
Differential depreciation
Annual depreciation on old machine:

$$\frac{\text{Cost} - \text{Salvage}}{\text{Expected life}} = \frac{\$4,000 - \$0}{10} = \$400$$

Annual depreciation on new machine:

$$\frac{\text{Cost} - \text{Salvage}}{\text{Expected life}} = \frac{\$6,000 - \$500}{5} = \$1,100$$

Differential depreciation = $1,100 − $400 = $700
Yearly net increase in cash flow into the firm:

Cost savings		$1,200
Deduct: Taxes at 40%	$480	
Add: Advantage of increase in depreciation		
(0.4 × $700)	280	200
Yearly increase in cash flow		$1,000
Determine total present value of the investment:		

The five-year cash flow of $1,000 per year is an annuity.
Discounted at 12 percent, the cost of capital, the present value is

3.605 × $1,000 = $3,605

The present value of the new machine, if sold at its salvage value of $500 at the end of the fifth year, is

0.567 × $500 = $284

Total present value of the expected cash flows:

$3,605 + $284 = $3,889

Determine whether net present value is positive:

Total present value	$3,889
Cost of investment	3,700
Net present value	$ 189

Decision

Bennie's Brewery should make the purchase because the investment will return slightly more than the cost of capital.

Note: The importance of depreciation has been shown in this example. The present value of the yearly cash flow resulting from operations is *only*

(Cost savings − Taxes) × (Present value factor)
    ($1,200 − $480)   ×   (3.605)   = $2,596

This figure is $1,104 less than the $3,700 cost of the investment. Only a very large depreciation advantage makes this investment worthwhile. The total present value of the advantage is $1,009:

(Tax rate × Differential depreciation) × (P.V. factor)
        (0.4 × $700)   ×   (3.605)   = $1,009

A Make-or-Buy Decision

Problem

The Triple X Company manufactures and sells refrigerators. It makes some of the parts for the refrigerators and purchases others. The engineering department believes it might be possible to cut costs by manufacturing one of the parts currently being purchased for $8.25 each. The firm uses 100,000 of these parts each year, and the accounting department compiles the following list of costs based on engineering estimates.

Fixed costs will increase by $50,000.

Labor costs will increase by $125,000.

Factory overhead, currently running $500,000 per year, may be expected to increase 12 percent.

Raw materials used to make the part will cost $600,000.

Given the preceding estimates, should Triple X make the part or continue to buy it?

Solution
Find total cost incurred if the part were manufactured:

Additional fixed costs	$ 50,000
Additional labor costs	125,000
Raw materials cost	600,000
Additional overhead costs = 0.12 × $500,000	60,000
Total cost to manufacturer	$835,000

Find cost per unit to manufacture:

$$\frac{\$835,000}{100,000} = \$8.35 \text{ per unit}$$

Decision
Triple X should continue to buy the part. Manufacturing costs exceed the present cost to purchase by $0.10 per unit.

REVIEW AND DISCUSSION QUESTIONS

1. List three examples of capital investments in production and operations management.

2. Define the following terms: *fixed, variable, opportunity,* and *avoidable* costs; *risk* and *expected value; obsolescence* and *depreciation.*

3. How do taxes affect profits? Why?

4. How does depreciation affect capital investment? Why?

5. If a firm is short of capital, what action might it take to conserve the capital it has and to obtain more?

6. What are the reasons for using present-value analysis rather than "future-value" analysis?

7. Why might a decision maker like to see the payback analysis as well as the rate of return and the net present value?

8. Discuss why the comparison of alternative investment decisions is especially difficult when the investment choices have different life lengths.

9. Compare the advantages and disadvantages of each depreciation method.

PROBLEMS

1. What is the depreciation expense for the third year, using the sum-of-the-years'-digit method for the following cost of a new machine?

Cost of machine	$35,000
Estimated life	6 years
Estimated salvage value	$ 5,000

2. Disregarding tax considerations, is it cheaper to buy or to lease a piece of equipment with the following costs for a five-year term? (Interest value of money is 10 percent.)

	To Buy	To Lease
Purchase (or lease) cost	$50,000	$10,000/yr.
Annual operating cost	4,000/yr.	4,000/yr.
Maintenance cost	2,000/yr.	0
Salvage value at end of 5 years	$20,000	0

3. A new piece of office equipment must be purchased, and the choice has been narrowed down to two styles, each capable of meeting the intended needs. With a 10-year horizon and an interest rate of 8 percent, which equipment should be purchased?

	Equipment A	Equipment B
Initial cost	$10,000	$7,000
Salvage value (10 years hence)	4,000	2,000
Estimated annual operation and maintenance cost	1,000	1,500

4. The university is accepting bids for the hot dog and cold drink concession at the new stadium. The contract is for a five-year period, and it is your feeling that a bid of $40,000 will win the contract. A preliminary analysis indicates that annual operating costs will be $35,000 and average annual sales will be $50,000. The contract can be written off during the five years. Taxes are at the 40 percent rate, and your goal is to make a 20 percent return on your investment.
    a. Will you meet your goal if you use straight-line depreciation?
    b. Would you meet your goal using sum-of-the-years'-digits depreciation?

5. In adding a new product line, a firm needs a new piece of machinery. An investigation of suitable equipment for the production process has narrowed the choice to the two machines listed.

	Machine A	Machine B
Type of equipment	General purpose	Special purpose
Installed cost	$8,000	$13,000
Salvage value	800	3,000
Annual labor cost	6,000	3,600
Estimated life (years)	10	5

Assume that at the end of five years, a comparable replacement for Machine B will be available. Using present-value analysis with a 10 percent interest rate, which machine would you choose?

6. ABC's business has been going so well that the firm decides to diversify with a sideline business. Ballard, a partner and an experienced cabinetmaker, has a great deal of know-how in making cabinets for kitchens and vanities for bathrooms. (Countertops would be subcontracted because of the specialized equipment needed for molding and pressing.) The company is anticipating putting out a standard line of cabinets available in birch, walnut, mahogany, or oak veneer at no extra charge.

Three manufacturing methods are feasible for producing the cabinets. The first is largely manual, the second uses some semiautomated equipment, and the third is largely automatic. The semiautomatic equipment requires an investment of $45,000. ABC expects this equipment to generate incremental after-tax cash flows of $15,000 for each of the next four years. What is the net present value for this equipment? What is the payback period? What should ABC do?

SELECTED BIBLIOGRAPHY

Brigham, Eugene F. *Fundamentals of Financial Management.* New York: Dryden Press, 1986.

Hodder, James E., and Henry E. Riggs. "Pitfalls in Evaluating Risky Projects." *Harvard Business Review,* January–February 1985, pp. 128–35.

Gitman, Lawrence J. *Principles of Managerial Finance,* 4th ed. New York: Harper & Row, 1985.

Gup, Benton E. *Principles of Financial Management,* 2nd ed. New York: John Wiley & Sons, 1987.

Pringle, John J., and Robert S. Harris. *Essentials of Managerial Finance.* Glenview, Ill.: Scott, Foresman, 1984.

Soloman, Eyra, and John J. Pringle. *An Introduction to Financial Management.* Santa Monica, Calif.: Goodyear Publishing, 1980.

Van Horne, James C. *Financial Management and Policy,* 7th ed. Englewood Cliffs, N.J.: Prentice Hall, 1986.

———. *Fundamentals of Financial Management.* 6th ed. Englewood Cliffs, N.J.: Prentice Hall, 1986.

Welsch, Glenn A., and Robert N. Anthony. *Fundamentals of Financial Accounting.* Homewood, Ill.: Richard D. Irwin, 1984.

APPENDIX B Uniformly Distributed Random Digits

56970	10799	52098	04184	54967	72938	50834	23777	08392
83125	85077	60490	44369	66130	72936	69848	59973	08144
55503	21383	02464	26141	68779	66388	75242	82690	74099
47019	06683	33203	29603	54553	25971	69573	83854	24715
84828	61152	79526	29554	84580	37859	28504	61980	34997
08021	31331	79227	05748	51276	57143	31926	00915	45821
36458	28285	30424	98420	72925	40729	22337	48293	86847
05752	96045	36847	87729	81679	59126	59437	33225	31280
26768	02513	58454	56958	20575	76746	40878	06846	32828
42613	72456	43030	58085	06766	60227	96414	32671	45587
95457	12176	65482	25596	02678	54592	63607	82096	21913
95276	67524	63564	95958	39750	64379	46059	51666	10433
66954	53574	64776	92345	95110	59448	77249	54044	67942
17457	44151	14113	02462	02798	54977	48340	66738	60184
03704	23322	83214	59337	01695	60666	97410	55064	17427
21538	16997	33210	60337	27976	70661	08250	69509	60264
57178	16730	08310	70348	11317	71623	55510	64750	87759
31048	40058	94953	55866	96283	40620	52087	80817	74533
69799	83300	16498	80733	96422	58078	99643	39847	96884
90595	65017	59231	17772	67831	33317	00520	90401	41700
33570	34761	08039	78784	09977	29398	93896	78227	90110
15340	82760	57477	13898	48431	72936	78160	87240	52710
64079	07733	36512	56186	99098	48850	72527	08486	10951
63491	84886	67118	62063	74958	20946	28147	39338	32109
92003	76568	41034	28260	79708	00770	88643	21188	01850
52360	46658	66511	04172	73085	11795	52594	13287	82531
74622	12142	68355	65635	21828	39539	18988	53609	04001
04157	50070	61343	64315	70836	82857	35335	87900	36194
86003	60070	66241	32836	27573	11479	94114	81641	00496
41208	80187	20351	09630	84668	42486	71303	19512	50277
06433	80674	24520	18222	10610	05794	37515	48619	62866
39298	47829	72648	37414	75755	04717	29899	78817	03509
89884	59651	67533	68123	17730	95862	08034	19473	63971
61512	32155	51906	61662	64430	16688	37275	51262	11569
99653	47635	12506	88535	36553	23757	34209	55803	96275
95913	11085	13772	76638	48423	25018	99041	77529	81360
55804	44004	13122	44115	01601	50541	00147	77685	58788
35334	82410	91601	40617	72876	33967	73830	15405	96554
57729	88646	76487	11622	96297	24160	09903	14047	22917
86648	89317	63677	70119	94739	25875	38829	68377	43918
30574	06039	07967	32422	76791	30725	53711	93385	13421
81307	13114	83580	79974	45929	85113	72268	09858	52104
02410	96385	79067	54939	21410	86980	91772	93307	34116
18969	87444	52233	62319	08598	09066	95288	04794	01534
87863	80514	66860	62297	80198	19347	73234	86265	49096
08397	10538	15438	62311	72844	60203	46412	65943	79232
28520	45247	58729	10854	99058	18260	38765	90038	94209
44285	09452	15867	70418	57012	72122	36634	97283	95943
86299	22510	33571	23309	57040	29285	67870	21913	72958
84842	05748	90894	61658	15001	94005	36308	41161	37341

APPENDIX C Normally Distributed Random Digits

An entry in the table is the value z from a normal distribution with a mean of 0 and a standard deviation of 1.

1.98677	1.23481	−.28360	.99217	−.87919	−.21600
−.59341	1.54221	−.65806	1.08372	1.68560	1.14899
.11340	.19126	−.65084	.12188	.02338	−.61545
.89783	−.54929	−.03663	−1.89506	.15158	−.20061
−.50790	1.14463	1.30917	1.26528	.09459	.16423
−1.63968	−.63248	.21482	−1.16241	−.60015	−.55233
1.14081	−.29988	−.48053	−1.21397	−.34391	−1.84881
−.43354	−.32855	.67115	.52289	−1.42796	−.14181
.05707	.35331	.20470	.01847	1.71086	−1.44738
.77153	.72576	−.29833	.26139	1.25845	−.35468
−1.38286	.04406	−.75499	.61068	.61903	−.96845
1.60166	−1.66161	.70886	−.20302	−.28373	2.07219
−.48781	.02629	−.34306	2.00746	−1.12059	.07943
−1.10632	1.18250	−.60065	.09737	.63297	1.00659
.77000	−.87214	−.63584	−.39546	−.72776	.45594
−.56882	−.23153	−2.03852	−.28101	.30384	−.14246
.27721	−.04776	.11740	−.17211	1.63483	1.34221
−.40251	−.31052	−1.04834	−.23243	−1.52224	.85903
1.27086	−.93166	−.03766	1.21016	.13451	.81941
1.14464	.56176	.89824	1.54670	1.48411	.14422
.04172	1.49672	−.15490	.77084	−.29064	2.87643
−.36795	1.22318	−1.05084	−1.05409	.82052	.09670
1.94110	1.00826	−.85411	−1.31341	−1.85921	.74578
.14946	−2.75470	−.10830	1.02845	.69291	−.78579
.32512	1.11241	.45138	.79940	−.91803	−1.35919
.66748	−.55806	.27694	.80928	−.18061	1.26569
−1.23681	−.49094	.34951	1.66404	.30419	−1.32670
−.57808	−.04187	2.01897	.92651	.10518	−.34227
1.24924	−.98726	−.24277	−.48852	1.14221	−.43447
.38640	−.26990	−.21369	.65047	.27436	−2.30590
.47191	.52304	−1.16670	1.11789	−.10954	1.17787
−1.12401	.24826	.03741	−.72132	−.44131	−1.10636
−.04997	−1.19941	−.63591	1.27889	.69289	−.27419
−.08265	1.08497	.12277	−.61647	−2.74235	1.10660
.28522	.04496	−1.53535	.42616	−.54092	−1.99089
−.60318	−.00926	−1.57852	−.68966	−1.07899	−2.26274
1.66247	−.94171	−1.84672	.14506	−1.79616	−.03350
−.06993	.82752	−1.79937	−.58224	.38834	1.17421
.22572	−.23812	1.38760	.97453	−.48264	.42092
2.12500	.18124	.22034	1.06353	−.84988	−1.40673
−.51185	−1.35882	1.34636	−.03440	.31133	−1.63670
.35724	−1.45402	.16793	1.16726	−.76094	−.38834
−1.29352	−.28185	.86607	.68714	2.16262	1.82108
.34521	1.16515	−.11361	−1.35778	.16051	.93119
−1.33783	−.28278	−.09756	1.38268	−1.74537	.76566

APPENDIX D Areas of the Standard Normal Distribution

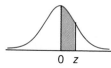

0 z

An entry in the table is the proportion under the entire curve which is between z = 0 and a positive value of z. Areas for negative values of z are obtained by symmetry.

z	.00	.01	.02	.03	.04	.05	.06	.07	.08	.09
0.0	.0000	.0040	.0080	.0120	.0160	.0199	.0239	.0279	.0319	.0359
0.1	.0398	.0438	.0478	.0517	.0557	.0596	.0636	.0675	.0714	.0753
0.2	.0793	.0832	.0871	.0910	.0948	.0987	.1026	.1064	.1103	.1141
0.3	.1179	.1217	.1255	.1293	.1331	.1368	.1406	.1443	.1480	.1517
0.4	.1554	.1591	.1628	.1664	.1700	.1736	.1772	.1808	.1844	.1879
0.5	.1915	.1950	.1985	.2019	.2054	.2088	.2123	.2157	.2190	.2224
0.6	.2257	.2291	.2324	.2357	.2389	.2422	.2454	.2486	.2517	.2549
0.7	.2580	.2611	.2642	.2673	.2703	.2734	.2764	.2794	.2823	.2852
0.8	.2881	.2910	.2939	.2967	.2995	.3023	.3051	.3078	.3106	.3133
0.9	.3159	.3186	.3212	.3238	.3264	.3289	.3315	.3340	.3365	.3389
1.0	.3413	.3438	.3461	.3485	.3508	.3531	.3554	.3577	.3599	.3621
1.1	.3643	.3665	.3686	.3708	.3729	.3749	.3770	.3790	.3810	.3830
1.2	.3849	.3869	.3888	.3907	.3925	.3944	.3962	.3980	.3997	.4015
1.3	.4032	.4049	.4066	.4082	.4099	.4115	.4131	.4147	.4162	.4177
1.4	.4192	.4207	.4222	.4236	.4251	.4265	.4279	.4292	.4306	.4319
1.5	.4332	.4345	.4357	.4370	.4382	.4394	.4406	.4418	.4429	.4441
1.6	.4452	.4463	.4474	.4484	.4495	.4505	.4515	.4525	.4535	.4545
1.7	.4554	.4564	.4573	.4582	.4591	.4599	.4608	.4616	.4625	.4633
1.8	.4641	.4649	.4656	.4664	.4671	.4678	.4686	.4693	.4699	.4706
1.9	.4713	.4719	.4726	.4732	.4738	.4744	.4750	.4756	.4761	.4767
2.0	.4772	.4778	.4783	.4788	.4793	.4798	.4803	.4808	.4812	.4817
2.1	.4821	.4826	.4830	.4834	.4838	.4842	.4846	.4850	.4854	.4857
2.2	.4861	.4864	.4868	.4871	.4875	.4878	.4881	.4884	.4887	.4890
2.3	.4893	.4896	.4898	.4901	.4904	.4906	.4909	.4911	.4913	.4916
2.4	.4918	.4920	.4922	.4925	.4927	.4929	.4931	.4932	.4934	.4936
2.5	.4938	.4940	.4941	.4943	.4945	.4946	.4948	.4949	.4951	.4952
2.6	.4953	.4955	.4956	.4957	.4959	.4960	.4961	.4962	.4963	.4964
2.7	.4965	.4966	.4967	.4968	.4969	.4970	.4971	.4972	.4973	.4974
2.8	.4974	.4975	.4976	.4977	.4977	.4978	.4979	.4979	.4980	.4981
2.9	.4981	.4982	.4982	.4983	.4984	.4984	.4985	.4985	.4986	.4986
3.0	.4987	.4987	.4987	.4988	.4988	.4989	.4989	.4989	.4990	.4990

Source: Paul G. Hoel, *Elementary Statistics* (New York: John Wiley & Sons, 1960), p. 240.

APPENDIX E Areas of the Cumulative Standard Normal Distribution

An entry in the table is the proportion under the curve cumulated from the negative tail.

z	G(z)	z	G(z)	z	G(z)
−4.00	0.00003	−3.60	0.00016	−3.20	0.00069
−3.99	0.00003	−3.59	0.00017	−3.19	0.00071
−3.98	0.00003	−3.58	0.00017	−3.18	0.00074
−3.97	0.00004	−3.57	0.00018	−3.17	0.00076
−3.96	0.00004	−3.56	0.00019	−3.16	0.00079
−3.95	0.00004	−3.55	0.00019	−3.15	0.00082
−3.94	0.00004	−3.54	0.00020	−3.14	0.00084
−3.93	0.00004	−3.53	0.00021	−3.13	0.00087
−3.92	0.00004	−3.52	0.00022	−3.12	0.00090
−3.91	0.00005	−3.51	0.00022	−3.11	0.00094
−3.90	0.00005	−3.50	0.00023	−3.10	0.00097
−3.89	0.00005	−3.49	0.00024	−3.09	0.00100
−3.88	0.00005	−3.48	0.00025	−3.08	0.00104
−3.87	0.00005	−3.47	0.00026	−3.07	0.00107
−3.86	0.00006	−3.46	0.00027	−3.06	0.00111
−3.85	0.00006	−3.45	0.00028	−3.05	0.00114
−3.84	0.00006	−3.44	0.00029	−3.04	0.00118
−3.83	0.00006	−3.43	0.00030	−3.03	0.00122
−3.82	0.00007	−3.42	0.00031	−3.02	0.00126
−3.81	0.00007	−3.41	0.00032	−3.01	0.00131
−3.80	0.00007	−3.40	0.00034	−3.00	0.00135
−3.79	0.00008	−3.39	0.00035	−2.99	0.00139
−3.78	0.00008	−3.38	0.00036	−2.98	0.00144
−3.77	0.00008	−3.37	0.00038	−2.97	0.00149
−3.76	0.00008	−3.36	0.00039	−2.96	0.00154
−3.75	0.00009	−3.35	0.00040	−2.95	0.00159
−3.74	0.00009	−3.34	0.00042	−2.94	0.00164
−3.73	0.00010	−3.33	0.00043	−2.93	0.00169
−3.72	0.00010	−3.32	0.00045	−2.92	0.00175
−3.71	0.00010	−3.31	0.00047	−2.91	0.00181
−3.70	0.00011	−3.30	0.00048	−2.90	0.00187
−3.69	0.00011	−3.29	0.00050	−2.89	0.00193
−3.68	0.00012	−3.28	0.00052	−2.88	0.00199
−3.67	0.00012	−3.27	0.00054	−2.87	0.00205
−3.66	0.00013	−3.26	0.00056	−2.86	0.00212
−3.65	0.00013	−3.25	0.00058	−2.85	0.00219
−3.64	0.00014	−3.24	0.00060	−2.84	0.00226
−3.63	0.00014	−3.23	0.00062	−2.83	0.00233
−3.62	0.00015	−3.22	0.00064	−2.82	0.00240
−3.61	0.00015	−3.21	0.00066	−2.81	0.00248

z	G(z)	z	(Gz)	z	G(z)
−2.80	0.00256	−2.30	0.01072	−1.80	0.03593
−2.79	0.00264	−2.29	0.01101	−1.79	0.03673
−2.78	0.00272	−2.28	0.01130	−1.78	0.03754
−2.77	0.00280	−2.27	0.01160	−1.77	0.03836
−2.76	0.00289	−2.26	0.01191	−1.76	0.03920
−2.75	0.00298	−2.25	0.01222	−1.75	0.04006
−2.74	0.00307	−2.24	0.01255	−1.74	0.04093
−2.73	0.00317	−2.23	0.01287	−1.73	0.04182
−2.72	0.00326	−2.22	0.01321	−1.72	0.04272
−2.71	0.00336	−2.21	0.01355	−1.71	0.04363
−2.70	0.00347	−2.20	0.01390	−1.70	0.04457
−2.69	0.00357	−2.19	0.01426	−1.69	0.04551
−2.68	0.00368	−2.18	0.01463	−1.68	0.04648
−2.67	0.00379	−2.17	0.01500	−1.67	0.04746
−2.66	0.00391	−2.16	0.01539	−1.66	0.04846
−2.65	0.00402	−2.15	0.01578	−1.65	0.04947
−2.64	0.00415	−2.14	0.01618	−1.64	0.05050
−2.63	0.00427	−2.13	0.01659	−1.63	0.05155
−2.62	0.00440	−2.12	0.01700	−1.62	0.05262
−2.61	0.00453	−2.11	0.01743	−1.61	0.05370
−2.60	0.00466	−2.10	0.01786	−1.60	0.05480
−2.59	0.00480	−2.09	0.01831	−1.59	0.05592
−2.58	0.00494	−2.08	0.01876	−1.58	0.05705
−2.57	0.00508	−2.07	0.01923	−1.57	0.05821
−2.56	0.00523	−2.06	0.01970	−1.56	0.05938
−2.55	0.00539	−2.05	0.02018	−1.55	0.06057
−2.54	0.00554	−2.04	0.02068	−1.54	0.06178
−2.53	0.00570	−2.03	0.02118	−1.53	0.06301
−2.52	0.00587	−2.02	0.02169	−1.52	0.06426
−2.51	0.00604	−2.01	0.02222	−1.51	0.06552
−2.50	0.00621	−2.00	0.02275	−1.50	0.06681
−2.49	0.00639	−1.99	0.02330	−1.49	0.06811
−2.48	0.00657	−1.98	0.02385	−1.48	0.06944
−2.47	0.00676	−1.97	0.02442	−1.47	0.07078
−2.46	0.00695	−1.96	0.02550	−1.46	0.07215
−2.45	0.00714	−1.95	0.02559	−1.45	0.07353
−2.44	0.00734	−1.94	0.02619	−1.44	0.07493
−2.43	0.00755	−1.93	0.02680	−1.43	0.07636
−2.42	0.00776	−1.92	0.02743	−1.42	0.07780
−2.41	0.00798	−1.91	0.02807	−1.41	0.07927
−2.40	0.00820	−1.90	0.02872	−1.40	0.08076
−2.39	0.00842	−1.89	0.02938	−1.39	0.08226
−2.38	0.00866	−1.88	0.03005	−1.38	0.08379
−2.37	0.00889	−1.87	0.03074	−1.37	0.08534
−2.36	0.00914	−1.86	0.03144	−1.36	0.08691
−2.35	0.00939	−1.85	0.03216	−1.35	0.08851
−2.34	0.00964	−1.84	0.03288	−1.34	0.09012
−2.33	0.00990	−1.83	0.03362	−1.33	0.09176
−2.32	0.01017	−1.82	0.03438	−1.32	0.09342
−2.31	0.01044	−1.81	0.03515	−1.31	0.09510

z	G(z)	z	(Gz)	z	G(z)
−1.30	0.09680	−0.85	0.19766	−0.40	0.34458
−1.29	0.09853	−0.84	0.20045	−0.39	0.34827
−1.28	0.10027	−0.83	0.20327	−0.38	0.35197
−1.27	0.10204	−0.82	0.20611	−0.37	0.35569
−1.26	0.10383	−0.81	0.20897	−0.36	0.35942
−1.25	0.10565	−0.80	0.21186	−0.35	0.36317
−1.24	0.10749	−0.79	0.21476	−0.34	0.36693
−1.23	0.10935	−0.78	0.21770	−0.33	0.37070
−1.22	0.11123	−0.77	0.22065	−0.32	0.37448
−1.21	0.11314	−0.76	0.22363	−0.31	0.37828
−1.20	0.11507	−0.75	0.22663	−0.30	0.38209
−1.19	0.11702	−0.74	0.22965	−0.29	0.38591
−1.18	0.11900	−0.73	0.23270	−0.28	0.38974
−1.17	0.12100	−0.72	0.23576	−0.27	0.39358
−1.16	0.12302	−0.71	0.23885	−0.26	0.39743
−1.15	0.12507	−0.70	0.24196	−0.25	0.40129
−1.14	0.12714	−0.69	0.24510	−0.24	0.40517
−1.13	0.12924	−0.68	0.24825	−0.23	0.40905
−1.12	0.13136	−0.67	0.25143	−0.22	0.41294
−1.11	0.13350	−0.66	0.25463	−0.21	0.41683
−1.10	0.13567	−0.65	0.25785	−0.20	0.42074
−1.09	0.13786	−0.64	0.26109	−0.19	0.42465
−1.08	0.14007	−0.63	0.26435	−0.18	0.42858
−1.07	0.14231	−0.62	0.26763	−0.17	0.43251
−1.06	0.14457	−0.61	0.27093	−0.16	0.43644
−1.05	0.14686	−0.60	0.27425	−0.15	0.44038
−1.04	0.14917	−0.59	0.27760	−0.14	0.44433
−1.03	0.15150	−0.58	0.28096	−0.13	0.44828
−1.02	0.15386	−0.57	0.28434	−0.12	0.45224
−1.01	0.15625	−0.56	0.28774	−0.11	0.45620
−1.00	0.15866	−0.55	0.29116	−0.10	0.46017
−0.99	0.16109	−0.54	0.29460	−0.09	0.46414
−0.98	0.16354	−0.53	0.29806	−0.08	0.46812
−0.97	0.16602	−0.52	0.30153	−0.07	0.47210
−0.96	0.16853	−0.51	0.30503	−0.06	0.47608
−0.95	0.17106	−0.50	0.30854	−0.05	0.48006
−0.94	0.17361	−0.49	0.31207	−0.04	0.48405
−0.93	0.17619	−0.48	0.31561	−0.03	0.48803
−0.92	0.17879	−0.47	0.31918	−0.02	0.49202
−0.91	0.18141	−0.46	0.32276	−0.01	0.49601
−0.90	0.18406	−0.45	0.32636	0.00	0.50000
−0.89	0.18673	−0.44	0.32997	0.01	0.50399
−0.88	0.18943	−0.43	0.33360	0.02	0.50798
−0.87	0.19215	−0.42	0.33724	0.03	0.51197
−0.86	0.19489	−0.41	0.34090	0.04	0.51595

z	G(z)	z	(Gz)	z	G(z)
0.05	0.51994	0.50	0.69146	0.95	0.82894
0.06	0.52392	0.51	0.69497	0.96	0.83147
0.07	0.52790	0.52	0.69847	0.97	0.83398
0.08	0.53188	0.53	0.70194	0.98	0.83646
0.09	0.53586	0.54	0.70540	0.99	0.83891
0.10	0.53983	0.55	0.70884	1.00	0.84134
0.11	0.54380	0.56	0.71226	1.01	0.84375
0.12	0.54776	0.57	0.71566	1.02	0.84614
0.13	0.55172	0.58	0.71904	1.03	0.84850
0.14	0.55567	0.59	0.72240	1.04	0.85083
0.15	0.55962	0.60	0.72575	1.05	0.85314
0.16	0.56356	0.61	0.72907	1.06	0.85543
0.17	0.56749	0.62	0.73237	1.07	0.85769
0.18	0.57142	0.63	0.73565	1.08	0.85993
0.19	0.57535	0.64	0.73891	1.09	0.86214
0.20	0.57926	0.65	0.74215	1.10	0.86433
0.21	0.58317	0.66	0.74537	1.11	0.86650
0.22	0.58706	0.67	0.74857	1.12	0.86864
0.23	0.59095	0.68	0.75175	1.13	0.87076
0.24	0.59483	0.69	0.75490	1.14	0.87286
0.25	0.59871	0.70	0.75804	1.15	0.87493
0.26	0.60257	0.71	0.76115	1.16	0.87698
0.27	0.60642	0.72	0.76424	1.17	0.87900
0.28	0.61026	0.73	0.76730	1.18	0.88100
0.29	0.61409	0.74	0.77035	1.19	0.88298
0.30	0.61791	0.75	0.77337	1.20	0.88493
0.31	0.62172	0.76	0.77637	1.21	0.88686
0.32	0.62552	0.77	0.77935	1.22	0.88877
0.33	0.62930	0.78	0.78230	1.23	0.89065
0.34	0.63307	0.79	0.78524	1.24	0.89251
0.35	0.63683	0.80	0.78814	1.25	0.89435
0.36	0.64058	0.81	0.79103	1.26	0.89617
0.37	0.64431	0.82	0.79389	1.27	0.89796
0.38	0.64803	0.83	0.79673	1.28	0.89973
0.39	0.65173	0.84	0.79955	1.29	0.90147
0.40	0.65542	0.85	0.80234	1.30	0.90320
0.41	0.65910	0.86	0.80511	1.31	0.90490
0.42	0.66276	0.87	0.80785	1.32	0.90658
0.43	0.66640	0.88	0.81057	1.33	0.90824
0.44	0.67003	0.89	0.81327	1.34	0.90988
0.45	0.67364	0.90	0.81594	1.35	0.91149
0.46	0.67724	0.91	0.81859	1.36	0.91309
0.47	0.68082	0.92	0.82121	1.37	0.91466
0.48	0.68439	0.93	0.82381	1.38	0.91621
0.49	0.68793	0.94	0.82639	1.39	0.91774

z	G(z)	z	G(z)	z	G(z)
1.40	0.91924	1.85	0.96784	2.30	0.98928
1.41	0.92073	1.86	0.96856	2.31	0.98956
1.42	0.92220	1.87	0.96926	2.32	0.98983
1.43	0.92364	1.88	0.96995	2.33	0.99010
1.44	0.92507	1.89	0.97062	2.34	0.99036
1.45	0.92647	1.90	0.97128	2.35	0.99061
1.46	0.92785	1.91	0.97193	2.36	0.99086
1.47	0.92922	1.92	0.97257	2.37	0.99111
1.48	0.93056	1.93	0.97320	2.38	0.99134
1.49	0.93189	1.94	0.97381	2.39	0.99158
1.50	0.93319	1.95	0.97441	2.40	0.99180
1.51	0.93448	1.96	0.97500	2.41	0.99202
1.52	0.93574	1.97	0.97558	2.42	0.99224
1.53	0.93699	1.98	0.97615	2.43	0.99245
1.54	0.93822	1.99	0.97670	2.44	0.99266
1.55	0.93943	2.00	0.97725	2.45	0.99286
1.56	0.94062	2.01	0.97778	2.46	0.99305
1.57	0.94179	2.02	0.97831	2.47	0.99324
1.58	0.94295	2.03	0.97882	2.48	0.99343
1.59	0.94408	2.04	0.97932	2.49	0.99361
1.60	0.94520	2.05	0.97982	2.50	0.99379
1.61	0.94630	2.06	0.98030	2.51	0.99396
1.62	0.94738	2.07	0.98077	2.52	0.99413
1.63	0.94845	2.08	0.98124	2.53	0.99430
1.64	0.94950	2.09	0.98169	2.54	0.99446
1.65	0.95053	2.10	0.98214	2.55	0.99461
1.66	0.95154	2.11	0.98257	2.56	0.99477
1.67	0.95254	2.12	0.98300	2.57	0.99492
1.68	0.95352	2.13	0.98341	2.58	0.99506
1.69	0.95449	2.14	0.98382	2.59	0.99520
1.70	0.95543	2.15	0.98422	2.60	0.99534
1.71	0.95637	2.16	0.98461	2.61	0.99547
1.72	0.95728	2.17	0.98500	2.62	0.99560
1.73	0.95818	2.18	0.98537	2.63	0.99573
1.74	0.95907	2.19	0.98574	2.64	0.99585
1.75	0.95994	2.20	0.98610	2.65	0.99598
1.76	0.96080	2.21	0.98645	2.66	0.99609
1.77	0.96164	2.22	0.98679	2.67	0.99621
1.78	0.96246	2.23	0.98713	2.68	0.99632
1.79	0.96327	2.24	0.98745	2.69	0.99643
1.80	0.96407	2.25	0.98778	2.70	0.99653
1.81	0.96485	2.26	0.98809	2.71	0.99664
1.82	0.96562	2.27	0.98840	2.72	0.99674
1.83	0.96638	2.28	0.98870	2.73	0.99683
1.84	0.96712	2.29	0.98899	2.74	0.99693

z	G(z)	z	G(z)	z	G(z)
2.75	0.99702	3.20	0.99931	3.65	0.99987
2.76	0.99711	3.21	0.99934	3.66	0.99987
2.77	0.99720	3.22	0.99936	3.67	0.99988
2.78	0.99728	3.23	0.99938	3.68	0.99988
2.79	0.99736	3.24	0.99940	3.69	0.99989
2.80	0.99744	3.25	0.99942	3.70	0.99989
2.81	0.99752	3.26	0.99944	3.71	0.99990
2.82	0.99760	3.27	0.99946	3.72	0.99990
2.83	0.99767	3.28	0.99948	3.73	0.99990
2.84	0.99774	3.29	0.99950	3.74	0.99991
2.85	0.99781	3.30	0.99952	3.75	0.99991
2.86	0.99788	3.31	0.99953	3.76	0.99992
2.87	0.99795	3.32	0.99955	3.77	0.99992
2.88	0.99801	3.33	0.99957	3.78	0.99992
2.89	0.99807	3.34	0.99958	3.79	0.99992
2.90	0.99813	3.35	0.99960	3.80	0.99993
2.91	0.99819	3.36	0.99961	3.81	0.99993
2.92	0.99825	3.37	0.99962	3.82	0.99993
2.93	0.99831	3.38	0.99964	3.83	0.99994
2.94	0.99386	3.89	0.99965	3.84	0.99994
2.95	0.99841	3.40	0.99966	3.85	0.99994
2.96	0.99846	3.41	0.99968	3.86	0.99994
2.97	0.99851	3.42	0.99969	3.87	0.99995
2.98	0.99856	3.43	0.99970	3.88	0.99995
2.99	0.99861	3.44	0.99971	3.89	0.99995
3.00	0.99865	3.45	0.99972	3.90	0.99995
3.01	0.99869	3.46	0.99973	3.91	0.99995
3.02	0.99874	3.47	0.99974	3.92	0.99996
3.03	0.99878	3.48	0.99975	3.93	0.99996
3.04	0.99882	3.49	0.99976	3.94	0.99996
3.05	0.99886	3.50	0.99977	3.95	0.99996
3.06	0.99889	3.51	0.99978	3.96	0.99996
3.07	0.99893	3.52	0.99978	3.97	0.99996
3.08	0.99897	3.53	0.99979	3.98	0.99997
3.09	0.99900	3.54	0.99980	3.99	0.99997
3.10	0.99903	3.55	0.99981	4.00	0.99997
3.11	0.99906	3.56	0.99981		
3.12	0.99910	3.57	0.99982		
3.13	0.99913	3.58	0.99983		
3.14	0.99916	3.59	0.99983		
3.15	0.99918	3.60	0.99984		
3.16	0.99921	3.61	0.99985		
3.17	0.99924	3.62	0.99985		
3.18	0.99926	3.63	0.99986		
3.19	0.99929	3.64	0.99986		

Source: Bernard Ostle, *Statistics in Research*, 2nd ed. (Ames: Iowa State University Press, 1967).

APPENDIX F Negative Exponential Distribution: Values of e^{-x}

x	e^{-x} (value)	x	e^{-x} (value)	x	e^{-x} (value)	x	e^{-x} (value)
0.00	1.00000	0.50	0.60653	1.00	0.36788	1.50	0.22313
0.01	0.99005	0.51	.60050	1.01	.36422	1.51	.22091
0.02	.98020	0.52	.59452	1.02	.36060	1.52	.21871
0.03	.97045	0.53	.58860	1.03	.35701	1.53	.21654
0.04	.96079	0.54	.58275	1.04	.35345	1.54	.21438
0.05	.95123	0.55	.57695	1.05	.34994	1.55	.21225
0.06	.94176	0.56	.57121	1.06	.34646	1.56	.21014
0.07	.93239	0.57	.56553	1.07	.34301	1.57	.20805
0.08	.92312	0.58	.55990	1.08	.33960	1.58	.20598
0.09	.91393	0.59	.55433	1.09	.33622	1.59	.20393
0.10	.90484	0.60	.54881	1.10	.33287	1.60	.20190
0.11	.89583	0.61	.54335	1.11	.32956	1.61	.19989
0.12	.88692	0.62	.53794	1.12	.32628	1.62	.19790
0.13	.87809	0.63	.53259	1.13	.32303	1.63	.19593
0.14	.86936	0.64	.52729	1.14	.31982	1.64	.19398
0.15	.86071	0.65	.52205	1.15	.31664	1.65	.19205
0.16	.87514	0.66	.51685	1.16	.31349	1.66	.19014
0.17	.84366	0.67	.51171	1.17	.31037	1.67	.18825
0.18	.83527	0.68	.50662	1.18	.30728	1.68	.18637
0.19	.82696	0.69	.50158	1.19	.30422	1.69	.18452
0.20	.81873	0.70	.49659	1.20	.30119	1.70	.18268
0.21	.81058	0.71	.49164	1.21	.29820	1.71	.18087
0.22	.80252	0.72	.48675	1.22	.29523	1.72	.17907
0.23	.79453	0.73	.48191	1.23	.29229	1.73	.17728
0.24	.78663	0.74	.47711	1.24	.28938	1.74	.17552
0.25	.77880	0.75	.47237	1.25	.28650	1.75	.17377
0.26	.77105	0.76	.46767	1.26	.28365	1.76	.17204
0.27	.76338	0.77	.46301	1.27	.28083	1.77	.17033
0.28	.75578	0.78	.45841	1.28	.27804	1.78	.16864
0.29	.74826	0.79	.45384	1.29	.27527	1.79	.16696
0.30	.74082	0.80	.44933	1.30	.27253	1.80	.16530
0.31	.73345	0.81	.44486	1.31	.26982	1.81	.16365
0.32	.72615	0.82	.44043	1.32	.26714	1.82	.16203
0.33	.71892	0.83	.43605	1.33	.26448	1.83	.16041
0.34	.71177	0.84	.43171	1.34	.26185	1.84	.15882
0.35	.70469	0.85	.42741	1.35	.25924	1.85	.15724
0.36	.69768	0.86	.42316	1.36	.25666	1.86	.15567
0.37	.69073	0.87	.41895	1.37	.25411	1.87	.15412
0.38	.68386	0.88	.41478	1.38	.25158	1.88	.15259
0.39	.67706	0.89	.41066	1.39	.24908	1.89	.15107

x	e^{-x} (value)	x	e^{-x} (value)	x	e^{-x} (value)	x	e^{-x} (value)
0.40	.67032	0.90	.40657	1.40	.24660	1.90	.14957
0.41	.66365	0.91	.40252	1.41	.24414	1.91	.14808
0.42	.65705	0.92	.39852	1.42	.24171	1.92	.14661
0.43	.65051	0.93	.39455	1.43	.23931	1.93	.14515
0.44	.64404	0.94	.39063	1.44	.23693	1.94	.14370
0.45	.63763	0.95	.38674	1.45	.23457	1.95	.14227
0.46	.63128	0.96	.38289	1.46	.23224	1.96	.14086
0.47	.62500	0.97	.37908	1.47	.22993	1.97	.13946
0.48	.61878	0.98	.37531	1.48	.22764	1.98	.13807
0.49	.61263	0.99	.37158	1.49	.22537	1.99	.13670
0.50	.60653	1.00	.36788	1.50	.22313	2.00	.13534

APPENDIX G Interest Tables

TABLE 1 Compound Sum of $1

Year	1%	2%	3%	4%	5%	6%	7%
1	1.010	1.020	1.030	1.040	1.050	1.060	1.070
2	1.020	1.040	1.061	1.082	1.102	1.124	1.145
3	1.030	1.061	1.093	1.125	1.158	1.191	1.225
4	1.041	1.082	1.126	1.170	1.216	1.262	1.311
5	1.051	1.104	1.159	1.217	1.276	1.338	1.403
6	1.062	1.126	1.194	1.265	1.340	1.419	1.501
7	1.072	1.149	1.230	1.316	1.407	1.504	1.606
8	1.083	1.172	1.267	1.369	1.477	1.594	1.718
9	1.094	1.195	1.305	1.423	1.551	1.689	1.838
10	1.105	1.219	1.344	1.480	1.629	1.791	1.967
11	1.116	1.243	1.384	1.539	1.710	1.898	2.105
12	1.127	1.268	1.426	1.601	1.796	2.012	2.252
13	1.138	1.294	1.469	1.665	1.886	2.133	2.410
14	1.149	1.319	1.513	1.732	1.980	2.261	2.579
15	1.161	1.346	1.558	1.801	2.079	2.397	2.759
16	1.173	1.373	1.605	1.873	2.183	2.540	2.952
17	1.184	1.400	1.653	1.948	2.292	2.693	3.159
18	1.196	1.428	1.702	2.026	2.407	2.854	3.380
19	1.208	1.457	1.754	2.107	2.527	3.026	3.617
20	1.220	1.486	1.806	2.191	2.653	3.207	3.870
25	1.282	1.641	2.094	2.666	3.386	4.292	5.427
30	1.348	1.811	2.427	3.243	4.322	5.743	7.612

Year	8%	9%	10%	12%	14%	15%	16%
1	1.080	1.090	1.100	1.120	1.140	1.150	1.160
2	1.166	1.188	1.210	1.254	1.300	1.322	1.346
3	1.260	1.295	1.331	1.405	1.482	1.521	1.561
4	1.360	1.412	1.464	1.574	1.689	1.749	1.811
5	1.469	1.539	1.611	1.762	1.925	2.011	2.100
6	1.587	1.677	1.772	1.974	2.195	2.313	2.436
7	1.714	1.828	1.949	2.211	2.502	2.660	2.826
8	1.851	1.993	2.144	2.476	2.853	3.059	3.278
9	1.999	2.172	2.358	2.773	3.252	3.518	3.803
10	2.159	2.367	2.594	3.106	3.707	4.046	4.411
11	2.332	2.580	2.853	3.479	4.226	4.652	5.117
12	2.518	2.813	3.138	3.896	4.818	5.350	5.936
13	2.720	3.066	3.452	4.363	5.492	6.153	6.886
14	2.937	3.342	3.797	4.887	6.261	7.076	7.988
15	3.172	3.642	4.177	5.474	7.138	8.137	9.266
16	3.426	3.970	4.595	6.130	8.137	9.358	10.748
17	3.700	4.328	5.054	6.866	9.276	10.761	12.468
18	3.996	4.717	5.560	7.690	10.575	12.375	14.463
19	4.316	5.142	6.116	8.613	12.056	14.232	16.777
20	4.661	5.604	6.728	9.646	13.743	16.367	19.461
25	6.848	8.623	10.835	17.000	26.462	32.919	40.874
30	10.063	13.268	17.449	29.960	50.950	66.212	85.850

TABLE 1 (Concluded)

Year	18%	20%	24%	28%	32%	36%
1	1.180	1.200	1.240	1.280	1.320	1.360
2	1.392	1.440	1.538	1.638	1.742	1.850
3	1.643	1.728	1.907	2.067	2.300	2.515
4	1.939	2.074	2.364	2.684	3.036	3.421
5	2.288	2.488	2.932	3.436	4.007	4.653
6	2.700	2.986	3.635	4.398	5.290	6.328
7	3.185	3.583	4.508	5.629	6.983	8.605
8	3.759	4.300	5.590	7.206	9.217	11.703
9	4.435	5.160	6.931	9.223	12.166	15.917
10	5.234	6.192	8.594	11.806	16.060	21.647
11	6.176	7.430	10.657	15.112	21.199	29.439
12	7.288	8.916	13.215	19.343	27.983	40.037
13	8.599	10.699	16.386	24.759	36.937	54.451
14	10.147	12.839	20.319	31.691	48.757	74.053
15	11.974	15.407	25.196	40.565	64.359	100.712
16	14.129	18.488	31.243	51.923	84.954	136.97
17	16.672	22.186	38.741	66.461	112.14	186.28
18	19.673	26.623	48.039	85.071	148.02	253.34
19	23.214	31.948	59.568	108.89	195.39	344.54
20	27.393	38.338	73.864	139.38	257.92	468.57
25	62.669	95.396	216.542	478.90	1033.6	2180.1
30	143.371	237.376	634.820	1645.5	4142.1	10143.

Year	40%	50%	60%	70%	80%	90%
1	1.400	1.500	1.600	1.700	1.800	1.900
2	1.960	2.250	2.560	2.890	3.240	3.610
3	2.744	3.375	4.096	4.913	5.832	6.859
4	3.842	5.062	6.544	8.352	10.498	13.032
5	5.378	7.594	10.486	14.199	18.896	24.761
6	7.530	11.391	16.777	24.138	34.012	47.046
7	10.541	17.086	26.844	41.034	61.222	89.387
8	14.758	25.629	42.950	69.758	110.200	169.836
9	20.661	38.443	68.720	118.588	198.359	322.688
10	28.925	57.665	109.951	201.599	357.047	613.107
11	40.496	86.498	175.922	342.719	642.684	1164.902
12	56.694	129.746	281.475	582.622	1156.831	2213.314
13	79.372	194.619	450.360	990.457	2082.295	4205.297
14	111.120	291.929	720.576	1683.777	3748.131	7990.065
15	155 568	437.894	1152.921	2862.421	6746.636	15181.122
16	217.795	656.84	1844.7	4866.1	12144.	28844.0
17	304.914	985.26	2951.5	8272.4	21859.	54804.0
18	426.879	1477.9	4722.4	14063.0	39346.	104130.0
19	597.630	2216.8	7555.8	23907.0	70824.	197840.0
20	836.683	3325.3	12089.0	40642.0	127480.	375900.0
25	4499.880	25251.	126760.0	577060.0	2408900.	9307600.0
30	24201.432	191750.	1329200.	8193500.0	45517000.	230470000.0

TABLE 2 Sum of an Annuity of $1 for *N* Years

Year	1%	2%	3%	4%	5%	6%
1	1.000	1.000	1.000	1.000	1.000	1.000
2	2.010	2.020	2.030	2.040	2.050	2.060
3	2.030	3.060	3.091	3.122	3.152	3.184
4	4.060	4.122	4.184	4.246	4.310	4.375
5	5.101	5.204	5.309	5.416	5.526	5.637
6	6.152	6.308	6.468	6.633	6.802	6.975
7	7.214	7.434	7.662	7.898	8.142	8.394
8	8.286	8.583	8.892	9.214	9.549	9.897
9	9.369	9.755	10.159	10.583	11.027	11.491
10	10.462	10.950	11.464	12.006	12.578	13.181
11	11.567	12.169	12.808	13.486	14.207	14.972
12	12.683	13.412	14.192	15.026	15.917	16.870
13	13.809	14.680	15.618	16.627	17.713	18.882
14	14.947	15.974	17.086	18.292	19.599	21.051
15	16.097	17.293	18.599	20.024	21.579	23.276
16	17.258	18.639	20.157	21.825	23.657	25.673
17	18.430	20.012	21.762	23.698	25.840	28.213
18	19.615	21.412	23.414	25.645	28.132	30.906
19	20.811	22.841	25.117	27.671	30.539	33.760
20	22.019	24.297	26.870	29.778	33.066	36.786
25	28.243	32.030	36.459	41.646	47.727	54.865
30	34.785	40.568	47.575	56.085	66.439	79.058

Year	7%	8%	9%	10%	12%	14%
1	1.000	1.000	1.000	1.000	1.000	1.000
2	2.070	2.080	2.090	2.100	2.120	2.140
3	3.215	3.246	3.278	3.310	3.374	3.440
4	4.440	4.506	4.573	4.641	4.770	4.921
5	5.751	5.867	5.985	6.105	6.353	6.610
6	7.153	7.336	7.523	7.716	8.115	8.536
7	8.654	8.923	9.200	9.487	10.089	10.730
8	10.260	10.637	11.028	11.436	12.300	13.233
9	11.978	12.488	13.021	13.579	14.776	16.085
10	13.816	14.487	15.193	15.937	17.549	19.337
11	15.784	16.645	17.560	18.531	20.655	23.044
12	17.888	18.977	20.141	21.384	24.133	27.271
13	20.141	21.495	22.953	24.523	28.029	32.089
14	22.550	24.215	26.019	27.975	32.393	37.581
15	25.129	27.152	29.361	31.772	37.280	43.842
16	27.888	30.324	33.003	35.950	42.753	50.980
17	30.840	33.750	36.974	40.545	48.884	59.118
18	33.999	37.450	41.301	45.599	55.750	68.394
19	37.379	41.446	46.018	51.159	63.440	78.969
20	40.995	45.762	51.160	57.275	72.052	91.025
25	63.249	73.106	84.701	93.347	133.334	181.871
30	94.461	113.283	136.308	164.494	241.333	356.787

TABLE 2 (Concluded)

Year	16%	18%	20%	24%	28%	32%
1	1.000	1.000	1.000	1.000	1.000	1.000
2	2.160	2.180	2.200	2.240	2.280	2.320
3	3.506	3.572	3.640	3.778	3.918	4.062
4	5.066	5.215	5.368	5.684	6.016	6.362
5	6.877	7.154	7.442	8.048	8.700	9.398
6	8.977	9.442	9.930	10.980	12.136	13.406
7	11.414	12.142	12.916	14.615	16.534	18.696
8	14.240	15.327	16.499	19.123	22.163	25.678
9	17.518	19.086	20.799	24.712	29.369	34.895
10	21.321	23.521	25.959	31.643	38.592	47.062
11	25.733	28.755	32.150	40.238	50.399	63.122
12	30.850	34.931	39.580	50.985	65.510	84.320
13	36.786	42.219	48.497	64.110	84.853	112.303
14	43.672	50.818	59.196	80.496	109.612	149.240
15	51.660	60.965	72.035	100.815	141.303	197.997
16	60.925	72.939	87.442	126.011	181.87	262.36
17	71.673	87.068	105.931	157.253	233.79	347.31
18	84.141	103.740	128.117	195.994	300.25	459.45
19	98.603	123.414	154.740	244.033	385.32	607.47
20	115.380	146.628	186.688	303.601	494.21	802.86
25	249.214	342.603	471.981	898.092	1706.8	3226.8
30	530.312	790.948	1181.882	2640.916	5873.2	12941.0

Year	36%	40%	50%	60%	70%	80%
1	1.000	1.000	1.000	1.000	1.000	1.000
2	2.360	2.400	2.500	2.600	2.700	2.800
3	4.210	4.360	4.750	5.160	5.590	6.040
4	6.725	7.104	8.125	9.256	10.503	11.872
5	10.146	10.846	13.188	15.810	18.855	22.370
6	14.799	16.324	20.781	26.295	33.054	41.265
7	21.126	23.853	32.172	43.073	57.191	75.278
8	29.732	34.395	49.258	69.916	98.225	136.500
9	41.435	49.153	74.887	112.866	167.983	246.699
10	57.352	69.814	113.330	181.585	286.570	445.058
11	78.998	98.739	170.995	291.536	488.170	802.105
12	108.437	139.235	257.493	467.458	830.888	1444.788
13	148.475	195.929	387.239	748.933	1413.510	2601.619
14	202.926	275.300	581.859	1199.293	2403.968	4683.914
15	276.979	386.420	873.788	1919.869	4087.745	8432.045
16	377.69	541.99	1311.7	3072.8	6950.2	15179.0
17	514.66	759.78	1968.5	4917.5	11816.0	27323.0
18	700.94	1064.7	2953.8	7868.9	20089.0	49182.0
19	954.28	1491.6	4431.7	12591.0	34152.0	88528.0
20	1298.8	2089.2	6648.5	20147.0	58059.0	159350.0
25	6053.0	11247.0	50500.0	211270.0	824370.0	3011100.0
30	28172.0	60501.0	383500.0	2215400.0	11705000.0	56896000.0

TABLE 3 Present Value of $1

Year	1%	2%	3%	4%	5%	6%	7%	8%	9%	10%	12%	14%	15%
1	.990	.980	.971	.962	.952	.943	.935	.926	.917	.909	.893	.877	.870
2	.980	.961	.943	.925	.907	.890	.873	.857	.842	.826	.797	.769	.756
3	.971	.942	.915	.889	.864	.840	.816	.794	.772	.751	.712	.675	.658
4	.961	.924	.889	.855	.823	.792	.763	.735	.708	.683	.636	.592	.572
5	.951	.906	.863	.822	.784	.747	.713	.681	.650	.621	.567	.519	.497
6	.942	.888	.838	.790	.746	.705	.666	.630	.596	.564	.507	.456	.432
7	.933	.871	.813	.760	.711	.665	.623	.583	.547	.513	.452	.400	.376
8	.923	.853	.789	.731	.677	.627	.582	.540	.502	.467	.404	.351	.327
9	.914	.837	.766	.703	.645	.592	.544	.500	.460	.424	.361	.308	.284
10	.905	.820	.744	.676	.614	.558	.508	.463	.422	.386	.322	.270	.247
11	.896	.804	.722	.650	.585	.527	.475	.429	.388	.350	.287	.237	.215
12	.887	.788	.701	.625	.557	.497	.444	.397	.356	.319	.257	.208	.187
13	.879	.773	.681	.601	.530	.469	.415	.368	.326	.290	.229	.182	.163
14	.870	.758	.661	.577	.505	.442	.388	.340	.299	.263	.205	.160	.141
15	.861	.743	.642	.555	.481	.417	.362	.315	.275	.239	.183	.140	.123
16	.853	.728	.623	.534	.458	.394	.339	.292	.252	.218	.163	.123	.107
17	.844	.714	.605	.513	.436	.371	.317	.270	.231	.198	.146	.108	.093
18	.836	.700	.587	.494	.416	.350	.296	.250	.212	.180	.130	.095	.081
19	.828	.686	.570	.475	.396	.331	.276	.232	.194	.164	.116	.083	.070
20	.820	.673	.554	.456	.377	.312	.258	.215	.178	.149	.104	.073	.061
25	.780	.610	.478	.375	.295	.233	.184	.146	.116	.092	.059	.038	.030
30	.742	.552	.412	.308	.231	.174	.131	.099	.075	.057	.033	.020	.015

Year	16%	18%	20%	24%	28%	32%	36%	40%	50%	60%	70%	80%	90%
1	.862	.847	.833	.806	.781	.758	.735	.714	.667	.625	.588	.556	.526
2	.743	.718	.694	.650	.610	.574	.541	.510	.444	.391	.346	.309	.277
3	.641	.609	.579	.524	.477	.435	.398	.364	.296	.244	.204	.171	.146
4	.552	.516	.482	.423	.373	.329	.292	.260	.198	.153	.120	.095	.077
5	.476	.437	.402	.341	.291	.250	.215	.186	.132	.095	.070	.053	.040
6	.410	.370	.335	.275	.227	.189	.158	.133	.088	.060	.041	.029	.021
7	.354	.314	.279	.222	.178	.143	.116	.095	.059	.037	.024	.016	.011
8	.305	.266	.233	.179	.139	.108	.085	.068	.039	.023	.014	.009	.006
9	.263	.226	.194	.144	.108	.082	.063	.048	.026	.015	.008	.005	.003
10	.227	.191	.162	.116	.085	.062	.046	.035	.017	.009	.005	.003	.002
11	.195	.162	.135	.094	.066	.047	.034	.025	.012	.006	.003	.002	.001
12	.168	.137	.112	.076	.052	.036	.025	.018	.008	.004	.002	.001	.001
13	.145	.116	.093	.061	.040	.027	.018	.013	.005	.002	.001	.001	.000
14	.125	.099	.078	.049	.032	.021	.014	.009	.003	.001	.001	.000	.000
15	.108	.084	.065	.040	.025	.016	.010	.006	.002	.001	.000	.000	.000
16	.093	.071	.054	.032	.019	.012	.007	.005	.002	.001	.000	.000	
17	.080	.060	.045	.026	.015	.009	.005	.003	.001	.000	.000		
18	.069	.051	.038	.021	.012	.007	.004	.002	.001	.000	.000		
19	.060	.043	.031	.017	.009	.005	.003	.002	.000	.000			
20	.051	.037	.026	.014	.007	.004	.002	.001	.000	.000			
25	.024	.016	.010	.005	.002	.001	.000	.000					
30	.012	.007	.004	.002	.001	.000	.000						

TABLE 4 Present Value of an Annuity of $1

Year	1%	2%	3%	4%	5%	6%	7%	8%	9%	10%
1	0.990	0.980	0.971	0.962	0.952	0.943	0.935	0.926	0.917	0.909
2	1.970	1.942	1.913	1.886	1.859	1.833	1.808	1.783	1.759	1.736
3	2.941	2.884	2.829	2.775	2.723	2.673	2.624	2.577	2.531	2.487
4	3.902	3.808	3.717	3.630	3.546	3.465	3.387	3.312	3.240	3.170
5	4.853	4.713	4.580	4.452	4.329	4.212	4.100	3.993	3.890	3.791
6	5.795	5.601	5.417	5.242	5.076	4.917	4.766	4.623	4.486	4.355
7	6.728	6.472	6.230	6.002	5.786	5.582	5.389	5.206	5.033	4.868
8	7.652	7.325	7.020	6.733	6.463	6.210	6.971	5.747	5.535	5.335
9	8.566	8.162	7.786	7.435	7.108	6.802	6.515	6.247	5.985	5.759
10	9.471	8.983	8.530	8.111	7.722	7.360	7.024	6.710	6.418	6.145
11	10.368	9.787	9.253	8.760	8.306	7.887	7.449	7.139	6.805	6.495
12	11.255	10.575	9.954	9.385	8.863	8.384	7.943	7.536	7.161	6.814
13	12.134	11.348	10.635	9.986	9.394	8.853	8.358	7.904	7.487	7.103
14	13.004	12.106	11.296	10.563	9.899	9.295	8.745	8.244	7.786	7.367
15	13.865	12.849	11.938	11.118	10.380	9.712	9.108	8.559	8.060	7.606
16	14.718	13.578	12.561	11.652	10.838	10.106	9.447	8.851	8.312	7.824
17	15.562	14.292	13.166	12.166	11.274	10.477	9.763	9.122	8.544	8.022
18	16.398	14.992	13.754	12.659	11.690	10.828	10.059	9.372	8.756	8.201
19	17.226	15.678	14.324	13.134	12.085	11.158	10.336	9.604	8.950	8.365
20	18.046	16.351	14.877	13.590	12.462	11.470	10.594	9.818	9.128	8.514
25	22.023	19.523	17.413	15.622	14.094	12.783	11.654	10.675	9.823	9.077
30	25.808	22.397	19.600	17.292	15.373	13.765	12.409	11.258	10.274	9.427

Year	12%	14%	16%	18%	20%	24%	28%	32%	36%
1	0.893	0.877	0.862	0.847	0.833	0.806	0.781	0.758	0.735
2	1.690	1.647	1.605	1.566	1.528	1.457	1.392	1.332	1.276
3	2.402	2.322	2.246	2.174	2.106	1.981	1.868	1.766	1.674
4	3.037	2.914	2.798	2.690	2.589	2.404	2.241	2.096	1.966
5	3.605	3.433	3.274	3.127	2.991	2.745	2.532	2.345	2.181
6	4.111	3.889	3.685	3.498	3.326	3.020	2.759	2.534	2.339
7	4.564	4.288	4.039	3.812	3.605	3.242	2.937	2.678	2.455
8	4.968	4.639	4.344	4.078	3.837	3.421	3.076	2.786	2.540
9	5.328	4.946	4.607	4.303	4.031	3.566	3.184	2.868	2.603
10	5.650	5.216	4.833	4.494	4.193	3.682	3.269	2.930	2.650
11	5.988	5.453	5.029	4.656	4.327	3.776	3.335	2.978	2.683
12	6.194	5.660	5.197	4.793	4.439	3.851	3.387	3.013	2.708
13	6.424	5.842	5.342	4.910	4.533	3.912	3.427	3.040	2.727
14	6.628	6.002	5.468	5.008	4.611	3.962	3.459	3.061	2.740
15	6.811	6.142	5.575	5.092	4.675	4.001	3.483	3.076	2.750
16	6.974	6.265	5.669	5.162	4.730	4.033	3.503	3.088	2.758
17	7.120	6.373	5.749	5.222	4.775	4.059	3.518	3.097	2.763
18	7.250	6.467	5.818	5.273	4.812	4.080	3.529	3.104	2.767
19	7.366	6.550	5.877	5.316	4.844	4.097	3.539	3.109	2.770
20	7.469	6.623	5.929	5.353	4.870	4.110	3.546	3.113	2.772
25	7.843	6.873	6.097	5.467	4.948	4.147	3.564	3.122	2.776
30	8.055	7.003	6.177	5.517	4.979	4.160	3.569	3.124	2.778

APPENDIX H Answers to Selected Problems

Supplement to Chapter 4   Waiting Line Theory

1. Quick Lube Inc.

   $\lambda = 3,\ \mu = 4$

   a. Utilization $(\rho) = \dfrac{\lambda}{\mu} = \dfrac{3}{4} = 75\%$.

   b. $\bar{n}_1 = \dfrac{\lambda^2}{\mu(\mu - \lambda)} = \dfrac{3^2}{4(4 - 3)} = \dfrac{9}{4} = 2.25$ cars in line.

   c. $\bar{t}_1 = \dfrac{\lambda}{\mu(\mu - \lambda)} = \dfrac{3}{4(4 - 3)} = \dfrac{3}{4} = 45$ minutes in line.

   d. $\bar{t}_s = \dfrac{1}{\mu - \lambda} = \dfrac{1}{1} = 1$ hour (waiting + lube).

2. American Vending Inc.
   Case I: One worker.

   $\lambda = 3/\text{hour Poisson},\ \mu = 5/\text{hour exponential}$

   There is an average number of machines in the system of:

   $\bar{n}_s = \dfrac{\lambda}{\mu - \lambda} = \dfrac{3}{5 - 3} = \dfrac{3}{2} = 1\frac{1}{2}$ machines

   Downtime cost is $\$25 \times 1.5 = \$37.50$ per hour; repair cost is $\$4.00$ per hour; and total cost per hour for 1 worker is $\$37.50 + \$4.00 = \$41.50$.

   Downtime $(1.5 \times \$25) = \$37.50$
   Labor (1 worker $\times$ \$4) = $\underline{4.00}$
   $\overline{\underline{\$41.50}}$

   Case II: Two workers.

   $\lambda = 3,\ \mu = 7$

   $\bar{n}_s = \dfrac{\lambda}{\mu - \lambda} = \dfrac{3}{7 - 3} = .75$ machines

   Downtime $(.75 \times \$25) = \$18.75$
   Labor (2 workers $\times$ \$4.00) = $\underline{8.00}$
   $\overline{\underline{\$26.75}}$

   Case III: Three workers.

   $\lambda = 3,\ \mu = 8$

   $\bar{n}_s = \dfrac{\lambda}{\mu - \lambda} = \dfrac{3}{8 - 3} = \dfrac{3}{5} = .60$ machines

Downtime (.60 × $25) = $15.00
Labor (3 workers × $4) = 12.00
                          $27.00

Comparing the costs for one, two, or three workers, we see that Case II with two workers is the optimal decision.

CHAPTER 5   Design for Total Quality Management

1.   Insurance company forms.

   a. $\bar{p} = \dfrac{46}{15(100)} = .031$

   $S_p = \sqrt{\dfrac{\bar{p}(1 - \bar{p})}{n}} = \sqrt{\dfrac{.0307(1 - .0307)}{100}} = \sqrt{.0003} = .017$

   $\text{UCL} = \bar{p} + 1.96S_p = .031 + 1.96(.017) = .064$
   $\text{LCL} = \bar{p} - 1.96S_p = .031 - 1.96(.017) = -.002 \text{ or zero}$

   b.   The defectives are plotted here.

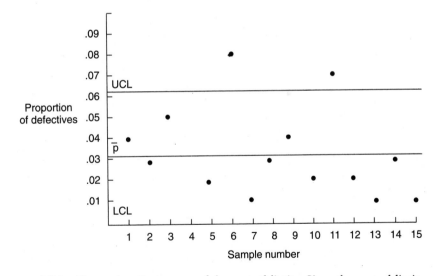

   c.   Of the 15 samples, 2 were out of the control limits. Since the control limits were established as 95 percent, or 1 out of 20, we would say that the process is out of control. It needs to be examined to find the cause of such widespread variation.

2.   Should Part A be inspected?

   .03 defective with no inspection.
   .02 defective with inspection.

    a. This problem can be solved simply by looking at the opportunity for 1 percent improvement.

       Benefit = .01($4.00) = $0.04

       Cost of inspection = $0.01

    Therefore, inspect and save $0.03 per unit.

    b. A cost of $0.05 per unit to inspect would be $0.01 greater than the savings, and therefore, inspection should not be performed.

CHAPTER 7 Forecasting

1. *a.* Simple moving average, 4-week.

Monday $\dfrac{2,400 + 2,300 + 2,400 + 2,200}{4} = \dfrac{9,300}{4} = 2,325$ doz.

Tuesday $= \dfrac{8,500}{4} = 2,125$ doz.

Wednesday $= \dfrac{9,500}{4} = 2,375$ doz.

Thursday $= \dfrac{7,500}{4} = 1,875$ doz.

Friday, Saturday, and Sunday $= \dfrac{19,200}{4} = 4,800$ doz.

b. Weighted average with weights of .40, .30, .20, and .10.

	(.10)		(.20)		(.30)		(.40)		
Monday	220	+	480	+	690	+	960	=	2,350
Tuesday	200	+	420	+	660	+	880	=	2,160
Wednesday	230	+	480	+	690	+	1,000	=	2,400
Thursday	180	+	380	+	540	+	800	=	1,900
Friday, Saturday, and Sunday	470	+	900	+	1,530	+	1,960	=	4,860
	1,300	+	2,660	+	4,110	+	5,600	=	13,670

c. $F_t = F_{t-1} + \alpha(A_{t-1} - F_{t-1})$
$= 22,000 + 0.10(21,000 - 22,000)$
$= 22,000 - 100$
$= 21,900$ loaves

d. $F_{t+1} = 21,900 + \alpha(22,500 - 21,900)$
$= 21,900 + .10(600)$
$= 21,960$ loaves

2. The demands for the past six quarters, as given in the problem, were:

	I	II	III	IV
Last year	1,200	700	900	1,100
This year	1,400	1,000		

Strategy 1: Next 3 months' demand = last 3 months' demand.

Testing this on the last 3 months, $F_{II} = A_I$; therefore $F_{II} = 1,400$.

Actual demand was 1,000, so $\dfrac{1,000}{1,400} = 71.4\%$

Strategy 2: This quarter's demand = demand same quarter last year.
The forecast for the second quarter this year will therefore be 700, the amount for that quarter last year.

Actual demand was 1,000, so $\dfrac{1,000}{700} = 142.9\%$.

Strategy 3: 10% more than last quarter.

$F_{II} = 1,400 \times 1.10 = 1,540$.

Actual was 1,000, so $\dfrac{1,000}{1,540} = 64.9\%$

Strategy 4: 50% more than same quarter last year.

$F_{II} = 700 \times 1.50 = 1,050$.

Actual was 1,000, so $\dfrac{1,000}{1,050} = 95.2\%$.

Strategy 5: Same rate of increase or decrease as last 3 months.

$\dfrac{1,400}{1,200} = 1.167$.

$F_{II} = 700 \times 1.167 = 816.9$

Actual was 1,000 so $\dfrac{1,000}{816.9} = 122.49\%$.

Strategy 4 was the closest in predicting the recent quarter—95.2% or just 4.8% under. Using this strategy (50% more than the same quarter last year), we would forecast the third quarter this year as 50% more than the third quarter last year, or

This year $F_{III} = 1.50 \, A_{III}$ (last year)

$F_{III} = 1.50 \, (900) = 1,450$ units

3. Evaluate the forecasting model using MAD end tracking signal.

Month	Actual Demand	Forecast Demand	Actual Deviation	Cumulative Deviation (RSFE)	Absolute Deviation
October	700	40	40	40	40
November	760	840	−80	−40	40
December	780	750	30	−10	10
January	790	835	−45	−55	55
February	850	910	−60	−115	115
March	950	890	60	−55	15
				Total Dev. =	315

$$\text{MAD} = \frac{315}{.6} = 52.5$$

$$\text{Tracking signal} = \frac{-55}{52.5} = -1.05$$

-1.05 0

Forecast model is well within the distribution.

4.

(1) X Period	(2) Y Actual	(3) Period Average	(4) Seasonal Factor	(5) Deseasoned Demand
1	300	358	0.527	568.99
2	540	650	0.957	564.09
3	885	1,038	1.529	578.92
4	580	670	0.987	587.79
5	416		0.527	789.01
6	760		0.957	793.91
7	1,191		1.529	779.08
8	760		0.987	770.21
Total	5,432	2,716	8.0	
Average	679	679	1	

Column 3 is seasonal average. For example, the first quarter average is

$$\frac{300 + 416}{2} = 358$$

Column 4 is the quarter average (column 3) divided by the overall average (679). Column 5 is the actual data multiplied by the seasonal index.

X Period	Deseasoned Demand	X^2	XY
1	568.99	1	569.0
2	564.09	4	1128.2
3	578.92	9	1736.7
4	587.79	16	2351.2
5	789.01	25	3945.0
6	793.91	36	4763.4
7	779.08	49	5453.6
8	770.21	64	6161.7
Sums	36	5,432	204	26,108.8
Average	4.5	679		

Regression results for deseasonalized data.

$$b = \frac{(26108) - (8)(4.5)(679)}{(204) - (8)(4.5)^2}$$

$$= 39.64$$

$$d = \bar{y} - b\bar{x}$$

$$a = 679 - 39.64(4.5)$$

$$= 500$$

Therefore, the deseasonalized regression results are

$$Y = 500 + 39.64X$$

Period	Trend Forecast	Seasonal Factor	Final Forecast
9	857.4	0.527	452.0
10	897.0	0.957	858.7
11	936.7	1.529	1431.9
12	976.3	0.987	963.3

CHAPTER 8   Capacity Planning and Location

1.   Banana Computers

a.

	SKU	Current Year	Year 2	Year 3	Year 4	Year 5	Year 6	Planning Values
Product Family A forecasts	1	5,700.0	6,042.0	6,344.1	6,661.3	7,061.0	7,555.3	
	2	4,200.0	4,452.0	4,674.6	4,908.3	5,202.8	5,567.0	
	3	2,900.0	3,074.0	3,227.7	3,389.1	3,592.4	3,843.9	
Equipment demand	1	0.6	0.6	0.6	0.7	0.7	0.8	10,000
	2	0.6	0.6	0.7	0.7	0.7	0.8	7,000
	3	0.5	0.5	0.5	0.6	0.6	0.6	6,000
Total		1.7	1.8	1.8	1.9	2.0	2.2	
Labor demand	1	6.8	7.3	7.6	8.0	8.5	9.1	12
	2	7.2	7.6	8.0	8.4	8.9	9.5	12
	3	4.8	5.1	5.4	5.6	6.0	6.4	10
Total		18.9	20.0	21.0	22.1	23.4	25.0	

b.

	SKU	Current Year	Year 2	Year 3	Year 4	Year 5	Year 6	Planning Values
Product Family B forecasts	1	1,200.0	1,296.0	1,399.7	1,525.7	1,663.0	1,779.4	
	2	5,400.0	5,832.0	6,298.6	6,865.4	7,483.3	8.007.2	
	3	2,800.0	3,024.0	3,265.9	3,559.9	3,880.2	4,151.9	
Equipment demand	1	0.4	0.4	0.5	0.5	0.6	0.6	3,000
	2	0.5	0.6	0.6	0.7	0.7	0.8	10,000
	3	0.4	0.4	0.5	0.5	0.6	0.6	7,000
Total		1.3	1.4	1.6	1.7	1.9	2.0	
Labor demand	1	4.8	5.2	5.6	6.1	6.7	7.1	12
	2	6.5	7.0	7.6	8.2	9.0	9.6	12
	3	4.0	4.3	4.7	5.1	5.5	5.9	10
Total		15.3	16.5	17.8	19.4	21.2	22.7	

2.   Sam Malone owner of Cheers:

Lease decision

@D   Revenue for 8 years =

8[.5(700,000) + 0.3(500,000) + 0.2(300,000)]		$4,480,000
Lease cost for 8 years = 8(250,000)	$2,000,000	
Operating cost for 8 years = (200,000)	1,600,000	3,600,000
Net income		$ 880,000

@E   Revenue for 8 years =

8[.5(700,000) + 0.3(500,000) + 0.2(300,000)]		$4,480,000
Lease cost 30 percent greater or		
1.30(250,000)	$ 325,000	
Lease for 8 years = 8(325,000)	2,600,000	
Operating cost for 8 years =		
8(200,000)	1,600,000	4,200,000
Net income		$ 280,000

@C   Net income = 0.5(880,000) + 0.5(280,000) = 580,000

@B   Net income = Revenue for 2 years − Operating cost for 2 years
         − Lease cost for 2 years + Value of node C
       = 2[.5(700,000) + 0.3(500,000) + 0.2(300,000)]
         − 2(250,000) − 2(200,000) + $580,000
       = $800,000

Build Inglewood

@F   Revenue for 10 years =

10[0.5(400,000) + 0.3(300,000) + 0.2(200,000)]	$3,300,000
Operating costs for 10 years = 10(200,000)	−2,000,000
Plus salvage value	−0−
	1,300,000
@A Less cost to build	−1,000,000
Net income	$ 300,000

The best decision is to lease, with a net income of $800,000; building would produce a net income of only $300,000.

Supplement to Chapter 8   Linear Programming

1. The optimal point, as shown on the next page, is $X = 67$ and $Y = 133$. Profit at this point would be $10(67) + 5(133) = \$1,335$.

$$X + Y \leq 200$$
$$4X + Y \leq 400$$

Maximize $10X + 5Y$

(1) $X + Y = 200$
   @$X = 0$ $Y = 200$
   @$Y = 0$ $X = 200$

(2) $4X + Y \leq 400$
   @$X = 0$ $Y = 400$
   @$Y = 0$ $X = 100$

Assume:

   $10X + 5Y = 500$
   @$X = 0$ $Y = 100$
   @$Y = 0$ $X = 50$

To fit the graph scale and area of interest, double the values to $Y = 200$, $X = 100$.

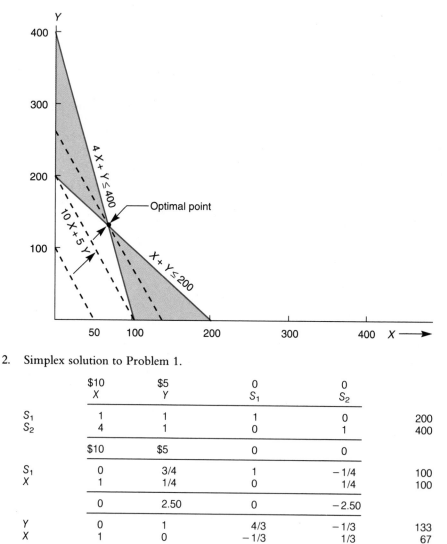

2. Simplex solution to Problem 1.

	$10 X	$5 Y	0 S_1	0 S_2	
S_1	1	1	1	0	200
S_2	4	1	0	1	400
	$10	$5	0	0	
S_1	0	3/4	1	−1/4	100
X	1	1/4	0	1/4	100
	0	2.50	0	−2.50	
Y	0	1	4/3	−1/3	133
X	1	0	−1/3	1/3	67
			$−3.33	$−1.66	

With $X = 67$ and $Y = 133$, the value of the objective function would be $Z = 10(67) + 5(133) = $1,335$.

CHAPTER 9 Facility Layout

1. University office layout.
   a. Evaluate this layout according to one of the methods in the chapter.

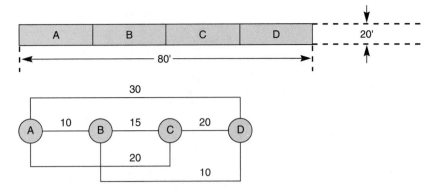

Using the material handling cost method shown in the toy company example we obtain the following costs, assuming that every nonadjacency doubles the initial cost/unit distance:

$$AB = 10 \times 1 = 10$$
$$AC = 20 \times 2 = 40$$
$$AD = 30 \times 3 = 90$$
$$BC = 15 \times 1 = 15$$
$$BD = 10 \times 2 = 20$$
$$CD = 20 \times 1 = 20$$

Current cost = 195

b. Improve the layout by exchanging functions within rooms. Show your amount of improvement using the same method as in (a). A better layout would be BCDA.

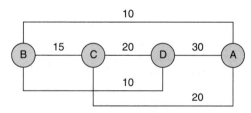

AB = 10 X 3 = 30
AC = 20 X 2 = 40
AD = 30 X 1 = 30
BC = 15 X 1 = 15
BD = 10 X 2 = 20
CD = 20 X 1 = 20
Improved cost = 155

2. Assembly line balancing.
    a. Draw the schematic diagram.

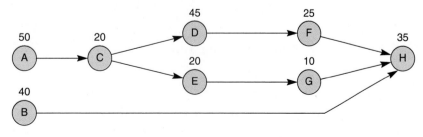

b. Theoretical minimum number of stations to meet D = 400 is:

$$N_t = \frac{T}{C} = \frac{245 \text{ seconds}}{\left(\dfrac{60 \text{ seconds} \times 480 \text{ minutes}}{400 \text{ units}}\right)} = \frac{245}{72} = 3.4 \text{ stations}$$

c. Use the longest operating time rule and balance the line in the minimum number of stations to produce 400 units per day.

	Task	Task Time (seconds)	Remaining Unassigned Time	Feasible Remaining Tasks
Station 1	A	50	22	C
	C	20	2	None
Station 2	D	45	27	E, F
	F	25	2	None
Station 3	B	40	32	E
	E	20	12	G
	G	10	2	None
Station 4	H	35	37	None

CHAPTER 10   Job Design and Work Measurement

1. Felix Unger time study (assume minutes).

	ST	$\bar{T}$	Performance Rating	NT
Get shoeshine kit	.50	.50/2 = .25	125%	.31
Polish shoes (2 pair)	3.40	3.40/2 = 1.70	110	1.87
Put away kit	.75	.75/2 = .375	80	.30
Normal time for one pair of shoes				2.48

Standard time for the pair = 2.48 × 1.05 = 2.61 minutes.

2. Work sampling of head baker.

To calculate the number of observations, use the formula at the bottom of Exhibit 10.16, since the 95 percent confidence is required (i.e., $Z \cong 2$).

p = "Doing" = 6/15 = 40%

E = 5% (given)

$$N = \frac{4p(1 - p)}{E^2} = \frac{4(.4)(1 - .4)}{(.05)(.05)} = \frac{.96}{.0025} = 384$$

CHAPTER 11   Project Planning and Control

1. CPM problem.

The answers to a, b, and c are shown in the following diagram.

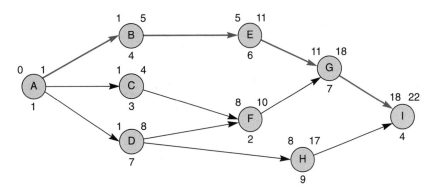

d. New critical path: A, D, F, G, I. Time of completion = 23 days.

2. Crashing a construction project.

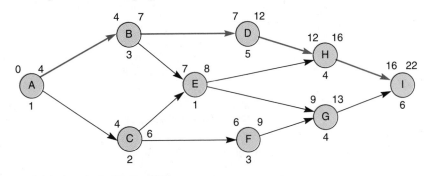

a. Critical path A, B, D, H, I.
Normal completion time = 22 weeks.

b.

Activity	Crash Cost	Normal Cost	Normal Time	Crash Time	Cost per Weeks	Weeks
A	$11,000	$10,000	4	2	$ 500	2
B	9,000	6,000	3	2	3,000	1
C	6,000	4,000	2	1	2,000	1
D	18,000	14,000	5	3	2,000	2
E	9,000	9,000	1	1		0
F	8,000	7,000	3	2	1,000	1
G	25,000	13,000	4	2	6,000	2
H	18,000	11,000	4	1	2,333	3
I	29,000	20,000	6	5	9,000	1

1. 1st week: CP = A B D H I. Cheapest is A at $500. Critical path stays the same.

2. 2nd week: A is still the cheapest at $500. Critical path stays the same.

3. 3rd week: Since A is no longer available, the choices are B (at $3,000), D (at $2,000), H (at $2,333), or I (at $9,000).

Therefore, choose D at $2,000.

Total Project Cost shortened 3 weeks is

A	$11,000
B	6,000
C	4,000
D	16,000
E	9,000
F	7,000
G	13,000
H	11,000
I	20,000
	$97,000

Supplement to Chapter 11   Learning Curves

1. Computing the price for two additional subs for the Loch Ness Monster search team.

The solution is found by applying learning curve (LC) values to labor costs for the 11th and 12th subs and adding these amounts to the material requirements. A 10 percent markup is then added to the sum. LC of the 11th is estimated as the average of the 10th and 12th.

Cost of the 11th sub:

Materials	$200,000
Labor: 300,000 (.3058 + .2784) ÷ 2	87,630
	$287,630

Cost of the 12th sub:

Materials	$200,000
Labor: .2784 × 300,000	83,520
	$283,520

Selling price: 1.10 × (287,630 + 283,520) $628,265

2. a. Learning rate $= \dfrac{9 \text{ minutes}}{10 \text{ minutes}} = 90\%$

From Exhibit S11.5, the time for the 1,000th unit is .3499 × 10 minutes = 3.499 minutes.

Yes, hire the person.

b. From Exhibit S11.5, unit 10 at 90% is .7047. Therefore, time for 10th unit = .7047 × 10 = 7.047 minutes.

CHAPTER 12   Aggregate Planning

1. *Plan 1: Exact production; vary work force* (assume 10 in work force to start).

Month	(1) Production Required	(2) Production Hours Required (1) × 4	(3) Hours/Month per Worker 22 × 8	(4) Workers Required (2) ÷ (3)	(5) WORKERS Hired	(6) WORKERS Fired
January	300	1,200	176	7	0	3
February	600	2,400	176	14	7	0
March	650	2,600	176	15	1	0
April	800	3,200	176	19	4	0
May	900	3,600	176	21	2	0
June	800	3,200	176	19	0	2

Month	(7) Hiring Cost (5) × $50	(8) Layoff Cost (6) × $100	(9) Straight-Time Cost (2) × $12.50
January	0	$300	$ 15,000
February	350	0	30,000
March	50	0	32,500
April	200	0	40,000
May	100	0	45,000
June	0	200	40,000
	$700	$500	$202,500

Total cost for plan:

Hiring cost	$ 700
Layoff cost	500
Straight-time cost	202,500
Total	$203,700

Plan 2: Constant work force; vary inventory and stockout only.

Month	(1) Cumulative Production Requirement	(2) Production Hours Available 22 × 8 × 10	(3) Units Produced (2) ÷ 4	(4) Cumulative Production
January	300	1,760	440	440
February	900	1,760	440	880
March	1,550	1,760	440	1,320
April	2,350	1,760	440	1,760
May	3,250	1,760	440	2,200
June	4,050	1,760	440	2,640

Month	(5) Units Short (1) − (4)	(6) Shortage Cost (5) × $20	(7) Units Excess (4) − (1)	(8) Inventory Cost (7) × $10	(9) Straight-Time Cost (2) × $12.50
January	$ 0	0	140	1,400	$ 22,000
February	20	400	0	0	22,000
March	230	4,600	0	0	22,000
April	590	11,800	0	0	22,000
May	1,050	21,000	0	0	22,000
June	1,410	28,200	0	0	22,000
		$66,000		$1,400	$132,000

Total cost for plan:

Shortage cost	$ 66,000
Inventory cost	1,400
Straight-time cost	132,000
Total	$199,400

Plan 3A: Constant work force of 10; vary overtime only; inventory carryover permitted.

Month	(1) Production Requirement	(2) Standard-Time Production Hours Available 22 × 8 × 10	(3) Standard-Time Units Produced (2) ÷ 4	(4) Overtime Required in Units (1) − (3)
January	300	1,760	440	0
February	460*	1,760	440	20
March	650	1,760	440	210
April	800	1,760	440	360
May	900	1,760	440	460
June	800	1,760	440	360
				1,410

Month	(5) Overtime Required Hours (4) × 4	(6) Overtime Cost (5) × $18.75	(7) Straight-Time Cost (2) × $12.50	(8) Excess Inventory Costs (3) − (1) × $10
January	0	$ 0	$ 22,000	$1,400
February	80	1,500	22,000	
March	840	15,750	22,000	
April	1,440	27,000	22,000	
May	1,840	34,500	22,000	
June	1,440	27,000	22,000	
		$105,750	$132,000	$1,400

*600 − 140 units of beginning inventory in February.

Total cost for plan:

Straight-time cost	$132,000
Overtime cost	105,750
Inventory cost	1,400
Total	$239,150

Plan 3B: Constant work force of 10; vary overtime only; no inventory carryover.

Month	(1) Production Requirement	(2) Standard-Time Hours Available 22 × 8 × 10	(3) Standard-Time Units Produced Min. [(2) ÷ 4; (1)]	(4) Overtime Required in Units (1) − (3)
January	300	1,760	300	0
February	600	1,760	440	160
March	650	1,760	440	210
April	800	1,760	440	360
May	900	1,760	440	460
June	800	1,760	440	360

Month	(5) Overtime Required in Hours (4) × 4 Hours	(6) Overtime Cost (5) × $18.75	(7) Standard-Time Cost (2) × $12.50	(8) Excess Inventory Cost (3) − (1) × $10
January	0	$ 0	$ 22,000	$1,400
February	640	12,000	22,000	
March	840	15,750	22,000	
April	1,440	27,000	22,000	
May	1,840	34,500	22,000	
June	1,440	27,000	22,000	
		$116,250	$132,000	$1,400

Total cost for plan:

Straight time cost	$132,000
Overtime cost	116,250
Excess inventory cost	1,400
	$249,650

Summary.

			COSTS			
Plan Description	Hiring	Layoff	Straight Time	Shortage	Excess Inventory	Total Cost
1 Exact production; vary work force	$700	$500	$202,500	—	—	$203,700
2 Constant work force; vary inventory and shortages		—	132,000	$66,000	$1,400	199,400
3A Constant work force; vary overtime with carryover of inventory		Overtime 105,750	132,000	—	1,400	239,150
3B Constant work force; vary overtime (carryover not permitted)		— 116,250	132,000	—	1,400	249,650

CHAPTER 13 Inventory Systems for Independent Demand

1. The quantity to be ordered each time is:

$$Q = \sqrt{\frac{2DS}{H}} = \sqrt{\frac{2(1,000)5}{4}} = 50 \text{ units}$$

   a. The total ordering cost for a year is:

$$\frac{D}{Q}S = \frac{1,000}{50}(\$5) = \$100$$

   b. The storage cost for a year is:

$$\frac{Q}{2}H = \frac{50}{2}(\$4) = \$100$$

2. $\sigma_{T+L} = \sqrt{(14 + 7)(30)^2} = \sqrt{18,900} = 137.5$

   $E(z) = \dfrac{120(14)(1 - .99)}{137.5} = 0.122$

   From Exhibit 13.6, $z = .80$;

   $q = \bar{d}(T + L) + z\sigma_{T+L} - I$
   $= 120(14 + 7) + .80(137.5) - 130$
   $= 2,500 \text{ units}$

3. $q = \bar{d}(T + L) + z\sigma_{T+L} - I$

   $\sigma_{T+L} = \sqrt{21(5)^2} = \boxed{23} \qquad \bar{d} = 20$
   $T = 14$

   $E(z) = \dfrac{D_T(1 - P)}{\sigma_{T+L}} = \dfrac{20(14)(1 - .99)}{23} = \boxed{.1217}$

   From Table 13.6 $z = \boxed{.80}$

$$q = \overline{d}(T + L) + z\sigma_{T+L} - I$$
$$= 20(14 + 7) + .80(23) - 180$$
$$= 420 + 18.4 - 180$$
$$q = 258.4 \text{ units}$$

CHAPTER 14   Inventory Systems for Dependent Demand: Materials Requirements Planning

1. *a.*

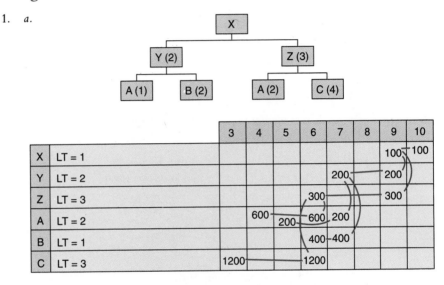

		3	4	5	6	7	8	9	10
X	LT = 1							100	100
Y	LT = 2					200		200	
Z	LT = 3				300			300	
A	LT = 2		600	200	600	200			
B	LT = 1				400	400			
C	LT = 3	1200			1200				

2. *a.*

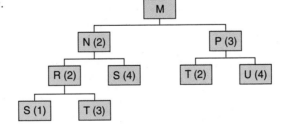

b.   M = 100
       N = 200
       P = 300
       R = 400
       S = 800 + 400 = 1,200
       T = 600 + 1,200 = 1,800
       U = 1,200

c.

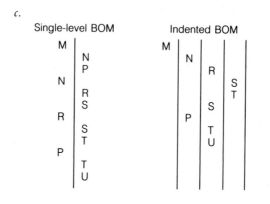

Single-level BOM   Indented BOM

CHAPTER 15   Job Shop Scheduling and Control

1. Runout problem of allocating expense money.

	(1) Expense Money on Hand	(2) Daily Expenses
Eldest son	$3.20	$1.95
Daughter	2.40	1.65
Youngest son	1.80	.55
	$7.40	$4.15

$$\text{Aggregate runout time} = \frac{\text{Inventory on hand} + \text{New amount}}{\text{Daily demand}}$$

$$= \frac{7.40 + 20}{4.15} = 6.60 \text{ days}$$

	(3) Total Expense Money Required (2) × 6.60	(4) Net Amount to Be Allocated (3) − (1)
Eldest son	$12.87	$ 9.67
Daughter	10.89	8.49
Youngest son	3.63	1.83
	$27.39	$19.99

The allocations are $9.67, $8.49, and $1.83. Rounding accounts for the 1 cent difference between the $20 and $19.99 allocated.

2. This problem can be viewed as a two-machine flow shop and can be easily solved using "Johnson's method."

ORIGINAL DATA			JOHNSON METHOD	
Car	Refitting Time (hours)	Repainting Time (hours)	Order of Selection	Position in Sequence
A	6	3	4th	3rd
B	0	4	1st	1st
C	5	2	3rd	4th
D	8	6	5th	2nd
E	2	1	2nd	5th

Graph of Johnson solution:

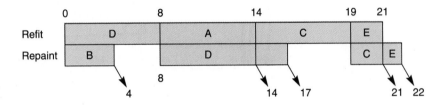

Supplement to Chapter 15   Simulation

1. Assign random numbers to the balls to correspond to the percentage present in the urn.

	Random Number
10 green balls	00–09
40 red balls	10–49
50 spotted balls	50–99

Many possible answers exist, depending on how the random numbers were assigned and which numbers were used from the list provided in the problem.

For the random number sequence above and using the first two numbers of those given we obtain the following:

RN	Color
26	Red
42	Red
95	Spotted
95	Spotted
66	Spotted
17	Red
3	Green
56	Spotted
83	Spotted
55	Spotted

For the 10 there were 1 green, 3 red, and 6 spotted balls—a good estimate based on a sample of only 10!

2. Demand for blood.

DELIVERY			NUMBER OF PATIENTS			PATIENT DEMAND		
Pints	Frequency	Random Number	Blood	Frequency	Random Number	Pints	Frequency	Random Number
4	.15	00–14	0	.25	00–24	1	.40	00–39
5	.20	15–34	1	.25	25–49	2	.30	40–69
6	.25	35–59	2	.30	50–79	3	.20	70–89
7	.15	60–74	3	.15	80–94	4	.10	90–99
8	.15	75–89	4	.05	95–99			
9	.10	90–99						

Week No.	Beginning Inventory	QUANTITY DELIVERED		Total Blood on Hand	PATIENTS NEEDING BLOOD		QUANTITY NEEDED			Number of Pints Remaining
		RN	Pints		RN	Patients	Patient	RN	Pints	
1	0	74	7	7	85	3	First	21	1	6
							Second	06	1	5
							Third	71	3	2
2	2	31	5	7	28	1		96	4	3
3	3	02	4	7	72	2	First	12	1	6
							Second	67	2	4
4	4	53	6	10	44	1		23	1	9
5	9	16	5	14	16	0				14
6	14	40	6	20	83	3	First	65	2	18
							Second	34	1	17
							Third	82	3	14
7	14									

At the end of 6 weeks, there were 14 pints on hand.

Name Index

Subject Index